808.8

Corder, Jimmie Wayne          C794f
AUTHOR

Finding a voice
TITLE

112867
DATE D~

808.8                    C794f
Corder, Jimmie Wayne
Finding a voice
112867


MAR 1 0 '78

# Finding a Voice

# Finding a Voice

**Jim W. Corder**
*Texas Christian University*

**Scott, Foresman and Company**
Glenview, Illinois    Brighton, England

## Acknowledgments

"The Heiligenstadt Testament" from "The Letters of Beethoven" translated by Emily
Anderson. Reprinted by the permission of St. Martin's Press, Inc., The Macmillan
Company of Canada, and Macmillan London and Basingstoke.    "Mr. Flood's Par-
ty" from Collected Poems by Edwin Arlington Robinson. Reprinted with permission of
The Macmillan Company. Copyright 1921 by Edwin Arlington Robinson, renewed
1949 by Ruth Nivison.    "Hearthside" from The Portable Dorothy Parker. Copyright
1926, 1954 by Dorothy Parker. Reprinted by permission of The Viking Press,
Inc.    "Sailing to Byzantium" from The Varioum Edition of the Poems of W. B.
Yeats, ed. by Peter Allt and Russell K. Alspach. Copyright 1928 by The Macmillan
Company, renewed © 1956 by Georgie Yeats. Reprinted with permission of The
Macmillan Company, Mr. M. B. Yeats and the Macmillan Co. of Canada.    "A Rose
for Emily" Copyright 1930 and renewed 1958 by William Faulkner. Reprinted from
Collected Stories of William Faulkner, by permission of Random House,
Inc.    "Desert Places" from The Poetry of Robert Frost edited by Edward Connery
Lathem. Copyright 1936 by Robert Frost. Copyright © 1964 by Lesley Frost Ballan-
tine. Copyright © 1969 by Holt, Rinehart and Winston, Inc. Reprinted by permission
of Holt, Rinehart and Winston, Inc.    "The Green Hills of Earth" by Robert A. Hein-
lein from The Saturday Evening Post, February 8, 1947. Copyright 1947 by The Curtis
Publishing Company. Reprinted by permission of the author's agent, Lurton Blassin-
game.    From Goodbye to a River, by John Graves. Copyright © 1959 by Curtis
Publishing Company. Copyright © 1960 by John Graves. Reprinted by permission of
Alfred A. Knopf, Inc.    "One Home" from The Rescued Year by William Stafford.
Copyright © 1960 by William E. Stafford. Reprinted by permission of Harper & Row,
Publishers, Inc.    "The Rescued Year" from The Rescued Year by William Stafford.
Copyright © 1964 by William E. Stafford. Reprinted by permission of Harper & Row,
Publishers, Inc.    "Goodbye, Old Paint, I'm Leaving Cheyenne" from For A Bitter
Season by George Garrett. Copyright © 1967 by George Garrett. By permission of the
copyright holder and the publisher, University of Missouri Press, Columbia, Missouri.
Introduction from The Way to Rainy Mountain by N. Scott Momaday. First published
in The Reporter, January 26, 1967. Reprinted from The Way to Rainy Mountain, copy-
right 1969, The University of New Mexico Press. Reprinted by permission.    "Half
Past Home" Copyright © 1967 by Marge Piercy. Reprinted from Hard Loving, by
Marge Piercy, by permission of Wesleyan University Press.    From The Death
and Life of Great American Cities, by Jane Jacobs. Copyright © 1961 by Jane Jacobs.
Reprinted by permission of Random House, Inc.    "Retrospect and Prospect" from
The City in History, © 1961 by Lewis Mumford. Reprinted by permission of Harcourt
Brace Jovanovich, Inc.    "Man and Animal: The City and the Hive" by Susanne K.
Langer. Copyright © 1958 by The Antioch Review, Inc. First published in The Antioch
Review, Volume 18, no. 3; reprinted by permission of the editors.    "The City May
Be as Lethal as the Bomb," by Barbara Ward from The New York Times Magazine,
(April 19, 1964). Copyright © 1964 by The New York Times Company. Reprinted

Darkness" from *Europe and Elsewhere* by Mark Twain. (Harper & Row.) "Speech at Meeting of the Petrograd Soviet of Workers' and Soldiers' Deputies" from *The Russian Revolution: Writing and Speeches from the February Revolution to the October Revolution* by V.I. Lenin and Joseph Stalin. Copyright 1938 by International Publishers Co., Inc. Reprinted by permission of International Publishers Co., Inc. "Speech Before the Reichstag" from *My New Order* by Adolf Hitler, edited with Commentary by Raoul de Roussy de Sales. Reprinted by permission of Mary Euyang Shen. "On Becoming Prime Minister" and "Dunkirk" ("A Colossal Military Disaster") by Winston Churchill from *Blood, Sweat, and Tears.* (British Title: *War Speeches*.) Reprinted by permission of The Canadian Publishers, McClelland and Stewart Limited, Toronto, and Cassell and Company, Ltd., Publishers. "The Portable Phonograph" by Walter Van Tilburg Clark from *Watchful Gods and Other Stories.* Copyright 1941, © 1969 by Walter Van Tilburg Clark. Reprinted by permission of International Famous Agency. "The Machinery for Peace" (pp. 103–118) from *Tomorrow is Now* by Eleanor Roosevelt. Copyright © 1963 by the Estate of Anna Eleanor Roosevelt. Reprinted by permission of Harper & Row, Publishers, Inc. "Now Don't Try to Reason with Me: Rhetoric Today, Left, Right, and Center," from *Now Don't Try to Reason With Me* by Wayne C. Booth. Copyright © 1970 University of Chicago Press. Reprinted by permission. "A Yippie Manifesto by Jerry Rubin from *Evergreen Review.* Reprinted by permission of Lubell, Lubell, Fine and Schaap. "Can We Survive Nihilism?" Copyright © 1967 by The Trustees for the Merton Legacy Trust, c/o New Directions Publishing Corporation. Reprinted by permission of the copyright holders. "What the Year 2000 Won't Be Like" by Joseph Wood Krutch from *Saturday Review* (January 20, 1968). Copyright © 1968 by Saturday Review. Reprinted by permission. "Funeral Oration" by Pericles from *The Peloponnesian War* by Thucydides, translated by Rex Warner. Reprinted by permission of the publisher, Penguin Books Ltd. and the copyright holder, The Bodley Head Ltd.

## Picture Credits

Cover     Abstract: hand painted cotton. From *Objects: USA*, the Johnson Collection of Contemporary Crafts.

Page x     Arabbito sketch of a caravan from a wall of D-E. Courtesy of Dura-Europos Publications.

Page xii     Veraulius woodcut from Anatomy Bark, 1543 by John of Oajcar. Courtesy the Metropolitan Museum of Art.

Page 14     Skyscrapers with bird. Photography by Jan Lukas, Rapho Guillumette Pictures.

Page 16     Sioux moving their tents. Painting by George Catlin. Courtesy of the American Museum of Natural History.

Page 100     Hiroshige: General view of the Nihonbashi Fishmarket. Courtesy Victoria and Albert Museum, photograph by John Webb, Brompton Studio.

Page 208     Lord and Peasant in the Nile Valley: Hunting scene from 19th Dynasty. Courtesy of the Trustees, The British Museum.

Page 264     Sculpture of woman with book. Photograph by Lars Werner Thieme.

Page 266     Title Page from Ogilby's Brittania 1675. Photograph by John R. Freeman and Co.

Page 301     Pompeiian painting showing girl musing over book. Courtesy Alinari-Art Reference Bureau.

Page 387     The money lender and his wife. Courtesy of the Louvre-Service de Documentation Photographique de la Reunion des Musees Nationaux.

Page 458     Sequence Picture. Detail of photograph by Ray Metzker.

Page 460     German Family. Courtesy "WALLRAF-RICHARTZ-MUSEUM, Koln"

Page 522     The second Lahore Durbar: December 26, 1846. Coutesy of the Trustees, The British Museum.

Page 650     The siege and capture of Saragossa in 1809. Photograph courtesy of the Bibliotheque Nationale.

# Preface

*Finding a Voice* uses many questions to focus on a single question: How can we justly and decently make our voices, at best imperfect instruments given to saying things only incompletely, worth hearing? It seeks to promote answers to that question by providing a wide variety of statements in which people have found good voices, or failed to do so, or have flailed about, sometimes rising, sometimes falling. While the urgency of the question scarcely seems to need authentication, the particular form in which I have put it and its apparent usurpation of the entire book do require some accounting; this the Introduction attempts to give. If the question is urgent and general, the answers must seem sometimes plodding and always specific: this person succeeds just here, and here; that person fails just there, and there.

For this reason—and for others—*Finding a Voice* includes a wide variety of forms and genres from a wide range of time. The exigencies of time and place and the needs of speaker and audience (reader and writer) make a shifting burden; a human voice speaks for good or ill through the possibilities of the form it takes and out of the premises and silent colorings of its backgrounds. It seems likely, then, that we may learn more about human voices, and discover more good answers to that initial question, if we hear many voices taking many forms in many times than if we listen only to the voices of a single time, a single form, or a single prevailing set of ideas and assumptions, however complex.

The readings are in three groups, each identified by a question that has been often, or always, crucial to human concerns. I have tried to frame the questions in language that would make them native to many times and places and not just our own. The readings in each section are arranged in smaller groups, each addressed to a more specific version of the same general question. Being varied in perspective and method, yet related to a common question, the readings will enable us to remind ourselves, I hope, that today we speak out of a history, our words hooking onto or being colored by other people's words; that if we speak in ways unlike those of others, we nevertheless speak, much as they did, in some context, whether or not fully recognized; that while we may have escaped what seem to us the naive presuppositions of earlier people, we too have our presuppositions; that our voices may be emboldened, enlarged, or otherwise made more fit by our knowledge of how others have spoken; and that if we do not know these things, we must someday grow shrill in our pride, or fall into silent despair, or succumb to delusion.

But so varied a collection of readings will not answer always or only to a single question, or to a small set of questions, however flexibly they may be put. In the various genres here represented, in the other themes that develop in the readings (some of which are suggested in the part introductions) and in the traditional and emergent concerns of rhetoric there are other questions and other interests that may be pertinent to composition courses. Because they are samples of our history, the readings may afford some opportunities for study of shifts in premises and philosophies in the history of ideas, for example, and shifts in value systems that take away the import of voices that once led multitudes or that give import to voices that once were alone in some wilderness.

I am indebted for many kindnesses to Mr. John Miller and Mr. Richard Welna. To Patsy I gladly owe a share of what her hands have worked for.

J. W. C.

# Contents

## How large is our community?    100

## How can our Earth survive?    208

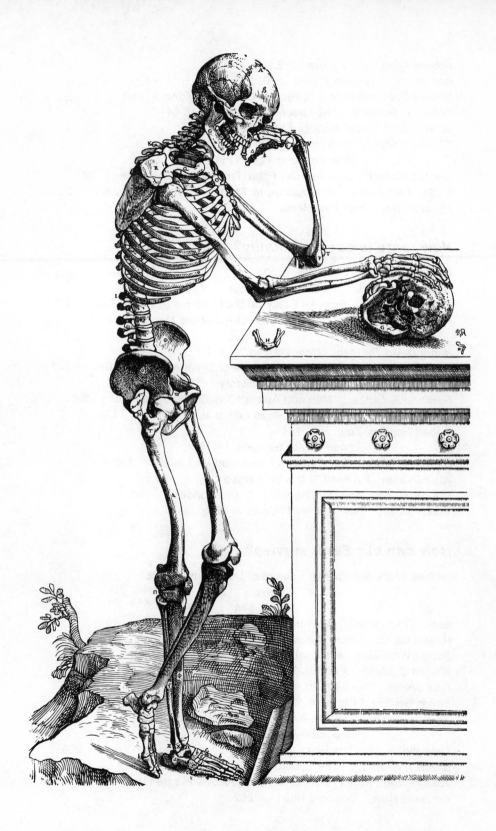

# Part Two.   How Shall We Learn?   264

Arhats bestowing alms upon beggars. Courtesy Museum of Fine Arts, Boston.

# Part Three.   With Whom Can We Live?   458

## How shall we choose among competing social systems? 650

## Alternate Table of Contents    793

# *Introduction*

## Some Observations on the Book

Whatever else it may claim to be or to do, *Finding a Voice* is a collection of readings. If they have any worth at all, the readings can stand alone, requiring no analysis to substantiate their merit. Analysis, even analysis for its own sake, to be sure, has many clear and certain virtues and values. Presumably objective analysis that has no goal except to be analysis can make possible the discovery of new ideas or the rediscovery of old ideas, and can help us to understand certain strategies and styles and ways of organizing experience. These are things that ought to happen.

Yet to be faced with a thick book of readings waiting to be analyzed one after the other is a prospect with scant comfort, another sometimes bewildering grab bag of experiences in a world that already too quickly brings us to clusters of experience, or thrusts us from experience to experience, pinball style, with neither prior warning nor time for adjustment afterward. The family circle has grown, Marshall McLuhan has told us, and almost from their beginnings the children who will be students are hurried into varied, highly disparate experiences. All the world's their teacher, and as they go mewling and toddling about the house, the television set, not the family, may be the first, and foremost, teacher. With television and newspapers and magazines available at home, particularly the quick-draw news bulletin, and tapes and movies and a hundred retrieval machines at school, they are zoomed here to there to there, from the late movie to a kitchen in Los Angeles, from the Popeye cartoons to a motel in Memphis, from Romper Room to the streets of Dallas. And they grow older and zoom from a class on Shelley to an off-campus tutoring session with hungry kids and back to work on an underground newspaper and thence to a class in medieval history and on to a committee meeting on the perils and promises of open visitation in the dormitories. A large pile of readings, largely unsorted and undiscriminated, may seem only an unappealing model of a world already filled with more experiences than we can grasp.

But each reading—like each experience—is a human thing having the breath of some life in it. Just living at a normal, sometimes regularly accel-

1

erating, pace may not enable us to catch that breath; the cursory or casual or even dutiful confrontation with experience or with reading may not make that breath ours, or at least touch us. It has consequently been common, when a large group of readings is presented to an audience, to make some arrangement of them beforehand, to discriminate among them according to some question that has already been asked and answered. Readings can be arranged, for example, in structural sequences, or in substantive sequences. That is, they can be arranged so that they illustrate patterns and styles and genres to be seen, understood, and accumulated, or they can be arranged so that they show views and aspects of previously determined themes. I have chosen the latter method, using certain critical questions to set themes for the readings.

Still, it is not always easy to grant the worth of a poem or an essay, even when the rest of the world already agrees upon its merit. A genre or a pattern may remain just a genre or a pattern, a theme just a theme, an essay just an essay—unless it somehow gets into our lives, makes certain demands upon us, or fulfills certain needs. "A writer's style," it has been suggested, "is the characteristic route he takes through all the choices presented in both the writing and prewriting stages. It is the manifestation of his conception of the topic, modified by his audience, situation, and intention— what we might call his 'universe of discourse.'"[1] Why should another person's "universe of discourse" matter? How does that universe impinge upon ours, or bear upon the shaping of ours?

The question is, then, if we are not simply to fall in and start analyzing, and not to be limited to the study of previously set themes and structures, how will a grab bag of experiences, this book, matter? How will it come to have worth?

Readings will justifiably come to have worth for us, it seems likely, and matter to us, if we learn to ask a good question of them. To be sure, we don't always have a good question to ask, whether for insufficiency of our own or of the readings; but it is true, as John Ciardi put it recently, that "No man can have his questions answered until he has thought how to ask them."[2] To ask a question is to signal a need; in the fulfillment of the need we earn something for ourselves:

To be fully human means in part to think one's own thoughts, to reach a point at which, whether one's ideas are different from or similar to other men's, they are truly one's own.

The art of asking oneself critical questions that lead either to new answers or to genuine revitalizing of old answers, the art of making thought live anew in each generation, may not be entirely amenable to instruction. But it is a necessary art, nonetheless, for any man who wants to be free.[3]

[1]Richard E. Young and Alton L. Becker, "Toward a Modern Theory of Rhetoric: A Tagmemic Consideration," in Martin Steinman, ed., *New Rhetorics* (New York, 1967), p. 104.

[2]John Ciardi, "Term Paper Time and No Thanks," *Saturday Review* (April 5, 1969), p. 14.

[3]Wayne C. Booth, "Is There Any Knowledge That a Man *Must* Have?" in Wayne C. Booth, ed., *The Knowledge Most Worth Having* (Chicago, 1967), p. 23.

And there are good questions to ask, as well as questions yet unfound, that touch our reading and our writing. In our *writing*, for example, we may need to ask, "Why write an essay by Monday?"—that is, what is there in the situation that suggests an essay rather than a sermon or song lyric, that determines that it must be written, and not spoken in some way, that declares it must happen by Monday?

Because it is a question that needs to be asked, and because the answers to it are numerous and provocative, the question I want to ask is this: *How can we justly and decently make our voices, at best imperfect instruments given to saying only incomplete things, worth hearing?* Nothing in this book proposes a single answer to the question; the readings seem likely to furnish a variety of answers in a variety of contexts. But I should say something to explain why I think this a good question.

## On Finding a Voice

An individual utterance is always a part of a total reality which seeks expression in this utterance.

Dietrich Bonhoeffer, *Ethics*

There is always more to say than can be said. The word is not the thing, the phrase not the idea. Our language functions as a synecdoche, the figure of speech, functions. That is, what we say is a part standing for a whole, something standing for something more. What we say is always less than what might be said. Our statements are incomplete.

How, then, can we make the truth, or something like the truth, out of what is incomplete? How can statements be both inadequate, in the sense just mentioned, *and* worth someone's time for listening or reading? These are ancient questions, even if particularly urgent in our time when so often in the streets and in the halls of government—and of universities—language intended to persuade instead antagonizes, when language-users alienate both friends and enemies, and each is left alone again, his discourse finding no community. What is it that endows a voice with worth? Why do we listen to one person and not to another? How shall we learn to discriminate among the voices we hear? How shall we find voices?

These are not questions we are accustomed to asking ourselves. It seems clear that sometimes ideas and assumptions deep in our character and in the character of our culture, and of inestimable importance and meaning to us, lead us away from such questions, paradoxically to our great loss. Our belief in the individuality of a person and in his dignity and worth, for example, can lead us, through miscalculations of the capacities of people, to a kind of pride that defines one individuality at the cost of all others. This pride, ironically, can generate both extravagant expectations about our language capacities and a marked diminution of the possibilities of language. On the one hand, the right to speak, naturally ours, we think, as a part of our individuality, is also, we are likely to think, the right to be heard. We have only to be sincere, and our natural voice can say all things, can "tell it like it is." On the other hand, we are led sometimes to think that there can be no use for language. Given the intricate texture of all that we are, we often seem to think that we invest our words with such meanings, bred over the long years and in a thousand ways, that no one can possibly understand us and read all the nuances of our discourse. "If there were any way for you to understand me," I say to my antagonist, "you would agree with me, but there is no way for you to understand me." Led to this extreme, we eventually distrust argument, debate, and all the uses of language itself. This, I should say incidentally, is one of many reasons for what we have often seen recently—activists of one inclination or another turning to some mode other than language for persuasion.

But not even perfect sincerity gives us a voice worth hearing, and at the other extreme the flight from language is a surrender of our humanity. The drive to say it all and the drive to say none of it are both delusive and destructive, the one, it seems likely, resulting from an overestimate of our own capacities, the other resulting from a marked underestimate of the capacities of language. For it is still possible to use language toward communion. It is not easy, but then it never was. It requires of us the perpetual effort to recover from incompleteness.

Good discourse is ever moving toward completeness. What complicates and intensifies the process is that discourse is a closure, a stopping, hence an incompleteness in itself. We do not speak *these* words unless we have already chosen or been directed not to speak *those*. This means, so far as I can see, that as discourse is a closure, and yet as it is good discourse will move toward completeness, the language that finds and deserves hearing reaches somehow beyond its synecdochic—its incomplete—nature. This brings us back to the question I started with: How do we earn an audience? What voice gets a justified hearing?

In classical rhetoric texts, among the explorations of the inventive processes by means of which a person searches out an argument, works to formulate a predication, and ransacks all possible good resources to shape and strengthen a work, it is common to find great and thoughtful consideration given to how an argument gets to an audience. Persuasion may be effected, Aristotle said, through the audience, by the arguments, or by the character of the speaker. For the moment at least using *persuasion* to mean earning, if not winning over, an audience, let us consider these three possibilities.

Of the first, little need be said. Emotional appeal, the arousal of feelings in the audience, is and has been common in all kinds of discourse, from advertisements and sermons to political speeches and on to quiet and thoughtful poems. If the blatant and dishonest cigarette commercial depends upon emotional appeal, so too does Goldsmith's "The Deserted Village." Emotional appeal is not inherently reprehensible, and can never be simply abandoned. Still, we have already more supply than need of emotional arguments—shouting, lying, cheating, using others as objects to be manipulated—in whatever form they appear.

More crucial to the question of finding a voice are those other modes: Persuasion can be effected by the nature of the argument itself and by the character of the speaker.

"Persuasion," Aristotle said, "is effected by the arguments, when we demonstrate the truth, real or apparent, by such means as inhere in particular cases." Logical argument, to be sure, is under pronounced and growing attack: "The simple painful task of putting ideas together logically, so that they 'track' or 'follow' each other, as we say, doesn't seem to appeal to many of us any more."[4] We have heard reason attacked as a mask for the preservation of injustice and the status quo; yet, as Wayne C. Booth has remarked, "even if the older forms of rationality were limited, our need for them is as great as ever,"[5] for surely "wherever men find themselves too impatient to think together about their problems, wherever immediate action based on unity becomes more important than men's determination to achieve genuine unity by discovering the truth together,"[6] there honest inquiry and honest language must soon or late disappear.

Our ideas, we hope, will be lucid; they will "track," we hope, from first principles critically won and not thoughtlessly assumed. Only so may we *give* ourselves "with the truth adhering."[7] Beyond the range of certitude particularly, it is crucial that we give ourselves in our utterances. Given the synecdochic character of our statements, we may expect that there will be many versions of truth; some may earn hearing by the nature of their argument; others may earn hearing by the honesty of their giving, shaped and informed by the lucidity of their thinking. Of this last kind of argument, appeal through the character of the speaker, Aristotle wrote in *Rhetoric:*

The character of the speaker is a cause of persuasion when the speech is so uttered as to make him worthy of belief; for as a rule we trust men of probity more, and more quickly, about things in general, while on points outside the realm of exact knowledge, where opinion is divided, we trust them absolutely. This trust, however, should be created by the speech itself, and not left to depend upon an antecedent impression that the speaker is this or that kind of man. It is not true, as some writers on the art maintain, that the probity of the speaker contributes nothing to his persuasiveness; on the contrary, we might almost affirm that his character is the most potent of all the means to persuasion.

This trust, we should note again, "should be created by the speech itself." All that can save sentences, Robert Frost once said, "is the speaking tone of voice somehow entangled in the words and fastened to the page for the ear of the imagination. That is all that can save poetry from sing-song,

[4]Wayne C. Booth, "Now Don't Try to Reason with Me: Rhetoric Today, Left, Right, and Center," *The University of Chicago Magazine,* LX (November 1967), 12.

[5]*Ibid.,* p. 13.

[6]*Ibid.,* p. 18.

[7]F. J. Sheed, "My Life on the Street Corner," *Saturday Review* (May 10, 1969), p. 22.

all that can save prose from itself."[8] It has been put in other ways: "Genuine speech is the expression of a genuine personality. . . . Because it takes pains to make itself intelligible, it assumes that the hearer is a genuine personality too—in other words, wherever it is spoken it creates a community."[9]

Against the community achievable through *logical argument* (lucid, "tracking" ideas) and *ethical argument* (not argument from some ethical system, but from the appeal of *ethos*, a genuine person speaking), uncreating words resonate about us. Word piles on word, ill-shaped meaning on ill-shaped meaning, assumed meaning on assumed meaning until we are deafened by the sound, all too often the sound of pride, or of ignorance, or of rampant feeling. To some extent, confusion of meaning and ambiguity of meaning may be both inevitable and desirable. They may be inevitable in the sense I have already pointed out, that our utterances are always incomplete, and in the sense that Geoffrey Wagner has mentioned, that "we are, in short, our own enchanted listeners."[10] We may hear ourselves, not another; *his* words may act only as a trigger to release *our* words, unlocking not his meaning, but one we already possessed. And this ambiguity and confusion may be desirable in the sense that the provisionary quality of words is a stay against absolutism.

Still, people caught forever in their own meanings scarcely find communion; people in a crowded world can scarcely take wholly virtuous action when they are caught in meanings that are only theirs.

How, then, may we recover from our own incompleteness? How shall we learn to listen to others who seek to do so? The provisionary quality of words determines that there shall be no single answer. Indeed, discourse most often fails because speakers and writers assume that they have a single answer, that their voices are already endowed with all worth.

## On the Form of the Book

Many cannot conceive why form should be allowed to impede the expression of honest hearts. The reason lies in one of the limitations imposed upon man: unformed expression is ever tending toward ignorance. Good intention is primary, but it is never enough. . . .

Richard M. Weaver, *Ideas Have Consequences*

The matter is not simple. Countless voices, both worthy and otherwise, have won hearings, some gaining an audience in their own time, some only after the passage of time had brought new versions of truth, new audiences with new needs who would listen. It would be good, and easier for us, if we

---

[8]From the introduction to "A Way Out," quoted in "The Speaking Voice," Reuben Brower, reprinted in *The Study of Literature*, Sylvan Barnet, Morton Berman, William Burto, eds. (Boston, 1960), p. 160.

[9]Northrop Frye, *The Well-Tempered Critic* (Bloomington, Ind., 1963), p. 41.

[10]Geoffrey Wagner, *On the Wisdom of Words* (Princeton, 1968), p. 218.

could look about us, hear and read human statements, and discover that only those statements of cohesive, tracking logic earn a hearing. Desirable as that may be, it is not the case. It would be good, and in some ways easier for us, if we could look about us, hear and read human statements, and discover that only good people earn a hearing. But neither is that the case. Aristotle based ethical appeal on intelligence, character, and goodwill, but as Otis M. Walter has said, "The trinity of Aristotle cannot explain many whose styles of thought, styles of living, and styles of hair-do are cherished and imitated. Aristotle's analysis may be a good statement of whom we *ought* to believe, but it is inadequate to account for many in whom we *do* believe."[11] Many have found ethical appeal in and believed pathological speakers: witness the following attracted by Adolf Hitler.

Indeed, the virtuous and the vicious speaker may make similar appeals to any audience they gain. Otis Walter suggests that the person having ethos for us fulfills a strong need that we perceive as worthy or moral but are unable to fulfill ourselves, the speaker having some sort of exclusive ability to fulfill the need: "Ethos arises only when there is a strong need, only when the need can be best gratified by another, and only when such needs are perceived to be (correctly or incorrectly) worthy."[12] To the extent that this is true, we need not only good voices in that great range beyond certainty, but also defenses against voices:

If ethos arises in seemingly hopeless situations where needs are desperate, then one defense must be to *reduce the needs* that pave the road down which the man on horseback rides. One strong defense against ethos is to reduce starvation, hopelessness, and degradation. In a word, we must prevent the uniform frustration of a whole people. When needs are too strong, people may abandon democratic problem-solving and turn to the father-figure. The process can be stymied by seeing that no single need provides enough fertilizer to nourish the malignant growth of the single "savior.". . . When needs are relatively well satisfied we have a defense against the social pathology of ethos.

Secondly, we may help a society develop immunity to pathological ethos by the educational process of *developing sophistication about which needs are worthy and which are superficial or neurotic*. To whatever extent the human being can refine his own needs, criticize them, suppress some and develop others, to this extent he can existentially create himself and help determine the kinds of people he will admire. One great objective of education should be to create people who will not be subject to neurotic needs. A second defense against the pathology of ethos lies in creating people with a conscious and sophisticated sense of values.

A third defense is that societies must produce *many men who can meet the needs of people*. Ethos does not become strong unless the agent possessing it seems to have some sort of exclusive power to gratify needs. . . . This third defense, that of producing many men who are sensitive to human need and who search for ways of meeting needs, is partly, again, a matter of education.[13]

[11]Otis M. Walter, "Toward an Analysis of Ethos," *Pennsylvania Speech Annual*, XXI (1964), 37.
[12]*Ibid.*, p. 43.
[13]*Ibid.*, p. 44.

Which brings us back to the matter of this book. To the tuning of our own voices and ears, we must bring the knowledge of many voices, of the overt and covert assumptions that guide them, of the substance of what they say, and of their ways of making substance through structure and style, with a fastidious awareness of contexts. To these ends, the book includes many kinds of writing—essays, speeches, poems, fiction, varieties of journalistic writing, and other forms. If it should be objected that poems and short stories, for example, in some ways unlike essays and speeches, exist for their own sake and are not in the usual sense meant as arguments to gain an audience, we should remember that a poem or story emerges from its time and place as a speech does, if for different reasons, that it grows out of assumptions and received versions of truth as a speech does, that it is a voice speaking, to be heard or not.

The readings in each section make some kind of response—thorough or tangential, private or public—to the question that labels the section, thus providing perspectives on a common controversy, necessarily an incomplete survey. In this way, we can observe how people have found voices to speak, or have failed to speak, or have spoken to no avail; it should also be easier for us to understand contexts and to know that language has antecedents and consequences.

Not all of the selections here will speak to us now; not all spoke to an audience when first formulated. Some of the selections that found an audience originally will not find an audience now. Some will find an audience now that did not originally. Not all of the selections will speak directly to the questions set out as labels for the various sections, though all will in some way or other, however indirectly. And they will, in some way, speak to *our* responses to any one of the questions. Our words are not ours alone. Our arguments in a sense are not ours alone. Their fabric is made of threads of meaning laid over and under and around and plaited through the words, of colorings given to words long before we used them, of premises attached to words whether we will it or not. If I use words, then, as if they were only mine, and have not reasoned through my words from first principles, have not heard the words of others, and am oblivious to the meanings others have made, then it seems likely that my statements, while they may contain my meanings, will also contain other meanings that I don't intend, own, control, or understand. Thus, what any person says impinges upon what I say, and all the selections, albeit indirectly, speak to our responses.

I do not pretend that such a variety of readings belongs to any single kind of study. The book begins with a question out of rhetoric and continues to focus on that question, and so belongs to the study of English composition, rhetoric, and speech. But the central question, like the art of rhetoric from which it grows, can act both as a center of study in its own right and as an organizing agency for other kinds of study. Thus, to study how we have spoken over a long period of time, how we have found our subject and made predications, how we have or have not exploited the resources available to us, how we have responded to each other, how we have filled needs in our own time or later, is to enter into the province of history and the humanities in a particularly interesting way, I think, for it seems likely there could be no more revealing history than the history of how we have taken the universe of experience and made predications about it.

Since the book belongs to no single kind of study, I have not adorned it with any of the apparatus peculiar to a single discipline—such things as study questions and theme assignments. I have, however, added two things that may be of some use. The first, Toward Understanding and Responding: Some Exploratory Questions, consists chiefly of a series of specific questions that can usefully be asked of the readings. The questions are pertinent to any selection in the book, and are of such nature that all of them, any part of them, or any single one of them may be asked of a single reading selection. The second guide to study is an alternate table of contents, appearing at the end of the book, that identifies genres and rhetorical structures among the selections.

Otherwise, I think the direction of the book pretty clearly indicates many questions, topics for writing, and possibilities for discussion: Why do we listen to one person rather than to another? How does what one person says enter into what another says? In what ways does the predication of one period of history differ from that of another? How do people accept and use or reject the resources (including assumptions) that their time gives? How do the resources of one time differ from those of another? What kinds of thinking make a predication possible? What kind of relationship exists between the writer and the work?

The questions go on. I have tried to suggest in the introductory notes to the three parts further kinds of questions that might well be asked, further ways of getting into the materials of that part; I have also suggested other themes that emerge in the readings.

To the question originally posed here—How may we make our voices worth hearing?—there is no single answer. There are some things we know, but cannot cleanly grasp except in specific incidents. Emotional appeal, we know, is not in itself reprehensible; but we must look to particular cases to know how an emotional appeal happens, why an emotional appeal is fit or unfit, and specifically, how it seems to work. We know, or should know, the great and primary value of the tracking, logical argument, but again must look to cases to discover how such an argument works and whether it has been found worth hearing. In the great arena of experience beyond the range of certain proof, we know that people and audiences are won by the ethos of a speaker or writer, by the character demonstrated within the discourse itself; but we can only say how this happens by scrutinizing a piece of writing. We know that there will be many combinations of logical, emotional, and ethical arguments, and we know that versions of experience and of the whole creation are presented to us in literary modes not overtly aimed at winning us over, yet still the modes of people speaking to us.

We know that we are what we are because of the voices of many people and so should listen closely to those voices and hear them well. And we should come to know, from hearing good voices and bad, that as we respect our own thoughts, we may feel a responsibility to share them.[14] Finally, we know that those who set out to share their ideas, if they are to do so decently and well, with good cause and virtuous effects, must accept certain responsibilities: *to own* the experience or idea they speak of, fastidiously aware of its background and foreground, thoughtful of its past and future, and *to guarantee* the expression of the experience or idea, giving it the backing of such a history of searching and thinking as will stand scrutiny.[15] They must, that is to say, come and be present in their work, with the truth adhering.

## Toward Understanding and Responding:
## Some Exploratory Questions

The title and introduction to this book suggest a particular and rather extensive line of questions that can and should be raised about the readings here. But not everyone is interested in the same line of questioning, no single line of questioning is ever wholly sufficient, and the readings gathered here are full enough and rich enough to be receptive to many sorts of inquiry. The questions below, then, afford opportunities to explore the readings in directions other than that suggested by the title and introduction. It may be that working out the answer to a single question will lead you to what you need to know about one of the readings. It may be, on some occasions, that you will need to work at a selection through all of the questions raised here, or through some particular sequence of related questions. Such sequences are easily discoverable; the questions often bring up other questions, and the answer to one may lead you backward or forward to another.

### On the Origin of the Work

1.  Can you tell how the subject developed? Does it have the character of a subject already established and accepted as a matter of interest, now to be amplified in a literary work of some kind, or does the subject emerge only as the work itself develops?

2.  Is it possible to discover what ways of thinking led the author—or one of the characters—into the subject and its development?

3.  Is the subject reduced to its parts for discussion or presentation? If so,

[14]See S. Leonard Rubinstein, "From Need to Desire," *College English*, XXIX (November 1967), 126–128.

[15]See Harry H. Crosby and George F. Estey, *College Writing, the Rhetorical Imperative* (New York, 1968), pp. 18ff.

are you still able to track the subject while you are being invited to consider its parts?

4.  In your view is the subject explored for all its potential? Does the author's premise, whether stated or implied or silently present, enable him to see things that we do not see? Does it prevent him from seeing things he should see?

5.  How does the author take his subject? Or look at it? What is his relationship to it? From what point of view does he see it?

6.  Who speaks to you in the selection, an author, a character, some benevolent editorial personage? If the selection is not one having characters in the fictional sense, are we to assume that the author is always speaking in his own right? Has he set out to create in his work a presence who speaks? Is he speaking ironically?

7.  If you know who is speaking, then can you discover what his resources are? What equips him for this work? What resources of his own does he exploit—feelings, beliefs, assumptions both examined and unexamined? What resources does he bring from outside—information, authority, testimony?

8.  If you are able to discover something about the speaker's resources, then see if you can determine why he uses certain kinds of resources and not others. Do his resources, whether internal or external, allow him to fulfill his work, or do they prevent him from doing so?

9.  Who is the audience for the work? What difference does it make? Is the nature of the audience discernible in the text? Does the author accommodate his audience in any way?

10. How does the speaker seek to take his subject to his audience? Does he wish to move us, to sway our feelings, or to inform us? Does he speak directly or indirectly to us, or to whatever audience he has?

## On the Structure of the Work

1.  Is there a locatable, recognizable thesis that can be isolated, or are the selection and its thesis identical, the whole work being required to work out a thesis, or predication of some kind? Does it make any difference?

2.  Where does the speaker slow down to give fuller attention to some things, and where does he speed up to move quickly by others? What effect has this tempo on the mood and quality of the work?

3.  Does the work belong to some established literary genre? If so, to what ends does it use the conventions of that genre?

4.  If not of a particular literary genre, does the work utilize a traditional or common form of organization? If so, why? What is gained for the work by the use of a known and previously used structure?

5.  Is the structure of the work instead entirely unique? If so, what is gained for the work?

## On the Style of the Work

1. What simple information can you gather about the language of the work? Is the diction sententious, Latinate, curt, pompous, denotative, connotative, figurative, sober, plain?

2. Of what consequence is this information? What is gained or lost for the work by the qualities of diction you have discovered?

3. What simple information can you gather about the sentences? How long are they? In what ways, if any, do they vary? What kinds of sentences are they? Can you account for variations in complexity? How do they begin? Are there sentences that control the development of a whole selection or of parts of a whole selection?

4. Of what consequence is this information? What qualities does it enable us to see in the work?

5. How do parts of the work fit together? Why do they fit together in one way rather than in another?

6. How do these stylistic features reveal the stance and character of the speaker? What do they reveal about him? If the speaker is a character within a work, does he know what his style reveals about him?

## On the Occasion of the Work

1. Is the work in your view intended as persuasion?

2. Does the work seem to be an expository account of or an emotional celebration of something in the present, a critical or historical or persuasive exploration of something that happened in the past, or an argumentative exhortation for or against something yet to happen? In other words, to what time does it address itself? Does its style fit its time?

3. Can you discover how the work was received in its own time? If there is a difference between the way it was originally received and the way it is presently received, how do you account for it?

Where Can We Live?

We have been fugitives on the earth, and now elsewhere, seeking out our place, sometimes deliberately and adventurously, sometimes accidentally and meekly, sometimes alone, sometimes caught up in great migrations, finding it sometimes here close by, sometimes out there in a far blue distance, finding it to settle for a moment or an era, only to move on with change and new need. As we move on to new places, the tempo of our life changes and with it all that we do and all that we are. The families that left Sweet Auburn for the city, Goldsmith knew, did not simply change their addresses; they moved from a world dominated by people and the rhythms of nature to a world dominated by things, and so, for better or worse, became different from what they had been.

Involved in this central question, "Where Can We Live?" there are, then, many vital and vexatious questions, many themes growing and shifting, some of which are specified as section headings. The speakers in some of the readings that follow will seem to ask the central question again and again — Where has our place been? Where will our place be hereafter? Certainly *The Book of Ruth* and *Wanderer* and the poems of William Stafford give themselves to the question. In other readings speakers will seem sure of their place and therefore free to think more intently about what they will make of it — for example, in the essays by Wernick and Udall. Others, from Thoreau to Jane Jacobs, along with their many interests, will speculate upon how big a place and a society can be and upon how much or how little will suffice to organize and govern the places where we live, and some (for example, Glenn T. Seaborg) in their exploration of the places where we live will introduce the intricate issues of technological development. In some way or other all will speak of the sometime rural, sometime urban organization of our societies and of what it means to shift from one to the other; some, including Goldsmith and Crane, will speak directly of our transition from a rural to an urban society; and occasionally one, Paul Simon for instance, will show how our landscape changes. Some of the readings that follow examine change itself. Miss Emily in Faulkner's story refuses to admit change, but some, especially Joseph Wood Krutch, Edwin Godsey, and John Graves, will know in their bones, however sadly, that the world does change, that the place where we live is not the last place on earth or in the cosmos, and that when we find a new place we will find with it some good things and some bad things and will have left forever behind some good things and some bad things.

There are, then, in the central question that labels this group of readings, many other questions, and so, of course, there are many ways of speaking to these questions, and many voices speaking. As they speak, there are many opportunities to investigate what a person is like in the place where he is — whether he be Ulysses, or Mr. Flood, or Rhysling, and there are many moods, from the happy acquiescence of Robert Wernick to the elegiac if undeceived awareness of John Graves and George Garrett. For the issue is complex, and many voices have asked where we shall live and what we shall be like, whether in some happy spot near Auburn or in the great reaches of space, or only in those desert places that stretch on inside us all.

15

# Where do we belong?

# Genesis

## Chapter 3

Now the serpent was more subtil than any beast of the field which the LORD God had made. And he said unto the woman, Yea, hath God said, Ye shall not eat of every tree of the garden?

2 And the woman said unto the serpent, We may eat of the fruit of the trees of the garden:

3 But of the fruit of the tree which *is* in the midst of the garden, God hath said, Ye shall not eat of it, neither shall ye touch it, lest ye die.

4 And the serpent said unto the woman, Ye shall not surely die:

5 For God doth know that in the day ye eat thereof, then your eyes shall be opened, and ye shall be as gods, knowing good and evil.

6 And when the woman saw that the tree *was* good for food, and that it *was* pleasant to the eyes, and a tree to be desired to make *one* wise, she took of the fruit thereof, and did eat, and gave also unto her husband with her; and he did eat.

7 And the eyes of them both were opened, and they knew that they *were* naked; and they sewed fig leaves together, and made themselves aprons.

8 And they heard the voice of the LORD God walking in the garden in the cool of the day: and Adam and his wife hid themselves from the presence of the LORD God amongst the trees of the garden.

9 And the LORD God called unto Adam, and said unto him, Where *art* thou?

10 And he said, I heard thy voice in the garden, and I was afraid, because I *was* naked; and I hid myself.

11 And he said, Who told thee that thou *wast* naked? Hast thou eaten of the tree, whereof I commanded thee that thou shouldest not eat?

12 And the man said, The woman whom thou gavest *to be* with me, she gave me of the tree, and I did eat.

13 And the Lord God said unto the woman, What *is* this *that* thou hast done? And the woman said, The serpent beguiled me, and I did eat.

14 And the Lord God said unto the serpent, Because thou hast done this, thou *art* cursed above all cattle, and above every beast of the field; upon thy belly shalt thou go, and dust shalt thou eat all the days of thy life:

15 And I will put enmity between thee and the woman, and between thy seed and her seed; it shall bruise thy head, and thou shalt bruise his heel.

16 Unto the woman he said, I will greatly multiply thy sorrow and thy conception; in sorrow thou shalt bring forth children; and thy desire *shall be* to thy husband, and he shall rule over thee.

17 And unto Adam he said, Because thou hast hearkened unto the voice of thy wife, and hast eaten of the tree, of which I commanded thee, saying, Thou shalt not eat of it: cursed *is* the ground for thy sake; in sorrow shalt thou eat *of* it all the days of thy life;

18 Thorns also and thistles shall it bring forth to thee; and thou shalt eat the herb of the field;

19 In the sweat of thy face shalt thou eat bread, till thou return unto the ground; for out of it wast thou taken: for dust thou *art*, and unto dust shalt thou return.

20 And Adam called his wife's name Eve; because she was the mother of all living.

21 Unto Adam also and to his wife did the Lord God make coats of skins, and clothed them.

22 And the Lord God said, Behold, the man is become as one of us, to know good and evil: and now, lest he put forth his hand, and take also of the tree of life, and eat, and live for ever:

23 Therefore the Lord God sent him forth from the garden of Eden, to till the ground from whence he was taken.

24 So he drove out the man; and he placed at the east of the garden of Eden Cherubims, and a flaming sword which turned every way, to keep the way of the tree of life.

## Chapter 4

And Adam knew Eve his wife; and she conceived, and bare Cain, and said, I have gotten a man from the Lord.

2 And she again bare his brother Abel. And Abel was a keeper of sheep, but Cain was a tiller of the ground.

3 And in process of time it came to pass, that Cain brought of the fruit of the ground an offering unto the Lord.

4 And Abel, he also brought of the firstlings of his flock and of the fat thereof. And the Lord had respect unto Abel and to his offering:

5 But unto Cain and to his offering he had not respect. And Cain was very wroth, and his countenance fell.

6 And the Lord said unto Cain, Why art thou wroth? and why is thy countenance fallen?

7 If thou doest well, shalt thou not be accepted? and if thou doest not well, sin lieth at the door. And unto thee *shall be* his desire, and thou shalt rule over him.

8 And Cain talked with Abel his brother: and it came to pass, when they were in the field, that Cain rose up against Abel his brother, and slew him.

9 And the Lord said unto Cain, Where *is* Abel thy brother? And he said, I know not: *Am* I my brother's keeper?

10 And he said, What hast thou done? the voice of thy brother's blood crieth unto me from the ground.

11 And now *art* thou cursed from the earth, which hath opened her mouth to receive thy brother's blood from thy hand;

12 When thou tillest the ground, it shall not henceforth yield unto thee her strength; a fugitive and a vagabond shalt thou be in the earth.

13 And Cain said unto the Lord, My punishment *is* greater than I can bear.

14 Behold, thou hast driven me out this day from the face of the earth; and from thy face shall I be hid; and I shall be a fugitive and a vagabond in the earth; and it shall come to pass, *that* every one that findeth me shall slay me.

15 And the Lord said unto him, Therefore whosoever slayeth Cain, vengeance shall be taken on him sevenfold. And the Lord set a mark upon Cain, lest any finding him should kill him.

16 And Cain went out from the presence of the Lord, and dwelt in the land of Nod, on the east of Eden.

17 And Cain knew his wife; and she conceived, and bare Enoch: and he builded a city, and called the name of the city, after the name of his son, Enoch.

18 And unto Enoch was born Irad: and Irad begat Mehujael: and Mehujael begat Methusael: and Methusael begat Lamech.

19 And Lamech took unto him two wives: the name of the one *was* Adah, and the name of the other Zillah.

20 And Adah bare Jabal: he was the father of such as dwell in tents, and *of such as have* cattle.

21 And his brother's name *was* Jubal: he was the father of all such as handle the harp and organ.

22 And Zillah, she also bare Tubal-cain, an instructor of every artificer in brass and iron: and the sister of Tubal-cain *was* Naamah.

23 And Lamech said unto his wives, Adah and Zillah, Hear my

voice; ye wives of Lamech, hearken unto my speech: for I have slain a man to my wounding, and a young man to my hurt.

24 If Cain shall be avenged sevenfold, truly Lamech seventy and sevenfold.

25 And Adam knew his wife again; and she bare a son, and called his name Seth: For God, *said she*, hath appointed me another seed instead of Abel, whom Cain slew.

26 And to Seth, to him also there was born a son; and he called his name Enos: then began men to call upon the name of the LORD.

(c. 950 B.C.)

# Psalm 137

By the rivers of Babylon, there we sat down, yea, we wept, when we remembered Zion.

2 We hanged our harps upon the willows in the midst thereof.

3 For there they that carried us away captive required of us a song; and they that wasted us *required of us* mirth, *saying*, Sing us *one* of the songs of Zion.

4 How shall we sing the LORD's song in a strange land?

5 If I forget thee, O Jerusalem, let my right hand forget *her cunning.*

6 If I do not remember thee, let my tongue cleave to the roof of my mouth; if I prefer not Jerusalem above my chief joy.

7 Remember, O LORD, the children of Edom in the day of Jerusalem; who said, Rase *it*, rase *it*, *even* to the foundation thereof.

8 O daughter of Babylon, who art to be destroyed; happy *shall he be*, that rewardeth thee as thou hast served us.

9 Happy *shall he be*, that taketh and dasheth thy little ones against the stones.

(c. 900 B.C.)

# The Book of Ruth

### Chapter 1

Now it came to pass in the days when the judges ruled, that there was a famine in the land. And a certain man of Bethlehem-judah went to sojourn in the country of Moab, he, and his wife, and his two sons.

2 And the name of the man *was* Elimelech, and the name of his wife Naomi, and the name of his sons Mahlon and Chilion, Ephrathites of Bethlehem-judah. And they came into the country of Moab, and continued there.

3 And Elimelech Naomi's husband died; and she was left, and her two sons.

4 And they took them wives of the women of Moab: the name of the one *was* Orpah, and the name of the other Ruth: and they dwelled there about ten years.

5 And Mahlon and Chilion died also both of them; and the woman was left of her two sons and her husband.

6 Then she arose with her daughters in law, that she might return from the country of Moab: for she had heard in the country of Moab how that the Lord had visited his people in giving them bread.

7 Wherefore she went forth out of the place where she was, and her two daughters in law with her; and they went on the way to return unto the land of Judah.

8 And Naomi said unto her two daughters in law, Go, return each to her mother's house: the Lord deal kindly with you, as ye have dealt with the dead, and with me.

9 The Lord grant you that ye may find rest, each *of you* in the house of her husband. Then she kissed them; and they lifted up their voice, and wept.

10 And they said unto her, Surely we will return with thee unto thy people.

11 And Naomi said, Turn again, my daughters: why will ye go with me? *are* there yet *any more* sons in my womb, that they may be your husbands?

12 Turn again, my daughters, go *your way;* for I am too old to have an husband. If I should say, I have hope, *if* I should have an husband also to night, and should also bear sons;

13 Would ye tarry for them till they were grown? would ye stay for them from having husbands? nay, my daughters; for it grieveth me much for your sakes that the hand of the Lord is gone out against me.

14 And they lifted up their voice, and wept again: and Orpah kissed her mother in law; but Ruth clave unto her.

15 And she said, Behold, thy sister in law is gone back unto her people, and unto her gods: return thou after thy sister in law.

16 And Ruth said, Intreat me not to leave thee, *or* to return from following after thee: for whither thou goest, I will go; and where thou lodgest, I will lodge: thy people *shall be* my people, and thy God my God:

17 Where thou diest, will I die, and there will I be buried: the Lord do so to me, and more also, *if ought* but death part thee and me.

18 When she saw that she was stedfastly minded to go with her, then she left speaking unto her.

19 So they two went until they came to Bethlehem. And it came to

pass, when they were come to Bethlehem, that all the city was moved about them, and they said, *Is* this Naomi?

20 And she said unto them, Call me not Naomi, call me Mara: for the Almighty hath dealt very bitterly with me.

21 I went out full, and the LORD hath brought me home again empty: why *then* call ye me Naomi, seeing the LORD hath testified against me, and the Almighty hath afflicted me?

22 So Naomi returned, and Ruth the Moabitess, her daughter in law, with her, which returned out of the country of Moab: and they came to Bethlehem in the beginning of barley harvest.

## Chapter 2

And Naomi had a kinsman of her husband's, a mighty man of wealth, of the family of Elimelech; and his name *was* Boaz.

2 And Ruth the Moabitess said unto Naomi, Let me now go to the field, and glean ears of corn after *him* in whose sight I shall find grace. And she said unto her, Go, my daughter.

3 And she went, and came, and gleaned in the field after the reapers: and her hap was to light on a part of the field *belonging* unto Boaz, who *was* of the kindred of Elimelech.

4 And, behold, Boaz came from Bethlehem, and said unto the reapers, The LORD *be* with you. And they answered him, The LORD bless thee.

5 Then said Boaz unto his servant that was set over the reapers, Whose damsel *is* this?

6 And the servant that was set over the reapers answered and said, It *is* the Moabitish damsel that came back with Naomi out of the country of Moab:

7 And she said, I pray you, let me glean and gather after the reapers among the sheaves: so she came, and hath continued even from the morning until now, that she tarried a little in the house.

8 Then said Boaz unto Ruth, Hearest thou not, my daughter? Go not to glean in another field, neither go from hence, but abide here fast by my maidens:

9 *Let* thine eyes *be* on the field that they do reap, and go thou after them: have I not charged the young men that they shall not touch thee? and when thou art athirst, go unto the vessels, and drink of *that* which the young men have drawn.

10 Then she fell on her face, and bowed herself to the ground, and said unto him, Why have I found grace in thine eyes, that thou shouldest take knowledge of me, seeing I *am* a stranger?

11 And Boaz answered and said unto her, It hath fully been shewed me, all that thou hast done unto thy mother in law since the death of thine husband: and *how* thou hast left thy father and thy mother, and

the land of thy nativity, and art come unto a people which thou knewest not heretofore.

12 The LORD recompense thy work, and a full reward be given thee of the LORD God of Israel, under those wings thou art come to trust.

13 Then she said, Let me find favour in thy sight, my lord; for that thou hast comforted me, and for that thou hast spoken friendly unto thine handmaid, though I be not like unto one of thine handmaidens.

14 And Boaz said unto her, At mealtime come thou hither, and eat of the bread, and dip thy morsel in the vinegar. And she sat beside the reapers: and he reached her parched *corn,* and she did eat, and was sufficed, and left.

15 And when she was risen up to glean, Boaz commanded his young men, saying, Let her glean even among the sheaves, and reproach her not:

16 And let fall also *some* of the handfuls of purpose for her, and leave *them,* that she may glean *them,* and rebuke her not.

17 So she gleaned in the field until even, and beat out that she had gleaned: and it was about an ephah of barley.

18 And she took *it* up, and went into the city: and her mother in law saw what she had gleaned: and she brought forth, and gave to her that she had reserved after she was sufficed.

19 And her mother in law said unto her, Where hast thou gleaned to day? and where wroughtest thou? blessed be he that did take knowledge of thee. And she shewed her mother in law with whom she had wrought, and said, The man's name with whom I wrought to day *is* Boaz.

20 And Naomi said unto her daughter in law, Blessed *be* he of the LORD, who hath not left off his kindness to the living and to the dead. And Naomi said unto her, The man *is* near of kin unto us, one of our next kinsmen.

21 And Ruth the Moabitess said, He said unto me also, Thou shalt keep fast by my young men, until they have ended all my harvest.

22 And Naomi said unto Ruth her daughter in law, *It is* good, my daughter, that thou go out with his maidens, that they meet thee not in any other field.

23 So she kept fast by the maidens of Boaz to glean unto the end of barley harvest and of wheat harvest; and dwelt with her mother in law.

## Chapter 3

Then Naomi her mother in law said unto her, My daughter, shall I not seek rest for thee, that it may be well with thee?

2 And now *is* not Boaz of our kindred, with whose maidens thou wast? Behold, he winnoweth barley to night in the threshingfloor.

3 Wash thyself therefore, and anoint thee, and put thy raiment upon thee, and get thee down to the floor: *but* make not thyself known unto the man, until he shall have done eating and drinking.

4 And it shall be, when he lieth down, that thou shalt mark the place where he shall lie, and thou shalt go in, and uncover his feet, and lay thee down; and he will tell thee what thou shalt do.

5 And she said unto her, All that thou sayest unto me I will do.

6 And she went down unto the floor, and did according to all that her mother in law bade her.

7 And when Boaz had eaten and drunk, and his heart was merry, he went to lie down at the end of the heap of corn: and she came softly, and uncovered his feet, and laid her down.

8 And it came to pass at midnight, that the man was afraid, and turned himself: and, behold, a woman lay at his feet.

9 And he said, Who *art* thou? And she answered, I *am* Ruth thine handmaid: spread therefore thy skirt over thine handmaid; for thou *art* a near kinsman.

10 And he said, Blessed *be* thou of the LORD, my daughter: *for* thou hast shewed more kindness in the latter end than at the beginning, inasmuch as thou followedst not young men, whether poor or rich.

11 And now, my daughter, fear not; I will do to thee all that thou requirest: for all the city of my people doth know that thou *art* a virtuous woman.

12 And now it is true that I *am thy* near kinsman: howbeit there is a kinsman nearer than I.

13 Tarry this night, and it shall be in the morning, *that* if he will perform unto thee the part of a kinsman, well; let him do the kinsman's part: but if he will not do the part of a kinsman to thee, then will I do the part of a kinsman to thee, *as* the LORD liveth: lie down until the morning.

14 And she lay at his feet until the morning: and she rose up before one could know another. And he said, Let it not be known that a woman came into the floor.

15 Also he said, Bring the vail that *thou hast* upon thee, and hold it. And when she held it, he measured six *measures* of barley, and laid *it* on her: and she went into the city.

16 And when she came to her mother in law, she said, Who *art* thou, my daughter? And she told her all that the man had done to her.

17 And she said, These six *measures* of barley gave he me; for he said to me, Go not empty unto thy mother in law.

18 Then said she, Sit still, my daughter, until thou know how the matter will fall: for the man will not be in rest, until he have finished the thing this day.

## Chapter 4

Then went Boaz up to the gate, and sat him down there: and, behold, the kinsman of whom Boaz spake came by; unto whom he said, Ho, such a one! turn aside, sit down here. And he turned aside, and sat down.

2 And he took ten men of the elders of the city, and said, Sit ye down here. And they sat down.

3 And he said unto the kinsman, Naomi, that is come again out of the country of Moab, selleth a parcel of land, which *was* our brother Elimelech's:

4 And I thought to advertise thee, saying, Buy *it* before the inhabitants, and before the elders of my people. If thou wilt redeem *it*, redeem *it:* but if thou wilt not redeem *it, then* tell me, that I may know: for *there is* none to redeem *it* beside thee; and I *am* after thee. And he said, I will redeem *it.*

5 Then said Boaz, What day thou buyest the field of the hand of Naomi, thou must buy *it* also of Ruth the Moabitess, the wife of the dead, to raise up the name of the dead upon his inheritance.

6 And the kinsman said, I cannot redeem *it* for myself, lest I mar mine own inheritance: redeem thou my right to thyself; for I cannot redeem *it.*

7 Now this *was the manner* in former time in Israel concerning redeeming and concerning changing, for to confirm all things; a man plucked off his shoe, and gave *it* to his neighbour: and this *was* a testimony in Israel.

8 Therefore the kinsman said unto Boaz, Buy *it* for thee. So he drew off his shoe.

9 And Boaz said unto the elders, and *unto* all the people, Ye *are* witnesses this day, that I have bought all that *was* Elimelech's, and all that *was* Chilion's and Mahlon's, of the hand of Naomi.

10 Moreover Ruth the Moabitess, the wife of Mahlon, have I purchased to be my wife, to raise up the name of the dead upon his inheritance, that the name of the dead be not cut off from among his brethren, and from the gate of his place: ye *are* witnesses this day.

11 And all the people that *were* in the gate, and the elders, said, *We are* witnesses. The Lord make the woman that is come into thine house like Rachel and like Leah, which two did build the house of Israel: and do thou worthily in Ephratah, and be famous in Bethlehem:

12 And let thy house be like the house of Pharez, whom Tamar bare unto Judah, of the seed which the Lord shall give thee of this young woman.

13 So Boaz took Ruth, and she was his wife: and when he went in unto her, the Lord gave her conception, and she bare a son.

14 And the women said unto Naomi, Blessed *be* the Lord, which hath not left thee this day without a kinsman, that his name may be famous in Israel.

15 And he shall be unto thee a restorer of *thy* life, and a nourisher of thine old age: for thy daughter in law, which loveth thee, which is better to thee than seven sons, hath born him.

16 And Naomi took the child, and laid it in her bosom, and became nurse unto it.

17 And the women her neighbours gave it a name, saying, There is a son born to Naomi; and they called his name Obed: he *is* the father of Jesse, the father of David.

18 Now these *are* the generations of Pharez: Pharez begat Hezron,

19 And Hezron begat Ram, and Ram begat Amminadab,

20 And Amminadab begat Nahshon, and Nahshon begat Salmon,

21 And Salmon begat Boaz, and Boaz begat Obed,

22 And Obed begat Jesse, and Jesse begat David.

(c. 500 B.C.)

# The Wanderer*

Oft the lone man learns the favor,
the grace of God, though go he must
his ways on the deep, dreary and long,
arouse with hands the rime-cold sea,
fare far from home; fate is unswerving.
So quoth the wanderer, of woes mindful,
of fell slaughters, fall of dear ones:
　　"Oft at each daybreak I am doomed alone
to bewail my cares. Not one now is alive
that I to him openly dare
to say my mind. For sooth I know
that is a worthy wont in a kemp
that fast he bind his breast and keep
his thoughts to himself, think as he will.
No weary mood can ward a man,
no hot head can give help against fate;
therefore he that holds high his good name
oft binds in his bosom the bitter thought.
So I must fetter, lock fast my mood,
oft hounded with care, of home bereft,
far from fellows, friends and kinsmen,
since that day by-gone when the dark, the earth,
hid my gold-friend, and I got me thence,
outcast, winter-sad, over ice-bound waves,
with heavy mood a hearth to seek
where I far or nigh might find a lord,

*Translation by Kemp Malone.

a man in mead-hall mindful of me,
one to befriend me, the friendless waif,
treat me kindly. They ken, the wise,
how grim a mate grief is to him
who lives without a loved master.
The wanderer's path, not wound gold, holds him,
a breast frozen, not bliss of earth.
He minds the guests in hall, the gift-taking,
how at the board in years of youth his gold-friend
gave him tokens; gone is kindness, all.
For that he learns who long must fare without
his beloved leader's lore, wise sayings,
when sorrow and sleep at the same time together
press oft and bind the poor lone one:
to him it seems in mood that his sweet master
he clips and kisses, and clasps at knee
with hands and head, as whilom then
when in days of yore he yet held the throne.
The friendless wight awakes at last,
the fallow flood before him sees,
the birds bathing, broadening their feathers,
frost, snow and hail falling mingled.
Then are the heavier the heart's death-wounds,
sore for the loved one; sorrow is renewed.
Then the mood becomes mindful of kinsmen,
greets them with gladness, gazes fondly
at sight of his fellows; they swim oft away;
the life of the fleeting ones brings little there
of the words he kens; care is renewed
for him who must send his soul wandering
over the ice-bound waves, his weary heart.
Therefore I cannot this world besee
without thinking thoughts of darkness,
when I the life wholly behold of kemps,
how the hall they in haste gave up,
the mood-bold thanes. So this middle-earth
with every day down sinks and falls.
Not one can be wise at once, ere he own
winters in the world. The wise man is patient,
not too hot-headed nor too hasty-tongued,
nor too weak a fighter, nor too foolish-minded,
nor too fearful nor too fain nor too fee-greedy,
never too bold at boasting ere he know the better rede.
The spearman, moved to speak a vow,
must wait, bide his time, till well he know

what turn his mood will take at last.
The tried kemp must grasp how ghastly it will be
when the weal of this world stands waste wholly,
as now in many a spot through this middle-earth
the wind-blown walls stand waste, befrosted,
the abodes of men lie buried in snow,
the wine-halls are dust in the wind, the rulers
dead, stripped of glee; — the dright all fell,
by the wall the proud sought shield. War took off some,
brought some away; a bird took one
over the high sea-flood; the hoar-grey wolf
dealt death to one; with dreary cheer
a kemp hid one in a cave of earth.
So the Maker of men made this borough waste
till all stood idle, the old work of giants,
without the din of dwellers in hall."
    He then, wise in soul, with weighty thought
thinks deeply upon this darksome life,
this fallen fastness, far and oft minds
much spilling of blood, and speaks these words:
    "Where came the horse, where the rider, where the ring-giver?
Where came the house of feasting? Where is hall-gladness?
Alas, the bright mead-cup! Alas, the mailed fighter!
Alas, the prince's power! Past is that time,
grown dark in the night, as if it never were!
Where the tried warriors once trod stands now
a wall wondrous high, with worm-shapes dight.
The might of spears, of maces death-greedy,
and fate, that famed one, they felled the kemps,
and the storm beats down upon these stone shelters,
the falling snow binds fast the ground,
the blaring winter. Then blackness comes,
night-shades darken, the north sends out
fierce falls of hail to the fright of kemps.
Altogether hard is this earthly kingdom,
the word of the fates shifts the world under heaven.
Here kine are fleeting, here kin are fleeting,
here men are fleeting, here mates are fleeting,
all this earthly frame grows idle at last."
    So quoth the sage, sat apart in thought.
He is good who holds troth, his grief must he never
from his breast speak too soon, unless boot first he know
to win boldly. He does well to seek help
of his Father above, where our bliss all stands.

                                                     (c. 750 A.D.)

*Ludwig van Beethoven*

# The Heiligenstadt Testament

To Caspar Anton Carl and [Nikolaus Johann] van Beethoven

Heiligenstadt, October 6, 1802

For my Brothers Carl and [Johann] Beethoven

O my fellow men, who consider me, or describe me as, unfriendly, peevish or even misanthropic, how greatly do you wrong me. For you do not know the secret reason why I appear to you to be so. Ever since my childhood my heart and soul have been imbued with the tender feeling of goodwill; and I have always been ready to perform even great actions. But just think, for the last six years I have been afflicted with an incurable complaint which has been made worse by incompetent doctors. From year to year my hopes of being cured have gradually been shattered and finally I have been forced to accept the prospect of a *permanent infirmity* (the curing of which may perhaps take years or may even prove to be impossible). Though endowed with a passionate and lively temperament and even fond of the distractions offered by society I was soon obliged to seclude myself and live in solitude. If at times I decided just to ignore my infirmity, alas! how cruelly was I then driven back by the intensified sad experience of my poor hearing. Yet I could not bring myself to say to people: "Speak up, shout, for I am deaf." Alas! how could I possibly refer to the impairing *of a sense* which in me should be more perfectly developed than in other people, a sense which at one time I possessed in the greatest perfection, even to a degree of perfection such as assuredly few in my profession possess or have ever possessed—Oh, I cannot do it; so forgive me, if you ever see me withdrawing from your company which I used to enjoy. Moreover my misfortune pains me doubly, inasmuch as it leads to my being misjudged. For me there can be no relaxation in human society, no refined conversations, no mutual confidences. I must live quite alone and may creep into society only as often as sheer necessity demands; I must live like an outcast. If I appear in company I am overcome by a burning anxiety, a fear that I am running the risk of letting people notice my condition—And that has been my experience during the last six months which I have spent in the country. My sensible doctor by suggesting that I should spare my hearing as much as possible has more or less encouraged my present natural inclination, though indeed when carried away now and then by my instinctive desire for human society, I have let myself be tempted to seek it. But how humiliated I have felt if somebody standing beside me heard the sound of a flute in the distance and *I heard nothing*, or if somebody heard *a shepherd sing* and again I heard nothing—Such experiences almost made me despair, and I was on the point of putting an end to my life—The only thing that held me back was *my art*. For indeed it seemed to me impossible to leave this world before I had produced all the works that I felt the urge to compose; and thus I have dragged on this miserable existence — a truly miserable existence, seeing that I have such a sensitive body that any fairly sudden change can plunge me from the best spirits into the worst of humours — *Patience* — that is the virtue, I am told, which I must now choose for my guide; and I now possess it — I hope that I shall persist in my resolve to endure to the end, until it pleases the inexorable Parcae to cut the thread; perhaps my condition will improve, perhaps not; at any rate I am now resigned — At the early age of 28 I was obliged to become a philosopher, though this was not easy; for indeed this is more difficult for an artist than for anyone else — Almighty God, who look down into my innermost soul, you see into my heart and you know that it is filled with love for humanity and a desire to do good. Oh my fellow men, when some day you read this statement, remember that you have done me wrong; and let some unfortunate man derive comfort from the thought that he has found another equally unfortunate who, notwithstanding all the obstacles imposed by nature, yet did everything in his power to be raised to the rank of noble artists and human beings. — And you, my brothers Carl and [Johann], when I am dead, request on my behalf Professor Schmidt, if he is still living, to describe my disease, and attach this written document to his record, so that after my death at any rate the world and I may be reconciled as far as possible — At the same time I herewith nominate you both heirs to my small property (if I may so describe it) — Divide it honestly, live in harmony and help one another. You know that you have long ago been forgiven for the harm you did me. I again thank you, my brother Carl, in particular, for the affection you have shown me of late years. My wish is that you should have a better and more carefree existence than I have had. Urge your children to be *virtuous*, for virtue alone can make a man happy. Money cannot do this. I speak from experience. It was virtue that sustained me in my misery. It was thanks to virtue and also to my art that I did not put an end to my life by suicide — Farewell and love one another — I thank all my friends, and especially *Prince Lichnowsky* and *Professor Schmidt*. I would like Prince L[ichnowsky]'s instruments to be preserved by one of you, provided this does not lead to a quarrel between you. But as soon as they can serve a more useful purpose, just sell them; and how glad I shall be if in my grave I can still be of some use to you both — Well, that is all — Joyfully I go to meet Death — should it come before I have had an opportunity of developing all my artistic gifts, then in spite of my hard fate it would still come too soon, and no doubt I would like it to postpone its coming — Yet even so I should be content, for would it not free me from a condition of continual suffering? Come then, Death, *whenever* you like, and with courage I will go to meet you — Farewell; and when I am dead, do not wholly forget me. I deserve to be remembered by you, since during my lifetime I have often thought of you and tried to make you happy — Be happy —

Ludwig van Beethoven

For my brothers Carl and [Johann]
To be read and executed after my death —
Heiligenstadt, October 10, 1802 — Thus I take leave of you — and, what is
more, rather sadly — yes, the hope I cherished — the hope I brought with
me here of being cured to a certain extent at any rate — that hope I must
now abandon completely. As the autumn leaves fall and wither, likewise — that hope has faded for me. I am leaving here — almost in the same
condition as I arrived — Even that high courage — which has often inspired me on fine summer days — has vanished — Oh Providence — do but
grant me one day *of pure joy* — For so long now the inner echo of real joy
has been unknown to me — Oh when — oh when, Almighty God — shall I be
able to hear and feel this echo again in the temple of Nature and in
contact with humanity — Never? — No! — Oh, that would be too hard.

Ludwig van Beethoven

### *Alfred, Lord Tennyson*

# Ulysses

It little profits that an idle king,
By this still hearth, among these barren crags,
Matched with an aged wife, I mete and dole
Unequal laws unto a savage race,
That hoard, and sleep, and feed, and know not me.

I cannot rest from travel; I will drink
Life to the lees: all times I have enjoyed
Greatly, have suffered greatly, both with those
That loved me, and alone; on shore, and when
Through scudding drifts the rainy Hyades
Vexed the dim sea: I am become a name;
For always roaming with a hungry heart
Much have I seen and known: cities of men
And manners, climates, councils, governments,
Myself not least, but honored of them all;
And drunk delight of battle with my peers,
Far on the ringing plains of windy Troy.
I am a part of all that I have met;
Yet all experience is an arch wherethrough
Gleams that untraveled world, whose margin fades

For ever and for ever when I move.
How dull it is to pause, to make an end,
To rust unburnished, not to shine in use!
As though to breathe were life. Life piled on life
Were all too little, and of one to me
Little remains; but every hour is saved
From that eternal silence, something more,
A bringer of new things; and vile it were
For some three suns to store and hoard myself,
And this gray spirit yearning in desire
To follow knowledge like a sinking star,
Beyond the utmost bound of human thought.

    This is my son, mine own Telemachus,
To whom I leave the scepter and the isle —
Well-loved of me, discerning to fulfill
This labor, by slow prudence to make mild
A rugged people, and through soft degrees
Subdue them to the useful and the good.
Most blameless is he, centered in the sphere
Of common duties, decent not to fail
In offices of tenderness, and pay
Meet adoration to my household gods,
When I am gone. He works his work, I mine.

    There lies the port; the vessel puffs her sail;
There gloom the dark broad seas. My mariners,
Souls that have toiled, and wrought, and thought with me —
That ever with a frolic welcome took
The thunder and the sunshine, and opposed
Free hearts, free foreheads — you and I are old;
Old age hath yet his honor and his toil;
Death closes all; but something ere the end,
Some work of noble note, may yet be done,
Not unbecoming men that strove with Gods.
The lights begin to twinkle from the rocks;
The long day wanes; the slow moon climbs; the deep
Moans round with many voices. Come, my friends,
'Tis not too late to seek a newer world.
Push off, and sitting well in order smite
The sounding furrows; for my purpose holds
To sail beyond the sunset, and the baths
Of all the western stars, until I die.
It may be that the gulfs will wash us down;
It may be we shall touch the Happy Isles,
And see the great Achilles, whom we knew.

Though much is taken, much abides; and though
We are not now that strength which in old days
Moved earth and heaven, that which we are, we are;
One equal temper of heroic hearts,
Made weak by time and fate, but strong in will
To strive, to seek, to find, and not to yield.

(1842)

## Robert Browning

# Fra Lippo Lippi

I am poor brother Lippo, by your leave!
You need not clap your torches to my face.
Zooks, what's to blame? you think you see a monk!
What, 'tis past midnight, and you go the rounds,
And here you catch me at an alley's end
Where sportive ladies leave their doors ajar?
The Carmine's my cloister; hunt it up,
Do—harry out, if you must show your zeal,
Whatever rat, there, haps on his wrong hole,
And nip each softling of a wee white mouse,
*Weke, weke*, that's crept to keep him company!
Aha, you know your betters! Then, you'll take
Your hand away that's fiddling on my throat,
And please to know me likewise. Who am I?
Why, one, sir, who is lodging with a friend
Three streets off—he's a certain . . . how d' ye call?
Master—a . . . Cosimo of the Medici,
I' the house that caps the corner. Boh! you were best!
Remember and tell me, the day you're hanged,
How you affected such a gullet's gripe!
But you, sir, it concerns you that your knaves
Pick up a manner nor discredit you;
Zooks, are we pilchards, that they sweep the streets
And count fair prize what comes into their net?
He's Judas to a tittle, that man is!
Just such a face! Why, sir, you make amends.
Lord, I'm not angry! Bid your hangdogs go

Drink out this quarter-florin to the health
Of the munificent House that harbors me
(And many more beside, lads! more beside!)
And all's come square again! I'd like his face—
His, elbowing on his comrade in the door
With the pike and lantern—for the slave that holds
John Baptist's head a-dangle by the hair
With one hand ("Look you, now," as who should say)
And his weapon in the other, yet unwiped!
It's not your chance to have a bit of chalk,
A wood-coal or the like? or you should see!
Yes, I'm the painter, since you style me so.
What, brother Lippo's doings, up and down,
You know them and they take you? like enough!
I saw the proper twinkle in your eye—
Tell you, I liked your looks at very first.
Let's sit and set things straight now, hip to haunch.
Here's spring come, and the nights one makes up bands
To roam the town and sing out carnival,
And I've been three weeks shut within my mew,
A-painting for the great man, saints and saints
And saints again. I could not paint all night—
Ouf! I leaned out of window for fresh air.
There came a hurry of feet and little feet,
A sweep of lute strings, laughs, and whifts of song—
*Flower o' the broom,*
*Take away love, and our earth is a tomb!*
*Flower o' the quince,*
*I let Lisa go, and what good in life since?*
*Flower o' the thyme*—and so on. Round they went.
Scarce had they turned the corner when a titter
Like the skipping of rabbits by moonlight—three slim shapes,
And a face that looked up . . . zooks, sir, flesh and blood,
That's all I'm made of! Into shreds it went,
Curtain and counterpane and coverlet,
All the bed furniture—a dozen knots,
There was a ladder! Down I let myself,
Hands and feet, scrambling somehow, and so dropped,
And after them. I came up with the fun
Hard by Saint Laurence, hail fellow, well met—
*Flower o' the rose,*
*If I've been merry, what matter who knows?*
And so as I was stealing back again
To get to bed and have a bit of sleep
Ere I rise up tomorrow and go work
On Jerome knocking at his poor old breast

With his great round stone to subdue the flesh,
You snap me of a sudden. Ah, I see!
Though your eye twinkles still, you shake your head—
Mine's shaved—a monk, you say—the sting's in that!
If Master Cosimo announced himself,
Mum's the word naturally; but a monk!
Come, what am I a beast for? tell us, now!
I was a baby when my mother died
And father died and left me in the street.
I starved there, God knows how, a year or two
On fig skins, melon parings, rinds, and shucks,
Refuse and rubbish. One fine frosty day,
My stomach being empty as your hat,
The wind doubled me up, and down I went.
Old Aunt Lapaccia trussed me with one hand
(Its fellow was a stinger as I knew),
And so along the wall, over the bridge,
By the straight cut to the convent. Six words there,
While I stood munching my first bread that month:
"So, boy, you're minded," quoth the good fat father,
Wiping his own mouth—'twas refection time—
"To quit this very miserable world?
Will you renounce" . . . "the mouthful of bread?" thought I;
By no means! Brief, they made a monk of me;
I did renounce the world, its pride and greed,
Palace, farm, villa, shop, and banking house,
Trash, such as these poor devils of Medici
Have given their hearts to—all at eight years old.
Well, sir, I found in time, you may be sure,
'Twas not for nothing—the good bellyful,
The warm serge, and the rope that goes all round,
And day-long blessed idleness beside!
"Let's see what the urchin's fit for"—that came next.
Not overmuch their way, I must confess.
Such a to-do! They tried me with their books;
Lord, they'd have taught me Latin in pure waste!
*Flower o' the clove,*
*All the Latin I construe is "amo," I love!*
But, mind you, when a boy starves in the streets
Eight years together, as my fortune was,
Watching folk's faces to know who will fling
The bit of half-stripped grape-bunch he desires,
And who will curse or kick him for his pains—
Which gentleman processional and fine,
Holding a candle to the Sacrament,
Will wink and let him lift a plate and catch

The droppings of the wax to sell again,
Or holla for the Eight and have him whipped—
How say I?—nay, which dog bites, which lets drop
His bone from the heap of offal in the street—
Why, soul and sense of him grow sharp alike;
He learns the look of things, and none the less
For admonition from the hunger pinch.
I had a store of such remarks, be sure,
Which, after I found leisure, turned to use.
I drew men's faces on my copy books,
Scrawled them within the antiphonary's marge,
Joined legs and arms to the long music-notes,
Found eyes and nose and chin for A's and B's,
And made a string of pictures of the world
Betwixt the ins and outs of verb and noun,
On the wall, the bench, the door. The monks looked black.
"Nay," quoth the Prior, "turn him out, d'ye say?
In no wise. Lose a crow and catch a lark.
What if at last we get our man of parts,
We Carmelites, like those Camaldolese
And Preaching Friars, to do our church up fine
And put the front on it that ought to be!"
And hereupon he bade me daub away.
Thank you! my head being crammed, the walls a blank,
Never was such prompt disemburdening.
First, every sort of monk, the black and white,
I drew them, fat and lean; then, folk at church,
From good old gossips waiting to confess
Their cribs of barrel droppings, candle ends—
To the breathless fellow at the altar foot,
Fresh from his murder, safe and sitting there
With the little children round him in a row
Of admiration, half for his beard and half
For that white anger of his victim's son
Shaking a fist at him with one fierce arm,
Signing himself with the other because of Christ
(Whose sad face on the cross sees only this
After the passion of a thousand years),
Till some poor girl, her apron o'er her head
(Which the intense eyes looked through), came at eve
On tiptoe, said a word, dropped in a loaf,
Her pair of earrings, and a bunch of flowers
(The brute took growling), prayed, and so was gone.
I painted all, then cried, " 'Tis ask and have;
Choose, for more's ready!"—laid the ladder flat,
And showed my covered bit of cloister wall.

The monks closed in a circle and praised loud
Till checked, taught what to see and not to see,
Being simple bodies—"That's the very man!
Look at the boy who stoops to pat the dog!
That woman's like the Prior's niece who comes
To care about his asthma; it's the life!"
But there my triumph's straw-fire flared and funked;
Their betters took their turn to see and say;
The Prior and the learned pulled a face
And stopped all that in no time. "How? what's here?
Quite from the mark of painting, bless us all!
Faces, arms, legs, and bodies like the true
As much as pea and pea! It's devil's game!
Your business is not to catch men with show,
With homage to the perishable clay,
But lift them over it, ignore it all,
Make them forget there's such a thing as flesh.
Your business is to paint the souls of men—
Man's soul, and it's a fire, smoke . . . no, it's not . . .
It's vapor done up like a new-born babe
(In that shape when you die it leaves your mouth)—
It's . . . well, what matters talking, it's the soul!
Give us no more of body than shows soul!
Here's Giotto, with his Saint a-praising God,
That sets us praising—why not stop with him?
Why put all thoughts of praise out of our head
With wonder at lines, colors, and what not?
Paint the soul, never mind the legs and arms!
Rub all out, try at it a second time.
Oh, that white smallish female with the breasts,
She's just my niece . . . Herodias, I would say—
Who went and danced and got men's heads cut off!
Have it all out!" Now, is this sense, I ask?
A fine way to paint soul, by painting body
So ill the eye can't stop there, must go further
And can't fare worse! Thus, yellow does for white
When what you put for yellow's simply black,
And any sort of meaning looks intense
When all beside itself means and looks naught.
Why can't a painter lift each foot in turn,
Left foot and right foot, go a double step,
Make his flesh liker and his soul more like,
Both in their order? Take the prettiest face,
The Prior's niece . . . patron saint—is it so pretty
You can't discover if it means hope, fear,
Sorrow, or joy? won't beauty go with these?

Suppose I've made her eyes all right and blue,
Can't I take breath and try to add life's flash,
And then add soul and heighten them three-fold?
Or say there's beauty with no soul at all
(I never saw it—put the case the same);
If you get simple beauty and naught else,
You get about the best thing God invents—
That's somewhat; and you'll find the soul you have missed,
Within yourself, when you return him thanks.
"Rub all out!" Well, well, there's my life, in short,
And so the thing has gone on ever since.
I'm grown a man no doubt, I've broken bounds;
You should not take a fellow eight years old
And make him swear to never kiss the girls.
I'm my own master, paint now as I please—
Having a friend, you see, in the Corner-house!
Lord, it's fast holding by the rings in front—
Those great rings serve more purposes than just
To plant a flag in, or tie up a horse!
And yet the old schooling sticks, the old grave eyes
Are peeping o'er my shoulder as I work,
The heads shake still—"It's art's decline, my son!
You're not of the true painters, great and old;
Brother Angelico's the man, you'll find;
Brother Lorenzo stands his single peer—
Fag on at flesh, you'll never make the third!"
*Flower o' the pine,*
*You keep your mistr . . . manners, and I'll stick to mine!*
I'm not the third, then; bless us, they must know!
Don't you think they're the likeliest to know,
They with their Latin? So, I swallow my rage,
Clench my teeth, suck my lips in tight, and paint
To please them—sometimes do and sometimes don't;
For, doing most, there's pretty sure to come
A turn, some warm eve finds me at my saints—
A laugh, a cry, the business of the world
(*Flower o' the peach,*
*Death for us all, and his own life for each!*)—
And my whole soul revolves, the cup runs over,
The world and life's too big to pass for a dream,
And I do these wild things in sheer despite,
And play the fooleries you catch me at,
In pure rage! The old mill-horse, out at grass
After hard years, throws up his stiff heels so,
Although the miller does not preach to him
The only good of grass is to make chaff.

What would men have? Do they like grass or no—
May they or mayn't they? All I want's the thing
Settled forever one way. As it is,
You tell too many lies and hurt yourself;
You don't like what you only like too much,
You do like what, if given you at your word,
You find abundantly detestable.
For me, I think I speak as I was taught;
I always see the garden and God there
A-making man's wife; and, my lesson learned—
The value and significance of flesh—
I can't unlearn ten minutes afterwards.

You understand me; I'm a beast, I know.
But see, now—why, I see as certainly
As that the morning star's about to shine,
What will hap some day. We've a youngster here
Comes to our convent, studies what I do,
Slouches and stares and lets no atom drop.
His name is Guidi—he'll not mind the monks—
They call him Hulking Tom; he lets them talk;
He picks my practice up—he'll paint apace,
I hope so—though I never live so long,
I know what's sure to follow. You be judge!
You speak no Latin more than I, belike;
However, you're my man, you've seen the world—
The beauty and the wonder and the power,
The shapes of things, their colors, lights, and shades,
Changes, surprises—and God made it all!
—For what? Do you feel thankful, aye or no,
For this fair town's face, yonder river's line,
The mountain round it and the sky above,
Much more the figures of man, woman, child,
These are the frame to? What's it all about?
To be passed over, despised? or dwelt upon,
Wondered at? Oh, this last of course!—you say.
But why not do as well as say—paint these
Just as they are, careless what comes of it?
God's works—paint any one, and count it crime
To let a truth slip. Don't object, "His works
Are here already; nature is complete:
Suppose you reproduce her—which you can't—
There's no advantage! you must beat her, then."
For, don't you mark? we're made so that we love
First when we see them painted, things we have passed
Perhaps a hundred times nor cared to see;

And so they are better, painted—better to us,
Which is the same thing. Art was given for that;
God uses us to help each other so,
Lending our minds out. Have you noticed, now,
Your cullion's hanging face? A bit of chalk,
And trust me but you should, though! How much more,
If I drew higher things with the same truth!
That were to take the Prior's pulpit-place,
Interpret God to all of you! Oh, oh,
It makes me mad to see what men shall do
And we in our graves! This world's no blot for us,
Nor blank; it means intensely, and means good—
To find its meaning is my meat and drink.
"Aye, but you don't so instigate to prayer!"
Strikes in the Prior; "when your meaning's plain,
It does not say to folk—remember matins,
Or, mind you fast next Friday!" Why, for this
What need of art at all? A skull and bones,
Two bits of stick nailed crosswise, or, what's best,
A bell to chime the hour with does as well.
I painted a Saint Laurence six months since
At Prato, splashed the fresco in fine style;
"How looks my painting, now the scaffold's down?"
I ask a brother. "Hugely," he returns—
"Already not one phiz of your three slaves
Who turn the Deacon off his toasted side,
But's scratched and prodded to our heart's content,
The pious people have so eased their own
With coming to say prayers there in a rage;
We get on fast to see the bricks beneath.
Expect another job this time next year,
For pity and religion grow i' the crowd—
Your painting serves its purpose!" Hang the fools!

     —That is—you'll not mistake an idle word
Spoke in a huff by a poor monk, God wot,
Tasting the air this spicy night, which turns
The unaccustomed head like Chianti wine!
Oh, the church knows! don't misreport me, now!
It's natural a poor monk out of bounds
Should have his apt word to excuse himself;
And hearken how I plot to make amends.
I have bethought me: I shall paint a piece
. . . There's for you! Give me six months, then go, see
Something in Sant' Ambrogio's! Bless the nuns!
They want a cast o' my office. I shall paint

God in the midst, Madonna and her babe,
Ringed by a bowery, flowery angel brood,
Lilies and vestments and white faces, sweet
As puff on puff of grated orris root
When ladies crowd to Church at midsummer.
And then i' the front, of course a saint or two—
Saint John, because he saves the Florentines,
Saint Ambrose, who puts down in black and white
The convent's friends and gives them a long day,
And Job, I must have him there past mistake,
The man of Uz (and Us without the z,
Painters who need his patience). Well, all these
Secured at their devotion, up shall come
Out of a corner when you least expect,
As one by a dark stair into a great light,
Music and talking, who but Lippo! I!—
Mazed, motionless, and moonstruck—I'm the man!
Back I shrink—what is this I see and hear?
I, caught up with my monk's-things by mistake,
My old serge gown and rope that goes all round,
I, in this presence, this pure company!
Where's a hole, where's a corner for escape?
Then steps a sweet angelic slip of a thing
Forward, puts out a soft palm: "Not so fast!"
—Addresses the celestial presence, "Nay,
He made you and devised you, after all,
Though he's none of you! Could Saint John there draw—
His camel-hair make up a painting-brush?
We come to brother Lippo for all that,
*Iste perfecit opus!"* So, all smile—
I shuffle sideways with my blushing face
Under the cover of a hundred wings
Thrown like a spread of kirtles when you're gay
And play hot cockles, all the doors being shut,
Till, wholly unexpected, in there pops
The hothead husband! Thus I scuttle off
To some safe bench behind, not letting go
The palm of her, the little lily thing
That spoke the good word for me in the nick,
Like the Prior's niece . . . Saint Lucy, I would say.
And so all's saved for me, and for the church
A pretty picture gained. Go, six months hence!
Your hand, sir, and good-by; no lights, no lights!
The street's hushed, and I know my own way back,
Don't fear me! There's the gray beginning. Zooks!

(1855)

**Stephen Crane**

# The Bride Comes to Yellow Sky

## 1

The great Pullman was whirling onward with such dignity of motion that a glance from the window seemed simply to prove that the plains of Texas were pouring eastward. Vast flats of green grass, dull-hued spaces of mesquit and cactus, little groups of frame houses, woods of light and tender trees, all were sweeping into the east, sweeping over the horizon, a precipice.

A newly married pair had boarded this coach at San Antonio. The man's face was reddened from many days in the wind and sun, and a direct result of his new black clothes was that his brick-coloured hands were constantly performing in a most conscious fashion. From time to time he looked down respectfully at his attire. He sat with a hand on each knee, like a man waiting in a barber's shop. The glances he devoted to other passengers were furtive and shy.

The bride was not pretty, nor was she very young. She wore a dress of blue cashmere, with small reservations of velvet here and there, and with steel buttons abounding. She continually twisted her head to regard her puff sleeves, very stiff, straight, and high. They embarrassed her. It was quite apparent that she had cooked, and that she expected to cook, dutifully. The blushes caused by the careless scrutiny of some passengers as she had entered the car were strange to see upon this plain, under-class countenance, which was drawn in placid, almost emotionless lines.

They were evidently very happy. "Ever been in a parlour-car before?" he asked, smiling with delight.

"No," she answered; "I never was. It's fine, ain't it?"

"Great! And then after a while we'll go forward to the diner, and get a big lay-out. Finest meal in the world. Charge a dollar."

"Oh, do they?" cried the bride. "Charge a dollar? Why, that's too much—for us—ain't it, Jack?"

"Not this trip, anyhow," he answered bravely. "We're going to go the whole thing."

Later he explained to her about the trains. "You see, it's a thousand miles from one end of Texas to the other; and this train runs right across it, and never stops but four times." He had the pride of an owner. He pointed out to her the dazzling fittings of the coach; and in truth her eyes opened wider as she contemplated the sea-green figured velvet, the shining brass, silver, and glass, the wood that gleamed as darkly brilliant as the surface of a pool of oil. At one end a bronze figure sturdily held a support for a separated chamber, and at convenient places on the ceiling were frescos in olive and silver.

To the minds of the pair, their surroundings reflected the glory of their marriage that morning in San Antonio; this was the environment of their new estate; and the man's face in particular beamed with an elation that made him appear ridiculous to the negro porter. This individual at times surveyed them from afar with an amused and superior grin. On other occasions he bullied them with skill in ways that did not make it exactly plain to them that they were being bullied. He subtly used all the manners of the most unconquerable kind of snobbery. He oppressed them; but of this oppression they had small knowledge, and they speedily forgot that infrequently a number of travellers covered them with stares of derisive enjoyment. Historically there was supposed to be something infinitely humorous in their situation.

"We are due in Yellow Sky at 3:42," he said, looking tenderly into her eyes.

"Oh, are we?" she said, as if she had not been aware of it. To evince surprise at her husband's statement was part of her wifely amiability. She took from a pocket a little silver watch; and as she held it before her, and stared at it with a frown of attention, the new husband's face shone.

"I bought it in San Anton' from a friend of mine," he told her gleefully.

"It's seventeen minutes past twelve," she said, looking up at him with a kind of shy and clumsy coquetry. A passenger, noting this play, grew excessively sardonic, and winked at himself in one of the numerous mirrors.

At last they went to the dining-car. Two rows of negro waiters, in glowing white suits, surveyed their entrance with the interest, and also the equanimity, of men who had been forewarned. The pair fell to the lot of a waiter who happened to feel pleasure in steering them through their meal. He viewed them with the manner of a fatherly pilot, his countenance radiant with benevolence. The patronage, entwined with the ordinary deference, was not plain to them. And yet, as they returned to their coach, they showed in their faces a sense of escape.

To the left, miles down a long purple slope, was a little ribbon of mist where moved the keening Rio Grande. The train was approaching it at an angle, and the apex was Yellow Sky. Presently it was apparent that, as the distance from Yellow Sky grew shorter, the husband became commensurately restless. His brick-red hands were more insistent in their prominence. Occasionally he was even rather absent-minded and far-away when the bride leaned forward and addressed him.

As a matter of truth, Jack Potter was beginning to find the shadow of a deed weigh upon him like a leaden slab. He, the town marshal of Yellow Sky, a man known, liked, and feared in his corner, a prominent person, had gone to San Antonio to meet a girl he believed he loved, and there, after the usual prayers, had actually induced her to marry him, without consulting Yellow Sky for any part of the transaction. He was now bringing his bride before an innocent and unsuspecting community.

Of course people in Yellow Sky married as it pleased them, in accordance with a general custom; but such was Potter's thought of his duty to his friends, or of their idea of his duty, or of an unspoken form which does not control men in these matters, that he felt he was heinous. He had committed an extraordinary crime. Face to face with this girl in San Antonio, and spurred by his sharp impulse, he had gone headlong over all the social hedges. At San Antonio he was like a man hidden in the dark. A knife to sever any friendly duty, any form, was easy to his hand in that remote city. But the hour of Yellow Sky—the hour of daylight—was approaching.

He knew full well that his marriage was an important thing to his town. It could only be exceeded by the burning of the new hotel. His friends could not forgive him. Frequently he had reflected on the advisability of telling them by telegraph, but a new cowardice had been upon him. He feared to do it. And now the train was hurrying him toward a scene of amazement, glee, and reproach. He glanced out of the window at the line of haze swinging slowly in toward the train.

Yellow Sky had a kind of brass band, which played painfully, to the delight of the populace. He laughed without heart as he thought of it. If the citizens could dream of his prospective arrival with his bride, they would parade the band at the station and escort them, amid cheers and laughing congratulations, to his adobe home.

He resolved that he would use all the devices of speed and plainscraft in making the journey from the station to his house. Once within that safe citadel, he could issue some sort of vocal bulletin, and then not go among the citizens until they had time to wear off a little of their enthusiasm.

The bride looked anxiously at him. "What's worrying you, Jack?"

He laughed again. "I'm not worrying, girl; I'm only thinking of Yellow Sky."

She flushed in comprehension.

A sense of mutual guilt invaded their minds and developed a finer tenderness. They looked at each other with eyes softly aglow. But Potter often laughed the same nervous laugh; the flush upon the bride's face seemed quite permanent.

The traitor to the feelings of Yellow Sky narrowly watched the speeding landscape. "We're nearly there," he said.

Presently the porter came and announced the proximity of Potter's home. He held a brush in his hand, and, with all his airy superiority gone, he brushed Potter's new clothes as the latter slowly turned this way and that way. Potter fumbled out a coin and gave it to the porter, as he had seen others do. It was a heavy and muscle-bound business, as that of a man shoeing his first horse.

The porter took their bag, and as the train began to slow they moved forward to the hooded platform of the car. Presently the two engines and their long string of coaches rushed into the station of Yellow Sky.

"They have to take water here," said Potter, from a constricted throat and in mournful cadence, as one announcing death. Before the train stopped his eye had swept the length of the platform, and he was glad and astonished to see there was none upon it but the station-agent, who, with a slightly hurried and anxious air, was walking toward the water-tanks. When the train had halted, the porter alighted first, and placed in position a little temporary step.

"Come on, girl," said Potter, hoarsely. As he helped her down they each laughed on a false note. He took the bag from the negro, and bade his wife cling to his arm. As they slunk rapidly away, his hang-dog glance perceived that they were unloading the two trunks, and also that the station-agent, far ahead near the baggage-car, had turned and was running toward him, making gestures. He laughed, and groaned as he laughed, when he noted the first effect of his marital bliss upon Yellow Sky. He gripped his wife's arm firmly to his side, and they fled. Behind them the porter stood, chuckling fatuously.

## 2

The California express on the Southern Railway was due at Yellow Sky in twenty-one minutes. There were six men at the bar of the Weary Gentleman saloon. One was a drummer who talked a great deal and rapidly; three were Texans who did not care to talk at that time; and two were Mexican sheep-herders, who did not talk as a general practice in the Weary Gentleman saloon. The barkeeper's dog lay on the board walk that crossed in front of the door. His head was on his paws, and he glanced drowsily here and there with the constant vigilance of a dog that is kicked on occasion. Across the sandy street were some vivid green grass-plots, so wonderful in appearance, amid the sands that burned near them in a blazing sun, that they caused a doubt in the mind. They exactly resembled the grass mats used to represent lawns on the stage. At the cooler end of the railway station, a man without a coat sat in a tilted chair and smoked his pipe. The fresh-cut bank of the Rio Grande circled near the town, and there could be seen beyond it a great plum-coloured plain of mesquite.

Save for the busy drummer and his companions in the saloon, Yellow Sky was dozing. The new-comer leaned gracefully upon the bar, and recited many tales with the confidence of a bard who has come upon a new field.

"—and at the moment that the old man fell downstairs with the bureau in his arms, the old woman was coming up with two scuttles of coal, and of course——"

The drummer's tale was interrupted by a young man who suddenly appeared in the open door. He cried: "Scratchy Wilson's drunk, and has turned loose with both hands." The two Mexicans at once set down their glasses and faded out of the rear entrance of the saloon.

The drummer, innocent and jocular, answered: "All right, old man. S'pose he has? Come in and have a drink, anyhow."

But the information had made such an obvious cleft in every skull in the room that the drummer was obliged to see its importance. All had become instantly solemn. "Say," said he, mystified, "what is this?" His three companions made the introductory gesture of eloquent speech; but the young man at the door forestalled them.

"It means, my friend," he answered, as he came into the saloon, "that for the next two hours this town won't be a health resort."

The barkeeper went to the door, and locked and barred it; reaching out of the window, he pulled in heavy wooden shutters, and barred them. Immediately a solemn, chapel-like gloom was upon the place. The drummer was looking from one to another.

"But say," he cried, "what is this, anyhow? You don't mean there is going to be a gun-fight?"

"Don't know whether there'll be a fight or not," answered one man, grimly; "but there'll be some shootin'—some good shootin'."

The young man who had warned them waved his hand. "Oh, there'll be a fight fast enough, if any one wants it. Anybody can get a fight out there in the street. There's a fight just waiting."

The drummer seemed to be swayed between the interest of a foreigner and a perception of personal danger.

"What did you say his name was?" he asked.

"Scratchy Wilson," they answered in chorus.

"And will he kill anybody? What are you going to do? Does this happen often? Does he rampage around like this once a week or so? Can he break in that door?"

"No; he can't break down that door," replied the barkeeper. "He's tried it three times. But when he comes you'd better lay down on the floor, stranger. He's dead sure to shoot at it, and a bullet may come through."

Thereafter the drummer kept a strict eye upon the door. The time had not yet been called for him to hug the floor, but, as a minor precaution, he sidled near to the wall. "Will he kill anybody?" he said again.

The men laughed low and scornfully at the question.

"He's out to shoot, and he's out for trouble. Don't see any good in experimentin' with him."

"But what do you do in a case like this? What do you do?"

A man responded: "Why, he and Jack Potter——"

"But," in chorus the other men interrupted, "Jack Potter's in San Anton'."

"Well, who is he? What's he got to do with it?"

"Oh, he's the town marshal. He goes out and fights Scratchy when he gets on one of these tears."

"Wow!" said the drummer, mopping his brow. "Nice job he's got."

The voices had toned away to mere whisperings. The drummer wished to ask further questions, which were born of an increasing anxiety and bewilderment; but when he attempted them, the men merely looked at him in irritation and motioned him to remain silent. A tense waiting hush was upon them. In the deep shadows of the room their eyes shone as they listened for sounds from the street. One man made three gestures at the barkeeper; and the latter, moving like a ghost, handed him a glass and a bottle. The man poured a full glass of whisky, and set down the bottle noiselessly. He gulped the whisky in a swallow, and turned again toward the door in immovable silence. The drummer saw that the barkeeper, without a sound, had taken a Winchester from beneath the bar. Later he saw this individual beckoning to him, so he tiptoed across the room.

"You better come with me back of the bar."

"No, thanks," said the drummer, perspiring; "I'd rather be where I can make a break for the back door."

Whereupon the man of bottles made a kindly but peremptory gesture. The drummer obeyed it, and, finding himself seated on a box with his head below the level of the bar, balm was laid upon his soul at sight of various zinc and copper fittings that bore a resemblance to armour-plate. The barkeeper took a seat comfortably upon an adjacent box.

"You see," he whispered, "this here Scratchy Wilson is a wonder with a gun — a perfect wonder; and when he goes on the war-trail, we hunt our holes — naturally. He's about the last one of the old gang that used to hang out along the river here. He's a terror when he's drunk. When he's sober he's all right — kind of simple — wouldn't hurt a fly — nicest fellow in town. But when he's drunk — whoo!"

There were periods of stillness. "I wish Jack Potter was back from San Anton'," said the barkeeper. "He shot Wilson up once — in the leg — and he would sail in and pull out the kinks in this thing."

Presently they heard from a distance the sound of a shot, followed by three wild yowls. It instantly removed a bond from the men in the darkened saloon. There was a shuffling of feet. They looked at each other. "Here he comes," they said.

## 3

A man in a maroon-coloured flannel shirt, which had been purchased for purposes of decoration, and made principally by some Jewish women on the East Side of New York, rounded a corner and walked into the middle of the main street of Yellow Sky. In either hand the man held a long, heavy, blue-black revolver. Often he yelled, and these cries rang through a semblance of a deserted village, shrilly flying over the roofs in a volume that seemed to have no relation to the ordinary vocal strength of a man. It was as if the surrounding stillness formed the arch of a tomb over him. These cries of ferocious challenge rang against walls of silence. And his boots had red tops with gilded imprints, of the kind beloved in winter by little sledding boys on the hillsides of New England.

The man's face flamed in a rage begot of whisky. His eyes, rolling, and yet keen for ambush, hunted the still doorways and windows. He walked with the creeping movement of the midnight cat. As it occurred to him, he roared menacing information. The long revolvers in his hands were as easy as straws; they were moved with an electric swiftness. The little fingers of each hand played sometimes in a musician's way. Plain from the low collar of the shirt, the cords of his neck straightened and sank, straightened and sank, as passion moved him. The only sounds were his terrible invitations. The calm adobes preserved their demeanour at the passing of this small thing in the middle of the street.

There was no offer of fight—no offer of fight. The man called to the sky. There were no attractions. He bellowed and fumed and swayed his revolvers here and everywhere.

The dog of the barkeeper of the Weary Gentleman saloon had not appreciated the advance of events. He yet lay dozing in front of his master's door. At sight of the dog, the man paused and raised his revolver humorously. At sight of the man, the dog sprang up and walked diagonally away, with a sullen head, and growling. The man yelled, and the dog broke into a gallop. As it was about to enter an alley, there was a loud noise, a whistling, and something spat the ground directly before it. The dog screamed, and, wheeling in terror, galloped headlong in a new direction. Again there was a noise, a whistling, and sand was kicked viciously before it. Fear-stricken, the dog turned and flurried like an animal in a pen. The man stood laughing, his weapons at his hips.

Ultimately the man was attracted by the closed door of the Weary Gentleman saloon. He went to it and, hammering with a revolver, demanded drink.

The door remaining imperturbable, he picked a bit of paper from the walk, and nailed it to the framework with a knife. He then turned his back contemptuously upon this popular resort and, walking to the opposite side of the street and spinning there on his heel quickly and lithely, fired at the bit of paper. He missed it by a half-inch. He swore at himself, and went away. Later he comfortably fusilladed the windows of his most intimate friend. The man was playing with this town; it was a toy for him.

But still there was no offer of fight. The name of Jack Potter, his ancient antagonist, entered his mind, and he concluded that it would be a glad thing if he should go to Potter's house, and by bombardment induce him to come out and fight. He moved in the direction of his desire, chanting Apache scalp-music.

When he arrived at it, Potter's house presented the same still front as had the other adobes. Taking up a strategic position, the man howled a challenge. But this house regarded him as might a great stone god. It gave no sign. After a decent wait, the man howled further challenges, mingling with them wonderful epithets.

Presently there came the spectacle of a man churning himself into deepest rage over the immobility of a house. He fumed at it as the winter wind attacks a prairie cabin in the North. To the distance there should have gone the sound of a tumult like the fighting of two hundred Mexicans. As necessity bade him, he paused for breath or to reload his revolvers.

### 4

Potter and his bride walked sheepishly and with speed. Sometimes they laughed together shamefacedly and low.

"Next corner, dear," he said finally.

They put forth the efforts of a pair walking bowed against a strong wind. Potter was about to raise a finger to point the first appearance of the new home when, as they circled the corner, they came face to face with a man in a maroon-coloured shirt, who was feverishly pushing cartridges into a large revolver. Upon the instant the man dropped his revolver to the ground and, like lightning, whipped another from its holster. The second weapon was aimed at the bridegroom's chest.

There was a silence. Potter's mouth seemed to be merely a grave for his tongue. He exhibited an instinct to at once loosen his arm from the woman's grip, and he dropped the bag to the sand. As for the bride, her face had gone as yellow as old cloth. She was a slave to hideous rites, gazing at the apparitional snake.

The two men faced each other at a distance of three paces. He of the revolver smiled with a new and quiet ferocity.

"Tried to sneak up on me," he said. "Tried to sneak up on me!" His eyes grew more baleful. As Potter made a slight movement, the man thrust his revolver venomously forward. "No; don't you do it, Jack Potter. Don't you move a finger toward a gun just yet. Don't you move an eyelash. The time has come for me to settle with you, and I'm goin' to do it my own way, and loaf along with no interferin'. So if you don't want a gun bent on you, just mind what I tell you."

Potter looked at his enemy. "I ain't got a gun on me, Scratchy," he said. "Honest, I ain't." He was stiffening and steadying, but yet somewhere at the back of his mind a vision of the Pullman floated: the sea-green figured velvet, the shining brass, silver, and glass, the wood that gleamed as darkly brilliant as the surface of a pool of oil—all the glory of the marriage, the environment of the new estate. "You know I fight when it comes to fighting, Scratchy Wilson; but I ain't got a gun on me. You'll have to do all the shootin' yourself."

His enemy's face went livid. He stepped forward, and lashed his weapon to and fro before Potter's chest. "Don't you tell me you ain't got no gun on you, you whelp. Don't tell me no lie like that. There ain't a man in Texas ever seen you without no gun. Don't take me for no kid." His eyes blazed with light, and his throat worked like a pump.

"I ain't takin' you for no kid," answered Potter. His heels had not moved an inch backward. "I'm takin' you for a damn fool. I tell you I ain't got a gun, and I ain't. If you're goin' to shoot me up, you better begin now; you'll never get a chance like this again."

So much enforced reasoning had told on Wilson's rage; he was calmer. "If you ain't got a gun, why ain't you got a gun?" he sneered. "Been to Sunday-school?"

"I ain't got a gun because I've just come from San Anton' with my wife. I'm married," said Potter. "And if I'd thought there was going to be any galoots like you prowling around when I brought my wife home, I'd had a gun, and don't you forget it."

"Married!" said Scratchy, not at all comprehending.

"Yes, married. I'm married," said Potter, distinctly.

"Married?" said Scratchy. Seemingly for the first time, he saw the drooping, drowning woman at the other man's side. "No!" he said. He was like a creature allowed a glimpse of another world. He moved a pace backward, and his arm, with the revolver, dropped to his side. "Is this the lady?" he asked.

"Yes; this is the lady," answered Potter.

There was another period of silence.

"Well," said Wilson at last, slowly, "I s'pose it's all off now."

"It's all off if you say so, Scratchy. You know I didn't make the trouble." Potter lifted his valise.

"Well, I 'low it's off, Jack," said Wilson. He was looking at the ground. "Married!" He was not a student of chivalry; it was merely that in the presence of this foreign condition he was a simple child of the earlier plains. He picked up his starboard revolver, and, placing both weapons in their holsters, he went away. His feet made funnel-shaped tracks in the heavy sand.

(1898)

*Edwin Arlington Robinson*

# Mr. Flood's Party

Old Eben Flood, climbing alone one night
Over the hill between the town below
And the forsaken upland hermitage
That held as much as he should ever know
On earth again of home, paused warily.
The road was his with not a native near;
And Eben, having leisure, said aloud;
For no man else in Tilbury Town to hear:

"Well, Mr. Flood, we have the harvest moon
Again, and we may not have many more;
The bird is on the wing, the poet says,
And you and I have said it here before.
Drink to the bird." He raised up to the light
The jug that he had gone so far to fill,
And answered huskily: "Well, Mr. Flood,
Since you propose it, I believe I will."

Alone, as if enduring to the end
A valiant armor of scarred hopes outworn,
He stood there in the middle of the road
Like Roland's ghost winding a silent horn.
Below him, in the town among the trees,
Where friends of other days had honored him,
A phantom salutation of the dead
Rang thinly till old Eben's eyes were dim.

Then, as a mother lays her sleeping child
Down tenderly, fearing it may awake,
He set the jug down slowly at his feet
With trembling care, knowing that most things break;
And only when assured that on firm earth
It stood, as the uncertain lives of men
Assuredly did not, he paced away,
And with his hand extended paused again:

"Well, Mr. Flood, we have not met like this
In a long time; and many a change has come
To both of us, I fear, since last it was
We had a drop together. Welcome home!"
Convivially returning with himself,

50

Again he raised the jug up to the light;
And with an acquiescent quaver said:
"Well, Mr. Flood, if you insist, I might.

"Only a very little, Mr. Flood—
For auld lang syne. No more, sir; that will do."
So, for the time, apparently it did,
And Eben evidently thought so too;
For soon amid the silver loneliness
Of night he lifted up his voice and sang,
Secure, with only two moons listening,
Until the whole harmonious landscape rang—

"For auld lang syne." The weary throat gave out,
The last word wavered; and the song being done,
He raised again the jug regretfully
And shook his head, and was again alone.
There was not much that was ahead of him,
And there was nothing in the town below—
Where strangers would have shut the many doors
That many friends had opened long ago.

(1920)

**Dorothy Parker**

# Hearthside

Half across the world from me
Lie the lands I'll never see—
I, whose longing lives and dies
Where a ship has sailed away;
I, that never close my eyes
But to look upon Cathay.

Things I may not know nor tell
Wait, where older waters swell;
Ways that flowered at Sappho's tread,
Winds that sighed in Homer's strings,
Vibrant with the singing dead,
Golden with the dust of wings.

Under deeper skies than mine,
Quiet valleys dip and shine.
Where their tender grasses heal
Ancient scars of trench and tomb
I shall never walk; nor kneel
Where the bones of poets bloom.

If I seek a lovelier part,
Where I travel goes my heart;
Where I stray my thought must go;
With me wanders my desire.
Best to sit and watch the snow,
Turn the lock, and poke the fire.

(1926)

### *William Butler Yeats*

# Sailing to Byzantium

## 1

That is no country for old men. The young
In one another's arms, birds in the trees,
— Those dying generations — at their song,
The salmon-falls, the mackerel-crowded seas,
Fish, flesh, or fowl, commend all summer long
Whatever is begotten, born, and dies.
Caught in that sensual music all neglect
Monuments of unaging intellect.

## 2

An aged man is but a paltry thing,
A tattered coat upon a stick, unless
Soul clap its hands and sing, and louder sing
For every tatter in its mortal dress,
Nor is there singing school but studying
Monuments of its own magnificence;
And therefore I have sailed the seas and come
To the holy city of Byzantium.

**3**

O sages standing in God's holy fire
As in the gold mosaic of a wall,
Come from the holy fire, perne in a gyre,
And be the singing-masters of my soul.
Consume my heart away; sick with desire
And fastened to a dying animal
It knows not what it is; and gather me
Into the artifice of eternity.

**4**

Once out of nature I shall never take
My bodily form from any natural thing,
But such a form as Grecian goldsmiths make
Of hammered gold and gold enamelling
To keep a drowsy Emperor awake;
Or set upon a golden bough to sing
To lords and ladies of Byzantium
Of what is past, or passing, or to come.

                                        (1928)

### William Faulkner

# A Rose for Emily

**1**

When Miss Emily Grierson died, our whole town went to her funeral:
the men through a sort of respectful affection for a fallen monument,
the women mostly out of curiosity to see the inside of her house, which
no one save an old manservant—a combined gardener and cook—had
seen in at least ten years.

It was a big, squarish frame house that had once been white, decorated with cupolas and spires and scrolled balconies in the heavily light-
some style of the seventies, set on what had once been our most select
street. But garages and cotton gins had encroached and obliterated even
the august names of that neighborhood; only Miss Emily's house was
left, lifting its stubborn and coquettish decay above the cotton wagons

and the gasoline pumps—an eyesore among eyesores. And now Miss Emily had gone to join the representatives of those august names where they lay in the cedar-bemused cemetery among the ranked and anonymous graves of Union and Confederate soldiers who fell at the battle of Jefferson.

Alive, Miss Emily had been a tradition, a duty, and a care; a sort of hereditary obligation upon the town, dating from that day in 1894 when Colonel Sartoris, the mayor—he who fathered the edict that no Negro woman should appear on the streets without an apron—remitted her taxes, the dispensation dating from the death of her father on into perpetuity. Not that Miss Emily would have accepted charity. Colonel Sartoris invented an involved tale to the effect that Miss Emily's father had loaned money to the town, which the town, as a matter of business, preferred this way of repaying. Only a man of Colonel Sartoris' generation and thought could have invented it, and only a woman could have believed it.

When the next generation, with its more modern ideas, became mayors and aldermen, this arrangement created some little dissatisfaction. On the first of the year they mailed her a tax notice. February came, and there was no reply. They wrote her a formal letter, asking her to call at the sheriff's office at her convenience. A week later the mayor wrote her himself, offering to call or to send his car for her, and received in reply a note on paper of an archaic shape, in a thin, flowing calligraphy in faded ink, to the effect that she no longer went out at all. The tax notice was also enclosed, without comment.

They called a special meeting of the Board of Aldermen. A deputation waited upon her, knocked at the door through which no visitor had passed since she ceased giving china-painting lessons eight or ten years earlier. They were admitted by the old Negro into a dim hall from which a stairway mounted into still more shadow. It smelled of dust and disuse—a close, dank smell. The Negro led them into the parlor. It was furnished in heavy, leather-covered furniture. When the Negro opened the blinds of one window, they could see that the leather was cracked; and when they sat down, a faint dust rose sluggishly about their thighs, spinning with slow motes in the single sun-ray. On a tarnished gilt easel before the fireplace stood a crayon portrait of Miss Emily's father.

They rose when she entered—a small, fat woman in black, with a thin gold chain descending to her waist and vanishing into her belt, leaning on an ebony cane with a tarnished gold head. Her skeleton was small and spare; perhaps that was why what would have been merely plumpness in another was obesity in her. She looked bloated, like a body long submerged in motionless water, and of that pallid hue. Her eyes, lost in the fatty ridges of her face, looked like two small pieces of coal pressed into a lump of dough as they moved from one face to another while the visitors stated their errand.

She did not ask them to sit. She just stood in the door and listened quietly until the spokesman came to a stumbling halt. Then they could hear the invisible watch ticking at the end of the gold chain.

Her voice was dry and cold. "I have no taxes in Jefferson. Colonel Sartoris explained it to me. Perhaps one of you can gain access to the city records and satisfy yourselves."

"But we have. We are the city authorities, Miss Emily. Didn't you get a notice from the sheriff, signed by him?"

"I received a paper, yes," Miss Emily said. "Perhaps he considers himself the sheriff . . . I have no taxes in Jefferson."

"But there is nothing on the books to show that, you see. We must go by the—"

"See Colonel Sartoris. I have no taxes in Jefferson."

"But, Miss Emily—"

"See Colonel Sartoris." (Colonel Sartoris had been dead almost ten years.) "I have no taxes in Jefferson. Tobe!" The Negro appeared. "Show these gentlemen out."

## 2

So she vanquished them, horse and foot, just as she had vanquished their fathers thirty years before about the smell. That was two years after her father's death and a short time after her sweetheart—the one we believed would marry her—had deserted her. After her father's death she went out very little; after her sweetheart went away, people hardly saw her at all. A few of the ladies had the temerity to call, but were not received, and the only sign of life about the place was the Negro man—a young man then—going in and out with a market basket.

"Just as if a man—any man—could keep a kitchen properly," the ladies said; so they were not surprised when the smell developed. It was another link between the gross, teeming world and the high and mighty Griersons.

A neighbor, a woman, complained to the mayor, Judge Stevens, eighty years old.

"But what will you have me do about it, madam?" he said.

"Why, send her word to stop it," the woman said. "Isn't there a law?"

"I'm sure that won't be necessary," Judge Stevens said. "It's probably just a snake or a rat that nigger of hers killed in the yard. I'll speak to him about it."

The next day he received two more complaints, one from a man who came in diffident deprecation. "We really must do something about it, Judge. I'd be the last one in the world to bother Miss Emily, but we've got to do something." That night the Board of Aldermen met—three graybeards and one younger man, a member of the rising generation.

"It's simple enough," he said. "Send her word to have her place cleaned up. Give her a certain time to do it in, and if she don't . . ."

"Dammit, sir," Judge Stevens said, "will you accuse a lady to her face of smelling bad?"

So the next night, after midnight, four men crossed Miss Emily's lawn and slunk about the house like burglars, sniffing along the base of the brickwork and at the cellar openings while one of them performed a regular sowing motion with his hand out of a sack slung from his shoulder. They broke open the cellar door and sprinkled lime there, and in all the outbuildings. As they recrossed the lawn, a window that had been dark was lighted and Miss Emily sat in it, the light behind her, and her upright torso motionless as that of an idol. They crept quietly across the lawn and into the shadow of the locusts that lined the street. After a week or two the smell went away.

That was when people had begun to feel really sorry for her. People in our town, remembering how old lady Wyatt, her great-aunt, had gone completely crazy at last, believed that the Griersons held themselves a little too high for what they really were. None of the young men were quite good enough for Miss Emily and such. We had long thought of them as a tableau, Miss Emily a slender figure in white in the background, her father a spraddled silhouette in the foreground, his back to her and clutching a horsewhip, the two of them framed by the back-flung front door. So when she got to be thirty and was still single, we were not pleased exactly, but vindicated; even with insanity in the family she wouldn't have turned down all of her chances if they had really materialized.

When her father died, it got about that the house was all that was left to her; and in a way, people were glad. At last they could pity Miss Emily. Being left alone, and a pauper, she had become humanized. Now she too would know the old thrill and the old despair of a penny more or less.

The day after his death all the ladies prepared to call at the house and offer condolence and aid, as is our custom. Miss Emily met them at the door, dressed as usual and with no trace of grief on her face. She told them that her father was not dead. She did that for three days, with the ministers calling on her, and the doctors, trying to persuade her to let them dispose of the body. Just as they were about to resort to law and force, she broke down, and they buried her father quickly.

We did not say she was crazy then. We believed she had to do that. We remembered all the young men her father had driven away, and we knew that with nothing left, she would have to cling to that which had robbed her, as people will.

## 3

She was sick for a long time. When we saw her again, her hair was cut short, making her look like a girl, with a vague resemblance to those angels in colored church windows — sort of tragic and serene.

The town had just let the contracts for paving the sidewalks, and in the summer after her father's death they began the work. The construction company came with niggers and mules and machinery, and a foreman named Homer Barron, a Yankee—a big, dark, ready man, with a big voice and eyes lighter than his face. The little boys would follow in groups to hear him cuss the niggers, and the niggers singing in time to the rise and fall of picks. Pretty soon he knew everybody in town. Whenever you heard a lot of laughing anywhere about the square, Homer Barron would be in the center of the group. Presently we began to see him and Miss Emily on Sunday afternoons driving in the yellow-wheeled buggy and the matched team of bays from the livery stable.

At first we were glad that Miss Emily would have an interest, because the ladies all said, "Of course a Grierson would not think seriously of a Northerner, a day laborer." But there were still others, older people, who said that even grief could not cause a real lady to forget *noblesse oblige*—without calling it *noblesse oblige*. They just said, "Poor Emily. Her kinsfolk should come to her." She had some kin in Alabama; but years ago her father had fallen out with them over the estate of old lady Wyatt, the crazy woman, and there was no communication between the two families. They had not even been represented at the funeral.

And as soon as the old people said, "Poor Emily," the whispering began. "Do you suppose it's really so?" they said to one another. "Of course it is. What else could . . ." This behind their hands; rustling of craned silk and satin behind jalousies closed upon the sun of Sunday afternoon as the thin, swift clop-clop-clop of the matched team passed: "Poor Emily."

She carried her head high enough—even when we believed that she was fallen. It was as if she demanded more than ever the recognition of her dignity as the last Grierson; as if it had wanted that touch of earthiness to reaffirm her imperviousness. Like when she bought the rat poison, the arsenic. That was over a year after they had begun to say "Poor Emily," and while the two female cousins were visiting her.

"I want some poison," she said to the druggist. She was over thirty then, still a slight woman, though thinner than usual, with cold, haughty black eyes in a face the flesh of which was strained across the temples and about the eye-sockets as you imagine a lighthouse-keeper's face ought to look. "I want some poison," she said.

"Yes, Miss Emily. What kind? For rats and such? I'd recom—"

"I want the best you have. I don't care what kind."

The druggist named several. "They'll kill anything up to an elephant. But what you want is—"

"Arsenic," Miss Emily said. "Is that a good one?"

"Is . . . arsenic? Yes, ma'am. But what you want—"

"I want arsenic."

The druggist looked down at her. She looked back at him, erect, her face like a strained flag. "Why, of course," the druggist said. "If that's what you want. But the law requires you to tell what you are going to use it for."

Miss Emily just stared at him, her head tilted back in order to look him eye for eye, until he looked away and went and got the arsenic and wrapped it up. The Negro delivery boy brought her the package; the druggist didn't come back. When she opened the package at home there was written on the box, under the skull and bones: "For rats."

## 4

So the next day we all said, "She will kill herself"; and we said it would be the best thing. When she had first begun to be seen with Homer Barron, we had said, "She will marry him." Then we said, "She will persuade him yet," because Homer himself had remarked—he liked men, and it was known that he drank with the younger men in the Elks' Club—that he was not a marrying man. Later we said, "Poor Emily" behind the jalousies as they passed on Sunday afternoon in the glittering buggy, Miss Emily with her head high and Homer Barron with his hat cocked and a cigar in his teeth, reins and whip in a yellow glove.

Then some of the ladies began to say that it was a disgrace to the town and a bad example to the young people. The men did not want to interfere, but at last the ladies forced the Baptist minister—Miss Emily's people were Episcopal—to call upon her. He would never divulge what happened during that interview, but he refused to go back again. The next Sunday they again drove about the streets, and the following day the minister's wife wrote to Miss Emily's relations in Alabama.

So she had blood-kin under her roof again and we sat back to watch developments. At first nothing happened. Then we were sure that they were to be married. We learned that Miss Emily had been to the jeweler's and ordered a man's toilet set in silver, with the letters H. B. on each piece. Two days later we learned that she had bought a complete outfit of men's clothing, including a nightshirt, and we said, "They are married." We were really glad. We were glad because the two female cousins were even more Grierson than Miss Emily had ever been.

So we were not surprised when Homer Barron—the streets had been finished some time since—was gone. We were a little disappointed that there was not a public blowing-off, but we believed that he had gone on to prepare for Miss Emily's coming, or to give her a chance to get rid of the cousins. (By that time it was a cabal, and we were all Miss Emily's allies to help circumvent the cousins.) Sure enough, after another week they departed. And, as we had expected all along, within three days Homer Barron was back in town. A neighbor saw the Negro man admit him at the kitchen door at dusk one evening.

And that was the last we saw of Homer Barron. And of Miss Emily for some time. The Negro man went in and out with the market basket, but the front door remained closed. Now and then we would see her at a window for a moment, as the men did that night when they sprinkled the lime, but for almost six months she did not appear on the streets. Then we knew that this was to be expected too; as if that quality of her father which had thwarted her woman's life so many times had been too virulent and too furious to die.

When we next saw Miss Emily, she had grown fat and her hair was turning gray. During the next few years it grew grayer and grayer until it attained an even pepper-and-salt iron-gray, when it ceased turning. Up to the day of her death at seventy-four it was still that vigorous iron-gray, like the hair of an active man.

From that time on her front door remained closed, save for a period of six or seven years, when she was about forty, during which she gave lessons in china-painting. She fitted up a studio in one of the downstairs rooms, where the daughters and granddaughters of Colonel Sartoris' contemporaries were sent to her with the same regularity and in the same spirit that they were sent to church on Sundays with a twenty-five-cent piece for the collection plate. Meanwhile her taxes had been remitted.

Then the newer generation became the backbone and the spirit of the town, and the painting pupils grew up and fell away and did not send their children to her with boxes of color and tedious brushes and pictures cut from the ladies' magazines. The front door closed upon the last one and remained closed for good. When the town got free postal delivery, Miss Emily alone refused to let them fasten the metal numbers above her door and attach a mailbox to it. She would not listen to them.

Daily, monthly, yearly we watched the Negro grow grayer and more stooped, going in and out with the market basket. Each December we sent her a tax notice, which would be returned by the post office a week later, unclaimed. Now and then we would see her in one of the downstairs windows – she had evidently shut up the top floor of the house – like the carven torso of an idol in a niche, looking or not looking at us, we could never tell which. Thus she passed from generation to generation – dear, inescapable, impervious, tranquil, and perverse.

And so she died. Fell ill in the house filled with dust and shadows, with only a doddering Negro man to wait on her. We did not even know she was sick; we had long since given up trying to get any information from the Negro. He talked to no one, probably not even to her, for his voice had grown harsh and rusty, as if from disuse.

She died in one of the downstairs rooms, in a heavy walnut bed with a curtain, her gray head propped on a pillow yellow and moldy with age and lack of sunlight.

**5**

The Negro met the first of the ladies at the front door and let them in, with their hushed, sibilant voices and their quick, curious glances, and then he disappeared. He walked right through the house and out the back and was not seen again.

The two female cousins came at once. They held the funeral on the second day, with the town coming to look at Miss Emily beneath a mass of bought flowers, with the crayon face of her father musing profoundly above the bier and the ladies sibilant and macabre; and the very old men — some in their brushed Confederate uniforms — on the porch and the lawn, talking of Miss Emily as if she had been a contemporary of theirs, believing that they had danced with her and courted her perhaps, confusing time with its mathematical progression, as the old do, to whom all the past is not a diminishing road but, instead, a huge meadow which no winter ever quite touches, divided from them now by the narrow bottleneck of the most recent decade of years.

Already we knew that there was one room in that region above stairs which no one had seen in forty years, and which would have to be forced. They waited until Miss Emily was decently in the ground before they opened it.

The violence of breaking down the door seemed to fill this room with pervading dust. A thin, acrid pall as of the tomb seemed to lie every-where upon this room decked and furnished as for a bridal: upon the valance curtains of faded rose color, upon the rose-shaded lights, upon the dressing table, upon the delicate array of crystal and the man's toilet things backed with tarnished silver, silver so tarnished that the mono-gram was obscured. Among them lay a collar and tie, as if they had just been removed, which, lifted, left upon the surface a pale crescent in the dust. Upon a chair hung the suit, carefully folded; beneath it the two mute shoes and the discarded socks.

The man himself lay in the bed.

For a long while we just stood there, looking down at the profound and fleshless grin. The body had apparently once lain in the attitude of an embrace, but now the long sleep that outlasts love, that conquers even the grimace of love, had cuckolded him. What was left of him, rotted beneath what was left of the nightshirt, had become inextricable from the bed in which he lay; and upon him and upon the pillow beside him lay that even coating of the patient and biding dust.

Then we noticed that in the second pillow was the indentation of a head. One of us lifted something from it, and leaning forward, that faint and invisible dust dry and acrid in the nostrils, we saw a long strand of iron-gray hair.

(1930)

Robert Frost

# Desert Places

Snow falling and night falling fast, oh, fast
In a field I looked into going past,
And the ground almost covered smooth in snow,
But a few weeds and stubble showing last.

The woods around it have it—it is theirs.
All animals are smothered in their lairs.
I am too absent-spirited to count;
The loneliness includes me unawares.

And lonely as it is, that loneliness
Will be more lonely ere it will be less—
A blanker whiteness of benighted snow
With no expression, nothing to express.

They cannot scare me with their empty spaces
Between stars—on stars where no human race is.
I have it in me so much nearer home
To scare myself with my own desert places.

(1934)

Dwight D. Eisenhower

# Speech in London Guildhall

June 12, 1945

My Lord Mayor, My Lords, Ladies and Gentlemen: The high sense of distinction I feel in receiving this great honor from the City of London is inescapably mingled with feelings of profound sadness. All of us must always regret that your country and mine were ever faced with the tragic situation that compelled the appointment of an Allied commander-in-chief, the capacity in which I have just been so extravagantly commended.

Humility must always be the portion of any man who receives acclaim earned in the blood of his followers and the sacrifices of his

61

friends. Conceivably a commander may have been professionally superior. He may have given everything of his heart and mind to meet the spiritual and physical needs of his comrades. He may have written a chapter that will glow forever in the pages of military history. Still, even such a man, if he existed, would sadly face the facts that his honors cannot hide in his memories the crosses marking the resting places of the dead. They cannot soothe the anguish of the widow or the orphan whose husband or father will not return.

The only attitude in which a commander may with satisfaction receive the tributes of his friends is in humble acknowledgment that, no matter how unworthy he may be, his position is a symbol of great human forces that have labored arduously and successfully for a righteous cause. Unless he feels this symbolism and this rightness in what he has tried to do, then he is disregardful of the courage, the fortitude and devotion of the vast multitudes he has been honored to command. If all the Allied men and women that have served with me in this war can only know that it is they this august body is really honoring today then, indeed, will I be content.

This feeling of humility cannot erase, of course, my great pride in being tendered the Freedom of London. I am not a native of this land. I come from the very heart of America. In the superficial aspects by which we ordinarily recognize family relationships the town where I was born and the one where I was reared are far separated from this great city. Abilene, Kansas, and Denison, Texas, would together add in size to possibly one five hundredth part of Greater London. By your standards those towns are young, without your aged traditions that carry the roots of London back into the uncertainties of unrecorded history. To those people I am proud to belong, but I find myself today five thousand miles from that countryside, the honored guest of a city whose name stands for grandeur and size throughout the world. Hardly would it seem possible for the London Council to have gone farther afield to find a man to honor with its priceless gift of token citizenship.

Yet kinship among nations is not determined in such measurements as proximity, size and age. Rather we should turn to those inner things, call them what you will—I mean those intangibles that are the real treasures free men possess. To preserve his freedom of worship, his equality before the law, his liberty to speak and act as he sees fit, subject only to the provision that he trespass not upon similar rights of others—the Londoner will fight! So will the citizen of Abilene! When we consider these things then the valley of the Thames draws closer to the farms of Kansas and the plains of Texas. To my mind it is clear that when two peoples will face the tragedies of war to defend the same spiritual values, the same treasured rights, then, in deepest sense those two are truly related. So, even as I proclaim my undying Americanism, I am bold enough, and exceedingly proud to claim, basic kinship to you of London.

And what man who has followed the history of this war could fail to experience inspiration from the example of this city? When the British Empire stood – alone but unconquered, almost naked but unafraid – to defy the Hitler hordes, it was on this devoted city that the first terroristic blows were launched.

Five years and eight months of war, much of it on the actual battle-line! Blitzes, big and little, fly-bombs, V-bombs; all of them you took in your stride. You worked – from your needed efforts you would not be deterred. You carried on, and from your midst arose no cry for mercy, no wail of defeat. The Battle of Britain will take its place as another of your deathless traditions. And your faith and endurance have finally been rewarded.

You had been more than two years in war when Americans, in numbers, began swarming into your country. Most were mentally unprepared for the realities of war – especially as waged by the Nazis. Others believed that tales of British sacrifice had been exaggerated. Still others failed to recognize the difficulties of the task ahead.

All such doubts, questions and complacencies could not endure a single casual tour through your scarred streets and avenues. With awe our men gazed upon empty spaces where once had stood buildings erected by the toil and sweat of peaceful folk. Our eyes rounded as we saw your women serving quietly and efficiently in almost every kind of war effort, even flak batteries. We became accustomed to the warning sirens, which seemed to compel, from the native Londoner, not a single hurried step. Gradually we drew closer together until we became true partners in the war.

In London, my associates and I planned two great expeditions, that to invade the Mediterranean and later that to cross the Channel. London's hospitality to Americans, her good-humored acceptance of the added inconveniences we brought, her example of fortitude and quiet confidence in the final outcome – all these helped to make the supreme headquarters of two Allied expeditions the smooth-working organizations they became! They were composed of chosen representatives of two proud and independent peoples, each noted for its initiative and for its satisfaction with its own customs, manners and methods. Many feared that these representatives could never combine together in efficient fashion to solve the complex problems presented by modern war.

I hope you believe we proved the doubters wrong! Moreover, I hold that we proved this point not only for war, we proved that it can always be done by our two peoples, provided only both show the same good will, the same forbearance, the same objective attitude that British and Americans so amply demonstrated in nearly three years of bitter campaigning.

No one man could, alone, have brought about this result. Had I possessed the military skill of a Marlborough, the wisdom of Solomon, the understanding of Lincoln, I still would have been helpless without the loyalty, the vision, the generosity of thousands upon thousands of

British and Americans. Some of them were my companions in the high command, many were enlisted men and junior officers carrying the fierce brunt of the battle, and many others were back in the U.S. and here in Great Britain, in London. Moreover, back of us were always our great national war leaders and their civil and military staffs that supported and encouraged us through every trial, every test. The whole was one great team. I know that on this special occasion, the three million American men and women serving in the Allied Expeditionary Force would want me to pay the tribute of admiration, respect and affection to their British comrades of this war.

My most cherished hope is that, after Japan joins the Nazi in utter defeat, neither my country nor yours need ever again summon its sons and daughters from their peaceful pursuits to face the tragedies of battle. But—a fact important for both of us to remember—neither London nor Abilene, sisters under the skin, will sell her birthright for physical safety, her liberty for mere existence.

No petty differences in the world of trade, traditions or national pride should ever blind us to identities in priceless values. If we keep our eyes on this guidepost then no difficulties along our path of mutual co-operation can ever be insurmountable. Moreover, when this truth has permeated to the remotest hamlet and heart of all peoples, then indeed may we beat our swords into plowshares and all nations can enjoy the fruitfulness of the earth.

My Lord Mayor, I thank you once again for an honor to me and to the American forces that will remain one of the proudest in my memories.

### Robert A. Heinlein

# The Green Hills of Earth

This is the story of Rhysling, the Blind Singer of the Spaceways—but not the official version. You sang his words in school:

> "I pray for one last landing
> On the globe that gave me birth;
> Let me rest my eyes on the fleecy skies
> And the cool, green hills of Earth."

Or perhaps you sang in French, or German. Or it might have been Esperanto, while Terra's rainbow banner rippled over your head.

The language does not matter—it was certainly an *Earth* tongue.

No one has ever translated *"Green Hills"* into the lisping Venerian speech; no Martian ever croaked and whispered it in the dry corridors. This is ours. We of Earth have exported everything from Hollywood crawlies to synthetic radioactives, but this belongs solely to Terra, and to her sons and daughters wherever they may be.

We have all heard many stories of Rhysling. You may even be one of the many who have sought degrees, or acclaim, by scholarly evaluations of his published works—*Songs of the Spaceways, The Grand Canal, and other Poems, High and Far,* and *"UP SHIP!"*

Nevertheless, although you have sung his songs and read his verses, in school and out your whole life, it is at least an even money bet—unless you are a spaceman yourself—that you have never even heard of most of Rhysling's unpublished songs, such items as *Since the Pusher Met My Cousin, That Red-Headed Venusburg Gal, Keep Your Pants On, Skipper,* or *A Space Suit Built for Two.*

Nor can we quote them in a family magazine.

Rhysling's reputation was protected by a careful literary executor and by the happy chance that he was never interviewed. *Songs of the Spaceways* appeared the week he died; when it became a best seller, the publicity stories about him were pieced together from what people remembered about him plus the highly colored handouts from his publishers.

The resulting traditional picture of Rhysling is about as authentic as George Washington's hatchet or King Alfred's cakes.

In truth you would not have wanted him in your parlor; he was not socially acceptable. He had a permanent case of sun itch, which he scratched continually, adding nothing to his negligible beauty.

Van der Voort's portrait of him for the Harriman Centennial edition of his works shows a figure of high tragedy, a solemn mouth, sightless eyes concealed by black silk bandage. He was never solemn! His mouth was always open, singing, grinning, drinking, or eating. The bandage was any rag, usually dirty. After he lost his sight he became less and less neat about his person.

"Noisy" Rhysling was a jetman, second class, with eyes as good as yours, when he signed on for a loop trip to the Jovian asteroids in the R.S. *Goshawk.* The crew signed releases for everything in those days; a Lloyd's associate would have laughed in your face at the notion of insuring a spaceman. The Space Precautionary Act had never been heard of, and the Company was responsible only for wages, if and when. Half the ships that went further than Luna City never came back. Spacemen did not care; by preference they signed for shares, and any one of them would have bet you that he could jump from the 200th floor of Harriman Tower and ground safely, if you offered him three to two and allowed him rubber heels for the landing.

Jetmen were the most carefree of the lot and the meanest. Compared with them the masters, the radarmen, and the astrogators (there were no supers or stewards in those days) were gentle vegetarians. Jetmen knew too much. The others trusted the skill of the captain to get them down safely; jetmen knew that skill was useless against the blind and fitful devils chained inside their rocket motors.

The *Goshawk* was the first of Harriman's ships to be converted from chemical fuel to atomic power-piles — or rather the first that did not blow up. Rhysling knew her well; she was an old tub that had plied the Luna City run, Supra-New York space station to Leyport and back, before she was converted for deep space. He had worked the Luna run in her and had been along on the first deep space trip, Drywater on Mars — and back, to everyone's surprise.

He should have made chief engineer by the time he signed for the Jovian loop trip, but, after the Drywater pioneer trip, he had been fired, blacklisted, and grounded at Luna City for having spent his time writing a chorus and several verses at a time when he should have been watching his gauges. The song was the infamous *The Skipper is a Father to his Crew*, with the uproariously unprintable final couplet.

The blacklist did not bother him. He won an accordion from a Chinese barkeep in Luna City by cheating at one-thumb and thereafter kept going by singing to the miners for drinks and tips until the rapid attrition in spacemen caused the Company agent there to give him another chance. He kept his nose clean on the Luna run for a year or two, got back into deep space, helped give Venusburg its original ripe reputation, strolled the banks of the Grand Canal when a second colony was established at the ancient Martian capital, and froze his toes and ears on the second trip to Titan.

Things moved fast in those days. Once the power-pile drive was accepted the number of ships that put out from the Luna-Terra system was limited only by the availability of crews. Jetmen were scarce; the shielding was cut to a minimum to save weight and few married men cared to risk possible exposure to radioactivity. Rhysling did not want to be a father, so jobs were always open to him during the golden days of the claiming boom. He crossed and recrossed the system, singing the doggerel that boiled up in his head and chording it out on his accordion.

The master of the *Goshawk* knew him; Captain Hicks had been astrogator on Rhysling's first trip in her. "Welcome home, Noisy," Hicks had greeted him. "Are you sober, or shall I sign the book for you?"

"You can't get drunk on the bug juice they sell here, Skipper." He signed and went below, lugging his accordion.

Ten minutes later he was back. "Captain," he stated darkly, "that number two jet ain't fit. The cadmium dampers are warped."

"Why tell me? Tell the Chief."

"I did, but he says they will do. He's wrong."

The captain gestured at the book. "Scratch out your name and scram. We raise ship in thirty minutes."

Rhysling looked at him, shrugged, and went below again.

It is a long climb to the Jovian planetoids; a Hawk-class clunker had to blast for three watches before going into free flight. Rhysling had the second watch. Damping was done by hand then, with a multiplying vernier and a danger gauge. When the gauge showed red, he tried to correct it—no luck.

Jetmen don't wait; that's why they are jetmen. He slapped the emergency discover and fished at the hot stuff with the tongs. The lights went out, he went right ahead. A jetman has to know his power room the way your tongue knows the inside of your mouth.

He sneaked a quick look over the top of the lead baffle when the lights went out. The blue radioactive glow did not help him any; he jerked his head back and went on fishing by touch.

When he was done he called over the tube, "Number two jet out. And for crissake get me some light down here!"

There was light—the emergency circuit—but not for him. The blue radioactive glow was the last thing his optic nerve ever responded to.

## 2

"As Time and Space come bending back to shape this star-specked scene,
The tranquil tears of tragic joy still spread their silver sheen;
Along the Grand Canal still soar the fragile Towers of Truth;
Their fairy grace defends this place of Beauty, calm and couth.

"Bone-tired the race that raised the Towers, forgotten are their lores;
Long gone the gods who shed the tears that lap these crystal shores.
Slow beats the time-worn heart of Mars beneath this icy sky;
The thin air whispers voicelessly that all who live must die—

"Yet still the lacy Spires of Truth sing Beauty's madrigal
And she herself will ever dwell along the Grand Canal!"

—from *The Grand Canal*, by permission of
Lux Transcriptions, Ltd., London and Luna City

On the swing back they set Rhysling down on Mars at Drywater; the boys passed the hat and the skipper kicked in a half month's pay. That was all—*finish*—just another space bum who had not had the good fortune to finish it off when his luck ran out. He holed up with the prospectors and archeologists at How-Far? for a month or so, and could probably have stayed forever in exchange for his songs and his accordion playing. But spacemen die if they stay in one place; he hooked a crawler over to Drywater again and thence to Marsopolis.

The capital was well into its boom; the processing plants lined the Grand Canal on both sides and roiled the ancient waters with the filth of the run-off. This was before the Tri-Planet Treaty forbade disturbing cultural relics for commerce; half the slender, fairylike towers had been torn down, and others were disfigured to adapt them as pressurized buildings for Earthmen.

Now Rhysling had never seen any of these changes and no one described them to him; when he "saw" Marsopolis again, he visualized it as it had been, before it was rationalized for trade. His memory was good. He stood on the riparian esplanade where the ancient great of Mars had taken their ease and saw its beauty spreading out before his blinded eyes—ice blue plain of water unmoved by tide, untouched by breeze, and reflecting serenely the sharp, bright stars of the Martian sky, and beyond the water the lacy buttresses and flying towers of an architecture too delicate for our rumbling, heavy planet.

The result was *Grand Canal*.

The subtle change in his orientation which enabled him to see beauty at Marsopolis where beauty was not now began to affect his whole life. All women became beautiful to him. He knew them by their voices, and fitted their appearances to the sounds. It is a mean spirit indeed who will speak to a blind man other than in gentle friendliness; scolds who had given their husbands no peace sweetened their voices to Rhysling.

It populated his world with beautiful women and gracious men. *Dark Star Passing, Berenice's Hair, Death Song of a Wood's Colt,* and his other love songs of the wanderers, the womenless men of space, were the direct result of the fact that his conceptions were unsullied by tawdry truths. It mellowed his approach, changed his doggerel to verse, and sometimes even to poetry.

He had plenty of time to think now, time to get all the lovely words just so, and to worry a verse until it sang true in his head. The monotonous beat of *Jet Song*—

> When the field is clear, the reports all seen,
> When the lock sighs shut, when the lights wink green,
> When the check-off's done, when it's time to pray,
> When the Captain nods, when she blasts away—

> Hear the jets!
> Hear them snarl at your back
> When you're stretched on the rack;
> Feel your ribs clamp your chest,
> Feel your neck grind its rest.
> Feel the pain in your ship,
> Feel her strain in their grip.
> Feel her rise! Feel her drive!
> Straining steel, come alive,
> On her jets!

—came to him not while he himself was a jetman but later while he was hitchhiking from Mars to Venus and sitting out a watch with an old shipmate.

At Venusburg he sang his new songs and some of the old, in the bars. Someone would start a hat around for him; it would come back with a minstrel's usual take doubled or tripled in recognition of the gallant spirit behind the bandaged eyes.

It was an easy life. Any space port was his home and any ship his private carriage. No skipper cared to refuse to lift the extra mass of blind Rhysling and his squeeze box; he shuttled from Venusburg to Leyport to Drywater to New Shanghai, or back again, as the whim took him.

He never went closer to Earth than Supra-New York Space Station. Even when signing the contract for *Songs of the Spaceways* he made his mark in a cabin-class liner somewhere between Luna City and Ganymede. Horowitz, the original publisher, was aboard for a second honeymoon and heard Rhysling sing at a ship's party. Horowitz knew a good thing for the publishing trade when he heard it; the entire contents of *Songs* were sung directly into the tape in the communications room of the ship before he let Rhysling out of his sight. The next three volumes were squeezed out of Rhysling at Venusburg, where Horowitz had sent an agent to keep him liquored up until he had sung all he could remember.

*UP SHIP!* is not certainly authentic Rhysling throughout. Much of it is Rhysling's, no doubt, and *Jet Song* is unquestionably his, but most of the verses were collected after his death from people who had known him during his wanderings.

*The Green Hills of Earth* grew through twenty years. The earliest form we know about was composed before Rhysling was blinded, during a drinking bout with some of the indentured men on Venus. The verses were concerned mostly with the things the labor clients intended to do back on Earth if and when they ever managed to pay their bounties and thereby be allowed to go home. Some of the stanzas were vulgar, some were not, but the chorus was recognizably that of *Green Hills*.

We know exactly where the final form of *Green Hills* came from, and when.

There was a ship in at Venus Ellis Isle which was scheduled for the direct jump from there to Great Lakes, Illinois. She was the old *Falcon*, youngest of the Hawk class and the first ship to apply the Harriman Trust's new policy of extra-fare express service between Earth cities and any colony with scheduled stops.

Rhysling decided to ride her back to Earth. Perhaps his own song had gotten under his skin—or perhaps he just hankered to see his native Ozarks one more time.

The Company no longer permitted deadheads; Rhysling knew this but it never occurred to him that the ruling might apply to him. He was getting old, for a spaceman, and just a little matter of fact about his privileges. Not senile—he simply knew that he was one of the landmarks in space, along with Halley's Comet, the Rings, and Brewster's Ridge. He walked in the crew's port, went below, and made himself at home in the first empty acceleration couch.

The Captain found him there while making a last minute tour of his ship. "What are you doing here?" he demanded.

"Dragging it back to Earth, Captain," Rhysling needed no eyes to see a skipper's four stripes.

"You can't drag in this ship; you know the rules. Shake a leg and get out of here. We raise ship at once." The Captain was young; he had come up after Rhysling's active time, but Rhysling knew the type—five years at Harriman Hall with only cadet practice trips instead of solid, deep space experience. The two men did not touch in background nor spirit; space was changing.

"Now, Captain, you wouldn't begrudge an old man a trip home."

The officer hesitated—several of the crew had stopped to listen. "I can't do it. 'Space Precautionary Act, Clause Six: No one shall enter space save as a licensed member of a crew of a chartered vessel, or as a paying passenger of such a vessel under such regulations as may be issued pursuant to this act.' Up you get and out you go."

Rhysling lolled back, his hands under his head. "If I've got to go, I'm damned if I'll walk. Carry me."

The Captain bit his lip and said, "Master-at-Arms! Have this man removed."

The ship's policeman fixed his eyes on the overhead struts. "Can't rightly do it, Captain. I've sprained my shoulder." The other crew members, present a moment before, had faded into the bulkhead paint.

"Well, get a working party!"

"Aye, aye, sir." He, too, went away.

Rhysling spoke again. "Now look, Skipper—let's not have any hard feelings about this. You've got an out to carry me if you want to—the 'Distressed Spaceman' clause."

"'Distressed Spaceman,' my eye! You're no distressed spaceman; you're a space-lawyer. I know who you are; you've been bumming around the system for years. Well, you won't do it in my ship. That clause was intended to succor men who had missed their ships, not to let a man drag free all over space."

"Well, now, Captain, can you properly say I haven't missed my ship? I've never been back home since my last trip as a signed-on crew member. The law says I can have a trip back."

"But that was years ago. You've used up your chance."

"Have I now? The clause doesn't say a word about how soon a man has to take his trip back; it just says he's got it coming to him. Go look it up, Skipper. If I'm wrong, I'll not only walk out on my two legs, I'll beg your humble pardon in front of your crew. Go on—look it up. Be a sport."

Rhysling could feel the man's glare, but he turned and stomped out of the compartment. Rhysling knew that he had used his blindness to place the Captain in an impossible position, but this did not embarrass Rhysling—he rather enjoyed it.

Ten minutes later the siren sounded, he heard the orders on the bull horn for Up-Stations. When the soft sighing of the locks and the slight pressure change in his ears let him know that take-off was imminent he got up and shuffled down to the power room, as he wanted to be near the jets when they blasted off. He needed no one to guide him in any ship of the Hawk class.

Trouble started during the first watch. Rhysling had been lounging in the inspector's chair, fiddling with the keys of his accordion and trying out a new version of *Green Hills.*

> "Let me breathe unrationed air again
> Where there's no lack nor dearth

And something, something, something 'Earth'"—it would not come out right. He tried again.

> "Let the sweet fresh breezes heal me
> As they rove around the girth
> Of our lovely mother planet,
> Of the cool green hills of Earth."

That was better, he thought. "How do you like that, Archie?" he asked over the muted roar.

"Pretty good. Give out with the whole thing." Archie Macdougal, Chief Jetman, was an old friend, both spaceside and in bars; he had been an apprentice under Rhysling many years and millions of miles back.

Rhysling obliged, then said, "You youngsters have got it soft. Everything automatic. When I was twisting her tail you had to stay awake."

"You still have to stay awake." They fell to talking shop and Macdougal showed him the direct response damping rig which had replaced the manual vernier control which Rhysling had used. Rhysling felt out the controls and asked questions until he was familiar with the new installation. It was his conceit that he was still a jetman and that his present occupation as a troubadour was simply an expedient during one of the fusses with the company that any man could get into.

"I see you still have the old hand damping plates installed," he remarked, his agile fingers flitting over the equipment.

"All except the links. I unshipped them because they obscure the dials."

"You ought to have them shipped. You might need them."

"Oh, I don't know. I think—" Rhysling never did find out what Macdougal thought for it was at that moment the trouble tore loose. Macdougal caught it square, a blast of radioactivity that burned him down where he stood.

Rhysling sensed what had happened. Automatic reflexes of old habit came out. He slapped the discover and rang the alarm to the control room simultaneously. Then he remembered the unshipped links. He had to grope until he found them, while trying to keep as low as he could to get maximum benefit from the baffles. Nothing but the links bothered him as to location. The place was as light to him as any place could be; he knew every spot, every control, the way he knew the keys of his accordion.

"Power room! Power room! What's the alarm?"

"Stay out!" Rhysling shouted. "The place is 'hot.'" He could feel it on his face and in his bones, like desert sunshine.

The links he got into place, after cursing someone, anyone, for having failed to rack the wrench he needed. Then he commenced trying to reduce the trouble by hand. It was a long job and ticklish. Presently he decided that the jet would have to be spilled, pile and all.

First he reported. "Control!"

"Control aye aye!"

"Spilling jet three—emergency."

"Is this Macdougal?"

"Macdougal is dead. This is Rhysling, on watch. Stand by to record."

There was no answer; dumbfounded the Skipper may have been, but he could not interfere in a power room emergency. He had the ship to consider, and the passengers and crew. The doors had to stay closed.

The Captain must have been still more surprised at what Rhysling sent for record. It was:

> "We rot in the molds of Venus,
> We retch at her tainted breath.
> Foul are her flooded jungles,
> Crawling with unclean death."

Rhysling went on cataloguing the Solar System as he worked, "—harsh bright soil of Luna—," "—Saturn's rainbow rings—," "—the frozen night of Titan—," all the while opening and spilling the jet and fishing it clean. He finished with an alternate chorus—

> "We've tried each spinning space mote
> And reckoned its true worth:
> Take us back again to the homes of men
> On the cool, green hills of Earth."

—then, almost absentmindedly remembered to tack on his revised first verse:

> "The arching sky is calling
> Spacemen back to their trade.
> All hands! Stand by! Free falling!
> And the lights below us fade.
> Out ride the sons of Terra,
> Far drives the thundering jet,
> Up leaps the race of Earthmen,
> Out, far, and onward yet—"

The ship was safe now and ready to limp home shy one jet. As for himself, Rhysling was not so sure. That "sunburn" seemed sharp, he thought. He was unable to see the bright, rosy fog in which he worked but he knew it was there. He went on with the business of flushing the air out through the outer valve, repeating it several times to permit the level of radioaction to drop to something a man might stand under suitable armor. While he did this he sent one more chorus, the last bit of authentic Rhysling that ever could be:

> "We pray for one last landing
> On the globe that gave us birth;
> Let us rest our eyes on fleecy skies
> And the cool, green hills of Earth."

(1951)

### John Graves

## from **Goodbye to a River**

### Chapter 9

Behind the wide blue roll of cloud the Canadian air moved down frigid but crisp and clear, and in the mornings by the fire, when I would set my coffee cup aside nearly empty and pick it up again a few minutes later, the sugary dregs would have become mush ice. Yelping flights of geese, convinced now of winter's imminence, V-cut the blue sky. At the caprice of the little man at Possum Kingdom, or of his bosses, the river dropped three feet; channel became a study, and the pup developed a stubborn habit of leaping ashore at shallow and difficult places. In John Hittson Bend dropping-splotches painted the high red-and-gold sandstone cliffs white below ledges. Eagle's nests? Falcons? I should check, some spring, and get my head ripped open by a defensive parent. . . . One day the big cold wind blew from morning until late afternoon, and under its bleak sweep there were only I and the pup and the canoe and the river and frost-dead leaves whipping across the air, and from time to time a great blue heron gliding away from a perch before us with a cry of protestant rancor. A dozen dead foxes lay heaped on the bank at one place, victims of the new squeak-squawk callers that lure them at night within reach of spotlights and shotguns; the hound people, ritualists, hate that innovation. . . . In a sand-bottomed canyon once, a stallion and two mares and a big colt, alert under the season's spur, came pounding down the beach at the strange thing that was the boat, then threw sand high stopping and pounded away as the strange thing broke in two and I began to lead it through a shallows.

Change. Autumn. Maybe — certainly — there was melancholy in it, but it was a good melancholy. I've never been partial to the places where the four seasons are one. If the sun shines all year long at La Jolla, and the water stays warm enough for swimming over rocks that wave moss like green long hair, that is pleasant, but not much else. Sunshine and warm water seem to me to have full meaning only when they come after winter's bite; green is not so green if it doesn't follow the months of brown and gray. And the scheduled inevitable death of green carries its own exhilaration; in that change is the promise of all the rebirths to come, and the deaths, too. In it is the only real unchangingness, solidity, and in the alternation of bite and caress, of fat and lean, of song and silence, is the reward and punishment that life has always been, and the punishment itself becomes good, maybe because it promises reward, maybe because after much honey the puckering acid of acorns tastes right. Without the year's changes, for me, there is little morality.

If you tell me that that is a poisonous northern puritanism and has no validity for the sun-warmed mass of the world's peoples, and remind me that the Greeks sired our cycle in a climate much like southern California's, I won't argue. I'm only talking about what is mine.

Looming over the outer edge of a bend called Poke Stalk is a line of high bluffs, an escarpment where the mountain country falls abruptly away to farming land. I camped beneath them that night near a place where, in an October years before, Hale and I had stopped and had eaten fat bluebills out of season, shot by kids upstream who had run off with their guilty consciences and left the ducks on the water when they saw us paddling down. Skinning them out that night, we broiled the breasts over drift-mesquite coals and burned the evidence, feeling guilty, too, but having eaten well. . . .

The wind died at sunset. The night, its wisp of a moon not yet out, was clear, with stars, and so still that I found myself resenting the fire's hoarse whisper and snapping against a boulder that bounced its heat into the little tent. Screech owls, rare in that country since the big drouth, were quavering tentatively to one another near where I'd seen a deserted flagstone house across the river. Masses of tangled dead timber overhung the tiny flat I was camped on; six inches from one of the rear tent stakes the earth fell away into an eroded pit eight feet deep, eaten out by the river in flood.

A truck's working-groan to the east, where Two Eighty-one climbed the scarp . . . Southward, a freight train threaded the T. & P., and sounded faintly the Cadillac honk of its Diesel, importunate, lacking the lonesomeness of the old steam wails we had once listened to from there. The day's wind and bright light and paddling had washed me with clean fatigue, and my muscles felt good, in tone. A week it had taken, seventy unhurried miles, longer than it had used to, but I was older now. The skin of my hands from work and from the alternate wetting and drying and the cold had chapped hornily, and at the knuckles of my thumbs and forefingers had broken in bloody stinging cracks. Cuts and little sore knots where sandbur tips had embedded themselves finished the disfigurement. . . . If one had a modern-tragic viewpoint like—oh, Graham Greene's, one might make symbols out of those fingers. But one didn't. One felt damned good. One was for the moment a simple puritan, soaking reward from the glow of a fire on one's front while at one's tail the creeping cold of night only italicized (puritanically?) one's simple comfort, and in the embers one's simple supper, a potato, lay baking. . . .

The pup wanted play. It was his main trouble and the root of the insubordination that had invaded him. After gnawing neurotically for a time on the blanket, which since the norther was becoming important for warmth at night on top of the sleeping bag, he tried to make love to it, and yipped with rebellious despair when I made him stop, and came to chew on my raw hands.

After eating, I walked around behind the tent to look at the night and, forgetting the big pit, fell into it. I landed flat in slimy mud, stunned, a tangle of old barbed wire six inches from my forehead, and when I'd pulled up onto all fours, still a little faint with the feeling you have after falls and wounds, the pup scrambled down to me and began to lick my face. I pushed him away, and a whole memory came back to me of a lost two or three months after the war when I'd stayed at a ramshackle hacienda in the uplands of Vera Cruz state, with the slightly crazy old recluse whose people had owned the place since the seventeenth century. We had drunk habanero one night, and had discussed loudly, and I'd wandered out the back door to fall into an unroofed cellar pit among broken glass, and had come back to consciousness with a little dog licking my face. Like an old man's repertory of stories, experience begins to repeat itself after a time, even or maybe especially in its meaningless phases. On the fringes of the middle age and after, the déjà-vu is likely not to be illusory.

No worse off than before except for another layer of filth on my clothes, I climbed out of the pit and went to bed and slept hard, half hearing things that screamed on the heights above us and once, as though in a dream, the tearing, splintering progress of a frost-freed boulder that bounded down through brush and trees and came to its next eon's resting place in the river, with a splash. . . .

When I got up, the thinnest of horned moons hung in the east and stars were bright all over the sky. Under the cold air a rounded roll of fog followed the river's course exactly down its twists and bends, and when light came the day had a windless clarity that would have been worth undergoing ten blue northers to see. It was old Parson Herbert's sweet day so cool, so calm, so bright, and I even had a small catfish on the throwline. I skinned and gutted it by the waterside, and when I was back at the tent feeding twigs to the embers left over, under ashes, from the night's fire, a man of about fifty carrying a thirty-thirty Winchester came picking his way among the boulders of the shore. He wore a Stetson, brogans, and striped bib overalls under a denim jacket, and looked embarrassed when I told him good morning.

"I guess you got permission to be here?"

I had to answer no, embarrassed myself. Though the tangle of barbed wire I'd fallen beside in the pit served no purpose, it was part of a fence, flood-flattened, on whose unpublic side I had camped. There hadn't been any other level ground. I told the man what I was doing.

He stared at me, then smiled. "I was thinkin' it was somebody slipped in for a deer," he said. "Found one last week with just a ham cut off. It makes you mad."

I offered him coffee and he took it, black, refusing anything to eat but staying to talk while I fried and ate the catfish. He was not a loquacious sort, but he liked the look of what I was doing, and people will open sometimes to a stranger, met strangely, whom they find partly sympathetic and whom they will not likely see again. It is a principle that gets one into involvements in the third-class carriages of French trains. . . . He'd run away from home down the country a way when he'd been seventeen, and had come to work for a rancher in that bend, tending cattle, batching in the flagstone house across the river. He'd met his wife there one day, when she had come to the river picnicking with a party of people.

"Looked at her," he said. "Liked her. Guess she liked me. Still both do."

When he had just about consolidated his own small ranch there (cheap land or no, it's a tough thing to get done), the big drouth had burned in and had shrunk his few head of cattle to sway-backed racks of bones before he'd sold them at canner-and-cutter prices, and he'd thought he'd have to sell the place, too. But mohair goats and a long stint at the Fort Worth Convair plant that draws much of its labor from that region had scrooched him by, he said.

The passenger brought a rock and dropped it at his feet, hoping for play. With a slanting grin the rancher looked at him and reached down to pull his ear.

"Son-of-a-gun dogs," he said. "Run out here from Mineral Wells at night. Kilt me thirty-five goats oncet from sundown to sunup. Two of the worst was hounds, and I knowed who they belonged to, but he said they wouldn't run no goats. Laid a load of number two shot into one of 'em one night, and the next time I seen that fellow, he said: 'Know that blue dog of mine? Bobcat clawed him up turble, other night.' And I said: 'You don't tell me? Rough outfits, bobcats . . .'"

I said I doubted that the passenger was going to get big enough to do much slaughter among people's livestock.

"Sha," he said. "Tell me. I've seen Pekes out there a-runnin'."

Though he said he scarcely ever killed deer, he had a passion for squirrel shooting and for hunting what he called "short varmints." He said the things screaming on the hill the night before had been ringtails, which were more numerous than he'd ever known them to be and which he blamed for a local shortage of squirrels: in the spring, he claimed, they went into the holes and ate the young ones on the nests. Of the projected Brazos dams—one is to be slapped up against those bluffs—he said: "I've learned to get along with her pretty good the way she is. Don't know how I'll like her when she's a lake. Good bottomland, them fish'll be grazin' on."

He was one of the quiet, tough, unprofane types that that country still breeds from time to time, close in type to the best of the old ones, or to what nostalgia says the best of them were like. He had blue eyes with seamed corners, brown skin, a strong nose, and thin lips that shaped themselves stiffly, thoughtfully, around his words. . . . He told me about a field full of Indian debris, and corn-pounding holes along a high ledge, and a kind of cave where he'd once let a hermit live for five years, occasionally bringing him coffee and beans and flour from town. The hermit had always stayed hidden until he could see who had come, and at the river had kept a big chicken-wire box full of live catfish.

"Give me one oncet weighed thirty-two pounds," the rancher said. "Up and left one spring, never said why."

He took a look at the canoe, and said he'd always thought he'd like to do a little floating himself.

"Come on," I said.

He looked at me. "Dang if I wouldn't," he said. "Dang if I wouldn't."

But then he grinned and shook his head, and after drinking half a cup more coffee wished me luck and continued his patrol along the bank. I washed pots and scraped off some whiskers and rolled my gear into bundles ready for loading, then climbed for a look at the hermit's hole. It was under a block of conglomerate forty or fifty feet tall, in a grove of live oaks beneath the bluffs. Age-long surface drainage had chewed out a chamber between the earth and the boulder's cuspate base, and the hermit, whoever he had been, had laid walls of sandstone blocks at either opening of the cavity, mortaring with mud, leaving a door at the big lower end and a chimney hole at the upper. The domed ceiling, blackened by smoke, was tall enough to stand under; it was a snug retreat, and if I'd known about it the night before I would have stayed there, though the floor was littered with the droppings of exploratory goats. In the live oaks outside titmice were whistling *peter-peter-peter*, and down the hill the river sparkled blue, and I found myself thinking that you wouldn't have to be a really peculiar old misanthrope, at that, to want to live in such a place for five years, or for a lifetime. . . .

A river has few "views." It seeks the lowest line of its country, straight or crooked, and what you see when you travel along it are mostly river and sky and trees, water and clouds and sun and shore. Things a quarter-mile away exist for you only because you know they are there; your consciousness of them is visual only if you walk ashore to see them. For a man who likes rivers, most of the time that is all right; for a man who seeks sharp solitude, it's special. But sometimes, too, the shores close in a bit as room walls will, and you crave more space.... Now, without having thought about doing so, I clambered beyond the hermit's hole up ledges, hoisting the pup at spots, to the top of the bluff.

I was out of breath when I got there, but it was a fine spot and worth the climb. I knew it from before. People drive out to it from Mineral Wells for picnics, on a dirt road running past Baptist crossroads churches and log ruins. As you stand there on weathered solid stone, the lowlands roll south and east from below you to the horizon; your eye can trace fifteen miles or so of the river's course as it meanders over sand, slower and flattened, between tall bright cottonwoods and oaks and pecans, and where you can't see it you can guess it, and can guess too the things around it, knowing them. Though it's nothing much in comparison to the vistas you get in real mountains, after a week in the Brazos's winding trough, it dizzied me a little; it made fun of what I had been doing. Heights have that kind of humor.

Likely that bluff had a good name once before some dullard called it Inspiration Point. The nation's map is measled with names like that, pocks from the old nineteenth-century plague that made people build gazebos and well-tops of rough masonry with oaken buckets on ropes but no well beneath (unless it was a "wishing well"), and sing "Annie Laurie," and read Scott for his worst qualities, and long to own paintings by Bouguereau or Landseer or Alma-Tadema, and, disregarding the guts and soul in the old nomenclature of American places, rename them Inspiration Point and Lovers' Retreat (there's one of those up Eagle Creek) and Maiden's Leap. It was worse in the interior than on the East Coast, where the old names had rooted themselves before that frame of mind came along. It was worst of all in the South, because the South yearned hardest to believe Scott, but the whole hinterland had the disease; in the Midwest it got flavored with Hiawatha.... Though it has its own cachet now — yes, I like gingerbreaded houses, and old pictures of women with buns and with big breasts under stiff shirtwaists — it was, for me, a flouting of real ghosts and genii, an unimaginative lamina of Greco-Scotch-English never-neverism on the surface of a land that seemed too new to would-be-cultured sensibilities. You don't have to line up too solidly with the America shouters to resent it.

Now that the land looks a little older and we don't have to stare directly at the tobacco juice on the haired chins of those who made its past, the grandchildren of the Gothicists are likely to be enchanted to find that the streamlet below their house used to be called Dead Nigger Draw, but they have a hard fight with the real-estate men, staunchly Gothic all, if they try to cancel out its present title of Bonnie Brae.... And the effort, somehow, seems little more praiseworthy or genuine than their grandparents' was.

One digresses? Certainly.

That whole arc of country below the Point is ghost-laden. Violent, obscure history piles in on you as you look off over the lowlands. They were richer than the mountain country; therefore more people wanted them and came there. People make trouble; trouble makes history, or anyhow tales, since not much of the history is reliable. After the trouble, little of weight happened in that piece of country—no oil booms, no industry to speak of until the Fort Worth factories began to suck the people away—so that for a long time remembrance of the frontier was strong on the slowly eroding farms and the ranches, and in the little bypassed towns. It sat on the land. It still does, a little, if the land means anything to you.

Two miles below the bluff you can see a railroad bridge where the Texas & Pacific main line crosses to hill-hidden Brazos town, which weed-shot to existence in the eighties when the railroad came. It is a dusty spraddle of small frame houses now, with a brick post office and an empty store or two; a few countrymen eye you with faint astonishment if you drive out there; as well they may. No one goes there by accident since their highway bridge washed out and made them a dead end, and if anyone goes there except by accident he makes ripples in that quietness. An old man lived there for a long time who used to hint of dark and pleasurable past connections with the Jameses and the Youngers and Quantrell. Since his death I'm unaware of even any refracted drama in Brazos, Texas, though there is fair fishing by the stark piers of the vanished road bridge.

A mile down from there is the Highway 281 bridge by the mouth of Palo Pinto Creek for which the county was named; no one knows what painted stick it was that gave the creek *its* name, but that kind of haziness perhaps beats Gothicism. Like Keechi and Elm and the other creeks, it drains history into the Brazos along with silt and leaves and drift and water. It has a hundred hidden valleys; The People loved it. In the fall of 1837 the ineffable Bigfoot Wallace came there with a wilderness surveying party—he was twenty years old, huge, and a year out of Virginia whence he had traveled to take Mexican toll for the deaths of a brother and a cousin at Goliad. Up the Palo Pinto (mostly they called it a river then) he strayed from his companions and got lost, fought some Indians, sprained his ankle, lived in a cave. . . . In good-humored old age, when he liked to talk, he told John Duval that other Comanches had taken him prisoner one day, and back at their camp had tied him to a pole with firewood around him in preparation for a redskin-style auto-da-fé. Things looked black, but—inevitably—"just at this moment the old squaw I had seen in the lodge rushed through the crowd of painted warriors, and began to throw the wood from around me. . . ." With like inevitability, he was adopted into the tribe, and stayed with them for three educational months before slipping away and going back to the settlements.

The fact is, there was probably truth in it. He was nearly everywhere that counted, Bigfoot Wallace, with enough vitality and humor to have seen four or five ordinary men through life. Though he was no half-horse, half-alligator sort of a liar, he sometimes told things a little big, but why not?

Port Smythe, M.D., on the other hand, modeled himself on the tradition of the clear-eyed scientific amateur when he visited the Palo Pinto in 1852, still before many whites had been there. As a kind of last bachelor fling, he rode horseback up the Brazos from the settled country to the south, hiring Indian guides to show him the way. He expected no trouble and found none, Latinized every scrap of weed that his horse's hoof bruised, and exclaimed over nature's grandeurs in unscientific tones that echoed Cooper and Scott: old, low, flat Comanche Peak down in Hood County was "the crowning Glory of the Landscape, . . . the Hoary Monarch of this wide domain," and his Indians could only be "the Sons and Daughters of the forest." Having attained the Palo Pinto, he noted:

. . . sundry specimens of Natural History, among which were the Raven, (*Corvus-corax*) Red Bird, (*Loxia-cardinalis*) the Humming Bird, (*Trochilus*—***) &c., besides innumerable Rattle Snakes, (*Crotalus-horridus*) Tarantula, (*Lycosia-tarantula*) and Scorpion, (*Scorpio*).

and, without climbing the bluffs to see where he'd been, rode back home again to write a pleasant, earnest journal of the trip, inconsequential from this range, though its newspaper publication may have lured some lackland South Texans up the river.

Up the Palo Pinto also, during the Civil War, settlers clustered against the Comanches, and while few details of that time have come down, a rhyme has that implies the details behind it:

White's town, and Burnett's street,
Stubblefield's fort, and nothing to eat. . . .

(Tip Seay rode out from that fort on a half-broken black horse one day, against good advice, and never rode back again. Maybe somebody repeated the good advice to his scalped corpse when they found it.)

From the creek mouth the river drops down and loops back north, making the great Christmas-stocking shape of the Dobbs Valley Bend, named for old Chesley Dobbs, who ranched there till his luck ran out and the Indians got his long hair (against good counsel, too, he'd ridden out homeward from Palo Pinto town), even though the tracks showed that his pony had given them a run. There seem always to have been those mournful post-mortem trail cuttings, since hoofprints and bruised bushes and tatters of cloth had voices for men both red and white in those days; I know a few for whom they still do, but not many. Chesley Dobbs was the one whose scalp they'd found at the Old Painted Campground, on Keechi. . . . Where the Brazos breaks south still again, forming the Littlefield Bend and piercing the invisible skin of Parker County, my merchant friend's bailiwick, stands a lonely, rusty-faced hill called Red Bluff, where the Comanches (I can't help it; the stories are there; I'm not telling even a fourth of them) hid once before making a reasonably bloody raid on Webb Gilbert's remuda and wounding Roe Littlefield in a place that nobody, for some reason, will mention.

Beyond that, Rock Creek comes in past the brick kilns at Bennett, draining the country where Fuller Millsap ranched and fought Indians and shouted but backed down from a shotgun duel with Charles Goodnight, and George McCleskey died at Blue Springs pumping bullets out of his Henry between the cabin logs even after his legs were paralyzed, and Old Lady Rippy reached in between her sagging breasts and hauled out a plug and bit a chew when The People tried to make her run so they could shoot her more amusingly, and cursed them in their own language, so that nonplused they went away, but got her later along with the crusty old man she was married to—howling like wolves down at his traps. . . . And Owl Head Johnson lived alone and got lynched for stealing hogs. . . .

When you see Rock Creek after a rain, you know what is happening to that country, and has been for a century. Above it, even in wet times, the river is likely to run fairly clear, since most of the tributary streams up to Possum Kingdom drain sandstone country without much rich dirt. But Rock Creek carries the runoff from the steeply up-and-down western part of Parker County which used to be an oak forest with grassed glades, and since the whites moved in with axes and moldboard plows and too many chattel ruminants, the western part of Parker County has been flowing down Rock Creek to the Brazos, and down the Brazos to the Gulf. After rain, the creek and the river below its mouth run thick as black-bean soup; it was the old men from up that way who could brag the loudest later, in front of the feed stores, about the farms they'd worn out. Now the S. C. S. tells them how to terrace, and a lot of them do, but that barn's door gaped wide for a long long time.

Rock Creek was a main avenue for Indian depredations into the richer low country. Dozens of people died up its valley, most of them interestingly, if your interests run so. But maybe Mrs. Sherman's story will suffice to give the tone of that warfare. . . .

They rode up to the cabin while the Shermans were at dinner on November 27, 1860—dinner in rural Texas then and up into my young years being the noontime meal. There were half a hundred of them, painted, devil-ugly in look and mood. It was the year after the humiliating march up across the Red under good, dead Neighbors; the frontier country was not yet strange to The People, nor were they yet convinced they had lost it. They wanted rent-pay for it in horses, and trophies, and blood, and boasting-fuel for around the prairie campfires in the years to come. Horses they had taken in plenty—300 or so of them by the time they reached the Shermans'—and they had just lanced John Brown to death among his ponies to the east, and the day before had raped and slaughtered and played catch-ball with babies' bodies at the Landmans' and the Gages' to the north.

Though the Shermans did not know about any of that, their visitors lacked the aspect that a man would want to see in his luncheon guests — even a sharper frontiersman than Ezra Sherman, who, in that particular time and place, with a wife and four kids for a responsibility, had failed to furnish himself with firearms.

The oldest boy, Mrs. Sherman's by an earlier husband who had died, said: "Papa . . ."

But by the time Ezra Sherman turned around, they were inside the one-room cabin, a half-dozen of them, filling it with hard tarnished-copper bodies and the flash of flat eyes and a smell of woodsmoke and horse sweat and leather and wild armpits and crotches. Behind them, through the door, were the urgent jostle and gabble and snickering of the rest.

"God's Heaven!" Sherman said, gripping the table's edge.

Martha Sherman said: "Don't show nothin'. Don't scare."

She had come to the frontier young with a brother and his family, but even if she'd only come the year before she'd have known more about it than her husband. There was sense in her, and force. Her youngest started bawling at the Indians; she took his arm and squeezed it hard until he shushed, looking up the while into the broad face, slash-painted diagonally in scarlet and black, of the big one who moved grinning toward the table. He wore two feathers slanting up from where a braid fanned into the hair of his head, and held a short lance.

"Hey," he said.

"Hey," Ezra Sherman answered.

The Indian said something.

"No got whisky," Ezra Sherman said. "No got horse. Want 'lasses? *Good* 'lasses."

"You're fixin' to have us kilt," his wife said, and stood up. "Git!" she told the big Indian.

He grinned still, and gabbled at her. She shook her head and pointed to the door, and behind her heard the youngest begin again to cry. The Indian's gabble changed timbre; it was Spanish now, she knew, but she didn't understand that either.

"Git out!" she repeated.

"*Hambre*," he said, rubbing his bare belly and pointing to the bacon and greens and cornbread and buttermilk on the table.

"No, you ain't," she said, and snatched up a willow broom that was leaned against the wall. But her eye caught motion to the left and she spun, swinging the broom up and down and whack against the ear of the lean, tall, bowlegged one who had hold of her bolt of calico. She swung again and again, driving him back with his hands raised, and then one of the hands was at a knife in his belt, and Two-feathers's lance came down like a fence between them. Her broom hit it and bounced up. The three of them stood there. . . .

Two-feathers was laughing. The lean Indian wasn't. The calico lay on the floor, trampled; she bent and picked it up, and her nervous fingers plucked away its wrinkles and rolled it again into a bolt.

"Martha, you're gonna rile 'em," her husband said.

"Be quiet," she told him without looking away from Two-feathers's laughing eyes.

"Good," the big Indian's mouth said in English from out of the black-and-red smear. With his hand he touched the long chestnut hair at her ear; she tossed her head away from the touch, and he laughed again. *"Mucha mujer,"* he said.

The lean one jabbered at him spittingly.

Martha Sherman's oldest said calmly: "That's red hair."

It was. In the cabin's windowless gloom she had not noticed, but now she saw that the lean one's dirty braids glinted auburn, and that his eyes, flicking from her to the authoritative big one, were green like her own. Finally he nodded sulkily to something that Two-feathers said. Two-feathers waved the other warriors back and turned to where Ezra Sherman stood beside the dinner table.

"No hurt," he said, and jerked his head toward the door. "Vamoose."

"Yes," Ezra Sherman said, and stuck out his hand. "Friend. Good fellow."

The big Indian glanced ironically at the hand and touched it with his own. "Vamoose," he repeated.

Ezra Sherman said: "You see? He don't mean no trouble. I bet if I dip up some molasses they'll just . . ."

"He means go," Martha Sherman said levelly. "You bring Alfie."

"Go where?"

*"Come on!"* she said, and the force of her utterance bent him down and put his callus-crusted farmer's hands beneath his baby's arms and straightened him and pulled him along behind her as she walked, holding the hands of the middle children, out the door into the stir and murmur of the big war party. It was misting lightly, grayly. . . . The solemn oldest boy came last, and as he left the cabin he was still looking back at the green-eyed, lean, redheaded Comanche.

Two-feathers shouted from the door and the gabble died, and staring straight ahead Martha Sherman led her family across the bare wet dirt of the yard and through the gate, past ponies' tossing hackamored heads and the bristle of bows and muskets and lances and the flat dark eyes of fifty Comanches. She took the road toward the creek. In a minute they were in brush, out of sight of the house, and they heard the voices begin loud again behind them. Martha Sherman began to trot, dragging the children.

"Where we goin' to?" Ezra Sherman said.

"Pottses'."

He said: "I don't see how you could git so ugly about a little old hank of cloth and then leave the whole house with—"

"Don't talk, Ezra," she said. "Move. Please, please move."

But then there was the thudding rattle of unshod hooves on the road behind them, and a hard-clutching hand in her chestnut hair, and a ring of ponies dancing around them, with brown riders whose bodies gave and flexed with the dancing like joined excrescences of the ponies' spines.

Before she managed to twist her head and see him, she knew it was the redheaded one who had her; he gabbled contemptuously at Ezra Sherman, and with the musket in his other hand pointed down the road toward the creek. The pony shied at the motion, yanking her off balance. She did not fight now, knowing it pointless or worse.

"Durn you, let her be!" Ezra Sherman yelled, moving, but a sharp lancepoint pricked his chest two inches from the baby's nose and he stopped, looking up.

"Go on, Ezra," his wife said. "They'll let you go."

"Ain't right," he said. The lancepoint jabbed; he backed away a half-foot.

"Go on."

He went, trailing stumbling children, and the last she saw of them was the back-turned face of her oldest, but one of the horsemen made a plunging run at him, and he turned and followed the family. . . . The redhead's pony spun and started dancing back up the road. The hand jerked her hair, and she went half down, and a hoof caught her ankle; then she was running to keep from dragging. Snow was drifting horizontally against the chinaberries she had planted around her dooryard, though it was not cold; she saw finally that it was feathers from her bed, which one of them had ripped open and was shaking in the doorway while others laughed. In a shed some of them had found the molasses barrel and had axed its top and were drinking from tin cups and from their hands, throwing the ropy liquid over each other with yells. The old milk cow came loping and bawling grotesquely from behind the house, a Comanche astride her neck, three arrows through her flopping bag. . . .

Deftly, without loosening his grip, the redhead swung his leg across his pony's neck and slid to the ground and in one long strong motion, like laying out a rope or a blanket, threw her flat. Two of the others took her legs, pulling them apart. She kicked. The flame-pain of a lance knifed into her ribs and through her chest and out the back and into the ground and was withdrawn; she felt each inch of its thrust and retreat, and in a contraction of shock there relaxed elsewhere, and her legs were clamped out wide, and the lean redhead had let go of her hair and stood above her, working at his waistband.

Spread-eagled, she twisted her head and saw Two-feathers a few yards away, her big Bible in his hands, watching. Her eyes spoke, and maybe her mouth; he shrugged and turned toward the shed where the molasses barrel stood, past a group that was trying to light fire against the wet cabin wall. . . .

The world was a wild yell, and the redhead was first, and the third one, grunting, had molasses smeared over his chest and bed feathers stuck in it, and after that she didn't count; though trying hard she could not slip over into the blackness that lay just beyond an uncrossable line. Still conscious, and that part over, she knew when one on horseback held her arms up and another worked a steel-pointed arrow manually, slowly, into her body under her shoulderblade, and left it there. Knew, too, when the knife made its hot circumcision against the bone of her skull, and when a horseman meshed his fingers into her long hair again and she was dragging beside his panicked, snorting pony. But the hair was good and held, and finally a stocky warrior had to stand with a foot on each of her shoulders as she lay in the plowed field before the house, and peel off her scalp by main force.

For a time after that they galloped back and forth across her body, yelling—one thing she recalled with a crystallinity that the rest of it lost, or never had, was that no hoof touched her—and shot two or three more arrows into her, and went away. She lived for four days (another writer says three, and another still says one, adding the detail that she gave birth to a dead child; take your pick), tended by neighbor women, and if those days were anything but a continuing fierce dream for her, no record of it has come down.

In delirium, she kept saying she wouldn't have minded half so much if it hadn't been for that red hair. . . .

The oldest boy had quit his stepfather and had circled back through the brush and had watched it all from hiding. No record, either, states how he felt about Comanches afterward, or the act of love, or anything.

It seems clear that The People were good haters. So were the whites, though, and that was a year before a war unconnected with Indians was to draw away many of the tough young ones. The Brazos frontier stewed; citizens and Rangers and soldiers joined into a pursuit to follow the party and its big herd of horses (500 or 600 by the time they left the settlements) to the Comanche winter villages in the northwest. Charles Goodnight was along, and Sul Ross, and Captain Jack Cureton, and nearly everybody else, and most of them left accounts of it which flatly conflict. What is sure is that they found Comanches on the Pease, and smote them hip and thigh, man and woman and child, and took back Mrs. Sherman's Bible and a blue-eyed, sullen squaw who turned out to be Cynthia Ann Parker, kidnapped twenty-four years previously on the Navasota. Her Uncle Isaac (Parker County is named for him, and he died there) journeyed up to Camp Cooper to identify her when the expedition returned. She lived for four captive years among relatives, scarcely ever breaking silence except to beg brokenly that they let her go back to her husband and her children and the free, dirty, shifting life of the plains. Since of course they wouldn't, she died in the damp windless forests of East Texas. But Peta Nocona had sired a son on her, Quanah, who was to be one of the great chiefs in the last years of the fighting, and who survived to wear black suits on visits to Fort Worth and to be friends with Theodore Roosevelt.

(That story trails on: Theodore Roosevelt gave Quanah land in perpetuity in Oklahoma, pretty land along Cache Creek, and just last year —perpetuity, as is its wont with Indians, having expired—his children and grandchildren and the last of his wives came protestingly into the news again when the Field Artillery had the place condemned and grabbed it.)

Maybe the redheaded Comanche had been another one like Cynthia Ann, or maybe like Quanah the half-white son of another woman captured long before. The bag of fragmentary, jumbled, contradictory tales left over from the frontier is lumpy with mysteries like that, and no one will ever solve them now. The reason Cynthia Ann's story is famous, besides her relation to Quanah, is that it came to the surface again, and had an end, whereas most of the others didn't. Captive children, renegades white and black, Mexicans by the hundreds—The People weren't exclusive in terms of race. They'd been winners for too long to be a pure blood, anyhow; women go to winners. They were a spirit, another on the roster of the world's proud savages who had to win totally or lose totally, like Zulus and Araucanians and Moros and Pathans and Fuzzy-Wuzzies. All colonial and imperial histories are smoky with their fighting. There's more pathos in the defeat of gentle and reasonable peoples, but the fall of pride strikes more sparks.

If the river has meaning for you, you can see all of that from the sandstone bluffs where the mountains drop away. You don't have to strain to impose the tales on the landscape; they're there. . . . Margaret Barton at Brannon's Crossing with an arrow next to her heart which they were afraid to pull out, throbbing in the air with her blood beat, all night long . . . Bill Youngblood, whose cohorts gave chase and killed the Indian who had his scalp, and galloped to the graveyard just in time to put it back on his head—their literal, Calvinistic application of the doctrine of corporeal resurrection agreeing with the Comanches that it was bad to go to your earthly resting place in more than one piece, or for that matter less . . . Dignified Mr. Couts, later the big man at Weatherford, who ranched in the early days opposite Palo Pinto mouth and refused to take guff from the four hairiest white bully-boys in the neighborhood; they waited for him with shotguns between the spring and the church door at Soda Springs one Sunday morning, and, knowing them there, he walked on into them with a bucket of cool water in his hand and a Colt's Navy in his waistband. When they opened fire, he got the first one through the heart, the second one through the trigger hand and then the shoulder, and the third in the hip. ("The reason I didn't kill him as he went in at the door," he told Mr. Holland analytically later, "was that he jumped up about two feet getting in and I hit him that much below where I aimed.") The fourth, comprehensibly spooked, piled his horse into a ditch and smashed up his face and shoulder. Mr. Couts counted the bullet holes in his hat and his black silk vest, and the neighborhood was reasonably lawful for a time after that. . . . In '66 he drove 1,000 longhorns to California, rode back alone across the plains and down the Platte to the Missouri with $50,000 in gold in his saddlebags, caught a boat south, and opened a bank.

Most of those stories are recorded, though only a few are recorded well. In what scholars call "primary sources"—pioneers' memoirs and little county histories with a genealogical slant—they're likely to be a bit prejudiced and fragmentary, with the choicest details left out either from delicacy or because cowards and scoundrels have descendants. In the Texas brag-books and their ilk, a teeming species, they're most often contorted beyond recognition. Only in the work of a few people who for the past score or so of years have been trying, literately and otherwise, to see shape in the too turbulent century behind us, do they come out straight—or fairly straight, since the old folks those historians talked to had written nothing down when things were popping, and only spoke of them later when memory was playing its dirty tricks.

There is consequently a mistiness. . . . Take Andrew Berry. The People caught him down the river a way from the Point with a wagon-load of pumpkins, and after killing him scalped him and broke the pumpkins over his bloody skull. But one version of the story has him killed just below Lazy Bend, and another far down by Spring Creek, and a third, more dramatic but just as likely to be true, has two little redheaded sons along with him who were scalped and crowned with pumpkins, too.

The fact is, the stories have been retreating into fog for a long time, as maybe they should. Boosters in compulsory beards stage centennials in the little towns and resurrect the old bloodshed in pamphlets and festivals, and have high times dunking one another in reconstructed horse troughs. Some towns maintain annual pageants, and museums. But the significances are transmuted there, more often than not, by what Hollywood and television and the *Post* and who-not have said the general West was like, and by the Texas paranoia (petroleum and carved belts and bourbon and country clubs and nickeled six-guns and aircraft factories and the excessive regional glee of the newly arrived: mingle them with the old leathery thing if you can), so that the rough-edged realities of the past have faded dimmer each year.

Probably a man from that bump of the country who has soaked the tales in runs a danger of overappraising their worth. In kind, they don't differ sharply from the lore most regions west of the Mississippi can muster. In weight—in, say, the number of people killed or the human glory or shame manifested in their slaughter—they're dustmote-sized when you compare them to the violences two wars in two generations have wrought among our race. I once saw 4,000 Japanese stacked like cordwood, the harvest of two days' fighting, on one single islet of one single atoll awaiting bulldozer burial, more dead than the Brazos country could show for its whole two or three decades of travail, and just as brave. Almost daily for years, Belsen or Dachau could have matched the flavor of Mrs. Sherman's agony. . . .

What it amounts to is that a short segment of the American frontier, distinctive in its way but not as distinctive as a local might be tempted to think, paused in the Brazos country, crackled and smoked for a few years like fire in underbrush while the Indians were being fought out of existence and the cattle were being harried north, and then moved on, carrying most of the vigorous frontiersmen with it.

Nothing that happened in this segment, then or later, made any notable dent in human history. From one very possible point of view, the stories tell of a partly unnecessary, drawn-out squabble between savages and half-illiterate louts constituting the fringes of a culture which, two and a half centuries before, had spawned Shakespeare, and which even then was reading Dickens and Trollope and Thoreau and considering the thoughts of Charles Darwin. They tell too—the stories—of the subsequent squabbles among the louts themselves: of cattle thievery, corn whisky, Reconstruction, blood feuds, lynchings, splinter sectarianism, and further illiteracy.

Can they then have any bearing on mankind's adventure?

Maybe, a little. They don't all tell of louts. There was something of a showing-through; meanings floated near the surface which have relevance to the murkier thing Americans have become. It didn't happen just on the Brazos, certainly, but all along the line of that moving brush fire. There's nothing new in the idea that the frontier had continuing impact on our character, or that one slice of that frontier, examined, may to some degree explain the whole. . . .

But in truth such gravities were not what salted the tales I could read, looking off over the low country from the point atop the bluffs. Mankind is one thing; a man's self is another. What that self is tangles itself knottily with what his people were, and what they came out of. Mine came out of Texas, as did I. If those were louts, they were my own louts.

Origin being as it is an accident outside the scope of one's will, I tend not to seek much credit for being a Texan. Often (breathes there a man?) I can work up some proud warmth about the fact that I indubitably am one. A lot of the time, though, I'd as soon be forty other kinds of men I've known. I've lived much away from that region, and have liked most of the places I've lived in. I used to know who the good bullfighters were and why they were good. I'm familiar with the washed silent streets of Manhattan at five o'clock in the morning, and what Los Angeles promises in the evening when you're young with money on your hip, and once almost saw the rats change sewers swarmingly in Paris, and did see dawn wash the top of the old wall at Avila. . . . I've waked in the green freshness of mountain mornings in tropical lands, and have heard the strange birds cry, and the street venders, and maybe music somewhere, and have felt the hit of it like a fist in my stomach, going sleepy-eyed out onto a balcony under the green mountains and above flame-flower trees to thank God for life and for being there. And I'm glad I have.

If a man couldn't escape what he came from, we would most of us still be peasants in Old World hovels. But if, having escaped or not, he wants in some way to know himself, define himself, and tries to do it without taking into account the thing he came from, he is writing without any ink in his pen. The provincial who cultivates only his roots is in peril, potato-like, of becoming more root than plant. The man who cuts his roots away and denies that they were ever connected with him withers into a half a man. . . . It's not necessary to like being a Texan, or a Midwesterner, or a Jew, or an Andalusian, or a Negro, or a hybrid child of the international rich. It is, I think, necessary to know in that crystal chamber of the mind where one speaks straight to oneself that one is or was that thing, and for any understanding of the human condition it's probably necessary to know a little about what the thing consists of.

And Mrs. Sherman and Bigfoot Wallace and Charlie Goodnight and Old Lady Rippy and the rest of them, haunting the country they'd known below the Point, were a part of my thing. They weren't all of it, but they were a part. In mere fact, they were. Much of the good and bad and beside-the-point of what they'd been was stuck in me as certainly as the canyon wren's song, as surely as were the memories, looking down toward Brazos town, of the times we'd misread the wild zigzagging channel in those sandy stretches and had ended on bars and had had to get out to tug the loaded boat over, up to our knees in shaking, sucking quicksand. That it all meant much was doubtful, and that I'd ever understand a half of what it did mean was more doubtful still, but the effort seemed worth while.

Such, as Port Smythe, M.D., might have written if he hadn't been too tired for climbing when he got there, were the Conflicting Sentiments with which my Bosom was inspired as I gazed out from that Noble Eminence.

I inched and skidded back down the bluff, tossed my gear and my dog into the aged Old Town, and took off paddling down the river toward the T. & P. bridge. . . .

(1960)

*William Stafford*

## One Home

Mine was a Midwest home—you can keep your world.
Plain black hats rode the thoughts that made our code.
We sang hymns in the house; the roof was near God.

The light bulb that hung in the pantry made a wan light,
but we could read by it the names of preserves—
outside, the buffalo grass, and the wind in the night.

A wildcat sprang at Grandpa on the Fourth of July
when he was cutting plum bushes for fuel,
before Indians pulled the West over the edge of the sky.

To anyone who looked at us we said, "My friend";
liking the cut of a thought, we could say, "Hello."
(But plain black hats rode the thoughts that made our code.)

The sun was over our town; it was like a blade.
Kicking cottonwood leaves we ran toward storms.
Wherever we looked the land would hold us up.

(1966)

## The Rescued Year

Take a model of the world so big
it is the world again, pass your hand,
press back that area in the west where no one lived,
the place only your mind explores. On your thumb
that smudge becomes my ignorance, a badge
the size of Colorado: toward that state by train
we crossed our state like birds and lodged—
the year my sister gracefully
grew up—against the western boundary
where my father had a job.

Time should go the way it went
that year: we weren't at war; we had

each day a treasured unimportance;
the sky existed, so did our town;
the library had books we hadn't read;
every day at school we learned and sang,
or at least hummed and walked in the hall.

In church I heard the preacher; he said
"Honor!" with a sound like empty silos
repeating the lesson. For a minute I held
Kansas Christian all along the Santa Fe.
My father's mean attention, though, was busy — this
I knew — and going home his wonderfully level gaze
would hold the state I liked, where little happened
and much was understood. I watched my father's finger
mark off huge eye-scans of what happened in the creed.

Like him, I tried. I still try,
send my sight like a million pickpockets
up rich people's drives: it is time
when I pass for every place I go to be alive.
Around any corner my sight is a river,
and I let it arrive: rich by those brooks
his thought poured for hours
into my hand. His creed: the greatest ownership
of all is to glance around and understand.

That Christmas Mother made paper
presents; we colored them with crayons
and hung up a tumbleweed for a tree.
A man from Hugoton brought my sister
a present (his farm was tilted near oil
wells; his car ignored the little
bumps along our drive: nothing
came of all this — it was just part of the year).

I walked out where a girl I knew would be;
we crossed the plank over the ditch
to her house. There was popcorn on the stove,
and her mother recalled the old days, inviting me back.
When I walked home in the cold evening,
snow that blessed the wheat had roved
along the highway seeking furrows,
and all the houses had their lights —
oh, that year did not escape me: I rubbed
the wonderful old lamp of our dull town.

That spring we crossed the state again,
my father soothing us with stories:
the river lost in Utah, underground—
"They've explored only the ones they've found!"—
and that old man who spent his life knowing,
unable to tell how he knew—
"I've been sure by smoke, persuaded
by mist, or a cloud, or a name:
once the truth was ready"—my father smiled
at this—"it didn't care how it came."

In all his ways I hold that rescued year—
comes that smoke like love into the broken
coal, that forms to chunks again and lies
in the earth again in its dim folds, and comes a sound,
then shapes to make a whistle fade,
and in the quiet I hold no need, no hurry:
any day the dust will move, maybe settle;
the train that left will roll back into our station,
the name carved on the platform unfill with rain,
and the sound that followed the couplings back
will ripple forward and hold the train.

                                                            (1966)


## George Garrett

# Goodbye, Old Paint, I'm Leaving Cheyenne

From the television set come shots and cries,
a hollow drum of hooves and then,
emerging from snowy chaos, the tall riders
plunging in a tumultuous surf of dust.
The Stage, it seems, is overdue.
My children, armed to the teeth, enchanted,
are, for the moment at least, quiet.
I see the Badmen riding for the Gulch,
all grins, not knowing as we do
("The rest of you guys follow me!")
the Hero's going to get there first.
And as the plot like a lariat spins out
a tricky noose, I shrink and become

a boy with a sweaty nickel in his palm
waiting to see two features and the serial
at the Rialto on a Saturday morning:
Buck Jones, the taciturn, Tom Mix
of silver spinning guns and a white horse,
and somebody left face to face with a buzz saw,
to writhe into next Saturday morning.

But how you have changed, my cavaliers,
how much we have had to grow up!
No Hero now is anything but cautious.
(We know the hole a .45 can make.)
No Badman's born that way.
("My mother loved me but she died.")
No buzz saw frightens like the whine
of a mind gone wild. No writhing's like
the spirit's on its bed of nails.
I clench my nickel tighter in my fist.
Children, this plot is new to me.
I watch the Hero take the wrong road
at the Fork and gallop away, grim-faced,
worn out from the exercise of choice.
I see the Badmen safely reach the Gulch,
then fight among themselves and die,
proving good luck is worse than any wound.
My spellbound children stare and couldn't care
less about my fit of raw nostalgia
or all the shabby ghosts I loved and lost.

(1967)

**N. Scott Momaday**

## *from* The Way to Rainy Mountain

### Introduction

A single knoll rises out of the plain in Oklahoma, north and west of the
Wichita Range. For my people, the Kiowas, it is an old landmark, and
they gave it the name Rainy Mountain. The hardest weather in the world
is there. Winter brings blizzards, hot tornadic winds arise in the spring,

and in summer the prairie is an anvil's edge. The grass turns brittle and brown, and it cracks beneath your feet. There are green belts along the rivers and creeks, linear groves of hickory and pecan, willow and witch hazel. At a distance in July or August the steaming foliage seems almost to writhe in fire. Great green and yellow grasshoppers are everywhere in the tall grass, popping up like corn to sting the flesh, and tortoises crawl about on the red earth, going nowhere in the plenty of time. Loneliness is an aspect of the land. All things in the plain are isolate; there is no confusion of objects in the eye, but *one* hill or *one* tree or *one* man. To look upon that landscape in the early morning, with the sun at your back, is to lose the sense of proportion. Your imagination comes to life, and this, you think, is where Creation was begun.

I returned to Rainy Mountain in July. My grandmother had died in the spring, and I wanted to be at her grave. She had lived to be very old and at last infirm. Her only living daughter was with her when she died, and I was told that in death her face was that of a child.

I like to think of her as a child. When she was born, the Kiowas were living the last great moment of their history. For more than a hundred years they had controlled the open range from the Smoky Hill River to the Red, from the headwaters of the Canadian to the fork of the Arkansas and Cimarron. In alliance with the Comanches, they had ruled the whole of the southern Plains. War was their sacred business, and they were among the finest horsemen the world has ever known. But warfare for the Kiowas was preeminently a matter of disposition rather than of survival, and they never understood the grim, unrelenting advance of the U.S. Cavalry. When at last, divided and ill-provisioned, they were driven onto the Staked Plains in the cold rains of autumn, they fell into panic. In Palo Duro Canyon they abandoned their crucial stores to pillage and had nothing then but their lives. In order to save themselves, they surrendered to the soldiers at Fort Sill and were imprisoned in the old stone corral that now stands as a military museum. My grandmother was spared the humiliation of those high gray walls by eight or ten years, but she must have known from birth the affliction of defeat, the dark brooding of old warriors.

Her name was Aho, and she belonged to the last culture to evolve in North America. Her forebears came down from the high country in western Montana nearly three centuries ago. They were a mountain people, a mysterious tribe of hunters whose language has never been positively classified in any major group. In the late seventeenth century they began a long migration to the south and east. It was a journey toward the dawn, and it led to a golden age. Along the way the Kiowas were befriended by the Crows, who gave them the culture and religion of the Plains. They acquired horses, and their ancient nomadic spirit was suddenly free of the ground. They acquired Tai-me, the sacred Sun Dance doll, from that moment the object and symbol of their worship, and so shared in the divinity of the sun. Not least, they acquired the sense of destiny, therefore courage and pride. When they entered upon the southern Plains they had been transformed. No longer were they slaves to the simple necessity of survival; they were a lordly and dangerous society of fighters and thieves, hunters and priests of the sun. According to their origin myth, they entered the world through a hollow log. From one point of view, their migration was the fruit of an old prophecy, for indeed they emerged from a sunless world.

Although my grandmother lived out her long life in the shadow of Rainy Mountain, the immense landscape of the continental interior lay like memory in her blood. She could tell of the Crows, whom she had never seen, and of the Black Hills, where she had never been. I wanted to see in reality what she had seen more perfectly in the mind's eye, and traveled fifteen hundred miles to begin my pilgrimage.

Yellowstone, it seemed to me, was the top of the world, a region of deep lakes and dark timber, canyons and waterfalls. But, beautiful as it is, one might have the sense of confinement there. The skyline in all directions is close at hand, the high wall of the woods and deep cleavages of shade. There is a perfect freedom in the mountains, but it belongs to the eagle and the elk, the badger and the bear. The Kiowas reckoned their stature by the distance they could see, and they were bent and blind in the wilderness.

Descending eastward, the highland meadows are a stairway to the plain. In July the inland slope of the Rockies is luxuriant with flax and buckwheat, stonecrop and larkspur. The earth unfolds and the limit of the land recedes. Clusters of trees, and animals grazing far in the distance, cause the vision to reach away and wonder to build upon the mind. The sun follows a longer course in the day, and the sky is immense beyond all comparison. The great billowing clouds that sail upon it are shadows that move upon the grain like water, dividing light. Farther down, in the land of the Crows and Blackfeet, the plain is yellow. Sweet clover takes hold of the hills and bends upon itself to cover and seal the soil. There the Kiowas paused on their way; they had come to the place where they must change their lives. The sun is at home on the plains. Precisely there does it have the certain character of a god. When the Kiowas came to the land of the Crows, they could see the dark lees of the hills at dawn across the Bighorn River, the profusion of light on the grain shelves, the oldest deity ranging after the solstices. Not yet would they veer southward to the caldron of the land that lay below; they must wean their blood from the northern winter and hold the mountains a while longer in their view. They bore Tai-me in procession to the east.

A dark mist lay over the Black Hills, and the land was like iron. At the top of a ridge I caught sight of Devil's Tower upthrust against the gray sky as if in the birth of time the core of the earth had broken through its crust and the motion of the world was begun. There are things in nature that engender an awful quiet in the heart of man; Devil's Tower is one of them. Two centuries ago, because they could not do otherwise, the Kiowas made a legend at the base of the rock. My grandmother said:

Eight children were there at play, seven sisters and their brother. Suddenly the boy was struck dumb; he trembled and began to run upon his hands and feet. His fingers became claws, and his body was covered with fur. Directly there was a bear where the boy had been. The sisters were terrified; they ran, and the bear after them. They came to the stump of a great tree, and the tree spoke to them. It bade them climb upon it, and as they did so it began to rise into the air. The bear came to kill them, but they were just beyond its reach. It reared against the tree and scored the bark all around with its claws. The seven sisters were borne into the sky, and they became the stars of the Big Dipper.

From that moment, and so long as the legend lives, the Kiowas have kinsmen in the night sky. Whatever they were in the mountains, they could be no more. However tenuous their well-being, however much they had suffered and would suffer again, they had found a way out of the wilderness.

My grandmother had a reverence for the sun, a holy regard that now is all but gone out of mankind. There was a wariness in her, and an ancient awe. She was a Christian in her later years, but she had come a long way about, and she never forgot her birthright. As a child she had been to the Sun Dances; she had taken part in those annual rites, and by them she had learned the restoration of her people in the presence of Tai-me. She was about seven when the last Kiowa Sun Dance was held in 1887 on the Washita River above Rainy Mountain Creek. The buffalo were gone. In order to consummate the ancient sacrifice – to impale the head of a buffalo bull upon the medicine tree – a delegation of old men journeyed into Texas, there to beg and barter for an animal from the Goodnight herd. She was ten when the Kiowas came together for the last time as a living Sun Dance culture. They could find no buffalo; they had to hang an old hide from the sacred tree. Before the dance could begin, a company of soldiers rode out from Fort Sill under orders to disperse the tribe. Forbidden without cause the essential act of their faith, having seen the wild herds slaughtered and left to rot upon the ground, the Kiowas backed away forever from the medicine tree. That was July 20, 1890, at the great bend of the Washita. My grandmother was there. Without bitterness, and for as long as she lived, she bore a vision of deicide.

Now that I can have her only in memory, I see my grandmother in the several postures that were peculiar to her: standing at the wood stove on a winter morning and turning meat in a great iron skillet; sitting at the south window, bent above her beadwork, and afterwards, when her vision failed, looking down for a long time into the fold of her hands; going out upon a cane, very slowly as she did when the weight of age came upon her; praying. I remember her most often at prayer. She made long, rambling prayers out of suffering and hope, having seen many things. I was never sure that I had the right to hear, so exclusive were they of all mere custom and company. The last time I saw her she prayed standing by the side of her bed at night, naked to the waist, the light of a kerosene lamp moving upon her dark skin. Her long, black hair, always drawn and braided in the day, lay upon her shoulders and against her breasts like a shawl. I do not speak Kiowa, and I never understood her prayers, but there was something inherently sad in the sound, some merest hesitation upon the syllables of sorrow. She began in a high and descending pitch, exhausting her breath to silence; then again and again — and always the same intensity of effort, of something that is, and is not, like urgency in the human voice. Transported so in the dancing light among the shadows of her room, she seemed beyond the reach of time. But that was illusion; I think I knew then that I should not see her again.

Houses are like sentinels in the plain, old keepers of the weather watch. There, in a very little while, wood takes on the appearance of great age. All colors wear soon away in the wind and rain, and then the wood is burned gray and the grain appears and the nails turn red with rust. The windowpanes are black and opaque; you imagine there is nothing within, and indeed there are many ghosts, bones given up to the land. They stand here and there against the sky, and you approach them for a longer time than you expect. They belong in the distance; it is their domain.

Once there was a lot of sound in my grandmother's house, a lot of coming and going, feasting and talk. The summers there were full of excitement and reunion. The Kiowas are a summer people; they abide the cold and keep to themselves, but when the season turns and the land becomes warm and vital they cannot hold still; an old love of going returns upon them. The aged visitors who came to my grandmother's house when I was a child were made of lean and leather, and they bore themselves upright. They wore great black hats and bright ample shirts that shook in the wind. They rubbed fat upon their hair and wound their braids with strips of colored cloth. Some of them painted their faces and carried the scars of old and cherished enmities. They were an old council of warlords, come to remind and be reminded of who they were. Their wives and daughters served them well. The women might indulge themselves; gossip was at once the mark and compensation of their servitude. They made loud and elaborate talk among themselves, full of jest and gesture, fright and false alarm. They went abroad in fringed and flowered shawls, bright beadwork and German silver. They were at home in the kitchen, and they prepared meals that were banquets.

There were frequent prayer meetings, and great nocturnal feasts. When I was a child I played with my cousins outside, where the lamplight fell upon the ground and the singing of the old people rose up around us and carried away into the darkness. There were a lot of good things to eat, a lot of laughter and surprise. And afterwards, when the quiet returned, I lay down with my grandmother and could hear the frogs away by the river and feel the motion of the air.

Now there is a funeral silence in the rooms, the endless wake of some final word. The walls have closed in upon my grandmother's house. When I returned to it in mourning, I saw for the first time in my life how small it was. It was late at night, and there was a white moon, nearly full. I sat for a long time on the stone steps by the kitchen door. From there I could see out across the land; I could see the long row of trees by the creek, the low light upon the rolling plains, and the stars of the Big Dipper. Once I looked at the moon and caught sight of a strange thing. A cricket had perched upon the handrail, only a few inches away from me. My line of vision was such that the creature filled the moon like a fossil. It had gone there, I thought, to live and die, for there, of all places, was its small definition made whole and eternal. A warm wind rose up and purled like the longing within me.

The next morning I awoke at dawn and went out on the dirt road to Rainy Mountain. It was already hot, and the grasshoppers began to fill the air. Still, it was early in the morning, and the birds sang out of the shadows. The long yellow grass on the mountain shone in the bright light, and a scissortail hied above the land. There, where it ought to be, at the end of a long and legendary way, was my grandmother's grave. Here and there on the dark stones were ancestral names. Looking back once, I saw the mountain and came away.

(1967, 1969)

**Marge Piercy**

# Half Past Home

Morning rattles the tall spike fence.
Already the old are set out to get dirty in the sun
spread like drying coverlets around the garden
by straggly hedges smelling of tomcat.
From the steep oxblood hospital
hunched under its miser's frown of roof,
dishes mutter, pumps work, an odor
of disinfectant slops into the street
toward the greygreen quadrangles of the university.
Pickets with the facts of their poverty hoisted on sticks

turn in the street like a tattered washing.
The trustees decline to negotiate
for this is a charitable institution.

Among the houses of the poor and black nearby
a crane nods waisthigh among broken bedrooms.
Already the university digs foundations
to be hallowed with the names of old trustees.
The dish and bottle washers, the orderlies march
carrying the crooked sick toward death on their backs.
The neighborhood is being cured of poverty.
Busses will carry the moppushers in and out.

Are the old drying too slowly in their garden?
Under elms spacious and dusty
as roominghouse porches the old men mutter
that they are closing the north wing,
for the land is valuable when you get down to it
and they will, down to the prairie dog bones.

This is the Home for Incurables: and the old are.
Many are the diseases that trustees are blind to,
or call incurable, like their own blindness
wide as the hoarse wind blows, mile after mile
where the city smokes sweetly as a barbecue
or sizzles like acid under nobody's sun.

(1970)

# How large is our community?

*Pericles*

## Funeral Oration*

Many of those who have spoken here in the past have praised the institution of this speech at the close of our ceremony. It seemed to them a mark of honour to our soldiers who have fallen in war that a speech should be made over them. I do not agree. These men have shown themselves valiant in action, and it would be enough, I think, for their glories to be proclaimed in action, as you have just seen it done at this funeral organized by the State. Our belief in the courage and manliness of so many should not be hazarded on the goodness or badness of one man's speech. Then it is not easy to speak with a proper sense of balance, when a man's listeners find it difficult to believe in the truth of what one is saying. The man who knows the facts and loves the dead may well think that an oration tells less than what he knows and what he would like to hear: others who do not know so much may feel envy for the dead, and think the orator overpraises them, when he speaks of exploits that are beyond their own capacities. Praise of other people is tolerable only up to a certain point, the point where one still believes that one could do oneself some of the things one is hearing about. Once you get beyond this point, you will find people becoming jealous and incredulous. However, the fact is that this institution was set up and approved by our forefa-

*Translation by Rex Warner.

thers, and it is my duty to follow the tradition and do my best to meet the wishes and the expectations of every one of you.

I shall begin by speaking about our ancestors, since it is only right and proper on such an occasion to pay them the honour of recalling what they did. In this land of ours there have always been the same people living from generation to generation up till now, and they, by their courage and their virtues, have handed it on to us, a free country. They certainly deserve our praise. Even more so do our fathers deserve it. For to the inheritance they had received they added all the empire we have now, and it was not without blood and toil that they handed it down to us of the present generation. And then we ourselves, assembled here to-day, who are mostly in the prime of life, have, in most directions, added to the power of our empire and have organized our State in such a way that it is perfectly well able to look after itself both in peace and in war.

I have no wish to make a long speech on subjects familiar to you all: so I shall say nothing about the warlike deeds by which we acquired our power or the battles in which we or our fathers gallantly resisted our enemies, Greek or foreign. What I want to do is, in the first place, to discuss the spirit in which we faced our trials and also our constitution and the way of life which has made us great. After that I shall speak in praise of the dead, believing that this kind of speech is not inappropriate to the present occasion, and that this whole assembly, of citizens and foreigners, may listen to it with advantage.

Let me say that our system of government does not copy the institutions of our neighbours. It is more the case of our being a model to others, than of our imitating anyone else. Our constitution is called a democracy because power is in the hands not of a minority but of the whole people. When it is a question of settling private disputes, everyone is equal before the law; when it is a question of putting one person before another in positions of public responsibility, what counts is not membership of a particular class, but the actual ability which the man possesses. No one, so long as he has it in him to be of service to the state, is kept in political obscurity because of poverty. And, just as our political life is free and open, so is our day-to-day life in our relations with each other. We do not get into a state with our next-door neighbour if he enjoys himself in his own way, nor do we give him the kind of black looks which, though they do no real harm, still do hurt people's feelings. We are free and tolerant in our private lives; but in public affairs we keep to the law. This is because it commands our deep respect.

We give our obedience to those whom we put in positions of authority, and we obey the laws themselves, especially those which are for the protection of the oppressed, and those unwritten laws which it is an acknowledged shame to break.

And here is another point. When our work is over, we are in a position to enjoy all kinds of recreation for our spirits. There are various kinds of contests and sacrifices regularly throughout the year; in our own homes we find a beauty and a good taste which delight us every day and which drive away our cares. Then the greatness of our city brings it about that all the good things from all over the world flow in to us, so that to us it seems just as natural to enjoy foreign goods as our own local products.

Then there is a great difference between us and our opponents, in our attitude towards military security. Here are some examples: Our city is open to the world, and we have no periodical deportations in order to prevent people observing or finding out secrets which might be of military advantage to the enemy. This is because we rely, not on secret weapons, but on our own real courage and loyalty. There is a difference, too, in our educational systems. The Spartans, from their earliest boyhood, are submitted to the most laborious training in courage; we pass our lives without all these restrictions, and yet are just as ready to face the same dangers as they are. Here is a proof of this: When the Spartans invade our land, they do not come by themselves, but bring all their allies with them; whereas we, when we launch an attack abroad, do the job by ourselves, and, though fighting on foreign soil, do not often fail to defeat opponents who are fighting for their own hearths and homes. As a matter of fact none of our enemies has ever yet been confronted with our total strength, because we have to divide our attention between our navy and the many missions on which our troops are sent on land. Yet, if our enemies engage a detachment of our forces and defeat it, they give themselves credit for having thrown back our entire army; or, if they lose, they claim that they were beaten by us in full strength. There are certain advantages, I think, in our way of meeting danger voluntarily, with an easy mind, instead of with a laborious training, with natural rather than with state-induced courage. We do not have to spend our time practising to meet sufferings which are still in the future; and when they are actually upon us we show ourselves just as brave as these others who are always in strict training. This is one point in which, I think, our city deserves to be admired. There are also others:

Our love of what is beautiful does not lead to extravagance; our love of the things of the mind does not make us soft. We regard wealth as something to be properly used, rather than as something to boast about. As for poverty, no one need be ashamed to admit it: the real shame is in not taking practical measures to escape from it. Here each individual is interested not only in his own affairs but in the affairs of the state as well: even those who are mostly occupied with their own business are extremely well-informed on general politics – this is a peculiarity of ours: we do not say that a man who takes no interest in politics is a man who minds his own business; we say that he has no business here at all. We Athenians, in our own persons, take our decisions on policy or submit them to proper discussions: for we do not think that there is an incompatibility between words and deeds; the worst thing is to rush into action before the consequences have been properly debated. And this is another point where we differ from other people. We are capable at the same time of taking risks and of estimating them beforehand. Others are brave out of ignorance; and, when they stop to think, they begin to fear. But the man who can most truly be accounted brave is he who best knows the meaning of what is sweet in life and of what is terrible, and then goes out undeterred to meet what is to come.

Again, in questions of general good feeling there is a great contrast between us and most other people. We make friends by doing good to others, not by receiving good from them. This makes our friendship all the more reliable, since we want to keep alive the gratitude of those who are in our debt by showing continued goodwill to them: whereas the feelings of one who owes us something lack the same enthusiasm, since he knows that, when he repays our kindness, it will be more like paying back a debt than giving something spontaneously. We are unique in this. When we do kindnesses to others, we do not do them out of any calculations of profit or loss: we do them without afterthought, relying on our free liberality. Taking everything together then, I declare that our city is an education to Greece, and I declare that in my opinion each single one of our citizens, in all the manifold aspects of life, is able to show himself the rightful lord and owner of his own person, and do this, moreover, with exceptional grace and exceptional versatility. And to show that this is no empty boasting for the present occasion, but real tangible fact, you have only to consider the power which our city possesses and which has been won by those very qualities which I have mentioned. Athens, alone of the states we know, comes to her testing time in a greatness that surpasses what was imagined of her. In her case, and in her case alone, no invading enemy is ashamed at being defeated, and no subject can complain of being governed by people unfit for their responsibilities. Mighty indeed are the marks and monuments of our empire which we have left. Future ages will wonder at us, as the present age wonders at us now. We do not need the praises of a Homer, or of anyone else whose words may delight us for the moment, but whose estimation of facts will fall short of what is really true. For our adventurous spirit has forced an entry into every sea and into every land; and everywhere we have left behind us everlasting memorials of good done to our friends or suffering inflicted on our enemies.

This, then, is the kind of city for which these men, who could not bear the thought of losing her, nobly fought and nobly died. It is only natural that every one of us who survive them should be willing to undergo hardships in her service. And it was for this reason that I have spoken at such length about our city, because I wanted to make it clear that for us there is more at stake than there is for others who lack our advantages; also I wanted my words of praise for the dead to be set in the bright light of evidence. And now the most important of these words has been spoken. I have sung the praises of our city; but it was the courage and gallantry of these men, and of people like them, which made her splendid. Nor would you find it true in the case of many of the Greeks, as it is true of them, that no words can do more than justice to their deeds.

To me it seems that the consummation which has overtaken these men shows us the meaning of manliness in its first revelation and in its final proof. Some of them, no doubt, had their faults; but what we ought to remember first is their gallant conduct against the enemy in defence of their native land. They have blotted out evil with good, and done more service to the commonwealth than they ever did harm in their private lives. No one of these men weakened because he wanted to go on enjoying his wealth: no one put off the awful day in the hope that he might live to escape his poverty and grow rich. More to be desired than such things, they chose to check the enemy's pride. This, to them, was a risk most glorious, and they accepted it, willing to strike down the enemy and relinquish everything else. As for success or failure, they left that in the doubtful hands of Hope, and when the reality of battle was before their faces, they put their trust in their own selves. In the fighting, they thought it more honourable to stand their ground and suffer death than to give in and save their lives. So they fled from the reproaches of men, abiding with life and limb the brunt of battle; and, in a small moment of time, the climax of their lives, a culmination of glory, not of fear, were swept away from us.

So and such they were, these men — worthy of their city. We who remain behind may hope to be spared their fate, but must resolve to keep the same daring spirit against the foe. It is not simply a question of estimating the advantages in theory. I could tell you a long story (and you know it as well as I do) about what is to be gained by beating the enemy back. What I would prefer is that you should fix your eyes every day on the greatness of Athens as she really is, and should fall in love with her. When you realize her greatness, then reflect that what made her great was men with a spirit of adventure, men who knew their duty, men who were ashamed to fall below a certain standard. If they ever failed in an enterprise, they made up their minds that at any rate the city should not find their courage lacking to her, and they gave to her the best contribution that they could. They gave her their lives, to her and to all of us, and for their own selves they won praises that never grow old, the most splendid of sepulchres — not the sepulchre in which their bodies are laid, but where their glory remains eternal in men's minds, always there on the right occasion to stir others to speech or to action. For famous men have the whole earth as their memorial: it is not only the inscriptions on their graves in their own country that mark them out; no, in foreign lands also, not in any visible form but in people's hearts, their memory abides and grows. It is for you to try to be like them. Make up your minds that happiness depends on being free, and freedom depends on being courageous. Let there be no relaxation in face of the perils of the war.

The people who have most excuse for despising death are not the wretched and unfortunate, who have no hope of doing well for themselves, but those who run the risk of a complete reversal in their lives, and who would feel the difference most intensely, if things went wrong for them. Any intelligent man would find a humiliation caused by his own slackness more painful to bear than death, when death comes to him unperceived, in battle, and in the confidence of his patriotism.

For these reasons I shall not commiserate with those parents of the dead, who are present here. Instead I shall try to comfort them. They are well aware that they have grown up in a world where there are many changes and chances. But this is good fortune—for men to end their lives with honour, as these have done, and for you honourably to lament them: their life was set to a measure where death and happiness went hand in hand. I know that it is difficult to convince you of this. When you see other people happy you will often be reminded of what used to make you happy too. One does not feel sad at not having some good thing which is outside one's experience: real grief is felt at the loss of something which one is used to. All the same, those of you who are of the right age must bear up and take comfort in the thought of having more children. In your own homes these new children will prevent you from brooding over those who are no more, and they will be a help to the city, too, both in filling the empty places, and in assuring her security. For it is impossible for a man to put forward fair and honest views about our affairs if he has not, like everyone else, children whose lives may be at stake. As for those of you who are now too old to have children, I would ask you to count as gain the greater part of your life, in which you have been happy, and remember that what remains is not long, and let your hearts be lifted up at the thought of the fair fame of the dead. One's sense of honour is the only thing that does not grow old, and the last pleasure, when one is worn out with age, is not, as the poet said, making money, but having the respect of one's fellow men.

As for those of you here who are sons or brothers of the dead, I can see a hard struggle in front of you. Everyone always speaks well of the dead, and, even if you rise to the greatest heights of heroism, it will be a hard thing for you to get the reputation of having come near, let alone equalled, their standard. When one is alive, one is always liable to the jealousy of one's competitors, but when one is out of the way, the honour one receives is sincere and unchallenged.

Perhaps I should say a word or two on the duties of women to those among you who are now widowed. I can say all I have to say in a short word of advice. Your great glory is not to be inferior to what God has made you, and the greatest glory of a woman is to be least talked about by men, whether they are praising you or criticizing you. I have now, as the law demanded, said what I had to say. For the time being our offerings to the dead have been made, and for the future their children will be supported at the public expense by the city, until they come of age.

This is the crown and prize which she offers, both to the dead and to their children, for the ordeals which they have faced. Where the rewards of valour are the greatest, there you will find also the best and bravest spirits among the people. And now, when you have mourned for your dear ones, you must depart.

(430 B.C.)

*Oliver Goldsmith*

# The Deserted Village

Sweet Auburn! loveliest village of the plain,
Where health and plenty cheered the laboring swain,
Where smiling spring its earliest visit paid,
And parting summer's lingering blooms delayed;
Dear lovely bowers of innocence and ease,
Seats of my youth, when every sport could please;
How often have I loitered o'er thy green,
Where humble happiness endeared each scene!
How often have I paused on every charm,
The sheltered cot, the cultivated farm,
The never-failing brook, the busy mill,
The decent church that topped the neighboring hill;
The hawthorn bush, with seats beneath the shade,
For talking age and whispering lovers made!
How often have I blessed the coming day,
When toil, remitting, lent its turn to play,
And all the village train, from labor free,
Led up their sports beneath the spreading tree!
While many a pastime circled in the shade,
The young contending as the old surveyed;
And many a gambol frolicked o'er the ground,
And sleights of art and feats of strength went round;
And still, as each repeated pleasure tired,
Succeeding sports the mirthful band inspired—
The dancing pair that simply sought renown,
By holding out to tire each other down;
The swain mistrustless of his smutted face,
While secret laughter tittered round the place;
The bashful virgin's side-long looks of love;

The matron's glance, that would those looks reprove.
These were thy charms, sweet village! sports like these,
With sweet succession, taught e'en toil to please;
These round thy bowers their cheerful influence shed;
These were thy charms—but all these charms are fled.

   Sweet smiling village, loveliest of the lawn,
Thy sports are fled, and all thy charms withdrawn;
Amidst thy bowers the tyrant's hand is seen,
And desolation saddens all thy green;
One only master grasps the whole domain,
And half a tillage stints thy smiling plain.
No more thy glassy brook reflects the day,
But, choked with sedges, works its weedy way;
Along thy glades, a solitary guest,
The hollow-sounding bittern guards its nest;
Amidst thy desert walks the lapwing flies,
And tires their echoes with unvaried cries;
Sunk are thy bowers in shapeless ruin all,
And the long grass o'ertops the moldering wall;
And, trembling, shrinking from the spoiler's hand,
Far, far away thy children leave the land.

   Ill fares the land, to hastening ills a prey,
Where wealth accumulates, and men decay.
Princes and lords may flourish, or may fade;
A breath can make them, as a breath has made;
But a bold peasantry, their country's pride,
When once destroyed, can never be supplied.

   A time there was, ere England's griefs began,
When every rood of ground maintained its man;
For him light labor spread her wholesome store,
Just gave what life required, but gave no more:
His best companions, innocence and health;
And his best riches, ignorance of wealth.

   But times are altered; trade's unfeeling train
Usurp the land, and dispossess the swain;
Along the lawn, where scattered hamlets rose,
Unwieldy wealth and cumbrous pomp repose;
And every want to opulence allied,
And every pang that folly pays to pride.
Those gentle hours that plenty bade to bloom,
Those calm desires that asked but little room,
Those healthful sports that graced the peaceful scene,

Lived in each look, and brightened all the green —
These, far departing, seek a kinder shore,
And rural mirth and manners are no more.

Sweet Auburn! parent of the blissful hour,
Thy glades forlorn confess the tyrant's power.
Here, as I take my solitary rounds,
Amidst thy tangling walks and ruined grounds,
And, many a year elapsed, return to view
Where once the cottage stood, the hawthorn grew —
Remembrance wakes with all her busy train,
Swells at my breast, and turns the past to pain.

In all my wanderings round this world of care,
In all my griefs — and God has given my share —
I still had hopes, my latest hours to crown,
Amidst these humble bowers to lay me down;
To husband out life's taper at the close,
And keep the flame from wasting by repose;
I still had hopes, for pride attends us still,
Amidst the swains to show my book-learned skill,
Around my fire an evening group to draw,
And tell of all I felt, and all I saw;
And, as a hare, whom hounds and horns pursue,
Pants to the place from whence at first she flew,
I still had hopes, my long vexations past,
Here to return — and die at home at last.

O blest retirement, friend to life's decline,
Retreats from care, that never must be mine,
How happy he who crowns, in shades like these,
A youth of labor with an age of ease;
Who quits a world where strong temptations try,
And, since 'tis hard to combat, learns to fly!
For him no wretches, born to work and weep,
Explore the mine, or tempt the dangerous deep;
No surly porter stands, in guilty state,
To spurn imploring famine from the gate;
But on he moves to meet his latter end,
Angels around befriending virtue's friend;
Bends to the grave with unperceived decay,
While resignation gently slopes the way;
And, all his prospects brightening to the last,
His heaven commences ere the world be past!

Sweet was the sound, when oft, at evening's close,
Up yonder hill the village murmur rose.

There, as I passed with careless steps and slow,
The mingled notes came softened from below;
The swain responsive as the milkmaid sung,
The sober herd that lowed to meet their young;
The noisy geese that gabbled o'er the pool,
The playful children just let loose from school;
The watch-dog's voice that bayed the whispering wind,
And the loud laugh that spoke the vacant mind; —
These all in sweet confusion sought the shade,
And filled each pause the nightingale had made.
But now the sounds of population fail,
No cheerful murmurs fluctuate in the gale,
No busy steps the grass-grown footway tread,
For all the bloomy flush of life is fled —
All but yon widowed, solitary thing,
That feebly bends beside the plashy spring;
She, wretched matron — forced, in age for bread,
To strip the brook with mantling cresses spread,
To pick her wintry faggot from the thorn,
To seek her nightly shed, and weep till morn —
She only left of all the harmless train,
The sad historian of the pensive plain.

    Near yonder copse, where once the garden smiled,
And still where many a garden-flower grows wild,
There, where a few torn shrubs the place disclose,
The village preacher's modest mansion rose.
A man he was to all the country dear,
And passing rich with forty pounds a year.
Remote from towns he ran his godly race,
Nor e'er had changed, nor wished to change, his place;
Unpracticed he to fawn, or seek for power,
By doctrines fashioned to the varying hour;
Far other aims his heart had learned to prize,
More skilled to raise the wretched than to rise.
His house was known to all the vagrant train;
He chid their wanderings, but relieved their pain;
The long-remembered beggar was his guest,
Whose beard descending swept his aged breast;
The ruined spendthrift, now no longer proud,
Claimed kindred there, and had his claims allowed;
The broken soldier, kindly bade to stay,
Sat by his fire, and talked the night away; —
Wept o'er his wounds, or, tales of sorrow done,
Shouldered his crutch, and showed how fields were won.
Pleased with his guests, the good man learned to glow,
And quite forgot their vices in their woe;

Careless their merits or their faults to scan,
His pity gave ere charity began.

Thus to relieve the wretched was his pride,
And e'en his failings leaned to virtue's side;
But in his duty prompt at every call,
He watched and wept, he prayed and felt for all;
And, as a bird each fond endearment tries
To tempt its new-fledged offspring to the skies,
He tried each art, reproved each dull delay,
Allured to brighter worlds, and led the way.

Beside the bed where parting life was laid,
And sorrow, guilt, and pain, by turns dismayed,
The reverend champion stood. At his control,
Despair and anguish fled the struggling soul;
Comfort came down the trembling wretch to raise,
And his last faltering accents whispered praise.

At church, with meek and unaffected grace,
His looks adorned the venerable place;
Truth from his lips prevailed with double sway,
And fools, who came to scoff, remained to pray.
The service past, around the pious man
With steady zeal, each honest rustic ran;
Ten children followed, with endearing wile,
And plucked his gown, to share the good man's smile;
His ready smile a parent's warmth expressed;
Their welfare pleased him, and their cares distressed:
To them his heart, his love, his griefs were given,
But all his serious thoughts had rest in heaven.
As some tall cliff that lifts its awful form,
Swells from the vale, and midway leaves the storm,
Though round its breast the rolling clouds are spread,
Eternal sunshine settles on its head.

Beside yon straggling fence that skirts the way,
With blossomed furze unprofitably gay,
There, in his noisy mansion, skilled to rule,
The village master taught his little school.
A man severe he was, and stern to view;
I knew him well, and every truant knew;
Well had the boding tremblers learned to trace
The day's disasters in his morning face;
Full well they laughed with counterfeited glee
At all his jokes, for many a joke had he;

Full well the busy whisper, circling round,
Conveyed the dismal tidings when he frowned.
Yet he was kind, or if severe in aught,
The love he bore to learning was in fault.
The village all declared how much he knew;
'Twas certain he could write, and cipher too;
Lands he could measure, terms and tides presage,
And e'en the story ran that he could gauge.
In arguing, too, the parson owned his skill,
For e'en though vanquished, he could argue still;
While words of learned length and thundering sound
Amazed the gazing rustics ranged around;
And still they gazed, and still the wonder grew,
That one small head could carry all he knew.
But past is all his fame;—the very spot,
Where many a time he triumphed, is forgot.

Near yonder thorn, that lifts its head on high,
Where once the sign-post caught the passing eye,
Low lies that house where nut-brown drafts inspired,
Where gray-beard mirth and smiling toil retired,
Where village statesmen talked with looks profound,
And news much older than their ale went round.
Imagination fondly stoops to trace
The parlor splendors of that festive place;
The whitewashed wall, the nicely-sanded floor,
The varnished clock that clicked behind the door,
The chest, contrived a double debt to pay,
A bed by night, a chest of drawers by day,
The pictures placed for ornament and use,
The twelve good rules, the royal game of goose,
The hearth, except when winter chilled the day,
With aspen boughs, and flowers, and fennel, gay;—
While broken teacups, wisely kept for show,
Ranged o'er the chimney, glistened in a row.

Vain transitory splendors! could not all
Reprieve the tottering mansion from its fall?
Obscure it sinks, nor shall it more impart
An hour's importance to the poor man's heart.
Thither no more the peasant shall repair,
To sweet oblivion of his daily care;
No more the farmer's news, the barber's tale,
No more the woodman's ballad shall prevail;
No more the smith his dusky brow shall clear,
Relax his ponderous strength, and lean to hear;

The host himself no longer shall be found
Careful to see the mantling bliss go round;
Nor the coy maid, half willing to be pressed,
Shall kiss the cup to pass it to the rest.

Yes! let the rich deride, the proud disdain,
These simple blessings of the lowly train;
To me more dear, congenial to my heart,
One native charm, than all the gloss of art.
Spontaneous joys, where nature has its play,
The soul adopts, and owns their first-born sway;
Lightly they frolic o'er the vacant mind,
Unenvied, unmolested, unconfined:
But the long pomp, the midnight masquerade,
With all the freaks of wanton wealth arrayed,
In these, ere triflers half their wish obtain,
The toiling pleasure sickens into pain;
And, e'en while fashion's brightest arts decoy,
The heart distrusting asks, if this be joy.

Ye friends to truth, ye statesmen, who survey
The rich man's joys increase, the poor's decay,
'Tis yours to judge how wide the limits stand
Between a splendid and a happy land.
Proud swells the tide with loads of freighted ore,
And shouting folly hails them from her shore;
Hoards e'en beyond the miser's wish abound,
And rich men flock from all the world around.
Yet count our gains. This wealth is but a name
That leaves our useful products still the same.
Not so the loss. The man of wealth and pride
Takes up a space that many poor supplied;
Space for his lake, his park's extended bounds,
Space for his horses, equipage, and hounds;
The robe that wraps his limbs in silken sloth,
Has robbed the neighboring fields of half their growth;
His seat, where solitary sports are seen,
Indignant spurns the cottage from the green;
Around the world each needful product flies,
For all the luxuries the world supplies;
While thus the land, adorned for pleasure all,
In barren splendor feebly waits the fall.

As some fair female, unadorned and plain,
Secure to please while youth confirms her reign,
Slights every borrowed charm that dress supplies,

Nor shares with art the triumph of her eyes;
But when those charms are past, for charms are frail,
When time advances, and when lovers fail,
She then shines forth, solicitous to bless,
In all the glaring impotence of dress;
Thus fares the land by luxury betrayed;
In nature's simplest charms at first arrayed; —
But verging to decline, its splendors rise,
Its vistas strike, its palaces surprise;
While, scourged by famine, from the smiling land
The mournful peasant leads his humble band;
And while he sinks, without one arm to save,
The country blooms — a garden and a grave!

    Where, then, ah! where shall poverty reside,
To 'scape the pressure of contiguous pride?
If to some common's fenceless limits strayed,
He drives his flock to pick the scanty blade,
Those fenceless fields the sons of wealth divide,
And e'en the bare-worn common is denied.

    If to the city sped — what waits him there?
To see profusion that he must not share;
To see ten thousand baneful arts combined
To pamper luxury and thin mankind;
To see those joys the sons of pleasure know
Extorted from his fellow-creature's woe;
Here while the courtier glitters in brocade,
There the pale artist plies the sickly trade;
Here while the proud their long-drawn pomps display,
There the black gibbet glooms beside the way;
The dome where pleasure holds her midnight reign,
Here, richly decked, admits the gorgeous train;
Tumultuous grandeur crowds the blazing square,
The rattling chariots clash, the torches glare.
Sure scenes like these no troubles e'er annoy!
Sure these denote one universal joy! —
Are these thy serious thoughts? — ah, turn thine eyes
Where the poor houseless shivering female lies;
She once, perhaps, in village plenty blessed,
Has wept at tales of innocence distressed;
Her modest looks the cottage might adorn,
Sweet as the primrose peeps beneath the thorn;
Now lost to all, her friends, her virtue, fled,
Near her betrayer's door she lays her head,
And, pinched with cold, and shrinking from the shower,

With heavy heart deplores that luckless hour,
When idly first, ambitious of the town,
She left her wheel, and robes of country brown.

Do thine, sweet Auburn, thine, the loveliest train,
Do thy fair tribes participate her pain?
E'en now, perhaps, by cold and hunger led,
At proud men's doors they ask a little bread!

Ah, no. To distant climes, a dreary scene,
Where half the convex world intrudes between,
Through torrid tracts with fainting steps they go,
Where wild Altama murmurs to their woe.
Far different there from all that charmed before,
The various terrors of that horrid shore;
Those blazing suns that dart a downward ray,
And fiercely shed intolerable day;
Those matted woods where birds forget to sing,
But silent bats in drowsy clusters cling;
Those poisonous fields, with rank luxuriance crowned,
Where the dark scorpion gathers death around;
Where at each step the stranger fears to wake
The rattling terrors of the vengeful snake;
Where crouching tigers wait their hapless prey,
And savage men more murderous still than they;
While oft in whirls the mad tornado flies,
Mingling the ravaged landscape with the skies.
Far different these from every former scene,
The cooling brook, the grassy-vested green,
The breezy covert of the warbling grove,
That only sheltered thefts of harmless love.

Good Heaven! what sorrows gloomed that parting day,
That called them from their native walks away;
When the poor exiles, every pleasure past,
Hung round their bowers, and fondly looked their last,
And took a long farewell, and wished in vain,
For seats like these beyond the western main;
And shuddering still to face the distant deep,
Returned and wept, and still returned to weep!
The good old sire the first prepared to go
To new-found worlds, and wept for others' woe;
But for himself, in conscious virtue brave,
He only wished for worlds beyond the grave.
His lovely daughter, lovelier in her tears,
The fond companion of his helpless years,

Silent went next, neglectful of her charms,
And left a lover's for a father's arms.
With louder plaints the mother spoke her woes,
And blessed the cot where every pleasure rose,
And kissed her thoughtless babes with many a tear,
And clasped them close, in sorrow doubly dear;
Whilst her fond husband strove to lend relief
In all the silent manliness of grief.

    O luxury, thou cursed by Heaven's decree,
How ill exchanged are things like these for thee!
How do thy potions, with insidious joy,
Diffuse their pleasures only to destroy!
Kingdoms by thee to sickly greatness grown,
Boast of a florid vigor not their own;
At every draft more large and large they grow,
A bloated mass of rank unwieldy woe;
Till sapped their strength, and every part unsound,
Down, down they sink, and spread a ruin round.

    E'en now the devastation is begun,
And half the business of destruction done;
E'en now, methinks, as pondering here I stand,
I see the rural virtues leave the land.
Down where yon anchoring vessel spreads the sail,
That idly waiting flaps with every gale,
Downward they move, a melancholy band,
Pass from the shore, and darken all the strand;
Contented toil, and hospitable care,
And kind connubial tenderness are there;
And piety with wishes placed above,
And steady loyalty, and faithful love.

    And thou, sweet Poetry, thou loveliest maid,
Still first to fly where sensual joys invade!
Unfit, in these degenerate times of shame,
To catch the heart, or strike for honest fame;
Dear charming nymph, neglected and decried,
My shame in crowds, my solitary pride;
Thou source of all my bliss and all my woe,
That found'st me poor at first and keep'st me so;
Thou guide by which the nobler arts excel,
Thou nurse of every virtue, fare thee well!
Farewell! and oh! where'er thy voice be tried,
On Torno's cliffs, or Pambamarca's side,
Whether where equinoctial fervors glow,

Or winter wraps the polar world in snow,
Still let thy voice, prevailing over time,
Redress the rigors of th' inclement clime;
Aid slighted truth with thy persuasive strain;
Teach erring man to spurn the rage of gain;
Teach him that states, of native strength possessed,
Though very poor, may still be very blest;
That trade's proud empire hastes to swift decay,
As ocean sweeps the labored mole away;
While self-dependent power can time defy,
As rocks resist the billows and the sky.

(1770)

## *Thomas Malthus*

# *from* An Essay on the Principle of Population

Book I   Of the Checks to Population in the Less Civilised Parts of the World
and in Past Times

## Chapter 1   Statement of the Subject. Ratios of the Increase of Population and Food

In an inquiry concerning the improvement of society, the mode of conducting the subject which naturally presents itself, is,

1. To investigate the causes that have hitherto impeded the progress of mankind towards happiness; and,

2. To examine the probability of the total or partial removal of these causes in future.

To enter fully into this question, and to enumerate all the causes that have hitherto influenced human improvement, would be much beyond the power of an individual. The principal object of the present essay is to examine the effects of one great cause intimately united with the very nature of man; which, though it has been constantly and powerfully operating since the commencement of society, has been little noticed by the writers who have treated this subject. The facts which establish the existence of this cause have, indeed, been repeatedly stated and acknowledged; but its natural and necessary effects have been almost totally overlooked; though probably among these effects may be reckoned a very considerable portion of that vice and misery, and of that unequal distribution of the bounties of nature, which it has been the unceasing object of the enlightened philanthropist in all ages to correct.

The cause to which I allude, is the constant tendency in all animated life to increase beyond the nourishment prepared for it.

It is observed by Dr. Franklin, that there is no bound to the prolific nature of plants or animals, but what is made by their crowding and interfering with each other's means of subsistence. Were the face of the earth, he says, vacant of other plants, it might be gradually sowed and overspread with one kind only, as for instance with fennel: and were it empty of other inhabitants, it might in a few ages be replenished from one nation only, as for instance with Englishmen.

This is incontrovertibly true. Through the animal and vegetable kingdoms Nature has scattered the seeds of life abroad with the most profuse and liberal hand; but has been comparatively sparing in the room and the nourishment necessary to rear them. The germs of existence contained in this earth, if they could freely develop themselves, would fill millions of worlds in the course of a few thousand years. Necessity, that imperious, all-pervading law of nature, restrains them within the prescribed bounds. The race of plants and the race of animals shrink under this great restrictive law; and man cannot by any efforts of reason escape from it.

In plants and irrational animals, the view of the subject is simple. They are all impelled by a powerful instinct to the increase of their species; and this instinct is interrupted by no doubts about providing for their offspring. Wherever therefore there is liberty, the power of increase is exerted; and the superabundant effects are repressed afterwards by want of room and nourishment.

The effects of this check on man are more complicated. Impelled to the increase of his species by an equally powerful instinct, reason interrupts his career, and asks him whether he may not bring beings into the world, for whom he cannot provide the means of support. If he attend to this natural suggestion, the restriction too frequently produces vice. If he hear it not, the human race will be constantly endeavouring to increase beyond the means of subsistence. But as, by that law of our nature which makes food necessary to the life of man, population can never actually increase beyond the lowest nourishment capable of supporting it, a strong check on population, from the difficulty of acquiring food, must be constantly in operation. This difficulty must fall somewhere, and must necessarily be severely felt in some or other of the various forms of misery, or the fear of misery, by a large portion of mankind.

That population has this constant tendency to increase beyond the means of subsistence, and that it is kept to its necessary level by these causes, will sufficiently appear from a review of the different states of society in which man has existed. But, before we proceed to this review, the subject will, perhaps, be seen in a clearer light, if we endeavour to ascertain what would be the natural increase of population, if left to exert itself with perfect freedom; and what might be expected to be the rate of increase in the productions of the earth, under the most favourable circumstances of human industry.

It will be allowed that no country has hitherto been known, where the manners were so pure and simple, and the means of subsistence so abundant, that no check whatever has existed to early marriages from the difficulty of providing for a family, and that no waste of the human species has been occasioned by vicious customs, by towns, by unhealthy occupations, or too severe labour. Consequently in no state that we have yet known, has the power of population been left to exert itself with perfect freedom.

Whether the law of marriage be instituted, or not, the dictate of nature and virtue seems to be an early attachment to one woman; and where there were no impediments of any kind in the way of an union to which such an attachment would lead, and no causes of depopulation afterwards, the increase of the human species would be evidently much greater than any increase which has been hitherto known.

In the northern states of America, where the means of subsistence have been more ample, the manners of the people more pure, and the checks to early marriages fewer, than in any of the modern states of Europe, the population has been found to double itself, for above a century and a half successively, in less than twenty-five years. Yet, even during these periods, in some of the towns, the deaths exceeded the births, a circumstance which clearly proves that, in those parts of the country which supplied this deficiency, the increase must have been much more rapid than the general average.

In the back settlements, where the sole employment is agriculture, and vicious customs and unwholesome occupations are little known, the population has been found to double itself in fifteen years. Even this extraordinary rate of increase is probably short of the utmost power of population. Very severe labour is requisite to clear a fresh country; such situations are not in general considered as particularly healthy; and the inhabitants, probably, are occasionally subject to the incursions of the Indians, which may destroy some lives, or at any rate diminish the fruits of industry.

According to a table of Euler, calculated on a mortality of 1 in 36, if the births be to the deaths in the proportion of 3 to 1, the period of doubling will be only 12 years and $\frac{4}{5}$ths. And this proportion is not only a possible supposition, but has actually occurred for short periods in more countries than one.

Sir William Petty supposes a doubling possible in so short a time as ten years.

But, to be perfectly sure that we are far within the truth, we will take the slowest of these rates of increase, a rate in which all concurring testimonies agree, and which has been repeatedly ascertained to be from procreation only.

It may safely be pronounced, therefore, that population, when un-checked, goes on doubling itself every twenty-five years, or increases in a geometrical ratio.

The rate according to which the productions of the earth may be supposed to increase, it will not be so easy to determine. Of this, however, we may be perfectly certain, that the ratio of their increase in a limited territory must be of a totally different nature from the ratio of the increase of population. A thousand millions are just as easily doubled every twenty-five years by the power of population as a thousand. But the food to support the increase from the greater number will by no means be obtained with the same facility. Man is necessarily confined in room. When acre has been added to acre till all the fertile land is occupied, the yearly increase of food must depend upon the melioration of the land already in possession. This is a fund, which, from the nature of all soils, instead of increasing, must be gradually diminishing. But population, could it be supplied with food, would go on with unexhausted vigour; and the increase of one period would furnish the power of a greater increase the next, and this without any limit.

From the accounts we have of China and Japan, it may be fairly doubted, whether the best-directed efforts of human industry could double the produce of these countries even once in any number of years. There are many parts of the globe, indeed, hitherto uncultivated, and al-most unoccupied; but the right of exterminating, or driving into a corner where they must starve, even the inhabitants of these thinly-peopled regions, will be questioned in a moral view. The process of improving their minds and directing their industry would necessarily be slow; and during this time, as population would regularly keep pace with the in-creasing produce, it would rarely happen that a great degree of knowl-edge and industry would have to operate at once upon rich unappropri-ated soil. Even where this might take place, as it does sometimes in new colonies, a geometrical ratio increases with such extraordinary rapidity, that the advantage could not last long. If the United States of America continue increasing, which they certainly will do, though not with the same rapidity as formerly, the Indians will be driven further and further back into the country, till the whole race is ultimately exterminated, and the territory is incapable of further extension.

These observations are, in a degree, applicable to all the parts of the earth, where the soil is imperfectly cultivated. To exterminate the in-habitants of the greatest part of Asia and Africa, is a thought that could not be admitted for a moment. To civilise and direct the industry of the various tribes of Tartars and Negroes, would certainly be a work of con-siderable time, and of variable and uncertain success.

Europe is by no means so fully peopled as it might be. In Europe there is the fairest chance that human industry may receive its best di-rection. The science of agriculture has been much studied in England and Scotland; and there is still a great portion of uncultivated land in these countries. Let us consider at what rate the produce of this island might be supposed to increase under circumstances the most favourable to improvement.

If it be allowed that by the best possible policy, and great encouragements to agriculture, the average produce of the island could be doubled in the first twenty-five years, it will be allowing, probably, a greater increase than could with reason be expected.

In the next twenty-five years, it is impossible to suppose that the produce could be quadrupled. It would be contrary to all our knowledge of the properties of land. The improvement of the barren parts would be a work of time and labour; and it must be evident to those who have the slightest acquaintance with agricultural subjects, that in proportion as cultivation extended, the additions that could yearly be made to the former average produce must be gradually and regularly diminishing. That we may be the better able to compare the increase of population and food, let us make a supposition, which, without pretending to accuracy, is clearly more favourable to the power of production in the earth, than any experience we have had of its qualities will warrant.

Let us suppose that the yearly additions which might be made to the former average produce, instead of decreasing, which they certainly would do, were to remain the same; and that the produce of this island might be increased every twenty-five years, by a quantity equal to what it at present produces. The most enthusiastic speculator cannot suppose a greater increase than this. In a few centuries it would make every acre of land in the island like a garden.

If this supposition be applied to the whole earth, and if it be allowed that the subsistence for man which the earth affords might be increased every twenty-five years by a quantity equal to what it at present produces, this will be supposing a rate of increase much greater than we can imagine that any possible exertions of mankind could make it.

It may be fairly pronounced, therefore, that, considering the present average state of the earth, the means of subsistence, under circumstances the most favourable to human industry, could not possibly be made to increase faster than in an arithmetical ratio.

The necessary effects of these two different rates of increase, when brought together, will be very striking. Let us call the population of this island eleven millions; and suppose the present produce equal to the easy support of such a number. In the first twenty-five years the population would be twenty-two millions, and the food being also doubled, the means of subsistence would be equal to this increase. In the next twenty-five years, the population would be forty-four millions, and the means of subsistence only equal to the support of thirty-three millions. In the next period the population would be eighty-eight millions, and the means of subsistence just equal to the support of half that number. And, at the conclusion of the first century, the population would be a hundred and seventy-six millions, and the means of subsistence only equal to the support of fifty-five millions, leaving a population of a hundred and twenty-one millions totally unprovided for.

Taking the whole earth, instead of this island, emigration would of course be excluded; and, supposing the present population equal to a thousand millions, the human species would increase as the numbers, 1, 2, 4, 8, 16, 32, 64, 128, 256, and subsistence as 1, 2, 3, 4, 5, 6, 7, 8, 9. In two centuries the population would be to the means of subsistence as 256 to 9; in three centuries as 4096 to 13, and in two thousand years the difference would be almost incalculable.

In this supposition no limits whatever are placed to the produce of the earth. It may increase for ever and be greater than any assignable quantity; yet still the power of population being in every period so much superior, the increase of the human species can only be kept down to the level of the means of subsistence by the constant operation of the strong law of necessity, acting as a check upon the greater power.

### Chapter 2   Of the general Checks to Population, and the Mode of their Operation

The ultimate check to population appears then to be a want of food, arising necessarily from the different ratios according to which population and food increase. But this ultimate check is never the immediate check, except in cases of actual famine.

The immediate check may be stated to consist in all those customs, and all those diseases, which seem to be generated by a scarcity of the means of subsistence; and all those causes, independent of this scarcity, whether of a moral or physical nature, which tend prematurely to weaken and destroy the human frame.

These checks to population, which are constantly operating with more or less force in every society, and keep down the number to the level of the means of subsistence, may be classed under two general heads – the preventive, and the positive checks.

The preventive check, as far as it is voluntary, is peculiar to man, and arises from that distinctive superiority in his reasoning faculties, which enables him to calculate distant consequences. The checks to the indefinite increase of plants and irrational animals are all either positive, or, if preventive, involuntary. But man cannot look around him, and see the distress which frequently presses upon those who have large families; he cannot contemplate his present possessions or earnings, which he now nearly consumes himself, and calculate the amount of each share, when with very little addition they must be divided, perhaps, among seven or eight, without feeling a doubt whether, if he follow the bent of his inclinations, he may be able to support the offspring which he will probably bring into the world. In a state of equality, if such can exist, this would be the simple question. In the present state of society other considerations occur. Will he not lower his rank in life, and be obliged to give up in great measure his former habits? Does any mode of employment present itself by which he may reasonably hope to maintain a family? Will he not at any rate subject himself to greater difficulties, and more severe labour, than in his single state? Will he not be unable to transmit to his children the same advantages of education and improvement that he had himself possessed? Does he even feel secure that, should he have a large family, his utmost exertions can save them from rags and squalid poverty, and their consequent degradation in the community? And may he not be reduced to the grating necessity of forfeiting his independence, and of being obliged to the sparing hand of Charity for support?

These considerations are calculated to prevent, and certainly do prevent, a great number of persons in all civilised nations from pursuing the dictate of nature in an early attachment to one woman.

If this restraint do not produce vice, it is undoubtedly the least evil that can arise from the principle of population. Considered as a restraint on a strong natural inclination, it must be allowed to produce a certain degree of temporary unhappiness; but evidently slight, compared with the evils which result from any of the other checks to population; and merely of the same nature as many other sacrifices of temporary to permanent gratification, which it is the business of a moral agent continually to make.

When this restraint produces vice, the evils which follow are but too conspicuous. A promiscuous intercourse to such a degree as to prevent the birth of children, seems to lower, in the most marked manner, the dignity of human nature. It cannot be without its effect on men, and nothing can be more obvious than its tendency to degrade the female character, and to destroy all its most amiable and distinguishing characteristics. Add to which, that among those unfortunate females, with which all great towns abound, more real distress and aggravated misery are, perhaps, to be found, than in any other department of human life.

When a general corruption of morals, with regard to the sex, pervades all the classes of society, its effects must necessarily be, to poison the springs of domestic happiness, to weaken conjugal and parental affection, and to lessen the united exertions and ardour of parents in the care and education of their children: — effects which cannot take place without a decided diminution of the general happiness and virtue of the society; particularly as the necessity of art in the accomplishment and conduct of intrigues, and in the concealment of their consequences necessarily leads to many other vices.

The positive checks to population are extremely various, and include every cause, whether arising from vice or misery, which in any degree contributes to shorten the natural duration of human life. Under this head, therefore, may be enumerated all unwholesome occupations, severe labour and exposure to the seasons, extreme poverty, bad nursing of children, great towns, excesses of all kinds, the whole train of common diseases and epidemics, wars, plague, and famine.

On examining these obstacles to the increase of population which I have classed under the heads of preventive and positive checks, it will appear that they are all resolvable into moral restraint, vice, and misery.

Of the preventive checks, the restraint from marriage which is not followed by irregular gratifications may properly be termed moral restraint.

Promiscuous intercourse, unnatural passions, violations of the marriage bed, and improper arts to conceal the consequences of irregular connexions, are preventive checks that clearly come under the head of vice.

Of the positive checks, those which appear to arise unavoidably from the laws of nature, may be called exclusively misery; and those which we obviously bring upon ourselves, such as wars, excesses, and many others which it would be in our power to avoid, are of a mixed nature. They are brought upon us by vice, and their consequences are misery.

The sum of all these preventive and positive checks, taken together, forms the immediate check to population; and it is evident that, in every country where the whole of the procreative power cannot be called into action, the preventive and the positive checks must vary inversely as each other; that is, in countries either naturally unhealthy, or subject to a great mortality, from whatever cause it may arise, the preventive check will prevail very little. In those countries, on the contrary, which are naturally healthy, and where the preventive check is found to prevail with considerable force, the positive check will prevail very little, or the mortality be very small.

In every country some of these checks are, with more or less force, in constant operation; yet, notwithstanding their general prevalence, there are few states in which there is not a constant effort in the population to increase beyond the means of subsistence. This constant effort as constantly tends to subject the lower classes of society to distress, and to prevent any great permanent melioration of their condition.

These effects, in the present state of society, seem to be produced in the following manner. We will suppose the means of subsistence in any country just equal to the easy support of its inhabitants. The constant effort towards population, which is found to act even in the most vicious societies, increases the number of people before the means of subsistence are increased. The food, therefore, which before supported eleven millions, must now be divided among eleven millions and a half. The poor consequently must live much worse, and many of them be reduced to severe distress. The number of labourers also being above the proportion of work in the market, the price of labour must tend to fall, while the price of provisions would at the same time tend to rise. The labourer therefore must do more work, to earn the same as he did before. During this season of distress, the discouragements to marriage and the difficulty of rearing a family are so great, that the progress of population is retarded. In the mean time, the cheapness of labour, the plenty of labourers, and the necessity of an increased industry among them, encourage cultivators to employ more labour upon their land, to turn up fresh soil, and to manure and improve more completely what is already in tillage, till ultimately the means of subsistence may become in the same proportion to the population, as at the period from which we set out. The situation of the labourer being then again tolerably comfortable, the restraints to population are in some degree loosened; and, after a short period, the same retrograde and progressive movements, with respect to happiness, are repeated.

This sort of oscillation will not probably be obvious to common view; and it may be difficult even for the most attentive observer to calculate its periods. Yet that, in the generality of old states, some alternation of this kind does exist though in a much less marked, and in a much more irregular manner, than I have described it, no reflecting man, who considers the subject deeply, can well doubt.

One principal reason why this oscillation has been less remarked, and less decidedly confirmed by experience than might naturally be expected, is, that the histories of mankind which we possess are, in general, histories only of the higher classes. We have not many accounts that can be depended upon, of the manners and customs of that part of mankind, where these retrograde and progressive movements chiefly take place. A satisfactory history of this kind, of one people and of one period, would require the constant and minute attention of many observing minds in local and general remarks on the state of the lower classes of society, and the causes that influenced it; and to draw accurate inferences upon this subject, a succession of such historians for some centuries would be necessary. This branch of statistical knowledge has, of late years, been attended to in some countries, and we may promise ourselves a clearer insight into the internal structure of human society from the progress of these inquiries. But the science may be said yet to be in its infancy, and many of the objects, on which it would be desirable to have information, have been either omitted or not stated with sufficient accuracy. Among these, perhaps, may be reckoned the proportion of the number of adults to the number of marriages; the extent to which vicious customs have prevailed in consequence of the restraints upon matrimony; the comparative mortality among the children of the most distressed part of the community, and of those who live rather more at their ease; the variations in the real price of labour; the observable differences in the state of the lower classes of society, with respect to ease and happiness, at different times during a certain period; and very accurate registers of births, deaths, and marriages, which are of the utmost importance in this subject.

A faithful history, including such particulars, would tend greatly to elucidate the manner in which the constant check upon population acts;

and would probably prove the existence of the retrograde and progressive movements that have been mentioned; though the times of their vibration must necessarily be rendered irregular from the operation of many interrupting causes; such as, the introduction or failure of certain manufacturers; a greater or less prevalent spirit of agricultural enterprise; years of plenty, or years of scarcity; wars, sickly seasons, poor-laws, emigrations and other causes of a similar nature.

A circumstance which has, perhaps, more than any other, contributed to conceal this oscillation from common view, is the difference between the nominal and real price of labour. It very rarely happens that the nominal price of labour universally falls; but we well know that it frequently remains the same, while the nominal price of provisions has been gradually rising. This, indeed, will generally be the case, if the increase of manufactures and commerce be sufficient to employ the new labourers that are thrown into the market, and to prevent the increased supply from lowering the money-price. But an increased number of labourers receiving the same money-wages will necessarily, by their competition, increase the money-price of corn. This is, in fact, a real fall in the price of labour; and, during this period, the condition of the lower classes of the community must be gradually growing worse. But the farmers and capitalists are growing rich from the real cheapness of labour. Their increasing capitals enable them to employ a greater number of men; and, as the population had probably suffered some check from the greater difficulty of supporting a family, the demand for labour, after a certain period, would be great in proportion to the supply, and its price would of course rise, if left to find its natural level; and thus the wages of labour, and consequently the condition of the lower classes of society, might have progressive and retrograde movements, though the price of labour might never nominally fall.

In savage life, where there is no regular price of labour, it is little to be doubted that similar oscillations took place. When population has increased nearly to the utmost limits of the food, all the preventive and the positive checks will naturally operate with increased force. Vicious habits with respect to the sex will be more general, the exposing of children more frequent, and both the probability and fatality of wars and epidemics will be considerably greater; and these causes will probably continue their operation till the population is sunk below the level of the food; and then the return to comparative plenty will again produce an increase, and, after a certain period, its further progress will again be checked by the same causes.

But without attempting to establish these progressive and retrograde movements in different countries, which would evidently require more minute histories than we possess, and which the progress of civilisation naturally tends to counteract, the following propositions are intended to be proved: —

1. Population is necessarily limited by the means of subsistence.

2. Population invariably increases where the means of subsistence increase, unless prevented by some very powerful and obvious checks.

3. These checks, and the checks which repress the superior power of population, and keep its effects on a level with the means of subsistence, are all resolvable into moral restraint, vice and misery.

The first of these propositions scarcely needs illustration. The second and third will be sufficiently established by a review of the immediate checks to population in the past and present state of society.

(1803)

## *Robert Owen*

# Observations on the Effect of the Manufacturing System

Those who were engaged in the trade, manufactures, and commerce of this country thirty or forty years ago formed but a very insignificant portion of the knowledge, wealth, influence, or population of the Empire.

Prior to that period, Britain was essentially agricultural. But, from that time to the present, the home and foreign trade have increased in a manner so rapid and extraordinary as to have raised commerce to an importance, which it never previously attained in any country possessing so much political power and influence.

(By the returns to the Population Act in 1811, it appears that in England, Scotland and Wales there are 895,998 families chiefly employed in agriculture – 1,129,049 families chiefly employed in trade and manufactures – 640,500 individuals in the army and navy – and 519,168 families not engaged in any of these employments. It follows that nearly half as many more persons are engaged in trade as in agriculture – and that of the whole population the agriculturists are about 1 to 3.)

This change has been owing chiefly to the mechanical inventions which introduced the cotton trade into this country, and to the cultivation of the cotton tree in America. The wants which this trade created for the various materials requisite to forward its multiplied operations, caused an extraordinary demand for almost all the manufactures previously established, and, of course, for human labour. The numerous fanciful and useful fabrics manufactured from cotton soon became objects of desire in Europe and America: and the consequent extension of the British foreign trade was such as to astonish and confound the most enlightened statesmen both at home and abroad.

The immediate effects of this manufacturing phenomenon were a rapid increase of the wealth, industry, population, and political influence of the British Empire; and by the aid of which it has been enabled to contend for five-and-twenty years against the most formidable military and *immoral* power that the world perhaps ever contained.

These important results, however, great as they really are, have not been obtained without accompanying evils of such a magnitude as to raise a doubt whether the latter do not preponderate over the former.

Hitherto, legislators have appeared to regard manufactures only in one point of view, as a source of national wealth.

The other mighty consequences which proceed from extended manufactures *when left to their natural progress*, have never yet engaged the attention of any legislature. Yet the political and moral effects to which we allude, well deserve to occupy the best faculties of the greatest and the wisest statesmen.

The general diffusion of manufactures throughout a country generates a new character in its inhabitants; and as this character is formed upon a principle quite unfavourable to individual or general happiness, it will produce the most lamentable and permanent evils, unless its tendency be counteracted by legislative inteference and direction.

The manufacturing system has already so far extended its influence over the British Empire, as to effect an essential change in the general character of the mass of the people. This alteration is still in rapid progress; and ere long, the comparatively happy simplicity of the agricultural peasant will be wholly lost amongst us. It is even now scarcely anywhere to be found without a mixture of those habits which are the offspring of trade, manufactures, and commerce.

The acquisition of wealth, and the desire which it naturally creates for a continued increase, have introduced a fondness for essentially injurious luxuries among a numerous class of individuals who formerly never thought of them, and they have also generated a disposition which strongly impels its possessors to sacrifice the best feelings of human nature to this love of accumulation. To succeed in this career, the industry of the lower orders, from whose labour this wealth is now drawn, has been carried by new competitors striving against those of longer standing, to a point of real oppression, reducing them by successive changes, as the spirit of competition increased and the ease of acquiring wealth diminished, to a state more wretched than can be imagined by those who have not attentively observed the changes as they have gradually occurred. In consequence, they are at present in a situation infinitely more degraded and miserable than they were before the introduction of these manufactories, upon the success of which their bare subsistence now depends.

To support the additional population which this increased demand for labour has produced, it now becomes necessary to maintain the present extent of our foreign trade, or, under the existing circumstances of our population, it will become a serious and alarming evil.

It is highly probable, however, that the export trade of this country has attained its utmost height, and that by the competition of other states, possessing equal or greater local advantage, it will now gradually diminish.

The direct effect of the Corn Bill lately passed will be to hasten this decline and prematurely to destroy that trade. In this view it is deeply to be regretted that the Bill passed into a law; and I am persuaded its promoters will ere long discover the absolute necessity for its repeal, to prevent the misery which must ensue to the great mass of the people.

The inhabitants of every country are trained and formed by its great leading existing circumstances, and the character of the lower orders in Britain is now formed chiefly by circumstances arising from trade, manufactures, and commerce; and the governing principle of trade, manufactures, and commerce is immediate pecuniary gain, to which on the great scale every other is made to give way. All are sedulously trained to buy cheap and to sell dear; and to succeed in this art, the parties must be taught to acquire strong powers of deception; and thus a spirit is generated through every class of traders, destructive of that open, honest sincerity, without which man cannot make others happy, nor enjoy happiness himself.

Strictly speaking, however, this defect of character ought not to be attributed to the individuals possessing it, but to the overwhelming effect of the system under which they have been trained.

But the effects of this principle of gain, unrestrained, are still more lamentable on the working classes, those who are employed in the operative parts of the manufactures; for most of these branches are more or less unfavourable to the health and morals of adults. Yet parents do not hesitate to sacrifice the well-being of their children by putting them to occupations by which the constitution of their minds and bodies is rendered greatly inferior to what it might and ought to be under a system of common foresight and humanity.

Not more than thirty years since, the poorest parents thought the age of fourteen sufficiently early for their children to commence regular labour: and they judged well; for by that period of their lives they had acquired by play and exercise in the open air, the foundation of a sound robust constitution; and if they were not all initiated in book learning, they had been taught the far more useful knowledge of domestic life, which could not but be familiar to them at the age of fourteen, and which, as they grew up and became heads of families, was of more value to them (as it taught them economy in the expenditure of their earnings) than one half of their wages under the present circumstances.

It should be remembered also that twelve hours per day, including the time for regular rest and meals, were then thought sufficient to extract all the working strength of the more robust adult; when it may be remarked local holidays were much more frequent than at present in most parts of the kingdom.

At this period, too, they were generally trained by the example of some landed proprietor, and in such habits as created a mutual interest between the parties, by which means even the lowest peasant was generally considered as belonging to, and forming somewhat of a member of, a respectable family. Under these circumstances the lower orders experienced not only a considerable degree of comfort, but they had also frequent opportunities of enjoying healthy rational sports and amusements; and in consequence they became strongly attached to those on whom they depended; their services were willingly performed; and mutual good offices bound the parties by the strongest ties of human nature to consider each other as friends in somewhat different situations; the servant indeed often enjoying more solid comfort and ease than his master.

Contrast this state of matters with that of the lower orders of the present day; — with human nature trained as it now is, under the new manufacturing system.

In the manufacturing districts it is common for parents to send their children of both sexes at seven or eight years of age, in winter as well as summer, at six o'clock in the morning, sometimes of course in the dark, and occasionally amidst frost and snow, to enter the manufactories, which are often heated to a high temperature, and contain an atmosphere far from being the most favourable to human life, and in which all those employed in them very frequently continue until twelve o'clock at noon, when an hour is allowed for dinner, after which they return to remain, in a majority of cases, till eight o'clock at night.

The children now find they must labour incessantly for their bare subsistence: they have not been used to innocent, healthy, and rational amusement; they are not permitted the requisite time, if they had been previously accustomed to enjoy them. They know not what relaxation means, except by the actual cessation from labour. They are surrounded by others similarly circumstanced with themselves; and thus passing on from childhood to youth, they become gradually initiated, the young men in particular, but often the young females also, in the seductive pleasures of the pot-house and inebriation: for which their daily hard labour, want of better habits, and the general vacuity of their minds, tend to prepare them.

Such a system of training cannot be expected to produce any other than a population weak in bodily and mental faculties, and with habits generally destructive of their own comforts, of the well-being of those around them, and strongly calculated to subdue all the social affections. Man so circumstanced sees all around him hurrying forward, at a mail-coach speed, to acquire individual wealth, regardless of him, his comforts, his wants, or even his sufferings, except by way of a *degrading parish charity*, fitted only to steel the heart of man against his fellows, or to form the tyrant and the slave. To-day he labours for one master, to-morrow for a second, then for a third, and a fourth, until all ties between employers and employed are frittered down to the consideration of what immediate gain each can derive from the other.

The employer regards the employed as mere instruments of gain, while these acquire a gross ferocity of character, which, if legislative measures shall not be judiciously devised to prevent its increase, and ameliorate the condition of this class, will sooner or later plunge the country into a formidable and perhaps inextricable state of danger.

The direct object of these observations is to effect the amelioration and avert the danger. The only mode by which these objects can be accomplished is to obtain an Act of Parliament—

First,—To limit the regular hours of labour in mills of machinery to twelve per day, including one hour and a half for meals.

Second,—To prevent children from being employed in mills of machinery until they shall be ten years old, or that they shall not be employed more than six hours per day until they shall be twelve years old.

Third,—That children of either sex shall not be admitted into any manufactory,—after a time to be named,—until they can read and write in an useful manner, understand the first four rules of arithmetic, and the girls be likewise competent to sew their common garments of clothing.

These measures, when influenced by no party feelings or narrow mistaken notions of immediate self-interest, but considered solely in a national view, will be found to be beneficial to the child, to the parent, to the employer, and to the country. Yet, as we are now trained, many individuals cannot detach general subjects from party considerations, while others can see them only through the medium of present pecuniary gain. It may thence be concluded, that individuals of various descriptions will disapprove of some or all of these measures. I will therefore endeavour to anticipate their objections, and reply to them.

The child cannot be supposed to make any objection to the plans proposed: he may easily be taught to consider them, as they will prove to be by experience, essentially beneficial to him in childhood, youth, manhood, and old age.

Parents who have grown up in ignorance and bad habits, and who consequently are in poverty, may say "We cannot afford to maintain our children until they shall be twelve years of age, without putting them to employment by which they may earn wages, and we therefore object to that part of the plan which precludes us from sending them to manufactories until they shall be of that age."

If the poorest and most miserable of the people formerly supported their children without regular employment until they were fourteen, why may they not now support them until they shall be twelve years old? If parents who decline this duty had not been ignorant and trained in bad habits which render their mental faculties inferior to the instinct of many animals, they would understand that by forcing their children to labour in such situations at a premature age, they place their offspring in circumstances calculated to retard their growth, and make them peculiarly liable to bodily disease and mental injury, while they debar them the chance of acquiring that sound robust constitution which otherwise they would possess, and without which they cannot enjoy much happiness, but must become a burthen to themselves, their friends, and their country. Parents by so acting also deprive their children of the opportunity of acquiring the habits of domestic life, without a knowledge of which high nominal wages can procure them but few comforts, and without which among the working classes very little domestic happiness can be enjoyed.

Children thus prematurely employed are prevented from acquiring any of the common rudiments of book learning; but in lieu of this useful and valuable knowledge, they are likely to acquire the most injurious habits by continually associating with those as ignorant and as ill instructed as themselves. And thus it may be truly said, that for every penny gained by parents from the premature labour of their offspring, they sacrifice not only future pounds, but also the future health, comfort, and good conduct of their children; and unless this pernicious system shall be arrested by the introduction of a better, the evil is likely to extend, and to become worse through every succeeding generation.

I do not anticipate any objection from employers to the age named for the admittance of children into their manufactories; or to children being previously trained in good habits and the rudiments of common learning; for, upon an experience abundantly sufficient to ascertain the fact, I have uniformly found it to be more profitable to admit children to constant daily employment at ten years old, than at any earlier period; and that those children, or adults, who had been the best taught, made the best servants, and were by far the most easily directed to do every thing that was right and proper for them to perform. The proprietors of expensive establishments may object to the reduction of the *now* customary hours of labour. The utmost extent, however, of their argument is, that the rent or interest of the capital expended in forming the establishment is chargeable on the quantity of its produce;—and if, instead of being permitted to employ their work-people within their manufactories so long as human nature can be tempted to continue its exertions, say for fourteen or fifteen hours per day, they shall be restricted to twelve hours of labour per day from their work-people, then the prime cost of the article which they manufacture will be increased by the greater proportion of rent or interest which attaches to the smaller quantity produced. If, however, this law shall be, as it is proposed, general over England, Scotland, and Ireland, whatever difference may ultimately arise in the prime cost of the articles produced in these manufactories, will be borne by the consumers, and not by the proprietors of such establishments. And, in a national view, the labour which is exerted twelve hours per day will be obtained more economically than if stretched to a longer period.

I doubt, however, whether any manufactory, so arranged as to occupy the hands employed in it twelve hours per day, will not produce its fabric, even to the immediate proprietor, nearly if not altogether as cheap as those in which the exertions of the employed are continued to fourteen or fifteen hours per day.

Should this, however, not prove to be the case to the extent mentioned, the improved health, the comforts, useful acquirements of the population, and the diminution of poor-rates, naturally consequent on this change in the manners and habits of the people, will amply compensate to the country for a mere fractional addition to the prime cost of any commodity.

And is it to be imagined that the British Government will ever put the chance of a trivial pecuniary gain of a few, in competition with the solid welfare of so many millions of human beings?

The employer cannot be injured by being obliged so to act towards his labourers as, for the interest of the country, he should act. Since the general introduction of expensive machinery, human nature has been forced far beyond its average strength; and much, very much private misery and public injury are the consequences.

It is indeed a measure more to be deplored in a national view than almost any other that has occurred for many centuries past. It has deranged the domestic habits of the great mass of the people. It has deprived them of the time in which they might acquire instruction, or enjoy rational amusements. It has robbed them of their substantial advantages, and, by leading them into habits of the pot-house and inebriation, it has poisoned all their social comforts.

Shall we then make laws to imprison, transport, or condemn to death those who purloin a few shillings of our property, injure any of our domestic animals, or even a growing twig; and shall we *not* make laws to restrain those who otherwise will not be restrained in their desire for gain, from robbing, in the pursuit of it, millions of our fellow-creatures of their health, – their time for acquiring knowledge and future improvement, – of their social comforts, – and of every rational enjoyment? This system of proceeding cannot continue long; – it will work its own cure by the practical evils which it creates, and that in a most dangerous way to the public welfare, if the Government shall not give it a proper direction.

The public, however, are perhaps most interested in that part of the plan which recommends the training and educating of the lower orders under the direction and at the expense of the country. And it is much to be wished that the extended substantial advantages to be derived from this measure were more generally considered and understood, in order that the mistaken ideas which now exist regarding it, in the most opposite quarters, may be entirely removed.

A slight general knowledge of the past occurrences of the world, with some experience of human nature as it appears in the little sects and parties around us, is sufficient to make it evident to those not very much misinstructed from infancy, that children may be taught any habits and any sentiments; and that these, with the bodily and mental propensities and faculties existing at birth in each individual, combined with the general circumstances in which he is placed, constitute the whole character of man.

It is thence evident that human nature can be improved and formed into the character which it is for the interest and happiness of all it should possess, solely by directing the attention of mankind to the adoption of legislative measures judiciously calculated to give the best habits and most just and useful sentiments to the rising generation; and in an especial manner to those who are placed in situations which, without such measures, render them liable to be taught the worst habits and the most useless and injurious sentiments.

I ask those who have studied the science of government upon those enlightened principles which alone ought to influence the statesman — What is the difference, in a national view, between an individual trained in habits which give him health, temperance, industry, correct principles of judging, foresight, and general good conduct; and one trained in ignorance, idleness, intemperance, defective powers of judging, and in general vicious habits? Is not one of the former of more real worth and political strength to the State than many of the latter?

Are there not many millions in the British dominions in whom this difference can be made? And if a change which so essentially affects the well-being of those individuals, and, through them, of every member of the empire, *may* be made, is it not the first duty of the Government and the country to put into immediate practice the means which *can* effect the change?

Shall then such important measures be waived, and the best interests of this country compromised, because one party wishes its own peculiar principles to be forced on the young mind; or because another is afraid that the advantages to be derived from this improved system of legislation will be so great as to give too much popularity and influence to the Ministers who shall introduce it?

The termination of such errors in practice is, I trust, near at hand, and then Government will be no longer compelled to sacrifice the well-doing and the well-being of the great mass of the people and of the empire, to the prejudices of comparatively a few individuals, trained to mistake even their own security and interests.

Surely a measure most obviously calculated to render a greater benefit to millions of our fellow-creatures than any other ever yet adopted, cannot be much longer suspended because one party in the State may erroneously suppose it would weaken their influence over the public mind unless that party shall alone direct that plan; but which direction, it is most obvious, the intelligence of the age will not commit to any party exclusively. Or because others, trained in very opposite principles, may imagine that a national system of education for the poor and lower orders, under the sanction of Government, but superintended and directed in its details by the country, would place a dangerous power in the hands of Ministers of the Crown.

Such sentiments as these cannot exist in minds divested of party considerations, who sincerely desire to benefit their fellow-men, who have no private views to accomplish, and who wish to support and strengthen the Government, that the Government may be the better enabled to adopt decisive and effectual measures for the general amelioration of the people.

I now therefore, in the name of the millions of the neglected poor and ignorant, whose habits and sentiments have been hitherto formed to render them wretched, call upon the British Government and the British Nation to unite their efforts to arrange a system to train and instruct those who, for any good or useful purpose, are now untrained and uninstructed; and to arrest by a clear, easy, and practical system of prevention, the ignorance and consequent poverty, vice, and misery which are rapidly increasing throughout the empire; for, "Train up a child in the way he should go, and when he is old he will not depart from it."

(1815)

# Henry David Thoreau

## from **Walden**

### Economy

When I wrote the following pages, or rather the bulk of them, I lived alone, in the woods, a mile from any neighbor, in a house which I had built myself, on the shore of Walden Pond, in Concord, Massachusetts, and earned my living by the labor of my hands only. I lived there two years and two months. At present I am a sojourner in civilized life again.

I should not obtrude my affairs so much on the notice of my readers if very particular inquiries had not been made by my townsmen concerning my mode of life, which some would call impertinent, though they do not appear to me at all impertinent, but, considering the circumstances, very natural and pertinent. Some have asked what I got to eat; if I did not feel lonesome; if I was not afraid; and the like. Others have been curious to learn what portion of my income I devoted to charitable purposes; and some, who have large families, how many poor children I maintained. I will therefore ask those of my readers who feel no particular interest in me to pardon me if I undertake to answer some of these questions in this book. In most books, the I, or first person, is omitted; in this it will be retained; that, in respect to egotism, is the main difference. We commonly do not remember that it is, after all, always the first person that is speaking. I should not talk so much about myself if there were anybody else whom I knew as well. Unfortunately, I am confined to this theme by the narrowness of my experience. Moreover, I, on my side, require of every writer, first or last, a simple and sincere account of his own life, and not merely what he has heard of other men's lives; some such account as he would send to his kindred from a distant land; for if he has lived sincerely, it must have been in a distant land to me. Perhaps these pages are more particularly addressed to poor students. As for the rest of my readers, they will accept such portions as apply to them. I trust that none will stretch the seams in putting on the coat, for it may do good service to him whom it fits.

I would fain say something, not so much concerning the Chinese and Sandwich Islanders as you who read these pages, who are said to live in New England; something about your condition, especially your outward condition or circumstances in this world, in this town, what it is, whether it is necessary that it be as bad as it is, whether it cannot be improved as well as not. I have travelled a good deal in Concord; and everywhere, in shops, and offices, and fields, the inhabitants have appeared to me to be doing penance in a thousand remarkable ways. What I have heard of Bramins sitting exposed to four fires and looking in the face of the sun; or hanging suspended, with their heads downward, over flames; or looking at the heavens over their shoulders "until it becomes impossible for them to resume their natural position, while from the twist of the neck nothing but liquids can pass into the stomach;" or dwelling, chained for life, at the foot of a tree; or measuring with their bodies, like caterpillars, the breadth of vast empires; or standing on one leg on the tops of pillars, — even these forms of conscious penance are hardly more incredible and astonishing than the scenes which I daily witness. The twelve labors of Hercules were trifling in comparison with those which my neighbors have undertaken; for they were only twelve, and had an end; but I could never see that these men slew or captured any monster or finished any labor. They have no friend Iolaus to burn with a hot iron the root of the hydra's head, but as soon as one head is crushed, two spring up.

I see young men, my townsmen, whose misfortune it is to have inherited farms, houses, barns, cattle, and farming tools; for these are more easily acquired than got rid of. Better if they had been born in the open pasture and suckled by a wolf, that they might have seen with clearer eyes what field they were called to labor in. Who made them serfs of the soil? Why should they eat their sixty acres, when man is condemned to eat only his peck of dirt? Why should they begin digging their graves as soon as they are born? They have got to live a man's life, pushing all these things before them, and get on as well as they can. How many a poor immortal soul have I met well-nigh crushed and smothered under its load, creeping down the road of life, pushing before it a barn seventy-five feet by forty, its Augean stables never cleansed, and one hundred acres of land, tillage, mowing, pasture, and wood-lot! The portionless, who struggle with no such unnecessary inherited encumbrances, find it labor enough to subdue and cultivate a few cubic feet of flesh.

But men labor under a mistake. The better part of the man is soon plowed into the soil for compost. By a seeming fate, commonly called necessity, they are employed, as it says in an old book, laying up treasures which moth and rust will corrupt and thieves break through and steal. It is a fool's life, as they will find when they get to the end of it, if not before. It is said that Deucalion and Pyrrha created men by throwing stones over their heads behind them: —

Inde genus durum sumus, experiensque laborum,
Et documenta damus quâ simus origine nati.

Or, as Raleigh rhymes it in his sonorous way, —

"From thence our kind hard-hearted is, enduring pain and care,
 Approving that our bodies of a stony nature are."

So much for a blind obedience to a blundering oracle, throwing the stones over their heads behind them, and not seeing where they fell.

Most men, even in this comparatively free country, through mere ignorance and mistake, are so occupied with the factitious cares and superfluously coarse labors of life that its finer fruits cannot be plucked by them. Their fingers, from excessive toil, are too clumsy and tremble too much for that. Actually, the laboring man has not leisure for a true integrity day by day; he cannot afford to sustain the manliest relations to men; his labor would be depreciated in the market. He has no time to be anything but a machine. How can he remember well his ignorance — which his growth requires — who has so often to use his knowledge? We should feed and clothe him gratuitously sometimes, and recruit him with our cordials, before we judge of him. The finest qualities of our nature, like the bloom on fruits, can be preserved only by the most delicate handling. Yet we do not treat ourselves nor one another thus tenderly.

Some of you, we all know, are poor, find it hard to live, are sometimes, as it were, gasping for breath. I have no doubt that some of you who read this book are unable to pay for all the dinners which you have actually eaten, or for the coats and shoes which are fast wearing or are already worn out, and have come to this page to spend borrowed or stolen time, robbing your creditors of an hour. It is very evident what mean and sneaking lives many of you live, for my sight has been whetted by experience; always on the limits, trying to get into business and trying to get out of debt, a very ancient slough, called by the Latins *aes alienum*, another's brass, for some of their coins were made of brass; still living, and dying, and buried by this other's brass; always promising to pay, promising to pay, to-morrow, and dying to-day, insolvent; seeking to curry favor, to get custom, by how many modes, only not state-prison offences; lying, flattering, voting, contracting yourselves into a nutshell of civility, or dilating into an atmosphere of thin and vaporous generosity, that you may persuade your neighbor to let you make his shoes, or his hat, or his coat, or his carriage, or import his groceries for him; making yourselves sick, that you may lay up something against a sick day, something to be tucked away in an old chest, or in a stocking behind the plastering, or, more safely, in the brick bank; no matter where, no matter how much or how little.

I sometimes wonder that we can be so frivolous, I may almost say, as to attend to the gross but somewhat foreign form of servitude called Negro Slavery, there are so many keen and subtle masters that enslave both North and South. It is hard to have a Southern overseer; it is worse to have a Northern one; but worst of all when you are the slave-driver of yourself. Talk of a divinity in man! Look at the teamster on the highway, wending to market by day or night; does any divinity stir within him? His highest duty to fodder and water his horses! What is his destiny to him compared with the shipping interests? Does not he drive for Squire Make-a-stir? How godlike, how immortal, is he? See how he cowers and sneaks, how vaguely all the day he fears, not being immortal nor divine, but the slave and prisoner of his own opinion of himself, a fame won by his own deeds. Public opinion is a weak tyrant compared with our own private opinion. What a man thinks of himself, that it is which determines, or rather indicates, his fate. Self-emancipation even in the West Indian provinces of the fancy and imagination, – what Wilberforce is there to bring that about? Think, also, of the ladies of the land weaving toilet cushions against the last day, not to betray too green an interest in their fates! As if you could kill time without injuring eternity.

The mass of men lead lives of quiet desperation. What is called resignation is confirmed desperation. From the desperate city you go into the desperate country, and have to console yourself with the bravery of minks and muskrats. A stereotyped but unconscious despair is concealed even under what are called the games and amusements of mankind. There is no play in them, for this comes after work. But it is a characteristic of wisdom not to do desperate things.

When we consider what, to use the words of the catechism, is the chief end of man, and what are the true necessaries and means of life, it appears as if men had deliberately chosen the common mode of living because they preferred it to any other. Yet they honestly think there is no choice left. But alert and healthy natures remember that the sun rose clear. It is never too late to give up our prejudices. No way of thinking or doing, however ancient, can be trusted without proof. What everybody echoes or in silence passes by as true to-day may turn out to be falsehood to-morrow, mere smoke of opinion, which some had trusted for a cloud that would sprinkle fertilizing rain on their fields. . . .

Near the end of March, 1845, I borrowed an axe and went down to the woods by Walden Pond, nearest to where I intended to build my house, and began to cut down some tall, arrowy white pines, still in their youth, for timber. It is difficult to begin without borrowing, but perhaps it is the most generous course thus to permit your fellow-men to have an interest in your enterprise. The owner of the axe, as he released his hold on it, said that it was the apple of his eye; but I returned it sharper than I received it. It was a pleasant hillside where I worked, covered with pine woods, through which I looked out on the pond, and a small open field in the woods where pines and hickories were springing up. The ice in the pond was not yet dissolved, though there were some open spaces, and it was all dark-colored and saturated with water. There were some slight flurries of snow during the days that I worked there; but for the most part when I came out on to the railroad, on my way home, its yellow sand-heap stretched away gleaming in the hazy atmosphere, and the rails shone in the spring sun, and I heard the lark and pewee and other birds already come to commence another year with us. They were pleasant spring days, in which the winter of man's discontent was thawing as well as the earth, and the life that had lain torpid began to stretch itself. One day, when my axe had come off and I had cut a green hickory for a wedge, driving it with a stone, and had placed the whole to soak in a pond-hole in order to swell the wood, I saw a striped snake run into the water, and he lay on the bottom, apparently without inconvenience, as long as I stayed there, or more than a quarter of an hour; perhaps because he had not yet fairly come out of the torpid state. It appeared to me that for a like reason men remain in their present low and primitive condition; but if they should feel the influence of the spring of springs arousing them, they would of necessity rise to a higher and more ethereal life. I had previously seen the snakes in frosty mornings in my path with portions of their bodies still numb and inflexible, waiting for the sun to thaw them. On the 1st of April it rained and melted the ice, and in the early part of the day, which was very foggy, I heard a stray goose groping about over the pond and cackling as if lost, or like the spirit of the fog.

So I went on for some days cutting and hewing timber, and also studs and rafters, all with my narrow axe, not having many communicable or scholar-like thoughts, singing to myself,—

Men say they know many things;
But lo! they have taken wings,—
The arts and sciences,
And a thousand appliances;
The wind that blows
Is all that anybody knows.

I hewed the main timbers six inches square, most of the studs on two sides only, and the rafters and floor timbers on one side, leaving the rest of the bark on, so that they were just as straight and much stronger than sawed ones. Each stick was carefully mortised or tenoned by its stump, for I had borrowed other tools by this time. My days in the woods were not very long ones; yet I usually carried my dinner of bread and butter, and read the newspaper in which it was wrapped, at noon, sitting amid the green pine boughs which I had cut off, and to my bread was imparted some of their fragrance, for my hands were covered with a thick coat of pitch. Before I had done I was more the friend than the foe of the pine tree, though I had cut down some of them, having become better acquainted with it. Sometimes a rambler in the wood was attracted by the sound of my axe, and we chatted pleasantly over the chips which I had made.

By the middle of April, for I made no haste in my work, but rather made the most of it, my house was framed and ready for the raising. I had already bought the shanty of James Collins, an Irishman who worked on the Fitchburg Railroad, for boards. James Collins' shanty was considered an uncommonly fine one. When I called to see it he was not at home. I walked about the outside, at first unobserved from within, the window was so deep and high. It was of small dimensions, with a peaked cottage roof, and not much else to be seen, the dirt being raised five feet all around as if it were a compost heap. The roof was the soundest part, though a good deal warped and made brittle by the sun. Doorsill there was none, but a perennial passage for the hens under the doorboard. Mrs. C. came to the door and asked me to view it from the inside. The hens were driven in by my approach. It was dark, and had a dirt floor for the most part, dank, clammy, and aguish, only here a board and there a board which would not bear removal. She lighted a lamp to show me the inside of the roof and the walls, and also that the board floor extended under the bed, warning me not to step into the cellar, a sort of dust hole two feet deep. In her own words, they were "good boards overhead, good boards all around, and a good window," — of two whole squares originally, only the cat had passed out that way lately. There was a stove, a bed, and a place to sit, an infant in the house where it was born, a silk parasol, gilt-framed looking-glass, and a patent new coffee-mill nailed to an oak sapling, all told. The bargain was soon concluded, for James had in the meanwhile returned. I to pay four dollars and twenty-five cents to-night, he to vacate at five to-morrow morning, selling to nobody else meanwhile: I to take possession at six. It were well, he said, to be there early, and anticipate certain indistinct but wholly unjust claims on the score of ground rent and fuel. This he assured me was the only encumbrance. At six I passed him and his family on the road. One large bundle held their all, — bed, coffee-mill, looking-glass, hens, — all but the cat; she took to the woods and became a wild cat, and, as I learned afterward, trod in a trap set for woodchucks, and so became a dead cat at last.

I took down this dwelling the same morning, drawing the nails, and removed it to the pond-side by small cartloads, spreading the boards on the grass there to bleach and warp back again in the sun. One early thrush gave me a note or two as I drove along the woodland path. I was informed treacherously by a young Patrick that neighbor Seeley, an

Irishman, in the intervals of the carting, transferred the still tolerable, straight, and drivable nails, staples, and spikes to his pocket, and then stood when I came back to pass the time of day, and look freshly up, unconcerned, with spring thoughts, at the devastation; there being a dearth of work, as he said. He was there to represent spectatordom, and help make this seemingly insignificant event one with the removal of the gods of Troy.

I dug my cellar in the side of a hill sloping to the south, where a woodchuck had formerly dug his burrow, down through sumach and blackberry roots, and the lowest stain of vegetation, six feet square by seven deep, to a fine sand where potatoes would not freeze in any winter. The sides were left shelving, and not stoned; but the sun having never shone on them, the sand still keeps its place. It was but two hours' work. I took particular pleasure in this breaking of ground, for in almost all latitudes men dig into the earth for an equable temperature. Under the most splendid house in the city is still to be found the cellar where they store their roots as of old, and long after the superstructure has disappeared posterity remark its dent in the earth. The house is still but a sort of porch at the entrance of a burrow.

At length, in the beginning of May, with the help of some of my acquaintances, rather to improve so good an occasion for neighborliness than from any necessity, I set up the frame of my house. No man was ever more honored in the character of his raisers than I. They are destined, I trust, to assist at the raising of loftier structures one day. I began to occupy my house on the 4th of July, as soon as it was boarded and roofed, for the boards were carefully feather-edged and lapped, so that it was perfectly impervious to rain, but before boarding I laid the foundation of a chimney at one end, bringing two cartloads of stones up the hill from the pond in my arms. I built the chimney after my hoeing in the fall, before a fire became necessary for warmth, doing my cooking in the meanwhile out of doors on the ground, early in the morning: which mode I still think is in some respects more convenient and agreeable than the usual one. When it stormed before my bread was baked, I fixed a few boards over the fire, and sat under them to watch my loaf, and passed some pleasant hours in that way. In those days, when my hands were much employed, I read but little, but the least scraps of paper which lay on the ground, my holder, or tablecloth, afforded me as much entertainment, in fact answered the same purpose as the Iliad.

It would be worth the while to build still more deliberately than I did, considering, for instance, what foundation a door, a window, a cellar, a garret, have in the nature of man, and perchance never raising any superstructure until we found a better reason for it than our temporal necessities even. There is some of the same fitness in a man's building his own house that there is in a bird's building its own nest. Who knows but if men constructed their dwellings with their own hands, and provided food for themselves and families simply and honestly enough, the poetic faculty would be universally developed, as birds universally sing when they are so engaged? But alas! we do like cowbirds and cuckoos, which lay their eggs in nests which other birds have built, and cheer no traveller with their chattering and unmusical notes. Shall we forever resign the pleasure of construction to the carpenter? What does architecture amount to in the experience of the mass of men? I never in all my walks came across a man engaged in so simple and natural an occupation as building his house. We belong to the community. It is not the tailor alone who is the ninth part of a man; it is as much the preacher, and the merchant, and the farmer. Where is this division of labor to end? and what object does it finally serve? No doubt another *may* also think for me; but it is not therefore desirable that he should do so to the exclusion of my thinking for myself.

True, there are architects so called in this country, and I have heard of one at least possessed with the idea of making architectural ornaments have a core of truth, a necessity, and hence a beauty, as if it were a revelation to him. All very well perhaps from his point of view, but only a little better than the common dilettantism. A sentimental reformer in architecture, he began at the cornice, not at the foundation. It was only how to put a core of truth within the ornaments, that every sugarplum, in fact, might have an almond or caraway seed in it,— though I hold that almonds are most wholesome without the sugar,— and not how the inhabitant, the indweller, might build truly within and without, and let the ornaments take care of themselves. What reasonable man ever supposed that ornaments were something outward and in the skin merely,—that the tortoise got his spotted shell, or the shellfish its mother-o'-pearl tints, by such a contract as the inhabitants of Broadway their Trinity Church? But a man has no more to do with the style of architecture of his house than a tortoise with that of its shell: nor need the soldier be so idle as to try to paint the precise *color* of his virtue on his standard. The enemy will find it out. He may turn pale when the trial comes. This man seemed to me to lean over the cornice, and timidly whisper his half truth to the rude occupants who really knew it better than he. What of architectural beauty I now see, I know has gradually grown from within outward, out of the necessities and character of the indweller, who is the only builder,—out of some unconscious truthfulness, and nobleness, without ever a thought for the appearance; and whatever additional beauty of this kind is destined to be produced will be preceded by a like unconscious beauty of life. The most interesting dwellings in this country, as the painter knows, are the most unpretending, humble log huts and cottages of the poor commonly; it is the life of the inhabitants whose shells they are, and not any peculiarity in their surfaces merely, which makes them *picturesque;* and equally interesting will be the citizen's suburban box, when his life shall be as simple and as agreeable to the imagination, and there is as little straining after effect in the style of his dwelling. A great proportion of architectural ornaments are literally hollow, and a September gale would strip them off, like borrowed plumes, without injury to the substantials. They can do without *architecture* who have no olives nor wines in the cellar. What if an equal ado were made about the ornaments of style in literature, and the architects of our bibles spent as much time about their cornices as the architects of our churches do? So are made the *belles-lettres* and the *beaux-arts* and their professors. Much it concerns a man, forsooth, how a few sticks are slanted over him or under him, and what colors are daubed upon his box. It would signify somewhat, if, in any earnest sense, *he* slanted them and daubed it; but the spirit having departed out of the tenant, it is of a piece with constructing his own coffin,—the architecture of the grave, and "carpenter" is but another name for "coffin-maker." One man says, in his despair or indifference to life, take up a handful of the earth at your feet, and paint your house that color. Is he thinking of his last and narrow house? Toss up a copper for it as well. What an abundance of leisure he must have! Why do you take up a handful of dirt? Better paint your house your own complexion; let it turn pale or blush for you. An enterprise to improve the style of cottage architecture! When you have got my ornaments ready, I will wear them.

Before winter I built a chimney, and shingled the sides of my house, which were already impervious to rain, with imperfect and sappy shingles made of the first slice of the log, whose edges I was obliged to straighten with a plane.

I have thus a tight shingled and plastered house, ten feet wide by fifteen long, and eight-feet posts, with a garret and a closet, a large window on each side, two trap-doors, one door at the end, and a brick fireplace opposite. The exact cost of my house, paying the usual price for such materials as I used, but not counting the work, all of which was done by myself, was as follows; and I give the details because very few are able to tell exactly what their houses cost, and fewer still, if any, the separate cost of the various materials which compose them:—

| | | |
|---|---|---|
| Boards . . . . . . . . . . . . . . . . . . . . . . | $ 8 03½, | mostly shanty boards. |
| Refuse shingles for roof and sides . . . | 4 00 | |
| Laths . . . . . . . . . . . . . . . . . . . . . | 1 25 | |
| Two second-hand windows with glass . | 2 43 | |
| One thousand old brick . . . . . . . . . . | 4 00 | |
| Two casks of lime . . . . . . . . . . . . . | 2 40 | That was high. |
| Hair . . . . . . . . . . . . . . . . . . . . . . | 0 31 | More than I needed. |
| Mantle-tree iron . . . . . . . . . . . . . . . | 0 15 | |
| Nails . . . . . . . . . . . . . . . . . . . . . . | 3 90 | |
| Hinges and screws . . . . . . . . . . . . . | 0 14 | |
| Latch . . . . . . . . . . . . . . . . . . . . . | 0 10 | |
| Chalk . . . . . . . . . . . . . . . . . . . . . | 0 01 | |
| Transportation . . . . . . . . . . . . . . . | 1 40 | { I carried a good part on my back. |
| In all . . . . . . . . . . . . . . . . . . . . . | $28 12½ | |

These are all the materials, excepting the timber, stones, and sand, which I claimed by squatter's right. I have also a small woodshed adjoining, made chiefly of the stuff which was left after building the house. . . .

## Where I Lived

I went to the woods because I wished to live deliberately, to front only the essential facts of life, and see if I could not learn what it had to teach, and not, when I came to die, discover that I had not lived. I did not wish to live what was not life, living is so dear; nor did I wish to practise resignation, unless it was quite necessary. I wanted to live deep and suck out all the marrow of life, to live so sturdily and Spartan-like as to put to rout all that was not life, to cut a broad swath and shave close, to drive life into a corner, and reduce it to its lowest terms, and, if it proved to be mean, why then to get the whole and genuine meanness of it, and publish its meanness to the world; or if it were sublime, to know it by experience, and be able to give a true account of it in my next excursion. For most men, it appears to me, are in a strange uncertainty about it, whether it is of the devil or of God, and have *somewhat hastily* concluded that it is the chief end of man here to "glorify God and enjoy him forever."

Still we live meanly, like ants; though the fable tells us that we were long ago changed into men; like pygmies we fight with cranes; it is error upon error, and clout upon clout, and our best virtue has for its occasion a superfluous and evitable wretchedness. Our life is frittered away by detail. An honest man has hardly need to count more than his ten fingers, or in extreme cases he may add his ten toes, and lump the rest. Simplicity, simplicity, simplicity! I say, let your affairs be as two or three, and not a hundred or a thousand; instead of a million count half a dozen, and keep your accounts on your thumb-nail. In the midst of this chopping sea of civilized life, such are the clouds and storms and quicksands and thousand-and-one items to be allowed for, that a man has to live, if he would not founder and go to the bottom and not make his port at all, by dead reckoning, and he must be a great calculator indeed who succeeds. Simplify, simplify. Instead of three meals a day, if it be necessary eat but one; instead of a hundred dishes, five; and reduce other things in proportion. Our life is like a German Confederacy, made up of petty states, with its boundary forever fluctuating, so that even a German cannot tell you how it is bounded at any moment. The nation itself, with all its so-called internal improvements, which, by the way are all external and superficial, is just such an unwieldy and overgrown establishment, cluttered with furniture and tripped up by its own traps, ruined by luxury and heedless expense, by want of calculation and a worthy aim, as the million households in the land; and the only cure for it, as for them, is in a rigid economy, a stern and more than Spartan simplicity of life and elevation of purpose. It lives too fast. Men think that it is essential that the *Nation* have commerce, and export ice, and talk through a telegraph, and ride thirty miles an hour, without a doubt, whether *they* do or not; but whether we should live like baboons or like men, is a little uncertain. If we do not get out sleepers, and forge rails, and devote days and nights to the work, but go to tinkering upon our *lives* to improve *them*, who will build railroads? And if railroads are not built, how shall we get to heaven in season? But if we stay at home and mind our business, who will want railroads? We do not ride on the railroad; it rides upon us. Did you ever think what those sleepers are that underlie the railroad? Each one is a man, an Irishman, or a Yankee man. The rails are laid on them, and they are covered with sand, and the cars run smoothly over them. They are sound sleepers, I assure you. And every few years a new lot is laid down and run over; so that, if some have the pleasure of riding on a rail, others have the misfortune to be ridden upon. And when they run over a man that is walking in his sleep, a supernumerary sleeper in the wrong position, and wake him up, they suddenly stop the cars, and make a hue and cry about it, as if this were an exception. I am glad to know that it takes a gang of men for every five miles to keep the sleepers down and level in their beds as it is, for this is a sign that they may sometime get up again.

Why should we live with such hurry and waste of life? We are determined to be starved before we are hungry. Men say that a stitch in time saves nine, and so they take a thousand stitches to-day to save nine to-morrow. As for *work*, we have n't any of any consequence. We have the Saint Vitus' dance, and cannot possibly keep our heads still. If I should only give a few pulls at the parish bell-rope, as for a fire, that is, without setting the bell, there is hardly a man on his farm in the outskirts of Concord, notwithstanding that press of engagements which was his excuse so many times this morning, nor a boy, nor a woman, I might almost say, but would forsake all and follow that sound, not mainly to save property from the flames, but, if we will confess the truth, much more to see it burn, since burn it must, and we, be it known, did not set it on fire,—or to see it put out, and have a hand in it, if that is done as handsomely; yes, even if it were the parish church itself. Hardly a man takes a half-hour's nap after dinner, but when he wakes he holds up his head and asks, "What's the news?" as if the rest of mankind had stood his sentinels. Some give directions to be waked every half-hour, doubtless for no other purpose; and then, to pay for it, they tell what they have dreamed. After a night's sleep the news is as indispensable as the breakfast. "Pray tell me anything new that has happened to a man anywhere on this globe,"—and he reads it over his coffee and rolls, that a man has had his eyes gouged out this morning on the Wachito River; never dreaming the while that he lives in the dark unfathomed mammoth cave of this world, and has but the rudiment of an eye himself.

For my part, I could easily do without the post-office. I think that there are very few important communications made through it. To speak critically, I never received more than one or two letters in my life —I wrote this some years ago—that were worth the postage. The penny-post is, commonly, an institution through which you seriously offer a man that penny for his thoughts which is so often safely offered in jest. And I am sure that I never read any memorable news in a newspaper. If we read of one man robbed, or murdered, or killed by accident, or one house burned, or one vessel wrecked, or one steamboat blown up, or one cow run over on the Western Railroad, or one mad dog killed, or one lot of grasshoppers in the winter,—we never need read of another. One is enough. If you are acquainted with the principle, what do you care for a myriad instances and applications? To a philosopher all *news*, as it is called, is gossip, and they who edit and read it are old women over their tea. Yet not a few are greedy after this gossip. There was such a rush, as I hear, the other day at one of the offices to learn the foreign news by the last arrival, that several large squares of plate glass belonging to the establishment were broken by the pressure,—news which I seriously think a ready wit might write a twelvemonth, or twelve years, before-hand with sufficient accuracy. As for Spain, for instance, if you know how to throw in Don Carlos and the Infanta, and Don Pedro and Seville and Granada, from time to time in the right proportions,—they may have changed the names a little since I saw the papers,—and serve up a bull-fight when other entertainments fail, it will be true to the letter, and give us as good an idea of the exact state or ruin of things in Spain as the most succinct and lucid reports under this head in the newspapers: and as for England, almost the last significant scrap of news from that quarter was the revolution of 1649; and if you have learned the history of her crops for an average year, you never need attend to that thing again, unless your speculations are of a merely pecuniary character. If one may judge who rarely looks into the newspapers, nothing new does ever happen in foreign parts, a French revolution not excepted.

What news! how much more important to know what that is which was never old! "Kieou-he-yu (great dignitary of the state of Wei) sent a man to Khoung-tseu to know his news. Khoung-tseu caused the messenger to be seated near him, and questioned him in these terms: What is your master doing? The messenger answered with respect: My master desires to diminish the number of his faults, but he cannot come to the end of them. The messenger being gone, the philosopher remarked: What a worthy messenger! What a worthy messenger!" The preacher, instead of vexing the ears of drowsy farmers on their day of rest at the end of the week,—for Sunday is the fit conclusion of an ill-spent week, and not the fresh and brave beginning of a new one,—with this one other draggle-tail of a sermon, should shout with thundering voice, "Pause! Avast! Why so seeming fast, but deadly slow?"

Shams and delusions are esteemed for soundest truths, while reality is fabulous. If men would steadily observe realities only, and not allow themselves to be deluded, life, to compare it with such things as we know, would be like a fairy tale and the Arabian Nights' Entertainments. If we respected only what is inevitable and has a right to be, music and poetry would resound along the streets. When we are unhurried and wise, we perceive that only great and worthy things have any permanent and absolute existence, that petty fears and petty pleasures are but the shadow of the reality. This is always exhilarating and sublime. By closing the eyes and slumbering, and consenting to be deceived by shows, men establish and confirm their daily life of routine and habit everywhere, which still is built on purely illusory foundations. Children, who play life, discern its true law and relations more clearly than men, who fail to live it worthily, but who think that they are wiser by experience, that is, by failure. I have read in a Hindoo book, that "there was a king's son, who, being expelled in infancy from his native city, was brought up by a forester, and, growing up to maturity in that state, imagined himself to belong to the barbarous race with which he lived. One of his father's ministers having discovered him, revealed to him what he was, and the misconception of his character was removed, and he knew himself to be a prince. So soul," continues the Hindoo philosopher, "from the circumstances in which it is placed, mistakes its own character, until the truth is revealed to it by some holy teacher, and then it knows itself to be *Brahme*." I perceive that we inhabitants of New England live this mean life that we do because our vision does not penetrate the surface of things. We think that that *is* which *appears* to be. If a man should walk through this town and see only the reality, where, think you, would the "Mill-dam" go to? If he should give us an account of the realities he beheld there, we should not recognize the place in his description. Look at a meeting-house, or a court-house, or a jail, or a shop, or a dwelling-house, and say what that thing really is before a true gaze, and they would all go to pieces in your account of them. Men esteem truth remote, in the outskirts of the system, behind the farthest star, before Adam and after the last man. In eternity there is indeed something true and sublime. But all these times and places and occasions are now and here. God himself culminates in the present moment, and will never be more divine in the lapse of all the ages. And we are enabled to apprehend at all what is sublime and noble only by the perpetual instilling and drenching of the reality that surrounds us. The universe constantly and obediently answers to our conceptions; whether we travel fast or slow, the track is laid for us. Let us spend our lives in conceiving then. The poet or the artist never yet had so fair and noble a design but some of his posterity at least could accomplish it.

Let us spend one day as deliberately as Nature, and not be thrown off the track by every nutshell and mosquito's wing that falls on the rails. Let us rise early and fast, or break fast, gently and without perturbation; let company come and let company go, let the bells ring and the children cry,—determined to make a day of it. Why should we knock under and go with the stream? Let us not be upset and overwhelmed in that terrible rapid and whirlpool called a dinner, situated in the meridian shallows. Weather this danger and you are safe, for the rest of the way is down hill. With unrelaxed nerves, with morning vigor, sail by it, looking another way, tied to the mast like Ulysses. If the engine whistles, let it whistle till it is hoarse for its pains. If the bell rings, why should we run? We will consider what kind of music they are like. Let us settle ourselves, and work and wedge our feet downward through the mud and slush of opinion, and prejudice, and tradition, and delusion, and appearance, that alluvion which covers the globe, through Paris and London, through New York and Boston and Concord, through Church and State, through poetry and philosophy and religion, till we come to a hard bottom and rocks in place, which we can call *reality*, and say, This is, and no mistake; and then begin, having a *point d'appui*, below freshet and frost and fire, a place where you might found a wall or a state, or set a lamp-post safely, or perhaps a gauge, not a Nilometer, but a Realometer, that future ages might know how deep a freshet of shams and appearances had gathered from time to time. If you stand right fronting and face to face to a fact, you will see the sun glimmer on both its surfaces, as if it were a cimeter, and feel its sweet edge dividing you through the heart and marrow, and so you will happily conclude your mortal career. Be it life or death, we crave only reality. If we are really dying, let us hear the rattle in our throats and feel cold in the extremities; if we are alive, let us go about our business.

(1854)

## Jane Jacobs

## *from* **The Death and Life of Great American Cities**
Visual Order: Its Limitations and Possibilities

When we deal with cities we are dealing with life at it most complex and intense. Because this is so, there is a basic esthetic limitation on what can be done with cities: *A city cannot be a work of art.*

We need art, in the arrangements of cities as well as in the other realms of life, to help explain life to us, to show us meanings, to illuminate the relationship between the life that each of us embodies and the life outside us. We need art most, perhaps, to reassure us of our own humanity. However, although art and life are interwoven, they are not the same things. Confusion between them is, in part, why efforts at city design are so disappointing. It is important, in arriving at better design strategies and tactics, to clear up this confusion.

Art has its own peculiar forms of order, and they are rigorous. Artists, whatever their medium, *make selections* from the abounding materials of life, and organize these selections into works that are under the control of the artist. To be sure, the artist has a sense that the demands of the work (i.e., of the selections of material he has made) control him. The rather miraculous result of this process – if the selectivity, the organization and the control are consistent within themselves – can be art. But the essence of this process is disciplined, highly discriminatory selectivity *from* life. In relation to the inclusiveness and the literally endless intricacy of life, art is arbitrary, symbolic and abstracted. That is its value and the source of its own kind of order and coherence.

To approach a city, or even a city neighborhood, as if it were a larger architectural problem, capable of being given order by converting it into a disciplined work of art, is to make the mistake of attempting to substitute art for life.

The results of such profound confusion between art and life are neither life nor art. They are taxidermy. In its place, taxidermy can be a useful and decent craft. However, it goes too far when the specimens put on display are exhibitions of dead, stuffed cities.

Like all attempts at art which get far away from the truth and which lose respect for what they deal with, this craft of city taxidermy becomes, in the hands of its master practitioners, continually more picky and precious. This is the only form of advance possible to it.

All this is a life-killing (and art-killing) misuse of art. The results impoverish life instead of enriching it.

To be sure, it is possible for the creation of art not to be so individualistic a process as it usually is in our society.

Under certain circumstances, the creation of art can apparently be done by general, and in effect anonymous, consensus. For instance, in a closed society, a technologically hampered society, or an arrested society, either hard necessity or tradition and custom can enforce on everyone a disciplined selectivity of purposes and materials, a discipline by consensus on what those materials demand of their organizers, and a disciplined control over the forms thereby created. Such societies can produce villages, and maybe even their own kinds of cities, which look to us like works of art in their physical totality.

But this is not the case with us. For us, such societies may be interesting to ponder; and we may regard their harmonious works with admiration or a kind of nostalgia, and wonder wistfully why we can't be like that.

We can't be like that because the limitations on possibilities and the strictures on individuals in such societies extend much beyond the materials and conceptions used in creating works of art from the grist of everyday life. The limitations and strictures extend into every realm of opportunity (including intellectual opportunity) and into relationships among people themselves. These limitations and strictures would seem to us an unnecessary and intolerable stultification of life. For all our conformity, we are too adventurous, inquisitive, egoistic and competitive to be a harmonious society of artists by consensus, and, what is more, we place a high value upon the very traits that prevent us from being so. Nor is this the constructive use we make of cities or the reason we find them valuable: to embody tradition or to express (and freeze) harmonious consensus.

Nineteenth-century Utopians, with their rejection of urbanized society, and with their inheritance of eighteenth-century romanticism about the nobility and simplicity of "natural" or primitive man, were much attracted to the idea of simple environments that were works of art by harmonious consensus. To get back to this condition has been one of the hopes incorporated in our tradition of Utopian reform.

This futile (and deeply reactionary) hope tinctured the Utopianism of the Garden City planning movement too and, at least ideologically, somewhat gentled its more dominant theme of harmony and order imposed and frozen by authoritarian planning.

The hope for an eventual, simple environment formed of art by consensus—or rather, a ghostly vestige of that hope—has continued to flit through Garden City planning theory when it has kept itself pure from Radiant City and City Beautiful planning. Thus, as late as the 1930's, Lewis Mumford in *The Culture of Cities* gave an importance, which would be puzzling indeed in the absence of this tradition, to pursuits like basket weaving, pottery making and blacksmithing in the planned communities he envisioned for us. As late as the 1950's, Clarence Stein, the leading American Garden City planner, on the occasion of receiving the American Institute of Architects' gold medal for his contributions to architectural progress, was casting about for some object which might suitably be created by harmonious consensus in the ideal communities he envisioned. He suggested that citizens could be allowed to build a nursery school, of course with their own hands. But the gist of Stein's message was that, aside from the conceded nursery school, the complete physical environment of a community and all the arrangements that comprise it must be in the total, absolute and unchallenged control of the project's architects.

This is, of course, no different from the Radiant City and City Beautiful assumptions. These always were primarily architectural design cults, rather than cults of social reform.

Indirectly through the Utopian tradition, and directly through the more realistic doctrine of art by imposition, modern city planning has been burdened from its beginnings with the unsuitable aim of converting cities into disciplined works of art.

Like the housers who face a blank if they try to think what to do besides income-sorting projects, or the highwaymen who face a blank if
they try to think what to do besides accommodate more cars, just so,
architects who venture into city design often face a blank in trying to
create visual order in cities except by substituting the order of art for
the very different order of life. They cannot do anything else much. They
cannot develop alternate tactics, for they lack a strategy for design that
will help cities.

Instead of attempting to substitute art for life, city designers should
return to a strategy ennobling both to art and to life: a strategy of illuminating and clarifying life and helping to explain to us its meanings
and order – in this case, helping to illuminate, clarify and explain the
order of cities.

We are constantly being told simple-minded lies about order in cities,
talked down to in effect, assured that duplication represents order. It is
the easiest thing in the world to seize hold of a few forms, give them a
regimented regularity, and try to palm this off in the name of order. However, simple regimented regularity and significant systems of functional
order are seldom coincident in this world.

To see complex systems of functional order as order, and not as
chaos, takes understanding. The leaves dropping from the trees in the
autumn, the interior of an airplane engine, the entrails of a dissected
rabbit, the city desk of a newspaper, all appear to be chaos if they are
seen without comprehension. Once they are understood as systems of
order, they actually *look* different.

Because we use cities, and therefore have experience with them,
most of us already possess a good groundwork for understanding and
appreciating their order. Some of our trouble in comprehending it, and
much of the unpleasant chaotic effect, comes from lack of enough visual
reinforcements to underscore the functional order, and, worse still, from
unnecessary visual contradictions.

It is fruitless, however, to search for some dramatic key element or
kingpin which, if made clear, will clarify all. No single element in a city
is, in truth, the kingpin or the key. The mixture itself is kingpin, and its
mutual support is the order.

The murk has no shape or pattern except where it is carved into
space by the light. Where the murk between the lights becomes deep and
undefinable and shapeless, the only way to give it form or structure is to
kindle new fires in the murk or sufficiently enlarge the nearest existing
fires.

Only intricacy and vitality of use give, to the parts of a city, appropriate structure and shape. Kevin Lynch, in his book *The Image of the
City*, mentions the phenomenon of "lost" areas, places that the people
he interviewed completely ignored and were actually unaware of unless
reminded, although it would seem the locations of these "lost" places

by no means merited this oblivion, and sometimes his observers had just traversed them in actuality or in imagination.[1]

Wherever the fires of use and vitality fail to extend in a city is a place in the murk, a place essentially without city form and structure. Without that vital light, no seeking for "skeletons" or "frameworks" or "cells" on which to hang the place can bring it into a city form.

These metaphoric space-defining fires are formed — to get back to tangible realities — by areas where diverse city uses and users give each other close-grained and lively support.

This is the essential order which city design can assist. These areas of vitality need to have their remarkable functional order clarified. As cities get more such areas, and less gray area or murk, the need and the opportunities for clarification of this order will increase.

Whatever is done to clarify this order, this intricate life, has to be done mainly by tactics of emphasis and suggestion.

Suggestion — the part standing for the whole — is a principal means by which art communicates; this is why art often tells us so much with such economy. One reason we understand this communication of suggestion and symbol is that, to a certain extent, it is the way all of us see life and the world. We constantly make organized selections of what we consider relevant and consistent from among all the things that cross our senses. We discard, or tuck into some secondary awareness, the impressions that do not make sense for our purposes of the moment — unless those irrelevant impressions are too strong to ignore. Depending on our purposes, we even vary our selections of what we take in and organize. To this extent, we are all artists.

This attribute of art, and this attribute in the way we see, are qualities on which the practice of city design can bank and which it can turn to advantage.

Designers do not need to be in literal control of an entire field of vision to incorporate visual order in cities. Art is seldom ploddingly literal, and if it is, it is poor stuff. Literal visual control in cities is usually a bore to everybody but the designers in charge, and sometimes after it is done, it bores them too. It leaves no discovery or organization or interest for anybody else.

The tactics needed are suggestions that help people make, for themselves, order and sense, instead of chaos, from what they see.

Streets provide the principal visual scenes in cities.

However, too many streets present our eyes with a profound and confusing contradiction. In the foreground, they show us all kinds of

---

[1]About a similar phenomenon, regarding highways, Professor Lynch makes this comment: "Many [Los Angeles] subjects had difficulty in making a mental connection between the fast highway and the remainder of the city structure, just as in the Boston case. They would, in imagination, even walk across the Hollywood Freeway as if it did not exist. A high-speed artery may not necessarily be the best way of visually delimiting a central district."

detail and activity. They make a visual announcement (very useful to us for understanding the order of cities) that this is an intense life and that into its composition go many different things. They make this announcement to us not only because we may see considerable activity itself, but because we see, in different types of buildings, signs, store fronts or other enterprises or institutions, and so on, the inanimate evidences of activity and diversity. However, if such a street goes on and on into the distance, with the intensity and intricacy of the foreground apparently dribbling into endless amorphous repetitions of itself and finally petering into the utter anonymity of distance, we are also getting a visual announcement that clearly says endlessness.

In terms of all human experience, these two announcements, one telling of great intensity, the other telling of endlessness, are hard to combine into a sensible whole.

One or the other of these two conflicting sets of impressions has to take precedence. The viewer has to combat or try to suppress the other set of impressions. Either way, it is difficult not to sense confusion and disorder. The more lively and varied the foreground (that is, the better its innate order of diversity), the sharper, and therefore the more disturbing, the contradiction of the two announcements can be. If too many streets embody this conflict, if they stamp a district or a whole city with this equivocation, the general effect is bound to be chaotic.

There are, of course, two ways of trying to see such a street. If a person gives the long view precedence, with its connotations of repetition and infinity, then the close-up scene and the intensity it conveys seems superfluous and offensive. I think this is the way that many architecturally trained viewers see city streets, and this is one reason for the impatience, and even contempt, that many (not all) of those who are architecturally trained express for the physical evidences of city diversity, freedom and life.

If the foreground view, on the other hand, takes precedence, then the endless repetition and continuation into lost, indefinite distances becomes the superfluous, offensive and senseless element. I think this is the way most of us look at city streets most of the time, because this is the viewpoint of a person whose purpose it is to use what exists on that street, rather than to look at it in detachment. Looking at the street in this way, the viewer makes sense, and at least a minimum amount of order, from the intimate view, but only at the price of considering the distance as a deplorable mishmash, better dismissed from mind if possible.

To bring even a chance for visual order to most such streets – and to districts in which such streets predominate – this basic contradiction of strong visual impressions has to be dealt with. I think this is what European visitors are getting at when they remark, as they often do, that the ugliness of our cities is owing to our gridiron street systems.

The functional order of the city demands that the intensity and diversity be there; their evidences can be removed from the street only at the cost of destroying necessary functional order. On the other hand, however, the order of the city does not demand the impression of endlessness; this impression can be minimized without interfering with functional order. Indeed, by so doing, the really significant attribute of intensity is reinforced.

Therefore a good many city streets (not all) need visual interruptions, cutting off the indefinite distant view and at the same time visually heightening and celebrating intense street use by giving it a hint of enclosure and entity.

Old parts of our cities which have irregular street patterns frequently do this. However, they have the disadvantage of being difficult to understand as street systems; people easily get lost in them and have a difficult time keeping them mapped out in their heads.

Where the basic street pattern is a gridiron plan, which has many advantages, there are two main ways, nevertheless, of introducing sufficient visual irregularities and interruptions into the city scene.

The first means is by adding additional streets where the streets of the gridiron plan are too far apart from each other—as on the West Side of Manhattan, for example: in short, where additional streets are necessary in any case for the functional purpose of helping to generate diversity.

If such new streets are added economically, with a decent respect and restraint for saving the most valuable, the most handsome, or the most various among buildings that lie in their potential paths, and also with the aim of incorporating sides or rears of existing buildings into their frontages wherever possible, to give a mixture of age, then these new streets are seldom going to be straight for great length. They are going to have bends in them and sometimes a considerable tangent. Even a straight street cutting one former large block into two small blocks will not likely form a continuous straight line with its extensions through the next block and the next and next, indefinitely. There are certain to be T junctures where these offset street segments meet intersecting streets at right angles. Ordinary prudence and respect for city variety, combined with an awareness that irregularity in these cases is an advantage in itself, can determine the best of various potential alternative paths for new extra streets. The least material destruction should be combined with maximum visual gain; these two aims are not in conflict.

Subsidiary irregularity within a dominant grid system is not difficult to understand. Extra streets like these, introduced in between the grid streets, could even be named in recognition of their relationship to the grid.

The combination of a basic, easily understandable grid system, together with purposely irregular streets dropped in where the grid is too large for good city functioning, could be, I think, a distinctive and most valuable American contribution to the tactics of city design.

The second means for introducing irregularities and visual interruptions where they are insufficient, is on grid streets themselves.

San Francisco is a city with many natural visual interruptions in a gridiron street pattern. San Francisco's streets, in general, are regular gridiron arrangements in two-dimensional plan; however, in three-dimensional topography they are masterpieces of visual interruption. The many and abrupt hills constantly make separations between the nearby scene and the distance, and this is true whether one is looking along a street toward a rise, or looking down a slope. This arrangement greatly emphasizes the intimate and immediate street scenes, without sacrificing the clarity of gridiron organization.

Cities without such topography cannot reproduce any such happy accident by natural means. However, they too can introduce visual interruptions into straight and regular street patterns without sacrificing clarity of organization and movement. Bridges that connect two buildings up above a street sometimes do this service; so do buildings which themselves bridge a street. Occasional large buildings (preferably with public significance) can be placed across straight streets at ground level. Grand Central Terminal in New York is a well-known example.[2]

Straight, "endless" streets can be interrupted and the street itself divided around a square or plaza forming the interruption; this square can be occupied by a building. In cases where vehicular traffic can actually be dead-ended on straight streets, small parks could be thrown across from sidewalk to sidewalk; the visual interruption or diversion would be provided here by groves of trees or by small (and, let us hope, cheerful) park structures.

In still other cases, a visual diversion need not extend across a straight street, but can be in the form of a building or group of buildings set forward from the normal building line to make a jog, with the sidewalk cut underneath. Another form of jog is a plaza at one side of the street, which makes the building beyond stand out as a visual interruption.

It might be supposed that all this visual emphasis on intensity of street use would be rather overwhelming or even inhuman. But this is not so. Districts with many visual street interruptions do not, in real life, tend to intimidate or overwhelm people; they are more apt to be characterized as "friendly" and also to be comprehensible as districts. After all, this is intensity of human life which is being acknowledged

[2]It also provides an example of an extra street, Vanderbilt Avenue, with T terminations, and at Vanderbilt's northern T is a handsome new building, Union Carbide, which in effect bridges the sidewalk; the short blocks between Vanderbilt and Madison are illustrative, by the way, of the liveliness and pedestrian convenience natural to short blocks in cities.

and emphasized and, what is more, emphasized in its understandable, close-up aspect. It is city infinity and repetition which generally seem overwhelming, inhuman and incomprehensible.

There can be pitfalls, however, in the use of visual street interruptions.

First, there is little point in using them where there is no visual tale of street intensity and detail to tell. If a street is, in truth, a long repetition of one kind of use, providing thin activity, then visual interruption does not clarify the existing form of order here. Visual enclosure of practically nothing (in terms of city intensity) can hardly be more than a design affectation. Visual interruptions and vistas will not, in themselves, *bring* city vitality and intensity or their accompaniments of safety, interest, casual public life and economic opportunity. Only the four basic generators of diversity can do that.

Second, it is unnecessary, and would even become boring in its own way, for all city streets to have visual interruptions. After all, a big city is a big place, and there is nothing wrong in acknowledging or stating this fact too from time to time. (Another of the advantages of San Francisco's hills, for instance, is that the views from them do precisely this, and they do it at the same time as they are separating the distance from the immediate street view.) Occasional endlessness, or else focal endings far in the distance on streets, lend variety. Some streets that run into borders such as bodies of water, campuses or large sports grounds should be left without visual interruptions. Not every street that terminates in a border need reveal this fact, but some of them should, both to introduce distant glimpses of what is different, and to convey casual messages about the whereabouts of the border—a form of orientation clue, incidentally, that Lynch found very important to the people he interviewed for his study of city "imageability."

Third, visual street interruptions should be, in functional terms, not dead ends, but "corners." Actual physical cut-offs to foot traffic in particular are destructive in cities. There should always be a way around the visual interruption or through it, a way that is obvious as a person reaches it, and that then lays out before the eyes a new street scene. This seductive attribute of designed interruptions to the eye was summed up neatly by the late architect Eliel Saarinen, who is reported to have said, in explaining his own design premises, "There must always be an end in view, and the end must not be final."

Fourth, visual interruptions get their force partially from being exceptions to the rule. Too many of the same kind can cancel themselves out. For instance, if plazas along the side of a street are plentiful, the street disintegrates visually as a street, to say nothing of going dead functionally. Jogs with arcades beneath, if they are plentiful instead of exceptional, just give us a narrower street and can even become claustrophobic in their effect.

Fifth, a visual street interruption is a natural eye-catcher and its own character has much to do with the impressions made by the entire scene. If it is banal, vacuous or merely messy, it might better not exist. A gas station or a bunch of billboards or a vacant and neglected building in such a place casts a pall out of all proportion to its size. A visual street interruption which is also beautiful is great luck, but when we go after beauty too solemnly in cities we usually seem to end up with pomposity. Beauty is not around for the asking, but we can ask that visual interruptions be decent and even interesting.

Landmarks, as their name says, are prime orientation clues. But good landmarks in cities also perform two other services in clarifying the order of cities. First, they emphasize (and also dignify) the diversity of cities; they do this by calling attention to the fact that they are different from their neighbors, and important because they are different. This explicit statement about themselves carries an implicit statement about the composition and order of cities. Second, in certain instances landmarks can make important to our eyes city areas which are important in functional fact but need to have that fact visually acknowledged and dignified.

By understanding these other services, we can understand why many different uses are eligible and useful as city landmarks, depending on their contexts in the city.

Let us first consider the role of landmarks as announcers and dignifiers of diversity. One reason a landmark can be a landmark is, of course, that it is in a spot where it shows to advantage. But in addition, it is necessary that the landmark be distinctive as a thing itself, and it is this point with which we are now concerned.

Not all city landmarks are buildings. However, buildings are the principal landmarks in cities and the principles which make them serve well or ill apply also to most other kinds of landmarks, such as monuments, dramatic fountains, and so on.

Satisfying distinction in the appearance of a building almost always grows out of distinction in its use, as discussed in Chapter Twelve. The same building can be physically distinctive in one matrix because its use is distinctive in that context, but can be undistinctive in another setting where its use is the rule rather than the exception. The distinctiveness of a landmark depends considerably on reciprocity between the landmark and its neighbors.

In New York, Trinity Church, at the head of Wall Street, is a well-known and effective landmark. But Trinity would be relatively pallid as an element of city design if it were merely one among an assemblage of churches or even of other symbolic-looking institutions. Trinity's physical distinction, which is anything but pallid in its setting, depends partly on its good landmark site—at a T intersection and a rise in ground—but it also depends greatly on Trinity's functional distinction in its context of office buildings. So dominant is this fact of difference that

Trinity makes a satisfying climax for its street scene, even though it is much smaller than its neighbors. An office building of this size (or any size) at this same advantageous spot, in this context, simply could not perform this service nor convey this degree of visual order, let alone do it with such unlabored and "natural" rightness.

Just so, the New York Public Library building, set in its commercial matrix at Fifth Avenue and Forty-second Street, forms an excellent landmark, but this is not true of the public libraries of San Francisco, Pittsburgh and Philadelphia, as examples. These have the disadvantage of being set among institutions which contrast insufficiently in function or—inevitably—in appearance.

Back in Chapter Eight, which deals with the need for mixed primary uses, I discussed the functional value of dotting important civic buildings within the workaday city, instead of assembling them into cultural or civic projects. In addition to the functional awkwardnesses and the economic waste of primary diversity that these projects cause, the buildings assembled into such islands of pomp are badly underused as landmarks. They pale each other, although each one, by itself, could make a tremendously effective impression and symbol of city diversity. This is serious, because we badly need more, not fewer, city landmarks—great landmarks and small.

Sometimes attempts are made to give a building landmark quality simply by making it bigger than its neighbors, or by turning it out with stylistic differences. Usually, if the use of such a building is essentially the same as the uses of its neighbors, it is pallid—try as it might. Nor does such a building do us that extra service of clarifying and dignifying diversity of uses. Indeed, it tries to tell us that what is important in the order of cities are mere differences in size or outward dress. Except in very rare cases of real architectural masterpieces, this statement that style or size is everything gets from city users, who are not so dumb, about the affection and attention it deserves.

However, it should be noted that some buildings which depend on size for their distinction do provide good landmark orientation service and visual interest for people *at a distance*. In New York, the Empire State Building and the Consolidated Edison Tower with its great illuminated clock are examples. For people seeing them from the streets close by, these same buildings, inconsequential in their differences from neighboring buildings, are inconsequential as landmarks. Philadelphia City Hall, with its tower surmounted by the statue of William Penn, makes a splendid landmark from afar; and its true, not superficial, difference within its intimate matrix of city also makes it a splendid landmark from close by. For distant landmarks, size can sometimes serve. For intimate landmarks, distinction of use and a statement about the importance of differences are of the essence.

These principles apply to minor landmarks too. A grade school can be a local landmark, by virtue of its special use in its surroundings, combined with visibility. Many different uses can serve as landmarks, provided they are special in their own context. For instance, people from Spokane, Washington, say that a physically distinctive and beloved landmark there is the Davenport Hotel, which serves, as hotels sometimes do, also as a unique and major center of city public life and assembly. In a place that is mainly residential, working places that are well seen can make landmarks, and often do.

Some outdoor spaces that are focal centers, or, as they are sometimes called, nodes, behave very much like landmarks and get much of their power as clarifiers of order from the distinctiveness of their use, just as in the case of landmark buildings. The plaza at Rockefeller Center in New York is such a place; to users of the city on the ground in its vicinity it is much more of a "landmark" than the towering structure behind it or the lesser towers further enclosing it.

Now let us consider that second extra service which landmarks can perform to clarify the order of cities: their ability to help state explicitly and visually that a place is important which is in truth functionally important.

Centers of activity, where the paths of many people come together in concentrated fashion, are important places economically and socially in cities. Sometimes they are important in the life of a city as a whole, sometimes to a particular district or neighborhood. Yet such centers may not have the visual distinction or importance merited by the functional truth. When this is the case, a user is being given contradictory and confusing information. The sight of the activity and the intensity of land use says Importance. The absence of any visual climax or dignifying object says Unimportance.

Because commerce is so predominant in most city centers of activity, an effective landmark in such a place usually needs to be overtly uncommercial.

People become deeply attached to landmarks that occur in centers of activity and in this their instincts about city order are correct. In Greenwich Village, the old Jefferson Market Courthouse, now abandoned as a courthouse, occupies a prominent site abutting on one of the community's busiest areas. It is an elaborate Victorian building, and opinions differ radically as to whether it is architecturally handsome or architecturally ugly. However, there is a remarkable degree of unanimity, *even among those who do not like the building as a building*, that it must be retained and used for something. Citizens from the area, as well as architectural students working under their direction, have devoted immense amounts of time to detailed study of the building interior, its condition and its potentialities. Existing civic organizations have put time, effort and pressure into the job of saving it, and a new organization was even started to finance the repair of the public clock on the tower and get it going! The Public Library system, having been shown the architectural and economic practicality, has now asked the city for funds to convert the building to a major branch library.

Why all the to-do over a peculiar building on a centrally located site which could make a lot of quick money for somebody and some extra taxes for the city, if it were used for commerce and residences, like most sites around it?

Functionally, it happens that just such a difference in use as a library is needed here, to help counter the self-destruction of diversity. However, few people are aware of this functional need, or conscious that just such a building can help to anchor diversity. Rather, there seems to be a strong popular agreement that *visually* the whole busy neighborhood of this landmark will lose its point—in short, its order will blur rather than clarify—if this landmark is replaced by a duplication of the uses that already exist around it.

Even an inherently meaningless landmark in a center of activity seems to contribute to the users' satisfaction. For instance, in St. Louis there stands a tall concrete column in the middle of a down-at-heel commercial center in declining, gray area surroundings. It once served as a water tower. Many years ago, when the water tank was removed, the local citizens prevailed on City Hall to save the pedestal, which they themselves then repaired. It still gives to the district its name, "The Watertower," and it still gives a bit of pathetic distinction to its district too, which would otherwise hardly even be recognizable as a place.

As clarifiers of city order, landmarks do best when they are set right amidst their neighbors, as in the case of all the examples I have mentioned. If they are buffered off and isolated from the generalized scene, they are contradicting, instead of explaining and visually reinforcing, an important fact about city differences: that they support each other. This too needs to be said by suggestion.

Eye-catchers, as already mentioned in the case of visual street interruptions, have an importance in city appearance out of all proportion to the physical space they occupy.

Some eye-catchers are eye-catchers just by virtue of *what* they are, rather than because of precisely *where* they are: an odd building for instance, or a little group of differing buildings standing out, because of themselves, in the wide-angle view across a park space. I think it is neither necessary nor desirable to try deliberately to create or to control this category of eye-catchers. Where diversity is generated, where there is mixture in building ages and types, and where there are opportunity and welcome for many people's plans and tastes, eye-catchers of this kind always turn up, and they are more surprising, various and interesting than anyone, aiming primarily at city design, could deliberately plan. Truth is stranger than fiction.

Other eye-catchers, however, are eye-catchers because of *precisely where* they are, and these are necessary to consider as a deliberate part of city design. First of all, there must be spots that, simply as locations, do catch the eye—for example, visual street interruptions. Second, these spots must count for something. These highly visible spots are few and exceptional; they are only one or two among many scores of buildings and locations comprising a street scene. We cannot therefore depend on the law of averages or on chance alone to deliver us visual accents in exactly these natural eye-catcher spots. Often, no more is needed than a good paint color (and a subtraction of billboards) on a building that already exists. Sometimes a new building or new use is needed in these spots—even a landmark. By taking care with the relatively very few spots that are inevitable eye-catchers, much character, interest and accent can be given to a whole scene by suggestion, and with the least design regimentation and the greatest economy of means and tactics.

The importance of such places, and the importance of making them count are points well made in *Planning and Community Appearance,* a booklet prepared by a committee of New York planners and architects formed to investigate the problems of municipal design control. The committee's principal recommendation was that the crucial visual spots in a community be identified, and that *these small spots be zoned to require exceptional treatment.* No good can come, said the committee's report, of blandly including such eye-catching locations in general schemes of zoning and planning.[3] Their locations alone give buildings on these few sites special and exceptional significance, and when we ignore that fact we are ignoring the most tangible realities.

There are some city streets which, in the absence of excellent eye-catchers, or even in addition to eye-catchers, need another kind of design help too. They need unifying devices, to suggest that the street, with all its diversity, is also an entity.

I have mentioned, in Chapter Twelve, a tactic suitable for some streets of mixed residences and commerce, to prevent them from being visually exploded or disintegrated by incongruously large uses. The suitable tactic for visual unity on these streets, as already explained, is to zone a limit on the length of street frontage permitted any single enterprise.

For another family of street unifying tactics, we can exploit the principle that a strong, but otherwise unobtrusive, design element can tie together in orderly fashion much happenstance detail. This kind of unification can be useful on streets that are heavily used, much seen and contain much detail without much real variety of use—streets almost entirely commercial, for instance.

One of the simplest such devices is trees along the stretch to be unified, but trees planted close enough together to give a look of continuity when they are seen close up, as well as when the space between them is elided by distance. Pavements have possibilities as unifiers; that is, sidewalk pavements with strong, simple patterns. Awnings in strong colors have possibilities.

[3]This booklet, obtainable from the New York Regional Plan Association, also discusses the legislative, regulatory and tax arrangements required by such an approach, and is thus valuable to anyone seriously interested in city visual order.

Each street that needs this kind of help is its own problem, and probably needs its own solution.[4] There is a pitfall inherent in unification devices. One reason for a unifier's power is that it is special to a place. The sky itself, in a way, ties together nearly every scene, but its very ubiquity makes it an ineffective visual unifier of most scenes. A unifier supplies only the visual suggestion of entity and order; the viewer does most of the job of unifying by using the hint to help him organize what he sees. If he sees exactly the same unifier in otherwise disparate places and scenes, he will soon unconsciously discount it.

All these various tactics for capturing city visual order are concerned with bits and pieces in the city—bits and pieces which are, to be sure, knit into a city fabric of use that is as continuous and little cut apart as possible. But emphasis on bits and pieces is of the essence: this is what a city is, bits and pieces that supplement each other and support each other.

Perhaps this all seems very commonplace compared with the sweep and swoop of highways, or the eerily beautiful beehive huts of tribal kraals. But what we have to express in expressing our cities is not to be scorned. Their intricate order—a manifestation of the freedom of countless numbers of people to make and carry out countless plans—is in many ways a great wonder. We ought not to be reluctant to make this living collection of interdependent uses, this freedom, this life, more understandable for what it is, nor so unaware that we do not know what it is.

(1961)

**Lewis Mumford**

## *from* **The City in History**

Retrospect and Prospect

In taking form, the ancient city brought together many scattered organs of the common life, and within its walls promoted their interaction and fusion. The common functions that the city served were important; but the common purposes that emerged through quickened methods of com-

[4]The effects of various kinds of unifiers—as well as of visual interruptions good and bad, landmarks and much else—are pictured and explained in two remarkable books on design in English cities, towns and countryside, *Outrage* and *Counter Attack*, both by Gordon Cullen and Ian Nairn.

munication and co-operation were even more significant. The city mediated between the cosmic order, revealed by the astronomer priests, and the unifying enterprises of kingship. The first took form within the temple and its sacred compound, the second within the citadel and the bounding city wall. By polarizing hitherto untapped human aspirations and drawing them together in a central political and religious nucleus, the city was able to cope with the immense generative abundance of neolithic culture.

By means of the order so established, large bodies of men were for the first time brought into effective co-operation. Organized in disciplined work groups, deployed by central command, the original urban populations in Mesopotamia, Egypt, and the Indus Valley controlled flood, repaired storm damage, stored water, remodelled the landscape, built up a great water network for communication and transportation, and filled the urban reservoirs with human energy available for other collective enterprises. In time, the rulers of the city created an internal fabric of order and justice that gave to the mixed populations of cities, by conscious effort, some of the moral stability and mutual aid of the village. Within the theater of the city new dramas of life were enacted.

But against these improvements we must set the darker contributions of urban civilization: war, slavery, vocational over-specialization, and in many places, a persistent orientation toward death. These institutions and activities, forming a 'negative symbiosis,' have accompanied the city through most of its history, and remain today in markedly brutal form, without their original religious sanctions, as the greatest threat to further human development. Both the positive and the negative aspects of the ancient city have been handed on, in some degree, to every later urban structure.

Through its concentration of physical and cultural power, the city heightened the tempo of human intercourse and translated its products into forms that could be stored and reproduced. Through its monuments, written records, and orderly habits of association, the city enlarged the scope of all human activities, extending them backwards and forwards in time. By means of its storage facilities (buildings, vaults, archives, monuments, tablets, books), the city became capable of transmitting a complex culture from generation to generation, for it marshalled together not only the physical means but the human agents needed to pass on and enlarge this heritage. That remains the greatest of the city's gifts. As compared with the complex human order of the city, our present ingenious electronic mechanisms for storing and transmitting information are crude and limited.

From the original urban integration of shrine, citadel, village, workshop, and market, all later forms of the city have, in some measure, taken their physical structure and their institutional patterns. Many parts of this fabric are still essential to effective human association, not least those that sprang originally from the shrine and the village.

Without the active participation of the primary group, in family and neighborhood, it is doubtful if the elementary moral loyalties – respect for the neighbor and reverence for life – can be handed on, without savage lapses, from the old to the young.

At the other extreme, it is doubtful, too, whether those multifarious co-operations that do not lend themselves to abstraction and symbolization can continue to flourish without the city, for only a small part of the contents of life can be put on the record. Without the superposition of many different human activities, many levels of experience, within a limited urban area, where they are constantly on tap, too large a portion of life would be restricted to record-keeping. The wider the area of communication and the greater the number of participants, the more need there is for providing numerous accessible permanent centers for face-to-face intercourse and frequent meetings at every human level.

The recovery of the essential activities and values that first were incorporated in the ancient cities, above all those of Greece, is accordingly a primary condition for the further development of the city in our time. Our elaborate rituals of mechanization cannot take the place of the human dialogue, the drama, the living circle of mates and associates, the society of friends. These sustain the growth and reproduction of human culture, and without them the whole elaborate structure becomes meaningless – indeed actively hostile to the purposes of life.

Today the physical dimensions and the human scope of the city have changed; and most of the city's internal functions and structures must be recast to promote effectively the larger purposes that shall be served: the unification of man's inner and outer life, and the progressive unification of mankind itself. The city's active role in future is to bring to the highest pitch of development the variety and individuality of regions, cultures, personalities. These are complementary purposes: their alternative is the current mechanical grinding down of both the landscape and the human personality. Without the city modern man would have no effective defenses against those mechanical collectives that, even now, are ready to make all veritably human life superfluous, except to perform a few subservient functions that the machine has not yet mastered.

Ours is an age in which the increasingly automatic processes of production and urban expansion have displaced the human goals they are supposed to serve. Quantitative production has become, for our mass-minded contemporaries, the only imperative goal: they value quantification without qualification. In physical energy, in industrial productivity, in invention, in knowledge, in population the same vacuous expansions and explosions prevail. As these activities increase in volume and in tempo, they move further and further away from any humanly desirable objectives. As a result, mankind is threatened with far more formidable inundations than ancient man learned to cope with. To save himself he must turn his attention to the means of controlling, directing, organizing, and subordinating to his own biological functions and cultural purposes the insensate forces that would, by their very superabundance, undermine his life. He must curb them and even eliminate them completely when, as in the case of nuclear and bacterial weapons, they threaten his very existence.

Now it is not a river valley, but the whole planet, that must be brought under human control: not an unmanageable flood of water, but even more alarming and malign explosions of energy that might disrupt the entire ecological system on which man's own life and welfare depends. The prime need of our age is to contrive channels for excessive energies and impetuous vitalities that have departed from organic norms and limits: cultural flood control in every field calls for the erection of embankments, dams, reservoirs, to even out the flow and spread it into the final receptacles, the cities and regions, the groups, families, and personalities, who will be able to utilize this energy for their own growth and development. If we were prepared to restore the habitability of the earth and cultivate the empty spaces in the human soul, we should not be so preoccupied with sterile escapist projects for exploring interplanetary space, or with even more rigorously dehumanized policies based on the strategy of wholesale collective extermination. It is time to come back to earth and confront life in all its organic fecundity, diversity, and creativity, instead of taking refuge in the under-dimensioned world of Post-historic Man.

Modern man, unfortunately, has still to conquer the dangerous aberrations that took institutional form in the cities of the Bronze Age and gave a destructive destination to our highest achievements. Like the rulers of the Bronze Age, we still regard power as the chief manifestation of divinity, or if not that, the main agent of human development. But 'absolute power,' like 'absolute weapons,' belongs to the same magico-religious scheme as ritual human sacrifice. Such power destroys the symbiotic co-operation of man with all other aspects of nature, and of men with other men. Living organisms can use only limited amounts of energy. 'Too much' or 'too little' is equally fatal to organic existence. Organisms, societies, human persons, not least, cities, are delicate devices for regulating energy and putting it to the service of life.

The chief function of the city is to convert power into form, energy into culture, dead matter into the living symbols of art, biological reproduction into social creativity. The positive functions of the city cannot be performed without creating new institutional arrangements, capable of coping with the vast energies modern man now commands: arrangements just as bold as those that originally transformed the overgrown village and its stronghold into the nucleated, highly organized city.

These necessary changes could hardly be envisaged, were it not for the fact that the negative institutions that accompanied the rise of the city have for the last four centuries been falling into decay, and seemed until recently to be ready to drop into limbo. Kingship by divine right has all but disappeared, even as a moribund idea; and the political functions that were once exercised solely by the palace and the temple, with the coercive aid of the bureaucracy and the army, were during the nineteenth century assumed by a multitude of organizations, corporations, parties, associations, and committees. So, too, the conditions laid down by Aristotle for the abolition of slave labor have now been largely met, through the harnessing of inorganic sources of energy and the invention of automatic machines and utilities. Thus slavery, forced labor, legalized expropriation, class monopoly of knowledge, have been giving way to free labor, social security, universal literacy, free education, open access to knowledge, and the beginnings of universal leisure, such as is necessary for wide participation in political duties. If vast masses of people in Asia, Africa, and South America still live under primitive conditions and depressing poverty, even the ruthless colonialism of the nineteenth century brought to these peoples the ideas that would release them. 'The heart of darkness,' from Livingstone on to Schweitzer, was pierced by a shaft of light.

In short, the oppressive conditions that limited the development of cities throughout history have begun to disappear. Property, caste, even vocational specialization have—through the graded income tax and the 'managerial revolution'—lost most of their hereditary fixations. What Alexis de Tocqueville observed a century ago is now more true than ever: the history of the last eight hundred years is the history of the progressive equalization of classes. This change holds equally of capitalist and communist systems, in a fashion that might have shocked Karl Marx, but would not have surprised John Stuart Mill. For the latter foresaw the conditions of dynamic equilibrium under which the advances of the machine economy might at last be turned to positive human advantage. Until but yesterday, then, it seemed that the negative symbiosis that accompanied the rise of the city was doomed. The task of the emerging city was to give an ideal form to these radically superior conditions of life.

Unfortunately, the evil institutions that accompanied the rise of the ancient city have been resurrected and magnified in our own time: so the ultimate issue is in doubt. Totalitarian rulers have reappeared, sometimes elevated, like Hitler, into deities, or mummified in Pharaoh-fashion after death, for worship, like Lenin and Stalin. Their methods of coercion and terrorism surpass the vilest records of ancient rulers, and the hoary practice of exterminating whole urban populations has even been exercised by the elected leaders of democratic states, wielding powers of instantaneous destruction once reserved to the gods. Everywhere secret knowledge has put an end to effective criticism and democratic control; and the emancipation from manual labor has brought about a new kind of enslavement: abject dependence upon the machine. The monstrous gods of the ancient world have all reappeared, hugely magnified, demanding total human sacrifice. To appease their super-Moloch in the Nuclear Temples, whole nations stand ready, supinely, to throw their children into his fiery furnace.

If these demoralizing tendencies continue, the forces that are now at work will prove uncontrollable and deadly; for the powers man now commands must, unless they are detached from their ancient ties to the citadel, and devoted to human ends, lead from their present state of paranoid suspicion and hatred to a final frenzy of destruction. On the other hand, if the main negative institutions of civilization continue to crumble—that is, if the passing convulsions of totalitarianism mark in fact the death-throes of the old order—is it likely that war will escape the same fate? War was one of the 'lethal genes' transmitted by the city from century to century, always doing damage but never yet widely enough to bring civilization itself to an end. That period of tolerance is now over. If civilization does not eliminate war as an open possibility, our nuclear agents will destroy civilization—and possibly exterminate mankind. The vast village populations that were once reservoirs of life will eventually perish with those of the cities.

Should the forces of life, on the other hand, rally together, we shall stand on the verge of a new urban implosion. When cities were first founded, an old Egyptian scribe tells us, the mission of the founder was to "put the gods in their shrines." The task of the coming city is not essentially different: its mission is to put the highest concerns of man at the center of all his activities: to unite the scattered fragments of the human personality, turning artificially dismembered men—bureaucrats, specialists, 'experts,' depersonalized agents—into complete human beings, repairing the damage that has been done by vocational separation, by social segregation, by the over-cultivation of a favored function, by tribalisms and nationalisms, by the absence of organic partnerships and ideal purposes.

Before modern man can gain control over the forces that now threaten his very existence, he must resume possession of himself. This sets the chief mission for the city of the future: that of creating a visible regional and civic structure, designed to make man at home with his deeper self and his larger world, attached to images of human nurture and love.

We must now conceive the city, accordingly, not primarily as a place of business or government, but as an essential organ for expressing and actualizing the new human personality—that of 'One World Man.' The old separation of man and nature, of townsman and countryman, of Greek and barbarian, of citizen and foreigner, can no longer be maintained: for communication, the entire planet is becoming a village; and as a result, the smallest neighborhood or precinct must be planned as a working model of the larger world. Now it is not the will of a single deified ruler, but the individual and corporate will of its citizens, aiming at self-knowledge, self-government, and self-actualization, that must be embodied in the city. Not industry but education will be the center of their activities; and every process and function will be evaluated and approved just to the extent that it furthers human development, whilst the city itself provides a vivid theater for the spontaneous encounters and challenges and embraces of daily life.

Apparently, the inertia of current civilization still moves toward a worldwide nuclear catastrophe; and even if that fatal event is postponed, it may be a century or more before the possibility can be written off. But happily life has one predictable attribute: it is full of surprises. At the last moment – and our generation may in fact be close to the last moment – the purposes and projects that will redeem our present aimless dynamism may gain the upper hand. When that happens, obstacles that now seem insuperable will melt away; and the vast sums of money and energy, the massive efforts of science and technics, which now go into the building of nuclear bombs, space rockets, and a hundred other cunning devices directly or indirectly attached to dehumanized and demoralized goals, will be released for the recultivation of the earth and the rebuilding of cities: above all, for the replenishment of the human personality. If once the sterile dreams and sadistic nightmares that obsess the ruling élite are banished, there will be such a release of human vitality as will make the Renascence seem almost a stillbirth.

It would be foolish to predict when or how such a change may come about; and yet it would be even more unrealistic to dismiss it as a possibility, perhaps even an imminent possibility, despite the grip that the myth of the machine still holds on the Western World. Fortunately, the preparations for the change from a power economy to a life economy have been long in the making; and once the reorientation of basic ideas and purposes takes place, the necessary political and physical transformations may swiftly follow. Many of the same forces that are now oriented toward death will then be polarized toward life.

In discussing the apparent stabilization of the birthrate, as manifested throughout Western civilization before 1940, the writer of 'The Culture of Cities' then observed: "One can easily imagine a new cult of family life, growing up in the face of some decimating catastrophe, which would necessitate a swift revision in plans for housing and city development: a generous urge toward procreation might clash in policy with the views of the prudent, bent on preserving a barely achieved equilibrium."

To many professional sociologists, captivated by the smooth curves of their population graphs, that seemed a far-fetched, indeed quite unimaginable possibility before the Second World War. But such a spontaneous reaction actually took place shortly after the war broke out, and has continued, despite various 'expert' predictions to the contrary, for the last twenty years. Many people who should be vigilantly concerned over the annihilation of mankind through nuclear explosions have concealed that dire possibility from themselves by excessive anxiety over the 'population explosion' – without the faintest suspicion, apparently, that the threat of de-population and that of over-population might in fact be connected.

As of today, this resurgence of reproductive activity might be partly explained as a deep instinctual answer to the premature death of scores of millions of people throughout the planet. But even more possibly, it may be the unconscious reaction to the likelihood of an annihilating outburst of nuclear genocide on a planetary scale. As such, every new baby is a blind desperate vote for survival: people who find themselves unable to register an effective political protest against extermination do so by a biological act. In countries where state aid is lacking, young parents often accept a severe privation of goods and an absence of leisure, rather than accept privation of life by forgoing children. The automatic response of every species threatened with extirpation takes the form of excessive reproduction. This is a fundamental observation of ecology.

No profit-oriented, pleasure-dominated economy can cope with such demands: no power-dominated economy can permanently suppress them. Should the same attitude spread toward the organs of education, art, and culture, man's super-biological means of reproduction, it would alter the entire human prospect: for public service would take precedence over private profit, and public funds would be available for the building and rebuilding of villages, neighborhoods, cities, and regions, on more generous lines than the aristocracies of the past were ever able to afford for themselves. Such a change would restore the discipline and the delight of the garden to every aspect of life; and it might do more to balance the birthrate, by its concern with the quality of life, than any other collective measure.

As we have seen, the city has undergone many changes during the last five thousand years; and further changes are doubtless in store. But the innovations that beckon urgently are not in the extension and perfection of physical equipment: still less in multiplying automatic electronic devices for dispersing into formless sub-urban dust the remaining organs of culture. Just the contrary: significant improvements will come only through applying art and thought to the city's central human concerns, with a fresh dedication to the cosmic and ecological processes that enfold all being. We must restore to the city the maternal, life-nurturing functions, the autonomous activities, the symbiotic associations that have long been neglected or suppressed. For the city should be an organ of love; and the best economy of cities is the care and culture of men.

The city first took form as the home of a god: a place where eternal values were represented and divine possibilities revealed. Though the symbols have changed the realities behind them remain. We know now, as never before, that the undisclosed potentialities of life reach far beyond the proud algebraics of contemporary science; and their promises for the further transformations of man are as enchanting as they are inexhaustible. Without the religious perspectives fostered by the city, it is doubtful if more than a small part of man's capacities for living and learning could have developed. Man grows in the image of his gods, and up to the measure they have set. The mixture of divinity, power, and personality that brought the ancient city into existence must be weighed out anew in terms of the ideology and the culture of our own time, and poured into fresh civic, regional, and planetary molds. In order to defeat the insensate forces that now threaten civilization from within, we must transcend the original frustrations and negations that have dogged the city throughout its history. Otherwise the sterile gods of power, unrestrained by organic limits or human goals, will remake man in their own faceless image and bring human history to an end.

The final mission of the city is to further man's conscious participation in the cosmic and the historic process. Through its own complex and enduring structure, the city vastly augments man's ability to interpret these processes and take an active, formative part in them, so that every phase of the drama it stages shall have, to the highest degree possible, the illumination of consciousness, the stamp of purpose, the color of love. That magnification of all the dimensions of life, through emotional communion, rational communication, technological mastery, and above all, dramatic representation, has been the supreme office of the city in history. And it remains the chief reason for the city's continued existence.

(1961)

*Susanne K. Langer*

# Man and Animal: The City and the Hive*

Within the past five or six decades, the human scene has probably changed more radically than ever before in history. The outward changes in our own setting are already an old story: the disappearance of horse-drawn vehicles, riders, children walking to school, and the advent of the long, low, powerful Thing in their stead; the transformation of the mile-wide farm into a ticktacktoe of lots, each sprouting a split-level dream home. These are the obvious changes, more apparent in the country than in the city. The great cities have grown greater,

*This paper, read at the Cooper Union in New York, was published in *The Antioch Review* (Fall, 1958) and reprinted in *Society Today and Tomorrow*, E. F. Hunt and Jules Karlin, eds. N. Y.: Macmillan, 1961.

brighter, more mechanized, but their basic patterns seem less shaken by the new power and speed in which the long industrial revolution culminates.

The deepest change, however, is really a change in our picture of mankind, and that is most spectacular where mankind is teeming and concentrated – in the city. Our old picture of human life was a picture of local groups, each speaking its mother tongue, observing some established religion, following its own customs. It might be a civilized community or a savage tribe, but it had its distinct traditions. And in it were subdivisions, usually families, with their more special local ties and human relations.

Today, natural tribes and isolated communities have all but disappeared. The ease and speed of travel, the swift economic changes that send people in search of new kinds of work, the two wars that swept over all boundaries, have wiped out most of our traditions. The old family structure is tottering. Society tends to break up into new and smaller units – in fact, into its ultimate units, the human individuals that compose it.

This atomization of society is most obvious in a great cosmopolitan city. The city seems to be composed of millions of unrelated individuals, each scrambling for himself, yet each caught in the stream of all the others.

Discerning eyes saw this a hundred years ago, especially in industrial cities, where individuals from far or near came to do what other individuals from far or near had also come to do – each a cog in the new machine. Most of the cogs had no other relation to each other. And ever since this shake-up in society began, a new picture of society has been in the making – the picture of *human masses*, brought together by some outside force, some imposed function, into a superpersonal unit – masses of people, each representing an atom of "manpower" in a new sort of organism, the industrial state.

The idea of the state as a higher organism – the state as a superindividual – is old. But our conception of such a state is new, because our industrial civilization, which begets our atomized society, is new. The old picture was not one of masses driven by some imposed economic power, or any other outside power. The superindividual was a rational being, directed by a mind within it. The guardians of the state, the rulers, were its mind. Plato described the state as "the man writ large." Hobbes, two thousand years later, called it "Leviathan," the great creature. A city-state like ancient Athens or Sparta might be "a man writ large," but England was too big for that. It was the big fish in the big pond. The mind of Hobbes's fish was perhaps subhuman, but it was still single and sovereign in the organism.

Another couple of centuries later, Rudyard Kipling, faced with a democratic, industrialized civilization, called his allegory of England, "The Mother Hive." Here, a common will, dictated by complicated instincts, replaced even Leviathan's mind; each individual was kept in line by the blind forces of the collective life.

The image of the hive has had a great success as an ideal of collaborative social action. Every modern utopia (except the completely wishful Shangri-La) reflects the beehive ideal. Even a statesman of highest caliber, Jan Smuts, has praised it as a pattern for industrial society. Plato's personified state and Hobbes's sea monster impress us as fantasies, but the hive looks like more than a poetic figure; it seems really to buzz around us.

I think the concept of the state as a collective organism, composed of multitudes of little workers, guided by social forces that none of the little workers can fathom, and accomplishing some greater destiny, is supported by a factor other than our mechanized industry; that other factor is a momentous event in our intellectual history: the spread of the theory of evolution.

First biologists, then psychologists, and finally sociologists and moralists have become newly aware that man belongs to the animal kingdom. The impact of the concept of evolution on scientific discovery has been immense, and it has not stopped at laboratory science; it has also produced some less sober and sound inspirations. The concept of continuous animal evolution has made most psychologists belittle the differences between man and his nonhuman relatives, and led some of them, indeed, to think of *Homo sapiens* as just one kind of primate among others, like the others in all essential respects – differing from apes and monkeys not much more than they differ from species to species among themselves. Gradually the notion of the human animal became common currency, questioned only by some religious minds. This in turn has made it natural for social theorists with scientific leanings to model their concepts of human society on animal societies, the anthill and the beehive.

Perhaps it were well, at this point, to say that I myself stand entirely in the scientific camp. I do not argue against any religious or even vitalistic doctrines; such things are not arguable. I speak not *for*, but *from*, a naturalist's point of view, and anyone who does not share it can make his own reservations in judging what I say.

Despite man's zoological status, which I wholeheartedly accept, there is a deep gulf between the highest animal and the most primitive normal human being: a difference in mentality that is fundamental. It stems from the development of one new process in the human brain – a process that seems to be entirely peculiar to that brain: the use of *symbols for ideas*. By "symbols" I mean all kinds of signs that can be used and understood whether the things they refer to are there or not. The word "symbol" has, unfortunately, many different meanings for different people. Some people reserve it for mystic signs, like Rosicrucian symbols; some mean by it *significant images*, such as Keats' "Huge cloudy symbols of a high romance"; some use it quite the opposite way and speak of "mere symbols," meaning empty gestures, signs that have lost their meanings; and some, notably logicians, use the term for mathematical signs, marks that constitute a code, a brief, concise language. In their sense, ordinary words are symbols, too. Ordinary language is a symbolism.

When I say that the distinctive function of the human brain is the use of symbols, I mean any and all of these kinds. They are all different from signs that animals use. Animals interpret signs, too, but only as pointers to actual things and events, cues to action or expectation, threats and promises, landmarks and earmarks in the world. Human beings use such signs, too, but above all they use symbols — especially words — to think and talk about things that are neither present nor expected. The words convey *ideas*, that may or may not have counterparts in actuality. This power of thinking *about* things expresses itself in language, imagination, and speculation — the chief products of human mentality that animals do not share.

Language, the most versatile and indispensable of all symbolisms, has put its stamp on all our mental functions, so that I think they always differ from even their closest analogues in animal life. Language has invaded our feeling and dreaming and action, as well as our reasoning, which is really a product of it. The greatest change wrought by language is the increased scope of awareness in speech-gifted beings. An animal's awareness is always of things in its own place and life. In human awareness, the present, actual situation is often the least part. We have not only memories and expectations; we have *a past* in which we locate our memories, and *a future* that vastly overreaches our own anticipations. Our past is a story, our future a piece of imagination. Likewise our ambient is a place in a wider, symbolically conceived place, the universe. We live in *a world*.

This difference of mentality between man and animal seems to me to make a cleft between them almost as great as the division between animals and plants. There is continuity between the orders, but the division is real nevertheless. Human life differs radically from animal life. By virtue of our incomparably wider awareness, of our power of envisagement of things and events beyond any actual perception, we have acquired needs and aims that animals do not have; and even the most savage human society, having to meet those needs and implement those aims, is not really comparable to any animal society. The two may have some analogous functions, but the essential structure must be different, because man and beast live differently in every way.

Probably the profoundest difference between human and animal needs is made by one piece of human awareness, one fact that is not present to animals, because it is never learned in any direct experience: that is our foreknowledge of death. The fact that we ourselves must die is not a simple and isolated fact. It is built on a wide survey of facts that discloses the structure of history as a succession of overlapping brief lives, the patterns of youth and age, growth and decline; and above all that, it is built on the logical insight that *one's own life is a case in point*. Only a creature that can think symbolically *about* life can conceive of its own death. Our knowledge of death is part of our knowledge of life.

What, then, do we—all of us—know about life?

Every life that we know is generated from other life. Each living thing springs from some other living thing or things. Its birth is a process of new individuation, in a life stream whose beginning we do not know.

*Individuation* is a word we do not often meet. We hear about individuality, sometimes spoken in praise, sometimes as an excuse for someone's being slightly crazy. We hear and read about "the individual," a being that is forever adjusting, like a problem child, to something called "society." But how does individuality arise? What makes an individual? A fundamental, biological process of *individuation*, that marks the life of every stock, plant or animal. Life is a series of individuations, and these can be of various sorts, and reach various degrees.

Most people would agree, offhand, that every creature lives its life and then dies. This might, indeed, be called a truism. But, like some other truisms, it is not true. The lowest forms of life, such as the amoebae, normally (that is, barring accidents) do not die. When they grow very large and might be expected to lay eggs, or in some other way raise a family, they do no such thing; they divide, and make two small ones ready to grow. Well now, where is the old one? It did not die. But it is gone. Its individuation was only an episode in the life of the stock, a phase, a transient form that changed again. Amoebae are individuated in space—they move and feed as independent, whole organisms—but in time they are not self-identical individuals. They do not generate young ones while they themselves grow old; they grow old and *become* young ones.

All the higher animals, however, are final individuations that end in death. They spring from a common stock, but they do not merge back into it. Each one is an end. Somewhere on its way toward death it usually produces a new life to succeed it, but its own story is finished by death.

That is our pattern, too. Each human individual is a culmination of an inestimably long line—its ancestry—and each is destined to die. The living stock is like a palm tree, a trunk composed of its own past leaves. Each leaf springs from the trunk, unfolds, grows, and dies off; its past is incorporated in the trunk, where new life has usually arisen from it. So there constantly are ends, but the stock lives on, and each leaf has that whole life behind it.

The momentous difference between us and our animal cousins is that they do not know they are going to die. Animals spend their lives avoiding death, until it gets them. They do not know it is going to. Neither do they know that they are part of a greater life, but pass on the torch without knowing. Their aim, then, is simply to keep going, to function, to escape trouble, to live from moment to moment in an endless Now.

Our power of symbolic conception has given us each a glimpse of himself as one final individuation from the great human stock. We do not know when or what the end will be, but we know that there will be one. We also envisage a past and future, a stretch of time so vastly longer than any creature's memory, and a world so much richer than any world of sense, that it makes our time in that world seem infinitesimal. This is the price of the great gift of symbolism.

In the face of such uncomfortable prospects (probably conceived long before the dawn of any religious ideas), human beings have evolved aims different from those of any other creatures. Since we cannot have our fill of existence by going on and on, we want to have *as much life as possible* in our short span. If our individuation must be brief, we want to make it complete; so we are inspired to think, act, dream our desires, create things, express our ideas, and in all sorts of ways make up by concentration what we cannot have by length of days. We seek the greatest possible individuation, or development of personality. In doing this, we have set up a new demand, not for mere continuity of existence, but for *self-realization*. That is a uniquely human aim.

But obviously, the social structure could not arise on this principle alone. Vast numbers of individualists realizing themselves with a vengeance would not make up an ideal society. A small number might try it; there is a place, far away from here, called the Self-Realization Golden World Colony. But most of us have no golden world to colonize. You can only do that south of Los Angeles.

Seriously, however, an ideal is not disposed of by pointing out that it cannot be implemented under existing conditions. It may still be a true ideal; and if it is very important we may have to change the conditions, as we will have to for the ideal of world peace. If complete individuation were reallly the whole aim of human life, our society would be geared to it much more than it is. It is not the golden world that is wanting, but something else; the complete individualist is notoriously not the happy man, even if good fortune permits his antics.

The fact is that *the greatest possible individuation* is usually taken to mean, "as much as is possible without curtailing the rights of others." But that is not the real measure of how much is possible. The measure is provided in the individual himself, and is as fundamental as his knowledge of death. It is the other part of his insight into nature—his knowledge of life, of the great unbroken stream, the life of the stock from which his individuation stems.

One individual life, however rich, still looks infinitesimal; no matter how much self-realization is concentrated in it, it is a tiny atom—and we don't like to be tiny atoms, not even hydrogen atoms. We need more than fullness of personal life to counter our terrible knowledge of all it implies. And we have more; we have our history, our commitments made for us before we were born, our relatedness to the rest of mankind. The counterpart of individuation from the great life of the stock is our rootedness in that life, our involvement with the whole human race, past and present.

Each person is not only a free, single end, like the green palm leaf that unfolds, grows in a curve of beauty, and dies in its season; he is like the whole palm leaf, the part inside the trunk, too. He is the culmination of his entire ancestry, and *represents* that whole human past. In his brief individuation he is an *expression* of all humanity. That is what makes each person's life sacred and all-important. A single ruined life is the bankruptcy of a long line. This is what I mean by the individual's involvement with all mankind.

All animals are unconsciously involved with their kind. Heredity governs not only their growth, color, and form, but their actions, too. They carry their past about with them in everything they do. But they do not know it. They don't need to, because they never could lose it. Their involvement with the greater life of the race is implicit in their limited selfhood.

Our knowledge that life is finite, and, in fact, precarious and brief, drives us on to greater individuation than animals attain. Our mental talents have largely freed us from that built-in behavior called instinct. The scope of our imagination gives each of us a separate world, and a separate consciousness, and threatens to break the instinctual ties of brotherhood that make all the herrings swim into one net, and all the geese turn their heads at the same moment. Yet we cannot afford to lose the feeling of involvement with our kind; for if we do, personal life shrinks up to nothingness.

The sense of involvement is our social sense. We have it by nature, originally just as animals do, and just as unconsciously. It is the direct feeling of needing our own kind, caring what happens. Social sense is an instinctive sense of being somehow one with all other people – a feeling that reflects the rootedness of our existence in a human past. Human society rests on this feeling. It is often said to rest on the need of collaboration, or on domination of the weak by the strong, or some other circumstance, but I think such theories deal with its modes, and ignore its deeper structure; at the bottom of it is the feeling of involvement, or social sense. If we lose that, no coercion will hold us to our duties, because they do not feel like commitments, and no achievements will matter, because they are doomed to be snuffed out with the individual, without being laid to account in the continuity of life.

Great individual development, such as human beings are driven by their intellectual insights to seek, does of course always threaten to break the bond of direct social involvement, that give animal life its happy unconscious continuity. When the strain gets hard, we have social turmoil, anarchy, irresponsibility, and in private lives the sense of loneliness and infinite smallness that lands some people in nihilism and cynicism, and leads others to existentialism or less intellectual cults.

It is then that social philosophers look on animal societies as models for human society. There is no revolt, no strike, no competition, no anti-Anything party, in a beehive. As Kipling, fifty years or more ago, represented his British utopia, which he called the Mother Hive, that ideal state had a completely co-operative economy, an army that went into action without a murmur, each man with the same impulse the moment an enemy threatened to intrude, and a populace of such tribal solidarity that it would promptly run out any stranger that tried to become established in the state and disrupt its traditions. Any native individual that could not fit into the whole had to be liquidated; the loss was regrettable, but couldn't be helped, and would be made up.

Yet the beehive really has no possible bearing on human affairs, for it owes its harmonious existence to the fact that its members are *incompletely individuated*, even as animals go. None of them performs all of a creature's essential functions: feeding, food getting, nest building, mating, and procreating. The queen has to be fed and tended; she has only procreative functions. She doesn't even bring up her own children; they have nurses. The drones are born and reared only as her suitors, and when the romance is finished they are killed, like proper romantic heroes. The building, nursing, food getting, and fighting are done by sterile females who cannot procreate, amazons who do all their own housework. So there is not only division of labor, but division of organs, functional and physical incompleteness. The direct involvement of each bee with the whole lets the hive function with an organic rhythm that makes its members appear wonderfully socialized. But they are really not socialized at all, any more than the cells in our tissues are socialized; they are associated, by being unindividuated.

This is as far away from a human ideal as one can get. We need, above all, a world in which we can realize our capacities, develop and act as personalities. That means giving up our instinctive pattern of habit and prejudice, our herd instincts. Yet we need the emotional security of the greater, continuous life—the awareness of our involvement with all mankind. How can we eat that cake, and have it too?

The same mental talent that makes us need so much individuation comes to the rescue of our social involvement: I mean the peculiarly human talent of holding ideas in the mind by means of symbols. Human life, even in the simplest forms we know, is shot through and through with *social symbols*. All fantastic beliefs in a great ancestor are symbolic of the original and permanent life of the stock from which every individual life stems. The totem, the hero, the sacred cow, these are the most elementary social symbols. With a maturer view of the world, and the development of religious ideas, the symbolic image of man is usually taken up into the greater view of a divine world order and a moral law. We are sons of Adam and daughters of Eve. If Adam and Eve were simply some human couple supposed to have lived in the

Near East before it was so difficult, this would be an odd way of speaking; we don't ordinarily refer to our neighbor's children as Mr. Brown's boys and Mrs. Brown's girls. But Adam is Man, and Eve is Woman (the names even mean that): and among us transient little mites, every man is Man, every woman is Woman. That is the source of human dignity, the sense of which has to be upheld at all levels of social life.

Most people have some religious ritual that supports their knowledge of a greater life, but even in purely secular affairs we constantly express our faith in the continuity of human existence. Animals provide lairs or nests for their immediate offspring. Man builds for the future — often for nothing else. His earliest great buildings were not mansions, but monuments. And not only physical edifices, but above all laws and institutions are intended for the future, and often justified by showing that they have a precedent, or are in accord with the past. They are conveniences of their day, but symbols of more than their day. They are symbols of society, and of each individual's inalienable membership in society.

What, then, is the measure of our possible individuation, without loss of social sense? It is the power of social symbolism. We can give up our actual, instinctual involvements with our kind just to the extent that we can replace them by symbolic ones. This is the prime function of social symbols, from a handshake, to the assembly of robed judges in a Supreme Court. In protocol and ritual, in the investment of authority, in sanctions and honors, lies our security against loss of involvement with mankind; in such bonds lies our freedom to be individuals.

It has been said that an animal society, like a beehive, is really an organism, and the separate bees its organic parts. I think this statement requires many reservations, but it contains some truth. The hive is an organic structure, a superindividual, something like an organism. A human city, however, is an *organization*. It is above all a symbolic structure, a mental reality. Its citizens are the whole and only individuals. They are not a "living mass," like a swarm of semi-individuated bees. The model of the hive has brought with it the concept of human masses, to be cared for in times of peace, deployed in times of war, educated for use or sacrificed for the higher good of their state. In the specious analogy of animal and human society, the hive and the city, lies, I think, the basic philosophical fallacy of all totalitarian theory, even the most sincere and idealistic — even the thoroughly noble political thought of Plato.

We are like leaves of the palm tree, each deeply embedded in the tree, a part of the trunk, each opening to the light in a final, separate life. Our world is a human world, organized to implement our highest individuation. There may be ten thousand of us working in one factory. There are several millions of us living in a city like New York. But we are not the masses; we are the public.

(1958, 1962)

*Barbara Ward*

# The City May Be as Lethal as the Bomb

Most people in North America and Western Europe are probably aware that something fairly drastic is happening to their cities. They grow. They congest. One has the feeling that if it were possible to train some gigantic, extraterrestrial slow-motion camera on the whole process, one would see what looks like a strange, agitated, rugous membrane spreading densely and more and more rapidly over wider and wider areas of the planet's surface.

And the camera would not lie. Behind the average citizen's vague awareness of constant and possibly uncontrollable change lie some formidable facts. They spring from the three vast movements of revolutionary change in which the whole human race is involved. The first is the revolution of rising population; the second, the technological revolution; the third, "the revolution of rising expectations." All three have converged on the old static city and blown it to smithereens.

The modern economic system is overwhelmingly urban. Economic factors—patterns of transport, concentrated labor markets, quick communication, access to suppliers, minimum costs in getting goods to consumers—set the trend to large urban concentrations in motion and, once it has started, the apparent conveniences of largeness make the areas larger still. Then to these new cities stream the men and women stirred from rural stagnation by the bright lights and the "sidewalks paved with gold." And as the world's population has moved onward to a rate of growth of some 2 per cent a year, the stream of aspiring humanity has become a flood. Urban population grows at twice the general rate, and big cities grow faster still. Some of the largest are growing by 8 per cent a year. São Paulo, heading for the 5 million mark, receives 5,000 new inhabitants a day. If Bombay were to follow Japanese patterns, it could grow to 35 million within decades.

From one end of the world to the other, the countryside empties its people into the cities. Southern Italians to Turin and Milan, Southern Negroes to Chicago and New York, Ibos and Yorubas to Lagos, Puerto Ricans to San Juan, Soviet peasants to Moscow, Bantu into the purlieus of Johannesburg—year by year, the urban flood goes on until, some 80 years from now, the proportion of the human race depending wholly on farming may be no greater than the 4 or 5 per cent who live on the land in England. Irretrievably, inescapably we are heading toward an urban world. But, on present showing, it may not be a world worth living in.

Downright satisfaction with the present city is already scarce. Not many people in London today would echo Dr. Johnson's robust statement that "when a man is tired of London, he is tired of life." In fact, one can argue that much in the present pattern of urbanism has been created by *dissatisfaction*. The move to the suburbs is an escape from the city. When people can afford it, they move away and, as others catch up with them, move farther still. Meanwhile, in a city center deprived of leadership and wealth, people stay not because they will but because they must, and around them the rural migrants, arriving fresh from the countryside, fill in the gaps and, through ignorance, bewilderment and poverty, depress standards still further.

This pattern, naturally, is variable. In cities built before the industrial revolution, the center may still wear the magnificence of monarchical society. London, Madrid, Rome have a certain ceremonial spaciousness that Manchester or Detroit never possessed. The genius of Baron Haussman is preserved in Paris. In these cities, meaner quarters are not a solid core but scattered through the city and out into the first ring of suburbs—the *banlieue rouge* of Paris, for instance. But even here, there is suburban sprawl and decline at the center.

This underlying pattern, created in large measure by the movements of people in search of something else, is not a happy model for mankind's urban future. Its economic costs are high. To give only a few examples, within the city itself, any abandonment of existing areas means enormous loss in the shape of expensive urban capital underused while sewers, power lines, roads and so forth are duplicated elsewhere.

One has also to count the "dead time" absorbed in distant commuting and the cost of maintaining a vast web of public commuter transport. Private traffic, often absorbing for one driver the space of four travelers, swells uncontrollably the cost of road programs.

The word "uncontrollably" is not inaccurate since modern traffic, like flood water, tends to fill completely the channels opened for it, however often they are enlarged. Last summer, the British Government rejected a handsome scheme for redesigning the rather undistinguished heart of London at Piccadilly on the ground that it underestimated the future flow of traffic. The Government's critics pointed out that no plan can satisfy future flows since the size of the roads will itself determine the scale of the traffic flow which will choke them. Even Los Angeles has not solved this dilemma, although, in trying to do so, it has virtually ceased to be a city and is now a place where catering for the automobile takes up some 70 per cent of urban space.

But economic losses involved in the provision or duplication of expensive physical plant are only the tip of the iceberg. The social costs of the modern city spread out underneath the surface of urban life, not always fully visible below the ebb and flow of daily living but cold, hard, menacing and capable of producing deadly banks of intellectual fog.

The city, after all, is not just a collection of buildings and services.

It is, or should be, a community in which human beings are civilized and enriched. "Civility," "urbanity" were once the words used to express the virtues and manners by which men could be raised above crude self-concern and the blind clash of competitive instinct. Throughout most of Western civilization, in time and space, the city has been the school of the nation in the sense that Athens claimed to be "the education of Hellas." At this highest level of function, what can we say of it today?

Its vast physical dispersal must lessen its cultural impact simply because meeting, learning and exchanging experience are at the core of culture. When the leaders in wealth and education leave the city, it is not only the tax revenues that dwindle, important as they are to civic standards. Stimulus, variety, experiment wane as well. Nor does the single-class, single-culture suburb, with its predominantly female occupancy over long stretches of time, seem to make for a very vigorous cultural achievement, in spite of sincere efforts in that direction.

If this were all, the matter might not be too disturbing. There has, after all, been some recovery of civic culture in many Western centers in the last two decades. The real crisis lies in the degree to which parts of the modern city produce the opposite of culture—brutality, delinquency, antisocial behavior of every sort.

The rural populations move in with more rapidity than any present program of urban construction can match. In Lagos, in Nigeria, for instance, the effect of almost universal primary education in the up-country villages has been to send a spate of 12-year-olds, barely literate, educated to little beyond distaste for country pursuits, into a city where even unskilled jobs are scarce and possibilities of further education scarcer still. By 1970, there may be half a million unemployed school leavers concentrated in Lagos. There are already 20,000 prowling around Nairobi, and perhaps 80,000—thieving, demonstrating, despairing—in the towns of the Copper Belt.

This combustible material is already the recruiting ground of the Congo's disruptive movements, and it is increasingly available for any form of violence. Thus the cities become the centers of irresponsible pressure, and aggravate enormously Africa's gravest risk—the breakdown of civil order.

Or take the bursting cities—every one ringed with barrios and *favellas*, filthy concentrations of grass and tin huts offering, without water or light, a pretense of shelter to migrant families. At times, these settlements reach fantasies of squalor. Outside San Juan in Puerto Rico, the huts are built on piles over water. The tide brings all the scum and excrement of the city to the doorstep. On a rough day, unsuspecting health visitors sometimes even become seasick as wave and wind rock the swaying houses.

Once arrived in the city, the migrant begins the search for work, for the "golden pavements." In developing countries, the stumbling block is usually the degree to which the economy is not growing fast enough to absorb so much raw new urban labor. In many developed cities, the decline of unskilled employment as automation moves in and businesses move out has a comparable effect of high urban worklessness. The plight of the unskilled American Negro in a dozen of America's big cities can be repeated in a hundred others around the globe. There is a difference, however – an explosive one: the degree to which in America the line of misfortune follows the line of race. But even this is not unique. The Malayan migrant resents the able Chinese city dweller, the East African laborer hates the Asian middle class.

It is at this point that the dispersal of the new city adds to the social pressures. Too often those with the means, the self-confidence and the influence to confront the despair and revolt at the cities' core grow up and live in tree-lined suburbs where, from nursery to maturity, they have face-to-face contact only with their own kind. Their imagination is little nourished by the sense of a "diversity of creatures." They know little directly about the plight of not-so-distant neighbors. And all too often lack of knowledge is the beginning of fear.

One sees this segregation by residence undermining political confidence in new African states. One sees it in New Delhi, where ministers and senior civil servants live coolly and spaciously in the old imperial enclave. It is a burning, searing element in the Negro struggle for emancipation in America, since the color bar takes away an important safety valve available in other cities – the ability of anyone to move out, once a leafy, lawngirt villa is within his economic grasp.

Wherever it is found – in new countries or old, in developing continents or the wealthy West – it is dynamite in the foundations of any urban order. And if, in the next four or five decades of headlong urban expansion, no better models emerge, the world is condemning itself to go through the most socially unstable era it has ever had to face.

Can we, from our present failures, draw some conclusions about better urban models? One proviso must be that the range and interconnection of urban problems are such that any attempt at definition risks leaving out more than it puts in – and one must begin with a general point. Whatever the particular patterns of urban order that are adopted, the cities of the future, in which most of mankind will live, depend for their health on a strong steady rhythm of economic expansion.

The point may seem obvious, yet the degree to which pockets of *urban* unemployment as high as 10 to 15 per cent of the work force are tolerated is a reminder of how easy it is, where *general* employment is fairly satisfactory, to forget the dynamite of neglected urban worklessness. Even welfare services tend to show this blind spot. Much more time, money and trained man power are spent on countering the consequences of extreme poverty and the broken home—which again and again are caused by the unemployment of parents—than upon strengthening placement and retraining services or, at a higher level, relating man power to the availability of jobs on a regional basis. America's "war on poverty" is an attempt to counter misery in this way—by jobs and opportunities, not by handouts.

To return to urban specifics, here are one or two. There are many more but these seem basic. A first one relates to access to work and access to other than urban life. Neither, ideally, should demand so much traveling time that the commuter or holidaymaker arrives stunned with the effort of reaching his goal.

A second objective is closely linked with this—a more rational approach to traffic. The mixing of man and machine in quite different types of purpose and movement is one of the most dehumanizing factors in modern cities. The child going to school and the woman going shopping have to face the roaring flood of commercial intercity traffic. Trucks, delivering goods, stop the circulation of shoppers coming to buy them. Short car trips to the suburbs hold up transcontinental bus lines. And at certain times, day after day, everything stops everything. Sane urban order would, therefore, depend upon much more imaginative disentangling of the city's movements.

In the British context, the Buchanan Report, published last year, is the systematic attempt to devise traffic plans for modern urban life and to assess their cost. It is high—$252 million for a city of 400,000, like Leeds. But it offers hope of separating traffic from man and allowing cities, like houses, to distinguish between "corridors" for movement and "rooms" for living.

This division would make a vital contribution to a further goal—an urban community built to a *human* scale. The primary cell or unit or neighborhood—the building block of urban order—in which the fundamental social task of bringing up children takes place needs to be a place in which young people can securely learn their own culture and yet be prepared to recognize and accept the varied cultures of others. Security means the human scale—a decent family home, enjoyment and stimulus to be had within walking distance, meeting and playing without the shadow of street accidents. Variety means diversity of ages and occupations to give the full scope of living, church and school and corner store to bring families together, assured access to other parts of the city, an accepted and dignified city center round which revolve the great concerns of urban life in politics, in education, in art.

The search for human scale, within reach of man's five senses, is capable of almost infinite variety. The essential point is to accept its primacy; otherwise, as in Puerto Rico, a heroic effort of rehousing can end in the melancholy fact that 60 per cent of the slum dwellers like their surroundings and nearly 80 per cent of the families rehoused in the modern *caserios* do not.

Yet one must add that, having laid down one or two sane norms for better urban living, most experts so far agree very little on specific ways of putting them into effect. So when we ask the question, "What are the chances of checking the present accelerating slide toward urban disaster?" the answer has to be that an essential aspect of it—the achievement of new decisions—presents very real difficulties.

Citizens, political decision makers, experts—all find great difficulty in focusing on the urban crisis. The man in the street suffers first of all from his dispersal. In the fragmented city, it is hard for him to think of an "urban" problem as such. He may know what he wants for his own corner of the city. Zoning laws, for instance, are understood and accepted. But he does not see the city as a whole. For him, the blight at the core is not a threat to a whole urban region or—when it has such racial overtones as in America—to a whole way of life.

In an even wider perspective men and women who know to the marrow of their bones that nuclear war means destruction, and feel quite sincerely that the growth of population can menace food supplies, have no sense at all that uncontrolled urban explosion could do more harm to man's psyche than would inadequate food to his body. In short, there is still no real focus on our perilous urbanism.

If the citizen is not concerned, the politician tends not to be either. And he faces profounder difficulties. Little pressure comes up from below to urge him toward comprehensive and humane solutions. But a number of lateral pressures are tremendous. Some critics pin all the blame for urban evil on private interests, real-estate lobbies, profiteering landlords and the like. The degree to which Moscow and Odessa face the same urban explosion suggests caution in this attribution of blame. But it is true that many of the solutions—control of land use, taxing of land values, diversions of traffic, low-cost housing, open spaces—cut across commercial interests and that, while these interests are active and vocal, the citizen is not.

Moreover, his chosen instrument, local government, often lacks authority to deal with problems which are regional and even national in scope. In fact, local governments all too often fight regional solutions in the name of their own autonomy.

Even at the level of skilled practitioners in the urban arts, universities, institutes, centers of learning of all kinds still need to recognize the variety of skills that must be brought together to build a decent community, and to accept as normative a concept of ecology, of a total environment molding urban life, of a new "science of human settlements" within which planner, economist, architect, engineer, administrator, social scientist and artist could work together – and in turn inspire public opinion and begin to influence political thought.

For, provided people know *how* to think about the urban future, physical limitations are not too inhibiting. There will be tough choices to be made in the use of land. There will be limits on the height water can be pumped. But there are some cheering prospects as well. Taking the likely growth of population over the next century, not more than 4 or 5 per cent of the future human race is already housed. In fact, in the next 40 years, as many houses will have to be built as hitherto in the whole history of man. Provided we can devise better urban models over the next decade, most of humanity has the prospect of living in better cities than ours.

And the necessary resources are not lacking. Once urban grace and convenience are felt by the voter and his representative to be as urgently necessary as defense or mobility are today, the means will not be found lacking. The Western world spends some $80 billion a year on arms – and grows richer in the process. No one has much questioned the millions devoted these days to roads in America – a program which has sent the bulldozers slicing through a hundred cities and ripping out scores of urban slums. An outright onslaught on urban renewal and expansion would not cost half the arms bill and would demand no more forceful action than the highway program. In fact, it could supplement both – and perhaps one day replace them – as a dynamic sustainer of domestic demand.

Resources are not the problem. It is the shaping imagination, the liberating idea. With it, man's abundance can be used to make his urban life worth living. Without it, the city may be, in its slower way, as lethal as the bomb.

(1964)

## Robert Hayden

# Tour 5

The road winds down through autumn hills
in blazonry of farewell scarlet
and recessional gold,
past cedar groves, through static villages
whose names are all that's left
of Choctaw, Chickasaw.

We stop a moment in a town
watched over by Confederate sentinels,
buy gas and ask directions of a rawboned man
whose eyes revile us as the enemy.

Shrill gorgon silence breathes behind
his taut civility
and in the ever-tautening air,
dark for us despite its Indian summer glow.
We drive on, following the route
of highwaymen and phantoms,

Of slaves and armies.
Children, wordless and remote,
wave at us from kindling porches.
And now the land is flat for miles,
the landscape lush, metallic, flayed,
its brightness harsh as bloodstained swords.

(1966)

# Those Winter Sundays

Sundays too my father got up early
and put his clothes on in the blueblack cold,
then with cracked hands that ached
from labor in the weekday weather made
banked fires blaze. No one ever thanked him.

I'd wake and hear the cold splintering, breaking.
When the rooms were warm, he'd call,
and slowly I would rise and dress,
fearing the chronic angers of that house,

Speaking indifferently to him,
who had driven out the cold
and polished my good shoes as well.
What did I know, what did I know
of love's austere and lonely offices?

(1966)

**Stewart L. Udall**

# Our Perilous Population Implosion

In recent years, no nation has been more inclined to preach at the world about the perils of overpopulation, nor less concerned over the impact of unplanned human and industrial proliferation on the quality of life at home than has the United States. As headlong growth has eroded the American environment, we have substituted international rhetoric for national action.

Not long after the results of the 1960 census were published I happened to be in Vermont, at a press conference with Senator George Aiken. The Green Mountain State had no population increase in the decade of the 1950s, and a reporter asked Senator Aiken whether he was disturbed by this circumstance. The Senator smiled a wry smile and shot back: "No, we Vermonters have looked at the country and noted what some people call 'growth,' and we're not disturbed. We are going to wait a while and grow right!"

At a time when the U.S. birthrate has taken a sharp dip I, too, have an Aiken-like reaction. Shouldn't we, after all the unsettling predictions of a doubling and quadrupling of our numbers, positively welcome the slower growth trends of the Sixties? Why not hope that our population will actually level off for a few years—and give us a "breather" in which to learn the art of growing right?

The turmoil in our cities is, in part, a result of the disordered growth policies fostered in an era when a cardinal article of the American faith was that all growth was good—that population increase and prosperity were intertwined.

It is peculiar that, despite the grow-slow signs of the Sixties, our census experts, demographers, and sociologists continue to parrot the prediction that our present population of 200 million will about double itself by the year 2000. While nobody really knows exactly what the effects of such a population will be on the entire American environment, it is not the absence of precise information that is disturbing. Rather, the troubling thing about these oft-repeated forecasts is that they bid us accept the inevitable and thus overwhelm our creativity and conscience. No isolated example is a recent *New York Times* editorial on "Planning for Regional Growth":

How can the metropolitan area best provide satisfactory living space for the enormous growth in population predicted by the turn of the century? The tri-state area, roughly bounded by Trenton, Poughkeepsie, and New Haven, now has about 18,000,000 residents, expected to increase to nearly 30,000,000 by the year 2000.

Acquiescence to these assumptions is wrong, not simply because we will be unable to adequately feed a doubled population, but because of another, more invidious hunger—a starvation of the human spirit. The urban uprisings of our time tell us that parts of our cities are simply unlivable. We are now paying the price of a century of neglect and poor planning. If we permit the outdated growth policies of the past to further overpower prescience, this will ensure an increasingly ugly, overcrowded, unclean, joyless environment for the American people.

But this need *not* happen . . . civilization, after all, is an act of will. If we *now* would pause and ponder—as a rich and powerful nation should and can afford to—the elemental and elementary issues which have so long been beclouded by the dust of our haste, we might escape the growth-gospel that grips and motivates the American mind.

What *are* some of these questions?

First, *what is the optimum population—is there an ideal land-people ratio—for our nation?* At our first census, in 1790, the area of the nation was 900,000 square miles; today, the fifty states have an area of 3,500,000 square miles. But while our land area has increased *four-fold* (not all of it habitable), our population has increased *fifty times* over. From the Colonial (primarily agricultural) period, when population density was five persons per square mile, we have imploded toward the cities so that, today, 70 per cent of our people live on just 1 per cent of the land. This means an average population density, for our urban areas, of about 4,000 people per square mile (in New York City it is 25,000 per square mile). One does not need to be a trained psychiatrist to conclude, for example, that congested, polluted living conditions sicken the senses and make slum dwellers less humane toward themselves and even their own neighbors.

Other questions flow from this basic and complex issue. Some of them are:

*What environment—what balance between the works of nature and the works of man—should we seek?* "Society will somehow demand controls to keep life bearable," the *Wall Street Journal* suggested airily in its 1966 analysis of the meaning of a population of 300 million Americans. This is precisely the rationalization that has led to the environmental erosion of twentieth-century America. A Federal Aviation Agency pamphleteer recently offered this explanation of the not-so-subtle process whereby the public would eventually accept sonic booms as the price of technological supremacy:

. . . Individuals tend to accommodate themselves to an initially disturbing noise once it becomes a pattern of daily life. There are noises today in cities and in small towns that are taken for granted which, if they were introduced as new noises, would cause disturbance for an initial period of time. . . . People living near Air Force bases, where sonic booms are a common occurrence, don't find them unacceptable, and this may be a sound indication that widespread public tolerance will grow as booms become more a part of daily living.

This is the insidious logic of a different, diminished America. It implies that men must adapt to machines, not machines to men; that production, speed, novelty, progress at any price must come first, and people second; that mechanization may be pushed as far as human endurance will allow. It ignores experience—which should tell us we should not add new strains and pressures and discomforts to a high-pressure world. Jet engines at close range reach 150 decibels, but two-thirds of all deafness in working males is caused by occupational noise which rarely exceeds 130 decibels. In any case, is it right to permit 300 people in an SST, hurtling across the land faster than sound, to interrupt the sleep of 30,000,000? Must the travel of a few mean travail for the many?

*What manner of cities should we create?* Shall private transportation and highways dominate the city, as in Los Angeles, or shall mass transportation navigate the city and its environs, as in the Bay Area Rapid Transit District nearing completion around San Francisco? Shall technological, or human engineering dominate? Regrettably, a segment of the scientific community abets the formation of a bearable world of teeming billions. Certain brilliant men are so engrossed in engineering techniques that they have seemingly lost sight of their own species. Buckminster Fuller, one of the most creative of our designers, has proposed that we build gargantuan geodesic domes over our cities. These great greenhouses would enclose a mechanized, man-controlled climate: the stars, the seasons, and the sun would be walled out in a triumph of technology. Air pollution *and* weather would disappear; yet these domes would deny the instinct of man to coexist with nature, and affirm his tendency—rare among higher animals—to foul his nest.

*How best can we conserve the countryside?* This goes beyond mere questions of billboard controls and anti-litter campaigns; it goes to the issue of land use itself. In Santa Clara County, California, Charles Abrams pointed out not long ago, ". . . one dairy farm a week has been lost to subdivisions." Frontier individualism has caused us to abhor planning. Most of our land-use policies, as well as our decisions about modes of transportation and the design of cities, have been dictated by the short-term economics of the marketplace.

Since Detroit accepted no responsibility for air pollution, and the builders of freeways showed no concern for conservation, it should hardly surprise us that the climates of whole regions—as well as the landscapes—have been sacrificed to galloping growth. In the absence of restraint or guidelines for growth, the single-minded, speculative, build-for-today-and-let-tomorrow-fend-for-itself approach has left us with a man-made mess of staggering proportions. It is not bureaucracy expanding itself, but need, that caused President Johnson to recommend—and Congress to approve—a Department of Housing and Urban Development.

*How can we accomplish both full production and the full life? How can we achieve a material prosperity that will also promote the prosperity of the human spirit?* Gross National Product is our Holy Grail; the economists and statisticians its keepers. Statistics concerning auto output, steel production, heavy construction, housing starts, freight-car loadings have become the indices of the American advance. We have had no environmental index, no census statistic to measure whether the country is more or less livable from year to year. A tranquility index, a cleanliness index, a privacy index, might have told us something about the condition of man, but a fast-growing country bent on piling up material things has been indifferent to the "little things" that add joy to everyday living.

The environment has not been undone by the errors or inroads of a single segment of society. The innumerable fumes and poisons and defacements were not, taken one by one, outrageous, but, like resentments, they accumulated until they were too many and the impact was intolerable. No floods or forest fires or great dust storms warned us of impending bankruptcy. It is hard to say just when San Francisco lost its bay, Los Angeles its salubrious air, Lake Erie its whitefish, or New York its lordly Hudson. There was no cry of alarm, and the reason was subversively simple: the common belief that the blight of a pleasant land was the price of "progress."

For a rational nation proud of its scientific prowess, we are remarkably fatalistic about the future. In regard to our legacy of natural resources, we have shown little long-range resourcefulness. In regard to our production of goods and services, we generally have made "Will it sell?"—not "Is it useful?"—our test. The long debate over automotive safety features is a perfect case in point.

But, as virtually all problems on earth are people problems, as we know that the environment can dehumanize man as it deteriorates and becomes oppressive, the critical issue comes down to population—and in this regard there is a strong streak of determinism in our attitude. If we want an improved environment, if we aspire to a social and physical setting that enlarges, not narrows, individual choice, then we must understand that each increment of population erodes our options and increases the role which the supertechnocrats and mechanistic planners will play in our lives. Why? For the simple reason that our continued implosion toward the cities, our annual population growth of 4,000,000 people, increases the physical and social pressures, causes us to seek quick remedies, leads us to waste too much wealth on quick-fix projects that provide at best a temporary respite from yesterday's mistakes. The razing of tenements, their instant replacement by high-rise slums, changes the facade—not the features—of the ghetto. And yet, because the cures and comforts and scientific spectaculars of the postwar period have made us optimists, unafraid of the future, there will be a growing tendency to rely more on science than on social planning as population increases and implodes. And this is wrong, for our failures are social, not scientific.

Without a slow-growth population policy *and* practice, we will find it difficult to eliminate slums, to build attractive cities, to expand education, to control crime, to create an equal-opportunity society. And with each new difficulty, with each new defeat (no matter how partial), the tendency will be to turn toward the panaceas of engineering, the creations of computers, the strong right arm of the bulldozer, the steadfastness of the piledriver. All this tends to be circular: more social problems because of increased answers which are not answers at all . . . more pressure and more technical response to human needs. Out of this we would achieve an asphalt America with nature overwhelmed. If our recent past counts for anything, it should convince us this new America will, at best, be functional; at worst, it will be unattractive, mechanized, messy, and inhuman. We would have little freedom of movement in our polynucleated cities. Creative play, contemplation under a big sky, would be whittled away.

In the anthill world of megalopolis, we would become an indoor people: hunting, fishing, hiking would be the avocations of the hardy few and the wealthy elite, and silence would be found only by those whose wanderings were to the farthest of shores or the white paths of winter. From our soundproof rooms we would lament the passing of the solitude we still can enjoy today—an elixir of space, the immanence of nature. Indeed, these might well become the amenities most scarce, the "luxuries" most missed in so much of our tomorrow-filled, flat-faced country where stream valleys, swamps, and estuaries would be used as dumping grounds—as waste receptacles—for the profligacy of our plenty.

Many years ago Sherwood Anderson wrote to his friend Waldo Frank:

Is it not likely that when the country was new and men were often alone in the fields and the forest they got a sense of bigness outside themselves that has now in some way been lost? . . . Mystery whispered in the grass, played in the branches of trees overhead, was caught up and blown across the American land in clouds of dust at evening on the prairies . . . I am old enough to remember tales that strengthen my belief in a deep semi-religious influence that was formerly at work among our people. The flavor of it hangs over the best work of Mark Twain . . . I can remember old fellows in my home town speaking feelingly of an evening spent on the big empty plains. It had taken the shrillness out of them. They had learned the trick of quiet.

A half-century later we have unlearned, and all but lost, the trick of quiet.

Overpopulation would drive wildlife to the wall; the eagle and the elk would become memories; the smell of pine already is synthesized and marketed in pressurized cans for use in deodorizing our apartments and — who knows — perhaps someday our cities. Many would eat fish-flour, but few would know the taste of brook trout or fresh-caught salmon.

And beyond 2000? Well, some predict an America of one billion souls in 2080. China and India together today have that many people. What is the quality of life — even questions of hunger aside — where elbow room is gone, forever? No matter what the level of our goods-and-gadgets "standard of living," that sort of overpopulation would mean poverty. Pearl Buck may have indulged in overstatement when she observed that "Democracy is impossible in an overpopulated country." It is no overstatement, however, to say that the full life, as we like to think of it today, is impossible in an overpopulated nation.

The inhibitions of old cultures and outdated religious and economic doctrines have retarded the development of wise priorities for worldwide population planning. In 1967, despite the amazing advances of science, the approach to our overall world effort at human betterment is most unscientific. We have long since perfected the concept of the land's carrying capacity for animals, and we practice the principle of sustained yield in the management of trees and plants. Yet we abandon the idea of natural balance when we come to our own species. We have mastered the arts of animal husbandry, we know the life laws of crops and insects, we know how to plan our agricultural output. In effect, we have enhanced the future of everything — except the overall future of the human race. The time has come to take to heart the humanistic counsel of Lewis Mumford:

The balanced economy we must now seek will place its emphasis not on the horsepower it consumes but on the manpower it releases: It will translate energy into leisure and leisure into life.

In short, we must evolve an ecology of man in harmony with the constantly unfolding ecologies of other living things. We need a man-centered science which will seek to determine the interrelationships of life, interrelationships whose understanding will enhance the condition of man.

There is no better place to begin enlarging life, I believe, than through a higher, more responsible attitude toward parenthood. There has been too much nonsense written and spoken about the unlimited right of couples to have children, and too little sense about the primal responsibilities of child-rearing. The nightmares of overpopulation (exploding *and* imploding) would subside if we applied the conservation concept to our own kind. What we call "conservation" is rooted in the nature of man and the inner order of his universe. It puts the future first, and expedience second. It makes the fullness of life the overriding objective of all social planning.

Science has now made it simple for us to plan the conservation of our most precious resource—the human child. Parents can elect to have only those children they want—and wise men and women should want only the number they personally are psychologically and financially ready to rear; yet even those who, by this definition, are able must take cognizance of the fact that *beyond* the private creation of life are pub-lic—social—consequences. Beyond love, beyond ability, beyond the be-stowals of time and attention required by true parenthood, there are the considerations of our interactions with our fellow man and our institu-tions. Certainly, levels of health care, educational opportunities, and a clean, life-giving environment must affect decisions as to parenthood.

One could contemplate the United States a century from now with equanimity if our growth rates and growth patterns reflected a mature, purposeful national will. Arrogant events and the headlong pace of material progress have left us little time to ask what people are for, or to agree on long-term societal aspirations. We have learned neither how to grow, nor at what pace, and *that* is our failing and our future trouble.

The bright upland of a better world will not come into view until we bring population and human planning into balance. I would have no fear for my country's tomorrows if we would turn toward creative par-enthood and creative education, if we already had established the se-cure foundations of an equal-opportunity society and mastered the sen-sitive arts of building a life-encouraging environment. At this moment in history we need to realize that:

Bigger is not better;

Slower may be faster;

Less may well mean more.

(1967)

**Joan Didion**

# Farewell to the Enchanted City

> How many miles to Babylon?
> Three score miles and ten —
> Can I get there by candlelight?
> Yes, and back again —
> If your feet are nimble and light,
> You can get there by candlelight.

It is easy to see the beginnings of things, and harder to see the ends. I can remember now, with a clarity that makes the nerves in the back of my neck constrict, when New York began for me, but I cannot lay my finger upon the moment it ended, can never cut through the ambiguities and second starts and broken resolves to the exact place on the page where the heroine is no longer as optimistic as she once was. When I first saw New York I was 20, and it was summertime, and I got off a DC-7 at the old Idlewild temporary terminal in a new dress which had seemed very smart in Sacramento but seemed less smart already, even in the old Idlewild temporary terminal, and the warm air smelled of mildew, and some instinct, programmed by all the movies I had ever seen and all the songs I had ever heard sung and all the stories I had ever read about New York, informed me that it would never be quite the same again. In fact it never was. Some time later there was a song on all the jukeboxes on the upper East Side that went, *but where is the schoolgirl who used to be me?* and if it was late enough at night I used to wonder that. I know now that almost every woman wonders it, wherever she is and whatever she is doing, but one of the mixed blessings of being 20 and 21 and even 23 is the conviction that nothing like this, all evidence to the contrary notwithstanding, has ever happened to anyone before.

Of course it might have been some other city, had circumstances been different and the time been different and had I been different, might have been Paris or Chicago or even San Francisco, but because I am talking about myself I am talking here about New York. That first night I opened my window on the bus into town and watched for the skyline, but all I could see were the wastes of Queens and the big signs that said MIDTOWN TUNNEL THIS LANE and then a flood of summer rain, and for the next three days I sat wrapped in blankets in a hotel room air-conditioned to 35 degrees and tried to get over a bad cold and a high fever. It did not occur to me to call a doctor, because I knew none, and although it did occur to me to call the desk and ask that the air conditioner be turned off, I never called, because I did not know how much to tip whoever might come — was anyone ever so young? I am here to tell you that someone was. All I could do during those three days was talk long distance to the boy I already knew I would never marry in the spring. I would stay in New York, I told him, just six months, and I could see the Brooklyn Bridge from my window. As it turned out the bridge was the Triborough, and I stayed eight years.

In retrospect it seems to me that those days before I knew the names of all the bridges were happier than the ones that came later, but perhaps you will see that as we go along. Part of what I want to tell you is what it is like to be young in New York, how six months can become eight years with the deceptive ease of a film dissolve, for that is how those years appear to me now, in a long sequence of sentimental dissolves and old-fashioned trick shots—the Seagram Building fountains dissolve into snowflakes, I enter a revolving door at 20 and come out a good deal older. But most particularly I want to explain to you, and in the process perhaps explain to myself, why I no longer live in New York. It is often said that New York is a city for only the very rich and the very poor. It is less often said that New York is also, at least for those of us who came there from somewhere else, a city for only the very young.

I remember once, one cold bright December evening in New York, suggesting to a friend who complained of having been around too long that he come with me to a party where there would be, I assured him with the bright resourcefulness of 23, "new faces." He laughed literally until he choked, and I had to roll down the taxi window and hit him on the back. "New faces," he said finally, "don't tell me about *new faces.*" It seemed that the last time he had gone to a party where he had been promised "new faces," there had been 15 people in the room, and he had already slept with five of the women and owed money to all but two of the men. I laughed with him, but the first snow had just begun to fall, and the big Christmas trees glittered yellow and white as far as I could see up Park Avenue, and I had a new dress, and it would be a long while before I would come to understand the particular moral of the story.

It would be a long while because, quite simply, I was in love with New York. I do not mean "love" in any colloquial way, I mean that I was in love with the city, the way you love the first person who ever touches you and never love anyone quite that way again. I remember walking across 62nd Street one twilight that first spring, or the second spring, they were all alike for a while. I was late to meet someone, but I stopped at Lexington Avenue and bought a peach and stood on the corner eating it, and knew that I had come out of the West and reached the mirage. I could taste the peach and feel the soft air blowing up from a subway grating on my legs, and I could smell lilac and garbage and expensive perfume, and I knew that it would cost something sooner or later—because I did not belong there, did not come from there—but when you are 22 or 23 you figure that later you will have a high emotional balance, and be able to pay whatever it costs. I still believed in possibilities then, still had the sense, so peculiar to New York, that something remarkable would happen any minute, any day, any month. I was making only $65 or $70 a week then, so little money that some weeks I had to charge food at Bloomingdale's gourmet shop in order to eat, a fact which went unmentioned in the letters I wrote to California. I never told my father that I needed money, because then he would have sent it, and I would never know if I could do it by myself. At that time making a living seemed a game to me, with arbitrary but quite flexible rules. And except on a certain kind of winter evening—6:30 in the 70's, say, already dark and bitter with a wind off the river, when I would be walking very fast toward a bus and would look in the bright windows of brownstones and see cooks working in clean kitchens and imagine women lighting candles on the floor above and beautiful children being bathed on the floor above that—except on nights like those, I never felt poor; I had the feeling that if I needed money I could always get it. I could write a syndicated column for teen-agers under the name "Debbi Lynn," or I could smuggle gold into India, or I could become a $100 call girl, and none of it would matter.

Nothing was irrevocable; everything was within reach. Just around every corner lay something curious and interesting, something I had never before seen or done or known about. I could go to a party and meet someone who called himself Mr. Emotional Appeal and ran The Emotional Appeal Institute or Tina Onassis Blandford or a Florida cracker who was then a regular on what he called "the Big C," the Southampton—El Morocco circuit ("I'm well-connected on the Big C, honey," he would tell me over collard greens on his vast borrowed terrace), or the widow of the celery king of the Harlem market or a piano salesman from Bonne Terre, Mo., or someone who had already made and lost two fortunes in Midland, Tex. I could make promises to myself and to other people, and there would be all the time in the world to keep them. I could stay up all night and make mistakes, and none of it would count.

You see, I was in a curious position in New York; it never occurred to me that I was living a real life there. In my imagination I was always there for just another few months, just until Christmas or Easter or the first warm day in May. For that reason I was most comfortable in the company of Southerners. They seemed to be in New York as I was, on some indefinitely extended leave from wherever they belonged, disinclined to consider the future, temporary exiles who always knew when the flights left for New Orleans or Memphis or Richmond or, in my case, California. Someone who lives always with a plane schedule in the drawer lives on a slightly different calendar. Christmas, for example, was a difficult season. Other people could take it in stride, going to Stowe or going abroad, or going for the day to their mothers' places in

Connecticut; those of us who believed that we lived somewhere else would spend it making and canceling airline reservations, waiting for weatherbound flights as if for the last plane out of Lisbon in 1940, and finally comforting one another, those of us who were left, with the oranges and mementoes and smoked-oyster stuffings of childhood, gathering close, colonials in an exotic country.

Which is precisely what we were. I am not sure that it is possible for anyone brought up in the East to entirely appreciate what New York, the idea of New York, means to those of us who come out of the West and the South. To an Eastern child, particularly one who has always had an uncle on Wall Street and who has spent several hundred Saturdays first at F.A.O. Schwarz and being fitted for shoes at Best's, and then waiting under the Biltmore clock and dancing to Lester Lanin, New York is just a city, albeit *the* city, a plausible place for people to live. But to those of us who came from places where no one had heard of Lester Lanin, and *Grand Central Station* was a Saturday radio program, where Wall Street and Fifth Avenue and Madison Avenue were not places at all but abstractions ("Money" and "High Fashion" and "The Hucksters"), New York was no mere city. It was instead an infinitely romantic notion, the mysterious nexus of all love and money and power, the shining and perishable dream itself. To think of "living" there was to reduce the miraculous to the mundane; one does not "live" at Xanadu.

In fact it was difficult in the extreme for me to understand those young women for whom New York was not simply an ephemeral Estoril but a real place, girls who bought toasters and installed new cabinets in their apartments and committed themselves to some reasonable future. I never bought any furniture in New York. For a year or so I lived in other people's apartments; after that I lived in the 90's in an apartment furnished entirely with things taken from storage by a friend whose wife had moved away. And when I left the apartment in the 90's (that was when I was leaving everything, when it was all breaking up), I left everything in it, even my winter clothes and the map of Sacramento County I had hung on the bedroom wall to remind me who I was, and I moved into a monastic four-room floor-through on 75th Street. "Monastic" is perhaps misleading here, implying some chic severity; until after I was married and my husband moved some furniture in, there was nothing at all in those four rooms except a cheap double mattress and box springs, ordered by telephone the day I decided to move, and two French garden chairs lent me by a friend who imported them.

All I ever did to the apartment was hang 50 yards of yellow theatrical silk across the bedroom windows, because I had some idea that the gold light would make me feel better, but I did not bother to weight the curtains correctly, and all that summer the long panels of transparent golden silk would blow out the windows and get tangled and drenched in the afternoon thunderstorms. That was the year, my 28th, when I was discovering that not all of the promises would be kept, that some things are in fact irrevocable and that it had counted after all, every evasion and every procrastination, every mistake, every word, all of it.

That is what it was all about, wasn't it? Promises? Now, when New York comes back to me, it comes in hallucinatory flashes, so clinically detailed that I sometimes wish that memory would effect the distortion with which it is so commonly credited. For a lot of the time in New York I used a perfume called *Fleurs de Rocaille*, and *L'Air du Temps*, and now the slightest trace of either can short-circuit my connections for the rest of the day. Nor can I smell Henri Bendel jasmine soap without falling back into the past, or the particular mixtures of spices used for boiling crabs. There were barrels of crab boil in a Czech place in the 80's where I once stopped. Smells, of course, are notorious memory stimuli but there are other things which affect me the same way. Blue-and-white-striped sheets. Vermouth cassis. Some faded nightgowns which were new in 1959 or 1960, and some chiffon scarves I bought about the same time.

I suppose that a lot of us who have been young in New York have the same scenes on our home screens. I remember sitting in a lot of apartments with a slight headache about five o'clock in the morning. I had a friend who could not sleep, and he knew a few other people who had the same trouble, and we would watch the sky lighten and have a last drink with no ice and then go home in the early morning light, when the streets were clean and wet (had it rained in the night? we never knew), and the few cruising taxis still had their headlights on, and the only color was the red and green of traffic signals.

It is relatively hard to fight at six-thirty or seven in the morning without any sleep, which was perhaps one reason we stayed up all night, and it seemed to me a pleasant time of day. The windows were shuttered in that apartment in the 90's, and I could sleep a few hours and then go to work. I liked going to work, liked the soothing and satisfactory rhythm of getting out a magazine, liked the orderly progression of four-color closings and two-color closings and black-and-white closings and then The Product, no abstraction but something which looked effortlessly glossy and could be picked up on a newsstand and weighed in the hand. I liked all the minutiae of proofs and layouts, liked working late on the nights the magazine went to press, sitting and reading *Variety* and waiting for the copy desk to call. From my office I could look across town to the weather signal on the Mutual of New York Building and the lights that alternately spelled out Time and Life above Rockefeller Plaza; that pleased me obscurely, and so did walking uptown in the mauve eight o'clocks of early summer evenings and looking at things: Lowestoft tureens in 57th Street windows, people in evening clothes trying to get taxis, the trees just coming into full leaf, the lambent air, all the sweet promises of money and summer.

Some years passed, but I still did not lose that sense of wonder about New York. I began to cherish the loneliness of it, the sense that at any given time no one need know where I was or what I was doing. I liked walking, from the East River over to the Hudson and back on brisk days, down around the Village on warm days. A friend would leave me the key to her apartment in the West Village when she was out of town, and sometimes I would just move down there, because by that time the telephone was beginning to bother me (the canker, you see, was already in the rose), and not many people had that number. I remember one day when someone who did have the West Village number came to pick me up for lunch there, and we both had hangovers, and I cut my finger opening him a beer and burst into tears, and we walked to a Spanish restaurant and drank Bloody Marys and *gazpacho* until we felt better. I was not then guilt-ridden about spending afternoons that way, because I still had all the afternoons in the world.

And even that late in the game I still liked going to parties, all parties, bad parties, Saturday-afternoon parties given by recently married couples who lived in Stuyvesant Town, West Side parties given by unpublished or failed writers who served cheap red wine and talked about going to Guadalajara, Village parties where all the guests worked for advertising agencies and voted for Reform Democrats, press parties at Sardi's, the worst kinds of parties. You will have perceived by now that I was not one to profit by the experience of others, that it was a very long time indeed before I stopped believing in new faces and began to understand the lesson in that story, which was that it is distinctly possible to stay too long at the fair.

I could not tell you when I began to understand that. All I know is that it was very bad when I was 28. Everything that was said to me I seemed to have heard before, and I could no longer listen. I could no longer sit in little bars near Grand Central and listen to someone complaining of his wife's inability to cope with the help while he missed another train to Connecticut. I no longer had any interest in hearing about the advances other people had received from their publishers, about plays which were having second-act trouble in Philadelphia, or about people I would like very much if only I would come out and meet them. I had already met them, always. There were certain parts of the city which I had to avoid. I could not bear upper Madison Avenue on weekday mornings (this was a particularly inconvenient aversion, since I then lived just 50 or 60 feet east of Madison), because I would see women walking Yorkshire terriers and shopping at Gristede's, and some Veblenesque gorge would rise in my throat. I could not go to Times Square in the afternoon, or to the New York Public Library for any reason whatsoever. One day I could not go into a Schrafft's; the next day it would be Bonwit Teller.

I hurt the people I cared about, and insulted those I did not. I cut myself off from the one person who was closer to me than any other. I cried until I was not even aware when I was crying and when I was not, cried in elevators and in taxis and in Chinese laundries, and when I went to the doctor he said only that I seemed to be depressed and should see a "specialist." He wrote down a psychiatrist's name and address for me, but I did not go.

Instead I got married, which as it turned out was a very good thing to do but badly timed, since I still could not walk on upper Madison Avenue in the mornings and still could not listen to people and still cried in Chinese laundries. I had never before understood what "despair" meant, and I am not sure that I understand now, but I understood that year. Of course I could not work. I could not even get dinner with any degree of certainty, and I would sit in the apartment paralyzed until my husband would call from his office and say gently that I did not have to get dinner, that I could meet him at Michael's Pub or at Toots Shor's or at Sardi's East. And then one morning in April (we had been married in January), he telephoned and told me that he wanted to get out of New York for a while, that he would take a six-month leave of absence, that we would go somewhere.

It was almost three years ago when he told me that, and we have lived in Los Angeles since. Many of the people we knew in New York think this a curious aberration, and in fact tell us so. There is no possible, no adequate answer to that, and so we give certain stock answers, the answers everyone gives. I talk about how difficult it would be for us to "afford" to live in New York right now, about how much "space" we need. All I mean is that I was very young in New York, and that at some point the golden rhythm was broken, and I am not that young anymore. The last time I was in New York was in a cold January, and everyone was ill and tired. Many of the people I used to know there had moved to Dallas or had bought a farm in New Hampshire. We stayed 10 days, and then we took an afternoon flight back to Los Angeles, and on the way home from the airport that night I could see the moon on the Pacific and smell jasmine all around, and we both knew that there was no longer any point in keeping the apartment we still kept in New York. There were years when I called Los Angeles "the Coast," but they seem a long time ago.

(1967)

**C. A. Doxiadis**

# The Coming Era of Ecumenopolis

We must face the fact that modern man has failed to build adequate cities. In the past his problems were simpler, and he solved them by trial and error. Now human forces and mechanical ones are mixed and man is confused. He tries and fails. We say he will become adapted. Yes, he is running the danger of becoming adapted, since adaptation is only meaningful if it means the welfare of man. Prisoners, too, become adapted to conditions! For man to adapt to our present cities would be a mistake, since he is the great prisoner. Not only is man unsafe in his prison, but he is facing a great crisis and heading for disaster.

Confused by the danger, man behaves unwisely. He takes the new conditions of a hostile habitat for granted, and, for example, builds new cities in the image of those that failed or, in the countryside, builds air-conditioned schools with no windows because he is accustomed to doing it in industrial areas. Sometimes he attempts to turn to the past, or dreams of Utopias which have no place in our world. What man needs is an Entopia, an "in-place" which he *can* build, a place which satisfies the dreamer and is acceptable to the scientist, a place where the projections of the artist and the builder merge.

How can man achieve this?

Man and the space surrounding him are connected in many ways within a very complex system. Man's space is just a thin layer on the crust of the earth, consisting of the five elements which shape man and are shaped by him: nature, in which he lives; man himself; society, which he has formed; the shells (or structures) which he builds; and the networks he constructs. This is the real world of man, the *anthropo-cosmos* halfway between the electron and the universe. But only one subject is of primary importance: man as an individual. The subjects of secondary importance are nature and society. Shells and networks come last. Every element of the anthropocosmos has to serve man; otherwise our endeavor would have no justification.

So how can we best serve our basic subject, man? What is our goal? At this point we have to admit that we have no goals. We are developing a technology that is changing our life, yet we have set no goal for it. No businessman would buy machinery at random when building a factory, no housewife would collect furniture at random for her home. Yet this is exactly what we are doing in the case of our cities, the physical expressions of our life. For them we are producing and collecting at random.

What will our goal be? Aristotle said that the aim of the city is to make man happy and safe. I can find no better definition. So if, in the

chaos of our present situation, we can accept this, then we have something firm to stand on, provided we can define what we mean by man,
happiness, safety, and city.

I shall begin with man, so close to us and still "man the unknown."
But which man are we talking about? Which one is it who best represents the nature of man? Is it primitive man, to whom some romantics
want us to return, or the ancient Greek? The medieval or Renaissance
man, or the modern technocrat? The only possible answer is the contemporary man. He is our starting point.

Which man, then, is our ideal? To answer we have to look at man
from every possible angle. We have to look at the body, and, when we
see people stretching or youngsters rock 'n' rolling, realize that their
bodies are revolting against the inactivity we have condemned them to.
We have to realize how ignorant we are as to whether the taller, larger
people which our children are becoming are more resistant to the hardships of life than are their shorter, smaller forebears. And we must look
beyond the body. Man transcends this sphere by many other concentric
ones defined by his senses. No sensation can be overlooked: a sweet or
bitter taste, the caressing of a marble carving or a loved one, walking
on sand with bare feet, the smells, the sounds, the sights—all physical
sensations, and then all metaphysical ones such as faith and religion.

The mind of man carries him into areas which cannot be reached
through the senses. So does his soul, by way of sentiments, for sentiments, too, are shaping factors. Body, senses, mind, and soul are only
partial aspects of man, but they cannot be separated; they all operate
together in health and in sickness. A dancer may find his motivation
through stimulation of his senses, or mind, or sentiments. The mind
can be stimulated through the rhythmical movement of the body walking or swimming. We must not forget the example of the peripatetic
philosophers.

Science is beginning to merge the separate images of man that it
had set up and see him again as a whole. Common man finds perfection
in the *complete* man. When, for example, one is contemplating marriage, not one aspect of the prospective mate is overlooked. And history
demonstrates how in his great eras man believed in developing all his
capacities harmoniously.

At present we are at a disadvantage since we have not been studying man properly and have formed no concept of our ideal man. Because of this, man's body and soul are developing in a nonharmonious
way, according to the mind rather than the senses. And even the mind
is not developing harmoniously in all its areas, but only in some, which
are expanding much more than before, while others become atrophic.
What kind of creature is this man going to be? The risks we are running
by allowing the present trends to continue are very great. We may be
turning out monsters without proper balance between their different
parts, monsters who may annihilate one another or mankind.

Confronted with such a threat, I think we have a twofold obligation: first, to study man as a whole, without rejecting anything that he has learned throughout his history unless we can prove scientifically that it is harmful. This we can achieve not by coordinating existing sciences—man does not consist of externally coordinated parts, since he forms a whole—but by Anthropics, the Science of Man. Second, in the absence of any proof that we can produce a better man by changing the relationship between the body, the senses, the mind, and the soul, we should work toward a complete man with a harmonious development of all his elements, a total man whom I cannot name anything but *human man*.

Now I turn to the second term in Aristotle's definition, happiness. I beg the skeptics to forgive me, but I cannot omit dealing with this aspect of life. Happiness cannot be measured, but it is still happiness that the common man dreams of and which represents the fulfillment of his goals, the satisfaction of his interests.

One can be unhappy if one's trousers are too tight, the ceiling too low, or the temperature uncomfortable—also because of other similar physiological reasons. But one can be equally unhappy if the senses suffer—in a room painted red, for example, since one's eyes are not used to it, or through noise, smell, coarse clothes, or bad food. Also through stresses on his mind or soul. Man's happiness depends on the alleviation of the stresses he is subject to within his social environment or within himself.

These stresses can be relieved. There is, for example, the story about the man who always wore tight shoes so that when he'd take them off at home the physical relief would help him put up with an unhappy home life. But man can also learn to enjoy these stresses. As the balance between man and his environment changes continuously, his chances for happiness change, too. So what is of major importance is man's capacity for happiness. This capacity man is either born with—we could perhaps express it by an HQ, or Happiness Quotient—or he acquires or loses it by training. A proper science of Anthropics can develop a scientific HQ which will be of the greatest importance to man.

By such approaches man can hope not only to alleviate or enjoy stresses, as the case might be, but also to work toward his further betterment by drawing from within himself something better than himself. This can be gradually achieved when he begins to understand how to coordinate his internal rhythm with that of his environment by changing one or the other. He will have a variety of choices, ranging from harmony with the physical world (matching his footsteps to the pavement slabs) to harmony with nature (swimming along with the waves) to harmony with others (in the rhythmical marching of parades or in work for the amelioration of his society) to harmony with external influences (dancing to a certain tune) to the complete freedom of climbing a mountain or lying on its slopes as it pleases his internal personal rhythm.

The next term in Aristotle's definition—safety—is a concept just as difficult to understand as is happiness, and just as indispensable. Civilization started when man first felt safe within his city. Today, for the first time in history since then, he is no longer safe, and this constitutes the greatest problem to be faced by him and his civilization.

How can the city be made safe once more? This question has to be answered through an analysis of all five elements of the anthropocosmos, since the neglect of any one would upset the whole system. Nature has to be preserved, since without the proper development of all its resources there can be no hope for man's safety. The survival of man depends on his evolutionary resources and on his inborn diversity; consequently, he needs a free democratic society which will allow for the survival of the greatest variety of individuals, since we don't yet know which type is going to lead to a better total human man.

Every individual must feel and be safe, which means that personal safety within a safe society can regulate personal and group conflicts. The question is, at what cost can this be achieved? A man would be much safer if he never left his home, but he wouldn't be happy and he wouldn't develop further. We cannot sacrifice happiness and evolution in the cause of safety, nor safety in the cause of happiness. So we come to the conclusion that what we need is a safety which can guarantee a basis from which to begin our endeavors toward happiness and the fulfillment of our duties to society. This leads to the concept of a system which will allow for different environments offering all degrees of safety, ranging from the absolute one, if possible, for newborn babies and invalids, to a completely natural environment which young people will have to conquer; ranging from sterilized rooms to jungles. In such a habitat we can hope for the best balance between controlled and uncontrolled environment that will offer man the maximum safety and allow the dynamic balance of man and environment which is indispensable for lasting happiness, which is the only goal.

We can now turn to the city of man, but not with preconceived notions about limiting the operation of forces which are independent of man, as people very often do. We must understand that, unlike Utopia, our Entopia depends on forces which are dynamic and which are either uncontrollable or controllable only in the long run. It is these forces which create a new frame for the city to come.

The dynamic forces of developing humanity show that we must be prepared for a continuing increase of population which may well reach 20 to 30 billion people by the end of the next century, at which time it may level off. This will mean a universal city, Ecumenopolis, which will cover the earth with a continuous network of minor and major urban concentrations of different forms. This means that urbanization will continue and that eventually farming may be carried out from urban settlements. This also means that the pressure of population on resources will be such that important measures will have to be taken so that a balance can be retained between the five elements of the anthropocosmos in a universal scale.

But, more than with all separate phenomena, we should be concerned with the survival of man, who, long before the earth has exhausted its capacity for production, will be subjected to great forces pressing him to the point of extinction – forces caused by the elimination of human values in his settlements. If we realize only that at that point the average urban area will have twenty to thirty times more people and a hundred times more machines, and that difficulties grow much faster than the forces causing them, we will understand that this new frame is going to be inhuman in dimensions. If we understand how far the dynamic forces reach, we will see that our real challenge lies not in changing these historical trends – something we cannot do anyway – but in using them for the benefit of man by shaping this universal city in such a way that not only will it not crush man, but so that it will provide him with a human settlement much better than those of today. In order to do this we have to build the city of inhuman dimensions on the measure of man. We don't have to invent the human solutions, since they already exist – we have to understand them and use them within the new frame.

As an example, a careful study of the cities of the past proves that the maximum distance from their centers was ten minutes, and the average one six minutes meaning that people walking for a total of thirty minutes a day could visit the center or other places two or three times. This shows that there was a human dimension influencing social and other contacts, and it also gives one example of how it may be possible to measure a fundamental aspect of the human city – on the basis of the time dimension and not that of physical dimensions, since we now have new means of transportation and communications.

Up to now, measurements in cities have been based on economic criteria, but these define feasibility more than goals. It is time for man to define goals and their feasibility at the same time. Man's most precious commodity, the one which cannot be replaced and which we don't yet know how to expand, is his own life, which is expressed by its length, or lifetime. This is the basic commodity as qualified by the satisfaction and safety man enjoys and as limited by economic considerations, upon which our formula for the city will have to be based.

Man, in this case the average American citizen, spends 76 per cent of his lifetime at home (males 69 per cent and females 83 per cent), and 24 per cent away from it. He spends 36 per cent sleeping, 20 per cent working, and 10 per cent eating, dressing, and bathing. He is left with 34 per cent, or one-third of his life, for leisure, pleasure, thought, etc. It is this one-third which constitutes the basic difference between man and animal. But males ages twenty to fifty-nine have only 20 per cent of free time, of which one-third is spent in commuting. This means ninety minutes; but for some people it means three hours, or two-thirds of their free time.

On the basis of such calculations we can develop a time budget which is more important than any other budget for man, and estimate how much time each man can afford to spend on each of his activities. We can then qualify the satisfaction that man gets at every time length. Is it better for him, for example, to walk for twenty minutes, drive in a Volkswagen for ten, or in a Cadillac for two hours? We can also try to measure the degree of safety at every time length. In principle, then, total satisfaction would be the product of time multiplied by satisfaction. A happy life would be the product of time multiplied by satisfaction multiplied by safety. If we now insert into the picture the factor of economic feasibility for satisfaction, we have the formula of feasible happiness, which is leading to the human city that we can build, our common Entopia which should include all our personal Entopias in a balanced whole, the Entopia which is the common denominator of our feasible dreams.

If we have managed to define human man, natural happiness, and reasonable safety, and measure them, we can define the human city. It will be very big, but it will consist of two categories of parts, the cells and the networks. The cells are going to be the size of the cities of the past—no larger than 50,000 inhabitants, no larger than 2,000 by 2,000 yards, no larger than a ten-minute average walk. They will be built on a human scale on the basis of human experience. The networks are going to be absolutely mechanical and automatic, interconnecting the cells by transportation and communications, forming enormous organisms with the cells as basic units. Their vehicles will reach speeds of many hundreds of miles an hour; their arteries will be underground, not highways but deepways, as they are in the bodies of all mammals. The higher the speed the deeper they will go. In the cells man will be offered all choices, from isolation and solitude to very intense participation in social and political life. (The fact that we need TV should not lead us to the elimination of the marketplace. We don't need only one-way communications, we need a natural human dialogue as well.)

The surface of the city will allow the flora to spread again, beginning from small gardens within the cells, to major zones of forests above the tunnels of the networks, to big farming areas and natural reserves where man will find the rough conditions which he also needs. Society will operate much more efficiently, and people will come together in a multitude of both natural and artificial ways.

Houses will be the natural environment, not formally specified, since there the individual will want to express himself. Normal multistory residence buildings will need much greater areas per floor so that a whole community will be able to operate at each level—a community with its shopping center, playgrounds, and public squares. Automated factories will be placed within the earth, especially in hills and mountains.

Man will be free to move over the surface of the whole city, and even though the buildings will be as pleasant as possible, he will have many chances of walking or staying out without shelter or protection, since his whole organism must be kept fit for all sorts of adjustments that the future may necessitate. In this city we can hope that man, relieved of all stresses that arise from his conflict with the machine, will allow his body to dance, his senses to express themselves through the arts, his mind to dedicate itself to philosophy or mathematics, and his soul to love and to dream.

It has often been said that man may exterminate himself through science. What we must also say is that man's hopes for a much better evolution lie in science, which, after all, is the only acquisition of a proved universal value that he can transmit from generation to generation. The whole difference between extermination and evolution lies in the goal that science will set.

The task is hard. People must learn to recognize that they must be very conservative when dealing with man, and very revolutionary when dealing with new systems and networks. The task is also hard because many expect magical solutions overnight, or formulas for the immediate solution of the problems. They actually like to talk about sufferings, and they do not understand that cities face such acute problems because man does not have a system of values with which to define what a good life is. Personally, I am convinced that the root of all problems in our cities lies in our minds, in our loss of belief in man and in his ability to set goals and to implement them.

We can never solve problems and tackle diseases unless we conceive the whole. We cannot build a cathedral by carving stones but only by dreaming of it, conceiving it as a whole, developing a systematic approach, and only then working out the details. But dreaming and conceiving are not enough. We have to carve the stones and lift them.

(1967)

**Vassar Miller**

# The Calling of the Names

I move from room to room.
No one is here to haunt my empty house
except the small dog dancing at my feet,
brown shadow of a loneliness,

which has no other name,
so like a child that cannot tell you his,
or else will not (who knows the difference?)
and sulks and will not say his prayers;

or like an old, old man
who has long since forgotten what he was
assuming that he ever knew, for he
was the demoniac whose name was Legion.

So, I have ceased to call.
No name has magic, summons not one ghost,
which never was, as quiet haunts my house,
Pan's pipe to which the small dog dances.

                                        (1968)

## How can our Earth survive?

**Indians of the Southwest**

## Songs of Dawn Boy

1

Where my kindred dwell,
> *There I wander.*

The Red Rock House,
> *There I wander.*

Where dark kethawns are at the doorway,
> *There I wander.*

With the pollen of dawn upon my trail,
> *There I wander.*

At the yuni, the striped cotton hangs with pollen.
> *There I wander.*

Going around with it.
> *There I wander.*

Taking another, I depart with it.
> *With it I wander.*

In the house of long life,
> *There I wander.*

In the house of happiness,
> *There I wander.*

Beauty before me,
> *With it I wander.*

Beauty behind me,
> *With it I wander.*

Beauty below me,
> With it I *wander*.
Beauty above me,
> With it I *wander*.
Beauty all around me,
> With it I *wander*.
In old age traveling,
> With it I *wander*.
On the beautiful trail I am,
> With it I *wander*.

## 2

In Kininaéki.
In the house made of dawn.
In the story made of dawn.
On the trail of dawn.
O, Talking God!
His feet, my feet, restore.
His limbs, my limbs, restore.
His body, my body, restore.
His mind, my mind, restore.
His voice, my voice, restore.
His plumes, my plumes, restore.
With beauty before him, with beauty before me.
With beauty behind him, with beauty behind me.
With beauty above him, with beauty above me.
With beauty below him, with beauty below me.
With beauty around him, with beauty around me.
With pollen beautiful in his voice, with pollen beautiful in my voice.
It is finished in beauty.
It is finished in beauty.
In the house of evening light.
From the story made of evening light.
On the trail of evening light.
O, House God![1]

## 3

To the house of my kindred,
> *There I return.*
Child of the yellow corn am I.

---

[1]The rest as in 1, except that lines 12 and 13 are transposed.

To the Red Rock House,
> *There I return.*

Where the blue kethawns are by the doorway,
> *There I return.*

The pollen of evening light on my trail,
> *There I return.*

At the yuni the haliotis shell hangs with the pollen,
Going around,
> *With it I return.*

Taking another, I walk out with it.
> *With it I return.*

To the house of old age,
> *Up there I return.*

To the house of happiness,
> *Up there I return.*

Beauty behind me,
> *With it I return.*

Beauty before me,
> *With it I return.*

Beauty above me,
> *With it I return.*

Beauty below me,
> *With it I return.*

Beauty all around me,
> *With it I return.*

Now in old age wandering,
> *I return.*

Now on the trail of beauty, I am.
> *There I return.*


# A Prayer

For Second Day of the Night Chant


From the base of the east.
From the base of the Pelado Peak.
From the house made of mirage,
From the story made of mirage,
From the doorway of rainbow,
The path out of which is the rainbow,
The rainbow passed out with me.
The rainbow raised up with me.

Through the middle of broad fields,
The rainbow returned with me.
To where my house is visible,
The rainbow returned with me.
To the roof of my house,
The rainbow returned with me.
To the entrance of my house.
The rainbow returned with me.
To just within my house,
The rainbow returned with me.
To my fireside,
The rainbow returned with me.
To the center of my house,
The rainbow returned with me.
At the fore part of my house with the dawn,
The Talking God sits with me.
The House God sits with me.
Pollen Boy sits with me.
Grasshopper Girl sits with me.
In beauty Estsánatlehi, my mother, for her I return.
Beautifully my fire to me is restored.
Beautifully my possessions are to me restored.
Beautifully my soft goods to me are restored.
Beautifully my hard goods to me are restored.
Beautifully my horses to me are restored.
Beautifully my sheep to me are restored.
Beautifully my old men to me are restored.
Beautifully my old women to me are restored.
Beautifully my young men to me are restored.
Beautifully my women to me are restored.
Beautifully my children to me are restored.
Beautifully my wife to me is restored.
Beautifully my chiefs to me are restored.
Beautifully my country to me is restored.
Beautifully my fields to me are restored.
Beautifully my house to me is restored.
Talking God sits with me.
House God sits with me.
Pollen Boy sits with me.
Grasshopper Girl sits with me.
Beautifully white corn to me is restored.
Beautifully yellow corn to me is restored.
Beautifully blue corn to me is restored.
Beautifully corn of all kinds to me is restored.
In beauty may I walk.
All day long may I walk.

Through the returning seasons may I walk.
On the trail marked with pollen may I walk.
With grasshoppers about my feet may I walk.
With dew about my feet may I walk.
With beauty may I walk.
With beauty before me, may I walk.
With beauty behind me, may I walk.
With beauty above me, may I walk.
With beauty below me, may I walk.
With beauty all around me, may I walk.
In old age wandering on a trail of beauty, lively, may I walk.
In old age wandering on a trail of beauty, living again, may I walk.
  It is finished in beauty.
  It is finished in beauty.


# Night Chant

For the Ninth Song


In Tsegihi,
In the house made of dawn,
In the house made of evening twilight,
In the house made of dark cloud,
In the house made of rain and mist, of pollen, of grasshoppers,
Where the dark mist curtains the doorway,
The path to which is on the rainbow,
Where the zig-zag lightning stands high on top,
Where the he-rain stands high on top,
Oh, male divinity!
With your moccasins of dark cloud, come to us,
With your mind enveloped in dark cloud, come to us,
With the dark thunder above you, come to us soaring,
With the shapen cloud at your feet, come to us soaring.
With the far darkness made of the dark cloud over your head, come to
    us soaring,
With the far darkness made of the rain and the mist over your head,
    come to us soaring,
With the far darkness made of the rain and the mist over your head,
    come to us soaring.
With the zig-zag lightning flung out high over your head,
With the rainbow hanging high over your head, come to us soaring.
With the far darkness made of the dark cloud on the ends of your wings,

With the far darkness made of the rain and the mist on the ends of your
  wings, come to us soaring,
With the zig-zag lightning, with the rainbow hanging high on the ends
  of your wings, come to us soaring.
With the near darkness made of dark cloud of the rain and the mist,
  come to us,
With the darkness on the earth, come to us.


With these I wish the foam floating on the flowing water over the roots
  of the great corn,
I have made your sacrifice,
I have prepared a smoke for you,
My feet restore for me.
My limbs restore, my body restore, my mind restore, my voice restore for
  me.
Today, take out your spell for me,
Today, take away your spell for me.
Away from me you have taken it,
Far off from me it is taken,
Far off you have done it.


Happily I recover,
Happily I become cool,
My eyes regain their power, my head cools, my limbs regain their
  strength, I hear again.
Happily for me the spell is taken off,
Happily I walk; impervious to pain, I walk; light within, I walk; joyous,
  I walk.
Abundant dark clouds I desire,
An abundance of vegetation I desire,
An abundance of pollen, abundant dew, I desire.
Happily may fair white corn, to the ends of the earth, come with you,
Happily may fair yellow corn, fair blue corn, fair corn of all kinds,
  plants of all kinds, goods of all kinds, jewels of all kinds, to the ends
  of the earth, come with you.
With these before you, happily may they come with you,
With these behind, below, above, around you, happily may they come
  with you,
Thus you accomplish your tasks.


Happily the old men will regard you,
Happily the old women will regard you,
The young men and the young women will regard you,
The children will regard you,
The chiefs will regard you,

Happily, as they scatter in different directions, they will regard you,
Happily, as they approach their homes, they will regard you.

May their roads home be on the trail of peace,
Happily may they all return.
In beauty I walk,
With beauty before me, I walk,
With beauty behind me, I walk,
With beauty above and about me, I walk,
It is finished in beauty,
It is finished in beauty.

(Dates unknown)

**Sarah Orne Jewett**

# A White Heron

1

The woods were already filled with shadows one June evening, just before eight o'clock, though a bright sunset still glimmered faintly among the trunks of the trees. A little girl was driving home her cow, a plodding, dilatory, provoking creature in her behavior, but a valued companion for all that. They were going away from the western light, and striking deep into the dark woods, but their feet were familiar with the path, and it was no matter whether their eyes could see it or not.

There was hardly a night the summer through when the old cow could be found waiting at the pasture bars; on the contrary, it was her greatest pleasure to hide herself away among the high huckleberry bushes, and though she wore a loud bell she had made the discovery that if one stood perfectly still it would not ring. So Sylvia had to hunt for her until she found her, and call Co'! Co'! with never an answering Moo, until her childish patience was quite spent. If the creature had not given good milk and plenty of it, the case would have seemed very different to her owners. Besides, Sylvia had all the time there was, and very little use to make of it. Sometimes in pleasant weather it was a consolation to look upon the cow's pranks as an intelligent attempt to play hide and seek, and as the child had no playmates she lent herself to this amusement with a good deal of zest. Though this chase had been so long that the wary animal herself had given an unusual signal of her whereabouts, Sylvia had only laughed when she came upon Mistress Moolly at the swamp-side, and urged her affectionately homeward with a twig of birch leaves. The old cow was not inclined to wander farther, she even turned in the right direction for once as they left the pasture, and stepped along the road at a good pace. She was quite ready to be milked now, and seldom stopped to browse. Sylvia wondered what her grandmother would say because they were so late. It was a great while since she had left home at half past five o'clock, but everybody knew the difficulty of making this errand a short one. Mrs. Tilley had chased the hornéd torment too many summer evenings herself to blame any one else for lingering, and was only thankful as she waited that she had Sylvia, nowadays, to give such valuable assistance. The good woman suspected that Sylvia loitered occasionally on her own account; there never was such a child for straying about out-of-doors since the world was made! Everybody said that it was a good change for a little maid who had tried to grow for eight years in a crowded manufacturing town, but, as for Sylvia herself, it seemed as if she never had been alive at all before she came to live at the farm. She thought often with wistful compassion of a wretched dry geranium that belonged to a town neighbor.

"'Afraid of folks,'" old Mrs. Tilley said to herself, with a smile, after she had made the unlikely choice of Sylvia from her daughter's houseful of children, and was returning to the farm. "'Afraid of folks,' they said! I guess she won't be troubled no great with 'em up to the old place!" When they reached the door of the lonely house and stopped to unlock it, and the cat came to purr loudly, and rub against them, a deserted pussy, indeed, but fat with young robins, Sylvia whispered that this was a beautiful place to live in, and she never should wish to go home.

The companions followed the shady woodroad, the cow taking slow steps, and the child very fast ones. The cow stopped long at the brook to drink, as if the pasture were not half a swamp, and Sylvia stood still and waited, letting her bare feet cool themselves in the shoal water, while the great twilight moths struck softly against her. She waded on through the brook as the cow moved away, and listened to the thrushes with a heart that beat fast with pleasure. There was a stirring in the great boughs overhead. They were full of little birds and beasts that seemed to be wide-awake, and going about their world, or else saying good-night to each other in sleepy twitters. Sylvia herself felt sleepy as she walked along. However, it was not much farther to the house, and the air was soft and sweet. She was not often in the woods so late as this, and it made her feel as if she were a part of the gray shadows and the moving leaves. She was just thinking how long it seemed since she first came to the farm a year ago, and wondering if everything went on in the noisy town just the same as when she was there; the thought of the great red-faced boy who used to chase and frighten her made her hurry along the path to escape from the shadow of the trees.

Suddenly this little woods-girl is horror-stricken to hear a clear whistle not very far away. Not a bird's whistle, which would have a sort of friendliness, but a boy's whistle, determined, and somewhat aggressive. Sylvia left the cow to whatever sad fate might await her, and stepped discreetly aside into the bushes, but she was just too late. The enemy had discovered her, and called out in a very cheerful and persuasive tone, "Halloa, little girl, how far is it to the road?" and trembling Sylvia answered almost inaudibly, "A good ways."

She did not dare to look boldly at the tall young man, who carried a gun over his shoulder, but she came out of her bush and again followed the cow, while he walked alongside.

"I have been hunting for some birds," the stranger said kindly, "and I have lost my way, and need a friend very much. Don't be afraid," he added gallantly. "Speak up and tell me what your name is, and whether you think I can spend the night at your house, and go out gunning early in the morning."

Sylvia was more alarmed than before. Would not her grandmother consider her much to blame? But who could have foreseen such an accident as this? It did not appear to be her fault, and she hung her head as if the stem of it were broken, but managed to answer "Sylvy," with much effort when her companion again asked her name.

Mrs. Tilley was standing in the doorway when the trio came into view. The cow gave a loud moo by way of explanation.

"Yes, you'd better speak up for yourself, you old trial! Where'd she tuck herself away this time, Sylvy?" Sylvia kept an awed silence; she knew by instinct that her grandmother did not comprehend the gravity of the situation. She must be mistaking the stranger for one of the farmer-lads of the region.

The young man stood his gun beside the door, and dropped a heavy game-bag beside it; then he bade Mrs. Tilley good-evening, and repeated his wayfarer's story, and asked if he could have a night's lodging.

"Put me anywhere you like," he said. "I must be off early in the morning, before day; but I am very hungry, indeed. You can give me some milk at any rate, that's plain."

"Dear sakes, yes," responded the hostess, whose long slumbering hospitality seemed to be easily awakened. "You might fare better if you went out on the main road a mile or so, but you're welcome to what we've got. I'll milk right off, and you make yourself at home. You can sleep on husks or feathers," she proffered graciously. "I raised them all myself. There's good pasturing for geese just below here towards the ma'sh. Now step round and set a plate for the gentleman, Sylvy!" And Sylvia promptly stepped. She was glad to have something to do, and she was hungry herself.

It was a surprise to find so clean and comfortable a little dwelling in this New England wilderness. The young man had known the horrors of its most primitive housekeeping, and the dreary squalor of that level of society which does not rebel at the companionship of hens. This was the best thrift of an old-fashioned farmstead, though on such a small scale that it seemed like a hermitage. He listened eagerly to the old woman's quaint talk, he watched Sylvia's pale face and shining gray eyes with ever growing enthusiasm, and insisted that this was the best supper he had eaten for a month; then, afterward, the new-made friends sat down in the doorway together while the moon came up.

Soon it would be berry-time, and Sylvia was a great help at picking. The cow was a good milker, though a plaguy thing to keep track of, the hostess gossiped frankly, adding presently that she had buried four children, so that Sylvia's mother, and a son (who might be dead) in California were all the children she had left. "Dan, my boy, was a great hand to go gunning," she explained sadly. "I never wanted for pa'tridges or gray squer'ls while he was to home. He's been a great wand'rer, I expect, and he's no hand to write letters. There, I don't blame him, I'd ha' seen the world myself if it had been so I could.

"Sylvia takes after him," the grandmother continued affectionately, after a minute's pause. "There ain't a foot o' ground she don't know her way over, and the wild creatur's counts her one o' themselves. Squer'ls she'll tame to come an' feed right out o' her hands, and all sorts o' birds. Last winter she got the jay-birds to bangeing here, and I believe she'd 'a' scanted herself of her own meals to have plenty to throw out amongst 'em, if I hadn't kep' watch. Anything but crows, I tell her, I'm willin' to help support,—though Dan he went an' tamed one o' them that did seem to have reason same as folks. It was round here a good spell after he went away. Dan an' his father they didn't hitch,—but he never held up his head ag'in after Dan had dared him an' gone off."

The guest did not notice this hint of family sorrows in his eager interest in something else.

"So Sylvy knows all about birds, does she?" he exclaimed, as he looked round at the little girl who sat, very demure but increasingly sleepy, in the moonlight. "I am making a collection of birds myself. I have been at it ever since I was a boy." (Mrs. Tilley smiled.) "There are two or three very rare ones I have been hunting for these five years. I mean to get them on my own ground if they can be found."

"Do you cage 'em up?" asked Mrs. Tilley doubtfully, in response to this enthusiastic announcement.

"Oh, no, they're stuffed and preserved, dozens and dozens of them," said the ornithologist, "and I have shot or snared every one myself. I caught a glimpse of a white heron three miles from here on Saturday, and I have followed it in this direction. They have never been found in this district at all. The little white heron, it is," and he turned again to look at Sylvia with the hope of discovering that the rare bird was one of her acquaintances.

But Sylvia was watching a hop-toad in the narrow footpath.

"You would know the heron if you saw it," the stranger continued eagerly. "A queer tall white bird with soft feathers and long thin legs. And it would have a nest perhaps in the top of a high tree, made of sticks, something like a hawk's nest."

Sylvia's heart gave a wild beat; she knew that strange white bird, and had once stolen softly near where it stood in some bright green swamp grass, away over at the other side of the woods. There was an open place where the sunshine always seemed strangely yellow and hot, where tall, nodding rushes grew, and her grandmother had warned her that she might sink in the soft black mud underneath and never be heard of more. Not far beyond were the salt marshes and beyond those was the sea, the sea which Sylvia wondered and dreamed about, but never had looked upon, though its great voice could often be heard above the noise of the woods on stormy nights.

"I can't think of anything I should like so much as to find that heron's nest," the handsome stranger was saying. "I would give ten dollars to anybody who could show it to me," he added desperately, "and I mean to spend my whole vacation hunting for it if need be. Perhaps it was only migrating, or had been chased out of its own region by some bird of prey."

Mrs. Tilley gave amazed attention to all this, but Sylvia still watched the toad, not divining, as she might have done at some calmer time, that the creature wished to get to its hole under the doorstep, and was much hindered by the unusual spectators at that hour of the evening. No amount of thought, that night, could decide how many wished-for treasures the ten dollars, so lightly spoken of, would buy.

The next day the young sportsman hovered about the woods, and Sylvia kept him company, having lost her first fear of the friendly lad, who proved to be most kind and sympathetic. He told her many things about the birds and what they knew and where they lived and what they did with themselves. And he gave her a jack-knife, which she thought as great a treasure as if she were a desert-islander. All day long he did not once make her troubled or afraid except when he brought down some unsuspecting singing creature from its bough. Sylvia would have liked him vastly better without his gun; she could not understand why he killed the very birds he seemed to like so much. But as the day waned, Sylvia still watched the young man with loving admiration. She had never seen anybody so charming and delightful; the woman's heart, asleep in the child, was vaguely thrilled by a dream of love. Some premonition of that great power stirred and swayed these young foresters who traversed the solemn woodlands with soft-footed silent care. They stopped to listen to a bird's song; they pressed forward again eagerly, parting the branches, – speaking to each other rarely and in whispers; the young man going first and Sylvia following, fascinated, a few steps behind, with her gray eyes dark with excitement.

She grieved because the longed-for white heron was elusive, but she did not lead the guest, she only followed, and there was no such thing as speaking first. The sound of her own unquestioned voice would have terrified her,—it was hard enough to answer yes or no when there was need of that. At last evening began to fall, and they drove the cow home together, and Sylvia smiled with pleasure when they came to the place where she heard the whistle and was afraid only the night before.

## 2

Half a mile from home, at the farther edge of the woods, where the land was highest, a great pine-tree stood, the last of its generation. Whether it was left for a boundary mark, or for what reason, no one could say; the woodchoppers who had felled its mates were dead and gone long ago, and a whole forest of sturdy trees, pines and oaks and maples, had grown again. But the stately head of this old pine towered above them all and made a landmark for sea and shore miles and miles away. Sylvia knew it well. She had always believed that whoever climbed to the top of it could see the ocean; and the little girl had often laid her hand on the great rough trunk and looked up wistfully at those dark boughs that the wind always stirred, no matter how hot and still the air might be below. Now she thought of the tree with a new excitement, for why, if one climbed it at break of day, could not one see all the world, and easily discover whence the white heron flew, and mark the place, and find the hidden nest?

What a spirit of adventure, what wild ambition! What fancied triumph and delight and glory for the later morning when she could make known the secret! It was almost too real and too great for the childish heart to bear.

All night the door of the little house stood open, and the whippoor-wills came and sang upon the very step. The young sportsman and his old hostess were sound asleep, but Sylvia's great design kept her broad awake and watching. She forgot to think of sleep. The short summer night seemed as long as the winter darkness, and at last when the whippoorwills ceased, and she was afraid the morning would after all come too soon, she stole out of the house and followed the pasture path through the woods, hastening toward the open ground beyond, listening with a sense of comfort and companionship to the drowsy twitter of a half-awakened bird, whose perch she had jarred in passing. Alas, if the great wave of human interest which flooded for the first time this dull little life should sweep away the satisfactions of an existence heart to heart with nature and the dumb life of the forest!

There was the huge tree asleep yet in the paling moonlight, and small and hopeful Sylvia began with utmost bravery to mount to the top of it, with tingling, eager blood coursing the channels of her whole frame, with her bare feet and fingers, that pinched and held like bird's claws to the monstrous ladder reaching up, up, almost to the sky itself. First she must mount the white oak tree that grew alongside, where she was almost lost among the dark branches and the green leaves heavy and wet with dew; a bird fluttered off its nest, and a red squirrel ran to and fro and scolded pettishly at the harmless housebreaker. Sylvia felt her way easily. She had often climbed there, and knew that higher still one of the oak's upper branches chafed against the pine trunk, just where its lower boughs were set close together. There, when she made the dangerous pass from one tree to the other, the great enterprise would really begin.

She crept out along the swaying oak limb at last, and took the daring step across into the old pine-tree. The way was harder than she thought; she must reach far and hold fast, the sharp dry twigs caught and held her and scratched her like angry talons, the pitch made her thin little fingers clumsy and stiff as she went round and round the tree's great stem, higher and higher upward. The sparrows and robins in the woods below were beginning to wake and twitter to the dawn, yet it seemed much lighter there aloft in the pine-tree, and the child knew that she must hurry if her project were to be of any use.

The tree seemed to lengthen itself out as she went up, and to reach farther and farther upward. It was like a great main-mast to the voyaging earth; it must truly have been amazed that morning through all its ponderous frame as it felt this determined spark of human spirit creeping and climbing from higher branch to branch. Who knows how steadily the least twigs held themselves to advantage this light, weak creature on her way! The old pine must have loved his new dependent. More than all the hawks, and bats, and moths, and even the sweet-voiced thrushes, was the brave, beating heart of the solitary gray-eyed child. And the tree stood still and held away the winds that June morning while the dawn grew bright in the east.

Sylvia's face was like a pale star, if one had seen it from the ground, when the last thorny bough was past, and she stood trembling and tired but wholly triumphant, high in the tree-top. Yes, there was the sea with the dawning sun making a golden dazzle over it, and toward that glorious east flew two hawks with slow-moving pinions. How low they looked in the air from that height when before one had only seen them far up, and dark against the blue sky. Their gray feathers were as soft as moths; they seemed only a little way from the tree, and Sylvia felt as if she too could go flying away among the clouds. Westward, the woodlands and farms reached miles and miles into the distance; here and there were church steeples, and white villages; truly it was a vast and awesome world.

The birds sang louder and louder. At last the sun came up bewilderingly bright. Sylvia could see the white sails of ships out at sea, and the clouds that were purple and rose-colored and yellow at first began to fade away. Where was the white heron's nest in the sea of green branches, and was this wonderful sight and pageant of the world the only reward for having climbed to such a giddy height? Now look down again, Sylvia, where the green marsh is set among the shining birches and dark hemlocks; there where you saw the white heron once you will see him again; look, look! a white spot of him like a single floating feather comes up from the dead hemlock and grows larger, and rises, and comes close at last, and goes by the landmark pine with steady sweep of wing and outstretched slender neck and crested head. And wait ! wait! do not move a foot or a finger, little girl, do not send an arrow of light and consciousness from your two eager eyes, for the heron has perched on a pine bough not far beyond yours, and cries back to his mate on the nest, and plumes his feathers for the new day!

The child gives a long sigh a minute later when a company of shouting cat-birds comes also to the tree, and vexed by the fluttering and lawlessness the solemn heron goes away. She knows his secret now, the wild, light, slender bird that floats and wavers, and goes back like an arrow presently to his home in the green world beneath. Then Sylvia, well satisfied, makes her perilous way down again, not daring to look far below the branch she stands on, ready to cry sometimes because her fingers ache and her lamed feet slip. Wondering over and over again what the stranger would say to her, and what he would think when she told him how to find his way straight to the heron's nest.

"Sylvy, Sylvy!" called the busy old grandmother again and again, but nobody answered, and the small husk bed was empty, and Sylvia had disappeared.

The guest waked from a dream, and remembering his day's pleasure hurried to dress himself that it might sooner begin. He was sure from the way the shy little girl looked once or twice yesterday that she had at least seen the white heron, and now she must really be persuaded to tell. Here she comes now, paler than ever, and her worn old frock is torn and tattered, and smeared with pine pitch. The grandmother and the sportsman stand in the door together and question her, and the splendid moment has come to speak of the dead hemlock-tree by the green marsh.

But Sylvia does not speak after all, though the old grandmother fretfully rebukes her, and the young man's kind appealing eyes are looking straight in her own. He can make them rich with money; he has promised it, and they are poor now. He is so well worth making happy, and he waits to hear the story she can tell.

No, she must keep silence! What is it that suddenly forbids her and makes her dumb? Has she been nine years growing, and now, when the great world for the first time puts out a hand to her, must she thrust it aside for a bird's sake? The murmur of the pine's green branches is in her ears, she remembers how the white heron came flying through the golden air and how they watched the sea and the morning together, and Sylvia cannot speak; she cannot tell the heron's secret and give its life away.

Dear loyalty, that suffered a sharp pang as the guest went away disappointed later in the day, that could have served and followed him and loved him as a dog loves! Many a night Sylvia heard the echo of his whistle haunting the pasture path as she came home with the loitering cow. She forgot even her sorrow at the sharp report of his gun and the piteous sight of thrushes and sparrows dropping silent to the ground, their songs hushed and their pretty feathers stained and wet with blood. Were the birds better friends than their hunter might have been,—who can tell? Whatever treasures were lost to her, woodlands and summertime, remember! Bring your gifts and graces and tell your secrets to this lonely country child!

(1886)

## Rachel Carson

### *from* Silent Spring

The sedge is wither'd from the lake,
  And no birds sing.
                    Keats

I am pessimistic about the human race because it is too ingenious for its own good. Our approach to nature is to beat it into submission. We would stand a better chance of survival if we accommodated ourselves to this planet and viewed it appreciatively instead of skeptically and dictatorially.
                    E. B. White

### Chapter 1. A Fable for Tomorrow

There was once a town in the heart of America where all life seemed to live in harmony with its surroundings. The town lay in the midst of a checkerboard of prosperous farms, with fields of grain and hillsides of orchards where, in spring, white clouds of bloom drifted above the green fields. In autumn, oak and maple and birch set up a blaze of color that flamed and flickered across a backdrop of pines. Then foxes barked in the hills and deer silently crossed the fields, half hidden in the mists of the fall mornings.

Along the roads, laurel, viburnum and alder, great ferns and wild-flowers delighted the traveler's eye through much of the year. Even in winter the roadsides were places of beauty, where countless birds came to feed on the berries and on the seed heads of the dried weeds rising above the snow. The countryside was, in fact, famous for the abundance and variety of its bird life, and when the flood of migrants was pouring through in spring and fall people traveled from great distances to observe them. Others came to fish the streams, which flowed clear and cold out of the hills and contained shady pools where trout lay. So it had been from the days many years ago when the first settlers raised their houses, sank their wells, and built their barns.

Then a strange blight crept over the area and everything began to change. Some evil spell had settled on the community: mysterious maladies swept the flocks of chickens; the cattle and sheep sickened and died. Everywhere was a shadow of death. The farmers spoke of much illness among their families. In the town the doctors had become more and more puzzled by new kinds of sickness appearing among their patients. There had been several sudden and unexplained deaths, not only among adults but even among children, who would be stricken suddenly while at play and die within a few hours.

There was a strange stillness. The birds, for example—where had they gone? Many people spoke of them, puzzled and disturbed. The feeding stations in the backyards were deserted. The few birds seen anywhere were moribund; they trembled violently and could not fly. It was a spring without voices. On the mornings that had once throbbed with the dawn chorus of robins, catbirds, doves, jays, wrens, and scores of other bird voices there was now no sound; only silence lay over the fields and woods and marsh.

On the farms the hens brooded, but no chicks hatched. The farmers complained that they were unable to raise any pigs—the litters were small and the young survived only a few days. The apple trees were coming into bloom but no bees droned among the blossoms, so there was no pollination and there would be no fruit.

The roadsides, once so attractive, were now lined with browned and withered vegetation as though swept by fire. These, too, were silent, deserted by all living things. Even the streams were now lifeless. Anglers no longer visited them, for all the fish had died.

In the gutters under the eaves and between the shingles of the roofs, a white granular powder still showed a few patches; some weeks before it had fallen like snow upon the roofs and the lawns, the fields and streams.

No witchcraft, no enemy action had silenced the rebirth of new life in this stricken world. The people had done it themselves.

This town does not actually exist, but it might easily have a thousand counterparts in America or elsewhere in the world. I know of no community that has experienced all the misfortunes I describe. Yet every one of these disasters has actually happened somewhere, and many real communities have already suffered a substantial number of them. A grim specter has crept upon us almost unnoticed, and this imagined tragedy may easily become a stark reality we all shall know.

What has already silenced the voices of spring in countless towns in America? This book is an attempt to explain.

## Chapter 2. The Obligation to Endure

The history of life on earth has been a history of interaction between living things and their surroundings. To a large extent, the physical form and the habits of the earth's vegetation and its animal life have been molded by the environment. Considering the whole span of earthly time, the opposite effect, in which life actually modifies its surroundings, has been relatively slight. Only within the moment of time represented by the present century has one species—man—acquired significant power to alter the nature of his world.

During the past quarter century this power has not only increased to one of disturbing magnitude but it has changed in character. The most alarming of all man's assaults upon the environment is the contamination of air, earth, rivers, and sea with dangerous and even lethal materials. This pollution is for the most part irrecoverable; the chain of evil it initiates not only in the world that must support life but in living tissues is for the most part irreversible. In this now universal contamination of the environment, chemicals are the sinister and little-recognized partners of radiation in changing the very nature of the world—the very nature of its life. Strontium 90, released through nuclear explosions into the air, comes to earth in rain or drifts down as fallout, lodges in soil, enters into the grass or corn or wheat grown there, and in time takes up its abode in the bones of a human being, there to remain until his death. Similarly, chemicals sprayed on croplands or forests or gardens lie long in soil, entering into living organisms, passing from one to another in a chain of poisoning and death. Or they pass mysteriously by underground streams until they emerge and, through the alchemy of air and sunlight, combine into new forms that kill vegetation, sicken cattle, and work unknown harm on those who drink from once-pure wells. As Albert Schweitzer has said, "Man can hardly even recognize the devils of his own creation."

It took hundreds of millions of years to produce the life that now inhabits the earth—eons of time in which that developing and evolving and diversifying life reached a state of adjustment and balance with its surroundings. The environment, rigorously shaping and directing the life it supported, contained elements that were hostile as well as supporting. Certain rocks gave out dangerous radiation; even within the light of the sun, from which all life draws its energy, there were short-wave radiations with power to injure. Given time—time not in years but in millennia—life adjusts, and a balance has been reached. For time is the essential ingredient; but in the modern world there is no time.

The rapidity of change and the speed with which new situations are created follow the impetuous and heedless pace of man rather than the deliberate pace of nature. Radiation is no longer merely the background radiation of rocks, the bombardment of cosmic rays, the ultraviolet of the sun that have existed before there was any life on earth; radiation is now the unnatural creation of man's tampering with the atom. The chemicals to which life is asked to make its adjustment are no longer merely the calcium and silica and copper and all the rest of the minerals washed out of the rocks and carried in rivers to the sea; they are the synthetic creations of man's inventive mind, brewed in his laboratories, and having no counterparts in nature.

To adjust to these chemicals would require time on the scale that is nature's; it would require not merely the years of a man's life but the life of generations. And even this, were it by some miracle possible, would be futile, for the new chemicals come from our laboratories in an endless stream; almost five hundred annually find their way into actual use in the United States alone. The figure is staggering and its implications are not easily grasped—500 new chemicals to which the bodies of men and animals are required somehow to adapt each year, chemicals totally outside the limits of biologic experience.

Among them are many that are used in man's war against nature. Since the mid-1940's over 200 basic chemicals have been created for use in killing insects, weeds, rodents, and other organisms described in the modern vernacular as "pests"; and they are sold under several thousand different brand names.

These sprays, dusts, and aerosols are now applied almost universally to farms, gardens, forests, and homes—nonselective chemicals that have the power to kill every insect, the "good" and the "bad," to still the song of birds and the leaping of fish in the streams, to coat the leaves with a deadly film, and to linger on in soil—all this though the intended target may be only a few weeds or insects. Can anyone believe it is possible to lay down such a barrage of poisons on the surface of the earth without making it unfit for all life? They should not be called "insecticides," but "biocides."

The whole process of spraying seems caught up in an endless spiral. Since DDT was released for civilian use, a process of escalation has been going on in which ever more toxic materials must be found. This has happened because insects, in a triumphant vindication of Darwin's principle of the survival of the fittest, have evolved super races immune to the particular insecticide used, hence a deadlier one has always to be developed—and then a deadlier one than that. It has happened also because, for reasons to be described later, destructive insects often undergo a "flareback," or resurgence, after spraying, in numbers greater than before. Thus the chemical war is never won, and all life is caught in its violent crossfire.

Along with the possibility of the extinction of mankind by nuclear war, the central problem of our age has therefore become the contamination of man's total environment with such substances of incredible potential for harm—substances that accumulate in the tissues of plants and animals and even penetrate the germ cells to shatter or alter the very material of heredity upon which the shape of the future depends.

Some would-be architects of our future look toward a time when it will be possible to alter the human germ plasm by design. But we may easily be doing so now by inadvertence, for many chemicals, like radiation, bring about gene mutations. It is ironic to think that man might determine his own future by something so seemingly trivial as the choice of an insect spray.

All this has been risked—for what? Future historians may well be amazed by our distorted sense of proportion. How could intelligent beings seek to control a few unwanted species by a method that contaminated the entire environment and brought the threat of disease and death even to their own kind? Yet this is precisely what we have done. We have done it, moreover, for reasons that collapse the moment we examine them. We are told that the enormous and expanding use of pesticides is necessary to maintain farm production. Yet is our real problem not one of *overproduction*? Our farms, despite measures to remove acreages from production and to pay farmers *not* to produce, have yielded such a staggering excess of crops that the American taxpayer in 1962 is paying out more than one billion dollars a year as the total carrying cost of the surplus-food storage program. And is the situation helped when one branch of the Agriculture Department tries to reduce production while another states, as it did in 1958, "It is believed generally that reduction of crop acreages under provisions of the Soil Bank will stimulate interest in use of chemicals to obtain maximum production on the land retained in crops."

All this is not to say there is no insect problem and no need of control. I am saying, rather, that control must be geared to realities, not to mythical situations, and that the methods employed must be such that they do not destroy us along with the insects.

The problem whose attempted solution has brought such a train of disaster in its wake is an accompaniment of our modern way of life.

Long before the age of man, insects inhabited the earth—a group of extraordinarily varied and adaptable beings. Over the course of time since man's advent, a small percentage of the more than half a million species of insects have come into conflict with human welfare in two principal ways: as competitors for the food supply and as carriers of human disease.

Disease-carrying insects become important where human beings are crowded together, especially under conditions where sanitation is poor, as in time of natural disaster or war or in situations of extreme poverty and deprivation. Then control of some sort becomes necessary. It is a sobering fact, however, as we shall presently see, that the method of massive chemical control has had only limited success, and also threatens to worsen the very conditions it is intended to curb.

Under primitive agricultural conditions the farmer had few insect problems. These arose with the intensification of agriculture—the devotion of immense acreages to a single crop. Such a system set the stage for explosive increases in specific insect populations. Single-crop farming does not take advantage of the principles by which nature works; it is agriculture as an engineer might conceive it to be. Nature has introduced great variety into the landscape, but man has displayed a passion for simplifying it. Thus he undoes the built-in checks and balances by which nature holds the species within bounds. One important natural check is a limit on the amount of suitable habitat for each species. Obviously then, an insect that lives on wheat can build up its population to much higher levels on a farm devoted to wheat than on one in which wheat is intermingled with other crops to which the insect is not adapted.

The same thing happens in other situations. A generation or more ago, the towns of large areas of the United States lined their streets with the noble elm tree. Now the beauty they hopefully created is threatened with complete destruction as disease sweeps through the elms, carried by a beetle that would have only limited chance to build up large populations and to spread from tree to tree if the elms were only occasional trees in a richly diversified planting.

Another factor in the modern insect problem is one that must be viewed against a background of geologic and human history: the spreading of thousands of different kinds of organisms from their native homes to invade new territories. This worldwide migration has been studied and graphically described by the British ecologist Charles Elton in his recent book *The Ecology of Invasions*. During the Cretaceous Period, some hundred million years ago, flooding seas cut many land bridges between continents and living things found themselves confined in what Elton calls "colossal separate nature reserves." There, isolated from others of their kind, they developed many new species. When some of the land masses were joined again, about 15 million years ago, these species began to move out into new territories—a movement that is not only still in progress but is now receiving considerable assistance from man.

The importation of plants is the primary agent in the modern spread of species, for animals have almost invariably gone along with the plants, quarantine being a comparatively recent and not completely effective innovation. The United States Office of Plant Introduction alone has introduced almost 200,000 species and varieties of plants from all over the world. Nearly half of the 180 or so major insect enemies of plants in the United States are accidental imports from abroad, and most of them have come as hitchhikers on plants.

In new territory, out of reach of the restraining hand of the natural enemies that kept down its numbers in its native land, an invading plant or animal is able to become enormously abundant. Thus it is no accident that our most troublesome insects are introduced species.

These invasions, both the naturally occurring and those dependent on human assistance, are likely to continue indefinitely. Quarantine and massive chemical campaigns are only extremely expensive ways of buying time. We are faced, according to Dr. Elton, "with a life-and-death need not just to find new technological means of suppressing this plant or that animal"; instead we need the basic knowledge of animal populations and their relations to their surroundings that will "promote an even balance and damp down the explosive power of outbreaks and new invasions."

Much of the necessary knowledge is now available but we do not use it. We train ecologists in our universities and even employ them in our governmental agencies but we seldom take their advice. We allow the chemical death rain to fall as though there were no alternative, whereas in fact there are many, and our ingenuity could soon discover many more if given opportunity.

Have we fallen into a mesmerized state that makes us accept as inevitable that which is inferior or detrimental, as though having lost the will or the vision to demand that which is good? Such thinking, in the words of the ecologist Paul Shepard, "idealizes life with only its head out of water, inches above the limits of toleration of the corruption of its own environment . . . Why should we tolerate a diet of weak poisons, a home in insipid surroundings, a circle of acquaintances who are not quite our enemies, the noise of motors with just enough relief to prevent insanity? Who would want to live in a world which is just not quite fatal?"

Yet such a world is pressed upon us. The crusade to create a chemically sterile, insect-free world seems to have engendered a fanatic zeal on the part of many specialists and most of the so-called control agencies. On every hand there is evidence that those engaged in spraying operations exercise a ruthless power. "The regulatory entomologists . . . function as prosecutor, judge and jury, tax assessor and collector and sheriff to enforce their own orders," said Connecticut entomologist Neely Turner. The most flagrant abuses go unchecked in both state and federal agencies.

It is not my contention that chemical insecticides must never be used. I do contend that we have put poisonous and biologically potent chemicals indiscriminately into the hands of persons largely or wholly ignorant of their potentials for harm. We have subjected enormous numbers of people to contact with these poisons, without their consent and often without their knowledge. If the Bill of Rights contains no guarantee that a citizen shall be secure against lethal poisons distributed either by private individuals or by public officials, it is surely only because our forefathers, despite their considerable wisdom and foresight, could conceive of no such problem.

I contend, furthermore, that we have allowed these chemicals to be used with little or no advance investigation of their effect on soil, water, wildlife, and man himself. Future generations are unlikely to condone our lack of prudent concern for the integrity of the natural world that supports all life.

There is still very limited awareness of the nature of the threat. This is an era of specialists, each of whom sees his own problem and is unaware of or intolerant of the larger frame into which it fits. It is also an era dominated by industry, in which the right to make a dollar at whatever cost is seldom challenged. When the public protests, confronted with some obvious evidence of damaging results of pesticide applications, it is fed little tranquilizing pills of half truth. We urgently need an end to these false assurances, to the sugar coating of unpalatable facts. It is the public that is being asked to assume the risks that the insect controllers calculate. The public must decide whether it wishes to continue on the present road, and it can do so only when in full possession of the facts. In the words of Jean Rostand, "The obligation to endure gives us the right to know."

(1962)

### Robert Wernick

# Let's Spoil the Wilderness

A rancher in the hills north of San Francisco saw two bald eagles, one day last spring, killing his lambs. He did what King Agamemnon, or King David, or any other sheepman mentioned favorably in our history books would have done. He killed the eagles. But this is 20th-century

America, and there is a law against harming any feather on a bald eagle. The rancher was arrested, and for days he was subjected to vile abuse in the press. Right-thinking people rained down such vituperation that you would have thought he had been caught molesting little girls or sending parcels to the Viet Cong. For right-thinking people he was guilty of a gruesome crime. What crime? He was spoiling the wilderness.

The trumpeting voice of the wilderness lover is heard at great distances these days. He is apt to be a perfectly decent person, if hysterical. And the causes which excite him so are generally worthy. Who can really find a harsh word for him as he strives to save Lake Erie from the sewers of Cleveland, save the redwoods from the California highway engineers, save the giant rhinoceros from the Somali tribesmen who kill those noble beasts to powder their horns into what they fondly imagine is a wonder-working aphrodisiac?

Worthy causes, indeed, but why do those who espouse them have to be so shrill and intolerant and sanctimonious? What right do they have to insinuate that anyone who does not share their passion for the whooping crane is a Philistine and a slob? From the gibberish they talk, you would think the only way to save the bald eagle is to dethrone human reason.

I would like to ask what seems to me an eminently reasonable question: *Why shouldn't we spoil the wilderness?*

Have these people ever stopped to think what the wilderness is? It is precisely what man has been fighting against since he began his painful, awkward climb to civilization. It is the dark, the formless, the terrible, the old chaos which our fathers pushed back, which surrounds us yet, which will engulf us all in the end. It is held at bay by constant vigilance, and when the vigilance slackens it swoops down for a melodramatic revenge, as when the jungle took over Chichen Itza in Yucatán or lizards took over Jamshid's courtyard in Persia. It lurks in our own hearts, where it breeds wars and oppressions and crimes. Spoil it! Don't you wish we could?

Of course, when the propagandists talk about unspoiled wilderness, they don't mean anything of that sort. What they mean by wilderness is a kind of grandiose picnic ground, in the Temperate Zone, where the going is rough enough to be challenging but not literally murderous, where hearty folk like Supreme Court Justice Douglas and Interior Secretary Udall can hike and hobble through spectacular scenery, with a helicopter hovering in the dirty old civilized background in case a real emergency comes up.

Well, the judge and the Secretary and their compeers are all estimable people, and there is no reason why they should not be able to satisfy their urge for primitive living. We ought to recognize, however, that other people have equally strong and often equally legitimate urges to build roads, dig mines, plow up virgin land, erect cities. Such people used to be called pioneers; now they are apt to be called louts. At all events, we are faced with sets of conflicting drives, and it is up to us to make a rational choice among them.

The trouble is, it is difficult to make a rational choice when one of the parties insists on wrapping all its discourse in a vile metaphysical fog.

One cannot talk of eagles, for instance, without being told by the wilderness folk that man, vile man, has no right to destroy one of God's beautiful creatures; that the bald eagle, besides being the symbol of the United States of America, represents all the will to be free and wide-ranging quest which made life worth living for our forefathers; and finally, that killing eagles upsets the balance of nature.

These aren't arguments; they are 100 percent nonsense. The most savage nature lover thinks nothing of vindictively squashing one of God's beautiful creatures when the creature happens to be an anopheles mosquito. And yet the mosquito in every respect but size is just as awe-inspiring, just as beautiful, just as free as any eagle. The individual eagle you see stretching his great wings as he searches for a fish or a lamb to eat is quite unaware that he is a symbol of anything. And quite rightly too: The eagle on our Great Seal is a perfectly mythical creature, and could go on being a symbol even if all eagles in the land were exterminated. The British, after all, have got on quite well without Acts of Parliament to protect lions and unicorns.

As for the balance of nature, this is simply an arty phrase to denote the status quo, whatever exists in a certain place at a certain time. In truth, the status quo is always changing. On our Great Plains, for example, the balance of nature consisted for centuries of immense herds of bison browsing thunderously on buffalo grass. In the late 18th century the balance consisted of Indians, who had acquired Spanish horses, slaughtering bison. Nowadays it consists of strip-farming, beauty shops, filling stations, beer cans, etc.

Naturally some balances are more desirable for interested parties than others. From the point of view of the bison, the balance of 1750 was infinitely preferable to any balance afterward; the Indians might have preferred the balance of 1800. From the point of view of Mother Nature, it doesn't seem to make the slightest difference. In her bloody, blundering way, she has been lurching along for millions of years, wiping out whole species, drowning whole continents, burning, ravaging, destroying. Our rifles and DDT are puny compared to the forces that annihilated dinosaurs and the multicolored world of the trilobites.

The most we can do, it seems to me, is to look after our own interests as best we can, and no more consider the feelings of the eagle and the rhinoceros than they consider ours.

Of course, we make mistakes, and hurt our own interests, as when ranchers kill off coyotes and are then visited with plagues of jackrabbits. But conservationists can make mistakes too. When they saved the beaver in Montana not long ago, the busy little creatures chewed down so many trees that they caused disastrous floods.

There is actually one legitimate reason for saving the wilderness, and that is that some people enjoy it and feel thrilled and ennobled by it. They have a taste for desolate landscapes and lonely nights under the stars. There is nothing wrong with such a taste. Everyone, everywhere, in whatever culture or society, needs something to help transcend the daily round of work and grief and boredom. Some find such transcendence by driving at illegal speeds on freeways, some by chomping on sacred mushrooms. An exultant thrashing through the wilderness may be a rich human experience—not quite so rich perhaps as reading the book of Isaiah or visiting the Parthenon, but certainly more varied, and more deeply satisfying than sniffing glue.

However, let us not lose sight of the fact that the wilderness taste is definitely a minority taste. Tamed and sanitized as modern wilderness areas are apt to be, with their almost total lack of large predatory animals and hostile Indians, they are still much too sharp of fang and claw for the vast majority of people—people who have worked hard for their comforts and don't see why they should give them up for a mosquito-clouded view and an icy dip in a mountain stream.

Wilderness lovers are a phenomenon of modern time; they are not tolerated in primitive cultures; the Bible doesn't have a good word to say for Ishmael. They breed in highly developed civilizations, where men have become bored with excessive cultivation and refinement. They affect old rumpled clothes, unshaved jaws, salty language; they spit and sweat and boast of their friendship with aborigines. But this is all veneer: Underneath, they are decadents, aristocrats, snobs.

I find something quite appealing about this particular form of snobbery. Compared to folk-song snobs, foreign-movie snobs and plain old social snobs, wilderness snobs present a fine manly appearance, and I wish them all joy as they follow the spoor of the wolverine and unroll their sleeping bags under the giant ponderosa.

But I urge them to avoid the great vice of their kind, which is megalomania. A man who has been infected with the wilderness lust is not satisfied with one stretch of forest, or one uncluttered mountainside. He wants hundreds of square miles of thicket and coulee and beaver dam and white water; and he wants them all for himself.

In the full euphoria which attends this fever, all ordinary human connections are apt to be broken. You struggle, slipping angrily through chalky rock and prickly pear, to the top of a ridge, and before you are miles of sagebrush flats, with white streaks of alkali, dry lakes, purple rocks, an immensity of desolation. Your heart fills with delight and then you catch sight of a rickety service station at a forsaken crossroads, and all the beauty drains out of the scene. A single beer can will spoil a square mile of woods; and as for the lovers' initials and fraternity Greek letters painted on rocks, it takes but one such pitiful imprint of humanity to spoil a mountain.

This is very wrongheaded, though it must be admitted that there is something grandiose about the wilderness lover in full flight. No one who reads it can forget the passage in which John Muir, the great American naturalist, describes how, at the height of a tempest in the high Sierras, he lashed himself to the trunk of a giant pine and for hours heaved and swung with the great tree, while the wind howled and whole forested mountainsides quivered to its blasts. The scene has a splendid absurdity about it.

I am reliably informed that it is impossible to duplicate Muir's experience in present-day California. There is not a high tree left in the state from which you can't see the lights of cars stabbing through the night on some freeway or other. And of course that spoils everything. For the particular sensation, the *frisson*, that John Muir was after, was not simply a physical one—you could get the same by lashing yourself to the mast on the Empire State Building. It was the exultant triumphant feeling of riding the blasts, of soaring over a vast stretch of pure convulsed nature, and doing it alone, without another human soul in reach of sight or sound.

I am sure that in losing opportunities for this sensation, Californians have suffered a great loss. It is, however, a loss which I am afraid we will have to put up with. The population of California, as of the world, is growing; this population is becoming more affluent and more mobile, and as it expands and covers the land with its detritus of motels and soda bottles, there are just not enough square miles left to satisfy the wilderness lovers.

I suggest to these worthy people that they bow gracefully to the inevitable and model their conduct on that of the kings of England. William the Conqueror and his descendants were great wilderness lovers, and they turned half of England into royal forests where, through the brambles and under giant oaks, they could ride for giddy days chasing the red stag and the wild boar; and any Saxon hind who came sneaking in looking for firewood or a rabbit had his ears, or worse, chopped off.

Grudgingly over the centuries the kings gave up this demi-paradise to the uncouth people of England, who insisted on parceling it out into grubby farms and grimy factories. The loss was irreparable, but the royal huntsmen prudently swallowed their grief, and sought a replica of their old pleasures on safaris in East Africa.

Just so our modern wilderness lovers may soon have to abandon the whole North American continent to the suburbanite hordes. Barring a nuclear war, which would bring back the wilderness with a vengeance, they will have to spread their wings a little, and indulge their special tastes in Spitzbergen and the mountains of New Guinea. And if the tides of civilization lap eventually over these too, there will soon be available excursion rockets to Mars and Alpha Centauri. And there should be enough unspoiled wilderness out there for anybody's taste.

(1965)

*William Stafford*

# A Family Turn

All her Kamikaze friends admired my aunt,
their leader, charmed in vinegar,
a woman who could blaze with such white blasts
as Lawrence's that lit Arabia.
Her mean opinions bent her hatpins.

We'd take a ride in her old car
that ripped like Sherman through society:
Main Street's oases sheltered no one
when she pulled up at Thirty-first
and whirled that Ford for another charge.

We swept headlines from under rugs, names
all over town, which I learned her way, by heart,
and blazed with love that burns because it's real.
With a turn that's our family's own,
she'd say, "Our town is not the same" —

Pause — "And it's never been."

(1966)

*Paul Simon*

# The 59th Street Bridge Song (Feelin' Groovy)

Slow down,
You move too fast.
You got to make the morning last.
Just kickin' down the cobble stones,
Lookin' for fun and feelin' Groovy.

Hello lamppost,
What-cha knowin'
I've come to watch your flowers growin'.
Ain't-cha got no rhymes for me?
Doot'in' doo-doo, feelin' Groovy.

Got no deeds to do,
No promises to keep.
I'm dappled and drowsy and ready to sleep.
Let the morningtime drop all its petals on me.
Life, I love you.
All is Groovy.

(1966)

**Edwin Godsey**

# Hoppy

When Mary pulled the sorrel's reins from Stephen
The stunt man's hands, swung her buckskin squaw's skirt
Over, leaned up into his neck and by God
Was gone, Morris began shouting: "What are
You doing? Is she ruining me? Cut!
Hey, Sweetheart! Somebody grab that woman. Cut!
She shouldn't be galloping in it here! Cut!"
I was the camera jockey on this series.
We took her last frames going over the rise.
Guitars were to volume up there for *The End*
With boys back here all lithe as cats, leaning
Against the fence and singing "Tumbleweed"
While Hoppy turned, waved, and rode away.

It was his riding off like that that got her,
I guess. It must have made the girl forget
Hoppy was phony. It's hard to understand, though.
She'd been around. She knew the camera angles.
You would say this one had quit pulling taffy.
One time I took her out myself. Just once.
She was O.K. – a little hard is all.
But that was back before they disappeared.
Way back before the war. You never know
About a person. Some people get mixed up.

I could have used a Hoppy – Oh, my God –
At Anzio. Oh, you'd have been great, Hoppy,
The way you jingle-jumped from boulders, bullets
Whining in ricochet but plugged your ten

And came out clean ("Move in for the close-up, William"),
And gee-whiz coursed the outlaws through the hills,
Leaped on them horseback, rolled into the gulches
And whipped them silly in the sound effects.


Maybe she thought he was the real thing or
Something like that. It's hard to understand, though—
Conestoga wagons, whiskey brawls,
Gold miners, Sioux with smuggled Winchesters
(Who'd take your scalp), the gunfights at high noon.
But she was safe there, even in that wild land.


It's interesting to think what they said when
She caught up with him. Hoppy would grin and nod:
"You keep a sharp eye out for Indians, Ma'am."
And she, "At last, I've found you, Hoppy. Hoppy,
I love you." "But Ma'am," he'd say, "no epic heroes
Have time for love—I mean, the family kind.
I can't be different. It's mostly killing here.
A hard country, here, to live in." "Better,"
She'd say. And he, "But this is no place for a
Woman or child." "Why it's a good place, Hoppy,
A good place. We'll have sons—trust me—more than
The sands of the desert. And every one a hero.
I've seen the signs." "We ought to make camp soon . . ."
(What could he say?) "You understand you'll have
To keep a sharp eye out." They'd build a campfire,
Drink coffee, eat sourdough hotcakes, and hear coyotes.
It wouldn't be as easy as a motel.


So all in buckskin love went riding on
Somewhere. At least they never reappeared.
Old actors say they ride the desert still
(At times they see a family resemblance
In one of the young crew but never so soft-
Spoken or beautiful as Hoppy was)—
She and the hero with the tall black Stetson
And easy grin of a boy, on the white steed.
They say they ride toward sunset by the mesquite,
Through the arroyos and beneath saguaros
That stand like giants in the land: Clip-clop,
Clippity, clippity, clippity, where the dust
Splashes like pools of water from those hoofs,
And twilight coming on in El Dorado.

It's nice to think like that, but what I think is
They ran into trouble at Los Alamos
Back in the forties, and needed to move fast
("Ma'am, what in hell is that?") and didn't make it—
And lost the way I lost at Anzio.

(1967)

## Zulfikar Ghose

# The Preservation of Landscapes

Again summer journeys across England
take me past landscapes become familiar
with five years' travelling. The country comes
alive again with its beeches and elms,
composing its prettiness in my mind
with a fleeting abstraction of colour.

Gliders, pinned to the sky above Cambridge,
are still as eagles for a moment, then
are swift as the homeward flight of swallows.
I drive across the flat Cambridgeshire farms
and find the sun absorbed in a lonely
colloquy with the land, bargaining growth.

The train does ninety on the run between
Leicester and Derby, leaps across the Trent,
and, as a plane overshoots a runway,
briefly avoids industrial Midlands
to nibble through pastureland, devouring
the coarse grass with the quickness of locusts.

Dark pine-forests on the road to Portsmouth;
aspens, whose leaves catch the breeze and the light
as do sequins on a hat at Ascot,
and the gay ash-trees on the road to Bath;
and the fields, the fields are like coloured bits
of paper pasting England on my mind.

I share the anxiety of Englishmen
about England, prizing each field, each tree,
each tuft of grass above the incursions
of concrete and steel. O, sad, sad, England!
The beeches in East Riding, too, among the moors,
are yellow with the dust from upturned roads.

And yet I would rather have steel, rather
go giddy on winding car-park buildings
than look at the fiercely sunlit landscapes
of Southeast Asia where foreign jets
have cut the jungle for airstrips and the earth
is cleaved at the centre, deflowered with bombs.

(1967)

# Geography Lesson

When the jet sprang into the sky,
it was clear why the city
had developed the way it had,
seeing it scaled six inches to the mile.

There seemed an inevitability
about what on ground had looked haphazard,
unplanned and without style
when the jet sprang into the sky.

When the jet reached ten thousand feet,
it was clear why the country
had cities where rivers ran
and why the valleys were populated.
The logic of geography —
that land and water attracted man —
was clearly delineated
when the jet reached ten thousand feet.

When the jet rose six miles high,
it was clear that the earth was round
and that it had more sea than land.

But it was difficult to understand
that the men on the earth found
causes to hate each other, to build
walls across cities and to kill.
From that height, it was not clear why.

(1967)

*Lynn White, Jr.*

# The Historical Roots of Our Ecological Crisis

A conversation with Aldous Huxley not infrequently put one at the receiving end of an unforgettable monologue. About a year before his lamented death he was discoursing on a favorite topic: Man's unnatural treatment of nature and its sad results. To illustrate his point he told how, during the previous summer, he had returned to a little valley in England where he had spent many happy months as a child. Once it had been composed of delightful grassy glades; now it was becoming overgrown with unsightly brush because the rabbits that formerly kept such growth under control had largely succumbed to a disease, myxomatosis, that was deliberately introduced by the local farmers to reduce the rabbits' destruction of crops. Being something of a Philistine, I could be silent no longer, even in the interests of great rhetoric. I interrupted to point out that the rabbit itself had been brought as a domestic animal to England in 1176, presumably to improve the protein diet of the peasantry.

All forms of life modify their contexts. The most spectacular and benign instance is doubtless the coral polyp. By serving its own ends, it has created a vast undersea world favorable to thousands of other kinds of animals and plants. Ever since man became a numerous species he has affected his environment notably. The hypothesis that his fire-drive method of hunting created the world's great grasslands and helped to exterminate the monster mammals of the Pleistocene from much of the globe is plausible, if not proved. For 6 millennia at least, the banks of the lower Nile have been a human artifact rather than the swampy African jungle which nature, apart from man, would have made it. The Aswan Dam, flooding 5000 square miles, is only the latest stage in a long process. In many regions terracing or irrigation, overgrazing, the cutting of forests by Romans to build ships to fight Carthaginians or by Crusaders to solve the logistics problems of their expeditions, have profoundly changed some ecologies. Observation that the French land-scape falls into two basic types, the open fields of the north and the *bocage* of the south and west, inspired Marc Bloch to undertake his classic study of medieval agricultural methods. Quite unintentionally, changes in human ways often affect nonhuman nature. It has been noted, for example, that the advent of the automobile eliminated huge flocks of sparrows that once fed on the horse manure littering every street.

The history of ecologic change is still so rudimentary that we know little about what really happened, or what the results were. The extinction of the European aurochs as late as 1627 would seem to have been a simple case of overenthusiastic hunting. On more intricate matters it often is impossible to find solid information. For a thousand years or more the Frisians and Hollanders have been pushing back the North Sea, and the process is culminating in our own time in the reclamation of the Zuider Zee. What, if any, species of animals, birds, fish, shore life, or plants have died out in the process? In their epic combat with Neptune have the Netherlanders overlooked ecological values in such a way that the quality of human life in the Netherlands has suffered? I cannot discover that the questions have ever been asked, much less answered.

People, then, have often been a dynamic element in their own environment, but in the present state of historical scholarship we usually do not know exactly when, where, or with what effects man-induced changes came. As we enter the last third of the 20th century, however, concern for the problem of ecologic backlash is mounting feverishly. Natural science, conceived as the effort to understand the nature of things, had flourished in several eras and among several peoples. Similarly there had been an age-old accumulation of technological skills, sometimes growing rapidly, sometimes slowly. But it was not until about four generations ago that Western Europe and North America arranged a marriage between science and technology, a union of the theoretical and the empirical approaches to our natural environment. The emergence in widespread practice of the Baconian creed that scientific knowledge means technological power over nature can scarcely be dated before about 1850, save in the chemical industries, where it is anticipated in the 18th century. Its acceptance as a normal pattern of action may mark the greatest event in human history since the invention of agriculture, and perhaps in nonhuman terrestrial history as well.

Almost at once the new situation forced the crystallization of the novel concept of ecology; indeed, the word *ecology* first appeared in the English language in 1873. Today, less than a century later, the impact of our race upon the environment has so increased in force that it has changed in essence. When the first cannons were fired, in the early 14th century, they affected ecology by sending workers scrambling to the forests and mountains for more potash, sulfur, iron ore, and charcoal, with some resulting erosion and deforestation. Hydrogen bombs are of a different order: a war fought with them might alter the genetics of all life on this planet. By 1285 London had a smog problem arising from the burning of soft coal, but our present combustion of fossil fuels threatens to change the chemistry of the globe's atmosphere as a whole, with consequences which we are only beginning to guess. With the population explosion, the carcinoma of planless urbanism, the now geological deposits of sewage and garbage, surely no creature other than man has ever managed to foul its nest in such short order.

There are many calls to action, but specific proposals, however worthy as individual items, seem too partial, palliative, negative: ban the bomb, tear down the billboards, give the Hindus contraceptives and tell them to eat their sacred cows. The simplest solution to any suspect change is, of course, to stop it, or, better yet, to revert to a romanticized past: make those ugly gasoline stations look like Anne Hathaway's cottage or (in the Far West) like ghost-town saloons. The "wilderness area" mentality invariably advocates deep-freezing an ecology, whether San Gimignano or the High Sierra, as it was before the first Kleenex was dropped. But neither atavism nor prettification will cope with the ecologic crisis of our time.

What shall we do? No one yet knows. Unless we think about fundamentals, our specific measures may produce new backlashes more serious than those they are designed to remedy.

As a beginning we should try to clarify our thinking by looking, in some historical depth, at the presuppositions that underlie modern technology and science. Science was traditionally aristocratic, speculative, intellectual in intent; technology was lower-class, empirical, action-oriented. The quite sudden fusion of these two, towards the middle of the 19th century, is surely related to the slightly prior and contemporary democratic revolutions which, by reducing social barriers, tended to assert a functional unity of brain and hand. Our ecologic crisis is the product of an emerging, entirely novel, democratic culture. The issue is whether a democratized world can survive its own implications. Presumably we cannot unless we rethink our axioms.

## The Western Traditions of Technology and Science

One thing is so certain that it seems stupid to verbalize it: both modern technology and modern science are distinctively *Occidental*. Our technology has absorbed elements from all over the world, notably from China; yet everywhere today, whether in Japan or in Nigeria, successful technology is Western. Our science is the heir to all the sciences of the past, especially perhaps to the work of the great Islamic scientists of the Middle Ages, who so often outdid the ancient Greeks in skill and perspicacity: al-Rāzī in medicine, for example; or ibn-al-Haytham in optics; or Omar Khayyám in mathematics. Indeed, not a few works of such geniuses seem to have vanished in the original Arabic and to survive only in medieval Latin translations that helped to lay the foundations for later Western developments. Today, around the globe, all significant science is Western in style and method, whatever the pigmentation or language of the scientists.

A second pair of facts is less well recognized because they result from quite recent historical scholarship. The leadership of the West, both in technology and in science, is far older than the so-called Scientific Revolution of the 17th century or the so-called Industrial Revolution of the 18th century. These terms are in fact outmoded and obscure the true nature of what they try to describe—significant stages in two long and separate developments. By A.D. 1000 at the latest—and perhaps, feebly, as much as 200 years earlier—the West began to apply water power to industrial processes other than milling grain. This was followed in the late 12th century by the harnessing of wind power. From simple beginnings, but with remarkable consistency of style, the West rapidly expanded its skills in the development of power machinery, labor-saving devices, and automation. Those who doubt should contemplate that most monumental achievement in the history of automation: the weight-driven mechanical clock, which appeared in two forms in the early 14th century. Not in craftsmanship but in basic technological capacity, the Latin West of the later Middle Ages far outstripped its elaborate, sophisticated, and esthetically magnificent sister cultures, Byzantium and Islam. In 1444 a great Greek ecclesiastic, Bessarion, who had gone to Italy, wrote a letter to a prince in Greece. He is amazed by the superiority of Western ships, arms, textiles, glass. But above all he is astonished by the spectacle of waterwheels sawing timbers and pumping the bellows of blast furnaces. Clearly, he had seen nothing of the sort in the Near East.

By the end of the 15th century the technological superiority of Europe was such that its small, mutually hostile nations could spill out over all the rest of the world, conquering, looting, and colonizing. The symbol of this technological superiority is the fact that Portugal, one of the weakest states of the Occident, was able to become, and to remain for a century, mistress of the East Indies. And we must remember that the technology of Vasco da Gama and Albuquerque was built by pure empiricism, drawing remarkably little support or inspiration from science.

In the present-day vernacular understanding, modern science is supposed to have begun in 1543, when both Copernicus and Vesalius published their great works. It is no derogation of their accomplishments, however, to point out that such structures as the *Fabrica* and the *De revolutionibus* do not appear overnight. The distinctive Western tradition of science, in fact, began in the late 11th century with a massive movement of translation of Arabic and Greek scientific works into

Latin. A few notable books—Theophrastus, for example—escaped the West's avid new appetite for science, but within less than 200 years effectively the entire corpus of Greek and Muslim science was available in Latin, and was being eagerly read and criticized in the new European universities. Out of criticism arose new observation, speculation, and increasing distrust of ancient authorities. By the late 13th century Europe had seized global scientific leadership from the faltering hands of Islam. It would be as absurd to deny the profound originality of Newton, Galileo, or Copernicus as to deny that of the 14th century scholastic scientists like Buridan or Oresme on whose work they built. Before the 11th century, science scarcely existed in the Latin West, even in Roman times. From the 11th century onward, the scientific sector of Occidental culture has increased in a steady crescendo.

Since both our technological and our scientific movements got their start, acquired their character, and achieved world dominance in the Middle Ages, it would seem that we cannot understand their nature or their present impact upon ecology without examining fundamental medieval assumptions and developments.

## Medieval View of Man and Nature

Until recently, agriculture has been the chief occupation even in "advanced" societies; hence, any change in methods of tillage has much importance. Early plows, drawn by two oxen, did not normally turn the sod but merely scratched it. Thus, cross-plowing was needed and fields tended to be squarish. In the fairly light soils and semiarid climates of the Near East and Mediterranean, this worked well. But such a plow was inappropriate to the wet climate and often sticky soils of northern Europe. By the latter part of the 7th century after Christ, however, following obscure beginnings, certain northern peasants were using an entirely new kind of plow, equipped with a vertical knife to cut the line of the furrow, a horizontal share to slice under the sod, and a moldboard to turn it over. The friction of this plow with the soil was so great that it normally required not two but eight oxen. It attacked the land with such violence that cross-plowing was not needed, and fields tended to be shaped in long strips.

In the days of the scratch-plow, fields were distributed generally in units capable of supporting a single family. Subsistence farming was the presupposition. But no peasant owned eight oxen: to use the new and more efficient plow, peasants pooled their oxen to form large plow-teams, originally receiving (it would appear) plowed strips in proportion to their contribution. Thus, distribution of land was based no longer on the needs of a family but, rather, on the capacity of a power machine to till the earth. Man's relation to the soil was profoundly changed. Formerly man had been part of nature; now he was the exploiter of nature. Nowhere else in the world did farmers develop any analogous agricultural implement. Is it coincidence that modern technology, with its ruthlessness toward nature, has so largely been produced by descendants of these peasants of northern Europe?

This same exploitive attitude appears slightly before A.D. 830 in Western illustrated calendars. In older calendars the months were shown as passive personifications. The new Frankish calendars, which set the style for the Middle Ages, are very different: they show men coercing the world around them – plowing, harvesting, chopping trees, butchering pigs. Man and nature are two things, and man is master.

These novelties seem to be in harmony with larger intellectual patterns. What people do about their ecology depends on what they think about themselves in relation to things around them. Human ecology is deeply conditioned by beliefs about our nature and destiny – that is, by religion. To Western eyes this is very evident in, say, India or Ceylon. It is equally true of ourselves and of our medieval ancestors.

The victory of Christianity over paganism was the greatest psychic revolution in the history of our culture. It has become fashionable today to say that, for better or worse, we live in "the post-Christian age." Certainly the forms of our thinking and language have largely ceased to be Christian, but to my eye the substance often remains amazingly akin to that of the past. Our daily habits of action, for example, are dominated by an implicit faith in perpetual progress which was unknown either to Greco-Roman antiquity or to the Orient. It is rooted in, and is indefensible apart from, Judeo-Christian teleology. The fact that Communists share it merely helps to show what can be demonstrated on many other grounds: that Marxism, like Islam, is a Judeo-Christian heresy. We continue today to live, as we have lived for about 1700 years, very largely in a context of Christian axioms.

What did Christianity tell people about their relations with the environment?

While many of the world's mythologies provide stories of creation, Greco-Roman mythology was singularly incoherent in this respect. Like Aristotle, the intellectuals of the ancient West denied that the visible world had had a beginning. Indeed, the idea of a beginning was impossible in the framework of their cyclical notion of time. In sharp contrast, Christianity inherited from Judaism not only a concept of time as nonrepetitive and linear but also a striking story of creation. By gradual stages a loving and all-powerful God had created light and darkness, the heavenly bodies, the earth and all its plants, animals, birds, and fishes. Finally, God had created Adam and, as an afterthought, Eve to keep man from being lonely. Man named all the animals, thus establishing his dominance over them. God planned all of this explicitly for man's benefit and rule: no item in the physical creation had any purpose save to serve man's purposes. And, although man's body is made of clay, he is not simply part of nature: he is made in God's image.

Especially in its Western form, Christianity is the most anthropocentric religion the world has seen. As early as the 2nd century both Tertullian and Saint Irenaeus of Lyons were insisting that when God shaped Adam he was foreshadowing the image of the incarnate Christ, the Second Adam. Man shares, in great measure, God's transcendence of nature. Christianity, in aboslute contrast to ancient paganism and Asia's religions (except, perhaps, Zoroastrianism), not only established a dualism of man and nature but also insisted that it is God's will that man exploit nature for his proper ends.

At the level of the common people this worked out in an interesting way. In Antiquity every tree, every spring, every stream, every hill had its own *genius loci*, its guardian spirit. These spirits were accessible to men, but were very unlike men; centaurs, fauns, and mermaids show their ambivalence. Before one cut a tree, mined a mountain, or dammed a brook, it was important to placate the spirit in charge of that particular situation, and to keep it placated. By destroying pagan animism, Christianity made it possible to exploit nature in a mood of indifference to the feelings of natural objects.

It is often said that for animism the Church substituted the cult of saints. True; but the cult of saints is functionally quite different from animism. The saint is not *in* natural objects; he may have special shrines, but his citizenship is in heaven. Moreover, a saint is entirely a man; he can be approached in human terms. In addition to saints, Christianity of course also had angels and demons inherited from Judaism and perhaps, at one remove, from Zoroastrianism. But these were all as mobile as the saints themselves. The spirits *in* natural objects, which formerly had protected nature from man, evaporated. Man's effective monopoly on spirit in this world was confirmed, and the old inhibitions to the exploitation of nature crumbled.

When one speaks in such sweeping terms, a note of caution is in order. Christianity is a complex faith, and its consequences differ in differing contexts. What I have said may well apply to the medieval West, where in fact technology made spectacular advances. But the Greek East, a highly civilized realm of equal Christian devotion, seems to have produced no marked technological innovation after the late 7th century, when Greek fire was invented. The key to the contrast may perhaps be found in a difference in the tonality of piety and thought which students of comparative theology find between the Greek and the Latin Churches. The Greeks believed that sin was intellectual blindness, and that salvation was found in illumination, orthodoxy—that is, clear thinking. The Latins, on the other hand, felt that sin was moral evil, and that salvation was to be found in right conduct. Eastern theology has been intellectualist. Western theology has been voluntarist. The Greek saint contemplates; the Western saint acts. The implications of Christianity for the conquest of nature would emerge more easily in the Western atmosphere.

The Christian dogma of creation, which is found in the first clause of all the Creeds, has another meaning for our comprehension of today's ecologic crisis. By revelation, God had given man the Bible, the Book of Scripture. But since God had made nature, nature also must reveal the divine mentality. The religious study of nature for the better understanding of God was known as natural theology. In the early Church, and always in the Greek East, nature was conceived primarily as a symbolic system through which God speaks to men: the ant is a sermon to sluggards; rising flames are the symbol of the soul's aspiration. This view of nature was essentially artistic rather than scientific. While Byzantium preserved and copied great numbers of ancient Greek scientific texts, science as we conceive it could scarcely flourish in such an ambience.

However, in the Latin West by the early 13th century natural theology was following a very different bent. It was ceasing to be the decoding of the physical symbols of God's communication with man and was becoming the effort to understand God's mind by discovering how his creation operates. The rainbow was no longer simply a symbol of hope first sent to Noah after the Deluge: Robert Grosseteste, Friar Roger Bacon, and Theodoric of Freiberg produced startlingly sophisticated work on the optics of the rainbow, but they did it as a venture in religious understanding. From the 13th century onward, up to and including Leibnitz and Newton, every major scientist, in effect, explained his motivations in religious terms. Indeed, if Galileo had not been so expert an amateur theologian he would have got into far less trouble: the professionals resented his intrusion. And Newton seems to have regarded himself more as a theologian than as a scientist. It was not until the late 18th century that the hypothesis of God became unnecessary to many scientists.

It is often hard for the historian to judge, when men explain why they are doing what they want to do, whether they are offering real reasons or merely culturally acceptable reasons. The consistency with which scientists during the long formative centuries of Western science said that the task and the reward of the scientist was "to think God's thoughts after him" leads one to believe that this was their real motivation. If so, then modern Western science was cast in a matrix of Christian theology. The dynamism of religious devotion, shaped by the Judeo-Christian dogma of creation, gave it impetus.

## An Alternative Christian View

We would seem to be headed toward conclusions unpalatable to many Christians. Since both *science* and *technology* are blessed words in our contemporary vocabulary, some may be happy at the notions, first, that, viewed historically, modern science is an extrapolation of natural theology and, second, that modern technology is at least partly to be explained as an Occidental, voluntarist realization of the Christian dogma of man's transcendence of, and rightful mastery over, nature. But, as we now recognize, somewhat over a century ago science and technology—hitherto quite separate activities—joined to give mankind powers which, to judge by many of the ecologic effects, are out of control. If so, Christianity bears a huge burden of guilt.

I personally doubt that disastrous ecologic backlash can be avoided simply by applying to our problems more science and more technology. Our science and technology have grown out of Christian attitudes toward man's relation to nature which are almost universally held not only by Christians and neo-Christians but also by those who fondly regard themselves as post-Christians. Despite Copernicus, all the cosmos rotates around our little globe. Despite Darwin, we are *not*, in our hearts, part of the natural process. We are superior to nature, contemptuous of it, willing to use it for our slightest whim. The newly elected Governor of California, like myself a churchman but less troubled than I, spoke for the Christian tradition when he said (as is alleged), "when you've seen one redwood tree, you've seen them all." To a Christian a tree can be no more than a physical fact. The whole concept of the sacred grove is alien to Christianity and to the ethos of the West. For nearly 2 millennia Christian missionaries have been chopping down sacred groves, which are idolatrous because they assume spirit in nature.

What we do about ecology depends on our ideas of the man-nature relationship. More science and more technology are not going to get us out of the present ecologic crisis until we find a new religion, or rethink our old one. The beatniks, who are the basic revolutionaries of our time, show a sound instinct in their affinity for Zen Buddhism, which conceives of the man-nature relationship as very nearly the mirror image of the Christian view. Zen, however, is as deeply conditioned by Asian history as Christianity is by the experience of the West, and I am dubious of its viability among us.

Possibly we should ponder the greatest radical in Christian history since Christ: Saint Francis of Assisi. The prime miracle of Saint Francis is the fact that he did not end at the stake, as many of his left-wing followers did. He was so clearly heretical that a General of the Franciscan Order, Saint Bonaventura, a great and perceptive Christian, tried to suppress the early accounts of Franciscanism. The key to an understanding of Francis is his belief in the virtue of humility—not merely for the individual but for man as a species. Francis tried to depose man from his monarchy over creation and set up a democracy of all God's creatures. With him the ant is no longer simply a homily for the lazy, flames a sign of the thrust of the soul toward union with God; now they are Brother Ant and Sister Fire, praising the Creator in their own ways as Brother Man does in his.

Later commentators have said that Francis preached to the birds as a rebuke to men who would not listen. The records do not read so: he urged the little birds to praise God, and in spiritual ecstasy they flapped their wings and chirped rejoicing. Legends of saints, especially the Irish saints, had long told of their dealings with animals but always, I believe, to show their human dominance over creatures. With Francis it is different. The land around Gubbio in the Apennines was being ravaged by a fierce wolf. Saint Francis, says the legend, talked to the wolf and persuaded him of the error of his ways. The wolf repented, died in the odor of sanctity, and was buried in consecrated ground.

What Sir Steven Ruciman calls "the Franciscan doctrine of the animal soul" was quickly stamped out. Quite possibly it was in part inspired, consciously or unconsciously, by the belief in reincarnation held by the Cathar heretics who at that time teemed in Italy and southern France, and who presumably had got it originally from India. It is significant that at just the same moment, about 1200, traces of metempsychosis are found also in western Judaism, in the Provençal *Cabbala*. But Francis held neither to transmigration of souls nor to pantheism. His view of nature and of man rested on a unique sort of pan-psychism of all things animate and inanimate, designed for the glorification of their transcendent Creator, who, in the ultimate gesture of cosmic humility, assumed flesh, lay helpless in a manger, and hung dying on a scaffold.

I am not suggesting that many contemporary Americans who are concerned about our ecologic crisis will be either able or willing to counsel with wolves or exhort birds. However, the present increasing disruption of the global environment is the product of a dynamic technology and science which were originating in the Western medieval world against which Saint Francis was rebelling in so original a way. Their growth cannot be understood historically apart from distinctive attitudes toward nature which are deeply grounded in Christian dogma. The fact that most people do not think of these attitudes as Christian is irrelevant. No new set of basic values has been accepted in our society to displace those of Christianity. Hence we shall continue to have a worsening ecologic crisis until we reject the Christian axiom that nature has no reason for existence save to serve man.

The greatest spiritual revolutionary in Western history, Saint Francis, proposed what he thought was an alternative Christian view of nature and man's relation to it: he tried to substitute the idea of the equality of all creatures, including man, for the idea of man's limitless rule of creation. He failed. Both our present science and our present technology are so tinctured with orthodox Christian arrogance toward nature that no solution for our ecologic crisis can be expected from them alone. Since the roots of our trouble are so largely religious, the remedy must also be essentially religious, whether we call it that or not.

We must rethink and refeel our nature and destiny. The profoundly religious, but heretical, sense of the primitive Franciscans for the spiritual autonomy of all parts of nature may point a direction. I propose Francis as a patron saint for ecologists.

(1967)

*Glenn T. Seaborg*

# The Cybernetic Age: An Optimist's View

What we need is a computer that will tell us where all other computers are leading us. We have computers that make up corporation payrolls, review a nation's tax returns, diagnose diseases, help design, produce, and market new products, control air and auto traffic, operate bakeries, hire and fire, read and write, learn and teach, and even play Cupid — though fortunately not yet to other computers, just among people. But the ultimate computer that can assess the significance of all this has yet to be built and programed. This task is still left to humans.

And it is an incredibly difficult task. Why? Because the ultimate potential of the computer puts us to the test as human beings. It brings up questions we have lived with for centuries, but never have been asked to answer fully or act upon if we believed we knew the answers. It gives us new freedom and yet tremendous responsibilities which, if not acted upon, could result in a loss of almost all freedom. It presents us with choices and decisions of enormous consequences. It offers man a remarkable new chance to shape his own destiny, but asks him to be Godlike enough to select that destiny without much margin for error.

Let me project a few thoughts on how the computer may forge our future — and, more important, on some of the ideas and alternatives with which we must come to grips if we are going to control the direction of that future.

To begin with, I believe that cybernation — the complete adaptation of computer-like equipment to industrial, economic, and social activity — will represent a quantum jump in the extension of man. The Industrial Revolution amplified (and to a large extent replaced) man's muscle as a productive force. Still, a large percentage of our production resulted from the energies of man and beast. Today in the United States, only a fraction of 1 per cent of our productive power results from the physical energy of human beings or animals.

Springing from our Scientific Revolution of recent decades is what is being called a "Cybernetic Revolution." This revolution, which, comparatively speaking, is only in its infancy, amplifies (and will to a large extent replace) man's nervous system. Actually, this is an understatement because computers amplify the collective intelligence of men — the intelligence of society — and, while the effect of the sum of men's physical energies may be calculated, a totally different and compounded effect results from combining facts and ideas — the knowledge generated within a society or civilization. Add this effect to the productive capacity of the machine driven by an almost limitless energy source like the nucleus of the atom, and the resulting system can perform feats almost staggering to our imagination. With the fullest development of cybernation we could be faced with prospects that challenge our very relationships to such basic concepts as freedom and the nature of work and leisure.

Let me suggest a few random scenes from the coming Cybernetic Age which contain some significant implications. I will not vouch for the accuracy of these forecasts or try to predict the year they might occur, but perhaps you can imagine yourself in one of these three situations:

Situation No. 1: You have flown out of town on a business trip and upon arrival at your destination have a few spare hours in which to visit an old friend. At the airport you rent a car, or some other type of ground vehicle. The procedure for putting you in the driver's seat is simple and efficient. You place an identifying card containing your bank account number and a microfiche of your fingerprints in a slot, and the fingers of your free hand over a flat, innocent-looking plate. Within seconds you have been identified as the owner of the card and your credit rating has been checked. The keys to your rented car are released to you and you are on your way.

Driving through town you encounter a minimum of delay at the busiest hour because the traffic lights are controlled by computers. But, anxious to see your old friend, you step up your speed once you are on the outskirts of town and, without realizing it, you exceed the speed limit by a few miles an hour. You remain unaware of this violation until you return home, at which time you receive a notice of it and learn that the violation calls for a fine, which, you also learn, has already been charged to your bank account.

How did this happen? It was almost as simple as renting the car. An inconspicuous device clocked your speed and recorded your auto tags. It reported the violation to the owner of the vehicle whose own computer had your records at hand and instantly "turned you in." The computer operated by the long arm of the law had no difficulty in tracking down both you and your bank account, so justice was swift and complete.

You are fairly well conditioned to this sort of situation by now, but sometimes you have moments of doubt and anxiety about what happened. If someone, or something, was watching you that closely on the road, where else might they be watching you? What if the system was in error—if someone, somewhere, was "adjusting" it so as to create more violators and bring in a little more revenue? But paying the fine was far easier than trying to investigate that possibility, so you give up what you once considered a legitimate right. Furthermore, you've heard that next year they're installing systems which will automatically regulate your speed on those roads, so you won't have to worry about exceeding the limit. You won't have that worry—or choice.

I will not belabor the implications of this situation. I believe they speak for themselves. Let me move on to situation No. 2:

For several days you have not been feeling well, and you call your local health center for an appointment. You can remember when you used to call your doctor, but it's been many years since he's bothered with initial diagnoses, and he would be the first to admit he could not be as thorough or accurate as the health center.

At the center you give all the necessary information to a medical secretary, whose typewriter feeds it into a computer system. First comes your identification number, which automatically supplies the system with your previous medical history, then all your new complaints and symptoms. On the basis of the information given so far and a comparison with your previous history, the computer may venture an immediate diagnosis, but if it has any doubts— and it is a highly conservative computer—it recommends one or several diagnostic tests. The tests are conducted simply and efficiently with the aid of one or two capable medical technicians and a battery of equipment.

The battery of diagnostic equipment programs its findings into the central computer which already has your previous medical history and your current complaints. Within seconds, after the tests are completed, the system presents its full diagnosis. At the same time it also makes recommendation for treatment, perhaps printing out a prescription which can be filled before you leave the center.

Does your doctor ever see patients? The computer refers a few cases to him because of their unusual interest. The high level of medicine he practices now enables him to help these patients. Their cases also help him in his work with engineers to improve the design of diagnostic and treatment systems and to train the many medical technicians who are needed to handle the increased population.

As in the first situation, there are a multitude of implications in this project. But let me proceed to situation No. 3:

You are a key man in a company that produces certain products for the home. You feel quite fortunate because you have a creative job in a highly automated plant. Market surveys analyzed by computers tell the company of the need for a new product. You sit at a desk containing a large fluorescent screen and with an electronic "lightpen" draw your conception of the new product. As you design the product you "tell" the computerized screen what materials you want the product to be made of. The system coordinates the information from the lightpen with your other instructions. As you work, it guides you in your design by making recommendations, by showing you on command the stress and strain in various points of your design, by correcting your errors, by recommending alternatives and improvements.

When both you and the system are satisfied with your handiwork, you release the design for manufacture. The system has theoretically tested the product so that no initial sample or test model is necessary. It turns the design over to another department—probably other computers—which calculates and orders the materials necessary to produce it, sets up the required manufacturing equipment, and prepares the production schedule. You never see the product, but you know it has been turned out just the way you envisioned it. And how long will it be before the computer will make it without you?

To some people these three examples sound like science fiction. Others will refer to them as "windy futurism." But they are far from being either. Some of the devices and methods mentioned are already in existence and in practical use. Others are in the development stages. And many more are not only technically feasible but may someday become economically and socially acceptable.

What are some of the implications in these examples, and what bearing will they have on our future? Running through all three examples were many common features: depersonalization, a separation of man and product, a collapse of time, a further reduction of human work, and a shift of needs and skills. All of these offer both threats and promises. I believe that the promises will eventually override the threats, but not before they have made us face and solve a great many problems we have not had to face before. This in itself is going to account for a great deal of human growth.

There is no doubt that the Cybernetic Revolution is going to make us reexamine the relationship between our freedoms and our responsibilities within the framework of society and find ways to guarantee a maximum of freedom for the individual within a highly organized society.

Another way in which the Cybernetic Revolution is going to force considerable human growth is in making us take a more rational, long-range approach in handling our affairs—our relationships with our fellow man and with nature. We are beginning to learn that the crisis-to-crisis approach that we have been using to carry on will no longer work. Science and technology have shrunk time by increasing the rate of change and have forged the world into a global civilization capable of exerting tremendous forces in a highly interrelated sphere of activity. We must make the fullest use of tools like the computer to help us prevent chaos and self-annihilation in such a complex world.

Looking at the most positive aspects of the computer, and projecting how its growing applications might control and multiply the forces of science and technology, one can foresee some remarkable "alternative futures." The most promising among these would be an era of abundance for all mankind—one in which most goods and services are provided by cybernated systems. And this brings us to the most striking aspect of human growth that could take place as a result of the Cybernetic Revolution—the change in our relationship to labor and leisure.

For a good part of our history we have been shaping through the manipulation of wealth what Peter Drucker calls "economic man." Perhaps the Cybernetic Revolution will carry us to a new level of man—a higher level—at which we will enjoy different values. On this subject it is interesting to recall what the great economist John Maynard Keynes wrote in 1932 in his *Essays in Persuasion:*

When the accumulation of wealth is no longer of high social importance there will be great changes in the code of morals. We shall be able to rid ourselves of many of the pseudo-moral principles which have hag-ridden us for 200 years, by which we have exalted some of the most distasteful of human qualities into the position of highest values.

If the Cybernetic Revolution produces such a social millennium, a radical change in man's relationship to work would take place and the growth of leisure time would pose new problems to be solved.

As a result, our ideas on leisure would change drastically. Most people today do not recognize the true value of leisure. A little leisure has always been treasured, and there have been societies in which certain men and women lived in almost complete leisure, though at the expense of others' labor. But the idea of almost an entire civilization living in even relative leisure is beyond the comprehension of many of us and still frowned upon by most others.

A civilization equipped and educated to live in an era of relative leisure can bring about a new Golden Age—one without a slave base, other than those mechanical and cybernetic slaves produced by the ingenuity of a higher level of man. Such an age does not have to be, as a few predict, a civilization of drugged, purposeless people controlled by a small elite. But it could tragically become that, if we did nothing but let ourselves be swept along by some of the forces in motion today.

There are indications that some of these forces are just that overwhelming. There are also indications, however, that society is reacting to the "feedback" of certain personal and social effects of technology. This feedback is coming from more and more people in all levels of society and all walks of life. It is expressing an increasing uneasiness about the state of our personal and community lives in a highly materialistic society, a concern over the individual's role in the growing complexity and impersonalization of that society, a groping for "national purpose," and a feeling that the unity of man, referred to by poets and philosophers throughout the ages, is becoming a reality with immense psychological and physical implications.

To me, these feelings forecast the need for a huge re-evaluation of our goals and values, and it will be in our universities where such a re-evaluation will take place. Perhaps its seeds have already been sown in the current unrest on the campuses of many of our universities. From this re-evaluation, from the debates and soul-searching that take place, will evolve both a new understanding and reinforcement of those old ideals which are still valid, and new ideals and goals. Together they may provide us with something like a comprehensive philosophy of life to match the physical unity of mankind rapidly being fostered by today's science and technology.

If we can use this new philosophy to guide the great scientific and technological forces we have created, we could witness, possibly within a few decades, the equivalent of a new "human breakthrough"—an advance to a new stage of social development—one that was initiated by our reactions to today's trends.

In such a development the university, the greatest depository and dispenser of man's knowledge, should play a major role. In fact, I can see no other institution more logically equipped to be the central force in this evolutionary process, to develop, refine, and pass on to the new generations a new heritage of a higher level of mankind.

But if we are to carry out such a monumental task, many changes will probably have to take place in the universities and our educational system in general. One such change will involve reconciling the continuing importance of specialization with a growing need for interdisciplinary thinking—not only in science and technology, but in all areas of our economic, social, and human development. Specialization has been giving us increasing amounts of knowledge, but the world cries out today for more of something beyond knowledge—for *wisdom*.

All of this demands a new role of leadership from our educational system. Most of today's schools are involved to a great degree in serving the requirements of an industrial age, in fulfilling the needs of a society which has been only partly and indirectly of their making. In the future, this role will shift to one in which the nature of society is determined more by the thinking of the university, and in which the industrial community will tend to serve goals created by that thinking.

What we must look for from the universities is the development of an education that turns out individuals of the highest intellect and broadest outlook, able to understand man and machine, and live creatively with both. Such an education could not be expected in a four-year curriculum or even a six- or eight-year one. It would start as early as the beginning of school or sooner and involve continuing education of one type or another throughout a person's lifetime. And, as Robert Theobald indicates, education in the age of the Cybernetic Revolution would not be directed toward "earning a living" but toward "total living."

This is a big order involving imagination, energy, and bold leadership from the academic world. But the time is certainly ripe for this kind of leadership.

The coming Cybernetic Revolution which calls forth these new goals for education will also give education valuable new tools and technologies for pursuing them. The computer will make knowledge more accessible. It will perform miracles in compiling, organizing, and analyzing information. It should link the knowledge of the world's libraries and depositories of information into networks responding like a giant brain. And it should put at the fingertips of anyone who wishes to be a modern-day Faust all the knowledge he desires without selling his soul to the Devil.

Some believe that, in a cybernated utopia, human incentives will diminish and we will completely stagnate. I don't believe this will happen at all. New incentives will arise as man moves up to higher levels of needs. The quest for new knowledge will always grow. The domain of science is practically boundless. We are only beginning our adventures in space, and we still have a long way to go in understanding many things about this planet and the life on it.

Much has been said about the impersonalization caused by the growth of machines, but as a result of this growth I can see a new and better relationship arising among men. If in the past we have spent most of our time working with machines, serving and being served by them, naturally we feel a sense of isolation and alienation among them. But when machines have truly freed us from the necessity of physical work, perhaps we can better accept them for what they are and have the time to see and relate to other people in a different light. When we have more time to be with other people—not accidentally, on crowded buses, in elevators, in markets and offices, but in places of our own choosing at our own leisure—we may feel differently toward one another.

When we are less likely to be in competition with one another, much of the hypocrisy of society will vanish and more honest relationships will be formed. And, finally, when we can walk down the street—anywhere in the world—in a community free from want, where every human being has a sense of dignity not gained at the expense of others, we might not only walk free from fear but with a great feeling of exaltation.

If we can make the transition of living with and using the complex machines of the future in a *human-oriented* society, the rewards will be worth any effort we can make. As everyone knows, such a transition will not be easy, because it involves so much of what Eric Hoffer has called "The Ordeal of Change." But I think we will have to make such a transition eventually. We may have already begun to do so.

(1967)

*Joseph Wood Krutch*

# What the Year 2000 Won't Be Like

The end of a millennium doesn't come around very often. When the last one approached, many people are said to have believed that the world would come to an end in the year 1000. It didn't. But now that 2000 is only thirty-two years away, prophecy is again an active business – and it is upsetting to realize that had these prophecies been made in 1900 rather than in 1967, they would have been far less disturbed by problems then undreamed of. Neither World War I – in 1900 only fourteen, not thirty-two years away – nor World War II would have been anticipated, much less their consequences. Those of us who were alive then did not realize that we were living in a brief Indian summer, and this fact does not encourage confidence in the prophecies now being made.

Unless some of the more extravagant predictions concerning the near-abolition of death are fulfilled, I personally have no stake in any world even thirty-two years away. If, therefore, I have spent two or three weeks examining and comparing a number of serious prophecies, it is only out of curiosity – reinforced by such concern as one can have for that posterity which, as a cynic once remarked, "never did anything for me."

The prophecies are surprisingly numerous and elaborate, some from interdisciplinary teams, some from one or two bold individuals. Among the first are the ambitious symposium published in the Spring 1966 issue of *American Scholar* and the even more ambitious one reported in the 300 pages of the Summer 1967 issue of *Daedalus*, the journal of the American Academy of Arts and Sciences. Also known to me, though only in summary, are contributions from the American Institute of Planners. Notable among individual pronouncements are those by Buckminster Fuller in both the *American Scholar* and *Saturday Review* ["Report on the 'Geosocial Revolution,'"]; by René Dubos of the Rockefeller Institute; by Robert Sinsheimer, professor of biophysics at California Institute of Technology; by Vladimir Engelhardt, director of the biology section of the Russian Academy of Sciences; and a substantial volume by Anthony J. Wiener and Herman Kahn.

At a less sophisticated level there are the perennial articles in the women's magazines promising such contributions to the good life as cooking by electronic ovens and telephones with TV attachments. There is also the assurance given by an avant-garde magazine that we won't have to wait until the year 2000 for "festivals of pornographic films at Lincoln Center" – which the magazine promises to achieve by 1970. Nevertheless, I had best say right here that, having listened to the confident voices of at least a score of intelligent and informed men, I am no more sure than I was before what the future has in store for us.

There are so many conflicting forces making for so many possibilities that there are a dozen possible futures, no one of which seems certain enough to justify saying, "This is what it is going to be like."

Almost without exception, these prophecies depend upon projections or extrapolations which consist essentially of prolonging the curve with a dotted line on some chart. And though each prophet tends to concern himself almost exclusively with trends observable in his own field of study—with very little attention to the possibility that they will be increasingly influenced by other trends in other fields—I suppose that the majority would accept the list of those tendencies expected to continue as it was drawn up by a contributor to *Daedalus*. It includes the following: "an increasingly sensate (empirical, this-worldly, secular-humanistic, pragmatic, utilitarian, hedonistic) culture; world-wide industrialization and modernization; increasing affluence and (recently) leisure; population growth; urbanization and (soon) the growth of megalopolises; increased literacy and education; increased capacity for mass destruction."

Undoubtedly, these are, at the moment, trends which nearly anybody could have listed. But as soon as one begins to consider them critically, it becomes apparent that they are far from a reliable basis for predicting the future. The method itself disregards the fact that—fortunately—trends do not always continue. If they did, we would be justified in concluding, for instance, that smog and water pollution have obviously been increasing at a rate which makes it inevitable that we will either suffocate or die of intestinal disorders by the year so-and-so. Maybe we will, but possibly we won't. Conscious determination to resist the trend can be effective, though most of the prophets leave that out of consideration. In the second place, even if some of these trends continue to follow the curve drawn by the past and even if no new ones develop, the fact still remains that one trend may collide so disruptively with another that both cannot possibly continue. Surely, the consequences of "increased capacity for mass destruction" might reverse several of the other trends—including that toward population growth. And if certain other prophets are right in assuming that we will not use our increased capacity for mass destruction, then population growth might reverse other trends—for instance, the trend toward affluence.

Consider for a moment the contradictory estimates of the extent to which population pressures are a dominating factor. Secretary of the Interior Stewart Udall, in the article "Our Perilous Population Implosion" [see p. 186], protested eloquently against the fatalism which considers only how an overpopulated earth might be fed and housed, rather than how it might be controlled. Paul Sears pointed out several years ago that the most important problem in connection with space is not how to get to the moon but how to avoid running out of it here on earth, and he warned that "no known form of life has been observed to multiply without bumping up against limitations imposed by the space it occupies." Then he added that those who brush the problem aside by assuring us that technology will solve it forget that "the limitations involve not only quantity but quality."

All the projections of the population curve give us stupefying numbers expected to be reached even before the year 2000. A recent study of animal behavior proved that overcrowding produces psychotic behavior and certainly suggests that the reaction of human beings is probably similar—even that the crime explosion may be the result of the overcrowding to which we are already subject. René Dubos, microbiologist and experimental psychologist, warns us that survival depends not so much on our ability to avoid famine and sustain a minimal standard of living as on the quality and diversity of our urban environment. "Just as important [as physical requirements] for maintaining human life is an environment in which it is possible to satisfy the longing for quiet, privacy, independence, initiative, and open space. These are not luxuries but constitute real biological necessities." Yet not a single prophet that I have heard predicts that there will be any successful effort to contain population growth in the near future.

Just to add to our worries, Jean Bourgeis-Pichat, director of the French National Institute of Demographic Studies, declares that medical science will certainly raise problems other than increasing population pressures:

We are on the eve of an era in which society will have to decide who will survive and who will die. The new medical techniques are becoming so expensive that it soon will be impossible to give the benefit of them to everybody, and society will certainly not let money decide the issue. We will soon be confronted with a problem of choice, and when we say choice we mean a moral problem. Is our cultural state ready for that? I think this is open to doubt.

Compare these thoughts with Bernard Shaw's *Doctor's Dilemma.* On the other hand, all this is waved aside by one of the contributors to the *American Scholar*'s symposium with the casual pronouncement that "in hedonic potential, megalopolis is no more and no less a natural environment for man than Athens or a peasant village," and in the same issue of the magazine an assistant dean at Carnegie Tech assures us that the abundance produced by the "productivity revolution" is an assurance that the prospect for world-wide abundance and leisure "will not be delayed by more than a few generations by the population explosion." Buckminster Fuller makes this even simpler by assuring us that "the only real world problem is that of the performance per pound of the world's metals and other resources."

The probable incompatibility of the recognized trends is enough to make them a very shaky basis for predictions that claim to be more than a guess, but there is another reason why existing trends do not necessarily—in fact, very often do not—define the future. How safe is it to assume that something totally unexpected will not create some trend of the times more important than any now recognized? Would anyone have predicted Pasteur's great discovery thirty years before he made it—or insulin, or penicillin? Very few physicists would have predicted thirty-two years before Pearl Harbor that atomic fission would be achieved so soon. Yet this last development was probably the most fateful of all the events of the twentieth century—as well as, perhaps, one of the most horrible of all of the possible solutions of the population problem.

And what of the so-called conquest of space? To some, including educator and writer Willy Ley, it promises the solution of most of our problems. Others may be more inclined to agree with Loren Eiseley that the wealth and creative intelligence being invested in it may constitute a public sacrifice equal to the building of the pyramids. They may then remember that the pyramids were responsible for the otherwise incomprehensible fact that, though what we would now call the national income of Egypt was very great, the majority of its people lived in abject poverty. On the other hand, it is perhaps equally probable that the recognition of the economic burden, or even simple disillusion with the results, may, even before the year 2000, make the obsession with outer space remembered only as a temporary folly.

For all I or anybody else can know, the increasing taste for violence, both public and private—both for gain and for fun—may tell us more about the future than any of the other trends, though I do not remember that it was ever cited as being significant by any of the prophets I read. What of LSD as an invention possibly as important as Pasteur's discovery or penicillin or insulin? The prophets, moreover, for the most part take no account of those intangibles—mental, moral, or emotional—which some are probably quite apt to dismiss as mere by-products of economic and social conditions. Are McLuhanism and the hippie philosophies only, as I assume, fleeting phenomena? If they are not, who can measure the possible effect of the hippies' rejection of society or the McLuhanites' scorn for the word?

Based on most of the prophecies I have consulted, one would hardly suspect the existence of such phenomena as the existentialist's denial of meaning in the universe and of external sanctions for any moral code. Neither, to descend to a lower level, would one meet with any recognition of the possible significance and consequences of that enormous appetite for pornography, the mere existence of which seems to me to be more important than the question of whether it should or should not be regulated by law. Nevertheless, the quality of life in the year 2000 may depend as much upon such beliefs, attitudes, and faiths as it does upon the trends recognized by most of the prophets.

The quality of life—that is precisely what seems to be almost entirely left out of consideration in many prophecies. In many of them, the nearest that one comes to even a reference to the concept of a good life is that declaration previously quoted concerning the "hedonic potential of megalopolis," and, even in this case, the acceptance of such a term as more meaningful than, say, either "the prospect for happiness" or "the possibility of a good life" seems to me in itself likely to have an influence upon the kind of life we are preparing for the future.

So, too, I suspect, might be the persistence of two trends which I have observed in the majority of the prophets which are often characteristic of those who are afraid of being accused of unscientific attitudes unless they assume: 1) that the past not only suggests but actually determines the future; and 2) that, although one may attempt to describe that future, one should avoid judging it. These two assumptions lead, sometimes unintentionally, to a sort of fatalism. Since the future is going to be determined by certain known factors, one is compelled to say simply that what will be will be.

Many of those who use the method of projection talk about planning for the future. Probably at least some of them would reject rigid determinism. Yet planning does not mean planning a main outline for the future, but merely planning ways of meeting and perhaps alleviating what cannot be avoided. So far as I can recall, the only direct and adequate recognition of this necessary result of the method of projection was by two of the participants in the *Daedalus* symposium. The first, Lawrence Frank, social psychologist and retired foundation official, remarked that whereas our ancestors often accepted a theological fatalism, "today we seem to be relinquishing this theological conception as we accept a new kind of fatalism expressed in a series of trends." The second, Matthew Meselson, professor of biology at Harvard, suggested that he would prefer "normative forecasting" to the kind which most of his fellow members of the *Daedalus* symposium seemed to practice. The last session reported is, therefore, headed: "The Need for Normative Studies." But the speeches seem for the most part to suggest postponing that for a future meeting.

Normative is a word which many—perhaps most—scientists are more than merely suspicious of, for it implies a rejection of complete relativism and it accepts the distinction they refuse to make between the normal and the average, between what is and what ought to be. But there seems little reason for wanting to know what the future threatens to be like unless there is some possibility of changing it and some willingness to assume that some futures would be better than others.

If sociology seems somewhat too completely content to describe and predict without attempting either to judge or control, that is certainly not a charge which can be leveled against some of the biologists, who also have been inspired to prophecy by the approaching end of a millennium. The Russian biochemist, Vladimir Engelhardt, is relatively unsensational compared to at least some of his American colleagues. He assures us only that science, having moved on from its concern with the management of the inanimate, has now learned how to apply the same successful methods to living creatures, including man. By the year 2000, he says, we will have pep pills which have no after-effects and which banish fatigue entirely; cancer will be no more serious than a nose cold; and defective organs will be replaced by spare parts as routinely as is now the case with other machines.

Perhaps even Dr. Engelhardt is somewhat guilty of that hubris to which many scientists are prone, but he is humility itself compared to Robert Sinsheiner, professor of biophysics at Cal Tech, who declared before his institution's 75th anniversary conference that the scientist has now in effect become both Nature with a capital N and God with a capital G. Until today, he stated, prophecy has been a very chancy business, but now that science has become "the prime mover of change," it is not unreasonable to hope that the race of prophets employing its method may have become reliable. Science has now proved beyond question that there is no qualitative difference between the animate and the inanimate, and though we don't yet know exactly how the inanimate becomes conscious, there is every reason to believe that we will soon be rid of that bothersome mystery also. "It has become increasingly clear," Professor Sinsheiner said, "that all the properties of life can be understood to be simply inherent in the material properties of the complex molecule which comprises the cell." Already we make proteins; soon we will make viruses, and then living cells — which will be, as he calls it, "the second Genesis."

In their new book, *The Year 2000*, Anthony J. Wiener (formerly of the Massachusetts Institute of Technology) and Herman Kahn (formerly of the RAND Corporation) issue a solemn warning against just such unlimited confidence in the benefits of mankind's increasing power and such blindness to the threat inherent in its lagging wisdom:

Practically all of the major technological changes since the beginning of industrialization have resulted in unforeseen consequences. . . . Our very power over nature threatens to become itself a source of power that is out of control. . . . Choices are posed that are too large, too complex, important, uncertain, or comprehensive to be safely left to fallible humans.

Sinsheiner, on the other hand, has no such doubts. He is willing to entrust "fallible human beings" with powers, not only over man's physical and social environment, but over his physiology and his personality. Now that we are beginning to understand the role of DNA, he says, we are masters not only of the human body, but also of the future human being. "Would you like to control the sex of your offspring? Would you like your son to be six feet tall? Seven feet? . . . We know of no intrinsic limits to the lifespan. How long would you like to live?"

How would *you* like to be able to determine this or that? To me, it seems that a more pertinent question would be: "How would you like *someone else* to answer these questions for you?" And it most certainly would be *someone else*. Is there — will there ever be — a someone who should be entrusted with that ultimate power which Sinsheiner then goes on to describe as follows?

Essentially we will surely come to the time when man will have the power to alter, specifically and consciously, his very genes. This will be a new event in the universe. No longer need nature wait for the chance to be patient and the slow process of selection. Intelligence can be applied to evolution.

Does the use made by man of the powers he has achieved suggest that he is ready to merit another such stupendous development? Should we not wait until he has become a little wiser before he holds the whole future of mankind in his hands? Not long ago I was told that the October 1967 issue of the British journal *Science* predicts that within half a century we will be breeding unusually intelligent animals for low grade labor. Wouldn't unusually stupid human beings prove more useful and easier to create?

(1968)

## Adrienne Rich

# Concord River

The turtles on the ledges of July
Heard our approach and splashed. Now in the mud
Lie like the memory of fecund summer
Their buried eggs. The river, colder now,
Has other, autumn tales to carry on
Between the banks where lovers used to lie.

Lovers, or boys escaped from yard and farm
To drown in sensual purities of sun—
No matter which; for single fisherman
Casting into the shade, or those absorbed
In human ardor, summer was the same,
Impervious to weariness or alarm.

The fisherman, by craft and love removed
From meanness, has an almanac at home
Saying the season will be brief this year
And ice strike early; yet upon its shelf
The book is no despoiler of this day
In which he moves and ponders, most himself.

That boy, watching for turtles by the shore,
Steeped in his satisfactory loneliness,

If asked could tell us that the sun would set,
Or autumn drive him back to games and school—
Tell us at second-hand, believing then
Only midsummer and the noonstruck pool.

And we, who floated through the sunlit green,
Indolent, voluntary as the dance
Of dragon-flies above the skimming leaves—
For us the landscape and the hour became
A single element, where our drifting silence
Fell twofold, like our shadows on the water.

This is the Concord River, where the ice
Will hold till April: this is the willowed stream
Much threaded by the native cogitators
Who wrote their journals calmly by its shore,
Observing weather and the swing of seasons
Along with personal cosmologies.

Henry Thoreau most nearly learned to live
Within a world his soul could recognize—
Unshaken by accounts of any country
He could not touch with both his hands. He saw
The river moving past the provincial town
And knew each curve of shoreline for his own.

He travelled much, he said—his wayward speech
Sounding always a little insolent,
Yet surer than the rest; they, like ourselves,
Ran off to dabble in a world beyond
While he exalted the geography
He lived each day: a river and a pond.

For him there was no turning of the ear
To rumored urgencies that sought to rouse
The fisher from his pool, the serious child
From his unconscious wandering: the sound
Of desperate enterprises rang to him
Fictive as ghosts upon old Indian ground.

Lover and child and fisherman, alike
Have in their time been native to this shore
As he would have it peopled: all entranced
By such concerns in their perfected hour
That in their lives the river and the tree
Are absolutes, no longer scenery.

(1967)

How Shall We Learn?

In *Rambler* 154, included here, Samuel Johnson remarks that "The mental disease of the present generation, is impatience of study, contempt of the great masters of ancient wisdom, and a disposition to rely wholly upon un-assisted genius and natural sagacity." He introduces thereby, though in 1751, a controversy as current as those of this morning, one of the many controversies embedded in the central question of this section: in our schooling, should we first be concerned to think for ourselves and to ex-press ourselves, or should we first be concerned to recover for ourselves as much as possible of what the world has known; do we re-invent the wheel on our own, or start with the wheel already made; or can there be some happy reconciliation of the two positions? Much as it is debated in our own time, this is not a new controversy; it figures indirectly in many of the read-ings that follow and importantly in some, from Augustine through Pope and Reynolds and on to Weaver in our own time.

But many other questions have arisen, and more are to come, in what is plainly one of the most controversial enterprises of all, education. One question that might be pursued in almost all of the readings that follow, for example, is why and how such radically polarized arguments develop in a field where one might expect to find quiet discourse and sharing. On almost every educational issue that emerges, one is likely to find protagonists of contrary views asserting that affairs must go either this way or that, with all too few to affirm that so crucial and interesting an enterprise as education should never reduce itself to a single view, that it should admit, embrace, and be larger than contrary views.

Some questions that develop are of particular interest to us now. Writ-ers as disparate as Cardinal Newman and Milton Mayer, debate, as many others do, whether the focus of our schooling shall be on the presumably timeless or on the presumably immediate. Others—Alfred North Whitehead for one—consider whether education is first a service to the larger com-munity or a value self-contained. In some of the documents included here we hear various questions of freedom under discussion; again in some of the documents, as well as in such pieces as those by Jefferson and Woll-stonecraft, we see approaches to the question, *Who* shall be schooled? Other writers—George Garrett, Nathan Glazer—will consider both what should be taught and how it should be taught. Questions of dissent and what appear to be instances of obvious educational failures figure in the articles by Weaver, Arendt, and Schrag. Indeed, there are many questions, for as such studies of the present state of and expectations for education as those by Wayne C. Booth and Peter Schrag will show, there are occasions for both disturbed edginess and intense excitement.

# What shall we learn?

**Roger Ascham**

*from* **The Schoolmaster**

Book 1

Learning teacheth more in one year, than experience in twenty; and learning teacheth safely, when experience maketh more miserable than wise. He hazardeth sore, that waxeth wise by experience. An unhappy master is he, that is made cunning by many shipwrecks; a miserable merchant, that is neither rich nor wise, but after some bankrupts. It is costly wisdom that is bought by experience. We know by experience itself, that it is a marvelous pain, to find out but a short way by long wandering. And surely, he that would prove wise by experience, he may be witty indeed, but even like a swift runner, that runneth fast out of the way, and upon the night, he knoweth not whither. And verily they be fewest in number, that be happy or wise by unlearned experience. And look well upon the former life of those few, whether your example be old or young, who without learning have gathered by long experience a little wisdom, and some happiness; and when you do consider, what mischief they have committed, what dangers they have escaped (and yet twenty for one do perish in the adventure), then think well with yourself, whether ye would, that your own son should come to wisdom and happiness by the way of such experience, or no.

\* \* \* \* \* \*

Erasmus, the honor of learning of all our time, said wisely, "That experience is the common schoolhouse of fools, and ill men. Men of wit, and honesty be otherwise instructed. For there be, that keep them out of fire, and yet was never burned; that beware of water, and yet was never nigh drowning; that hate harlots, and was never at the stews; that abhor falsehood, and never brake promise themselves."

But will ye see a fit similitude of this adventured experience. A father that doth let loose his son to all experiences, is most like a fond hunter, that letteth slip a whelp to the whole herd; twenty to one, he shall fall upon a rascal, and let go the fair game. Men that hunt so be either ignorant persons, privy stealers, or nightwalkers.

Learning therefore, ye wise fathers, and good bringing up, and not blind and dangerous experience, is the next and readiest way that must lead your children, first to wisdom, and then to worthiness, if ever ye purpose they shall come there.

And to say all in short, though I lack authority to give counsel, yet I lack not good will to wish that the youth in England, specially gentlemen, and namely nobility, should be by good bringing up so grounded in judgment of learning, so founded in love of honesty, as when they should be called forth to the execution of great affairs, in service of their Prince and country, they might be able to use, and to order all experiences, were they good, were they bad, and that according to the square, rule, and line, of wisdom, learning, and virtue.

And I do not mean by all this my talk that young gentlemen should always be poring on a book, and by using good studies, should lose honest pleasure, and haunt no good pastime; I mean nothing less. For it is well known that I both like and love, and have always, and do yet still use all exercises and pastimes, that befit for my nature and ability. And beside natural disposition, in judgment also I was never, either stoic in doctrine, or Anabaptist in religion to mislike a merry, pleasant, and playful nature, if no outrage be committed against law, measure, and good order.

Therefore I would wish, that beside some good time fitly appointed, and constantly kept, to increase by reading the knowledge of the tongues, and learning; young gentlemen should use, and delight in all courtly exercises, and gentlemanlike pastimes. And good cause why: For the self same noble city of Athens, justly commended of me before, did wisely, and upon great consideration, appoint the Muses, Apollo, and Pallas, to be patrons of learning to their youth. For the Muses, besides learning, were also ladies of dancing, mirth, and minstrelsy: Apollo was god of shooting, and author of cunning playing upon instruments; Pallas also was lady mistress in wars. Whereby was nothing else meant, but that learning should be always mingled with honest mirth, and comely exercises; and that war also should be governed by learning, and moderated by wisdom; as did well appear in those captains of Athens named by me before, and also in Scipio and Caesar, the two diamonds of Rome. And Pallas was no more feared in wearing Aegida, than she was praised for choosing Olivam; whereby shineth the glory of learning, which thus was governor and mistress in the noble city of Athens, both of war and peace.

Therefore to ride comely, to run fair at the tilt, or ring; to play at all weapons, to shoot fair in bow, or surely in gun; to vault lustily, to run, to leap, to wrestle, to swim; to dance comely, to sing, and to play on instruments cunningly; to hawk, to hunt; to play at tennis, and all pastimes generally, which be joined with labor, used in open place, and on the daylight, containing either some fit exercise for war, or some pleasant pastime for peace, be not only comely and decent, but also very necessary for a courtly gentleman to use.

*     *     *     *     *

Present examples of this present time I list not to touch; yet there is one example for all the gentlemen of this court to follow, that may well satisfy them, or nothing will serve them, nor no example move them to goodness and learning.

It is your shame (I speak to you all, you young gentlemen of England) that one maid should go beyond you all in excellency of learning, and knowledge of divers tongues. Point forth six of the best given gentlemen of this court, and all they together show not so much good will, spend not so much time, bestow not so many hours daily, orderly, and constantly, for the increase of learning and knowledge, as doth the Queen's Majesty herself. Yea I believe, that beside her perfect readiness in Latin, Italian, French, and Spanish, she readeth here now at Windsor more Greek every day, than some prebendary of this Church doth read Latin in a whole week. And that which is most praiseworthy of all, within the walls of her privy chamber, she hath obtained that excellency of learning to understand, speak, and write both wittily with head, and fair with hand, as scarce one or two rare wits in both the universities have in many years reached unto. Amongst all the benefits that God has blessed me withal, next the knowledge of Christ's true religion, I count this the greatest, that it pleased God to call me to be one poor minister in setting forward these excellent gifts of learning in this most excellent prince; whose only example if the rest of our nobility would follow, then might England be for learning and wisdom in nobility, a spectacle to all the world beside. But see the mishap of men; the best examples have never such force to move to any goodness, as the bad, vain, light, and fond have to all illness.

(1570)

**Alexander Pope**

# An Essay on Criticism

## 1

'Tis hard to say, if greater want of skill
Appear in writing or in judging ill;
But, of the two, less dangerous is th' offence
To tire our patience, than mislead our sense.
Some few in that, but numbers err in this,
Ten censure wrong for one who writes amiss;
A fool might once himself alone expose,
Now one in verse makes many more in prose.
    'Tis with our judgments as our watches, none
Go just alike, yet each believes his own.
In Poets as true genius is but rare,
True Taste as seldom is the Critic's share;
Both must alike from Heaven derive their light,
These born to judge, as well as those to write.
Let such teach others who themselves excel,
And censure freely who have written well.
Authors are partial to their wit, 'tis true,
But are not Critics to their judgment too?
    Yet if we look more closely, we shall find
Most have the seeds of judgment in their mind:
Nature affords at least a glimmering light;
The lines, though touched but faintly, are drawn right.
But as the slightest sketch, if justly traced,
Is by ill colouring but the more disgraced,
So by false learning is good sense defaced:
Some are bewildered in the maze of schools,
And some made coxcombs Nature meant but fools.
In search of wit these lose their common sense,
And then turn Critics in their own defence:
Each burns alike, who can, or cannot write,
Or with a Rival's, or an Eunuch's spite.
All fools have still an itching to deride,
And fain would be upon the laughing side.
If Mevius scribble in Apollo's spite,
There are who judge still worse than he can write.
    Some have at first for Wits, then Poets past,
Turned Critics next, and proved plain fools at last.
Some neither can for Wits nor Critics pass,
As heavy mules are neither horse nor ass.

Those half-learned witlings, numerous in our isle,
As half-formed insects on the banks of Nile;
Unfinished things, one knows not what to call,
Their generation's so equivocal:
To tell 'em, would a hundred tongues require,
Or one vain wit's, that might a hundred tire.
    But you who seek to give and merit fame,
And justly bear a Critic's noble name,
Be sure yourself and your own reach to know,
How far your genius, taste, and learning go;
Launch not beyond your depth, but be discreet,
And mark that point where sense and dulness meet.
    Nature to all things fixed the limits fit,
And wisely curbed proud man's pretending wit.
As on the land while here the ocean gains,
In other parts it leaves wide sandy plains;
Thus in the soul while memory prevails,
The solid power of understanding fails;
Where beams of warm imagination play,
The memory's soft figures melt away.
One science only will one genius fit;
So vast is art, so narrow human wit:
Not only bounded to peculiar arts,
But oft in those confined to single parts.
Like Kings we lose the conquests gained before,
By vain ambition still to make them more;
Each might his several province well command,
Would all but stoop to what they understand.
    First follow Nature, and your judgment frame
By her just standard, which is still the same:
Unerring NATURE, still divinely bright,
One clear, unchanged, and universal light,
Life, force, and beauty, must to all impart,
At once the source, and end, and test of Art.
Art from that fund each just supply provides,
Works without show, and without pomp presides:
In some fair body thus th' informing soul
With spirits feeds, with vigour fills the whole,
Each motion guides, and every nerve sustains;
Itself unseen, but in the effects, remains.
Some, to whom Heaven in wit has been profuse,
Want as much more, to turn it to its use;
For wit and judgment often are at strife,
Though meant each other's aid, like man and wife.
'Tis more to guide, than spur the Muse's steed;
Restrain his fury, than provoke his speed;

The wingèd courser, like a generous horse,
Shows most true mettle when you check his course.
 Those RULES of old discovered, not devised,
Are Nature still, but Nature methodized;
Nature, like Liberty, is but restrained
By the same LAWS which first herself ordained.
 Hear how learned Greece her useful rules indites,
When to repress, and when indulge our flights:
High on Parnassus' top her sons she showed,
And pointed out those arduous paths they trod;
Held from afar, aloft, th' immortal prize,
And urged the rest by equal steps to rise.
Just precepts thus from great examples given,
She drew from them what they derived from Heaven.
The generous Critic fanned the Poet's fire,
And taught the world with reason to admire.
Then Criticism the Muses' handmaid proved,
To dress her charms, and make her more beloved:
But following wits from that intention strayed,
Who could not win the mistress, wooed the maid;
Against the Poets their own arms they turned,
Sure to hate most the men from whom they learned.
So modern 'Pothecaries, taught the art
By Doctor's bills to play the Doctor's part,
Bold in the practice of mistaken rules,
Prescribe, apply, and call their masters fools.
Some on the leaves of ancient authors prey,
Nor time nor moths e'er spoiled so much as they.
Some drily plain; without invention's aid,
Write dull receipts how poems may be made.
These leave the sense, their learning to display,
And those explain the meaning quite away.
 You then whose judgment the right course would steer,
Know well each ANCIENT's proper character;
His Fable, Subject, scope in every page;
Religion, Country, genius of his Age:
Without all these at once before your eyes,
Cavil you may, but never criticize.
Be Homer's works your study and delight,
Read them by day, and meditate by night;
Thence form your judgment, thence your maxims bring,
And trace the Muses upward to their spring.
Still with itself compared, his text peruse;
And let your comment be the Mantuan Muse.
 When first young Maro in his boundless mind
A work t' outlast immortal Rome designed,

Perhaps he seemed above the Critic's law,
And but from Nature's fountains scorned to draw:
But when t' examine every part he came,
Nature and Homer were, he found, the same.
Convinced, amazed, he checks the bold design;
And rules as strict his laboured work confine,
As if the Stagirite o'erlooked each line.
Learn hence for ancient rules a just esteem;
To copy nature is to copy them.
    Some beauties yet no Precepts can declare,
For there's a happiness as well as care.
Music resembles Poetry, in each
Are nameless graces which no methods teach,
And which a master hand alone can reach.
If, where the rules not far enough extend,
(Since rules were made but to promote their end)
Some lucky License answer to the full
Th' intent proposed, that License is a rule.
Thus Pegasus, a nearer way to take,
May boldly deviate from the common track;
From vulgar bounds with brave disorder part,
And snatch a grace beyond the reach of art,
Which without passing through the judgment, gains
The heart, and all its end at once attains.
In prospects thus, some objects please our eyes,
Which out of nature's common order rise,
The shapeless rock, or hanging precipice.
Great Wits sometimes may gloriously offend,
And rise to faults true Critics dare not mend.
But though the Ancients thus their rules invade,
(As Kings dispense with laws themselves have made)
Moderns, beware! or if you must offend
Against the precept, ne'er transgress its End;
Let it be seldom, and compelled by need;
And have, at least, their precedent to plead.
The Critic else proceeds without remorse,
Seizes your fame, and puts his laws in force.
    I know there are, to whose presumptuous thoughts
Those freer beauties, even in them, seem faults.
Some figures monstrous and misshaped appear,
Considered singly, or beheld too near,
Which, but proportioned to their light, or place,
Due distance reconciles to form and grace.
A prudent chief not always must display
His powers in equal ranks, and fair array,
But with th' occasion and the place comply,
Conceal his force, nay seem sometimes to fly.

Those oft are stratagems which error seem,
Nor is it Homer nods, but we that dream.
    Still green with bays each ancient Altar stands,
Above the reach of sacrilegious hands;
Secure from Flames, from Envy's fiercer rage,
Destructive War, and all-involving Age.
See, from each clime the learned their incense bring!
Hear, in all tongues consenting Pæans ring!
In praise so just let every voice be joined,
And fill the general chorus of mankind.
Hail, Bards triumphant! born in happier days;
Immortal heirs of universal praise!
Whose honours with increase of ages grow,
As streams roll down, enlarging as they flow;
Nations unborn your mighty names shall sound,
And worlds applaud that must not yet be found!
Oh may some spark of your celestial fire,
The last, the meanest of your sons inspire,
(That on weak wings, from far, pursues your flights;
Glows while he reads, but trembles as he writes)
To teach vain Wits a science little known,
T' admire superior sense, and doubt their own!


## 2

    Of all the Causes which conspire to blind
Man's erring judgment, and misguide the mind,
What the weak head with strongest bias rules,
Is *Pride*, the never-failing vice of fools.
Whatever Nature has in worth denied,
She gives in large recruits of needful Pride;
For as in bodies, thus in souls, we find
What wants in blood and spirits, swelled with wind:
Pride, where Wit fails, steps in to our defence,
And fills up all the mighty Void of sense.
If once right reason drives that cloud away,
Truth breaks upon us with resistless day.
Trust not yourself; but your defects to know,
Make use of every friend—and every foe.
    A *little learning* is a dangerous thing;
Drink deep, or taste not the Pierian spring:
There shallow draughts intoxicate the brain,
And drinking largely sobers us again.
Fired at first sight with what the Muse imparts,
In fearless youth we tempt the heights of Arts,

While from the bounded level of our mind,
Short views we take, nor see the lengths behind;
But more advanced, behold with strange surprise
New distant scenes of endless science rise!
So pleased at first the towering Alps we try,
Mount o'er the vales, and seem to tread the sky,
Th' eternal snows appear already past,
And the first clouds and mountains seem the last;
But, those attained, we tremble to survey
The growing labours of the lengthened way,
Th' increasing prospect tires our wandering eyes,
Hills peep o'er hills, and Alps on Alps arise!
    A perfect Judge will read each work of Wit
With the same spirit that its author writ:
Survey the WHOLE, nor seek slight faults to find
Where nature moves, and rapture warms the mind;
Nor lose, for that malignant dull delight,
The generous pleasure to be charmed with wit.
But in such lays as neither ebb, nor flow,
Correctly cold, and regularly low,
That shunning faults, one quiet tenour keep;
We cannot blame indeed——but we may sleep.
In Wit, as Nature, what affects our hearts
Is not th' exactness of peculiar parts;
'Tis not a lip, or eye, we beauty call,
But the joint force and full result of all.
Thus when we view some well-proportioned dome,
(The world's just wonder, and even thine, O Rome!)
No single parts unequally surprise,
All comes united to th' admiring eyes;
No monstrous height, or breadth, or length appear;
The Whole at once is bold, and regular.
    Whoever thinks a faultless piece to see,
Thinks what ne'er was, nor is, nor e'er shall be.
In every work regard the writer's End,
Since none can compass more than they intend;
And if the means be just, the conduct true,
Applause, in spite of trivial faults, is due.
As men of breeding, sometimes men of wit,
T' avoid great errors, must the less commit:
Neglect the rules each verbal Critic lays,
For not to know some trifles, is a praise.
Most Critics, fond of some subservient art,
Still make the Whole depend upon a Part:
They talk of principles, but notions prize,
And all to one loved Folly sacrifice.

Once on a time, La Mancha's Knight, they say,
A certain Bard encountering on the way,
Discoursed in terms as just, with looks as sage,
As e'er could Dennis of the Grecian stage;
Concluding all were desperate sots and fools,
Who durst depart from Aristotle's rules.
Our Author, happy in a judge so nice,
Produced his Play, and begged the Knight's advice;
Made him observe the subject, and the plot,
The manners, passions, unities; what not?
All which, exact to rule, were brought about,
Were but a Combat in the lists left out.
"What! leave the Combat out?" exclaims the Knight;
Yes, or we must renounce the Stagirite.
"Not so by Heaven" (he answers in a rage)
"Knights, squires, and steeds, must enter on the stage."
So vast a throng the stage can ne'er contain.
"Then build a new, or act it in a plain."
　　Thus Critics, of less judgment than caprice,
Curious not knowing, not exact but nice,
Form short Ideas; and offend in arts
(As most in manners) by a love to parts.
　　Some to *Conceit* alone their taste confine,
And glittering thoughts struck out at every line;
Pleased with a work where nothing's just or fit;
One glaring Chaos and wild heap of wit.
Poets like painters, thus, unskilled to trace
The naked nature and the living grace,
With gold and jewels cover every part,
And hide with ornaments their want of art.
True Wit is Nature to advantage dressed,
What oft was thought, but ne'er so well expressed;
Something, whose truth convinced at sight we find,
That gives us back the image of our mind.
As shades more sweetly recommend the light,
So modest plainness sets off sprightly wit.
For works may have more wit than does 'em good,
As bodies perish through excess of blood.
　　Others for *Language* all their care express,
And value books, as women men, for Dress:
Their praise is still, — the Style is excellent:
The Sense, they humbly take upon content.
Words are like leaves; and where they most abound,
Much fruit of sense beneath is rarely found.
False Eloquence, like the prismatic glass,
Its gaudy colours spreads on every place;

The face of Nature we no more survey,
All glares alike, without distinction gay:
But true Expression, like th' unchanging Sun,
Clears, and improves whate'er it shines upon,
It gilds all objects, but it alters none.
Expression is the dress of thought, and still
Appears more decent, as more suitable;
A vile conceit in pompous words expressed,
Is like a clown in regal purple dressed:
For different styles with different subjects sort,
As several garbs with country, town, and court.
Some by old words to fame have made pretence,
Ancients in phrase, mere moderns in their sense;
Such laboured nothings, in so strange a style,
Amaze th' unlearned, and make the learnèd smile.
Unlucky, as Fungoso in the Play,[1]
These sparks with awkward vanity display
What the fine gentleman wore yesterday;
And but so mimic ancient wits at best,
As apes our grandsires, in their doublets drest.
In words, as fashions, the same rule will hold;
Alike fantastic, if too new, or old:
Be not the first by whom the new are tried,
Nor yet the last to lay the old aside.
    But most by Numbers judge a Poet's song;
And smooth or rough, with them is right or wrong:
In the bright Muse though thousand charms conspire,
Her Voice is all these tuneful fools admire;
Who haunt Parnassus but to please their ear,
Not mend their minds; as some to Church repair,
Not for the doctrine, but the music there.
These equal syllables alone require,
Though oft the ear the open vowels tire;
While expletives their feeble aid do join;
And ten low words oft creep in one dull line:
While they ring round the same unvaried chimes,
With sure returns of still expected rhymes;
Where'er you find "the cooling western breeze,"
In the next line, it "whispers through the trees:"
If crystal streams "with pleasing murmurs creep,"
The reader's threatened (not in vain) with "sleep:"
Then, at the last and only couplet fraught
With some unmeaning thing they call a thought,
A needless Alexandrine ends the song,
That, like a wounded snake, drags its slow length along.

---

[1]See Ben Jonson's *Every Man out of his Humour.* Pope.

Leave such to tune their own dull rhymes, and know
What's roundly smooth, or languishingly slow;
And praise the easy vigour of a line,
Where Denham's strength, and Waller's sweetness join.
True ease in writing comes from art, not chance,
As those move easiest who have learned to dance.
'Tis not enough no harshness gives offence,
The sound must seem an Echo to the sense:
Soft is the strain when Zephyr gently blows,
And the smooth stream in smoother numbers flows;
But when loud surges lash the sounding shore,
The hoarse, rough verse should like the torrent roar:
When Ajax strives some rock's vast weight to throw,
The line too labours, and the words move slow;
Not so, when swift Camilla scours the plain,
Flies o'er th' unbending corn, and skims along the main.
Hear how Timotheus' varied lays surprise,[2]
And bid alternate passions fall and rise!
While, at each change, the son of Libyan Jove
Now burns with glory, and then melts with love;
Now his fierce eyes with sparkling fury glow,
Now sighs steal out, and tears begin to flow:
Persians and Greeks like turns of nature found,
And the World's victor stood subdued by Sound!
The power of Music all our hearts allow,
And what Timotheus was, is DRYDEN now.

    Avoid Extremes; and shun the fault of such,
Who still are pleased too little or too much.
At every trifle scorn to take offence,
That always shows great pride, or little sense;
Those heads, as stomachs, are not sure the best,
Which nauseate all, and nothing can digest.
Yet let not each gay Turn thy rapture move;
For fools admire, but men of sense approve:
As things seem large which we through mists descry,
Dulness is ever apt to magnify.

    Some foreign writers, some our own despise;
The Ancients only, or the Moderns prize.
Thus Wit, like Faith, by each man is applied
To one small sect, and all are damned beside.
Meanly they seek the blessing to confine,
And force that sun but on a part to shine,
Which not alone the southern wit sublimes,
But ripens spirits in cold northern climes;

---

[2]See *Alexander's Feast, or the Power of Music*; an Ode by Mr. Dryden. Pope.

Which from the first has shone on ages past,
Enlights the present, and shall warm the last;
Though each may feel increases and decays,
And see now clearer and now darker days.
Regard not then if Wit be old or new,
But blame the false, and value still the true.
    Some ne'er advance a Judgment of their own,
But catch the spreading notion of the Town;
They reason and conclude by precedent,
And own stale nonsense which they ne'er invent.
Some judge of authors' names, not works, and then
Nor praise nor blame the writings, but the men.
Of all this servile herd, the worst is he
That in proud dulness joins with Quality.
A constant Critic at the great man's board,
To fetch and carry nonsense for my Lord.
What woeful stuff this madrigal would be,
In some starved hackney sonneteer, or me?
But let a Lord once own the happy lines,
How the wit brightens! how the style refines!
Before his sacred name flies every fault,
And each exalted stanza teems with thought!
    The Vulgar thus through Imitation err;
As oft the Learned by being singular;
So much they scorn the crowd, that if the throng
By chance go right, they purposely go wrong:
So Schismatics the plain believers quit,
And are but damned for having too much wit.
Some praise at morning what they blame at night;
But always think the last opinion right.
A Muse by these is like a mistress used,
This hour she's idolized, the next abused;
While their weak heads like towns unfortified,
Twixt sense and nonsense daily change their side.
Ask them the cause; they're wiser still, they say;
And still tomorrow's wiser than today.
We think our fathers fools, so wise we grow;
Our wiser sons, no doubt, will think us so.
Once School divines this zealous isle o'erspread;
Who knew most Sentences, was deepest read;
Faith, Gospel, all, seemed made to be disputed,
And none had sense enough to be confuted:
Scotists and Thomists, now, in peace remain,
Amidst their kindred cobwebs in Duck Lane.[3]

---

[3]A place where old and secondhand books were sold formerly, near Smithfield. Pope.

If Faith itself has different dresses worn,
What wonder modes in Wit should take their turn?
Oft, leaving what is natural and fit,
The current folly proves the ready wit;
And authors think their reputation safe,
Which lives as long as fools are pleased to laugh.
  Some valuing those of their own side or mind,
Still make themselves the measure of mankind:
Fondly we think we honour merit then,
When we but praise ourselves in other men.
Parties in Wit attend on those of State,
And public faction doubles private hate.
Pride, Malice, Folly, against Dryden rose,
In various shapes of Parsons, Critics, Beaus;
But sense survived, when merry jests were past;
For rising merit will buoy up at last.
Might he return, and bless once more our eyes,
New Blackmores and new Milbourns must arise:
Nay should great Homer lift his awful head,
Zoilus again would start up from the dead.
Envy will merit, as its shade, pursue;
But like a shadow, proves the substance true;
For envied Wit, like Sol eclipsed, makes known
Th' opposing body's grossness, not its own.
When first that sun too powerful beams displays,
It draws up vapours which obscure its rays;
But even those clouds at last adorn its way,
Reflect new glories, and augment the day.
  Be thou the first true merit to befriend;
His praise is lost, who stays till all commend.
Short is the date, alas, of modern rhymes,
And 'tis but just to let them live betimes.
No longer now that golden age appears,
When Patriarch wits survived a thousand years:
Now length of Fame (our second life) is lost,
And bare threescore is all even that can boast;
Our sons their fathers' failing language see,
And such as Chaucer is, shall Dryden be.
So when the faithful pencil has designed
Some bright Idea of the master's mind,
Where a new world leaps out at his command,
And ready Nature waits upon his hand;
When the ripe colours soften and unite,
And sweetly melt into just shade and light;
When mellowing years their full perfection give,
And each bold figure just begins to live,

The treacherous colours the fair art betray,
And all the bright creation fades away!
     Unhappy Wit, like most mistaken things,
Atones not for that envy which it brings.
In youth alone its empty praise we boast,
But soon the short-lived vanity is lost:
Like some fair flower the early spring supplies,
That gaily blooms, but even in blooming dies.
What is this Wit, which must our cares employ?
The owner's wife, that other men enjoy;
Then most our trouble still when most admired,
And still the more we give, the more required;
Whose fame with pains we guard, but lose with ease,
Sure some to vex, but never all to please;
'Tis what the vicious fear, the virtuous shun,
By fools 'tis hated, and by knaves undone!
     If Wit so much from Ignorance undergo,
Ah let not Learning too commence its foe!
Of old, those met rewards who could excel,
And such were praised who but endeavoured well:
Though triumphs were to generals only due,
Crowns were reserved to grace the soldiers too.
Now, they who reach Parnassus' lofty crown,
Employ their pains to spurn some others down;
And while self-love each jealous writer rules,
Contending wits become the sport of fools:
But still the worst with most regret commend,
For each ill Author is as bad a Friend.
To what base ends, and by what abject ways,
Are mortals urged through sacred lust of praise!
Ah ne'er so dire a thirst of glory boast,
Nor in the Critic let the Man be lost.
Good nature and good sense must ever join;
To err is human, to forgive, divine.
     But if in noble minds some dregs remain
Not yet purged off, of spleen and sour disdain;
Discharge that rage on more provoking crimes,
Nor fear a dearth in these flagitious times.
No pardon vile Obscenity should find,
Though wit and art conspire to move your mind;
But Dulness with Obscenity must prove
As shameful sure as Impotence in love.
In the fat age of pleasure, wealth and ease,
Sprung the rank weed, and thrived with large increase:
When love was all an easy Monarch's care;
Seldom at council, never in a war:

Jilts ruled the state, and statesmen farces writ;
Nay wits had pensions, and young Lords had wit:
The Fair sat panting at a Courtier's play,
And not a Mask went unimproved away:
The modest fan was lifted up no more,
And Virgins smiled at what they blushed before.
The following licence of a Foreign reign
Did the dregs of bold Socinus drain;
Then unbelieving Priests reformed the nation,
And taught more pleasant methods of salvation;
Where Heaven's free subjects might their rights dispute,
Lest God himself should seem to absolute;
Pulpits their sacred satire learned to spare,
And Vice admired to find a flatterer there!
Encouraged thus, Wit's Titans braved the skies,
And the press groaned with licensed blasphemies.
These monsters, Critics! with your darts engage,
Here point your thunder, and exhaust your rage!
Yet shun their fault, who, scandalously nice,
Will needs mistake an author into vice;
All seems infected that th' infected spy,
As all looks yellow to the jaundiced eye.

### 3

Learn then what MORALS Critics ought to show,
For 'tis but half a Judge's task, to know.
'Tis not enough, taste, judgment, learning, join;
In all you speak, let truth and candour shine:
That not alone what to your sense is due
All may allow; but seek your friendship too.
    Be silent always when you doubt your sense;
And speak, though sure, with seeming diffidence:
Some positive, persisting fops we know,
Who, if once wrong, will needs be always so;
But you, with pleasure own your errors past,
And make each day a Critic on the last.
    'Tis not enough, your counsel still be true;
Blunt truths more mischief than nice falsehoods do;
Men must be taught as if you taught them not,
And things unknown proposed as things forgot.
Without Good Breeding, truth is disapproved;
That only makes superior sense beloved.
    Be niggards of advice on no pretence;
For the worst avarice is that of sense.

With mean complacence ne'er betray your trust,
Nor be so civil as to prove unjust.
Fear not the anger of the wise to raise;
Those best can bear reproof, who merit praise.
    'Twere well might Critics still this freedom take,
But Appius reddens at each word you speak,
And stares, tremendous, with a threatening eye,[4]
Like some fierce Tyrant in old tapestry.
Fear most to tax an Honourable fool,
Whose right it is, uncensured, to be dull;
Such, without wit, are Poets when they please,
As without learning they can take Degrees.
Leave dangerous truths to unsuccessful Satires,
And flattery to fulsome Dedicators,
Whom, when they praise, the world believes no more,
Than when they promise to give scribbling o'er.
'Tis best sometimes your censure to restrain,
And charitably let the dull be vain:
Your silence there is better than your spite,
For who can rail so long as they can write?
Still humming on, their drowsy course they keep,
And lashed so long, like tops, are lashed asleep.
False steps but help them to renew the race,
As, after stumbling, Jades will mend their pace.
What crowds of these, impenitently bold,
In sounds and jingling syllables grown old,
Still run on Poets, in a raging vein,
Even to the dregs and squeezings of the brain,
Strain out the last dull droppings of their sense,
And rhyme with all the rage of Impotence.
    Such shameless Bards we have; and yet 'tis true,
There are as mad abandoned Critics too.
The bookful blockhead, ignorantly read,
With loads of learnèd lumber in his head,
With his own tongue still edifies his ears,
And always listening to himself appears.
All books he reads, and all he reads assails,
From Dryden's Fables down to Durfey's Tales.
With him, most authors steal their works, or buy;
Garth did not write his own Dispensary.[5]

[4] This picture was taken to himself by *John Dennis*, a furious old Critic by profession, who, upon no other provocation, wrote against this Essay and its author, in a manner perfectly lunatic: For, as to the mention made of him in l. 270, he took it as a Compliment, and said it was treacherously meant to cause him to overlook this *Abuse* of his *Person*. Pope.

[5] A common slander at that time in prejudice of that deserving Author. Our Poet did him this justice, when that slander most prevailed; and it is now (perhaps the sooner for this very verse) dead and forgotten. Pope.

Name a new Play, and he's the Poet's friend,
Nay showed his faults — but when would Poets mend?
No place so sacred from such fops is barred,
Nor is Paul's church more safe than Paul's churchyard:
Nay, fly to Altars; there they'll talk you dead:
For Fools rush in where Angels fear to tread.
Distrustful sense with modest caution speaks,
It still looks home, and short excursions makes;
But rattling nonsense in full volleys breaks,
And never shocked, and never turned aside,
Bursts out, resistless, with a thundering tide.

    But where's the man, who counsel can bestow,
Still pleased to teach, and yet not proud to know?
Unbiased, or by favour, or by spite;
Not dully prepossessed, nor blindly right;
Though learned, well-bred; and though well-bred, sincere;
Modestly bold, and humanly severe:
Who to a friend his faults can freely show,
And gladly praise the merit of a foe?
Blest with a taste exact, yet unconfined;
A knowledge both of books and human kind;
Generous converse; a soul exempt from pride;
And love to praise, with reason on his side?

    Such once were Critics; such the happy few,
Athens and Rome in better ages knew.
The mighty Stagirite first left the shore,
Spread all his sails, and durst the deeps explore;
He steered securely, and discovered far,
Led by the light of the Mæonian Star.
Poets, a race long unconfined, and free,
Still fond and proud of savage liberty,
Received his laws; and stood convinced 'twas fit,
Who conquered Nature, should preside o'er Wit.

    Horace still charms with graceful negligence,
And without method talks us into sense,
Will, like a friend, familiarly convey
The truest notions in the easiest way.
He, who supreme in judgment, as in wit,
Might boldly censure, as he boldly writ,
Yet judged with coolness, though he sung with fire;
His Precepts teach but what his works inspire.
Our Critics take a contrary extreme,
They judge with fury, but they write with fle'me:
Nor suffers Horace more in wrong Translations
By Wits, than Critics in as wrong Quotations.

    See Dionysius Homer's thoughts refine,
And call new beauties forth from every line!

Fancy and art in gay Petronius please,
The scholar's learning, with the courtier's ease.
In grave Quintilian's copious work, we find
The justest rules, and clearest method joined:
Thus useful arms in magazines we place,
All ranged in order, and disposed with grace,
But less to please the eye, than arm the hand,
Still fit for use, and ready at command.
Thee, bold Longinus! all the Nine inspire,
And bless their Critic with a Poet's fire.
An ardent Judge, who zealous in his trust,
With warmth gives sentence, yet is always just;
Whose own example strengthens all his laws;
And is himself that great Sublime he draws.
Thus long succeeding Critics justly reigned,
License repressed, and useful laws ordained.
Learning and Rome alike in empire grew;
And Arts still followed where her Eagles flew;
From the same foes, at last, both felt their doom,
And the same age saw Learning fall, and Rome.
With Tyranny, then Superstition joined,
As that the body, this enslaved the mind;
Much was believed, but little understood,
And to be dull was construed to be good;
A second deluge Learning thus o'errun,
And the Monks finished what the Goths begun.
At length Erasmus, the great injured name,
(The glory of the Priesthood, and the shame!)
Stemmed the wild torrent of a barbarous age,
And drove those holy Vandals off the stage.
But see! each Muse, in Leo's golden days,
Starts from her trance, and trims her withered bays,
Rome's ancient Genius, o'er its ruins spread,
Shakes off the dust, and rears his reverend head.
Then Sculpture and her sister arts revive;
Stones leaped to form, and rocks began to live;
With sweeter notes each rising Temple rung;
A Raphael painted, and a Vida sung.
Immortal Vida: on whose honoured brow
The Poet's bays and Critic's ivy grow:
Cremona now shall ever boast thy name,
As next in place to Mantua, next in fame!
But soon by impious arms from Latium chased,
Their ancient bounds the banished Muses passed;
Thence Arts o'er all the northern world advance,
But Critic learning flourished most in France:

The rules a nation, born to serve, obeys;
And Boileau still in right of Horace sways.
But we, brave Britons, foreign laws despised,
And kept unconquered, and uncivilized;
Fierce for the liberties of wit, and bold,
We still defied the Romans, as of old.
Yet some there were, among the sounder few
Of those who less presumed, and better knew,
Who durst assert the juster ancient cause,
And here restored Wit's fundamental laws.
Such was the Muse, whose rules and practice tell,[6]
"Nature's chief Masterpiece is writing well."
Such was Roscommon, not more learned than good,
With manners generous as his noble blood;
To him the wit of Greece and Rome was known,
And every author's merit, but his own.
Such late was Walsh – the Muse's judge and friend,
Who justly knew to blame or to commend;
To failings mild, but zealous for desert;
The clearest head, and the sincerest heart.
This humble praise, lamented shade! receive,
This praise at least a grateful Muse may give:
The Muse, whose early voice you taught to sing,
Prescribed her heights, and pruned her tender wing,
(Her guide now lost) no more attempts to rise,
But in low numbers short excursions tries:
Content, if hence th' unlearned their wants may view,
The learned reflect on what before they knew:
Careless of censure, nor too fond of fame;
Still pleased to praise, yet not afraid to blame;
Averse alike to flatter, or offend;
Not free from faults, nor yet too vain to mend.

(1711)

[6]*Essay on Poetry* by the Duke of Buckingham. . . . Our Author . . . was honoured very young with his friendship, and it continued till his death in all the circumstances of a familiar esteem. Pope.

*from* # The Rambler

No. 154. Saturday, 7 September 1751

> —Tibi res antiquae laudis & artis
> Aggredior, sanctos ausus recludere fontes.
>
> > Virgil, Georgics, II. 174–75

> For thee my tuneful accents will I raise,
> And treat of arts disclos'd in ancient days;
> Once more unlock for thee the sacred spring.
>
> > Dryden

The direction of Aristotle to those that study politicks, is, first to examine and understand what has been written by the ancients upon government; then to cast their eyes round upon the world, and consider by what causes the prosperity of communities is visibly influenced, and why some are worse, and others better administered.

The same method must be pursued by him who hopes to become eminent in any other part of knowledge. The first task is to search books, the next to contemplate nature. He must first possess himself of the intellectual treasures which the diligence of former ages has accumulated, and then endeavour to encrease them by his own collections.

The mental disease of the present generation, is impatience of study, contempt of the great masters of ancient wisdom, and a disposition to rely wholly upon unassisted genius and natural sagacity. The wits of these happy days have discovered a way to fame, which the dull caution of our laborious ancestors durst never attempt; they cut the knots of sophistry which it was formerly the business of years to untie, solve difficulties by sudden irradiations of intelligence, and comprehend long processes of argument by immediate intuition.

Men who have flattered themselves into this opinion of their own abilities, look down on all who waste their lives over books, as a race of inferior beings condemned by nature to perpetual pupillage, and fruitlessly endeavouring to remedy their barrenness by incessant cultivation, or succour their feebleness by subsidiary strength. They presume that none would be more industrious than they, if they were not more sensible of deficiencies, and readily conclude, that he who places no confidence in his own powers, owes his modesty only to his weakness.

It is however certain that no estimate is more in danger of erroneous calculations than those by which a man computes the force of his own genius. It generally happens at our entrance into the world, that by the natural attraction of similitude, we associate with men like ourselves young, sprightly, and ignorant, and rate our accomplishments by comparison with theirs; when we have once obtained an acknowledged superiority over our acquaintances, imagination and desire easily extend it over the rest of mankind, and if no accident forces us into new emulations, we grow old, and die in admiration of ourselves.

Vanity, thus confirmed in her dominion, readily listens to the voice of idleness, and sooths the slumber of life with continual dreams of excellence and greatness. A man elated by confidence in his natural vigour of fancy and sagacity of conjecture, soon concludes that he already possesses whatever toil and enquiry can confer. He then listens with eagerness to the wild objections which folly has raised against the common means of improvement; talks of the dark chaos of indigested knowledge; describes the mischievous effects of heterogeneous sciences fermenting in the mind; relates the blunders of lettered ignorance; expatiates on the heroic merit of those who deviate from prescription, or shake off authority; and gives vent to the inflations of his heart by declaring that he owes nothing to pedants and universities.

All these pretensions, however confident, are very often vain. The laurels which superficial acuteness gains in triumphs over ignorance unsupported by vivacity, are observed by Locke to be lost whenever real learning and rational diligence appear against her; the sallies of gaiety are soon repressed by calm confidence, and the artifices of subtilty are readily detected by those who having carefully studied the question, are not easily confounded or surprised.

But though the contemner of books had neither been deceived by others nor himself, and was really born with a genius surpassing the ordinary abilities of mankind; yet surely such gifts of providence may be more properly urged as incitements to labour, than encouragements to negligence. He that neglects the culture of ground, naturally fertile, is more shamefully culpable than he whose field would scarcely recompence his husbandry.

Cicero remarks, that not to know what has been transacted in former times is to continue always a child. If no use is made of the labours of past ages, the world must remain always in the infancy of knowledge. The discoveries of every man must terminate in his own advantage, and the studies of every age be employed on questions which the past generation had discussed and determined. We may with as little reproach borrow science as manufactures from our ancestors; and it is as rational to live in caves till our own hands have erected a palace, as to reject all knowledge of architecture, which our understandings will not supply.

To the strongest and quickest mind it is far easier to learn than to invent. The principles of arithmetic and geometry may be comprehended by a close attention in a few days; yet who can flatter himself that the study of a long life would have enabled him to discover them, when he sees them yet unknown to so many nations, whom he cannot suppose less liberally endowed with natural reason, than the Grecians or Egyptians?

Every science was thus far advanced towards perfection, by the emulous diligence of contemporary students, and the gradual discoveries of one age improving on another. Sometimes unexpected flashes of instruction were struck out by the fortuitous collision of happy incidents, or an involuntary concurrence of ideas, in which the philosopher to whom they happened had no other merit than that of knowing their value, and transmitting unclouded to posterity that light which had been kindled by causes out of his power. The happiness of these casual illuminations no man can promise to himself, because no endeavours can procure them; and therefore, whatever be our abilities or application, we must submit to learn from others what perhaps would have lain hid for ever from human penetration, had not some remote enquiry brought it to view; as treasures are thrown up by the ploughman and the digger in the rude exercise of their common occupations.

The man whose genius qualifies him for great undertakings, must at least be content to learn from books the present state of human knowledge; that he may not ascribe to himself the invention of arts generally known; weary his attention with experiments of which the event has been long registered; and waste, in attempts which have already succeeded or miscarried, that time which might have been spent with usefulness and honour upon new undertakings.

But though the study of books is necessary, it is not sufficient to constitute literary eminence. He that wishes to be counted among the benefactors of posterity, must add by his own toil to the acquisitions of his ancestors, and secure his memory from neglect by some valuable improvement. This can only be effected by looking out upon the wastes of the intellectual world, and extending the power of learning over regions yet undisciplined and barbarous; or by surveying more exactly her ancient dominions, and driving ignorance from the fortresses and retreats where she skulks undetected and undisturbed. Every science has its difficulties which yet call for solution before we attempt new systems of knowledge; as every country has its forests and marshes, which it would be wise to cultivate and drain, before distant colonies are projected as a necessary discharge of the exuberance of inhabitants.

No man ever yet became great by imitation. Whatever hopes for the veneration of mankind must have invention in the design or the execution; either the effect must itself be new, or the means by which it is produced. Either truths hitherto unknown must be discovered, or those which are already known enforced by stronger evidence, facilitated by clearer method, or elucidated by brighter illustrations.

Fame cannot spread wide or endure long that is not rooted in nature, and manured by art. That which hopes to resist the blast of malignity, and stand firm against the attacks of time, must contain in itself some original principle of growth. The reputation which arises from the detail or transposition of borrowed sentiments, may spread for a while, like ivy on the rind of antiquity, but will be torn away by accident or contempt, and suffered to rot unheeded on the ground.

## Joshua Reynolds

## from Discourses on Art

Discourse Two

I congratulate you on the honour which you have just received. I have the highest opinion of your merits, and could wish to show my sense of them in something which possibly may be more useful to you than barren praise. I could wish to lead you into such a course of study as may render your future progress unanswerable to your past improvement; and, whilst I applaud you for what has been done, remind you how much yet remains to attain perfection.

I flatter myself, that from the long experience I have had, and the unceasing assiduity with which I have pursued those studies, in which, like you, I have been engaged, I shall be acquitted of vanity in offering some hints to your consideration. They are indeed in a great degree founded upon my own mistakes in the same pursuit. But the history of errors, properly managed, often shortens the road to truth. And although no method of study that I can offer, will of itself conduct to excellence, yet it may preserve industry from being misapplied.

In speaking to you of the Theory of the Art, I shall only consider it as it has a relation to the *method* of your studies.

Dividing the study of painting into three distinct periods, I shall address you as having passed through the first of them, which is confined to the rudiments; including a facility of drawing any object that presents itself, a tolerable readiness in the management of colours, and an acquaintance with the most simple and obvious rules of composition.

This first degree of proficiency is, in painting, what grammar is in literature, a general preparation for whatever species of the art the student may afterwards choose for his more particular application. The power of drawing, modelling, and using colours, is very properly called the Language of the art; and in this language, the honours you have just received, prove you to have made no inconsiderable progress.

When the Artist is once enabled to express himself with some degree of correctness, he must then endeavour to collect subjects for expression; to amass a stock of ideas, to be combined and varied as occasion may require. He is now in the second period of study, in which his business is to learn all that has been known and done before his own time. Having hitherto received instructions from a particular master, he is now to consider the Art itself as his master. He must extend his capacity to more sublime and general instructions. Those perfections which lie scattered among various masters, are now united in one general idea, which is henceforth to regulate his taste, and enlarge his imagination. With a variety of models thus before him, he will avoid that narrowness and poverty of conception which attends a bigotted admiration of a single master, and will cease to follow any favourite where he ceases to excel. This period is, however, still a time of subjection and discipline. Though the Student will not resign himself blindly to any single authority, when he may have the advantage of consulting many, he must still be afraid of trusting his own judgment, and of deviating into any track where he cannot find the footsteps of some former master.

The third and last period emancipates the Student from subjection to any authority, but what he shall himself judge to be supported by reason. Confiding now in his own judgment, he will consider and separate those different principles to which different modes of beauty owe their original. In the former period he sought only to know and combine excellence, wherever it was to be found, into one idea of perfection: in this, he learns, what requires the most attentive survey and the most subtle disquisition, to discriminate perfections that are incompatible with each other.

He is from this time to regard himself as holding the same rank with those masters whom he before obeyed as teachers, and as exercising a sort of sovereignty over those rules which have hitherto restrained him. Comparing now no longer the performance of the Art with each other, but examining the Art itself by the standard of Nature, he corrects what is erroneous, supplies what is scanty, and adds by his own observation what the industry of his predecessors may have yet left wanting to perfection. Having well established his judgment, and stored his memory, he may now without fear try the power of his imagination. The mind that has been thus disciplined, may be indulged in the warmest enthusiasm, and venture to play on the borders of the wildest extravagance. The habitual dignity which long converse with the greatest minds has imparted to him, will display itself in all his attempts; and he will stand among his instructors, not as an imitator, but a rival.

These are the different stages of the Art. But as I now address myself particularly to those Students who have been this day rewarded for their happy passage through the first period, I can with no propriety suppose they want any help in the initiatory studies. My present design is to direct your view to distant excellence, and to show you the readiest path that leads to it. Of this I shall speak with such latitude, as may leave the province of the professor uninvaded; and shall not anticipate those precepts, which it is his business to give, and your duty to understand.

It is indisputably evident that a great part of every man's life must be employed in collecting materials for the exercise of genius. Invention, strictly speaking, is little more than a new combination of those images which have been previously gathered and deposited in the memory: nothing can come of nothing: he who has laid up no materials, can produce no combinations.

A Student unacquainted with the attempts of former adventurers, is always apt to over-rate his own abilities; to mistake the most trifling excursions for discoveries of moment, and every coast new to him, for a new-found country. If by chance he passes beyond his usual limits, he congratulates his own arrival at those regions which they who have steered a better course have long left behind them.

The productions of such minds are seldom distinguished by an air of originality: they are anticipated in their happiest efforts; and if they are found to differ in any thing from their predecessors, it is only in irregular sallies, and trifling conceits. The more extensive therefore your acquaintance is with the works of those who have excelled, the more extensive will be your powers of invention; and what may appear still more like a paradox, the more original will be your conceptions. But the difficulty on this occasion is to determine who ought to be proposed as models of excellence, and who ought to be considered as the properest guides.

To a young man just arrived in *Italy*, many of the present painters of that country are ready enough to obtrude their precepts, and to offer their own performances as examples of that perfection which they affect to recommend. The Modern, however, who recommends *himself* as a standard, may justly be suspected as ignorant of the true end, and unacquainted with the proper object, of the art which he professes. To follow such a guide, will not only retard the Student, but mislead him.

On whom then can he rely, or who shall show him the path that leads to excellence? the answer is obvious: those great masters who have travelled the same road with success, are the most likely to conduct others. The works of those who have stood the test of ages, have a claim to that respect and veneration to which no modern can pretend. The duration and stability of their fame, is sufficient to evince that it has not been suspended upon the slender thread of fashion and caprice, but bound to the human heart by every tie of sympathetic approbation.

There is no danger of studying too much the works of those great men; but how they may be studied to advantage is an enquiry of great importance.

Some who have never raised their minds to the consideration of the real dignity of the Art, and who rate the works of an Artist in proportion as they excel or are defective in the mechanical parts, look on theory as something that may enable them to talk but not to paint better; and confining themselves entirely to mechanical practice, very assiduously toil on in the drugery of copying; and think they make a rapid progress while they faithfully exhibit the minutest part of a favourite picture. This appears to me a very tedious, and I think a very erroneous method of proceeding. Of every large composition, even of those which are most admired, a great part may be truly said to be *common-place*. This, though it takes up much time in copying, conduces little to improvement. I consider general copying as a delusive kind of industry; the Student satisfies himself with the appearance of doing something; he falls into the dangerous habit of imitating without selecting, and of labouring without any determinate object; as it requires no effort of the mind, he sleeps over his work; and those powers of invention and composition which ought particularly to be called out, and put in action, lie torpid, and lose their energy for want of exercise.

How incapable those are of producing any thing of their own, who have spent much of their time in making finished copies, is well known to all who are conversant with our art.

To suppose that the complication of powers, and variety of ideas necessary to that mind which aspires to the first honours in the art of Painting, can be obtained by the frigid contemplation of a few single models, is no less absurd, than it would be in him who wishes to be a Poet, to imagine that by translating a tragedy he can acquire to himself sufficient knowledge of the appearances of nature, the operations of the passions, and the incidents of life.

The great use in copying, if it be at all useful, should seem to be in learning to colour; yet even colouring will never be perfectly attained by servilely copying the model before you. An eye critically nice can only be formed by observing well-coloured pictures with attention: and by close inspection, and minute examination, you will discover, at last, the manner of handling, the artifices of contrast, glazing, and other expedients, by which good colourists have raised the value of their tints, and by which nature has been so happily imitated.

I must inform you, however, that old pictures deservedly celebrated for their colouring, are often so changed by dirt and varnish, that we ought not to wonder if they do not appear equal to their reputation in the eyes of unexperienced painters, or young students. An artist whose judgment is matured by long observation, considers rather what the picture once was, than what it is at present. He has by habit acquired a power of seeing the brilliancy of tints through the cloud by which it is obscured. An exact imitation, therefore, of those pictures, is likely to fill the student's mind with false opinions; and to send him back a colourist of his own formation, with ideas equally remote from nature and from art, from the genuine practice of the masters, and the real appearances of things.

Following these rules, and using these precautions, when you have clearly and distinctly learned in what good colouring consists, you cannot do better than have recourse to nature herself, who is always at hand, and in comparison of whose true splendour the best coloured pictures are but faint and feeble.

However, as the practice of copying is not entirely to be excluded, since the mechanical practice of painting is learned in some measure by it, let those choice parts only be selected which have recommended the work to notice. If its excellence consists in its general effort, it would be proper to make slight sketches of the machinery and general management of the picture. Those sketches should be kept always by you for the regulation of your style. Instead of copying the touches of those great masters, copy only their conceptions. Instead of treading in their footsteps, endeavour only to keep the same road. Labour to invent on their general principles and way of thinking. Possess yourself with their spirit. Consider with yourself how a Michael Angelo or a Raffaelle would have treated this subject: and work yourself into a belief that your picture is to be seen and criticised by them when completed. Even an attempt of this kind will rouse your powers.

But as mere enthusiasm will carry you but a little way, let me recommend a practice that may be equivalent to and will perhaps more efficaciously contribute to your advancement, than even the verbal corrections of those masters themselves, could they be obtained. What I would propose is, that you should enter into a kind of competition, by painting a similar subject, and making a companion to any picture that you consider as a model. After you have finished your work, place it near the model, and compare them carefully together. You will then not only see, but feel your own deficiencies more sensibly than by precepts, or any other means of instruction. The true principles of painting will mingle with your thoughts. Ideas thus fixed by sensible objects, will be certain and definitive; and sinking deep into the mind, will not only be more just, but more lasting than those presented to you by precepts only; which will always be fleeting, variable, and undetermined.

This method of comparing your own efforts with those of some great master, is indeed a severe and mortifying task, to which none will submit, but such as have great views, with fortitude sufficient to forego the gratifications of present vanity for future honour. When the Student has succeeded in some measure to his own satisfaction, and has felicitated himself on his success, to go voluntarily to a tribunal where he knows his vanity must be humbled, and all self-approbation must vanish, requires not only great resolution, but great humility. To him, however, who has the ambition to be a real master, the solid satisfaction which proceeds from a consciousness of his advancement (of which seeing his own faults is the first step), will very abundantly compensate for the mortification of present disappointment. There is, besides, this alleviating circumstance. Every discovery he makes, every acquisition of knowledge he attains, seems to proceed from his own sagacity; and thus he acquires a confidence in himself sufficient to keep up the resolution of perseverance.

We all must have experienced how lazily, and consequently how ineffectually, instruction is received when forced upon the mind by others. Few have been taught to any purpose who have not been their own teachers. We prefer those instructions which we have given ourselves, from our affection to the instructor; and they are more effectual, from being received into the mind at the very time when it is most open and eager to receive them.

With respect to the pictures that you are to choose for your models, I could wish that you would take the world's opinion rather than your own. In other words, I would have you choose those of established reputation, rather than follow your own fancy. If you should not admire them at first, you will, by endeavouring to imitate them, find that the world has not been mistaken.

It is not an easy task to point out those various excellencies for your imitation which lie distributed amongst the various schools. An endeavour to do this may perhaps be the subject of some future discourse. I will, therefore, at present only recommend a model for Style in Painting, which is a branch of the art more immediately necessary to the young student. Style in painting is the same as in writing, a power over materials, whether words or colours, by which conceptions or sentiments are conveyed. And in this Lodovico Carrache (I mean in his best works) appears to me to approach the nearest to perfection. His unaffected breadth of light and shadow, the simplicity of colouring, which holding its proper rank, does not draw aside the least part of the attention from the subject, and the solemn effect of that twilight which seems diffused over his pictures, appear to me to correspond with grave and dignified subjects, better than the more artificial brilliancy of sunshine which enlightens the pictures of Titian: though Tintoret thought that Titian's colouring was the model of perfection, and would correspond even with the sublime of Michael Angelo; and that if Angelo had coloured like Titian, or Titian designed like Angelo, the world would once have had a perfect painter.

It is our misfortune, however, that those works of Carrache which I would recommend to the Student, are not often found out of *Bologna*. The *St. Francis in the midst of his Friars, The Transfiguration, The Birth of St. John the Baptist, The Calling of St. Matthew, The St. Jerome, The Fresco Paintings* in the Zampieri palace, are all worthy the attention of the student. And I think those who travel would do well to allot a much greater portion of their time to that city than it has been hitherto the custom to bestow.

In this art, as in others, there are many teachers who profess to show the nearest way to excellence, and many expedients have been invented by which the toil of study might be saved. But let no man be seduced to idleness by specious promises. Excellence is never granted to man, but as the reward of labour. It argues indeed no small strength of mind to persevere in habits of industry, without the pleasure of perceiving those advances; which, like the hand of a clock, whilst they make hourly approaches to their point, yet proceed so slowly as to escape observation. A facility of drawing, like that of playing upon a musical instrument, cannot be acquired but by an infinite number of acts. I need not, therefore, enforce by many words the necessity of continual application; nor tell you that the porte-crayon ought to be for ever in your hands. Various methods will occur to you by which this power may be acquired. I would particularly recommend, that after your return from the Academy (where I suppose your attendance to be constant) you would endeavour to draw the figure by memory. I will even venture to add, that by perseverance in this custom, you will become able to draw the human figure tolerably correct, with as little effort of the mind as is required to trace with a pen the letters of the alphabet.

That this facility is not unattainable, some members in this Academy give a sufficient proof. And be assured, that if this power is not acquired whilst you are young, there will be no time for it afterwards: at least the attempt will be attended with as much difficulty as those experience who learn to read or write after they have arrived to the age of maturity.

But while I mention the porte-crayon as the student's constant companion, he must still remember, that the pencil is the instrument by which he must hope to obtain eminence. What, therefore, I wish to impress upon you is, that whenever an opportunity offers, you paint your studies instead of drawing them. This will give you such a facility in using colours, that in time they will arrange themselves under the pencil, even without the attention of the hand that conducts it. If one act excluded the other, this advice could not with any propriety be given. But if Painting comprises both drawing and colouring, and if by a short struggle of resolute industry, the same expedition is attainable in painting as in drawing on paper. I cannot see what objection can justly be made to the practice; or why that should be done by parts, which may be done all together.

If we turn our eyes to the several Schools of Painting, and consider their respective excellencies, we shall find that those who excel most in colouring, pursued this method. The *Venetian* and *Flemish* schools, which owe much of their fame to colouring, have enriched the cabinets of the collectors of drawings, with very few examples. Those of Titian, Paul Veronese, Tintoret, and the Bassans, are in general slight and undetermined. Their sketches on paper are as rude as their pictures are excellent in regard to harmony of colouring. Correggio and Barocci have left few, if any finished drawings behind them. And in the *Flemish* school, Rubens and Vandyck made their designs for the most part either in colours, or in chiaro oscuro. It is as common to find studies of the *Venetian* and *Flemish* Painters on canvas, as of the schools of

*Rome* and *Florence* on paper. Not but that many finished drawings are sold under the names of those masters. Those, however, are undoubtedly the productions either of engravers or of their scholars, who copied their works.

These instructions I have ventured to offer from my own experience, but as they deviate widely from received opinions, I offer them with diffidence; and when better are suggested, shall retract them without regret.

There is one precept, however, in which I shall only be opposed by the vain, the ignorant, and the idle. I am not afraid that I shall repeat it too often. You must have no dependence on your own genius. If you have great talents, industry will improve them; if you have but moderate abilities, industry will supply their deficiency. Nothing is denied to well directed labour: nothing is to be obtained without it. Not to enter into metaphysical discussion on the nature or essence of genius, I will venture to assert, that assiduity unabated by difficulty, and a disposition eagerly directed to the object of its pursuit, will produce effects similar to those which some call the result of *natural powers*.

Though a man cannot at all times, and in all places, paint or draw, yet the mind can prepare itself by laying in proper materials, at all times, and in all places. Both Livy and Plutarch, in describing Philopoemen, one of the ablest generals of antiquity, have given us a striking picture of a mind always intent on its profession, and by assiduity obtaining those excellencies which some all their lives vainly expect from Nature. I shall quote the passage in Livy at length, as it runs parallel with the practice I would recommend to the Painter, Sculptor, and Architect.

"Philopoemen was a man eminent for his sagacity and experience in choosing ground, and in leading armies; to which he formed his mind by perpetual meditation, in times of peace as well as war. When, in any occasional journey, he came to a strait official passage, if he was alone, he considered with himself, and if he was in company he asked his friends, what it would be best to do if in this place they had found an enemy, either in the front, or in the rear, on the one side, or on the other. 'It might happen,' says he, 'that the enemy to be opposed might come on drawn up in regular lines, or in a tumultuous body, formed only by the nature of the place.' He then considered a little what ground he should take; what number of soldiers he should use, and what arms he should give them; where he should lodge his carriages, his baggage, and the defenceless followers of his camp; how many guards, and of what kind, he should sent to defend them; and whether it would be better to press forward along the pass, or recover by retreat his former station: he would consider likewise where his camp could most commodiously be formed; how much ground he should inclose within his trenches; where he should have the convenience of water, and where he might find plenty of wood and forage; and when he should break up his camp on the following day, through what road he could most safely pass, and in what form he should dispose his troops. With such thoughts and disquisitions he had from his early years so exercised his mind, that on these occasions nothing could happen which he had not been already accustomed to consider."

I cannot help imagining that I see a promising young painter, equally vigilant, whether at home, or abroad, in the streets, or in the fields. Every object that presents itself, is to him a lesson. He regards all Nature with a view to his profession, and combines her beauties, or corrects her defects. He examines the countenance of men under the influence of passion; and often catches the most pleasing hints from subjects of turbulence or deformity. Even bad pictures themselves supply him with useful documents; and as Leonardo da Vinci has observed, he improves upon the fanciful images that are sometimes seen in the fire, or are accidentally sketched upon a discoloured wall.

The artist who has his mind thus filled with ideas, and his hand made expert by practice, works with ease and readiness; whilst he who would have you believe that he is waiting for the inspirations of Genius, is in reality at a loss how to begin; and is at last delivered of his monsters, with difficulty and pain.

The well-grounded painter, on the contrary, has only maturely to consider his subject, and all the mechanical parts of his art follow without his exertion. Conscious of the difficulty of obtaining what he possesses, he makes no pretensions to secrets, except those of closer application. Without conceiving the smallest jealousy against others, he is contented that all shall be as great as himself, who have undergone the same fatigue; and as his pre-eminence depends not upon a trick, he is free from the painful suspicions of a juggler, who lives in perpetual fear lest his trick should be discovered.

(1769)

*A. A. Milne*

# The End

When I was One,
I had just begun.

When I was Two,
I was nearly new.

When I was Three,
I was hardly Me.

When I was Four,
I was not much more.

When I was Five,
I was just alive.

But now I am Six, I'm as clever as clever.
So I think I'll be six now for ever and ever.

(1927)

### George Garrett

# Excursion

We wandered in a half-lit chilly dark.

Half-lit because the light was sieved
through chinks and cracks and holes.
Chilly because it was already winter.
The tombs, in fact, were closed;
but *lire* seem to be the magic key
to anything this side of heaven's gate.

We stumbled in a half-lit chilly dark
and saw their implements,
(symbolic, of course and nothing like
Egyptian ones I've heard about,
real ships, real swords, real beds)
carved into the living rock.
And we saw their frescoes too,
the sad, wide-eyed, two-dimensional people
we could scarcely believe in,
but there they were, their dark eyes answering
no questions, telling no secrets at all.
There are times when even lovers share this look.

We move into another chamber
where someone giggled

"Well, they knew how to live,"
our host and guide, a Philadelphian,
Harvard- and museum-trained, said.

What glowed on the walls was *erotica*,
the daydreams and the night thoughts,
the pinned-up wishes of the ancients.
One in particular caught our eyes,
(the light fell on it best).

A slave on all fours is the lady's couch,
and she, thus mounted, lies
back, knees high, to receive
("receive," I believe is the word we use
nowadays, the proper euphemism)
a standing lover
whom nature or art has hugely gifted.
She is no more of flesh and blood
than a playing-card queen,
but still her false face is alive with joy.
She seems to like her shaky perch.
Her lover is much more solemn and intent,
gripping a mighty instrument.
The slave is stolid in his pose.
What is he thinking? God knows.

And we, the creatures of another culture,
one where truth is seldom in the nude,
whose tombs are plots of silence
and whose dreams are fugitive as spies,
to be caught and shot at first light?
Someone has giggled, somebody joked,
and now in separate privacy we creep
into a crazy house of mirrors
where the self-disguised, assumes
a shiver of swift lewd poses
like a gambler's shuffled deck.

Does it seem strange to go to the dead
for the facts of life?
Orpheus, Virgil, Dante, Christ
descended in the dark and stirred
the troubled bones. And we,
with all hell in our heads,
must follow or go mad.
"Love, let us be true . . . ,"

old Matthew Arnold sang,
who couldn't have meant what he said.
Or maybe he did. . . .
I have seen a Victorian gentleman's
boot-remover made of brass —
a naked woman whose spread legs
catch and pull off the boot.

We move along and pretty soon
are outside in the open air again.

"Places like this have the kind of truth
that the public monuments conceal,"
an archeologist says.
"Boy, I wouldn't want to be that slave,"
the shy sociologist tells me.

But what I like best is
the classicist from Vassar.
She's suddenly bright-eyed and wordy
like somebody with a fever.
"Until I went down in these tombs
I never really *believed* in ancient times."
She babbles of bones and artifacts
(meanwhile avoids the subject of
the tomb assigned to human love)
and bounces like a little girl
on the back seat all the way home.

(1967)

# Can our schools change?

*Bernard Mandeville*

*from* **An Essay on Charity and Charity Schools**

Enlightened England

The rise then and original of all the bustle and clamor that is made throughout the kindgom in behalf of charity schools is chiefly built on frailty and human passion; at least it is more than possible that a nation should have the same fondness and feel the same zeal for them as are shown in ours, and yet not be prompted to it by any principle of virtue or religion. Encouraged by this consideration, I shall with the greater liberty attack this vulgar error, and endeavor to make it evident that far from being beneficial, this forced education is pernicious to the public, the welfare whereof, as it demands of us a regard superior to all other laws and considerations, so it shall be the only apology I intend to make for differing from the present sentiments of the learned and reverent body of our divines, and venturing plainly to deny what I have just now owned to be openly asserted by most of our bishops as well as inferior clergy. As our Church pretends to no infallibility even in spirituals, her proper province, so it cannot be an affront to her to imagine that she may err in temporals, which are not so much under her immediate care. – But to my task.

The whole earth being cursed and no bread to be had but what we eat in the sweat of our brows, vast toil must be undergone before man can provide himself with necessaries for his sustenance and the bare support of his corrupt and defective nature as he is a single creature; but infinitely more to make life comfortable in a civil society, where men are become taught animals, and great numbers of them have by mutual compact framed themselves into a body politic; and the more man's knowledge increases in this state, the greater will be the variety of labor required to make him easy. It is impossible that a society can long subsist and suffer many of its members to live in idleness, and enjoy all the ease and pleasure they can invent, without having at the same time great multitudes of people that to make good this defect, will condescend to be quite the reverse, and by use and patience inure their bodies to work for others and themselves besides.

The plenty and cheapness of provisions depends in a great measure on the price and value that is set upon this labor, and consequently the welfare of all societies, even before they are tainted with foreign luxury, requires that it should be performed by such of their members as in the first place are sturdy and robust and never used to ease or idleness, and in the second, soon contented as to the necessaries of life; such as are glad to take up with the coarsest manufacture in everything they wear, and in their diet have no other aim than to feed their bodies when their stomachs prompt them to eat, and, with little regard to taste or relish, refuse no wholesome nourishment that can be swallowed when men are hungry, or ask anything for their thirst but to quench it.

As the greatest part of the drudgery is to be done by daylight, so it is by this only that they actually measure the time of their labor without any thought of the hours they are employed or the weariness they feel; and the hireling in the country must get up in the morning not because he has rested enough, but because the sun is going to rise. This last article alone would be an intolerable hardship to grown people under thirty who during nonage had been used to lie abed as long as they could sleep; but all three together make up such a condition of life as a man more mildly educated would hardly choose, though it should deliver him from a jail or a shrew.

If such people there must be, as no great nation can be happy without vast numbers of them, would not a wise legislature cultivate the breed of them with all imaginable care, and provide against their scarcity as he would prevent the scarcity of provision itself? No man would be poor and fatigue himself for a livelihood if he could help it. The absolute necessity all stand in for victuals and drink, and in cold climates for clothes and lodging, makes them submit to anything that can be born with. If nobody did want, nobody would work; but the greatest hardships are looked upon as solid pleasures when they keep a man from starving.

From what has been said, it is manifest that in a free nation, where slaves are not allowed of, the surest wealth consists in a multitude of laborious poor; for besides that they are the never-failing nursery of fleets and armies, without them there could be no enjoyment, and no product of any country could be valuable. To make the society happy and people easy under the meanest circumstances, it is requisite that great numbers of them should be ignorant as well as poor. Knowledge both enlarges and multiplies our desires, and the fewer things a man wishes for, the more easily his necessities may be supplied.

The welfare and felicity, therefore, of every state and kingdom require that the knowledge of the working poor should be confined within the verge of their occupations, and never extended (as to things visible) beyond what relates to their calling. The more a shepherd, a plowman, or any other peasant knows of the world and the things that are foreign to his labor or employment, the less fit he'll be to go through the fatigues and hardships of it with cheerfulness and content.

Reading, writing, and arithmetic are very necessary to those whose business requires such qualifications, but where people's livelihood has no dependence on these arts, they are very pernicious to the poor, who are forced to get their daily bread by their daily labor. Few children make any progress at school, but at the same time they are capable of being employed in some business or other, so that every hour those of poor people spend at their book is so much time lost to the society. Going to school in comparison to working is idleness, and the longer boys continue in this easy sort of life, the more unfit they'll be when grown up for downright labor, both as to strength and inclination. Men who are to remain and end their days in a laborious, tiresome, and painful station of life, the sooner they are put upon it at first, the more patiently they'll submit to it forever after. Hard labor and the coarsest diet are a proper punishment to several kinds of malefactors, but to impose either on those that have not been used and brought up to both is the greatest cruelty when there is no crime you can charge them with.

Reading and writing are not attained to without some labor of the brain and assiduity, and before people are tolerably versed in either, they esteem themselves infinitely above those who are wholly ignorant of them, often with so little justice and moderation as if they were of another species. As all mortals have naturally an aversion to trouble and painstaking, so we are all fond of, and apt to overvalue, those qualifications we have purchased at the expense of our ease and quiet for years together. Those who spent a great part of their youth in learning to read, write, and cipher expect, and not unjustly, to be employed where those qualifications may be of use to them; the generality of them will look upon downright labor with the utmost contempt—I mean labor performed in the service of others in the lowest station of life, and for the meanest consideration. A man who has had some education may follow husbandry by choice, and be diligent at the dirtiest and most laborious work; but then the concern must be his own; and avarice, the care of a family, or some other pressing motive must put him upon it; but he won't make a good hireling and serve a farmer for a pitiful reward; at least he is not so fit for it as a day laborer that has always been employed about the plow and dung cart, and remembers not that ever he has lived otherwise.

When obsequiousness and mean services are required, we shall always observe that they are never so cheerfully nor so heartily performed as from inferiors to superiors; I mean inferiors, not only in riches and quality, but likewise in knowledge and understanding. A servant can have no unfeigned respect for his master as soon as he has sense enough to find out that he serves a fool. When we are to learn or to obey, we shall experience in ourselves that the greater opinion we have of the wisdom and capacity of those that are either to teach or command us, the greater deference we pay to their laws and instructions. No creatures submit contentedly to their equals, and should a horse know as much as a man, I should not desire to be his rider. . . .

I would not be thought cruel, and am well assured if I know anything of myself that I abhor inhumanity; but to be compassionate to excess where reason forbids it, and the general interest of the society requires steadiness of thought and resolution, is an unpardonable weakness. I know it will be ever urged against me that it is barbarous the children of the poor should have no opportunity of exerting themselves as long as God has not debarred them from natural parts and genius more than the rich. But I cannot think this is harder than it is that they should not have money as long as they have the same inclinations to spend as others. That great and useful men have sprung from hospitals, I don't deny; but it is likewise very probable that when they were first employed, many as capable as themselves not brought up in hospitals were neglected that with the same good fortune would have done as well as they, if they had been made use of instead of them.

There are many examples of women that have excelled in learning, and even in war, but this is no reason we should bring 'em all up to Latin and Greek or else military discipline, instead of needlework and housewifery. But there is no scarcity of sprightliness or natural parts among us, and no soil or climate has human creatures to boast of better formed either inside or outside than this island generally produces. But it is not wit, genius, or docility we want, but diligence, application, and assiduity.

Abundance of hard and dirty labor is to be done, and coarse living is to be complied with. Where shall we find a better nursery for these necessities than the children of the poor? None certainly are nearer to it or fitter for it. Besides that, the things I called hardships neither seem nor are such to those who have been brought up to 'em and know no better. There is not a more contented people amongst us than those who work the hardest and are the least acquainted with the pomp and delicacies of the world.

These are truths that are undeniable; yet I know few people will be pleased to have them divulged; what makes them odious is an unreasonable vein of petty reverence for the poor that runs through most multitudes, and more particularly in this nation, and arises from a mixture of pity, folly, and superstition. It is from a lively sense of this compound that men cannot endure to hear or see anything said or acted against the poor, without considering how just the one or insolent the other. So a beggar must not be beat though he strikes you first. Journeymen tailors go to law with their masters and are obstinate in a wrong cause; yet they must be pitied; and murmuring weavers must be relieved, and have fifty silly things done to humor them, though in the midst of their poverty they insult their betters, and on all occasions appear to be more prone to make holidays and riots than they are to working or sobriety.

This puts me in mind of our wool, which, considering the posture of our affairs and the behavior of the poor, I sincerely believe ought not upon any account to be carried abroad. But if we look into the reason why suffering it to be fetched away is so pernicious, our heavy complaint and lamentations that it is exported can be no great credit to us. Considering the mighty and manifold hazards that must be run before it can be got off the coast and safely landed beyond sea, it is manifest that the foreigners, before they can work our wool, must pay more for it very considerably than what we can have it for at home. Yet, notwithstanding this great difference in the prime cost, they can afford to sell the manufactures made of it cheaper at foreign markets than ourselves. This is the disaster we groan under, the intolerable mischief, without which the exportation of that commodity could be no greater prejudice to us than that of tin or lead, as long as our hands were fully employed and we had still wool to spare.

There is no people yet come to higher perfection in the woolen manufacture, either as to dispatch or goodness of work, at least in the most considerable branches, than ourselves, and therefore what we complain of can only depend on the difference in the management of the poor between other nations and ours. If the laboring people in one country will work twelve hours in a day, and six days in a week, and in another they are employed but eight hours in a day, and not above four days in a week, the one is obliged to have nine hands for what the other does with four. But if moreover the living, the food and raiment, and what is consumed by the workmen of the industrious costs but half the money of what is expended among an equal number of the other, the consequence must be that the first will have the work of eighteen men for the same price as the other gives for the work of four. I would not insinuate, neither do I think, that the difference either in diligence or necessaries of life between us and any neighboring nation is near so great as what I speak of; yet I would have it considered that half of that difference and much less is sufficient to overbalance the disadvantage they labor under as to the price of wool.

Nothing to me is more evident than that no nation in any manufacture whatever can undersell their neighbors with whom they are at best but equals as to skill and dispatch, and the conveniency for working, more especially when the prime cost of the thing to be manufactured is not in their favor, unless they have provisions and whatever is relating to their sustenance cheaper, or else workmen that are either more assiduous, and will remain longer at their work, or be content with a meaner and coarser way of living than those of their neighbors. This is certain: that where numbers are equal, the more laborious people are, and the fewer hands the same quantity of work is performed by, the greater plenty there is in a country of the necessaries for life, the more considerable and the cheaper that country may render its exports.

It being granted, then, that abundance of work is to be done, the next thing which I think to be likewise undeniable is that the more cheerfully it is done the better, as well for those that perform it as for the rest of the society. To be happy is to be pleased, and the less notion a man has of a better way of living, the more content he'll be with his own; and on the other hand, the greater a man's knowledge and experience is in the world, the more exquisite the delicacy of his taste, and the more consummate judge he is of things in general, certainly the more difficult it will be to please him. I would not advance anything that is barbarous or inhuman. But when a man enjoys himself, laughs and sings, and in his gesture and behavior shows me all the tokens of content and satisfaction, I pronounce him happy, and have nothing to do with his wit or capacity. I never enter into the reasonableness of his mirth; at least I ought not to judge of it by my own standard, and argue from the effect which the thing that makes him merry would have upon me. At that rate a man that hates cheese must call me a fool for loving blue mold. *De gustibus non est disputandum* is as true in a metaphorical as it is in the literal sense, and the greater the distance is between people as to their condition, their circumstances, and manner of living, the less capable they are of judging of one another's troubles or pleasures.                                    (1723)

*Mary Wollstonecraft*

## *from* Vindication of the Rights of Woman

CHAPTER XII ON NATIONAL EDUCATION

The good effects resulting from attention to private education will ever be very confined, and the parent who really puts his own hand to the plough, will always, in some degree, be disappointed, till education becomes a grand national concern. A man cannot retire into a desert with his child, and if he did he could not bring himself back to childhood, and become the proper friend and playfellow of an infant or youth. And when children are confined to the society of men and women, they very soon acquire that kind of premature manhood which stops the growth of every vigorous power of mind or body. In order to open their faculties they should be excited to think for themselves; and this can only be done by mixing a number of children together, and making them jointly pursue the same objects.

A child very soon contracts a benumbing indolence of mind, which he has seldom sufficient vigour afterwards to shake off, when he only asks a question instead of seeking for information, and then relies implicitly on the answer he receives. With his equals in age this could never be the case, and the subjects of inquiry, though they might be influenced, would not be entirely under the direction of men, who frequently damp, if not destroy, abilities, by bringing them forward too hastily: and too hastily they will infallibly be brought forward, if the child be confined to the society of a man, however sagacious that man may be.

Besides, in youth the seeds of every affection should be sown, and the respectful regard, which is felt for a parent, is very different from the social affections that are to constitute the happiness of life as it advances. Of these equality is the basis, and an intercourse of sentiments unclogged by that observant seriousness which prevents disputation, though it may not enforce submission. Let a child have ever such an affection for his parent, he will always languish to play and prattle with children; and the very respect he feels, for filial esteem always has a dash of fear mixed with it, will, if it do not teach him cunning, at least prevent him from pouring out the little secrets which first open the heart to friendship and confidence, gradually leading to more expansive benevolence. Added to this, he will never acquire that frank ingenuousness of behaviour, which young people can only attain by being frequently in society where they dare to speak what they think; neither afraid of being reproved for their presumption, nor laughed at for their folly.

Forcibly impressed by the reflections which the sight of schools, as they are at present conducted, naturally suggested, I have formerly delivered my opinion rather warmly in favour of a private education; but further experience has led me to view the subject in a different light. I still, however, think schools, as they are now regulated, the hot-beds of vice and folly, and the knowledge of human nature, supposed to be attained there, merely cunning selfishness.

At school boys become gluttons and slovens, and, instead of cultivating domestic affections, very early rush into the libertinism which destroys the constitution before it is formed; hardening the heart as it weakens the understanding.

I should, in fact, be averse to boarding-schools, if it were for no other reason than the unsettled state of mind which the expectation of the vacations produces. On these the children's thoughts are fixed with eager anticipating hopes, for, at least, to speak with moderation, half of the time, and when they arrive they are spent in total dissipation and beastly indulgence.

But, on the contrary, when they are brought up at home, though they may pursue a plan of study in a more orderly manner than can be adopted when near a fourth part of the year is actually spent in idleness, and as much more in regret and anticipation; yet they there acquire too high an opinion of their own importance, from birth, allowed to tyrannise over servants, and from the anxiety expressed by most mothers, on the score of manners, who, eager to teach the accomplishments of a gentleman, stifle, in their birth, the virtues of a man. Thus brought into company when they ought to be seriously employed, and treated like men when they are still boys, they become vain and effeminate.

The only way to avoid two extremes equally injurious to morality, would be to contrive some way of combining a public and private education. Thus to make men citizens two natural steps might be taken, which seem directly to lead to the desired point; for the domestic affections, that first open the heart to the various modifications of humanity, would be cultivated, whilst the children were nevertheless allowed to spend great part of their time, on terms of equality, with other children.

I still recollect, with pleasure, the country day-school; where a boy trudged in the morning, wet or dry, carrying his books, and his dinner, if it were at a considerable distance; a servant did not then lead master by the hand, for, when he had once put on coat and breeches, he was allowed to shift for himself, and return alone in the evening to recount the feats of the day close at the parental knee. His father's house was his home, and was ever after fondly remembered; nay, I appeal to many superior men, who were educated in this manner, whether the recollection of some shady lane where they conned their lesson; or, of some stile, where they sat making a kite, or mending a bat, has not endeared their country to them?

But, what boy ever recollected with pleasure the years he spent in close confinement, at an academy near London? unless, indeed, he should, by chance, remember the poor scarecrow of an usher, whom he tormented; or, the tartman, from whom he caught a cake, to devour it with a cattish appetite of selfishness. At boarding-schools of every description, the relaxation of the junior boys is mischief; and of the senior, vice. Besides, in great schools, what can be more prejudicial to the moral character than the system of tyranny and abject slavery which is established amongst the boys, to say nothing of the slavery to forms, which makes religion worse than a farce? For what good can be expected from the youth who receives the sacrament of the Lord's Supper, to avoid forfeiting half a guinea, which he probably afterwards spends in some sensual manner? Half the employment of the youths is to elude the necessity of attending public worship; and well they may, for such a constant repetition of the same thing must be a very irksome restraint on their natural vivacity. As these ceremonies have the most fatal effect on their morals, and as a ritual performed by the lips, when the heart and mind are far away, is not now stored up by our Church as a bank to draw on for the fees of the poor souls in purgatory, why should they not be abolished?

But the fear of innovation, in this country, extends to everything. This is only a covert fear, the apprehensive timidity of indolent slugs, who guard, by sliming it over, the snug place, which they consider in the light of an hereditary estate; and eat, drink, and enjoy themselves, instead of fulfilling the duties, excepting a few empty forms, for which it was endowed. These are the people who most strenuously insist on the will of the founder being observed, crying out against all reformation, as if it were a violation of justice. I am now alluding particularly to the relics of Popery retained in our colleges, when the Protestant members seem to be such sticklers for the Established Church; but their zeal never makes them lose sight of the spoil of ignorance, which rapacious priests of superstitious memory have scraped together. No, wise in their generation, they venerate the prescriptive right of possession, as a stronghold, and still let the sluggish bell tinkle to prayers, as during the days when the elevation of the host was supposed to atone for the sins of the people, lest one reformation should lead to another, and the spirit kill the letter. These Romish customs have the most baneful effect on the morals of our clergy; for the idle vermin who two or three times a day perform in the most slovenly manner a service which they think useless, but call their duty, soon lose a sense of duty. At college, forced to attend or evade public worship, they acquire an habitual contempt for the very service, the performance of which is to enable them to live in idleness. It is mumbled over as an affair of business, as a stupid boy repeats his talk, and frequently the college cant escapes from the preacher the moment after he has left the pulpit, and even whilst he is eating the dinner which he earned in such a dishonest manner.

Nothing, indeed, can be more irreverent than the cathedral service as it is now performed in this country, neither does it contain a set of weaker men than those who are the slaves of this childish routine. A disgusting skeleton of the former state is still exhibited; but all the solemnity that interested the imagination, if it did not purify the heart, is stripped off. The performance of high mass on the Continent must impress every mind, where a spark of fancy glows, with that awful melancholy, that sublime tenderness, so near akin to devotion. I do not say that these devotional feelings are of more use, in a moral sense, than any other emotion of taste; but I contend that the theatrical pomp which gratifies our senses, is to be preferred to the cold parade that insults the understanding without reaching the heart.

Amongst remarks on national education, such observations cannot be misplaced, especially as the supporters of these establishments, degenerated into puerilities, affect to be the champions of religion. Religion, pure source of comfort in this vale of tears! how has thy clear stream been muddied by the dabblers, who have presumptuously endeavoured to confine in one narrow channel, the living waters that ever flow towards God—the sublime ocean of existence! What would life be without that peace which the love of God, when built on humanity, alone can impart? Every earthly affection turns back, at intervals, to prey upon the heart that feeds it; and the purest effusions of benevolence, often rudely damped by man, must mount as a free-will offering to Him who gave them birth, whose bright image they faintly reflect.

In public schools, however, religion, confounded with irksome ceremonies and unreasonable restraints, assumes the most ungracious aspect: not the sober austere one that commands respect whilst it inspires fear; but a ludicrous cast, that serves to point a pun. For, in fact, most of the good stories and smart things which enliven the spirits that have been concentrated at whist, are manufactured out of the incidents to which the very men labour to give a droll turn who countenance the abuse to live on the spoil.

There is not, perhaps, in the kingdom, a more dogmatical, or luxurious set of men, than the pedantic tyrants who reside in colleges and preside at public schools. The vacations are equally injurious to the morals of the masters and pupils, and the intercourse, which the former keep up with the nobility, introduces the same vanity and extravagance into their families, which banish domestic duties and comforts from the lordly mansion, whose state is awkwardly aped. The boys, who live at a great expense with the masters and assistants, are never domesticated, though placed there for that purpose; for, after a silent dinner, they swallow a hasty glass of wine, and retire to plan some mischievous trick, or to ridicule the person or manners of the very people they have just been cringing to, and whom they ought to consider as the representatives of their parents.

Can it then be a matter of surprise that boys become selfish and vicious who are thus shut out from social converse? or that a mitre often graces the brow of one of these diligent pastors?

The desire of living in the same style, as the rank just above them, infects each individual and every class of people, and meanness is the concomitant of this ignoble ambition; but those professions are most debasing whose ladder is patronage; yet, out of one of these professions the tutors of youth are, in general, chosen. But, can they be expected to inspire independent sentiments, whose conduct must be regulated by the cautious prudence that is ever on the watch for preferment?

So far, however, from thinking of the morals of boys, I have heard several masters of schools argue, that they only undertook to teach Latin and Greek; and that they had fulfilled their duty, by sending some good scholars to college.

A few good scholars, I grant, may have been formed by emulation and discipline; but, to bring forward these clever boys, the health and morals of a number have been sacrificed. The sons of our gentry and wealthy commoners are mostly educated at these seminaries, and will anyone pretend to assert that the majority, making every allowance, come under the description of tolerable scholars?

It is not for the benefit of society that a few brilliant men should be brought forward at the expense of the multitude. It is true, that great men seem to start up, as great revolutions occur, at proper intervals, to restore order, and to blow aside the clouds that thicken over the face of truth; but let more reason and virtue prevail in society, and these strong winds would not be necessary. Public education, of every denomination, should be directed to form citizens; but if you wish to make good citizens, you must first exercise the affections of a son and a brother. This is the only way to expand the heart; for public affections, as well as public virtues must ever grow out of the private character, or they are merely meteors that shoot athwart a dark sky, and disappear as they are gazed at and admired.

Few, I believe, have had much affection for mankind, who did not first love their parents, their brothers, sisters, and even the domestic brutes, whom they first played with. The exercise of youthful sympathies forms the moral temperature; and it is the recollection of these first affections and pursuits that gives life to those that are afterwards more under the direction of reason. In youth, the fondest friendships are formed, the genial juices mounting at the same time, kindly mix; or, rather the heart, tempered for the reception of friendship, is accustomed to seek for pleasure in something more noble than the churlish gratification of appetite.

In order then to inspire a love of home and domestic pleasures, children ought to be educated at home, for riotous holidays only make them fond of home for their own sakes. Yet, the vacations, which do not foster domestic affections, continually disturb the course of study, and render any plan of improvement abortive which includes temperance; still, were they abolished, children would be entirely separated from their parents, and I question whether they would become better citizens by sacrificing the preparatory affections, by destroying the force of relationships that render the marriage state as necessary as respectable. But, if a private education produce self-importance, or insulate a man in his family, the evil is only shifted, not remedied.

This train of reasoning brings me back to a subject, on which I mean to dwell, the necessity of establishing proper day-schools.

But, these should be national establishments, for whilst schoolmasters are dependent on the caprice of parents, little exertion can be expected from them, more than is necessary to please ignorant people. Indeed, the necessity of a master's giving the parents some sample of the boy's abilities, which during the vacation is shown to every visitor,[1] is productive of more mischief than would at first be supposed. For it is

[1] I now particularly allude to the numerous academies in and about London, and to the behaviour of the trading part of this great city.

seldom done entirely, to speak with moderation, by the child itself; thus the master countenances falsehood, or winds the poor machine up to some extraordinary exertion, that injures the wheels, and stops the progress of gradual improvement. The memory is loaded with unintelligible words, to make a show of, without the understanding's acquiring any distinct ideas: but only that education deserves emphatically to be termed cultivation of mind, which teaches young people how to begin to think. The imagination should not be allowed to debauch the understanding before it gained strength, or vanity will become the forerunner of vice: for every way of exhibiting the acquirements of a child is injurious to its moral character.

How much time is lost in teaching them to recite what they do not understand? whilst, seated on benches, all in their best array, the mammas listen with astonishment to the parrotlike prattle, uttered in solemn cadences, with all the pomp of ignorance and folly. Such exhibitions only serve to strike the spreading fibres of vanity through the whole mind; for they neither teach children to speak fluently, nor behave gracefully. So far from it, that these frivolous pursuits might comprehensively be termed the study of affectation; for we now rarely see a simple, bashful boy, though few people of taste were ever disgusted by that awkward sheepishness so natural to the age, which schools and an early introduction into society, have changed into impudence and apish grimace.

Yet, how can these things be remedied whilst schoolmasters depend entirely on parents for a subsistence; and, when so many rival schools hang out their lures, to catch the attention of vain fathers and mothers, whose parental affection only leads them to wish that their children should outshine those of their neighbours?

Without great good luck, a sensible, conscientious man, would starve before he could raise a school, if he disdained to bubble weak parents by practising the secret tricks of the craft.

In the best regulated schools, however, where swarms are not crammed together, many bad habits must be acquired; but, at common schools, the body, heart, and understanding, are equally stunted, for parents are often only in quest of the cheapest school, and the master could not live, if he did not take a much greater number than he could manage himself; nor will the scanty pittance, allowed for each child, permit him to hire ushers sufficient to assist in the discharge of the mechanical part of the business. Besides, whatever appearance the house and garden may make, the children do not enjoy the comfort of either, for they are continually reminded by irksome restrictions that they are not at home, and the state-rooms, garden, etc., must be kept in order for the recreation of the parents; who, of a Sunday, visit the school, and are impressed by the very parade that renders the situation of their children uncomfortable.

With what disgust have I heard sensible women, for girls are more restrained and cowed than boys, speak of the wearisome confinement, which they endured at school. Not allowed, perhaps, to step out of one broad walk in a superb garden, and obliged to pace with steady deportment stupidly backwards and forwards, holding up their heads and turning out their toes, with shoulders braced back, instead of bounding, as Nature directs to complete her own design, in the various attitudes so conducive to health.[2] The pure animal spirits, which make both mind and body shoot out, and unfold the tender blossoms of hope, are turned sour, and vented in vain wishes or pert repinings, that contract the faculties and spoil the temper; else they mount to the brain, and sharpening the understanding before it gains proportionable strength, produce that pitiful cunning which disgracefully characterises the female mind—and I fear will ever characterise it whilst women remain the slaves of power!

The little respect paid to chastity in the male world is, I am persuaded, the grand source of many of the physical and moral evils that torment mankind, as well as of the vices and follies that degrade and destroy women; yet, at school, boys infallibly lose that decent bashfulness, which might have ripened into modesty, at home.

And what nasty indecent tricks do they not also learn from each other, when a number of them pig together in the same bedchamber, not to speak of the vices, which render the body weak, whilst they effectually prevent the acquisition of any delicacy of mind. The little attention paid to the cultivation of modesty, amongst men, produces great depravity in all the relationships of society; for, not only love—love that ought to purify the heart, and first call forth all the youthful powers, to prepare the man to discharge the benevolent duties of life, is sacrificed to premature lust; but, all the social affections are deadened by the selfish gratifications, which very early pollute the mind, and dry up the generous juices of the heart. In what an unnatural manner is innocence often violated; and what serious consequences ensue to render private vices a public pest. Besides, an habit of personal order, which has more effect on the moral character, than is, in general, supposed, can only be acquired at home, where that respectable reserve is kept up which checks the familiarity that, sinking into beastliness, undermines the affection it insults.

I have already animadverted on the bad habits which females acquire when they are shut up together; and, I think, that the observation

---

[2] I remember a circumstance that once came under my own observation, and raised my indignation. I went to visit a little boy at a school where young children were prepared for a large one. The master took me into the schoolroom, etc., but whilst I walked down a broad gravel walk, I could not help observing that the grass grew very luxuriantly on each side of me. I immediately asked the child some questions, and found that the poor boys were not allowed to stir off the walk, and that the master sometimes permitted sheep to be turned in to crop the untrodden grass. The tyrant of this domain used to sit by a window that overlooked the prison yard, and one nook turning from it, where the unfortunate babes could sport freely, he enclosed, and planted it with potatoes. The wife likewise was equally anxious to keep the children in order, lest they should dirty or tear their clothes.

may fairly be extended to the other sex, till the natural inference is drawn which I have had in view throughout – that to improve both sexes they ought, not only in private families, but in public schools, to be educated together. If marriage be the cement of society, mankind should all be educated after the same model, or the intercourse of the sexes will never deserve the name of fellowship, nor will women ever fulfil the peculiar duties of their sex, till they become enlightened citizens, till they become free by being enabled to earn their own subsistence, independent of men; in the same manner, I mean, to prevent misconstruction, as one man is independent of another. Nay, marriage will never be held sacred till women, by being brought up with men, are prepared to be their companions rather than their mistresses; for the mean doublings of cunning will ever render them contemptible, whilst oppression renders them timid. So convinced am I of this truth, that I will venture to predict that virtue will never prevail in society till the virtues of both sexes are founded on reason; and, till the affections common to both are allowed to gain their due strength by the discharge of mutual duties.

Were boys and girls permitted to pursue the same studies together, those graceful decencies might early be inculcated which produce modesty without those sexual distinctions that taint the mind. Lessons of politeness, and that formulary of decorum, which treads on the heels of falsehood, would be rendered useless by habitual propriety of behavior. Not indeed put on for visitors, like the courtly robe of politeness, but the sober effect of cleanliness of mind. Would not this simple elegance of sincerity be a chaste homage paid to domestic affections, far surpassing the meretricious compliments that shine with false lustre in the heartless intercourse of fashionable life? But till more understanding preponderates in society, there will ever be a want of heart and taste, and the harlot's *rouge* will supply the place of that celestial suffusion which only virtuous affections can give to the face. Gallantry, and what is called love, may subsist without simplicity of character; but the main pillars of friendship are respect and confidence – esteem is never founded on it cannot tell what!

A taste for the fine arts requires great cultivation, but not more than a taste for the virtuous affections, and both suppose that enlargement of mind which opens so many sources of mental pleasure. Why do people hurry to noisy scenes and crowded circles? I should answer, because they want activity of mind, because they have not cherished the virtues of the heart. They only therefore see and feel in the gross, and continually pine after variety, finding everything that is simple insipid.

This argument may be carried further than philosophers are aware of, for if nature destined woman, in particular, for the discharge of domestic duties, she made her susceptible of the attached affections in a great degree. Now women are notoriously fond of pleasure, and naturally must be so according to my definition, because they cannot enter into the minutiae of domestic taste, lacking judgment, the foundation of all taste; for the understanding, in spite of sensual cavillers, reserves to itself the privilege of conveying pure joy to the heart.

With what a languid yawn have I seen an admirable poem thrown down that a man of true taste returns to again and again with rapture; and whilst melody has almost suspended respiration, a lady has asked me where I bought my gown. I have seen also an eye glanced coldly over a most exquisite picture rest, sparkling with pleasure, on a caricature rudely sketched; and whilst some terrific feature in nature has spread a sublime stillness through my soul, I have been desired to observe the pretty tricks of a lap-dog that my perverse fate forced me to travel with. Is it surprising that such a tasteless being should rather caress this dog than her children? Or that she should prefer the rant of flattery to the simple accents of sincerity?

To illustrate this remark I must be allowed to observe that men of the first genius and most cultivated minds have appeared to have the highest relish for the simple beauties of nature; and they must have forcibly felt, what they have so well described, the charm which natural affections and unsophisticated feelings spread round the human character. It is this power of looking into the heart, and responsively vibrating with each emotion, that enables the poet to personify each passion, and the painter to sketch with a pencil of fire.

True taste is ever the work of the understanding employed in observing natural effects; and till women have more understanding, it is vain to expect them to possess domestic taste. Their lively senses will ever be at work to harden their hearts, and the emotions struck out of them will continue to be vivid and transitory, unless a proper education store their mind with knowledge.

It is the want of domestic taste, and not the acquirement of knowledge, that takes women out of their families, and tears the smiling babe from the breast that ought to afford it nourishment. Women have been allowed to remain in ignorance and slavish dependence many, very many, years, and still we hear of nothing but their fondness of pleasure and sway, their preference of rakes and soldiers, their childish attachment to toys, and the vanity that makes them value accomplishments more than virtues.

History brings forward a fearful catalogue of the crimes which their cunning has produced, when the weak slaves have had sufficient address to overreach their masters. In France, and in how many other countries, have men been the luxurious despots, and women the crafty ministers? Does this prove that ignorance and dependence domesticate them? Is not their folly the byword of the libertines, who relax in their society? and do not men of sense continually lament that an immoderate fondness for dress and dissipation carries the mother of a family for ever from home? Their hearts have not been debauched by knowledge, or their minds led away by scientific pursuits, yet they do not fulfil the peculiar duties which, as women, they are called upon by Nature to fulfil. On the contrary, the state of warfare which subsists between the sexes makes them employ those wiles that often frustrate the more open designs of force.

When therefore I call women slaves, I mean in a political and civil sense; for indirectly they obtain too much power, and are debased by their exertions to obtain illicit sway.

Let an enlightened nation[3] then try what effect reason would have to bring them back to nature, and their duty; and allowing them to share the advantages of education and government with man, see whether they will become better, as they grow wiser and become free. They cannot be injured by the experiment, for it is not in the power of man to render them more insignificant than they are at present.

To render this practicable, day-schools for particular ages should be established by Government, in which boys and girls might be educated together. The school for the younger children, from five to nine years of age, ought to be absolutely free and open to all classes.[4] A sufficient number of masters should also be chosen by a select committee in each parish, to whom any complaint of negligence, etc., might be made, if signed by six of the children's parents.

Ushers would then be unnecessary; for I believe experience will ever prove that this kind of subordinate authority is particularly injurious to the morals of youth. What, indeed, can tend to deprave the character more than outward submission and inward contempt? Yet how can boys be expected to treat an usher with respect, when the master seems to consider him in the light of a servant, and almost to countenance the ridicule which becomes the chief amusement of the boys during the play hours?

But nothing of this kind could occur in an elementary day-school, where boys and girls, the rich and poor, should meet together. And to prevent any of the distinctions of vanity, they should be dressed alike, and all obliged to submit to the same discipline, or leave the school. The schoolroom ought to be surrounded by a large piece of ground, in which the children might be usefully exercised, for at this age they should not be confined to any sedentary employment for more than an hour at a time. But these relaxations might all be rendered a part of elementary education, for many things improve and amuse the senses, when introduced as a kind of show, to the principles of which, dryly laid down, children would turn a deaf ear. For instance, botany, mechanics, and astronomy; reading, writing, arithmetic, natural history, and some simple experiments in natural philosophy, might fill up the day; but these pursuits should never encroach on gymnastic plays in the open air. The ele-

---

[3]France.

[4]Treating this part of the subject, I have borrowed some hints from a very sensible pamphlet, written by the late Bishop of Autun, on "Public Education."

ments of religion, history, the history of man, and politics, might also be taught by conversations in the Socratic form.

After the age of nine, girls and boys, intended for domestic employments, or mechanical trades, ought to be removed to other schools, and receive instruction in some measure appropriated to the destination of each individual, the two sexes being still together in the morning; but in the afternoon the girls should attend a school, where plain work, mantua-making, millinery, etc., would be their employment.

The young people of superior abilities, or fortune, might now be taught, in another school, the dead and living languages, the elements of science, and continue the study of history and politics, on a more extensive scale, which would not exclude polite literature.

Girls and boys still together? I hear some readers ask. Yes. And I should not fear any other consequence than that some early attachment might take place; which, whilst it had the best effect on the moral character of the young people, might not perfectly agree with the views of the parents, for it will be a long time, I fear, before the world will be so far enlightened that parents, only anxious to render their children virtuous, shall allow them to choose companions for life themselves.

Besides, this would be a sure way to promote early marriages, and from early marriages the most salutary physical and moral effects naturally flow. What a different character does a married citizen assume from the selfish coxcomb, who lives but for himself, and who is often afraid to marry lest he should not be able to live in a certain style. Great emergencies excepted, which would rarely occur in a society of which equality was the basis, a man can only be prepared to discharge the duties of public life, by the habitual practice of those inferior ones which form the man.

In this plan of education the constitution of boys would not be ruined by the early debaucheries, which now make men so selfish, or girls rendered weak and vain, by indolence, and frivolous pursuits. But, I presuppose, that such a degree of equality should be established between the sexes as would shut out gallantry and coquetry, yet allow friendship and love to temper the heart for the discharge of higher duties.

These would be schools of morality—and the happiness of man, allowed to flow from the pure springs of duty and affection, what advances might not the human mind make? Society can only be happy and free in proportion as it is virtuous; but the present distinctions, established in society, corrode all private, and blast all public virtue.

I have already inveighed against the custom of confining girls to their needle, and shutting them out from all political and civil employments; for by thus narrowing their minds they are rendered unfit to fulfil the peculiar duties which Nature has assigned them.

Only employed about the little incidents of the day, they necessarily grow up cunning. My very soul has often sickened at observing the sly tricks practised by women to gain some foolish thing on which their silly hearts were set. Not allowed to dispose of money, or call anything their own, they learn to turn the market penny; or, should a husband offend, by staying from home, or give rise to some emotions of jealousy—a new gown, or any pretty bauble, smooths Juno's angry brow.

But these *littlenesses* would not degrade their character, if women were led to respect themselves, if political and moral subjects were opened to them; and, I will venture to affirm, that this is the only way to make them properly attentive to their domestic duties. An active mind embraces the whole circle of its duties, and finds time enough for all. It is not, I assert, a bold attempt to emulate masculine virtues; it is not the enchantment of literary pursuits, or the steady investigation of scientific subjects, that leads women astray from duty. No, it is indolence and vanity—the love of pleasure and the love of sway, that will reign paramount in an empty mind. I say empty emphatically, because the education which women now receive scarcely deserves the name. For the little knowledge that they are led to acquire, during the important years of youth, is merely relative to accomplishments; and accomplishments without a bottom, for unless the understanding be cultivated, superficial and monotonous is every grace. Like the charms of a made-up face, they only strike the senses in a crowd; but at home, wanting mind, they want variety. The consequence is obvious; in gay scenes of dissipation we meet the artificial mind and face, for those who fly from solitude dread, next to solitude, the domestic circle; not having it in their power to amuse or interest, they feel their own insignificance, or find nothing to amuse or interest themselves.

Besides, what can be more indelicate than a girl's *coming out* in the fashionable world? Which, in other words, is to bring to market a marriageable miss, whose person is taken from one public place to another, richly caparisoned. Yet, mixing in the giddy circle under restraint, these butterflies long to flutter at large, for the first affection of their souls is their own persons, to which their attention has been called with the most sedulous care whilst they were preparing for the period that decides their fate for life. Instead of pursuing this idle routine, fighting for tasteless show, and heartless state, with what dignity would the youths of both sexes form attachments in the schools that I have cursorily pointed out; in which, as life advanced, dancing, music, and drawing might be admitted as relaxations, for at these schools young people of fortune ought to remain, more or less, till they were of age. Those who were designed for particular professions might attend, three or four mornings in the week, the schools appropriated for their immediate instruction.

I only drop these observations at present, as hints; rather, indeed, as an outline of the plan I mean, than a digested one; but I must add, that I highly approve of one regulation mentioned in the pamphlet[5] al-

---

[5]The Bishop of Autun's.

ready alluded to, that of making the children and youths independent of the masters respecting punishments. They should be tried by their peers, which would be an admirable method of fixing sound principles of justice in the mind, and might have the happiest effect on the temper, which is very early soured or irritated by tyranny, till it becomes peevishly cunning, or ferociously overbearing.

My imagination darts forward with benevolent fervour to greet these amiable and respectable groups, in spite of the sneering of cold hearts, who are at liberty to utter, with frigid self-importance, the damning epithet—romantic; the force of which I shall endeavour to blunt by repeating the words of an eloquent moralist: "I know not whether the allusions of a truly humane heart, whose zeal renders everything easy, be not preferable to that rough and repulsing reason, which always finds an indifference for the public good, the first obstacle to whatever would promote it."

I know that libertines will also exclaim, that woman would be unsexed by acquiring strength of body and mind, and that beauty, soft bewitching beauty! would no longer adorn the daughters of men. I am of a very different opinion, for I think that, on the contrary, we should then see dignified beauty and true grace; to produce which, many powerful physical and moral causes would concur. Not relaxed beauty, it is true, or the graces of helplessness; but such as appears to make us respect the human body as a majestic pile fit to receive a noble inhabitant, in the relics of antiquity.

I do not forget the popular opinion that the Grecian statues were not modelled after nature. I mean, not according to the proportions of a particular man; but that beautiful limbs and features were selected from various bodies to form an harmonious whole. This might, in some degree, be true. The fine ideal picture of an exalted imagination might be superior to the materials which the statuary found in nature, and thus it might with propriety be termed rather the model of mankind than of a man. It was not, however, the mechanical selection of limbs and features; but the ebullition of an heated fancy that burst forth, and the fine senses and enlarged understanding of the artist selected the solid matter, which he drew into this glowing focus.

I observed that it was not mechanical because a whole was produced—a model of that grand simplicity, of those concurring energies, which arrest our attention and command our reverence. For only insipid lifeless beauty is produced by a servile copy of even beautiful nature. Yet, independent of these observations, I believe that the human form must have been far more beautiful than it is at present, because extreme indolence, barbarous ligatures, and many causes, which forcibly act on it, in our luxurious state of society, did not retard its expansion, or render it deformed. Exercise and cleanliness appear to be not only the surest means of preserving health, but of promoting beauty, the physical causes only considered; yet this is not sufficient, moral ones must concur, or beauty will be merely of that rustic kind which blooms on the innocent, wholesome countenances of some country people, whose minds have not been exercised. To render the person perfect, physical and moral beauty ought to be attained at the same time; each lending and receiving force by the combination. Judgment must reside on the brow, affection and fancy beam in the eye, and humanity curve the cheek, or vain is the sparkling of the finest eye or the elegantly turned finish of the fairest features; whilst in every motion that displays the active limbs and well-knit joints, grace and modesty should appear. But this fair assemblage is not to be brought together by chance; it is the reward of exertions calculated to support each other; for judgment can only be acquired by reflection, affection by the discharge of duties, and humanity by the exercise of compassion to every living creature.

Humanity to animals should be particularly inculcated as a part of national education, for it is not at present one of our national virtues. Tenderness for their humble dumb domestics, amongst the lower class, is oftener to be found in a savage than a civilised state. For civilisation prevents that intercourse which creates affection in the rude hut, or mud hovel, and leads uncultivated minds who are only depraved by the refinements which prevail in the society, where they are trodden under foot by the rich, to domineer over them to revenge the insults that they are obliged to bear from their superiors.

This habitual cruelty is first caught at school, where it is one of the rare sports of the boys to torment the miserable brutes that fall in their way. The transition, as they grow up, from barbarity to brutes to domestic tyranny over wives, children, and servants, is very easy. Justice, or even benevolence, will not be a powerful spring of action unless it extend to the whole creation; nay, I believe that it may be delivered as an axiom, that those who can see pain, unmoved, will soon learn to inflict it.

The vulgar are swayed by present feelings, and the habits which they have accidentally acquired; but on partial feelings much dependence cannot be placed, though they be just; for, when they are not invigorated by reflection, custom weakens them, till they are scarcely perceptible. The sympathies of our nature are strengthened by pondering cogitations, and deadened by thoughtless use. Macbeth's heart smote him more for one murder, the first, than for a hundred subsequent ones, which were necessary to back it.

But, when I used the epithet vulgar, I did not mean to confine my remark to the poor, for partial humanity, founded on present sensations, or whim, is quite as conspicuous, if not more so, amongst the rich.

The lady who sheds tears for the bird starved in a snare, and execrates the devils in the shape of men, who goad to madness the poor ox, or whip the patient ass, tottering under a burden above its strength, will nevertheless keep her coachman and horses whole hours waiting for her, when the sharp frost bites, or the rain beats against the well-closed windows which do not admit a breath of air to tell her how roughly the wind blows without. And she who takes her dogs to bed, and nurses them with a parade of sensibility, when sick, will suffer her babes to grow up crooked in a nursery. This illustration of my argument is drawn from a matter of fact. The woman whom I allude to was handsome, reckoned very handsome, by those who do not miss the mind when the face is plump and fair; but her understanding had not been led from female duties by literature, nor her innocence debauched by knowledge. No, she was quite feminine, according to the masculine acceptation of the word; and, so far from loving these spoiled brutes that filled the place which her children ought to have occupied, she only lisped out a pretty mixture of French and English nonsense, to please the men who flocked round her. The wife, mother, and human creature, were all swallowed up by the factitious character which an improper education and the selfish vanity of beauty had produced.

I do not like to make a distinction without a difference, and I own that I have been as much disgusted by the fine lady who took her lapdog to her bosom instead of her child; as by the ferocity of a man, who, beating his horse, declared, that he knew as well when he did wrong, as a Christian.

This brood of folly shows how mistaken they are who, if they allow women to leave their harems, do not cultivate their understandings, in order to plant virtues in their hearts. For had they sense, they might acquire that domestic taste which would lead them to love with reasonable subordination their whole family, from their husband to the house dog; nor would they ever insult humanity in the person of the most menial servant by paying more attention to the comfort of a brute, than to that of a fellow-creature.

My observations on national education are obviously hints; but I principally wish to enforce the necessity of educating the sexes together to perfect both, and of making children sleep at home that they may learn to love home; yet to make private support, instead of smothering, public affections, they should be sent to school to mix with a number of equals, for only by the jostlings of equality can we form a just opinion of ourselves.

To render mankind more virtuous, and happier of course, both sexes must act from the same principle; but how can that be expected when only one is allowed to see the reasonableness of it? To render also the social compact truly equitable, and in order to spread those enlightening principles, which alone can ameliorate the fate of man, women must be allowed to found their virtue on knowledge, which is scarcely possible unless they be educated by the same pursuits as men. For they are now made so inferior by ignorance and low desires, as not to deserve to be ranked with them; or, by the serpentine wrigglings of cunning, they mount the tree of knowledge, and only acquire sufficient to lead men astray.

It is plain from the history of all nations, that women cannot be confined to merely domestic pursuits, for they will not fulfil family duties, unless their minds take a wider range, and whilst they are kept in ignorance they become in the same proportion the slaves of pleasure as they are the slaves of man. Nor can they be shut out of great enterprises, though the narrowness of their minds often make them mar, what they are unable to comprehend.

The libertinism, and even the virtues of superior men, will always give women, of some description, great power over them; and these weak women, under the influence of childish passions and selfish vanity, will throw a false light over the objects which the very men view with their eyes, who ought to enlighten their judgment. Men of fancy, and those sanguine characters who mostly hold the helm of human affairs, in general, relax in the society of women; and surely I need not cite to the most superficial reader of history the numerous examples of vice and oppression which the private intrigues of female favourites have produced; not to dwell on the mischief that naturally arises from the blundering interposition of well-meaning folly. For in the transactions of business it is much better to have to deal with a knave than a fool, because a knave adheres to some plan; and any plan of reason may be seen through much sooner than a sudden flight of folly. The power which vile and foolish women have had over wise men, who possessed sensibility, is notorious; I shall only mention one instance.

Whoever drew a more exalted female character than Rousseau? though in the lump he constantly endeavoured to degrade the sex. And why was he thus anxious? Truly to justify to himself the affection which weakness and virtue had made him cherish for that fool Theresa. He could not raise her to the common level of her sex; and therefore he laboured to bring woman down to hers. He found her a convenient humble companion, and pride made him determine to find some superior virtues in the being whom he chose to live with; but did not her conduct during his life, and after his death, clearly show how grossly he was mistaken who called her a celestial innocent? Nay, in the bitterness of his heart, he himself laments that when his bodily infirmities made him no longer treat her like a woman, she ceased to have an affection for him. And it was very natural that she should, for having so few sentiments in common, when the sexual tie was broken, what was to hold her? To hold her affection whose sensibility was confined to one sex, nay, to one man, it requires sense to turn sensibility into the broad channel of humanity. Many women have not mind enough to have an affection for a woman, or a friendship for a man. But the sexual weakness that makes woman depend on man for a subsistence, produces a kind of cattish affection, which leads a wife to purr about her husband as she would about any man who fed and caressed her.

Men are, however, often gratified by this kind of fondness, which is confined in a beastly manner to themselves; but should they ever become more virtuous, they will wish to converse at their fireside with a friend after they cease to play with a mistress.

Besides, understanding is necessary to give variety and interest to sensual enjoyments, for low indeed in the intellectual scale is the mind that can continue to love when neither virtue nor sense give a human appearance to an animal appetite. But sense will always preponderate; and if women be not, in general, brought more on a level with men, some superior women, like the Greek courtesans, will assemble the men of abilities around them, and draw from their families many citizens, who would have stayed at home had their wives had more sense, or the graces which result from the exercise of the understanding and fancy, the legitimate parents of taste. A woman of talents, if she be not absolutely ugly, will always obtain great power—raised by the weakness of her sex; and in proportion as men acquire virtue and delicacy, by the exertion of reason, they will look for both in women, but they can only acquire them in the same way that men do.

In France or Italy, have the women confined themselves to domestic life? Though they have not hitherto had a political existence, yet have they not illicitly had great sway, corrupting themselves and the men with whose passions they played? In short, in whatever light I view the subject, reason and experience convince me that the only method of leading women to fulfil their peculiar duties is to free them from all restraint by allowing them to participate the inherent rights of mankind.

Make them free, and they will quickly become wise and virtuous, as men become more so, for the improvement must be mutual, or the injustice which one-half of the human race are obliged to submit to retorting on their oppressors, the virtue of man will be worm-eaten by the insect whom he keeps under his feet.

Let men take their choice. Man and woman were made for each other, though not to become one being; and if they will not improve women, they will deprave them.

I speak of the improvement and emancipation of the whole sex, for I know that the behaviour of a few women, who, by accident, or following a strong bent of nature, have acquired a portion of knowledge superior to that of the rest of their sex, has often been overbearing; but there have been instances of women who, attaining knowledge, have not discarded modesty, nor have they always pedantically appeared to despise the ignorance which they laboured to disperse in their own minds. The exclamations then which any advice respecting female learning commonly produces, especially from pretty women, often arise from envy. When they chance to see that even the lustre of their eyes, and the flippant sportiveness of refined coquetry, will not always secure them attention during a whole evening, should a woman of a more cultivated understanding endeavour to give a rational turn to the conversation, the common source of consolation is that such women seldom get husbands. What arts have I not seen silly women use to interrupt by *flirtation* – a very significant word to describe such a manoeuvre – a rational conversation, which made the men forget that they were pretty women.

But, allowing what is very natural to man, that the possession of rare abilities is really calculated to excite over-weening pride, disgusting in both men and women, in what a state of inferiority must the female faculties have rusted when such a small portion of knowledge as those women attained, who have sneeringly been termed learned women, could be singular? – sufficiently so to puff up the possessor, and excite envy in her contemporaries, and some of the other sex. Nay, has not a little rationality exposed many women to the severest censure? I advert to well-known facts, for I have frequently heard women ridiculed, and every little weakness exposed, only because they adopted the advice of some medical men, and deviated from the beaten track in their mode of treating their infants. I have actually heard this barbarous aversion to innovation carried still further, and a sensible woman stigmatised as an unnatural mother, who has thus been wisely solicitous to preserve the health of her children, when in the midst of her care she has lost one by some of the casualties of infancy, which no prudence can ward off. Her acquaintance have observed that this was the consequence of new-fangled notions – the new-fangled notions of ease and cleanliness. And those who pretending to experience, though they have long adhered to prejudices that have, according to the opinion of the most sagacious physicians, thinned the human race, almost rejoiced at the disaster that gave a kind of sanction to prescription.

Indeed, if it were only on this account, the national education of women is of the utmost consequence, for what a number of human sacrifices are made to that Moloch prejudice! And in how many ways are children destroyed by the lasciviousness of man? The want of natural affection in many women, who are drawn from their duty by the admiration of men, and the ignorance of others, render the infancy of man a much more perilous state than that of brutes; yet men are unwilling to place women in situations proper to enable them to acquire sufficient understanding to know how even to nurse their babes.

So forcibly does this truth strike me that I would rest the whole tendency of my reasoning upon it, for whatever tends to incapacitate the maternal character, takes woman out of her sphere.

But it is vain to expect the present race of weak mothers either to take that reasonable care of a child's body, which is necessary to lay the foundation of a good constitution, supposing that it do not suffer for the sins of its fathers; or to manage its temper so judiciously that the child will not have, as it grows up, to throw off all that its mother, its first instructor, directly or indirectly taught; and unless the mind have uncommon vigour, womanish follies will stick to the character throughout life. The weakness of the mother will be visited on the children. And whilst women are educated to rely on their husbands for judgment, this must ever be the consequence, for there is no improving an understanding by halves, nor can any being act wisely from imitation, because in every circumstance of life there is a kind of individuality, which requires an exertion of judgment to modify general rules. The being who can think justly in one track will soon extend its intellectual empire; and she who has sufficient judgment to manage her children will not submit, right or wrong, to her husband, or patiently to the social laws which make a nonentity of a wife.

In public schools women, to guard against the errors of ignorance, should be taught the elements of anatomy and medicine, not only to enable them to take proper care of their own health, but to make them rational nurses of their infants, parents, and husbands; for the bills of mortality are swelled by the blunders of self-willed old women, who give nostrums of their own without knowing anything of the human frame. It is likewise proper, only in a domestic view, to make women acquainted with the anatomy of the mind, by allowing the sexes to associate together in every pursuit, and by leading them to observe the progress of the human understanding in the improvement of the sciences and arts—never forgetting the science of morality, or the study of the political history of mankind.

A man has been termed a microcosm, and every family might also be called a state. States, it is true, have mostly been governed by arts that disgrace the character of man, and the want of a just constitution and equal laws have so perplexed the notions of the worldly wise, that they more than question the reasonableness of contending for the rights of humanity. Thus morality, polluted in the national reservoir, sends off streams of vice to corrupt the constituent parts of the body politic; but should more noble, or rather more just, principles regulate the laws, which ought to be the government of society, and not those who execute them, duty might become the rule of private conduct.

Besides, by the exercise of their bodies and minds women would acquire that mental activity so necessary in the maternal character, united with the fortitude that distinguishes steadiness of conduct from the obstinate perverseness of weakness. For it is dangerous to advise the indolent to be steady, because they instantly become rigorous, and to save themselves trouble, punish with severity faults that the patient fortitude of reason might have prevented.

But fortitude presupposes strength of mind, and is strength of mind to be acquired by indolent acquiescence? by asking advice instead of exerting the judgment? by obeying through fear, instead of practising the forbearance which we all stand in need of ourselves? The conclusion which I wish to draw is obvious. Make women rational creatures and free citizens, and they will quickly become good wives and mothers—that is, if men do not neglect the duties of husbands and fathers.

Discussing the advantages which a public and private education combined, as I have sketched, might rationally be expected to produce, I have dwelt most on such as are particularly relative to the female world, because I think the female world oppressed; yet the gangrene, which the vices engendered by oppression have produced, is not confined to the morbid part, but pervades society at large; so that when I wish to see my sex become more like moral agents, my heart bounds with the anticipation of the general diffusion of that sublime contentment which only morality can diffuse.

(1792)

*Thomas Jefferson*

# On the Education of Women

Letter to Nathaniel Burwell

Monticello, March 14, 1818

Dear Sir,

Your letter of February 17th found me suffering under an attack of rheumatism, which has but now left me at sufficient ease to attend to the letters I have received. A plan of female education has never been a subject of systematic contemplation with me. It has occupied my attention so far only as the education of my own daughters occasionally required. Considering that they would be placed in a country situation, where little aid could be obtained from abroad, I thought it essential to give them a solid education, which might enable them, when become mothers, to educate their own daughters, and even to direct the course for sons, should their fathers be lost, or incapable, or inattentive. My surviving daughter accordingly, the mother of many daughters as well as sons, has made their education the object of her life, and being a better judge of the practical part than myself, it is with her aid and that of her élèves that I shall subjoin a catalogue of the books for such a course of reading as we have practiced.

A great obstacle to good education is the inordinate passion prevalent for novels, and the time lost in that reading which should be instructively employed. When this poison infects the mind, it destroys its tone and revolts it against wholesome reading. Reason and fact, plain and unadorned, are rejected. Nothing can engage attention unless dressed in all the figments of fancy, and nothing so bedecked comes amiss. The result is a bloated imagination, sickly judgment, and disgust toward all the real businesses of life. This mass of trash, however, is not without some distinction; some few modelling their narratives, although fictitious, on the incidents of real life, have been able to make them interesting and useful vehicles of a sound morality. Such, I think, are Marmontel's new moral tales, but not his old ones, which are really immoral. Such are the writings of Miss Edgeworth, and some of those of Madame Genlis. For a like reason, too, much poetry should not be indulged. Some is useful for forming style and taste. Pope, Dryden, Thompson, Shakespeare, and of the French, Molière, Racine, the Corneilles, may be read with pleasure and improvement.

The French language, become that of the general intercourse of nations, and from their extraordinary advances, now the depository of all science, is an indispensable part of education for both sexes. In the subjoined catalogue, therefore, I have placed the books of both languages indifferently, according as the one or the other offers what is best.

The ornaments too, and the amusements of life, are entitled to their portion of attention. These, for a female, are dancing, drawing, and music. The first is a healthy exercise, elegant and very attractive for young people. Every affectionate parent would be pleased to see his daughter qualified to participate with her companions, and without awkwardness at least, in the circles of festivity, of which she occasionally becomes a part. It is a necessary accomplishment, therefore, although of short use, for the French rule is wise, that no lady dances after marriage. This is founded in sound physical reasons, gestation and nursing leaving little time to a married lady when this exercise can be safe or innocent. Drawing is thought less of in this country than in Europe. It is an innocent and engaging amusement, often useful, and a qualification not to be neglected in one who is to become a mother and instructor. Music is invaluable where a person has an ear. Where they have not, it should not be attempted. It furnishes a delightful recreation for the hours of respite from the cares of the day, and lasts us through life. The taste of this country, too, calls for this accomplishment more strongly than for either of the others.

I need say nothing of household economy, in which the mothers of our country are generally skilled, and generally careful to instruct their daughters. We all know know its value, and that diligence and dexterity in all its processes are inestimable treasures. The order and economy of a house are as honorable to the mistress as those of the farm to the master, and if either be neglected, ruin follows, and children destitute of the means of living.

This, Sir, is offered as a summary sketch on a subject on which I have not thought much. It probably contains nothing but what has already occurred to yourself, and claims your acceptance on no other ground than as a testimony of my respect for your wishes, and of my great esteem and respect.

*W. D. Snodgrass*

# The Campus on the Hill

Up the reputable walks of old established trees
They stalk, children of the *nouveaux riches*; chimes
Of the tall Clock Tower drench their heads in blessing:
"I don't wanna play at your house;
I don't like you any more."
My house stands opposite, on the other hill,
 Among meadows, with the orchard fences down and falling;
Deer come almost to the door.
You cannot see it, even in this clearest morning.
White birds hang in the air between
Over the garbage landfill and those homes thereto adjacent,
Hovering slowly, turning, settling down
Like the flakes sifting imperceptibly onto the little town
In a waterball of glass.
And yet, this morning, beyond this quiet scene,
The floating birds, the backyards of the poor,
Beyond the shopping plaza, the dead canal, the hillside lying tilted in
      the air,
Tomorrow has broken out today:
Riot in Algeria, in Cyprus, in Alabama;
Aged in wrong, the empires are declining,
And China gathers, soundlessly, like evidence.
What shall I say to the young on such a morning? —
Mind is the one salvation? — also grammar? —
No; my little ones lean not toward revolt. They
Are the Whites, the vaguely furiously driven, who resist
Their souls with such passivity
As would make Quakers swear. All day, dear Lord, all day
They wear their godhead lightly.
They look out from their hill and say,
To themselves, "We have nowhere to go but down;
The great destination is to stay."
Surely the nations will be reasonable;
They look at the world — don't they? — the world's way?
The clock just now has nothing more to say.

                                                        (1959)

*Nathan Glazer*

# The Wasted Classroom

It is understandable that there should be so little fundamental criticism of our colleges and universities. Most original thinking still comes from them, but this is less because they are such good places for it than because there is hardly any place else with even the minor advantages they afford. Few students are unbiased or competent critics. Journalists too often today reproduce others' views rather than develop their own— and the views they would reproduce on colleges and universities would be those naturally of the "experts"—presidents and admissions officers and professors. Perhaps most important, most people are too worried about getting their children into college to be concerned much about what goes on once they get there.

But there are extremely serious problems in the colleges. And despite the millions of dollars now being spent on research in higher education, we are not doing much to make college education more than a huge boondoggle—which is what most of it is today.

From where do I draw my evidence for this view? Aside from my own experience as a student (City College in New York, the University of Pennsylvania, Columbia University), I have been a college teacher: I taught sociology for a year at the University of California in Berkeley, a year at Bennington College in Vermont, a half-year at Smith College—a crude sampling of our better universities and colleges. I have lectured or engaged in research at a half-dozen more colleges and universities, and have friends with whom I have talked about teaching and its problems at almost every important university in the country. Of course I am aware of exceptions, but I am confident that my general conclusion about college holds.

And that conclusion, a sober and not extremist one, is that a very large part of what students and teachers do in the best colleges and universities is sheer waste. It is not particularly vicious waste, except insofar as it dulls minds and irritates and frustrates students and teachers. Nor does it prevent useful and necessary things from being done in the colleges. But it is worth speaking about the waste, not only because it is vast, but because, despite the common awareness that this is so, so little is done about it.

There are, I found, three main sources of waste in college teaching: the classroom system, the examination system, the departmental system.

No doubt certain college subjects do require both classroom teaching and as many classroom hours as are now given to them. But this is not the case with most college subjects. As to what goes on in the sciences, I cannot say—the fact that the radios work, the bridges stand,

and the atom bombs explode, that this complicated technical system works, suggests that teaching in the sciences and technical subjects is not waste, and I will say nothing about them (although I suspect a great deal could, and should, be done to improve the teaching of fundamental scientific concepts to nonspecialists). But I know how classes in literature, in history, in political science and psychology and anthropology and sociology are conducted. In these subjects a single classic mode of organization dominates our schools. Classes meet for three hours a week, some for more, some for less. These classes are conducted by the teacher in a lecture-discussion style – that is, informal lecturing (or in large classes, more formal lecturing), which is often accompanied by some "discussion" initiated by students or teachers. In fact, during most of the class time, the teacher talks to the students.

There are, however, few college subjects in the humanities and the social sciences in which forty-five hours of the teacher lecturing and the students listening can be useful. Perhaps some individual courses may require groups of 15 to 125 students to meet three hours a week for fifteen weeks with a teacher. But when we realize that most students are expected to take four or five such courses, and most teachers to give three of them, it is perfectly clear what actually goes on. Teachers can perhaps (if they are good) give one or two series of good lectures a year; students, unless they are brilliant, may have something to contribute to an occasional discussion. As a matter of fact, however, most teachers give lectures that are not as good as the average texts in their fields – which are not very good – and most students have not read enough or heard enough to make the kind of contribution that is worth making in a class of fifty students. But both accept with amazingly little complaint the strait jacket of the "course."

Now it is true that this strait jacket is broken at certain times – particularly by seminars in which smaller groups meet only once a week with teachers. The seminar system is an enormous step forward: (a) the teacher generally lectures only once a week (and can consequently lecture better), and (b) the students work in small groups, on a single subject, and their personal confusion about some matter – which is normally suppressed or, if raised, is a waste of time in a large class – can be carefully dealt with in a small group. More important, the students have a better chance to discover that true education can only result from their own attempts to organize and clarify a problem, something which is seldom encouraged by lectures to large classes which read textbooks.

In other words, the seminar is the obvious and proper model for education in the humanities and social sciences. But it is rare. It is generally reserved for the graduate school and the graduate students (as if only they really have to learn anything); it is available only to seniors in most colleges, and even then is often reserved for honors students (again, as if only they need to learn).

But let us come back to the problem of the course meeting for forty-five hours a semester (and never forget—there are four or five of these for each student, two or three, in the best schools, for each teacher, and quite often four or even five). The advantage of talking or lecturing to someone is that he gets something in a form he cannot get from reading a book or listening to the radio or looking at television. If lecturing is to be worthwhile it should be personal, fresh, original. Perhaps at the beginning of European university education, students were willing to listen to the same lecture repeated year after year because books were in manuscript and rare, and one in effect had to record one's own book in the form of notes from the lips of the teacher. Perhaps too in an earlier epoch there was the feeling that knowledge was esoteric and should be communicated orally. Obviously such considerations no longer prevail, although thousands of students still scrawl endless pages of notes, often while sitting in a vacant daze.

This is not to say that there are no justifications at all for lecturing. There are teachers who are in effect writing their book as they lecture—if it is an important book (like the books Hegel was writing), then scholars will come to listen, rather than wait for the book itself. On the continent today a course of lectures, I understand, is often this book in process—it is the work that a man is doing, being presented to minds ready to understand and profit from it. And it can be argued that lecturing has its value as stimulation and entertainment—the art of lecturing is one that every academician appreciates, and that many students do too, and it certainly has a place in the university.

A teacher can indeed perform useful functions in his lectures: he may argue with what the students have been given to read; he may supplement it or arrange it for them. But he does not need forty-five hours a semester to do this—the students would be better off reading more books, thinking more, working more, and taking fewer notes. I have heard a lot of lectures in my lifetime as a student, researcher, and teacher, and I would ask college teachers to honestly consider in how many courses a dozen good lectures would not do all that could be done—in the form of *lecturing*—for a class.

But the timetable traditionally called for forty-five hours, and now the students expect it, administrations demand it, and even teachers have become convinced there's no harm in it, although many are hard put to fill up the forty-five hours usefully. Hardly anyone thinks of beginning at the beginning, forgetting the system, and deciding when and where this form of course organization is best.

In the sciences, with their special laboratory periods, the courses are somewhat better arranged. And recently, one of the worst victims of the standard course arrangement, the teaching of languages, has also been freeing itself from the three-hours-a-week standard. But no such revolution in the arrangement of the course seems imminent in the social sciences and humanities, though the need is just as great.

Fortunately for the system this first skeleton is propped up by a second – the examination system. If there is no other way of making fruitful use of forty-five hours of class time, at least one can use this time to prepare the students for an equally fruitless practice required by the system – the examinations. Once again I remind the reader that I have limited myself to the humanities and social sciences. In technical subjects – sciences, mathematics, languages – subjects which develop specific skills and transmit (for the moment) a fixed body of laws, principles and procedures, examinations are not only possible but necessary. One can arrange a language (I mean in learning it as a skill to use – not its literature) or a science or mathematical discipline into sections of hierarchal levels of complexity so that one must pass a test in step one before taking step two, and so on.

But in the humanities and the social sciences this kind of ordering often is literally not possible. I recall once being asked by the college administration what were the "prerequisites" for two courses I was going to teach in sociology. Since the students had to take Math I before Math II, it was assumed that Sociology I – whatever that is – must come before Sociology II. But in fact I saw no reason why the students could not take the courses I was giving – one on American ethnic groups, another on cities and their problems – without having taken any other course in sociology. (Of course, it may be useful and illuminating to have studied one aspect of philosophy or history, or literature, or the social sciences, before another; but this is not a prerequisite in the way Math I is a prerequisite.)

The nature of examinations in the humanities and the social sciences must be different. For what are the examinations to contain? We do not transmit fixed bodies of law, principle, or skill in which students can be drilled and then examined by a simple and unambiguous test. Plenty of information is transmitted, but, in general, the mastery of pure facts or methods is not the essential skill in question. The aim in these disciplines is understanding, appreciation, discrimination, reasoning; and drill in them is only possible if they are taught badly, in catechistic fashion. When drill occurs in the social sciences and the humanities – as it often does – the teachers and students are likely to feel that they are still in high school, and they are right.

I have been told that if you ask a Soviet philosophy student what pragmatism is – or who Dewey or William James was – he can recite to you the definitions and brief one-sentence accounts from a Soviet philosophical dictionary. It is possible to drill the Soviet students in these subjects only because they are not learning them. And once again, we see the cold hand of the medieval university in the notion of examinations in the humanities and social sciences, for there too one could be drilled catechistically in received knowledge. But how silly to ask for the "right" answers to questions about poems or complicated movements in history or literature or complex social problems! However, one teaching skeleton props up the next. Since teachers are required to give courses and grades, they too often run their courses by feeding out neat interpretations which can be properly regurgitated at exam times, and marked "right."

Certainly not all courses are conducted like this. In some colleges, the requirements for grades are met by something far more adequate than the usual examinations—the student's own work. He is asked to apply what he learns from reading and discussion to the analysis of a piece of literature or the consideration of a problem, and in answering such an essay question the student may theoretically have an opportunity for a modulated presentation of a subject which catches up some of its complexity.

But the matter is not so simple. Many of the elementary courses in college are given in large lecture rooms, supplemented by discussion groups conducted by graduate students. How can the essay questions presented to large classes be graded so that equality and justice can prevail? What often happens is that factual questions are presented in essay form. The graduate students or assistants who administer and mark the tests get together and decide that in answering a particular question a student will have to refer to, say, four or five points, each to be given so much credit. This settled, they begin plowing through the stacks of papers.

But how can this bureaucratic system of marking take account of what is essentially important in an essay—understanding, a general grasp of the material, a capacity to see it freshly and originally? For teachers of the sciences, engineering, and languages, these qualities, of course, may not be essential. They want the students to get it right. But what good teacher in the humanities merely wants it "right"—wants, in effect, a textbooky reproduction of his lecture which will be forgotten in a few weeks? Since the teacher is, in fact, forced to lecture, and forced to give examinations and grades, he will too often settle for this and could not in all justice give it a bad mark—but it is not what he is looking for. If it is, he is a bad teacher.

There is an obvious answer to this problem. For the examination, there could be substituted the demanding paper, the job of work, just as for the class there could be substituted the seminar. And yet, just as the seminar is something special and reserved for the graduate student, so too the paper is something special—the student may do one, but he still generally must take a meaningless examination, and somehow it must be graded. Since the system demands grades, no one questions them— and no one asks whether it really was worth it to have spent all that time deciding the marks for a hundred students. (Suppose this time was spent in going over a student's research paper with him—something that is seldom done.)

Observing the examination system in operation, I have become more and more persuaded that it is fundamentally unjust to the student, for it assumes that the student is being graded for his work in the course. There is a certain rough truth to this when technical subjects, scientific skills, languages, and the like, are being studied. In the social sciences and humanities, this is simply not so. The student's grades reflect his general ability to use language, to organize, to think rapidly, at least as much as they show what he has gained from the course. Indeed, after working in schools where the atmosphere is dominated by the rituals of examinations and grades, I have often thought that it would be useful to give the examination the first day of the course and get that stupidity out of the way. This would at least turn the attention of the students to the substance of the course itself. For in fact, as the system now operates in most colleges, those who are gifted in the art of taking exams—who can write fluently, think quickly, regurgitate systematically—will generally do well in any case, and the relation of the amount of time and interest invested in the course to final grades is often accidental.

The entire concept of college examinations, in short, needs radical review. Even when students taking courses in the humanities and social sciences are asked challenging essay questions, and marked carefully, their performance must depend not simply on the specific matter that has been presented to them but on the entire world of reading and experience and perception they bring to the subject. In effect, they are being tested not on the specific course but on the sum of their work in the broad area of knowledge in question. Why bother, then, with specific course examinations and grades—why not give the student a limited number of general tests toward the end of his college career, with a few over-all grades? If colleges emphasized intensive reading and seminars rather than lectures—and individual papers rather than sterile course exams—this kind of examination would seem natural—if examinations were required at all.

Finally, we come to the third evil of college teaching today—the departments. If the classroom system needs grades to justify its existence, it also needs the departmental system to fill up the class time and decide what to ask on the examinations. Once again, let us divide what is necessary and useful from its distortion. The departments of knowledge have a long and honorable history. To be a member of a department means that a man owes his loyalty to his field of knowledge as well as to his university. Indeed, the department, or rather the discipline (which is expressed in the form of the department in each college or university), is more important to him generally than the school in which he happens to teach. He may shift schools but scarcely ever will he be able to shift departments. His advancement, within his college or from a job in one college to another, will depend not on his virtues as a teacher (who is to judge that?) but on his standing in his discipline, and this standing is measured by (a) his doctoral degree (granted by a group of people who have such degrees in the same discipline); (b) his publications (in the journals of his discipline); and (c) his research grants (given by persons drawn from his discipline). And of course he has been trained in that discipline, in a graduate school.

What this means is that it is much easier for a man to think of himself as a psychologist, a historian, a sociologist, a classicist, a specialist in Elizabethan drama than as someone who is engaged in liberal education. And he is more concerned in *communicating his discipline* to the students than in *educating* them. Obviously this is a large and general charge and there are exceptions. But since it is the discipline that has prestige, the professor is oriented generally to what is most characteristic of the discipline. This means the newest thinking in his specialty, the most abstract concepts, the things about which scholars do research and publish papers. In psychology, for example, he would think he was engaged in the worst kind of sellout if he paid attention to the psychological problems that concern the students rather than to those that concern psychologists.

In effect, the making of scholars in the graduate schools, while it does produce some good scholars, certainly makes many poor teachers. But there are more pernicious effects of the system of departments than the role of the discipline itself. There is first of all the competition among the departments, for status, for students, for prestige. This means that there is constant bickering over how many courses a student must be required to take in this or in that subject. And the central concern of such arguments, unfortunately, is not what the student needs for a good education (though certainly such a motivation does play a role), but the interests of the department: Can we require fewer courses in our department than others require in their departments? Can we accept the fact that our discipline plays a less essential role in education than others? (The answer is usually no—departments fiercely insist on equal status.) Can we (and this is a most important consideration) accept the fact that if we allow this or that course to be dropped from the list of requirements, we will have to let a man go, or not be able to make a new appointment?

These questions are the very stuff of academic life. The question of building and teaching a curriculum relevant to the needs of the college-educated citizen is far less pressing.

Departmentalization thus means that liberal education is hurt in another and crucial way—educational programs that cannot be fitted into the departmental scheme are shortchanged. Everyone knows that sociology, anthropology, social psychology, political science, and history today deal in large part with a common subject matter. But joint courses in this general field must usually be conducted by people whose primary loyalty is to their discipline. Indeed, it is almost impossible to find distinguished people who are ready to devote themselves to interdepartmental courses in the social sciences. Professor Lewis Feuer, who conducts such a joint course in the social sciences at the University of California in Berkeley, is able to transcend these silly battles between disciplinary representatives, in part because he is a philosopher; Professor David Riesman, who gives a general course in the social sciences at Harvard, is also able to transcend them in part, because he has been formally trained in none of the competing disciplines. (He is a lawyer who trained himself in them.) But even when one finds such rare individuals to take over the so-called interdisciplinary courses, they are hampered in finding assistants and associates—for all advancement, as I have pointed out, is made through achievement in the disciplines. And if a graduate student or professor should devote himself to acquiring and teaching what everyone agrees is most important for a liberal education—the broad grounding that is common to a number of disciplines—how would he achieve advancement?

The predictable result of departmentalization—and I have not even begun to analyze the reasons for the strength of the departments—has been that the great experiments in liberal education of the 'twenties and 'thirties have been grinding to a close.

Let us see what has happened. For many years the University of Chicago gave perhaps the best undergraduate education in the United States. Departments were entirely abolished in the College and all students were required to take broad courses in the Social Sciences (sociology, anthropology, political science, economics, etc.); the Humanities (drama, fiction, poetry, philosophy, etc.); the Natural Sciences (physics, biology, geology, astronomy, etc.); as well as Mathematics. Much of the instruction took place in seminars. It emphasized the intensive reading of original texts (not textbooks), and some of the most distinguished scholars in the University were willing to conduct small classes in the College. The admirable premise here was that the college-educated citizen should be exposed to important ideas and methods in the major fields of knowledge, whatever his ultimate choice of specialty, within the university or without. But now the College is succumbing to the power of research-oriented departments, and it is becoming more traditional in its approach.

Similarly, the Contemporary Civilization Course of Columbia College—another famous attempt at interdepartmental education—recently abandoned its second year. And, as Christopher Jencks' article in this supplement makes clear, Harvard's once ambitious General Education courses have failed to challenge the domination of its departments.

Indeed, as one looks over the American college scene, it becomes clear that American education has never been more conservative than it is today. Why is this so? It is not because the experiments in changing the undergraduate program have failed. It cannot be said that the students at Antioch, Bennington, and Sarah Lawrence are worse educated than those from more traditional schools. Nor have general-education courses at Columbia, Harvard, and Chicago produced inferior students. Quite the contrary. What has happened is that the emphasis on achievement in the traditional departmental disciplines has become nearly irresistible. In recent years it has been reinforced by the enormous research funds which have been made available to the departments by government, industry, and foundations. As a result, the numbers and effectiveness of those men and women who might be interested in new approaches to undergraduate education have been radically reduced. For a young scholar to devote time, thought, and energy to developing general-education programs may well involve risk to his career. Thus the general-education movement is being crushed, and the plague of departmentalization now grows even in the small progressive colleges.

No doubt, a good deal more is wrong with higher education. I speak from an intermediate level, higher than the students and lower than the administrators, and this is what I have seen, and I am not alone.

Recently, for example, a group of college teachers drawn from four colleges in the Connecticut Valley—Smith, Mt. Holyoke, Amherst, and the University of Massachusetts—spent some time thinking of how to set up a new college that would give an education as good as these colleges are reputed to give, at lower cost. They proposed a New College, one of whose main principles is the elimination of the usual classroom lecturing, in favor of seminars on the one hand and a few lectures on the other. The expectation is that in such a program students could do a better job educating themselves (with the serious help of their teachers) than in one where they were spending the best hours of the day going through the ritual of the classroom. Another major proposal for the New College was that it should not try to have a full roster of departments, with all the evil effects that this must entail in undergraduate education.

Perhaps it is another straw in the wind that the University of the Pacific in Stockton, California, has announced a radical reorganization in which students will take only three courses a semester, each course meeting five hours a week. Students' eligibility for graduation will be based on final examinations of proficiency and on the recommendations of tutors. Except for the fact that the new plan—apparently concerned that students and teachers will not put in enough time—assigns *five* hours to each course, it seems a hopeful one. One new experimental college, Monteith, recently founded at Wayne State University in Detroit, is carrying on the general-education approach that is declining at the University of Chicago. One of the most serious efforts to establish a strong general-education curriculum is being made by the new York University in Toronto. And while it is true that general education is declining in the big universities, some of the small experimental colleges of the past—Antioch, Sarah Lawrence, Bennington—with their individual and nontraditional approaches, still seem strong. Their problem, however, is to find young teachers who do not have a narrow disciplinary approach.

Unfortunately, no one has suggested any way of dealing with this problem, which I believe is the crux of the matter. Educational reform must be the work of the administrators and the professors who are truly concerned about the minds of undergraduates. A few have indicated what they implicitly think of most American college education. But the rest . . . alas, the pleasures of research are real, the disciplinary training is powerful, and not many of them think that much is wrong with college education. Nor does the general public seem worried. Higher education does after all train technicians, enough to keep things going; it does hand out diplomas that qualify people for higher status and better jobs. But the fact that it is largely a huge waste for our young people who spent some of their best years there, and for the thousands of teachers who spend most of their lives there, does not seem to bother many people. It should.

(1961)

*Hannah Arendt*

# The Crisis in Education*

## 1

The general crisis that has overtaken the modern world everywhere and in almost every sphere of life manifests itself differently in each country, involving different areas and taking on different forms. In America, one of its most characteristic and suggestive aspects is the recurring crisis in education that, during the last decade at least, has become a political problem of the first magnitude, reported on almost daily in the newspapers. To be sure, no great imagination is required to detect the dangers of a constantly progressing decline of elementary standards throughout the entire school system, and the seriousness of the trouble has been properly underlined by the countless unavailing efforts of the educational authorities to stem the tide. Still, if one compares this crisis in education with the political experiences of other countries in the twentieth century, with the revolutionary turmoil after the First World War, with concentration and extermination camps, or even with the profound malaise which, appearances of prosperity to the contrary notwithstanding, has spread throughout Europe ever since the end of the Second World War, it is somewhat difficult to take a crisis in education as seriously as it deserves. It is tempting indeed to regard it as a

*Translation by Denver Lindley.

local phenomenon, unconnected with the larger issues of the century, to be blamed on certain peculiarities of life in the United States which are not likely to find a counterpart in other parts of the world.

Yet, if this were true, the crisis in our school system would not have become a political issue and the educational authorities would not have been unable to deal with it in time. Certainly more is involved here than the puzzling question of why Johnny can't read. Moreover, there is always a temptation to believe that we are dealing with specific problems confined within historical and national boundaries and of importance only to those immediately affected. It is precisely this belief that in our time has consistently proved false. One can take it as a general rule in this century that whatever is possible in one country may in the foreseeable future be equally possible in almost any other.

Aside from these general reasons that would make it seem advisable for the layman to be concerned with trouble in fields about which, in the specialist's sense, he may know nothing (and this, since I am not a professional educator, is of course my case when I deal with a crisis in education), there is another even more cogent reason for his concerning himself with a critical situation in which he is not immediately involved. And that is the opportunity, provided by the very fact of crisis—which tears away façades and obliterates prejudices—to explore and inquire into whatever has been laid bare of the essence of the matter, and the essence of education is natality, the fact that human beings are *born* into the world. The disappearance of prejudices simply means that we have lost the answers on which we ordinarily rely without even realizing they were originally answers to questions. A crisis forces us back to the questions themselves and requires from us either new or old answers, but in any case direct judgments. A crisis becomes a disaster only when we respond to it with preformed judgments, that is, with prejudices. Such an attitude not only sharpens the crisis but makes us forfeit the experience of reality and the opportunity for reflection it provides.

However clearly a general problem may present itself in a crisis, it is nevertheless impossible ever to isolate completely the universal element from the concrete and specific circumstances in which it makes its appearance. Though the crisis in education may affect the whole world, it is characteristic that we find its most extreme form in America, the reason being that perhaps only in America could a crisis in education actually become a factor in politics. In America, as a matter of fact, education plays a different and, politically, incomparably more important role than in other countries. Technically, of course, the explanation lies in the fact that America has always been a land of immigrants; it is obvious that the enormously difficult melting together of the most diverse ethnic groups—never fully successful but continuously succeeding beyond expectation—can only be accomplished through the schooling, education, and Americanization of the immigrants' children. Since for most of these children English is not their mother tongue but has to be learned in school, schools must obviously assume functions which in a nation-state would be performed as a matter of course in the home.

More decisive, however, for our considerations is the role that continuous immigration plays in the country's political consciousness and frame of mind. America is not simply a colonial country in need of immigrants to populate the land, though independent of them in its political structure. For America the determining factor has always been the motto printed on every dollar bill: *Novus Ordo Seclorum*, A New Order of the World. The immigrants, the newcomers, are a guarantee to the country that it represents the new order. The meaning of this new order, this founding of a new world against the old, was and is the doing away with poverty and oppression. But at the same time its magnificence consists in the fact that from the beginning this new order did not shut itself off from the outside world—as has elsewhere been the custom in the founding of utopias—in order to confront it with a perfect model, nor was its purpose to enforce imperial claims or to be preached as an evangel to others. Rather its relation to the outside world has been characterized from the start by the fact that this republic, which planned to abolish poverty and slavery, welcomed all the poor and enslaved of the earth. In the words spoken by John Adams in 1765—that is, before the Declaration of Independence—"I always consider the settlement of America as the opening of a grand scheme and design in Providence for the illumination and emancipation of the slavish part of mankind all over the earth." This is the basic intent or the basic law in accordance with which America began her historical and political existence.

The extraordinary enthusiasm for what is new, which is shown in almost every aspect of American daily life, and the concomitant trust in an "indefinite perfectibility"—which Tocqueville noted as the credo of the common "uninstructed man" and which as such antedates by almost a hundred years the development in other countries of the West—would presumably have resulted in any case in greater attention paid and greater significance ascribed to the newcomers by birth, that is, the children, whom, when they had outgrown their childhood and were about to enter the community of adults as young people, the Greeks simply called οἱ νέοι, the new ones. There is the additional fact, however, a fact that has become decisive for the meaning of education, that this pathos of the new, though it is considerably older than the eighteenth century, only developed conceptually and politically in that century. From this source there was derived at the start an educational ideal, tinged with Rousseauism and in fact directly influenced by Rousseau, in which education became an instrument of politics, and political activity itself was conceived of as a form of education.

The role played by education in all political utopias from ancient times onward shows how natural it seems to start a new world with those who are by birth and nature new. So far as politics is concerned, this involves of course a serious misconception: instead of joining with one's equals in assuming the effort of persuasion and running the risk of failure, there is dictatorial intervention, based upon the absolute superiority of the adult, and the attempt to produce the new as a *fait accompli*, that is, as though the new already existed. For this reason, in Europe, the belief that one must begin with the children if one wishes to produce new conditions has remained principally the monopoly of revolutionary movements of tyrannical cast which, when they came to power, took the children away from their parents and simply indoctrinated them. Education can play no part in politics, because in politics we always have to deal with those who are already educated. Whoever wants to educate adults really wants to act as their guardian and prevent them from political activity. Since one cannot educate adults, the word "education" has an evil sound in politics; there is a pretense of education, when the real purpose is coercion without the use of force. He who seriously wants to create a new political order through education, that is, neither through force and constraint nor through persuasion, must draw the dreadful Platonic conclusion: the banishment of all older people from the state that is to be founded. But even the children one wishes to educate to be citizens of a utopian morrow are actually denied their own future role in the body politic, for, from the standpoint of the new ones, whatever new the adult world may propose is necessarily older than they themselves. It is in the very nature of the human condition that each new generation grows into an old world, so that to prepare a new generation for a new world can only mean that one wishes to strike from the newcomers' hands their own chance at the new.

All this is by no means the case in America, and it is exactly this fact that makes it so hard to judge these questions correctly here. The political role that education actually plays in a land of immigrants, the fact that the schools not only serve to Americanize the children but affect their parents as well, that here in fact one helps to shed an old world and to enter into a new one, encourages the illusion that a new world is being built through the education of the children. Of course the true situation is not this at all. The world into which children are introduced, even in America, is an old world, that is, a pre-existing world, constructed by the living and the dead, and it is new only for those who have newly entered it by immigration. But here illusion is stronger than reality because it springs directly from a basic American experience, the experience that a new order can be founded, and what is more, founded with full consciousness of a historical continuum, for the phrase "New World" gains its meaning from the Old World, which, however admirable on other scores, was rejected because it could find no solution for poverty and oppression.

Now in respect to education itself the illusion arising from the pathos of the new has produced its most serious consequences only in our own century. It has first of all made it possible for that complex of modern educational theories which originated in Middle Europe and consists of an astounding hodgepodge of sense and nonsense to accomplish, under the banner of progressive education, a most radical revolution in the whole system of education. What in Europe has remained an experiment, tested out here and there in single schools and isolated educational institutions and then gradually extending its influences in certain quarters, in America about twenty-five years ago completely overthrew, as though from one day to the next, all traditions and all the established methods of teaching and learning. I shall not go into details, and I leave out of account private schools and especially the Roman Catholic parochial school system. The significant fact is that for the sake of certain theories, good or bad, all the rules of sound human reason were thrust aside. Such a procedure is always of great and pernicious significance, especially in a country that relies so extensively on common sense in its political life. Whenever in political questions sound human reason fails or gives up the attempt to supply answers we are faced by a crisis; for this kind of reason is really that common sense by virtue of which we and our five individual senses are fitted into a single world common to us all and by the aid of which we move about in it. The disappearance of common sense in the present day is the surest sign of the present-day crisis. In every crisis a piece of the world, something common to us all, is destroyed. The failure of common sense, like a divining rod, points to the place where such a cave-in has occurred.

In any case the answer to the question of why Johnny can't read or to the more general question of why the scholastic standards of the average American school lag so very far behind the average standards in actually all the countries of Europe is not, unfortunately, simply that this country is young and has not yet caught up with the standards of the Old World but, on the contrary, that this country in this particular field is the most "advanced" and most modern in the world. And this is true in a double sense: nowhere have the education problems of a mass society become so acute, and nowhere else have the most modern theories in the realm of pedagogy been so uncritically and slavishly accepted. Thus the crisis in American education, on the one hand, announces the bankruptcy of progressive education and, on the other, presents a problem of immense difficulty because it has arisen under the conditions and in response to the demands of a mass society.

In this connection we must bear in mind another more general factor which did not, to be sure, cause the crisis but which has aggravated it to a remarkable degree, and this is the unique role the concept of equality plays and always has played in American life. Much more is involved in this than equality before the law, more too than the leveling of class distinctions, more even than what is expressed in the phrase "equality of opportunity," though that has a greater significance in this connection because in the American view a right to education is one of the inalienable civic rights. This last has been decisive for the structure of the public-school system in that secondary schools in the European sense exist only as exceptions. Since compulsory school attendance extends to the age of sixteen, every child must enter high school, and the high school therefore is basically a kind of continuation of primary school. As a result of this lack of a secondary school the preparation for the college course has to be supplied by the colleges themselves, whose curricula therefore suffer from a chronic overload, which in turn affects the quality of the work done there.

At first glance one might perhaps think that this anomaly lies in the very nature of a mass society in which education is no longer a privilege of the wealthy classes. A glance at England, where, as everyone knows, secondary education has also been made available in recent years to all classes of the population, will show that this is not the case. For there at the end of primary school, with students at the age of eleven, has been instituted the dreaded examination that weeds out all but some ten per cent of the scholars suited for higher education. The rigor of this selection was not accepted even in England without protest; in America it would have been simply impossible. What is aimed at in England is "meritocracy," which is clearly once more the establishment of an oligarchy, this time not of wealth or of birth but of talent. But this means, even though people in England may not be altogether clear about it, that the country even under a socialist government will continue to be governed as it has been from time out of mind, that is, neither as a monarchy nor as a democracy but as an oligarchy or aristocracy— the latter in case one takes the view that the most gifted are also the best, which is by no means a certainty. In America such an almost physical division of the children into gifted and ungifted would be considered intolerable. Meritocracy contradicts the principle of equality, of an equalitarian democracy, no less than any other oligarchy.

Thus what makes the educational crisis in America so especially acute is the political temper of the country, which of itself struggles to equalize or to erase as far as possible the difference between young and old, between the gifted and the ungifted, finally between children and adults, particularly between pupils and teachers. It is obvious that such an equalization can actually be accomplished only at the cost of the teacher's authority and at the expense of the gifted among the students. However, it is equally obvious, at least to anyone who has ever come in contact with the American educational system, that this difficulty, rooted in the political attitude of the country, also has great advantages, not simply of a human kind but educationally speaking as well; in any case these general factors cannot explain the crisis in which we presently find ourselves nor justify the measures through which that crisis has been precipitated.

**2**

These ruinous measures can be schematically traced back to three basic assumptions, all of which are only too familiar. The *first* is that there exist a child's world and a society formed among children that are autonomous and must insofar as possible be left to them to govern. Adults are only there to help with this government. The authority that tells the individual child what to do and what not to do rests with the child group itself – and this produces, among other consequences, a situation in which the adult stands helpless before the individual child and out of contact with him. He can only tell him to do what he likes and then prevent the worst from happening. The real and normal relations between children and adults, arising from the fact that people of all ages are always simultaneously together in the world, are thus broken off. And so it is of the essence of this first basic assumption that it takes into account only the group and not the individual child.

As for the child in the group, he is of course rather worse off than before. For the authority of a group, even a child group, is always considerably stronger and more tyrannical than the severest authority of an individual person can ever be. If one looks at it from the standpoint of the individual child, his chances to rebel or to do anything on his own hook are practically nil; he no longer finds himself in a very unequal contest with a person who has, to be sure, absolute superiority over him but in contest with whom he can nevertheless count on the solidarity of other children, that is, of his own kind; rather he is in the position, hopeless by definition, of a minority of one confronted by the absolute majority of all the others. There are very few grown people who can endure such a situation, even when it is not supported by external means of compulsion; children are simply and utterly incapable of it.

Therefore by being emancipated from the authority of adults the child has not been freed but has been subjected to a much more terrifying and truly tyrannical authority, the tyranny of the majority. In any case the result is that the children have been so to speak banished from the world of grown-ups. They are either thrown back upon themselves or handed over to the tyranny of their own group, against which, because of its numerical superiority, they cannot rebel, with which, because they are children, they cannot reason, and out of which they cannot flee to any other world because the world of adults is barred to them. The reaction of the children to this pressure tends to be either conformism or juvenile delinquency, and is frequently a mixture of both.

The *second* basic assumption which has come into question in the present crisis has to do with teaching. Under the influence of modern psychology and the tenets of pragmatism, pedagogy has developed into a science of teaching in general in such a way as to be wholly emancipated from the actual material to be taught. A teacher, so it was thought, is a man who can simply teach anything; his training is in teaching, not in the mastery of any particular subject. This attitude, as we shall presently see, is naturally very closely connected with a basic assumption about learning. Moreover, it has resulted in recent decades in a most serious neglect of the training of teachers in their own subjects, especially in the public high schools Since the teacher does not need to know his own subject, it not infrequently happens that he is just one hour ahead of his class in knowledge. This in turn means not only that the students are actually left to their own resources but that the most legitimate source of the teacher's authority as the person who, turn it whatever way one will, still knows more and can do more than oneself is no longer effective. Thus the non-authoritarian teacher, who would like to abstain from all methods of compulsion because he is able to rely on his own authority, can no longer exist.

But this pernicious role that pedagogy and the teachers' colleges are playing in the present crisis was only possible because of a modern theory about learning. This was, quite simply, the logical application of the *third* basic assumption in our context, an assumption which the modern world has held for centuries and which found its systematic conceptual expression in pragmatism. This basic assumption is that you can know and understand only what you have done yourself, and its application to education is as primitive as it is obvious: to substitute, insofar as possible, doing for learning. The reason that no importance was attached to the teacher's mastering his own subject was the wish to compel him to the exercise of the continuous activity of learning so that he would not, as they said, pass on "dead knowledge" but, instead, would constantly demonstrate how it is produced. The conscious intention was not to teach knowledge but to inculcate a skill, and the result was a kind of transformation of institutes for learning into vocational institutions which have been as successful in teaching how to drive a car or how to use a typewriter or, even more important for the "art" of living, how to get along with other people and to be popular, as they have been unable to make the children acquire the normal prerequisites of a standard curriculum.

However, this description is at fault, not only because it obviously exaggerates in order to drive home a point, but because it fails to take into account how in this process special importance was attached to obliterating as far as possible the distinction between play and work—in favor of the former. Play was looked upon as the liveliest and most appropriate way for the child to behave in the world, as the only form of activity that evolves spontaneously from his existence as a child. Only what can be learned through play does justice to this liveliness. The child's characteristic activity, so it was thought, lies in play; learning in the old sense, by forcing a child into an attitude of passivity, compelled him to give up his own playful initiative.

The close connection between these two things—the substitution of doing for learning and of playing for working—is directly illustrated by the teaching of languages: the child is to learn by speaking, that is by doing, not by studying grammar and syntax; in other words he is to learn a foreign language in the same way that as an infant he learned his own language: as though at play and in the uninterrupted continuity of simple existence. Quite apart from the question of whether this is possible or not—it is possible, to a limited degree, only when one can keep the child all day long in the foreign-speaking environment—it is perfectly clear that this procedure consciously attempts to keep the older child as far as possible at the infant level. The very thing that should prepare the child for the world of adults, the gradually acquired habit of work and of not-playing, is done away with in favor of the autonomy of the world of childhood.

Whatever may be the connection between doing and knowing, or whatever the validity of the pragmatic formula, its application to education, that is, to the way the child learns, tends to make absolute the world of childhood in just the same way that we noted in the case of the first basic assumption. Here, too, under the pretext of respecting the child's independence, he is debarred from the world of grown-ups and artifically kept in his own, so far as that can be called a world. This holding back of the child is artificial because it breaks off the natural relationship between grown-ups and children, which consists among other things in teaching and learning, and because at the same time it belies the fact that the child is a developing human being, that childhood is a temporary stage, a preparation for adulthood.

The present crisis in America results from the recognition of the destructiveness of these basic assumptions and a desperate attempt to reform the entire educational system, that is, to transform it completely. In doing this what is actually being attempted—except for the plans for an immense increase in the facilities for training in the physical sciences and in technology—is nothing but restoration: teaching will once more be conducted with authority; play is to stop in school hours, and serious work is once more to be done; emphasis will shift from extracurricular skills to knowledge prescribed by the curriculum; finally there is even talk of transforming the present curricula for teachers so that the teachers themselves will have to learn something before being turned loose on the children.

These proposed reforms, which are still in the discussion state and are of purely American interest, need not concern us here. Nor can I discuss the more technical, yet in the long run perhaps even more important question of how to reform the curricula of elementary and secondary schools in all countries so as to bring them up to the entirely new requirements of the present world. What is of importance to our argument is a twofold question. Which aspects of the modern world and its crisis have actually revealed themselves in the educational crisis, that is, what are the true reasons that for decades things could be said and done in such glaring contradiction to common sense? And, second, what can we learn from this crisis for the essence of education—not in the sense that one can always learn from mistakes what ought not to be done, but rather by reflecting on the role that education plays in every civilization, that is on the obligation that the existence of children entails for every human society. We shall begin with the second question.

## 3

A crisis in education would at any time give rise to serious concern even if it did not reflect, as in the present instance it does, a more general crisis and instability in modern society. For education belongs among the most elementary and necessary activities of human society, which never remains as it is but continuously renews itself through birth, through the arrival of new human beings. These newcomers, moreover, are not finished but in a state of becoming. Thus the child, the subject of education, has for the educator a double aspect: he is new in a world that is strange to him and he is in process of becoming, he is a new human being and he is a becoming human being. This double aspect is by no means self-evident and it does not apply to the animal forms of life; it corresponds to a double relationship, the relationship to the world on the one hand and to life on the other. The child shares the state of becoming with all living things; in respect to life and its development, the child is a human being in process of becoming, just as a kitten is a cat in process of becoming. But the child is new only in relation to a world that was there before him, that will continue after his death, and in which he is to spend his life. If the child were not a newcomer in this human world but simply a not yet finished living creature, education would be just a function of life and would need to consist in nothing save that concern for the sustenance of life and that training and practice in living that all animals assume in respect to their young.

Human parents, however, have not only summoned their children into life through conception and birth, they have simultaneously introduced them into a world. In education they assume responsibility for both, for the life and development of the child and for the continuance of the world. These two responsibilities do not by any means coincide; they may indeed come into conflict with each other. The responsibility for the development of the child turns in a certain sense against the world: the child requires special protection and care so that nothing destructive may happen to him from the world. But the world, too, needs protection to keep it from being overrun and destroyed by the onslaught of the new that bursts upon it with each new generation.

Because the child must be protected against the world, his traditional place is in the family, whose adult members daily return back from the outside world and withdraw into the security of private life within four walls. These four walls, within which people's private family life is lived, constitute a shield against the world and specifically against the public aspect of the world. They enclose a secure place, without which no living thing can thrive. This holds good not only for the life of childhood but for human life in general. Wherever the latter is consistently exposed to the world without the protection of privacy and security its vital quality is destroyed. In the public world, common to all, persons count, and so does work, that is, the work of our hands that each of us contributes to our common world; but life *qua* life does not matter there. The world cannot be regardful of it, and it has to be hidden and protected from the world.

Everything that lives, not vegetative life alone, emerges from darkness and, however strong its natural tendency to thrust itself into the light, it nevertheless needs the security of darkness to grow at all. This may indeed be the reason that children of famous parents so often turn out badly. Fame penetrates the four walls, invades their private space, bringing with it, especially in present-day conditions, the merciless glare of the public realm, which floods everything in the private lives of those concerned, so that the children no longer have a place of security where they can grow. But exactly the same destruction of the real living space occurs wherever the attempt is made to turn the children themselves into a kind of world. Among these peer groups then arises public life of a sort and, quite apart from the fact that it is not a real one and that the whole attempt is a sort of fraud, the damaging fact remains that children—that is, human beings in process of becoming but not yet complete—are thereby forced to expose themselves to the light of a public existence.

That modern education, insofar as it attempts to establish a world of children, destroys the necessary conditions for vital development and growth seems obvious. But that such harm to the developing child should be the result of modern education strikes one as strange indeed, for this education maintained that its exclusive aim was to serve the child and rebelled against the methods of the past because these had not sufficiently taken into account the child's inner nature and his needs. "The Century of the Child," as we may recall, was going to emancipate the child and free him from the standards derived from the adult world. Then how could it happen that the most elementary conditions of life necessary for the growth and development of the child were overlooked or simply not recognized? How could it happen that the child was exposed to what more than anything else characterized the adult world, its public aspect, after the decision had just been reached that the mistake in all past education had been to see the child as nothing but an undersized grown-up?

The reason for this strange state of affairs has nothing directly to do with education; it is rather to be found in the judgments and prejudices about the nature of private life and public world and their relation to each other which have been characteristic of modern society since the beginning of modern times and which educators, when they finally began, relatively late, to modernize education, accepted as self-evident assumptions without being aware of the consequences they must necessarily have for the life of the child. It is the peculiarity of modern society, and by no means a matter of course, that it regards life, that is, the earthly life of the individual as well as the family, as the highest good; and for this reason, in contrast to all previous centuries, emancipated this life and all the activities that have to do with its preservation and enrichment from the concealment of privacy and exposed them to the light of the public world. This is the real meaning of the emancipation of workers and women, not as persons, to be sure, but insofar as they fulfill a necessary function in the life-process of society.

The last to be affected by this process of emancipation were the children, and the very thing that had meant a true liberation for the workers and the women—because they were not only workers and women but persons as well, who therefore had a claim on the public world, that is, a right to see and be seen in it, to speak and be heard— was an abandonment and betrayal in the case of the children, who are still at the stage where the simple fact of life and growth outweighs the factor of personality. The more completely modern society discards the distinction between what is private and what is public, between what can thrive only in concealment and what needs to be shown to all in the full light of the public world, the more, that is, it introduces between the private and the public a social sphere in which the private is made public and vice versa, the harder it makes things for its children, who by nature require the security of concealment in order to mature undisturbed.

However serious these infringements of the conditions for vital growth may be, it is certain that they were entirely unintentional; the central aim of all modern education efforts has been the welfare of the child, a fact that is, of course, no less true even if the efforts made have not always succeeded in promoting the child's welfare in the way that was hoped. The situation is entirely different in the sphere of educational tasks directed no longer toward the child but toward the young person, the newcomer and stranger, who has been born into an already existing world which he does not know. These tasks are primarily, but not exclusively, the responsibility of the schools; they have to do with teaching and learning; the failure in this field is the most urgent problem in America today. What lies at the bottom of it?

Normally the child is first introduced to the world in school. Now school is by no means the world and must not pretend to be; it is rather the institution that we interpose between the private domain of home and the world in order to make the transition from the family to the world possible at all. Attendance there is required not by the family but by the state, that is by the public world, and so, in relation to the child, school in a sense represents the world, although it is not yet actually the world. At this stage of education adults, to be sure, once more assume a responsibility for the child, but by now it is not so much responsibility for the vital welfare of a growing thing as for what we generally call the free development of characteristic qualities and talents. This, from the general and essential point of view, is the uniqueness that distinguishes every human being from every other, the quality by virtue of which he is not only a stranger in the world but something that has never been here before.

Insofar as the child is not yet acquainted with the world, he must be gradually introduced to it; insofar as he is new, care must be taken that this new thing comes to fruition in relation to the world as it is. In any case, however, the educators here stand in relation to the young as representatives of a world for which they must assume responsibility although they themselves did not make it, and even though they may, secretly or openly, wish it were other than it is. This responsibility is not arbitrarily imposed upon educators; it is implicit in the fact that the young are introduced by adults into a continuously changing world. Anyone who refuses to assume joint responsibility for the world should not have children and must not be allowed to take part in educating them.

In education this responsibility for the world takes the form of authority. The authority of the educator and the qualifications of the teacher are not the same thing. Although a measure of qualification is indispensable for authority, the highest possible qualification can never by itelf beget authority. The teacher's qualification consists in knowing the world and being able to instruct others about it, but his authority rests on his assumption of responsibility for that world. Vis-à-vis the child it is as though he were a representative of all adult inhabitants, pointing out the details and saying to the child: This is our world.

Now we all know how things stand today in respect to authority. Whatever one's attitude toward this problem may be, it is obvious that in public and political life authority either plays no role at all—for the violence and terror exercised by the totalitarian countries have, of course, nothing to do with authority—or at most plays a highly contested role. This, however, simply means, in essence, that people do not wish to require of anyone or to entrust to anyone the assumption of responsibility for everything else, for wherever true authority existed it was joined with responsibility for the course of things in the world. If we remove authority from political and public life, it may mean that from now on an equal responsibility for the course of the world is to be required of everyone. But it may also mean that the claims of the world and the requirements of order in it are being consciously or unconsciously repudiated; all responsibility for the world is being rejected, the responsibility for giving orders no less than for obeying them. There is no doubt that in the modern loss of authority both intentions play a part and have often been simultaneously and inextricably at work together.

In education, on the contrary, there can be no such ambiguity in regard to the present-day loss of authority. Children cannot throw off educational authority, as though they were in a position of oppression by an adult majority—though even this absurdity of treating children as an oppressed minority in need of liberation has actually been tried out in modern educational practice. Authority has been discarded by the adults, and this can mean only one thing: that the adults refuse to assume responsibility for the world into which they have brought the children.

There is of course a connection between the loss of authority in public and political life and in the private pre-political realms of the family and the school. The more radical the distrust of authority becomes in the public sphere, the greater the probability naturally becomes that the private sphere will not remain inviolate. There is this additional fact, and it is very likely the decisive one, that from time out of mind we have been accustomed in our tradition of political thought to regard the authority of parents over children, of teachers over pupils, as the model by which to understand political authority. It is just this model, which can be found as early as Plato and Aristotle, that makes the concept of authority in politics so extraordinarily ambiguous. It is based, first of all, on an absolute superiority such as can never exist among adults and which, from the point of view of human dignity, must never exist. In the second place, following the model of the nursery, it is based on a purely temporary superiority and therefore becomes self-contradictory if it is applied to relations that are not temporary by nature—such as the relations of the rulers and the ruled. Thus it lies in the nature of the matter—that is, both in the nature of the present crisis in authority and in the nature of our traditional political thought—that the loss of authority which began in the political sphere should end in the private one; and it is naturally no accident that the place where political authority was first undermined, that is, in America, should be the place where the modern crisis in education makes itself most strongly felt.

The general loss of authority could, in fact, hardly find more radical expression than by its intrusion into the pre-political sphere, where authority seemed dictated by nature itself and independent of all historical changes and political conditions. On the other hand, modern man could find no clearer expression for his dissatisfaction with the world, for his disgust with things as they are, than by his refusal to assume, in respect to his children, responsibility for all this. It is as though parents daily said: "In this world even we are not very securely at home; how to move about in it, what to know, what skills to master, are mysteries to us too. You must try to make out as best you can; in any case you are not entitled to call us to account. We are innocent, we wash our hands of you."

This attitude has, of course, nothing to do with that revolutionary desire for a new order in the world—*Novus Ordo Seclorum*—which once animated America; it is rather a symptom of that modern estrangement from the world which can be seen everywhere but which presents itself in especially radical and desperate form under the conditions of a mass society. It is true that modern educational experiments, not in America alone, have struck very revolutionary poses, and this has, to a certain degree, increased the difficulty of clearly recognizing the situation and caused a certain degree of confusion in the discussion of the problem; for in contradiction to all such behavior stands the unquestionable fact that so long as America was really animated by that spirit she never dreamed of initiating the new order with education but, on the contrary, remained conservative in educational matters.

To avoid misunderstanding: it seems to me that conservatism, in the sense of conservation, is of the essence of the educational activity, whose task is always to cherish and protect something—the child against the world, the world against the child, the new against the old, the old against the new. Even the comprehensive responsibility for the world that is thereby assumed implies, of course, a conservative attitude. But this holds good only for the realm of education, or rather for the relations between grown-ups and children, and not for the realm of politics, where we act among and with adults and equals. In politics this conservative attitude—which accepts the world as it is, striving only to preserve the status quo—can only lead to destruction, because the world, in gross and in detail, is irrevocably delivered up to the ruin of time unless human beings are determined to intervene, to alter, to create what is new. Hamlet's words, "The time is out of joint. O cursed spite that ever I was born to set it right," are more or less true for every new generation, although since the beginning of our century they have perhaps acquired a more persuasive validity than before.

Basically we are always educating for a world that is or is becoming out of joint, for this is the basic human situation, in which the world is created by mortal hands to serve mortals for a limited time as home. Because the world is made by mortals it wears out; and because it continuously changes its inhabitants it runs the risk of becoming as mortal as they. To preserve the world against the mortality of its creators and inhabitants it must be constantly set right anew. The problem is simply to educate in such a way that a setting-right remains actually possible, even though it can, of course, never be assured. Our hope always hangs on the new which every generation brings; but precisely because we can base our hope only on this, we destory everything if we so try to control the new that we, the old, can dictate how it will look. Exactly for the sake of what is new and revolutionary in every child, education must be conservative; it must preserve this newness and introduce it as a new thing into an old world, which, however revolutionary its actions may be, is always, from the standpoint of the next generation, superannuated and close to destruction.

## 4

The real difficulty in modern education lies in the fact that, despite all the fashionable talk about a new conservatism, even that minimum of conservation and the conserving attitude without which education is simply not possible is in our time extraordinarily hard to achieve. There are very good reasons for this. The crisis of authority in education is most closely connected with the crisis of tradition, that is with the crisis in our attitude toward the realm of the past. This aspect of the modern crisis is especially hard for the educator to bear, because it is his task to mediate between the old and the new, so that his very profession requires of him an extraordinary respect for the past. Through long centuries, i.e., throughout the combined period of Roman-Christian civilization, there was no need for him to become aware of this special quality in himself because reverence for the past was an essential part of the Roman frame of mind, and this was not altered or ended by Christianity, but simply shifted onto different foundations.

It was of the essence of the Roman attitude (though this was by no means true of every civilization or even of the Western tradition taken as a whole) to consider the past *qua* past as a model, ancestors, in every instance, as guiding examples for their descendants; to believe that all greatness lies in what has been, and therefore that the most fitting human age is old age, the man grown old, who, because he is already almost an ancestor, may serve as a model for the living. All this stands in contradiction not only to our world and to the modern age from the Renaissance on, but, for example, to the Greek attitude toward life as well. When Goethe said that growing old is "the gradual withdrawal from the world of appearances," his was a comment made in the spirit of the Greeks, for whom being and appearing coincide. The Roman attitude would have been that precisely in growing old and slowly disappearing from the community of mortals man reaches his most characteristic form of being, even though, in respect to the world of appearances, he is in the process of disappearing; for only now can he approach the existence in which he will be an authority for others.

With the undisturbed background of such a tradition, in which education has a political function (and this was a unique case), it is in fact comparatively easy to do the right thing in matters of education without even pausing to consider what one is really doing, so completely is the specific ethos of the educational principle in accord with the basic ethical and moral convictions of society at large. To educate, in the words of Polybius, was simply "to let you see that you are altogether worthy of your ancestors," and in this business the educator could be a "fellow-contestant" and a "fellow-workman" because he too, though on a different level, went through life with his eyes glued to the past. Fellowship and authority were in this case indeed but the two sides of the same matter, and teacher's authority was firmly grounded in the encompassing authority of the past as such. Today, however, we are no longer in that position; and it makes little sense to act as though we still were and had only, as it were, accidentally strayed from the right path and were free at any moment to find our way back to it. This means that wherever the crisis has occurred in the modern world, one cannot simply go on nor yet simply turn back. Such a reversal will never bring us anywhere except to the same situation out of which the crisis has just arisen. The return would simply be a repeat performance – though perhaps different in form, since there are no limits to the possibilities of nonsense and capricious notions that can be decked out as the last word in science. On the other hand, simple, unreflective perseverance, whether it be pressing forward in the crisis or adhering to the routine that blandly believes the crisis will not engulf its particular sphere of life, can only, because it surrenders to the course of time, lead to ruin; it can only, to be more precise, increase that estrangement from the world by which we are already threatened on all sides. Consideration of the principles of education must take into account this process of estrangement from the world; it can even admit that we are here presumably confronted by an automatic process, provided only that it does not forget that it lies within the power of human thought and action to interrupt and arrest such processes.

The problem of education in the modern world lies in the fact that by its very nature it cannot forgo either authority or tradition, and yet must proceed in a world that is neither structured by authority nor held together by tradition. That means, however, that not just teachers and educators, but all of us, insofar as we live in one world together with our children and with young people, must take toward them an attitude radically different from the one we take toward one another. We must decisively divorce the realm of education from the others, most of all from the realm of public, political life, in order to apply to it alone a concept of authority and an attitude toward the past which are appropriate to it but have no general validity and must not claim a general validity in the world of grown-ups.

In practice the first consequence of this would be a clear understanding that the function of the school is to teach children what the world is like and not to instruct them in the art of living. Since the world is old, always older than they themselves, learning inevitably turns toward the past, no matter how much living will spend itself in the present. Second, the line drawn between children and adults should signify that one can neither educate adults nor treat children as though they were grown up; but this line should never be permitted to grow into a wall separating children from the adult community as though they were not living in the same world and as though childhood were an autonomous human state, capable of living by its own laws. Where the line between childhood and adulthood falls in each instance cannot be determined by a general rule; it changes often, in respect to age, from country to country, from one civilization to another, and also from individual to individual. But education, as distinguished from learning, must have a predictable end. In our civilization this end probably coincides with graduation from college rather than with graduation from high school, for the professional training in universities or technical schools, though it always has something to do with education, is nevertheless in itself a kind of specialization. It no longer aims to introduce the young person to the world as a whole, but rather to a particular, limited segment of it. One cannot educate without at the same time teaching; an education without learning is empty and therefore degenerates with great ease into moral-emotional rhetoric. But one can quite easily teach without educating, and one can go on learning to the end of one's days without for that reason becoming educated. All these are particulars, however, that must really be left to the experts and the pedagogues.

What concerns us all and cannot therefore be turned over to the special science of pedagogy is the relation between grown-ups and children in general or, putting it in even more general and exact terms, our attitude toward the fact of natality: the fact that we have all come into the world by being born and that this world is constantly renewed through birth. Education is the point at which we decide whether we love the world enough to assume responsibility for it and by the same token save it from that ruin which, except for renewal, except for the coming of the new and young, would be inevitable. And education, too, is where we decide whether we love our children enough not to expel them from our world and leave them to their own devices, nor to strike from their hands their chance of undertaking something new, something unforeseen by us, but to prepare them in advance for the task of renewing a common world.

(1961)

# Gnostics of Education

More than any other nation the United States has chosen to look upon its schools at all levels as means of education rather than mere instruction. The difference is an important one, since education means not merely the imparting of information to the mind but the shaping of the mind and of the personality. Instruction may be limited to the transmission of facts and principles it is desirable to know as a body of knowledge, but education is unavoidably a training for a way of life. Education comprises instruction, of course, but it goes beyond instruction to a point that makes it intimately related with the preservation of a culture. Under normal conditions the points of view that an educator instills are the points of view of the culture, and actually nothing else is possible as a settled thing because an education and a culture working at cross purposes can only produce a conflict which has to be resolved. A conflict of this kind of serious proportions has developed in our country with the ascension to influence of the "progressive" theory of education.

There are by now many hopeful signs that the battle has been essentially decided and that the danger carried by progressivism is drawing to an end. The threat of Russian technological rivalry, symbolized especially by the sputniks, and other more healthful pressures may before long produce far-reaching changes in the dominant American educational philosophy. What I propose to discuss in this chapter may therefore before long be history. But since it is the kind of history from which one may learn a great deal about philosophical dead ends and educational follies, the story needs telling in perspective, and the moral needs to be drawn.

It is not too much to say that in the past fifty years public education in the United States has been in the hands of revolutionaries. To grasp the nature of their attempted revolution, we need only realize that in the past every educational system has reflected to a great extent the social and political constitution of the society which supported it. This was assumed to be a natural and proper thing, since the young were to be trained to take places in the world that existed around them. They were "indoctrinated" with this world because its laws and relations were those by which they were expected to order their lives. In the period just mentioned, however, we have witnessed something never before seen in the form of a systematic attempt to undermine a society's traditions and beliefs through the educational establishment which is usually employed to maintain them. There had been an extraordinary occurrence, a virtual educational *coup d'état* carried out by a specially inclined minority. This minority has been in essence a cabal, with objectives radically different from those of the state which employed them. An amazing feature of the situation has been how little they have cared to conceal these objectives. On more than one occasion they have issued a virtual call to arms to use publicly created facilities for the purpose of actualizing a concept of society not espoused by the people. The result has been an educational system not only intrinsically bad but increasingly at war with the aims of the community which authorizes it, as we are not forced to recognize.

Although the history of how this situation came about is not the principal inquiry here, a little background may make the facts seem less incredible.

Public education was an outgrowth of the reasonable idea that a people cannot remain self-governing and free if they are untaught. It grew slowly during the nineteenth century until the coming of industrialism created demands for certain practical branches of it. In this growth few saw anything alarming, except perhaps a tendency to look upon universal literacy as a panacea. At one point in the development, however, there occurred a sinister change. This came about when state bureaucracies were created to set the terms and supervise the working of the expanding public school system. State legislators felt that they had to turn the actual administration of affairs over to a body of "experts." In course of time these state departments of education became virtually autonomous in their power to define the goals, methods, and materials of public instruction. The final step came when they were able to require all prospective public school teachers through the high school level to take a set number of courses in a subject called "Education," wherein the philosophical premises and aims of the new educators were taught. This is where the doctrinal revolution referred to above really took place. Here was an educational system within the educational system, committed to a body of methodology whose goals were defined by a philosophical sect.

I have said that the new education, for which the name "progressive" has been pre-empted by its advocates, is in marked conflict with our basic traditions and culture. It is not something based upon American experience or European experience or any perceptive view of the history of man. It is rather something dreamed up by romantic enthusiasts, political fanatics, and unreflective acolytes of positive science. These are all people "looking to the future," and the future, as with all who try to protect themselves with this phrase, is their subjective feeling about the way things ought to go. We are told by them that we are "living in a world of change"; but the "catch" is that they are in charge of the change. They are the prophets of the new future, which is going to look very unlike the past.

There is no difficulty at all in specifying reasons for the above charge. I list below some of the chief assumptions and tenets of progressive education. The conflict between them and the principal teachings of the Judeo-Christian—classical heritage of the West will be immediately apparent.

1. There is no such thing as a body of knowledge which reflects the structure of reality and which everyone therefore needs to learn. Knowledge is viewed as an instrumentality which is true or false according to the way it is applied to concrete situations or the way it serves the needs of the individual. Since these educators have embraced the notion that the essence of the world is change, there is no final knowledge about anything. The truths of yesterday are the falsehoods of today and the truths of today will be the falsehoods of tomorrow.

2. This being so, the object of education is not to teach knowledge, but to "teach students." As they translate this into practice, it means that everything should be adapted to the child as child, to the youth as youth, and to the particular group according to its limitations. There are no ideals or standards of performance which these are bound to measure themselves by or to respect.

3. As a corollary of the above principle, the child should be encouraged to follow his own desires in deciding what he should study, and what aspects of what subjects, and at what times.

4. The teacher must not think of himself as being in authority, because authority is evil. The teacher is there as a "leader," but the duty of the leader is only to synchronize and cooperate with the work of the group.

5. The student should never be made afraid of anything connected with the school. Marks and competitions are bad because they instill feelings of superiority and inferiority, which are "undemocratic."

6. The mind is not to be exalted over the senses: democracy requires that sensory and "activist" learning be valued on a par with intellectual learning. The mentally slow or retarded are not to be made to feel that they are lacking; it is better to impugn the whole tradition of intellectual education than to injure the feelings of the less bright and the lazy.

7. Consequently there should be less education through symbols like language and figures and more through using the hands on concrete objects. It is more important to make maps than to learn them, said John Dewey, the grand pundit of the revolutionary movement.

8. The general aim is to train the student so that he will adjust himself not simply to the existing society, as is sometimes inferred from their words, but to society conceived as social democracy.

A few other propositions equally startling can be deduced from the writings of the new school of educationists, but these should be enough to indicate what a complete reversal the progressivist theory represents. However, just in case the meaning of this is too revolutionary to reach the consciousness all at once, let me rephrase two or three of the central ideas. Knowledge, which has been the traditional reason for instituting schools, does not exist in any absolute or binding sense. The mind, which has always been regarded as the distinguishing possession of the human race, is now viewed as a tyrant which has been denying the rights of the body as a whole. It is to be "democratized" or reduced to an equality with the rest. Discipline, that great shaper of mind and body, is to be discarded because it carries elements of fear and compulsion. The student is to be prepared not to save his soul, or to inherit the wisdom and usages of past civilizations, or even to get ahead in life, but to become a member of a utopia resting on a false view of both nature and man.

This set of propositions practically inverts our traditional idea of education, which venerates mind, recognizes the moral and practical value of discipline, and regards competition as the indispensable spur to outstanding achievement. Yet these are the very propositions which have been systematically taught by educationists for about fifty years and which have strongly affected education on all but the university levels (and even there in some areas). In fact they have been more than taught; they have been enforced as dogmas in the schools and departments of education, and more than one prospective teacher has been advised that he must accept them or be rejected by the profession.

Where should one look to find the real sources of so profound a revolt against the long-accepted premises of education? Since we are dealing here with a change of great depth, it seems best not to spend time on intermediate causes, but to look for some major parallel in history and see whether this will not point to the ultimate cause. Progressive education is a wholesale apostasy, involving abandonment of fundamental and long-held beliefs about man and the world. If we are to account for it, we shall have to seek further than the pressures of industrialism and other modern-day phenomena. The analysis will concern basic attitudes toward existence, so that if we search for the root of the progressivist outlook, we shall perforce be dealing with questions of faith and of interpretation of historical experience.

There is one apostasy of a nature and a magnitude to warrant comparison with this one, and it affords a great deal of illumination, even though it happened at a remote time and even though its content cannot be precisely delineated. It was a subversive force in much the same way as our progressivism in education, and although it was finally put down, it lasted long enough to produce a large amount of confusion and to cause the thoughtful to search out its fundamental errors. This was the Gnosticism of the first and second centuries A.D.

Gnosticism may be described as an attempt to reinterpret annalistic Christianity in terms suited to the "enlightenment" of the contemporary era. It was a highly speculative system, which differed from what has become canonical Christianity in two important features: its attitude toward creation, and its doctrine of the nature of man.

According to the Gnostics, creation was not the work of an omnipotent and benevolent creator, but rather of a Demiurge of limited power, who necessarily left it finite and incomplete. Evil was therefore represented by them as congenital with creation. The important consequence of this doctrine was that it taught a dualism of good and evil, in which spirit, represented by man, was good and in which the world at least partly represented evil. Man was therefore superior to the created universe and – although this cannot be set forth in very exact terms – was somehow charged with its improvement. The opponents of Gnosticism, both Christian and neo-Platonic, attacked the Gnostics for the presumptuousness of this attitude toward creation. For example, Tertullian, in his *Five Books Against Marcion*, scored that famous Gnostic for his position on this matter. He wrote: "You, however, are a disciple above his master, and a servant above his lord; you have a higher level of discernment than his; you destroy what he requires. . . . You are an enemy to the sky, and yet you are glad to catch its freshness in your houses. You disparage the earth, although the elemental parent of your flesh, as if it were your undoubted enemy, and yet you abstract from it all its fatness for your food." In much the same vein Plotinus in the *Enneads* criticizes the "human audacity" of the Gnostics. "Two people inhabit the one stately house; one of them declaims against its plan and against its architect, but none the less maintains his residence in it. The other makes no complaint, asserts the entire competence of the architect and waits cheerfully for the day when he may leave it, having no further need of a house." Thus the Gnostics were consistently seen as setting themselves above creation and holding that the material universe, for which they were not responsible, was the real source of evil.

With regard to man himself, the Gnostics taught a doctrine of perfectionism. Man did not require salvation, for he was already in a state of "Messianic blessedness." Since he was in this state, it was not necessary for him to submit to external authority. Gnosticism therefore tended strongly toward antinomianism. This view of the natural blessedness of man, coupled with the feeling of his lack of responsibility for evil, made the Gnostics antiauthoritarian. When they were asked by the Christian Fathers where they got their doctrines, they said that they got them from themselves. As a matter of fact, they taught that every individual has a "hidden Deep," from which there well up thoughts, notions, and impulses. A modern student of the Gnostic movement has noted that this resembles in a number of ways the "Subliminal Self" of modern psychology. We could go on to remark that all this has a parallel in the attempts of our "progressive" educationists to base everything upon psychology.

The decision of the Fathers to reject Gnostic teachings was crucial for the future of Christianity. For the world of the Gnostics was "a fanciful world, 'moulded to the heart's desire,' in which the religious imagination was not tied down to religious facts." Furthermore, such sociology and science as Gnosticism presumed to incorporate were not elements of strength; these consisted of the fashionable doctrines of the day and would have proved an increasing liability with the passage of time. The Fathers were not seduced by the "modernism" of their age. The decision which they made was not only wise for their time but wise for any time in which this kind of choice has to be made. What they did was repudiate theorizing and adhere to annalistic and historical religion. Thus they retained on their side the powerful support of historicity with its facts and traditions. These were of course the fruit of experience, not of conjecture and speculation. The word of a prophet is a deed, it has been said, and they adhered to the word. Debate might range far, but there were always the records, the experiences, and the traditions to return to.

Today we are in a strikingly comparable situation, as enthusiasts and fanciful thinkers call upon us to abandon what we know through the annals of our education and erect a brave new world out of sanguine speculation. Just as the very authority and power of Christianity depended upon rejecting these overtures, so the authority and viability of education today depend upon our rejecting the often plausible appeals of the progressives to give up what we know historically about man and commit ourselves to their utopia.

In sum, it is the contention here that the progressive educationists of our time, while not Gnostics in the sense of historical descent, are gnostics in their thinking. It is a further contention that their gnosticism exhibits the same kind of delusion, fantasy, unreality, and unacceptable metaphysics which the Church Fathers, speaking out of tradition and true insight, challenged and put an end to. Finally, it is my own conviction that the doctrines of the new educationists are at least as menacing to the survival of our culture as were the Gnostic heresies of the first and second centuries to the great religious and cultural tradition which has streamed down to our time. For the essence of Gnosticism is a kind of irresponsibility—an irresponsiblity to the past and to the structure of reality in the present. Its teachings cannot serve as the foundations of a culture because the fact that its advocates are out of line with what is, inevitably reveals itself. Where they are allowed to provide foundations, they imperil the whole structure.

The following are a number of specific ways in which our educationists of the new order parallel the Gnostics of antiquity.

Let us note before taking them up that education at any level will reflect the primary assumptions that we make about reality, and for this reason no education is innocent of an attitude toward the existing world. In the way that it explains the interrelationships of phenomena and our relationships toward them, education will reveal beliefs about creation. Even if it denies that the world is something created by a creator, it thereby invokes a theory and prepares ground for an attitude. Of great significance here is the Gnostic account of creation. For the Gnostics, let us remember, creation was the work of a Demiurge who, for lack of omnipotence, had to leave his production finite and incomplete. This doctrine had the effect of introducing a principle of evil (in the sense of incompleteness or a less than perfect realization) with creation itself and of leaving man in opposition to this. Man was good, but creation contained both good and evil, or a world of light and a world of darkness, and the rectification had to come somehow through man himself. On this last point Gnostic theory is somewhat cloudy and confused, but the ideas of a divinized man and a partly evil creation emerge with enough clearness to be considered focal doctrines.

The new educationists do not deal with anything as "remote and academic" (favorite words of condemnation with them) as theories of creation. But they are under the same necessity which requires our ideas to reflect anterior suppositions, and we can gather from their utterances what these suppositions are. For them the universe is not a work of divine omnipotence. All we know about it, they say in effect, is that it is here and that it leaves unsatisfied many of man's wants. This is the reason for holding it bad or incomplete. The completing of it will be brought about through the natural process of evolution plus the efforts that man makes through his science. It is in this reliance upon science and scientism that modern education shows its tendency to hitch itself to a cultural fashion, as Gnosticism showed its disposition to adjust Christianity to a contemporary sophistical world view. Eliseo Vivas has pointed out that "Dewey and his disciples would substitute an education for 'modern man' which instills in the pupil an idolatry toward scientific method and contempt for the achievements of the past, thus fitting him to yield uncritically to the thorough mechanization of his life" [*The Moral Life and the Ethical Life*].

How widely this attitude has been spread through our channels of education can be seen by the frequency with which men now speak of the "conquest of nature." If nature is something ordained by a creator, one does not speak of "conquering" it. The creation of a benevolent creator is something good, and conquest implies enmity and aggression. If by the same token the world is good and is ordained for man, there are certainly suggestions of Pyrrhic victory in the idea of "triumphing" over nature. The man of the new education, however, feels it is his duty to be an invader of nature, breaking her "resistance" as in war.

We have just seen how both Tertullian and Plotinus attacked the attitude of scorning that which has been created while continuing to enjoy its benefits. We find further that St. Irenaeus, in his writings against the Gnostics, insists that some mysteries be left unsolved. This expresses the deep feeling, found also in the book of Genesis and in Aristotle, that there are some things it is better for man not to know than to know. Modern man, however, has reached the critical point at which he feels no qualms about demanding that nature give up all her secrets. There no longer exists any doubt in his mind as to whether he is competent to order and dispose of creation. A kind of moral self-modesty which was once present has been lost by his acceptance of a gnostic theory of creation.

A contemporary incident related in the annals of atomic science serves to illustrate this well. Among the observers of the first atomic bomb at Los Alamos in 1945 was William L. Laurence, science editor of the New York *Times*. This correspondent wrote a full account of the terrifying event and closed it, as one would expect a representative modern to do, on a note of jubilation. He told how the group of observers danced with joy following the great flash and boom. "They clapped their hands as they leaped from the ground — earth-bound man symbolizing the birth of a new force that for the first time gives man means to free himself from the gravitational pull of the earth that holds him down." Later, his report goes on to say, one of those present remarked: "The sun can't hold a candle to it." There are two assumptions worthy of note in this passage by the learned science editor. One is that man is the *victim* of the gravitational force that keeps him from flying off into space, and now at last this victim has the chance to do something about his situation. He is going to end this oppression by nature. The other is that man has now improved upon the sun. The original creator did the best he could when he produced this great luminary, but at last man has surpassed him and has made something exceeding it.

At once we recognize how closely this conforms with the Gnostic view that defect lies not in the nature of man, but in the finiteness of creation, which must be overcome by man. The concept of an original disposition for man's good is now made to appear quite archaic. Man is now in the saddle and can ride anywhere.

The connection between this attitude toward creation or nature and the philosophy underlying the kind of school which the Deweyite educators propose is not difficult to discern. The school is of course to be secular because a religious attitude toward the *donnée* of the world is ruled out. Questions of first and final cause are regarded as not within the scope of education, which means that education is confined to intermediate causes. Intermediate causes are of course the subject matter of science, and hence this attitude has the effect of orienting all education toward science. Furthermore, since industrialism is the offspring of applied science, such education fits one ideally for the industrial order. Still further, industrialism is constantly making war upon nature, disfiguring and violating her, and the products of our educational plants can be relied on to bring the right attitude toward this work.

Of equally evil consequence is the Gnostic attitude toward man, which is, obviously, related to the foregoing. The Gnostic belief was that man is not sinful, but divine. The real evil in the universe cannot be imputed to him; his impulses are good, and there is no ground for restraining him from anything which he wants to do. The mere supposal of such a ground would mean invoking an arbiter which Gnostic thinking does not recognize. By divinizing man, Gnostic thinking says that what he wants to do, he should do. Restraints upon human nature now become blasphemous; whereas in the older thinking it was action of human nature which was blasphemous when it contravened law and ethics. Thus the whole system of ethics becomes man-centered, and there is no sanction above man to which anything can be appealed. What man wants is considered right, and it is what, with the aid of his science, he is supposedly going to get.

I suggest that this radical view of man's nature would never have gained acceptance among so many in this country had not the way been prepared for it by an influential phase of American literature. The New England Transcendentalists of a century ago are a link between ancient Gnosticism and the new gnostic educators. Ralph Waldo Emerson, the leading exponent of Transcendentalism, taught forthrightly that man is divine and that his instincts are oracular. From the "Divinity School Address" through "Self Reliance" and to "The Over Soul" he developed the theme that man has a divine self-sufficiency and that he does not need to look beyond himself. He instilled in the many thousands who read him as "the American philosopher" belief not only that man bears no responsiblity for evil but even that evil is illusory. This was Emerson's rebellion against the Calvinism of his New England forbears, who had taught and acted out of a contrary belief—that man is responsible for the evil which most certainly exists in the world and that he is consequently involved in a curse for which every individual must suffer. As Calvinism with its stern morality and its rigorous intellectualism began to lose ground, its place was taken largely by the expansive optimism which Emerson devised—an optimism which, with its devotion to romantic illusions, was destined to take the sinew out of New England thought and culture.

I mention the Transcendentalists because they, as the most articulate group of radicals in nineteenth-century America, must bear the blame for undermining the previous realism of American thinking. Their influence has been very pervasive, and the progressivist educators have made use of that influence to put forward their heresies as expressive of the American mind and the American political spirit.[1]

We can now safely say that in progressive educational theory we have a gnostic version of the image of man. It is a picture which leaves out of account his original sin, his tendency to love evil and to wreak it, and his daily sinning through egotism. It leaves out of account the dark

---

[1] A related fact which cannot be overlooked is that a public school system supported by tax money was a New England conception. Tracing back to a statute enacted in Massachusetts in 1647, this system spread through the other New England colonies and states and later over the country as a whole, although it was resisted by most of the Southern states until after the Civil War. Thus at the very time that these latter-day gnostics were coming to dominate New England thinking, the New England school system was being imitated by one state after another, including finally the Southern states. That it would serve as a pipeline for the gnostic philosophy of the leaders of New England opinion was virtually inevitable.

recesses of his psyche, which even so "modern" a study as psychology has had to restore. The man of the gnostics is the child of his own good nature, confusing his sentiments with the structure of the world, and inclined, when he meets obstacles that do not yield, to blame other men rather than to recognize the limitations of man.

The modern gnostics further resemble the ancient ones in their attitude toward authority. If the ancient type tended toward antinomianism, the modern type works toward a theoretical undermining of responsibility. Because human nature is so good that it is not constrainable, laws and traditions are not to be respected. The Gnostics opposed the authority of the Church and the authority of the state under the impulse of their speculative picture of the universe. Again one might mark a parallel with Transcendentalism, for the individual and social protest of Emerson and Thoreau went theoretically to the point of anarchism. Both institutions and traditions were unceasingly attacked by them in the name of the liberty of the individual to follow his naturally good impulses.

The opposition of the present-day gnostics goes about the same length, although for special reasons they do not direct their attack against the state. Many of them seem to carry concealed a Marxist hope that the state may be utilized to gain their ends, after which it will "wither away," or perhaps it will serve as a final target in the attack upon "authoritarianism." As matters stand now, authoritarianism is the principle they chiefly decry. Because all men are equally good, no one is entitled by superior goodness to stand in authority. There are no higher degrees of virtue which authorize some individuals to lay down rules for others. Everybody "cooperates," and what the generality expresses a desire for is what should be done. They overlook the contradiction in this, which is that we always have majorities and dissenters, with the ensuing problem of effecting a resolution. Their position is, however, that no external moral absolute exists by which degrees of rightness and wrongness may be determined. Where no conception of a moral absolute exists, authority has no real basis.

Such are the views implied in the gnostics' dogmatic optimism about the nature of man. As we saw in the historical survey, the ancient Gnostics denied the need of salvation because they considered man to be already in a state of blessedness. Today this translates itself into the doctrine that human beings do not stand in need of correction, to say nothing of conversion. Obviously, if you regard man as already divine, you do not need a discipline for improving him ethically. It has been the general and indeed immemorial practice of the human race to set up some ideal type—"One Perfect Man"—and to judge the moral and intellectual worth of every human being by him. Sometimes the type was presented through religion, sometimes through mythology, and sometimes through the speculations of thinkers. In Christian lands Christ of course serves as the great exemplar and standard. But what the modern educator does is take empirical man, arrive at a type through averaging, and then posit this as what man "ought" to be. What should be merely descriptive thus becomes prescriptive. If you believe that man is already in a "saved" condition, you of course base your ideal on what he generally has been. Then extremes, even of goodness, become "deviants," and need to be pulled back toward the average. The saint is but an eccentric. Such acceptance of man in his average condition must keep down the standard of development and achievement, and the result is a complacency which refuses to believe that man needs to surpass himself.

It is now possible to trace the effects of this system of radical thought upon the education which the progressivists intend to give our children. Not every phase, of course, of the new gnosticism shows a full and equal effect upon educational theory. But that the main tenets of its philosophy exert a strong influence upon the ideals and programs with which we are now confronted becomes clear enough.

First we may turn to the objects of learning. Traditional education has always been based on the assumption that there is a world of data, a fixed reality, which is worth knowing and even worth reverencing. The content of education therefore reflected the structure of an antecedent reality. This, in fact, was education, and everything required for its communication to learners was ancillary. Clearly this presumes a certain respect for the world as creation, a belief in it and a trust in its providence, rather than a view (as if out of ancient Gnosticism) positing its essential incompleteness or badness. The world is there a priori; the learner has the duty of familiarizing himself with its nature and its sets of relations.

Now all of this has been reversed. The main concern of the modern educationists is not knowledge of an existent reality, but rather the mastery of a methodology. The aim of the methodology is to enable the learner "to grow through experience." These are key terms requiring some examination. The purpose of education is alleged to be growth, and growth is conceived as a natural unfolding of the individual. It is not growth toward something or away from something, because there are no ideal standards in mind. Sometimes the word "richness" is brought in to indicate the direction of "growth," but it is necessarily and probably deliberately vague. The concealed premise of the doctrine is that the individual is naturally good and that any kind of development of him will therefore be desirable. There is no regulative body of knowledge to impose a pattern; the individual needs only to increase the divinity that is in him by the process of growth. As for experience, it need not be qualified; all experience is good and is more rewarding than knowledge in the abstract. When Dewey declares that it is more important to make maps than to learn them, he exalts activity over thinking. While few will deny that something is gained through the practical handling of a problem, if the principle of learning solely by doing were applied exclusively, it would cut the learner off from the great body of traditional knowledge and wisdom of the race. This he cannot hope to get by experience alone. A number of progressive educators have shown by the trend of their utterances that they are quite willing to effect such a severance. This willingness is further evidenced by their attitude toward the use of symbols. On this subject Dewey has written in *The School and Society*: "The relegation of the merely symbolic and formal to a secondary position is not a mere accident but is part of the larger social evolution." Here as elsewhere one is forced to recognize that these revolutionaries are prepared to state their proposals if not their basic premises in unabashed terms. Their audaciousness, however, should not be allowed to disarm us. What Dewey is insisting upon is nothing less than a denigration of the intellect. For thousands of years education through concepts and the symbols expressing them has been recognized as the education of the mind to which all other education is subsidiary. Through his ability to symbolize and to make use of signs such as letters and figures, man has created practically all that goes by the name of culture. Ernst Cassirer points out that symbol making and using is the most specifically human activity. That culture and civilization depend on an elaborate network of symbols and that the more the human being "advances" the more complex these symbolic media become should be obvious. Now their use is to be de-emphasized in the name of "the larger social evolution," which is a cant phrase standing for the political aims of the progressivists.

It is a strange thing in this day of "progress" and almost universal literacy to have to plead for the rights of the mind, and especially against educators. But as Vivas has shown, the Deweyite school is actually a group of fanatical partisans who are determined to spread their special theory of human nature in opposition to all that history and the humanities have taught us.

The Gnostic belief that man is divine and already in a state of salvation displays itself very clearly in the new theory of "child-centered" education. The upshot of this is not merely to divinize man, which is bad enough, but to divinize the child. The progressivists worship the child as child and make concessions to him where traditional education makes demands upon him. One is compelled to infer from their statements not that the child is the probationer, but that the world of learning is. This is stated by Dewey writing in *Schools of Tomorrow*:

Are we to believe, with the strict disciplinarians, that education is the process of making a little savage into a man, that there are many virtues as well as facts that have to be taught to all children so that they may as nearly as possible approach the adult standard? Or are we to believe, with Rousseau, that education is the process of making up the discrepancy between the child at his birth and the man as he will need to be, "that childhood has its own way of seeing, thinking and feeling," and that the method of training these ways to what the man will need is to let the child test them upon the world about him?

To commence the reply, why should we believe with the romanticist Rousseau, rather than with the "strict disciplinarians"? It is the experience of most parents and teachers that the child is not a little angel, but in some degree a little savage, and that he needs to be educated out of this condition. There is nothing divine about his imperfections. As for "the man as he will need to be," how do we prepare anyone to become this except by initiating him, with due allowance for his limitations, into the demands and standards of the adult world? Finally, Dewey seems to be overlooking the fact that the real desire of every youngster is "to be a man" and not a perfect little angel of a child.

In *The School and Society* Dewey cites with approval the view of the educator Friedrich Froebel that "the primary root of all educative activity is in the instinctive, impulsive attitudes of children, and not in the presentation and application of external material, whether through the ideas of others or through the senses. . . ." Again like the Gnostics of old, these two see something sacred in instinctive attitudes and in the content of immature consciousness. These are to be venerated above that objectified body of learning which has been produced by systematic study and handed down by our cultural institutions. In brief, learning is to be foregone in favor of the child's spontaneous desires and unreflective thoughts.

Conspicuously absent from all of this is the discipline of the negative. It is invariably assumed that the child can be depended on to develop serious interests without pressure from outside. If this were true, we would have to concede that the child is in a state of grace. The inescapable fact is, however, that the child exhibits no sustained interests or his interests are in trivial or objectionable things. There is no more widely attested fact than that interest usually develops under pressure, and a major part of education consists of our being made to take an interest in things that ought to interest us or will require our interest as we attain adulthood.[2] Effective education often demands the rigorous suppressing of a present, desultory interest so that we can focus on things that have a real, enduring, and sanctioned interest. Indeed, this is identical with the act of concentration. When we concentrate, we rule out the lesser, the peripheral, the seductive interest so that we can get on with the problem we are obliged to solve. I believe it could be demonstrated that progressive techniques of education have done a good deal to lessen the powers of concentration of the present generation of students who have been exposed to them.

This belief in the natural goodness of the child and the rightness of

---

[2]A striking illustration of this truth came to my attention some years ago. A young engineer, an ordinary member of his profession, with an indifference toward the fine arts, obtained a job with a radio broadcasting station. .This station put half an hour of classical music on the air every day, and this young man had the duty of controlling volume. Naturally he had to listen very carefully in order to maintain this at a uniform level. This very circumstance of having to listen carefully to classical music in discharge of his duty caused him to hear in it things he had been unaware of, with the result that he became a devotee. If this accidental outside pressure had not forced him to give careful attention to these programs, he probably never would have been recruited into the ranks of music appreciators.

spontaneous expression leads to the progressivists' assault upon virtually all forms of authority and discipline in the classroom. They proceed on the assumptions that fear is never a good thing and that authority must produce fear. There are two important exceptions to be taken to such assumptions. The first is that although authority does sometimes induce fear, it also provides protection, support, and confirmation. It may hold together the organization on which we depend for the exercise of opportunities. Second, not all fear is bad. There are fears that are normal and salutary. We need to fear constantly a variety of dangers, some of which arise from our own nature: we need to fear sloth, carelessness, indifference, and the temptations of appetite. The possibility of ignominy keeps a healthful fear hanging over us, and it is authority which maintains this fear by enforcing the appropriate penalties if we succumb to indolence or to positive evil doing.

Accordingly the gnostics of education feel that they can bring their dream world nearer to reality by introducing "democracy in the classroom." Under this weird conception the teacher is not to be viewed as one in authority commissioned to instruct, but as a kind of moderator whose function is merely to conduct a meeting. Especially resented is the idea that the teacher has any advantage of knowledge or wisdom which entitles him to stand above his students. This would be a recognition of inequality, and equality must reign, *ruat caelum!* The resultant undermining of the authority and prestige of the teacher in public schools is a long story, and the story is now being told by a number of teachers who have experienced it.[3] It is important to show the theoretical objections to this "democratic" maneuver.

Not only is the teacher supposed to be apologetic about his superior knowledge, he is expected to give up one of the most valuable of pedagogical devices, which is the dramatic confrontation of master and pupil. Our traditional means of education has a most important resource in this situation. That one is admitted to be master and the other learner is a circumstance of good effect because it works to tone up the performance of both—the teacher stays on his toes trying to justify by superior knowledge and skill the office that is vested in him; the learner tries to earn the good opinion of the teacher by matching his performance as nearly as he can. In this way a vital tension is set up, and the powerful force of emulation is brought into play. The teacher is going to give the best that he has, and he is going to ask the ordinary mortal sitting there in row three to rise above his ordinary mortality and to excel. A healthful rivalry thus creates standards of criticism.

How the progressivists expect to compensate for this with a kind of relaxed, "democratic," shoulder-rubbing camaraderie in which the teacher is just "one of the boys" is another mystery of the assault upon criteria; for the teacher requires the magisterial stance in order to get

[3]See for example Joan Dunn, *Retreat from Learning: Why Teachers Can't Teach* (New York, 1955).

the most from his pupils. The old New Englanders, although they developed a number of democratic forms, knew where democracy was in place and where not. The ministers of their churches they called "teachers," and the teacher in the school was a kind of minister in the classroom. There was no sentimental blurring of the roles of instructor and learner. I suspect the fact that New England had thus established a firm intellectual tradition enabled the gnostic thinkers, when they came into ascendancy there, to exert much more influence than their doctrines otherwise would have secured for them.

In review, we see in this startling revolution the substitution of fantasy for historicity. Not only the traditional educator but also the "man in the street" when he is apprised of these facts knows that the progressive educators are not dealing in truth. The reason is that they have set themselves up as Messianic prophets, whose prophecy is of a special political world; therefore they are not primarily educators. An educator is a man inspired with deference toward the world's knowledge and prepared to communicate some phase of it to oncoming generations. One does not have to strip off many wrappings to see that the progressive educators are, by contrast, political ideologues. They are determined to destroy the organic society which we have inherited by postulating an equalitarian natural man as the grand end of all endeavor. Appreciating this fact enables us to understand their attack upon discipline and authority, their opposition to systems of grading and promotion, and their resistance to formal intellectual learning. Almost any question about their assumptions and their methods, if pushed far enough, will bring the defense that these are vindicated by their contribution to democracy. Their writings are filled with references to democracy as a "way of life." This in turn has led to strange cant about "education for democratic living."

There are several things to be said about this piece of sentimental affectation. For one thing, as we have pointed out elsewhere, democracy is not a way of life but a form of government. Government is not the substance of a people's life, although modern collectivism would persuade us to think so. Government in all free societies is a regulative machinery, whose task it is to provide protection and to preserve enough order for people to do what they can do for themselves as individual members of society. This identification of democracy with life is a rhetorical way of sneaking in the totalitarian concept.

For another, democracy is not the only conceivable form of government, although it has virtually become dogma to say so. It was not so regarded by Aristotle, who made aim rather than form the criterion of true government. The most that can be said is that democracy seems to be the best of the available choices for us today, and it is well for the student to be taught in what ways democracy is practical for us. But training for a form of government is neither the sole nor the primary object of education. Man may, by one classification, be a political animal, but political activity is not his highest expression. He is also a contemplative animal, and a creature with aesthetic and cultural yearnings. His very restlessness is a sign that he is a spiritual being with intimations about his origin and destiny. The matters with which education should deal include all these and not merely his political orientation and allegiance. Liberal education has flourished under and contributed to many forms of government, although there may be grave doubt as to whether it is compatible with the current concept of mass democracy. Insistence upon a political theory as the principle by which all educational policies are to be adjudicated is totalitarian radicalism.

Sentimentalism about the nature of the human being and this political fanaticism have thus combined to produce a concept of education treacherous to our regime. It represents the most overweening attempt of gnostic thinking to replace the natural structure of our society with their dream world, which is to substitute a subjective wishfulness for an historical reality.

From the beginning I have spoken of the progressive movement in education as an apostasy out of conviction that this classifies it accurately. An apostate is properly defined as one who, after making profession of a belief, falls away from or abandons it. So with the progressive educators. They profess before society a belief in education, and they are in fact supported by society for this profession. In reality, they are attackers and saboteurs of education. This truth I have tried to show by two lines of proof: namely, that the apostates do not have faith in the existence of knowledge, and that their real aim is the educationally illicit one of conditioning the young for political purposes. The fact that they do not believe in knowledge makes them manipulators or trainers rather than teachers, and this is the light in which we should understand their instrumentalist philosophy. The world for which the progressivists are conditioning their students is not the world espoused by general society, but by a rather small minority of radical doctrinaires and social faddists. They are doing things which the great majority of plain, uncorrupted individuals, from a standpoint in history and common sense, would repudiate if they could see their tendency.

This subversion has gone so far that gnostics of education until very recently constituted the greatest single threat to our culture. In the discredit that they have cast upon the higher faculties, in the way they have cut the young off from knowledge of the excellencies achieved in the past, and in the way they have turned attention toward transient externals and away from the central problem of man, they have no equal as an agency of subversion. Their schemes are exactly fitted, if indeed they are not designed, to produce citizens for the secular communist state, which is the millennial dream of the modern gnostic. To put an end to this adventure into fantasy and to prevent the cruel awakening which would follow, we should do all we can, educationally and politically, to hasten the decline of their influence.

(1964)

*Peter Schrag*

# The End of the Great Tradition

Higher education has gone mainstream; the old distinctions have vanished; one can no longer determine where "higher education" ends and the rest of the world begins: peripatetic professors, government contracts, political students. The 1960s represented the last decade of the traditional rhetoric about the enterprise: Was the institution public or private? How many students were enrolled? What was the student-faculty ratio? How much student power should there be in university government? What was the proper "role" (God help us) of the university? We're going to look back a few years from now and think: "How quaint, how naïve." Many of us will hope that nobody remembers the vast amount of nonsense we published about what's bugging the students, or how we could be "relevant," or how we could combine "breadth with depth." What we are going to ask—if we still have a voice to do so—is whether it is possible to organize knowledge and understanding in such a way as to keep all of education—indeed all of society—from being divided between the emotional and the technical, between mystics and tinkerers.

The division is not between Snow's two cultures, or students vs. faculty (or administration) or even the generation gap. The point is whether the idea of discipline—the way we used to talk about literature or history or mathematics—still makes sense or whether all education will be devoted either to technical questions (the building of economic models, or conflict resolution, or molecular biology) or to questions such as "Who am I?" and "How can I touch you?" For the radicals, the rallying cries are relationship, and confrontation, and engagement, and doing your own thing. Computers do the reasoning, and human beings *feel*. Does the book enable you to control spirits, like Prospero? Hell, no. The book enslaves, entraps, deludes, equivocates. "I don't want to read Augustine," says the kid to the professor, "because I don't like Augustine." The kid is a feeler. He already *knows*—doesn't want to know anything more. History is not his bag; history is a cop-out. He knows what it's like. He has the true faith. He is not merely a romantic; he has flipped back to sixth-century mysticism.

Don't blame him, or consider him as an example of "students" or the "young." By now, the star professor is back on the plane, off to do a little consulting or to check with the Institute of Applied Linguistics. The other students are grinding out the papers, or maybe trying to figure out how to put experience into machines, or what conflict-resolution has to do with poverty in Harlem. And everybody feeling guilty about feeling, or else proud that they feel more than anybody else. It is not the young against the old, but deciding where the young *and* the old are to go—how to keep abstraction from running away with passion, and vice versa.

A few years ago, Jacques Barzun declared that the liberal arts college is dead or dying because the high school had co-opted the first two years (general education) and the graduate school the last two (specialization). What he should have said is that the liberal arts are dead or dying, not because literature and history aren't being taught, but because the common cultural assumptions in which they were rooted have been shattered. We have talked for years about the fact that the ideal of the Renaissance man was unattainable. Leibnitz, it has been said, was probably the last man to know everything: We know about the explosion of knowledge and all that. The point, however, is more significant. We have begun to lose faith in rational possibilities. Knowing we can't know, we have given up trying. The questions, therefore, are technical and the culture existential. The way to the frontier is a narrow path through the jungle. The way to establish one's sense of himself is by way of emotional sensibilities. "I feel, therefore I am." The dilemma is real. The problem is not merely that a few professors have sold out to the Defense Department, the CIA, or the corporations, or that students are obstreperous or slovenly or weak from pot. The problem is that lacking common cultural assumptions—about freedom or religion or the good life—there is no common ground for discourse.

Let's be absolutely clear about this. The university was founded on Renaissance assumptions even if—as in America—it often became a vocational institution. The Renaissance assumptions were fairly simple, even after we had discovered (surely also a Renaissance kind of word) that nobody could know all about everything: belief in reason, a sense that the world—the world of God and man—was knowable, that the *terra incognita* of whatever sort would be explored eventually, that there were certain universal principles, and that "culture" was a unitary concept, not something that changed as one hopped from place to place or continent to continent. Yes, there were "higher" and "lower" cultures, but always on a linear scale with ourselves somewhere near the top. The Chinese were highly civilized while the West was still in the Dark Ages (catch them loaded words) because the Chinese had invented gunpowder. Wasn't that an achievement? And among the highest of the cultures was—naturally—the German, with Beethoven and Goethe and Schiller. But all of that evaporated at Auschwitz and Dachau, along with some of our self-assurance, when we had finally absorbed the impact of Hiroshima. Slaveholders, imperialists, repressors, the white devil, that's us. Who's to know what's good and for whom? Do your own thing, because only you know. We used to call it anti-intellectualism.

Surely there are extremes, minorities, and all that. But just as surely, the problem is to tame and reform the disciplines, to keep every field in some realm between applied mathematics or symbolic logic and some form of narcissistic breast-beating. Here are all these sophisticated people who have analyzed the world to death, whose whole sense of themselves as intellectuals is a critical sense, arriving at a point where the wisest men are tinkerers, and where the tinkerers earn all the rewards. The student radicals aren't revolting merely against the institution or even against the faculty, but against a system in which all of society, including the majority of students, are involved. The universities, let's face it, haven't been standing in the way of the educational demands of most undergraduates; they've been delivering. The majority—the business students, the ed students, the engineers and agronomists and dental technicians—have been *using* the system to get the emoluments. The disaffected, most of them humanists and social scientists, have been engaging in a kind of status revolt (like the Progressives once did against the industrial robber barons) to keep the university from being used that way. Give the students—*all* the students—full power to determine the curriculum, and it won't take long before they establish something remarkably similar to what they already have.

It is probably for this reason that debates about "relevance" are confusing. There's plenty of relevance in balancing books, learning to run computers, and nuclear physics. What's irrelevant is the liberal arts. (By this time, of course, many of the traditional liberal arts subjects—mathematics, political science, economics, psychology, the foreign languages—have become vocational; many of those who study them are, in some sense, already on the job.) The subjects appear under the old names in the catalogue, but they involve—or, rather, should involve—new questions, new sorts of activities, and bear a different relationship to the rest of the world. It is not simply that the professor is interested in his research, or not interested in anything but apprentices and disciples for his own field (although that is a common source of student complaint); it is also that learning has lost its mystery. The traditional liberal arts program (indeed, the traditional university) was something for a small minority, usually an elite, that was being "educated"—and hence initiated—into the temple. Rank and position were not derived from learning, but learning justified them. The doctor from the university was no more able to command spirits than the cobbler, but he thought he could. The common culture was therefore not only small, but its Latin hocus-pocus provided the happy illusion that it was learning, rather than the shared attitudes of a class, which made discourse possible and allowed the world to revolve in its orderly circuit.

The illusion of magic evaporated when the club became too big. Teach an ordinary seaman to use a sextant, and he begins to lose respect for the officers; now he, too, can determine where the hell he is. At the same time, either the status of officer starts to lose its glow or the search begins for a new way to pull rank. Hence, the rush for new problems, new specialties, new techniques. The growth of knowledge may be a cultural imperative—and it may make life better for us in the long run—but the solution of problems, and the imagination to distinguish the significant from the trivial is still a matter of individual choice. The production of silly papers is no more defensible than the manufacture of useless gadgets—though it is often rationalized with the same sort of argument. The pressure to publish is illiberal, not only because it steals time from the students, but also because it forces the professors to become technicians. Hence the trip to the Institute of Applied Linguistics. In a system where there are only a handful of real doctors (of English, or history, or whatever), the holders of chairs can afford to be liberal, can take time to be introspective and humane. Where the pressure is intense (either for students or professors), everybody must run to keep his seat.

The difficulty for the traditional disciplines in the humanities and social sciences (and here the natural scientists may be far ahead) is that they still behave, in large measure, as if there were nothing but Western culture—no television, no electronic circuits, no psychoanalysis, and no way of knowing about anything except through books. I'm not referring here to "teaching techniques"—which are obviously antediluvian—but to intellectual techniques, subject matter, and ways of organizing experience. What, for example, happens to our understanding of history when we can analyze not only what the man said, but the way he looked—his facial expressions, his laugh, his private off-the-cuff remarks? Will there be disciplinary techniques to handle such problems without making it necessary to become entangled in endless detail? Are there concepts to handle ambiguity or even what now seems absurd? If Hubert Humphrey is privately for a bombing halt but makes no public declarations, who is Hubert Humphrey? What is his *real* position? What is real? Do we have concepts for contradictions and ambivalence?

The mystery has suffered other blows. When the university and its scholars lost their monopoly as disseminators of news and ideas—as purveyors of information—the halo began to tarnish. What printing and the Bible did to the church, mass media are doing to the university. The Indies? The East? Outer space? See it on television; take a plane; someone's been there. The professor tells the kids about civil liberties, search and seizure, habeas corpus. Hell, that's not the way it was in Selma, at the Pentagon, in Chicago. The cops bust in; the sheriff is in with the KKK; the university has sold out to the Pentagon; the scholarly paper about rural development was financed by the CIA. Africa is going modern, sir. There are skyscrapers in Lagos. What do the professors know that isn't accessible to anyone who can travel, read, turn on the tube? Yes, they can deal endlessly with technical questions, or with remote matters of scholarship, but can they apply their disciplines to say something valid about the human condition? At the same time, are their ethics any higher, more noble than those of anyone else?

As the lines between the university and the rest of society became blurred, as the academy became more worldly, and as the world became more academic, the university necessarily came to be regarded as a center for technical training, social validation, and special services to government and industry. It is becoming less and less possible to distinguish professors from corporate technicians, government managers, and free-lance intellectuals. This isn't all bad, but it is new and different and confusing. Most of all, it justifies the students' demands for a voice in university government. The conservative charge—like Barzun's—that the students don't know enough to make proper judgments is misleading because it is now apparent most professors don't know anything either. Which is to say that they don't know very much about what people should learn, should be interested in, or should be in order to have some comfort in their lives. (And, needless to say, don't know anything about teaching.) Technical questions, yes, but a man who has established his mastery as a molecular biologist is no more qualified to establish a curriculum—that is, to tell a student what he should know—than the student himself (except, of course, in the field of molecular biology).

The point is simple, but the implications are substantial. The more specialized the disciplines become, the more its practitioners become journeymen rather than doctors of philosophy. And anyone who is going to enter an apprentice relationship with a journeyman should have absolute choice about the journeyman with whom he wishes to work. (The journeyman, if he has established his credentials in his craft, should, of course, have the full right to determine the course of study in his field. He offers the goods, the apprentice can accept or reject.) At the same time, a faculty of journeymen (specialists in disciplines) does not possess any demonstrated collective wisdom of which the students are innocent. In a world of cultural relativism, the notion that a Ph.D. in linguistics is a higher claim to wisdom than four years with the Beatles is both atavistic and arrogant. The medieval structure remains (and it remains only in the university), but the Renaissance ideal that gave it justification in the academy has vanished. A university should be a community, but in establishing "rights," the problem of student power (or even the distinction of "student" as against "faculty") is clouded by the fact that in most things everybody on the campus is an amateur.

Still, the central problem remains, and that is, establishing some ground for disciplined discourse. This may be a hopeless ideal, both for the university and for the world of which the university is increasingly becoming an indistinguishable part, but it is worth trying for. Part of the task is to stop denying the emotional, to recognize how much of "reason" covers feelings, sensibilities, and attitudes that are not now subject to the disciplinary arsenal. Everyone knows—as has sometimes been said—that even college professors put on their pants one leg at a time. Only the professors (and only some of them, at that) still pretend otherwise. This is not to suggest that the campus should become one huge T-group. Nonetheless, there is a major task in developing courses of inquiry, styles of discourse, methods of study and investigation that cut the jungle broadside, that begin with *this* world, and not in the undergrowth and safety of an established field. Where the disciplines have a contribution to make, let's invite them in, but don't let them monopolize the membership list.

Robert Hutchins and Jerome Wiesner have both used the phrase "the learning society," which one can take as a prediction about the future: The university, says the crystal ball, will be disestablished. It will lose not only its repute as the prime center of intellectual and social wisdom, it will also begin to lose its grip on the accrediting and certifying functions of the larger world. As we have already noted, the mass media, and a lot of other things, are making the news available to any interested citizen, and thus "higher education" – via special institutes, books, tapes, film, and travel – will not only be democratized, it will become, in a society that has solved its major production problems, a way of life. (If professors devoted less time to disseminating information, which can be disseminated a lot more efficiently in other ways, they might have more time and energy for discourse and for real questions and research. In many instances, the lecture is a sort of tribal ritual affirming the ancient, vestigial eminence of the doctor.)

Management in the more affluent and modern corporations is already a kind of institutional organism for the gathering and dissemination of information: new markets and products, yes, but surely also urban and race problems, pollution, politics, and even philosophy. Government and corporate managements are going to find their way of disciplining the world – of controlling spirits. But insofar as they don't represent the individual – the human being with his particular problems, desires, wishes, fears, and hopes – some other institution must. One of the major criticisms of the university during the past decade is that it has said yes too often – yes to government, to industry, to weapons research. What it will have to do now is to re-establish some autonomous identity, and some way, therefore, of knowing when to say no. But in the process of establishing that identity, it will also have to decide just what it, as a university, can do that someone else can't do just as well. Classical languages and medieval history by themselves aren't enough. Neither is physics. The matter is to invent new intellectual tools that can enable men to re-establish a sense of control over the universe, or at least a sense of themselves within it. Most of all, it must help to re-establish belief in that most utopian of ideals: that there are still things to learn which are really worth knowing.

(1969)

*David Stansfield*

# The Importance of Being Different

The Case for Diversity in Education

It's not so much that diversity is good as that its opposite, uniformity, is bad. Not that uniformity doesn't have its advantages. It does. It is the hallmark of the mass society, and of mass-production techniques which brought that society into being. Mass-production makes more goods available to more people. McDonald's Hamburgers may taste like cardboard, but they do only cost 20¢. Supermarkets may be impersonal and sterile, but they are cheaper to shop in than the friendly little store round the corner. Most of the western world may be covered with identical plastic Holiday Inns, but even that is better than sleeping in a ditch. Many people would rather watch bad television programs sandwiched between dogfood and deodorant commercials than have no entertainment at all they could either afford or understand.

The trouble is, mass-production of identical goods inevitably entails mass-production of very *similar,* if not identical, people to consume these goods. This is why our educational system has to try to turn out as standardized a product as possible. This has its disadvantages. One of which is that an education based on uniformity rather than diversity tends to make students excessively competitive.

Buckminster Fuller writes about this in *I seem to be a verb.* "Formerly, education's task was simple: Decide what society needs, then knead the fill. The effect of this pigeonhole training was to control the process of personal growth, rather than to encourage exploration. Perceptions were standardized. Specialization and standardization in the curriculum produced close resemblance, creating hot competition between individuals. A student could only differentiate himself from his fellow specialists by doing the same thing better—and faster. This competition became the chief motive force in mass education, as it was in the whole of society."

An over-competitive society makes it very difficult for us to do anything for its own sake. There's no such thing as "just for fun" in North America. Margaret Mead wrote something about this in her book *And Keep Your Powder Dry:* "American parents send their children to school, to nursery school or kindergarten or first grade, to measure up and to be measured against their contemporaries. 'How does John compare with the other children, Miss Jones?' That is the question, not: 'Has my child the tongue of a poet, or the eye of a painter, or the voice of a leader?'"

Fortunately, this desire to be "one-up" on everyone else at all costs is not shared by all cultures. But the sad thing is, when we do come across societies less competitive than our own, we do our best to "educate" their members to behave like us. A recent article in a Canadian newspaper by a ski coach who was trying to train Indians to compete in races is a typical example. "My biggest disappointment this season has been that Fred and Shirley aren't training as hard as I'd like them to. It's an interesting situation. Both are Indians and the custom is that no Indian likes to rise above the others. If he does, they quickly cut him back down to their own size. So Shirley and Fred won't train. They can beat the rest without training. My biggest problem will be to motivate them to greater things. If an Indian is behind, he wants to catch up, but when he's ahead, he sort of waits for the rest. That's why it is so important to get these kids against top competition."

In spite of the fact that Indians do not like to rise above their fellows, there is plenty of evidence to suggest that it is much easier to be "different" in most Indian societies than it is in White society. The only differences we can tolerate easily, it seems, are the differences between coming first or second or third or fourth and so on in some race or other. Paradoxically, conformity seems to breed competition, and vice versa; whereas truly individualistic people do not appear to have the same need to compete with one another as we have.

The most obvious objection to uniformity, of course, is that it is *boring*. Lewis Mumford warns us about this in a book called *Man's Role in Changing the Face of the Earth*. He writes:

If the goal is uniformity, why should we seek to preserve any of the richness of environmental and cultural individuality that still exists on the earth, and, in turn, widens the range of human choice? Why should we not, on these terms, create by mechanical processes one single climate, uniform from the pole to the equator? Why should we not grind down the mountains, whether to obtain granite and uranium and soil, or just for the pleasure of bulldozing and grinding, until the whole round earth becomes planed down to one level platform? Then let us, if we need trees at all, reduce them to a few marketable varieties, as we have already reduced the six hundred varieties of pear that were commonly cultivated in the United States only a century ago. Let us remove, as a constant temptation for man to sin against his god, the machine, any memory of things that are wild and untamable, pied and dappled, unique and precious: mountains one might be tempted to climb, deserts where one might seek solitude and inner peace, jungles whose living creatures would remind us of nature's original prodigality in creating a grand diversity of habitats and habits of life out of the primeval protoplasm with which it began. If the goal is a uniform type of man, reproducing at a uniform rate, in a uniform environment, kept at a constant temperature, pressure, and humidity, living a uniform life, without internal change or choice, from incubator to incinerator, most of our historic problems concerning man's relation to the earth will disappear. Only one problem will remain: Why should anyone, even a machine, bother to keep this kind of creature alive?

The less diversity there is in our society, the less tolerant we are when we do occasionally meet somebody who does not conform. Our treatment of blacks, homosexuals, cripples, hippies, Eskimos, mental patients, fat people and just about anyone else who differs from us in the slightest degree makes this point only too clear.

Ecologists not only tell us about pollution, they tell us much more significantly about the trend toward uniformity today which is one of the root causes of the deterioration of our environment. In his book *Another Country*, Raymond Dasmann writes:

Diversity has always characterized the biosphere to which man belonged . . . In living systems, complexity brings stability and ability to withstand change. The future survival of man may well depend on the continuing complexity of the biosphere . . . To consider the characteristics of diversity it is best to have a look at the natural world, relatively unmodified by man, and then to consider how human activities tend to affect it. If you were to roam over the globe looking for the place most favorable to the greatest variety of animal and plant life, you would end up, without question, somewhere within the humid tropics, in a biotic community known as tropical rain forest. Here the conditions for life are most nearly ideal . . . It is a long jump from rain forests . . . to cities, but the principle of diversity seems to hold equally well. Our suburbs are the equivalent of a monoculture, a single-species, even-aged stand of uniform housing. They lack natural viability because they lack the variety that would keep them alive and interesting. A little economic blight can sweep through them, decimating their populations, causing their houses to grow gray from lack of paint, to sag and decay. An industrial shutdown could start the process in many an area.

The key word is *Monoculture*. Just as the rows of identical trees that we plant to replace the old mixed forests that were chopped down to make lavatory paper are a form of living death, so the rows of identical children turned out by our schools will end inevitably in the extinction of our species. Monoculture is just as disastrous for humans as it is for trees. In *Tristes Tropiques*, Claude Levi-Strauss looks at monoculture from an anthropologist's point of view:

I understand how it is that people delight in travel-books and ask only to be misled by them. Such books preserve the illusion of something that no longer exists, but yet must be assumed to exist if we are to escape from the appalling indictment that has been piling up against us through twenty thousand years of history. There's nothing to be done about it; civilization is no longer a fragile flower, to be carefully preserved and reared with great difficulty here and there in sheltered corners of a territory rich in natural resources: too rich, almost, for there was an element of menace in their very vitality; yet they allowed us to put fresh life and variety into our cultivations. All that is over: humanity has taken to monoculture, once and for all, and is preparing to produce civilization in bulk, as if it were sugarbeet. The same dish will be served to us every day.

## Diversity In Education

The new Social Studies, Math, Physics and Language programs; much of educational television; Information Retrieval Television; Computer-Assisted Instruction; Individually Prescribed Instruction; Inquiry programs; Head Start programs; a host of so-called "discovery" multimedia kits—nearly all these new developments in education make available a greater *diversity* of experience to the student. But if we examine them more closely we find they have something else in common too: the great majority of them are designed to teach *all* the students the *same* things. They nearly all have pre-determined learning goals. And it isn't the students who do the determining.

Most of the educators who devise these programs are willing to give students more freedom to choose *how* they are going to learn, but they are just as authoritarian as ever when it comes to *what* they are going to learn. The students may be allowed to move toward their learning goals by way of different paths and at different rates, but they are all expected to end up in the same place.

It is very difficult for the natural differences between children and their ways of thinking to flourish if their heads are all filled with precisely the same set of facts and ideas. Just because the ways in which these facts and ideas are presented are diverse, it does not follow that the effect on the children will be one that encourages *them* to be diverse.

In other words, the educational programs we've mentioned do not really promote diversity at all. Rather, they *use* diversity as a technique to bring about uniformity. Currently there are two very obvious categories of pseudo-diversity programs. They suggest some of the reasons why *real* diversity in our educational system so rarely has a chance to develop. The first category usually has the word "individualization" somewhere in its title. At first glance one would imagine an individualization program to be concerned with helping children to be individuals. Unhappily this is seldom the case. All too often the word "individualization" should really be translated: "How to become the same as everybody else at your own pace." It's a judo technique. Use the child's individuality as a weapon in the battle to stamp out his individuality. Children have different learning styles? They learn in different ways, at different times, at different rates? All right. We'll design individual, tailormade courses for every child. We'll let them learn in any way they wish: in seminars, in lectures, in large groups, in small groups, on their own, from films, or books, or television, or computers, or talking typewriters. We won't even mind if some of them take years and years to learn subject-matter which is normally mastered in a few months. As long as they all get there in the end. And "there," of course, is always the same place, always the same subject-matter. We're turning out the same product as we always did. The only difference is that now we have—or will have very soon—hundreds of little custom-made assembly lines for every type of child instead of just one big assembly line for everybody.

The second, and perhaps more sinister, category of pseudo-diversity program we would like to discuss consists of those projects concerned with so-called "disadvantaged" children. The children involved are usually of pre-school age, and are usually black or brown or red—or just poor. They are not handicapped physically or mentally in any medical sense. Their only handicap—their "disadvantage"—is simply that they are not white middle-class Americans. They are *different*.

The people who organize the new programs for the disadvantaged children have the best intentions. They reason that since education is essentially on an obstacle course with hurdles designed to be success-fully jumped by one type of student only—namely, the white, middle-class, preferably Americanized student—it's not really fair on the others. They are faced with two alternatives. Either they can change the rules of the race so that all sorts of off-white or poor or Latin types will have a chance too, or else they can catch these oddballs when they are very, very young, and try to turn them into approximations of white, middle-class Americans before the race has even started. In other words, they can either change the race to fit the children, or change the children to fit the race.

Most of these educators reject the first alternative as too difficult. We must be realistic, they say. Ideally, of course, we should change the race (or even stop racing altogether), but we have to face the fact that the race is actually on *now,* and something has to be done right away about the "disadvantaged" children who aren't doing very well in it. We have to give them a head start.

Without realizing it, what the headstarters are really saying is: "We are very liberal, we don't mind any more that your skin is black or brown, or that you come from Calabria, or that you live in a ghetto. We will give you all the fruits of our wonderful civilization provided only that you learn to *think* like us." Physical racism has been replaced by intellectual racism.

Instead of trying to wash their faces white, we wash their brains white. We call this the "development of conceptual skills." Of course, the ghetto children have plenty of conceptual skills of their own, the only trouble is, they are not the same as ours. Once again, we have plumped for uniformity rather than diversity. Once again, imaginative, diverse new programs and techniques are being used to reduce diversi-ty and increase conformity.

There are a number of reasons why many educators feel students should all be taught the same things. One is simple inertia. The system has been teaching the same things for so long, it's difficult to change. Another reason is perhaps the hypnotic effect of all the new gadgets and techniques now available. All the computers and teaching ma-chines and closed-circuit television systems; the programmed learning, systems analysis and operations research techniques—the whole brave new world of "educational technology"; all this tends to leave little time to think about *why* it is necessary to set the same learning goals for all children. A third reason is the belief that every child should be equipped with the same set of "basic skills."

When pressed to explain just what is meant by basic skills, most people have to admit that probably only the Three R's are really essential for every student. At first, this seems reasonable. But then one wonders, is it really still necessary for *everyone* to know even elementary arithmetic? The sort of arithmetic, that is, that they wouldn't pick up anyway in their day-to-day living? No one bothers even to do addition, let alone multiplication, in stores any more. Calculating machines are universal.

John Holt has some things to say on this subject in *The Underachieving School:*

> . . . it seems to me that we have to think very carefully about the question of whether mathematics is some kind of necessity or whether it's an entertainment. I think a very good case can be made for it as an entertainment, rather like music. I happen to love music. But I think that a person who loves chess, or doing mathematics puzzles or proofs, is getting the kind of aesthetic satisfaction that I get listening to great music, and as far as I'm concerned it's as good as mine, and every bit as much worth encouraging. But when we talk about mathematics, whether arithmetic or in some loftier form, as a necessity for intelligent human life in the twentieth century, I part company. I think arithmetic in my country is largely a useless skill. Almost all the figuring done in the United States is done by machines and will be done so increasingly.

That leaves reading and writing. Apart from the fact that—as Holt points out in another section of his book—if we'd only leave them alone, children would nearly all learn this by themselves sooner or later anyway, since learning to read is so much easier than learning to talk, a skill in which children receive no formal instruction whatever—apart from all this, universal literacy would seem to be a somewhat mixed blessing.

There follow two quotations that raise the question of just how important it is that everyone learn to read. The first is from a book by Jacques Ellul called *Propaganda*, the second is from Sebastian de Grazia's book *Of Time, Work, & Leisure.*

> People used to think that learning to read evidenced human progress; they still celebrate the decline of illiteracy as a great victory; they condemn countries with a large proportion of illiterates; they think that reading is a road to freedom. All this is debatable, for the important thing is not to be able to read, but to understand what one reads, to reflect on and judge what one reads. Outside of that, reading has no meaning (and even destroys certain automatic qualities of memory and observation). But to talk about critical faculties and discernment is to talk about something far above primary education and to consider a very small minority. The vast majority of people, perhaps 90 percent, know how to read, but do not exercise their intelligence beyond this. They attribute authority and eminent value to the printed word, or, conversely, reject it altogether. As these people do not possess enough knowledge to reflect and discern, they believe—or disbelieve—*in toto* what they read. And as such people, moreover, will select the

easiest, not the hardest, reading matter, they are precisely on the level at which the printed word can seize and convince them without opposition. They are perfectly adapted to propaganda.

Reading and writing have become an index of educational progress. Doubtless they help increase the size of the community and enable a man to serve in the factory and army and to know what's on sale today, and what's going on in town tonight. Is this the knowledge the philosophers of democracy were interested in? Socrates was against writing, Plato expressed a similar aversion, Sicilian noblemen for a long time refused to read, holding that as with numerals the job is one for servants. Does reading serve as anything today but a bulletin board, a function largely reduced by radio and television, which do not call for reading? At one time a writer wrote a book for readers he knew almost personally and on whom he could count to read the book with care and thought. Today, and a hundred years ago too, a large proportion of Americans read, but few read anything better than the newspaper, that daily letter from the world to which they never write back. At one time poor people read well enough to read the Bible. Today the Bible is read by priests, students in theology and some in archaeology.

All this may not convince everyone that it is a waste of time to teach children the Three R's, but it does at least make us wonder if these "basic skills" are quite as basic as we thought.

We have tried to show that diversity is important, to discuss some of the reasons why there is so little of it in education at the moment, and finally to make the point that there is really no good reason why there should not be a great deal more diversity in education if we want it. It is *not* so very necessary that the same learning goals be set for all students. The philosophy behind many of the individualization and head start type programs is really rather short-sighted. Even the basic skill argument seems a little shaky on close inspection. So what do we do? The last section of this paper will attempt to answer that question.

## Encouraging Diversity

One of the favorite tests used by the "conceptual skills" people is the "pick-the-odd-one-out" quiz. They put a small ghetto child down in front of an excruciatingly badly drawn picture of a banana, an apple, an orange and a baseball. The child is supposed to point immediately to the baseball as the odd one out, because it's the only one you can't eat (if he points to the banana because it's the only one that isn't round, he is Wrong).

"Picking the odd one out" is both a cause and an effect of uniformity. The most important change that must be brought about if we want more diversity in education is a change from this *exclusive* attitude to an *inclusive* attitude. This can also be thought of as a switch from thinking in terms of what is present which should be absent (negative), to thinking in terms of what is absent which should be present (positive).

Some of the questions people working for diversity should ask most frequently about education are: "What is missing?" "How can we *add* to the range of materials or activities available?" "How can we *broaden* the educational spectrum?"

The habit many educators have of saying "*the* child needs such-and-such" or "*the* way to do this is so-and-so" reveals how strong a hold uniformity has over us. Which child? Which way? If we believe in diversity, we should continually be asking children to see how many *different* ways they can do their sums or draw their pictures or write their stories, rather than telling them *the* way to do all of these things.

The reader may be reminded of "creativity" tests at this point ("How many uses can you think of for a tin can?"). Unfortunately, the reason for devising these tests was not to foster diversity or divergency, but rather to find a *formula* for divergent thinking so that masses of children could henceforth be trained to diverge in precisely the same way. In other words, most programs in the so-called creativity field must really be classed with the other pseudo-diversity programs we have already mentioned; their real goal is uniformity. Trying to categorize and structure the ways in which children diverge is the same kind of absurdity as that exhibited by one teacher we saw recently who gave the following command to a group of children: "All of you go over now to the overhead projector and be *spontaneous.*" We would *not* like our reasons for asking "how many ways . . . ?" to be confused with the reasons of most of the creativity enthusiasts.

Just as it is impossible to make rules about creativity, so it is impossible to make rules about diversity. By its very nature, a rule is something which increases uniformity: "write on one side of the paper only" (everybody, always), "no running in the corridors" (no one, never), "learn the following dates by heart" (all of you). Some rules are good, of course; the laws of the land prevent us from hurting one another, and by and large give us more freedom than we would have in a lawless society. But many educational rules have nothing to do with behavior which affects other people. They merely serve to decrease diversity.

If we do try to make a rule which would increase diversity, we soon get bogged down in qualifications: "learn what you like—if you want to, that is, of course, if you don't want to learn what you like, then say so, and ask someone to tell you what you must learn, at least, ask someone if you wish, but if you'd prefer, just don't do anything at all . . .," and so on. Or else, the diversity "rule" becomes nothing but a suggestion that some people—if they wish, disobey a uniformity rule: "write on one or both sides of the paper," "do run in the corridors," "don't learn the following dates by heart." These are all obviously redundant things to say; like the notice "Please walk on the grass," simply reminds people of their freedom.

It seems that increasing diversity is more a question of what we should *stop* doing rather than of what we should *start* doing. It is much easier to think of specific things we should *not* do—such as make rules, watch television, read newspapers, obey fashion designers, believe commercials, dislike people who are "different," teach everyone the same subject—than of specific things we *should* do.

We can talk of general diversity principles, such as providing broad spectrums of educational experience, and so on, but even these must be much less precise and concrete than most uniformity principles or we'll inevitably wind up with enforced "spontaneity," "having a good time whether you want to or not," and so forth. Any diversity that is regimented is not diversity and really makes no difference at all.

(1971)

# Why shall we learn?

*Augustine*

## *from* On Christian Doctrine

Book IV

### Chapter 1. This work not intended as a treatise on rhetoric

This work of mine, which is entitled *On Christian Doctrine*, was at the commencement divided into two parts. For, after a preface, in which I answered by anticipation those who were likely to take exception to the work, I said, "There are two things on which all interpretation of Scripture depends: the mode of ascertaining the proper meaning, and the mode of making known the meaning when it is ascertained. I shall treat first of the mode of ascertaining, next of the mode of making known, the meaning." As, then, I have already said a great deal about the mode of ascertaining the meaning, and have given three books to this one part of the subject, I shall only say a few things about the mode of making known the meaning, in order if possible to bring them all within the compass of one book, and so finish the whole work in four books.

In the first place, then, I wish by this preamble to put a stop to the expectations of readers who may think that I am about to lay down rules of rhetoric such as I have learnt, and taught too, in the secular schools, and to warn them that they need not look for any such from me. Not that I think such rules of no use, but that whatever use they have is to be learnt elsewhere; and if any good man should happen to have leisure for learning them, he is not to ask me to teach them either in this work or any other.

## Chapter 2. It is lawful for a Christian teacher to use the art of rhetoric

Now, the art of rhetoric being available for the enforcing either of truth or falsehood, who will dare to say that truth in the person of its defenders is to take its stand unarmed against falsehood? For example, that those who are trying to persuade men of what is false are to know how to introduce their subject, so as to put the hearer into a friendly, or attentive, or teachable frame of mind, while the defenders of the truth shall be ignorant of that art? That the former are to tell their falsehoods briefly, clearly, and plausibly, while the latter shall tell the truth in such a way that it is tedious to listen to, hard to understand, and, in fine, not easy to believe it? That the former are to oppose the truth and defend falsehood with sophistical arguments, while the latter shall be unable either to defend what is true, or to refute what is false? That the former, while imbuing the minds of their hearers with erroneous opinions, are by their power of speech to awe, to melt, to enliven, and to rouse them, while the latter shall in defence of the truth be sluggish, and frigid, and somnolent? Who is such a fool as to think this wisdom? Since, then, the faculty of eloquence is available for both sides, and is of very great service in the enforcing either of wrong or right, why do not good men study to engage it on the side of truth, when bad men use it to obtain the triumph of wicked and worthless causes, and to further injustice and error?

## Chapter 3. The proper age and the proper means for acquiring rhetorical skill

But the theories and rules on this subject (to which, when you add a tongue thoroughly skilled by exercise and habit in the use of many words and many ornaments of speech, you have what is called *eloquence* or *oratory*) may be learnt apart from these writings of mine, if a suitable space of time be set aside for the purpose at a fit and proper age. But only by those who can learn them quickly; for the masters of Roman eloquence themselves did not shrink from saying that any one who cannot learn this art quickly can never thoroughly learn it at all. Whether this be true or not, why need we inquire? For even if this art can occasionally be in the end mastered by men of slower intellect, I do not think it of so much importance as to wish men who have arrived at mature age to spend time in learning it. It is enough that boys should give attention to it; and even of these, not all who are to be fitted for usefulness in the Church, but only those who are not yet engaged in any occupation of more urgent necessity, or which ought evidently to take precedence of it. For men of quick intellect and glowing temperament find it easier to become eloquent by reading and listening to eloquent speakers than by following rules for eloquence. And even outside the canon, which to our great advantage is fixed in a place of secure authority, there is no want of ecclesiastical writings, in reading which a man of ability will acquire a tinge of the eloquence with which they are written, even though he does not aim at this, but is solely intent on the matters treated of; especially, of course, if in addition he practise himself in writing, or dictating, and at last also in speaking, the opinions he has formed on grounds of piety and faith. If, however, such ability be wanting, the rules of rhetoric are either not understood, or if, after great labour has been spent in enforcing them, they come to be in some small measure understood, they prove of no service. For even those who have learnt them, and who speak with fluency and elelgance, cannot always think of them when they are speaking so as to speak in accordance with them, unless they are discussing the rules themselves. Indeed, I think there are scarcely any who can do both things – that is, speak well, and, in order to do this, think of the rules of speaking while they are speaking. For we must be careful that what we have got to say does not escape us whilst we are thinking about saying it according to the rules of art. Nevertheless, in the speeches of eloquent men, we find rules of eloquence carried out which the speakers did not think of as aids to eloquence at the time when they were speaking, whether they had ever learnt them, or whether they had never even met with them. For it is because they are eloquent that they exemplify these rules; it is not that they use them in order to be eloquent.

And, therefore, as infants cannot learn to speak except by learning words and phrases from those who do speak, why should not men become eloquent without being taught any art of speech, simply by reading and learning the speeches of eloquent men, and by imitating them as far as they can? And what do we find from the examples themselves to be the case in this respect? We know numbers who, without acquaintance with rhetorical rules, are more eloquent than many who have learnt these; but we know no one who is eloquent without having read and listened to the speeches and debates of eloquent men. For even the art of grammar, which teaches correctness of speech, need not be learnt by boys, if they have the advantage of growing up and living among men who speak correctly. For without knowing the names of any of the faults, they will, from being accustomed to correct speech, lay hold upon whatever is faulty in the speech of any one they listen to, and aovid it; just as citybred men, even when illiterate, seize upon the faults of rustics.

## Chapter 4. The duty of the Christian teacher

It is the duty, then, of the interpreter and teacher of Holy Scripture, the defender of the true faith and the opponent of error, both to teach what is right and to refute what is wrong, and in the performance of this task to conciliate the hostile, to rouse the careless, and to tell the ignorant both what is occurring at present and what is probable in the future. But once that his hearers are friendly, attentive, and ready to learn, whether he has found them so, or has himself made them so, the remaining objects are to be carried out in whatever way the case requires. If the hearers need teaching, the matter treated of must be made fully known by means of narrative. On the other hand, to clear up points that are doubtful requires reasoning and the exhibition of proofs. If, however, the hearers require to be roused rather than instructed, in order that they may be diligent to do what they already know, and to bring their feelings into harmony with the truths they admit, greater vigour of speech is needed. Here entreaties and reproaches, exhortations and upbraidings, and all the other means of rousing the emotions, are necessary.

And all the methods I have mentioned are constantly used by nearly every one in cases where speech is the agency employed.

## Chapter 5. Wisdom of more importance than eloquence to the Christian teacher

But as some men employ these coarsely, inelegantly, and frigidly, while others use them with acuteness, elegance, and spirit, the work that I am speaking of ought to be undertaken by one who can argue and speak with wisdom, if not with eloquence, and with profit to his hearers, even though he profit them less than he would if he could speak with eloquence too. But we must beware of the man who abounds in eloquent nonsense, and so much the more if the hearer is pleased with what is not worth listening to, and thinks that because the speaker is eloquent what he says must be true. And this opinion is held even by those who think that the art of rhetoric should be taught: for they confess that "though wisdom without eloquence is of little service to states, yet eloquence without wisdom is frequently a positive injury, and is of service never." If, then, the men who teach the principles of eloquence have been forced by truth to confess this in the very books which treat of eloquence, though they were ignorant of the true, that is, the heavenly wisdom which comes down from the Father of Lights, how much more ought we to feel it who are the sons and the ministers of this higher wisdom! Now a man speaks with more or less wisdom just as he has made more or less progress in the knowledge of Scripture; I do not mean by reading them much and committing them to memory, but by understanding them aright and carefully searching into their meaning. For there are those who read and yet neglect them; they read to remember the words, but are careless about knowing the meaning. It is plain we must set far above these the men who are not so retentive of the words, but see with the eyes of the heart into the heart of Scripture. Better than either of these, however, is the man who, when he wishes, can repeat the words, and at the same time correctly apprehends their meaning.

Now it is especially necessary for the man who is bound to speak wisely, even though he cannot speak eloquently, to retain in memory the words of Scripture. For the more he discerns the poverty of his own speech, the more he ought to draw on the riches of Scripture, so that what he says in his own words he may prove by the words of Scripture; and he himself, though small and weak in his own words, may gain strength and power from the confirming testimony of great men. For his proof gives pleasure when he cannot please by his mode of speech. But if a man desire to speak not only with wisdom, but with eloquence also (and assuredly he will prove of greater service if he can do both), I would rather send him to read, and listen to, and exercise himself in imitating, eloquent men, than advise him to spend time with the teachers of rhetoric; especially if the men he reads and listens to are justly praised as having spoken, or as being accustomed to speak, not only with eloquence, but with wisdom also. For eloquent speakers are heard with pleasure; wise speakers with profit. And, therefore, Scripture does not say that the multitude of the eloquent but "the multidue of the wise is the welfare of the world."[1] And as we must often swallow wholesome bitters, so we must always avoid unwholesome sweets. But what is better than wholesome sweetness or sweet wholesomeness? For the sweeter we try to make such things, the easier it is to make their wholesomeness serviceable. And so there are writers of the Church who have expounded the Holy Scriptures, not only with wisdom, but with eloquence as well; and there is not more time for the reading of these than is sufficient for those who are studious and at leisure to exhaust them.

## Chapter 6. The sacred writers unite eloquence with wisdom

Here, perhaps, some one inquires whether the authors whose divinely inspired writings constitute the canon, which carries with it a most wholesome authority, are to be considered wise only, or eloquent as well. A question which to me, and to those who think with me, is very easily settled. For where I understand these writers, it seems to me not only that nothing can be wiser, but also that nothing can be more eloquent. And I venture to affirm that all who truly understand what these

[1]Wisdom 6:24.

writers say, perceive at the same time that it could not have been properly said in any other way. For as there is a kind of eloquence that is more becoming in youth, and a kind that is more becoming in old age, and nothing can be called eloquence if it be not suitable to the person of the speaker, so there is a kind of eloquence that is becoming in men who justly claim the highest authority, and who are evidently inspired of God. With this eloquence they spoke; no other would have been suitable for them; and this itself would be unsuitable in any other, for it is in keeping with their character, while it mounts as far above that of others (not from empty inflation, but from solid merit) as it seems to fall below them. Where, however, I do not understand these writers, though their eloquence is then less apparent, I have no doubt but that it is of the same kind as that I do understand. The very obscurity, too, of these divine and wholesome words was a necessary element in eloquence of a kind that was designed to profit our understandings, not only by the discovery of truth, but also by the exercise of their powers.

I could, however, if I had time, show those men who cry up their own form of language as superior to that of our authors (not because of its majesty, but because of its inflation), that all those powers and beauties of eloquence which they make their boast, are to be found in the sacred writings which God in His goodness has provided to mould our characters and to guide us from this world of wickedness to the blessed world above. But it is not the qualities which these writers have in common with the heathen orators and poets that give me such unspeakable delight in their eloquence; I am more struck with admiration at the way in which, by an eloquence peculiarly their own, they so use this eloquence of ours that it is not conspicuous either by its presence or its absence: for it did not become them either to condemn it or to make an ostentatious display of it; and if they had shunned it, they would have done the former; if they had made it prominent, they might have appeared to be doing the latter. And in those passages where the learned do note its presence, the matters spoken of are such that the words in which they are put seem not so much to be sought out by the speaker as spontaneously to suggest themselves; as if wisdom were walking out of its house, that is, the breast of the wise man, and eloquence, like an inseparable attendant, followed it without being called for.

## Chapter 7. Examples of true eloquence drawn from the epistles of Paul and the prophecies of Amos

For who would not see what the apostle meant to say, and how wisely he has said it, in the following passage: "We glory in tribulations also: knowing that tribulation worketh patience; and patience, experience; and experience, hope: and hope maketh not ashamed; because the love of God is shed abroad in our hearts by the Holy Ghost which is given unto us"?[2] Now were any man unlearnedly learned (if I may use the expression) to contend that the apotle had here followed the rules of rhetoric, would not every Christian, learned or unlearned, laugh at him? And yet here we find the figure which is called in Greek κγίμαζ (climax), and by some in Latin *gradatio*, for they do not care to call it *scala* (a ladder), when the words and ideas have a connection of dependency the one upon the other, as we see here that patience arises out of tribulation, experience out of patience, and hope out of experience. Another ornament, too, is found here; for after certain statements finished in a single tone of voice, which we call clauses and sections (*membra et caesa*), but the Greeks κῶλα and κόμματα, there follows a rounded sentence (*ambitus sive circuitus*) which the Greeks call περίοεος, the clauses of which are suspended on the voice of the speaker till the whole is completed by the last clause. For of the statements which precede the period, this is the first clause, "knowing that tribulation worketh patience"; the second, "and patience, experience"; the third, "and experience, hope." Then the period which is subjoined is completed in three clauses of which the first is, "and hope maketh not ashamed"; the second, "because the love of God is shed abroad in our hearts"; the third, "by the Holy Ghost which is given unto us." But these and other matters of the same kind are taught in the art of elocution. As then I do not affirm that the apostle was guided by the rules of eloquence, so I do not deny that his wisdom naturally produced, and was accompanied by, eloquence.

In the Second Epistle to the Corinthians, again, he refutes certain false apostles who had gone out from the Jews, and had been trying to injure his character; and being compelled to speak of himself, though he ascribes this as folly to himself, how wisely and how eloquently he speaks! But wisdom is his guide, eloquence his attendant; he follows the first, the second follows him, and yet he does not spurn it when it comes after him. "I say again," he says, "Let no man think me a fool: if otherwise, yet as a fool receive me, that I may boast myself a little. That which I speak, I speak it not after the Lord, but as it were foolishly, in this confidence of boasting. Seeing that many glory after the flesh, I will glory also. For ye suffer fools gladly, seeing ye yourselves are wise. For ye suffer, if a man bring you into bondage, if a man devour you, if a man take of you, if a man exalt himself, if a man smite you on the face. I speak as concerning reproach, as though we had been weak. Howbeit, whereinsoever any is bold (I speak foolishly), I am bold also. Are they Hebrews? so am I. Are they Israelites? so am I. Are they the seed of Abraham? so am I. Are they ministers of Christ? (I speak as a fool), I am more: in labours more abundant, in stripes above measure, in prisons more frequent, in deaths oft. Of the Jews five times received I forty stripes save one, thrice was I beaten with rods, once was I stoned,

---

[2]Romans 5:3–5.

thrice I suffered shipwreck, a night and a day I have been in the deep; in journeyings often, in perils of waters, in perils of robbers, in perils by mine own countrymen, in perils by the heathen, in perils in the city, in perils in the wilderness, in perils in the sea, in perils among false brethren; in weariness and painfulness, in watchings often, in hunger and thirst, in fastings often, in cold and nakedness. Besides those things which are without, that which cometh upon me daily, the care of all the churches. Who is weak, and I am not weak? who is offended, and I burn not? If I must needs glory, I will glory of the things which concern my infirmities."[3] The thoughtful and attentive perceive how much wisdom there is in these words. And even a man sound asleep must notice what a stream of eloquence flows through them.

Further still, the educated man observes that those sections which the Greeks call κόμματα, and the clauses and periods of which I spoke a short time ago, being intermingled in the most beautiful variety, make up the whole form and features (so to speak) of that diction by which even the unlearned are delighted and affected. For, from the place where I commenced to quote, the passage consists of periods: the first the smallest possible, consisting of two members; for a period cannot have less than two members, though it may have more: "I say again, let no man think me a fool." The next has three members: "if otherwise, yet as a fool receive me, that I may boast myself a little." The third has four members: "That which I speak, I speak it not after the Lord, but as it were foolishly, in this confidence of boasting." The fourth has two: "Seeing that many glory after the flesh, I will glory also." And the fifth has two: "For ye suffer fools gladly, seeing ye yourselves are wise." The sixth again has two members: "for ye suffer, if a man bring you into bondage." Then follow three sections *(caesa)*: "if a man devour you, if a man take of you, if a man exalt himself." Next three clauses *(membra)*: "if a man smite you on the face. I speak as concerning reproach, as though we had been weak." Then is subjoined a period of three members: "Howbeit, whereinsoever any is bold (I speak foolishly), I am bold also." After this, certain separate sections being put in the interrogatory form, separate sections are also given as answers, three to three: "Are they Hebrews? so am I. Are they Israelites? so am I. Are they the seed of Abraham? so am I." But a fourth section being put likewise in the interrogatory form, the answer is given not in another section *(caesum)* but in a clause *(membrum)*: "Are they the ministers of Christ? (I speak as a fool.) I am more." Then the next four sections are given continuously, the interrogatory form being most elegantly suppressed: "in labours more abundant, in stripes above measure, in prisons more frequent, in deaths oft." Next is interposed a short period; for, by a suspension of the voice, "of the Jews five times" is to be marked off as constituting one member, to which is joined the second, "received I forty stripes save one." Then he returns to sections, and three are set down: "Thrice

[3]2 Corinthians 11:16–30.

was I beaten with rods, once was I stoned, thrice I suffered shipwreck."
Next comes a clause: "a night and a day I have been in the deep." Next
fourteen sections burst forth with a vehemence which is most appropriate: "In journeyings often, in perils of waters, in perils of robbers, in
perils by mine own countrymen, in perils by the heathen, in perils in the
city, in perils in the wilderness, in perils in the sea, in perils among
false brethren, in weariness and painfulness, in watchings often, in
hunger and thirst, in fastings often, in cold and nakedness." After this
comes in a period of three members: "Besides those things which are
without, that which cometh upon me daily, the care of all the churches." And to this he adds two clauses in a tone of inquiry: "Who is weak,
and I am not weak? who is offended, and I burn not?" In fine, this
whole passage, as if panting for breath, winds up with a period of two
members: "If I must needs glory, I will glory of the things which concern mine infirmities." And I cannot sufficiently express how beautiful
and delightful it is when after this outburst he rests himself, and gives
the hearer rest, by interposing a slight narrative. For he goes on to say:
"The God and Father of our Lord Jesus Christ, which is blessed for evermore, knoweth that I lie not." And then he tells, very briefly the danger he had been in, and the way he escaped it.

It would be tedious to pursue the matter further, or to point out the
same facts in regard to other passages of Holy Scripture. Suppose I had
taken the further trouble, at least in regard to the passages I have quoted from the apostle's writings, to point out figures of speech which are
taught in the art of rhetoric? Is it not more likely that serious men
would think I had gone too far, than that any of the studious would
think I had done enough? All these things when taught by masters are
reckoned of great value; great prices are paid for them, and the vendors
puff them magniloquently. And I fear lest I too should smack of that
puffery while thus descanting on matters of this kind. It was necessary,
however, to reply to the ill-taught men who think our authors contemptible; not because they do not possess, but because they do not display,
the eloquence which these men value so highly.

But perhaps some one is thinking that I have selected the Apostle
Paul because he is our great orator. For when he says, "Though I be
rude in speech, yet not in knowledge,"[4] he seems to speak as if granting
so much to his detractors, not as confessing that he recognized its truth.
If he had said, "I am indeed rude in speech, but not in knowledge," we
could not in any way have put another meaning upon it. He did not hesitate plainly to assert his knowledge, because without it he could not
have been the teacher of the Gentiles. And certainly if we bring forward
anything of his as a model of eloquence, we take it from those epistles
which even his very detractors, who thought his bodily presence weak
and his speech contemptible, confessed to be weighty and powerful.[5]

[4]2 Corinthians 11:6.
[5]2 Corinthians 10:10.

I see, then, that I must say something about the eloquence of the prophets also, where many things are concealed under a metaphorical style, which the more completely they seem buried under figures of speech give the greater pleasure when brought to light. In this place, however, it is my duty to select a passage of such a kind that I shall not be compelled to explain the matter, but only to commend the style. And I shall do so, quoting principally from the book of that prophet who says that he was a shepherd or herdsman, and was called by God from that occupation, and sent to prophesy to the people of God.[6] I shall not, however, follow the Septuagint translators, who, being themselves under the guidance of the Holy Spirit in their translation, seem to have altered some passages with the view of directing the reader's attention more particularly to the investigation of the spiritual sense (and hence some passages are more obscure, because more figurative, in their translation); but I shall follow the translation made from the Hebrew into Latin by the presbyter Jerome, a man thoroughly acquainted with both tongues.

When, then, this rustic, or *quondam* rustic prophet, was denouncing the godless, the proud, the luxurious, and therefore the most neglectful of brotherly love, he called aloud, saying: "Woe to you who are at ease in Zion, and trust in the mountain of Samaria, who are heads and chiefs of the people, entering with pomp into the house of Israel! Pass ye unto Calneh, and see; and from thence go ye to Hamath the great; then go down to Gath of the Philistines, and to all the best kingdoms of these: is their border greater than your border? Ye that are set apart for the day of evil, and that come near to the seat of oppression; that lie upon beds of ivory, and stretch yourselves upon couches; that eat the lamb of the flock, and the calves out of the midst of the herd; that chant to the sound of the viol. They thought that they had instruments of music like David; drinking wine in bowls, and anointing themselves with the costliest ointment: and they were not grieved for the affliction of Joseph."[7] Suppose those men who, assuming to be themselves learned and eloquent, despise our prophets as untaught and unskilful of speech, had been obliged to deliver a message like this, and to men such as these, would they have chosen to express themselves in any respect differently—those of them, at least, who would have shrunk from raving like madmen?

For what is there that sober ears could wish changed in this speech? In the first place, the invective itself; with what vehemence it throws itself upon the drowsy senses to startle them into wakefulness: "Woe to you who are at ease in Zion, and trust in the mountains of Samaria, who are heads and chiefs of the people, entering with pomp into the house of Israel!" Next, that he may use the favours of God,

[6]Amos 1:1; 7:14.
[7]Amos 6:1–6.

Who has bestowed upon them ample territory, to show their ingratitude in trusting to the mountain of Samaria, where idols were worshipped: "Pass ye unto Calneh," he says, "and see; and from thence go ye to Hamath the great; then go down to Gath of the Philistines, and to all the best kingdoms of these: is their border greater than your border?" At the same time also that these things are spoken of, the style is adorned with names of places as with lamps, such as "Zion," "Samaria," "Calneh," "Hamath the great," and "Gath of the Philistines." Then the words joined to these places are most appropriately varied: "ye are at ease," "ye trust," "pass on," "go," "descend."

And then the future captivity under an oppressive king is announced as approaching, when it is added: "Ye that are set apart for the day of evil, and come near to the seat of oppression." Then are subjoined the evils of luxury: "ye that lie upon beds of ivory, and stretch yourselves upon couches; that eat the lamb from the flock, and the calves out of the midst of the herd." These six clauses form three periods of two members each. For he does not say: "Ye who are set apart for the day of evil, who come near to the seat of oppression, who sleep upon beds of ivory, who stretch yourselves upon couches, who eat the lamb from the flock, and calves out of the herd." If he had so expressed it, this would have had its beauty: six separate clauses running on, the same pronoun being repeated each time, and each clause finished by a single effort of the speaker's voice. But it is more beautiful as it is, the clauses being joined in pairs under the same pronoun, and forming three sentences, one referring to the prophecy of the captivity: "Ye that are set apart for the day of evil, and come near the seat of oppression"; the second to lasciviousness: "ye that lie upon beds of ivory, and stretch yourselves upon couches"; the third to gluttony: "who eat the lamb from the flock, and the calves out of the midst of the herd." So that it is at the discretion of the speaker whether he finish each clause separately and make six altogether, or whether he suspend his voice at the first, the third, and the fifth, and by joining the second to the first, the fourth to the third, and the sixth to the fifth, make three most elegant periods of two members each: one describing the imminent catastrophe; another, the lascivious couch; and the third, the luxurious table.

Next he reproaches them with their luxury in seeking pleasure for the sense of hearing. And here, when he had said, "Ye who chant to the sound of the viol," seeing that wise men may practice music wisely, he, with wonderful skill of speech, checks the flow of his invective, and not now speaking to, but of, these men, and to show us that we must distinguish the music of the wise from the music of the voluptuary, he does not say, "Ye who chant to the sound of the viol, and think that ye have instruments of music like David"; but he first addresses to themselves what it is right the voluptuaries should hear, "Ye who chant to the sound of the viol"; and then, turning to others, he intimates that these men have not even skill in their art: "they thought that they had instruments of music like David; drinking wine in bowls, and anointing themselves with the costliest ointment." These three clauses are best pronounced when the voice is suspended on the first two members of the period, and comes to a pause on the third.

But now as to the sentence which follows all these: "and they were not grieved for the affliction of Joseph." Whether this be pronounced continuously as one clause, or whether with more elegance we hold the words, "and they were not grieved," suspended on the voice and then add, "for the affliction of Joseph," so as to make a period of two members; in any case, it is a touch of marvellous beauty not to say, "and they were not grieved for the affliction of their brother"; but to put Joseph for brother, so as to indicate brothers in general by the proper name of him who stands out illustrious from among his brethren, both in regard to the injuries he suffered and the good return he made. And, indeed, I do not know whether this figure of speech, by which Joseph is put for brothers in general, is one of those laid down in that art which I learnt and used to teach. But how beautiful it is, and how it comes home to the intelligent reader, it is useless to tell any one who does not himself feel it.

And a number of other points bearing on the laws of eloquence could be found in this passage which I have chosen as an example. But an intelligent reader will not be so much instructed by carefully analysing it as kindled by reciting it with spirit. Nor was it composed by man's art and care, but it flowed forth in wisdom and eloquence from the Divine mind; wisdom not aiming at eloquence, yet eloquence not shrinking from wisdom. For if, as certain very eloquent and acute men have perceived and said, the rules which are laid down in the art of oratory could not have been observed, and noted, and reduced to system, if they had not first had their birth in the genius of orators, is it wonderful they should be found in the messengers of Him Who is the author of all genius? Therefore let us acknowledge that the canonical writers are not only wise but eloquent also, with an eloquence suited to a character and position like theirs.

(A.D. 427)

*from*  # The Prince

### Chapter 15. Of the Things for Which Men, and Especially Princes, Are Praised or Blamed

It now remains to be seen what are the methods and rules for a prince as regards his subjects and friends. And as I know that many have written of this, I fear that my writing about it may be deemed presumptuous, differing as I do, especially in this matter, from the opinions of others. But my intention being to write something of use to those who understand, it appears to me more proper to go to the real truth of the matter than to its imagination; and many have imagined republics and principalities which have never been seen or known to exist in reality; for how we live is so far removed from how we ought to live, that he who abandons what is done for what ought to be done, will rather learn to bring about his own ruin than his preservation. A man who wishes to make a profession of goodness in everything must necessarily come to grief among so many who are not good. Therefore it is necessary for a prince, who wishes to maintain himself, to learn how not to be good, and to use this knowledge and not use it, according to the necessity of the case.

Leaving on one side, then, those things which concern only an imaginary prince, and speaking of those that are real, I state that all men, and especially princes, who are placed at a greater height, are reputed for certain qualities which bring them either praise or blame. Thus one is considered liberal, another *misero* or miserly (using a Tuscan term, seeing that *avaro* with us still means one who is rapaciously acquisitive and *misero* one who makes grudging use of his own); one a free giver, another rapacious; one cruel, another merciful; one a breaker of his word, another trustworthy; one effeminate and pusillanimous, another fierce and high-spirited; one humane, another haughty; one lascivious, another chaste; one frank, another astute; one hard, another easy; one serious, another frivolous; one religious, another an unbeliever, and so on. I know that every one will admit that it would be highly praiseworthy in a prince to possess all the above-named qualities that are reputed good, but as they cannot all be possessed or observed, human conditions not permitting of it, it is necessary that he should be prudent enough to avoid the scandal of those vices which would lose him the state, and guard himself if possible against those which will not lose it him, but if not able to, he can indulge them with less scruple. And yet he must not mind incurring the scandal of those vices, without which it would be difficult to save the state, for if one considers well, it will be found that some things which seem virtues would, if followed, lead to one's ruin, and some others which appear vices result in one's greater security and wellbeing.

## Chapter 16. Of Liberality and Niggardliness

Beginning now with the first qualities above named, I say that it would be well to be considered liberal; nevertheless liberality such as the world understands it will injure you, because if used virtuously and in the proper way, it will not be known, and you will incur the disgrace of the contrary vice. But one who wishes to obtain the reputation of liberality among men, must not omit every kind of sumptuous display, and to such an extent that a prince of this character will consume by such means all his resources, and will be at last compelled, if he wishes to maintain his name for liberality, to impose heavy taxes on his people, become extortionate, and do everything possible to obtain money. This will make his subjects begin to hate him, and he will be little esteemed being poor, so that having by this liberality injured many and benefited but few, he will feel the first little disturbance and be endangered by every peril. If he recognises this and wishes to change his system, he incurs at once the charge of niggardliness.

A prince, therefore, not being able to exercise this virtue of liberality without risk if it be known, must not, if he be prudent, object to be called miserly. In course of time he will be thought more liberal, when it is seen that by his parsimony his revenue is sufficient, that he can defend himself against those who make war on him, and undertake enterprises without burdening his people, so that he is really liberal to all those from whom he does not take, who are infinite in number, and niggardly to all to whom he does not give, who are few. In our times we have seen nothing great done except by those who have been esteemed niggardly; the others have all been ruined. Pope Julius II, although he had made use of a reputation for liberality in order to attain the papacy, did not seek to retain it afterwards, so that he might be able to wage war. The present King of France has carried on so many wars without imposing an extraordinary tax, because his extra expenses were covered by the parsimony he had so long practised. The present King of Spain, if he had been thought liberal, would not have engaged in and been successful in so many enterprises.

For these reasons a prince must care little for the reputation of being a miser, if he wishes to avoid robbing his subjects, if he wishes to be able to defend himself, to avoid becoming poor and contemptible, and not to be forced to become rapacious; this niggardliness is one of those vices which enable him to reign. If it is said that Caesar attained the empire through liberality, and that many others have reached the highest positions through being liberal or being thought so, I would reply that you are either a prince already or else on the way to become one. In the first case, this liberality is harmful; in the second, it is certainly necessary to be considered liberal. Caesar was one of those who wished to attain the mastery over Rome, but if after attaining it he had lived and had not moderated his expenses, he would have destroyed that empire. And should any one reply that there have been many princes, who have done great things with their armies, who have been thought extremely liberal, I would answer by saying that the prince may either spend his own wealth and that of his subjects or the wealth of others. In the first case he must be sparing, but for the rest he must not neglect to be very liberal. The liberality is very necessary to a prince who marches with his armies, and lives by plunder, sack and ransom, and is dealing with the wealth of others, for without it he would not be followed by his soldiers. And you may be very generous indeed with what is not the property of yourself or your subjects, as were Cyrus, Caesar, and Alexander; for spending the wealth of others will not diminish your reputation, but increase it, only spending your own resources will injure you. There is nothing which destroys itself so much as liberality, for by using it you lose the power of using it, and become either poor and despicable, or, to escape poverty, rapacious and hated. And of all things that a prince must guard against, the most important are being despicable or hated, and liberality will lead you to one or the other of these conditions. It is, therefore, wiser to have the name of a miser, which produces disgrace without hatred, than to incur of necessity the name of being rapacious, which produces both disgrace and hatred.

### Chapter 17. Of Cruelty and Clemency, and Whether It Is Better to Be Loved or Feared

Proceeding to the other qualities before named, I say that every prince must desire to be considered merciful and not cruel. He must, however, take care not to misuse this mercifulness. Cesare Borgia was considered cruel, but his cruelty had brought order to the Romagna, united it, and reduced it to peace and fealty. If this is considered well, it will be seen that he was really much more merciful than the Florentine people, who, to avoid the name of cruelty, allowed Pistoia to be destroyed. A prince, therefore, must not mind incurring the charge of cruelty for the purpose of keeping his subjects united and faithful; for, with a very few examples, he will be more merciful than those who, from excess of tenderness, allow disorders to arise, from whence spring bloodshed and rapine; for these as a rule injure the whole community, while the executions carried out by the prince injure only individuals. And of all princes, it is impossible for a new prince to escape the reputation of cruelty, new states being always full of dangers. Wherefore Virgil through the mouth of Dido says:

Res dura, et regni novitas me talia cogunt
Moliri, et late fines custode tueri.

Nevertheless, he must be cautious in believing and acting, and must not be afraid of his own shadow, and must proceed in a temperate manner with prudence and humanity, so that too much confidence does not render him incautious, and too much diffidence does not render him intolerant.

From this arises the question whether it is better to be loved more than feared, or feared more than loved. The reply is, that one ought to be both feared and loved, but as it is difficult for the two to go together, it is much safer to be feared than loved, if one of the two has to be wanting. For it may be said of men in general that they are ungrateful, voluble, dissemblers, anxious to avoid danger, and covetous of gain; as long as you benefit them, they are entirely yours; they offer you their blood, their goods, their life, and their children, as I have before said, when the necessity is remote; but when it approaches, they revolt. And the prince who has relied solely on their words, without making other preparations, is ruined; for the friendship which is gained by purchase and not through grandeur and nobility of spirit is bought but not secured, and at a pinch is not to be expended in your service. And men have less scruple in offending one who makes himself loved than one who makes himself feared; for love is held by a chain of obligation which, men being selfish, is broken whenever it serves their purpose; but fear is maintained by a dread of punishment which never fails.

Still, a prince should make himself feared in such a way that if he does not gain love, he at any rate avoids hatred; for fear and the absence of hatred may well go together, and will be always attained by one who abstains from interfering with the property of his citizens and subjects or with their women. And when he is obliged to take the life of any one, let him do so when there is a proper justification and manifest reason for it; but above all he must abstain from taking the property of others, for men forget more easily the death of their father than the loss of their patrimony. Then also pretexts for seizing property are never wanting, and one who begins to live by rapine will always find some reason for taking the goods of others, whereas causes for taking life are rarer and more fleeting.

But when the prince is with his army and has a large number of soldiers under his control, then it is extremely necessary that he should not mind being thought cruel; for without this reputation he could not keep an army united or disposed to any duty. Among the noteworthy actions of Hannibal is numbered this, that although he had an enormous army, composed of men of all nations and fighting in foreign countries, there never arose any dissension either among them or against the prince, either in good fortune or in bad. This could not be due to anything but his inhuman cruelty, which together with his infinite other virtues, made him always venerated and terrible in the sight of his soldiers, and without it his other virtues would not have sufficed to produce that effect. Thoughtless writers admire on the one hand his actions, and on the other blame the principal cause of them.

And that it is true that his other virtues would not have sufficed may be seen from the case of Scipio (famous not only in regard to his own times, but all times of which memory remains), whose armies rebelled against him in Spain, which arose from nothing but his excessive kindness, which allowed more licence to the soldiers than was consonant with military discipline. He was reproached with this in the senate by Fabius Maximus, who called him a corrupter of the Roman militia. Locri having been destroyed by one of Scipio's officers was not revenged by him, nor was the insolence of that officer punished, simply by reason of his easy nature; so much so, that some one wishing to excuse him in the senate, said that there were many men who knew rather how not to err, than how to correct the errors of others. This disposition would in time have tarnished the fame and glory of Scipio had he persevered in it under the empire, but living under the rule of the senate this harmful quality was not only concealed but became a glory to him.

I conclude, therefore, with regard to being feared and loved, that men love at their own free will, but fear at the will of the prince, and that a wise prince must rely on what is in his power and not on what is in the power of others, and he must only contrive to avoid incurring hatred, as has been explained.

## Chapter 18. In What Way Princes Must Keep Faith

How laudable it is for a prince to keep good faith and live with integrity, and not with astuteness, every one knows. Still the experience of our times shows those princes to have done great things who have had little regard for good faith, and have been able by astuteness to confuse men's brains, and who have ultimately overcome those who have made loyalty their foundation.

You must know, then, that there are two methods of fighting, the one by law, the other by force: the first method is that of men, the second of beasts; but as the first method is often insufficient, one must have recourse to the second. It is therefore necessary for a prince to know well how to use both the beast and the man. This was covertly taught to rulers by ancient writers, who relate how Achilles and many others of those ancient princes were given to Chiron the centaur to be brought up and educated under his discipline. The parable of this semi-animal, semi-human teacher is meant to indicate that a prince must know how to use both natures, and that the one without the other is not durable.

A prince being thus obliged to know well how to act as a beast must imitate the fox and the lion, for the lion cannot protect himself from traps, and the fox cannot defend himself from wolves. One must therefore be a fox to recognize traps, and a lion to frighten wolves. Those that wish to be only lions do not understand this. Therefore, a prudent ruler ought not to keep faith when by so doing it would be against his interest, and when the reasons which made him bind himself no longer exist. If men were all good, this precept would not be a good one; but as they are bad, and would not observe their faith with you, so you are not bound to keep faith with them. Nor have legitimate grounds ever failed a prince who wished to show colourable excuse for the non-fulfilment of his promise. Of this one could furnish an infinite number of modern examples, and show how many times peace has been broken, and how many promises rendered worthless, by the faithlessness of princes, and those that have been best able to imitate the fox have succeeded best. But it is necessary to be able to disguise this character well, and to be a great feigner and dissembler; and men are so simple and so ready to obey present necessities, that one who deceives will always find those who allow themselves to be deceived.

I will only mention one modern instance. Alexander VI did nothing else but deceive men, he thought of nothing else, and found the occasion for it; no man was ever more able to give assurances, or affirmed things with stronger oaths, and no man observed them less; however, he always succeeded in his deceptions, as he well knew this aspect of things.

It is not, therefore, necessary for a prince to have all the above-named qualities, but it is very necessary to seem to have them. I would even be bold to say that to possess them and always to observe them is dangerous, but to appear to possess them is useful. Thus it is well to seem merciful, faithful, humane, sincere, religious, and also to be so; but you must have the mind so disposed that when it is needful to be otherwise you may be able to change to the opposite qualities. And it must be understood that a prince, and especially a new prince, cannot observe all those things which are considered good in men, being often obliged, in order to maintain the state, to act against faith, against charity, against humanity, and against religion. And, therefore, he must have a mind disposed to adapt itself according to the wind, and as the variations of fortune dictate, and, as I said before, not deviate from what is good, if possible, but be able to do evil if constrained.

A prince must take great care that nothing goes out of his mouth which is not full of the above-named five qualities, and, to see and hear him, he should seem to be all mercy, faith, integrity, humanity, and religion. And nothing is more necessary than to seem to have this last quality, for men in general judge more by the eyes than by the hands, for every one can see, but very few have to feel. Everybody sees what you appear to be, few feel what you are, and those few will not dare to oppose themselves to the many, who have the majesty of the state to defend them; and in the actions of men, and especially of princes, from which there is no appeal, the end justifies the means. Let a prince therefore aim at conquering and maintaining the state, and the means will always be judged honourable and praised by every one, for the vulgar is always taken by appearances and the issue of the event; and the world consists only of the vulgar, and the few who are not vulgar are isolated when the many have a rallying point in the prince. A certain prince of the present time, whom it is well not to name, never does anything but preach peace and good faith, but he is really a great enemy to both, and either of them, had he observed them, would have lost him state or reputation on many occasions.

(1513)

## John Henry Cardinal Newman

### *from* The Idea of a University

Knowledge Its Own End

A university may be considered with reference either to its students or to its studies; and the principle, that all knowledge is a whole and the separate sciences part of one, which I have hitherto been using in behalf of its studies, is equally important when we direct our attention to its students. Now then I turn to the students, and shall consider the education which, by virtue of this principle, a university will give them; and thus I shall be introduced, gentlemen, to the second question, which I proposed to discuss, viz. whether and in what sense its teaching, viewed relatively to the taught, carries the attribute of utility along with it.

### 1

I have said that all branches of knowledge are connected together, because the subject-matter of knowledge is intimately united in itself, as being the acts and the work of the Creator. Hence it is that the sciences, into which our knowledge may be said to be cast, have multiplied bearings one on another, and an internal sympathy, and admit, or rather demand, comparison and adjustment. They complete, correct, balance each other. This consideration, if well-founded, must be taken into account, not only as regards the attainment of truth, which is their common end, but as regards the influence which they exercise upon those whose education consists in the study of them. I have said already, that to give undue prominence to one is to be unjust to another; to neglect or supersede these is to divert those from their proper object. It is to unsettle the boundary lines between science and science, to disturb their action, to destroy the harmony which binds them together. Such a proceeding will have a corresponding effect when introduced into a place of education. There is no science but tells a different tale, when viewed as a portion of a whole, from what it is likely to suggest when taken by itself, without the safeguard, as I may call it, of others.

Let me make use of an illustration. In the combination of colours, very different effects are produced by a difference in their selection and juxtaposition; red, green, and white change their shades, according to the contrast to which they are submitted. And, in like manner, the drift and meaning of a branch of knowledge varies with the company in which it is introduced to the student. If his reading is confined simply to one subject, however such division of labour may favour the advancement of a particular pursuit, a point into which I do not here enter, certainly it has a tendency to contract his mind. If it is incorporated with others, it depends on those others as to the kind of influence which it exerts upon him. Thus the classics, which in England are the means of refining the taste, have in France subserved the spread of revolutionary and deistical doctrines. In metaphysics, again, Butler's *Analogy of Religion,* which has had so much to do with the conversion to the Catholic faith of members of the University of Oxford, appeared to Pitt and others, who had received a different training, to operate only in the direction of infidelity. And so again, Watson, Bishop of Llandaff, as I think he tells us in the narrative of his life, felt the science of mathematics to indispose the mind to religious belief, while others see in its investigations the best parallel, and thereby defence, of the Christian Mysteries. In like manner, I suppose, Arcesilas would not have handled logic as Aristotle, nor Aristotle have criticized poets as Plato; yet reasoning and poetry are subject to scientific rules.

It is a great point then to enlarge the range of studies which a university professes, even for the sake of the students; and, though they cannot pursue every subject which is open to them, they will be the gainers by living among those and under those who represent the whole circle. This I conceive to be the advantage of a seat of universal learning, considered as a place of education. An assemblage of learned men, zealous for their own sciences, and rivals of each other, are brought, by familiar intercourse and for the sake of intellectual peace, to adjust together the claims and relations of their respective subjects of investigation. They learn to respect, to consult, to aid each other. Thus is created a pure and clear atmosphere of thought, which the student also breathes, though in his own case he only pursues a few sciences out of the multitude. He profits by an intellectual tradition, which is independent of particular teachers, which guides him in his choice of subjects, and duly interprets for him those which he chooses. He apprehends the great outlines of knowledge, the principles on which it rests, the scale of its parts, its lights and its shades, its great points and its little, as he otherwise cannot apprehend them. Hence it is that his education is called "liberal." A habit of mind is formed which lasts through life, of which the attributes are, freedom, equitableness, calmness, moderation, and wisdom; or what in a former discourse I have ventured to call a philosophical habit. This then I would assign as the special fruit of the education furnished at a university, as contrasted with other places of teaching or modes of teaching. This is the main purpose of a university in its treatment of its students.

And now the question is asked me, What is the *use* of it? and my answer will constitute the main subject of the discourses which are to follow.

## 2

Cautious and practical thinkers, I say, will ask of me, what, after all, is the gain of this philosophy, of which I make such account, and from which I promise so much. Even supposing it to enable us to exercise the degree of trust exactly due to every science respectively, and to estimate precisely the value of every truth which is anywhere to be found, how are we better for this master view of things, which I have been extolling? Does it not reverse the principle of the division of labour? will practical objects be obtained better or worse by its cultivation? to what then does it lead? where does it end? what does it do? how does it profit? what does it promise? Particular sciences are respectively the basis of definite arts, which carry on to results tangible and beneficial the truths which are the subjects of the knowledge attained; what is the art of this science of sciences? what is the fruit of such a philosophy? what are we proposing to effect, what inducements do we hold out to the Catholic community, when we set about the enterprise of founding a university?

I am asked what is the end of university education, and of the liberal or philosophical knowledge which I conceive it to impart: I answer, that what I have already said has been sufficient to show that it has a very tangible, real, and sufficient end, though the end cannot be divided from that knowledge itself. Knowledge is capable of being its own end. Such is the constitution of the human mind, that any kind of knowledge, if it be really such, is its own reward. And if this is true of all knowledge, it is true also of that special philosophy, which I have made to consist in a comprehensive view of truth in all its branches, of the relations of science to science, of their mutual bearings, and their respective values. What the worth of such an acquirement is, compared with other objects which we seek,—wealth or power or honour or the conveniences and comforts of life, I do not profess here to discuss; but I would maintain, and mean to show, that it is an object, in its own nature so really and undeniably good, as to be the compensation of a great deal of thought in the compassing, and a great deal of trouble in the attaining.

Now, when I say that knowledge is, not merely a means to something beyond it, or the preliminary of certain arts into which it naturally resolves, but an end sufficient to rest in and to pursue for its own sake, surely I am uttering no paradox, for I am stating what is both intelligible in itself, and has ever been the common judgment of philosophers and the ordinary feeling of mankind. I am saying what at least the public opinion of this day ought to be slow to deny, considering how much we have heard of late years, in opposition to religion, of entertaining, curious, and various knowledge. I am but saying what whole volumes have been written to illustrate, viz. by a "selection from the records of philosophy, literature, and art, in all ages and countries, of a body of examples, to show how the most unpropitious circumstances have been unable to conquer an ardent desire for the acquisition of knowledge."[1] That further advantages accrue to us and redound to others by its possession, over and above what it is in itself, I am very far indeed from denying; but, independent of these, we are satisfying a direct need of our nature in its very acquisition; and, whereas our nature, unlike that of the inferior creation, does not at once reach its perfection, but depends, in order to it, on a number of external aids and appliances, knowledge, as one of the principal of these, is valuable for what its very presence in us does for us after the manner of a habit, even though it be turned to no further account, nor subserve any direct end.

### 3

Hence it is that Cicero, in enumerating the various heads of mental excellence, lays down the pursuit of knowledge for its own sake, as the first of them. "This pertains most of all to human nature," he says, "for we are all of us drawn to the pursuit of knowledge; in which to excel we consider excellent, whereas to mistake, to err, to be ignorant, to be deceived, is both an evil and a disgrace."[2] And he considers knowledge the very first object to which we are attracted, after the supply of our physical wants. After the calls and duties of our animal existence, as they may be termed, as regards ourselves, our family, and our neighbours,

[1] Pursuit of Knowledge under Difficulties. Introd. [Newman]
[2] Cicer. Offic. init. [Newman]

follows, he tells us, "the search after truth. Accordingly, as soon as we escape from the pressure of necessary cares, forthwith we desire to see, to hear, and to learn; and consider the knowledge of what is hidden or is wonderful a condition of our happiness."

This passage, though it is but one of many similar passages in a multitude of authors, I take for the very reason that it is so familiarly known to us; and I wish you to observe, gentlemen, how distinctly it separates the pursuit of knowledge from those ulterior objects to which certainly it can be made to conduce, and which are, I suppose, solely contemplated by the persons who would ask of me the use of a university or liberal education. So far from dreaming of the cultivation of knowledge directly and mainly in order to our physical comfort and enjoyment, for the sake of life and person, of health, of the conjugal and family union, of the social tie and civil security, the great orator implies, that it is only after our physical and political needs are supplied, and when we are "free from necessary duties and cares," that we are in a condition for "desiring to see, to hear, and to learn." Nor does he contemplate in the least degree the reflex or subsequent action of knowledge, when acquired, upon those material goods which we set out by securing before we seek it; on the contrary, he expressly denies its bearing upon social life altogether, strange as such a procedure is to those who live after the rise of the Baconian philosophy, and he cautions us against such a cultivation of it as will interfere with our duties to our fellow-creatures. "All these methods," he says, "are engaged in the investigation of truth; by the pursuit of which to be carried off from public occupations is a transgression of duty. For the praise of virtue lies altogether in action; yet intermissions often occur, and then we recur to such pursuits; not to say that the incessant activity of the mind is vigorous enough to carry us on in the pursuit of knowledge, even without any exertion of our own." The idea of benefiting society by means of "the pursuit of science and knowledge," did not enter at all into the motives which he would assign for their cultivation.

This was the ground of the opposition which the elder Cato made to the introduction of Greek philosophy among his countrymen, when Carneades and his companions, on occasion of their embassy, were charming the Roman youth with their eloquent expositions of it. The fit representative of a practical people, Cato estimated everything by what it produced; whereas the pursuit of knowledge promised nothing beyond knowledge itself. He despised that refinement or enlargement of mind of which he had no experience.

## 4

Things, which can bear to be cut off from everything else and yet persist in living, must have life in themselves; pursuits, which issue in nothing, and still maintain their ground for ages, which are regarded as admirable, though they have not as yet proved themselves to be useful, must have their sufficient end in themselves, whatever it turn out to be. And we are brought to the same conclusion by considering the force of the epithet, by which the knowledge under consideration is popularly designated. It is common to speak of *"liberal* knowledge," of the *"liberal* arts and studies," and of a *"liberal* education," as the especial characteristic or property of a university and of a gentleman; what is really meant by the word? Now, first, in its grammatical sense it is opposed to *servile;* and by "servile work" is understood, as our catechisms inform us, bodily labour, mechanical employment, and the like, in which the mind has little or no part. Parallel to such servile works are those arts, if they deserve the name, of which the poet speaks,[3] which owe their origin and their method to hazard, not to skill; as, for instance, the practice and operations of an empiric. As far as this contrast may be considered as a guide into the meaning of the word, liberal education and liberal pursuits are exercises of mind, of reason, of reflection.

But we want something more for its explanation, for there are bodily exercises which are liberal, and mental exercises which are not so. For instance, in ancient times the practitioners in medicine were commonly slaves; yet it was an art as intellectual in its nature, in spite of the pretence, fraud and quackery with which it might then, as now, be debased, as it was heavenly in its aim. And so in like manner, we contrast a liberal education with a commercial education or a professional; yet no one can deny that commerce and the professions afford scope for the highest and most diversified powers of mind. There is then a great variety of intellectual exercises, which are not technically called "liberal"; on the other hand, I say, there are exercises of the body which do receive that appellation. Such, for instance, was the palaestra, in ancient times; such the Olympic games, in which strength and dexterity of body as well as of mind gained the prize. In Xenophon we read of the young Persian nobility being taught to ride on horseback and to speak the truth; both being among the accomplishments of a gentleman. War, too, however rough a profession, has ever been accounted liberal, unless in cases when it becomes heroic, which would introduce us to another subject.

Now comparing these instances together, we shall have no difficulty in determining the principle of this apparent variation in the application of the term which I am examining. Manly games, or games of skill, or military prowess, though bodily, are, it seems, accounted liberal; on the other hand, what is merely professional, though highly intellectual, nay, though liberal in comparison of trade and manual labour, is not simply called liberal, and mercantile occupations are not liberal at all. Why this distinction? because that alone is liberal knowledge, which stands on its own pretensions, which is independent of sequel, expects

---

[3]Τέχνη τύχην 'εστερξε καί τύχη τέχνην. Vid. Arist. Nic. Ethic. vi. [Newman].

no complement, refuses to be *informed* (as it is called) by any end, or absorbed into any art, in order duly to present itself to our contemplation. The most ordinary pursuits have this specific character, if they are self-sufficient and complete; the highest lose it, when they minister to something beyond them. It is absurd to balance, in point of worth and importance, a treatise on reducing fractures with a game of cricket or a fox-chase; yet of the two the bodily exercise has that quality which we call "liberal," and the intellectual has it not. And so of the learned professions altogether, considered merely as professions; although one of them be the most popularly beneficial, and another the most politically important, and the third the most intimately divine of all human pursuits, yet the very greatness of their end, the health of the body, or of the commonwealth, or of the soul, diminishes, not increases, their claim to the appellation "liberal," and that still more, if they are cut down to the strict exigencies of that end. If, for instance, theology instead of being cultivated as a contemplation, be limited to the purposes of the pulpit or be represented by the catechism, it loses, — not its usefulness, not its divine character, not its meritoriousness, (rather it gains a claim upon these titles by such charitable condescension), — but it does lose the particular attribute which I am illustrating; just as a face worn by tears and fasting loses its beauty, or a labourer's hand loses its delicateness; — for theology thus exercised is not simple knowledge, but rather is an art or a business making use of theology. And thus it appears that even what is supernatural need not be liberal, nor need a hero be a gentleman, for the plain reason that one idea is not another idea. And in like manner the Baconian philosophy, by using its physical sciences in the service of man, does thereby transfer them from the order of liberal pursuits to, I do not say the inferior, but the distinct class of the useful. And, to take a different instance, hence again, as is evident, whenever personal gain is the motive, still more distinctive an effect has it upon the character of a given pursuit; thus racing, which was a liberal exercise in Greece, forfeits its rank in times like these, so far as it is made the occasion of gambling.

All that I have been now saying is summed up in a few characteristic words of the great philosopher. "Of possessions," he says, "those rather are useful, which bear fruit; those *liberal, which tend to enjoyment*. By fruitful, I mean, which yield revenue; by enjoyable, where *nothing accrues of consequence beyond the using*."[4]

## 5

Do not suppose, that in thus appealing to the ancients, I am throwing back the world two thousand years, and fettering philosophy with the reasonings of paganism. While the world lasts, will Aristotle's doctrine

[4]Aristot. Rhet. i. 5. [Newman]

on these matters last, for he is the oracle of nature and of truth. While we are men, we cannot help, to a great extent, being Aristotelians, for the great master does but analyze the thoughts, feelings, views, and opinions of human kind. He has told us the meaning of our own words and ideas, before we were born. In many subject-matters, to think correctly, is to think like Aristotle; and we are his disciples whether we will or no, though we may not know it. Now, as to the particular instance before us, the word "liberal" as applied to knowledge and education, expresses a specific idea, which ever has been, and ever will be, while the nature of man is the same, just as the idea of the beautiful is specific, or of the sublime, or of the ridiculous, or of the sordid. It is in the world now, it was in the world then; and, as in the case of the dogmas of faith, it is illustrated by a continuous historical tradition, and never was out of the world, from the time it came into it. There have indeed been differences of opinion from time to time, as to what pursuits and what arts came under that idea, but such differences are but an additional evidence of its reality. That idea must have a substance in it, which has maintained its ground amid these conflicts and changes, which has ever served as a standard to measure things withal, which has passed from mind to mind unchanged, when there was so much to colour, so much to influence any notion or thought whatever, which was not founded in our very nature. Were it a mere generalization, it would have varied with the subjects from which it was generalized: but though its subjects vary with the age, it varies not itself. The palaestra may seem a liberal exercise to Lycurgus, an illiberal to Seneca; coach-driving and prize-fighting may be recognized in Elis, and be condemned in England; music may be despicable in the eyes of certain moderns, and be in the highest place with Aristotle and Plato, – (and the case is the same in the particular application of the idea of beauty, or of goodness, or of moral virtue, there is a difference of tastes, a difference of judgments) – still these variations imply, instead of discrediting, the archetypal idea, which is but a previous hypothesis or condition, by means of which issue is joined between contending opinions and without which there would be nothing to dispute about.

I consider, then, that I am chargeable with no paradox, when I speak of a knowledge which is its own end, when I call it liberal knowledge, or a gentleman's knowledge, when I educate for it, and make it the scope of a university. And still less am I incurring such a charge, when I make this acquisition consist, not in knowledge in a vague and ordinary sense, but in that knowledge which I have especially called philosophy or, in an extended sense of the word, science; for whatever claims knowledge has to be considered as a good, these it has in a higher degree when it is viewed not vaguely, not popularly, but precisely and transcendently as philosophy. Knowledge, I say, is then especially liberal, or sufficient for itself, apart from every external and ulterior object, when and so far as it is philosophical, and this I proceed to show.

**6**

Now bear with me, gentlemen, if what I am about to say, has at first sight a fanciful appearance. Philosophy, then, or science, is related to knowledge in this way: — knowledge is called by the name of science or philosophy, when it is acted upon, informed, or if I may use a strong figure, impregnated by reason. Reason is the principle of that intrinsic fecundity of knowledge, which, to those who possess it, is its especial value, and which dispenses with the necessity of their looking abroad for any end to rest upon external to itself. Knowledge, indeed, when thus exalted into a scientific form, is also power; not only is it excellent in itself, but whatever such excellence may be, it is something more, it has a result beyond itself. Doubtless; but that is a further consideration, with which I am not concerned. I only say that, prior to its being a power, it is a good; that it is, not only an instrument, but an end. I know well it may resolve itself into an art, and terminate in a mechanical process, and in tangible fruit; but it also may fall back upon that reason which informs it, and resolve itself into philosophy. In one case it is called useful knowledge; in the other liberal. The same person may cultivate it in both ways at once; but this again is a matter foreign to my subject; here I do but say that there are two ways of using knowledge, and in matter of fact those who use it in one way are not likely to use it in the other, or at least in a very limited measure. You see, then, here are two methods of education; the end of the one is to be philosophical, of the other to be mechanical; the one rises towards general ideas, the other is exhausted upon what is particular and external. Let me not be thought to deny the necessity, or to decry the benefit, of such attention to what is particular and practical, as belongs to the useful or mechanical arts; life could not go on without them; we owe our daily welfare to them; their exercise is the duty of the many, and we owe to the many a debt of gratitude for fulfilling that duty. I only say that knowledge, in proportion as it tends more and more to be particular, ceases to be knowledge. It is a question whether knowledge can in any proper sense be predicated of the brute creation; without pretending to metaphysical exactness of phraseology, which would be unsuitable to an occasion like this, I say, it seems to me improper to call that passive sensation, or perception of things, which brutes seem to possess, by the name of knowledge. When I speak of knowledge, I mean something intellectual, something which grasps what it perceives through the senses; something which takes a view of things; which sees more than the senses convey; which reasons upon what it sees, and while it sees; which invests it with an idea. It expresses itself, not in a mere enunciation, but by an enthymeme: it is of the nature of science from the first, and in this consists its dignity. The principle of real dignity in knowledge, its worth, its desirableness, considered irrespectively of its results, is this germ within it of a scientific or a philosophical process. This is how it comes to be an end in itself; this is why it admits of being called liberal. Not to know the relative disposition of things is the state of slaves or children; to have mapped out the universe is the boast, or at least the ambition, of philosophy.

Moreover, such knowledge is not a mere extrinsic or accidental advantage, which is ours today and another's tomorrow, which may be got up from a book, and easily forgotten again, which we can command or communicate at our pleasure, which we can borrow for the occasion, carry about in our hand, and take into the market; it is an acquired illumination, it is a habit, a personal possession, and an inward endowment. And this is the reason why it is more correct, as well as more usual, to speak of a university as a place of education, than of instruction, though, when knowledge is concerned, instruction would at first sight have seemed the more appropriate word. We are instructed, for instance, in manual exercises, in the fine and useful arts, in trades, and in ways of business; for these are methods, which have little or no effect upon the mind itself, are contained in rules committed to memory, to tradition, or to use, and bear upon an end external to themselves. But education is a higher word; it implies an action upon our mental nature, and the formation of a character; it is something individual and permanent, and is commonly spoken of in connexion with religion and virtue. When, then, we speak of the communication of knowledge as being education, we thereby really imply that that knowledge is a state or condition of mind; and since cultivation of mind is surely worth seeking for its own sake, we are thus brought once more to the conclusion, which the word "liberal" and the word "philosophy" have already suggested, that there is a knowledge which is desirable, though nothing come of it, as being of itself a treasure, and a sufficient remuneration of years of labour.

### 7

This, then, is the answer which I am prepared to give to the question with which I opened this discourse. Before going on to speak of the object of the Church in taking up philosophy, and the uses to which she puts it, I am prepared to maintain that philosophy is its own end, and, as I conceive, I have now begun the proof of it. I am prepared to maintain that there is a knowledge worth possessing for what it is, and not merely for what it does; and what minutes remain to me today I shall devote to the removal of some portion of the indistinctness and confusion with which the subject may in some minds be surrounded.

It may be objected then, that, when we profess to seek knowledge for some end or other beyond itself, whatever it be, we speak intelligibly; but that, whatever men may have said, however obstinately the idea may have kept its ground from age to age, still it is simply unmeaning to say that we seek knowledge for its own sake, and for nothing else; for that it ever leads to something beyond itself, which therefore is its end, and the cause why it is desirable;—moreover, that this end is twofold, either of this world or of the next; that all knowledge is cultivated either for secular objects or for eternal; that if it is directed to secular objects, it is called useful knowledge, if to eternal, religious or Christian knowledge;—in consequence, that if, as I have allowed, this liberal knowledge does not benefit the body or estate, it ought to benefit the soul; but if the fact be really so, that it is neither a physical or a secular good on the one hand, nor a moral good on the other, it cannot be a good at all, and is not worth the trouble which is necessary for its acquisition.

And then I may be reminded that the professors of this liberal or philosophical knowledge have themselves, in every age, recognized this exposition of the matter, and have submitted to the issue in which it terminates; for they have ever been attempting to make men virtuous; or, if not, at least have assumed that refinement of mind was virtue, and that they themselves were the virtuous portion of mankind. This they have professed on the one hand; and on the other, they have utterly failed in their professions, so as ever to make themselves a proverb among men, and a laughing-stock both to the grave and the dissipated portion of mankind, in consequence of them. Thus they have furnished against themselves both the ground and the means of their own exposure, without any trouble at all to anyone else. In a word, from the time that Athens was the university of the world, what has philosophy taught men, but to promise without practising, and to aspire without attaining. What has the deep and lofty thought of its disciples ended in but eloquent words? Nay, what has its teaching ever meditated, when it was boldest in its remedies for human ill, beyond charming us to sleep by its lessons, that we might feel nothing at all? like some melodious air, or rather like those strong and transporting perfumes, which at first spread their sweetness over everything they touch, but in a little while do but offend in proportion as they once pleased us. Did Philosophy support Cicero under the disfavour of the fickle populace, or nerve Seneca to oppose an imperial tyrant? It abandoned Brutus, as he sorrowfully confessed, in his greatest need, and it forced Cato, as his panegyrist strangely boasts, into the false position of defying heaven. How few can be counted among its professors, who, like Polemo, were thereby converted from a profligate course, or like Anaxagoras, thought the world well lost in exchange for its possession? The philosopher in *Rasselas* taught a superhuman doctrine, and then succumbed without an effort to a trial of human affection.

"He had discoursed," we are told, "with great energy on the government of the passions. His look was venerable, his action graceful, his pronunciation clear, and his diction elegant. He showed, with great strength of sentiment and variety of illustration, that human nature is degraded and debased, when the lower faculties predominate over the higher. He communicated the various precepts given, from time to time, for the conquest of passion, and displayed the happiness of those who had obtained the important victory, after which man is no longer the slave of fear, nor the fool of hope . . . He enumerated many examples of heroes immovable by pain or pleasure, who looked with indifference on those modes or accidents to which the vulgar give the names of good and evil."

Rasselas in a few days found the philosopher in a room half darkened, with his eyes misty, and his face pale. "Sir," said he, "you have come at a time when all human friendship is useless; what I suffer cannot be remedied, what I have lost cannot be supplied. My daughter, my only daughter, from whose tenderness I expected all the comforts of my age, died last night of a fever." "Sir," said the prince, "mortality is an event by which a wise man can never be surprised; we know that death is always near, and it should therefore always be expected." "Young man," answered the philosopher, "you speak like one who has never felt the pangs of separation." "Have you, then, forgot the precept," said Rasselas, "which you so powerfully enforced? . . . consider that external things are naturally variable, but truth and reason are always the same." "What comfort," said the mourner, "can truth and reason afford me? Of what effect are they now, but to tell me that my daughter will not be restored?"

## 8

Better, far better, to make no professions, you will say, than to cheat others with what we are not, and to scandalize them with what we are. The sensualist, or the man of the world, at any rate, is not the victim of fine words, but pursues a reality and gains it. The philosophy of utility, you will say, gentlemen, has at least done its work; and I grant it,—it aimed low, but it has fulfilled its aim. If that man of great intellect who has been its prophet in the conduct of life played false to his own professions, he was not bound by his philosophy to be true to his friend or faithful in his trust. Moral virtue was not the line in which he undertook to instruct men; and though, as the poet calls him, he were the "meanest" of mankind, he was so in what may be called his private capacity and without any prejudice to the theory of induction. He had a right to be so, if he chose, for anything that the idols of the den or the theatre had to say to the contrary. His mission was the increase of physical enjoyment and social comfort;[5] and most wonderfully, most awful-

---

[5]It will be seen that on the whole I agree with Lord Macaulay in his Essay on Bacon's Philosophy. I do not know whether he would agree with me. [Newman]

ly has he fulfilled his conception and his design. Almost day by day have we fresh shoots, and buds, and blossoms, which are to ripen into fruit, on that magical tree of knowledge which he planted, and to which none of us perhaps, except the very poor, but owes, if not his present life, at least his daily food, his health, and general well-being. He was the divinely provided minister of temporal benefits to all of us so great, that, whatever I am forced to think of him as a man, I have not the heart, from mere gratitude, to speak of him severely. And, in spite of the tendencies of his philosophy, which, are, as we see at this day, to depreciate, or to trample on theology, he has himself, in his writings, gone out of his way, as if with a prophetic misgiving of those tendencies, to insist on it as the instrument of that beneficent Father,[6] who, when He came on earth in visible form, took on Him first and most prominently the office of assuaging the bodily wounds of human nature. And truly, like the old mediciner in the tale, "he sat diligently at his work, and hummed, with cheerful countenance, a pious song;" and then in turn "went out singing into the meadows so gaily, that those who had seen him from afar might well have thought it was a youth gathering flowers for his beloved, instead of an old physician gathering healing herbs in the morning dew."[7]

Alas, that men, in the action of life or in their heart of hearts, are not what they seem to be in their moments of excitement, or in their trances or intoxications of genius, — so good, so noble, so serene! Alas, that Bacon too in his own way should after all be but the fellow of those heathen philosophers who in their disadvantages had some excuse for their inconsistency, and who surprise us rather in what they did say than in what they did not do! Alas, that he too, like Socrates or Seneca, must be stripped of his holy-day coat, which looks so fair, and should be but a mockery amid his most majestic gravity of phrase; and, for all his vast abilities, should, in the littleness of his own moral being, but typify the intellectual narrowness of his school! However, granting all this, heroism after all was not his philosophy: — I cannot deny he has abundantly achieved what he proposed. His is simply a method whereby bodily discomforts and temporal wants are to be most effectually removed from the greatest number; and already, before it has shown any signs of exhaustion, the gifts of nature, in their most artificial shapes and luxurious profusion and diversity, from all quarters of the earth, are, it is undeniable, by its means brought even to our doors, and we rejoice in them.

[6]De Augment. iv. 2, vid. Macaulay's Essay; vid. also "In principio operis ad Deum Patrem, Deum Verbum, Deum Spiritum, preces fundimus humillimas et ardentissimas, ut humani generis aerumnarum memores, et peregrinationis istius vitae in quâ dies paucos et malos terimus, *novis suis eleemosynis, per manus nostras,* familiam humanam dotare dignentur. Atque illud insuper supplices rogamus, ne *humana divinis officiant;* neve *ex reseratione viarum sensûs,* et accensione majore luminis naturalis, *aliquid incredulitatis* et noctis, animis nostris erga divina mysteria oboriatur," etc. *Proef.* Instaur. Magn. [Newman]

[7]Fouque's *Unknown Patient.* [Newman]

**9**

Useful knowledge, then, I grant, has done its work; and liberal knowledge as certainly has not done its work,—that is, supposing, as the objectors assume, its direct end, like religious knowledge, is to make men better; but this, I will not for an instant allow, and, unless I allow it, those objectors have said nothing to the purpose. I admit, rather I maintain, what they have been urging, for I consider Knowledge to have its end in itself. For all its friends, or its enemies, may say, I insist upon it, that it is as real a mistake to burden it with virtue or religion as with the mechanical arts. Its direct business is not to steel the soul against temptation or to console it in affliction, any more than to set the loom in motion, or to direct the steam carriage; be it ever so much the means or the condition of both material and moral advancement, still, taken by and in itself, it as little mends our hearts as it improves our temporal circumstances. And if its eulogists claim for it such a power, they commit the very same kind of encroachment on a province not their own as the political economist who should maintain that his science educated him for casuistry or diplomacy. Knowledge is one thing, virtue is another; good sense is not conscience, refinement is not humility, nor is largeness and justness of view faith. Philosophy, however enlightened, however profound, gives no command over the passions, no influential motives, no vivifying principles. Liberal education makes not the Christian, not the Catholic, but the gentleman. It is well to be a gentleman, it is well to have a cultivated intellect, a delicate taste, a candid, equitable, dispassionate mind, a noble and courteous bearing in the conduct of life;—these are the connatural qualities of a large knowledge; they are the objects of a university; I am advocating, I shall illustrate and insist upon them; but still, I repeat, they are no guarantee for sanctity or even for conscientiousness, they may attach to the man of the world, to the profligate, to the heartless,—pleasant, alas, and attractive as he shows when decked out in them. Taken by themselves, they do but seem to be what they are not; they look like virtue at a distance, but they are detected by close observers, and on the long run; and hence it is that they are popularly accused of pretence and hypocrisy, not, I repeat, from their own fault, but because their professors and their admirers persist in taking them for what they are not, and are officious in arrogating for them a praise to which they have no claim. Quarry the granite rock with razors, or moor the vessel with a thread of silk; then may you hope with such keen and delicate instruments as human knowledge and human reason to contend against those giants, the passion and the pride of man.

Surely we are not driven to theories of this kind, in order to vindicate the value and dignity of liberal knowledge. Surely the real grounds on which its pretensions rest are not so very subtle or abstruse, so very strange or improbable. Surely it is very intelligible to say, and that is what I say here, that liberal education, viewed in itself, is simply the cultivation of the intellect, as such, and its object is nothing more or less than intellectual excellence. Everything has its own perfection, be it higher or lower in the scale of things; and the perfection of one is not the perfection of another. Things animate, inanimate, visible, invisible, all are good in their kind, and have a *best* of themselves, which is an object of pursuit. Why do you take such pains with your garden or your park? You see to your walks and turf and shrubberies; to your trees and drives; not as if you meant to make an orchard of the one, or corn or pasture land of the other, but because there is a special beauty in all that is goodly in wood, water, plain, and slope, brought all together by art into one shape, and grouped into one whole. Your cities are beautiful, your palaces, your public buildings, your territorial mansions, your churches; and their beauty leads to nothing beyond itself. There is a physical beauty and a moral: there is a beauty of person, there is a beauty of our moral being, which is natural virtue; and in like manner there is a beauty, there is a perfection, of the intellect. There is an ideal perfection in these various subject-matters, towards which individual instances are seen to rise, and which are the standards for all instances whatever. The Greek divinities and demigods, as the statuary has moulded them, with their symmetry of figure and their high forehead and their regular features, are the perfection of physical beauty. The heroes, of whom history tells, Alexander, or Caesar, or Scipio, or Saladin, are the representatives of that magnanimity or self-mastery which is the greatness of human nature. Christianity too has its heroes, and in the supernatural order, and we call them saints. The artist puts before him beauty of feature and form; the poet, beauty of mind; the preacher, the beauty of grace: then intellect too, I repeat, has its beauty, and it has those who aim at it. To open the mind, to correct it, to refine it, to enable it to know, and to digest, master, rule, and use its knowledge, to give it power over its own faculties, application, flexibility, method, critical exactness, sagacity, resource, address, eloquent expression, is an object as intelligible (for here we are inquiring, not what the object of a liberal education is worth, nor what use the Church makes of it, but what it is in itself), I say, an object as intelligible as the cultivation of virtue, while, at the same time, it is absolutely distinct from it.

## 10

This indeed is but a temporal object, and a transitory possession; but so are other things in themselves which we make much of and pursue. The moralist will tell us that man, in all his functions, is but a flower which blossoms and fades, except so far as a higher principle breathes upon him, and makes him and what he is immortal. Body and mind are carried on into an eternal state of being by the gifts of Divine Munificence; but at first they do but fail in a failing world; and if the powers of intellect decay, the powers of the body have decayed before them, and, as an hospital or an almshouse, though its end be ephemeral, may be sanctified to the service of religion, so surely may a university, even were it nothing more than I have as yet described it. We attain to heaven by using this world well, though it is to pass away; we perfect our nature, not by undoing it, but by adding to it what is more than nature, and directing it towards aims higher than its own.

(1852)

*Alfred North Whitehead*

# Universities and Their Function

## 1

The expansion of universities is one marked feature of the social life in the present age. All countries have shared in this movement, but more especially America, which thereby occupies a position of honor. It is, however, possible to be overwhelmed even by the gifts of good fortune; and this growth of universities, in number of institutions, in size, and in internal complexity of organisation, discloses some danger of destroying the very sources of their usefulness, in the absence of a widespread understanding of the primary functions which universities should perform in the service of a nation. These remarks, as to the necessity for reconsideration of the function of universities, apply to all the more developed countries. They are only more especially applicable to America, because this country has taken the lead in a development which, under wise guidance, may prove to be one of the most fortunate forward steps which civilisation has yet taken.

This article will only deal with the most general principles, though the special problems of the various departments in any university are, of course, innumerable. But generalities require illustration, and for this purpose I choose the business school of a university. This choice is dictated by the fact that business schools represent one of the newer developments of university activity. They are also more particularly relevant to the dominant social activities of modern nations, and for that reason are good examples of the way in which the national life should be affected by the activities of its universities. Also at Harvard, where I have the honour to hold office, the new foundation of a business school on a scale amounting to magnificence has just reached its completion.

There is a certain novelty in the provision of such a school of training, on this scale of magnitude, in one of the few leading universities of the world. It marks the culmination of a movement which for many years past has introduced analogous departments throughout American universities. This is a new fact in the university world; and it alone would justify some general reflections upon the purpose of a university education, and upon the proved importance of that purpose for the welfare of the social organism.

The novelty of business schools must not be exaggerated. At no time have universities been restricted to pure abstract learning. The University of Salerno in Italy, the earliest of European universities, was devoted to medicine. In England, at Cambridge, in the year 1316, a college was founded for the special purpose of providing "clerks for the King's service." Universities have trained clergy, medical men, lawyers, engineers. Business is now a highly intellectualised vocation, so it well fits into the series. There is, however, this novelty: the curriculum suitable for a business school, and the various modes of activity of such a school, are still in the experimental stage. Hence the peculiar importance of recurrence to general principles in connection with the moulding of these schools. It would, however, be an act of presumption on my part if I were to enter upon any consideration of details, or even upon types of policy affecting the balance of the whole training. Upon such questions I have no special knowledge, and therefore have no word of advice.

## 2

The universities are schools of education, and schools of research. But the primary reason for their existence is not to be found either in the mere knowledge conveyed to the students or in the mere opportunities for research afforded to the members of the faculty.

Both these functions could be performed at a cheaper rate, apart from these very expensive institutions. Books are cheap, and the system of apprenticeship is well understood. So far as the mere imparting of information is concerned, no university has had any justification for existence since the popularisation of printing in the fifteenth century. Yet the chief impetus to the foundation of universities came after that date, and in more recent times has even increased.

The justification for a university is that it preserves the connection between knowledge and the zest of life, by uniting the young and the old in the imaginative consideration of learning. The university imparts information, but it imparts it imaginatively. At least, this is the function which it should perform for society. A university which fails in this respect has no reason for existence. This atmosphere of excitement, arising from imaginative consideration, transforms knowledge. A fact is no longer a bare fact: it is invested with all its possibilities. It is no longer a burden on the memory: it is energising as the poet of our dreams, and as the architect of our purposes.

Imagination is not to be divorced from the facts: it is a way of illuminating the facts. It works by eliciting the general principles which apply to the facts, as they exist, and then by an intellectual survey of alternative possibilities which are consistent with those principles. It enables men to construct an intellectual vision of a new world, and it preserves the zest of life by the suggestion of satisfying purposes.

Youth is imaginative, and if the imagination be strengthened by discipline this energy of imagination can in great measure be preserved through life. The tragedy of the world is that those who are imaginative have but slight experience, and those who are experienced have feeble imaginations. Fools act on imagination without knowledge; pedants act on knowledge without imagination. The task of a university is to weld together imagination and experience.

The initial discipline of imagination in its period of youthful vigor requires that there be no responsibility for immediate action. The habit of unbiased thought, whereby the ideal variety of exemplifications is discerned in its derivation from general principles, cannot be acquired when there is the daily task of preserving a concrete organisation. You must be free to think rightly and wrongly, and free to appreciate the variousness of the universe undisturbed by its perils.

These reflections upon the general functions of a university can be at once translated in terms of the particular functions of a business school. We need not flinch from the assertion that the main function of such a school is to produce men with a greater zest for business. It is a libel upon human nature to conceive that zest for life is the product of pedestrian purposes directed toward the narrow routine of material comforts. Mankind by its pioneering instinct, and in a hundred other ways, proclaims falsehood of that lie.

In the modern complex social organism, the adventure of life cannot be disjoined from intellectual adventure. Amid simpler circumstances, the pioneer can follow the urge of his instinct, directed toward the scene of his vision from the mountain top. But in the complex organisations of modern business the intellectual adventure of analysis, and of imaginative reconstruction, must precede any successful reorganisation. In a simpler world, business relations were simpler, being based on the immediate contact of man with man and on immediate confrontation with all relevant material circumstances. To-day business organisation requires an imaginative grasp of the psychologies of populations engaged in differing modes of occupation; of populations scattered through cities, through mountains, through plains; of populations on the ocean, and of populations in mines, and of populations in forests. It requires an imaginative grasp of conditions in the tropics, and of conditions in temperate zones. It requires an imaginative grasp of the interlocking interests of great organisations, and of the reactions of the whole complex to any change in one of its elements. It requires an imaginative understanding of laws of political economy, not merely in the abstract, but also with the power to construe them in terms of the particular circumstances of a concrete business. It requires some knowledge of the habits of government, and of the variations of those habits under diverse conditions. It requires an imaginative vision of the binding forces of any human organisation, a sympathetic vision of the limits of human nature and of the conditions which evoke loyalty of service. It requires some knowledge of the laws of health, and of the laws of fatigue, and of the conditions for sustained reliability. It requires an imaginative understanding of the social effects of the conditions of factories. It requires a sufficient conception of the rôle of applied science in modern society. It requires that discipline of character which can say "yes" and "no" to other men, not by reason of blind obstinacy, but with firmness derived from a conscious evaluation of relevant alternatives.

The universities have trained the intellectual pioneers of our civilisation — the priests, the lawyers, the statesmen, the doctors, the men of science, and the men of letters. They have been the home of those ideals which lead men to confront the confusion of their present times. The Pilgrim Fathers left England to found a state of society according to the ideals of their religious faith; and one of their earlier acts was the foundation of Harvard University in Cambridge, named after that ancient mother of ideals in England, to which so many of them owed their training. The conduct of business now requires intellectual imagination of the same type as that which in former times has mainly passed into those other occupations; and the universities are the organisations which have supplied this type of mentality for the service of the progress of the European races.

In early mediaeval history the origin of universities was obscure and almost unnoticed. They were a gradual and natural growth. But their existence is the reason for the sustained, rapid progressiveness of European life in so many fields of activity. By their agency the adventure of action met the adventure of thought. It would not have been possible antecedently to have divined that such organisations would have been successful. Even now, amid the imperfections of all things human, it is sometimes difficult to understand how they succeed in their work. Of course there is much failure in the work of universities. But, if we take a broad view of history, their success has been remarkable and almost uniform. The cultural histories of Italy, of France, of Germany, of Holland, of Scotland, of England, of the United States, bear witness to the influence of universities. By "cultural history" I am not chiefly thinking of the lives of scholars; I mean the energising of the lives of those men who gave to France, to Germany, and to other countries that impress of types of human achievement which, by their addition to the zest of life, form the foundation of our patriotism. We love to be members of society which can do those things.

There is one great difficulty which hampers all the higher types of human endeavour. In modern times this difficulty has even increased in its possibilities for evil. In any large organisation the younger men, who are novices, must be set to jobs which consist in carrying out fixed duties in obedience to orders. No president of a large corporation meets his youngest employee at his office door with the offer of the most responsible job which the work of that corporation includes. The young men are set to work at a fixed routine, and only occasionally even see the president as he passes in and out of the building. Such work is a great discipline. It imparts knowledge, and it produces reliability of character; also it is the only work for which the young men, in that novice state, are fit, and it is the work for which they are hired. There can be no criticism of the custom, but there may be an unfortunate effect — prolonged routine work dulls the imagination.

The result is that qualities essential at a later stage of a career are apt to be stamped out in an earlier stage. This is only an instance of the more general fact, that necessary technical excellence can only be acquired by a training which is apt to damage those energies of mind which should direct the technical skill. This is the key fact in education, and the reason for most of its difficulties.

The way in which a university should function in the preparation for an intellectual career, such as modern business or one of the older professions, is by promoting the imaginative consideration of the various general principles underlying that career. Its students thus pass into their period of technical apprenticeship with their imaginations already practised in connecting details with general principles. The routine then receives its meaning, and also illuminates the principles which give it that meaning. Hence, instead of a drudgery issuing in a blind rule of thumb, the properly trained man has some hope of obtaining an imagination disciplined by detailed facts and by necessary habits.

Thus the proper function of a university is the imaginative acquisition of knowledge. Apart from this importance of the imagination, there is no reason why business men, and other professional men, should not pick up their facts bit by bit as they want them for particular occasions. A university is imaginative or it is nothing — at least nothing useful.

## 3

Imagination is a contagious disease. It cannot be measured by the yard, or weighed by the pound, and then delivered to the students by members of the faculty. It can only be communicated by a faculty whose members themselves wear their learning with imagination. In saying this, I am only repeating one of the oldest of observations. More than two thousand years ago the ancients symbolised learning by a torch passing from hand to hand down the generations. That lighted torch is the imagination of which I speak. The whole art in the organisation of a university is the provision of a faculty whose learning is lighted up with imagination. This is the problem of problems in university education; and unless we are careful the recent vast extension of universities in number of students and in variety of activities – of which we are so justly proud – will fail in producing its proper results, by the mishandling of this problem.

The combination of imagination and learning normally requires some leisure, freedom from restraint, freedom from harassing worry, some variety of experiences, and the stimulation of other minds diverse in opinion and diverse in equipment. Also there is required the excitement of curiosity, and the self-confidence derived from pride in the achievements of the surrounding society in procuring the advance of knowledge. Imagination cannot be acquired once and for all, and then kept indefinitely in an ice box to be produced periodically in stated quantities. The learned and imaginative life is a way of living, and is not an article of commerce.

It is in respect to the provision and utilisation of these conditions for an efficient faculty that the two functions of education and research meet together in a university. Do you want your teachers to be imaginative? Then encourage them to research. Do you want your researchers to be imaginative? Then bring them into intellectual sympathy with the young at the most eager, imaginative period of life, when intellects are just entering upon their mature discipline. Make your researchers explain themselves to active minds, plastic and with the world before them; make your young students crown their period of intellectual acquisition by some contact with minds gifted with experience of intellectual adventure. Education is discipline for the adventure of life; research is intellectual adventure; and the universities should be homes of adventure shared in common by young and old. For successful education there must always be a certain freshness in the knowledge dealt with. It must either be new in itself or it must be invested with some novelty of application to the new world of new times. Knowledge does not keep any better than fish. You may be dealing with knowledge of the old species, with some old truth; but somehow or other it must come to the students, as it were, just drawn out of the sea and with the freshness of its immediate importance.

It is the function of the scholar to evoke into life wisdom and beauty which, apart from his magic, would remain lost in the past. A progressive society depends upon its inclusion of three groups – scholars, discoverers, inventors. Its progress also depends upon the fact that its educated masses are composed of members each with a tinge of scholarship, a tinge of discovery, and a tinge of invention. I am here using the term "discovery" to mean the progress of knowledge in respect to truths of some high generality, and the term "invention" to mean the progress of knowledge in respect to the application of general truths in particular ways subservient to present needs. It is evident that these three groups merge into each other, and also that men engaged in practical affairs are properly to be called inventors so far as they contribute to the progress of society. But any one individual has his own limitation of function, and his own peculiar needs. What is important for a nation is that there shall be a very close relation between all types of its progressive elements, so that the study may influence the market place, and the market place the study. Universities are the chief agencies for this fusion of progressive activities into an effective instrument of progress. Of course they are not the only agencies, but it is a fact that today the progressive nations are those in which universities flourish.

It must not be supposed that the output of a university in the form of original ideas is solely to be measured by printed papers and books labeled with the names of their authors. Mankind is as individual in its mode of output as in the substance of its thoughts. For some of the most fertile minds composition in writing, or in a form reducible to writing, seems to be an impossibility. In every faculty you will find that some of the more brilliant teachers are not among those who publish. Their originality requires for its expression direct intercourse with their pupils in the form of lectures, or of personal discussion. Such men exercise an immense influence; and yet, after the generation of their pupils has passed away, they sleep among the innumerable unthanked benefactors of humanity. Fortunately, one of them is immortal — Socrates.

Thus it would be the greatest mistake to estimate the value of each member of a faculty by the printed work signed with his name. There is at the present day some tendency to fall into this error; and an emphatic protest is necessary against an attitude on the part of authorities which is damaging to efficiency and unjust to unselfish zeal.

But, when all such allowances have been made, one good test for the general efficiency of a faculty is that as a whole it shall be producing in published form its quota of contributions of thought. Such a quota is to be estimated in weight of thought, and not in number of words.

This survey shows that the management of a university faculty has no analogy to that of a business organisation. The public opinion of the faculty, and a common zeal for the purposes of the university, form the only effective safeguards for the high level of university work. The faculty should be a band of scholars, stimulating each other, and freely determining their various activities. You can secure certain formal requirements, that lectures are given at stated times and that instructors and students are in attendance. But the heart of the matter lies beyond all regulation.

The question of justice to the teachers has very little to do with the case. It is perfectly just to hire a man to perform any legal services under any legal conditions as to times and salary. No one need accept the post unless he so desires.

The sole question is, what sort of conditions will produce the type of faculty which will run a successful university? The danger is that it is quite easy to produce a faculty entirely unfit—a faculty of very efficient pedants and dullards. The general public will only detect the difference after the university has stunted the promise of youth for scores of years.

The modern university system in the great democratic countries will only be successful if the ultimate authorities exercise singular restraint, so as to remember that universities cannot be dealt with according to the rules and policies which apply to the familiar business corporations. Business schools are no exception to this law of university life. There is really nothing to add to what the presidents of many American universities have recently said in public on this topic. But whether the effective portion of the general public, in America or other countries, will follow their advice appears to be doubtful. The whole point of a university, on its educational side, is to bring the young under the intellectual influence of a band of imaginative scholars. There can be no escape from proper attention to the conditions which—as experience has shown—will produce such a band.

**4**

The two premier universities of Europe, in age and in dignity, are the University of Paris and the University of Oxford. I will speak of my own country because I know it best. The University of Oxford may have sinned in many ways. But, for all her deficiencies, she has throughout the ages preserved one supreme merit, beside which all failures in detail are as dust in the balance: for century after century, throughout the long course of her existence, she has produced bands of scholars who treated learning imaginatively. For that service alone, no one who loves culture can think of her without emotion.

But it is quite unnecessary for me to cross the ocean for my examples. The author of the Declaration of Independence, Mr. Jefferson, has some claim to be the greatest American. The perfection of his various achievements certainly places him among the few great men of all ages. He founded a university, and devoted one side of his complex genius to placing that university amid every circumstance which could stimulate the imagination—beauty of buildings, of situation, and every other stimulation of equipment and organisation.

There are many other universities in America which can point my moral, but my final example shall be Harvard—the representative university of the Puritan movement. The New England Puritans of the seventeenth and eighteenth centuries were the most intensely imaginative people, restrained in their outward expression, and fearful of symbolism by physical beauty, but, as it were, racked with the intensity of spiritual truths intellectually imagined. The Puritan faculties of those centuries must have been imaginative indeed, and they produced great men whose names have gone round the world. In later times Puritanism softened, and, in the golden age of literary New England, Emerson, Lowell, and Longfellow set their mark upon Harvard. The modern scientific age then gradually supervenes, and again in William James we find the typical imaginative scholar.

To-day business comes to Harvard; and the gift which the University has to offer is the old one of imagination, the lighted torch which passes from hand to hand. It is a dangerous gift, which has started many a conflagration. If we are timid as to that danger, the proper course is to shut down our universities. Imagination is a gift which has often been associated with great commercial peoples – with Greece, with Florence, with Venice, with the learning of Holland, and with the poetry of England. Commerce and imagination thrive together. It is a gift which all must pray for their country who desire for it that abiding greatness achieved by Athens: –

> Her citizens, imperial spirits,
> Rule the present from the past.

For American education no smaller ideal can suffice.

(1927)

*Stephen Spender*

# An Elementary School Class Room in a Slum

Far far from gusty waves, these children's faces.
Like rootless weeds the torn hair round their paleness.
The tall girl with her weighed-down head. The paper-seeming boy
    with rat's eyes. The stunted unlucky heir
Of twisted bones, reciting a father's gnarled disease,
His lesson from his desk. At back of the dim class,
One unnoted, sweet and young: his eyes live in a dream
Of squirrels' game, in tree room, other than this.

On sour cream walls, donations. Shakespeare's head
Cloudless at dawn, civilized dome riding all cities.
Belled, flowery, Tyrolese valley. Open-handed map
Awarding the world its world. And yet, for these
Children, these windows, not this world, are world,
Where all their future's painted with a fog,
A narrow street sealed in with a lead sky,
Far far from rivers, capes, and stars of words.

Surely Shakespeare is wicked, the map a bad example
With ships and sun and love tempting them to steal —
For lives that slyly turn in their cramped holes
From fog to endless night? On their slag heap, these children
Wear skins peeped through by bones and spectacles of steel
With mended glass, like bottle bits on stones.
All of their time and space are foggy slum
So blot their maps with slums as big as doom.

Unless, governor, teacher, inspector, visitor,
This map becomes their window and these windows
That open on their lives like crouching tombs
Break, O break open, till they break the town
And show the children to the fields and all their world
Azure on their sands, to let their tongues
Run naked into books, the white and green leaves open
The history theirs whose language is the sun.

(1942)

*Milton Mayer*

# To Know and to Do

The renaissance seems to have ended at Verdun, at least for the Europeans; and there are signs, only fifty years afterward, that the Americans are beginning to read the lesson that Europe learned on Mort Homme Hill: Man is not going to be an unqualified success. Progress is no longer axiomatic. Pessimism (or apathy, which is predigested pessimism) is becoming pervasive. Even the Communists' "new man" is nothing more than a ceremonial expression nowadays. This is the age — whatever else it is — of waning confidence.

As the age of confidence the Renaissance was more of a birth than a rebirth: Bacon's assertion that knowledge is power would have astounded all the men who had gone before him—the fallen Oedipus no less than the fallen Adam. They had been taught to expect Verdun. So had the prophet who said of the great nations of old, "They are wise to do evil, but to do good they have no knowledge."

Bacon was none the less right and the Renaissance none the less real. Knowledge *was* power. Man powered with knowledge was, and is, as a god. But the power is proving to be independent of its generator. Like the Sorcerer's Apprentice, it needs no command to fetch water faster and faster. The water rises, and knowledge is a consternation: Rare indeed the commencement orator who does not wag his head over the discrepancy between man's moral and intellectual progress.

But what if morality is not progressive? And what if there is no necessary, or even probable, connection between morality and knowledge? What if (*horrible dictu*) the human crisis is first and last and always a moral crisis and not an intellectual crisis in the least?

When the late President Kennedy said that "science has no conscience of its own," he was doing more than quoting Rabelais; he was saying something revolutionary about education. He was saying (if science includes the highest sciences) that education is of conditional service to man and of no service at all if the condition is not met.

Look at the general disorder of our time. When most men have less than a hundred dollars a year and the per capita expenditure on war in "peacetime" is forty, what is there that intelligence can tell us? When the most knowledgeable (and therefore the richest) societies, with the longest history of civilized institutions, lead the world in suicide, insanity, alcoholism, divorce, crime, and delinquency, what critical need have they (or, for that matter, the least knowledgeable societies) of knowledge? What is it the Communist needs to *know* who wants free elections in Mississippi but not in Germany, or the anti-Communist who wants bases ninety kilometers from Russia but not ninety miles from Florida?

The sovereign faith in education is everywhere in the world established now. What for Jefferson was the keystone of the democratic arch has become the keystone of the democratic and the nondemocratic arches. If we can find a way to make use of universal education in the universal crisis, it would seem that we should do so. We would not make any such demand of bingo or tap-dancing or swinging on the old front gate; we may make it of education because education is everywhere the great public enterprise.

We pedagogues have been willing to exploit the enterprise without examining its premise that the more of it there is the better off we shall be. Our trade secret consists in our being supposed to have a secret when we haven't. What we have is a skeleton in the multi-purpose closet in the form of the unexamined premise.

The public pressure that fills the schools with junk is irresistible, because we have nothing to resist it with. Why shouldn't driver training be compulsory? Driving is a moral problem, which the public thinks, mistakenly, can be solved by teaching. So, too, when the Russians launched their Sputnik: Out went the new humanities, in went the new technologies, and up went the preprofessional preparation of technicians. Why not? Had the schools been doing anything whose high purpose would justify their going on doing it? The Russians presented a moral problem—the *evil* of Communist success—and the American people wanted it solved. The schools stood ready to hand.

In the theocratic centuries the asserted object of teaching was morality as a means to salvation. The object continued to be asserted long after the age of the priests. Yale undertook to transmit not only *Veritas* but *Lux;* Oberlin was consecrated by its charter to "the total abolition of all forms of sin"; and the Haverford catalogue maintains the primacy of the moral capacity to use the skills of learning for worthwhile ends. Such private institutions have no legal impediment to their transcendant aims; they are over the wall of separation upon which the safety and security of the secular state rests like Humpty Dumpty. But public education, at all levels, is forbidden by the First Amendment to abolish sin, tamper with moral capacity, or ask which ends are worthwhile.

What ever made us suppose that it could do these things even if the law allowed? What evidence is there, now or ever, that even under the most sacred auspices education could produce morality? In its sacerdotal prime it made men good churchmen. Had the churchmen been especially good men, Dante would have had to do without the first two parts of his three-part comedy and Luther without all ninety-five of his Ninety-Five Theses.

The truly parochial schools still try to improve the adolescent soul that will be known by its fruits. They make no bones about meaning to make men good. And their alumni are all of them fine fellows. But I do not know that they are finer than the alumni of Yale, Oberlin, or Haverford—or of City College. And they should be, if morality can be taught. Indeed, a weighted analysis should show that college graduates are better behaved in later life than noncollege graduates and the top of the class than the bottom; and the Doctors than the Masters. *Hélas!* as Sarah Bernhardt used to say.

Morality is action, and we know that action and knowledge are wholly separable in, for instance, mathematics. But the separability appears in the practitioners of all the other disciplines besides—in the logician whose personal life is eccentric, in the gluttonous physiologist, in the physicist who rounds a sharp curve at 80 m.p.h. One of the great political scientists of our time dismisses civil disobedience as anarchy because law is the indispensable condition of community—and asks a friend to slip a Swiss watch in through Customs. "We imagined," said

G. A. Borgese of Italian Fascism, "that the universities would be the last to surrender. They were the first."

But mankind requires a moral purpose (or the color of one) in the institutions it supports, including war. There are no honest apostles of wickedness. Men want to be good and to live among good men, and if they have not found it feasible to be good themselves they want their children to be good. Al Capone, protesting that "Insull's doing it, everybody's doing it," was appealing his conduct to the moral standard of the community. For goodness alone is the bond of men, and unless knowledge can be shown to have a causal (or at least predisponent) connection with it, the best education is only an amenity.

Our search for the connection takes us at once to the epistemological commonplace that descriptive knowledge accumulates and normative knowledge does not. Twentieth Century man does not have to learn that the seat of fever is the blood—or that the world is flat—before he can learn that it isn't. He starts with the latest break-through. But there are no break-throughs in the moral realm: Relativity is new, but moral relativism is as old as Thrasymachus. The *Odyssey* takes us the long, long way home of the tired businessman who *really* loves his wife; the *Apology* assembles the Un-Athenian Activities Committee; and Sophocles owes his big Broadway hit to his study of Freud. Man the ingenious has no ethical or political ingenuity.

Why not? Why isn't moral advance as ineluctable as scientific, and moral fact as persuasive? Why isn't "righteousness by the Law"? The schoolmen thought that reason rules the intellect despotically but the appetite constitutionally; the appetite ("which moves the other powers to act") vetoes reason when reason threatens its closest interests. It is about *me* that I can't "think" straight—about me and my family and my friends, my race and my religion, my party and my country and my age. I insist upon comparing Albert Schweitzer with Attila instead of Bull Connor with Epictetus. I am the victim of what elementary psychology calls reflexivity, in which the subject and object of inquiry are one.

Whoever deals with himself deals unscientifically—including that hero of the endless serial, the Man in White. Not, of course, when we see him in Surgery. There he is working on an external organism. We stay the knife in his hand and ask him if this *man*—this Haman, this Hitler—ought to live or die. He says it is none of his business, and we ask him whose it is. He doesn't know; he suggests that we try the psychiatrist down the hall.

The psychiatrist down the hall replies by reading from his *New Introductory Lectures*. The physician "has no need to consider whether the patient is a good man, a suicide, or a criminal . . . It is not the business of the analyst to decide between parties." What is the business of the analyst? "To send them away"—he is still reading—"as healthy and efficient as possible." "But this is Haman! This is Hitler." The psychiatrist—τηs ψυχηs ιατροs, or doctor of the soul—shrugs and says, "Keep going down the hall."

Down the hall the judge is instructing the jury in that which is instructable: the law. But in that which is not—the good and evil of men that brings them into court—the jury is the judge. Twelve ordinary men whose only competence is their relative freedom from reflexivity. The petit juror, not the judge, is the judge of morals, just as the petit voter, and not the political scientist, is the judge of politics. What moral knowledge seems to want is the scientist's dispassion without the scientist's science.

With the Renaissance impact of secularism, pluralism, and science, moral doctrine lost the unity (and therefore the authority) with which it was so long advanced as the index, if not the compulsion, to action. Nowadays we have surveys of moral doctrines. The survey or peepshow has much to be said for it. It steers clear of the prerogative (no longer claimed by the church) to tell the child what is right and wrong. It avoids the parental storm that engulfs the teacher who presumes to teach (or even to have) *a* doctrine. And it keeps the moral philosopher out of the moral hole. The student in fourth (or fourteenth) grade who asks, "Why should I be honest?" or "Where do we go when we die?" can be sent down the long, long hall.

Natural science, unlike moral science, never did claim to be able to make men good. (To be sure, its practice fortifies such virtues as patience, initiative, and open-mindedness, but so do burglary, baby-sitting, and philosophy.) It teaches what it knows can be taught and delivers the goods—the goods that enable us in peace to live longer and less laboriously and in war to fight longer and more effectively. It doesn't try to tell us what to live or fight for, or whether labor is bad for us or longevity good. These are the "insoluble" problems that have to be taken to the man still further down the ever-lengthening hall.

Some of the designers of the atomic bomb pleaded secretly with Mr. Truman that it not be used, and some of them entrenched themselves behind the admirable scientific attitude of suspended judgment. (Mr. Truman, who had a sign on his desk reading, "The buck stops here," may have envied them their trench.) Apparently a scientific lifetime does not help a man decide whether or not to explode an atomic bomb. And in the summer of 1963 the nation's lawyers decided to straddle the civil rights issue as the only possible compromise between the Northern and Southern delegates to the American Bar Association. How learned must I be—and in what?—in order to know what to do about the atomic bomb and civil rights?

I am told that the modern world, with all its complexity, requires more learning of me than my forebears had. Not in my case; I recall none of the crises of my life (there have been more than six) that I might have met better had I known more. But a little of my great-grandfather's incorruptibility might have come in handy. I have lied as a matter of course and cheated and stolen when I "had to." I have jettisoned principle when the wind howled and thanked God that I am as other men are. And on the occasions of unavoidable moral choice I have mobilized my good reasons for doing bad things and emerged as a trimmer whose object all sublime is to get on in the modern world of A.D. or B.C. 1964.

I am told that the fortunate form of government under which I live requires a great deal of knowledge of me as a citizen. I have to understand public finance—which the public financiers, who don't have to understand anything else, dispute. I have to know whether Cambodia is east or west of North or South Vietnam and why we are fighting *there*. I have to have a judicious opinion on Guinea, Guiana, and Ghana. I am, in a word, producing more history than I can possibly consume. Without a righteous specialist in all these matters—or with an unrighteous one—I am lost.

Morality aside, I am told that I have to have more technological knowledge than my father, who didn't have an automatic transmission. Why isn't just the opposite true? The neighborhood crawls with automatic transmission men. And the work I am likely to get (if I am looking for work) requires me only to press the button every time the bell rings—a procedure which Pavlov's dog discovered long since is easier learned on the job than from books. When Herbert Hoover was asked about Telstar, he said, "I belong to a generation that just doesn't grasp all that." Don't we all? And what difference does it make?

True, the conversion of knowledge to precept and precept to action is said to take prudence, and a man wants some sort of head for it; but as an excuse for helplessness it is one with the suspended judgment of the scientist who devises the bomb. A man lies bleeding by the road. Shall I use my automatic transmission to stop my car? The priest and the Levite were graduates of the Harvard Medical School, as the Samaritan was not. He misplaced the tourniquet. Too bad; but he was the only hope of him who had fallen among thieves.

We are asked if we mean to dispense with natural science. We reply: only with as much of it as we absolutely have to. It is nice to know that the earth goes round the sun, that man and a candle flame both metabolize, and that the angle of reflection is equal to the angle of incidence. It is nicer to know these things than to have to depend upon those who do. But the competence I want *and for which I can not depend upon another* is moral competence, and I can not get it from science.

Shall we then put a little more of our student's time into, say, esthetics? Music is said to have an inordinate power to soothe the savage breast—which comes closer to the moral crisis than all your metabolism. But we must aim at appreciation, not at theory: It is not musicology that soothes the savage breast. The trouble with the arts—music no less than medicine—is that a man may be both an artist and a swine. And this is true of the liberal artist too. Why, then, shouldn't we exhaust the possibilities of teaching decency (or at least exhaust ourselves looking for them) before we do our student the dubious favor of putting tools, even the finest tools, in his hand?

Watch out with your liberal arts, your arts of reasoning, or you will have equipped a monster to rationalize his monstrosities. You will have beefed up a part of a man—the part unique to men and to angels, and to fallen angels. Dewey may have been wrong in many things, wrongest of all to proclaim a science of pedagogy (as if a man could be *taught* to be a Dewey); but he was righter than he was wrong. He was right to insist, with Carlyle, that the end of man is an action and not a thought, however noble, and righter still to resist the compartmentalization to which the liberal, no less than the servile, arts are susceptible.

What is left, then, that may be taught to some possible moral advantage? What is left are, preeminently, the true humanities, the disciplines that deal with man as man: ethics, politics, psychology, sociology, social anthropology, history, natural theology, and the principles of metaphysics, jurisprudence, and economics. These are the studies, and they alone, that speak to the human crisis. What makes us think that they will be heard? Haven't we argued that knowledge does not compel action? The answer is that our parlous case must be made on the precarious faith that there may be a kind of post-nasal drip by means of which some of what goes into the head will find its way to the heart.

In this faith a studied acquaintance with man's moral struggle may commend itself to our crisis curriculum in several ways. It may urge sensitivity upon our student and intensify such sensitivity as he already has. It may sharpen his ability (though he may not be any the better for it himself) to tell a good man from a bad one. It may somehow, as Plato suggested, "anchor" the good man's goodness. Finally, his intercourse with the goodness and badness of men living and dead may exemplarily endear the one and dishearten the other to him.

The ancients had too few books. We have too many. But good books are better than bad books, and great books are great even though the two words are capitalized. Some of our texts may be remote in time or place, but so is progress; and their very remotion (so Alec Meiklejohn found at Amherst) may help our student escape the *Teufelskreis* of reflexivity. They will be masterpieces of the liberal arts, those tools of the verbal trade whose mastery constitutes a kind of graduate literacy. Why not teach the arts exemplarily too and use morality (the way the *Dialogues* do) as the material of their instruction? Some of our texts will be in foreign languages, which we can use to read them and to communicate with our fellow-men confronted around the world with the common human crisis.

The ancients took a cyclical view of the human condition. Men, even gods, soared and plummeted in a lifetime, in a single day, and "those cities which once were great are now nothing, while those that are great were once nothing." With the Renaissance behind us, the invalidity of the cyclical view is still to be demonstrated. It will not be demonstrated by new methods—not even when they are called methodologies—for teaching the irrelevant or by the construction of more stately mansions to shelter our cyclotrons.

We are not visionary these days, no more so (if no less) than our fathers who stoned the prophets. And our children, unless they are black, reject neither the image we present nor our preoccupation with images. There must be a reality somewhere. But the faith of the more recent fathers that education would disclose it turns out to be sterile. And its sterility illuminates the situation in which we find ourselves.

We are amputated Greeks. We have been cut off—cut ourselves off—from the mysticism that threaded Greek rationalism. An Italian in Thirteenth Century Paris, Aquinas by name, was the liveliest of all the Greeks; he undertook to prove the existence of God by reason alone. We dying Greeks undertake to prove we-care-not-what by reason alone and we wind up in the thrall of Emerson's Things and *their* meaningless mystique.

We know what goodness is, and we always have; Machiavelli knew, and Moses. But we do not know how to make men good. It is going on two-and-a-half millenia since the first discussion of education opened with the question, "Can you tell me, Socrates, whether virtue is acquired by teaching or by practice . . . or in some other way?" Perhaps the question is not to be answered; in which case we may concentrate on a succession (better yet, a continuum) of gaieties in contented conscience. But perhaps another two-and-a-half millenia of unrelenting inquiry will produce the answer; all the more reason for getting started at once.

(1964)

*Wayne C. Booth*

# Is There Any Knowledge That a Man *Must* Have?

As you have no doubt already recognized, my topic is simply a more exasperating form of the general topic of this conference. All of the ambiguities and annoyances that are stirred up when we ask what is most worth knowing are brought to the boiling point when we ask whether some things really *must* be known.

Such questions are not faced cheerfully by most of us in this empirical generation. It is true, of course, that we regularly make choices that are based on implied standards of what is worth knowing. We set degree requirements, we organize courses, we give examinations, and we would scarcely want to say that what we do is entirely arbitrary. We conduct research on this rather than that subject, and we urge our students in this rather than that direction; though we may profess a happy relativism of goals, as if all knowledge were equally valuable, we cannot and do not run our lives or our universities on entirely relativistic assumptions. And yet we seem to be radically unwilling to discuss the ground for our choices; it is almost as if we expected that a close look would reveal a scandal at the heart of our academic endeavor. The journals are full, true enough, of breast-beating and soul-searching, especially since "Berkeley." But you will look a long while before you find any discussion of what is worth knowing. You will look even longer before you find anything written in the past ten years worthy of being entered into the great debate on liberal education,[1] as it is represented by the selections in the "syllabus" prepared for this conference.[2] When Herbert Spencer, for example, wrote the essay from which we paraphrased our title, he knew that he addressed a public steeped in a tradition of careful argument about "What Knowledge Is of Most Worth." Though he disagreed with the traditional practice of placing classical studies at the center of liberal education, he knew that he could not defend scientific education simply by asserting its superiority. The very tradition he was attacking had educated an audience that required him to argue his case as cogently as possible, and, at the same time, it gave him confidence that his readers would think his question both important and amenable to productive discussion.

We were able to feel no such confidence in calling for a similar debate within a major university in 1966. Even at the University of Chicago, which has been more hospitable than most universities to serious controversy about the aims of education, we expected that the threat of hierarchical judgment implied by our topic would make men nervous. And we were right. "You will simply stir up meaningless controversy," one faculty member complained. "Since nobody can say what is most worth knowing, you'll get as many opinions as there are people, and the debate will be pointless." One bright fourth-year student said, "In choosing my major I've already chosen the knowledge which *for me* is most worth having. Each man chooses his own answers to this question, and the right choice for you is not the right choice for me."

And then—curiously enough—he repeated what I had heard earlier from the faculty member: "You'll get as many answers as there are men discussing."

---

[1] Since the conference, one fine exception has appeared, Daniel Bell's *The Reforming of General Education* (New York: Columbia University Press, 1966).

[2] The "syllabus" contained works like the following: "Liberal Knowledge Its Own End" by Cardinal Newman; "What Knowledge Is of Most Worth" by Herbert Spencer; selections from *The Education of Henry Adams;* "Science As a Vocation" by Max Weber; and *The Great Conversation* by Robert M. Hutchins.

Well, first of all, even if we think of knowledge as inert information, something that we can *have,* this simply is not so. There are not enough opinions about what is worth knowing to provide each of us with a custom-built model of his own. In the past few months, I have heard hundreds of defenses of this or that body of information or pattern of skills as worth learning, but there have been nothing like hundreds of different views. I suspect that a bit of logical sorting would reveal no more than twenty or thirty distinct views in this community, and perhaps no more than a good round dozen.

I raise what may seem like little more than a quibble because I think it is important at the beginning of this conference to recognize what our topic asks of us. Taken seriously, it not only asks us to affirm what we think is educationally important; we're all ready enough to do that at the drop of a hat. What is troublesome is that it asks us to reason together about our various preferences, and it assumes that some answers to the question will be better than others—not just preferable to you or to me, because of the way we have been educated, but better, period (or as men used to say, better, absolutely). It does not, of course, assume that finding answers will be easy; we cannot, like some non-academics, discover an indictment of the "knowledge factories" simply by ferreting out thesis topics that sound ridiculous. But it does assume that there is something irrational in our contemporary neglect of systematic thought about educational goals. Scholars in the middle ages are often accused of having automatically assumed hierarchies in every subject. Many of us as automatically assume that value judgments among types or bits of knowledge are irrelevant. Yet we cannot escape implying, by our practice, that though all "knowledges" are equal, some are more equal than others. Our choice of topic asks us to attempt, during this conference, to think seriously about the ground for the hierarchies that our practical choices imply.

## 2

Everyone lives on the assumption that a great deal of knowledge is not worth bothering about; though we all know that what looks trivial in one man's hands may turn out to be earth-shaking in another's, we simply cannot know very much, compared with what might be known, and we must therefore choose. What is shocking is not the act of choice which we all commit openly but the claim that some choices are wrong. Especially shocking is the claim implied by my title: There is some knowledge that a man *must* have.

There clearly is no such thing, if by knowledge we mean mere acquaintance with this or that thing, fact, concept, literary work, or scientific law. When C. P. Snow and F. R. Leavis exchanged blows on whether knowledge of Shakespeare is more important than knowledge of the second law of thermodynamics, they were both, it seemed to me, much too ready to assume as indispensable what a great many wise and good men have quite obviously got along without. And it is not only non-professionals who can survive in happy ignorance of this or that bit of lore. I suspect that many successful scientists (in biology, say) have lost whatever hold they might once have had on the second law; I know that a great many literary scholars survive and even flourish without knowing certain "indispensable" classics. We all get along without vast loads of learning that other men take as necessary marks of an educated man. If we once begin to "reason the need" we will find, like Lear, that "our basest beggars/Are in the poorest thing superfluous." Indeed, we can survive, in a manner of speaking, even in the modern world, with little more than the bare literacy necessary to tell the "off" buttons from the "on."

Herbert Spencer would remind us at this point that we are interpreting *need* as if it were entirely a question of private survival. Though he talks about what a man must know to stay alive, he is more interested, in his defense of science, in what a *society* must know to survive: "Is there any knowledge that *man* must have?"—not *a* man, but *man*. This question is put to us much more acutely in our time than it was in Spencer's, and it is by no means as easy to argue now as it was then that the knowledge needed for man's survival is scientific knowledge. The threats of atomic annihilation, of engulfing population growth, of depleted air, water, and food must obviously be met, if man is to survive, and in meeting them man will, it is true, need more and more scientific knowledge; but it is not at all clear that more and more scientific knowledge will by itself suffice. Even so, a modern Herbert Spencer might well argue that a conference like this one, with its emphasis on the individual and his cognitive needs, is simply repeating the mistakes of the classical tradition. The knowledge most worth having would be, from his point of view, that of how to pull mankind through the next century or so without absolute self-destruction. The precise proportions of different kinds of knowledge—physical, biological, political, ethical, psychological, historical, or whatever—would be different from those prescribed in Spencer's essay, but the nature of the search would be precisely the same.

We can admit the relevance of this emphasis on social utility and at the same time argue that our business here is with other matters entirely. If the only knowledge a man *must* have is how to cross the street without getting knocked down—or, in other words, how to navigate the centuries without blowing himself up—then we may as well close the conference and go home. We may as well also roll up the college and mail it to a research institute, because almost any place that is not cluttered up with notions of liberal education will be able to discover and transmit practical bits of survival-lore better than we can. Our problem of survival is a rather different one, thrust at us as soon as we change our title slightly once again to "Is there any knowledge (other than the knowledge for survival) that *a* man must have?" That slight shift opens a new perspective on the problem, because the question of what it is to be a man, of what it is to be fully human, is the question at the heart of liberal education.

To be human, to be human, to be fully human. What does it mean? What is required? Immediately, we start feeling nervous again. Is the speaker suggesting that some of us are not fully human *yet*? Here come those hierarchies again. Surely in our pluralistic society we can admit an unlimited number of legitimate ways to be a man, without prescribing some outmoded aristocratic code!

## 3

Who–or what–is the creature we would educate? Our answer will determine our answers to educational questions, and it is therefore, I think, worth far more vigorous effort than it usually receives. I find it convenient, and only slightly unfair, to classify the educational talk I encounter these days under four notions of man, three of them metaphorical, only one literal. Though nobody's position, I suppose, fits my types neatly, some educators talk as if they were programming machines, some talk as if they were conditioning rats, some talk as if they were training ants to take a position in the anthill, and some–precious few–talk as if they thought of themselves as men dealing with men.

One traditional division of the human soul, you will remember, was into three parts: the vegetable, the animal, and the rational. Nobody, so far as I know, has devised an educational program treating students as vegetables, though one runs into the analogy used negatively in academic sermons from time to time. Similarly, no one ever really says that men are ants, though there is a marvelous passage in Kwame Nkrumah's autobiography in which he meditates longingly on the order and pure functionality of an anthill. Educators do talk of men as machines or as animals, but of course they always point out that men are much more complicated than any other known animals or machines. My point here is not so much to attack any one of these metaphors–dangerous as I think they are–but to describe briefly what answers to our question each of them might suggest.

Ever since Descartes, La Mettrie, and others explicitly called man a machine, the metaphor has been a dominant one in educational thinking. Some have thought of man as a very complex machine, needing very elaborate programming; others have thought of him as a very simple machine, requiring little more than a systematic pattern of stimuli to produce foretellable responses. I heard a psychologist recently repeat the old behaviorist claim (first made by John B. Watson, I believe) that if you would give him complete control over any normal child's life from birth, he could turn that child into a great musician or a great mathematician or a great poet—you name it and he could produce it. On being pressed, the professor admitted that this claim was only "in theory," because we don't yet have the necessary knowledge. When I pushed further by asking why he was so confident in advance of experimental proof, it became clear that his faith in the fundamental metaphor of man as a programmable machine was unshakable.

When the notion of man as machine was first advanced, the machine was a very simple collection of pulleys and billiard balls and levers. Such original simplicities have been badly battered by our growing awareness both of how complex real machines can be and of how much more complex man is than any known machine. Modern notions of stimulus-response patterns are immeasurably more complicated than anything Descartes imagined, because we are now aware of the fantastic variety of stimuli that the man-machine is subject to and of the even more fantastic complexity of the responding circuits.

But whether the machine is simple or complex, the educational task for those who think of man under this metaphor is to program the mechanism so that it will produce the results that we have foreordained. We do not simply fill the little pitchers, like Mr. Gradgrind in Dickens' *Hard Times;* we are much too sophisticated to want only undigested "pourback," as he might have called his product. But we still program the information channels so that the proper if-loops and do-loops will be followed and the right feedback produced. The "programming" can be done by human teachers, of course, and not only by machines; but it is not surprising that those whose thinking is dominated by this metaphor tend to discover that machines are better teachers than men. The more ambitious programmers do not hesitate to claim that they can teach both thought and creativity in this way. But I have yet to see a program that can deal effectively with any subject that cannot be reduced to simple yes and no answers, that is, to answers that are known in advance by the programmer and can thus be fixed for all time.

We can assume that subtler machines will be invented that can engage in simulated dialogue with the pupil, and perhaps even recognize when a particularly bright pupil has discovered something new that refutes the program. But even the subtlest teaching machine imaginable will still be subject, one must assume, to a final limitation: it can teach only what a machine can "learn." For those who believe that man is literally nothing but a very complicated machine, this is not in fact a limitation; machines will ultimately be able to duplicate all mental processes, thus "learning" everything learnable, and they will be able in consequence to teach everything.

I doubt this claim for many reasons, and I am glad to find the testimony of Norbert Wiener, the first and best known cyberneticist, to the effect that there will always remain a radical gap between computers and the human mind. But "ultimately" is a long way off, and I am not so much concerned with whether ultimately man's mind will closely resemble some ultimately inventable machine as I am with the effects, here and now, of thinking about men under the analogy with machines of today. Let me simply close this section with an illustration of how the mechanistic model can permeate our thought in destructive ways. Ask yourselves what picture of creature-to-be-educated emerges from this professor of teacher education:

To implement the TEAM Project new curriculum proposal . . . our first concerns are with instructional systems, materials to feed the system, and personnel to operate the system. We have defined an instructional system as the optimal blending of the demands of content, communication, and learning. While numerous models have been developed, our simplified model of an instructional system would look like Figure 2. . . . We look at the process of communication — communicating content to produce learning — as something involving the senses: . . . [aural, oral, tactile, visual]. And I think in teacher education we had better think of the communications aspect of the instructional system as a package that includes the teacher, textbook, new media, classroom, and environment. To integrate these elements to more effectively transmit content into permanent learning, new and better instructional materials are needed and a new focus on the teacher of teachers is required. The teacher of teachers must: (1) examine critically the content of traditional courses in relation to desired behavioral outcomes; (2) become more sophisticated in the techniques of communicating course content; and (3) learn to work in concert with media specialists to develop the materials and procedures requisite to the efficient instructional system. And if the media specialist were to be charged with the efficient operation of the system, his upgrading would demand a broad-based "media generalist" orientation.[3]

I submit that the author of this passage was thinking of human beings as stimulus-response systems on the simplest possible model, and that he was thinking of the purpose of education as the transfer of information from one machine to another. Though he would certainly deny it if we asked him, he has come to think about the human mind so habitually in the mechanistic mode that he doesn't even know he's doing it.[4]

But it is time to move from the machine metaphor to animal metaphors. They are closely related, of course, because everybody who believes that man is a machine also believes that animals are machines, only simpler ones. But many people who would resist the word "machine" do tend to analogize man to one or another characteristic of animals. Since man is obviously an animal in one sense, he can be studied

---

[3]Desmond P. Wedberg, *Teacher Education Looks to the Future,* Twelfth Biennial School for Executives (Washington, D.C.: American Association of Colleges for Teacher Education, 1964).

[4]I am not of course suggesting that *any* use of teaching machines implies a mechanistic reduction of persons to machines; programmers rightly point out that machines *can* free teachers from the mechanical and save time for the personal.

as an animal, and he can be taught as an animal is taught. Most of the fundamental research in learning theory underlying the use of teaching machines has been done, in fact, on animals like rats and pigeons. You can teach pigeons to play Ping-Pong rather quickly be rewarding every gesture thay make that moves them toward success in the game and refusing to reward those gestures that you want to efface. Though everybody admits that human beings are more complicated than rats and pigeons, just as everyone admits that human beings are more complicated than computers, the basic picture of the animal as a collection of drives or instincts, "conditioned" to learn according to rewards or punishments, has underlain much modern educational theory.

The notion of the human being as a collection of drives different from animal drives only in being more complex carries with it implications for educational planners. If you and I are motivated only by sex or hunger or more complex drives like desire for power or for ego-satisfaction, then of course all education depends on the provision of satisfactions along our route to knowledge. If our teachers can just program carrots along the path at the proper distance, we donkey-headed students will plod along the path from carrot to carrot and end up as educated men.

I cannot take time here to deal with this view adequately, but it seems to me that it is highly questionable even about animals themselves. What kind of thing, really, is a rat or a monkey? The question of whether animals have souls has been debated actively for at least nine centuries; now psychologists find themselves dealing with the same question under another guise: What *are* these little creatures that we kill so blithely for the sake of knowledge? What *are* these strangely resistant little bundles of energy that will prefer – as experiments with rats have shown – a complicated interesting maze without food to a dull one *with* food?

There are, in fact, many experiments by now showing that at the very least we must postulate, for animals, a strong independent drive for mastery of the environment or satisfaction of curiosity about it. All the more advanced animals will learn to push levers that produce interesting results – clicks or bells or flashing lights or sliding panels – when no other reward is offered.[5] It seems clear that even to be a fulfilled animal, as it were, something more than "animal satisfaction" is needed!

I am reminded here of the experiments on mother-love in monkeys reported by Harry F. Harlow in the *Scientific American* some years ago. Harlow called his article "Love in Infant Monkeys," and the subtitle of his article read, "Affection in infants was long thought to be generated by the satisfactions of feeding. Studies of young rhesus monkeys

[5] See Robert W. White, "Motivation Reconsidered: The Concept of Competence," *Psychological Review,* 66 (1959), 297–333.

now indicate that love derives mainly from close bodily contact." The experiment consisted of giving infant monkeys a choice between a plain wire figure that offered the infant milk and a terry-cloth covered figure without milk. There was a pathetic picture of an infant clinging to the terry-cloth figure, and a caption that read "The infants spent most of their time clinging to the soft cloth 'mother' even when nursing bottles were attached to the wire mother." The article concluded—rather prematurely, I thought—that "contact comfort" had been shown to be a "prime requisite in the formation of an infant's love for its mother," that the act of nursing had been shown to be unimportant if not totally irrelevant in forming such love (though it was evident to any reader, even at the time, that no genuine "*act* of nursing" had figured in the experiment at all), and that "our investigations have established a secure experimental approach to this realm of dramatic and subtle emotional relationships." The only real problem, Harlow said, was the availability of enough infant monkeys for experiment.

Now I would not want to underrate the importance of Harlow's demonstration to the scientific community that monkeys do not live by bread alone. But I think that most scientists and humanists reading that article would have been struck by two things. The first is the automatic assumption that the way to study a subject like love is to break it down into its component parts; nobody looking at that little monkey clinging to the terry-cloth could possibly have said, "This is love," unless he had been blinded by a hidden conviction that love in animals is—must be—a mere cumulative result of a collection of drive satisfactions. This assumption is given quite plainly in Harlow's concluding sentence: "Finally with such techniques established, there appears to be no reason why we cannot at some future time investigate the fundamental neurophysiological and biochemical variables underlying affection and love." For Harlow monkeys (and people) seem to be mere collections of neurophysiological and biochemical variables, and love will be best explained when we can explain the genesis of each of its parts. The second striking point is that for Harlow animals do not matter, except as they are useful for experiment. If he had felt that they mattered, he might have noticed the look on his infant's face—a look that predicted for me, and for other readers of the *Scientific American* I've talked with, that these monkeys were doomed.

And indeed they were. A year or so later another article appeared, reporting Harlow's astonished discovery that all of the little monkeys on which he had earlier experimented had turned out to be incurably psychotic. Not a single monkey could mate, not a single monkey could play, not a single monkey could in fact become anything more than the twisted half-creatures that Harlow's deprivations had made of them. Harlow's new discovery was that monkeys needed close association with their peers during infancy and that such association was even more important to their development than genuine mothering. There was no sign that Harlow had learned any fundamental lessons from his earlier gross mistakes; he had landed nicely on his feet, still convinced that the way to study love is to break it down into its component parts and that the way to study animals is to maim them or reduce them to something less than themselves. As Robert White says, summarizing his reasons for rejecting similar methods in studying human infancy, it is too often assumed that the scientific way is to analyze behavior until one can find a small enough unit to allow for detailed research, but in the process "very vital common properties" are lost from view.

I cite Harlow's two reports not, of course, to attack animal experimentation—though I must confess that I am horrified by much that goes on in its name—nor to claim that animals are more like human beings than they are. Rather, I want simply to suggest that the danger of thinking of men as animals is heightened if the animals we think of are reduced to machines on a simple model.

The effects of reducing education to conditioning can be seen throughout America today. Usually they appear in subtle forms, disguised with the language of personalism; you will look a long time before you find anyone (except a very few Skinnerians) saying that he thinks of education as exactly like conditioning pigeons. But there are plenty of honest, blunt folk around to let the cat out of the bag—like the author of an article this year in *College Composition and Communication:* "The Use of a Multiple Response Device in the Teaching of Remedial English." The author claimed to have evidence that if you give each student four buttons to be pushed on multiple-choice questions, with all the buttons wired into a lighted grid at the front of the room, the resulting "instantaneous feedback"—every child learning immediately whether he agrees with the rest of the class—speeds up the learning of grammatical rules considerably over the usual workbook procedures. I daresay it does—but meanwhile what has happened to education? Or take the author of an article on "Procedures and Techniques of Teaching," who wrote as follows: "If we expect students to learn skills, they have to practice, but practice doesn't make perfect. Practice works if the learner *learns the results* of his practice, i.e., if he receives feedback. Feedback is most effective when it is contiguous to the response being learned. One of the chief advantages of teaching machines is that the learner finds out quickly whether his response is right or wrong . . . [Pressey] has published the results of an extensive program of research with tests that students score for themselves by punching alternatives until they hit the correct one. . . . [Thus] teaching machines or workbooks have many theoretical advantages over lecturing or other conventional methods of instruction." But according to what theory, one must ask, *do* systematic feedback mechanisms, perfected to whatever degree, have "theoretical advantages" over human contact? Whatever else can be said for such a theory, it will be based on the simplest of comparisons with animal learning. Unfortunately, the author goes on, experimental evidence is on the whole rather discouraging: "Experiments at the Systems Development Corporation . . . suggest that teaching incorporating . . . human characteristics is more effective than the typical fixed-sequence machines. (In this experiment instead of using teaching machines to simulate human teachers, the experimenters used humans to simulate teaching machines!)"

So far I have dealt with analogies for man that apply only to individuals. My third analogy turns to the picture of men in groups, and it is given to me partly by discussions of education, like those of Admiral Rickover, that see it simply as filling society's needs. I know of only one prominent educator who has publicly praised the anthill as a model for the kind of society a university should serve—a society of specialists each trained to do his part. But the notion pervades many of the defenses of the emerging multiversities.

If knowledge is needed to enable men to function as units in society, and if the health of society is taken as the purpose of their existence, then there is nothing wrong in training the ants to fill their niches; it would be wrong not to. "Education is our first line of defense—make it strong," so reads the title of the first chapter of Admiral Rickover's book, *Education and Freedom* (New York: Dutton, 1959). "We must upgrade our schools" in order to "guarantee the future prosperity and freedom of the Republic." You can tell whether the ant-analogy is dominating a man's thinking by a simple test of how he orders his ends and means. In Admiral Rickover's statement, the schools must be upgraded in order to guarantee future prosperity, that is, we improve education for the sake of some presumed social good.

I seldom find anyone putting it the other way round: we must guarantee prosperity so that we can improve the schools, and the reason we want to improve the schools is that we want to insure the development of certain kinds of persons, both as teachers and as students. You cannot even say what I just said so long as you are really thinking of ants and anthills. Ants are not ends in themselves, ultimately more valuable than the hills they live in (I *think* they are not; maybe to themselves, or in the eyes of God, even ants are ultimate, self-justifying ends). At least from our point of view, ants are expendable, or to put it another way, their society is more beautiful, more interesting, more admirable than they are. And I would want to argue that too many people think of human beings in the same way when they think of educating them. The Communists make this quite explicit: the ends of Communist society justify whatever distortion or destruction of individual purposes is necessary to achieve them; men are educated for the state, not for their own well-being. They are basically political animals, not in the Aristotelian sense that they require society if they are to achieve their full natures and thus their own special, human kind of happiness, but in the sense that they exist, like ants, for the sake of the body politic.

If the social order is the final justification of what we do in education, then a certain attitude toward teaching and research will result: all of us little workmen, down inside the anthill, will go on happily contributing our tiny bit to the total scheme without worrying much about larger questions of the why and wherefore. I know a graduate student who says that she sometimes sees her graduate professors as an army of tiny industrious miners at the bottom of a vast mine, chipping away at the edges and shipping their bits of knowledge up to the surface, blindly hoping that someone up there will know what to do with it all. An order is received for such-and-such new organic compounds; society needs them. Another order is received for an atomic bomb; it is needed, and it is therefore produced. Often no orders come down, but the chipping goes on anyway, and the shipments are made, because everyone knows that the health of the mine depends on a certain tonnage of specialized knowledge each working day.

We have learned lately that "they" are going to establish a great new atom-smasher, perhaps near Chicago. The atom-smasher will employ two thousand scientists and technicians. I look out at you here, knowing that some of you are physics majors, and I wonder whether any of you will ultimately be employed in that new installation, and if you are, whether it will be as an ant or as a human being. Which it will be must depend not on your ultimate employers but on yourself and on what happens to your education between now and then: if you have been given nothing but training to be that ultimate unit in that ultimate system, only a miracle can save you from formic dissolution of your human lineaments.

## 4

But it is long past time for me to turn from these negative, truncated portraits of what man really is not and attempt to say what he is. And here we encounter a difficulty that I find very curious. You will note that each of these metaphors has reduced man to something less than man, or at least to a partial aspect of man. It is easy to say that man is not a machine, though he is in some limited respects organized like a machine and even to some degree "programmable." It is also easy to say that man is not simply a complicated rat or monkey, though he is in some ways like rats and monkeys. Nor is man an ant, though he lives and must function in a complicated social milieu. All these metaphors break down not because they are flatly false but because they *are* metaphors, and any metaphorical definition is inevitably misleading. The ones I have been dealing with are especially misleading, because in every case they have reduced something more complex to something much less complex. But even if we were to analogize man to something more complex, say, the universe, we would be dissatisfied. What we want is some notion of what man really *is*, so that we will know what or whom we are trying to educate.

And here it is that we discover something very important about man, something that even the least religious person must find himself mystified by: man is the one "thing" we know that is completely resistant to our efforts at metaphor or analogy or image-making. What seems to be the most important literal characteristic of man is his resistance to definitions in terms of anything else. If you call me a machine, even a very complicated machine, I know that you deny what I care most about, my selfhood, my sense of being a person, my consciousness, my conviction of freedom and dignity, my awareness of love, my laughter. Machines have none of these things, and even if we were generous to their prospects, and imagined machines immeasurably superior to the most complicated ones now in existence, we would still feel an infinite gap between them and what we know to be a basic truth about ourselves: machines are expendable, ultimately expendable, and men are mysteriously ends in themselves.

I hear people deny this, but when they do they always argue for their position by claiming marvelous feats of super-machine calculation that machines can now do or will someday be able to do. But that is not the point; of course machines can outcalculate us. The question to ask is entirely a different one: Will they ever outlove us, outlive us, out-value us? Do we build machines because machines are good things in themselves? Do we nurture them for their own good, as we nurture our children? An obvious way to test our sense of worth in men and machines is to ask ourselves whether we would ever campaign to liberate the poor downtrodden machines who have been enslaved. Shall we form a National Association for the Advancement of Machinery? Will anyone ever feel a smidgeon of moral indignation because this or that piece of machinery is not given equal rights before the law? Or put it another way: Does anyone value Gemini more than the twins? There may be men now alive who would rather "destruct," as we say, the pilot than the experimental rocket, but most of us still believe that the human being in the space ship is more important than the space ship.

When college students protest the so-called depersonalization of education, what they mean, finally, is not simply that they want to meet their professors socially or that they want small classes or that they do not want to be dealt with by IBM machines. All these things are but symptoms of a deeper sense of a violation of their literal reality as persons, ends in themselves rather than mere expendable things. Similarly, the current deep-spirited revolt against racial and economic injustice seems to me best explained as a sudden assertion that people, of whatever color or class, are not reducible to social conveniences. When you organize your labor force or your educational system as if men were mere social conveniences, "human resources," as we say, contributors to the gross national product, you violate something that we all know, in a form of knowledge much deeper than our knowledge of the times tables or the second law of thermodynamics: those field hands, those children crowded into the deadening classroom, those men laboring without dignity in the city anthills are *men,* creatures whose worth is mysteriously more than any description of it we might make in justifying what we do to them.

## 5

Ants, rats, and machines can all learn a great deal. Taken together, they "know" a very great part of what our schools and colleges are now designed to teach. But is there any kind of knowledge that a creature must have to qualify as a man? Is there any part of the educational task that is demanded of us by virtue of our claim to educate this curious entity, this *person* that cannot be reduced to mechanism or animality alone?

You will not be surprised, by now, to have me sound, in my answer, terribly traditional, not to say square: the education that a *man* must have is what has traditionally been called liberal education. The knowledge it yields is the knowledge or capacity or power of how to act freely as a man. That's why we call liberal education liberal: it is intended to liberate from whatever it is that makes animals act like animals and machines act like machines.

I'll return in a moment to what it means to act freely as a man. But we are already in a position to say something about what knowledge a man must have—he must first of all be able to learn for himself. If he cannot learn for himself, he is enslaved by his teachers' ideas, or by the ideas of his more persuasive contemporaries, or by machines programmed by other men. He may have what we call a good formal education, yet still be totally bound by whatever opinions happen to have come his way in attractive garb. One wonders how many of our graduates have learned how to take hold of a subject and "work it up," so that they can make themselves experts on what other men have concluded. In some ways this is not a very demanding goal, and it is certainly not very exciting. It says nothing about that popular concept, creativity, or about imagination or originality. All it says is that anyone who is dependent on his teachers *is* dependent, not free, and that anyone who knows how to learn for himself is less like animals and machines than anyone who does not know how to learn for himself.

We see already that a college is not being merely capricious or arbitrary when it insists that some kinds of learning are more important than some others. The world is overflowing with interesting subjects and valuable skills, but surely any college worth the name will put first things first: it will try to insure, as one inescapable goal, that every graduate can dig out from the printed page what he needs to know. And it will not let the desire to tamp in additional tidbits of knowledge, however delicious, interfere with training minds for whom a formal teacher is no longer required.

To put our first goal in this way raises some real problems — perhaps even problems that we cannot solve. Obviously no college can produce self-learners in very many subjects. Are we not lucky if a graduate can learn for himself even in one field, now that knowledge in all areas has advanced as far as it has? Surely we cannot expect our graduates to reach a stage of independence in mathematics and physics, in political science and psychology, in philosophy and English, *and* in all the other nice subjects that one would like to master.

Rather than answer this objection right away, let me make things even more difficult by saying that it is not enough to learn how to learn. The man who cannot *think* for himself, going beyond what other men have learned or thought, is still enslaved to other men's ideas. Obviously the goal of learning to think is even more difficult than the goal of learning to learn. But difficult as it is we must add it to our list. It is simply not enough to be able to get up a subject on one's own, like a good encyclopaedia employee, even though any college would take pride if all its graduates could do so. To be fully human means in part to think one's own thoughts, to reach a point at which, whether one's ideas are different from or similar to other men's, they are truly one's own.

The art of asking oneself critical questions that lead either to new answers or to genuine revitalizing of old answers, the art of making thought live anew in each new generation, may not be entirely amenable to instruction. But it is a necessary art nonetheless, for any man who wants to be free. It is an art that all philosophers have tried to pursue, and many of them have given direct guidance in how to pursue it. Needless to say, it is an art the pursuit of which is never fully completed. No one thinks for himself very much of the time or in very many subjects. Yet the habitual effort to ask the right critical questions and to apply rigorous tests to our hunches is a clearer mark than any other of an educated man.

But again we stumble upon the question, "Learn to think about *what*?" The modern world presents us with innumerable subjects to think about. Does it matter whether anyone achieves this rare and difficult point in more than one subject? And if not, won't the best education simply be the one that brings a man into mastery of a narrow specialty as soon as possible, so that he can learn to think for himself as soon as possible? Even at best most of us are enslaved to opinions provided for us by experts in *most* fields. So far, it might be argued, I still have not shown that there is any kind of knowledge that a man must have, only that there are certain skills that he must be able to exercise in at least one field.

To provide a proper grounding for my answer to that objection would require far more time than I have left, and I'm not at all sure that I could do so even with all the time in the world. The question of whether it is possible to maintain a human stance toward any more than a tiny fraction of modern knowledge is not clearly answerable at this stage in our history. It will be answered, if at all, only when men have learned how to store and retrieve all "machinable" knowledge, freeing themselves for distinctively human tasks. But in the meantime, I find myself unable to surrender, as it were, three distinct kinds of knowledge that seem to me indispensable to being human.

To be a man, a man must first know something about his own nature and his place in Nature, with a capital N—something about the truth of things, as men used to say in the old-fashioned days before the word "truth" was banned from academia. Machines are not curious, so far as I can judge; animals are, but presumably they never go, in their philosophies, even at the furthest, beyond a kind of solipsistic existentialism. But in science, in philosophy (ancient and modern), in theology, in psychology and anthropology, and in literature (of some kinds), we are presented with accounts of our universe and of our place in it that as men we can respond· to in only one manly way: by thinking about them, by speculating and testing our speculations.

We know before we start that our thought is doomed to incompleteness and error and downright chanciness. Even the most rigorously scientific view will be changed, we know, within a decade, or perhaps even by tomorrow. But to refuse the effort to understand is to resign from the human race; the unexamined life can no doubt be worth living in other respects—after all, it is no mean thing to be a vegetable, an oak tree, an elephant or a lion. But a man, a man will want to see, in this speculative domain, beyond his next dinner.

By putting it in this way, I think we can avoid the claim that to be a man I must have studied any one field—philosophy, science, theology. But to be a man, *I must speculate,* and I must learn how to test my speculations so that they are not simply capricious, unchecked by other men's speculations. A college education, surely, should throw every student into a regular torrent of speculation, and it should school him to recognize the different standards of validation proper to different kinds of claims to truth. You cannot distinguish a man who in this respect is educated from other men by whether or not he believes in God, or in UFOs. But you can tell an educated man by the way he takes hold of the question of whether God exists, or whether UFOs are from Mars. Do you know your own reasons for your beliefs, or do you absorb your beliefs from whatever happens to be in your environment, like plankton taking in nourishment?

Second, the man who has not learned how to make the great human achievements in the arts his own, who does not know what it means to *earn* a great novel or symphony or painting for himself, is enslaved either to caprice or to other men's testimony or to a life of ugliness. You will notice that as I turn thus to "beauty"—another old-fashioned term—I do not say that a man must know how to prove what is beautiful or how to discourse on aesthetics. Such speculative activities are pleasant and worthwhile in themselves, but they belong in my first domain. Here we are asking that a man be educated to the experience of beauty; speculation about it can then follow. My point is simply that a man is less than a man if he cannot respond to the art made by his fellow man.

Again I have tried to put the standard in a way that allows for the impossibility of any one man's achieving independent responses in very many arts. Some would argue that education should insure some minimal human competence in all of the arts, or at least in music, painting, and literature. I suppose I would be satisfied if all of our graduates had been "hooked" by at least one art, hooked so deeply that they could never get free. As in the domain of speculation, we could say that the more types of distinctively human activity a man can master, the better, but we are today talking about floors, not ceilings, and I shall simply rest content with saying that to be a man, a man must know artistic beauty, in some form, and know it in the way that beauty can be known. (The distinction between natural and man-made beauty might give me trouble if you pushed me on it here, but let me just say, dogmatically, that I would not be satisfied simply to know natural beauty—women and sunsets, say—as a substitute for art).

Finally, the man who has not learned anything about how to understand his own intentions and to make them effective in the world, who has not, through experience and books, learned something about what is possible and what impossible, what desirable and what undesirable, will be enslaved by the political and social intentions of other men, benign or malign. The domain of practical wisdom is at least as complex and troublesome as the other two, and at the same time it is even more self-evidently indispensable. How should a man live? How should a society be run? What direction should a university take in 1966? For that matter what should be the proportion, in a good university, of inquiry into truth, beauty, and "goodness"? What kind of knowledge of self or of society is pertinent to living the life proper to a man? In short, the very question of this conference falls within this final domain: What knowledge, if any, is most worthy of pursuit? You cannot distinguish the men from the boys according to any one set of conclusions, but you *can* recognize a man, in this domain, simply by discovering whether he can think for himself about practical questions, with some degree of freedom from blind psychological or political or economic compulsions. Ernest Hemingway tells somewhere of a man who had "moved one dollar's width to the [political] right for every dollar that he'd ever earned." Perhaps no man ever achieves the opposite extreme, complete freedom in his choices from irrelevant compulsions. But all of us who believe in education believe that it is possible for any man, through study and conscientious thought, to school his choices—that is, to free them through coming to understand the forces working on them.

**6**

Even from this brief discussion of the three domains, I think we are put in a position to see how it can be said that there is some knowledge that a man must have. The line I have been pursuing will not lead to a list of great books, or even to a list of indispensable departments in a university. Nor will it lead, in any clear-cut fashion, to a pattern of requirements in each of the divisions. Truth, beauty, and goodness (or "right choice") are relevant to study in every division within the university; the humanities, for example, have no corner on beauty or imagination or art, and the sciences have no corner on speculative truth. What is more, a man can be ignorant even of Shakespeare, Aristotle, Beethoven, and Einstein, and be a man for a' that—*if* he has learned how to think his own thoughts, experience beauty for himself, and choose his own actions.

It is not the business of a college to determine or limit what a man will know; if it tries to, he will properly resent its impositions, perhaps immediately, perhaps ten years later when the imposed information is outmoded. But I think that it *is* the business of a college to help teach a man how to use his mind for himself, in at least the three directions I have suggested. There has been a splendid tradition in the College of the University of Chicago of honoring these goals with hard planning and devoted teaching. To think for oneself is, as we all know, hard enough. To design a program and assemble faculty to assist rather than hinder students in their efforts to think for themselves is even harder. But in an age that is oppressed by huge accumulations of unassimilated knowledge, the task of discovering what it means to educate a man is perhaps more important than ever before.

(1967)

### Margaret Mead and Rhoda Metraux

# Education for Diversity

May, 1967

How can parents give their children a solid education today and at the same time prepare them for life in a racially diverse world?

Traveling around the country, I meet a great number of parents who are deeply troubled about what action to take to achieve both these ends. Should they try to stick it out in a changing neighborhood? Should they struggle with all the difficulties of a newly integrated school? Should they move to a different kind of community for the sake of the children's education? Should they decide in favor of private schools?

Urgency is part of the problem, because the time for children's education is always *now*.

Parents want schooling for their children that will give them access to the knowledge and the skills that will open the doors of the world to them in later years. But farsighted parents also realize that their children must acquire a readiness to move into a highly diversified world in which they will live and work with men and women of markedly different backgrounds. No one can predict where these children, just taking their first tentative steps away from home, will be working twenty years from now, on what continent or at what tasks. And it is this double demand on education that poses the parents' dilemma.

In the past, schools did prepare American children to move freely in what was then a more circumscribed world. Two factors seem to have been important in achieving this. Most American families lived in small communities, where rich and poor jostled elbows and the children of new immigrants learning to speak the language and eat the food of the new country mingled with those who had come before them. And most children attended public schools, where our fundamental belief in the value of free public education gave meaning to their meeting and learning together. However much they differed in their background and in the prospects for their future, their common experience in school taught them the easy give-and-take, the friendliness and trust that made them into people who were at home anywhere in the country.

There were, of course, regions of the country where this was not so. Schools in the southeast were segregated, and in our largest cities immigrants of one nationality often were crowded together in one grim reception slum. But for most Americans in small towns and in the mixed neighborhoods of larger cities, the public school was a good preparation for the kind of diversity they were likely to meet in later life. Children learned what we then understood to be democracy—how to get along comfortably with people of many different backgrounds.

But young children today will move into a world that is global in its dimensions. They will face a far more complex diversity. As adults they may have to learn to speak any one of forty or fifty languages, and they may find themselves working as supervisors or subordinates, colleagues or neighbors, with individuals of any of the world's races. Instead of learning what they must so that they can get along as well in Chicago as they can in Boston, whether with second-generation Italians, Germans, Irish or their parents' own ethnic group, today's children must learn how to live and work with people anywhere in the world.

And they are ill prepared to do so, for our schools long ago ceased to be small replicas of a larger world. Great numbers of Americans now live in neighborhoods and communities where their principal associations are with families very similar to their own, of the same class, color and religion, having the same kind of education and interests, and even, within a narrow range, the same kinds of occupations. Where those belonging to ethnically disadvantaged groups have become isolated, we speak of their crowded slum neighborhoods as ghettos, borrowing the term used to describe the old segregated Jewish settlements in Europe. Where the community is made up of more-privileged people, we call it a suburb or a "nice residential section." One result for the ghetto children has been an ever-increasing inequality of opportunity for good schooling. But from the point of view of human experience, segregation is equally damaging for the privileged, who are cut off from experiencing others – and themselves – as full human beings.

What we are facing now is the hard struggle to reverse this process. In most of what we are undertaking in rezoning neighborhoods, changing real-estate regulations, trying to integrate housing and schools, attempting to open up employment and to give everyone access to recreational facilities, the emphasis is on the rights and needs of those who have suffered from poverty and prejudice. However tardily, we have come to realize that it is devastatingly destructive for children to grow up trapped in ghettos. But we are much less clear that it is deeply damaging for children to grow up isolated in suburbs and in "select" sections of a city.

Instead, where privileged children are concerned our attention is focused on the more limited problem of how they will get a sound basic education. And in the midst of the uneasy process of transition and the pressures that are brought to bear on everyone, there is a real danger that the diversity we once valued for all children will come to be defined as a privilege for the deprived and as a penalty for the previously privileged.

Talking all these problems over with parents today, I have been struck both by the similarity and the contrast between their situation now and mine twenty years ago, when my own daughter was ready for school. I knew what I wanted for her. I wanted a school where she could learn all that we depend on schools to teach. But I also wanted her to grow up able to move freely, responsibly and with sophistication anywhere in the world. I wanted her to feel at home and welcome anywhere in the New World, where all the great races of man have mingled, and in the Old World, where so many groups have lived apart from one another. I wanted her to understand that skin color and eye color and hair form are signs of special ability and disability only where, temporarily, people have treated them as such.

Particularly I wanted her to overcome the peculiar American belief that African heritage, in whatever proportion, is determining as no other heritage, European or Asian, is. I wanted her to know members of other groups so that she would not classify individuals by such categories as skin color, language or religion, but would be able to respond to each of them as a person whom she liked or found uncongenial for individual reasons. I wanted her to experience living with others as full human beings.

But we lived in New York City, and there seemed to be no way of providing good schooling based on diversity within the then-deteriorating school system. I was faced, as parents now are faced, with the fact that children are young only once. If they are to have the right kind of education, they must have it now, not in some far future when we have reorganized the school system. And so, very reluctantly (for I grew up believing firmly in public schools), I joined with a group of parents in starting a new school where a few children, at least, could have the things we wanted for all children: a good formal education, a rich artistic experience and the daily give-and-take of growing up with children and with adults — teachers, trustees, maintenance staff — of diverse ethnic, religious and cultural backgrounds.

My conscience troubled me. A good school should be rooted in the community, and our children came from distant parts of the city. The long bus trips were hard on the children, and keeping the school going was hard on the parents. Most of them were young and had little money. They were scarcely able to afford tuition for their own children, much less contribute to the many scholarships that were needed.

The school often faced disaster. We paid the staff less than they could have earned in a different kind of school, and sometimes we couldn't pay them on time. The Negro families faced the greatest difficulties. Their children had the longest bus rides and the Negro parents made the greatest sacrifices in sharing the costs. No one now can count the hours everyone gave to make that school a living thing. Our children had a good education, but at great cost.

Today we have the legal framework for creating such diversity in all our public schools. But we are still a long way from having created the social climate in which each child can have both a good formal education and a happy experience of human diversity. Our attempts nationally to bring together children who differ from one another in color, religion, language and in ethnic, economic and social background are still clumsy and crude. Breaking old neighborhood patterns, bringing together children and teachers and parents who are strangers to one another, using old schools and new schools, finding methods of teaching the deprived and the privileged simultaneously — all this is hard on everyone, the children most of all.

Can we make it work? Can we give our children, all our children, the kind of education they will need? Some parents I know have given up and are sending their children to private schools; others are founding new private schools. Even the parents who care the most are discouraged. We are finding that what we want is expensive in time and money, and especially in effort. We are discovering that it is not enough to try to work toward our older, already existing standards. If a fully integrated school is to benefit all its students, it must have better teachers and better facilities than any ordinary school. And everyone will have to work much harder—the teachers, the school boards, the parents, the children themselves and the whole community. It will not be easy.

But I think we can succeed—on one condition: that is, that we continue to value diversity. Today this is not simply an ideal. It is the reality of our children's world.

With Whom Can We Live?

To put widely disparate selections together and thus testify to their kinship may seem to foster a foolish incongruity. Yet the readings in this section are not incongruous; all are specimen answers, in some way or another, to the question "With Whom Can We Live?"

In *A Rhetoric of Motives* Kenneth Burke suggests that our separateness may be all we have in common, but that even as we are divided, set over against each other, we are under a need to live together. "I do not expect the Union to be dissolved," Abraham Lincoln said in a speech included here, "I do not expect the house to fall—but I do expect it will cease to be divided." The quest for communion and the failure to achieve it take many forms. Some of the readings here speak directly to the central matter of how we shall live with each other. Some of the readings, along with their own hopes for community, describe our common failures and dramatize the urgent need upon us to live together fruitfully and well.

Still other readings are addressed to specific forms that the central question may take. How—or whether—a person can live with generations other than his own is a common enough question in our own time, and it is variously explored here. Other selections treat love and other relationships between the sexes. Any concern for the question "With whom can we live?" must include exploration of civil rights and the relationships among groups of people. And of course the question that heads this section can lead us to considerations of war and violence and the coexistence of nations.

Our success at living with anybody has been spasmodic. One reason, surely, for our many failures has been our inability or unwillingness to hear any voice save our own. A price we can gladly pay to live with others is to hear voices other than our own and to learn things other than what we presently know. As the Constitutional Convention was nearing its end in 1787, Benjamin Franklin, grown old, passed a speech to James Wilson, who read it to the Convention. It began:

I confess that there are several parts of this Constitution which I do not at present approve, but I am not sure I shall never approve them: for having lived long, I have experienced many instances of being obliged by better information, or further consideration, to change opinions even on important subjects, which I once thought right, but found to be otherwise. It is therefore that the older I grow, the more apt I am to doubt my own judgment, and to pay more respect to the judgment of others. Most men indeed, as well as most sects in religion, think themselves in possession of all truth, and that wherever others differ from them it is so far error.

A little later, Franklin concluded:

On the whole, sir, I cannot help expressing a wish that every member of the Convention who may still have objections to it would with me, on this occasion, doubt a little of his own infallibility and, to make manifest our unanimity, put his name to this instrument.

# How shall we live with our families?

## Edward

"Why dois your brand sae drap wi bluid,
            Edward, Edward,
Why dois your brand sae drap wi bluid,
  And why sae sad gang yee O?"
"O I hae killed my hauke sae guid,
            Mither, mither,
O I hae killed my hauke sae guid,
  And I had nae mair bot hee O."

"Your haukis bluid was nevir sae reid,
            Edward, Edward,
Your haukis bluid was nevir sae reid,
  My deir son I tell thee O."
"O I hae killed my reid-roan steid,
            Mither, mither,
O I hae killed my reid-roan steid,
  That erst was sae fair and frie O."

"Your steid was auld, and ye hae gat mair,
            Edward, Edward,
Your steid was auld, and ye hae gat mair,
  Sum other dule ye drie O."

"O I hae killed my fadir deir,
                    Mither, mither,
O I hae killed my fadir deir,
   Alas, and wae is mee O!"

"And whatten penance wul ye drie for that,
                    Edward, Edward?
And whatten penance will ye drie for that?
   My deir son, now tell me O."
"Ile set my feit in yonder boat,
                    Mither, mither,
Ile set my feit in yonder boat,
   And Ile fare ovir the sea O."

"And what wul ye doe wi your towirs and your ha,
                    Edward, Edward?
And what wul ye doe wi your towirs and your ha,
   That were sae fair to see O?"
"Ile let thame stand tul they doun fa,
                    Mither, mither,
Ile let thame stand tul they doun fa,
   For here nevir mair maun I bee O."

"And what wul ye leive to your bairns and your wife,
                    Edward, Edward?
And what wul ye leive to your bairns and your wife,
   Whan ye gang ovir the sea O?"
"The warldis room, late them beg thrae life,
                    Mither, mither,
The warldis room, late them beg thrae life,
   For thame nevir mair wul I see O."

"And what wul ye leive to your ain mither deir,
                    Edward, Edward?
And what wul ye leive to your ain mither deir?
   My deir son, now tell me O."
"The curse of hell frae me sall ye beir,
                    Mither, mither,
The curse of hell frae me sall ye beir,
   Sic counseils ye gave to me O."

                                        (c. 1300)

# The Wife of Bath's Tale

When good King Arthur ruled in ancient days,
A king that every Briton loves to praise,
This was a land brim-full of fairy folk.
The Elf-Queen and her courtiers joined and broke
Their elfin dance on many a green mead,
Or so was the opinion once, I read,
Hundreds of years ago, in days of yore.
But no one now sees fairies any more,
For now the saintly charity and prayer
Of holy friars seem to have purged the air;
They search the countryside through field and stream
As thick as motes that speckle a sun-beam,
Blessing the halls, the chambers, kitchens, bowers,
Cities and boroughs, castles, courts and towers,
Thorpes, barns and stables, outhouses and dairies,
And that's the reason why there are no fairies.
Wherever there was wont to walk an elf
To-day there walks the holy friar himself
As evening falls or when the daylight springs,
Saying his mattins and his holy things,
Walking his limit round from town to town.
Women can now go safely up and down,
By every bush or under every tree;
There is no other incubus but he,
So there is really no one else to hurt you
And he will do no more than take your virtue.

    Now it so happened, I began to say,
Long, long ago in good King Arthur's day,
There was a knight who was a lusty liver.
One day as he came riding from the river
He saw a maiden walking all forlorn
Ahead of him, alone as she was born.
And of that maiden, spite of all she said,
By very force he took her maidenhead.
    This act of violence made such a stir,
So much petitioning of the king for her,
That he condemned the knight to lose his head
By course of law. He was as good as dead
(It seems that then the statutes took that view)
But that the queen and other ladies too
Implored the king to exercise his grace
So ceaselessly, he gave the queen the case

And granted her his life, and she could choose
Whether to show him mercy or refuse.

  The queen returned him thanks with all her might,
And then she sent a summons to the knight
At her convenience, and expressed her will:
'Sir, your position is precarious still,'
She said, 'you're on the edge of an abyss.
Yet you shall live if you can tell me this.
What is the thing that women most desire?
Beware the ax and say as I require.

  'If you can't answer on the moment, though,
I will concede you this: you are to go
A twelvemonth and a day to seek and learn
Sufficient answer, then you shall return.
I shall take gages from you to extort
Surrender of your body to the court.'

  Sad was the knight and sorrowfully sighed,
But there! What option had he? He'd been tried.
And in the end he chose to go away
And to return after a year and day
Armed with such answer as there might be sent
To him by God. He took his leave and went.

  He knocked at every house, searched every place,
Yes, anywhere that offered hope of grace.
What could it be that women wanted most?
But all the same he never touched a coast,
Country or town in which there seemed to be
Any two people willing to agree.

  Some said that women wanted wealth and treasure,
Honor said some, some jollity and pleasure;
Some gorgeous clothes and others fun in bed
And 'to be widowed and remarried,' said
Yet others. Some the thing that really mattered
Was that we should be gratified and flattered.
That's very near the truth, it seems to me;
A man can win us best with flattery.
Attentiveness and making a great fuss
About a woman, that's what fetches us.

  But others said a woman's real passion
Was liberty, behaving in what fashion
Might please her best, and not be corrected
But told she's wise, encouraged and respected.
Truly there's not a woman in ten score
Who has a fault and someone rubs the sore
But she will kick if what he says is true;
You try it out and you will find so too.

However vicious we may be within
We like to be thought wise and void of sin.
    Some people said that what we women treasure
Is to be thought dependable in pleasure,
Steadfast in keeping secrets from the jealous,
Not prone to blab the things a man may tell us.
But that opinion isn't worth a rush!
Good Lord, a woman keep a secret? Tush!
Remember Midas? Will you hear the tale?
    Among some other little things now stale,
Ovid relates that Midas, it appears,
Had grown a great big pair of ass's ears
Under his flowing locks. As best he might
He kept this foul deformity from sight.
His wife – she was the only one that knew –
Was trusted by him, and he loved her too.
He begged her not to tell a living creature
That he possessed so horrible a feature.
    She wouldn't tell for all the world, she swore,
It would be villainy, a sin what's more,
To earn her husband such a filthy name,
Besides it would redound to her own shame.
Nevertheless she thought she would have died
Keeping this secret bottled up inside;
It seemed to swell her heart and she, no doubt,
Thought it was on the point of bursting out.
    Fearing to speak of it to woman or man,
Down to a reedy marsh she quickly ran
And reached the sedge. Her heart was all on fire
And, as a bittern bumbles in the mire,
She whispered to the water, near the ground,
'Betray me not, O water, with thy sound!
I have told no one yet, but it appears
My husband has a pair of ass's ears!
Ah! My heart's well again, the secret's out!
I couldn't have kept it longer, I don't doubt.'
So, as you see, we women can't keep mum
For very long, but out the secrets come.
For what became of Midas, if you care
To turn up Ovid you will find it there.
    This knight that I am telling you about
Perceived at last he never would find out
What it could be that women loved the best.
Faint was the soul within his sorrowful breast
As home he went, he dared no longer stay;
His year was up and now it was the day.

As he rode home in a dejected mood,
Suddenly, at the margin of a wood,
He saw a dance upon the leafy floor
Of four and twenty ladies, nay, and more.
Eagerly he approached, in hope to learn
Some words of wisdom ere he should return;
But lo! Before he came to where they were,
Dancers and dance all vanished into air!
There wasn't a living creature to be seen
Save one old woman crouched upon the green.
A fouler-looking creature I suppose
Could scarcely be imagined. She arose
And said, 'Sir knight, there's no way on from here.
Tell me what you are looking for, my dear,
For peradventure that were best for you;
We old, old women know a thing or two.'
    'Dear Mother,' said the knight, 'alack the day!
I am as good as dead if I can't say
What thing it is that women most desire;
If you could tell me I would pay your hire.'
'Give me your hand,' she said, 'and swear to do
Whatever I shall next require of you
—If so to do should lie within your might—
And you shall know the answer before night.'
'Upon my honor,' he answered, 'I agree.'
'Then,' said the crone, 'I dare to guarantee
Your life is safe, I shall make good my claim.
Upon my life the queen will say the same.
Show me the very proudest of them all
In costly coverchief or jeweled caul
That dare say no to what I have to teach.
Let us go forward without further speech.'
And then she crooned her gospel in his ear
And told him to be glad and not to fear.
    They came to court. This knight, in full array,
Stood forth and said, 'O Queen, I've kept my day
And kept my word and have my answer ready.'
    There sat the noble matrons and the heady
Young girls, and widows too, that have the grace
Of wisdom, all assembled in that place,
And there the queen herself was throned to hear
And judge his answer. Then the knight drew near
And silence was commanded through the hall.
    The queen then bade the knight to tell them all
What thing it was that women wanted most.
He stood not silent like a beast or post,

But gave his answer with the ringing word
Of a man's voice and the assembly heard:
    'My liege and lady, in general,' said he,
'Women desire the self-same sovereignty
On husbands as they have on those that love them,
And would be set in mastery above them;
That is your greatest wish. Now spare or kill
Me as you please, I stand here at your will.'
    In all the court not one that shook her head
Or contradicted what the knight had said;
Maid, wife and widow cried, 'He's saved his life!'
    And on the word up started the old wife,
The one the knight saw sitting on the green,
And cried, 'Your mercy, sovereign lady queen!
Before the court disperses, do me right!
'Twas I who taught this answer to the knight,
For which he swore, and pledged his honor to it,
That the first thing I asked of him he'd do it,
So far as it should lie within his might.
Before this court I ask you then, sir knight,
To keep your word and take me for your wife;
For well you know that I have saved your life.
If this be false, deny it on your sword!'
    'Alas!' he said, 'Old lady, by the Lord
I know indeed that such was my behest,
But for God's love think of a new request,
Take all my goods, but leave my body free.'
'A curse on us,' she said, 'if I agree!
I may be foul, I may be poor and old,
Yet will not choose to be, for all the gold
That's bedded in the earth or lies above,
Less than your wife, nay, than your very love!'
    'My love?' said he. 'By Heaven, my damnation!
Alas that any of my race and station
Should ever make so foul a misalliance!'
Yet in the end his pleading and defiance
All went for nothing, he was forced to wed.
He takes his ancient wife and goes to bed.
    Now peradventure some may well suspect
A lack of care in me since I neglect
To tell of the rejoicings and display
Made at the feast upon their wedding-day.
I have but a short answer to let fall;
I say there was no joy or feast at all,
Nothing but heaviness of heart and sorrow.
He married her in private on the morrow

And all day long stayed hidden like an owl,
It was such torture that his wife looked foul.

    Great was the anguish churning in his head
When he and she were piloted to bed;
He wallowed back and forth in desperate style.
His wife lay still and wore a quiet smile;
At last she said, 'Dear husband, bless my soul!
Is this how knights treat wives upon the whole?
Are these the laws of good King Arthur's house?
Is all his knighthood so contemptuous?
I am your own beloved and your wife,
And I am she, indeed, that saved your life;
And certainly I never did you wrong.
Then why, this first of nights, so sad a song?
You're carrying on as if you were half-witted!
Say, for God's love, what sin have I committed?
I'll put things right if you will tell me how.'

    'Put right?' he cried. 'That never can be now!
Nothing can ever be put right again!
You're old, and so abominably plain,
So poor to start with, so low-bred to follow;
It's little wonder if I twist and wallow!
God, that my heart would burst within my breast!'

    'Is that,' said she, 'the cause of your unrest?'

    'Yes, certainly,' he said, 'and can you wonder?'

    'I could set right what you suppose a blunder,
That's if I cared to, in a day or two,
If I were shown more courtesy by you.
Just now,' she said, 'you spoke of gentle birth,
Such as descends from ancient wealth and worth.
If that's the claim you make for gentlemen
Such arrogance is hardly worth a hen.
Whoever loves to work for virtuous ends,
Public and private, and who most intends
To do what deeds of gentleness he can,
Take him to be the greatest gentleman.
Christ wills we take our gentleness from Him,
Not from a wealth of ancestry long dim,
Though they bequeath their whole establishment
By which we claim to be of high descent.
Our fathers cannot make us a bequest
Of all those virtues that became them best
And earned for them the name of gentleman,
But bade us follow them as best we can.

    'Thus the wise poet of the Florentines,
Dante by name, has written in these lines,

For such is the opinion Dante launches:
"Seldom arises by these slender branches
Prowess of men, for it is God, no less,
Wills us to claim of Him our gentleness."
For of our parents nothing can we claim
Save temporal things, and these may hurt and maim.

   'But everyone knows this as well as I;
For if gentility were implanted by
The natural course of lineage down the line,
Public or not, it could not cease to shine
In doing the fair work of gentle deed.
No vice or villainy could then bear seed.

   'Take fire and carry it to the darkest house
Between this kingdom and the Caucasus,
And shut the doors on it and leave it there.
It will burn on, and it will burn as fair
As if ten thousand men were there to see,
For fire will keep its nature and degree,
I can assure you, sir, until it dies.

   'But gentleness, as you will recognize,
Is not annexed in nature to possessions,
Men fail in living up to their professions;
But fire never ceases to be fire.
God knows you'll often find, if you inquire,
Some lording full of villainy and shame.
If you would be esteemed for the mere name
Of having been by birth a gentleman
And stemming from some virtuous, noble clan,
And do not live yourself by gentle deed
Or take your fathers' noble code and creed,
You are no gentleman, though duke or earl.
Vice and bad manners are what make a churl.

   'Gentility is only the renown
For bounty that your fathers handed down,
Quite foreign to your person, not your own;
Gentility must come from God alone.
That we are gentle comes to us by grace
And by no means is it bequeathed with place.

   'Reflect how noble (says Valerius)
Was Tullius surnamed Hostilius,
Who rose from poverty to nobleness.
And read Boethius, Seneca no less,
Thus they express themselves and are agreed:
"Gentle is he that does a gentle deed."
And therefore, my dear husband, I conclude
That even if my ancestors were rude,

Yet God on high – and so I hope He will –
Can grant me grace to live in virtue still,
A gentlewoman only when beginning
To live in virtue and to shrink from sinning.

'As for my poverty which you reprove,
Almighty God Himself in whom we move,
Believe and have our being, chose a life
Of poverty, and every man or wife
And every child can see our Heavenly King
Would never stoop to choose a shameful thing.
No shame in poverty if the heart is gay,
As Seneca and all the learned say.
He who accepts his poverty unhurt
I'd say is rich although he lacked a shirt.
But truly poor are they who whine and fret
And covet what they cannot hope to get.
And he that having nothing covets not
Is rich, though you may think he is a sot.

'True poverty can find a song to sing.
Juvenal says a pleasant little thing:
"The poor can dance and sing in the relief
Of having nothing that will tempt a thief."
Though it be hateful, poverty is good,
A great incentive to a livelihood,
And a great help to our capacity
For wisdom, if accepted patiently.
Poverty is, though wanting in estate,
A kind of wealth that none calumniate.
Poverty often, when the heart is lowly,
Brings one to God and teaches what is holy,
Gives knowledge of oneself and even lends
A glass by which to see one's truest friends.
And since it's no offense, let me be plain;
Do not rebuke my poverty again.

'Lastly you taxed me, sir, with being old.
Yet even if you never had been told
By ancient books, you gentlemen engage
Yourselves in honor to respect old age.
To call an old man "father" shows good breeding,
And this could be supported from my reading.

'You say I'm old and fouler than a fen.
You need not fear to be a cuckold, then.
Filth and old age, I'm sure you will agree,
Are powerful wardens upon chastity.
Nevertheless, well knowing your delights,
I shall fulfill your worldly appetites.

'You have two choices; which one will you try?
To have me old and ugly till I die,
But still a loyal, true and humble wife
That never will displease you all her life,
Or would you rather I were young and pretty
And take your chance what happens in a city
Where friends will visit you because of me,
Yes, and in other places too, maybe.
Which would you have? The choice is all your own.'
　　The knight thought long, and with a piteous groan
At last he said with all the care in life,
'My lady and my love, my dearest wife,
I leave the matter to your wise decision.
You make the choice yourself, for the provision
Of what may be agreeable and rich
In honor to us both, I don't care which;
Whatever pleases you suffices me.'
　　'And have I won the mastery?' said she,
'Since I'm to choose and rule as I think fit?'
'Certainly, wife,' he answered her, 'that's it.'
'Kiss me,' she cried. 'No quarrels! On my oath
And word of honor you shall find me both,
That is both fair and faithful as a wife;
May I go howling mad and take my life
Unless I prove to be as good and true
As ever wife was since the world was new!
And if to-morrow when the sun's above
I seem less fair than any lady-love,
Than any queen or empress east or west,
Do with my life and death as you think best.
Cast up the curtain, husband. Look at me!'
　　And when indeed the knight had looked to see,
Lo, she was young and lovely, rich in charms.
In ecstasy he caught her in his arms,
His heart went bathing in a bath of blisses
And melted in a hundred thousand kisses,
And she responded in the fullest measure
With all that could delight or give him pleasure.
　　So they lived ever after to the end
In perfect bliss; and may Christ Jesus send
Us husbands meek and young and fresh in bed,
And grace to overbid them when we wed.
And – Jesu hear my prayer! – cut short the lives
Of those who won't be governed by their wives;
And all old, angry niggards of their pence,
God send them soon a very pestilence!

　　　　　　　　　　　　　　　　　　　　　　(c. 1390)

*Andrew Marvell*

# To His Coy Mistress

Had we but world enough, and time,
This coyness, lady, were no crime.
We would sit down, and think which way
To walk, and pass our long love's day.
Thou by the Indian Ganges' side
Shouldst rubies find; I by the tide
Of Humber would complain. I would
Love you ten years before the Flood,
And you should, if you please, refuse
Till the conversion of the Jews.
My vegetable love should grow
Vaster than empires, and more slow;
An hundred years should go to praise
Thine eyes and on thy forehead gaze,
Two hundred to adore each breast,
But thirty thousand to the rest:
An age at least to every part,
And the last age should show your heart.
For, lady, you deserve this state,
Nor would I love at lower rate.

    But at my back I always hear
Time's wingèd chariot hurrying near;
And yonder all before us lie
Deserts of vast eternity.
Thy beauty shall no more be found,
Nor in thy marble vault shall sound
My echoing song; then worms shall try
That long preserved virginity,
And your quaint honor turn to dust,
And into ashes all my lust.
The grave's a fine and private place,
But none, I think, do there embrace.

    Now, therefore, while the youthful hue
Sits on thy skin like morning dew,
And while thy willing soul transpires
At every pore with instant fires,
Now let us sport us while we may,
And now, like am'rous birds of prey,
Rather at once our time devour
Than languish in his slow-chapped power.

471

Let us roll all our strength and all
Our sweetness up into one ball,
And tear our pleasures with rough strife
Thorough the iron gates of life.
Thus, though we cannot make our sun
Stand still, yet we will make him run.

                                                    (1681)

*Robert Browning*

# My Last Duchess

### Ferrara

That 's my last Duchess painted on the wall,
Looking as if she were alive. I call
That piece a wonder, now: Frà Pandolf's hands
Worked busily a day, and there she stands.
Will 't please you sit and look at her? I said
"Frà Pandolf" by design, for never read
Strangers like you that pictured countenance,
The depth and passion of its earnest glance,
But to myself they turned (since none puts by
The curtain I have drawn for you, but I)
And seemed as they would ask me, if they durst,
How such a glance came there; so, not the first
Are you to turn and ask thus. Sir, 't was not
Her husband's presence only, called that spot
Of joy into the Duchess' cheek: perhaps
Frà Pandolf chanced to say "Her mantle laps
Over my lady's wrist too much," or "Paint
Must never hope to reproduce the faint
Half-flush that dies along her throat"; such stuff
Was courtesy, she thought, and cause enough
For calling up that spot of joy. She had
A heart—how shall I say?—too soon made glad,
Too easily impressed; she liked whate'er
She looked on, and her looks went everywhere.
Sir, 't was all one! My favour at her breast,
The dropping of the daylight in the West,

The bough of cherries some officious fool
Broke in the orchard for her, the white mule
She rode with round the terrace—all and each
Would draw from her alike the approving speech,
Or blush, at least. She thanked men,—good! but thanked
Somehow—I know not how—as if she ranked
My gift of a nine-hundred-years-old name
With anybody's gift. Who 'd stoop to blame
This sort of trifling? Even had you skill
In speech—(which I have not)—to make your will
Quite clear to such an one, and say, "Just this
Or that in you disgusts me; here you miss,
Or there exceed the mark"—and if she let
Herself be lessoned so, nor plainly set
Her wits to yours, forsooth, and made excuse,
—E'en then would be some stooping; and I choose
Never to stoop. Oh, sir, she smiled, no doubt,
Whene'er I passed her; but who passed without
Much the same smile? This grew; I gave commands;
Then all smiles stopped together. There she stands
As if alive. Will 't please you rise? We'll meet
The company below, then. I repeat,
The Count your master's known munificence
Is ample warrant that no just pretence
Of mine for dowry will be disallowed;
Though his fair daughter's self, as I avowed
At starting, is my object. Nay, we'll go
Together down, sir! Notice Neptune, though,
Taming a sea-horse, thought a rarity,
Which Claus of Innsbruck cast in bronze for me!

(1842)

## Alfred, Lord Tennyson

# Locksley Hall

Comrades, leave me here a little, while as yet 'tis early morn:
Leave me here, and when you want me, sound upon the bugle-horn.

'Tis the place, and all around it, as of old, the curlews call,
Dreary gleams about the moorland flying over Locksley Hall;

Locksley Hall, that in the distance overlooks the sandy tracts,
And the hollow ocean-ridges roaring into cataracts.

Many a night from yonder ivied casement, ere I went to rest,
Did I look on great Orion sloping slowly to the West.

Many a night I saw the Pleiads, rising thro' the mellow shade,
Glitter like a swarm of fire-flies tangled in a silver braid.

Here about the beach I wander'd, nourishing a youth sublime
With the fairy tales of science, and the long result of Time;

When the centuries behind me like a fruitful land reposed;
When I clung to all the present for the promise that it closed:

When I dipt into the future far as human eye could see;
Saw the Vision of the world, and all the wonder that would be.—

In the Spring a fuller crimson comes upon the robin's breast;
In the Spring the wanton lapwing gets himself another crest;

In the Spring a livelier iris changes on the burnish'd dove;
In the Spring a young man's fancy lightly turns to thoughts of love.

Then her cheek was pale and thinner than should be for one so young,
And her eyes on all my motions with a mute observance hung.

And I said, 'My cousin Amy, speak, and speak the truth to me,
Trust me, cousin, all the current of my being sets to thee.'

On her pallid cheek and forehead came a colour and a light,
As I have seen the rosy red flushing in the northern night.

And she turn'd—her bosom shaken with a sudden storm of sighs—
All the spirit deeply dawning in the dark of hazel eyes—

Saying, 'I have hid my feelings, fearing they should do me wrong;'
Saying, 'Dost thou love me, cousin?' weeping, 'I have loved thee long.'

Love took up the glass of Time, and turn'd it in his glowing hands;
Every moment, lightly shaken, ran itself in golden sands.

Love took up the harp of Life, and smote on all the chords with might;
Smote the chord of Self, that, trembling, pass'd in music out of sight.

Many a morning on the moorland did we hear the copses ring,
And her whisper throng'd my pulses with the fulness of the Spring.

Many an evening by the waters did we watch the stately ships,
And our spirits rush'd together at the touching of the lips.

O my cousin, shallow-hearted! O my Amy, mine no more!
O the dreary, dreary moorland! O the barren, barren shore!

Falser than all fancy fathoms, falser than all songs have sung,
Puppet to a father's threat, and servile to a shrewish tongue!

Is it well to wish thee happy? — having known me — to decline
On a range of lower feelings and a narrower heart than mine!

Yet it shall be: thou shalt lower to his level day by day,
What is fine within thee growing coarse to sympathise with clay.

As the husband is, the wife is: thou art mated with a clown,
And the grossness of his nature will have weight to drag thee down.

He will hold thee, when his passion shall have spent its novel force,
Something better than his dog, a little dearer than his horse.

What is this? his eyes are heavy: think not they are glazed with
    wine.
Go to him: it is thy duty: kiss him: take his hand in thine.

It may be my lord is weary, that his brain is overwrought:
Soothe him with thy finer fancies, touch him with thy lighter
    thought.

He will answer to the purpose, easy things to understand —
Better thou wert dead before me, tho' I slew thee with my hand!

Better thou and I were lying, hidden from the heart's disgrace,
Roll'd in one another's arms, and silent in a last embrace.

Cursed be the social wants that sin against the strength of youth!
Cursed by the social lies that warp us from the living truth!

Cursed be the sickly forms that err from honest Nature's rule!
Cursed be the gold that gilds the straiten'd forehead of the fool!

Well — 'tis well that I should bluster! — Hadst thou less unworthy
    proved —
Would to God — for I had loved thee more than ever wife was loved.

Am I mad, that I should cherish that which bears but bitter fruit?
I will pluck it from my bosom, tho' my heart be at the root.

Never, tho' my mortal summers to such length of years should come
As the many-winter'd crow that leads the clanging rookery home.

Where is comfort? in division of the records of the mind?
Can I part her from herself, and love her, as I knew her, kind?

I remember one that perish'd: sweetly did she speak and move:
Such a one do I remember, whom to look at was to love.

Can I think of her as dead, and love her for the love she bore?
No—she never loved me truly: love is love for evermore.

Comfort? comfort scorn'd of devils! this is truth the poet sings,
That a sorrow's crown of sorrow is remembering happier things.

Drug thy memories, lest thou learn it, lest thy heart be put to proof,
In the dead unhappy night, and when the rain is on the roof.

Like a dog, he hunts in dreams, and thou art staring at the wall,
Where the dying night-lamp flickers, and the shadows rise and fall.

Then a hand shall pass before thee, pointing to his drunken sleep,
To thy widow'd marriage-pillows, to the tears that thou wilt weep.

Thou shalt hear the 'Never, never,' whisper'd by the phantom
      years,
And a song from out the distance in the ringing of thine ears;

And an eye shall vex thee, looking ancient kindness on thy pain.
Turn thee, turn thee on thy pillow: get thee to thy rest again.

Nay, but Nature brings thee solace; for a tender voice will cry.
'Tis a purer life than thine; a lip to drain thy trouble dry.

Baby lips will laugh me down: my latest rival brings thee rest.
Baby fingers, waxen touches, press me from the mother's breast.

O, the child too clothes the father with a dearness not his due.
Half is thine and half is his: it will be worthy of the two.

O, I see thee old and formal, fitted to thy petty part,
With a little hoard of maxims preaching down a daughter's heart.

'They were dangerous guides the feelings—she herself was not ex-
      empt—
Truly, she herself had suffer'd'—Perish in thy self-contempt!

Overlive it—lower yet—be happy! wherefore should I care?
I myself must mix with action, lest I wither by despair.

What is that which I should turn to, lighting upon days like these?
Every door is barr'd with gold, and opens but to golden keys.

Every gate is throng'd with suitors, all the markets overflow.
I have but an angry fancy: what is that which I should do?

I had been content to perish, falling on the foeman's ground,
When the ranks are roll'd in vapour, and the winds are laid with
    sound.

But the jingling of the guinea helps the hurt that Honour feels,
And the nations do but murmur, snarling at each other's heels.

Can I but relive in sadness? I will turn that earlier page.
Hide me from my deep emotion, O thou wondrous Mother-Age!

Make me feel the wild pulsation that I felt before the strife,
When I heard my days before me, and the tumult of my life;

Yearning for the large excitement that the coming years would yield
Eager-hearted as a boy when first he leaves his father's field,

And at night along the dusky highway near and nearer drawn,
Sees in heaven the light of London flaring like a dreary dawn;

And his spirit leaps within him to be gone before him then,
Underneath the light he looks at, in among the throngs of men:

Men, my brothers, men the workers, ever reaping something new:
That which they have done but earnest of the things that they
    shall do:

For I dipt into the future, far as human eye could see,
Saw the Vision of the world, and all the wonder that would be;

Saw the heavens fill with commerce, argosies of magic sails,
Pilots of the purple twilight, dropping down with costly bales;

Heard the heavens fill with shouting, and there rain'd a ghastly dew
From the nations' airy navies grappling in the central blue;

Far along the world-wide whisper of the south-wind rushing warm,
With the standards of the peoples plunging thro' the thunder-storm;

Till the war-drum throbb'd no longer, and the battle-flags were furl'd
In the Parliament of man, the Federation of the world.

There the common sense of most shall hold a fretful realm in awe,
And the kindly earth shall slumber, lapt in universal law.

So I triumph'd ere my passion sweeping thro' me left me dry,
Left me with the palsied heart, and left me with the jaundiced eye;

Eye, to which all order festers, all things here are out of joint:
Science moves, but slowly slowly, creeping on from point to point:

Slowly comes a hungry people, as a lion creeping nigher,
Glares at one that nods and winks behind a slowly-dying fire.

Yet I doubt not thro' the ages one increasing purpose runs,
And the thoughts of men are widen'd with the process of the suns.

What is that to him that reaps not harvest of his youthful joys,
Tho' the deep heart of existence beat for ever like a boy's?

Knowledge comes, but wisdom lingers, and I linger on the shore,
And the individual withers, and the world is more and more.

Knowledge comes, but wisdom lingers, and he bears a laden breast,
Full of sad experience, moving toward the stillness of his rest.

Hark, my merry comrades call me, sounding on the bugle-horn,
They to whom my foolish passion were a target for their scorn:

Shall it not be scorn to me to harp on such a moulder'd string?
I am shamed thro' all my nature to have loved so slight a thing.

Weakness to be wroth with weakness! woman's pleasure, woman's
     pain—
Nature made them blinder motions bounded in a shallower brain:

Woman is the lesser man, and all thy passions, match'd with mine,
Are as moonlight unto sunlight, and as water unto wine—

Here at least, where nature sickens, nothing. Ah, for some retreat
Deep in yonder shining Orient, where my life began to beat;

Where in wild Mahratta-battle fell my father evil-starr'd;—
I was left a trampled orphan, and a selfish uncle's ward.

Or to burst all links of habit—there to wander far away,
On from island unto island at the gateways of the day.

Larger constellations burning, mellow moons and happy skies,
Breadths of tropic shade and palms in cluster, knots of Paradise.

Never comes the trader, never floats an European flag,
Slides the bird o'er lustrous woodland, swings the trailer from the crag;

Droops the heavy-blossom'd bower, hangs the heavy-fruited tree—
Summer isles of Eden lying in dark-purple spheres of sea.

There methinks would be enjoyment more than in this march of mind
In the steamship, in the railway, in the thoughts that shake mankind.

There the passions cramp'd no longer shall have scope and breathing
      space;
I will take some savage woman, she shall rear my dusky race.

Iron-jointed, supple-sinew'd, they shall dive, and they shall run,
Catch the wild goat by the hair, and hurl their lances in the sun;

Whistle back the parrot's call, and leap the rainbows of the brooks,
Not with blinded eyesight poring over miserable books—

Fool, again the dream, the fancy! but I *know* my words are wild,
But I count the gray barbarian lower than the Christian child.

I, to herd with narrow foreheads, vacant of our glorious gains,
Like a beast with lower pleasures, like a beast with lower pains!

Mated with a squalid savage—what to me were sun or clime?
I the heir of all the ages, in the foremost files of time—

I that rather held it better men should perish one by one,
Than that earth should stand at gaze like Joshua's moon in Ajalon!

Not in vain the distance beacons. Forward, forward let us range,
Let the great world spin for ever down the ringing grooves of change.

Thro' the shadow of the globe we sweep into the younger day:
Better fifty years of Europe than a cycle of Cathay.

Mother-Age (for mine I knew not) help me as when life begun:
Rift the hills, and roll the waters, flash the lightnings, weigh the Sun.

O, I see the crescent promise of my spirit hath not set.
Ancient founts of inspiration well thro' all my fancy yet.

Howsoever these things be, a long farewell to Locksley Hall!
Now for me the woods may wither, now for me the roof-tree fall.

Comes a vapour from the margin, blackening over heath and holt,
Cramming all the blast before it, in its breast a thunderbolt.

Let it fall on Locksley Hall, with rain or hail, or fire or snow;
For the mighty wind arises, roaring seaward, and I go.

(1842)

## Locksley Hall Sixty Years After

Late, my grandson! half the morning have I paced these sandy tracts,
Watch'd again the hollow ridges roaring into cataracts,

Wander'd back to living boyhood while I heard the curlews call,
I myself so close on death, and death itself in Locksley Hall.

So — your happy suit was blasted — she the faultless, the divine;
And you liken — boyish babble — this boy-love of yours with mine.

I myself have often babbled doubtless of a foolish past;
Babble, babble; our old England may go down in babble at last.

'Curse him!' curse your fellow-victim? call him dotard in your rage?
Eyes that lured a doting boyhood well might fool a dotard's age.

Jilted for a wealthier! wealthier? yet perhaps she was not wise;
I remember how you kiss'd the miniature with those sweet eyes.

In the hall there hangs a painting — Amy's arms about my neck —
Happy children in a sunbeam sitting on the ribs of wreck.

In my life there was a picture, she that clasp'd my neck had flown;
I was left within the shadow sitting on the wreck alone.

Yours has been a slighter ailment, will you sicken for her sake?
You, not you! your modern amourist is of easier, earthlier make.

Amy loved me, Amy fail'd me, Amy was a timid child;
But your Judith—but your worldling—*she* had never driven me wild.

She that holds the diamond necklace dearer than the golden ring,
She that finds a winter sunset fairer than a morn of Spring.

She that in her heart is brooding on his briefer lease of life,
While she vows 'till death shall part us,' she the would-be-widow wife.

She the worldling born of worldlings—father, mother—be content,
Ev'n the homely farm can teach us there is something in descent.

Yonder in that chapel, slowly sinking now into the ground,
Lies the warrior, my forefather, with his feet upon the hound.

Cross'd! for once he sail'd the sea to crush the Moslem in his pride;
Dead the warrior, dead his glory, dead the cause in which he died.

Yet how often I and Amy in the mouldering aisle have stood,
Gazing for one pensive moment on that founder of our blood.

There again I stood to-day, and where of old we knelt in prayer,
Close beneath the casement crimson with the shield of Locksley—there,

All in white Italian marble, looking still as if she smiled,
Lies my Amy dead in child-birth, dead the mother, dead the child.

Dead—and sixty years ago, and dead her aged husband now—
I this old white-headed dreamer stoopt and kiss'd her marble brow.

Gone the fires of youth, the follies, furies, curses, passionate tears,
Gone like fires and floods and earthquakes of the planet's dawning
    years.

Fires that shook me once, but now to silent ashes fall'n away.
Cold upon the dead volcano sleeps the gleam of dying day.

Gone the tyrant of my youth, and mute below the chancel stones,
All his virtues—I forgive them—black in white above his bones.

Gone the comrades of my bivouac, some in fight against the foe,
Some thro' age and slow diseases, gone as all on earth will go.

Gone with whom for forty years my life in golden sequence ran,
She with all the charm of woman, she with all the breadth of man,

Strong in will and rich in wisdom, Edith, yet so lowly-sweet,
Woman to her inmost heart, and woman to her tender feet,

Very woman of very woman, nurse of ailing body and mind,
She that link'd again the broken chain that bound me to my kind.

Here to-day was Amy with me, while I wander'd down the coast,
Near us Edith's holy shadow, smiling at the slighter ghost.

Gone our sailor son thy father, Leonard early lost at sea;
Thou alone, my boy, of Amy's kin and mine art left to me.

Gone thy tender-natured mother, wearying to be left alone,
Pining for the stronger heart that once had beat beside her own.

Truth, for Truth is Truth, he worshipt, being true as he was brave;
Good, for Good is Good, he follow'd, yet he look'd beyond the grave,

Wiser there than you, that crowning barren Death as lord of all,
Deem this over-tragic drama's closing curtain is the pall!

Beautiful was death in him, who saw the death, but kept the deck,
Saying women and their babes, and sinking with the sinking
     wreck,

Gone for ever! Ever? no—for since our dying race began,
Ever, ever, and for ever was the leading light of man.

Those that in barbarian burials kill'd the slave, and slew the wife
Felt within themselves the sacred passion of the second life.

Indian warriors dream of ampler hunting grounds beyond the night;
Ev'n the black Australian dying hopes he shall return, a white.

Truth for truth, and good for good! The Good, the True, the Pure, the
     Just
Take the charm 'For ever' from them, and they crumble into dust.

Gone the cry of 'Forward, Forward,' lost within a growing gloom;
Lost, or only heard in silence from the silence of a tomb.

Half the marvels of my morning, triumphs over time and space,
Staled by frequence, shrunk by usage into commonest commonplace!

'Forward' rang the voices then, and of the many mine was one.
Let us hush this cry of 'Forward' till ten thousand years have gone.

Far among the vanish'd races, old Assyrian kings would flay
Captives whom they caught in battle—iron-hearted victors they.

Ages after, while in Asia, he that led the wild Moguls,
Timur built his ghastly tower of eighty thousand human skulls,

Then, and here in Edward's time, an age of noblest English names,
Christian conquerors took and flung the conquer'd Christian into flames.

Love your enemy, bless your haters, said the Greatest of the great;
Christian love among the Churches look'd the twin of heathen hate.

From the golden alms of Blessing man had coin'd himself a curse:
Rome of Cæsar, Rome of Peter, which was crueller? which was worse?

France had shown a light to all men, preach'd a Gospel, all men's good;
Celtic Demos rose a Demon, shriek'd and slaked the light with blood.

Hope was ever on her mountain, watching till the day begun—
Crown'd with sunlight—over darkness—from the still unrisen sun.

Have we grown at last beyond the passions of the primal clan?
'Kill your enemy, for you hate him,' still, 'your enemy' was a man.

Have we sunk below them? peasants maim the helpless horse, and
    drive
Innocent cattle under thatch, and burn the kindlier brutes alive.

Brutes, the brutes are not your wrongers—burnt at midnight, found at
    morn,
Twisted hard in mortal agony with their offspring, born-unborn,

Clinging to the silent mother! Are we devils? are we men?
Sweet St. Francis of Assisi, would that he were here again,

He that in his Catholic wholeness used to call the very flowers
Sisters, brothers—and the beasts—whose pains are hardly less than
    ours!

Chaos, Cosmos! Cosmos, Chaos! who can tell how all will end?
Read the wide world's annals, you, and take their wisdom for your
    friend.

Hopes the best, but hold the Present fatal daughter of the Past,
Shape your heart to front the hour, but dream not that the hour will
    last.

Ay, if dynamite and revolver leave you courage to be wise:
When was age so cramm'd with menace? madness? written, spoken
    lies?

Envy wears the mask of Love, and, laughing sober fact to scorn,
Cries to Weakest as to Strongest, 'Ye are equals, equal-born.'

Equal-born? O yes, if yonder hill be level with the flat.
Charm us, Orator, till the Lion look no larger than the Cat,

Till the Cat thro' that mirage of overheated language loom
Larger than the Lion,—Demos end in working its own doom.

Russia bursts our Indian barrier, shall we fight her? shall we yield?
Pause! before you sound the trumpet, hear the voices from the field.

Those three hundred millions under one Imperial sceptre now,
Shall we hold them? shall we loose them? take the suffrage of the plow.

Nay, but these would feel and follow Truth if only you and you,
Rivals of realm-ruining party, when you speak were wholly true.

Plowmen, Shepherds, have I found, and more than once, and still could
    find,
Sons of God, and kings of men in utter nobleness of mind,

Truthful, trustful, looking upward to the practised hustings-liar;
So the Higher wields the Lower, while the Lower is the Higher.

Here and there a cotter's babe is royal-born by right divine;
Here and there my lord is lower than his oxen or his swine.

Chaos, Cosmos! Cosmos, Chaos! once again the sickening game;
Freedom, free to slay herself, and dying while they shout her name.

Step by step we gain'd a freedom known to Europe, known to all;
Step by step we rose to greatness,—thro' the tonguesters we may fall.

You that woo the Voices—tell them 'old experience is a fool,'
Teach your flatter'd kings that only those who cannot read can rule.

Pluck the mighty from their seat, but set no meek ones in their place;
Pillory Wisdom in your markets, pelt your offal at her face.

Tumble Nature heel o'er head, and, yelling with the yelling street,
Set the feet above the brain and swear the brain is in the feet.

Bring the old dark ages back without the faith, without the hope,
Break the State, the Church, the Throne, and roll their ruins down the
    slope.

Authors—essayist, atheist, novelist, realist, rhymester, play your part,
Paint the mortal shame of nature with the living hues of Art.

Rip your brothers' vices open, strip your own foul passions bare;
Down with Reticence, down with Reverence—forward—naked—let
    them stare.

Feed the budding rose of boyhood with the drainage of your sewer;
Send the drain into the fountain, lest the stream should issue pure.

Set the maiden fancies wallowing in the troughs of Zolaism,—
Forward, forward, ay and backward, downward too into the abysm.

Do your best to charm the worst, to lower the rising race of men;
Have we risen from out the beast, then back into the beast again?

Only 'dust to dust' for me that sicken at your lawless din,
Dust in wholesome old-world dust before the newer world begin.

Heated am I? you—you wonder—well, it scarce becomes mine age—
Patience! let the dying actor mouth his last upon the stage.

Cries of unprogressive dotage ere the dotard fall asleep?
Noises of a current narrowing, not the music of a deep?

Ay, for doubtless I am old, and think gray thoughts, for I am gray:
After all the stormy changes shall we find a changeless May?

After madness, after massacre, Jacobinism and Jacquerie,
Some diviner force to guide us thro' the days I shall not see?

When the schemes and all the systems, Kingdoms and Republics fall,
Something kindlier, higher, holier—all for each and each for all?

All the full-brain, half-brain races, led by Justice, Love, and Truth;
All the millions one at length with all the visions of my youth?

All diseases quench'd by Science, no man halt, or deaf or blind;
Stronger ever born of weaker, lustier body, larger mind?

Earth at last a warless world, a single race, a single tongue—
I have seen her far away—for is not Earth as yet so young?—

Every tiger madness muzzled, every serpent passion kill'd,
Every grim ravine a garden, every blazing desert till'd,

Robed in universal harvest up to either pole she smiles,
Universal ocean softly washing all her warless Isles.

Warless? when her tens are thousands, and her thousands millions, then—
All her harvest all too narrow—who can fancy warless men?

Warless? war will die out late then. Will it ever? late or soon?
Can it, till this outworn earth be dead as yon dead world the moon?

Dead the new astronomy calls her. . . . On this day and at this hour,
In the gap between the sandhills, whence you see the Locksley
     tower,

Here we met, our latest meeting—Amy—sixty years ago—
She and I—the moon was falling greenish thro' a rosy glow,

Just above the gateway tower, and even where you see her now—
Here we stood and claspt each other, swore the seeming-deathless
     vow. . . .

Dead, but how her living glory lights the hall, the dune, the grass!
Yet the moonlight is the sunlight, and the sun himself will pass.

Venus near her! smiling downward at this earthlier earth of ours,
Closer on the Sun, perhaps a world of never fading flowers.

Hesper, whom the poet call'd the Bringer home of all good things.
All good things may move in Hesper, perfect peoples, perfect kings.

Hesper—Venus—were we native to that splendour or in Mars,
We should see the Globe we groan in, fairest of their evening stars.

Could we dream of wars and carnage, craft and madness, lust and
     spite,
Roaring London, raving Paris, in that point of peaceful light?

Might we not in glancing heavenward on a star so silver-fair,
Yearn, and clasp the hands and murmur, 'Would to God that we were
     there'?

Forward, backward, backward, forward, in the immeasurable sea,
Sway'd by vaster ebbs and flows than can be known to you or me.

All the suns—are these but symbols of innumerable man,
Man or Mind that sees a shadow of the planner or the plan?

Is there evil but on earth? or pain in every peopled sphere?
Well be grateful for the sounding watchword 'Evolution' here.

Evolution ever climbing after some ideal good,
And Reversion ever dragging Evolution in the mud.

What are men that He should heed us? cried the king of sacred song;
Insects of an hour, that hourly work their brother insect wrong,

While the silent Heavens roll, and Suns along their fiery way,
All their planets whirling round them, flash a million miles a day.

Many an Æon moulded earth before her highest, man, was born,
Many an Æon too may pass when earth is manless and forlorn,

Earth so huge, and yet so bounded—pools of salt, and plots of land—
Shallow skin of green and azure—chains of mountain, grains of sand!

Only That which made us, meant us to be mightier by and by,
Set the sphere of all the boundless Heavens within the human eye,

Sent the shadow of Himself, the boundless, thro' the human soul;
Boundless inward, in the atom, boundless outward, in the Whole.

———————

Here is Locksley Hall, my grandson, here the lion-guarded gate.
Not to-night in Locksley Hall—to-morrow—you, you come so late.

Wreck'd—your train—or all but wreck'd? a shatter'd wheel? a vicious
    boy!
Good, this forward, you that preach it, is it well to wish you joy?

Is it well that while we range with Science, glorying in the Time,
City children soak and blacken soul and sense in city slime?

There among the glooming alleys Progress halts on palsied feet,
Crime and hunger cast our maidens by the thousand on the street.

There the Master scrimps his haggard sempstress of her daily bread,
There a single sordid attic holds the living and the dead.

There the smouldering fire of fever creeps across the rotted floor,
And the crowded couch of incest in the warrens of the poor.

Nay, your pardon, cry your 'forward,' yours are hope and youth, but I
Eighty winters leave the dog too lame to follow with the cry,

Lame and old, and past his time, and passing now into the night;
Yet I would the rising race were half as eager for the light.

Light the fading gleam of Even? light the glimmer of the dawn?
Aged eyes may take the growing glimmer for the gleam withdrawn.

Far away beyond her myriad coming changes earth will be
Something other than the wildest modern guess of you and me.

Earth may reach her earthly-worst, or if she gain her earthly-best,
Would she find her human offspring this ideal man at rest?

Forward then, but still remember how the course of Time will swerve,
Crook and turn upon itself in many a backward streaming curve.

Not the Hall to-night, my grandson! Death and Silence hold their own.
Leave the Master in the first dark hour of his last sleep alone.

Worthier soul was he than I am, sound and honest, rustic Squire,
Kindly landlord, boon companion—youthful jealousy is a liar.

Cast the poison from your bosom, oust the madness from your brain.
Let the trampled serpent show you that you have not lived in vain.

Youthful! youth and age are scholars yet but in the lower school,
Nor is he the wisest man who never proved himself a fool.

Yonder lies our young sea-village—Art and Grace are less and less:
Science grows and Beauty dwindles—roofs of slated hideousness!

There is one old Hostel left us where they swing the Locksley shield,
Till the peasant cow shall butt the 'Lion passant' from his field.

Poor old Heraldry, poor old History, poor old Poetry, passing hence,
In the common deluge drowning old political common-sense!

Poor old voice of eighty crying after voices that have fled!
All I loved are vanish'd voices, all my steps are on the dead.

All the world is ghost to me, and as the phantom disappears,
Forward far and far from here is all the hope of eighty years.

———————

In this Hostel – I remember – I repent it o'er his grave –
Like a clown – by chance he met me – I refused the hand he gave.

From that casement where the trailer mantles all the mouldering
    bricks –
I was then in early boyhood, Edith but a child of six –

While I shelter'd in this archway from a day of driving showers –
Peept the winsome face of Edith like a flower among the flowers.

Here to-night! the Hall to-morrow, when they toll the Chapel bell!
Shall I hear in one dark room a wailing, 'I have loved thee well.'

Then a peal that shakes the portal – one has come to claim his bride,
Her that shrank, and put me from her, shriek'd, and started from my
    side –

Silent echoes! You, my Leonard, use and not abuse your day,
Move among your people, know them, follow him who led the way,

Strove for sixty widow'd years to help his homelier brother men,
Served the poor, and built the cottage, raised the school, and drain'd the
    fen.

Hears he now the Voice that wrong'd him? who shall swear it cannot
    be?
Earth would never touch her worst, were one in fifty such as he.

Ere she gain her Heavenly-best, a God must mingle with the game:
Nay, there may be those about us whom we neither see nor name,

Felt within us as ourselves, the Powers of Good, the Powers of Ill,
Strowing balm, or shedding poison in the fountains of the Will.

Follow you the Star that lights a desert pathway, yours or mine.
Forward, till you see the highest Human Nature is divine.

Follow Light, and do the Right – for man can half-control his doom –
Till you find the deathless Angel seated in the vacant tomb.

Forward, let the stormy moment fly and mingle with the Past.
I that loathed, have come to love him. Love will conquer at the last.

Gone at eighty, mine own age, and I and you will bear the pall;
Then I leave thee Lord and Master, latest Lord of Locksley Hall.

                                    (1886)

*Alan Dugan*

# Love Song: I and Thou

Nothing is plumb, level or square:
    the studs are bowed, the joists
are shaky by nature, no piece fits
    any other piece without a gap
or pinch, and bent nails
    dance all over the surfacing
like maggots. By Christ
    I am no carpenter. I built
the roof for myself, the walls
    for myself, the floors
for myself, and got
    hung up in it myself. I
danced with a purple thumb
    at this house-warming, drunk
with my prime whiskey: rage.
    Oh I spat rage's nails
into the frame-up of my work:
    it held. It settled plumb,
level, solid, square and true
    for that great moment. Then
it screamed and went on through,
    skewing as wrong the other way.
God damned it. This is hell,
    but I planned it, I sawed it,
I nailed it, and I
    will live in it until it kills me.
I can nail my left palm
    to the left-hand cross-piece but
I can't do everything myself.
    I need a hand to nail the right,
a help, a love, a you, a wife.

                (1961)

# Portrait from the Infantry

He smelled bad and was red-eyed with the miseries
of being scared while sleepless when he said
this: "I want a private woman, peace and quiet,

and some green stuff in my pocket. Fuck
the rest." Pity the underwear and socks,
long burnt, of an accomplished murderer,
oh God, of germans and replacements, who
refused three stripes to keep his B.A.R.,
who fought, fought not to fight some days
like any good small businessman of war,
and dug more holes than an outside dog
to modify some Freudian's thesis: "No
man can stand three hundred days
of fear of mutilation and death." What he
theorized was a joke: "To keep a tight
ass-hole, dry socks and a you-deep hole
with you at all times." Afterwards,
met in a sports shirt with a round wife, he was
the clean slave of a daughter, a power brake
and beer. To me, he seemed diminished
in his dream, or else enlarged, who knows?,
by its accomplishment: personal life
wrung from mass issues in a bloody time
and lived out hiddenly. Aside from sound
baseball talk, his only interesting remark
was, in pointing to his wife's belly, "If
he comes out left foot first" (the way
you Forward March!), "I am going to stuff
him back up." "Isn't he awful?" she said.

(1961)

**Edward Field**

# A New Cycle

My father buying me the bicycle that time
Was an unusual thing for him to do.
He believed that a parent's duty meant the necessities:
Food, clothing, shelter, and music lessons.

I had hardly dared to ask him for the bike
And I didn't believe he really meant to buy me one
Until I saw him take out the money and hand it over—
Eight dollars secondhand, but newly painted, and good rubber.

And I couldn't thank him, a hug was out of the question with us,
So I just got up on it and rode a ways shakily
And then I made him ride it—
He didn't even know he was supposed to say it was a good bike.

I rode off on it into a new life, paper route, pocket money,
Dances in other towns where the girls found me attractive,
And sexual adventures that would have made my father's hair
Stand up in horror had he known.

Daddy I can thank you now for the bike you gave me
Which meant more to me than you knew, or could have stood to know.
I rode away to everywhere it could take me, until finally
It took me to this nowhere, this noplace I am now.

I just passed my thirty-fifth birthday,
The end of a seven-year cycle and the beginning of a new one,
And sure enough I woke up the first day quite empty,
Everything over, with nothing to do and no ideas for the future.

Daddy whom I now can hug and kiss
Who gives me money when I ask,
What shall I do with this life you gave me
That cannot be junked like a bicycle when it wears out?

Is it utterly ridiculous for a man thirty-five years old and graying
To sit in his father's lap and ask for a bike? Even if he needs one?
Whom shall he ask if not his father?
Daddy, darling daddy, please buy me a bicycle.

                                                        (1963)


**Harvey Cox**

# Sex and Secularization

No aspect of human life seethes with so many unexorcised demons as
does sex. No human activity is so hexed by superstition, so haunted by
residual tribal lore, and so harassed by socially induced fear. Within the
breast of urban-secular man, a toe-to-toe struggle still rages between
his savage and his bourgeois forebears. Like everything else, the im-

ages of sex which informed tribal and town society are expiring along with the eras in which they arose. The erosion of traditional values and the disappearance of accepted modes of behavior have left contemporary man free, but somewhat rudderless. Abhoring a vacuum, the mass media have rushed in to supply a new code and a new set of behavioral prototypes. They appeal to the unexorcised demons. Nowhere is the persistence of mythical and metalogical denizens more obvious than in sex, and the shamans of sales do their best to nourish them. Nowhere is the humanization of life more frustrated. Nowhere is a clear word of exorcism more needed.

How is the humanization of sex impeded? First it is thwarted by the parading of cultural-identity images for the sexually dispossessed, to make money. These images become the tyrant gods of the secular society, undercutting its liberation from religion and transforming it into a kind of neotribal culture. Second, the authentic secularization of sex is checkmated by an anxious clinging to the sexual standards of the town, an era so recent and yet so different from ours that simply to transplant its sexual ethos into our situation is to invite hypocrisy of the worst degree.

Let us look first at the spurious sexual models conjured up for our anxious society by the sorcerers of the mass media and the advertising guild. Like all pagan deities, these come in pairs—the god and his consort. For our purposes they are best symbolized by The Playboy and Miss America, the Adonis and Aphrodite of a leisure-consumer society which still seems unready to venture into full postreligious maturity and freedom. The Playboy and Miss America represent The Boy and The Girl. They incorporate a vision of life. They function as religious phenomena and should be exorcised and exposed.

## The Residue of Tribalism

Let us begin with Miss America. In the first century B.C., Lucretius wrote this description of the pageant of Cybele:

Adorned with emblem and crown . . . she is carried in awe-inspiring state. Tight-stretched tambourines and hollow cymbals thunder all round to the stroke of open hands, hollow pipes stir with Phrygian strain. . . . She rides in procession through great cities and mutely enriches mortals with a blessing not expressed in words. They strew all her path with brass and silver, presenting her with bounteous alms, and scatter over her a snow-shower of roses.

Now compare this with the annual twentieth-century Miss America pageant in Atlantic City, New Jersey. Spotlights probe the dimness like votive tapers, banks of flowers exude their varied aromas, the orchestra blends feminine strings and regal trumpets. There is a hushed moment of tortured suspense, a drumroll, then the climax—a young woman with carefully prescribed anatomical proportions and exemplary "personality" parades serenely with scepter and crown to her throne. At TV sets across the nation throats tighten and eyes moisten. "There she goes, Miss America—" sings the crooner. "There she goes, your ideal." A new queen in America's emerging cult of The Girl has been crowned.

Is it merely illusory or anachronistic to discern in the multiplying pageants of the Miss America, Miss Universe, Miss College Queen type a residuum of the cults of the pre-Christian fertility goddesses? Perhaps, but students of the history of religions have become less prone in recent years to dismiss the possibility that the cultural behavior of modern man may be significantly illuminated by studying it in the perspective of the mythologies of bygone ages. After all, did not Freud initiate a revolution in social science by utilizing the venerable myth of Oedipus to help make sense out of the strange behavior of his Viennese contemporaries? Contemporary man carries with him, like his appendix and his fingernails, vestiges of his tribal and pagan past.

In light of this fertile combination of insights from modern social science and the history of religions, it is no longer possible to see in the Miss America pageant merely an overpublicized prank foisted on us by the advertising industry. It certainly is this, but it is also much more. It represents the mass cultic celebration, complete with a rich variety of ancient ritual embellishments, of the growing place of The Girl in the collective soul of America.

This young woman—though she is no doubt totally ignorant of the fact—symbolizes something beyond herself. She symbolizes The Girl, the primal image, the one behind the many. Just as the Virgin appears in many guises—as our Lady of Lourdes or of Fatima or of Guadalupe— but is always recognizably the Virgin, so with The Girl.

The Girl is also the omnipresent icon of consumer society. Selling beer, she is folksy and jolly. Selling gems, she is chic and distant. But behind her various theophanies she remains recognizably The Girl. In Miss America's glowingly healthy smile, her openly sexual but officially virginal figure, and in the name-brand gadgets around her, she personifies the stunted aspirations and ambivalent fears of her culture. "There she goes, your ideal."

Miss America stands in a long line of queens going back to Isis, Ceres, and Aphrodite. Everything from the elaborate sexual taboos surrounding her person to the symbolic gifts at her coronation hints at her ancient ancestry. But the real proof comes when we find that the function served by The Girl in our culture is just as much a "religious" one as that served by Cybele in hers. The functions are identical—to provide a secure personal "identity" for initiates and to sanctify a particular value structure.

Let us look first at the way in which The Girl confers a kind of identity on her initiates. Simone de Beauvoir says in *The Second Sex* that "no one is *born* a woman." One is merely born a female, and *"becomes a woman"* according to the models and meanings provided by the civilization. During the classical Christian centuries, it might be argued, the Virgin Mary served in part as this model. With the Reformation and especially with the Puritans, the place of Mary within the symbol system of the Protestant countries was reduced or eliminated. There are those who claim that this excision constituted an excess of zeal that greatly impoverished Western culture, an impoverishment from which it has never recovered. Some would even claim that the alleged failure of American novelists to produce a single great heroine (we have no Phaedra, no Anna Karenina) stems from this self-imposed lack of a central feminine ideal.

Without entering into this fascinating discussion, we can certainly be sure that, even within modern American Roman Catholicism, the Virgin Mary provides an identity image for few American girls. Where then do they look for the "model" Simone de Beauvoir convincingly contends they need? For most, the prototype of feminity seen in their mothers, their friends, and in the multitudinous images to which they are exposed on the mass media is what we have called The Girl.

In his significant monograph *Identity and the Life Cycle*, Erik Erikson reminds us that the child's identity is not modeled simply on the parent but on the parent's "super-ego." Thus in seeking to forge her own identity the young girl is led beyond her mother to her mother's ideal image, and it is here that what Freud called "the ideologies of the superego . . . the traditions of the race and the people" become formative. It is here also that The Girl functions, conferring identity on those for whom she is—perhaps never completely consciously—the tangible incarnation of womanhood.

To describe the mechanics of this complex psychological process by which the fledgling American girl participates in the life of The Girl and thus attains a woman's identity would require a thorough description of American adolescence. There is little doubt, however, that such an analysis would reveal certain striking parallels to the "savage" practices by which initiates in the mystery cults shared in the magical life of their god.

For those inured to the process, the tortuous nightly fetish by which the young American female pulls her hair into tight bunches secured by metal clips may bear little resemblance to the incisions made on their arms by certain African tribesmen to make them resemble their totem, the tiger. But to an anthropologist comparing two ways of attempting to resemble the holy one, the only difference might appear to be that with the Africans the torture is over after initiation, while with the American it has to be repeated every night, a luxury only a culture with abundant leisure can afford.

In turning now to an examination of the second function of The Girl—supporting and portraying a value system—a comparison with the role of the Virgin in the twelfth and thirteenth centuries may be helpful. Just as the Virgin exhibited and sustained the ideals of the age that fashioned Chartres Cathedral, as Henry Adams saw, so The Girl symbolizes the values and aspirations of a consumer society. (She is crowned not in the political capital, remember, but in Atlantic City or Miami Beach, centers associated with leisure and consumption.) And she is not entirely incapable of exploitation. If men sometimes sought to buy with gold the Virgin's blessings on their questionable causes, so The Girl now dispenses her charismatic favor on watches, refrigerators, and razor blades—for a price. Though The Girl has built no cathedrals, without her the colossal edifice of mass persuasion would crumble. Her sharply stylized face and figure beckon us from every magazine and TV channel, luring us toward the beatific vision of a consumer's paradise.

The Girl is *not* the Virgin. In fact she is a kind of antiMadonna. She reverses most of the values traditionally associated with the Virgin— poverty, humility, sacrifice. In startling contrast, particularly, to the biblical portrait of Mary in Luke I:46–55, The Girl has nothing to do with filling the hungry with "good things," hawking instead an endless proliferation of trivia on TV spot commercials. The Girl exalts the mighty, extols the rich, and brings nothing to the hungry but added despair. So The Girl does buttress and bring into personal focus a value system, such as it is. In both social and psychological terms, The Girl, whether or not she is really a goddess, certainly acts that way.

Perhaps the most ironic element in the rise of the cult of The Girl is that Protestantism has almost completely failed to notice it, while Roman Catholics have at least given some evidence of sensing its significance. In some places, for instance, Catholics are forbidden to participate in beauty pageants, a ruling not entirely inspired by prudery. It is ironic that Protestants have traditionally been most opposed to lady cults while Catholics have managed to assimilate more than one at various points in history.

If we are correct in assuming that The Girl *functions* in many ways as a goddess, then the cult of The Girl demands careful Protestant theological criticism. Anything that functions, even in part, as a god when it is in fact not God, is an idol. When the Reformers and their Puritan offspring criticized the cult of Mary it was not because they were anti-feminist. They opposed anything—man, woman, or beast (or dogma or institution)—that usurped in the slightest the prerogatives that belonged alone to God Almighty. As Max Weber has insisted, when the prophets of Israel railed against fertility cults, they had nothing against fertility. It is not against sexuality but against a cult that protest is needed. Not, as it were, against the beauty but against the pageant.

Thus the Protestant objection to the present cult of The Girl must be based on the realization that The Girl is an *idol*. She functions as the source of value, the giver of personal identity. But the values she mediates and the identity she confers are both spurious. Like every idol she is ultimately a creation of our own hands and cannot save us. The values she represents as ultimate satisfactions—mechanical comfort, sexual success, unencumbered leisure—have no ultimacy. They lead only to endless upward mobility, competitive consumption, and anxious cynicism. The devilish social insecurities from which she promises to deliver us are, alas, still there, even after we have purified our breaths, our skins, and our armpits by applying her sacred oils. She is a merciless goddess who draws us farther and farther into the net of accelerated ordeals of obeisance. As the queen of commodities in an expanding economy, the fulfillment she promises must always remain just beyond the tips of our fingers.

Why has Protestantism kept its attention obsessively fastened on the development of Mariolatry in Catholicism and not noticed the sinister rise of this vampirelike cult of The Girl in our society? Unfortunately, it is due to the continuing incapacity of theological critics to recognize the religious significance of cultural phenomena outside the formal religious system itself. But the rise of this new cult reminds us that the work of the reformer is never done. Man's mind is indeed—as Luther said—a factory busy making idols. The Girl is a far more pervasive and destructive influence than the Virgin, and it is to her and her omnipresent altars that we should be directing our criticism.

Besides sanctifying a set of phony values, The Girl compounds her noxiousness by maiming her victims in a Procrustean bed of uniformity. This is the empty "identity" she panders. Take the Miss America pageant, for example. Are these virtually indistinguishable specimens of white, middleclass postadolescence really the best we can do? Do they not mirror the ethos of a mass-production society, in which genuine individualism somehow mars the clean, precision-tooled effect? Like their sisters, the finely calibrated Rockettes, these meticulously measured and pretested "beauties" lined up on the boardwalk bear an ominous similarity to the faceless retinues of goose-steppers and the interchangeable mass exercisers of explicitly totalitarian societies. In short, *who* says this is beauty?

The caricature becomes complete in the Miss Universe contest, when Miss Rhodesia is a blonde, Miss South Africa is white, and Oriental girls with a totally different tradition of feminine beauty are forced to display their thighs and appear in spike heels and Catalina swim suits. Miss Universe is as universal as an American adman's stereotype of what beauty should be.

The truth is that The Girl can*not* bestow the identity she promises. She forces her initiates to torture themselves with starvation diets and beauty-parlor ordeals, but still cannot deliver the satisfactions she holds out. She is young, but what happens when her followers, despite added hours in the boudoir, can no longer appear young? She is happy and smiling and loved. What happens when, despite all the potions and incantations, her disciples still feel the human pangs of rejection and loneliness? Or what about all the girls whose statistics, or "personality" (or color) do not match the authoritative "ideal"?

After all, it is God — not The Girl — who is God. He is the center and source of value. He liberates men and women from the bland uniformity of cultural deities so that they may feast on the luxurious diversity of life He has provided. The identity He confers frees men from all pseudo-identities to be themselves, to fulfill their human destinies regardless of whether their faces or figures match some predetermined abstract "ideal." As His gift, sex is freed from both fertility cults and commercial exploitation to become the thoroughly human thing He intended. And since it is one of the last items we have left that is neither prepackaged nor standardized, let us not sacrifice it too hastily on the omnivorous altar of Cybele.

The Playboy, illustrated by the monthly magazine of that name, does for the boys what Miss America does for the girls. Despite accusations to the contrary, the immense popularity of this magazine is not solely attributable to pinup girls. For sheer nudity its pictorial art cannot compete with such would-be competitors as *Dude* and *Escapade*. *Playboy* appeals to a highly mobile, increasingly affluent group of young readers, mostly between eighteen and thirty, who want much more from their drugstore reading than bosoms and thighs. They need a total image of what it means to be a man. And Mr. Hefner's *Playboy* has no hesitation in telling them.

Why should such a need arise? David Riesman has argued that the responsibility for character formation in our society has shifted from the family to the peer group and to the mass-media peer-group surrogates. Things are changing so rapidly that one who is equipped by his family with inflexible, highly internalized values becomes unable to deal with the accelerated pace of change and with the varying contexts in which he is called upon to function. This is especially true in the area of consumer values toward which the "other-directed person" is increasingly oriented.

Within the confusing plethora of mass media signals and peer-group values, *Playboy* fills a special need. For the insecure young man with newly acquired free time and money who still feels uncertain about his consumer skills, *Playboy* supplies a comprehensive and authoritative guidebook to this forbidding new world to which he now has access. It tells him not only who to be; it tells him *how* to be, and even provides consolation outlets for those who secretly feel that they have not quite made it.

In supplying for the other-directed consumer of leisure both the normative identity image and the means of achieving it, *Playboy* relies on a careful integration of copy and advertising material. The comic book that appeals to a younger generation with an analogous problem skillfully intersperses illustrations of incredibly muscled men and excessively mammalian women with advertisements for body-building gimmicks and foam-rubber brassière supplements. Thus the thin-chested comic-book readers of both sexes are thoughtfully supplied with both the ends and the means for attaining a spurious brand of maturity. *Playboy* merely continues the comic-book tactic for the next age group. Since within every identity crisis, whether in teens or twenties, there is usually a sexual identity problem, *Playboy* speaks to those who desperately want to know what it means to be a man, and more specifically a *male*, in today's world.

Both the image of man and the means for its attainment exhibit a remarkable consistency in *Playboy*. The skilled consumer is cool and unruffled. He savors sports cars, liquor, high fidelity, and book-club selections with a casual, unhurried aplomb. Though he must certainly *have* and *use* the latest consumption item, he must not permit himself to get too attached to it. The style will change and he must always be ready to adjust. His persistent anxiety that he may mix a drink incorrectly, enjoy a jazz group that is passé, or wear last year's necktie style is comforted by an authoritative tone in *Playboy* beside which papal encyclicals sound irresolute.

"Don't hesitate," he is told, "this assertive, self-assured weskit is what every man of taste wants for the fall season." Lingering doubts about his masculinity are extirpated by the firm assurance that "real men demand this ruggedly masculine smoke" (cigar ad). Though "the ladies will swoon for you, no matter what they promise, don't give them a puff. This cigar is for men only." A fur-lined canvas field jacket is described as "the most masculine thing since the cave man." What to be and how to be it are both made unambiguously clear.

Since being a male necessitates some kind of relationship to females, *Playboy* fearlessly confronts this problem too, and solves it by the consistent application of the same formula. Sex becomes one of the items of leisure activity that the knowledgeable consumer of leisure handles with his characteristic skill and detachment. The girl becomes a desirable—indeed an indispensable—"Playboy accessory."

In a question-answer column entitled "The Playboy Adviser," queries about smoking equipment (how to break in a meerschaum pipe), cocktail preparation (how to mix a Yellow Fever), and whether or not to wear suspenders with a vest alternate with questions about what to do with girls who complicate the cardinal principle of casualness either by suggesting marriage or by some other impulsive gesture toward a permanent relationship. The infallible answer from the oracle never varies: sex must be contained, at all costs, within the entertainment-recreation area. Don't let her get "serious."

After all, the most famous feature of the magazine is its monthly foldout photo of a *play*mate. She is the symbol par excellence of recreational sex. When playtime is over, the playmate's function ceases, so she must be made to understand the rules of the game. As the crew-cut young man in a *Playboy* cartoon says to the rumpled and disarrayed girl he is passionately embracing, "Why speak of love at a time like this?"

The magazine's fiction purveys the same kind of severely departmentalized sex. Although the editors have recently improved the *Playboy* contents with contributions by Hemingway, Bemelmans, and even a Chekhov translation, many of the stories still rely on a repetitious and predictable formula. A successful young man, either single or somewhat less than ideally married—a figure with whom readers have no difficulty identifying—encounters a gorgeous and seductive woman who makes no demands on him except sex. She is the prose duplication of the cool-eyed but hot-blooded playmate of the foldout.

Drawing heavily on the fantasy life of all young Americans, the writers utilize for their stereotyped heroines the hero's schoolteacher, his secretary, an old girl friend, or the girl who brings her car into the garage where he works. The happy issue is always a casual but satisfying sexual experience with no entangling alliances whatever. Unlike the women he knows in real life, the *Playboy* reader's fictional girl friends know their place and ask for nothing more. They present no danger of permanent involvement. Like any good accessory, they are detachable and disposable.

Many of the advertisements reinforce the sex-accessory identification in another way—by attributing female characteristics to the items they sell. Thus a full-page ad for the MG assures us that this car is not only "the smoothest pleasure machine" on the road and that having one is a "love affair," but most important, "you drive it—it doesn't drive you." The ad ends with the equivocal question "Is it a date?"

*Playboy* insists that its message is one of liberation. Its gospel frees us from captivity to the puritanical "hatpin brigade." It solemnly crusades for "frankness" and publishes scores of letters congratulating it for its unblushing "candor." Yet the whole phenomenon of which *Playboy* is only a part vividly illustrates the awful fact of a new kind of tyranny.

Those liberated by technology and increased prosperity to new worlds of leisure now become the anxious slaves of dictatorial taste makers. Obsequiously waiting for the latest signal on what is cool and what is awkward, they are paralyzed by the fear that they may hear pronounced on them that dread sentence occasionally intoned by "The Playboy Adviser": "You goofed!" Leisure is thus swallowed up in apprehensive competitiveness, its liberating potential transformed into a self-destructive compulsion to consume only what is *à la mode*. *Playboy* mediates the Word of the most high into one section of the consumer world, but it is a word of bondage, not of freedom.

Nor will *Playboy*'s synthetic doctrine of man stand the test of scrutiny. Psychoanalysts constantly remind us how deep-seated sexuality is in the human being. But if they didn't remind us, we would soon discover it ourselves anyway. Much as the human male might like to terminate his relationship with a woman as he would snap off the stereo, or store her for special purposes like a camel's-hair jacket, it really can't be done. And anyone with a modicum of experience with women knows it can't be done. Perhaps this is the reason *Playboy*'s readership drops off so sharply after the age of thirty.

*Playboy* really feeds on the existence of a repressed fear of involvement with women, which for various reasons is still present in many otherwise adult Americans. So *Playboy*'s version of sexuality grows increasingly irrelevant as authentic sexual maturity is achieved.

The male identity crisis to which *Playboy* speaks has at its roots a deeply set fear of sex, a fear that is uncomfortably combined with fascination. *Playboy* strives to resolve this antinomy by reducing the proportions of sexuality, its power and its passion, to a packageable consumption item. Thus in *Playboy*'s iconography the nude woman symbolizes total sexual accessibility but demands nothing from the observer. "You drive it—it doesn't drive you." The terror of sex, which cannot be separated from its ecstasy, is dissolved. But this futile attempt to reduce the *mysterium tremendum* of the sexual fails to solve the problem of being a man. For sexuality is the basic form of all human relationship, and therein lies its terror and its power.

Karl Barth has called this basic relational form of man's life *Mitmensch*, co-humanity. This means that becoming fully human, in this case a human male, requires not having the other totally exposed to me and my purposes—while I remain uncommitted—but exposing myself to the risk of encounter with the other by reciprocal self-exposure. The story of man's refusal to be so exposed goes back to the story of Eden and is expressed by man's desire to control the other rather than to *be with* the other. It is basically the fear to be one's self, a lack of the "courage to be."

Thus any theological critique of *Playboy* that focuses on its "lewdness" will misfire completely. *Playboy* and its less successful imitators are not "sex magazines" at all. They are basically antisexual. They dilute and dissipate authentic sexuality by reducing it to an accessory, by keeping it at a safe distance.

It is precisely because these magazines are antisexual that they deserve the most searching kind of theological criticism. They foster a heretical doctrine of man, one at radical variance with the biblical view. For *Playboy*'s man, others—especially women—are *for* him. They are his leisure accessories, his playthings. For the Bible, man only becomes fully man by being *for* the other.

Moralistic criticisms of *Playboy* fail because its antimoralism is one of the few places in which *Playboy* is right. But if Christians bear the name of one who was truly man because he was totally *for* the other, and if it is in him that we know who God is and what human life is for, then we must see in *Playboy* the latest and slickest episode in man's continuing refusal to be fully human.

Freedom for mature sexuality comes to man only when he is freed from the despotic powers which crowd and cower him into fixed patterns of behavior. Both Miss America and The Playboy illustrate such powers. When they determine man's sexual life, they hold him in captivity. They prevent him from achieving maturity. They represent the constant danger of relapsing into tribal thralldom which always haunts the secular society, a threat from which the liberating, secularizing word of the Gospel repeatedly recalls it.

(1965)

*Rollo May*

# Antidotes for the New Puritanism

There are several strange and interesting dilemmas in which we find ourselves with respect to sex and love in our culture. When psychoanalysis was born in Victorian times half a century ago, repression of sexual impulses, feelings, and drives was the accepted mode. It was not nice to feel sexual, one would not talk about sex in polite company, and an aura of sanctifying repulsiveness surrounded the whole topic. Freud was right in pointing out the varied neurotic symptoms to which this repression of sex gave birth.

Then, in the 1920s, a radical change occurred almost overnight. The belief became a militant conviction in liberal circles that the opposite of repression—sex education, freedom of talking, feeling, and expression—would have healthy effects, and was obviously the only stand for the enlightened person. According to Max Lerner, our society shifted from acting as though sex did not exist to placing the most emphasis on sex of any society since the Roman.

Partly as a result of this radical change, we therapists rarely get nowadays in our offices patients who exhibit repression of sex in the pre-World War I Freudian sense. In fact we find just the opposite in the people who come for help: a great deal of talk about sex, a great deal of sexual activity, practically no one complaining of any cultural prohibitions over his going to bed as often or with as many partners as he wishes.

But what our patients *do* complain of is lack of feeling and passion—so much sex and so little meaning or even fun in it! Whereas the Victorian person didn't want anyone to know that he or she had sexual feelings, now we are ashamed if we do not. Before 1910 if you called a lady "sexy," you insulted her; nowadays the lady accepts the adjective as a prized compliment. Our patients often have problems of impotence or frigidity, but they struggle desperately not to let anyone know they *don't* feel sexually. The Victorian nice man or woman was guilty if he or she did perform sexually; now we are guilty if we *don't*.

One dilemma, therefore, is that enlightenment has not at all solved the sexual problems in our culture. To be sure, there are important positive results of the new enlightenment, chiefly in increased freedom for the individual. And some external problems are eased—sexual knowledge can be bought in any bookstore, contraception is available almost everywhere outside Boston, and external societal anxiety has lessened. *But internalized anxiety and guilt have increased.* And in some ways these are more morbid, harder to handle, and impose a heavier burden upon the individual man and woman than external anxiety and guilt.

A second dilemma is that the new emphasis on technique in sex and love-making backfires. It often seems to me that there is an inverse relationship between the number of how-to-do-it books perused by a person, or rolling off the presses in a society, and the amount of sexual passion or even pleasure experienced by the persons involved. Nothing is wrong with technique as such, in playing golf or acting or making love. But the emphasis beyond a certain point on technique in sex makes for a mechanistic attitude toward love-making, and goes along with alienation, feelings of loneliness, and depersonalization.

The third dilemma I propose is that our highly vaunted sexual freedom has turned out to be a new form of puritanism. I define puritanism as a state of alienation from the body, separation of emotion from reason, and use of the body as a machine. These were the elements of moralistic puritanism in Victorian times; industrialism expressed these same characteristics of puritanism in economic guise. Our modern sexual attitudes have a new content, namely, full sexual expression, but in the same old puritan form—alienation from the body and feeling, and exploitation of the body as though it were a machine.

In our new puritanism bad health is equated with sin. Sin used to be "to give in to one's sexual desires"; now it is "not to have full sexual expression." A woman used to be guilty if she went to bed with a man; now she feels vaguely guilty if after a certain number of dates she still refrains. And her partner, who is always completely enlightened—or at least pretends to be—refuses to allay her guilt and does not get overtly angry at her sin of "morbid repression," her refusal to "give." This, of course, makes her "no" all the more guilt-producing for her.

All this means, of course, that people have to learn to perform sexually but at the same time not to let themselves go in passion or unseemly commitment—which latter may be interpreted as exerting an unhealthy demand on the partner. *The Victorian person sought to have love without falling into sex; the modern person seeks to have sex without falling into love.*

Recently I amused myself by drawing an impressionistic picture of the attitude of the contemporary enlightened person toward sex and love. I call it the portrait of the new sophisticate:

The new sophisticate is not castrated by society but, like Origen, is self-castrated. Sex and the body are for him not something to be and live out, but tools to be cultivated like a TV announcer's voice. And like all genuine Puritans (very passionate men underneath) the new sophisticate does it by devoting himself passionately to the moral principle of dispersing all passion, loving everybody until love has no power left to scare anyone. He is deathly afraid of his passions unless they are kept under leash, and the theory of total expression is precisely his leash. His dogma of liberty is his repression; and his principle of full libidinal health, full sexual satisfaction, are his puritanism and amount to the same thing as his New England forefathers' denial of sex. The first Puritans repressed sex and were passionate; our new man represses passion and is sexual. Both have the purpose of holding back the body, both are ways of trying to make nature a slave. The modern man's rigid principle of full freedom is not freedom at all but a new straitjacket, in some ways as compulsive as the old. He does all this because he is afraid of his body and his compassionate roots in nature, afraid of the soil and his procreative power. He is our latter-day Baconian devoted to gaining power *over* nature, gaining knowledge in order to get more power. And you gain power over sexuality (like working the slave until all zest for revolt is squeezed out of him) precisely by the role of full expression. Sex becomes our tool like the caveman's wheel, crowbar, or adz. Sex, the new machine, the *Machina Ultima*.

It is not surprising that, confronted by these dilemmas, people become more and more concerned about the technical, mechanical aspects of the sexual act. The questions typically asked about the act of love-making are not whether there was passion or meaning or even pleasure, but how well did one perform? Even the sexologists, whose attitude is generally the more the merrier, are raising their eyebrows these days about the anxious overemphasis on achieving the orgasm and the great importance attached to "satisfying" the partner. The man makes a point of asking the woman if she "made it," or is she "all right," or uses some other such euphemism for an experience for which obviously no euphemism is possible. We men are reminded by Simone de Beauvoir and other women who try to interpret the love act to us, that this is the last thing in the world a woman wants to be asked at that moment.

I often get the impression, amid the male flexing of sexual biceps, that men are in training to become sexual athletes. But what is the great prize of the game? Now it is well known in psychotherapeutic circles that the overconcern with potency is generally a compensation for feelings of impotence. Men and women both are struggling to prove their sexual power. Another motive of the game is to overcome their own solitariness. A third motive is often the desperate endeavor to escape feelings of emptiness and the threat of apathy: they pant and quiver to find an answering quiver in someone else's body to prove their own is not dead. Out of an ancient conceit we call this love.

The struggle to find an identity is also a central motive in acting out these sexual roles—a goal present in women as well as men, as Betty Friedan in *The Feminine Mystique* made clear. The point I wish to emphasize here is the connection between this dilemma about potency and the tendency in our society for us to become machines or ledger books even in bed. A psychiatrist colleague of mine tells me that one of his patients brought in the following dream. "I was in bed with my wife. Between us was my accountant. He was going to make love to my wife. Somehow it seemed all right."

Along with the overemphasis upon mechanism there goes, understandably enough, a lessening of passion and of feeling itself, which seems to take the form of a kind of anaesthesia in people who otherwise can perform the mechanical aspects of the sexual act very capably. This is one reason we therapists get a good number of patients these days with problems of impotence, frigidity, and simple lack of feeling in the sexual act. We psychiatrists often hear the disappointed refrain, "We made love, but it wasn't much good."

Sex is the "last frontier," David Riesman meaningfully wrote fifteen years ago in *The Lonely Crowd*. Gerald Sykes in the same vein spoke of sex as the "last green thing." It is surely true that the zest, adventure, the discovering of vast new areas of feeling and passion in one's self, the trying out of one's power to arouse feelings in others— these are indeed "frontier experiences." They are normally present as part of the psychosexual development of every individual, and the young person rightly gets a validation of himself from such experiences. Sex in our society did in fact have this power in the several recent decades since the 1920s, when almost every other activity was becoming "other-directed," jaded, emptied of zest and adventure.

But for various reasons—one of them being that sex had to carry by itself the weight for the validation of the personality on practically all other levels as well—the frontier freshness and newness and challenge of sex were more and more lost. We are now living in the post-Riesman age, and are experiencing the difficult implications of the "other-directed," radar behavior. The "last frontier" has become a teeming Las Vegas and no frontier at all.

Young people can no longer get a bootlegged feeling of personal identity out of the sexual revolt, since there is nothing left to revolt against. A study of drug addiction among young people, published recently in the *New York Times,* reports the young people are saying that the revolt against parents and society, the "kick" of feeling their own "oats" which they used to get from sex, they now have to get from drugs. It is not surprising that for many youngsters what used to be called love-making is now so often experienced as a futile "panting palm to palm," in Aldous Huxley's predictive phrase, and that they tell us that it is hard for them to understand what the poets were talking about.

Nothing to revolt against, did I say? Well, there is obviously one thing left to revolt against, and that is sex itself. The frontier, the establishing of identity, can be, and not infrequently is for the young people, a revolt against sexuality entirely. A modern Lysistrata in robot's dress is rumbling at the gates of our cities, or if not rumbling, at least hovering. As sex becomes more machine-like, with passion irrelevant and then even pleasure diminishing, the problem comes full circle, and we find, *mirabile dictu,* a progression from an *anaesthetic* attitude to an *antiseptic* one. Sexual contact itself then tends to be avoided. The sexual revolution comes finally back on itself not with a bang but a whimper.

This is another and surely least constructive aspect of the new puritanism: it returns, finally, to an ascetic attitude. This is said graphically in a charming limerick that seems to have sprung up on some sophisticated campus:

> The word has come down from the Dean,
> That with the aid of the teaching machine,
>> King Oedipus Rex
>> Could have learned about sex
> Without ever touching the Queen.

What are the sources of these dilemmas? Perhaps if we can get some idea of what went wrong, we shall rediscover values in sex and love that will have genuine relevance for our age.

The essential element, I propose, in the dilemmas we have been discussing is the *banalization of sex and love.* Does not the tendency to make sex and love banal and vapid run through our whole culture? The plethora of books on the subject have one thing in common—they oversimplify sex and love, treating the topic like a combination of learning to play tennis and buying life insurance.

I have said above, describing the modern sophisticated man's dilemmas about sex, that he castrates himself "because he is afraid of his body, afraid of his compassionate roots in nature, afraid of the soil and his procreative powers." That is to say, something much more potent is going on in sexuality than one would gather from the oversimplified books on sex and love—something that still has the power to scare people. I believe banalization serves as a defense against this anxiety.

The widespread tendency among young people to "go steady"—premature monogamy, as it has been called—is an egregious illustration of our point. In my frequent visits to different college campuses for lectures, I have discussed this phenomenon with students, and something like the following seems to be going on. In our insecure age when all values are in flux, at least "the steady" is steady. Always having a date with the same fellow or girl on Saturday night, dancing with this same person through the entire party at college dances, always knowing this one is available, allays the anxiety of aloneness. But it also gets boring. This leads naturally enough to early sexuality: sex at least is something we can do when we run out of conversation—which happens often when the partners have not developed enough in their own right to be interesting very long to each other as persons. It is a strange fact in our society that what goes into building a relationship—the sharing of tastes, fantasies, dreams, hopes for the future and fears from the past—seems to make people more shy and vulnerable than going to bed with each other. They are more wary of the tenderness that goes with psychological and spiritual nakedness than they are of the physical nakedness in sexual intimacy.

Now substituting premature sexuality for meaningful intimate relationship relieves the young person's anxiety, but at the price of bypassing opportunity for further development. It seems that going steady, paradoxically, is related to promiscuity. I define "promiscuity" with Webster as the indiscriminate practice of sexuality whether with one person or a number: sex is indiscriminate when used in the service of security, or to fill up an emotional vacuum. But promiscuity is a lonely and alienating business. This loneliness becomes one of the pushes toward early marriage. Grasping each other in marriage gives a kind of security—a legal and social security at least—which temporarily allays loneliness, but at the price of the haunting dread of a boring marital future. *Each step in this pattern has within it the banalization of sex and love.*

Now the question rarely asked is, are not these young people—possibly wiser in their innocence than their culture in its sophistication—fleeing from some anxiety that is only too real? I propose that what scares them, like what scares our "new sophisticate," is an element in sex and love which is almost universally repressed in our culture, namely the *tragic, daimonic element.*

By "daimonic"—which I hasten to say does not refer to little "demons"—I mean the natural element within an individual, such as the erotic drive, which has the power to take over the whole person. The erotic urge pushes toward a general physiological aim, namely sexual release. But it can push the individual into all kinds of relationships without relation to the totality of his self.

But the potentially destructive effects of the daimonic are only the reverse side of the person's constructive vitality, his passion and other potentially creative activities. The Greeks used the term "daimon" to describe the inspired urges of the poet. Socrates, indeed, speaks of his "daimon" as his conscience. When this power goes awry—when one element takes over the total personality and drives the person into disintegrative behavior—it becomes "demon possession," the historical term for psychosis. The daimonic can be either creative or destructive, but either way it certainly is the opposite to banalization. The repression of the daimonic, tragic aspects of sex and love is directly related to their banalization in our culture.

The daimonic is present in all nature as blind, ambiguous power. But only in man does it become allied with the tragic. For tragedy is the self-conscious, personal realization of being in the power of one element; thus the Greeks defined tragedy as "inordinate desire," "pride," "reaching beyond just boundaries." We have only to call to mind Romeo and Juliet, Abelard and Héloise, Tristan and Isolde, Helen of Troy, to see the power of sexual love to seize a man and woman, lift them up into a whirlwind that defies rational control and may destroy not only themselves but others at the same time. These stories are told over and over again in Western classic literature, and passed down from generation to generation, for they come from a depth of human experience in sexual love that is profoundly significant. It is a level largely unmentioned in our day, much to the impoverishment of our talk and writing about sex and love.

If we are to overcome banalization, we must take sex and love on several different dimensions at once. Consider, as an analogy, Mozart's music. In some portions of his music Mozart is engaged in elegant play. In other portions his music comes to us as pure sensuous pleasure, giving us a sheer delight. But in other portions, like the death music at the end of *Don Giovanni*, Mozart is profoundly shaking: we are gripped by fate and the daimonic as the inescapable tragedy rises before us. If Mozart had only the first element, play, he would sooner or later be banal and boring. If he presented only pure sensuality, he would become cloying; or if only the fire and death music, his creations would be too heavy. He is great because he writes on all three dimensions; and he must be listened to on all these levels at once.

Sexuality and love similarly have these three dimensions. Sex not only can be play, but probably an element of sheer play should be fairly regularly present. By this token, casual relationships in sex may have their gratification or meaning in the sharing of pleasure, tenderness, and so on. But if one's whole pattern and attitude toward sex is only casual, then sooner or later the playing itself becomes boring. The same is true about sensuality, obviously an element in any gratifying sex: if it has to carry the whole weight of the relationship, it becomes cloying. If sex is only sensuality, you sooner or later turn against sex itself. The third element, the daimonic and tragic, we emphasized here because that is the one almost wholly repressed in our culture, a fact that has much to do with the banalization of sex and love in our day. In a book like Erich Fromm's *Art of Loving*, for example, the daimonic, tragic element is completely missing.

An appreciation of the tragic and daimonic side of sex and love can help us not only to avoid oversimplification but to love better. Let me illustrate the constructive use of the daimonic. Every person, as a separate individual, experiences aloneness and strives to overcome his loneliness, this striving usually being some kind of love. Sexuality and love require self-assertion: if the person is not to some extent an individual in his own right, he will not only have nothing to give, nothing to relate with, but will be unable to assert himself and therefore unable to be genuinely part of the relationship. Both the man and woman need self-assertion in order to breach the separateness and make some kind of union with each other. Thus there is truth in the vernacular expressions about needing to "let oneself go" and "give oneself over" to the sexual act — or to any creative experience for that matter.

The psychotherapist Dr. Otto Rank once remarked in his latter years of practice that practically all the women who came to him had problems because their husbands were not assertive enough. Despite the oversimplified sound of this sentence, it contains a telling point: our effete cultivation of sex can make us so intellectual and detached about it that the simple power of the act evaporates, and we lose — and this loss is especially serious for women — the important elemental pleasure of "being taken," being "carried away." But the self-assertive power must be integrated with the other aspects of one's own personality, and with the total person of the mate; otherwise it becomes daimonic in the destructive sense.

Let us now summarize some values, potential and actual, in sexual love. There is, first, the overall value of enrichment and fulfilment of personality. This comes from expansion of one's awareness of one's self, one's feelings, one's experience of his capacity to give sexual pleasure and other feelings to the other person, and achieve thereby an expansion of meaning in interpersonal relationship. This fulfilment carries us beyond what we are at any given moment; I become in a literal sense more than I was. The most powerful symbol imaginable for this fulfilment is procreation — the possibility that a new being may be conceived and born. The "birth," however, can and does refer at the same time to the birth of new aspects of one's self.

Tenderness is a second value, a tenderness that is much more than indicated in that most unpoetic of all words, "togetherness." The experience of tenderness comes out of the fact that the two persons, longing as all individuals do to overcome the separateness and isolation to which we are all heir because we are individuals, can participate in a relationship that for the moment is not two isolated selves but a union. In this kind of sexual intercourse, the lover often does not know whether a particular sensation of delight is felt by him or by his loved one — and it doesn't make any difference anyway. A sharing takes place which is a new gestalt, a new being, a new field of magnetic force. A gratifying sexual relationship thus has the gestalt of a painting — the various parts, the colors, feelings, forms, unite to become a new whole.

There is the third value which occurs ideally at the moment of climax in sexual intercourse. This is the point when the lovers are carried not only beyond their personal isolation, but when a shift in consciousness seems to occur that unites them also with nature. In Hemingway's novel, *For Whom the Bell Tolls,* the older woman, Pilar, waits for the hero, Robert Jordan, and the girl he loves when they have gone ahead into the mountain to make love; and when they return, she asks, "Did the earth move?" The shaking of the earth seems to be a normal part of the momentary loss of awareness of the self and the surging up of a sudden consciousness that includes the "earth" as well. There is an accelerating experience of touch, contact, union to the point where for a moment the awareness of separateness is lost, blotted out in a cosmic feeling of oneness with nature. I do not wish this to sound too "ideal," for I think it is a quality, however subtle, in all love-making except the most depersonalized sort. And I also do not wish it to sound simply "mystic," for despite limitations in our awareness, I think it is an inseparable part of actual experience in the love act.

This leads us immediately to the fourth value, sex and love as the affirmation of the self. Despite the fact that many people in our culture use sex to get a short-circuited, ersatz sense of identity, sexual love can and ought to provide a sound and meaningful way to the sense of personal identity. We emerge from love-making normally with renewed vitality, a vitality which comes not from triumph or proof of one's strength but from the expansion of awareness. Probably in love-making there is always some element of sadness—as, to use our previous analogy, there is in practically all music no matter how joyful—in the reminder that we have not succeeded absolutely in losing our separateness, nor is the infantile hope that we could recover the womb made into reality, and even our increased self-awareness can also be a poignant reminder that none of us ever overcomes his loneliness completely. But by one's replenished sense of one's own significance in the love act he can accept these unavoidable human limitations.

A final value inheres in the curious phenomenon in love-making: that to be able to give to the other person is essential to one's own full pleasure in the act. This sounds like a banal moralism in our age of mechanization of sex and "release of tension" in sexual objects. But it is not sentimentality but a point which anyone can confirm in his own experience in the love act, that to give is essential to one's own pleasure. Many patients in psychotherapy find themselves discovering, generally with some surprise, that something is missing if they cannot "do something for," give something to the partner—the normal expression of which is the giving in the act of intercourse itself. Just as giving is essential to one's own full pleasure, the ability to receive is necessary in the love interrelationship also. If you cannot receive, your giving will be a domination of the partner. Conversely, if you cannot give, your receiving will leave you empty. The paradox is demonstrably true that the person who can only receive becomes empty, for he is unable actively to appropriate and make his own what he receives. I speak, thus, not of receiving as a passive phenomenon, but of *active receiving:* one knows he is receiving, feels it, absorbs it into his own experience whether he verbally acknowledges it or not, and is grateful for it.

(1966)

**Cecelia Holland**

# I Don't Trust Anyone Under Thirty

Militant, committed, articulate and radical, the generation under thirty claims to be the hope of the world. Our parents believe it. They contrast the purity of our motives and the energy of our commitments with their own corrupted morality and corroded traditions and decide that everything we say *must* be right. "Don't let the kids down," says an advertisement for Gene McCarthy. Not since the Children's Crusade in the early 13th century has an older generation entrusted so much of its salvation to the young. Not since the Renaissance have we wielded so much influence over our elders. (Did Cesare Borgia trust anybody over thirty?).

Much of the work in the civil-rights crusade is done by people under thirty years of age. Almost all the protesters of the Vietnam war (and the great majority of those fighting in it) are under thirty. There are very few hippies over thirty, and the hippie movement stands out as the single most visible protest against the syndrome commonly called the American Way of Life. My generation is the most idealistic, the most dynamic and the most liberal in history; just ask us, we'll tell you. We're strong on freedom and long on love, and there are enough of us around to change the very definitions of the words to make these statements fact.

Are we strong on freedom? It would be hard to find a young person outside the South who isn't all for the Negro revolution. The freedom to protest the Vietnam war—to protest anything (except the protesters)—is as hallowed as the bones of a saint. Yet to hold a conservative viewpoint, however honestly, can only be a sign of cowardice. Anybody over thirty will ask first what your opinion is on the war. Anybody under thirty will automatically assume you're against it; if you aren't, you're a heretic.

Freedom and free speech should mean that anyone can hold any opinion he wants on the Negro or the war in Vietnam, as long as he doesn't try to enforce his views on anybody else. But our generation's conception of freedom goes more like this: "Do your own thing and all will be well, as long as your own thing is certified pure by the rest of us."

But what if your own thing doesn't happen to conform to that of the hip world, the militant students, the nonstudents or any other faction? There are, after all, people in this world who manage to live entirely within the existing social structure, and who do so by choice. There are people who find it possible to go through life neither rebelling nor conforming. Are they all hypocrites? To the under-thirty group, nonalignment is as abhorrent as slavish devotion to the *status quo*.

Let's face it, my generation is *not* strong on freedom. Basically, we

511

simply want to do what we like, without being bothered by anything silly like antique conventions and laws. But why the devil can't we just say so and let it go at that? Why do we dress our preferences in the vestments of a quasi-religion?

Part of the reason, I suspect, is that we're still bound by at least one antique convention: doing things for the right reasons, the socially acceptable motives. We have a party line, certain things and opinions that must be professed under certain conditions. Deviation labels one unfit. Anybody who's ever ventured into the wilderness of conversation with more than one hip or militant student or political fanatic or fellow-traveler knows that there is a striking similarity, not only in the lines of argument taken on almost all subjects but in the words and slogans used, not only within each faction but across partisan lines. Doctrine has hardened into dogma. (I am a fellow-traveler with the "straights," which means that sometimes I'm self-consciously hip; and making the transition from one vernacular to the other is difficult enough to suggest that the differences are not merely linguistic. Hip-think doesn't require logic or clarity, which makes it easier, of course, to sound profound.)

The drug issue is a good example of our dogmatism. If you don't smoke or pop pills, you're narrow-minded, tradition-bound and a chicken. Your reasons for denying the Nirvana of drugs make no difference. There are people for whom "grass," "acid," "speed" and their relatives hold no interest, just as there are people who dislike roast beef. Usually they manage to commune with the infinite quite well without an interpreter. Yet these people are as square to the drug-user as the housewife who won't wear short skirts because the neighbors might talk.

What does love mean to the Love Generation? It can mean purging oneself of hatred and prejudice and welcoming everyone else as a brother, and it can mean preaching the gospel while pushing Methedrine. It can mean the L.A. Diggers, a group of well-off, sympathetic people who give runaway kids a place to stop and catch their breath, and it can mean the "rank sweat of an enseamèd bed." There's something of calf-love in all our uses of the word, and something else that's just a little weird. The widely published off-campus living arrangements of college students like Barnard's Linda Leclair is another indication, with *Playboy* magazine and Ingmar Bergman, that sex is rapidly becoming a spectator sport. Why is it we can't love without announcing it to the world in infinite detail?

Love, as the song-makers know, is a private thing, and those who proclaim it in public tend to slip a little in the practice. Whatever the Columbia students were thinking about when they threw rocks, mailboxes and desks at the cops during their recent fit of self-expression, it wasn't love. If it was, it lost a lot in the translation.

Actually, when you cut out the preaching and look at the action, we're all sharpshooters—in the old sense—and our major target is that famous bogeyman, the world we never made. We think our parents made it—the hypocrisy, the prejudice, the materialism, the hatred, the uncertainty—and we know we have the answers for improving it. It takes the wisdom that comes with some age to realize that if the solution looks simple you probably don't understand the problem. And it takes the kind of minds we haven't got to realize that what you say means less than what you do.

The hip world isn't the whole of our generation, but it's a good microcosm. Its values and flaws characterize us all. The hippie drops out of society. But luckily for him, society sticks around, because the hippie is a parasite. The straight world supports him. Without this country's prosperity, there could be no hippies. They'd have nobody to bum from, nobody to give them easy jobs to tide them over the winter. There would be no leisure time in which to practice being hip, and no straight public to be titillated and fleeced. The hip world is neither self-supporting nor self-perpetuating, and it's hypocritical to claim that it is.

This kind of hypocrisy creeps into almost all our debunking of the Bad World. The institutions that create the atmosphere conducive to protest are inextricably bound up with the institutions we protest against. If it weren't for the Establishment, what would we fight against? And if we couldn't fight, who knows but—horrors—we might become Establishment ourselves? History is full of rebellious crusades that demolished the *status quo* and wound up becoming the *status quo* themselves.

To protect ourselves, we try to cover the deck with protests—prove our unimpeachable nobility by knocking everything in sight as ignoble. How well do we listen to what we say?

Materialism in this country has taken the odd turn of becoming a form of idealism: things put aside for tomorrow. Our parents live for tomorrow, in a thingy kind of way. They dream of the bright world ahead, a utopia which we find rather pathetic because we quit believing in utopias a long time ago. We live for today. We grab what we can get, now. Tomorrow never comes anyway. And when it does, it's just like today. Actually we aren't even particularly cynical about it, just sad.

The deadly corollary to this kind of thinking is that what you have to work for isn't worth having. (A woman's magazine recently declared that the emphasis is on "roles, not goals," a decent square translation of "do your own thing.") We think knowledge that must be learned isn't valuable; only intuitive, revealed knowledge is worth while. The college "grind" is a pitiable figure. It's so much easier to fake your way through. College isn't a place where you learn; it's an object to be revolutionized. You don't find knowledge, it comes to you, complete with bright colors and dogs barking flowers.

If we work, we do just enough to survive. A job exists to keep one fed—we accept employment as a token reason for accepting a living. We're a generation of grasshoppers.

We love Marshall McLuhan because he makes it impossible, and therefore unnecessary, to think logically. Our passion for J. R. R. Tolkien is, I think, due not to the clear-cut moral position he espouses but to the blatantly mythological character of his books; they aren't about the real world, which makes them safe to handle. ("We can dig the morality, but we don't have to do anything about it, because we aren't mythological people," says my sister, who is seventeen.) The fads borrowed from Oriental and Indian cultures are deliberate archaisms. We long for the safe, still, dead worlds in which all values are only reflections of eternity. We don't like change, and we doubt we can cope with it, so we pretend it doesn't exist. Reality has become elusive, painful, a blind god that isn't dead but probably isn't human either, so we prefer ambiguity.

If we're grasshoppers, what about the ants? "Of course they're straight—they're parents." Nobody over thirty can possibly have access to the Truth. Actually, we don't dislike our parents so much as we resent them—their money-fever, their ability to muddle (and meddle in) almost everything and, above all, their timidity. J. Alfred Prufrocks, the batch of them. It's the lack of authority they display that revolts us, and their readiness to be fooled. If our parents were a bolder, tougher generation, we would be a meeker, sweeter pack of grasshoppers.

The harshness of our indictment of our parents stems from our essential innocence, and our innocence stems from ignorance. We're the best-educated generation around, judging by the number of years we spend in schools, but we really don't know much. Colleges insist on graduating students who can't write an intelligible English sentence, who don't speak three words of a foreign language, who have read neither Marx nor Keynes nor Freud nor Joyce, and who never will. It isn't necessarily the colleges' fault: The books and the professors are there, but we've lost the ability to take advantage of them. Nevertheless, we feel ourselves entitled to hold an opinion on everything, whether we know anything about it or not. And we've discovered that the less we know about something, the easier it is to hold a strong opinion about it.

The Berkeley sit-in in defense of free speech was followed by the protest against the presence of a Navy recruiting booth on campus; many of the same students (and non-students) took part in both. Isn't this in some small, tinny way inconsistent? This may be an unfair parallel, but this kind of behavior reminds me of the U.S.S.R., where Benjamin Spock is considered a hero because he defies the United States Government; and where Soviet writers who publish anything in opposition to the Party are tried and punished as traitors.

Heaven preserve us from our own children.

(1968)

*Marge Piercy*

# Breaking Camp

Now it begins,
the sprays of forsythia against wet brick,
under the sidewalks mud seethes,
the grass is moist and tender in Central Park,
the air smells of ammonia and drains,
cats howl their lean barbed sex.

Now we relinquish winter dreams.
In Thanksgiving snow we stood in my slum kitchen
and saw each other and began and were afraid.
I ran through snow to tell you I was free.
Snow swirled past the mattress on the floorboards,
snow on the bare wedding of our choice.
We drove very fast into a blizzard of fur.

Now we abandon winter hopes,
roasts and laughter of friends in a warm room,
fire and cognac and goose on a platter and baking bread,
cinnamon love under the silken feather quilt,
the meshing of our neat and slippery flesh
while the snow flits like moths around the streetlamps,
while the snow's long hair brushes the pane.

Changeable and violent and honest,
hard head, soft belly and sure in your sex,
stormy and sensible, groper and mapmaker and visionary,
you are rooted in me with pain.
You use me like somebody else's mule.
You are always setting me tasks:
to spoon away a mountain of New York *Times* soaked in Texas oil,
to dam rivers of sewerage with a paper towel,
to feed an army on stew from barbed wire and buttons,
to build a city of love on a garbage dump.
I come shuddering from the warm tangles of winter sleep
choosing you compulsively, repetitiously, dumbly as breath.
You will never subside into rest.

The grey Canadian geese and glossy mallards, like arrowheads
are pulled north and beat their powerful wings above the long valleys.
Soon we will be sleeping on rocks hard as axes.

Soon I will be setting up camp in gulleys, on moraine
drinking rusty water out of my shoe.

Peace was a winter hope
with down comforters and a wall of books and tawny pears.
You are headed into the iron north of resistance.
I am curing our roast meat to leathery pemmican.
We will lie in the whips of the grass under the wind's blade
fitting our bodies into emblems of stars,
of leaping fish, of waterfalls and morning glories and small death.
We will stumble into the red morning to walk our feet raw.

You go on and I follow, I choose and follow.
The mills of injustice darken the sky with their smoke,
ash floats on the streams.
Soon we will be setting up camp on a plain of nails.
Soon we will be drinking blood out of shattered bone.
The dead will be stacked like bricks.
The suns of power will dance on the black sky
and scorch us to dust.

You belong to me no more than the sun that pounds on my head.
I belong to nothing but my work carried like a prayer rug on my back.
Yet we are always traveling through each other,
we belong to the same story and the same laboring.
You call and I follow, I choose and follow
through all the ragged cycles of build and collapse,
of lunge and defeat,
epicycles on our long journey
toward the north star of your magnetic conscience.

(1968)

*Fred H. Schroeder*

# "And Now, a Word from the Silent Generation"

I remember Pearl Harbor. There are many alive today who do not, because they are too young. But those of my generation—the Silent Generation—remember Pearl Harbor in a different way from other Americans
who are old enough to remember. For most of the men and women of
my generation, it is our first "news" memory, our first real current

event, and that has made all the difference in the world. The event was specific for us, surrounded with the aerial sound imagery of the time: the interruption of Jack Benny's radio program, the sound of FDR's voice, and the howl of air raid sirens.

Moreover, we remember the Great Depression, but these memories are vague and inarticulate. In a recent book on the Depression, Caroline Bird gave a name to the effects of the Depression in the title of her book, *The Invisible Scar*. For us of the Silent Generation the scar is more invisible than for others who were alive during the Depression, for our impressions of the time were not received verbally from newspapers and radio, and our reactions to the events of the times were not verbalized either. As an infant is aware of discomfort, but cannot articulate his discomfort by naming it *hunger,* or *weariness,* or *dampness,* so we were aware that our culture was out of joint, but could not name it *Depression.* Those who were of high school age and older in the 1930's were able to define and express their concerns. They could view each day in a larger context, and they could assign labels to the symptoms, causes and panaceas: "Depression," "New Deal," "Wall Street," "Communism," "Share the Wealth," "FDR," "WPA," "Fascism," "America First," "Hooverville" were labels toward which they could direct their spleen. For us, though, the broader impressions were subliminal, and our memories but spotty domestic symbols of the times.

I, for example, remember putting cardboard in my shoes. I remember daily potato soup. I remember that bottles of milk were stolen from our porch and that my parents, aware of the plight of the have-nots, made no complaint. I remember the shame of neighbor families who went on relief. I remember unopened bills piling on the telephone table. I remember darned socks and patched knickers. And we weren't poor by the standards of the day. Many of my generation have far bleaker memories than mine.

Thus, we of the Silent Generation grew up in a period when there were no positive answers to the question: "what do you know for sure?" What we did know, vaguely, was that the only security was in the family, and that was an uneasy security at best. We grew invisible scars over wounds that had never been defined. But when Pearl Harbor occurred, we finally received specific confirmation: it was indeed a mutable, insecure world, governed by irrational motives and violent men.

We grew to young adulthood to enter college around 1950, and when older people played the national game of labelling college generations, they labelled us the Silent Generation, meaning us no compliment. You are Uncommitted, they said. You have no Ideals, no Mission. You are Materialistic and Conformist. You are Silent. It is easy to be right when labelling classes of people, and the older Americans were right enough. Now, I think, many of them long for the convenience of another Silent Generation, pressed as they are by an intensely vocal and fanatically committed generation.

We of the Silent Generation, however, look at today's college-age Americans with the affectionate and slightly amused melancholy of the prematurely old. We, the products of the Birth Dearth, look at the products of the Baby Boom, and find their windmilling frenetic up-and-downism a little sad, pathetically time-consuming and most inefficient. We look at those of the generation that preceded us – the professional liberals of the Depression years – and find their rebelling against victorian gentility and American capitalism a bit old fashioned: the horse is dead, let's kick it no longer. In college, they introduced us to the heroes of disillusionment of the twenties: Hemingway, Fitzgerald and company, but we had grown up wise to their messages, and to many of us they seemed mainly to be wallowing in self-pity at being born into a pretty rotten century.

Why were we silent? For one thing, there was not much reason to be a loud liberal: we were under no obligation to rebel against a genteel establishment. Further, there was no reason to be a noisy conservative: we had no embarrassing past of radicalism to overcompensate for with extreme conservatism. Neither did we have a touchstone of positive "normalcy" to live down or to resurrect. We were silent because there was no reason to shout about the obvious: there is evil in the world; there is inequality among men; madmen and egoists can and will be leaders. There is little reason to berate mankind for prejudice, conformity and inconsistency. Such things are indeed reprehensible, but we grew up aware that such things are in the nature of the tribe.

This is a melancholy world view, derived from the experience of three decades of Depression, World War, atomic bombs, sputnik, and explosive international tensions. But it has not made us defeatist, conformist or uncommitted. It has, however, made us silent, not only for the reasons above which can be condensed to the folksy concept that "talk is cheap," but also because we have not been in a position to speak out in tones of self-righteous accusation. We have not been in such a position because we were an *unwanted* generation and because we were an *overshadowed* generation.

Underlying our position of being both unwanted and overshadowed is the simple statistical fact that we were the smallest generation in American history. The birthrate per thousand population in America in 1920 was 27.7, and it remained high throughout the twenties. In 1930, the first Depression year, it dropped to 21.3 and in 1933 it reached a low of 18.4, not to rise above 20 per thousand until 1941, ultimately to reach a fairly constant 25 per thousand in the post-World War II years. The relative statistics are startling enough, but the absolute decline is even more significant: from 1909 to the present time there have been more babies born in every other single year than were born in each year of the 1930's. In those ten years, only about twenty-five million babies were born. Today there are about seventeen million senior citizens – and the number will continue to increase until we of the smallest generation, who are now entering our economically productive years (ages 35 to 55) will each be responsible for supporting at least one person over sixty-five. In other words, simple economic pressures have been and will continue to be strong on us and keep us from wasteful vocality.

However, the portion of the generation born in the thirties who came to be called the Silent Generation is not made up entirely of the products of the Birth Dearth. It is my contention that the most significant factor in making of us a "generation" is the subliminal effect on our minds of childhood exposure to Depression and world tensions. Thus, our generation includes those born between 1927 and 1937. For us, as a group, extreme economic insecurity has been a way of life. We were, in 1968, between the ages of 31 and 41. We graduated from high schools between 1945 and 1955, and, roughly speaking, high school graduation marks the time when adolescents become part of what is known as a "generation." Those who are younger than we are probably have not been exposed in childhood to the fearful distress of real and marginal poverty, of the undefinable shock of Pearl Harbor, of fear of invasion (remember the Japanese balloons? Attu? Incendiary bomb drill? Torpedoed ships in coastal shipyards?). Those who are younger will not remember the creeping unknown of the polio epidemics of 1946, 1948 and 1949 or the chilling brinkmanship of the days of the Berlin air lift. Older people cannot understand in the same way as I, the feelings of a twelve-year-old boy in wartime Florida, listening to the boom of the coast defense guns, watching the flotillas of LSTs on the bay one day, to find them gone the next; cowering under a sky thundering with bombers moving from Tyndall Field and Eglin Field to who knows where? War was as real to us in the vague mutability of men and fortunes as it was for children of Europe. Those of us who were in high school watched the firmament of honor rolls become studded with gold stars.

These gold stars are symbolic of another reason that we have been silent. Our generation was overshadowed by the generation before us. They were heroes who went to fight a righteous war. It was not our place to be conscientious objectors, malingerers, or demonstrators against warfare, industry or the government establishment. Between a sneak attack on one front and the unmitigated evil of a madman on the other, the issues were clear. Those who served, served country and mankind. And when our war came, in Korea, though the issues were remote and muddy, we were not in position to complain or to refuse to serve. Like Auden's Unknown Citizen, "when there was war, we went." However much we may have been silent, we were not fools, hypocrites, or dupes. But overshadowed by a generation of self-sacrificing heroes, it was not our place to abrogate the military duties of citizenship. So we served in silence.

When we came to college, we were again overshadowed by the veterans of the war. The colleges were overcrowded with these men who had justly been given the perquisites of the GI Bill of Rights, and whose maturity, experience and urgency overshadowed the adolescent aspirations of a little generation whose unwanted presence on earth was probably due to uneconomic moments of passion among the depressed couples of the thirties. Against the competition of the battle-scarred and world-wise war veterans, I don't think we showed up very well. Also, I suspect that by the time we got to graduate schools, some kind of disillusioned reaction had developed among the university faculties. Second-thoughts must have occurred about how much of the ex-GIs' ability was really solid competence, and how much was simply the greater sophistication of older men. Furthermore, a weariness settled on the men of the Ivory Tower, who had been forced to double, treble, and quadruple the sizes of seminars and the numbers of thesis advisees. In short, the children of the Silent Generation, few in numbers to begin with, were hidden behind the mass of older men whose maturity, whose lost time, and whose service to their country demanded attention and drew energetic interest from professors who had never before seen such numbers of sophisticated and intellectually challenging students. We of the Silent Generation knew our places, and were silent.

So much for the causes of our silence. With what kind of value system did we respond to the society that made us?

In a word, our response was *individualism*. In a few more words, our response was the separation of public life from private life. All of us have at one time or another toyed with some highly individualistic value system: Zen Buddhism, existentialism, transcendentalism, domestic sentimentality, and calling. Of these, the two former are exotic; the others intensely American. None of them shows commitment to a group, party or faction. The exotic -isms, Zen and existentialism, are associated with the Beats, who were the most vocal and deviant of our generation. An important thing about the Beats, however, is that their lives were individualistic and essentially conventionally moral: they were family men and women. From Zen they derived spiritual introspection, from existentialism they derived individual integrity, but in neither posture were they activist, virulent, demonstrative or factional. Far more important, however, are the much drabber-looking value systems of transcendentalism, domestic sentimentality and calling.

As a midwesterner, I am probably more aware than many others of the transcendental Thoreavianism of the Silent Generation. The generation that followed us exhibits the Thoreavianism of Thoreau's "Civil Disobedience," following the lead of Martin Luther King. But the Silent Generation follows the Thoreau of *Walden* — the apolitical transcendentalism set forth as strongly in Emerson's "Ode to Channing." We call it *individualism,* others call it *irresponsibility,* but either way it asserts the belief that faith in men, institutions and society is far secondary to faith in nature. At its most vulgarly materialistic, our transcendentalism manifested itself in the "camping movement" which has at once corrupted American parks and driven the sensitive into the utter wilderness. At its most spiritual, it has made us look for meaning in some kind of artificial frontier individualism. Hypothesizing primitive conditions, how do we measure up to man, nature and God? We of the Silent Generation are a cautious lot, but it is better to die as an individual pitted against God than as a *sabot* pitted against a machine. God's cards may be random, but they are not stacked.

Closer to the surface than transcendental pantheism is domestic sentimentality. It is this response which made us liable to accusations of being conformist and materialistic. We went to college to work toward degrees and professional licenses. The co-eds of the fifties, when interviewed, said they wanted large families. We wanted homes and job security. We asked, as did a pretty young thing of her Beat boy-friend in a cartoon in the University of Minnesota's *Daily:* "But wouldn't it be valid sometimes to want a house in Edina and an automatic washing machine?" For us of the Silent Generation, it would indeed be valid. In a world—an ethos—beset by insecurity and madness, there are values in the family which transcend higher social units. They are not irresponsible, merely materialistic values. To rant, to rave about the outside world; to correct a disjointed society with words, words, words is to apply an abstract poultice to very real local wounds. With Candide, we chose to till our own gardens; to improve our families and our well-being. With Charles Dickens, we can look with kindly irritation on the Mrs. Jellabys of the missionary generations before and after us, sweeping out the world without putting their homes to rights.

Shallow? I think not. Not so long as we preserve some conception of *calling.* Christian calling, *per se,* as we've long since learned from Max Weber, may be out of fashion, but the idea that each of us is called by our inherent abilities to serve mankind in a vocational capacity—as building blocks rather than architects—gives meaning to our local tasks. I contend that this is the materialism and conformity of the Silent Generation. In a world of corrupt, diseased, and irrational institutions, there is no philosopher's stone, no panacea, no ideology to correct the ills, but there are people who can in their callings and in their families set things to right on a small scale.

(1969)

# How shall we live with the world?

## Deuteronomy 5

And Moses called all Israel, and said unto them, Hear, O Israel, the statutes and judgments which I speak in your ears this day, that ye may learn them, and keep, and do them.

2 The LORD our God made a covenant with us in Hôr′-ĕb.

3 The LORD made not this covenant with our fathers, but with us, *even* us, who *are* all of us here alive this day.

4 The LORD talked with you face to face in the mount out of the midst of the fire,

5 (I stood between the LORD and you at that time, to shew you the word of the LORD: for ye were afraid by reason of the fire, and went not up into the mount;) saying,

6 I *am* the LORD thy God, which brought thee out of the land of Egypt, from the house of bondage.

7 Thou shalt have none other gods before me.

8 Thou shalt not make thee *any* graven image, *or* any likeness *of any thing* that *is* in heaven above, or that *is* in the earth beneath, or that *is* in the waters beneath the earth:

9 Thou shalt not bow down thyself unto them, nor serve them: for I the LORD thy God *am* a jealous God, visiting the iniquity of the fathers upon the children unto the third and fourth *generation* of them that hate me,

10 And shewing mercy unto thousands of them that love me and keep my commandments.

11 Thou shalt not take the name of the LORD thy God in vain: for the LORD will not hold *him* guiltless that taketh his name in vain.

12 Keep the sabbath day to sanctify it, as the LORD thy God hath commanded thee.

13 Six days thou shalt labour, and do all thy work:

14 But the seventh day *is* the sabbath of the LORD thy God: *in it* thou shalt not do any work, thou, nor thy son, nor thy daughter, nor thy manservant, nor thy maidservant, nor thine ox, nor thine ass, nor any of thy cattle, nor thy stranger that *is* within thy gates; that thy manservant and thy maidservant may rest as well as thou.

15 And remember that thou wast a servant in the land of Egypt, and *that* the LORD thy God brought thee out thence through a mighty hand and by a stretched out arm: therefore the LORD thy God commanded thee to keep the sabbath day.

16 Honour thy father and thy mother, as the LORD thy God hath commanded thee; that thy days may be prolonged, and that it may go well with thee, in the land which the LORD thy God giveth thee.

17 Thou shalt not kill.

18 Neither shalt thou commit adultery.

19 Neither shalt thou steal.

20 Neither shalt thou bear false witness against thy neighbour.

21 Neither shalt thou desire thy neighbour's wife, neither shalt thou covet thy neighbour's house, his field, or his manservant, or his maidservant, his ox, or his ass, or any *thing* that *is* thy neighbour's.

22 These words the LORD spake unto all your assembly in the mount out of the midst of the fire, of the cloud, and of the thick darkness, with a great voice: and he added no more. And he wrote them in two tables of stone, and delivered them unto me.

23 And it came to pass, when ye heard the voice out of the midst of the darkness, (for the mountain did burn with fire,) that ye came near unto me, *even* all the heads of your tribes, and your elders;

24 And ye said, Behold, the LORD our God hath shewed us his glory and his greatness, and we have heard his voice out of the midst of the fire: we have seen this day that God doth talk with man, and he liveth.

25 Now therefore why should we die? for this great fire will consume us: if we hear the voice of the LORD our God any more, then we shall die.

26 For who *is there of* all flesh, that hath heard the voice of the living God speaking out of the midst of the fire, as we *have*, and lived?

27 Go thou near, and hear all that the LORD our God shall say: and speak thou unto us all that the LORD our God shall speak unto thee; and we will hear *it*, and do *it*.

28 And the LORD heard the voice of your words, when ye spake unto me; and the LORD said unto me, I have heard the voice of the words of

this people, which they have spoken unto thee: they have well said all that they have spoken.

29 O that there were such an heart in them, that they would fear me, and keep all my commandments always, that it might be well with them, and with their children for ever!

30 Go say to them, Get you into your tents again.

31 But as for thee, stand thou here by me, and I will speak unto thee all the commandments, and the statutes, and the judgments, which thou shalt teach them, that they may do *them* in the land which I give them to possess it.

32 Ye shall observe to do therefore as the LORD your God hath commanded you: ye shall not turn aside to the right hand or to the left.

33 Ye shall walk in all the ways which the LORD your God hath commanded you, that ye may live, and *that it may be* well with you, and *that* ye may prolong *your* days in the land which ye shall possess.

(c. 950 B.C.)

# Romans 12

I beseech you therefore, brethren, by the mercies of God, that ye present your bodies a living sacrifice, holy, acceptable unto God, *which is* your reasonable service.

2 And be not conformed to this world: but be ye transformed by the renewing of your mind, that ye may prove what *is* that good, and acceptable, and perfect, will of God.

3 For I say, through the grace given unto me, to every man that is among you, not to think *of himself* more highly than he ought to think; but to think soberly, according as God hath dealt to every man the measure of faith.

4 For as we have many members in one body, and all members have not the same office:

5 So we, *being* many, are one body in Christ, and every one members one of another.

6 Having then gifts differing according to the grace that is given to us, whether prophecy, *let us prophesy* according to the proportion of faith;

7 Or ministry, *let us wait* on *our* ministering: or he that teacheth, on teaching;

8 Or he that exhorteth, on exhortation: he that giveth, *let him do it* with simplicity; he that ruleth, with diligence; he that sheweth mercy, with cheerfulness.

9 *Let* love be without dissimulation. Abhor that which is evil; cleave to that which is good.

10 *Be* kindly affectioned one to another with brotherly love; in honour preferring one another;

11 Not slothful in business; fervent in spirit; serving the Lord;

12 Rejoicing in hope; patient in tribulation; continuing instant in prayer;

13 Distributing to the necessity of saints; given to hospitality.

14 Bless them which persecute you: bless, and curse not.

15 Rejoice with them that do rejoice, and weep with them that weep.

16 *Be* of the same mind one toward another. Mind not high things, but condescend to men of low estate. Be not wise in your own conceits.

17 Recompense to no man evil for evil. Provide things honest in the sight of all men.

18 If it be possible, as much as lieth in you, live peaceably with all men.

19 Dearly beloved, avenge not yourselves, but *rather* give place unto wrath: for it is written, Vengeance *is* mine; I will repay, saith the Lord.

20 Therefore if thine enemy hunger, feed him; if he thirst, give him drink: for in so doing thou shalt heap coals of fire on his head.

21 Be not overcome of evil, but overcome evil with good.

(c. A.D. 56)

## Benjamin Franklin

# Speech in the Philadelphia Convention at Its Final Session

September 17, 1787

Mr. President, I confess that I do not entirely approve of this constitution at present; but, Sir, I am not sure I shall never approve it; for, having lived long, I have experienced many instances of being obliged, by better information or fuller consideration, to change my opinions even on important subjects, which I once thought right, but found to be otherwise. It is therefore that, the older I grow, the more apt I am to doubt my own judgment of others. Most men, indeed, as well as most sects in religion, think themselves in possession of all truth, and that wherever others differ from them, it is so far error. Steele, a Protestant, in a dedication, tells the Pope that the only difference between our two churches in their opinions of the certainty of their doctrine is, the Romish Church is *infallible,* and the Church of England is *never in the wrong.* But, though many private persons think almost as highly of their own infallibility as of that of their sect, few express it so naturally as a certain French lady, who, in a little dispute with her sister, said, "But I meet with nobody but myself that is *always* in the right." *"Je ne trouve que moi qui aie toujours raison."*

In these sentiments, Sir, I agree to this constitution, with all its faults—if they are such; because I think a general government necessary for us, and there is no *form* of government but what may be a blessing to the people, if well administered; and I believe, further, that this is likely to be well administered for a course of years, and can only end in despotism, as other forms have done before it, when the people shall become so corrupted as to need despotic government, being incapable of any other. I doubt, too, whether any other convention we can obtain may be able to make a better constitution; for, when you assemble a number of men, to have the advantage of their joint wisdom, you inevitably assemble with those men all their prejudices, their passions, their errors of opinion, their local interests, and their selfish views. From such an assembly can a *perfect* production be expected? It therefore astonishes me, Sir, to find this system approaching so near to perfection as it does; and I think it will astonish our enemies, who are waiting with confidence to hear that our councils are confounded like those of the builders of Babel, and that our states are on the point of separation, only to meet hereafter for the purpose of cutting one another's throats. Thus I consent, Sir, to this constitution, because I expect no better, and because I am not sure that it is not the best. The opinions I have had of its *errors* I sacrifice to the public good. I have never whispered a syllable of them abroad. Within these walls they were born, and here they shall die. If every one of us, in returning to our constituents, were to report the objections he has had to it, and endeavor to gain partisans in support of them, we might prevent its being generally received, and thereby lose all the salutary effects and great advantages resulting naturally in our favor among foreign nations, as well as among ourselves, from our real or apparent unanimity. Much of the strength and efficiency of any government, in procuring and securing happiness to the people, depends on *opinion,* on the general opinion of the goodness of that government, as well as of the wisdom and integrity of its governors. I hope, therefore, for our own sakes, as a part of the people, and for the sake of our posterity, that we shall act heartily and unanimously in recommending this constitution, wherever our influence may extend, and turn our future thoughts and endeavors to the means of having it *well administered.*

On the whole, Sir, I cannot help expressing a wish that every member of the convention who may still have objections to it would with me on this occasion doubt a little of his own infallibility, and, to make *manifest* our *unanimity,* put his name to this instrument.

(1787)

**Frederick Douglass**

# The Meaning of July Fourth for the Negro

Speech at Rochester, New York, July 5, 1852

Mr. President, Friends and Fellow Citizens: He who could address this audience without a quailing sensation, has stronger nerves than I have. I do not remember ever to have appeared as a speaker before any assembly more shrinkingly, nor with greater distrust of my ability, than I do this day. A feeling has crept over me quite unfavorable to the exercise of my limited powers of speech. The task before me is one which requires much previous thought and study for its proper performance. I know that apologies of this sort are generally considered flat and unmeaning. I trust, however, that mine will not be so considered. Should I seem at ease, my appearance would much misrepresent me. The little experience I have had in addressing public meetings, in country school houses, avails me nothing on the present occasion.

The papers and placards say that I am to deliver a Fourth of July Oration. This certainly sounds large, and out of the common way, for me. It is true that I have often had the privilege to speak in this beautiful Hall, and to address many who now honor me with their presence. But neither their familiar faces, nor the perfect gage I think I have of Corinthian Hall seems to free me from embarrassment.

The fact is, ladies and gentlemen, the distance between this platform and the slave plantation, from which I escaped, is considerable – and the difficulties to be overcome in getting from the latter to the former are by no means slight. That I am here to-day is, to me, a matter of astonishment as well as of gratitude. You will not, therefore, be surprised, if in what I have to say I evince no elaborate preparation, nor grace my speech with any high sounding exordium. With little experience and with less learning, I have been able to throw my thoughts hastily and imperfectly together; and trusting to your patient and generous indulgence, I will proceed to lay them before you.

This, for the purpose of this celebration, is the Fourth of July. It is the birthday of your National Independence, and of your political freedom. This, to you, is what the Passover was to the emancipated people of God. It carries your minds back to the day, and to the act of your great deliverance; and to the signs, and to the wonders, associated with that act, and that day. This celebration also marks the beginning of another year of your national life; and reminds you that the Republic of America is now 76 years old. I am glad, fellow-citizens, that your nation is so young. Seventy-six years, though a good old age for a man, is but a mere speck in the life of a nation. Three score years and ten is the allotted time for individual men; but nations number their years by thousands. According to this fact, you are, even now, only in the beginning of your national career, still lingering in the period of childhood. I repeat, I am glad this is so. There is hope in the thought, and hope is much needed, under the dark clouds which lower above the horizon. The eye of the reformer is met with angry flashes, portending disastrous times; but his heart may well beat lighter at the thought that America is young, and that she is still in the impressible stage of her existence. May he not hope that high lessons of wisdom, of justice and of truth, will yet give direction to her destiny? Were the nation older, the patriot's heart might be sadder, and the reformer's brow heavier. Its future might be shrouded in gloom, and the hope of its prophets go out in sorrow. There is consolation in the thought that America is young.— Great streams are not easily turned from channels, worn deep in the course of ages. They may sometimes rise in quiet and stately majesty, and inundate the land, refreshing and fertilizing the earth with their mysterious properties. They may also rise in wrath and fury, and bear away, on their angry waves, the accumulated wealth of years of toil and hardship. They, however, gradually flow back to the same old channel, and flow on as serenely as ever. But, while the river may not be turned aside, it may dry up, and leave nothing behind but the withered branch, and the unsightly rock, to howl in the abyss-sweeping wind, the sad tale of departed glory. As with rivers so with nations.

Fellow-citizens, I shall not presume to dwell at length on the associations that cluster about this day. The simple story of it is, that, 76 years ago, the people of this country were British subjects. The style and title of your "sovereign people" (in which you now glory) was not then born. You were under the British Crown. Your fathers esteemed the English Government as the home government; and England as the fatherland. This home government, you know, although a considerable distance from your home, did, in the exercise of its parental prerogatives, impose upon its colonial children, such restraints, burdens and limitations, as, in its mature judgment, it deemed wise, right and proper.

But your fathers, who had not adopted the fashionable idea of this day, of the infallibility of government, and the absolute character of its acts, presumed to differ from the home government in respect to the wisdom and the justice of some of those burdens and restraints. They went so far in their excitement as to pronounce the measures of government unjust, unreasonable, and oppressive, and altogether such as ought not to be quietly submitted to. I scarcely need say, fellow-citizens, that my opinion of those measures fully accords with that of your fathers. Such a declaration of agreement on my part would not be worth much to anybody. It would certainly prove nothing as to what part I might have taken had I lived during the great controversy of 1776. To say now that America was right, and England wrong, is exceedingly easy. Everybody can say it; the dastard, not less than the noble brave, can flippantly discant on the tyranny of England towards the American Colonies. It is fashionable to do so; but there was a time when, to pronounce against England, and in favor of the cause of the colonies, tried men's souls. They who did so were accounted in their day plotters of mischief, agitators and rebels, dangerous men. To side with the right against the wrong, with the weak against the strong, and with the oppressed against the oppressor! here lies the merit, and the one which, of all others, seems unfashionable in our day. The cause of liberty may be stabbed by the men who glory in the deeds of your fathers. But, to proceed.

Feeling themselves harshly and unjustly treated, by the home government, your fathers, like men of honesty, and men of spirit, earnestly sought redress. They petitioned and remonstrated; they did so in a decorous, respectful, and loyal manner. Their conduct was wholly unexceptionable. This, however, did not answer the purpose. They saw themselves treated with sovereign indifference, coldness and scorn. Yet they persevered. They were not the men to look back.

As the sheet anchor takes a firmer hold, when the ship is tossed by the storm, so did the cause of your fathers grow stronger as it breasted the chilling blasts of kingly displeasure. The greatest and best of British statesmen admitted its justice, and the loftiest eloquence of the British Senate came to its support. But, with that blindness which seems to be the unvarying characteristic of tyrants, since Pharaoh and his hosts were drowned in the Red Sea, the British Government persisted in the exactions complained of.

The madness of this course, we believe, is admitted now, even by England; but we fear the lesson is wholly lost on our present rulers.

Oppression makes a wise man mad. Your fathers were wise men, and if they did not go mad, they became restive under this treatment. They felt themselves the victims of grievous wrongs, wholly incurable in their colonial capacity. With brave men there is always a remedy for oppression. Just here, the idea of a total separation of the colonies from the crown was born! It was a startling idea, much more so than we, at this distance of time, regard it. The timid and the prudent (as has been intimated) of that day were, of course, shocked and alarmed by it.

Such people lived then, had lived before, and will, probably, ever have a place on this planet; and their course, in respect to any great change (no matter how great the good to be attained, or the wrong to be redressed by it), may be calculated with as much precision as can be the course of the stars. They hate all changes, but silver, gold and copper change! Of this sort of change they are always strongly in favor.

These people were called Tories in the days of your fathers; and the appellation, probably, conveyed the same idea that is meant by a more modern, though a somewhat less euphonious term, which we often find in our papers, applied to some of our old politicians.

Their opposition to the then dangerous thought was earnest and powerful; but, amid all their terror and affrighted vociferations against it, the alarming and revolutionary idea moved on, and the country with it.

On the 2d of July, 1776, the old Continental Congress, to the dismay of the lovers of ease, and the worshipers of property, clothed that dreadful idea with all the authority of national sanction. They did so in the form of a resolution; and as we seldom hit upon resolutions, drawn up in our day, whose transparency is at all equal to this, it may refresh your minds and help my story if I read it.

Resolved, That these united colonies are, and of right, ought to be free and Independent States; that they are absolved from all allegiance to the British Crown; and that all political connection between them and the State of Great Britain is, and ought to be, dissolved.

Citizens, your fathers made good that resolution. They succeeded; and to-day you reap the fruits of their success. The freedom gained is yours; and you, therefore, may properly celebrate this anniversary. The 4th of July is the first great fact in your nation's history—the very ring-bolt in the chain of your yet undeveloped destiny.

Pride and patriotism, not less than gratitude, prompt you to celebrate and to hold it in perpetual remembrance. I have said that the Declaration of Independence is the ringbolt to the chain of your nation's destiny; so, indeed, I regard it. The principles contained in that instrument are saving principles. Stand by those principles, be true to them on all occasions, in all places, against all foes, and at whatever cost.

From the round top of your ship of state, dark and threatening clouds may be seen. Heavy billows, like mountains in the distance, disclose to the leeward huge forms of flinty rocks! That bolt drawn, that chain broken, and all is lost. Cling to this day—cling to it, and to its principles, with the grasp of a storm-tossed mariner to a spar at midnight.

The coming into being of a nation, in any circumstances, is an interesting event. But, besides general considerations, there were peculiar circumstances which make the advent of this republic an event of special attractiveness.

The whole scene, as I look back to it, was simple, dignified and sublime. The population of the country, at the time, stood at the insignificant number of three millions. The country was poor in the munitions of war. The population was weak and scattered, and the country a wilderness unsubdued. There were then no means of concert and combination, such as exist now. Neither steam nor lightning had then been reduced to order and discipline. From the Potomac to the Delaware was a journey of many days. Under these, and innumerable other disadvantages, your fathers declared for liberty and independence and triumphed.

Fellow Citizens, I am not wanting in respect for the fathers of this republic. The signers of the Declaration of Independence were brave men. They were great men, too—great enough to give frame to a great age. It does not often happen to a nation to raise, at one time, such a number of truly great men. The point from which I am compelled to view them is not, certainly, the most favorable; and yet I cannot contemplate their great deeds with less than admiration. They were statesmen, patriots and heroes, and for the good they did, and the principles they contended for, I will unite with you to honor their memory.

They loved their country better than their own private interests; and, though this is not the highest form of human excellence, all will concede that it is a rare virture, and that when it is exhibited it ought to command respect. He who will, intelligently, lay down his life for his country is a man whom it is not in human nature to despise. Your fathers staked their lives, their fortunes, and their sacred honor, on the cause of their country. In their admiration of liberty, they lost sight of all other interests.

They were peace men; but they preferred revolution to peaceful submission to bondage. They were quiet men; but they did not shrink from agitating against oppression. They showed forbearance; but that they knew its limits. They believed in order; but not in the order of tyranny. With them, nothing was "settled" that was not right. With them, justice, liberty and humanity were "final"; not slavery and oppression. You may well cherish the memory of such men. They were great in their day and generation. Their solid manhood stands out the more as we contrast it with these degenerate times.

How circumspect, exact and proportionate were all their movements! How unlike the politicians of an hour! Their statesmanship looked beyond the passing moment, and stretched away in strength into the distant future. They seized upon eternal principles, and set a glorious example in their defence. Mark them!

Fully appreciating the hardships to be encountered, firmly believing in the right of their cause, honorably inviting the scrutiny of an onlooking world, reverently appealing to heaven to attest their sincerity, soundly comprehending the solemn responsibility they were about to assume, wisely measuring the terrible odds against them, your fathers, the fathers of this republic, did, most deliberately, under the inspiration of a glorious patriotism, and with a sublime faith in the great principles of justice and freedom, lay deep, the corner-stone of the national superstructure, which has risen and still rises in grandeur around you.

Of this fundamental work, this day is the anniversary. Our eyes are met with demonstrations of joyous enthusiasm. Banners and pennants wave exultingly on the breeze. The din of business, too, is hushed. Even mammon seems to have quitted his grasp on this day. The ear-piercing fife and the stirring drum unite their accents with the ascending peal of a thousand church bells. Prayers are made, hymns are sung, and sermons are preached in honor of this day; while the quick martial tramp of a great and multitudinous nation, echoed back by all the hills, valleys and mountains of a vast continent, bespeak the occasion one of thrilling and universal interest—a nation's jubilee.

Friends and citizens, I need not enter further into the causes which led to this anniversary. Many of you understand them better than I do. You could instruct me in regard to them. That is a branch of knowledge in which you feel, perhaps, a much deeper interest than your speaker. The causes which led to the separation of the colonies from the British crown have never lacked for a tongue. They have all been taught in your common schools, narrated at your firesides, unfolded from your pulpits, and thundered from your legislative halls, and are as familiar to you as household words. They form the staple of your national poetry and eloquence.

I remember, also, that, as a people, Americans are remarkably familiar with all facts which make in their own favor. This is esteemed by some as a national trait—perhaps a national weakness. It is a fact, that whatever makes for the wealth or for the reputation of Americans and can be had cheap! will be found by Americans. I shall not be charged with slandering Americans if I say I think the American side of any question may be safely left in American hands.

I leave, therefore, the great deeds of your fathers to other gentlemen whose claim to have been regularly descended will be less likely to be disputed than mine!

My business, if I have any here to-day, is with the present. The accepted time with God and His cause is the ever-living now.

> Trust no future, however pleasant,
>     Let the dead past bury its dead;
> Act, act in the living present,
>     Heart within, and God overhead.

We have to do with the past only as we can make it useful to the present and to the future. To all inspiring motives, to noble deeds which can be gained from the past, we are welcome. But now is the time, the important time. Your fathers have lived, died, and have done their work, and have done much of it well. You live and must die, and you must do your work. You have no right to enjoy a child's share in the labor of your fathers, unless your children are to be blest by your labors. You have no right to wear out and waste the hard-earned fame of your fathers to cover your indolence. Sydney Smith tells us that men seldom eulogize the wisdom and virtues of their fathers, but to excuse some folly or wickedness of their own. This truth is not a doubtful one. There are illustrations of it near and remote, ancient and modern. It was fashionable, hundreds of years ago, for the children of Jacob to boast, we have "Abraham to our father," when they had long lost Abraham's faith and spirit. That people contented themselves under the shadow of Abraham's great name, while they repudiated the deeds which made his name great. Need I remind you that a similar thing is being done all over this country to-day? Need I tell you that the Jews are not the only people who built the tombs of the prophets, and garnished the sepulchers of the righteous? Washington could not die till he had broken the chains of his slaves. Yet his monument is built up by the price of human blood, and the traders in the bodies and souls of men shout—"We have Washington to *our father.*"—Alas! that it should be so; yet so it is.

> The evil that men do, lives after them,
> The good is oft interred with their bones.

Fellow-citizens, pardon me, allow me to ask, why am I called upon to speak here to-day? What have I, or those I represent, to do with your national independence? Are the great principles of political freedom and of natural justice, embodied in that Declaration of Independence, extended to us? and am I, therefore, called upon to bring our humble offering to the national altar, and to confess the benefits and express devout gratitude for the blessings resulting from your independence to us?

Would to God, both for your sakes and ours, that an affirmative answer could be truthfully returned to these questions! Then would my task be light, and my burden easy and delightful. For *who* is there so cold, that a nation's sympathy could not warm him? Who so obdurate and dead to the claims of gratitude, that would not thankfully acknowledge such priceless benefits? Who so stolid and selfish, that would not give his voice to swell the hallelujahs of a nation's jubilee, when the chains of servitude had been torn from his limbs? I am not that man. In a case like that, the dumb might eloquently speak, and the "lame man leap as an hart."

But such is not the state of the case. I say it with a sad sense of the disparity between us. I am not included within the pale of this glorious anniversary! Your high independence only reveals the immeasurable distance between us. The blessings in which you, this day, rejoice, are not enjoyed in common.—The rich inheritance of justice, liberty, prosperity and independence, bequeathed by your fathers, is shared by you, not by me. The sunlight that brought light and healing to you, has brought stripes and death to me. This Fourth July is *yours,* not *mine.* *You* may rejoice, *I* must mourn. To drag a man in fetters into the grand illuminated temple of liberty, and call upon him to join you in joyous anthems, were inhuman mockery and sacrilegious irony. Do you mean, citizens, to mock me, by asking me to speak to-day? If so, there is a parallel to your conduct. And let me warn you that it is dangerous to copy the example of a nation whose crimes, towering up to heaven, were thrown down by the breath of the Almighty, burying that nation in irrevocable ruin! I can to-day take up the plaintive lament of a peeled and woe-smitten people!

"By the rivers of Babylon, there we sat down. Yea! we wept when we remembered Zion. We hanged our harps upon the willows in the midst thereof. For there, they that carried us away captive, required of us a song; and they who wasted us required of us mirth, saying, Sing us one of the songs of Zion. How can we sing the Lord's song in a strange land? If I forget thee, O Jerusalem, let my right hand forget her cunning. If I do not remember thee, let my tongue cleave to the roof of my mouth."

Fellow-citizens, above your national, tumultuous joy, I hear the mournful wail of millions! whose chains, heavy and grievous yesterday, are, to-day, rendered more intolerable by the jubilee shouts that reach them. If I do forget, if I do not faithfully remember those bleeding children of sorrow this day, "may my right hand forget her cunning, and may my tongue cleave to the roof of my mouth!" To forget them, to pass lightly over their wrongs, and to chime in with the popular theme, would be treason most scandalous and shocking, and would make me a reproach before God and the world. My subject, then, fellow-citizens, is American slavery. I shall see this day and its popular characteristics from the slave's point of view. Standing there identified with the American bondman, making his wrongs mine, I do not hesitate to declare, with all my soul, that the character and conduct of this nation never looked blacker to me than on this 4th of July! Whether we turn to the declarations of the past, or to the professions of the present, the conduct of the nation seems equally hideous and revolting. America is false to the past, false to the present, and solemnly binds herself to be false to the future. Standing with God and the crushed and bleeding slave on this occasion, I will, in the name of humanity which is outraged, in the name of liberty which is fettered, in the name of the constitution and the Bible which are disregarded and trampled upon, dare to call in question and to denounce, with all the emphasis I can command, everything that serves to perpetuate slavery—the great sin and shame of America! "I will not equivocate; I will not excuse"; I will use the severest language I can command; and yet not one word shall escape me that any man, whose judgment is not blinded by prejudice, or who is not at heart a slaveholder, shall not confess to be right and just.

But I fancy I hear some one of my audience say, "It is just in this circumstance that you and your brother abolitionists fail to make a favorable impression on the public mind. Would you argue more, and denounce less; would you persuade more, and rebuke less; your cause would be much more likely to succeed." But, I submit, where all is plain there is nothing to be argued. What point in the anti-slavery creed would you have me argue? On what branch of the subject do the people of this country need light? Must I undertake to prove that the slave is a man? That point is conceded already. Nobody doubts it. The slaveholders themselves acknowledge it in the enactment of laws for their government. They acknowledge it when they punish disobedience on the part of the slave. There are seventy-two crimes in the State of Virginia which, if committed by a black man (no matter how ignorant he be), subject him to the punishment of death; while only two of the same crimes will subject a white man to the like punishment. What is this but the acknowledgment that the slave is a moral, intellectual, and responsible being? The manhood of the slave is conceded. It is admitted in the fact that Southern statute books are covered with enactments forbidding, under severe fines and penalties, the teaching of the slave to read or to write. When you can point to any such laws in reference to the beasts of the field, then I may consent to argue the manhood of the slave. When the dogs in your streets, when the fowls of the air, when the cattle on your hills, when the fish of the sea, and the reptiles that crawl, shall be unable to distinguish the slave from a brute, *then* will I argue with you that the slave is a man!

For the present, it is enough to affirm the equal manhood of the Negro race. Is it not astonishing that, while we are ploughing, planting, and reaping, using all kinds of mechanical tools, erecting houses, constructing bridges, building ships, working in metals of brass, iron, copper, silver and gold; that, while we are reading, writing and ciphering, acting as clerks, merchants and secretaries, having among us lawyers, doctors, ministers, poets, authors, editors, orators and teachers; that, while we are engaged in all manner of enterprises common to other men, digging gold in California, capturing the whale in the Pacific, feeding sheep and cattle on the hill-side, living, moving, acting, thinking, planning, living in families as husbands, wives and children, and, above all, confessing and worshipping the Christian's God, and looking hopefully for life and immortality beyond the grave, we are called upon to prove that we are men!

Would you have me argue that man is entitled to liberty? that he is the rightful owner of his own body? You have already declared it. Must I argue the wrongfulness of slavery? Is that a question for Republicans? Is it to be settled by the rules of logic and argumentation, as a matter beset with great difficulty, involving a doubtful application of the principle of justice, hard to be understood? How should I look today, in the presence of Americans, dividing, and subdividing a discourse, to show that men have a natural right to freedom? speaking of it relatively and positively, negatively and affirmatively. To do so, would be to make myself ridiculous, and to offer an insult to your understanding. — There is not a man beneath the canopy of heaven that does not know that slavery is wrong *for him.*

What, am I to argue that it is wrong to make men brutes, to rob them of their liberty, to work them without wages, to keep them ignorant of their relations to their fellow men, to beat them with sticks, to flay their flesh with the lash, to load their limbs with irons, to hunt them with dogs, to sell them at auction, to sunder their families, to knock out their teeth, to burn their flesh, to starve them into obedience and submission to their masters? Must I argue that a system thus marked with blood, and stained with pollution, is *wrong*? No! I will not. I have better employment for my time and strength than such arguments would imply.

What, then, remains to be argued? Is it that slavery is not divine; that God did not establish it; that our doctors of divinity are mistaken? There is blasphemy in the thought. That which is inhuman, cannot be divine! *Who* can reason on such a proposition? They that can, may; I cannot. The time for such argument is passed.

At a time like this, scorching irony, not convincing argument, is needed. O! had I the ability, and could reach the nation's ear, I would, to-day, pour out a fiery stream of biting ridicule, blasting reproach, withering sarcasm, and stern rebuke. For it is not light that is needed, but fire; it is not the gentle shower, but thunder. We need the storm, the whirlwind, and the earthquake. The feeling of the nation must be quickened; the conscience of the nation must be roused; the propriety of the nation must be startled; the hypocrisy of the nation must be exposed; and its crimes against God and man must be proclaimed and denounced.

What, to the American slave, is your 4th of July? I answer; a day that reveals to him, more than all other days in the year, the gross injustice and cruelty to which he is the constant victim. To him, your celebration is a sham; your boasted liberty, an unholy license; your national greatness, swelling vanity; your sounds of rejoicing are empty and heartless; your denunciation of tyrants, brass fronted impudence; your shouts of liberty and equality, hollow mockery; your prayers and hymns, your sermons and thanksgivings, with all your religious parade and solemnity, are, to Him, mere bombast, fraud, deception, impiety, and hypocrisy—a thin veil to cover up crimes which would disgrace a nation of savages. There is not a nation on the earth guilty of practices more shocking and bloody than are the people of the United States, at this very hour.

Go where you may, search where you will, roam through all the monarchies and despotisms of the Old World, travel through South America, search out every abuse, and when you have found the last, lay your facts by the side of the everyday practices of this nation, and you will say with me, that, for revolting barbarity and shameless hypocrisy, America reigns without a rival.

Take the American slave-trade, which we are told by the papers, is especially prosperous just now. Ex-Senator Benton tells us that the price of men was never higher than now. He mentions the fact to show that slavery is in no danger. This trade is one of the peculiarities of American institutions. It is carried on in all the large towns and cities in one-half of this confederacy; and millions are pocketed every year by dealers in this horrid traffic. In several states this trade is a chief source of wealth. It is called (in contradistinction to the foreign slave-trade) *"the internal slave-trade."* It is, probably, called so, too, in order to divert from it the horror with which the foreign slave-trade is contemplated. That trade has long since been denounced by this government as piracy. It has been denounced with burning words from the high places of the nation as an execrable traffic. To arrest it, to put an end to it, this nation keeps a squadron, at immense cost, on the coast of Africa. Everywhere, in this country, it is safe to speak of this foreign slave-trade as a most inhuman traffic, opposed alike to the laws of God and of man. The duty to extirpate and destroy it, is admitted even by our doctors of divinity. In order to put an end to it, some of these last have consented that their colored brethren (nominally free) should leave this country, and establish themselves on the western coast of Africa! It is, however, a notable fact that, while so much execration is poured out by Americans upon all those engaged in the foreign slave-trade, the men engaged in the slave-trade between the states pass without condemnation, and their business is deemed honorable.

Behold the practical operation of this internal slave-trade, the American slave-trade, sustained by American politics and American religion. Here you will see men and women reared like swine for the market. You know what is a swine-drover? I will show you a man-drover. They inhabit all our Southern States. They perambulate the country, and crowd the highways of the nation, with droves of human stock. You will see one of these human flesh jobbers, armed with pistol, whip, and bowie-knife, driving a company of a hundred men, women, and children, from the Potomac to the slave market at New Orleans. These wretched people are to be sold singly, or in lots, to suit purchasers. They are food for the cotton-field and the deadly sugar-mill. Mark the sad procession, as it moves wearily along, and the inhuman wretch who drives them. Hear his savage yells and his blood-curdling oaths, as he hurries on his affrighted captives! There, see the old man with locks thinned and gray. Cast one glance, if you please, upon that young mother, whose shoulders are bare to the scorching sun, her briny tears falling on the brow of the babe in her arms. See, too, that girl of thirteen, weeping, *yes!* weeping, as she thinks of the mother from whom she has been torn! The drove moves tardily. Heat and sorrow have nearly consumed their strength; suddenly you hear a quick snap, like the discharge of a rifle; the fetters clank, and the chain rattles simultaneously; your ears are saluted with a scream, that seems to have torn its way to the centre of your soul! The crack you heard was the sound of the slave-whip; the scream you heard was from the woman you saw with the babe. Her speed had faltered under the weight of her child and her chains! that gash on her shoulder tells her to move on. Follow this drove to New Orleans. Attend the auction; see men examined like horses; see the forms of women rudely and brutally exposed to the shocking gaze of American slave-buyers. See this drove sold and separated forever; and never forget the deep, sad sobs that arose from that scattered multitude. Tell me, citizens, where, under the sun, you can witness a spectacle more fiendish and shocking. Yet this is but a glance at the American slave-trade, as it exists, at this moment, in the ruling part of the United States.

I was born amid such sights and scenes. To me the American slave-trade is a terrible reality. When a child, my soul was often pierced with a sense of its horrors. I lived on Philpot Street, Fell's Point, Baltimore, and have watched from the wharves the slave ships in the Basin, anchored from the shore, with their cargoes of human flesh, waiting for favorable winds to waft them down the Chesapeake. There was, at that time, a grand slave mart kept at the head of Pratt Street, by Austin Woldfolk. His agents were sent into every town and county in Maryland, announcing their arrival, through the papers, and on flaming *"handbills,"* headed cash for Negroes. These men were generally well dressed men, and very captivating in their manners; ever ready to drink, to treat, and to gamble. The fate of many a slave has depended upon the turn of a single card; and many a child has been snatched from the arms of its mother by bargains arranged in a state of brutal drunkenness.

The flesh-mongers gather up their victims by dozens, and drive them, chained, to the general depot at Baltimore. When a sufficient number has been collected here, a ship is chartered for the purpose of conveying the forlorn crew to Mobile, or to New Orleans. From the slave prison to the ship, they are usually driven in the darkness of night; for since the antislavery agitation, a certain caution is observed.

In the deep, still darkness of midnight, I have been often aroused by the dead, heavy footsteps, and the piteous cries of the chained gangs that passed our door. The anguish of my boyish heart was intense; and I was often consoled, when speaking to my mistress in the morning, to hear her say that the custom was very wicked; that she hated to hear the rattle of the chains and the heart-rending cries. I was glad to find one who sympathized with me in my horror.

Fellow-citizens, this murderous traffic is, to-day, in active operation in this boasted republic. In the solitude of my spirit I see clouds of dust raised on the highways of the South; I see the bleeding footsteps; I hear the doleful wail of fettered humanity on the way to the slave-markets, where the victims are to be sold like *horses, sheep,* and *swine,* knocked off to the highest bidder. There I see the tenderest ties ruthlessly broken, to gratify the lust, caprice and rapacity of the buyers and sellers of men. My soul sickens at the sight.

> Is this the land your Fathers loved,
> The freedom which they toiled to win?
> Is this the earth whereon they moved?
> Are these the graves they slumber in?

But a still more inhuman, disgraceful, and scandalous state of things remains to be presented. By an act of the American Congress, not yet two years old, slavery has been nationalized in its most horrible and revolting form. By that act, Mason and Dixon's line has been obliterated; New York has become as Virginia; and the power to hold, hunt, and sell men, women and children, as slaves, remains no longer a mere state institution, but is now an institution of the whole United States. The power is co-extensive with the star-spangled banner, and American Christianity. Where these go, may also go the merciless slave-hunter. Where these are, man is not sacred. He is a bird for the sportsman's gun. By that most foul and fiendish of all human decrees, the liberty and person of every man are put in peril. Your broad republican domain is hunting ground for *men*. *Not* for thieves and robbers, enemies of society, merely, but for men guilty of no crime. Your law-makers have commanded all good citizens to engage in this hellish sport. Your President, your Secretary of State, your *lords, nobles,* and ecclesiastics enforce, as a duty you owe to your free and glorious country, and to your God, that you do this accursed thing. Not fewer than forty Americans have, within the past two years, been hunted down and, without a moment's warning, hurried away in chains, and consigned to slavery and excruciating torture. Some of these have had wives and children, dependent on them for bread; but of this, no account was made. The right of the hunter to his prey stands superior to the right of marriage, and to *all* rights in this republic, the rights of God included! For black men there is neither law nor justice, humanity nor religion. The Fugitive Slave *Law* makes mercy to them a crime; and bribes the judge who tries them. An American judge gets ten dollars for every victim he consigns to slavery, and five, when he fails to do so. The oath of any two villains is sufficient, under this hell-black enactment, to send the most pious and exemplary black man into the remorseless jaws of slavery! His own testimony is nothing. He can bring no witnesses for himself. The minister of American justice is bound by the law to hear but *one* side; and *that* side is the side of the oppressor. Let this damning fact be perpetually told. Let it be thundered around the world that in tyrant-killing, king-hating, people-loving, democratic, Christian America the seats of justice are filled with judges who hold their offices under an open and palpable *bribe,* and are bound, in deciding the case of a man's liberty, *to hear only his accusers!*

In glaring violation of justice, in shameless disregard of the forms of administering law, in cunning arrangement to entrap the defenceless, and in diabolical intent this Fugitive Slave Law stands alone in the annals of tyrannical legislation. I doubt if there be another nation on the globe having the brass and the baseness to put such a law on the statute-book. If any man in this assembly thinks differently from me in this matter, and feels able to disprove my statements, I will gladly confront him at any suitable time and place he may select.

I take this law to be one of the grossest infringements of Christian

Liberty, and, if the churches and ministers of our country were not stupidly blind, or most wickedly indifferent, they, too, would so regard it.

At the very moment that they are thanking God for the enjoyment
of civil and religious liberty, and for the right to worship God according
to the dictates of their own consciences, they are utterly silent in respect to a law which robs religion of its chief significance and makes it
utterly worthless to a world lying in wickedness. Did this law concern
the *"mint, anise, and cummin"* – abridge the right to sing psalms, to
partake of the sacrament, or to engage in any of the ceremonies of religion, it would be smitten by the thunder of a thousand pulpits. A general shout would go up from the church demanding *repeal, repeal,
instant repeal!* – And it would go hard with that politician who presumed to solicit the votes of the people without inscribing this motto on
his banner. Further, if this demand were not complied with, another
Scotland would be added to the history of religious liberty, and the stern
old covenanters would be thrown into the shade. A John Knox would be
seen at every church door and heard from every pulpit, and Fillmore
would have no more quarter than was shown by Knox to the beautiful,
but treacherous, Queen Mary of Scotland. The fact that the church of
our country (with fractional exceptions) does not esteem "the Fugitive
Slave Law" as a declaration of war against religious liberty, implies
that that church regards religion simply as a form of worship, an empty
ceremony, and *not* a vital principle, requiring active benevolence, justice, love, and good will towards man. It esteems sacrifice above mercy;
psalm-singing above right doing; solemn meetings above practical righteousness. A worship that can be conducted by persons who refuse to
give shelter to the houseless, to give bread to the hungry, clothing to the
naked, and who enjoin obedience to a law forbidding these acts of mercy is a curse, not a blessing to mankind. The Bible addresses all such
persons as "scribes, pharisees, hypocrites, who pay tithe of *mint, anise,
and cummin,* and have omitted the weightier matters of the law, judgment, mercy, and faith."

But the church of this country is not only indifferent to the wrongs
of the slave, it actually takes sides with the oppressors. It has made itself the bulwark of American slavery, and the shield of American slave-
hunters. Many of its most eloquent Divines, who stand as the very
lights of the church, have shamelessly given the sanction of religion
and the Bible to the whole slave system. They have taught that man
may, properly, be a slave; that the relation of master and slave is ordained of God; that to send back an escaped bondman to his master is
clearly the duty of all the followers of the Lord Jesus Christ; and this
horrible blasphemy is palmed off upon the world for Christianity.

For my part, I would say, welcome infidelity! welcome atheism!
welcome anything! in preference to the gospel, *as preached by those
Divines!* They convert the very name of religion into an engine of tyranny and barbarous cruelty, and serve to confirm more infidels, in this

age, than all the infidel writings of Thomas Paine, Voltaire, and Boling-
broke put together have done! These ministers make religion a cold and
flinty-hearted thing, having neither principles of right action nor bowels
of compassion. They strip the love of God of its beauty and leave the
throne of religion a huge, horrible, repulsive form. It is a religion for
oppressors, tyrants, man-stealers, and *thugs*. It is not that *"pure and
undefiled religion"* which is from above, and which is *"first pure, then
peaceable, easy to be entreated,* full of mercy and good fruits, *without
partiality, and without hypocrisy."* But a religion which favors the
rich against the poor; which exalts the proud above the humble; which
divides mankind into two classes, tyrants and slaves; which says to the
man in chains, *stay there;* and to the oppressor, *oppress on;* it is a religion which may be professed and enjoyed by all the robbers and enslav-
ers of mankind; it makes God a respecter of persons, denies his father-
hood of the race, and tramples in the dust the great truth of the brotherhood of man. All this we affirm to be true of the popular church, and the
popular worship of our land and nation – a religion, a church, and a
worship which, on the authority of inspired wisdom, we pronounce to be
an abomination in the sight of God. In the language of Isaiah, the
American church might be well addressed, "Bring no more vain obla-
tions; incense is an abomination unto me: the new moons and Sab-
baths, the calling of assemblies, I cannot away with; it is iniquity, even
the solemn meeting. Your new moons, and your appointed feasts my
soul hateth. They are a trouble to me; I am weary to bear them; and
when ye spread forth your hands I will hide mine eyes from you. Yea!
when ye make many prayers, I will not hear. Your hands are full of
blood; cease to do evil, learn to do well; seek judgment; relieve the oppressed; judge for the fatherless; plead for the widow."

The American church is guilty, when viewed in connection with
what it is doing to uphold slavery; but it is superlatively guilty when
viewed in its connection with its ability to abolish slavery.

The sin of which it is guilty is one of omission as well as of commission. Albert Barnes but uttered what the common sense of every man at
all observant of the actual state of the case will receive as truth, when
he declared that "There is no power out of the church that could sustain slavery an hour, if it were not sustained in it."

Let the religious press, the pulpit, the Sunday School, the conference meeting, the great ecclesiastical, missionary, Bible and tract associations of the land array their immense powers against slavery, and
slave-holding; and the whole system of crime and blood would be scattered to the winds, and that they do not do this involves them in the
most awful responsibility of which the mind can conceive.

In prosecuting the anti-slavery enterprise, we have been asked to
spare the church, to spare the ministry; but *how*, we ask, could such a
thing be done? We are met on the threshold of our efforts for the redemption of the slave, by the church and ministry of the country, in

battle arrayed against us; and we are compelled to fight or flee. From *what* quarter, I beg to know, has proceeded a fire so deadly upon our ranks, during the last two years, as from the Northern pulpit? As the champions of oppressors, the chosen men of American theology have appeared—men honored for their so-called piety, and their real learning. The Lords of Buffalo, the Springs of New York, the Lathrops of Auburn, the Coxes and Spencers of Brooklyn, the Gannets and Sharps of Boston, the Deweys of Washington, and other great religious lights of the land have, in utter denial of the authority of *Him* by whom they professed to be called to the ministry, deliberately taught us, against the example of the Hebrews, and against the remonstrance of the Apostles, *that we ought to obey man's law before the law of God.*

My spirit wearies of such blasphemy; and how such men can be supported, as the "standing types and representatives of Jesus Christ," is a mystery which I leave others to penetrate. In speaking of the American church, however, let it be distinctly understood that I mean the *great mass* of the religious organizations of our land. There are exceptions, and I thank God that there are. Noble men may be found, scattered all over these Northern States, of whom Henry Ward Beecher, of Brooklyn; Samuel J. May, of Syracuse; and my esteemed friend (Rev. R. R. Raymond) on the platform, are shining examples; and let me say further, that, upon these men lies the duty to inspire our ranks with high religious faith and zeal, and to cheer us on in the great mission of the slave's redemption from his chains.

One is struck with the difference between the attitude of the American church towards the anti-slavery movement, and that occupied by the churches in England towards a similar movement in that country. There, the church, true to its mission of ameliorating, elevating and improving the condition of mankind, came forward promptly, bound up the wounds of the West Indian slave, and restored him to his liberty. There, the question of emancipation was a high religious question. It was demanded in the name of humanity, and according to the law of the living God. The Sharps, the Clarksons, the Wilberforces, the Buxtons, the Burchells, and the Knibbs were alike famous for their piety and for their philanthropy. The anti-slavery movement *there* was not an anti-church movement, for the reason that the church took its full share in prosecuting that movement: and the anti-slavery movement in this country will cease to be an anti-church movement, when the church of this country shall assume a favorable instead of a hostile position towards that movement.

Americans! your republican politics, not less than your republican religion, are flagrantly inconsistent. You boast of your love of liberty, your superior civilization, and your pure Christianity, while the whole political power of the nation (as embodied in the two great political parties) is solemnly pledged to support and perpetuate the enslavement of three millions of your countrymen. You hurl your anathemas at the crowned headed tyrants of Russia and Austria and pride yourselves on your Democratic institutions, while you yourselves consent to be the mere *tools* and *body-guards* of the tyrants of Virginia and Carolina. You invite to your shores fugitives of oppression from abroad, honor them with banquets, greet them with ovations, cheer them, toast them, salute them, protect them, and pour out your money to them like water; but the fugitives from your own land you advertise, hunt, arrest, shoot, and kill. You glory in your refinement and your universal education; yet you maintain a system as barbarous and dreadful as ever stained the character of a nation—a system begun in avarice, supported in pride, and perpetuated in cruelty. You shed tears over fallen Hungary, and make the sad story of her wrongs the theme of your poets, statesmen, and orators, till your gallant sons are ready to fly to arms to vindicate her cause against the oppressor; but, in regard to the ten thousand wrongs of the American slave, you would enforce the strictest silence, and would hail him as an enemy of the nation who dares to make those wrongs the subject of public discourse! You are all on fire at the mention of liberty for France or for Ireland; but are as cold as an iceberg at the thought of liberty for the enslaved of America. You discourse eloquently on the dignity of labor; yet, you sustain a system which, in its very essence, casts a stigma upon labor. You can bare your bosom to the storm of British artillery to throw off a three-penny tax on tea; and yet wring the last hard earned farthing from the grasp of the black laborers of your country. You profess to believe "that, of one blood, God made all nations of men to dwell on the face of all the earth," and hath commanded all men, everywhere, to love one another; yet you notoriously hate (and glory in your hatred) all men whose skins are not colored like your own. You declare before the world, and are understood by the world to declare that you *"hold these truths to be self-evident, that all men are created equal; and are endowed by their Creator with certain inalienable rights; and that among these are, life, liberty, and the pursuit of happiness;* and yet, you hold securely, in a bondage which, according to your own Thomas Jefferson, *"is worse than ages of that which your fathers rose in rebellion to oppose,"* a *seventh part* of the inhabitants of your country.

Fellow-citizens, I will not enlarge further on your national inconsistencies. The existence of slavery in this country brands your republicanism as a sham, your humanity as a base pretense, and your Christianity as a lie. It destroys your moral power abroad: it corrupts your politicians at home. It saps the foundation of religion; it makes your name a hissing and a bye-word to a mocking earth. It is the antagonistic force in your government, the only thing that seriously disturbs and endangers your *Union*. It fetters your progress; it is the enemy of improvement; the deadly foe of education; it fosters pride; it breeds insolence; it promotes vice; it shelters crime; it is a curse to the earth that supports it; and yet you cling to it as if it were the sheet anchor of all your hopes. Oh! be warned! be warned! a horrible reptile is coiled up in your nation's bosom; the venomous creature is nursing at the tender breast of your youthful republic; *for the love of God, tear away,* and fling from you the hideous monster, and *let the weight of twenty millions crush and destroy it forever!*

But it is answered in reply to all this, that precisely what I have now denounced is, in fact, guaranteed and sanctioned by the Constitution of the United States; that, the right to hold, and to hunt slaves is a part of that Constitution framed by the illustrious Fathers of this Republic.

Then, I dare to affirm, notwithstanding all I have said before, your fathers stooped, basely stooped

> To palter with us in a double sense:
> And keep the word of promise to the ear,
> But break it to the heart.

And instead of being the honest men I have before declared them to be, they were the veriest impostors that ever practised on mankind. This is the inevitable conclusion, and from it there is no escape; but I differ from those who charge this baseness on the framers of the Constitution of the United States. It is a slander upon their memory, at least, so I believe. There is not time now to argue the constitutional question at length; nor have I the ability to discuss it as it ought to be discussed. The subject has been handled with masterly power by Lysander Spooner, Esq., by William Goodell, by Samuel E. Sewall, Esq., and last, though not least, by Gerrit Smith, Esq. These gentlemen have, as I think, fully and clearly vindicated the Constitution from any design to support slavery for an hour.

Fellow-citizens! there is no matter in respect to which the people of the North have allowed themselves to be so ruinously imposed upon as that of the pro-slavery character of the Constitution. In that instrument I hold there is neither warrant, license, nor sanction of the hateful thing; but interpreted, as it ought to be interpreted, the Constitution is a glorious liberty document. Read its preamble, consider its purposes. Is slavery among them? Is it at the gateway? or is it in the temple? it is neither. While I do not intend to argue this question on the present occasion, let me ask, if it be not somewhat singular that, if the Constitution were intended to be, by its framers and adopters, a slaveholding instrument, why neither slavery, slaveholding, nor slave can anywhere be found in it. What would be thought of an instrument, drawn up, legally drawn up, for the purpose of entitling the city of Rochester to a tract of land, in which no mention of land was made? Now, there are certain rules of interpretation for the proper understanding of all legal instruments. These rules are well established. They are plain, common-sense rules, such as you and I, and all of us, can understand and apply, without having passed years in the study of law. I scout the idea that the question of the constitutionality, or unconstitutionality of slavery, is not a question for the people. I hold that every American citizen has a right to form an opinion of the constitution, and to propagate that opinion, and to use all honorable means to make his opinion the prevailing one. Without this right, the liberty of an American citizen would be as insecure as that of a Frenchman. Ex-Vice-President Dallas tells us that the constitution is an object to which no American mind can be too attentive, and no American heart too devoted. He further says, the Constitution, in its words, is plain and intelligible, and is meant for the home-bred, unsophisticated understandings of our fellow-citizens. Senator Berrien tells us that the Constitution is the fundamental law, that which controls all others. The charter of our liberties, which every citizen has a personal interest in understanding thoroughly. The testimony of Senator Breese, Lewis Cass, and many others that might be named, who are everywhere esteemed as sound lawyers, so regard the constitution. I take it, therefore, that it is not presumption in a private citizen to form an opinion of that instrument.

Now, take the Constitution according to its plain reading, and I defy the presentation of a single pro-slavery clause in it. On the other hand, it will be found to contain principles and purposes, entirely hostile to the existence of slavery.

I have detained my audience entirely too long already. At some future period I will gladly avail myself of an opportunity to give this subject a full and fair discussion.

Allow me to say, in conclusion, notwithstanding the dark picture I have this day presented, of the state of the nation, I do not despair of this country. There are forces in operation which must inevitably work the downfall of slavery. "The arm of the Lord is not shortened," and the doom of slavery is certain. I, therefore, leave off where I began, with hope. While drawing encouragement from "the Declaration of Independence," the great principles it contains, and the genius of American Institutions, my spirit is also cheered by the obvious tendencies of the age. Nations do not now stand in the same relation to each other that they did ages ago. No nation can now shut itself up from the surrounding world and trot round in the same old path of its fathers without interference. The time was when such could be done. Long established customs of hurtful character could formerly fence themselves in, and do their evil work with social impunity. Knowledge was then confined and enjoyed by the privileged few, and the multitude walked on in mental darkness. But a change has now come over the affairs of mankind. Walled cities and empires have become unfashionable. The arm of commerce has borne away the gates of the strong city. Intelligence is penetrating the darkest corners of the globe. It makes its pathway over and under the sea, as well as on the earth. Wind, steam, and lightning are its chartered agents. Oceans no longer divide, but link nations together. From Boston to London is now a holiday excursion. Space is comparatively annihilated. — Thoughts expressed on one side of the Atlantic are distinctly heard on the other.

The far off and almost fabulous Pacific rolls in grandeur at our feet. The Celestial Empire, the mystery of ages, is being solved. The fiat of the Almighty, "Let there be Light," has not yet spent its force. No abuse, no outrage whether in taste, sport or avarice, can now hide itself from the all-pervading light. The iron shoe, and crippled foot of China must be seen in contrast with nature. Africa must rise and put on her yet unwoven garment. "Ethiopia shall stretch out her hand unto God." In the fervent aspirations of William Lloyd Garrison, I say, and let every heart join in saying it:

> God speed the year of jubilee
>     The wide world o'er!
> When from their galling chains set free,
> Th' oppress'd shall vilely bend the knee,
> And wear the yoke of tyranny
>     Like brutes no more.
> That year will come, and freedom's reign,
> To man his plundered rights again
>     Restore.
>
> God speed the day when human blood
>     Shall cease to flow!
> In every clime be understood,
> The claims of human brotherhood,
> And each return for evil, good,
>     Not blow for blow;
> That day will come all feuds to end,
> And change into a faithful friend
>     Each foe.
>
> God speed the hour, the glorious hour,
>     When none on earth
> Shall exercise a lordly power,
> Nor in a tyrant's presence cower;
> But to all manhood's stature tower,
>     By equal birth!
> That hour will come, to each, to all,
> And from his prison-house, to thrall
>     Go forth.
>
> Until that year, day, hour, arrive,
> With head, and heart, and hand I'll strive,
> To break the rod, and rend the gyve,
> The spoiler of his prey deprive —
> So witness Heaven!
> And never from my chosen post,
> Whate'er the peril or the cost,
> Be driven.

# A House Divided

Speech Delivered at Springfield, Illinois, at the Close of the Republican State Convention

June 16, 1858

If we could first know where we are, and whither we are tending, we could better judge what to do, and how to do it.

We are now far into the fifth year, since a policy was initiated, with the avowed object, and confident promise, of putting an end to slavery agitation.

Under the operation of that policy, that agitation has not only, not ceased, but has constantly augmented.

In my opinion, it will not cease, until a crisis shall have been reached, and passed—

"A house divided against itself cannot stand."

I believe this government cannot endure, permanently half slave and half free.

I do not expect the Union to be dissolved—I do not expect the house to fall—but I do expect it will cease to be divided.

It will become all one thing, or all the other.

Either the opponents of slavery, will arrest the further spread of it, and place it where the public mind shall rest in the belief that it is in course of ultimate extinction; or its advocates will push it forward, till it shall become alike lawful in all the States, old as well as new—North as well as South.

Have we no tendency to the latter condition?

Let any one who doubts, carefully contemplate that now almost complete legal combination—piece of machinery so to speak—compounded of the Nebraska doctrine, and the Dred Scott decision. Let him consider not only what work the machinery is adapted to do, and how well adapted; but also, let him study the history of its construction, and trace, if he can, or rather fail, if he can, to trace the evidences of design, and concert of action, among its chief bosses, from the beginning.

The new year of 1854 found slavery excluded from more than half the States by State Constitutions, and from most of the national territory by congressional prohibition.

Four days later, commenced the struggle, which ended in repealing that congressional prohibition.

This opened all the national territory to slavery; and was the first point gained.

But, so far, Congress only, had acted; and an indorsement by the people, real or apparent, was indispensable, to save the point already gained, and give chance for more.

This necessity had not been overlooked; but had been provided for, as well as might be, in the notable argument of "squatter sovereignty," otherwise called "sacred right of self government," which latter phrase, though expressive of the only rightful basis of any government, was so perverted in this attempted use of it as the amount to just this: That if any one man, choose to enslave another, no third man shall be allowed to object.

That argument was incorporated into the Nebraska bill itself, in the language which follows.

It being the true intent and meaning of this act not to legislate slavery into any Territory or State, nor to exclude it therefrom; but to leave the people thereof perfectly free to form and regulate their domestic institutions in their own way, subject only to the Constitution of the United States.

Then opened the roar of loose declamation in favor of "Squatter Sovereignty," and "Sacred right of self government."

"But," said opposition members, "let us be more specific—let us amend the bill so as to expressly declare that the people of the Territory may exclude slavery." "Not we," said the friends of the measure; and down they voted the amendment.

While the Nebraska bill was passing through congress, a law case, involving the question of a negro's freedom, by reason of his owner having voluntarily taken him first into a free State and then a territory covered by the congressional prohibition, and held him as a slave for a long time in each, was passing through the U.S. Circuit Court for the District of Missouri; and both Nebraska bill and law suit were brought to a decision in the same month of May, 1854. The negro's name was "Dred Scott," which name now designates the decision finally made in the case.

Before the then next Presidential election, the law case came to, and was argued in the Supreme Court of the United States; but the decision of it was deferred until after the election. Still, before the election, Senator Trumbull, on the floor of the Senate, requests the leading advocate of the Nebraska bill to state his opinion whether the people of a territory can constitutionally exclude slavery from their limits; and the latter answers, "That is a question for the Supreme Court."

The election came. Mr. Buchanan was elected, and the indorsement, such as it was, secured. That was the second point gained. The indorsement, however, fell short of a clear popular majority by nearly four hundred thousand votes, and so, perhaps, was not over-whelmingly reliable and satisfactory.

The outgoing President, in his last annual message, as impressively as possible echoed back upon the people the weight and authority of the indorsement.

The Supreme Court met again; did not announce their decision, but ordered a re-argument.

The Presidential inauguration came, and still no decision of the court; but the incoming President, in his inaugural address, fervently exhorted the people to abide by the forthcoming decision, whatever it might be.

Then, in a few days, came the decision.

The reputed author of the Nebraska bill finds an early occasion to make a speech at this capitol indorsing the Dred Scott Decision, and vehemently denouncing all opposition to it.

The new President, too, seizes the early occasion of the Silliman letter to indorse and strongly construe that decision, and to express his astonishment that any different view had ever been entertained.

At length a squabble springs up between the President and the author of the Nebraska bill, on the mere question of fact, whether the Lecompton constitution was or was not, in any just sense, made by the people of Kansas; and in that quarrel the latter declares that all he wants is a fair vote for the people, and that he cares not whether slavery be voted down or voted up. I do not understand his declaration that he cares not whether slavery be voted down or voted up, to be intended by him other than as an apt definition of the policy he would impress upon the public mind — the principle for which he declares he has suffered much, and is ready to suffer to the end.

And well may he cling to that principle. If he has any parental feeling, well may he cling to it. That principle, is the only shred left of his original Nebraska doctrine. Under the Dred Scott decision, "squatter sovereignty" squatted out of existence, tumbled down like temporary scaffolding — like the mold at the foundry served through one blast and fell back into loose sand — helped to carry an election, and then was kicked to the winds. His late joint struggle with the Republicans, against the Lecompton Constitution, involves nothing of the original Nebraska doctrine. That struggle was made on a point, the right of a people to make their own constitution, upon which he and the Republicans have never differed.

The several points of the Dred Scott decision, in connection with Senator Douglas' "care not" policy, constitute the piece of machinery, in its present state of advancement.

The working points of that machinery are:

First, that no negro slave, imported as such from Africa, and no descendant of such slave can ever be a citizen of any State, in the sense of that term as used in the Constitution of the United States.

This point is made in order to deprive the negro, in every possible event, of the benefit of that provision of the United States Constitution, which declares that —

"the citizens of each State shall be entitled to all privileges and immunities of citizens in the several States."

Secondly, that "subject to the Constitution of the United States," neither Congress nor a Territorial Legislature can exclude slavery from any United States Territory.

This point is made in order that individual men may fill up the territories with slaves, without danger of losing them as property, and thus enhance the chances of permanency to the institution through all the future.

Thirdly, that whether the holding a negro in actual slavery in a free State, makes him free, as against the holder, the United States courts will not decide, but will leave to be decided by the courts of any slave State the negro may be forced into by the master.

This point is made, not to be pressed immediately; but, if acquiesced in for a while, and apparently indorsed by the people at an election, then to sustain the logical conclusion that what Dred Scott's master might lawfully do with Dred Scott, in the free State of Illinois, every other master may lawfully do with any other one or one thousand slaves, in Illinois, or in any other free State.

Auxiliary to all this, and working hand in hand with it, the Nebraska doctrine, or what is left of it, is to educate and mould public opinion, at least Northern public opinion, to not care whether slavery is voted down or voted up.

This shows exactly where we now are; and partially also, whither we are tending.

It will throw additional light on the latter, to go back, and run the mind over the string of historical facts already stated. Several things will now appear less dark and mysterious than they did when they were transpiring. The people were to be left "perfectly free" "subject only to the Constitution." What the Constitution had to do with it, outsiders could not then see. Plainly enough now, it was an exactly fitted nitch for the Dred Scott decision to afterward come in, and declare that perfect freedom of the people, to be just no freedom at all.

Why was the amendment, expressly declaring the right of the people to exclude slavery, voted down? Plainly enough now, the adoption of it, would have spoiled the nitch for the Dred Scott decision.

Why was the court decision held up? Why, even a Senator's individual opinion withheld, till after the Presidential election? Plainly enough now, the speaking out then would have damaged the "perfectly free" argument upon which the election was to be carried.

Why the outgoing President's felicitation on the indorsement? Why the delay of a reargument? Why the incoming President's advance exhortation in favor of the decision?

These things look like the cautious patting and petting of a spirited horse, preparatory to mounting him, when it is dreaded that he may give the rider a fall.

And why the hasty after indorsements of the decision by the President and others?

We cannot absolutely know that all these exact adaptations are the result of preconcert. But when we see a lot of framed timbers, different portions of which we know have been gotten out at different times and places and by different workmen—Stephen, Franklin, Roger, and

James, for instance — and we see these timbers joined together, and see they exactly make the frame of a house or a mill, all the tenons and mortises exactly fitting, and all the lengths and proportions of the different pieces exactly adapted to their respective places, and not a piece too many or too few — not omitting even scaffolding — or, if a single piece be lacking, we see the place in the frame exactly fitted and prepared to yet bring such piece in — in such a case, we find it impossible not to believe that Stephen and Franklin and Roger and James all understood one another from the beginning, and all worked upon a common plan or draft drawn up before the first lick was struck.

It should not be overlooked that, by the Nebraska bill, the people of a State as well as Territory, were to be left "perfectly free" "subject only to the Constitution."

Why mention a State? They were legislating for territories, and not for or about States. Certainly the people of a State are and ought to be subject to the Constitution of the United States; but why is mention of this lugged into this merely territorial law? Why are the people of a territory and the people of a state therein lumped together, and their relation to the Constitution therein treated as being precisely the same?

While the opinion of the Court, by Chief Justice Taney, in the Dred Scott case, and the separate opinions of all the concurring Judges, expressly declare that the Constitution of the United States neither permits Congress nor a territorial legislature to exclude slavery from any United States territory, they all omit to declare whether or not the same Constitution permits a state, or the people of a State, to exclude it.

Possibly, this is a mere omission; but who can be quite sure, if McLean or Curtis had sought to get into the opinion a declaration of unlimited power in the people of a state to exclude slavery from their limits, just as Chase and Mace sought to get such declaration, in behalf of the people of a territory, into the Nebraska bill — I ask, who can be quite sure that it would not have been voted down, in the one case, as it had been in the other?

The nearest approach to the point of declaring the power of a State over slavery, is made by Judge Nelson. He approaches it more than once, using the precise idea, and almost the language too, of the Nebraska act. On one occasion his exact language is, "except in cases where the power is restrained by the Constitution of the United States, the law of the State is supreme over the subject of slavery within its jurisdiction."

In what cases the power of the states is so restrained by the U.S. Constitution is left an open question, precisly [sic] as the same question, as to the restraint on the power of the territories was left open in the Nebraska act. Put that and that together, and we have another nice little nitch, which we may, ere long, see filled with another Supreme Court decision, declaring that the Constitution of the United States does not permit a state to exclude slavery from its limits.

And this may especially be expected if the doctrine of "care not whether slavery be voted down or voted up," shall gain upon the public mind sufficiently to give promise that such a decision can be maintained when made.

Such a decision is all that slavery now lacks of being alike lawful in all the States.

Welcome or unwelcome, such decision is probably coming, and will soon be upon us, unless the power of the present political dynasty shall be met and overthrown. We shall lie down pleasantly dreaming that the people of Missouri are on the verge of making their State free; and we shall awake to the reality, instead, that the Supreme Court has made Illinois a slave State.

To meet and overthrow the power of that dynasty, is the work now before all those who would prevent that consummation.

That is what we have to do.

But how can we best do it?

There are those who denounce us openly to their own friends, and yet whisper us softly, that Senator Douglas is the aptest instrument there is, with which to effect that object. They do not tell us, nor has he told us, that he wishes any such object to be effected. They wish us to infer all, from the facts, that he now has a little quarrel with the present head of the dynasty; and that he has regularly voted with us, on a single point, upon which, he and we, have never differed.

They remind us that he is a great man, and that the largest of us are very small ones. Let this be granted. But "a living dog is better than a dead lion." Judge Douglas, if not a dead lion for this work, is at least a caged and toothless one. How can he oppose the advances of slavery? He don't care anything about it. His avowed mission is impressing the "public heart" to care nothing about it.

A leading Douglas Democratic newspaper thinks Douglas' superior talent will be needed to resist the revival of the African slave trade.

Does Douglas believe an effort to revive that trade is approaching? He has not said so. Does he really think so? But if it is, how can he resist it? For years he has labored to prove it a sacred right of white men to take negro slaves into the new territories. Can he possibly show that it is less a sacred right to buy them where they can be bought cheapest? And, unquestionably they can be bought cheaper in Africa than in Virginia.

He has done all in his power to reduce the whole question of slavery to one of a mere right of property; and as such, how can he oppose the foreign slave trade—how can he refuse that trade in that "property" shall be "perfectly free"—unless he does it as a protection to the home production? And as the home producers will probably not ask the protection, he will be wholly without a ground of opposition.

Senator Douglas holds, we know, that a man may rightfully be wiser to-day than he was yesterday—that he may rightfully change when he finds himself wrong.

But, can we for that reason, run ahead, and infer that he will make any particular change, of which he, himself, has given no intimation? Can we safely base our action upon any such vague inference?

Now, as ever, I wish to not misrepresent Judge Douglas' position, question his motives, or do aught that can be personally offensive to him.

Whenever, if ever, he and we can come together on principle so that our great cause may have assistance from his great ability, I hope to have interposed no adventitious obstacle.

But clearly, he is not now with us – he does not pretend to be – he does not promise to ever be.

Our cause, then, must be intrusted to, and conducted by its own undoubted friends – those whose hands are free, whose hearts are in the work – who do care for the result.

Two years ago the Republicans of the nation mustered over thirteen hundred thousand strong.

We did this under the single impulse of resistance to a common danger, with every external circumstance against us.

Of strange, discordant, and even, hostile elements, we gathered from the four winds, and formed and fought the battle through, under the constant hot fire of a disciplined, proud, and pampered enemy.

Did we brave all then to falter now? – now – when that same enemy is wavering, dissevered, and belligerent?

The result is not doubtful. We shall not fail – if we stand firm, we shall not fail.

Wise counsels may accelerate or mistakes delay it, but sooner or later the victory is sure to come.

# Farewell at Springfield

February 11, 1861

My friends: No one, not in my situation, can appreciate my feeling of sadness at this parting. To this place, and the kindness of these people, I owe everything. Here I have lived a quarter of a century, and have passed from a young to an old man. Here my children have been born, and one is buried. I now leave, not knowing when or whether ever I may return, with a task before me greater than that which rested upon Washington. Without the assistance of that Divine Being who ever attended him, I cannot succeed. With that assistance, I cannot fail. Trusting in Him who can go with me, and remain with you, and be everywhere for good, let us confidently hope that all will yet be well. To His care commending you, as I hope in your prayers you will commend me, I bid you an affectionate farewell.

# First Inaugural Address

March 4, 1861

Fellow-citizens of the United States: In compliance with a custom as old as the government itself, I appear before you to address you briefly, and to take, in your presence, the oath prescribed by the Constitution of the United States, to be taken by the President "before he enters on the execution of his office."

I do not consider it necessary at present for me to discuss those matters of administration about which there is no special anxiety or excitement.

Apprehension seems to exist among the people of the Southern States, that by the accession of a Republican Administration, their property, and their peace, and personal security, are to be endangered. There has never been any reasonable cause for such apprehension. Indeed, the most ample evidence to the contrary has all the while existed, and been open to their inspection. It is found in nearly all the published speeches of him who now addresses you. I do but quote from one of those speeches when I declare that "I have no purpose, directly or indirectly, to interfere with the institution of slavery in the States where it exists. I believe I have no lawful right to do so, and I have no inclination to do so." Those who nominated and elected me did so with full knowledge that I had made this, and many similar declarations, and had never recanted them. And more than this, they placed in the platform, for my acceptance, and as a law to themselves, and to me, the clear and emphatic resolution which I now read:

*Resolved,* That the maintenance inviolate of the rights of the States, and especially the right of each State to order and control its own domestic institutions according to its own judgment exclusively, is essential to that balance of power on which the perfection and endurance of our political fabric depend; and we denounce the lawless invasion by armed force of the soil of any State or Territory, no matter under what pretext, as among the gravest of crimes.

I now reiterate these sentiments: and in doing so, I only press upon the public attention the most conclusive evidence of which the case is susceptible, that the property, peace and security of no section are to be in any wise endangered by the now incoming Administration. I add too, that all the protection which, consistently with the Constitution and the laws, can be given, will be cheerfully given to all the States when lawfully demanded, for whatever cause—as cheerfully to one section as to another.

There is much controversy about the delivering up of fugitives from service or labor. The clause I now read is as plainly written in the Constitution as any other of its provisions:

No person held to service or labor in one State, under the laws thereof, escaping into another, shall, in consequence of any law or regulation therein, be discharged from such service or labor, but shall be delivered up on claim of the party to whom such service or labor may be due.

It is scarcely questioned that this provision was intended by those who made it, for the reclaiming of what we call fugitive slaves; and the intention of the law-giver is the law. All members of Congress swear their support to the whole Constitution—to this provision as much as to any other. To the proposition, then, that slaves whose cases come within the terms of this clause, "shall be delivered up," their oaths are unanimous. Now, if they would make the effort in good temper, could they not, with nearly equal unanimity, frame and pass a law, by means of which to keep good that unanimous oath?

There is some difference of opinion whether this clause should be enforced by national or by state authority; but surely that difference is not a very material one. If the slave is to be surrendered, it can be of but little consequence to him, or to others, by which authority it is done. And should any one, in any case, be content that his oath shall go unkept, on a merely unsubstantial controversy as to *how* it shall be kept?

Again, in any law upon this subject, ought not all the safeguards of liberty known in civilized and humane jurisprudence to be introduced, so that a free man be not, in any case, surrendered as a slave? And might it not be well, at the same time to provide by law for the enforcement of that clause in the Constitution which guarantees that "the citizens of each State shall be entitled to all privileges and immunities of citizens in the several States"?

I take the official oath to-day, with no mental reservations, and with no purpose to construe the Constitution or laws, by any hypercritical rules. And while I do not choose now to specify particular acts of Congress as proper to be enforced, I do suggest that it will be much safer for all, both in official and private stations, to conform to, and abide by, all those acts which stand unrepealed, than to violate any of them, trusting to find impunity in having them held to be unconstitutional.

It is seventy-two years since the first inauguration of a President under our national Constitution. During that period fifteen different and greatly distinguished citizens, have, in succession, administered the executive branch of the government. They have conducted it through many perils; and, generally, with great success. Yet, with all this scope for [of] precedent, I now enter upon the same task for the brief constitutional term of four years, under great and peculiar difficulty. A disruption of the Federal Union, heretofore only menaced, is now formidably attempted.

I hold, that in contemplation of universal law, and of the Constitution, the Union of these States is perpetual. Perpetuity is implied, if not expressed, in the fundamental law of all national governments. It is safe to assert that no government proper, ever had a provision in its organic law for its own termination. Continue to execute all the express provisions of our national Constitution, and the Union will endure forever—it being impossible to destroy it, except by some action not provided for in the instrument itself.

Again, if the United States be not a government proper, but an association of States in the nature of contract merely, can it, as a contract, be peaceably unmade, by less than all the parties who made it? One party to a contract may violate it—break it, so to speak; but does it not require all to lawfully rescind it?

Descending from these general principles, we find the proposition that, in legal contemplation, the Union is perpetual, confirmed by the history of the Union itself. The Union is much older than the Constitution. It was formed in fact, by the Articles of Association in 1774. It was matured and continued by the Declaration of Independence in 1776. It was further matured and the faith of all the then thirteen States expressly plighted and engaged that it should be perpetual, by the Articles of Confederation in 1778. And finally, in 1787, one of the declared objects for ordaining and establishing the Constitution, was *"to form a more perfect Union."*

But if [the] destruction of the Union, by one, or by a part only, of the States, be lawfully possible, the Union is *less* perfect than before the Constitution, having lost the vital element of perpetuity.

It follows from these views that no State, upon its own mere motion, can lawfully get out of the Union,—that *resolves* and *ordinances* to that effect are legally void, and that acts of violence, within any State or States, against the authority of the United States, are insurrectionary or revolutionary, according to circumstances.

I therefore consider that in view of the Constitution and the laws, the Union is unbroken; and to the extent of my ability I shall take care, as the Constitution itself expressly enjoins upon me, that the laws of the Union be faithfully executed in all the States. Doing this I deem to be only a simple duty on my part; and I shall perform it, so far as practicable, unless my rightful masters, the American people, shall withhold the requisite means, or, in some authoritative manner, direct the contrary. I trust this will not be regarded as a menace, but only as the declared purpose of the Union that it will constitutionally defend and maintain itself.

In doing this there needs to be no bloodshed or violence; and there shall be none, unless it be forced upon the national authority. The power confided to me will be used to hold, occupy, and possess the property and places belonging to the government, and to collect the duties and imposts; but beyond what may be necessary for these objects, there will be no invasion—no using of force against or among the people anywhere. Where hostility to the United States, in any interior locality, shall be so great and so universal, as to prevent competent resident citizens from holding the Federal offices, there will be no attempt to force obnoxious strangers among the people for that object. While the strict legal right may exist in the government to enforce the exercise of these offices, the attempt to do so would be so irritating, and so nearly impracticable with all, that I deem it better to forego, for the time, the uses of such offices.

The mails, unless repelled, will continue to be furnished in all parts of the Union. So far as possible, the people everywhere shall have that sense of perfect security which is most favorable to calm thought and reflection. The course here indicated will be followed, unless current events and experience shall show a modification or change to be proper; and in every case and exigency my best discretion will be exercised according to circumstances actually existing, and with a view and a hope of a peaceful solution of the national troubles, and the restoration of fraternal sympathies and affections.

That there are persons in one section or another who seek to destroy the Union at all events, and are glad of any pretext to do it, I will neither affirm or deny; but if there be such, I need address no word to them. To those, however, who really love the Union, may I not speak?

Before entering upon so grave a matter as the destruction of our national fabric, with all its benefits, its memories and its hopes, would it not be wise to ascertain precisely why we do it? Will you hazard so desperate a step, while there is any possibility that any portion of the ills you fly from have no real existence? Will you, while the certain ills you fly to, are greater than all the real ones you fly from? Will you risk the commission of so fearful a mistake?

All profess to be content in the Union, if all constitutional rights can be maintained. Is it true, then, that any right, plainly written in the Constitution, has been denied? I think not. Happily the human mind is so constituted, that no party can reach to the audacity of doing this. Think, if you can, of a single instance in which a plainly written provision of the Constitution has ever been denied. If, by the mere force of numbers, a majority should deprive a minority of any clearly written constitutional right, it might, in a moral point of view, justify revolution — certainly would, if such a right were a vital one. But such is not our case. All the vital rights of minorities, and of individuals, are so plainly assured to them, by affirmations and negations, guarantees and prohibitions, in the Constitution, that controversies never arise concerning them. But no organic law can ever be framed with a provision specifically applicable to every question which may occur in practical administration. No foresight can anticipate, nor any document of reasonable length contain express provisions for all possible questions. Shall fugitives from labor be surrendered by national or by State authority? The Constitution does not expressly say. *May* Congress prohibit slavery in the territories? The Constitution does not expressly say. *Must* Congress protect slavery in the territories? The Constitution does not expressly say.

From questions of this class spring all our constitutional controversies, and we divide upon them into majorities and minorities. If the minority will not acquiesce, the majority must, or the government must cease. There is no other alternative; for continuing the government, is acquiescence on one side or the other. If a minority, in such case, will secede rather than acquiesce, they make a precedent which, in turn, will divide and ruin them; for a minority of their own will secede from them whenever a majority refuses to be controlled by such minority. For instance, why may not any portion of a new confederacy, a year or two hence, arbitrarily secede again, precisely as portions of the present Union now claim to secede from it? All who cherish disunion sentiments, are now being educated to the exact temper of doing this.

Is there such perfect identity of interests among the States to compose a new Union, as to produce harmony only, and prevent renewed secession?

Plainly, the central idea of secession, is the essence of anarchy. A majority, held in restraint by constitutional checks and limitations, and always changing easily with deliberate changes of popular opinions and sentiments is the only true sovereign of a free people. Whoever rejects it, does, of necessity, fly to anarchy or to despotism. Unanimity is impossible; the rule of a minority, as a permanent arrangement, is wholly inadmissible; so that, rejecting the majority principle, anarchy or despotism in some form is all that is left.

I do not forget the position assumed by some, that constitutional questions are to be decided by the Supreme Court; nor do I deny that such decisions must be binding in any case, upon the parties to a suit, as to the object of that suit, while they are also entitled to very high respect and consideration in all parallel cases by all other departments of the government. And while it is obviously possible that such decision may be erroneous in any given case, still the evil effect following it, being limited to that particular case, with the chance that it may be over-ruled, and never become a precedent for other cases, can better be borne than could the evils of a different practice. At the same time, the candid citizen must confess that if the policy of the government upon vital questions, affecting the whole people, is to be irrevocably fixed by decisions of the Supreme Court, the instant they are made, in ordinary litigation between parties, in personal actions, the people will have ceased to be their own rulers, having to that extent practically resigned their government into the hands of that eminent tribunal. Nor is there in this view any assault upon the court or the judges. It is a duty from which they may not shrink, to decide cases properly brought before them; and it is no fault of theirs if others seek to turn their decisions to political purposes.

One section of our country believes slavery is *right,* and ought to be extended, while the other believes it is *wrong,* and ought not to be extended. This is the only substantial dispute. The fugitive slave clause of the Constitution, and the law for the suppression of the foreign slave trade, are each as well enforced, perhaps, as any law can ever be in a community where the moral sense of the people imperfectly supports the law itself. The great body of the people abide by the dry legal obligation in both cases, and a few break over in each. This, I think, cannot be perfectly cured; and it would be worse in both cases *after* the separation of the sections, than before. The foreign slave trade, now imperfectly suppressed, would be ultimately revived without restriction, in one section; while fugitive slaves, now only partially surrendered, would not be surrendered at all, by the other.

Physically speaking, we cannot separate. We cannot remove our respective sections from each other, nor build an impassable wall between them. A husband and wife may be divorced, and go out of the presence, and beyond the reach of each other; but the different parts of our country cannot do this. They cannot but remain face to face; and intercourse, either amicable or hostile, must continue between them. Is it possible, then, to make that intercourse more advantageous or more satisfactory, *after* separation than *before*? Can aliens make treaties easier than friends can make laws? Can treaties be more faithfully enforced between aliens than laws can among friends? Suppose you go to war, you cannot fight always; and when, after much loss on both sides, and no gain on either, you cease fighting, the identical old questions, as to terms of intercourse, are again upon you.

This country, with its institutions, belongs to the people who inhabit it. Whenever they shall grow weary of the existing government, they can exercise their *constitutional* right of amending it, or their *revolutionary* right to dismember or overthrow it. I cannot be ignorant of the fact that many worthy and patriotic citizens are desirous of having the national Constitution amended. While I make no recommendation of amendments, I fully recognize the rightful authority of the people over the whole subject to be exercised in either of the modes prescribed in the instrument itself; and I should under existing circumstances favor rather than oppose a fair opportunity being afforded the people to act upon it.

I will venture to add that to me the Convention mode seems preferable, in that it allows amendments to originate with the people themselves, instead of only permitting them to take or reject propositions, originated by others, not especially chosen for the purpose, and which might not be precisely such as they would wish to either accept or refuse. I understand a proposed amendment to the Constitution, which amendment, however, I have not seen, has passed Congress, to the effect that the federal government shall never interfere with the domestic institutions of the States, including that of persons held to service. To avoid misconstruction of what I have said, I depart from my purpose not to speak of particular amendments, so far as to say that holding such a provision to now be implied constitutional law, I have no objection to its being made express and irrevocable.

The Chief Magistrate derives all his authority from the people, and they have conferred none upon him to fix terms for the separation of the States. The people themselves can do this also if they choose; but the executive, as such, has nothing to do with it. His duty is to administer the present government, as it came to his hands, and to transmit it, unimpaired by him, to his successor.

Why should there not be a patient confidence in the ultimate justice of the people? Is there any better or equal hope, in the world? In our present differences, is either party without faith of being in the right? If the Almighty Ruler of nations, with his eternal truth and justice, be on your side of the North or on yours of the South, that truth, and that justice, will surely prevail, by the judgment of this great tribunal, the American people.

By the frame of the government under which we live, this same people have wisely given their public servants but little power for mischief; and have, with equal wisdom, provided for the return of that little to their own hands at very short intervals.

While the people retain their virtue and vigilance, no administration, by any extreme of wickedness or folly, can very seriously injure the government in the short space of four years.

My countrymen, one and all, think calmly and *well,* upon this whole subject. Nothing valuable can be lost by taking time. If there be an object to *hurry* any of you, in hot haste, to a step which you would never take *deliberately,* that object will be frustrated by taking time; but no good object can be frustrated by it. Such of you as are now dissatisfied, still have the old Constitution unimpaired, and, on the sensitive point, the laws of your own framing under it; while the new administration will have no immediate power, if it would, to change either. If it were admitted that you who are dissatisfied, hold the right side in the dispute, there still is no single good reason for precipitate action. Intelligence, patriotism, Christianity, and a firm reliance on Him, who has never yet forsaken this favored land, are still competent to adjust, in the best way, all our present difficulty.

In *your* hands, my dissatisfied fellow countrymen, and not in *mine,* is the momentous issue of civil war. The government will not assail *you.* You can have no conflict, without being yourselves the aggressors. *You* have no oath registered in Heaven to destroy the government, while *I* shall have the most solemn one to "preserve, protect and defend" it.

I am loth to close. We are not enemies, but friends. We must not be enemies. Though passion may have strained, it must not break our bonds of affection. The mystic chords of memory, stretching from every battle-field, and patriot grave, to every living heart and hearth-stone, all over this broad land, will yet swell the chorus of the Union, when again touched, as surely they will be, by the better angels of our nature.

# The Gettysburg Address

November 19, 1863

Four score and seven years ago our fathers brought forth on this continent a new nation, conceived in liberty, and dedicated to the proposition that all men are created equal.

Now we are engaged in a great civil war, testing whether that nation, or any nation so conceived and so dedicated, can long endure. We are met on a great battlefield of that war. We have come to dedicate a portion of that field as a final resting-place for those who here gave their lives that that nation might live. It is altogether fitting and proper that we should do this.

But in a larger sense we cannot dedicate, we cannot consecrate, we cannot hallow this ground. The brave men, living and dead, who struggled here have consecrated it, far above our poor power to add or detract. The world will little note, nor long remember what we say here, but it can never forget what they did here. It is for us, the living, rather, to be dedicated here to the unfinished work which they who fought here have thus far so nobly advanced. It is rather for us to be here dedicated to the great task remaining before us,—that from these honored dead we take increased devotion to that cause for which they gave the last full measure of devotion; that we here highly resolve that these dead shall not have died in vain; that this nation, under God, shall have a new birth of freedom; and that government of the people, by the people, and for the people, shall not perish from the earth.

# Second Inaugural Address

March 4, 1865

At this second appearing to take the oath of the presidential office, there is less occasion for an extended address than there was at the first. Then a statement, somewhat in detail, of a course to be pursued, seemed fitting and proper. Now, at the expiration of four years, during which public declarations have been constantly called forth on every point and phase of the great contest which still absorbs the attention, and engrosses the energies of the nation, little that is new could be presented. The progress of our arms, upon which all else chiefly depends, is as well known to the public as to myself; and it is, I trust, reasonably satisfactory and encouraging to all. With high hope for the future, no prediction in regard to it is ventured.

On the occasion corresponding to this four years ago, all thoughts were anxiously directed to an impending civil war. All dreaded it—all sought to avert it. While the inaugural address was being delivered from this place, devoted altogether to *saving* the Union without war, insurgent agents were in the city seeking to *destroy* it without war— seeking to dissolve the Union, and divide effects, by negotiation. Both parties deprecated war; but one of them would *make* war rather than let the nation survive; and the other would *accept* war rather than let it perish. And the war came.

One eighth of the whole population were colored slaves, not distributed generally over the Union, but localized in the Southern part of it. These slaves constituted a peculiar and powerful interest. All knew that this interest was, somehow, the cause of the war. To strengthen, perpetuate, and extend this interest was the object for which the insurgents would rend the Union, even by war; while the government claimed no right to do more than to restrict the territorial enlargement of it. Neither party expected for the war, the magnitude, or the duration, which it has already attained. Neither anticipated that the *cause* of the conflict might cease with, or even before, the conflict itself should cease. Each looked for an easier triumph, and a result less fundamental and astounding. Both read the same Bible, and pray to the same God; and each invokes His aid against the other. It may seem strange that any men should dare to ask a just God's assistance in wringing their bread from the sweat of other men's faces; but let us judge not that we be not judged. The prayers of both could not be answered; that of neither has been answered fully. The Almighty has his own purposes. "Woe unto the world because of offences! for it must needs be that offences come; but woe to that man by whom the offence cometh!" If we shall suppose that American Slavery is one of those offences which, in the providence of God, must needs come, but which, having continued through His appointed time, He now wills to remove, and that He gives to both North and South, this terrible war, as the woe due to those by whom the offence came, shall we discern therein any departure from those divine attributes which the believers in a Living God always ascribe to Him? Fondly do we hope—fervently do we pray—that this mighty scourge of war may speedily pass away. Yet, if God wills that it continue, until all the wealth piled by the bond-man's two hundred and fifty years of unrequited toil shall be sunk, and until every drop of blood drawn with the lash, shall be paid by another drawn with the sword, as was said three thousand years ago, so still it must be said "the judgments of the Lord, are true and righteous altogether."

With malice toward none; with charity for all; with firmness in the right, as God gives us to see the right, let us strive on to finish the work we are in; to bind up the nation's wounds; to care for him who shall have borne the battle, and for his widow, and his orphan—to do all which may achieve and cherish a just and lasting peace, among ourselves, and with all nations.

## 435

Much Madness is divinest Sense –
To a discerning Eye –
Much Sense – the starkest Madness –
'Tis the Majority
In this, as All, prevail –
Assent – and you are sane –
Demur – you're straightway dangerous –
And handled with a Chain –

(c. 1862, 1890)

## 441

This is my letter to the World
That never wrote to Me –
The simple News that Nature told –
With tender Majesty

Her Message is committed
To Hands I cannot see –
For love of Her – Sweet – countrymen –
Judge tenderly – of Me

(c. 1862, 1890)

## 449

I died for Beauty – but was scarce
Adjusted in the Tomb
When One who died for Truth, was lain
In an adjoining Room –

He questioned softly "Why I failed"?
"For Beauty", I replied –
"And I – for Truth – Themself are One –
We Brethren, are", He said –

And so, as Kinsmen, met a Night—
We talked between the Rooms—
Until the Moss had reached our lips—
And covered up—our names—

                                        (c. 1862, 1890)


## *Rudyard Kipling*

# Fuzzy-Wuzzy

### (Sudan Expeditionary Force)

We've fought with many men acrost the seas,
    An' some of 'em was brave an' some was not:
The Paythan an' the Zulu an' Burmese;
    But the Fuzzy was the finest o' the lot.
We never got a ha'porth's change of 'im:
    'E squatted in the scrub an' 'ocked our 'orses,
'E cut our sentries up at Sua*kim*,
    An' 'e played the cat an' banjo with our forces.
    So 'ere's *to* you, Fuzzy-Wuzzy, at your 'ome in the Soudan;
    You're a pore benighted 'eathen but a first-class fightin' man;
    We gives you your certificate, an' if you want it signed
    We'll come an' 'ave a romp with you whenever you're inclined.


We took our chanst among the Kyber 'ills,
The Boers knocked us silly at a mile,
The Burman give us Irriwaddy chills,
An' a Zulu *impi* dished us up in style:
But all we ever got from such as they
    Was pop to what the Fuzzy made us swaller;
We 'eld our bloomin' own, the papers say,
    But man for man the Fuzzy knocked us 'oller.
        Then 'ere's *to* you, Fuzzy-Wuzzy, an' the missis and the kid;
        Our orders was to break you, an' of course we went an' did.
        We sloshed you with Martinis, an' it wasn't 'ardly fair;
        But for all the odds agin' you, Fuzzy-Wuz, you broke the square.

E 'asn't got no papers of 'is own,
    'E 'asn't got no medals nor rewards,
So *we* must certify the skill 'e's shown,
    In usin' of 'is long two-'anded swords:
When 'e's 'oppin' in an' out among the bush
    With 'is coffin-'eaded shield an' shovel-spear,
An 'appy day with Fuzzy on the rush
    Will last an 'ealthy Tommy for a year.
        So 'ere's *to* you, Fuzzy-Wuzzy, an' your friends which are no more,
        If we 'adn't lost some messmates we would 'elp you to deplore.
        But give an' take's the gospel, an' we'll call the bargain fair,
        For if you 'ave lost more than us, you crumpled up the square!

'E rushes at the smoke when we let drive,
    An', before we know, 'e's 'ackin' at our 'ead;
'E's all 'ot sand an' ginger when alive,
    An' 'e's generally shammin' when 'e's dead.
'E's a daisy, 'e's a ducky, 'e's a lamb!
    'E's a injia-rubber idiot on the spree,
'E's the on'y thing that doesn't give a damn
    For a Regiment o' British Infantree!
        So 'ere's *to* you, Fuzzy-Wuzzy, at your 'ome in the Soudan;
        You're a poor benighted 'eathen but a first-class fightin' man;
        An' 'ere's *to* you, Fuzzy-Wuzzy, with your 'ayrick 'ead of 'air—
        You big black boundin' beggar—for you broke a British square!

                        (1890)

## *Booker T. Washington*

# The Atlanta Exposition Address

The Atlanta Exposition, at which I had been asked to make an address as a representative of the Negro race, as stated in the last chapter, was opened with a short address from Governor Bullock. After other interesting exercises, including an invocation from Bishop Nelson, of Georgia, a dedicatory ode by Albert Howell, Jr., and addresses by the President of the Exposition and Mrs. Joseph Thompson, the President of the Woman's Board, Governor Bullock introduced me with the words, "We have with us to-day a representative of Negro enterprise and Negro civilization."

When I arose to speak, there was considerable cheering, especially from the coloured people. As I remember it now, the thing that was uppermost in my mind was the desire to say something that would cement the friendship of the races and bring about hearty coöperation between them. So far as my outward surroundings were concerned, the only thing that I recall distinctly now is that when I got up, I saw thousands of eyes looking intently into my face. The following is the address which I delivered: —

Mr. President and Gentlemen of the Board of Directors and Citizens: One-third of the population of the South is of the Negro race. No enterprise seeking the material, civil, or moral welfare of this section can disregard this element of our population and reach the highest success. I but convey to you, Mr. President and Directors, the sentiment of the masses of my race when I say that in no way have the value and manhood of the American Negro been more fittingly and generously recognized than by the managers of this magnificent Exposition at every stage of its progress. It is a recognition that will do more to cement the friendship of the two races than any occurrence since the dawn of our freedom.

Not only this, but the opportunity here afforded will awaken among us a new era of industrial progress. Ignorant and inexperienced, it is not strange that in the first years of our new life we began at the top instead of at the bottom; that a seat in Congress or the state legislature was more sought than real estate or industrial skill; that the political convention of stump speaking had more attractions than starting a dairy farm or truck garden.

A ship lost at sea for many days suddenly sighted a friendly vessel. From the mast of the unfortunate vessel was seen a signal, "Water, water; we die of thirst!" The answer from the friendly vessel at once came back, "Cast down your bucket where you are." A second time the signal, "Water, water; send us water!" ran up from the distressed vessel, and was answered, "Cast down your bucket where you are." And a third and fourth signal for water was answered, "Cast down your bucket where you are." The captain of the distressed vessel, at last heeding the injunction, cast down his bucket, and it came up full of fresh, sparkling water from the mouth of the Amazon River. To those of my race who depend on bettering their condition in a foreign land or who underestimate the importance of cultivating friendly relations with the Southern white man, who is their next-door neighbour, I would say: "Cast down your bucket where you are"—cast it down in making friends in every manly way of the people of all races by whom we are surrounded.

Cast it down in agriculture, mechanics, in commerce, in domestic service, and in the professions. And in this connection it is well to bear in mind that whatever other sins the South may be called to bear, when it comes to business, pure and simple, it is in the South that the Negro is given a man's chance in the commercial world, and in nothing is this Exposition more eloquent than in emphasizing this chance. Our greatest danger is that in the great leap from slavery to freedom we may overlook the fact that the masses of us are to live by the productions of our hands, and fail to keep in mind that we shall prosper in proportion as we learn to dignify and glorify common labour and put brains and skill into the common occupations of life; shall prosper in proportion as we learn to draw the line between the superficial and the substantial, the ornamental gewgaws of life and the useful. No race can prosper till it learns that there is as much dignity in tilling a field as in writing a poem. It is at the bottom of life we must begin, and not at the top. Nor should we permit our grievances to overshadow our opportunities.

To those of the white race who look to the incoming of those of foreign birth and strange tongue and habits for the prosperity of the South, were I permitted I would repeat what I say to my own race, "Cast down your bucket where you are." Cast it down among the eight millions of Negroes whose habits you know, whose fidelity and love you have tested in days when to have proved treacherous meant the ruin of your firesides. Cast down your bucket among these people who have, without strikes and labour wars, tilled your fields, cleared your forests, builded your railroads and cities, and brought forth treasures from the bowels of the earth, and helped make possible this magnificent representation of the progress of the South. Casting down your bucket among my people, helping and encouraging them as you are doing on these grounds, and to education of head, hand, and heart, you will find that they will buy your surplus land, make blossom the waste places in your fields, and run your factories. While doing this, you can be sure in the future, as in the past, that you and your families will be surrounded by the most patient, faithful, law-abiding, and unresentful people that the world has seen. As we have proved our loyalty to you in the past, in nursing your children, watching by the sick-bed of your mothers and fathers, and often following them with tear-dimmed eyes to their graves, so in the future, in our humble way, we shall stand by you with a devotion that no foreigner can approach, ready to lay down our lives, if need be, in defence of yours, interlacing our industrial, commercial, civil, and religious life with yours in a way that shall make the interests of both races one. In all things that are purely social we can be as separate as the fingers, yet one as the hand in all things essential to mutual progress.

There is no defence or security for any of us except in the highest intelligence and development of all. If anywhere there are efforts tending to curtail the fullest growth of the Negro, let these efforts be turned into stimulating, encouraging, and making him the most useful and intelligent citizen. Effort or means so invested will pay a thousand per cent. interest. These efforts will be twice blessed—"blessing him that gives and him that takes."

There is no escape through law of man or God from the inevitable:—

The laws of changeless justice bind
Oppressor with oppressed;
And close as sin and suffering joined
We march to fate abreast.

Nearly sixteen millions of hands will aid you in pulling the load upward, or they will pull against you the load downward. We shall constitute one-third and more of the ignorance and crime of the South, or one-third its intelligence and progress; we shall contribute one-third to the business and industrial prosperity of the South, or we shall prove a veritable body of death, stagnating, depressing, retarding every effort to advance the body politic.

Gentlemen of the Exposition, as we present to you our humble effort at an exhibition of our progress, you must not expect overmuch. Starting thirty years ago with ownership here and there in a few quilts and pumpkins and chickens (gathered from miscellaneous sources), remember the path that has led from these to the inventions and production of agricultural implements, buggies, steam-engines, newspapers, books, statuary, carving, paintings, the management of drugstores and banks, has not been trodden without contact with thorns and thistles. While we take pride in what we exhibit as a result of our independent efforts, we do not for a moment forget that our part in this exhibition would fall far short of your expectations but for the constant help that has come to our educational life, not only from the Southern states, but especially from Northern philanthropists, who have made their gifts a constant stream of blessing and encouragement.

The wisest among my race understand that the agitation of questions of social equality is the extremest folly, and that progress in the enjoyment of all the privileges that will come to us must be the result of severe and constant struggle rather than of artificial forcing. No race that has anything to contribute to the markets of the world is long in any degree ostracized. It is important and right that all privileges of the law be ours, but it is vastly more important that we be prepared for the exercises of these privileges. The opportunity to earn a dollar in a factory just now is worth infinitely more than the opportunity to spend a dollar in an opera-house.

In conclusion, may I repeat that nothing in thirty years has given us more hope and encouragement, and drawn us so near to you of the white race, as this opportunity offered by the Exposition; and here bending, as it were, over the altar that represents the results of the struggles of your race and mine, both starting practically empty-handed three decades ago, I pledge that in your effort to work out the great and intricate problem which God has laid at the doors of the South, you shall have at all times the patient, sympathetic help of my race; only let this be constantly in mind, that, while from representations in these buildings of the product of field, of forest, of mine, of factory, letters,

and art, much good will come, yet far above and beyond material benefits will be that higher good, that, let us pray God, will come, in a blot-
ting out of sectional differences and racial animosities and suspicions,
in a determination to administer absolute justice, in a willing obedience
among all classes to the mandates of law. This, this, coupled with our
material prosperity, will bring into our beloved South a new heaven and
a new earth.

The first thing that I remember, after I had finished speaking, was
that Governor Bullock rushed across the platform and took me by the
hand, and that others did the same. I received so many and such hearty
congratulations that I found it difficult to get out of the building. I did
not appreciate to any degree, however, the impression which my address seemed to have made, until the next morning, when I went into
the business part of the city. As soon as I was recognized, I was surprised to find myself pointed out and surrounded by a crowd of men
who wished to shake hands with me. This was kept up on every street
on to which I went, to an extent which embarrassed me so much that I
went back to my boarding-place. The next morning I returned to Tuskegee. At the station in Atlanta, and at almost all of the stations at which
the train stopped between that city and Tuskegee, I found a crowd of
people anxious to shake hands with me.

The papers in all parts of the United States published the address in
full, and for months afterward there were complimentary editorial references to it. Mr. Clark Howell, the editor of the Atlanta *Constitution*,
telegraphed to a New York paper, among other words, the following, "I
do not exaggerate when I say that Professor Booker T. Washington's
address yesterday was one of the most notable speeches, both as to
character and as to the warmth of its reception, ever delivered to a
Southern audience. The address was a revelation. The whole speech is
a platform upon which blacks and whites can stand with full justice to
each other."

The Boston *Transcript* said editorially: "The speech of Booker T.
Washington at the Atlanta Exposition, this week, seems to have
dwarfed all the other proceedings and the Exposition itself. The sensation that it has caused in the press has never been equalled."

I very soon began receiving all kinds of propositions from lecture
bureaus, and editors of magazines and papers, to take the lecture platform, and to write articles. One lecture bureau offered me fifty thousand dollars, or two hundred dollars a night and expenses, if I would
place my services at its disposal for a given period. To all these communications I replied that my life-work was at Tuskegee; and that whenever I spoke it must be in the interests of the Tuskegee school and my
race, and that I would enter into no arrangements that seemed to place
a mere commercial value upon my services.

Some days after its delivery I sent a copy of my address to the President of the United States, the Hon. Grover Cleveland. I received from him the following autograph reply: —

> Gray Gables, Buzzard's Bay, Mass.,
> October 6, 1895.
>
> Booker T. Washington, Esq.:
>
> My Dear Sir: I thank you for sending me a copy of your address delivered at the Atlanta Exposition.
>
> I thank you with much enthusiasm for making the address. I have read it with intense interest, and I think the Exposition would be fully justified if it did not do more than furnish the opportunity for its delivery. Your words cannot fail to delight and encourage all who wish well for your race; and if our coloured fellow-citizens do not from your utterances gather new hope and form new determinations to gain every valuable advantage offered them by their citizenship, it will be strange indeed.
>
> Yours very truly,
> Grover Cleveland.

Later I met Mr. Cleveland, for the first time, when, as President, he visited the Atlanta Exposition. At the request of myself and others he consented to spend an hour in the Negro Building, for the purpose of inspecting the Negro exhibit and of giving the coloured people in attendance an opportunity to shake hands with him. As soon as I met Mr. Cleveland I became impressed with his simplicity, greatness, and rugged honesty. I have met him many times since then, both at public functions and at his private residence in Princeton, and the more I see of him the more I admire him. When he visited the Negro Building in Atlanta he seemed to give himself up wholly, for that hour, to the coloured people. He seemed to be as careful to shake hands with some old coloured "auntie" clad partially in rags, and to take as much pleasure in doing so, as if he were greeting some millionaire. Many of the coloured people took advantage of the occasion to get him to write his name in a book or on a slip of paper. He was as careful and patient in doing this as if he were putting his signature to some great state document.

Mr. Cleveland has not only shown his friendship for me in many personal ways, but has always consented to do anything I have asked of him for our school. This he has done, whether it was to make a personal donation or to use his influence in securing the donations of others. Judging from my personal acquaintance with Mr. Cleveland, I do not believe that he is conscious of possessing any colour prejudice. He is too great for that. In my contact with people I find that, as a rule, it is only the little, narrow people who live for themselves, who never read good books, who do not travel, who never open up their souls in a way to permit them to come into contact with other souls — with the great outside world. No man whose vision is bounded by colour can come into contact with what is highest and best in the world. In meeting men, in many places, I have found that the happiest people are those who do the most for others; the most miserable are those who do the least. I have also found that few things, if any, are capable of making one so blind and narrow as race prejudice. I often say to our students, in the course of my talks to them on Sunday evenings in the chapel, that the longer I live and the more experience I have of the world, the more I am convinced that, after all, the one thing that is most worth living for—and dying for, if need be—is the opportunity of making some one else more happy and more useful.

The coloured people and the coloured newspapers at first seemed to be greatly pleased with the character of my Atlanta address, as well as with its reception. But after the first burst of enthusiasm began to die away, and the coloured people began reading the speech in cold type, some of them seemed to feel that they had been hypnotized. They seemed to feel that I had been too liberal in my remarks toward the Southern whites, and that I had not spoken out strongly enough for what they termed the "rights" of the race. For a while there was a reaction, so far as a certain element of my own race was concerned, but later these reactionary ones seemed to have been won over to my way of believing and acting.

While speaking of changes in public sentiment, I recall that about ten years after the school at Tuskegee was established, I had an experience that I shall never forget. Dr. Lyman Abbott, then the pastor of Plymouth Church, and also editor of the *Outlook* (then the *Christian Union*), asked me to write a letter for his paper giving my opinion of the exact condition, mental and moral, of the coloured ministers in the South, as based upon my observations. I wrote the letter, giving the exact facts as I conceived them to be. The picture painted was a rather black one—or, since I am black, shall I say "white"? It could not be otherwise with a race but a few years out of slavery, a race which had not had time or opportunity to produce a competent ministry.

What I said soon reached every Negro minister in the country, I think, and the letters of condemnation which I received from them were not few. I think that for a year after the publication of this article every association and every conference or religious body of any kind, of my race, that met, did not fail before adjourning to pass a resolution condemning me, or calling upon me to retract or modify what I had said. Many of these organizations went so far in their resolutions as to advise parents to cease sending their children to Tuskegee. One association even appointed a "missionary" whose duty it was to warn the people against sending their children to Tuskegee. This missionary had a son in the school, and I noticed that, whatever the "missionary" might have said or done with regard to others, he was careful not to take his son away from the institution. Many of the coloured papers, especially those that were the organs of religious bodies, joined in the general chorus of condemnation or demands for retraction.

During the whole time of the excitement, and through all the criticism, I did not utter a word of explanation or retraction. I knew that I was right, and that time and the sober second thought of the people would vindicate me. It was not long before the bishops and other church leaders began to make a careful investigation of the conditions of the ministry, and they found out that I was right. In fact, the oldest and most influential bishop in one branch of the Methodist Church said that my words were far too mild. Very soon public sentiment began making itself felt, in demanding a purifying of the ministry. While this is not yet complete by any means, I think I may say, without egotism, and I have been told by many of our most influential ministers, that my words had much to do with starting a demand for the placing of a higher type of men in the pulpit. I have had the satisfaction of having many who once condemned me thank me heartily for my frank words.

The change of the attitude of the Negro ministry, so far as regards myself, is so complete that at the present time I have no warmer friends among any class than I have among the clergymen. The improvement in the character and life of the Negro ministers is one of the most gratifying evidences of the progress of the race. My experience with them, as well as other events in my life, convince me that the thing to do, when one feels sure that he has said or done the right thing, and is condemned, is to stand still and keep quiet. If he is right, time will show it.

In the midst of the discussion which was going on concerning my Atlanta speech, I received the letter which I give below, from Dr. Gilman, the President of Johns Hopkins University, who had been made chairman of the judges of award in connection with the Atlanta Exposition: —

> Johns Hopkins University, Baltimore,
> President's Office, September 30, 1895.
>
> Dear Mr. Washington: Would it be agreeable to you to be one of the Judges of Award in the Department of Education at Atlanta? If so, I shall be glad to place your name upon the list. A line by telegraph will be welcomed.
>
> Yours very truly,
> D. C. Gilman.

I think I was even more surprised to receive this invitation than I had been to receive the invitation to speak at the opening of the Exposition. It was to be a part of my duty, as one of the jurors, to pass not only upon the exhibits of the coloured schools, but also upon those of the white schools. I accepted the position, and spent a month in Atlanta in performance of the duties which it entailed. The board of jurors was a large one, consisting in all of sixty members. It was about equally divided between Southern white people and Northern white people. Among them were college presidents, leading scientists and men of letters, and specialists in many subjects. When the group of jurors to which I was assigned met for organization, Mr. Thomas Nelson Page, who was one of the number, moved that I be made secretary of that division, and the motion was unanimously adopted. Nearly half of our division were Southern people. In performing my duties in the inspection of the exhibits of white schools I was in every case treated with respect, and at the close of our labours I parted from my associates with regret.

I am often asked to express myself more freely than I do upon the political condition and the political future of my race. These recollections of my experience in Atlanta give me the opportunity to do so briefly. My own belief is, although I have never before said so in so many words, that the time will come when the Negro in the South will be accorded all the political rights which his ability, character, and material possessions entitle him to. I think, though, that the opportunity to freely exercise such political rights will not come in any large degree through outside or artificial forcing, but will be accorded to the Negro by the Southern white people themselves, and that they will protect him in the exercise of those rights. Just as soon as the South gets over the old feeling that it is being forced by "foreigners," or "aliens," to do something which it does not want to do, I believe that the change in the direction that I have indicated is going to begin. In fact, there are indications that it is already beginning in a slight degree.

Let me illustrate my meaning. Suppose that some months before the opening of the Atlanta Exposition there had been a general demand from the press and public platform outside the South that a Negro be given a place on the opening programme, and that a Negro be placed upon the board of jurors of award. Would any such recognition of the race have taken place? I do not think so. The Atlanta officials went as far as they did because they felt it to be a pleasure, as well as a duty, to reward what they considered merit in the Negro race. Say what we will, there is something in human nature which we cannot blot out, which makes one man, in the end, recognize and reward merit in another, regardless of colour or race.

I believe it is the duty of the Negro — as the greater part of the race is already doing — to deport himself modestly in regard to political claims, depending upon the slow but sure influences that proceed from the possession of property, intelligence, and high character for the full recognition of his political rights. I think that the according of the full exercise of political rights is going to be a matter of natural, slow growth, not an over-night, gourd-vine affair. I do not believe that the Negro should cease voting, for a man cannot learn the exercise of self-government by ceasing to vote any more than a boy can learn to swim by keeping out of the water, but I do believe that in his voting he should more and more be influenced by those of intelligence and character who are his next-door neighbours.

I know coloured men who, through the encouragement, help, and advice of Southern white people, have accumulated thousands of dollars' worth of property, but who, at the same time, would never think of going to those same persons for advice concerning the casting of their ballots. This, it seems to me, is unwise and unreasonable, and should cease. In saying this I do not mean that the Negro should truckle, or not vote from principle, for the instant he ceases to vote from principle he loses the confidence and respect of the Southern white man even.

I do not believe that any state should make a law that permits an ignorant and poverty-stricken white man to vote, and prevents a black man in the same condition from voting. Such a law is not only unjust, but it will react, as all unjust laws do, in time; for the effect of such a law is to encourage the Negro to secure education and property, and at the same time it encourages the white man to remain in ignorance and poverty. I believe that in time, through the operation of intelligence and friendly race relations, all cheating at the ballot box in the South will cease. It will become apparent that the white man who begins by cheating a Negro out of his ballot soon learns to cheat a white man out of his, and that the man who does this ends his career of dishonesty by the theft of property or by some equally serious crime. In my opinion, the time will come when the South will encourage all of its citizens to vote. It will see that it pays better, from every standpoint, to have healthy, vigorous life than to have that political stagnation which always results when one-half of the population has no share and no interest in the Government.

As a rule, I believe in universal, free suffrage, but I believe that in the South we are confronted with peculiar conditions that justify the protection of the ballot in many of the states, for a while at least, either by an educational test, a property test, or by both combined; but whatever tests are required, they should be made to apply with equal and exact justice to both races.

(1895)

# *W . E . B . DuBois*

## *from* **The Souls of Black Folks**
Of Mr. Booker T. Washington and Others

Easily the most striking thing in the history of the American Negro since 1876 is the ascendancy of Mr. Booker T. Washington. It began at the time when war memories and ideals were rapidly passing; a day of astonishing commercial development was dawning; a sense of doubt and hesitation overtook the freedmen's sons, — then it was that his leading began. Mr. Washington came, with a simple definite programme, at the psychological moment when the nation was a little ashamed of having bestowed so much sentiment on Negroes, and was concentrating its energies on Dollars. His programme of industrial education, conciliation of the South, and submission and silence as to civil and political rights, was not wholly original; the Free Negroes from 1830 up to wartime had striven to build industrial schools, and the American Missionary Association had from the first taught various trades; and Price and others had sought a way of honorable alliance with the best of the Southerners. But Mr. Washington first indissolubly linked these things; he put enthusiasm, unlimited energy, and perfect faith into this programme, and changed it from a by-path into a veritable Way of Life. And the tale of the methods by which he did this is a fascinating study of human life.

It startled the nation to hear a Negro advocating such a programme after many decades of bitter complaint; it startled and won the applause of the South, it interested and won the admiration of the North; and after a confused murmur of protest, it silenced if it did not convert the Negroes themselves.

To gain the sympathy and coöperation of the various elements comprising the white South was Mr. Washington's first task; and this, at the time Tuskegee was founded, seemed, for a black man, well-nigh impossible. And yet ten years later it was done in the words spoken at Atlanta: "In all things purely social we can be as separate as the five fingers, and yet one as the hand in all things essential to mutual progress." This "Atlanta Compromise" is by all odds the most notable thing in Mr. Washington's career. The South interpreted it in different ways: the radicals received it as a complete surrender of the demand for civil and political equality; the conservatives, as a generously conceived working basis for mutual understanding. So both approved it, and to-day its author is certainly the most distinguished Southerner since Jefferson Davis, and the one with the largest personal following.

Next to this achievement comes Mr. Washington's work in gaining place and consideration in the North. Others less shrewd and tactful had formerly essayed to sit on these two stools and had fallen between them; but as Mr. Washington knew the heart of the South from birth and training, so by singular insight he intuitively grasped the spirit of the age which was dominating the North. And so thoroughly did he learn the speech and thought of triumphant commercialism, and the ideals of material prosperity, that the picture of a lone black boy poring over a French grammar amid the weeds and dirt of a neglected home soon seemed to him the acme of absurdities. One wonders what Socrates and St. Francis of Assisi would say to this.

And yet this very singleness of vision and thorough oneness with his age is a mark of the successful man. It is as though Nature must needs make men narrow in order to give them force. So Mr. Washington's cult has gained unquestioning followers, his work has wonderfully prospered, his friends are legion, and his enemies are confounded. To-day he stands as the one recognized spokesman of his ten million fel-lows, and one of the most notable figures in a nation of seventy mil-lions. One hesitates, therefore, to criticise a life which, beginning with so little, has done so much. And yet the time is come when one may speak in all sincerity and utter courtesy of the mistakes and shortcom-ings of Mr. Washington's career, as well as of his triumphs, without being thought captious or envious, and without forgetting that it is eas-ier to do ill than well in the world.

The criticism that has hitherto met Mr. Washington has not always been of this broad character. In the South especially has he had to walk warily to avoid the harshest judgments, — and naturally so, for he is dealing with the one subject of deepest sensitiveness to that section. Twice — once when at the Chicago celebration of the Spanish-American War he alluded to the color-prejudice that is "eating away the vitals of the South," and once when he dined with President Roosevelt — has the resulting Southern criticism been violent enough to threaten seriously his popularity. In the North the feeling has several times forced itself into words, that Mr. Washington's counsels of submission overlooked certain elements of true manhood, and that his educational programme was unnecessarily narrow. Usually, however, such criticism has not found open expression, although, too, the spiritual sons of the Abolition-ists have not been prepared to acknowledge that the schools founded before Tuskegee, by men of broad ideals and self-sacrificing spirit, were wholly failures or worthy of ridicule. While, then, criticism has not failed to follow Mr. Washington, yet the prevailing public opinion of the land has been but too willing to deliver the solution of a wearisome problem into his hands, and say, "If that is all you and your race ask, take it."

Among his own people, however, Mr. Washington has encountered the strongest and most lasting opposition, amounting at times to bitter-ness, and even to-day continuing strong and insistent even though largely silenced in outward expression by the public opinion of the na-tion. Some of this opposition is, of course, mere envy; the disappoint-ment of displaced demagogues and the spite of narrow minds. But aside from this, there is among educated and thoughtful colored men in all parts of the land a feeling of deep regret, sorrow, and apprehension at the wide currency and ascendancy which some of Mr. Washington's theories have gained. These same men admire his sincerity of purpose, and are willing to forgive much to honest endeavor which is doing something worth the doing. They coöperate with Mr. Washington as far as they conscientiously can; and, indeed, it is no ordinary tribute to this man's tact and power that, steering as he must between so many di-verse interests and opinions, he so largely retains the respect of all.

But the hushing of the criticism of honest opponents is a dangerous thing. It leads some of the best of the critics to unfortunate silence and paralysis of effort, and others to burst into speech so passionately and intemperately as to lose listeners. Honest and earnest criticism from those whose interests are most nearly touched, — criticism of writers by readers, of government by those governed, of leaders by those led, — this is the soul of democracy and the safeguard of modern society. If the best of the American Negroes receive by outer pressure a leader whom they had not recognized before, manifestly there is here a certain palpable gain. Yet there is also irreparable loss, — a loss of that peculiarly valuable education which a group receives when by search and criticism it finds and commissions its own leaders. The way in which this is done is at once the most elementary and the nicest problem of social growth. History is but the record of such group-leadership; and yet how infinitely changeful is its type and character! And of all types and kinds, what can be more instructive than the leadership of a group within a group? — that curious double movement where real progress may be negative and actual advance be relative retrogression. All this is the social student's inspiration and despair.

Now in the past the American Negro has had instructive experience in the choosing of group leaders, founding thus a peculiar dynasty which in the light of present conditions is worth while studying. When sticks and stones and beasts form the sole environment of a people, their attitude is largely one of determined opposition to and conquest of natural forces. But when to earth and brute is added an environment of men and ideas, then the attitude of the imprisoned group may take three main forms, — a feeling of revolt and revenge; an attempt to adjust all thought and action to the will of the greater group; or, finally, a determined effort at self-realization and self-development despite environing opinion. The influence of all of these attitudes at various times can be traced in the history of the American Negro, and in the evolution of his successive leaders.

Before 1750, while the fire of African freedom still burned in the veins of the slaves, there was in all leadership or attempted leadership but the one motive of revolt and revenge, — typified in the terrible Maroons, the Danish blacks, and Cato of Stono, and veiling all the Americas in fear of insurrection. The liberalizing tendencies of the latter half of the eighteenth century brought, along with kindlier relations between black and white, thoughts of ultimate adjustment and assimilation. Such aspiration was especially voiced in the earnest songs of Phyllis, in the martyrdom of Attucks, the fighting of Salem and Poor, the intellectual accomplishments of Banneker and Derham, and the political demands of the Cuffes.

Stern financial and social stress after the war cooled much of the previous humanitarian ardor. The disappointment and impatience of the Negroes at the persistence of slavery and serfdom voiced itself in two movements. The slaves in the South, aroused undoubtedly by vague rumors of the Haytian revolt, made three fierce attempts at insurrection,—in 1800 under Gabriel in Virginia, in 1822 under Vesey in Carolina, and in 1831 again in Virginia under the terrible Nat Turner. In the Free States, on the other hand, a new and curious attempt at self-development was made. In Philadelphia and New York color-prescription led to a withdrawal of Negro communicants from white churches and the formation of a peculiar socio-religious institution among the Negroes known as the African Church,—an organization still living and controlling in its various branches over a million of men.

Walker's wild appeal against the trend of the times showed how the world was changing after the coming of the cotton-gin. By 1830 slavery seemed hopelessly fastened on the South, and the slaves thoroughly cowed into submission. The free Negroes of the North, inspired by the mulatto immigrants from the West Indies, began to change the basis of their demands; they recognized the slavery of slaves, but insisted that they themselves were freemen, and sought assimilation and amalgamation with the nation on the same terms with other men. Thus, Forten and Purvis of Philadelphia, Shad of Wilmington, DuBois of New Haven, Barbadoes of Boston, and others, strove singly and together as men, they said, not as slaves; as "people of color," not as "Negroes." The trend of the times, however, refused them recognition save in individual and exceptional cases, considered them as one with all the despised blacks, and they soon found themselves striving to keep even the rights they formerly had of voting and working and moving as freemen. Schemes of migration and colonization arose among them; but these they refused to entertain, and they eventually turned to the Abolition movement as a final refuge.

Here, led by Remond, Nell, Wells-Brown, and Douglass, a new period of self-assertion and self-development dawned. To be sure, ultimate freedom and assimilation was the ideal before the leaders, but the assertion of the manhood rights of the Negro by himself was the main reliance, and John Brown's raid was the extreme of its logic. After the war and emancipation, the great form of Frederick Douglass, the greatest of American Negro leaders, still led the host. Self-assertion, especially in political lines, was the main programme, and behind Douglass came Elliot, Bruce, and Langston, and the Reconstruction politicians, and, less conspicuous but of greater social significance, Alexander Crummell and Bishop Daniel Payne.

Then came the Revolution of 1876, the suppression of the Negro votes, the changing and shifting of ideals, and the seeking of new lights in the great night. Douglass, in his old age, still bravely stood for the ideals of his early manhood,—ultimate assimilation *through* self-assertion, and on no other terms. For a time Price arose as a new leader, destined, it seemed, not to give up, but to re-state the old ideals in a form less repugnant to the white South. But he passed away in his prime. Then came the new leader. Nearly all the former ones had become leaders by the silent suffrage of their fellows, had sought to lead their own people alone, and were usually, save Douglass, little known outside their race. But Booker T. Washington arose as essentially the leader not of one race but of two,—a compromiser between the South, the North, and the Negro. Naturally the Negroes resented, at first bitterly, signs of compromise which surrendered their civil and political rights, even though this was to be exchanged for larger chances of economic development. The rich and dominating North, however, was not only weary of the race problem, but was investing largely in Southern enterprises, and welcomed any method of peaceful coöperation. Thus, by national opinion, the Negroes began to recognize Mr. Washington's leadership; and the voice of criticism was hushed.

Mr. Washington represents in Negro thought the old attitude of adjustment and submission; but adjustment at such a peculiar time as to make his programme unique. This is an age of unusual economic development, and Mr. Washington's programme naturally takes an economic cast, becoming a gospel of Work and Money to such an extent as apparently almost completely to overshadow the higher aims of life. Moreover, this is an age when the more advanced races are coming in closer contact with the less developed races, and the race-feeling is therefore intensified; and Mr. Washington's programme practically accepts the alleged inferiority of the Negro races. Again, in our own land, the reaction from the sentiment of war time has given impetus to race-prejudice against Negroes, and Mr. Washington withdraws many of the high demands of Negroes as men and American citizens. In other periods of intensified prejudice all the Negro's tendency to self-assertion has been called forth; at this period a policy of submission is advocated. In the history of nearly all other races and peoples the doctrine preached at such crises has been that manly self-respect is worth more than lands and houses, and that a people who voluntarily surrender such respect, or cease striving for it, are not worth civilizing.

In answer to this, it has been claimed that the Negro can survive only through submission. Mr. Washington distinctly asks that black people give up, at least for the present, three things,—

First, political power,

Second, insistence on civil rights,

Third, higher education of Negro youth,—and concentrate all their energies on industrial education, the accumulation of wealth, and the conciliation of the South. This policy has been courageously and insistently advocated for over fifteen years, and has been triumphant for perhaps ten years. As a result of this tender of the palm-branch, what has been the return? In these years there have occurred:

1. The disfranchisement of the Negro.

2. The legal creation of a distinct status of civil inferiority for the Negro.

3. The steady withdrawal of aid from institutions for the higher training of the Negro.

These movements are not, to be sure, direct results of Mr. Washington's teachings; but his propaganda has, without a shadow of doubt, helped their speedier accomplishment. The question then comes: Is it possible, and probable, that nine millions of men can make effective progress in economic lines if they are deprived of political rights, made a servile caste, and allowed only the most meagre chance for developing their exceptional men? If history and reason give any distinct answer to these questions, it is an emphatic *No.* And Mr. Washington thus faces the triple paradox of his career:

1. He is striving nobly to make Negro artisans business men and property-owners; but it is utterly impossible, under modern competitive methods, for workingmen and property-owners to defend their rights and exist without the right of suffrage.

2. He insists on thrift and self-respect, but at the same time counsels a silent submission to civic inferiority such as is bound to sap the manhood of any race in the long run.

3. He advocates common-school and industrial training, and depreciates institutions of higher learning; but neither the Negro common-schools, nor Tuskegee itself, could remain open a day were it not for teachers trained in Negro colleges, or trained by their graduates.

This triple paradox in Mr. Washington's position is the object of criticism by two classes of colored Americans. One class is spiritually descended from Toussaint the Savior, through Gabriel, Vesey, and Turner, and they represent the attitude of revolt and revenge; they hate the white South blindly and distrust the white race generally, and so far as they agree on definite action, think that the Negro's only hope lies in emigration beyond the borders of the United States. And yet, by the irony of fate, nothing has more effectually made this programme seem hopeless than the recent course of the United States toward weaker and darker peoples in the West Indies, Hawaii, and the Philippines,—for where in the world may we go and be safe from lying and brute force?

The other class of Negroes who cannot agree with Mr. Washington has hitherto said little aloud. They deprecate the sight of scattered counsels, of internal disagreement; and especially they dislike making their just criticism of a useful and earnest man an excuse for a general discharge of venom from small-minded opponents. Nevertheless, the questions involved are so fundamental and serious that it is difficult to see how men like the Grimkes, Kelly Miller, J. W. E. Bowen, and other representatives of this group, can much longer be silent. Such men feel in conscience bound to ask of this nation three things:

1. The right to vote.
2. Civic equality.
3. The education of youth according to ability.

They acknowledge Mr. Washington's invaluable service in counselling patience and courtesy in such demands; they do not ask that ignorant black men vote when ignorant whites are debarred, or that any reasonable restrictions in the suffrage should not be applied; they know that the low social level of the mass of the race is responsible for much discrimination against it, but they also know, and the nation knows, that relentless color-prejudice is more often a cause than a result of the Negro's degradation; they seek the abatement of this relic of barbarism, and not its systematic encouragement and pampering by all agencies of social power from the Associated Press to the Church of Christ. They advocate, with Mr. Washington, a broad system of Negro common schools supplemented by thorough industrial training; but they are surprised that a man of Mr. Washington's insight cannot see that no such educational system ever has rested or can rest on any other basis than that of the well-equipped college and university, and they insist that there is a demand for a few such institutions throughout the South to train the best of the Negro youth as teachers, professional men, and leaders.

This group of men honor Mr. Washington for his attitude of conciliation toward the white South; they accept the "Atlanta Compromise" in its broadest interpretation; they recognize, with him, many signs of promise, many men of high purpose and fair judgment, in this section; they know that no easy task has been laid upon a region already tottering under heavy burdens. But, nevertheless, they insist that the way to truth and right lies in straightforward honesty, not in indiscriminate flattery; in praising those of the South who do well and criticising uncompromisingly those who do ill; in taking advantage of the opportunities at hand and urging their fellows to do the same, but at the same time in remembering that only a firm adherence to their higher ideals and aspirations will ever keep those ideals within the realm of possibility. They do not expect that the free right to vote, to enjoy civic rights, and to be educated, will come in a moment; they do not expect to see the bias and prejudices of years disappear at the blast of a trumpet; but they are absolutely certain that the way for a people to gain their reasonable rights is not by voluntarily throwing them away and insisting that they do not want them; that the way for a people to gain respect is not by continually belittling and ridiculing themselves; that, on the contrary, Negroes must insist continually, in season and out of season, that voting is necessary to modern manhood, that color discrimination is barbarism, and that black boys need education as well as white boys.

In failing thus to state plainly and unequivocally the legitimate demands of their people, even at the cost of opposing an honored leader, the thinking classes of American Negroes would shirk a heavy responsibility,—a responsibility to themselves, a responsibility to the struggling masses, a responsibility to the darker races of men whose future depends so largely on this American experiment, but especially a responsibility to this nation,—this common Fatherland. It is wrong to encourage a man or a people in evil-doing; it is wrong to aid and abet a national crime simply because it is unpopular not to do so. The growing spirit of kindliness and reconciliation between the North and South after the frightful differences of a generation ago ought to be a source of deep congratulation to all, and especially to those whose mistreatment caused the war; but if that reconciliation is to be marked by the industrial slavery and civic death of those same black men, with permanent legislation into a position of inferiority, then those black men, if they are really men, are called upon by every consideration of patriotism and loyalty to oppose such a course by all civilized methods, even though such opposition involves disagreement with Mr. Booker T. Washington. We have no right to sit silently by while the inevitable seeds are sown for a harvest of disaster to our children, black and white.

First, it is the duty of black men to judge the South discriminatingly. The present generation of Southerners are not responsible for the past, and they should not be blindly hated or blamed for it. Furthermore, to no class is the indiscriminate endorsement of the recent course of the South toward Negroes more nauseating than to the best thought of the South. The South is not "solid"; it is a land in the ferment of social change, wherein forces of all kinds are fighting for supremacy; and to praise the ill the South is to-day perpetrating is just as wrong as to condemn the good. Discriminating and broad-minded criticism is what the South needs,—needs it for the sake of her own white sons and daughters, and for the insurance of robust, healthy mental and moral development.

To-day even the attitude of the Southern whites toward the blacks is not, as so many assume, in all cases the same; the ignorant Southerner hates the Negro, the workingmen fear his competition, the money-makers wish to use him as a laborer, some of the educated see a menace in his upward development, while others—usually the sons of the masters—wish to help him to rise. National opinion has enabled this last class to maintain the Negro common schools, and to protect the Negro partially in property, life, and limb. Through the pressure of the money-makers, the Negro is in danger of being reduced to semi-slavery, especially in the country districts; the workingmen, and those of the educated who fear the Negro, have united to disfranchise him, and some have urged his deportation; while the passions of the ignorant are easily aroused to lynch and abuse any black man. To praise this intricate whirl of thought and prejudice is nonsense; to inveigh indiscriminately against "the South" is unjust; but to use the same breath in praising Governor Aycock, exposing Senator Morgan, arguing with Mr. Thomas Nelson Page, and denouncing Senator Ben Tillman, is not only sane, but the imperative duty of thinking black men.

It would be unjust to Mr. Washington not to acknowledge that in several instances he has opposed movements in the South which were unjust to the Negro; he sent memorials to the Louisiana and Alabama constitutional conventions, he has spoken against lynching, and in other ways has openly or silently set his influence against sinister schemes and unfortunate happenings. Notwithstanding this, it is equally true to assert that on the whole the distinct impression left by

Mr. Washington's propaganda is, first, that the South is justified in its present attitude toward the Negro because of the Negro's degradation; secondly, that the prime cause of the Negro's failure to rise more quickly is his wrong education in the past; and, thirdly, that his future rise depends primarily on his own efforts. Each of these propositions is a dangerous half-truth. The supplementary truths must never be lost sight of: first, slavery and race-prejudice are potent if not sufficient causes of the Negro's position; second, industrial and common-school training were necessarily slow in planting because they had to await the black teachers trained by higher institutions, — it being extremely doubtful if any essentially different development was possible, and certainly a Tuskegee was unthinkable before 1880; and, third, while it is a great truth to say that the Negro must strive and strive mightily to help himself, it is equally true that unless his striving be not simply seconded, but rather aroused and encouraged, by the initiative of the richer and wiser environing group, he cannot hope for great success.

In his failure to realize and impress this last point, Mr. Washington is especially to be criticised. His doctrine has tended to make the whites, North and South, shift the burden of the Negro problem to the Negro's shoulders and stand aside as critical and rather pessimistic spectators; when in fact the burden belongs to the nation, and the hands of none of us are clean if we bend not our energies to righting these great wrongs.

The South ought to be led, by candid and honest criticism, to assert her better self and do her full duty to the race she has cruelly wronged and is still wronging. The North — her co-partner in guilt — cannot salve her conscience by plastering it with gold. We cannot settle this problem by diplomacy and suaveness, by "policy" alone. If worse come to worst, can the moral fibre of this country survive the slow throttling and murder of nine millions of men?

The black men of America have a duty to perform, a duty stern and delicate, — a forward movement to oppose a part of the work of their greatest leader. So far as Mr. Washington preaches Thrift, Patience, and Industrial Training for the masses, we must hold up his hands and strive with him, rejoicing in his honors and glorying in the strength of this Joshua called of God and of man to lead the headless host. But so far as Mr. Washington apologizes for injustice, North or South, does not rightly value the privilege and duty of voting, belittles the emasculating effects of caste distinctions, and opposes the higher training and ambition of our brighter minds, — so far as he, the South, or the Nation, does this, — we must unceasingly and firmly oppose them. By every civilized and peaceful method we must strive for the rights which the world accords to men, clinging unwaveringly to those great words which the sons of the Fathers would fain forget: "We hold these truths to be self-evident: That all men are created equal; that they are endowed by their Creator with certain unalienable rights; that among these are life, liberty, and the pursuit of happiness."                    (1903)

*from* **I and Thou***

The world is twofold for man in accordance with his twofold attitude.

The attitude of man is twofold in accordance with the two basic words he can speak.

The basic words are not single words but word pairs.

One basic word is the word pair I-You.

The other basic word is the word pair I-It; but this basic word is not changed when He or She takes the place of It.

Thus the I of man is also twofold.

For the I of the basic word I-You is different from that in the basic word I-It.

Basic words do not state something that might exist outside them; by being spoken they establish a mode of existence.

Basic words are spoken with one's being.

When one says You, the I of the word pair I-You is said, too.

When one says It, the I of the word pair I-It is said, too.

The basic word I-You can only be spoken with one's whole being.

The basic word I-It can never be spoken with one's whole being.

There is no I as such but only the I of the basic word I-You and the I of the basic word I-It.

When a man says I, he means one or the other. The I he means is present when he says I. And when he says You or It, the I of one or the other basic word is also present.

Being I and saying I are the same. Saying I and saying one of the two basic words are the same.

Whoever speaks one of the basic words enters into the word and stands in it.

The life of a human being does not exist merely in the sphere of goal-directed verbs. It does not consist merely of activities that have something for their object.

I perceive something. I feel something. I imagine something. I want something. I sense something. I think something. The life of a human being does not consist merely of all this and its like.

All this and its like is the basis of the realm of It.

But the realm of You has another basis.

*Translation by Walter Kaufmann.

584

Whoever says You does not have something for his object. For wherever there is something there is also another something; every It borders on other Its; It is only by virtue of bordering on others. But where You is said there is no something. You has no borders.

Whoever says You does not have something; he has nothing. But he stands in relation.


We are told that man experiences his world. What does this mean?

Man goes over the surfaces of things and experiences them. He brings back from them some knowledge of their condition—an experience. He experiences what there is to things.

But it is not experiences alone that bring the world to man.

For what they bring to him is only a world that consists of It and It and It, of He and He and She and She and It.

I experience something.

All this is not changed by adding "inner" experiences to the "external" ones, in line with the non-eternal distinction that is born of mankind's craving to take the edge off the mystery of death. Inner things like external things, things among things!

I experience something.

And all this is not changed by adding "mysterious" experiences to "manifest" ones, self-confident in the wisdom that recognizes a secret compartment in things, reserved for the initiated, and holds the key. O mysteriousness without mystery, O piling up of information! It, it, it!


Those who experience do not participate in the world. For the experience is "in them" and not between them and the world.

The world does not participate in experience. It allows itself to be experienced, but it is not concerned, for it contributes nothing, and nothing happens to it.


The world as experience belongs to the basic word I-It.

The basic word I-You establishes the world of relation.


Three are the spheres in which the world of relation arises.

The first: life with nature. Here the relation vibrates in the dark and remains below language. The creatures stir across from us, but they are unable to come to us, and the You we say to them sticks to the threshold of language.

The second: life with men. Here the relation is manifest and enters language. We can give and receive the You.

The third: life with spiritual beings. Here the relation is wrapped in a cloud but reveals itself, it lacks but creates language. We hear no You and yet feel addressed; we answer—creating, thinking, acting: with our being we speak the basic word, unable to say You with our mouth.

But how can we incorporate into the world of the basic word what lies outside language?

In every sphere, through everything that becomes present to us, we gaze toward the train of the eternal You; in each we perceive a breath of it; in every You we address the eternal You, in every sphere according to its manner.


I contemplate a tree.

I can accept it as a picture: a rigid pillar in a flood of light, or splashes of green traversed by the gentleness of the blue silver ground.

I can feel it as movement: the flowing veins around the sturdy, striving core, the sucking of the roots, the breathing of the leaves, the infinite commerce with earth and air—and the growing itself in its darkness.

I can assign it to a species and observe it as an instance, with an eye to its construction and its way of life.

I can overcome its uniqueness and form so rigorously that I recognize it only as an expression of the law—those laws according to which a constant opposition of forces is continually adjusted, or those laws according to which the elements mix and separate.

I can dissolve it into a number, into a pure relation between numbers, and eternalize it.

Throughout all of this the tree remains my object and has its place and its time span, its kind and condition.

But it can also happen, if will and grace are joined, that as I contemplate the tree I am drawn into a relation, and the tree ceases to be an It. The power of exclusiveness has seized me.

This does not require me to forego any of the modes of contemplation. There is nothing that I must not see in order to see, and there is no knowledge that I must forget. Rather is everything, picture and movement, species and instance, law and number included and inseparably fused.

Whatever belongs to the tree is included: its form and its mechanics, its colors and its chemistry, its conversation with the elements and its conversation with the stars—all this in its entirety.

The tree is no impression, no play of my imagination, no aspect of a mood; it confronts me bodily and has to deal with me as I must deal with it—only differently.

One should not try to dilute the meaning of the relation: relation is reciprocity.

Does the tree then have consciousness, similar to our own? I have no experience of that. But thinking that you have brought this off in your own case, must you again divide the indivisible? What I encounter is neither the soul of a tree nor a dryad, but the tree itself.

When I confront a human being as my You and speak the basic word I-You to him, then he is no thing among things nor does he consist of things.

He is no longer He or She, limited by other Hes and Shes, a dot in the world grid of space and time, nor a condition that can be experienced and described, a loose bundle of named qualities. Neighborless and seamless, he is You and fills the firmament. Not as if there were nothing but he; but everything else lives in *his* light.

Even as a melody is not composed of tones, nor a verse of words, nor a statue of lines — one must pull and tear to turn a unity into a multiplicity — so it is with the human being to whom I say You. I can abstract from him the color of his hair or the color of his speech or the color of his graciousness; I have to do this again and again; but immediately he is no longer You.

And even as prayer is not in time but time in prayer, the sacrifice not in space but space in the sacrifice — and whoever reverses the relation annuls the reality — I do not find the human being to whom I say You in any Sometime and Somewhere. I can place him there and have to do this again and again, but immediately he becomes a He or a She, an It, and no longer remains my You.

As long as the firmament of the You is spread over me, the tempests of causality cower at my heels, and the whirl of doom congeals.

The human being to whom I say You I do not experience. But I stand in relation to him, in the sacred basic word. Only when I step out of this do I experience him again. Experience is remoteness from You.

The relation can obtain even if the human being to whom I say You does not hear it in his experience. For You is more than It knows. You does more, and more happens to it, than It knows. No deception reaches this far: here is the cradle of actual life.


This is the eternal origin of art that a human being confronts a form that wants to become a work through him. Not a figment of his soul but something that appears to the soul and demands the soul's creative power. What is required is a deed that a man does with his whole being: if he commits it and speaks with his being the basic word to the form that appears, then the creative power is released and the work comes into being.

The deed involves a sacrifice and a risk. The sacrifice: infinite possibility is surrendered on the altar of the form; all that but a moment ago floated playfully through one's perspective has to be exterminated; none of it may penetrate into the work; the exclusiveness of such a confrontation demands this. The risk: the basic word can only be spoken with one's whole being; whoever commits himself may not hold back part of himself; and the work does not permit me, as a tree or man might, to seek relaxation in the It-world; it is imperious: if I do not serve it properly, it breaks, or it breaks me.

The form that confronts me I cannot experience nor describe; I can only actualize it. And yet I see it, radiant in the splendor of the confrontation, far more clearly than all clarity of the experienced world. Not as a thing among the "internal" things, not as a figment of the "imagination," but as what is present. Tested for its objectivity, the form is not "there" at all; but what can equal its presence? And it is an actual relation: it acts on me as I act on it.

Such work is creation, inventing is finding. Forming is discovery. As I actualize, I uncover. I lead the form across—into the world of It. The created work is a thing among things and can be experienced and described as an aggregate of qualities. But the receptive beholder may be bodily confronted now and again.

(1923)

## Langston Hughes

# I, Too

I, too, sing America.

I am the darker brother.
They send me to eat in the kitchen
When company comes,
But I laugh,
And eat well,
And grow strong.

Tomorrow,
I'll be at the table
When company comes.
Nobody'll dare
Say to me,
"Eat in the kitchen,"
Then.

Besides,
They'll see how beautiful I am
And be ashamed—

I, too, am America.

(1929)

James Weldon Johnson

## *from* Negro Americans, What Now?

The world today is in a state of semi-chaos. We Negro Americans as a part of the world are affected by that state. We are affected by it still more vitally as a special group. We are not so sanguine about our course and our goal as we were a decade ago. We are floundering. We are casting about for ways of meeting the situation, both as Americans and as Negroes. In this casting about we have discovered and rediscovered a number of ways to which we have given more or less consideration. Let us see if we cannot by elimination reduce confusion and narrow down the limits of choice to what might be shown to be the one sound and wise line to follow.

### Exodus

Exodus has for generations been recurrently suggested as a method for solving the race problem. . . .

A century and a quarter ago deportation of the free Negroes might have been feasible; a half century later *that* was not a practicable undertaking; today the deportation or exodus of the Negro American population is an utter impossibility. Not within a bounded period could twelve million people be transported; and before that period was over the total number would be well above twelve million. Nor is there any place to which to take them. There are no more "vacant" places on earth; and no government in the world, with the barest possibility of Brazil as the exception, would welcome even one-twelfth the whole number; Liberia would no doubt be as reluctant as any. None of the tribes of colonial Africa would relish sharing their best lands with us merely because we and they are of somewhat the same complexion. The United States government might purchase territory somewhere and deport us. But that would involve a pretty stiff political job and a financial expenditure that would make the figures of the National Recovery program look small.

We may cross out exodus as a possible solution. We and the white people may as well make up our minds definitely that we, the same as they, are in this country to stay. We may be causing white America some annoyance, but we ourselves are not passing the time in undisturbed comfort. White America will simply have to sustain a situation that is of its own making, not ours.

## Physical Force

Our history in the United States records a half-dozen major and a score of minor efforts at insurrection during the period of slavery. This, if they heard it, would be news to that big majority of people who believe that we have gone through three centuries of oppression without once thinking in terms of rebellion or lifting a finger in revolt. Even now there come times when we think in terms of physical force.

We must condemn physical force and banish it from our minds. But I do not condemn it on any moral or pacific grounds. The resort to force remains and will doubtless always remain the rightful recourse of oppressed peoples. Our own country was established upon that right. I condemn physical force because I know that in our case it would be futile.

We would be justified in taking up arms or anything we could lay hands on and fighting for the common rights we are entitled to and denied, if we had a chance to win. But I know and we all know there is not a chance. It is, I believe, among the certainties that some day, perhaps not very far off, native blacks of Africa will, by physical force if necessary, compel the whites to yield their extra privileges and immunities. The increasing inability of the great powers to spare the strength and resources necessary for maintaining imperialism will hasten the certainty. The situation of the African natives is, however, on one point at least, the reverse of our own — on the point of comparative numerical strength.

Yet, there is a phase of physical force that we in the United States should consider. When we are confronted by the lawless, pitiless, brutish mob, and we know that life is forfeit, we should not give it up; we should, if we can, sell it, and at the dearest price we are able to put on it.

## The Revolution

Communism is coming to be regarded as the infallible solution by an increasing number of us. Those who look to the coming revolution (and why they should believe it is coming in the United States I see no good reason) seem to think it will work some instantaneous and magical transformation of our condition. It appears to me that this infinite faith in Communism indicates extreme *naïveté*. Those who hold this faith point to Soviet Russia as a land in which there is absolutely no prejudice against Negroes. This is an unquestioned fact, but I can see no grounds on which to attribute it to Communism. There was no prejudice against Negroes in Tsarist Russia. Tsarist Russia was the country that could honor a black Hannibal; the country that could make a mulatto Pushkin its national poet; the country in which university students in St. Petersburg could unhitch the horses from the carriage of Ira Aldridge, the black American tragedian, after his performance of Othello, and themselves draw him back to his hotel. The simple truth is: the *Russian people* have no prejudice against Negroes.

In considering Communism with respect to the Negro, the question before us, of course, is not how it works in Russia, but how it would probably work in the United States. If the United States goes Communistic, where will the Communists come from? They certainly will not be imported from Russia. They will be made from the Americans here on hand. We might well pause and consider what variations Communism in the United States might undergo.

I hold no brief against Communism as a theory of government. I hope that the Soviet experiment will be completely successful. I know that it is having a strong influence on the principal nations of the world, including our own. I think it is a high sign of progress that Negro Americans have reached the point of holding independent opinions on political and social questions. What I am trying to do is to sound a warning against childlike trust in the miraculous efficacy on our racial situation of any economic or social theory of government—Communism or Socialism or Fascism or Nazism or New Deals. The solving of our situation depends principally upon an evolutionary process along two parallel lines: our own development and the bringing about of a change in the national attitude toward us. That outcome will require our persevering effort under whatever form the government might take on.

It may be argued that although there is not and has not been any anti-Negro feeling in Russia, it is the country in which anti-Semitism was stronger than in any other, and that oppression and repression of the Jews have been greatly abated or entirely wiped out by Communism. Such an argument goes to prove the possibility that Communism in the United States would wipe out oppression and repression of Negro Americans and give them a status of equality. I grant the possibility— what though it may not be realized miraculously and suddenly. I grant that if America should turn truly Communistic (by which I mean—if it should adopt and practice Communism without reservations, and not adapt it as it has adapted democracy and Christianity so as to allow every degree of inequality and cruelty to be practiced under them); that if the capitalistic system should be abolished and the dictatorship of the proletariat established, with the Negro aligned, as he naturally ought to be, with the proletariat, race discriminations would be officially banned and the reasons and feelings back of them would finally disappear.

But except to a visionary there are no indications that the present or prospective strength of Communism is able or will be able to work such a change, either by persuasion or by military coup. In the situation as it now exists it would be positively foolhardy for us, as a group, to take up the cause of Communistic revolution and thereby bring upon ourselves all of the antagonisms that are directed against it in addition to those we already have to bear. It seems to me that the wholesale allegiance of the Negro to Communistic revolution would be second in futility only to his individual resort to physical force. . . .

## Isolation or Integration?

By this process of elimination we have reduced choices of a way out to two. There remain, on the one hand, the continuation of our efforts to achieve integration and, on the other hand, an acknowledgment of our isolation and the determination to accept and make the best of it.

Throughout our entire intellectual history there has been a division of opinion as to which of these two divergent courses the race should follow. From early times there have been sincere thinkers among us who were brought to the conclusion that our only salvation lies in the making of the race into a self-contained economic, social, and cultural unit; in a word, in the building of an *imperium in imperio*.

All along, however, majority opinion has held that the only salvation worth achieving lies in the making of the race into a component part of the nation, with all the common rights and privileges, as well as duties, of citizenship. This attitude has been basic in the general policy of the race—so far as it has had a general policy—for generations, the policy of striving zealously to gain full admission to citizenship and guarding jealously each single advance made.

But this question of direction, of goal, is not a settled one. There is in us all a stronger tendency toward isolation than we may be aware of. There come times when the most persistent integrationist becomes an isolationist, when he curses the White world and consigns it to hell. This tendency toward isolation is strong because it springs from a deep-seated, natural desire—a desire for respite from the unremitting, grueling struggle; for a place in which refuge might be taken. We are again and again confronted by this question. It is ever present, though often dormant. Recently it was emphatically brought forward by the utterances of so authoritative a voice as that of Dr. DuBois.

The question is not one to be lightly brushed aside. Those who stand for making the race into a self-sufficient unit point out that after years of effort we are still Jim-Crowed, discriminated against, segregated, and lynched; that we are still shut out from industry, barred from the main avenues of business, and cut off from free participation in national life. They point out that in some sections of the country we have not even secured equal protection of life and property under the laws. They declare that entrance of the Negro into full citizenship is as distant as it was seventy years ago. And they ask: What is the Negro to do? Give himself over to wishful thinking? Stand shooting at the stars with a popgun? Is it not rather a duty and a necessity for him to face the facts of his condition and environment, to acknowledge them as facts, and to make the best use of them that he can? These are questions which the thinkers of the race should strive to sift clearly.

To this writer it seems that one of the first results of clear thinking is a realization of the truth that the making of the race into a self-sustaining unit, the creating of an *imperium in imperio,* does not offer an easier or more feasible task than does the task of achieving full citizenship. Such an *imperium* would have to rest upon a basis of separate group economic independence, and the trend of all present-day forces is against the building of any foundation of that sort.

After thoughtful consideration, I cannot see the slightest possibility of our being able to duplicate the economic and social machinery of the country. I do not believe that any other special group could do it. The isolationists declare that because of imposed segregation we have, to a large degree, already done it. But the situation they point to is more apparent than real. Our separate schools and some of our other race institutions, many of our race enterprises, the greater part of our employment, and most of our fundamental activities are contingent upon our interrelationship with the country as a whole.

Clear thinking reveals that the outcome of voluntary isolation would be a permanent secondary status, so acknowledged by the race. Such a status would, it is true, solve some phases of the race question. It would smooth away a good part of the friction and bring about a certain protection and security. The status of slavery carried some advantages of that sort. But I do not believe we shall ever be willing to pay such a price for security and peace.

If Negro Americans could do what reasonably appears to be impossible, and as a separate unit achieve self-sufficiency built upon group economic independence, does anyone suppose that that would abolish prejudice against them and allay opposition, or that the struggle to maintain their self-sufficiency would be in any degree less bitter than the present struggle to become an integral part of the nation? Taking into account human nature as it is, would not the achievement be more likely to arouse envy and bring on even more violent hatreds and persecutions?

Certainly, the isolationists are stating a truth when they contend that we should not, ostrich-like, hide our heads in the sand, making believe that prejudice is non-existent; but in so doing they are apostles of the obvious. Calling upon the race to realize that prejudice is an actuality is a needless effort; it is placing emphasis on what has never been questioned. The danger for us does not lie in a possible failure to acknowledge prejudice as a reality, but in acknowledging it too fully. We cannot ignore the fact that we are segregated, no matter how much we might wish to do so; and the smallest amount of common sense forces us to extract as much good from the situation as there is in it. Any degree of sagacity forces us at the same time to use all our powers to abolish imposed segregation; for it is an evil *per se* and the negation of equality either of opportunity or of awards. We should by all means make our schools and institutions as excellent as we can possibly make them – and by that very act we reduce the certainty that they will forever remain schools and institutions "for Negroes only." We should make our business enterprises and other strictly group undertakings as successful as we can possibly make them. We should gather all the strength and experience we can from imposed segregation. But any good we are able to derive from the system we should consider as a means, not an end. The strength and experience we gain from it should be applied to the objective of *entering into;* not *staying out of* the body politic.

Clear thinking shows, too, that, as bad as conditions are, they are not as bad as they are declared to be by discouraged and pessimistic isolationists. To say that in the past two generations or more Negro Americans have not advanced a single step toward a fuller share in the commonwealth becomes, in the light of easily ascertainable facts, an absurdity. Only the shortest view of the situation gives color of truth to such a statement; any reasonably long view proves it to be utterly false.

With our choice narrowed down to these two courses, wisdom and far-sightedness and possibility of achievement demand that we follow the line that leads to equal rights for us, based on the common terms and conditions under which they are accorded and guaranteed to the other groups that go into the making up of our national family. It is not necessary for our advancement that such an outcome should suddenly eradicate all prejudices. It would not, of course, have the effect of suddenly doing away with voluntary grouping in religious and secular organizations or of abolishing group enterprises – for example, Negro newspapers. The accordance of full civil and political rights has not in the case of the greater number of groups in the nation had that effect. Nevertheless, it would be an immeasurable step forward, and would place us where we had a fair start with the other American groups. More than that we do not need to ask. . . .

## The Correlation of All Forces

### A Super-Power

Now, these principal forces and resources that we have enumerated are far from negligible. Even at their weakest they are assets. Their actual strength is great. Their potential powers have not been estimated. . . .

How may we call these potential powers, these powers that will prove effective, into being? The simplicity of the process will probably throw doubt on the magnitude of the feat. It may be done through the complete correlation of the existing forces. The result will be not merely increased efficiency in all the various units and greater total strength; it will be the creation of an entirely new power, a super-power, a power that will be a fusion of all our energies. If we create this power and center its force upon the walls that stand between us and the common rights, guarantees, and privileges of citizenship, we can be confident of battering them down.

The practical method I suggest for the creation and utilization of this power is to channel our forces so that they will function through a central machine. I believe we have that machine at hand in the National Association for the Advancement of Colored People. I believe we could get the desired results by making that organization the nucleus, the synthesis, the clearing house, of our forces. It already has the experience, the skill, and, in good part, the machinery. It has proved itself honest, sincere, intelligent, and capable. For the purpose of achieving, maintaining, and safeguarding our citizenship rights, no other organization can be compared with it. Its policies and techniques have proved to be the most advantageous and effective that we have thus far been able to devise.

I know that this is not a wholly unanimous opinion. The statement I have made has been frequently put in the form of a question. I believe, however, that a study of the history and work of the association for the past twenty-five years and of the concurrent history of Negro Americans will furnish sufficient evidence to prove that the race has made positive gains through the efforts of the N.A.A.C.P. Its successful efforts to hold segregation within the limits of custom and prevent it from being put over into the realm of law; its leadership in the fight against lynching, and its keeping of that crime and other racial injustices before the conscience of the American people; and its half-dozen signal legal victories involving our constitutional rights are examples in point.

But there is another way of evaluating the work of the organization. When the N.A.A.C.P. was founded, the great danger facing us was that we should lose the vestiges of our rights by default. The organization checked that danger. It acted as a watchman on the wall, sounding the alarms that called us to defense. Its work would be of value if only for the reason that without it our status would be worse than it is. In cities where our numbers are large we still live grouped together in one or more "Negro sections." . . . in such cities Negro Americans by this time would all have been sentenced *by law* to live in black ghettos if the N.A.A.C.P. had not won the Louisville Segregation Case, in which the Supreme Court declared residential segregation on grounds of race to be unconstitutional. I am taking it for granted that no one will be so shallow as to ask if there is any difference between segregation by social conventions and segregation by legal enactment. I believe also that the National Association laid the foundation for the restoration of the ballot to Negro Americans in the South through its victories in the Texas Primary Cases. The Negro lost the right to vote conferred on him by the Fourteenth and Fifteenth Amendments because the Supreme Court through hair-splitting sophistry and astute evasion emasculated both amendments to the point of nullification. The signs are now that the right to vote will be re-established through the decisions of that same court. There is a school that holds that these legal victories are empty. They are not. At the very least, they provide the ground upon which we may make a stand for our rights. In the North we have a fair degree of civil rights and in the South we have the right to battle for those rights because the Fourteenth and Fifteenth Amendments are in the constitution. Let us suppose them not there, and we reach a quick realization of the material importance of legal enactments. Or note the effect of adverse laws.

If we correlate our numerical strength, the strength of our religious and fraternal organizations, such political and economic power as we have, and the power of our press in a way to make the National Association for the Advancement of Colored People the spearhead of our forces, in a way that will enable it to shift the emphasis more and more from protest to action and more fully to translate declarations into deeds, and to widen its field to include all the fundamental phases of life that affect us as citizens, there are Negro Americans now born who will live to see the race accorded the common rights of citizenship on the same terms upon which they are accorded to the other groups in the nation. . . .

## Conclusion

In these few pages I have made no attempt at a general consideration of social problems; rather have I sought to limit the discussion to the peculiar and immediate problems that confront us as a special group. . . .

I have tried to show that the most logical, the most feasible and most worthwhile choice for us is to follow the course that leads to our becoming an integral part of the nation, with the same rights and guarantees that are accorded to other citizens, and on the same terms. I have pointed out that common sense compels us to get whatever and all the good we can out of the system of imposed segregation, to gather all the experience and strength that can be got from it; but that we should use that experience and strength steadily and as rapidly as possible to destroy the system. The seeming advantages of imposed segregation are too costly to keep. I have enumerated our principal forces and resources and set forth that none of these factors is a panacea; that we must correlate all our elements of strength to form a super-power to be centered on our main objective; that, knowing the rights we are entitled to, we must persistently use this power to defend those rights we hold, so that none may go by default, and to secure those we have not yet gained. I have stressed the vital need of plans and steps for uniting

black and white workers. I have made plain the importance of interra-
cial contact. I have pointed out the necessity of enlisting the energies of
youth. I have shown that in addition to other factors there is an emotional factor to deal with. I have implied the fact that our policies
should include an intelligent opportunism; by which I mean the alert-
ness and ability to seize the advantage from every turn of circumstance
whenever it can be done without sacrifice of principle. We require a
sense of strategy as well as a spirit of determination.

To revolutionary elements it will no doubt appear that what I have
outlined is too conservative. If it does, it is not because I am unconscious of the need of fundamental social change, but because I am considering the realities of the situation. Conservatism and radicalism are
relative terms. It is as radical for a black American in Mississippi to
claim his full rights under the Constitution and the law as it is for a
white American in any state to advocate the overthrow of the existing
national government. The black American in many instances puts his
life in jeopardy, and anything more radical than that cannot reasonably
be required.

I have suggested no quick or novel cure-all, for there is none. There
is no one salient to be captured; our battle is along a wide front. What I
have outlined is a plan for a long, hard campaign. A campaign that will
demand courage, determination, and patience. Not, however, the patience to wait, but the patience to keep on working and fighting. This
may seem far from a cheerful prospect; but why should we utter wails
of despair? Our situation is luxuriously easy to what former generations
have endured. We ought to gain fortitude from merely thinking of what
they came through.

And we ought to gather inspiration from the fact that we are in the
right. We are contending for only what we are entitled to under the organic law of the land, and by any high standard of civilization, of morality, or of decency. Black America is called upon to stand as the protag-
onist of tolerance, of fair play, of justice, and of good will. Until white
America heeds, we shall never let its conscience sleep. For the responsibility for the outcome is not ours alone. White America cannot save itself if it prevents us from being saved. But, in the nature of things,
white America is not going to yield what rightfully belongs to us without a struggle kept up by us. In that struggle our watchword needs to
be, "Work, work, work!" and our rallying cry, "Fight, fight, fight!"

(1934)

# Letter from Birmingham Jail

April 16, 1963

Bishop C. C. J. Carpenter
Bishop Joseph A. Durick
Rabbi Milton L. Grafman
Bishop Paul Hardin
Bishop Nolan B. Harmon
The Rev. George M. Murray .
The Rev. Edward V. Ramage
The Rev. Earl Stallings

My Dear Fellow Clergymen: While confined here in the Birmingham city jail, I came across your recent statement calling my present activities "unwise and untimely." Seldom do I pause to answer criticism of my work and ideas. If I sought to answer all the criticisms that cross my desk, my secretaries would have little time for anything other than such correspondence in the course of the day, and I would have no time for constructive work. But since I feel that you are men of genuine good will and that your criticisms are sincerely set forth, I want to try to answer your statement in what I hope will be patient and reasonable terms.

I think I should indicate why I am here in Birmingham, since you have been influenced by the view which argues against "outsiders coming in." I have the honor of serving as president of the Southern Christian Leadership Conference, an organization operating in every southern state, with headquarters in Atlanta, Georgia. We have some eighty-five affiliated organizations across the South, and one of them is the Alabama Christian Movement for Human Rights. Frequently we share staff, educational and financial resources with our affiliates. Several months ago the affiliate here in Birmingham asked us to be on call to engage in a nonviolent direct-action program if such were deemed necessary. We readily consented, and when the hour came we lived up to our promise. So I, along with several members of my staff, am here because I was invited here. I am here because I have organizational ties here.

But more basically, I am in Birmingham because injustice is here. Just as the prophets of the eighth century B.C. left their villages and carried their "thus saith the Lord" far beyond the boundaries of their home towns, and just as the Apostle Paul left his village of Tarsus and carried the gospel of Jesus Christ to the far corners of the Greco-Roman world, so am I compelled to carry the gospel of freedom beyond my own home town. Like Paul, I must constantly respond to the Macedonian call for aid.

Moreover, I am cognizant of the interrelatedness of all communities and states. I cannot sit idly by in Atlanta and not be concerned about what happens in Birmingham. Injustice anywhere is a threat to justice everywhere. We are caught in an inescapable network of mutuality, tied in a single garment of destiny. Whatever affects one directly, affects all indirectly. Never again can we afford to live with the narrow, provincial "outside agitator" idea. Anyone who lives inside the United States can never be considered an outsider anywhere within its bounds.

You deplore the demonstrations taking place in Birmingham. But your statement, I am sorry to say, fails to express a similar concern for the conditions that brought about the demonstrations. I am sure that none of you would want to rest content with the superficial kind of social analysis that deals merely with effects and does not grapple with underlying causes. It is unfortunate that demonstrations are taking place in Birmingham, but it is even more unfortunate that the city's white power structure left the Negro community with no alternative.

In any nonviolent campaign there are four basic steps: collection of the facts to determine whether injustices exist; negotiation; self-purification; and direct action. We have gone through all these steps in Birmingham. There can be no gainsaying the fact that racial injustice engulfs this community. Birmingham is probably the most thoroughly segregated city in the United States. Its ugly record of brutality is widely known. Negroes have experienced grossly unjust treatment in the courts. There have been more unsolved bombings of Negro homes and churches in Birmingham than any other city in the nation. These are the hard, brutal facts of the case. On the basis of these conditions, Negro leaders sought to negotiate with the city fathers. But the latter consistently refused to engage in good-faith negotiation.

Then, last September, came the opportunity to talk with leaders of Birmingham's economic community. In the course of the negotiations, certain promises were made by the merchants—for example, to remove the stores' humiliating racial signs. On the basis of these promises, the Reverend Fred Shuttlesworth and the leaders of the Alabama Christian Movement for Human Rights agreed to a moratorium on all demonstrations. As the weeks and months went by, we realized that we were the victims of a broken promise. A few signs, briefly removed, returned; the others remained.

As in so many past experiences, our hopes had been blasted, and the shadow of deep disappointment settled upon us. We had no alternative except to prepare for direct action, whereby we would present our very bodies as a means of laying our case before the conscience of the local and the national community. Mindful of the difficulties involved, we decided to undertake a process of self-purification. We began a series of workshops on nonviolence, and we repeatedly asked ourselves: "Are you able to accept blows without retaliating?" "Are you able to endure the ordeal of jail?" We decided to schedule our direct-action program for the Easter season, realizing that except for Christmas, this is the main shopping period of the year. Knowing that a strong economic-withdrawal program would be the by-product of direct action, we felt that this would be the best time to bring pressure to bear on the merchants for the needed change.

Then it occurred to us that Birmingham's mayoral election was coming up in March, and we speedily decided to postpone action until after election day. When we discovered that the Commissioner of Public Safety, Eugene "Bull" Connor, had piled up enough votes to be in the run-off, we decided again to postpone action until the day after the run-off so that the demonstrations could not be used to cloud the issues. Like many others, we waited to see Mr. Connor defeated, and to this end we endured postponement after postponement. Having aided in this community need, we felt that our direct-action program could be delayed no longer.

You may well ask: "Why direct action? Why sit-ins, marches and so forth? Isn't negotiation a better path?" You are quite right in calling for negotiation. Indeed, this is the very purpose of direct action. Nonviolent direct action seeks to create such a crisis and foster such a tension that a community which has constantly refused to negotiate is forced to confront the issue. It seeks so to dramatize the issue that it can no longer be ignored. My citing the creation of tension as part of the work of the nonviolent-resister may sound rather shocking. But I must confess that I am not afraid of the word "tension." I have earnestly opposed violent tension, but there is a type of constructive, nonviolent tension which is necessary for growth. Just as Socrates felt that it was necessary to create a tension in the mind so that individuals could rise from the bondage of myths and half-truths to the unfettered realm of creative analysis and objective appraisal, so must we see the need for nonviolent gadflies to create the kind of tension in society that will help men rise from the dark depths of prejudice and racism to the majestic heights of understanding and brotherhood.

The purpose of our direct-action program is to create a situation so crisis-packed that it will inevitably open the door to negotiation. I therefore concur with you in your call for negotiation. Too long has our beloved Southland been bogged down in a tragic effort to live in monologue rather than dialogue.

One of the basic points in your statement is that the action that I and my associates have taken in Birmingham is untimely. Some have asked: "Why didn't you give the new city administration time to act?" The only answer that I can give to this query is that the new Birmingham administration must be prodded about as much as the outgoing one, before it will act. We are sadly mistaken if we feel that the election of Albert Boutwell as mayor will bring the millennium to Birmingham. While Mr. Boutwell is a much more gentle person than Mr. Connor, they are both segregationists, dedicated to maintenance of the status quo. I have hope that Mr. Boutwell will be reasonable enough to see the futility of massive resistance to desegregation. But he will not see this without pressure from devotees of civil rights. My friends, I must say to you that we have not made a single gain in civil rights without determined legal and nonviolent pressure. Lamentably, it is an historical fact that privileged groups seldom give up their privileges voluntarily. Individuals may see the moral light and voluntarily give up their unjust posture; but, as Reinhold Niebuhr has reminded us, groups tend to be more immoral than individuals.

We know through painful experience that freedom is never voluntarily given by the oppressor; it must be demanded by the oppressed. Frankly, I have yet to engage in a direct-action campaign that was "well timed" in the view of those who have not suffered unduly from the disease of segregation. For years now I have heard the word "Wait!" It rings in the ear of every Negro with piercing familiarity. This "Wait" has almost always meant "Never." We must come to see, with one of our distinguished jurists, that "justice too long delayed is justice denied."

We have waited for more than 340 years for our constitutional and God-given rights. The nations of Asia and Africa are moving with jet-like speed toward gaining political independence, but we still creep at horse-and-buggy pace toward gaining a cup of coffee at a lunch counter. Perhaps it is easy for those who have never felt the stinging darts of segregation to say, "Wait." But when you have seen vicious mobs lynch your mothers and fathers at will and drown your sisters and brothers at whim; when you have seen hate-filled policemen curse, kick and even kill your black brothers and sisters; when you see the vast majority of your twenty million Negro brothers smothering in an airtight cage of poverty in the midst of an affluent society; when you suddenly find your tongue twisted and your speech stammering as you seek to explain to your six-year-old daughter why she can't go to the public amusement park that has just been advertised on television, and see tears welling up in her eyes when she is told that Funtown is closed to colored children, and see ominous clouds of inferiority beginning to form in her little mental sky, and see her beginning to distort her personality by developing an unconscious bitterness toward white people; when you have to concoct an answer for a five-year-old son who is asking: "Daddy, why do white people treat colored people so mean?"; when you take a cross-country drive and find it necessary to sleep night after night in the uncomfortable corners of your automobile because no motel will accept you; when you are humiliated day in and day out by nagging signs reading "white" and "colored"; when your first name becomes "nigger," your middle name becomes "boy" (however old you are) and your last name becomes "John," and your wife and mother are never given the respected title "Mrs."; when you are harried by day and haunted by night by the fact that you are a Negro, living constantly at tiptoe stance, never quite knowing what to expect next, and are plagued with inner fears and outer resentments; when you are forever fighting a degenerating sense of "nobodiness" — then you will understand why we find it difficult to wait. There comes a time when the cup of endurance runs over, and men are no longer willing to be plunged into the abyss of despair. I hope, sirs, you can understand our legitimate and unavoidable impatience.

You express a great deal of anxiety over our willingness to break laws. This is certainly a legitimate concern. Since we so diligently urge people to obey the Supreme Court's decision of 1954 outlawing segregation in the public schools, at first glance it may seem rather paradoxical for us consciously to break laws. One may well ask: "How can you advocate breaking some laws and obeying others?" The answer lies in the fact that there are two types of laws: just and unjust. I would be the first to advocate obeying just laws. One has not only a legal but a moral responsibility to obey just laws. Conversely, one has a moral responsibility to disobey unjust laws. I would agree with St. Augustine that "an unjust law is no law at all."

Now, what is the difference between the two? How does one determine whether a law is just or unjust? A just law is a man-made code that squares with the moral law or the law of God. An unjust law is a code that is out of harmony with the moral law. To put it in the terms of St. Thomas Aquinas: An unjust law is a human law that is not rooted in eternal law and natural law. Any law that uplifts human personality is just. Any law that degrades human personality is unjust. All segregation statutes are unjust because segregation distorts the soul and damages the personality. It gives the segregator a false sense of superiority and the segregated a false sense of inferiority. Segregation, to use the terminology of the Jewish philosopher Martin Buber, substitutes an "I-it" relationship for an "I-thou" relationship and ends up relegating persons to the status of things. Hence segregation is not only politically, economically and sociologically unsound, it is morally wrong and sinful. Paul Tillich has said that sin is separation. Is not segregation an existential expression of man's tragic separation, his awful estrangement, his terrible sinfulness? Thus it is that I can urge men to obey the 1954 decision of the Supreme Court, for it is morally right; and I can urge them to disobey segregation ordinances, for they are morally wrong.

Let us consider a more concrete example of just and unjust laws. An unjust law is a code that a numerical or power majority group compels a minority group to obey but does not make binding on itself. This is *difference* made legal. By the same token, a just law is a code that a majority compels a minority to follow and that it is willing to follow itself. This is *sameness* made legal.

Let me give another explanation. A law is unjust if it is inflicted on a minority that, as a result of being denied the right to vote, had no part in enacting or devising the law. Who can say that the legislature of Alabama which set up that state's segregation laws was democratically elected? Throughout Alabama all sorts of devious methods are used to prevent Negroes from becoming registered voters, and there are some counties in which, even though Negroes constitute a majority of the population, not a single Negro is registered. Can any law enacted under such circumstances be considered democratically structured?

Sometimes a law is just on its face and unjust in its application. For instance, I have been arrested on a charge of parading without a permit. Now, there is nothing wrong in having an ordinance which requires a permit for a parade. But such an ordinance becomes unjust when it is used to maintain segregation and to deny citizens the First-Amendment privilege of peaceful assembly and protest.

I hope you are able to see the distinction I am trying to point out. In no sense do I advocate evading or defying the law, as would the rabid segregationist. That would lead to anarchy. One who breaks an unjust law must do so openly, lovingly, and with a willingness to accept the penalty. I submit that an individual who breaks a law that conscience tells him is unjust, and who willingly accepts the penalty of imprisonment in order to arouse the conscience of the community over its injustice, is in reality expressing the highest respect for law.

Of course, there is nothing new about this kind of civil disobedience. It was evidenced sublimely in the refusal of Shadrach, Meshach and Abednego to obey the laws of Nebuchadnezzar, on the ground that a higher moral law was at stake. It was practiced superbly by the early Christians, who were willing to face hungry lions and the excruciating pain of chopping blocks rather than submit to certain unjust laws of the Roman Empire. To a degree, academic freedom is a reality today because Socrates practiced civil disobedience. In our own nation, the Boston Tea Party represented a massive act of civil disobedience.

We should never forget that everything Adolf Hitler did in Germany was "legal" and everything the Hungarian freedom fighters did in Hungary was "illegal." It was "illegal" to aid and comfort a Jew in Hitler's Germany. Even so, I am sure that, had I lived in Germany at the time, I would have aided and comforted my Jewish brothers. If today I lived in a Communist country where certain principles dear to the Christian faith are suppressed, I would openly advocate disobeying that country's antireligious laws.

I must make two honest confessions to you, my Christian and Jewish brothers. First, I must confess that over the past few years I have been gravely disappointed with the white moderate. I have almost reached the regrettable conclusion that the Negro's great stumbling block in his stride toward freedom is not the White Citizen's Counciler or the Ku Klux Klanner, but the white moderate, who is more devoted to "order" than to justice; who prefers a negative peace which is the absence of tension to a positive peace which is the presence of justice; who constantly says: "I agree with you in the goal you seek, but I cannot agree with your methods of direct action"; who paternalistically believes he can set the timetable for another man's freedom; who lives by a mythical concept of time and who constantly advises the Negro to wait for a "more convenient season." Shallow understanding from people of good will is more frustrating than absolute misunderstanding from people of ill will. Lukewarm acceptance is much more bewildering than outright rejection.

I had hoped that the white moderate would understand that law and order exist for the purpose of establishing justice and that when they fail in this purpose they become the dangerously structured dams that block the flow of social progress. I had hoped that the white moderate would understand that the present tension in the South is a necessary phase of the transition from an obnoxious negative peace, in which the Negro passively accepted his unjust plight, to a substantive and positive peace, in which all men will respect the dignity and worth of human personality. Actually, we who engage in nonviolent direct action are not the creators of tension. We merely bring to the surface the hidden tension that is already alive. We bring it out in the open, where it can be seen and dealt with. Like a boil that can never be cured so long as it is covered up but must be opened with all its ugliness to the natural medicines of air and light, injustice must be exposed, with all the tension its exposure creates, to the light of human conscience and the air of national opinion before it can be cured.

In your statement you assert that our actions, even though peaceful, must be condemned because they precipitate violence. But is this a logical assertion? Isn't this like condemning a robbed man because his possession of money precipitated the evil act of robbery? Isn't this like condemning Socrates because his unswerving commitment to truth and his philosophical inquiries precipitated the act by the misguided populace in which they made him drink hemlock? Isn't this like condemning Jesus because his unique God-consciousness and neverceasing devotion to God's will precipitated the evil act of crucifixion? We must come to see that, as the federal courts have consistently affirmed, it is wrong to urge an individual to cease his efforts to gain his basic constitutional rights because the quest may precipitate violence. Society must protect the robbed and punish the robber.

I had also hoped that the white moderate would reject the myth concerning time in relation to the struggle for freedom. I have just received a letter from a white brother in Texas. He writes: "All Christians know that the colored people will receive equal rights eventually, but it is possible that you are in too great a religious hurry. It has taken Christianity almost two thousand years to accomplish what it has. The teachings of Christ take time to come to earth." Such an attitude stems from a tragic misconception of time, from the strangely irrational notion there there is something in the very flow of time that will inevitably cure all ills. Actually, time itself is neutral; it can be used either destructively or constructively. More and more I feel that the people of ill will have used time much more effectively than have the people of good will. We will have to repent in this generation not merely for the hateful words and actions of the bad people but for the appalling silence of the good people. Human progress never rolls in on wheels of inevitability; it comes through the tireless efforts of men willing to be co-workers with God, and without this hard work, time itself becomes an ally of the forces of social stagnation. We must use time creatively, in the knowledge that the time is always ripe to do right. Now is the time to make real the promise of democracy and transform our pending national elegy into a creative psalm of brotherhood. Now is the time to lift our national policy from the quicksand of racial injustice to the solid rock of human dignity.

You speak of our activity in Birmingham as extreme. At first I was rather disappointed that fellow clergymen would see my nonviolent efforts as those of an extremist. I began thinking about the fact that I stand in the middle of two opposing forces in the Negro community. One is a force of complacency, made up in part of Negroes who, as a result of long years of oppression, are so drained of self-respect and a sense of "somebodiness" that they have adjusted to segregation; and in part of a few middle-class Negroes who, because of a degree of academic and economic security and because in some ways they profit by segregation, have become insensitive to the problems of the masses. The other force is one of bitterness and hatred, and it comes perilously close to advocating violence. It is expressed in the various black nationalist groups that are springing up across the nation, the largest and best-known being Elijah Muhammad's Muslim movement. Nourished by the Negro's frustration over the continued existence of racial discrimination, this movement is made up of people who have lost faith in America, who have absolutely repudiated Christianity, and who have concluded that the white man is an incorrigible "devil."

I have tried to stand between these two forces, saying that we need emulate neither the "do-nothingism" of the complacent nor the hatred and despair of the black nationalist. For there is the more excellent way of love and nonviolent protest. I am grateful to God that, through the influence of the Negro church, the way of nonviolence became an integral part of our struggle.

If this philosophy had not emerged, by now many streets of the South would, I am convinced, be flowing with blood. And I am further convinced that if our white brothers dismiss as "rabble-rousers" and "outside agitators" those of us who employ nonviolent direct action, and if they refuse to support our nonviolent efforts, millions of Negroes will, out of frustration and despair, seek solace and security in black-nationalist ideologies—a development that would inevitably lead to a frightening racial nightmare.

Oppressed people cannot remain oppressed forever. The yearning for freedom eventually manifests itself, and that is what has happened to the American Negro. Something within has reminded him of his birthright of freedom, and something without has reminded him that it can be gained. Consciously or unconsciously, he has been caught up by the *Zeitgeist,* and with his black brothers of Africa and his brown and yellow brothers of Asia, South America and the Caribbean, the United States Negro is moving with a sense of great urgency toward the promised land of racial justice. If one recognizes this vital urge that has engulfed the Negro community, one should readily understand why public demonstrations are taking place. The Negro has many pent-up resentments and latent frustrations, and he must release them. So let him march; let him make prayer pilgrimages to the city hall; let him go on freedom rides—and try to understand why he must do so. If his repressed emotions are not released in nonviolent ways, they will seek expression through violence; this is not a threat but a fact of history. So I have not said to my people: "Get rid of your discontent." Rather, I have tried to say that this normal and healthy discontent can be channeled into the creative outlet of nonviolent direct action. And now this approach is being termed extremist.

But though I was initially disappointed at being categorized as an extremist, as I continued to think about the matter I gradually gained a measure of satisfaction from the label. Was not Jesus an extremist for love: "Love your enemies, bless them that curse you, do good to them that hate you, and pray for them which despitefully use you, and persecute you." Was not Amos an extremist for justice: "Let justice roll down like waters and righteousness like an ever-flowing stream." Was not Paul an extremist for the Christian gospel: "I bear in my body the marks of the Lord Jesus." Was not Martin Luther an extremist: "Here I stand; I cannot do otherwise, so help me God." And John Bunyan: "I will stay in jail to the end of my days before I make a butchery of my conscience." And Abraham Lincoln: "This nation cannot survive half slave and half free." And Thomas Jefferson: "We hold these truths to be self-evident, that all men are created equal . . ." So the question is not whether we will be extremists, but what kind of extremists we will be. Will we be extremists for hate or for love? Will we be extremists for the preservation of injustice or for the extension of justice? In that dramatic scene on Calvary's hill three men were crucified. We must never forget that all three were crucified for the same crime—the crime of extremism. Two were extremists for immorality, and thus fell below their environment. The other, Jesus Christ, was an extremist for love, truth and goodness, and thereby rose above his environment. Perhaps the South, the nation and the world are in dire need of creative extremists.

I had hoped that the white moderate would see this need. Perhaps I was too optimistic; perhaps I expected too much. I suppose I should have realized that few members of the oppressor race can understand the deep groans and passionate yearnings of the oppressed race, and still fewer have the vision to see that injustice must be rooted out by strong, persistent and determined action. I am thankful, however, that some of our white brothers in the South have grasped the meaning of this social revolution and committed themselves to it. They are still all too few in quantity, but they are big in quality. Some—such as Ralph McGill, Lillian Smith, Harry Golden, James McBride Dabbs, Ann Braden and Sarah Patton Boyle—have written about our struggle in eloquent and prophetic terms. Others have marched with us down nameless streets of the South. They have languished in filthy, roach-infested jails, suffering the abuse and brutality of policemen who view them as "dirty nigger-lovers." Unlike so many of their moderate brothers and sisters, they have recognized the urgency of the moment and sensed the need for powerful "action" antidotes to combat the disease of segregation.

Let me take note of my other major disappointment. I have been so greatly disappointed with the white church and its leadership. Of course, there are some notable exceptions. I am not unmindful of the fact that each of you has taken some significant stands on this issue. I commend you, Reverend Stallings, for your Christian stand on this past Sunday, in welcoming Negroes to your worship service on a nonsegregated basis. I commend the Catholic leaders of this state for integrating Spring Hill College several years ago.

But despite these notable exceptions, I must honestly reiterate that I have been disappointed with the church. I do not say this as one of those negative critics who can always find something wrong with the church. I say this as a minister of the gospel, who loves the church; who was nurtured in its bosom; who has been sustained by its spiritual blessings and who will remain true to it as long as the cord of life shall lengthen.

When I was suddenly catapulted into the leadership of the bus protest in Montgomery, Alabama, a few years ago, I felt we would be supported by the white church. I felt that the white ministers, priests and rabbis of the South would be among our strongest allies. Instead, some have been outright opponents, refusing to understand the freedom movement and misrepresenting its leaders; all too many others have been more cautious than courageous and have remained silent behind the anesthetizing security of stained-glass windows.

In spite of my shattered dreams, I came to Birmingham with the hope that the white religious leadership of this community would see the justice of our cause and, with deep moral concern, would serve as the channel through which our just grievances could reach the power structure. I had hoped that each of you would understand. But again I have been disappointed.

I have heard numerous southern religious leaders admonish their worshipers to comply with a desegregation decision because it is the law, but I have longed to hear white ministers declare: "Follow this decree because integration is morally right and because the Negro is your brother." In the midst of blatant injustices inflicted upon the Negro, I have watched white churchmen stand on the sideline and mouth pious irrelevancies and sanctimonious trivialities. In the midst of a mighty struggle to rid our nation of racial and economic injustice, I have heard many ministers say: "Those are social issues, with which the gospel has no real concern." And I have watched many churches commit themselves to a completely otherworldly religion which makes a strange, un-Biblical distinction between body and soul, between the sacred and the secular.

I have traveled the length and breadth of Alabama, Mississippi and all the other southern states. On sweltering summer days and crisp autumn mornings I have looked at the South's beautiful churches with their lofty spires pointing heavenward. I have beheld the impressive outlines of her massive religious-education buildings. Over and over I have found myself asking: "What kind of people worship here? Who is their God? Where were their voices when the lips of Governor Barnett dripped with words of interposition and nullification? Where were they when Governor Wallace gave a clarion call for defiance and hatred? Where were their voices of support when bruised and weary Negro men and women decided to rise from the dark dungeons of complacency to the bright hills of creative protest?"

Yes, these questions are still in my mind. In deep disappointment I have wept over the laxity of the church. But be assured that my tears have been tears of love. There can be no deep disappointment where there is not deep love. Yes, I love the church. How could I do otherwise? I am in the rather unique position of being the son, the grandson and the great-grandson of preachers. Yes, I see the church as the body of Christ. But, oh! How we have blemished and scarred that body through social neglect and through fear of being nonconformists.

There was a time when the church was very powerful—in the time when the early Christians rejoiced at being deemed worthy to suffer for what they believed. In those days the church was not merely a thermometer that recorded the ideas and principles of popular opinion; it was a thermostat that transformed the mores of society. Whenever the early Christians entered a town, the people in power became disturbed and immediately sought to convict the Christians for being "disturbers of the peace" and "outside agitators." But the Christians pressed on, in the conviction that they were "a colony of heaven," called to obey God rather than man. Small in number, they were big in commitment. They were too God-intoxicated to be "astronomically intimidated." By their effort and example they brought an end to such ancient evils as infanticide and gladiatorial contests.

Things are different now. So often the contemporary church is a weak, ineffectual voice with an uncertain sound. So often it is an arch-defender of the status quo. Far from being disturbed by the presence of the church, the power structure of the average community is consoled by the church's silent—and often even vocal—sanction of things as they are.

But the judgment of God is upon the church as never before. If today's church does not recapture the sacrificial spirit of the early church, it will lose its authenticity, forfeit the loyalty of millions, and be dismissed as an irrelevant social club with no meaning for the twentieth century. Every day I meet young people whose disappointment with the church has turned into outright disgust.

Perhaps I have once again been too optimistic. Is organized religion too inextricably bound to the status quo to save our nation and the world? Perhaps I must turn my faith to the inner spiritual church, the church within the church, as the true *ekklesia* and the hope of the world. But again I am thankful to God that some noble souls from the ranks of organized religion have broken loose from the paralyzing chains of conformity and joined us as active partners in the struggle for freedom. They have left their secure congregations and walked the streets of Albany, Georgia, with us. They have gone down the highways of the South on tortuous rides for freedom. Yes, they have gone to jail with us. Some have been dismissed from their churches, have lost the support of their bishops and fellow ministers. But they have acted in the faith that right defeated is stronger than evil triumphant. Their witness has been the spiritual salt that has preserved the true meaning of the gospel in these troubled times. They have carved a tunnel of hope through the dark mountain of disappointment.

I hope the church as a whole will meet the challenge of this decisive hour. But even if the church does not come to the aid of justice, I have no despair about the future. I have no fear about the outcome of our struggle in Birmingham, even if our motives are at present misunderstood. We will reach the goal of freedom in Birmingham and all over the nation, because the goal of America is freedom. Abused and scorned though we may be, our destiny is tied up with America's destiny. Before the pilgrims landed at Plymouth, we were here. Before the pen of Jefferson etched the majestic words of the Declaration of Independence across the pages of history, we were here. For more than two centuries our forebears labored in this country without wages; they made cotton king; they built the homes of their masters while suffering gross injustice and shameful humiliation—and yet out of a bottomless vitality they continued to thrive and develop. If the inexpressible cruelties of slavery could not stop us, the opposition we now face will surely fail. We will win our freedom because the sacred heritage of our nation and the eternal will of God are embodied in our echoing demands.

Before closing I feel impelled to mention one other point in your statement that has troubled me profoundly. You warmly commended the Birmingham police force for keeping "order" and "preventing violence." I doubt that you would have so warmly commended the police force if you had seen its dogs sinking their teeth into unarmed, nonviolent Negroes. I doubt that you would so quickly commend the policemen if you were to observe their ugly and inhumane treatment of Negroes here in the city jail; if you were to watch them push and curse old Negro women and young Negro girls; if you were to see them slap and kick old Negro men and young boys; if you were to observe them, as they did on two occasions, refuse to give us food because we wanted to sing our grace together. I cannot join you in your praise of the Birmingham police department.

It is true that the police have exercised a degree of discipline in handling the demonstrators. In this sense they have conducted themselves rather "nonviolently" in public. But for what purpose? To preserve the evil system of segregation. Over the past few years I have consistently preached that nonviolence demands that the means we use must be as pure as the ends we seek. I have tried to make clear that it is wrong to use immoral means to attain moral ends. But now I must affirm that it is just as wrong, or perhaps even more so, to use moral means to preserve immoral ends. Perhaps Mr. Connor and his policemen have been rather nonviolent in public, as was Chief Pritchett in Albany, Georgia, but they have used the moral means of nonviolence to maintain the immoral end of racial injustice. As T. S. Eliot has said: "The last temptation is the greatest treason: To do the right deed for the wrong reason."

I wish you had commended the Negro sit-inners and demonstrators of Birmingham for their sublime courage, their willingness to suffer and their amazing discipline in the midst of great provocation. One day the South will recognize its real heroes. They will be the James Merediths, with the noble sense of purpose that enables them to face jeering and hostile mobs, and with the agonizing loneliness that characterizes the life of the pioneer. They will be old, oppressed, battered Negro women, symbolized in a seventy-two-year-old woman in Montgomery, Alabama, who rose up with a sense of dignity and with her people decided not to ride segregated buses, and who responded with ungrammatical profundity to one who inquired about her weariness: "My feets is tired, but my soul is at rest." They will be the young high school and college students, the young ministers of the gospel and a host of their elders, courageously and nonviolently sitting in at lunch counters and willingly going to jail for conscience' sake. One day the South will know that when these disinherited children of God sat down at lunch counters, they were in reality standing up for what is best in the American dream and for the most sacred values in our Judaeo-Christian heritage, thereby bringing our nation back to those great wells of democracy which were dug deep by the founding fathers in their formulation of the Constitution and the Declaration of Independence.

Never before have I written so long a letter. I'm afraid it is much too long to take your precious time. I can assure you that it would have been much shorter if I had been writing from a comfortable desk, but what else can one do when he is alone in a narrow jail cell, other than write long letters, think long thoughts and pray long prayers?

If I have said anything in this letter that overstates the truth and indicates an unreasonable impatience, I beg you to forgive me. If I have said anything that understates the truth and indicates my having a patience that allows me to settle for anything less than brotherhood, I beg God to forgive me.

I hope this letter finds you strong in the faith. I also hope that circumstances will soon make it possible for me to meet each of you, not as an integrationist or a civil-rights leader but as a fellow clergyman and a Christian brother. Let us all hope that the dark clouds of racial prejudice will soon pass away and the deep fog of misunderstanding will be lifted from our fear-drenched communities, and in some not too distant tomorrow the radiant stars of love and brotherhood will shine over our great nation with all their scintillating beauty.

> Yours for the cause of Peace and Brotherhood,
> Martin Luther King, Jr.

# I Have a Dream

August 28, 1963

I am happy to join with you today in what will go down in history as the greatest demonstration for freedom in the history of our nation.

Five score years ago, a great American, in whose symbolic shadow we stand today, signed the Emancipation Proclamation. This momentous decree came as a great beacon light of hope to millions of Negro slaves, who had been seared in the flames of withering injustice. It came as a joyous daybreak to end the long night of their captivity.

But one hundred years later, the Negro is still not free. One hundred years later, the life of the Negro is still sadly crippled by the manacles of segregation and the chains of discrimination. One hundred years later, the Negro lives on a lonely island of poverty in the midst of a vast ocean of material prosperity. One hundred years later (*Applause*), the Negro is still languished in the corners of American society and finds himself an exile in his own land. So we have come here today to dramatize a shameful condition.

In a sense we've come to our nation's Capitol to cash a check. When the architects of our republic wrote the magnificent words of the Constitution and the Declaration of Independence, they were signing a promissory note to which every American was to fall heir. This note was a promise that all men—yes, black men as well as white men—would be guaranteed the unalienable rights of life, liberty, and the pursuit of happiness.

It is obvious today that America has defaulted on this promissory note in so far as her citizens of color are concerned. Instead of honoring this sacred obligation, America has given the Negro people a bad check; a check which has come back marked "insufficient funds" (*Applause*). But we refuse to believe that the bank of justice is bankrupt. We refuse to believe that there are insufficient funds in the great vaults of opportunity of this nation. So we've come to cash this check—a check that will give us upon demand the riches of freedom and the security of justice (*Applause*). We have also come to this hallowed spot to remind America of the fierce urgency of *now*. This is no time to engage in the luxury of cooling off or to take the tranquilizing drug of gradualism. *Now is the time* to make real the promises of Democracy. *Now is the time* to rise from the dark and desolate valley of segregation to the sunlit path of racial justice. *Now is the (Applause) time* to lift our nation from the quicksands of racial injustice to the solid rock of brotherhood. *Now is the time* to make justice a reality for all of God's children.

It would be fatal for the nation to overlook the urgency of the moment. This sweltering summer of the Negro's legitimate discontent will not pass until there is an invigorating autumn of freedom and equality. Nineteen sixty-three is not an end, but a beginning. Those who hope that the Negro needed to blow off steam and will now be content will have a rude awakening if the nation returns to business as usual (*Applause*). There will be neither rest nor tranquility in America until the Negro is granted his citizenship rights. The whirlwinds of revolt will continue to shake the foundations of our nation until the bright day of justice emerges.

But that is something that I must say to my people who stand on the warm threshold which leads into the palace of justice. In the process of gaining our rightful place we must not be guilty of wrongful deeds. Let us not seek to satisfy our thirst for freedom by drinking from the cup of bitterness and hatred (*Applause*).

We must forever conduct our struggle on the high plane of dignity and discipline. We must not allow our creative protest to degenerate into physical violence. Again and again we must rise to the majestic heights of meeting physical force with soul force. The marvelous new militancy which has engulfed the Negro community must not lead us to a distrust of all white people, for many of our white brothers, as evidenced by their presence here today, have come to realize that their destiny is tied up with our destiny (*Applause*). And they have come to realize that their freedom is inextricably bound to our freedom. We cannot walk alone.

And as we walk, we must make the pledge that we shall always march ahead. We cannot turn back. There are those who ask the devotees of civil rights, "When will you be satisfied?" We can never be satisfied as long as the Negro is the victim of the unspeakable horrors of police brutality. We can never be satisfied as long as our bodies, heavy with the fatigue of travel, cannot gain lodging in the motels of the highways and the hotels of the cities (*Applause*). We cannot be satisfied as long as the Negro's basic mobility is from a smaller ghetto to a larger one. We can never be satisfied as long as our children are stripped of their selfhood and robbed of their dignity by signs stating "For Whites Only" (*Applause*). We cannot be satisfied as long as a Negro in Mississippi cannot vote and a Negro in New York believes he has nothing for which to vote (*Applause*). No, no, we are not satisfied, and we will not be satisfied until justice rolls down like waters and righteousness like a mighty stream (*Applause*).

I am not unmindful that some of you have come here out of great trials and tribulations. Some of you have come fresh from narrow jail cells. Some of you have come from areas where your quest for freedom left you battered by the storms of persecution and staggered by the winds of police brutality. You have been the veterans of creative suffering. Continue to work with the faith that unearned suffering is redemptive.

Go back to Mississippi, go back to Alabama, go back to South Carolina, go back to Georgia, go back to Louisiana, go back to the slums and ghettos of our northern cities, knowing that somehow this situation can and will be changed. Let us not wallow in the valley of despair.

I say to you today, my friends (*Applause*), so even though we face the difficulties of today and tomorrow, I still have a dream. It is a dream deeply rooted in the American dream.

I have a dream that one day this nation will rise up and live out the true meaning of its creed: "We hold these truths to be self-evident; that all men are created equal" (*Applause*).

I have a dream that one day on the red hills of Georgia the sons of former slaves and the sons of former slaveowners will be able to sit down together at the table of brotherhood; I have a dream—

That one day even the state of Mississippi, a state sweltering with the heat of injustice, sweltering with the heat of oppression, will be transformed into an oasis of freedom and justice; I have a dream—

That my four little children will one day live in a nation where they will not be judged by the color of their skin but by the content of their character; I have a dream today (*Applause*).

I have a dream that one day, down in Alabama, with its vicious racists, with its governor having his lips dripping with the words of interposition and nullification, one day right there in Alabama little black boys and black girls will be able to join hands with little white boys and white girls as sisters and brothers; I have a dream today (*Applause*)—

I have a dream that one day every valley shall be exalted, every hill and mountain shall be made low, the rough places will be made plane and crooked places will be made straight, and the glory of the Lord shall be revealed, and all flesh shall see it together.

This is our hope. This is the faith that I go back to the South with. With this faith we will be able to hew out of the mountain of despair a stone of hope. With this faith we will be able to transform the jangling discords of our nation into a beautiful symphony of brotherhood. With this faith we will be able to work together, to pray together, to struggle together, to go to jail together, to stand up for freedom together, knowing that we will be free one day *(Applause)*.

This will be the day *(Applause)*. . . . This will be the day when all of God's children will be able to sing with new meaning "My country 'tis of thee, sweet land of liberty, of thee I sing. Land where my fathers died, land of the pilgrim's pride, from every mountainside, let freedom ring," and if America is to be a great nation — this must become true.

So let freedom ring — from the prodigious hilltops of New Hampshire, let freedom ring; from the mighty mountains of New York, let freedom ring — from the heightening Alleghenies of Pennsylvania!

Let freedom ring from the snowcapped Rockies of Colorado!

Let freedom ring from the curvaceous slopes of California!

But not only that; let freedom ring from Stone Mountain of Georgia!

Let freedom ring from Lookout Mountain of Tennessee!

Let freedom ring from every hill and mole hill of Mississippi. From every mountainside, let freedom ring, and when this happens *(Applause)*. . .

When we allow freedom to ring, when we let it ring from every village and every hamlet, from every state and every city, we will be able to speed up that day when all of God's children, black men and white men, Jews and Gentiles, Protestants and Catholics, will be able to join hands and sing in the words of the old Negro spiritual, "Free at last! Free at last! Thank God almighty, we are free at last!" *(Thunderous applause.)*

## Marya Mannes

# Memo to a Film Maker

Note: Earlier I spoke of the need to submerge the pursuit of private goals and forfeit a part of individual and national sovereignty in the interest of the survival — in peace and dignity — of all of us.

The United Nations is an attempt to do just this: an instrument, still far from perfect but without present alternative, for creating one world of law out of the anarchy of warring fragments.

The following parable speaks of another way, in another language. It also speaks of the artist who, of all of us, is most committed and best equipped to bring order out of chaos.

While you've been busy messing around with cameras under water, in the air, and back in B.C., you've missed a natural. I mean a picture about a big symphony orchestra: a portrait of one of the greatest human and artistic phenomena of our time. Believe me, this is no culture item for the art theaters. This is a gold mine: a hundred and five potential stories in one, and for once a way of using music legitimately and magnificently instead of dragging it in by the tail of some maestro's coat or the hair of some third-rate vocalist with a heart-throb past. What's more, this picture could pack a message that would make most of your Biblical Spectaculars look like children's colored picture books in large type—which is what they are.

I would start with the works: the whole orchestra, full screen; a hundred and four men and the conductor performing the last movement, let's say, of Brahms's First, or anything that uses the full potentialities of an orchestra, almost drowning the audience in sound. After a couple of minutes, I would close in on the conductor (don't have him too wild-eyed and hair-tossing—the best ones are intense but controlled) and then on his hand as he cues individual sections of the orchestra. You know how a conductor makes lifting motions toward the first violins to raise their volume, or diminishing motions, palm down, toward the brasses.

Well, follow him as he turns to the first violins on his left and then close in on the concertmaster as he plays. Let's call him Rossi; a lot of concertmasters are Italian these days, where a generation ago they were usually German. Rossi is about forty, has receding black hair, and wears glasses. He is wholly wrapped up in his playing, yet keeps a wary intermittent eye on the conductor, Lorentz—as he must. You dissolve then from the middle-aged Rossi playing at a concert to the very young Rossi winning a conservatory prize in Bologna as the prodigy hope of his region and possibly of his country. You follow his story, which is a familiar one. Rossi had great promise, Rossi wanted to be a violin virtuoso, Rossi couldn't quite make the grade in a world that turns out Rossis every month and Menuhins once in ten years. So, emigrating from Italy to the land of opportunity, he sacrifices the dream of personal fame for the security of collective employment; and it's only when a guest artist plays a violin concerto (and this can be shown in the picture) that the dream stirs and Rossi thinks bitterly: He is no better than I; he just got the breaks.

If you want to, you can bring in Rossi's wife, Maria; the girl he married at home who feels shy and uncomfortable in any worldly company. The kind of woman, the others say, who could never help a man get anywhere. If I were you, I would give a glimpse of Rossi's home life, showing him as a very ordinary man with no interests outside of his music and his food; a hard worker, a good family man and a "good fellow," in no way distinguished. And then I would switch back to him at the concert and show what music and responsibility do to enlarge a man, for here Rossi has the stature and purity of dedication.

Go back to Lorentz, the conductor, and follow his cue to the flutist, Renaudel. (They are often French, the wind players, but don't ask me why.) Now Renaudel is a real heller, mad for the women and wholly unreliable, except for his playing. At the moment, he happens to be having an affair with Lorentz's wife, but Lorentz doesn't know it. You could have fun with this, especially if you could lead off from "L'Après-midi d'un Faune" and Renaudel's exquisite fluting to his activities at other times of the day.

There is really no end to these explorations into the men who make the music, these human instruments whose lives form the counterpoint to the major theme of creation. There is Wagenecht, for instance, the double-bass player. His father and grandfather were double-bass players too; it never occurred to him to do anything else. Wagenecht is married to his bull fiddle, and when the orchestra first went on tour many years ago, he used to reserve a lower for it in the train, not trusting his love to the baggage car. He is a born comic and an ardent chess player, but on the whole he prefers solitude with his large vibrating companion, who never fails him—as once a woman did.

Somewhere along the line you'll have to include Brodsky, the timpanist. Catch him first at the concert, bending tenderly over his big kettledrums, his ear to the hide as he stretches or loosens it to the proper pitch; then at his moment of triumph when the tattoo of his felt-balled sticks makes a fine thunder and he stands like Zeus. As far as his home life is concerned, I think you might make him henpecked and perhaps overcome by his wife's family, so that he can assert himself only with his drums.

Toward the end, of course, you'll have to tackle Lorentz, the conductor, for in a sense he is the key to the meaning of the picture. Here you have a highly complicated man; an artist of the first order, with a phenomenal memory and understanding of the world's music and the power and skill to project it; a politician, required and able to reconcile the demands of Brodsky and Renaudel with each other, and the demands of his board of trustees with those of Local 802; a contemplative man, secluded for hours on end with his scores; an extrovert, needing a public; a nervous, petty, irascible man, very vain; a man humble in the service of music.

Here is where we get close to the message I spoke about at the beginning. Don't look disgusted; you're the one who's always talking about making a picture that Means Something, that Illuminates. This is really a picture about sovereignties. Each of these hundred and four men in the symphony orchestra is an entity, with his own life, function, and power. When he plays in the orchestra, however, he submerges his sovereignty to the whole, which is music. If he did not—if he played what he wanted, when he wanted, regardless of the others and regardless of direction—there would only be chaos.

What is more, each of these men, instead of losing himself in the collective whole, finds himself. He finds himself in participating in something greater than he is: the act of creation. He has become a master of music (and essentially every member of a fine symphony orchestra must be one) in order to be the servant of music.

The same goes for the conductor. For while our Lorentz seems to be a dictator, guiding and compelling all the diverse elements and sovereignties into one whole, he is in reality as much a servant as any of his men. His power is the by-product and not the goal of his devotion. His sole and ultimate function is to bring to others what he has heard in silence: the universal speech of music, in all its magnificence.

I think that you ought to get going on this soon. Because the thing we lack most desperately now is a universal language, not to mention the humility to submerge our sovereignties in the learning of it. What we have now is an orchestra without a conductor, each man playing as he chooses; and the resultant cacophony is violent enough to shatter the windows of the world.

(1964)

## *Claude Brown*

*from* **Manchild in the Promised Land**

"Run!"

Where?

Oh, hell! Let's get out of here!

"Turk! Turk! I'm shot!"

I could hear Turk's voice calling from a far distance, telling me not to go into the fish-and-chips joint. I heard, but I didn't understand. The only thing I knew was that I was going to die.

I ran. There was a bullet in me trying to take my life, all thirteen years of it.

I climbed up on the bar yelling, "Walsh, I'm shot. I'm shot." I could feel the blood running down my leg. Walsh, the fellow who operated the fish-and-chips joint, pushed me off the bar and onto the floor. I couldn't move now, but I was still completely conscious.

Walsh was saying, "Git outta here, kid. I ain't got no time to play."

A woman was screaming, mumbling something about the Lord, and saying, "Somebody done shot that poor child."

Mama ran in. She jumped up and down, screaming like a crazy woman. I began to think about dying. The worst part of dying was thinking about the things and the people that I'd never see again. As I lay there trying to imagine what being dead was like, the policeman who had been trying to control Mama gave up and bent over me. He asked who had shot me. Before I could answer, he was asking me if I could hear him. I told him that I didn't know who had shot me and would he please tell Mama to stop jumping up and down. Every time Mama came down on that shabby floor, the bullet lodged in my stomach felt like a hot poker.

Another policeman had come in and was struggling to keep the crowd outside. I could see Turk in the front of the crowd. Before the cops came, he asked me if I was going to tell them that he was with me. I never answered. I looked at him and wondered if he saw who shot me. Then his question began to ring in my head: "Sonny, you gonna tell 'em I was with you?" I was bleeding on a dirty floor in a fish-and-chips joint, and Turk was standing there in the doorway hoping that I would die before I could tell the cops that he was with me. Not once did Turk ask me how I felt.

Hell, yeah, I thought, I'm gonna tell 'em.

It seemed like hours had passed before the ambulance finally arrived. Mama wanted to go to the hospital with me, but the ambulance attendant said she was too excited. On the way to Harlem Hospital, the cop who was riding with us asked Dad what he had to say. His answer was typical: "I told him about hanging out with those bad-ass boys." The cop was a little surprised. This must be a rookie, I thought.

The next day, Mama was at my bedside telling me that she had prayed and the Lord had told her that I was going to live. Mama said that many of my friends wanted to donate some blood for me, but the hospital would not accept it from narcotics users.

This was one of the worst situations I had ever been in. There was a tube in my nose that went all the way to the pit of my stomach. I was being fed intravenously, and there was a drain in my side. Everybody came to visit me, mainly out of curiosity. The girls were all anxious to know where I had gotten shot. They had heard all kinds of tales about where the bullet struck. The bolder ones wouldn't even bother to ask: they just snatched the cover off me and looked for themselves. In a few days, the word got around that I was in one piece.

On my fourth day in the hospital, I was awakened by a male nurse at about 3 A.M. When he said hello in a very ladyish voice, I thought that he had come to the wrong bed by mistake. After identifying himself, he told me that he had helped Dr. Freeman save my life. The next thing he said, which I didn't understand, had something to do with the hours he had put in working that day. He went on mumbling something about how tired he was and ended up asking me to rub his back. I had already told him that I was grateful to him for helping the doctor save my life. While I rubbed his back above the beltline, he kept pushing my hand down and saying, "Lower, like you are really grateful to me." I told him that I was sleepy from the needle a nurse had given me. He asked me to pat his behind. After I had done this, he left.

The next day when the fellows came to visit me, I told them about my early-morning visitor. Dunny said he would like to meet him. Tito joked about being able to get a dose of clap in the hospital. The guy with the tired back never showed up again, so the fellows never got a chance to meet him. Some of them were disappointed.

After I had been in the hospital for about a week, I was visited by another character. I had noticed a woman visiting one of the patients on the far side of the ward. She was around fifty-five years old, short and fat, and she was wearing old-lady shoes. While I wondered who this woman was, she started across the room in my direction. After she had introduced herself, she told me that she was visiting her son. Her son had been stabbed in the chest with an ice pick by his wife. She said that his left lung had been punctured, but he was doing fine now, and that Jesus was so-o-o good.

Her name was Mrs. Ganey, and she lived on 145th Street. She said my getting shot when I did "was the work of the Lord." My gang had been stealing sheets and bedspreads off clotheslines for months before I had gotten shot. I asked this godly woman why she thought it was the work of the Lord or Jesus or whoever. She began in a sermonlike tone, saying, "Son, people was gitting tired-a y'all stealing all dey sheets and spreads." She said that on the night that I had gotten shot, she baited her clothesline with two brand-new bedspreads, turned out all the lights in the apartment, and sat at the kitchen window waiting for us to show.

She waited with a double-barreled shotgun.

The godly woman said that most of our victims thought that we were winos or dope fiends and that most of them had vowed to kill us. At the end of the sermon, the godly woman said, "Thank the Lord I didn't shoot nobody's child." When the godly woman had finally departed, I thought, Thank the Lord for taking her away from my bed.

Later on that night, I was feeling a lot of pain and couldn't get to sleep. A nurse who had heard me moaning and groaning came over and gave me a shot of morphine. Less than twenty minutes later, I was deep into a nightmare.

I was back in the fish-and-chips joint, lying on the floor dying. Only, now I was in more pain than before, and there were dozens of Mamas around me jumping up and screaming. I could feel myself dying in a rising pool of blood. The higher the blood rose the more I died.

I dreamt about the boy who Rock and big Stoop had thrown off that roof on 149th Street. None of us had stayed around to see him hit the ground, but I just knew that he died in a pool of blood too. I wished that he would stop screaming, and I wished that Mama would stop screaming. I wished they would let me die quietly.

As the screams began to die out — Mama's and the boy's — I began to think about the dilapidated old tenement building that I lived in, the one that still had the words "pussy" and "fuck you" on the walls where I had scribbled them years ago. The one where the super, Mr. Lawson, caught my little brother writing some more. Dad said he was going to kill Pimp for writing on that wall, and the way he was beating Pimp with that ironing cord, I thought he would. Mama was crying, I was crying, and Pimp had been crying for a long time. Mama said that he was too young to be beaten like that. She ran out of the house and came back with a cop, who stopped Dad from beating Pimp.

I told Pimp not to cry any more, just to wait until I got big: I was going to kill Dad, and he could help me if he wanted to.

This was the building where Mr. Lawson had killed a man for peeing in the hall. I remembered being afraid to go downstairs the morning after Mr. Lawson had busted that man's head open with a baseball bat. I could still see blood all over the hall. This was the building where somebody was always shooting out the windows in the hall. They were usually shooting at Johnny D., and they usually missed. This was the building that I loved more than anyplace else in the world. The thought that I would never see this building again scared the hell out of me.

I dreamt about waking up in the middle of the night seven years before and thinking that the Germans or the Japs had come and that the loud noises I heard were bombs falling. Running into Mama's room, I squeezed in between her and Dad at the front window. Thinking that we were watching an air raid, I asked Dad where the sirens were and why the street lights were on. He said, "This ain't no air raid — just a whole lotta niggers gone fool. And git the hell back in that bed!" I went back to bed, but I couldn't go to sleep. The loud screams in the street and the crashing sound of falling plate-glass windows kept me awake for hours. While I listened to the noise, I imagined bombs falling and people running through the streets screaming. I could see mothers running with babies in their arms, grown men running over women and children to save their own lives, and the Japs stabbing babies with bayonets, just like in the movies. I thought, Boy, I sure wish I was out there. I bet the Stinky brothers are out there. Danny and Butch are probably out there having all the fun in the world.

The next day, as I was running out of the house without underwear or socks on, I could hear Mama yelling, "Boy, come back here and put a hat or something on your head!" When I reached the stoop, I was knocked back into the hall by a big man carrying a ham under his coat. While I looked up at him, wondering what was going on, he reached down with one hand and snatched me up, still holding the ham under his coat with his other hand. He stood me up against a wall and ran into the hall with his ham. Before I had a chance to move, other men came running through the hall carrying cases of whiskey, sacks of flour, and cartons of cigarettes. Just as I unglued myself from the wall and started out the door for the second time, I was bowled over again. This time by a cop with a gun in his hand. He never stopped, but after he had gone a couple of yards into the hall, I heard him say, "Look out, kid." On the third try, I got out of the building. But I wasn't sure that this was my street. None of the stores had any windows left, and glass was everywhere. It seemed that all the cops in the world were on 145th Street and Eighth Avenue that day. The cops were telling everybody to move on, and everybody was talking about the riot. I went over to a cop and asked him what a riot was. He told me to go on home. The next cop I asked told me that a riot was what had happened the night before. Putting two and two together I decided that a riot was "a whole lotta niggers gone fool."

I went around the corner to Butch's house. After I convinced him that I was alone, he opened the door. He said that Kid and Danny were in the kitchen. I saw Kid sitting on the floor with his hand stuck way down in a gallon jar of pickled pigs' ears. Danny was cooking some bacon at the stove, and Butch was busy hiding stuff. It looked as though these guys had stolen a whole grocery store. While I joined the feast, they took turns telling me about the riot. Danny and Kid hadn't gone home the night before; they were out following the crowds and looting.

My only regret was that I had missed the excitement. I said, "Why don't we have another riot tonight? Then Butch and me can get in it."

Danny said that there were too many cops around to have a riot now. Butch said that they had eaten up all the bread and that he was going to steal some more. I asked if I could come along with him, and he said that I could if I promised to do nothing but watch. I promised, but we both knew that I was lying.

When we got to the street, Butch said he wanted to go across the street and look at the pawnshop. I tagged along. Like many of the stores where the rioters had been, the pawnshop had been set afire. The firemen had torn down a sidewall getting at the fire. So Butch and I just walked in where the wall used to be. Everything I picked up was broken or burned or both. My feet kept sinking into the wet furs that had been burned and drenched. The whole place smelled of smoke and was as dirty as a Harlem gutter on a rainy day. The cop out front yelled to us to get out of there. He only had to say it once.

After stopping by the seafood joint and stealing some shrimp and oysters, we went to what was left of Mr. Gordon's grocery store. Butch just walked in, picked up a loaf of bread, and walked out. He told me to come on, but I ignored him and went into the grocery store instead. I picked up two loaves of bread and walked out. When I got outside, a cop looked at me, and I ran into a building and through the backyard to Butch's house. Running through the backyard, I lost all the oysters that I had; when I reached Butch's house, I had only two loaves of bread and two shrimp in my pocket.

Danny, who was doing most of the cooking, went into the street to steal something to drink. Danny, Butch, and Kid were ten years old, four years older than I. Butch was busy making sandwiches on the floor, and Kid was trying to slice up a loaf of bologna. I had never eaten shrimp, but nobody seemed to care, because they refused to cook it for me. I told Butch that I was going to cook it myself. He said that there was no more lard in the house and that I would need some grease.

I looked around the house until I came up with some Vaseline hair pomade. I put the shrimp in the frying pan with the hair grease, waited until they had gotten black and were smoking, then took them out and made a sandwich. A few years later, I found out that shrimp were supposed to be shelled before cooking. I ate half of the sandwich and hated shrimp for years afterward.

The soft hand tapping on my face to wake me up was Jackie's. She and Della had been to a New Year's Eve party. Jackie wanted to come by the hospital and kiss me at midnight. This was the only time in my life that I ever admitted being glad to see Jackie. I asked them about the party, hoping that they would stay and talk to me for a while. I was afraid that if I went back to sleep, I would have another bad dream.

The next thing I knew, a nurse was waking me up for breakfast. I didn't recall saying good night to Jackie and Della, so I must have fallen asleep while they were talking to me. I thought about Sugar, how nice she was, and how she was a real friend. I knew she wanted to be my girl friend, and I liked her a lot. But what would everybody say if I had a buck-toothed girl friend. I remembered Knoxie asking me how I kissed her. That question led to the first fight I'd had with Knoxie in years. No, I couldn't let Sugar be my girl. It was hard enough having her as a friend.

The next day, I asked the nurse why she hadn't changed my bed linen, and she said because they were evicting me. I had been in the hospital for eleven days, but I wasn't ready to go home. I left the hospital on January 2 and went to a convalescent home in Valhalla, New York. After I had been there for three weeks, the activity director took me aside and told me that I was going to New York City to see a judge and that I might be coming back. The following morning, I left to see that judge, but I never got back to Valhalla.

I stood there before Judge Pankin looking solemn and lying like a professional. I thought that he looked too nice to be a judge. A half hour after I had walked into the courtroom, Judge Pankin was telling me that he was sending me to the New York State Training School for Boys. The judge said that he thought I was a chronic liar and that he hoped I would be a better boy when I came out. I asked him if he wanted me to thank him. Mama stopped crying just long enough to say, "Hush your mouth, boy."

Mama tried to change the judge's mind by telling him that I had already been to Wiltwyck School for Boys for two and a half years. And before that, I had been ordered out of the state for at least one year. She said that I had been away from my family too much; that was why I was always getting into trouble.

The judge told Mama that he knew what he was doing and that one day she would be grateful to him for doing it.

I had been sent away before, but this was the first time I was ever afraid to go. When Mama came up to the detention room in Children's Court, I tried to act as though I wasn't afraid. After I told her that Warwick and where I was going were one and the same, Mama began to cry, and so did I.

Most of the guys I knew had been to Warwick and were too old to go back. I knew that there were many guys up there I had mistreated. The Stinky brothers were up there. They thought that I was one of the guys who had pulled a train on their sister in the park the summer before. Bumpy from 144th Street was up there. I had shot him in the leg with a zip gun in a rumble only a few months earlier. There were many guys up there I used to bully on the streets and at Wiltwyck, guys I had sold tea leaves to as pot. There were rival gang members up there who just hated my name. All of these guys were waiting for me to show. The word was out that I couldn't fight any more—that I had slowed down since I was shot and that a good punch to the stomach would put my name in the undertaker's book.

When I got to the Youth House, I tried to find out who was up at Warwick that I might know. Nobody knew any of the names I asked about. I knew that if I went up to Warwick in my condition, I'd never live to get out. I had a reputation for being a rugged little guy. This meant that I would have at least a half-dozen fights in the first week of my stay up there.

It seemed the best thing for me to do was to cop out on the nut. For the next two nights, I woke up screaming and banging on the walls. On the third day, I was sent to Bellevue for observation. This meant that I wouldn't be going to Warwick for at least twenty-eight days.

While I was in Bellevue, the fellows would come down and pass notes to me through the doors. Tito and Turk said they would get bagged and sent to Warwick by the time I got there. They were both bagged a week later for smoking pot in front of the police station. They were both sent to Bellevue. Two weeks after they showed, I went home.

The judge still wanted to send me to Warwick, but Warwick had a full house, so he sent me home for two weeks.

The day before I went back to court, I ran into Turk, who had just gotten out of Bellevue. Tito had been sent to Warwick, but Turk had gotten a walk because his sheet wasn't too bad. I told him I would probably be sent to Warwick the next day. Turk said he had run into Bucky in Bellevue. He told me that he and Tito had voted Bucky out of the clique. I told him that I wasn't going for it because Bucky was my man from short-pants days. Turk said he liked him too, but what else could he do after Bucky had let a white boy beat him in the nutbox? When I heard this, there was nothing I could do but agree with Turk. Bucky had to go. That kind of news spread fast, and who wanted to be in a clique with a stud who let a paddy boy beat him?

The next day, I went to the Youth House to wait for Friday and the trip to Warwick. As I lay in bed that night trying to think of a way out, I began to feel sorry for myself. I began to blame Danny, Butch, and Kid for my present fate. I told myself that I wouldn't be going to Warwick if they hadn't taught me how to steal, play hookey, make homemades, and stuff like that. But then I thought, aw, hell, it wasn't their fault—as a matter of fact, it was a whole lotta fun.

I remembered sitting on the stoop with Danny, years before, when a girl came up and started yelling at him. She said that her mother didn't want her brother to hang out with Danny any more, because Danny had taught her brother how to play hookey. When the girl had gone down the street, I asked Danny what hookey was. He said it was a game he would teach me as soon as I started going to school.

Danny was a man of his word. He was my next-door neighbor, and he rang my doorbell about 7:30 A.M. on the second day of school. Mama thanked him for volunteering to take me to school. Danny said he would have taught me to play hookey the day before, but he knew that Mama would have to take me to school on the first day. As we headed toward the backyard to hide our books, Danny began to explain the great game of hookey. It sounded like lots of fun to me. Instead of going to school, we would go all over the city stealing, sneak into a movie, or go up on a roof and throw bottles down into the street. Danny suggested that we start the day off by waiting for Mr. Gordon to put out his vegetables; we could steal some sweet potatoes and cook them in the backyard. I was sorry I hadn't started school sooner, because hookey sure was a lot of fun.

Before I began going to school, I was always in the streets with Danny, Kid, and Butch. Sometimes, without saying a word, they would all start to run like hell, and a white man was always chasing them. One morning as I entered the backyard where all the hookey players went to draw up an activity schedule for the day, Butch told me that Danny and Kid had been caught by Mr. Sands the day before. He went on to warn me about Mr. Sands, saying Mr. Sands was that white man who was always chasing somebody and that I should try to remember what he looked like and always be on the lookout for him. He also warned me not to try to outrun Mr. Sands, "because that cat is fast." Butch said, "When you see him, head for a backyard or a roof. He won't follow you there."

During the next three months, I stayed out of school twenty-one days. Dad was beating the hell out of me for playing hookey, and it was no fun being in the street in the winter, so I started going to school regularly. But when spring rolled around, hookey became my favorite game again. Mr. Sands was known to many parents in the neighborhood as the truant officer. He never caught me in the street, but he came by my house many mornings to escort me to class. This was one way of getting me to school, but he never found a way to keep me there. The moment my teacher took her eyes off me, I was back on the street. Every time Dad got a card from Mr. Sands, I got bruises and welts from Dad. The beatings had only a temporary effect on me. Each time, the beatings got worse; and each time, I promised never to play hookey again. One time I kept that promise for three whole weeks.

The older guys had been doing something called "catting" for years. That catting was staying away from home all night was all I knew about the term. Every time I asked one of the fellows to teach me how to cat, I was told I wasn't old enough. As time went on, I learned that guys catted when they were afraid to go home and that they slept everywhere but in comfortable places. The usual places for catting were subway trains, cellars, unlocked cars, under a friend's bed, and in vacant newsstands.

One afternoon when I was eight years old, I came home after a busy day of running from the police, truant officer, and storekeepers. The first thing I did was to look in the mailbox. This had become a habit with me even though I couldn't read. I was looking for a card, a yellow card. That yellow card meant that I would walk into the house and Dad would be waiting for me with his razor strop. He would usually be eating and would pause just long enough to say to me, "Nigger, you got a ass whippin' comin'." My sisters, Carole and Margie, would cry almost as much as I would while Dad was beating me, but this never stopped him. After each beating I got, Carole, who was two years older than I, would beg me to stop playing hookey. There were a few times when I thought I would stop just to keep her and Margie, my younger sister, from crying so much. I decided to threaten Carole and Margie instead, but this didn't help. I continued to play hookey, and they continued to cry on the days that the yellow card got home before I did.

Generally, I would break open the mailbox, take out the card, and throw it away. Whenever I did this, I'd have to break open two or three other mailboxes and throw away the contents, just to make it look good.

This particular afternoon, I saw a yellow card, but I couldn't find anything to break into the box with. Having some matches in my pockets, I decided to burn the card in the box and not bother to break the box open. After I had used all the matches, the card was not completely burned. I stood there getting more frightened by the moment. In a little while, Dad would be coming home; and when he looked in the mailbox, anywhere would be safer than home for me.

This was going to be my first try at catting out. I went looking for somebody to cat with me. My crime partner, Buddy, whom I had played hookey with that day, was busily engaged in a friendly rock fight when I found him in Colonial Park. When I suggested that we go up on the hill and steal some newspapers, Buddy lost interest in the rock fight.

We stole papers from newsstands and sold them on the subway trains until nearly 1 A.M. That was when the third cop woke us and put us off the train with the usual threat. They would always promise to beat us over the head with a billy and lock us up. Looking back, I think the cops took their own threats more seriously than we did. The third cop put us off the Independent Subway at Fifty-ninth Street and Columbus Circle. I wasn't afraid of the cops, but I didn't go back into the subway—the next cop might have taken me home.

In 1945, there was an Automat where we came out of the subway. About five slices of pie later, Buddy and I left the Automat in search of a place to stay the night. In the center of the Circle, there were some old lifeboats that the Navy had put on display.

Buddy and I slept in the boat for two nights. On the third day, Buddy was caught ringing a cash register in a five-and-dime store. He was sent to Children's Center, and I spent the third night in the boat alone. On the fourth night, I met a duty-conscious cop, who took me home. That ended my first catting adventure.

Dad beat me for three consecutive days for telling what he called "that dumb damn lie about sleeping in a boat on Fifty-ninth Street." On the fourth day, I think he went to check my story out for himself. Anyhow, the beatings stopped for a while, and he never mentioned the boat again.

Before long, I was catting regularly, staying away from home for weeks at a time. Sometimes the cops would pick me up and take me to a Children's Center. The Centers were located all over the city. At some time in my childhood, I must have spent at least one night in all of them except the one on Staten Island.

The procedure was that a policeman would take me to the Center in the borough where he had picked me up. The Center would assign someone to see that I got a bath and was put to bed. The following day, my parents would be notified as to where I was and asked to come and claim me. Dad was always in favor of leaving me where I was and saying good riddance. But Mama always made the trip. Although Mama never failed to come for me, she seldom found me there when she arrived. I had no trouble getting out of Children's Centers, so I seldom stayed for more than a couple of days.

When I was finally brought home – sometimes after weeks of catting – Mama would hide my clothes or my shoes. This would mean that I couldn't get out of the house if I should take a notion to do so. Anyway, that's how Mama had it figured. The truth of the matter is that these measures only made getting out of the house more difficult for me. I would have to wait until one of the fellows came around to see me. After hearing my plight, he would go out and round up some of the gang, and they would steal some clothes and shoes for me. When they had the clothes and shoes, one of them would come to the house and let me know. About ten minutes later, I would put on my sister's dress, climb down the back fire escape, and meet the gang with the clothes.

If something was too small or too large, I would go and steal the right size. This could only be done if the item that didn't fit was not the shoes. If the shoes were too small or large, I would have trouble running in them and probably get caught. So I would wait around in the backyard while someone stole me a pair.

Mama soon realized that hiding my clothes would not keep me in the house. The next thing she tried was threatening to send me away until I was twenty-one. This was only frightening to me at the moment of hearing it. Ever so often, either Dad or Mama would sit down and have a heart-to-heart talk with me. These talks were very moving. I always promised to mend my bad ways. I was always sincere and usually kept the promise for about a week. During these weeks, I went to school every day and kept my stealing at a minimum. By the beginning of the second week, I had reverted back to my wicked ways, and Mama would have to start praying all over again.

The neighborhood prophets began making prophecies about my life-span. They all had me dead, buried, and forgotten before my twenty-first birthday. These predictions were based on false tales of policemen shooting at me, on truthful tales of my falling off a trolley car into the midst of oncoming automobile traffic while hitching a ride, and also on my uncontrollable urge to steal. There was much justification for these prophecies. By the time I was nine years old, I had been hit by a bus, thrown into the Harlem River (intentionally), hit by a car, severely beaten with a chain. And I had set the house afire.

While Dad was still trying to beat me into a permanent conversion, Mama was certain that somebody had worked roots on me. She was writing to all her relatives in the South for solutions, but they were only able to say, "that boy musta been born with the devil in him." Some of them advised Mama to send me down there, because New York was no place to raise a child. Dad thought this was a good idea, and he tried to sell it to Mama. But Mama wasn't about to split up her family. She said I would stay in New York, devil or no devil. So I stayed in New York, enjoying every crazy minute.

Mama's favorite question was, "Boy, why you so bad?" I tried many times to explain to Mama that I wasn't "so bad." I tried to make her understand that it was trying to be good that generally got me into trouble. I remember telling her that I played hookey to avoid getting into trouble in school. It seemed that whenever I went to school, I got into a fight with the teacher. The teacher would take me to the principal's office. After I had fought with the principal, I would be sent home and not allowed back in school without one of my parents. So to avoid all that trouble, I just didn't go to school. When I stole things, it was only to save the family money and avoid arguments or scoldings whenever I asked for money.

Mama seemed silly to me. She was bothered because most of the parents in the neighborhood didn't allow their children to play with me. What she didn't know was that I never wanted to play with them. My friends were all daring like me, tough like me, dirty like me, ragged like me, cursed like me, and had a great love for trouble like me. We took pride in being able to hitch rides on trolleys, buses, taxicabs and in knowing how to steal and fight. We knew that we were the only kids in the neighborhood who usually had more than ten dollars in their pockets. There were other people who knew this too, and that was often a problem for us. Somebody was always trying to shake us down or rob us. This was usually done by the older hustlers in the neighborhood or by storekeepers or cops. At other times, older fellows would shake us down, con us, or Murphy us out of our loot. We accepted this as the ways of life. Everybody was stealing from everybody else. And sometimes we would shake down newsboys and shoeshine boys. So we really had no complaints coming. Although none of my sidekicks was over twelve years of age, we didn't think of ourselves as kids. The other kids my age were thought of as kids by me. I felt that since I knew more about life than they did, I had the right to regard them as kids.

In the fall of 1945, I was expelled from school for the first time. By the time February rolled around, I had been expelled from three other schools in Harlem. In February, Mama sent me downtown to live with Grandpapa on Eldridge Street. Papa enrolled me in a public school on Forsythe and Stanton Streets. It was cold that winter, and I usually went to school to be warm.

For weeks, everybody thought things were going along fine. The first day I didn't come home from school, Papa ignored it, thinking that I had gone uptown. But the next day, Mama received a card from Bellevue Hospital's psychiatric division informing her that I was undergoing psychiatric observation and that she was allowed to visit me on Wednesdays and Sundays. My grandfather knew nothing about any of this, so when Mama (his oldest daughter) came to him wanting to know what her son was doing in Bellevue, Papa asked, "How did he get there?" They both came over to Bellevue believing I had gone crazy. Dad didn't bother to come, because, as he put it, "That's where he shoulda been years ago." I was glad Dad didn't come, because he might not have believed that I was falsely accused of trying to push a boy in school out of a five-story window. Mama had already heard my teacher's version of the window incident, and now I was trying to explain my side of the story. My teacher had told her that I persuaded a boy to look out of the window to see an accident that hadn't taken place. Because of the window's wide ledge, I was holding his legs while he leaned out of the window. The boy started screaming and calling for help. When he got down out of the window, the boy said that I had been trying to push him out of the window. Just because we had fought the day before and I was the only one who saw the accident, I ended up in the nutbox.

I don't think my story completely convinced Mama or Papa, but they gave me the benefit of the doubt. Mama told me that I would have to stay in the hospital for a few weeks. Her eyes were filled with tears when she said good-bye, and I tried to look sad too, but I was actually happy. I thought about how nice it was going to be away from Dad. Also, there were a few of my friends there, and we were sure to find something to get into. I had already had a couple of fights and won, so this was going to be a real ball.

I had lots of fun in the nutbox and learned a lot of new tricks, just as I thought. I didn't know it at the time, but many of the boys I met in Bellevue would also be with me at Wiltwyck and Warwick years later. Some of those I had bullied in the nutbox would try to turn the tables later on in life. Some would succeed.

There were a few things around to steal. There were plenty of guys to fight with and lots of adults to annoy. The one drawback that the nutbox had was school and teachers. But I found the nutbox to be such a nice place that I was sad when Mama came to take me home.

When I returned home, I was told that my former school had refused to readmit me. This was the best news I had heard since I started going to school. I thought that I had finally gotten out of going to school. But two weeks later, I was enrolled in another school in Harlem.

Within two months from the time I had left Bellevue, I found myself in Manhattan's Children Court for the first time. The reason was that I had been thrown out of two more schools, and there weren't any more in Manhattan that would accept me. The judge told Mama that if I was still in New York State when the fall semester began, he would send me someplace where I would be made to go to school. After Mama had promised the judge that I would not be in New York when September rolled around, we went home.

This was the first time that Mama had been in court, and she was pretty angry about the whole thing. All the way uptown on the bus, Mama kept telling me that I should be ashamed of myself for making her come down to that court and face those white people. Every ten or twelve blocks, Mama would stop preaching just long enough to look at me and say, "Child, maybe that head doctor was right about you," or, "Boy, why you so damn bad?" She didn't understand what the psychiatrist was talking about when he was telling her about my emotional problems. Since she couldn't understand the terms he was using, Mama thought he was trying to tell her in a nice way that I was crazy. Of course, she didn't believe him. "That ole big-nose, thick-eyeglasses white man, he looked kinda crazy his own self," she said. No, she didn't believe him, whatever it was that he had said—but sometimes she wondered if that man might have been right.

When we got back uptown, Mrs. Rogers, who lived next door to us, came over to find out how things had gone in court. Mrs. Rogers, Danny's mother, had made many trips to Manhattan's Children Court. Now she had come to sympathize with Mama. Mrs. Rogers—who was also a jackleg preacher (she did not have a church)—called everybody "child," "brother," or "sister." What a person was called by Mrs. Rogers depended on whether or not he was "saved." To be saved meant to live for the Lord. Mrs. Rogers was saved, and so was her husband; she couldn't understand why all her children had not yet been "hit by spirit."

Mrs. Rogers, a big, burly woman about fifteen years older than Mama, always called Mama "child." I can remember her saying to Mama when we came home from court that day, "Child, ain't that Lexington Avenue bus the slowest thing in this whole city?" I always found Mrs. Rogers' visits hard to take. She was a very nice meddlesome old woman, but too godly to have around constantly. Poor Danny, he had to live with it. Mrs. Rogers had told Mama that Danny was so bad because his behavior was the Lord's way of testing her faith. Dad called Mrs. Rogers the "preacher woman." He believed that Mrs. Rogers was going against the Lord's Word and that this was the reason for her son's behavior. He had often said that "the Lord never told no woman to go out and preach the Gospel to nobody." Dad said that if the Lord had wanted a woman to preach, he would have chosen a woman to be one of his apostles.

On this day, Mrs. Rogers' advice was no different from the other times. After Mama had told Mrs. Rogers about what had happened in court, Mrs. Rogers began her usual sermon, saying, "Child, you just gotta pray, you just gotta pray and trust in the Lord." I always left the house at this point, because our house would be used as a practice pulpit for the next two or three hours.

As I ran down the stairs, I tried to imagine what was going on in the house. In a little while, Mrs. Rogers would be patting her foot real fast, and she would start talking real loud, clapping her hands, shaking her head, and every other word would be "Jesus" or "Lord." I wondered why Mrs. Rogers never got tired of talking about the Lord. Before Mrs. Rogers finished her private sermon, she would have Mama talking about the Lord and patting her feet. By the time Mrs. Rogers was ready to leave, she would have Mama promising to come to a church where she was preaching next Sunday. Mama would promise, and Mrs. Rogers would start telling her how good it is to be saved, to walk with Jesus, and to let God into your soul. Even though Mama knew Dad wasn't going to let her go to a sanctified church with that "jackleg preacher woman," she still promised to go. Dad always said, "All those sanctified people is just a bunch of old hypocrites, and none of 'em ain't a bit more saved than nobody else."

Mrs. Rogers never talked about saving Dad. She said, "That man got the devil in him," and I believed it. As a matter of fact, I had suspected something like that long before Mrs. Rogers did.

We had all been to Mrs. Rogers' Sunday sermon once. All of us except Dad. She was preaching that time in what looked like a church-apartment to me and a church-store to Carole. I think most of the people there were relatives of Mrs. Rogers. All of her family was there except for Danny; he had escaped on the way to church. June, one of Mrs. Rogers' daughters, was playing an old, out-of-tune upright piano. Another one of Danny's sisters was banging two cymbals together and mumbling something about Jesus. She seemed to be in a trance. Mr. Rogers was shaking a tambourine and singing about Jesus with a faraway look in his eyes. Mrs. Rogers who was dressed in a white robe, got up and started preaching. After Mrs. Rogers had been preaching for about fifteen minutes, an old lady got up and started screaming and shouting, "Help me, Lord Jesus!" She was still throwing her arms up and shouting for Jesus to help her when a younger woman jumped up and hollered, "Precious Lord Jesus, save me!" Mrs. Rogers' voice was getting louder all the time.

For two hours, she preached — and for two hours, people were getting up, shouting, jumping up and down, calling to Jesus for help and salvation, and falling out exhausted. Some of these "Holy Rollers," as Dad called them, would fall to the floor and start trembling rapidly; some of them even began to slobber on themselves. When I asked Mama what was wrong with those people and what they were doing on the floor, she told me that the "spirit" had hit them. When Carole heard this, she began to cry and wanted to get out of there before the spirit hit us. Mrs. Rogers had gone over to a man who was rolling on the floor, slobbering on himself, and babbling as if he were talking to the Lord. She held the man's hand very tight and told him repeatedly to walk with the Lord and not to fear Jesus. She was saying to the man, "Brother, say, 'Yes, Jesus; yes, Jesus.'" After a while, the man calmed down, and Mrs. Rogers said he had been saved.

Carole and Margie were frightened by these strange goings-on. I had been fascinated until now. But now this spirit thing had Mama jumping up and shouting. I joined Carole and Margie in a crying chorus, and the three of us started pulling on Mama. After Mama had jumped, clapped her hands, and had her say about Jesus, she fell back in her chair, tired and sweating. One of Mrs. Rogers' blood sisters had started fanning Mama. Carole, Margie, and I had stopped crying, but we were still scared, because we didn't know if Mama was all right or not.

In the makeshift pulpit, Mrs. Rogers was looking real pleased with herself, probably thinking that she had saved a lot of people. I think Mrs. Rogers judged her sermon by the number of people who were hit by the spirit and fell down during her sermon. She cautioned the people who were saved about "backslidin'" and told them about how happy they were going to be with Jesus in their lives. She also asked some of the old saved souls to "testify." After three or four saved souls had told about what a good friend Jesus had been to them, Mrs. Rogers began her third request for money. The ushers, who were also relatives of Mrs. Rogers, passed a china bowl down each row. Carole and Margie dropped the nickel that Mama had given to each of them in the bowl, then they turned and looked at me. Although that was the first time we had ever been to church together, they would have been surprised if I had put my nickel in the bowl. I didn't surprise them that day.

While Carole and Margie were busy telling Mama about me not putting my nickel in the bowl, I was pulling a chair from the aisle behind us. All the chairs in the place were kitchen chairs, and they weren't all the same size. Before I could get the chair into our aisle, a big fat shiny dark-skinned woman with a man's voice said, "Boy, leave dat chair 'lone." I was frightened by the heavy, commanding voice, but not as much as I was after I looked up and saw that great big old woman giving me the evil eye. My first thought was that she was a witch or a hag, whatever that was. I knew she couldn't be the boogeyman; not in church. But the longer I looked, the more I doubted her being anything other than the boogeyman. About thirty seconds later, when I had gotten my voice back, I meekly said, "Dat ain't your chair." The next thing I heard was the sound of Mama's hand falling heavily across my mouth. As I started crying, I heard Mama say, "What I tole you about sassin' ole people?" While I went on crying, Mama was telling me about the dangers of talking back to old people. I remember her saying, "If one of these old people put the bad mouth on you, maybe you'll be satisfied."

For years afterward, the mention of church always reminded me of the day that we went to hear Mrs. Rogers preach. To me, a church was a church-apartment where somebody lined up a lot of kitchen chairs in a few rows, a preacher did a lot of shouting about the Lord, people jumped up and down until they got knocked down by the spirit, and Mrs. Rogers put bowls of money on a kitchen table and kept pointing to it and asking for more. It was a place where I had to stand up until I couldn't stand any more and then had to sit down on hard wooden chairs. The one good thing I got out of going to hear Mrs. Rogers preach was a new threat to use on Carole and Margie. Whenever Carole and Margie would threaten to tell on me, I told them that if they did, the spirit would hit them the way it hit those people in Mrs. Rogers' church-apartment.

Maybe Dad was right when he said Mrs. Rogers was just robbing people in the name of the Lord. Anyway, I felt pretty good about her not getting my nickel.

Even though Dad didn't care for preachers and churches, he had a lot of religion in his own way. Most of the time, his religion didn't show. But on Saturday night, those who didn't see it heard it. Sometimes Dad would get religious on Friday nights too. But Saturday night was a must. Because it always took liquor to start Dad to singing spirituals and talking about the Lord, I thought for years that this lordly feeling was something in a bottle of whiskey. To me, it was like castor oil or black draught. You drink it and the next thing you know, you're doing things.

I was introduced to religion on Saturday night. I don't recall just when, but as far back as I can remember, Saturday night was the Lord's night in our house. Whenever Dad was able to make it home on his own two feet, he would bring a recording of a spiritual, a plate of pigs' feet and potato salad from the corner delicatessen or a plate of fish-and-chips from the wine joint around the corner, and whatever was left of his last bottle of religion. He usually got home about three o'clock in the morning, and the moment he hit the block I could hear him singing (or yelling) the record he had. By the time he got upstairs, everybody in the building knew the song and hated it. Before Dad was in the house, I could hear him calling me.

By the time he finished unlocking and relocking the door at least six times, kicking on it, cursing out the lock and the neighbors who had tried to quiet him down, I was up and had already turned on the phonograph. On her way to the door, Mama would say, "Boy, turn that thing off and git back in that bed." While Mama told Dad how disgusting he was, I would be busily picking out the pigs' feet or fish-and-chips with the least amount of hot sauce on them. When Mama had gotten tired of competing with Dad's singing, she went back to bed. As Dad gave me the record—usually by Sister Rosetta Tharpe, the Dixie Hummingbirds, or the Four Blind Boys—he would tell me how somebody I had never heard of sang it in the cotton fields or at somebody's wedding or funeral "down home." After listening to the record at least a dozen times, Dad would turn the phonograph off, and we would sing the song a few times. Before dawn started sneaking through the windows, Dad and I had gone through his entire repertoire of spirituals. By daybreak, we were both drunk and had fallen on the floor, and we stayed there until we awoke later in the day.

(1965)

*James Baldwin*

# Unnameable Objects, Unspeakable Crimes

I have often wondered, and it is not a pleasant wonder, just what white Americans talk about with one another. I wonder this because they do not, after all, seem to find very much to say to *me*, and I concluded long ago that they found the color of my skin inhibitory. This color seems to operate as a most disagreeable mirror, and a great deal of one's energy is expended in reassuring white Americans that they do not see what *they* see. This is utterly futile, of course, since *they do* see what *they* see. And what they see is an appallingly oppressive and bloody history, known all over the world. What they see is a disastrous, continuing, present, condition which menaces them, and for which they bear an inescapable responsibility. But since, in the main, they appear to lack the energy to change this condition, they would rather not be reminded of it. Does this mean that, in their conversations with one another, they merely make reassuring sounds? It scarcely seems possible, and yet, on the other hand, it seems all too likely.

Whatever they bring to one another, it is certainly not *freedom from guilt.*

The guilt remains, more deeply rooted, more securely lodged, than the oldest of old trees; and it can be unutterably exhausting to deal with people who, with a really dazzling ingenuity, a tireless agility, are perpetually defending themselves against charges which one has not made.

One does not have to make them. The record is there for all to read. It resounds all over the world. It might as well be written in the sky.

One wishes that Americans, white Americans, would read, for their own sakes, this record, and stop defending themselves against it. Only then will they be enabled to change their lives. The fact that Americans, white Americans, have not yet been able to do this—to face their history, to change their lives—hideously menaces this country. Indeed, it menaces the entire world.

For history, as nearly no one seems to know, is not merely something to be read. And it does not refer merely, or even principally, to the past. On the contrary, the great force of history comes from the fact that we carry it within us, are unconsciously controlled by it in many ways, and history is literally *present* in all that we do. It could scarcely be otherwise, since it is to history that we owe our frames of reference, our identities, and our aspirations.

And it is with great pain and terror that one begins to realize this. In great pain and terror, one begins to assess the history which has placed one where one is, and formed one's point of view. In great pain and terror, because, thereafter, one enters into battle with that historical creation, oneself, and attempts to re-create oneself according to a principle more humane and more liberating; one begins the attempt to achieve a level of personal maturity and freedom which robs history of its tyrannical power, and also changes history.

But, obviously, I am speaking as an historical creation which has had bitterly to contest its history, to wrestle with it and finally accept it, in order to bring myself out of it. My point of view is certainly formed by my history, and it is probable that only a creature despised by history finds history a questionable matter. On the other hand, people who imagine that history flatters them (as it does, indeed, since they wrote it) are impaled on their history like a butterfly on a pin and become incapable of seeing or changing themselves or the world.

This is the place in which, it seems to me, most white Americans find themselves. They are dimly, or vividly, aware that the history they have fed themselves is mainly a lie, but they do not know how to release themselves from it, and they suffer enormously from the resulting personal incoherence. This incoherence is heard nowhere more plainly than in those stammering, terrified dialogues white Americans sometimes entertain with that black conscience, the black man in America.

The nature of this stammering can be reduced to a plea: Do not blame *me*. I was not there. I did not do it. My history has nothing to do with Europe or the slave trade. Anyway, it was *your* chiefs who sold *you* to *me*. I was not present on the middle passage. I am not responsible for the textile mills of Manchester, or the cotton fields of Mississippi. Besides, consider how the English, too, suffered in those mills and in those awful cities! I, also, despise the governors of Southern states and the sheriffs of Southern counties; and I also want your child to have a decent education and rise as high as his capabilities will permit. I have nothing against you, *nothing!* What have *you* got against *me? What do you want?*

But, on the same day, in another gathering, and in the most private chamber of his heart always, he, the white man, remains proud of that history for which he does not wish to pay, and from which, materially, he has profited so much. On that same day, in another gathering, and in the most private chamber of the black man's heart always, he finds himself facing the terrible roster of the lost: the dead, black junkie; the defeated, black father; the unutterably weary, black mother; the unutterably ruined black girl. And one begins to suspect an awful thing: that people believe that they *deserve* their history and that when they operate on this belief, they perish. But they can scarcely avoid believing that they deserve it—one's short time on this earth is very mysterious and very dark and hard. I have known many black men and women and black boys and girls, who really believed that it was better to be white than black, whose lives were ruined or ended by this belief; and I myself carried the seeds of this destruction within me for a long time.

Now, if I, as a black man, profoundly believe that I deserve my history and deserve to be treated as I am, then I must also, fatally, believe that white people deserve their history and deserve the power and the glory which their testimony and the evidence of my own senses assure me that they have. And if black people fall into this trap, the trap of believing that they deserve their fate, white people fall into the yet more stunning and intricate trap of believing that they deserve *their* fate, and their comparative safety; and that black people, therefore, need only do as white people have done to rise to where white people now are. But this simply cannot be said, not only for reasons of politeness or charity, but also because white people carry in them a carefully muffled fear that black people long to do to others what has been done to them. Moreover, the history of white people has led them to a fearful, baffling place where they have begun to lose touch with reality—to lose touch, that is, with themselves—and where they certainly are not happy. They do not know how this came about; they do not dare examine how this came about. On the one hand, they can scarcely dare to open a dialogue which must, if it is honest, become a personal confession—a cry for help and healing, which is really, I think, the basis of all dialogues— and, on the other hand, the black man can scarcely dare to open a dialogue which must, if it is honest, become a personal confession which, fatally, contains an accusation. And yet, if we cannot do this, each of us will perish in those traps in which we have been struggling for so long.

The American situation is very peculiar, and it may be without precedent in the world. No curtain under heaven is heavier than that curtain of guilt and lies behind which Americans hide: it may prove to be yet more deadly to the lives of human beings than that iron curtain of which we speak so much—and know so little. The American curtain is color. We have used this word, this concept, to justify unspeakable crimes, not only in the past, but in the present. One can measure very neatly the white American's distance from his conscience—from himself—by observing the distance between himself and black people. One has only to ask oneself who established this distance. Who is this distance designed to protect? And from what is this distance designed to protect him?

I have seen this very vividly, for example, in the eyes of Southern law enforcement officers barring, let us say, the door to the courthouse. There they stand, comrades all, invested with the authority of the community, with helmets, with sticks, with guns, with cattle prods. Facing them are unarmed black people—or, more precisely, they are faced by a group of unarmed people arbitrarily called black, whose color really ranges from the Russian steppes, to the Golden Horn, to Zanzibar. In a moment, because he can resolve the situation in no other way, this sheriff, this deputy, this honored American citizen, must begin to club these people down. Some of these people may be related to him by blood; they are assuredly related to the black Mammy of his memory, and the black playmates of his childhood. And for a moment, therefore, he seems nearly to be pleading with the people facing him not to force him to commit yet another crime and not to make yet deeper that ocean of blood in which his conscience is drenched, in which his manhood is perishing. The people do not go away, of course; once a people arise, they never go away, a fact which should be included in the Marine handbook; and the club rises, the blood comes down, and our crimes and our bitterness and our anguish are compounded. Or, one sees it in the eyes of rookie cops in Harlem, who are really among the most terrified people in the world, and who must pretend to themselves that the black mother, the black junkie, the black father, the black child are of a different human species than themselves. They can only deal with their lives and their duties by hiding behind the color curtain. This curtain, indeed, eventually becomes their principal justification for the lives they lead.

But it is not only on this level that one sees the extent of our disaster. Not so very long ago, I found myself in Montgomery, with many, many thousands, marching to the Capitol. Much has been written about this march—for example, the Confederate flag was flying from the Capitol dome; the Federalized National Guard, assigned to protect the marchers, wore Confederate flags on their jackets; if the late Mrs. Viola Liuzzo was avoiding the patrols on that deadly stretch of road that night, she had far sharper eyesight than mine, for I did not see any. Well, there we were, marching to that mansion from which authority had fled. All along that road—I pray that my countrymen will hear me— old, black men and women, who have endured an unspeakable oppression for so long, waved and cheered and sang and wept. They could not march, but they had done something else: they had brought us to the place where we could march. How many of us, after all, were brought up on the white folks leavings, and how mighty a price those old men and women paid to bring those leavings home to us!

We reached the white section of town. There the businessmen stood, on balconies, jeering; there stood their maids, in back doors, silent, not daring to wave, but nodding. I watched a black, or rather, a beige-colored woman, standing in the street, watching us thoughtfully; she looked as though she probably held a clerical job in one of those buildings; proof, no doubt, to the jeering white businessmen that the South was making progress. This woman decided to join us, for when we reached the Capitol, I noticed that she was there. But, while we were still marching, through the white part of town, the watching, the waiting, the frightened part of town, we lifted our small American flags, and we faced those eyes—which could not face ours—and we sang. I was next to Harry Belafonte. From upstairs office windows, white American secretaries were leaning out of windows, jeering and mocking, and using the ancient Roman sentence of death: thumbs down. Then they saw Harry, who is my very dear friend and a beautiful cat, and who is also, in this most desperately schizophrenic of republics, a major, a reigning matinée idol. One does not need to be a student of Freud to understand what buried forces create a matinée idol, or what he represents to that public which batters down doors to watch him (one need only watch the rise and fall of American politicians. This is a sinister observation. And I mean it very seriously). The secretaries were legally white—it was on that basis that they lived their lives, from this principle that they took, collectively, their values; which is, as I have tried to indicate, an interesting spiritual condition. But they were also young. In that ghastly town, they were certainly lonely. They could only, after all, look forward to an alliance, by and by, with one of the jeering businessmen; their boyfriends could only look forward to becoming one of them. And they were also female, a word, which, in the context of the color curtain, has suffered the same fate as the word, "male": it has become practically obscene. When the girls saw Harry Belafonte, a collision occurred in them so visible as to be at once hilarious and unutterably sad. At one moment, the thumbs were down, they were barricaded within their skins, at the next moment, those downturned thumbs flew to their mouths, their fingers pointed, their faces changed, and exactly like bobbysoxers, they oohed, and aahed and moaned. God knows what was happening in the minds and hearts of those girls. Perhaps they would like to be free.

The white man's guilt, which he pretends is due to the fact that the world is a place of many colors, has nothing to do with color. If one attempts to reduce his dilemma to its essence, it really does not have much to do with his crimes, except in the sense that he has locked himself into a place where he is doomed to continue repeating them. The great, unadmitted crime is what he has done to himself. A man is a man, a woman is a woman, and a child is a child. To deny these facts is to open the doors on a chaos deeper and deadlier, and, within the space of a man's lifetime, more timeless, more eternal, than the medieval vision of Hell. And we have arrived at this unspeakable blasphemy in order to acquire things, in order to make money. We cannot endure the things we acquire—the only reason we continually acquire them, like junkies on a hundred dollar a day habit—and our money exists mainly on paper. God help us on that day when the population demands to know what is behind the paper. But, beyond all this, it is terrifying to consider the precise nature of the things we buy with the flesh we sell.

In Henry James' novel *The Ambassadors* published not long before World War I, and not long before his death, he recounts the story of a middle-aged New Englander, assigned by his middle-aged bride-to-be—a widow— the task of rescuing from the flesh-pots of Paris her only son. She wants him to come home to take over the direction of the family factory. In the event, it is the middle-aged New Englander—*The Ambassador*—who is seduced, not so much by Paris, as by a new and less utilitarian view of life. He counsels the young man to "live. Live all you can. It is a mistake not to." Which I translate as meaning "Trust life,

and it will teach you, in joy and sorrow, all you need to know." Jazz
musicians know this. Those old men and women who waved and sang
and wept as we marched in Montgomery know this. White Americans,
in the main, do not know this. They are still trapped in that factory to
which, in Henry James' novel, the son returns. We never know what
this factory produces, for James never tells us. He only conveys to us
that the factory, at an unbelievable human expense, produces unname-
able objects.

(1965)

### Helen Chasin

# In Communication with a UFO

Objects clutter the shiny air and flash
through the night sky, parsing its darkness
into the telegraphic grammar of space:

Here! We are here! Believe!
We hover but will not fix, we wheel
in the skeptical atmosphere. Beyond the reach
of your vision we skim curves of the universe
and splash like otters in its large drafts,
uttering shrieks of light, bellywhopping
to where you hang. Each sighting irks you
into a flurry of hope. Blind
with anticipation, earthlings, you want us
to be serious, bring the good news, disclose
that we are what you want us to be.

(1968)

*Robert L. Scott and Donald K. Smith*

# The Rhetoric of Confrontation

"Confront" is a simple enough verb meaning to stand or to come in front of. Like many simple words, however, it has been used in diverse contexts for varied purposes and has developed complex meanings. Among these the most interesting, and perhaps the strongest, is the sense of standing in front of as a barrier or a threat. This sense is especially apparent in the noun "confrontation."

Repeatedly in his book *Essays in the Public Philosophy,* Walter Lippmann uses the word "confrontation" in the sense of face-to-face coming together of spokesmen for disparate views. Confrontation, as he saw it then, was the guarantee of open communication and fruitful dissent. But Lippmann's book was copyrighted in 1955. Today, his phrase "because the purpose of the confrontation is to discern truth" sounds a bit archaic. If so, the remainder of his sentence, "there are rules of evidence and parliamentary procedure, there are codes of fair dealing and fair comment, by which a loyal man will consider himself bound when he exercises the right to publish opinion,"[1] seems absolutely irrelevant to the notion of "confrontation" as we live with it in marches, sit-ins, demonstrations, and discourse featuring disruption, obscenity, and threats.

Although certainly some use the word "confrontation" moderately, we shall be concerned here with the radical and revolutionary suggestion which the word carries more and more frequently. Even obviously moderate circumstances today gain some of the revolutionary overtones when the word is applied, as it might be for example, in announcing a church study group as the "confrontation of sacred and secular morality."

Acts of confrontation are currently at hand in such profusion that no one will lack evidence to prove or disprove the generalizations we make.[2]

[1](New York, 1955), p. 128.

[2]Readers will find our generalizations more or less in harmony with other discussions of radical rhetoric which have appeared in the *QJS* recently, e.g., Parke G. Burgess, "The Rhetoric of Black Power: A Moral Demand?" LIV (April 1968), 122–133; Leland M. Griffin, "The Rhetorical Structure of the 'New Left' Movement: Part I," L (April 1964), 113–135; and Franklyn S. Haiman, "The Rhetoric of the Streets: Some Legal and Ethical Considerations," LIII (April 1967), 99–114.

These writers sense a corporate wholeness in the messages and methods of various men. An attempt to explain the combination of message and method which forms the wholeness gives rise in each case to a *rhetoric.* All these efforts seem to us impulses to examine the sufficiency of our traditional concepts in dealing with phenomena which are becoming characteristic of contemporary dissent. In seeing rhetoric as an amalgam of meaning and method, these writers break with a tradition that takes rhetoric to be amoral techniques of manipulating a message to fit various contexts.

Rhetoric has always been response-oriented, that is, the rationale of practical discourse, discourse designed to gain response for specific ends. But these writers see response differently. For them, the response of audiences is an integral part of the message-method that makes the rhet-

Confrontation crackles menacingly from every issue in our country (Black Power and Student Power, as examples), hemisphere (Castroism, for example), and globe (Radical Nationalism everywhere). But primary to every confrontation in any setting, radical or moderate, is the impulse to confront. From what roots does that impulse spring?

## Radical Division

Radical confrontation reflects a dramatic sense of division. The old language of the "haves" and the "have-nots" scarcely indicates the basis of the division, nor its depth. The old language evokes the history of staid, well-controlled concern on the part of those who have, for those who have not. It suggests that remedy can come from traditional means – the use of some part of the wealth and talent of those who have to ease the burden of those who have not, and perhaps open opportunities for some of them to enter the mainstream of traditional values and institutions. It recalls the missionary spirit of the voluntary associations of those who have – the legislative charity of the New Deal, the Fair Deal, the Welfare State, and the whole spectrum of international development missions.

A benevolent tone characterizes the old rhetoric of social welfare. The tone assumes that all men seek and should increasingly have more of the available wealth, or education, or security, or culture, or opportunities. The values of those who "have" are celebrated as the goals to which all should aspire, and effective social policy becomes a series of acts to extend opportunity to share in those values. If those who have can provide for others more of their own perquisites – more of the right to vote, or to find employment, or to go to college, or to consume goods – then progress is assured.

Although the terms "have" and "have-not" are still accurate enough descriptions of the conditions that divide people and groups, their evocation of a traditional past hides the depth and radical nature of current divisions. Those on the "have not" side of the division, or at least some of their theorists and leaders, no longer accept designation as an inert mass hoping to receive what they lack through action by the "haves." Neither do they accept any assumption that what they wish is membership in the institutions of those who have, or an opportunity to learn and join their value system. Rather the "have nots" picture themselves as radically divided from traditional society, questioning not simply the limitations of its benevolence but more fundamentally its purposes and modes of operation. Whether they experience deprivation

oric. Thus, rhetoric is shifted from a focus of reaction to one of interaction or transaction. (See especially Burgess, 132–133; Griffin, 121; and Haiman, 113.)

Although we believe we share the sense of *rhetoric* which permeates these essays, we claim to analyze a fundamental level of meaning which underlies them.

as poverty, or lack of political power, or disaffection from traditional values, the "have not" leaders and theorists challenge existing institutions. This radical challenge, and its accompanying disposition toward confrontation, marks the vague attitudinal web that links revolutionaries in emerging nations to Black Power advocates in America or to students and intellectuals of the New Left. Three statements will illustrate the similar disposition of men who serve rather different causes in varied circumstances.

For Frantz Fanon, Algerian revolutionary and author of *The Wretched of the Earth,* the symbol of deprivation is the term "colonisation," and the end of confrontation is "decolonisation": "In decolonisation there is therefore the need of a complete calling in question of the colonial situation. If we wish to describe it precisely, we might find it in the well-known words 'The last shall be first and the first last.' Decolonisation is the putting into practice of this statement. That is why, if we try to describe it, all decolonisation is successful"[3]

For Black Power advocate Stokely Carmichael, the enemy is white racism, which is to be confronted, not joined: "Our concern for black power addresses itself directly to this problem, the necessity to reclaim our history and our identity from the cultural terrorism and depredation of self-justifying white guilt. To do this we shall have to struggle for the right to create our own terms through which to define ourselves and our relationship to the society, and to have these terms recognized. This is the first necessity of a free people, and the first right that any oppressor must suspend."[4]

For students in the New Left, the enemy to be confronted is simply "the establishment," or often in the United States, "technocracy." As student Frederick Richman sees the division:

The world in which the older generation grew up, and which the political systems support, is no longer one which youth can accept. In a world of rampaging technology, racial turmoil, and poverty, they see a President whose program is constituted largely of finishing touches to the New Deal, and a Congress unwilling to accept even that. In a time when personal freedom is of increasing concern, they see a republic operated by an immense bureaucratic structure, geared more to cold war adventures than to domestic needs, stifling individual initiative along with that of states and cities. Finally, they see a political system obsessed with stability and loyalty instead of with social justice.[5]

Those have-nots who confront established power do not seek to share; they demand to supplant.

They must demand to supplant for they live in a Manichean world. Fanon, who features the term, argues that the settler (we may translate

---

[3]Tr. Constance Farrington (New York, 1963), p. 30.

[4]"Toward Black Liberation," *Massachusetts Review,* VII (Autumn 1966), 639–640.

[5]"The Disenfranchised Majority," *Students and Society,* report on a conference, Vol. 1, No. 1; an occasional paper published by the Center for the Study of Democratic Institutions (Santa Barbara, Calif., 1967), p. 4.

"settler" into other words, e.g., racist, establishment, or power structure) is responsible for the situation in which he must now suffer: "The colonial world is a Manichean world."[6] Those who rule and take the fruit of the system as their due create an equation that identifies themselves with the force of good (order, civilization, progress) which struggles with evil (chaos, the primitive, retrogression). In such a circumstance, established authority often crusades to eliminate the vessels of evil by direct action; but often its leaders work benignly and energetically to transform the others into worthy copies of themselves. At best, the process of transformation is slow, during which time the mass of the others must be carefully held apart to keep them from contaminating the system. Only a few can cross the great gulf to be numbered among the good. Claiming to recognize the reality of this process, which is always masked under exalted labels, black radicals in America cry that the traditional goal of integration masks and preserves racism. In an analogous posture, Students for a Democratic Society picture their educational system as a vast machine to recruit servants for a traditional society, perpetuating all of the injustices of that society.

Whether the force of "good" works energetically and directly or indirectly and somewhat benignly, those without caste must strive to supplant such holders of power. Forced to accept a Manichean struggle, they must reverse the equation, not simply to gain food, land, power, or whatever, but to survive. Reversing the equation will deny the justice of the system that has dehumanized them.

The process of supplanting will be violent for it is born of a violent system. To complete the long quotation introduced above from Fanon: "The naked truth of decolonisation evokes for us the searing bullets and bloodstained knives which emanate from it. For if the last shall be first, this will only come to pass after a murderous and decisive struggle between the two protagonists. That affirmed intention to place the last at the head of things . . . can only triumph if we use all means to turn the scale, including, of course, that of violence."[7]

As Eric Hoffer concludes in his study of mass movements, those who make revolutions are apt to see themselves as spoiled, degraded, and without hope as things exist. But they locate the genesis of their degradation in things, in others, in the world as it is organized around them.[8]

## The Rite of the Kill

The enemy is obvious, and it is he who has set the scene upon which the actors must play out the roles determined by the cleavage of exploitation. The situation shrieks kill-or-be-killed. "From here on in, if we

---

[6]Fanon, p. 33. The book is replete with references to "Manicheanism."
[7]*Ibid.*, p. 30.
[8]*The True Believer* (New York, 1951), pp. 19–20 and *passim.*

must die anyway, we will die fighting back and we will not die alone," Malcolm X wrote in his "Appeal to African Heads of State." "We intend to see that our racist oppressors also get a taste of death."[9]

Judgments like "the oppressor" cannot be made without concomitant judgments. If there are those who oppress, there are those who are oppressed. This much seems obvious, but beneath that surface is the accusation that those oppressed have been something less than men ought to be. If one stresses the cunning, tenacious brutality of the oppressor, he suggests that the oppressed has been less than wise, alert, and strong. If one feels the heritage of injustice, then he senses the ignominy of his patrimony. The blighted self must be killed in striking the enemy. By the act of overcoming his enemy, he who supplants demonstrates his own worthiness, effacing the mark, whatever it may be—immaturity, weakness, subhumanity—that his enemy has set upon his brow.

To satisfy the rite that destroys the evil self in the act of destroying the enemy that has made the self evil, the radical may work out the rite of kill symbolically.[10] Harassing, embarrassing, and disarming the enemy may suffice, especially if he is finally led to admit his impotence in the face of the superior will of the revolutionary. Symbolic destruction of some manifestation of evil is well illustrated by the outbursts on campuses across America directed toward Dow Chemical. As far as we know in every confrontation of authority centering around the presence on the campus of a recruiter from Dow Chemical, the demonstrators early announced their intention of paralyzing the process until the recruiter agrees on behalf of the company to contaminate the scene no further with his presence.

Michael Novak, a Stanford University professor, pictures student disruption as a tactic to remove the mask of respectability worn by the establishment and kept in place both by the centralized control of communication processes and the traditional canons of free speech.

The balance of power in the formation of public opinion has been altered by the advent of television. The society of independent, rational individuals envisaged by John Stuart Mill does not exist. The fate of all is bound up with the interpretation of events given by the mass media, by the image projected, and by the political power which results. . . . In a society with respect for its political institutions, officials have only to act with decorum and energy in order to benefit by such respect and to have their views established as true until proven false. . . .

What, then, does freedom of speech mean in a technological society? How can one defend oneself against McCarthyism on the one hand and official newspeak on the other? The solution of the students has been to violate the taboos of decorum and thus embrace Vice President Humphrey, the CIA, Dow Chemical, and other enemies in an ugly scene, hoping that the unpopularity of the radicals

---

[9]*Malcolm X Speaks*, ed. George Breitman (New York, 1966), p. 77.
[10]See Fanon, p. 73.

will rub off on those embraced. They want to make the heretofore bland and respectable wear that tag which most alarms American sensibilities: "controversial."[11]

Student Stephen Saltonstall of Yale University views coercive disruption as the obvious tactic by which "a small concentrated minority" group can bring society to heel and proposes use of this tactic by students to "destroy the university's capability to prop up our political institutions. By stalemating America's intellectual establishment," he continues, "we may be able to paralyze the political establishment as well." Saltonstall's specific recommendations are far-ranging: "A small, disciplined group of shock troops could pack classes, break up drills, and harass army professors. . . . Students could infiltrate the office staffs of the electronic accelerators and foreign policy institutes and hamper their efficiency. The introduction of a small quantity of LSD in only five or six government department coffee-urns might be a highly effective tactic. Students should prevent their universities from being used as forums for government apologists. Public figures like Humphrey and McNamara, when they appear, should be subject to intimidation and humiliation."[12]

Some who confront the oppressive authority seek to transform its representatives as well as themselves, working to wipe out the Manichean world. Such a stance is typical of the strongly Christian representatives of the Civil Rights Movement in this country. But those who advocate killing the enemy or degrading him symbolically act out more simply and more directly the dynamics dictated by the sense of radical division.

## Confrontation as a Totalistic Strategy

Part of the attraction of confrontation is the strong sense of success, so strong that it may be a can't-lose strategy. After all in the Christian text Fanon cites ironically, "The last *shall be* first." The last shall be first precisely because he is last. The feeling is that one has nowhere to go but up, that he has nothing to lose, that after having suffered being down so long, he deserves to move up. Aside from the innate logic of the situation, four reasons for success seem apparent. In them we can imagine the radical voice speaking.

a. *We are already dead.* In the world as it is, we do not count. We make no difference. We are not persons. "Baby, it don't mean shit if I burn in a rebellion, because my life ain't worth shit. Dig?"[13] There is no mistaking that idiom, nor the sense behind it. Some radicals take oaths,

---

[11]"An End of Ideology?" *Commonweal*, LXXXVII (March 8, 1968), 681–682.
[12]"Toward a Strategy of Disruption," from *Students and Society*, p. 29.
[13]Quoted by Jack Newfield, "The Biggest Lab in the Nation," *Life*, LXIV (March 8, 1968), 87.

changing their names, considering themselves as dead, without families, until the revolution succeeds. It is difficult to cow a dead orphan.

b. *We can be reborn.* Having accepted the evaluation of what is, agreeing to be the most worthless of things, we can be reborn. We have nothing to hang on to. No old identity to stop us from identifying with a new world, no matter how horrifying the prospect may seem at the outset; and a new world will certainly be born of the fire we shall create. You, the enemy, on the other hand, must cling to what is, must seek to stamp out the flames, and at best can only end sorrowing at a world that cannot remain the same. Eventually you will be consumed.

c. *We have the stomach for the fight; you don't.* Having created the Manichean world, having degraded humanity, you are overwhelmed by guilt. The sense of guilt stops your hand, for what you would kill is the world you have made. Every blow you strike is suicide and you know it. At best, you can fight only delaying actions. We can strike to kill for the old world is not ours but one in which we are already dead, in which killing injures us not, but provides us with the chance of rebirth.

d. *We are united and understand.* We are united in a sense of a past dead and a present that is valuable only to turn into a future free of your degrading domination. We have accepted our past as past by willing our future. Since you must cling to the past, you have no future and cannot even understand.

## Confrontation as a Non-Totalistic Tactic

Radical and revolutionary confrontation worries and bleeds the enemy to death or it engulfs and annihilates him. The logic of the situation that calls it forth bids it be total. But undoubtedly confrontation is brought about by those who feel only division, not radical division. For these the forces of good and evil pop in and out of focus, now clearly perceived, now not; now identified with this manifestation of established power and now that. These radicals may stop short of revolution because they have motives that turn them into politicians who at some point will make practical moves rather than toss every possible compromise and accommodation into the flaming jaws that would destroy the old order.

Student activists in the New Left vacillate in their demands between calls for "destruction" of universities as they are now known and tactical discussions of ways of "getting into the system" to make it more responsive to student goals.[14]

Drift toward non-totalistic goals seems consistent with both the

---

[14]*Students and Society.* A full reading of the conference proceedings reveals clearly this split among the most vocal and militant of New Left students.

general affluence of this group and its position as a small minority in a large student population generally committed to establishment goals and values. It may also reflect a latent response to the embarrassment of affluent students, beneficiaries of the establishment, who claim the language and motivations of the truly deprived.[15] Similarly, the perception of confrontation as a tactic for prying apart and thus remodeling the machines of established power seems evident in many adherents of the Black Power movement. In many ways, the power Stokely Carmichael and Charles V. Hamilton forecast in their book is quite conventional, drawing analogies from past, thoroughly American experiences.[16]

Finally, one should observe the possible use of confrontation as a tactic for achieving attention and an importance not readily attainable through decorum. In retiring temporarily from his task of writing a regular newspaper column, Howard K. Smith complained bitterly of a press which inflated Stokely Carmichael from a "nobody who . . . had achieved nothing and represented no one" into "a factor to be reckoned with."[17] But Carmichael knows, from bitter experience, the art of confrontation. Martin Luther King writes of meeting a group of small boys while touring Watts after the riot. "We won!" they shouted joyously. King says his group asked them, "How can you say you won when thirty-four Negroes are dead, your community is destroyed, and whites are using the riot as an excuse for inaction?" The reply was, "We won because we made them pay attention to us."[18]

Without doubt, for many the act of confrontation itself, the march, sit-in, or altercation with the police is enough. It is consummatory. Through it the radical acts out his drama of self-assertion and writes in smeary, wordless language all over the establishment, "We know you for what you are. And you know that we know." Justifying the sense of rightness and, perhaps, firing a sense of guilt in the other is the hopeful outcome of the many coy confrontations of some shy radicals.[19]

## Confrontation and Rhetorical Theory

We have talked of the *rhetoric* of confrontation, not merely confrontation, because this action, as diverse as its manifestations may be, is inherently symbolic. The act carries a message. It dissolves the lines between marches, sit-ins, demonstrations, acts of physical violence, and

[15]For an analysis of the structure and characteristics of the student left, see Richard E. Peterson, "The Student Left in American Higher Education," *Daedalus*, XCVII (Winter 1968), 293–317.

[16]*Black Power: The Politics of Liberation in America* (New York, 1967), see especially Chap. 5.

[17]"Great Age of Journalism Gone?" *Minneapolis Star*, February 19, 1968, p. 5B.

[18]*Where Do We Go From Here: Chaos or Community?* (New York, 1967), p. 112.

[19]See Norman Mailer, "The Steps of the Pentagon," *Harper's Magazine*, CCXXXVI (March 1968), 47–142 [published in book form as *Armies of the Night* (New York, 1968)]. It may seem difficult to believe but Mailer, who calls himself a "right radical," fits our adjectives, coy and shy.

aggressive discourse. In this way it informs us of the essential nature of discourse itself as human action.

The rhetoric of confrontation also poses new problems for rhetorical theory. Since the time of Aristotle, academic rhetorics have been for the most part instruments of established society, presupposing the "goods" of order, civility, reason, decorum, and civil or theocratic law. Challenges to the sufficiency of this theory and its presuppositions have been few, and largely proposed either by elusive theologians such as Kierkegaard or Buber, or by manifestly unsavory revolutionaries such as Hitler, whose degraded theories of discourse seemed to flow naturally from degraded values and paranoid ambitions.

But the contemporary rhetoric of confrontation is argued by theorists whose aspirations for a better world are not easily dismissed, and whose passion for action equals or exceeds their passion for theory. Even if the presuppositions of civility and rationality underlying the old rhetoric are sound, they can no longer be treated as self-evident.[20] A rhetorical theory suitable to our age must take into account the charge that civility and decorum serve as masks for the preservation of injustice, that they condemn the dispossessed to non-being, and that as transmitted in a technological society they become the instrumentalities of power for those who "have."

A broader base for rhetorical theory is also needed if only as a means of bringing up to date the traditional status of rhetoric as a theory of managing public symbolic transactions. The managerial advice implicit in current theories of debate and discussion scarcely contemplates the possibility that respectable people should confront disruption of reasonable or customary actions, obscenity, threats of violence, and the like. Yet the response mechanisms turned to by those whose presuppositions could not contemplate confrontation often seem to complete the action sought by those who confront, or to confirm their subjective sense of division from the establishment. The use of force to get students out of halls consecrated to university administration or out of holes dedicated to construction projects seems to confirm the radical analysis that the establishment serves itself rather than justice. In this sense, the confronter who prompts violence in the language or behavior of another has found his collaborator. "Show us how ugly you really are," he says, and the enemy with dogs and cattle prods, or police billies and mace, complies. How can administrators ignore the insurgency of those committed to jamming the machinery of whatever enterprise is supposed to be ongoing? Those who would confront have learned a brutal art, practiced sometimes awkwardly and sometimes skillfully,

---

[20]Herein lies a major problem for rhetorical theory. In a sense Haiman's essay (note 2) is a defense of these values accepting the responsibility implied by his analysis which shows a significant case made by the very existence of "A Rhetoric of the Streets" which demands a rebuttal. Burgess' essay (note 2) sees Black Power as a unique method of forcing conventional thought to take seriously its own criterion of rationality.

which demands response. But that art may provoke the response that confirms its presuppositions, gratifies the adherents of those presuppositions, and turns the power-enforced victory of the establishment into a symbolic victory for its opponents.

As specialists interested in communication, we who profess the field of rhetoric need to read the rhetoric of confrontation, seek understanding of its presuppositions, tactics, and purposes, and seek placement of its claim against a just accounting of the presuppositions and claims of our tradition. Often as we read and reflect we shall see only grotesque, childish posturings that vaguely act out the deeper drama rooted in radical division. But even so, we shall understand more, act more wisely, and teach more usefully if we open ourselves to the fundamental meaning of radical confrontation.

(1969)

# How shall we choose among competing social systems?

*Plato*

# Apology*

How you, O Athenians, have been affected by my accusers, I cannot tell; but I know that they almost made me forget who I was—so persuasively did they speak; and yet they have hardly uttered a word of truth. But of the many falsehoods told by them, there was one which quite amazed me;—I mean when they said that you should be upon your guard and not allow yourselves to be deceived by the force of my eloquence. To say this, when they were certain to be detected as soon as I opened my lips and proved myself to be anything but a great speaker, did indeed appear to me most shameless—unless by the force of eloquence they mean the force of truth; for if such is their meaning, I admit that I am eloquent. But in how different a way from theirs! Well, as I was saying, they have scarcely spoken the truth at all; from me you shall hear the whole truth, but not delivered after their manner in a set oration duly ornamented with fine words and phrases. No, by heaven! I shall use the words and arguments which occur to me at the moment, for I am confident in the justice of my cause: at my time of life I ought not to be appearing before you, O men of Athens, in the character of a boy inventing falsehoods—let no one expect it of me. And I must particularly beg of you to grant me this favour:—If I defend myself in my

*Translation by Benjamin Jowett.

accustomed manner, and you hear me using the words which many of you have heard me using habitually in the agora, at the tables of the money-changers, and elsewhere, I would ask you not to be surprised, and not to interrupt me on this account. For I am more than seventy years of age, and appearing now for the first time before a court of law, I am quite a stranger to the language of the place; and therefore I would have you regard me as if I were really a stranger, whom you would excuse if he spoke in his native tongue, and after the fashion of his country: – Am I making an unfair request of you? Never mind the manner, which may or may not be good; but think only of the truth of my words, and give heed to that: let the speaker speak truly and the judge decide justly.

And first, I have to reply to the older charges and to my first accusers, and then I will go on to the later ones. For of old I have had many accusers, who have accused me falsely to you during many years; and I am more afraid of them than of Anytus and his associates, who are dangerous, too, in their own way. But far more dangerous are the others, who began when most of you were children, and took possession of your minds with their falsehoods, telling of one Socrates, a wise man, who speculated about the heaven above, and searched into the earth beneath, and made the worse appear the better cause. The men who have besmeared me with this tale are the accusers whom I dread; for their hearers are apt to fancy that such inquirers do not believe in the existence of the gods. And they are many, and their charges against me are of ancient date, and they were made by them in the days when some of you were more impressible than you are now – in childhood, or it may have been in youth – and the cause went by default, for there was none to answer. And hardest of all, I do not know and cannot tell the names of my accusers; unless in the chance case of a comic poet. All who from envy and malice have persuaded you – some of them having first convinced themselves – all this class of men are most difficult to deal with; for I cannot have them up here, and cross-examine them, and therefore I must simply fight with shadows in my own defence, and argue when there is no one who answers. I will ask you then to take it from me that my opponents are of two kinds; one recent, the other ancient: and I hope that you will see the propriety of my answering the latter first, for these accusations you heard long before the others, and much oftener.

Well, then, I must make my defence, and endeavour to remove from your minds in a short time, a slander which you have had a long time to take in. May I succeed, if to succeed be for my good and yours, or likely to avail me in my cause! The task is not an easy one; I quite understand the nature of it. And so leaving the event with God, in obedience to the law I will now make my defence.

I will begin at the beginning, and ask what is the accusation which has given rise to the slander of me, and in fact has encouraged Meletus to prefer this charge against me. Well, what do the slanderers say? They shall be my prosecutors, and this is the information they swear against me: 'Socrates is an evildoer; a meddler who searches into things under the earth and in heaven, and makes the worse appear the better cause, and teaches the aforesaid practices to others.' Such is the nature of the accusation: it is just what you have yourselves seen in the comedy of Aristophanes, who has introduced a man whom he calls Socrates, swinging about and saying that he walks on air, and talking a deal of nonsense concerning matters of which I do not pretend to know either much or little—not that I mean to speak disparagingly of anyone who is a student of natural philosophy. May Meletus never bring so many charges against me as to make me do that! But the simple truth is, O Athenians, that I have nothing to do with physical speculations. Most of those here present are witnesses to the truth of this, and to them I appeal. Speak then, you who have heard me, and tell your neighbours whether any of you have ever known me hold forth in few words or in many upon such matters. . . . You hear their answer. And from what they say of this part of the charge you will be able to judge of the truth of the rest.

As little foundation is there for the report that I am a teacher, and take money; this accusation has no more truth in it than the other. Although, if a man were really able to instruct mankind, this too would, in my opinion, be an honour to him. There is Gorgias of Leontium, and Prodicus of Ceos, and Hippias of Elis, who go the round of the cities, and are able to persuade the young men to leave their own citizens by whom they might be taught for nothing, and come to them whom they not only pay, but are thankful if they may be allowed to pay them. There is at this time a Parian philosopher residing in Athens, of whom I have heard; and I came to hear of him in this way:—I came across a man who has spent more money on the sophists than the rest of the world put together, Callias, the son of Hipponicus, and knowing that he had sons, I asked him: 'Callias,' I said, 'if your two sons were foals or calves, there would be no difficulty in finding someone to put over them; we should hire a trainer of horses, or a farmer probably, who would improve and perfect them in the appropriate virtue and excellence; but as they are human beings, whom are you thinking of placing over them? Is there anyone who understands human and civic virtue? You must have thought about the matter, for you have sons; is there anyone?' 'There is,' he said. 'Who is he?' said I; 'and of what country? and what does he charge?' 'Evenus the Parian,' he replied; 'he is the man, and his charge is five minas.' Happy is Evenus, I said to myself, if he really has this wisdom, and teaches at such a moderate charge. Had I the same, I should have been very proud and conceited; but the truth is that I have no knowledge of the kind.

I dare say, Athenians, that someone among you will reply, 'Yes, Socrates, but what *is* your occupation? What is the origin of these accusations which are brought against you; there must have been something strange which you have been doing? All these rumours and this talk about you would never have arisen if you had been like other men: tell us, then, what is the cause of them, for we should be sorry to judge hastily of you.' Now I regard this as a fair challenge, and I will endeavour to explain to you the reason why I am called wise and have such an evil fame. Please to attend then. And although some of you may think that I am joking, I declare that I will tell you the entire truth. Men of Athens, this reputation of mine has come of a certain sort of wisdom which I possess. If you ask me what kind of wisdom, I reply, wisdom such as may perhaps be attained by man, for to that extent I am inclined to believe that I am wise; whereas the persons of whom I was speaking have a kind of superhuman wisdom, which I know not how to describe, because I have it not myself; and he who says that I have, speaks falsely, and is taking away my character. And here, O men of Athens, I must beg you not to interrupt me, even if I seem to say something extravagant. For the word which I will speak is not mine. I will refer you to a witness who is worthy of credit; that witness shall be the god of Delphi—he will tell you about my wisdom, if I have any, and of what sort it is. You must have known Chaerephon; he was early a friend of mine, and also a friend of yours, for he shared in the recent exile of the people, and returned with you. Well, Chaerephon, as you know, was very impetuous in all his doings, and he went to Delphi and boldly asked the oracle to tell him whether—as I was saying, I must beg you not to interrupt—he actually asked the oracle to tell him whether anyone was wiser than I was, and the Pythian prophetess answered that there was no man wiser. Chaerephon is dead himself; but his brother, who is in court, will confirm the truth of what I am saying.

Why do I mention this? Because I am going to explain to you why I have such an evil name. When I heard the answer, I said to myself, What can the god mean? and what is the interpretation of his riddle? for I know that I have no wisdom, small or great. What then can he mean when he says that I am the wisest of men? And yet he is a god, and cannot lie; that would be against his nature. After long perplexity, I thought of a method of trying the question. I reflected that if I could only find a man wiser than myself, then I might go to the god with a refutation in my hand. I should say to him, 'Here is a man who is wiser than I am; but you said that I was the wisest.' Accordingly I went to one who had the reputation of wisdom, and observed him—his name I need not mention, he was a politician; and in the process of examining him and talking with him, this, men of Athens, was what I found. I could not help thinking that he was not really wise, although he was thought wise by many, and still wiser by himself; and thereupon I tried to explain to him that he thought himself wise, but was not really wise; and the consequence was that he hated me, and his enmity was shared by several who were present and heard me. So I left him, saying to myself as I went away: Well, although I do not suppose that either of us knows anything really worth knowing, I am at least wiser than this fellow – for he knows nothing, and thinks that he knows; I neither know nor think that I know. In this one little point, then, I seem to have the advantage of him. Then I went to another who had still higher pretensions to wisdom, and my conclusion was exactly the same. Whereupon I made another enemy of him, and of many others besides him.

Then I went to one man after another, being not unconscious of the enmity which I provoked, and I lamented and feared this: but necessity was laid upon me, – the word of God, I thought, ought to be considered first. And I said to myself, Go I must to all who appear to know, and find out the meaning of the oracle. And I swear to you, Athenians, – for I must tell you the truth – the result of my mission was just this: I found that the men most in repute were nearly the most foolish; and that others less esteemed were really closer to wisdom. I will tell you the tale of my wanderings and of the 'Herculean' labours, as I may call them, which I endured only to find at last the oracle irrefutable. After the politicians, I went to the poets; tragic, dithyrambic, and all sorts. And there, I said to myself, you will be instantly detected; now you will find out that you are more ignorant than they are. Accordingly, I took them some of the most elaborate passages in their own writings, and asked what was the meaning of them – thinking that they would teach me something. Will you believe me? I am ashamed to confess the truth, but I must say that there is hardly a person present who would not have talked better about their poetry than they did themselves. So I learnt that not by wisdom do poets write poetry, but by a sort of genius and inspiration; they are like diviners or soothsayers who also say many fine things, but do not understand the meaning of them. The poets appeared to me to be much in the same case; and I further observed that upon the strength of their poetry they believed themselves to be the wisest of men in other things in which they were not wise. So I departed, conceiving myself to be superior to them for the same reason that I was superior to the politicians.

At last I went to the artisans, for I was conscious that I knew nothing at all, as I may say, and I was sure that they knew many fine things; and here I was not mistaken, for they did know many things of which I was ignorant, and in this they certainly were wiser than I was. But I observed that even the good artisans fell into the same error as the poets; – because they were good workmen they thought that they also knew all sorts of high matters, and this defect in them overshadowed their wisdom; and therefore I asked myself on behalf of the oracle, whether I would like to be as I was, neither having their knowledge nor their ignorance, or like them in both; and I made answer to myself and to the oracle that I was better off as I was.

This inquisition has led to my having many enemies of the worst and most dangerous kind, and has given rise also to many imputations, including the name of 'wise'; for my hearers always imagine that I myself possess the wisdom which I find wanting in others. But the truth is, O men of Athens, that God only is wise; and by his answer he intends to show that the wisdom of men is worth little or nothing; although speaking of Socrates, he is only using my name by way of illustration, as if he said, He, O men, is the wisest, who, like Socrates, knows that his wisdom is in truth worth nothing. And so I go about the world, obedient to the god, and search and make inquiry into the wisdom of anyone, whether citizen or stranger, who appears to be wise; and if he is not wise, then in vindication of the oracle I show him that he is not wise; and my occupation quite absorbs me, and I have had no time to do anything useful either in public affairs or in any concern of my own, but I am in utter poverty by reason of my devotion to the god.

There is another thing: — young men of the richer classes, who have not much to do, come about me of their own accord; they like to hear people examined, and they often imitate me, and proceed to do some examining themselves; there are plenty of persons, as they quickly discover, who think that they know something, but really know little or nothing; and then those who are examined by them instead of being angry with themselves are angry with me: This confounded Socrates, they say; this villainous misleader of youth! — and then if somebody asks them, Why, what evil does he practise or teach? they do not know, and cannot tell; but in order that they may not appear to be at a loss, they repeat the ready-made charges which are used against all philosophers about teaching things up in the clouds and under the earth, and having no gods, and making the worse appear the better cause; for they do not like to confess that their pretence of knowledge has been detected — which is the truth; and as they are numerous and ambitious and energetic, and speak vehemently with persuasive tongues, they have filled your ears with their loud and inveterate calumnies. And this is the reason why my three accusers, Meletus and Anytus and Lycon, have set upon me; Meletus, who has a quarrel with me on behalf of the poets; Anytus, on behalf of the craftsmen and politicians; Lycon, on behalf of the rhetoricians: and as I said at the beginning, I cannot expect to get rid of such a mass of calumny all in a moment. And this, O men of Athens, is the truth and the whole truth; I have concealed nothing, I have dissembled nothing. And yet, I feel sure that my plainness of speech is fanning their hatred of me, and what is their hatred but a proof that I am speaking the truth? — Hence has arisen the prejudice against me; and this is the reason of it, as you will find out either in this or in any future inquiry.

I have said enough in my defence against the first class of my accusers; I turn to the second class. They are headed by Meletus, that good man and true lover of his country, as he calls himself. Against these, too, I must try to make a defence: — Let their affidavit be read: it contains something of this kind: It says that Socrates is a doer of evil, inasmuch as he corrupts the youth, and does not receive the gods whom the state receives, but has a new religion of his own. Such is the charge; and now let us examine the particular counts. He says that I am a doer of evil, and corrupt the youth; but I say, O men of Athens, that Meletus is a doer of evil, in that he is playing a solemn farce, recklessly bringing men to trial from a pretended zeal and interest about matters in which he really never had the smallest interest. And the truth of this I will endeavour to prove to you.

Come hither, Meletus, and let me ask a question of you. You attach great importance to the improvement of youth?

Yes, I do.

Tell the judges, then, who is their improver; for you must know, as you take such interest in the subject, and have discovered their corrupter, and are citing and accusing me in this court. Speak, then, and tell the judges who is the improver of youth:—Observe, Meletus, that you are silent, and have nothing to say. But is this not rather disgraceful, and a very considerable proof of what I was saying, that you have no interest in the matter? Speak up, friend, and tell us who their improver is.

The laws.

But that, my good sir, is not my question: Can you not name some person—whose first qualification will be that he knows the laws?

The judges, Socrates, who are present in court.

What, do you mean to say, Meletus, that they are able to instruct and improve youth?

Certainly they are.

What, all of them, or some only and not others?

All of them.

Truly, that is good news! There are plenty of improvers, then. And what do you say of the audience,—do they improve them?

Yes, they do.

And the senators?

Yes, the senators improve them.

But perhaps the members of the assembly corrupt them?—or do they too improve them?

They improve them.

Then every Athenian improves and elevates them; all with the exception of myself; and I alone am their corrupter? Is that what you affirm?

That is what I stoutly affirm.

I am very unfortunate if you are right. But suppose I ask you a question: Is it the same with horses? Does one man do them harm and all the world good? Is not the exact opposite the truth? One man is able to do them good, or at least very few;—the trainer of horses, that is to say, does them good, but the ordinary man does them harm if he has to do with them? Is not that true, Meletus, of horses, or of any other animals? Most assuredly it is; whether you and Anytus say yes or no. Happy indeed would be the condition of youth if they had one corrupter only, and all the rest of the world were their benefactors. But you, Meletus, have sufficiently shown that you never had a thought about the young: your carelessness is plainly seen in your not caring about the very things which you bring against me.

And now, Meletus, I adjure you to answer me another question: Which is better, to live among bad citizens, or among good ones? Answer, friend, I say; the question is one which may be easily answered. Do not the good do their neighbours good, and the bad do them evil?

Certainly.

And is there anyone who would rather be injured than benefited by those who live with him? Answer, my good friend, the law requires you to answer—does anyone like to be injured?

Certainly not.

And when you accuse me of corrupting and deteriorating the youth, do you allege that I corrupt them intentionally or unintentionally?

Intentionally, I say.

But you have just admitted that the good do their neighbours good, and the evil do them evil. Now, is that a truth which your superior wisdom has recognized thus early in life, and am I, at my age, in such darkness and ignorance as not to know that if a man with whom I have to live is corrupted by me, I am very likely to be harmed by him; and yet I corrupt him, and intentionally, too—so you say, although neither I nor any other human being is ever likely to be convinced by you. But either I do not corrupt them, or I corrupt them unintentionally; and on either view of the case you lie. If my offence is unintentional, the law has no cognizance of unintentional offences: you ought to have taken me privately, and warned and admonished me; for if I had had instruction, I should have left off doing what I only did unintentionally—beyond doubt I should; but you would have nothing to say to me and refused to teach me. And now you bring me up in this court, which is a place not of instruction, but of punishment.

It will be very clear to you, Athenians, as I was saying, that Meletus has never had any care, great or small, about the matter. But still I should like to know, Meletus, in what I am affirmed to corrupt the young. I suppose you mean, as I infer from your indictment, that I teach them not to acknowledge the gods which the state acknowledges, but some other new divinities or spiritual agencies in their stead. These are the lessons by which I corrupt the youth, as you say.

Yes, that I say emphatically.

Then, by the gods, Meletus, of whom we are speaking, tell me and the court, in somewhat plainer terms, what you mean! for I do not as yet understand whether you affirm that I teach other men to acknowledge some gods, and therefore that I do believe in gods, and am not an entire atheist—this you do not lay to my charge,—but only you say that they are not the same gods which the city recognizes – the charge is that they are different gods. Or, do you mean that I am an atheist simply, and a teacher of atheism?

I mean the latter – that you are a complete atheist.

What an extraordinary statement! Why do you think so, Meletus? Do you mean that I do not believe in the god-head of the sun or moon, like the rest of mankind?

I assure you, judges, that he does not: for he says that the sun is stone, and the moon earth.

Friend Meletus, do you think that you are accusing Anaxagoras? Have you such a low opinion of the judges, that you fancy them so illiterate as not to know that these doctrines are found in the books of Anaxagoras the Clazomenian, which are full of them? And so, forsooth, the youth are said to be taught them by Socrates, when they can be bought in the book-market for one drachma at most; and they might pay their money, and laugh at Socrates if he pretends to father these extraordinary views. And so, Meletus, you really think that I do not believe in any god?

I swear by Zeus that you verily believe in none at all.

Nobody will believe you, Meletus, and I am pretty sure that you do not believe yourself. I cannot help thinking, men of Athens, that Meletus is reckless and impudent, and that he has brought this indictment in a spirit of mere wantonness and youthful bravado. Has he not compounded a riddle, thinking to try me? He said to himself: – I shall see whether the wise Socrates will discover my facetious self-contradiction, or whether I shall be able to deceive him and the rest of them. For he certainly does appear to me to contradict himself in the indictment as much as if he said that Socrates is guilty of not believing in the gods, and yet of believing in them – but this is not like a person who is in earnest.

I should like you, O men of Athens, to join me in examining what I conceive to be his inconsistency; and do you, Meletus, answer. And I must remind the audience of my request that they would not make a disturbance if I speak in my accustomed manner:

Did ever man, Meletus, believe in the existence of human things, and not of human beings? . . . I wish, men of Athens, that he would answer, and not be always trying to get up an interruption. Did ever any man believe in horsemanship, and not in horses? or in flute-playing, and not in flute-players? My friend, no man ever did; I answer to you and to the court, as you refuse to answer for yourself. But now please to answer the next question: Can a man believe in the existence of things spiritual and divine, and not in spirits or demigods?

He cannot.

How lucky I am to have extracted that answer, by the assistance of the court! But then you swear in the indictment that I teach and believe in divine or spiritual things (new or old, no matter for that); at any rate,

I believe in spiritual things,—so you say and swear in the affidavit; and yet if I believe in them, how can I help believing in spirits or demigods;—must I not? To be sure I must; your silence gives consent. Now what are spirits or demigods? are they not either gods or the sons of gods?

Certainly they are.

But this is what I call the facetious riddle invented by you: the demigods or spirits are gods, and you say first that I do not believe in gods, and then again that I do believe in gods; that is, if I believe in demigods. For if the demigods are the illegitimate sons of gods, whether by nymphs, or by other mothers, as some are said to be—what human being will ever believe that there are no gods when there are sons of gods? You might as well affirm the existence of mules, and deny that of horses and asses. Such nonsense, Meletus, could only have been intended by you to make trial of me. You have put this into the indictment because you could think of nothing real of which to accuse me. But no one who has a particle of understanding will ever be convinced by you that a man can believe in the existence of things divine and superhuman, and the same man refuse to believe in gods and demigods and heroes.

I have said enough in answer to the charge of Meletus: any elaborate defence is unnecessary. You know well the truth of my statement that I have incurred many violent enmities; and this is what will be my destruction if I am destroyed;—not Meletus, nor yet Anytus, but the envy and detraction of the world, which has been the death of many good men, and will probably be the death of many more; there is no danger of my being the last of them.

Someone will say: And are you not ashamed, Socrates, of a course of life which is likely to bring you to an untimely end? To him I may fairly answer: There you are mistaken: a man who is good for anything ought not to calculate the chance of living or dying; he ought only to consider whether in doing anything he is doing right or wrong—acting the part of a good man or of a bad. Whereas, upon your view, the heroes who fell at Troy were not good for much, and the son of Thetis above all, who altogether despised danger in comparison with disgrace; and when he was so eager to slay Hector, his goddess mother said to him that if he avenged his companion Patroclus, and slew Hector, he would die himself—'Fate,' she said, in these or the like words, 'waits for you next after Hector'; he, receiving this warning, utterly despised danger and death, and instead of fearing them, feared rather to live in dishonour, and not to avenge his friend. 'Let me die forthwith,' he replies, 'and be avenged of my enemy, rather than abide here by the beaked ships, a laughing-stock and a burden of the earth.' Had Achilles any thought of death and danger? For wherever a man's place is, whether the place which he has chosen or that in which he has been placed by a commander, there he ought to remain in the hour of danger, taking no account of death or of anything else in comparison with disgrace. And this, O men of Athens, is a true saying.

Strange, indeed, would be my conduct, O men of Athens, if I who, when I was ordered by the generals whom you chose to command me at Potidaea and Amphipolis and Delium, remained where they placed me, like any other man, facing death—if now, when, as I conceive and imagine, God orders me to fulfil the philosopher's mission of searching into myself and other men, I were to desert my post through fear of death, or any other fear; that would indeed be strange, and I might justly be arraigned in court for denying the existence of the gods, if I disobeyed the oracle because I was afraid of death, fancying that I was wise when I was not wise. For the fear of death is indeed the pretence of wisdom, and not real wisdom, being a pretence of knowing the unknown; and no one knows whether death, of which men are afraid because they apprehend it to be the greatest evil, may not be the greatest good. Is not this ignorance of a disgraceful sort, the ignorance which is the conceit that a man knows what he does not know? And in this respect only I believe myself to differ from men in general, and may perhaps claim to be wiser than they are:—that whereas I know but little of the world below, I do not suppose that I know: but I do know that injustice and disobedience to a better, whether God or man, is evil and dishonourable, and I will never fear or avoid a possible good rather than a certain evil. And therefore if you let me go now, and are not convinced by Anytus, who said that since I had been prosecuted I must be put to death; (or if not that I ought never to have been prosecuted at all); and that if I escape now, your sons will all be utterly ruined by practising what I teach—if you say to me, Socrates, this time we will not mind Anytus, and you shall be let off, but upon one condition, that you are not to inquire and speculate in this way any more, and that if you are caught doing so again you shall die;—if this was the condition on which you let me go, I should reply: Men of Athens, I honour and love you; but I shall obey God rather than you, and while I have life and strength I shall never cease from the practice and teaching of philosophy, exhorting any one of you whom I meet and saying to him after my manner: You, my friend,—a citizen of the great and mighty and wise city of Athens,—are you not ashamed of heaping up the largest amount of money and honour and reputation, and caring so little about wisdom and truth and the greatest improvement of the soul, which you never regard nor heed at all? And if the person with whom I am arguing, says: Yes, but I do care; then I shall not leave him nor let him go at once, but proceed to interrogate and examine and cross-examine him, and if I think that he has no virtue in him but only says that he has, I shall reproach him with undervaluing the most precious, and overvaluing the less. And I shall repeat the same words to everyone whom I meet, young and old, citizen and alien, but especially to you citizens, inasmuch as you are my brethren. For know that this is the command of God; and I believe that no greater good has ever happened in the state than my service to the God. For I do nothing but go about persuading you all, old and young alike, not to take thought for your persons or your properties, but first and chiefly to care about the greatest improvement of the soul. I tell you that virtue is not given by money, but that from virtue comes money and every other good of man, public as well as private. This is my teaching, and if it corrupts the young, it is mischievous; but if any-one says that this is not my teaching, he is speaking an untruth. Where-fore, O men of Athens, I say to you, do as Anytus bids or not as Anytus bids, and either acquit me or not; but whichever you do, understand that I shall never alter my ways, not even if I have to die many times.

Men of Athens, do not interrupt, but hear me; I begged you before to listen to me without interruption, and I beg you now to hear me to the end. I have something more to say, at which you may be inclined to cry out; but I believe that to hear me will be good for you, and therefore I beseech you to restrain yourselves. I would have you know, that if you kill such an one as I am, you will injure yourselves more than you will injure me. Nothing will injure me, not Meletus nor yet Anytus—they cannot, for a bad man is not permitted to injure a better than himself. I do not deny that Anytus may, perhaps, kill him, or drive him into exile, or deprive him of civil rights; and he may imagine, and others may imagine, that he is inflicting a great injury upon him: but there I do not agree. For the evil of doing as he is doing—the evil of seeking unjustly to take the life of another—is greater far.

And now, Athenians, I am not going to argue for my own sake, as you may think, but for yours, that you may not sin against God by con-demning me, who am his gift to you. For if you kill me you will not easi-ly find a successor to me, who, if I may use such a ludicrous figure of speech, am a sort of gadfly, given to the state by God; and the state is a great and noble steed who is tardy in his motions owing to his very size, and requires to be stirred into life. I am that gadfly which God has at-tached to the state, and all day long and in all places am always fasten-ing upon you, arousing and persuading and reproaching you. You will not easily find another like me, and therefore I would advise you to spare me. I dare say that you may feel out of temper (like a person who is suddenly awakened from sleep), and you think that you might easily strike me dead as Anytus advises, and then you would sleep on for the remainder of your lives, unless God in his care of you sent you another gadfly. When I say that I am given to you by God, the proof of my mis-sion is this:—if I had been like other men, I should not have neglected all my own concerns or patiently seen the neglect of them during all these years, and have been doing yours, coming to you individually like a father or elder brother, exhorting you to regard virtue; such conduct, I say, would be unlike human nature. If I gained anything, or if my ex-hortations were paid, there would be some sense in my doing so; but now, as you see for yourselves, not even the unfailing impudence of my accusers dares to say that I have ever exacted or sought pay of anyone; of that they can produce no witness. And I have a sufficient witness to the truth of what I say—my poverty.

Someone may wonder why I go about in private giving advice and busying myself with the concerns of others, but do not venture to come forward in public and advise the state. I will tell you why. You have heard me speak at sundry times and in divers places of a superhuman oracle or sign which comes to me, and is the divinity which Meletus ridicules in the indictment. This sign, which is a kind of voice, first began to come to me when I was a child; from time to time it forbids me to do something which I am going to do, but never commands anything. This is what deters me from being a politician. And rightly, as I think. For I am certain, O men of Athens, that if I had engaged in politics, I should have perished long ago, and done no good either to you or to myself. And do not be offended at my telling you the truth: for the truth is, that no man who sets himself firmly against you or any other multitude, honestly striving to keep the state from many lawless and unrighteous deeds, will save his life; he who will fight for the right, if he would live even for a brief space, must have a private station and not a public one.

I can give you convincing evidence of what I say, not words only, but what you value far more—actions. Let me relate to you a passage of my own life which will prove to you that to no man should I ever wrongly yield from fear of death, and that I should in fact be willing to perish for not yielding. I will tell you a tale of the courts, not very interesting perhaps, but nevertheless true. The only office of state which I ever held, O men of Athens, was that of senator: the tribe Antiochis, which is my tribe, had the presidency at the trial of the generals who had not taken up the bodies of the slain after the battle of Arginusae; and you proposed to try them in a body, contrary to law, as you all thought afterwards; but at the time I was the only one of the Prytanes who was opposed to the illegality, and I gave my vote against you; and when the orators threatened to impeach and arrest me, and you called and shouted, I made up my mind that I would run the risk, having law and justice with me, rather than take part in your injustice because I feared imprisonment and death. This happened in the days of the democracy. But when the oligarchy of the Thirty was in power, they sent for me and four others into the rotunda, and bade us bring Leon the Salaminian from Salamis, as they wanted to put him to death. This was a specimen of the sort of commands which they were always giving with the view of implicating as many as possible in their crimes; and then I showed again, not in word only but in deed, that, if I may be allowed to use such an expression, I care not a straw for death, and that my great and only care is lest I should do an unrighteous or unholy thing. For the strong arm of that oppressive power did not frighten me into doing wrong; and when we came out of the rotunda the other four went to Salamis and fetched Leon, but I went quietly home. For which I might have lost my life, had not the power of the Thirty shortly afterwards come to an end. And many will witness to my words.

Now do you really imagine that I could have survived all these years, if I had led a public life, supposing that like a good man I had always maintained the right and had made justice, as I ought, the first thing? No indeed, men of Athens, neither I nor any other man. But I have been always the same in all my actions, public as well as private, and never have I yielded any base compliance to those who are slanderously termed my disciples, or to any other. Not that I have ever had any regular disciples. But if anyone likes to come and hear me while I am pursuing my mission, whether he be young or old, he is not excluded. Nor do I converse only with those who pay; but anyone, whether he be rich or poor, may ask and answer me and listen to my words; and whether he turns out to be a bad man or a good one, neither result can be justly imputed to me; for I never taught nor professed to teach anything. And if anyone says that he has ever learned or heard anything from me in private which all the world has not heard, let me tell you that he is lying.

But I shall be asked, Why do people delight in continually conversing with you? I have told you already, Athenians, the whole truth about this matter: they like to hear the cross-examination of the pretenders to wisdom; there is amusement in it. Now this duty of cross-examining other men has been imposed upon me by God; and has been signified to me by oracles, dreams, and in every way in which the will of divine power was ever intimated to anyone. This is true, O Athenians; or, if not true, can easily be disproved. If I really am or have been corrupting the youth, those of them who are now grown up and have become sensible that I gave them bad advice in the days of their youth should of course come forward as accusers, and take their revenge; or if they do not like to come themselves, some of their relatives, fathers, brothers, or other kinsmen, should think of the evil their families have suffered at my hands. Now is their time. Many of them I see in the court. There is Crito, who is of the same age and of the same deme with myself, and there is Critobulus his son, whom I also see. Then again there is Lysanias of Sphettus, who is the father of Aeschines—he is present; and also there is Antiphon of Cephisus, who is the father of Epigenes; and there are the brothers of several who have associated with me. There is Nicostratus the son of Theodotides, and the brother of Theodotus (now Theodotus himself is dead, and therefore he, at any rate, will not seek to stop him); and there is Paralus the son of Demodocus, who had a brother Theages; and Adeimantus the son of Ariston, whose brother Plato is present; and Aeantodorus, who is the brother of Apollodorus, whom I also see. I might mention a great many others, some of whom Meletus should have produced as witnesses in the course of his speech; and let him still produce them, if he has forgotten—I will make way for him. And let him say, if he has any testimony of the sort which he can produce. Nay, Athenians, the very opposite is the truth. For all these are ready to witness on behalf of the corrupter, of the injurer of their kindred, as Meletus and Anytus call me; not the corrupted youth only— there might have been a motive for that—but their uncorrupted elder relatives. Why should they too support me with their testimony? Why, indeed, except for the sake of truth and justice, and because they know that I am speaking the truth, and that Meletus is a liar.

Well, Athenians, this and the like of this is all the defence which I have to offer. Yet a word more. Perhaps there may be someone who is offended at me, when he calls to mind how he himself on a similar, or even a less serious occasion, prayed and entreated the judges with many tears, and how he produced his children in court to excite compassion, together with a host of relations and friends; whereas I, who am probably in danger of my life, will do none of these things. The contrast may occur to his mind, and he may be set against me, and vote in anger because he is displeased at me on this account. Now if there be such a person among you,—mind, I do not say that there is,—to him I may fairly reply: My friend, I am a man, and like other men, a creature of flesh and blood, and not 'of wood or stone', as Homer says; and I have a family, yes, and sons, O Athenians, three in number, one almost a man, and two others who are still young; and yet I will not bring any of them hither in order to petition you for an acquittal. And why not? Not from any self-assertion or want of respect for you. Whether I am or am not afraid of death is another question, of which I will not now speak. But when I think of my own good name, and yours, and that of the whole state, I feel that such conduct would be discreditable. One who has reached my years, and has the name I have, ought not to demean himself. Whether this opinion of me be deserved or not, at any rate the world has decided that Socrates is in some way superior to other men. And if those among you who are said to be superior in wisdom or courage, or any other virtue, demean themselves in this way, how shameful is their conduct! I have seen men of reputation behaving in the strangest manner while they were being tried: they seemed to fancy that they were going to suffer something dreadful if they had to die, and that they would live for ever if you spared them; and I think that such are a dishonour to the state, and that any stranger coming in would have said of them that the most eminent men of Athens, to whom the Athenians themselves give office and honour, are no better than women. And I say that these things ought not to be done to you by those who have a reputation in any walk of life; and if they are done, you ought not to permit them; you ought rather to show that you are far more disposed to condemn the man who gets up a doleful scene and makes the city ridiculous, than him who holds his peace.

But, setting aside the question of honour, there seems to be something wrong in asking a favour of a judge, and thus procuring an acquittal, instead of informing and convincing him. For his duty is not to make a present of justice, but to give judgement; and he has sworn that he will judge according to the laws, and not according to his own good pleasure; and we ought not to encourage you, nor should you allow yourselves to be encouraged, in this habit of perjury—there can be no piety in that. Do not then require me to do what I consider dishonourable and impious and wrong, especially now, when I am being tried for impiety on the indictment of Meletus. For if, O men of Athens, by force of persuasion and entreaty I could overpower your oaths, then I should be teaching you to believe that there are no gods, and in defending should simply convict myself of the charge of not believing in them. But that is not so – far otherwise. For I do believe that there are gods, and in a sense higher than that in which any of my accusers believe in them. And to you and to God I commit my cause, to be determined as is best for you and me.

There are many reasons why I am not grieved, O men of Athens, at the vote of condemnation. I expected it, and am only surprised that the votes are so nearly equal; for I had thought that the majority against me would have been far larger; but now, had thirty votes gone over to the other side, I should have been acquitted. And I may say, I think, that I have escaped Meletus. I may say more; for without the assistance of Anytus and Lycon, anyone may see that he would not have had a fifth part of the votes, as the law requires, in which case he would have incurred a fine of a thousand drachmas.

And so he proposes death as the penalty. And what shall I propose on my part, O men of Athens? Clearly that which is my due. And what is my due? What ought I to have done to me, or to pay – a man who has never had the wit to keep quiet during his whole life; but has been careless of what the many care for – wealth, and family interests, and military offices, and speaking in the assembly, and magistracies, and plots, and parties. Reflecting that I was really too honest a man to be a politician and live, I did not go where I could do no good to you or to myself; but where I could do privately the greatest good (as I affirm it to be) to everyone of you, thither I went, and sought to persuade every man among you that he must look to himself, and seek virtue and wisdom before he looks to his private interests, and look to the state before he looks to the interests of the state; and that this should be the order which he observes in all his actions. What shall be done to such an one? Doubtless some good thing, O men of Athens, if he has his reward, and the good should be of a kind suitable to him. What would be a reward suitable to a poor man who is your benefactor, and who desires leisure that he may instruct you? There can be no reward so fitting as maintenance in the Prytaneum, O men of Athens, a reward which he deserves far more than the citizen who has won the prize at Olympia in the horse or chariot race, whether the chariots were drawn by two horses or by many. For I am in want, and he has enough; and he only gives you the appearance of happiness, and I give you the reality. And if I am to estimate the penalty fairly, I should say that maintenance in the Prytaneum is the just return.

Perhaps you think that I am braving you in what I am saying now, as in what I said before about the tears and prayers. But this is not so. I speak rather because I am convinced that I never intentionally wronged anyone, although I cannot convince you—the time has been too short; if there were a law at Athens, as there is in other cities, that a capital cause should not be decided in one day, then I believe that I should have convinced you. But I cannot in a moment refute great slanders; and, as I am convinced that I never wronged another, I will assuredly not wrong myself. I will not say of myself that I deserve any evil, nor propose any penalty. Why should I? Because I am afraid of the penalty of death which Meletus proposes? When I do not know whether death is a good or an evil, why should I propose a penalty which would certainly be an evil? Shall I say imprisonment? And why should I live in prison, and be the slave of the magistrates of the year—of the Eleven? Or shall the penalty be a fine, and imprisonment until the fine is paid? There is the same objection. I should have to lie in prison, for money I have none, and cannot pay. And if I say exile (and this may possibly be the penalty which you will affix), I must indeed be blinded by the love of life, if I am so irrational as to expect that when you, who are my own citizens, cannot endure my discourses and arguments, and have found them so grievous and odious that you will have no more of them, others are likely to endure them. No indeed, men of Athens, that is not very likely. And what a life should I lead, at my age, wandering from city to city, ever changing my place of exile, and always being driven out! For I am quite sure that wherever I go, there, as here, the young men will flock to listen to me; and if I drive them away, their elders will drive me out at their request; and if I let them come, their fathers and friends will drive me out for their sakes.

Someone will say: Yes, Socrates, but cannot you hold your tongue, and then you may go into a foreign city, and no one will interfere with you? Now I have great difficulty in making you understand my answer to this. For if I tell you that to do as you say would be a disobedience to God, and therefore that I cannot hold my tongue, you will not believe that I am serious; and if I say again that daily to discourse about virtue, and of those other things about which you hear me examining myself and others, is the greatest good of man, and that the unexamined life is no life for a human being, you are still less likely to believe me. Yet I say what is true, although a thing of which it is hard for me to persuade you. Also, I have never been accustomed to think that I deserve to suffer any harm. Had I money I might have estimated the offence at what I was able to pay, and not have been much the worse. But I have none, and therefore I must ask you to proportion the fine to my means. Well, perhaps I could afford a mina, and therefore I propose that penalty: Plato, Crito, Critobulus, and Apollodorus, my friends here, bid me say thirty minas, and they will be the sureties. Let thirty minas be the penalty; for which sum they will be ample security to you.

Not much time will be gained, O Athenians, in return for the evil name which you will get from the detractors of the city, who will say that you killed Socrates, a wise man; for they will call me wise, even although I am not wise, when they want to reproach you. If you had waited a little while, your desire would have been fulfilled in the course of nature. For I am far advanced in years, as you may perceive, and not far from death. I am speaking now not to all of you, but only to those who have condemned me to death. And I have another thing to say to them: You think that I was convicted because I had no words of the sort which would have procured my acquittal—I mean, if I had thought fit to leave nothing undone or unsaid. Not so; the deficiency which led to my conviction was not of words—certainly not. But I had not the boldness nor impudence nor inclination to address you as you would have liked me to do, weeping and wailing and lamenting, and saying and doing many things, such indeed as you have been accustomed to hear from others, but I maintain to be unworthy of myself. I thought at the time that I ought not to do anything common or mean when in danger: nor do I now repent of the style of my defence; I would rather die having spoken after my manner, than speak in your manner and live. For neither in war nor yet at law ought I or any man to use every way of escaping death. Often in battle there can be no doubt that if a man will throw away his arms, and fall on his knees before his pursuers, he may escape death; and in other dangers there are other ways of escaping death, if a man has the hardihood to say and do anything. The difficulty, my friends, is not to avoid death, but to avoid unrighteousness; for that runs faster than death. I am old and move slowly, and the slower runner has overtaken me; my accusers are keen and quick, and the faster runner, who is wickedness, has overtaken them. And now I depart hence condemned by you to suffer the penalty of death,—they too go their ways condemned by the truth to suffer the penalty of villainy and wrong; and I must abide by my award—let them abide by theirs. I suppose that these things may be regarded as fated,—and I think that they are well.

And now, O men who have condemned me, I would fain prophesy to you; for I am about to die, and in the hour of death men are gifted with prophetic power. And I prophesy to you who are my murderers, that immediately after my departure punishment far heavier than you have inflicted on me surely awaits you. Me you have killed because you wanted to escape the accuser, and not to give an account of your lives. But that will not be as you suppose: far otherwise. For I say that there will be more accusers of you than there are now; accusers whom hitherto I have restrained: and as they are younger they will be more severe with you, and you will be more offended at them. If you think that by killing men you will stop all censure of your evil lives, you are mistaken; that is not a way of escape which is either very possible, or honourable; the easiest and the noblest way is not to be disabling others, but to be improving yourselves. This is the prophecy which I utter before my departure to the judges who have condemned me.

Friends who would have acquitted me, I would like also to talk with you about the thing which has come to pass, while the magistrates are busy, and before I go to the place at which I must die. Stay then a little, for we may as well talk with one another while there is time. You are my friends, and I should like to show you the meaning of this event which has happened to me. O my judges—for you I may truly call judges—I should like to tell you of a wonderful circumstance. Hitherto the divine faculty of which the internal oracle is the source has constantly been in the habit of opposing me even about trifles, if I was going to make a slip or error in any matter; and now as you see there has come upon me that which may be thought, and is generally believed to be, the last and worst evil. But the oracle made no sign of opposition, either when I was leaving my house in the morning, or when I was on my way to the court, or while I was speaking, at anything which I was going to say; and yet I have often been stopped in the middle of a speech, but now in nothing I either said or did touching the matter in hand has the oracle opposed me. What do I take to be the explanation of this silence? I will tell you. It is an intimation that what has happened to me is a good, and therefore those of us who think that death is an evil must be in error. I have this conclusive proof; the customary sign would surely have opposed me had I been going to evil and not to good.

Let us reflect in another way, and we shall see that there is great reason to hope that death is a good; for one of two things—either death is a state of nothingness and utter unconsciousness, or, as men say, there is a change and migration of the soul from this world to another. Now if you suppose that there is no consciousness, but a sleep like the sleep of him who is undisturbed even by dreams, death will be an unspeakable gain. For if a person were to select the night in which his sleep was undisturbed even by dreams, and were to compare with this the other days and nights of his life, and then were to tell us how many days and nights he had passed in the course of his life better and more pleasantly than this one, I think that any man, I will not say a private man, but even the great king will not find many such days or nights, when compared with the others. Now if death be of such a nature, I say that to die is gain; for eternity is then only a single night. But if death is the journey to another place, and there, as men say, all the dead abide, what good, O my friends and judges, can be greater than this? If indeed when the pilgrim arrives in the world below, he is delivered from our earthly professors of justice, and finds the true judges who are said to give judgement there, Minos and Rhadamanthus and Aeacus and Triptolemus, and other sons of God who were righteous in their own life, that pilgrimage will be worth making. What would not a man give if he might converse with Orpheus and Musaeus and Hesiod and Homer? Nay, if this be true, let me die again and again. I myself, too, shall find a wonderful interest in there meeting and conversing with Palamedes, and Ajax the son of Telamon, and any other ancient hero who has suffered death through an unjust judgement; and there will be no small pleasure, as I think, in comparing my own experience with theirs. Above all, I shall then be able to continue my search into true and false knowledge, as in this world, so also in the next; and I shall find out who is wise, and who pretends to be wise, and is not. What would not a man give, O judges, to be able to examine the leader of the great Trojan expedition; or Odysseus or Sisyphus, or numberless others, men and women too! What infinite delight would there be in conversing with them and asking them questions! In another world they do not put a man to death for asking questions: assuredly not. For besides being happier than we are, they will be immortal, if what is said is true.

Wherefore, O judges, be of good cheer about death, and know of a certainty that no evil can happen to a good man, either in life or after death, and that he and his are not neglected by the gods. Nor has my own approaching end happened by mere chance; I see clearly that the time had arrived when it was better for me to die and be released from trouble; therefore the oracle gave no sign, and therefore also I am not at all angry with my condemners, or with my accusers. But although they have done me no harm, they intended it; and for this I may properly blame them.

Still I have a favour to ask of them. When my sons are grown up, I would ask you, O my friends, to punish them; I would have you trouble them, as I have troubled you, if they seem to care about riches, or anything, more than about virtue; or if they pretend to be something when they are really nothing, —then reprove them, as I have reproved you, for not caring about that for which they ought to care, and thinking that they are something when they are really nothing. And if you do this, I shall have received justice at your hands, and so will my sons.

The hour of departure has arrived, and we go our ways—I to die, and you to live. Which is better God only knows.

(c. 399 B.C.)

*John Donne*

# Meditation XVII

[The poet, confined to his bed with a serious illness, hears the bells of the church adjoining, and is thereby reminded of death and the transiency of human life.]

Perchance he for whom this bell tolls may be so ill, as that he knows not it tolls for him; and perchance I may think myself so much better than I am, as that they who are about me, and see my state, may have caused it to toll for me, and I know not that. The church is catholic, universal, so are all her actions; all that she does belongs to all. When she baptizes a child, that action concerns me; for that child is thereby connected to that head which is my head too, and ingrafted into that body whereof I am a member. And when she buries a man, that action concerns me: all mankind is of one author, and is one volume; when one man dies, one chapter is not torn out of the book, but translated into a better language; and every chapter must be so translated; God employs several translators; some pieces are translated by age, some by sickness, some by war, some by justice; but God's hand is in every translation, and his hand shall bind up all our scattered leaves again for that library where every book shall lie open to one another. As therefore the bell that rings to a sermon calls not upon the preacher only, but upon the congregation to come, so this bell calls us all; but how much more me, who am brought so near the door by this sickness. There was a contention as far as a suit (in which both piety and dignity, religion and estimation, were mingled), which of the religious orders should ring to prayers first in the morning; and it was determined, that they should ring first that rose earliest. If we understand aright the dignity of this bell that tolls for our evening prayer, we would be glad to make it ours by rising early, in that application, that it might be ours as well as his, whose indeed it is. The bell doth toll for him that thinks it doth; and though it intermit again, yet from that minute that that occasion wrought upon him, he is united to God. Who casts not up his eye to the sun when it rises? but who takes off his eye from a comet when that breaks out? Who bends not his ear to any bell which upon any occasion rings? but who can remove it from that bell which is passing a piece of himself out of this world? No man is an island, entire of itself; every man is a piece of the continent, a part of the main. If a clod be washed away by the sea, Europe is the less, as well as if a promontory were, as well as if a manor of thy friend's or of thine own were: any man's death diminishes me, because I am involved in mankind, and therefore never send to know for whom the bell tolls; it tolls for thee. Neither can we call this a begging of misery, or a borrowing of misery, as though we were not miserable enough of ourselves, but must fetch in more from the next house, in taking upon us the misery of our neighbors. Truly it were an excusable covetousness if we did, for affliction is a treasure, and scarce any man hath enough of it. No man hath affliction enough that is not matured and ripened by it, and made fit for God by that affliction. If a man carry treasure in bullion, or in a wedge of gold, and have none coined into current money, his treasure will not defray him as he travels. Tribulation is a treasure in the nature of it, but it is not current money in the use of it, except we get nearer and nearer our home, Heaven, by it. Another man may be sick too, and sick to death, and this affliction may lie in his bowels, as gold in a mine, and be of no use to him; but this bell, that tells me of his affliction, digs out and applies that gold to me: if by this consideration of another's danger I take mine own into contemplation, and so secure myself, by making my recourse to my God, who is our only security.

(c.1620)

## Jonathan Swift

# A Modest Proposal

It is a melancholy object to those who walk through this great town or travel in the country, when they see the streets, the roads, and cabin doors crowded with beggars of the female sex, followed by three, four, or six children, all in rags, and importuning every passenger for an alms. These mothers, instead of being able to work for their honest livelihood, are forced to employ all their time in strolling, to beg sustenance for their helpless infants, who, as they grow up, either turn thieves for want of work or leave their dear native country to fight for the Pretender in Spain, or sell themselves to the Barbados.

I think it is agreed by all parties that this prodigious number of children in the arms or on the backs or at the heels of their mothers, and frequently of their fathers, is in the present deplorable state of the kingdom a very great additional grievance; and therefore whoever could find out a fair, cheap, and easy method of making these children sound, useful members of the commonwealth would deserve so well of the public as to have his statue set up for a preserver of the nation.

But my intention is very far from being confined to provide only for the children of professed beggars; it is of a much greater extent, and shall take in the whole number of infants at a certain age who are born of parents in effect as little able to support them as those who demand our charity in the streets.

As to my own part, having turned my thoughts for many years upon this important subject and maturely weighed the several schemes of other projectors, I have always found them grossly mistaken in their computation. It is true a child just dropped from its dam may be supported by her milk for a solar year with little other nourishment, at most not above the value of two shillings, which the mother may certainly get, or the value in scraps, by her lawful occupation of begging; and it is exactly at one year old that I propose to provide for them in such a manner as, instead of being a charge upon their parents or the parish, or wanting food and raiment for the rest of their lives, they shall, on the contrary, contribute to the feeding and partly to the clothing of many thousands.

There is likewise another great advantage in my scheme, that it will prevent those voluntary abortions and that horrid practice of women murdering their bastard children, alas, too frequent among us, sacrificing the poor innocent babes, I doubt, more to avoid the expense than the shame, which would move tears and pity in the most savage and inhuman breast.

The number of souls in this kingdom being usually reckoned one million and a half, of these I calculate there may be about two hundred thousand couple whose wives are breeders; from which number I subtract thirty thousand couple who are able to maintain their own children, although I apprehend there cannot be so many under the present distresses of the kingdom; but this being granted, there will remain an hundred and seventy thousand breeders. I again subtract fifty thousand for those women who miscarry, or whose children die by accident or disease within the year. There only remain an hundred and twenty thousand children of poor parents annually born: the question therefore is how this number shall be reared and provided for, which, as I have already said, under the present situation of affairs, is utterly impossible by all the methods hitherto proposed; for we can neither employ them in handicraft or agriculture: we neither build houses (I mean in the country) nor cultivate land; they can very seldom pick up a livelihood by stealing till they arrive at six years old, except where they are of towardly parts; although I confess they learn the rudiments much earlier, during which time they can however be properly looked upon only as probationers, as I have been informed by a principal gentleman in the county of Cavan, who protested to me that he never knew above one or two instances under the age of six, even in a part of the kingdom so renowned for the quickest proficiency in that art.

I am assured by our merchants that a boy or a girl before twelve years old is no salable commodity, and even when they come to this age they will not yield above three pounds, or three pounds and half a crown at most, on the Exchange, which cannot turn to account either to the parents or kingdom, the charge of nutriment and rags having been at least four times that value.

I shall now therefore humbly propose my own thoughts, which I hope will not be liable to the least objection.

I have been assured by a very knowing American of my acquaintance in London, that a young healthy child well nursed is at a year old a most delicious, nourishing, and wholesome food, whether stewed, roasted, baked, or boiled; and I make no doubt that it will equally serve in a fricassee or a ragout.

I do therefore humbly offer it to public consideration that, of the hundred and twenty thousand children already computed, twenty thousand may be reserved for breed, whereof only one fourth part to be males, which is more than we allow to sheep, black cattle, or swine; and my reason is that these children are seldom the fruits of marriage, a circumstance not much regarded by our savages; therefore one male will be sufficient to serve four females. That the remaining hundred thousand may at a year old be offered in sale to the persons of quality and fortune through the kingdom, always advising the mother to let them suck plentifully in the last month, so as to render them plump and fat for a good table. A child will make two dishes at an entertainment for friends; and when the family dines alone, the fore or hind quarter will make a reasonable dish, and seasoned with a little pepper or salt will be very good boiled on the fourth day, especially in winter.

I have reckoned, upon a medium, that a child just born will weigh twelve pounds, and in a solar year if tolerably nursed increaseth to twenty-eight pounds.

I grant this food will be somewhat dear, and therefore very proper for landlords, who, as they have already devoured most of the parents, seem to have the best title to the children.

Infants' flesh will be in season throughout the year, but more plentiful in March and a little before and after; for we are told by a grave author, an eminent French physician, that, fish being a prolific diet, there are more children born in Roman Catholic countries about nine months after Lent than at any other season; therefore reckoning a year after Lent, the markets will be more glutted than usual, because the number of Popish infants is at least three to one in this kingdom, and therefore it will have one other collateral advantage by lessening the number of Papists among us.

I have already computed the charge of nursing a beggar's child (in which list I reckon all cottagers, laborers, and four-fifths of the farmers) to be about two shillings per annum, rags included; and I believe no gentleman would repine to give ten shillings for the carcass of a good fat child, which, as I have said, will make four dishes of excellent nutritive meat when he hath only some particular friend or his own family to dine with him. Thus the squire will learn to be a good landlord, and grow popular among his tenants; the mother will have eight shillings net profit, and be fit for work till she produces another child.

Those who are more thrifty (as I must confess the times require) may flay the carcass, the skin of which, artificially dressed, will make admirable gloves for ladies and summer boots for fine gentlemen.

As to our city of Dublin, shambles may be appointed for this purpose in the most convenient parts of it, and butchers we may be assured will not be wanting, although I rather recommend buying the children alive and dressing them hot from the knife, as we do roasting pigs.

A very worthy person, a true lover of his country, and whose virtues I highly esteem, was lately pleased in discoursing on this matter to offer a refinement upon my scheme. He said that many gentlemen of this kingdom having of late destroyed their deer, he conceived that the want of venison might be well supplied by the bodies of young lads and maidens, not exceeding fourteen years of age nor under twelve, so great a number of both sexes in every country being now ready to starve for want of work and service; and these to be disposed of by their parents if alive, or otherwise by their nearest relations. But with due deference to so excellent a friend and so deserving a patriot, I cannot be altogether in his sentiments; for as to the males, my American acquaintance assured me from frequent experience that their flesh was generally tough and lean, like that of our schoolboys, by continual exercise, and their taste disagreeable, and to fatten them would not answer the charge. Then as to the females, it would, I think with humble submission, be a loss to the public, because they soon would become breeders themselves. And besides, it is not improbable that some scrupulous people might be apt to censure such a practice (although indeed very unjustly) as a little bordering upon cruelty, which, I confess, hath always been with me the strongest objection against any project, however so well.

But in order to justify my friend, he confessed that this expedient was put into his head by the famous Psalmanazar, a native of the island Formosa, who came from thence to London above twenty years ago, and in conversation told my friend that in his country, when any young person happened to be put to death, the executioner sold the carcass to persons of quality, as a prime dainty, and that in his time the body of a plump girl of fifteen, who was crucified for an attempt to poison the emperor, was sold to his Imperial Majesty's prime minister of state and other great mandarins of the court, in joints from the gibbet, at four hundred crowns. Neither indeed can I deny that if the same use were made of several plump young girls in this town, who, without one single groat to their fortunes, cannot stir abroad without a chair, and appear at the playhouse and assemblies in foreign fineries, which they never will pay for, the kingdom would not be the worse.

Some persons of a desponding spirit are in great concern about the vast number of poor people who are aged, diseased, or maimed; and I have been desired to employ my thoughts what course may be taken to ease the nation of so grievous an encumbrance. But I am not in the least pain upon that matter, because it is very well known that they are every day dying and rotting by cold and famine and filth and vermin, as fast as can be reasonably expected. And as to the younger laborers, they are now in almost as hopeful a condition. They cannot get work, and consequently pine away for want of nourishment, to a degree that, if at any time they are accidentally hired to common labor, they have not strength to perform it; and thus the country and themselves are happily delivered from the evils to come.

I have too long digressed, and therefore shall return to my subject. I think the advantages by the proposal which I have made are obvious and many, as well as of the highest importance.

For first, as I have already observed, it would greatly lessen the number of Papists, with whom we are yearly overrun, being the principal breeders of the nation as well as our most dangerous enemies, and who stay at home on purpose with a design to deliver the kingdom to the Pretender, hoping to take their advantage by the absence of so many good Protestants who have chosen rather to leave their country than stay at home and pay tithes against their conscience to an episcopal curate.

Secondly, the poorer tenants will have something valuable of their own, which by law may be made liable to distress, and help to pay their landlord's rent, their corn and cattle being already seized, and money a thing unknown.

Thirdly, whereas the maintenance of an hundred thousand children, from two years old and upwards, cannot be computed at less than ten shillings apiece per annum, the nation's stock will be thereby increased fifty thousand pounds per annum, besides the profit of a new dish introduced to the tables of all gentlemen of fortune in the kingdom who have any refinement in taste; and the money will circulate among ourselves, the goods being entirely of our own growth and manufacture.

Fourthly, the constant breeders, besides the gain of eight shillings sterling per annum by the sale of their children, will be rid of the charge of maintaining them after the first year.

Fifthly, this food would likewise bring great custom to taverns, where the vintners will certainly be so prudent as to procure the best receipts for dressing it to perfection, and consequently have their houses frequented by all the fine gentlemen who justly value themselves upon their knowledge in good eating; and a skillful cook who understands how to oblige his guests will contrive to make it as expensive as they please.

Sixthly, this would be a great inducement to marriage, which all wise nations have either encouraged by rewards or enforced by laws and penalties. It would increase the care and tenderness of mothers toward their children, when they were sure of a settlement for life to the poor babes, provided in some sort by the public to their annual profit instead of expense. We should soon see an honest emulation among the married women, which of them could bring the fattest child to the market. Men would become as fond of their wives, during the time of their pregnancy, as they are now of their mares in foal, their cows in calf, or sows when they are ready to farrow, nor offer to beat or kick them (as is too frequent a practice) for fear of a miscarriage.

Many other advantages might be enumerated: for instance, the addition of some thousand carcasses in our exportation of barreled beef; the propagation of swine's flesh, and improvement in the art of making good bacon, so much wanted among us by the great destruction of pigs, too frequent at our tables, which are no way comparable in taste or magnificence to a well-grown, fat yearling child, which roasted whole will make a considerable figure at a lord mayor's feast or any other public entertainment. But this and many others I omit, being studious of brevity.

Supposing that one thousand families in this city would be constant customers for infants' flesh, besides other who might have it at merry meetings, particularly weddings and christenings, I compute that Dublin would take off annually about twenty thousand carcasses, and the rest of the kingdom (where probably they will be sold somewhat cheaper) the remaining eighty thousand.

I can think of no one objection that will possibly be raised against this proposal, unless it should be urged that the number of people will be thereby much lessened in the kingdom. This I freely own, and was indeed one principal design in offering it to the world. I desire the reader will observe that I calculate my remedy *for this one individual kingdom of Ireland, and for no other that ever was, is, or, I think, ever can be upon earth.* Therefore let no man talk to me of other expedients: *of taxing our absentees at five shillings a pound; of using neither clothes nor household furniture, except what is of our own growth and manufacture; of utterly rejecting the materials and instruments that promote foreign luxury; of curing the expensiveness of pride, vanity, idleness, and gaming in our women; of introducing a vein of parsimony, prudence, and temperance; of learning to love our country, wherein we differ even from Laplanders, and the inhabitants of Topinamboo; of quitting our animosities and factions, nor act any longer like the Jews who were murdering one another at the very moment their city was taken; of being a little cautious not to sell our country and consciences for nothing; of teaching landlords to have at least one degree of mercy toward their tenants. Lastly, of putting a spirit of honesty, industry, and skill into our shopkeepers, who, if a resolution could now be taken to buy only our native goods, would immediately unite to cheat and exact upon us in the price, the measure, and the goodness, nor could ever yet be brought to make one fair proposal of just dealing, though often and earnestly invited to it.*

Therefore, I repeat, let no man talk to me of these and the like expedients till he hath at least some glimpse of hope that there will ever be some hearty and sincere attempt to put them in practice.

But as to myself, having been wearied out for many years with offering vain, idle, visionary thoughts, and at length utterly despairing of success, I fortunately fell upon this proposal; which, as it is wholly new, so it hath something solid and real, of no expense and little trouble, full in our own power, and whereby we can incur no danger in *disobliging England.* For this kind of commodity will not bear exportation, the flesh being of too tender a consistence to admit a long continuance in salt, *although perhaps I could name a country which would be glad to eat up our whole nation without it.*

After all, I am not so violently bent upon my own opinion as to reject any offer proposed by wise men which shall be found equally innocent, cheap, easy, and effectual. But before something of that kind shall be advanced in contradiction to my scheme and offering a better, I desire the author or authors will be pleased maturely to consider two points. First, as things now stand, how they will be able to find food and raiment for an hundred thousand useless mouths and backs. And secondly, there being a round million of creatures in human figure throughout this kingdom, whose whole subsistence put into a common stock would leave them in debt two millions of pounds sterling, adding those who are beggars by profession to the bulk of farmers, cottagers, and laborers, with their wives and children, who are beggars in effect; I desire those politicians who dislike my overture, and may perhaps be so bold to attempt an answer, that they will first ask the parents of these mortals whether they would not at this day think it a great happiness to have been sold for food at a year old in the manner I prescribe, and thereby have avoided such a perpetual scene of misfortunes as they have since gone through by the oppression of landlords, the impossibility of paying rent without money or trade, the want of common sustenance, with neither house nor clothes to cover them from the inclemencies of the weather, and the most inevitable prospect of entailing the like or greater miseries upon their breed for ever.

I profess in the sincerity of my heart that I have not the least personal interest in endeavoring to promote this necessary work, having no other motive than the *public good of my country, by advancing our trade, providing for infants, relieving the poor, and giving some pleasure to the rich.* I have no children by which I can propose to get a single penny; the youngest being nine years old, and my wife past childbearing.

(1729)

# The Declaration of Independence
The Unanimous Declaration of the Thirteen United States of America

When in the Course of human events, it becomes necessary for one people to dissolve the political bands, which have connected them with another, and to assume among the powers of the earth, the separate and equal station to which the Laws of Nature and of Nature's God entitle them, a decent respect to the opinions of mankind requires that they should declare the causes which impel them to the separation. — We hold these truths to be self-evident, that all men are created equal, that they are endowed by the Creator with certain unalienable Rights,

that among these are Life, Liberty and the pursuit of Happiness. – That
to secure these rights, Governments are instituted among Men, deriving
their just powers from the consent of the governed, – That whenever
any Form of Government becomes destructive of these ends, it is the
Right of the People to alter or to abolish it, and to institute new Government laying its foundation on such principles and organizing its powers
in such form, as to them shall seem most likely to effect their Safety
and Happiness. Prudence, indeed, will dictate that Governments long
established should not be changed for light and transient causes; and
accordingly all experience hath shewn, that mankind are more disposed
to suffer, while evils are sufferable, than to right themselves by abolishing the forms to which they are accustomed. But when a long train of
abuses and usurpations, pursuing invariably the same Object evinces a
design to reduce them under absolute Despotism, it is their right, it is
their duty, to throw off such Government, and to provide new Guards
for their future security. – Such has been the patient sufferance of these
Colonies; and such is now the necessity which constrains them to alter
their former Systems of Government. The history of the present King of
Great Britain is a history of repeated injuries and usurpations, all having in direct object the establishment of an absolute Tyranny over these
States. To prove this, let Facts be submitted to a candid world. – He has
refused his Assent to Laws, the most wholesome and necessary for the
public good. – He has forbidden his Governors to pass Laws of immediate and pressing importance, unless suspended in their operation till his
Assent should be obtained; and when so suspended, he has utterly neglected to attend to them. – He has refused to pass other Laws for the
accommodation of large districts of people, unless those people would
relinquish the right of Representation in the Legislature, a right inestimable to them and formidable to tyrants only. – He has called together
legislative bodies at places unusual, uncomfortable, and distant from
the depository of their public Records, for the sole purpose of fatiguing
them into compliance with his measures. – He has dissolved Representative Houses repeatedly, for opposing with manly firmness his invasions on the rights of the people. – He has refused for a long time, after
such dissolutions, to cause others to be elected; whereby the Legislative
powers, incapable of Annihilation, have returned to the People at large
for their exercise; the State remaining in the meantime exposed to all
the dangers of invasion from without, and convulsions within. – He has
endeavoured to prevent the population of these States; for that purpose
obstructing the Laws for Naturalization of Foreigners; refusing to pass
others to encourage their migrations hither, and raising the conditions
of new Appropriations of Lands. – He has obstructed the Administration
of Justice, by refusing his Assent to Laws for establishing Judiciary
powers. – He has made Judges dependent on his Will alone, for the ten-
ure of their offices, and the amount and payment of their salaries. – He
has erected a multitude of New Offices, and sent hither swarms of

Officers to harrass our people, and eat out their substance. – He has kept among us, in times of peace, Standing Armies without the Consent of our legislatures. – He has affected to render the Military independent of and superior to the Civil power. – He has combined with others to subject us to a jurisdiction foreign to our constitution, and unacknowledged by our laws; giving his Assent to their Acts of pretended Legislation. – For quartering large bodies of armed troops among us: – For protecting them, by a mock Trial, from punishment for any Murders which they should commit on the Inhabitants of these States: – For cutting off our Trade with all parts of the world: – For imposing Taxes on us without our Consent: – For depriving us in many cases, of the benefits of Trial by Jury: – For transporting us beyond Seas to be tried for pretended offenses: – For abolishing the free System of English Laws in a neighboring Province, establishing therein an Arbitrary government, and enlarging its Boundaries so as to render it at once an example and fit instrument for introducing the same absolute rule into these Colonies: – For taking away our Charters, abolishing our most valuable Laws, and altering fundamentally the Forms of our Governments: – For suspending our own Legislatures, and declaring themselves invested with power to legislate for us in all cases whatsoever. – He has abdicated Government here, by declaring us out of his Protection and waging War against us. – He has plundered our seas, ravaged our Coasts, burnt our towns, and destroyed the lives of our people. – He is at this time transporting large Armies of foreign Mercenaries to compleat the works of death, desolation and tyranny, already begun with circumstances of Cruelty & perfidy scarcely paralleled in the most barbarous ages, and totally unworthy the Head of a civilized nation. – He has constrained our fellow Citizens taken Captive on the high Seas to bear Arms against their Country, to become the executioners of their friends and Brethren, or to fall themselves by their Hands. – He has excited domestic insurrections amongst us, and has endeavoured to bring on the inhabitants of our frontiers, the merciless Indian Savages, whose known rule of warfare, is an undistinguished destruction of all ages, sexes and conditions. In every stage of these Oppressions We have Petitioned for Redress in the most humble terms: Our repeated Petitions have been answered only by repeated injury. A Prince whose character is thus marked by every act which may define a Tyrant, is unfit to be the ruler of a free people. Nor have We been wanting in attentions to our British brethren. We have warned them from time to time of attempts by their legislature to extend an unwarrantable jurisdiction over us. We have reminded them of the circumstances of our emigration and settlement here. We have appealed to their native justice and magnanimity, and we have conjured them by the ties of our common kindred to disavow these usurpations, which would inevitably interrupt our connections and correspondence. They too have been deaf to the voice of justice and of consanguinity. We must, therefore, acquiesce in the necessity, which denounces our Separation, and hold them, as we hold the rest of mankind, Enemies in War, in Peace Friends. –

We, therefore, the Representatives of the United States of America, in General Congress, Assembled, appealing to the Supreme Judge of the world for the rectitude of our intentions do, in the Name, and by Authority of the good People of these Colonies, solemnly publish and declare, That these United Colonies are, and of Right ought to be Free and Independent States; that they are Absolved from all Allegiance to the British Crown, and that all political connection between them and the State of Great Britain, is and ought to be totally dissolved; and that as Free and Independent States, they have full Power to levy War, conclude Peace, contract Alliances, establish Commerce, and to do all other Acts and Things which Independent States may of right do. – And for the support of this Declaration, with a firm reliance on the protection of divine Providence, we mutually pledge to each other our Lives, our Fortunes and our sacred Honor.

(1776)

## Karl Marx and Friedrich Engels

### *from*   Manifesto of the Communist Party

A spectre is haunting Europe–the spectre of Communism. All the Powers of old Europe have entered into a holy alliance to exorcise this spectre; Pope and Czar, Metternich and Guizot, French Radicals and German police-spies.

Where is the party in opposition that has not been decried as communistic by its opponents in power? Where the Opposition that has not hurled back the branding reproach of Communism against the more advanced opposition parties, as well as against its reactionary adversaries?

Two things resuit from this fact.

I. Communism is already acknowledged by all European Powers to be itself a Power.

II. It is high time that Communists should openly, in the face of the whole world, publish their views, their aims, their tendencies, and meet this nursery tale of the spectre of Communism with a Manifesto of the party itself.

To this end, Communists of various nationalities have assembled in London and sketched the following Manifesto, to be published in the English, French, German, Italian, Flemish and Danish languages.

## Chapter 1. Bourgeois and Proletarians[1]

The history of all hitherto existing society[2] is the history of class struggles.

Freeman and slave, patrician and plebeian, lord and serf, guild-master[3] and journeyman, in a word, oppressor and oppressed, stood in constant opposition to one another, carried on uninterrupted, now hidden, now open fight, a fight that each time ended, either in a revolutionary re-constitution of society at large, or in the common ruin of the contending classes.

In the earlier epochs of history we find almost everywhere a complicated arrangement of society into various orders, a manifold gradation of social rank. In ancient Rome we have patricians, knights, plebeians, slaves; in the middle ages, feudal lords, vassals, guild-masters, journeymen, apprentices, serfs; in almost all of these classes, again, subordinate gradations.

The modern bourgeois society that has sprouted from the ruins of feudal society, has not done away with class antagonisms. It has but established new classes, new conditions of oppression, new forms of struggle in place of the old ones.

Our epoch, the epoch of the bourgeoisie, possesses, however, this distinctive feature; it has simplified the class antagonisms. Society as a whole is more and more splitting up into two great hostile camps, into two great classes directly facing each other: Bourgeoisie and Proletariat.

From the serfs of the middle ages sprang the chartered burghers of the earliest towns. From these burgesses the first elements of the bourgeoisie were developed.

The discovery of America, the rounding of the Cape, opened up fresh ground for the rising bourgeoisie. The East Indian and Chinese markets, the colonization of America, trade with the colonies, the increase in the means of exchange and in commodities generally, gave to commerce, to navigation, to industry, an impulse never before known, and thereby, to the revolutionary element in the tottering feudal society, a rapid development.

---

[1] By bourgeoisie is meant the class of modern Capitalists, owners of the means of social production and employers of wage-labor. By proletariat, the class of modern wage laborers who, having no means of production of their own, are reduced to selling their labor-power in order to live.

[2] That is, all written history. In 1847, the pre-history of society, the social organization existing previous to recorded history, was all but unknown. Since then Haxthausen discovered common ownership of land in Russia, Maurer proved it to be the social foundation from which all Teutonic races started in history, and bye and bye village communities were found to be, or to have been, the primitive form of society everywhere from India to Ireland. The inner organization of this primitive Communistic society was laid bare, in its typical form, by Morgan's crowning discovery of the true nature of the gens and its relation to the tribe. With the dissolution of these primeval communities society begins to be differentiated into separate and finally antagonistic classes. I have attempted to retrace this process of dissolution in: "Der Ursprung der Familie, des Privateigenthums und des Staats," 2nd edit., Stuttgart, 1886.

[3] Guild-master, that is, a full member of a guild, a master within, not a head.

The feudal system of industry, under which industrial production was monopolized by closed guilds, now no longer sufficed for the growing wants of the new market. The manufacturing system took its place. The guild-masters were pushed on one side by the manufacturing middle-class: division of labor between the different corporate guilds vanished in the face of division of labor in each single workshop.

Meantime the markets kept ever growing, the demand ever rising. Even manufacture no longer sufficed. Thereupon, steam and machinery revolutionized industrial production. The place of manufacture was taken by the giant, Modern Industry, the place of the industrial middle-class, by industrial millionaires, the leaders of whole industrial armies, the modern bourgeois.

Modern industry has established the world market, for which the discovery of America paved the way. This market has given an immense development to commerce, to navigation, to communication by land. This development has, in its turn, reacted on the extension of industry; and in proportion as industry, commerce, navigation, railways extended, in the same proportion the bourgeoisie developed, increased its capital, and pushed into the background every class handed down from the Middle Ages.

We see, therefore, how the modern bourgeoisie is itself the product of a long course of development, of a series of revolutions in the modes of production and of exchange.

Each step in the development of the bourgeoisie was accompanied by a corresponding political advance of that class. An oppressed class under the sway of the feudal nobility, an armed and self-governing association in the mediaeval commune,[4] here independent urban republic (as in Italy and Germany), there taxable "third estate" of the monarchy (as in France), afterwards, in the period of manufacture proper, serving either the semi-feudal or the absolute monarchy as a counterpoise against nobility, and, in fact, corner stone of the great monarchies in general, the bourgeoisie has at last, since the establishment of Modern Industry and of the world-market, conquered for itself, in the modern representative State, exclusive political sway. The executive of the modern State is but a committee for managing the common affairs of the whole bourgeoisie.

The bourgeoisie, historically, has played a most revolutionary part.

The bourgeoisie, wherever it has got the upper hand, has put an end to all feudal, patriarchal, idyllic relations. It has pitilessly torn asunder the motley feudal ties that bound man to his "natural superiors," and has left no other nexus between man and man than naked self-interest, than callous "cash payment." It has drowned the most heavenly ecsta-

---

[4] "Commune" was the name taken in France by the nascent towns even before they had conquered from their feudal lords and masters, local self-government and political rights as "the Third Estate." Generally speaking, for economical development of the bourgeoisie, England is here taken as the typical country, for its political development, France.

sies of religious fervor, of chivalrous enthusiasm, of Philistine sentimentalism, in the icy water of egotistical calculation. It has resolved
personal worth into exchange value, and in place of the numberless
indefeasible chartered freedoms, has set up that single, unconscionable
freedom—Free Trade. In one word, for exploitation, veiled by religious
and political illusions, it has substituted naked, shameless, direct, brutal exploitation.

The bourgeoisie has stripped of its halo every occupation hitherto
honored and looked up to with reverent awe. It has converted the physician, the lawyer, the priest, the poet, the man of science, into its paid
wage laborers.

The bourgeoisie has torn away from the family its sentimental veil,
and has reduced the family relation to a mere money relation.

The bourgeoisie has disclosed how it came to pass that the brutal
display of vigor in the Middle Ages, which reactionists so much admire,
found its fitting complement in the most slothful indolence. It has been
the first to show what man's activity can bring about. It has accomplished wonders far surpassing Egyptian pyramids, Roman aqueducts
and Gothic cathedrals; it has conducted expeditions that put in the
shade all former Exoduses of nations and crusades.

The bourgeoisie cannot exist without constantly revolutionizing the
instruments of production, and thereby the relations of production, and
with them the whole relations of society. Conservation of the old modes
of production in unaltered form was, in the contrary, the first condition
of existence for all earlier industrial classes. Constant revolutionizing
of production, uninterrupted disturbance of all social conditions, everlasting uncertainty and agitation distinguish the bourgeois epoch from
all earlier ones. All fixed, fast frozen relations, with their train of ancient and venerable prejudices and opinions, are swept away, all new
formed ones become antiquated before they can ossify. All that is solid
melts into the air, all that is holy is profaned, and man is at last compelled to face with sober senses, his real conditions of life, and his relations with his kind.

The need of a constantly expanding market for its products chases
the bourgeoisie over the whole surface of the globe. It must nestle
everywhere, settle everywhere, establish connections everywhere.

The bourgeoisie has through its exploitation of the world market
given a cosmopolitan character to production and consumption in every
country. To the great chagrin of reactionists, it has drawn from under
the feet of industry the national ground on which it stood. All old-estab-
lished national industries have been destroyed or are daily being destroyed. They are dislodged by new industries, whose introduction becomes a life and death question for all civilized nations, by industries
that no longer work up indigenous raw material, but raw material
drawn from the remotest zones; industries whose products are consumed, not only at home, but in every quarter of the globe. In place of

the old wants, satisfied by the productions of the country, we find new wants, requiring for their satisfaction the products of distant lands and climes. In place of the old local and national seclusion and self-sufficiency, we have intercourse in every direction, universal interdependence of nations. And as in material, so also in intellectual production. The intellectual creations of individual nations become common property. National onesiddedness and narrowmindedness become more and more impossible, and from the numerous national and local literatures there arises a world-literature.

The bourgeoisie, by the rapid improvement of all instruments of production, by the immensely facilitated means of communication, draws all, even the most barbarian nations into civilization. The cheap prices of its commodities are the heavy artillery with which it batters down all Chinese walls, with which it forces the barbarians' intensely obstinate hatred of foreigners to capitulate. It compels all nations, on pain of extinction, to adopt the bourgeois mode of production; it compels them to introduce what it calls civilization into their midst, *i.e.*, to become bourgeois themselves. In a word, it creates a world after its own image.

The bourgeoisie has subjected the country to the rule of the towns. It has created enormous cities, has greatly increased the urban population as compared with the rural, and has thus rescued a considerable part of the population from the idiocy of rural life. Just as it has made the country dependent on the towns, so it has made barbarian and semi-barbarian countries dependent on civilized ones, nations of peasants on nations of bourgeois, the East on the West.

The bourgeoisie keeps more and more doing away with the scattered state of the population, of the means of production, and of property. It has agglomerated population, centralized means of production, and has concentrated property in a few hands. The necessary consequence of this was political centralization. Independent, or but loosely connected provinces, with separate interests, laws, governments, and systems of taxation, became lumped together in one nation, with one government, one code of laws, one national class interest, one frontier and one customs tariff.

The bourgeoisie, during its rule of scarce one hundred years, has created more massive and more colossal productive forces than have all preceding generations together. Subjection of Nature's forces to man, machinery, application of chemistry to industry and agriculture, steam-navigation, railways, electric telegraphs, clearing of whole continents for cultivation, canalization of rivers, whole populations conjured out of the ground—what earlier century had even a presentiment that such productive forces slumbered in the lap of social labor?

We see then: the means of production and of exchange on whose foundation the bourgeoisie built itself up, were generated in feudal society. At a certain stage in the development of these means of production and of exchange, the conditions under which feudal society produced and exchanged, the feudal organization of agriculture and manufacturing industry, in one word, the feudal relations of property became no longer compatible with the already developed productive forces; they became so many fetters. They had to burst asunder; they were burst asunder.

Into their places stepped free competition, accompanied by social and political constitution adapted to it, and by economical and political sway of the bourgeois class.

A similar movement is going on before our own eyes. Modern bourgeois society with its relations of production, of exchange and of property, a society that has conjured up such gigantic means of production and of exchange, is like the sorcerer, who is no longer able to control the powers of the nether world whom he has called up by his spells. For many a decade past, the history of industry and commerce is but the history of the revolt of modern productive forces against modern conditions of production, against the property relations that are the conditions for the existence of the bourgeoisie and of its rule. It is enough to mention the commercial crises that by their periodical return put on its trial, each time more threateningly, the existence of the entire bourgeois society. In these crises a great part not only of the existing products, but also of the previously created productive forces, are periodically destroyed. In these crises there breaks out an epidemic that, in all earlier epochs, would have seemed an absurdity—the epidemic of overproduction. Society suddenly finds itself put back into a state of momentary barbarism; it appears as if a famine, a universal war of devastation, had cut off the supply of every means of subsistence; industry and commerce seem to be destroyed; and why? Because there is too much civilization, too much means of subsistence, too much industry, too much commerce. The productive forces at the disposal of society no longer tend to further the development of the conditions of the bourgeois property; on the contrary, they have become too powerful for these conditions by which they are fettered, and as soon as they overcome these fetters they bring disorder into the whole of bourgeois society, endanger the existence of bourgeois property. The conditions of bourgeois society are too narrow to comprise the wealth created by them. And how does the bourgeoisie get over these crises? On the one hand by enforced destruction of a mass of productive forces; on the other, by the conquest of new markets, and by the more thorough exploitation of the old ones. That is to say, by paving the way for more extensive and more destructive crises, and by diminishing the means whereby crises are prevented.

The weapons with which the bourgeoisie felled feudalism to the ground are now turned against the bourgeoisie itself.

But not only has the bourgeoisie forged the weapons that bring death to itself; it has also called into existence the men who are to wield those weapons—the modern working-class—the proletarians.

In proportion as the bourgeoisie, *i.e.*, capital, is developed, in the same proportion is the proletariat, the modern working-class, developed, a class of laborers who live only so long as they find work, and who find work only so long as their labor increases capital. These laborers, who must sell themselves piecemeal, are a commodity, like every other article of commerce, and are consequently exposed to all the vicissitudes of competition, to all the fluctuations of the market.

Owing to the extensive use of machinery and to division of labor, the work of the proletarians has lost all individual character, and, consequently, all charm for the workman. He becomes an appendage of the machine, and it is only the most simple, most monotonous and most easily acquired knack that is required of him. Hence, the cost of production of a workman is restricted almost entirely to the means of subsistence that he requires for his maintenance, and for the propagation of his race. But the price of a commodity, and also of labor, is equal to its cost of production. In proportion, therefore, as the repulsiveness of the work increases the wage decreases. Nay more, in proportion as the use of machinery and division of labor increases, in the same proportion the burden of toil increases, whether by prolongation of the working hours, by increase of the work enacted in a given time, or by increased speed of the machinery, etc.

Modern industry has converted the little workshop of the patriarchal master into the great factory of the industrial capitalist. Masses of laborers, crowded into factories, are organized like soldiers. As privates of the industrial army they are placed under the command of a perfect hierarchy of officers and sergeants. Not only are they the slaves of the bourgeois class and of the bourgeois state, they are daily and hourly enslaved by the machine, by the overlooker, and, above all, by the individual bourgeois manufacturer himself. The more openly this despotism proclaims gain to be its end and aim, the more petty, the more hateful and the more embittering it is.

The less the skill and exertion or strength implied in manual labor, in other words, the more modern industry becomes developed, the more is the labor of men superseded by that of women. Differences of age and sex have no longer any distinctive social validity for the working class. All are instruments of labor, more or less expensive to use, according to their age and sex.

No sooner is the exploitation of the laborer by the manufacturer, so far at an end, that he receives his wages in cash, than he is set upon by the other portions of the bourgeoisie, the landlord, the shopkeeper, the pawnbroker, etc.

The lower strata of the middle class — the small tradespeople, shopkeepers and retired tradesmen generally, the handicraftsmen and peasants — all these sink gradually into the proletariat, partly because their diminutive capital does not suffice for the scale on which Modern Industry is carried on, and is swamped in the competition with the large capitalists, partly because their specialized skill is rendered worthless by new methods of production. Thus the proletariat is recruited from all classes of the population.

The proletariat goes through various stages of development. With its birth begins its struggle with the bourgeoisie. At first the contest is carried on by individual laborers, then by the workpeople of a factory, then by operatives of one trade, in one locality, against the individual bourgeois who directly exploits them. They direct their attacks not against the bourgeois conditions of production, but against the instruments of production themselves; they destroy imported wares that compete with their labor, they smash to pieces machinery, they set factories ablaze, they seek to restore by force the vanished status of the workman of the Middle Ages.

At this stage the laborers still form an incoherent mass scattered over the whole country, and broken up by their mutual competition. If anywhere they unite to form more compact bodies, this is not yet the consequence of their own active union, but of the union of the bourgeoisie, which class, in order to attain its own political ends, is compelled to set the whole proletariat in motion, and is moreover yet, for a time, able to do so. At this stage, therefore, the proletarians do not fight their enemies, but the enemies of their enemies, the remnants of absolute monarchy, the landowners, the non-industrial bourgeois, the petty bourgeoisie. Thus the whole historical movement is concentrated in the hands of the bourgeoisie, every victory so obtained is a victory for the bourgeoisie.

But with the development of industry the proletariat not only increases in number; it becomes concentrated in greater masses, its strength grows and it feels that strength more. The various interests and conditions of life within the ranks of the proletariat are more and more equalized, in proportion as machinery obliterates all distinctions of labor, and nearly everywhere reduces wages to the same low level. The growing competition among the bourgeois, and the resulting commercial crisis, make the wages of the workers even more fluctuating. The unceasing improvement of machinery, ever more rapidly developing, makes their livelihood more and more precarious; the collisions between individual workmen and individual bourgeois take more and more the character of collisions between two classes. Thereupon the workers begin to form combinations (Trades' Unions) against the bourgeois; they club together in order to keep up the rate of wages; they found permanent associations in order to make provision beforehand for these occasional revolts. Here and there the contest breaks out into riots.

Now and then the workers are victorious, but only for a time. The real fruit of their battle lies not in the immediate result but in the ever-expanding union of workers. This union is helped on by the improved means of communication that are created by modern industry, and that places the workers of different localities in contact with one another. It was just this contact that was needed to centralize the numerous local struggles, all of the same character, into one national struggle between classes. But every class struggle is a political struggle. And that union, to attain which the burghers of the Middle Ages with their miserable highways, required centuries, the modern proletarians, thanks to railways, achieve in a few years.

This organization of the proletarians into a class, and consequently into a political party, is continually being upset again by the competition between the workers themselves. But it ever rises up again, stronger, firmer, mightier. It compels legislative recognition of particular interests of the workers by taking advantage of the divisions among the bourgeoisie itself. Thus the ten hours' bill in England was carried.

Altogether collisions between the classes of the old society further, in many ways, the course of development of the proletariat. The bourgeoisie finds itself involved in a constant battle. At first with the aristocracy; later on, with those portions of the bourgeoisie itself whose interests have become antagonistic to the progress of industry; at all times, with the bourgeoisie of foreign countries. In all these battles it sees itself compelled to appeal to the proletariat, to ask for its help, and thus, to drag it into the political arena. The bourgeoisie itself, therefore, supplies the proletariat with its own elements of political and general education; in other words, it furnishes the proletariat with weapons for fighting the bourgeoisie.

Further, as we have already seen, entire sections of the ruling classes are, by the advance of industry, precipitated into the proletariat, or are at least threatened in their conditions of existence. These also supply the proletariat with fresh elements of enlightenment and progress.

Finally, in times when the class-struggle nears the decisive hour, the process of dissolution going on within the ruling class—in fact, within the whole range of an old society—assumes such a violent, glaring character that a small section of the ruling class cuts itself adrift and joins the revolutionary class, the class that holds the future in its hands. Just as, therefore, at an earlier period, a section of the nobility went over to the bourgeoisie, so now a portion of the bourgeoisie goes over to the proletariat, and in particular, a portion of the bourgeois ideologists, who have raised themselves to the level of comprehending theoretically the historical movements as a whole.

Of all the classes that stand face to face with the bourgeoisie to-day the proletariat alone is a really revolutionary class. The other classes decay and finally disappear in the face of modern industry; the proletariat is its special and essential product.

The lower middle class, the small manufacturer, the shopkeeper, the artisan, the peasant, all these fight against the bourgeoisie, to save from extinction their existence as fractions of the middle class. They are therefore not revolutionary, but conservative. Nay, more; they are reactionary, for they try to roll back the wheel of history. If by chance they are revolutionary, they are so only in view of their impending transfer into the proletariat; they thus defend not their present, but their future interests; they desert their own standpoint to place themselves at that of the proletariat.

The "dangerous class," the social scum, that passively rotting mass thrown off by the lowest layers of old society, may, here and there, be swept into the movement by a proletarian revolution; its conditions of life, however, prepare it far more for the part of a bribed tool of reactionary intrigue.

In the conditions of the proletariat, those of the old society at large are already virtually swamped. The proletarian is without property; his relation to his wife and children has no longer anything in common with the bourgeois family relations; modern industrial labor, modern subjection to capital, the same in England as in France, in America as in Germany, has stripped him of every trace of national character. Law, morality, religion, are to him so many bourgeois prejudices, behind which lurk in ambush just as many bourgeois interests.

All the preceding classes that got the upper hand sought to fortify their already acquired status by subjecting society at large to their conditions of appropriation. The proletarians cannot become masters of the productive forces of society except by abolishing their own previous mode of appropriation, and thereby also every other previous mode of appropriation. They have nothing of their own to secure and to fortify; their mission is to destroy all previous securities for and insurances of individual property.

All previous historical movements were movements of minorities, or in the interest of minorities. The proletarian movement is the self-conscious, independent movement of the immense majority. The proletariat, the lowest stratum of our present society, cannot stir, cannot raise itself up without the whole superincumbent strata of official society being sprung into the air.

Though not in substance, yet in form, the struggle of the proletariat with the bourgeoisie is at first a national struggle. The proletariat of each country must, of course, first of all settle matters with its own bourgeoisie.

In depicting the most general phases of the development of the proletariat, we traced the more or less veiled civil war, raging within existing society, up to the point where that war breaks out into open revolution, and where the violent overthrow of the bourgeoisie, lays the foundations for the sway of the proletariat.

Hitherto every form of society has been based, as we have already seen, on the antagonism of oppressing and oppressed classes. But in order to oppress a class, certain conditions must be assured to it under which it can, at least, continue its slavish existence. The serf, in the period of serfdom, raised himself to membership in the commune, just as the petty bourgeois, under the yoke of feudal absolutism managed to develop into a bourgeois. The modern laborer on the contrary, instead of rising with the progress of industry, sinks deeper and deeper below the conditions of existence of his own class. He becomes a pauper, and pauperism develops more rapidly than population and wealth. And here it becomes evident that the bourgeoisie is unfit any longer to be the ruling class in society, and to impose its conditions of existence upon society as an over-riding law. It is unfit to rule, because it is incompetent to assure an existence to its slave within his slavery, because it cannot help letting him sink into such a state that it has to feed him, instead of being fed by him. Society can no longer live under this bourgeoisie; in other words, its existence is no longer compatible with society.

The essential condition for the existence, and for the sway of the bourgeois class, is the formation and augmentation of capital; the condition for capital is wage labor. Wage labor rests exclusively on competition between the laborers. The advance of industry, whose involuntary promoter is the bourgeoisie, replaces the isolation of the laborers, due to competition, by their involuntary combination, due to association. The development of Modern Industry, therefore, cuts from under its feet the very foundation on which the bourgeoisie produces and appropriates products. What the bourgeoisie therefore produces, above all, are its own grave diggers. Its fall and the victory of the proletariat are equally inevitable.

(1847)

## Samuel Clemens

# To the Person Sitting in Darkness

Christmas will dawn in the United States over a people full of hope and aspiration and good cheer. Such a condition means contentment and happiness. The carping grumbler who may here and there go forth will find few to listen to him. The majority will wonder what is the matter with him and pass on. — New York *Tribune,* on Christmas Eve.

From the *Sun,* of New York:

The purpose of this article is not to describe the terrible offenses against humanity committed in the name of Politics in some of the most notorious East Side districts. *They could not be described, even verbally.* But it is the intention to let the great mass of more or less careless citizens of this beautiful metropolis of the New World get some conception of the havoc and ruin wrought to man, woman, and child in the most densely populated and least-known section of the city. Name, date, and place can be supplied to those of little faith—or to any man who feels himself aggrieved. It is a plain statement of record and observation, written without license and without garnish.

Imagine, if you can, a section of the city territory completely dominated by one man, without whose permission neither legitimate nor illegitimate business can be conducted; *where illegitimate business is encouraged and legitimate business discouraged;* where the respectable residents have to fasten their doors and windows summer nights and sit in their rooms with asphyxiating air and 100-degree temperature, rather than try to catch the faint whiff of breeze in their natural breathing places, the stoops of their homes; *where naked women dance by night in the streets, and unsexed men prowl like vultures through the darkness on "business"* not only permitted but encouraged by the police; *where the education of infants begins with the knowledge of prostitution* and the training of little girls is training in the arts of Phryne; where *American* girls brought up with the refinements of *American* homes are imported from small towns upstate, Massachusetts, Connecticut, and New Jersey, and kept as virtually prisoners as if they were locked up behind jail bars until they have lost all semblance of womanhood; *where small boys are taught to solicit for the women of disorderly houses;* where there is an organized society of young men *whose sole business in life is to corrupt young girls and turn them over to bawdy houses;* where men walking with their wives along the street are openly insulted; *where children that have adult diseases are the chief patrons of the hospitals and dispensaries;* where it is the rule, rather than the exception, that *murder, rape, robbery, and theft go unpunished*—in short where the Premium of the most awful forms of Vice is the Profit of the politicians.

The following news from China appeared in the *Sun*, of New York, on Christmas Eve. The italics are mine:

The Rev. Mr. Ament, of the American Board of Foreign Missions, has returned from a trip which he made for the purpose of collecting indemnities for damages done by Boxers. *Everywhere he went he compelled the Chinese to pay.* He says that all his native Christians are now provided for. He had 700 of them under his charge, and 300 were killed. He has *collected 300 taels for each* of these murders, and has *compelled full payment for all the property belonging to Christians* that was destroyed. He also assessed *fines* amounting to THIRTEEN TIMES the amount of the indemnity. *This money will be used for the propagation of the Gospel.*

Mr. Ament declares that the compensation he has collected is *moderate* when compared with the amount secured by the Catholics, who demand, in addition to money, *head for head.* They collect 500 taels for each murder of a Catholic. In the Wenchiu country, 680 Catholics were killed, and for this the European Catholics here demand 750,000 strings of cash and 680 *heads.*

In the course of a conversation, Mr. Ament referred to the attitude of the missionaries toward the Chinese. He said:

"I deny emphatically that the missionaries are *vindictive,* that they *generally* looted, or that they have done anything *since* the siege that *the circum-*

*stances did not demand.* I criticize the Americans. *The soft hand of the Americans is not as good as the mailed fist of the Germans.* If you deal with the Chinese with a soft hand they will take advantage of it.

"The statement that the French government will return the loot taken by the French soldiers is the source of the greatest amusement here. The French soldiers were more systematic looters than the Germans, and it is a fact that to-day *Catholic Christians,* carrying French flags and armed with modern guns, *are looting villages* in the Province of Chili."

By happy luck, we get all these glad tidings on Christmas Eve—just in time to enable us to celebrate the day with proper gayety and enthusiasm. Our spirits soar, and we find we can even make jokes: Taels, I win, Heads you lose.

Our Reverend Ament is the right man in the right place. What we want of our missionaries out there is, not that they shall merely represent in their acts and persons the grace and gentleness and charity and loving-kindness of our religion, but that they shall also represent the American spirit. The oldest Americans are the Pawnees. Macallum's History says:

When a white Boxer kills a Pawnee and destroys his property, the other Pawnees do not trouble to seek *him* out, they kill any white person that comes along; also, they make some white village pay deceased's heirs the full cash value of deceased, together with full cash value of the property destroyed; they also make the village pay, in addition, *thirteen times* the value of that property into a fund for the dissemination of the Pawnee religion, which they regard as the best of all religions for the softening and humanizing of the heart of man. It is their idea that it is only fair and right that the innocent should be made to suffer for the guilty, and that it is better that ninety and nine innocent should suffer than that one guilty person should escape.

Our Reverend Ament is justifiably jealous of those enterprising Catholics, who not only get big money for each lost convert, but get "head for head" besides. But he should soothe himself with the reflections that the entirety of their exactions are for their own pockets, whereas he, less selfishly, devotes only 300 taels per head to that service, and gives the whole vast thirteen repetitions of the property-indemnity to the service of propagating the Gospel. His magnanimity has won him the approval of his nation, and will get him a monument. Let him be content with these rewards. We all hold him dear for manfully defending his fellow missionaries from exaggerated charges which were beginning to distress us, but which his testimony has so considerably modified that we can now contemplate them without noticeable pain. For now we know that, even before the siege, the missionaries were not "generally" out looting, and that, "since the siege," they have acted quite handsomely, except when "circumstances" crowded them. I am arranging for the monument. Subscriptions for it can be sent to the American

Board; designs for it can be sent to me. Designs must allegorically set forth the Thirteen Reduplications of the Indemnity, and the Object for which they were exacted; as Ornaments, the designs must exhibit 680 Heads, so disposed as to give a pleasing and pretty effect; for the Catholics have done nicely, and are entitled to notice in the monument. Mottoes may be suggested, if any shall be discovered that will satisfactorily cover the ground.

Mr. Ament's financial feat of squeezing a thirteen-fold indemnity out of the pauper peasants to square other people's offenses, thus condemning them and their women and innocent little children to inevitable starvation and lingering death, in order that the blood money so acquired might be *"used for the propagation of the Gospel,"* does not flutter my serenity; although the act and the words, taken together, concrete a blasphemy so hideous and so colossal that, without doubt, its mate is not findable in the history of this or of any other age. Yet, if a layman had done that thing and justified it with those words, I should have shuddered, I know. Or, if I had done the thing and said the words myself—However, the thought is unthinkable, irreverent as some imperfectly informed people think me. Sometimes an ordained minister sets out to be blasphemous. When this happens, the layman is out of the running; he stands no chance.

We have Mr. Ament's impassioned assurance that the missionaries are not "vindictive." Let us hope and pray that they will never become so, but will remain in the almost morbidly fair and just and gentle temper which is affording so much satisfaction to their brother and champion to-day.

The following is from the New York *Tribune* of Christmas Eve. It comes from that journal's Tokyo correspondent. It has a strange and impudent sound, but the Japanese are but partially civilized as yet. When they become wholly civilized they will not talk so:

The missionary question, of course, occupies a foremost place in the discussion. It is now felt as essential that the Western Powers take cognizance of the sentiment here, that religious invasions of Oriental countries by powerful Western organizations are tantamount to filibustering expeditions, and should not only be discountenanced, but that stern measures should be adopted for their suppression. The feeling here is that the missionary organizations constitute a constant menace to peaceful international relations.

*Shall we?* That is, shall we go on conferring our Civilization upon the peoples that sit in darkness, or shall we give those poor things a rest? Shall we bang right ahead in our oldtime, loud, pious way, and commit the new century to the game; or shall we sober up and sit down and think it over first? Would it not be prudent to get our Civilization tools together, and see how much stock is left on hand in the way of Glass Beads and Theology, and Maxim Guns and Hymn Books, and Trade Gin and Torches of Progress and Enlightenment (patent adjustable ones, good to fire villages with, upon occasion), and balance the books, and arrive at the profit and loss, so that we may intelligently decide whether to continue the business or sell out the property and start a new Civilization Scheme on the proceeds?

Extending the Blessings of Civilization to our Brother who Sits in Darkness has been a good trade and has paid well, on the whole; and there is money in it yet, if carefully worked – but not enough, in my judgment, to make any considerable risk advisable. The People that Sit in Darkness are getting to be too scarce – too scarce and too shy. And such darkness as is now left is really of but an indifferent quality, and not dark enough for the game. The most of those People that Sit in Darkness have been furnished with more light than was good for them or profitable for us. We have been injudicious.

The Blessings-of-Civilization Trust, wisely and cautiously administered, is a Daisy. There is more money in it, more territory, more sovereignty, and other kinds of emolument, than there is in any other game that is played. But Christendom has been playing it badly of late years, and must certainly suffer by it, in my opinion. She has been so eager to get every stake that appeared on the green cloth, that the People who Sit in Darkness have noticed it – they have noticed it, and have begun to show alarm. They have become suspicious of the Blessings of Civilization. More – they have begun to examine them. This is not well. The Blessings of Civilization are all right, and a good commercial property; there could not be a better, in a dim light. In the right kind of a light, and at a proper distance, with the goods a little out of focus, they furnish this desirable exhibit to the Gentlemen who Sit in Darkness:

| | |
|---|---|
| Love, | Law and Order, |
| Justice, | Liberty, |
| Gentleness, | Equality, |
| Christianity, | Honorable Dealing, |
| Protection to the Weak, | Mercy, |
| Temperance, | Education, |

– and so on.

There. Is it good? Sir, it is pie. It will bring into camp any idiot that sits in darkness anywhere. But not if we adulterate it. It is proper to be emphatic upon that point. This brand is strictly for Export – apparently. *Apparently.* Privately and confidentially, it is nothing of the kind. Privately and confidentially, it is merely an outside cover, gay and pretty and attractive, displaying the special patterns of our Civilization which we reserve for Home Consumption, while *inside* the bale is the Actual Thing that the Customer Sitting in Darkness buys with his blood and tears and land and liberty. That Actual Thing is, indeed,

Civilization, but it is only for Export. Is there a difference between the two brands? In some of the details, yes.

We all know that the Business is being ruined. The reason is not far to seek. It is because our Mr. McKinley, and Mr. Chamberlain, and the Kaiser, and the Tsar and the French have been exporting the Actual Thing *with the outside cover left off*. This is bad for the Game. It shows that these new players of it are not sufficiently acquainted with it.

It is a distress to look on and note the mismoves, they are so strange and so awkward. Mr. Chamberlain manufactures a war out of materials so inadequate and so fanciful that they make the boxes grieve and the gallery laugh, and he tries hard to persuade himself that it isn't purely a private raid for cash, but has a sort of dim, vague respectability about it somewhere, if he could only find the spot; and that, by and by, he can scour the flag clean again after he has finished dragging it through the mud, and make it shine and flash in the vault of heaven once more as it had shone and flashed there a thousand years in the world's respect until he laid his unfaithful hand upon it. It is bad play—bad. For it exposes the Actual Thing to Them that Sit in Darkness, and they say: "What! Christian against Christian? And only for money? Is *this* a case of magnanimity, forbearance, love, gentleness, mercy, protection of the weak—this strange and overshowy onslaught of an elephant upon a nest of field mice, on the pretext that the mice had squeaked an insolence at him—conduct which 'no self-respecting government could allow to pass unavenged'? as Mr. Chamberlain said. Was that a good pretext in a small case, when it had not been a good pretext in a large one?—for only recently Russia had affronted the elephant three times and survived alive and unsmitten. Is this Civilization and Progress? Is it something better than we already possess? These harryings and burnings and desert-makings in the Transvaal—is this an improvement on our darkness? Is it, perhaps, possible that there are two kinds of Civilization—one for home consumption and one for the heathen market?"

Then They that Sit in Darkness are troubled, and shake their heads; and they read this extract from a letter of a British private, recounting his exploits in one of Methuen's victories, some days before the affair of Magersfontein, and they are troubled again:

We tore up the hill and into the intrenchments, and the Boers saw we had them; so they dropped their guns and went down on their knees and put up their hands clasped, and begged for mercy. And we gave it them—*with the long spoon*.

The long spoon is the bayonet. See *Lloyd's Weekly*, London, of those days. The same number—and the same column—contained some quite unconscious satire in the form of shocked and bitter upbraidings of the Boers for their brutalities and inhumanities!

Next, to our heavy damage, the Kaiser went to playing the game without first mastering it. He lost a couple of missionaries in a riot in Shantung, and in his account he made an overcharge for them. China had to pay a hundred thousand dollars apiece for them, in money; twelve miles of territory, containing several millions of inhabitants and worth twenty million dollars; and to build a monument, and also a Christian church; whereas the people of China could have been depended upon to remember the missionaries without the help of these expensive memorials. This was all bad play. Bad, because it would not, and could not, and will not now or ever, deceive the Person Sitting in Darkness. He knows that it was an overcharge. He knows that a missionary is like any other man: he is worth merely what you can supply his place for, and no more. He is useful, but so is a doctor, so is a sheriff, so is an editor; but a just Emperor does not charge war prices for such. A diligent, intelligent, but obscure missionary, and a diligent, intelligent country editor are worth much, and we know it; but they are not worth the earth. We esteem such an editor, and we are sorry to see him go; but, when he goes, we should consider twelve miles of territory, and a church, and a fortune, overcompensation for his loss. I mean, if he was a Chinese editor, and we had to settle for him. It is no proper figure for an editor or a missionary; one can get shop-worn kings for less. It was bad play on the Kaiser's part. It got this property, true; but it *produced the Chinese revolt*, the indignant uprising of China's traduced patriots, the Boxers. The results have been expensive to Germany, and to the other Disseminators of Progress and the Blessings of Civilization.

The Kaiser's claim was paid, yet it was bad play, for it could not fail to have an evil effect upon Persons Sitting in Darkness in China. They would muse upon the event, and be likely to say: "Civilization is gracious and beautiful, for such is its reputation; but can we afford it? There are rich Chinamen, perhaps they can afford it; but this tax is not laid upon them, it is laid upon the peasants of Shantung; it is they that must pay this mighty sum, and their wages are but four cents a day. Is this a better civilization than ours, and holier and higher and nobler? Is not this rapacity? Is not this extortion? Would Germany charge America two hundred thousand dollars for two missionaries, and shake the mailed fist in her face, and send warships, and send soldiers, and say: 'Seize twelve miles of territory, worth twenty millions of dollars, as additional pay for the missionaries; and make those peasants build a monument to the missionaries, and a costly Christian church to remember them by?' And later would Germany say to her soldiers: 'March through America and slay, *giving no quarter;* make the German face there, as has been our Hun-face here, a terror for a thousand years; march through the Great Republic and slay, slay, slay, carving a road for our offended religion through its heart and bowels?' Would Germany do like this to America, to England, to France, to Russia? Or only to China, the helpless—imitating the elephant's assault upon the field mice? Had we better invest in this Civilization—this Civilization which called Napoleon a buccaneer for carrying off Venice's bronze horses, but which steals our ancient astronomical instruments from our walls, and goes looting like common bandits—that is, all the alien soldiers except America's; and (Americans again excepted) storms frightened villages and cables the result to glad journals at home every day: 'Chinese losses, 450 killed; ours, *one officer and two men wounded.* Shall proceed against neighboring village to-morrow, where a *massacre* is reported.' Can we afford Civilization?"

And next Russia must go and play the game injudiciously. She affronts England once or twice—with the Person Sitting in Darkness observing and noting; by moral assistance of France and Germany, she robs Japan of her hard-earned spoil, all swimming in Chinese blood— Port Arthur—with the Person again observing and noting; then she seizes Manchuria, raids its villages, and chokes its great river with the swollen corpses of countless massacred peasants—that astonished Person still observing and noting. And perhaps he is saying to himself: "It is yet *another* Civilized Power, with its banner of the Prince of Peace in one hand and its loot basket and its butcher knife in the other. Is there no salvation for us but to adopt Civilization and lift ourselves down to its level?"

And by and by comes America, and our Master of the Game plays it badly—plays it as Mr. Chamberlain was playing it in South Africa. It was a mistake to do that; also, it was one which was quite unlooked for in a Master who was playing it so well in Cuba. In Cuba, he was playing the usual and regular *American* game, and it was winning, for there is no way to beat it. The Master, contemplating Cuba, said: "Here is an oppressed and friendless little nation which is willing to fight to be free; we go partners, and put up the strength of seventy million sympathizers and the resources of the United States: play!" Nothing but Europe combined could call that hand: and Europe cannot combine on anything. There, in Cuba, he was following our great traditions in a way which made us very proud of him, and proud of the deep dissatisfaction which his play was provoking in continental Europe. Moved by a high inspiration, he threw out those stirring words which proclaimed that forcible annexation would be "criminal aggression"; and in the utterance fired another "shot heard round the world." The memory of that fine saying will be outlived by the remembrance of no act of his but one—that he forgot it within the twelvemonth, and its honorable gospel along with it.

For, presently, came the Philippine temptation. It was strong; it was too strong, and he made that bad mistake: he played the European game, the Chamberlain game. It was a pity; it was a great pity, that error; that one grievous error, that irrevocable error. For it was the very place and time to play the American game again. And at no cost. Rich winnings to be gathered in, too; rich and permanent; indestructible; a fortune transmissible forever to the children of the flag. Not land, not money, not dominion—no, something worth many times more than that dross: our share, the spectacle of a nation of long harassed and persecuted slaves set free through our influence; our posterity's share, the golden memory of that fair deed. The game was in our hands. If it had been played according to the American rules, Dewey would have sailed away from Manila as soon as he had destroyed the Spanish fleet—after putting up a sign on shore guaranteeing foreign property and life against damage by the Filipinos, and warning the Powers that interference with the emancipated patriots would be regarded as an act unfriendly to the United States. The Powers cannot combine, in even a bad cause, and the sign would not have been molested.

Dewey could have gone about his affairs elsewhere, and left the competent Filipino army to starve out the little Spanish garrison and send it home, and the Filipino citizens to set up the form of government they might prefer, and deal with the friars and their doubtful acquisitions according to Filipino ideas of fairness and justice—ideas which have since been tested and found to be of as high an order as any that prevail in Europe or America.

But we played the Chamberlain game, and lost the chance to add another Cuba and another honorable deed to our good record.

The more we examine the mistake, the more clearly we perceive that it is going to be bad for the Business. The Person Sitting in Darkness is almost sure to say: "There is something curious about this— curious and unaccountable. There must be two Americas: one that sets the captive free, and one that takes a once-captive's new freedom away from him, and picks a quarrel with him with nothing to found it on; then kills him to get his land."

The truth is, the Person Sitting in Darkness *is* saying things like that; and for the sake of the Business we must persuade him to look at the Philippine matter in another and healthier way. We must arrange his opinions for him. I believe it can be done; for Mr. Chamberlain has arranged England's opinion of the South African matter, and done it most cleverly and successfully. He presented the facts—some of the facts—and showed those confiding people what the facts meant. He did it statistically, which is a good way. He used the formula: "Twice 2 are 14, and 2 from 9 leaves 35." Figures are effective; figures will convince the elect.

Now, my plan is a still bolder one than Mr. Chamberlain's, though apparently a copy of it. Let us be franker than Mr. Chamberlain; let us audaciously present the whole of the facts, shirking none, then explain them according to Mr. Chamberlain's formula. This daring truthfulness will astonish and dazzle the Person Sitting in Darkness, and he will take the Explanation down before his mental vision has had time to get back into focus. Let us say to him:

"Our case is simple. On the first of May, Dewey destroyed the Spanish fleet. This left the Archipelago in the hands of its proper and rightful owners, the Filipino nation. Their army numbered 30,000 men, and they were competent to whip out or starve out the little Spanish garrison; then the people could set up a government of their own devising.

Our traditions required that Dewey should now set up his warning sign, and go away. But the Master of the Game happened to think of another plan—the European plan. He acted upon it. This was, to send out an army—ostensibly to help the native patriots put the finishing touch upon their long and plucky struggle for independence, but really to take their land away from them and keep it. That is, in the interest of Progress and Civilization. The plan developed, stage by stage, and quite satisfactorily. We entered into a military alliance with the trusting Filipinos, and they hemmed in Manila on the land side, and by their valuable help the place, with its garrison of 8,000 or 10,000 Spaniards, was captured—a thing which we could not have accomplished unaided at that time. We got their help by—by ingenuity. We knew they were fighting for their independence, and that they had been at it for two years. We knew they supposed that we also were fighting in their worthy cause—just as we had helped the Cubans fight for Cuban independence—and we allowed them to go on thinking so. *Until Manila was ours and we could get along without them.* Then we showed our hand. Of course, they were surprised—that was natural; surprised and disappointed; disappointed and grieved. To them it looked un-American; uncharacteristic; foreign to our established traditions. And this was natural, too; for we were only playing the American Game in public—in private it was the European. It was neatly done, very neatly, and it bewildered them. They could not understand it; for we had been so friendly—so affectionate, even—with those simple-minded patriots! We, our own selves, had brought back out of exile their leader, their hero, their hope, their Washington—Aguinaldo; brought him in a warship, in high honor, under the sacred shelter and hospitality of the flag; brought him back and restored him to his people, and got their moving and eloquent gratitude for it. Yes, we had been so friendly to them, and had heartened them up in so many ways! We had lent them guns and ammunition; advised with them; exchanged pleasant courtesies with them; placed our sick and wounded in their kindly care; intrusted our Spanish prisoners to their humane and honest hands; fought shoulder to shoulder with them against 'the common enemy' (our own phrase); praised their courage, praised their gallantry, praised their mercifulness, praised their fine and honorable conduct; borrowed their trenches, borrowed strong positions which they had previously captured from the Spaniards; petted them, lied to them—officially proclaiming that our land and naval forces came to give them their freedom and displace the bad Spanish Government—fooled them, used them until we needed them no longer; then derided the sucked orange and threw it away. We kept the positions which we had beguiled them of; by and by, we moved a force forward and overlapped patriot ground—a clever thought, for we needed trouble, and this would produce it. A Filipino soldier, crossing the ground, where no one had a right to forbid him, was shot by our sentry. The badgered patriots resented this with arms, without waiting to know whether Aguinaldo, who was absent, would approve or not.

Aguinaldo did not approve; but that availed nothing. What we wanted, in the interest of Progress and Civilization, was the Archipelago, unencumbered by patriots struggling for independence; and War was what we needed. We clinched our opportunity. It is Mr. Chamberlain's case over again—at least in its motive and intention; and we played the game as adroitly as he played it himself."

At this point in our frank statement of fact to the Person Sitting in Darkness, we should throw in a little trade taffy about the Blessings of Civilization—for a change, and for the refreshment of his spirit—then go on with our tale:

"We and the patriots have captured Manila, Spain's ownership of the Archipelago and her sovereignty over it were at an end—obliterated—annihilated—not a rag or shred of either remaining behind. It was then that we conceived the divinely humorous idea of *buying* both of the specters from Spain! [It is quite safe to confess this to the Person Sitting in Darkness, since neither he nor any other sane person will believe it.] In buying those ghosts for twenty millions, we also contracted to take care of the friars and their accumulations. I think we also agreed to propagate leprosy and smallpox, but as to this there is doubt. But it is not important; persons afflicted with the friars do not mind other diseases.

"With our Treaty ratified, Manila subdued, and our Ghosts secured, we had no further use for Aguinaldo and the owners of the Archipelago. We forced a war, and we have been hunting America's guest and ally through the woods and swamps ever since."

At this point in the tale, it wil be well to boast a little of our war work and our heroisms in the field, so as to make our performance look as fine as England's in South Africa; but I believe it will not be best to emphasize this too much. We must be cautious. Of course, we must read the war telegrams to the Person, in order to keep up our frankness; but we can throw an air of humorousness over them, and that will modify their grim eloquence a little, and their rather indiscreet exhibitions of gory exultation. Before reading to him the following display heads of the dispatches of November 18, 1900, it will be well to practice on them in private first, so as to get the right tang of lightness and gayety into them:

ADMINISTRATION WEARY OF
PROTRACTED HOSTILITIES!

REAL WAR AHEAD FOR FILIPINO
REBELS![1]

WILL SHOW NO MERCY!
KITCHENER'S PLAN ADOPTED!

[1]"Rebels!" Mumble that funny word—don't let the Person catch it distinctly.

Kitchener knows how to handle disagreeable people who are fighting for their homes and their liberties, and we must let on that we are merely imitating Kitchener, and have no national interest in the matter, further than to get ourselves admired by the Great Family of Nations, in which august company our Master of the Game has bought a place for us in the back row.

Of course, we must not venture to ignore our General MacArthur's reports—oh, why do they keep on printing those embarrassing things?—we must drop them trippingly from the tongue and take the chances:

During the last ten months our losses have been 268 killed and 750 wounded; Filipino loss, *three thousand two hundred and twenty-seven killed,* and 694 wounded.

We must stand ready to grab the Person Sitting in Darkness, for he will swoon away at this confession, saying: "Good God! those 'niggers' spare their wounded, and the Americans massacre theirs!"

We must bring him to, and coax him and coddle him, and assure him that the ways of Providence are best, and that it would not become us to find fault with them; and then, to show him that we are only imitators, not originators, we must read the following passage from the letter of an American soldier lad in the Philippines to his mother, published in *Public Opinion,* of Decorah, Iowa, describing the finish of a victorious battle: *"We never left one alive. If one was wounded, we would run our bayonets through him."*

Having now laid all the historical facts before the Person Sitting in Darkness, we should bring him to again, and explain them to him. We should say to him:

"They look doubtful, but in reality they are not. There have been lies; yes, but they were told in a good cause. We have been treacherous; but that was only in order that real good might come out of apparent evil. True, we have crushed a deceived and confiding people; we have turned against the weak and the friendless who trusted us; we have stamped out a just and intelligent and well-ordered republic; we have stabbed an ally in the back and slapped the face of a guest; we have bought a Shadow from an enemy that hadn't it to sell; we have robbed a trusting friend of his land and his liberty; we have invited our clean young men to shoulder a discredited musket and do bandits' work under a flag which bandits have been accustomed to fear, not to follow; we have debauched America's honor and blackened her face before the world; but each detail was for the best. We know this. The Head of every State and Sovereignty in Christendom and 90 per cent of every legislative body in Christendom, including our Congress and our fifty state legislatures, are members not only of the church, but also of the Blessings-of-Civilization Trust. This world-girdling accumulation of trained morals, high principles, and justice cannot do an unright thing, an unfair thing, an ungenerous thing, an unclean thing. It knows what it is about. Give yourself no uneasiness; it is all right."

Now then, that will convince the Person. You will see. It will restore the Business. Also, it will elect the Master of the Game to the vacant place in the Trinity of our national gods; and there on their high thrones the Three will sit, age after age, in the people's sight, each bearing the Emblem of his service: Washington, the Sword of the Liberator; Lincoln, the Slave's Broken Chains; the Master, the Chains Repaired.

It will give the Business a splendid new start. You will see.

Everything is prosperous, now; everything is just as we should wish it. We have got the Archipelago, and we shall never give it up. Also, we have every reason to hope that we shall have an opportunity before very long to slip out of our congressional contract with Cuba and give her something better in the place of it. It is a rich country, and many of us are already beginning to see that the contract was a sentimental mistake. But now—right now—is the best time to do some profitable rehabilitating work—work that will set us up and make us comfortable, and discourage gossip. We cannot conceal from ourselves that, privately, we are a little troubled about our uniform. It is one of our prides; it is acquainted with honor; it is familiar with great deeds and noble; we love it, we revere it; and so this errand it is on makes us uneasy. And our flag—another pride of ours, our chiefest! We have worshiped it so; and when we have seen it in far lands—glimpsing it unexpectedly in that strange sky, waving its welcome and benediction to us—we have caught our breaths, and uncovered our heads, and couldn't speak, for a moment, for the thought of what it was to us and the great ideals it stood for. Indeed, we *must* do something about these things; it is easily managed. We can have a special one—our states do it: we can have just our usual flag, with the white stripes painted black and the stars replaced by the skull and crossbones.

And we do not need that Civil Commission out there. Having no powers, it has to invent them, and that kind of work cannot be effectively done by just anybody; an expert is required. Mr. Croker can be spared. We do not want the United States represented there, but only the Game.

By help of these suggested amendments, Progress and Civilization in that country can have a boom, and it will take in the Persons who are Sitting in Darkness, and we can resume Business at the old stand.

(1901)

*Nikolai Lenin*

# Speech at Meeting of the Petrograd Soviet of Workers' and Soldiers' Deputies

November 7, 1917

Comrades, the workers' and peasants' revolution, about the necessity of which the Bolsheviks have always spoken, has taken place.

What is the significance of this workers' and peasants' revolution? The significance of this revolution is, first of all, that we shall have a Soviet government, our own organ of power, in which the bourgeoisie will have no share whatever. The oppressed masses will themselves create a power. The old state apparatus will be shattered to its foundations and a new administrative apparatus set up in the shape of the Soviet organisations.

From now on, a new phase in the history of Russia begins, and this revolution, the third Russian revolution, should in the end lead to the victory of socialism.

One of our next tasks is to put an immediate end to the war. But in order to end this war, which is closely bound up with the present capitalist system, it is clear to everybody that capital itself must be overcome.

We shall be helped in this by the world working class movement, which is already beginning to develop in Italy, England and Germany.

The proposal for a just and immediate peace made by us to the international democracy will awaken an ardent response among the international proletarian masses everywhere. In order to strengthen this confidence of the proletariat, all the secret treaties must be published immediately.

Within Russia a huge section of the peasantry have said: We have played enough with the capitalists, we will now march with the workers. We shall secure the confidence of the peasants by a single decree putting an end to landed proprietorship. The peasants will understand that the salvation of the peasantry lies only in an alliance with the workers. We shall institute genuine workers' control over production.

We have now learnt to work harmoniously. This is attested by the revolution that has just taken place. We possess the force of mass organisation which will overcome everything and which will lead the proletariat to the world revolution.

In Russia we must now set about building a proletarian socialist state.

Long live the world socialist revolution!

*from* **Speech before the Reichstag**

July 13, 1934

Commissioned thereto by the Government the President of the Reichstag, Hermann Goering, has called you together today to give me the possibility of explaining before this best-qualified Forum of the Nation events which may well remain for all time in our history as a memory alike of sorrow and of warning. Out of a sum of material causes and personal guilt, from human inadequacy and human defects, there arose for our young Reich a crisis which only too easily might for an incalculable period have produced consequences completely disastrous. To make clear to you and thereby to the nation how this crisis arose and how it was overcome is the aim of my speech. The content of this speech will be of ruthless frankness. Only in its scope do I feel bound to impose upon myself some limitation, and that limitation is on the one side conditioned by the interests of the Reich and on the other side by bounds which are set by the sentiment of shame.

When on January 30, 1933, Field Marshal and President of the Reich von Hindenburg entrusted me with the leadership of the newly formed German Government, the National Socialist party took over a State which both politically and economically was in complete decline. All political forces of the former state of affairs which had just been brought to a close had their share in this decline, and consequently a share in guilt. Since the abdication of the Kaiser and the German princes the German people had been delivered into the hands of men who, as the representatives of our past world of parties, had either consciously induced this decline or had weakly suffered it to continue. Beginning with the Marxist revolutionaries and proceeding by way of the Center till one reached the Bourgeois Nationalists—all parties and their leaders were given an opportunity to prove their capacity to govern Germany. Endless coalitions allowed them to put to the test their political arts and their economic skill. They have all failed miserably. January 30 [1933] was therefore not the day when our Government formally took over responsibility from the hands of another Government, it was rather the final liquidation, long desired by the nation, of an intolerable state of affairs.

It is essential that this should be clearly stated since, as subsequent events have proved, some individuals would seem to have forgotten that previously they were given full opportunity for demonstrating their political capacities. There is no one in Germany who could have any ground, even did he so wish, to charge the National Socialist Movement with having obstructed or even blocked the way to political forces which offered any hope of success. Fate, for reasons which we cannot fathom, condemned our people for fifteen years to serve as the field on which these politicians could make their experiments – as the rabbit in the hands of the vivisector.

It may have been interesting and pleasurable for the outside world – especially for the world that is ill-disposed toward us – to follow these experiments; for the German people they were as painful as they were humiliating. Look back on this period and before your eyes let all those figures pass who succeeded each other as Chancellors of the Reich. In what land were the scales of providence more often brought into use, and where more frequently was the verdict passed that the object weighed had fallen short of the due weight? No! We National Socialists have the right to refuse to be counted as members of this line. On January 30, 1933, it was not a case of a new government being formed as had happened times without number before, but a new regime had superseded an old and sick age.

This historic act of the liquidation of that most melancholy period in our nation's life which now lies behind us was legalized by the German people itself. For we have not seized possession of power as usurpers, as did the men of November 1918; we have received power constitutionally and legally. We have not made a revolution as uprooted anarchists, but, as executing the nation's will, we have set aside a regime born of rebellion, and we have seen our task to lie not in maintaining power at the point of the bayonet, but in finding that power in the heart of our people, and anchoring it there.

When today I read in a certain foreign newspaper that at the present time I am filled with profound anxieties, and at this moment in particular with economic anxieties, I have only one answer for these scribblers: assuredly that is true, but it is not merely today that anxiety tortures me; it has done so for a long time past. If it was formerly the anxiety for our people which led us to protect our people in the war which, despite its innocence, had been forced upon it, after the collapse it was the far greater anxiety for the future which turned us into revolutionaries. And when after fifteen years of struggle at last we received the leadership of the nation, this torturing anxiety not only did not loosen its hold upon us, but on the contrary did but embrace us the more closely. I may be believed when I assure you that never yet in my life have I allowed myself to be anxious for my own personal fate. But I confess that from the day when the confidence of the Field Marshal appointed for me my place I have borne the burden of that heavy anxiety which the present and the future of our people lays upon us all. . . .

When I as Chancellor of the Reich came into the Wilhelmstrasse, the authority of the Reich had become a worthless phantom. The spirit of revolt and insubordination dominated the German States and communes. The shadows of the most melancholy political past of the German people rose alarmingly before us. Particularism and Separatism insolently proclaimed themselves as the new German conception of the

State. From the internal weakness of the Reich sprang its undignified attitude toward the world without. It had once more become a humiliation to confess publicly that one was a German. The spirit of insubordination and of internal revolt within a few months we exterminated and destroyed. While fully respecting the essential character of our German tribes we have strengthened the authority of the Reich as the expression of the common will of our people's life and have made it supreme. The German Reich is today no longer a merely geographical conception: it has become a political unity. We have directed our people's development on to lines which only two years ago were regarded as unattainable. And just as within the Reich we firmly secured the unity and therewith the future of the German people, so in the sphere of foreign policy we have resolutely championed the rights of our people. . . .

The features which marked our former political confusion have not been set aside because we destroyed them, but because the German people removed them from its heart. And I must—today and in this place—confess that assuredly our work would have been utterly vain, and must have been vain, had not the German people given us its confidence and its loyal cooperation in so large a measure. Our success is due to the 41½ million men and women from all walks of life who gave us no merely superficial 'Yes,' but devoted themselves with all their hearts to the new regime.

To them our success is mainly due. Without their confiding trust, without their patient forbearance, without their devotion and readiness for sacrifice, the work of German recovery would never have succeeded. They are, as the supporters of the people's rebirth, at the same time the best representatives of the people. They are in truth the German people. . . .

And over against this positive world of the German spirit, the incorporation of the true values of our people, there stands also, it is true, a small negative world. They take no part in their hearts in the work of German recovery and restoration. First there is the small body of those international disintegrators of a people who as apostles of the *Weltanschauung* of communism alike in the political and economic sphere systematically incite the peoples, break up established order, and endeavor to produce chaos. We see evidence of the activity of these international conspirators all about us. Up and down the countries the flames of revolt run over the peoples. Streets riots, fights at the barricades, mass terrorism, and the individualistic propaganda of disintegration disturb today nearly all the countries of the world. Even in Germany some single fools and criminals of this type still again and again seek to exercise their destructive activity. Since the destruction of the Communist party we experience one attempt after another, though growing ever weaker as time passes, to found and to sustain the work of communistic organizations of a more or less anarchistic character. Their method is always the same. . . .

The second group of the discontented consists of those political leaders who feel that their political future has been closed since January 30, but yet are still unable to accept the irrevocability of this fact. The more time veils with the gracious mantle of forgetfulness their own incapacity, the more do they think themselves entitled gradually to bring themselves back into the people's memory. But since their incapacity was not formerly limited to any special period but was born in them by nature, they are today, too, unable to prove their value in any positive and useful work, but they see the fulfillment of their life's task to lie in a criticism which is as treacherous as it is mendacious. With them, too, the people has no sympathy. The National Socialist State can neither be seriously threatened by them nor in any way damaged.

A third group of destructive elements is formed of those revolutionaries whose former relation to the State was shattered by the events of 1918; they became uprooted and thereby lost altogether all sympathy with any ordered human society. They became revolutionaries who favored revolution for its own sake and desired to see revolution established as a permanent condition. We all formerly suffered under the frightful tragedy that we, as disciplined and loyal soldiers, were suddenly faced with a revolt of mutineers who managed to seize possession of the State. Each of us had been brought up to respect the laws and to reverence authority, we had been trained in obedience to the commands and regulations issued by the authorities, in a subordination of our wills in face of the State's representatives. Now the revolution of deserters and mutineers forced upon us in our thought the abandonment of these conceptions. . . .

Amongst the numberless documents which during the last week it was my duty to read, I have discovered a diary with the notes of a man who, in 1918, was thrown into the path of resistance to the laws and who now lives in a world in which law in itself seems to be a provocation to resistance. It is an unnerving document—an unbroken tale of conspiracy and continual plotting: it gives one an insight into the mentality of men who, without realizing it, have found in nihilism their final confession of faith. Incapable of any true cooperation, with a desire to oppose all order, filled with hatred against every authority, their unrest and disquietude can find satisfaction only in some conspiratorial activity of the mind perpetually plotting the disintegration of whatever at any moment may exist. Many of them in the early days of our struggle have together with us fulminated against the State which is now no more, but their inner lack of discipline led most of them, even during the course of the struggle, away from the disciplined National Socialist Movement.

The last remnant appeared to have separated itself from us after January 30. The link with the National Socialist Movement was severed at the moment when the Movement itself, now representing the State, became the object of their pathological aversion. They are on principle enemies of every authority, and therefore there can be no hope at all of their conversion. . . .

This third group of pathological enemies of the State is dangerous because they represent a reservoir of those ready to co-operate in every attempt at a revolt, at least just for so long as a new order does not begin to crystallize out of the state of chaotic confusion.

I must now mention the fourth group, which often perhaps even against its own will does in fact carry on a truly destructive activity. The group is composed of those persons who belong to a comparatively small section of society and who, having nothing to do, find time and opportunity to report orally everything that has happened in order thus to bring some interesting and important variety into their otherwise completely purposeless lives. For while the overwhelming majority of the nation has to earn its daily bread in toilsome work, in certain strata of life there are still folk whose sole activity it is to do nothing, only to need afterwards a rest-cure from doing nothing. The more paltry is the life of such a drone, the more eagerly will he seize upon anything which may give some interesting content to the vacuity of his mind. Personal and political gossip is eagerly swallowed and even more eagerly handed on. Since these men as a result of doing nothing do not possess any living relation to the millions which form the mass of the nation, their life is confined in its range to the circle within which they move. Every bit of gossip which strays into this circle reverberates backwards and forwards like figures reflected in two distorting mirrors. Because their whole ego is full of nothingness, and since they find a similar nothingness amongst their like, they look upon the whole world as equally empty; they come to think that the outlook of their own circle is the outlook of everyone. Their anxieties, they imagine, form the cares of the whole nation. In reality this little cloud of drones is but a State within the State; it has no contact with the life, the sentiments, the hopes and cares of the rest of the people. They are, however, dangerous because they are veritable bacillus-carriers of unrest and uncertainty, of rumors, assertions, lies and suspicions, of slanders and fears, and thus they contribute to produce gradually a state of nervousness which spreads amongst the people so that in the end it is hard to find or recognize where its influence stops. . . .

The first idle talk which one heard here and there of a new revolution, of a new upheaval, of a new revolt, gradually grew in intensity to such an extent that only an irresponsible statesmanship could afford to ignore it. One could no longer simply dismiss as silly chatter all the information which came to us in hundreds and at last in thousands of reports both orally and in writing. Only three months ago the leaders of the Party were still convinced that it was simply the irresponsible gossip of political reactionaries, of Marxist anarchists, or of all sorts of idlers with which they had to deal—gossip which had no support in fact.

In the middle of March I took steps to have preparations made for a new wave of propaganda which was to render the German people immune from any attempt to spread fresh poison. At the same time I gave orders to certain departments of the Party administration to trace the rumors of a new revolution which were continually cropping up and to find out, if possible, the sources from which they came. The result was that certain tendencies appeared in the ranks of some of the higher leaders of the SA which were bound to cause the gravest anxiety. At first it was a case of general symptoms, the inner connections of which were not at once clear:

1. Against my express order, and in despite of declarations made to me through the Chief of Staff, Roehm, there had been such an increase in the numbers of the SA that the internal homogeneity of this unique organization must be endangered.

2. Education in the National Socialist *Weltanschauung* in the above-mentioned sections of individual higher SA authorities had been more and more neglected.

3. The natural relationship between the Party and the SA began slowly to be weakened. We were able to establish that efforts were being made, as it seemed systematically, to withdraw the SA more and more from the mission appointed for it by me and to use it in the service of other tasks or other interests.

4. Promotions to posts of leadership in the SA when they were tested showed that a completely one-sided valuation had been set on purely external skill or often only on a supposed intellectual capacity. The great body of the oldest and most loyal SA men was always more and more neglected when appointments to the post of leader were made or when vacancies had to be filled, while a quite incomprehensible preference was shown for those who had been enlisted in the year 1933 who were not specially highly respected in the Movement. Often only a few months' membership in the Party or even only in the SA was enough to secure promotion to a high position in the SA which the old SA leader could not reach after years of service.

5. The behavior of these individual SA leaders who had for the greater part not grown up with the Movement at all was false to National Socialist standards and often positively revolting. It could not be overlooked that it was precisely in these circles that one source of the unrest in the Movement was discovered, in that their incomplete practical National Socialism sought to veil itself in very unseemly demands for a new revolution.

I drew the attention of the Chief of Staff, Roehm, to these abuses and to a number of others without meeting with any appreciable help in their removal, indeed without any recognizable concurrence on his part with my objections.

In the months of April and May there was a constant increase in these complaints, and it was then that I received for the first time reports, confirmed by official documents, of conversations which had been held by individual higher leaders of the SA and which can only be described as "gross impropriety." For the first time in some official documents we obtained irrefutable evidence that in these conversations references had been made to the necessity for a new revolution and that leaders had received instructions to prepare themselves both materially and in spirit for such a new revolution. The Chief of Staff, Roehm, endeavored to maintain that these conversations had not in fact been held and that the reports were to be explained as veiled attacks upon the SA.

The confirmation of some of these cases through the statements of those who had been present led to the more serious ill-treatment of these witnesses who for the most part came from the ranks of the old SA. Already by the end of April the leaders of the Party and a number of State institutions concerned in the matter were convinced that a certain group of the higher SA leaders was consciously contributing toward the alienation of the SA from the Party as well as from the other institutions of the State, or at least was not opposing this alienation. The attempt to remedy this state of affairs through the normal official channels always remained unsuccessful. The Chief of Staff, Roehm, promised me personally over and over again that he would inquire into these cases and that he would remove or punish the guilty parties. But no visible change in the situation resulted.

In the month of May numerous charges of offenses committed by SA leaders, both those of high rank and of intermediate position, were received by officials of the Party and of the State; these offenses were supported by official documents and could not be denied. Provocative speeches led directly to intolerable excesses. The Minister-President Goering had already previously endeavored, so far as Prussia was concerned, to maintain the authority of the will of the National Socialist State over the self-will of individual elements. In some other German States, meanwhile, the authorities of the Party and the officials had been compelled to oppose single intolerable excesses. Some of the responsible parties were taken into custody. I have before this always stressed the fact that an authoritarian regime is under special obligations. When one demands of a people that it should put blind confidence in its leaders, then for their part these leaders must deserve this confidence through their achievement and through specially good behavior. Mistakes and errors may in individual cases slip in, but they are to be eradicated. Bad behavior, drunken excesses, the molestation of peaceful decent folk—these are unworthy of a leader, they are not National Socialist, and they are in the highest degree detestable.

I have for this reason always insisted that in their conduct and behavior higher demands should be made of National Socialist leaders than of the rest of the people. He who desires to receive higher respect than others must meet this demand by a higher achievement. The most elementary demand that can be made of him is that in his life he should not give a shameful example to those about him. I do not desire, therefore, that National Socialists guilty of such offenses should be judged and punished more leniently than are other fellow-countrymen of theirs; rather, I expect that a leader who forgets himself in this way should be punished with greater rigor than would be an unknown man in a like case. And here I would make no distinction between leaders of the political organizations and leaders of the formations of our SA, SS, Hitler Youth, etc.

The resolution of the National Socialist Government to put an end to such excesses of individual unworthy elements which did but cover with shame the Party and the SA led to a very violent counter-activity on the part of the Chief of Staff. National Socialist fighters of the earliest days, some of whom had striven for nearly fifteen years for the victory of the Movement and now as high State officials in leading positions in our State represented the Movement, were called to account for the action which they had taken against such unworthy elements: that is to say, that through Courts of Honor, composed in part of some of the youngest members of the Party or even at times of those who were not members of the Party at all, the Chief of Staff, Roehm, sought to secure the punishment of these oldest Party combatants.

These disagreements led to very serious exchanges of views between the Chief of Staff and myself, and it was in these interviews that for the first time doubts of the loyalty of this man began to rise in my mind. Though for many months I had rejected every such idea, though previously through the years I had protected this man with my person in unswerving loyalty and comradeship, now gradually warnings which I received—especially from my deputy in the leadership of the Party, Rudolf Hess—began to induce suspicions which even with the best of will I was not able to stifle.

After the month of May there could be no further doubt that the Chief of Staff, Roehm, was busied with ambitious schemes which, if they were realized, could lead only to the most violent disturbances.

If during these months I hesitated again and again before taking a final decision that was due to two considerations:

1. I could not lightly persuade myself to believe that a relation which I thought to be founded on loyalty could be only a lie.

2. I still always cherished the secret hope that I might be able to spare the Movement and my SA the shame of such a disagreement, and that it might be possible to remove the mischief without severe conflicts. It must be confessed that the last days of May continuously brought to light more and more disquieting facts.

The Chief of Staff now began to alienate himself from the Party not only in spirit but also in his whole external manner of life. All the principles through which we had grown to greatness lost their validity. The life which the Chief of Staff and with him a certain circle began to lead was from any National Socialist point of view intolerable. It was not only terrible that he himself and the circle of those who were devoted to him should violate all laws of decency and modest behavior, it was still worse that now this poison began to spread in ever wider circles. The worst of all was that gradually out of a certain common disposition of character there began to be formed within the SA a party which became the kernel of a conspiracy directed not only against the normal views of a healthy people but also against the security of the State. The review which took place in the month of May of promotions in certain SA districts led to the horrible realization that men without regard to services rendered to the National Socialist party or to the SA had been promoted to positions in the SA solely because they belonged to the circle of those possessing this special disposition. Individual cases with which you are familiar, such, for example, as that of the Standard-Leader Schmidt in Breslau, disclosed a picture of conditions which could only be regarded as intolerable. My order to proceed against the offenders was followed in theory, but in fact it was sabotaged.

Gradually from amongst the leaders of the SA there emerged three groups: a small group of elements which were held together through a like disposition, men who were ready for any action and who had given themselves blindly into the hands of the Chief of Staff, Roehm. The principal members of this group were the SA leaders Ernst from Berlin, Heines in Silesia, Hayn in Saxony, and Heydebreck in Pomerania. Besides these there was a second group of SA leaders who did not belong to the former group in spirit but felt themselves bound to obey the Chief of Staff, Roehm, solely from a simple conception of a soldier's duty. Over against these stood a third group of leaders who made no secret of their inner disgust and reprobation and were in consequence in part removed from responsible posts, in part thrust aside, and in many respects left out of account.

At the head of this group of SA leaders, who because of their fundamental decency had been hardly treated, stood the present Chief of Staff, Lutze, and the leader of the SS, Himmler.

Without ever informing me, and when at first I never dreamt of any such action, the Chief of Staff, Roehm, through the agency of an utterly corrupt swindler—a certain Herr von A—, entered into relations with General Schleicher. General Schleicher was the man who gave external expression to the secret wish of the Chief of Staff, Roehm. He it was who defined the latter's views in concrete form and maintained that:

1. The present regime in Germany cannot be supported.

2. Above all the Army and all national associations must be united in a single band.

3. The only man who could be considered for such a position was the Chief of Staff, Roehm.

4. Herr von Papen must be removed and he himself would be ready

to take the position of Vice-Chancellor, and that in addition further important changes must be made in the Cabinet of the Reich.

As always happens in such cases there now began the search after the men for the new Government, always under the view that I myself should at least for the present be left in the position which I now hold.

The execution of these proposals of General von Schleicher was bound, as soon as Point 2 was reached, to come up against my unalterable opposition. Both from a consideration of the facts and from a consideration of personal character it would never have been possible for me to consent to a change in the Reich Ministry of War and to the appointment of the Chief of Staff, Roehm, to that Ministry.

Firstly: the consideration of the facts: for fourteen years I have stated consistently that the fighting organizations of the Party are political institutions and that they have nothing to do with the army. On the facts of the case it would be, in my opinion, to disavow this view of mine and my fourteen years of political life if I were now to summon to the head of the army the leader of the SA. In November, 1923, I proposed that an officer should lead the army and not the man who was then the leader of my SA, Captain Goering.

Secondly: the consideration of human character. On this point it would have been impossible for me ever to concur in the proposal of General von Schleicher. When these plans became known to me my picture of the value of the character of the Chief of Staff, Roehm, was already such that before my conscience and for the sake of the honor of the army I could no longer under any circumstances contemplate admitting him to this post: above all, the supreme head of the army is the Field Marshal and President of the Reich. As Chancellor I gave my oath into his keeping. His person is for us all inviolate. The promise which I gave him that I would preserve the army as a non-political instrument of the Reich is for me binding, both from my inmost conviction and also from the word which I have given. But further, any such act would have been impossible for me on the human side in the face of the War Minister of the Reich. Both I myself and all of us are happy to be able to see in him a man of honor from the crown of his head to the soles of his feet. He reconciled the army with those who were once revolutionaries and has linked it up with their Government today and he has done this from the deepest convictions of his heart. He has made his own in truest loyalty the principle for which I myself will stand to my last breath.

In the State there is only one bearer of arms, and that is the army; there is only one bearer of the political will, and that is the National Socialist party. Any thought of consenting to the plans of General von Schleicher would be, so far as I am concerned, not only disloyalty to the Field Marshal and the War Minister, but also disloyalty to the army. For just as General von Blomberg as War Minister in the National Socialist State fulfills his duty in the highest sense of the word, so do, also, the other officers and the soldiers. I cannot demand from them that as individuals each of them should take up a definite position towards our Movement, but not one of them has lost the true position of loyal service to the National Socialist State. And, further, I could not without the most compelling cause have permitted the removal of men who as a united body on January 30 gave me their promise to co-operate in the salvation of the Reich and of the people. . . .

Since the Chief of Staff, Roehm, was himself uncertain whether any attempt on the lines which I have described might not well meet with resistance from me, the first plan was devised in order to achieve the desired result by compulsion. Extensive preparations were made, in the first place:

1. Psychological conditions which should favor the outbreak of a second revolution were to be systematically created. For this end by means of the SA propaganda authorities themselves the assertion was spread through the ranks of the SA that the army intended to disband the SA, and it was later added that unfortunately I myself had been won over to the support of this plan. A wretched and infamous lie!

2. The SA must forthwith anticipate this attack, and in a second revolution must remove the reactionary elements on the one hand and the opposition of the Party on the other. Authority in the State must be entrusted to the leaders of the SA.

3. To this end the SA should make as rapidly as possible all the necessary material preparations. Through different pretexts, e.g. by the lying statement that he was anxious to carry through a scheme of social relief for the benefit of the SA, the Chief of Staff, Roehm, succeeded in collecting contributions running into millions of marks. Twelve million marks were raised for these objects.

4. In order to be in a position to deliver ruthlessly the most decisive blows there were formed under the title of "Staff-Guards" groups of terrorists specially sworn in for the purpose. The old SA man had for more than a decade gone starving in the service of the Movement; now these new formations were paid troops, and the personal character and the purpose for which they were enlisted cannot be more clearly shown than by the truly fearful list of the punishments which they had previously incurred; indeed the old, true SA leader and SA man now very quickly were thrust into the background in favor of those elements which had enjoyed no political training but were better qualified for the kind of work for which they were intended. At certain gatherings of leaders as well as on holiday-trips gradually the SA leaders concerned in the plan were brought together and dealt with individually, that is to say, that while the members of the inner circle systematically prepared the main action, the second and larger circle of SA leaders was only given general information to the effect that a second revolution was on the way, that this second revolution had no other object than to restore to me personally my freedom of action, and that therefore the new—

and this time bloody – rising – "The Night of the Long Knives" was their ghastly name for it – was exactly what I myself desired. The necessity for the initiative of the SA was explained by reference to my own inability to come to any decision: that disability would be removed only when I was faced with an accomplished fact. Presumably it was by means of these untrue pretexts that the preparation for the scheme so far as foreign policy was concerned was given to Herr von Detten. General von Schleicher saw to this aspect of the scheme in part personally, but left the practical side of the negotiations to his intermediary General von Bredow. Gregor Strasser was brought in.

At the beginning of June I made a last attempt and had yet another talk with Roehm which lasted nearly five hours and was prolonged until midnight. I informed him that from numberless rumors and from numerous assurances and statements of old, loyal comrades and SA leaders I had gained the impression that by certain unscrupulous elements a national-bolshevist rising was being prepared which could only bring untold misery upon Germany. . . . The Chief of Staff left this interview after assuring me that the reports were partly untrue and partly exaggerated, and that moreover he would for the future do everything in his power to set things to rights.

The result of the interview, however, was that the Chief of Staff, Roehm, recognizing that for the undertaking which he was planning he could in no circumstances count on my personal support, now prepared to remove me personally from the scene. To this end it was explained to the larger circle of SA leaders who had been drawn into the plot that I myself was in thorough agreement with the proposed undertaking, but that I personally must know nothing about it or else that I wished on the outbreak of the rising immediately to be arrested and kept in custody for some twenty-four or forty-eight hours in order thus through the *fait accompli* to be relieved from an awkward responsibility which must otherwise arise for me in the sphere of our foreign relations. This explanation is conclusively illustrated by the fact that meanwhile care had been taken to bribe the man whose task it was later to carry through my removal. Standard-leader Uhl, a few hours before his death, confessed that he had been ready to execute such an order.

The first plan for the revolution was founded on the idea of granting leave to the SA. During this period of leave, since any plausible excuse was lacking, inexplicable riots were to break out similar to the conditions in August, 1932. These would compel me to summon the Chief of Staff, who alone would be in a position to restore order; for this purpose I should have to entrust him with full executive authority. But when meanwhile it had been clearly shown that in no circumstances could my willingness to give such an order be relied upon, this plan was abandoned and direct action was now contemplated.

That action was to begin by a blow struck without any warning in Berlin: there was to be an assault upon the Government building, I myself was to be taken into custody so that further steps, as though ordered by me, could follow without any hindrance. The conspirators calculated that commands given in my name to the SA would immediately call into action the SA throughout the Reich, and also that thereby there would result automatically a division in all the other forces of the State ranged in opposition to the rising.

The Chief of Staff, Roehm, the Gruppenführer (Group-leader) Ernst, the Obergruppenführer Heines, Hayn, and a number of others declared in the presence of witnesses that immediately there was to follow a conflict of the bloodiest kind, lasting several days, with their opponents. The economic side of such a development was dismissed with positively insane irresponsibility: bloody terrorism in one way or another was to provide the necessary means. Here I must deal with the view that every successful revolution provides in itself its own justification. The Chief of Staff, Roehm, and his followers declared their revolution to be a necessity because only so could the victory of pure National Socialism receive its full justification. But at this point I must assert, both in the interest of the present and of posterity, that these men no longer had any right at all to appeal to National Socialism as their *Weltanschauung*. Their lives had become as evil as the lives of those whom we defeated in 1933 and whose places we took. The behavior of these men made it impossible for me to ask them to my house or, even if it were once only, to enter the house of the Chief of Staff in Berlin. It is difficult to conceive what would have become of Germany if these people had won the day. The greatness of the danger could not be fully realized until we received the communications which now reached Germany from abroad. English and French papers began with increasing frequency to speak of an upheaval which would shortly take place in Germany, and from the ever-growing stream of communications it was clear that the conspirators had systematically sought to foster the view in foreign countries that the revolution of the genuine National Socialists was at hand and that the existing regime was now incapable of action. General von Bredow, who as political agent in foreign affairs for General von Schleicher looked after these connections, worked in sympathy with those reactionary circles who—though not perhaps standing in any direct connection with this conspiracy—yet readily allowed themselves to be misused as subterranean purveyors of information for foreign Powers.

Thus at the end of June I had made up my mind to put an end to this impossible development, and that, too, before the blood of ten thousand innocent folk should seal the catastrophe. . . . I decided that on Saturday, June 30, I would deprive the Chief of Staff of his office and for the time being keep him in custody and would arrest a number of SA leaders whose crimes were unquestioned. Since it was doubtful, when things had reached so threatening a climax, whether the Chief of Staff, Roehm, would have come to Berlin at all, or indeed anywhere else, I decided to go in person to a discussion amongst SA leaders which had been announced to be held at Wiessee. Relying on the authority of my own personality and on my power of decision which had never failed me in the hour of need, I determined that there at twelve o'clock midday I would deprive the Chief of Staff of his office, I would arrest those SA leaders who were principally responsible, and in an earnest appeal to the others I would recall them to their duty. However, in the course of June 29, I received such threatening intelligence concerning the last preparations for action that I was forced at midday to interrupt an inspection of a workers' camp in Westphalia in order to hold myself in readiness for all emergencies. At one o'clock in the night I received from Berlin and Munich two urgent messages concerning alarm-summonses: firstly that for Berlin an alarm-muster had been ordered for four o'clock in the afternoon, that for the transport of the regular shock-formations the requisition of lorries had been ordered, and that this requisition was now proceeding, and that promptly at five o'clock action was to begin with a surprise attack: the Government building was to be occupied. Gruppenführer Ernst with this end in view had not after all gone to Wiessee but had remained behind in Berlin to undertake the conduct of operations there.

Secondly: in Munich the alarm-summons had already been given to the SA; they had been ordered to assemble at nine o'clock in the evening. The SA formations had not been dismissed to their homes, they were already stationed in their alarm-quarters. That is mutiny! I and no one else am the commander of the SA!

In these circumstances I could make but one decision. If disaster was to be prevented at all, action must be taken with lightning speed. Only a ruthless and bloody intervention might still perhaps stifle the spread of the revolt. And then there could be no question that it was better that a hundred mutineers, plotters, and conspirators should be destroyed than that ten thousand innocent SA men should be allowed to shed their blood. For if once criminal activity was set in motion in Berlin, then the consequences were indeed unthinkable. The effect which had been produced by the fact that the conspirators purported to act in my name was proved by the distressing fact that, for instance, these mutineers in Berlin had succeeded through citing my authority in securing for their plot four armored cars from unsuspecting police-officers and further by the fact that the plotters Heines and Hayn in Saxony and Silesia through their appeals had made police-officers doubtful which side they should support in the coming conflict between the SA and the enemies of Hitler. It was at last clear to me that only one man could oppose and must oppose the Chief of Staff. It was to me that he had pledged his loyalty and broken that pledge, and for that I alone must call him to account!

At one o'clock in the night I received the last dispatches telling me of the alarm-summonses; at two o'clock in the morning I flew to Munich. Meanwhile Minister-President Goering had previously received from me the commission that if I proceeded to apply a purge he was to take similar measures at once in Berlin and in Prussia. With an iron fist he beat down the attack on the National Socialist State before it could develop. The necessity for acting with lightning speed meant that in this decisive hour I had very few men with me. In the presence of the Minister Goebbels and of the new Chief of Staff the action of which you are already informed was executed and brought to a close in Munich. Although only a few days before I had been prepared to exercise clemency, at this hour there was no place for any such consideration. Mutinies are suppressed in accordance with laws of iron which are eternally the same. *If anyone reproaches me and ask why I did not resort to the regular courts of justice for conviction of the offenders, then of that I can say to him is this: in this hour I was responsible for the fate of the German people, and thereby I became* the *supreme Justiciar of the German people!*

Mutinous divisions have in all periods been recalled to order by decimation. Only one State has failed to make any use of its Articles of War and this State paid for that failure by collapse—Germany. I did not wish to deliver up the young Reich to the fate of the old Reich. I gave the order to shoot those who were the ringleaders in this treason, and I further gave the order to burn out down to the raw flesh the ulcers of this poisoning of the wells in our domestic life and of the poisoning of the outside world. And I further ordered that if any of the mutineers should attempt to resist arrest, they were immediately to be struck down with armed force. The nation must know that its existence—and that is guaranteed through its internal order and security—can be threatened by no one with impunity! And everyone must know for all future time that if he raises his hand to strike the State, then certain death is his lot. And every National Socialist must know that no rank and no position can protect him from his personal responsibility and therefore from his punishment. I have prosecuted thousands of our former opponents on account of their corruption. I should in my own mind reproach myself if I were now to tolerate similar offences in our own ranks. No people and no Government can help it if creatures arise such as we once knew in Germany, a Kutisker for example, such as France came to know in a Stavisky, or such as we today have once more experienced—men whose aim is to sin against a nation's interests. But every people is itself guilty if it does not find the strength to destroy such noxious creatures. If people bring against me the objection that only a judicial procedure could precisely weigh the measure of the guilt and of its expiation, then against this view I lodge my most solemn protest. He who rises against Germany is a traitor to his country: and the traitor to his country is not to be punished according to the range and the extent of his act, but according to the purpose which that act has revealed. He who in his heart purposes to raise a mutiny and thereby breaks loyalty, breaks faith, breaks sacred pledges, he can expect nothing else than that he himself will be the first sacrifice. I have no intention to have the little culprits shot and to spare the great criminals. It is not my duty to inquire whether it was too hard a lot which was inflicted on those conspirators, these agitators and destroyers, these poisoners of the well-springs of German public opinion and in a wider sense of world opinion: it is not mine to consider which of them suffered too severely: I have only to see to it that Germany's lot should not be intolerable. A foreign journalist, who enjoys the privileges of a guest in our midst, protests in the name of the wives and children of those who have been shot and awaits the day when from their ranks there will come vengeance. To this gentleman I can say only one thing in answer: women and children have ever been the innocent victims of the criminal acts of men. I, too, have pity for them, but I believe that the suffering inflicted on them through the guilt of these men is but a minute fraction in comparison with the suffering that perhaps ten thousand German women would have had to endure if this act had been successful. A foreign diplomat explains that the meeting with Schleicher and Roehm was of course of an entirely harmless character. That matter I need not discuss with anyone. In the political sphere conceptions of what is harmless and what is not will never coincide. But when three traitors in Germany arrange and effect a meeting with a foreign statesman which they themselves characterize as "serviceable," when they effect this meeting after excluding every member of their staff, when they give strict orders that no word of this meeting shall reach me, then I shall have such men shot dead even when it should prove true that at a consultation which was thus kept secret from me they talked of nothing save the weather, old coins, and like topics.

*The penalty for these crimes was hard and severe. Nineteen higher SA leaders, thirty-one leaders and members of the SA, were shot, and further, for complicity in the plot, three leaders of the SS, while thirteen SA leaders and civilians who attempted to resist arrest lost their lives. Three more committed suicide. Five who did not belong to the SA but were members of the Party were shot for taking part in the plot. Finally there were also shot three members of the SS who had been guilty of scandalous ill-treatment of those who had been taken into protective custody.*

In order to prevent political passion and exasperation venting itself in lynch justice on further offenders when the danger was removed and the revolt could be regarded as suppressed, still on Sunday, July 1, strictest orders were given that all further retribution should cease. Thereby from the night of Sunday, July 1, the normal state of affairs was reestablished. A number of acts of violence which do not stand in any connection with the plot will be brought before the ordinary courts for judgment.

These sacrifices may indeed be heavy, but they will not be vain if from them once and for all results the conviction that every attempt at treason will be broken down without respect of person. If at some hour or another fate should summon me from my place, then I confidently hope that my successor will not act otherwise, and if he too must give place to another, that the third after us will be ready to protect the security of people and of nation with no less resolution.

If in the two weeks that now lie behind us a part of the foreign press in place of any objective and just report of events has flooded the world with untrue and incorrect assertions and communications, I cannot admit the validity of the excuse that it was impossible to obtain any other information. In most cases it needed only a short telephone call to the authorities concerned in order to show that most of these assertions could not be sustained. When in particular the report was spread that among the victims of the conspiracy there were included even members of the Cabinet of the Reich, it would not have been difficult to establish that the contrary was the case. The assertion that the Vice-Chancellor, von Papen, that the Minister Seldte, or other members of the Cabinet of the Reich had been connected with the mutineers is most strongly contradicted by the fact that one of the first intentions of the mutineers was the murder of these men. Similarly all reports of any complicity in the plot on the part of any one of the German princes or of any pursuit of them is free invention. If finally during the last few days an English paper can report that I was at present suffering from a nervous breakdown, it would have needed only a small inquiry to establish the truth. I can only assure these anxious reporters that neither in the War nor after the War have I ever suffered such a breakdown, but this time I have indeed suffered the severest breakdown of the trust and faith which I had placed in a man for whose protection I had done everything in my power, for whom I had actually sacrificed myself. . . .

In these days which have been days of severe trial both for me and for its members the SA has preserved the spirit of loyalty. Thus for the third time the SA has proved that it is mine, just as I will prove at any time that I belong to my SA men. In a few weeks' time the brown shirt will once more dominate the streets of Germany and will give to one and all clear evidence that because it has overcome its grievous distress the life of National Socialist Germany is only the more vigorous. . . .

*Winston Churchill*

# On Becoming Prime Minister

May 13, 1940

On Friday evening last I received His Majesty's Commission to form a new Administration. It was the evident wish and will of Parliament and the nation that this should be conceived on the broadest possible basis and that it should include all Parties, both those who supported the late Government and also the Parties of the Opposition. I have completed the most important part of this task. A War Cabinet has been formed of five Members, representing, with the Opposition Liberals, the unity of the nation. The three Party Leaders have agreed to serve, either in the War Cabinet or in high executive office. The three Fighting Services have been filled. It was necessary that this should be done in one single day, on account of the extreme urgency and rigor of events. A number of other key positions were filled yesterday, and I am submitting a further list to His Majesty tonight. I hope to complete the appointment of the principal Ministers during tomorrow. The appointment of the other Ministers usually takes a little longer, but I trust that, when Parliament meets again, this part of my task will be completed, and that the Administration will be complete in all respects.

I considered it in the public interest to suggest that the House should be summoned to meet today. Mr. Speaker agreed, and took the necessary steps, in accordance with the powers conferred upon him by the Resolution of the House. At the end of the proceedings today, the Adjournment of the House will be proposed until Tuesday, 21st May, with, of course, provision for earlier meeting if need be. The business to be considered during that week will be notified to Members at the earliest opportunity. I now invite the House, by the Resolution which stands in my name, to record its approval of the steps taken and to declare its confidence in the new Government.

To form an Administration of this scale and complexity is a serious undertaking in itself, but it must be remembered that we are in the preliminary stage of one of the greatest battles in history, that we are in action at many points in Norway and in Holland, that we have to be prepared in the Mediterranean, that the air battle is continuous, and that many preparations have to be made here at home. In this crisis I hope I may be pardoned if I do not address the House at any length today. I hope that any of my friends and colleagues, or former colleagues, who are affected by the political reconstruction, will make all allowance for any lack of ceremony with which it has been necessary to act. I would say to the House, as I said to those who have joined this Government: "I have nothing to offer but blood, toil, tears, and sweat."

We have before us an ordeal of the most grievous kind. We have before us many, many long months of struggle and of suffering. You ask, What is our policy? I will say: "It is to wage war, by sea, land and air, with all our might and with all the strength that God can give us: to wage war against a monstrous tyranny, never surpassed in the dark, lamentable catalogue of human crime. That is our policy." You ask, What is our aim? I can answer in one word: Victory—victory at all costs, victory in spite of all terror, victory however long and hard the road may be; for without victory there is no survival. Let that be realized; no survival for the British Empire; no survival for all that the British Empire has stood for; no survival for the urge and impulse of the ages, that mankind will move forward towards its goal. But I take up my task with buoyancy and hope. I feel sure that our cause will not be suffered to fail among men. At this time I feel entitled to claim the aid of all, and I say, "Come, then, let us go forward together with our united strength."

# Dunkirk

June 4, 1940

From the moment that the French defenses at Sedan and on the Meuse were broken at the end of the second week of May, only a rapid retreat to Amiens and the south could have saved the British and French Armies who had entered Belgium at the appeal of the Belgian King; but this strategic fact was not immediately realized. The French High Command hoped they would be able to close the gap, and the Armies of the north were under their orders. Moreover, a retirement of this kind would have involved almost certainly the destruction of the fine Belgian Army of over 20 divisions and the abandonment of the whole of Belgium. Therefore, when the force and scope of the German penetration were realized and when a new French Generalissimo, General Weygand, assumed command in place of General Gamelin, an effort was made by the French and British Armies in Belgium to keep on holding the right hand of the Belgians and to give their own right hand to a newly created French Army which was to have advanced across the Somme in great strength to grasp it.

However, the German eruption swept like a sharp scythe around the right and rear of the Armies of the north. Eight or nine armored divisions, each of about four hundred armored vehicles of different kinds, but carefully assorted to be complementary and divisible into small self-contained units, cut off all communications between us and the main French Armies. It severed our own communications for food and ammunition, which ran first to Amiens and afterwards through Abbeville, and it shore its way up the coast to Boulogne and Calais, and almost to Dunkirk. Behind this armored and mechanized onslaught came a number of German divisions in lorries, and behind them again there plodded comparatively slowly the dull brute mass of the ordinary German Army and German people, always so ready to be led to the trampling down in other lands of liberties and comforts which they have never known in their own.

I have said this armored scythe-stroke almost reached Dunkirk — almost but not quite. Boulogne and Calais were the scenes of desperate fighting. The Guards defended Boulogne for a while and were then withdrawn by orders from this country. The Rifle Brigade, the 60th Rifles, and the Queen Victoria's Rifles, with a battalion of British tanks and 1,000 Frenchmen, in all about four thousand strong, defended Calais to the last. The British Brigadier was given an hour to surrender. He spurned the offer, and four days of intense street fighting passed before silence reigned over Calais, which marked the end of a memorable resistance. Only 30 unwounded survivors were brought off by the Navy, and we do not know the fate of their comrades. Their sacrifice, however, was not in vain. At least two armored divisions, which otherwise would have been turned against the British Expeditionary Force, had to be sent to overcome them. They have added another page to the glories of the light divisions, and the time gained enabled the Graveline water lines to be flooded and to be held by the French troops.

Thus it was that the port of Dunkirk was kept open. When it was found impossible for the Armies of the north to reopen their communications to Amiens with the main French Armies, only one choice remained. It seemed, indeed, forlorn. The Belgian, British and French Armies were almost surrounded. Their sole line of retreat was to a single port and to its neighboring beaches. They were pressed on every side by heavy attacks and far outnumbered in the air.

When, a week ago today, I asked the House to fix this afternoon as the occasion for a statement, I feared it would be my hard lot to announce the greatest military disaster in our long history. I thought — and some good judges agreed with me — that perhaps 20,000 or 30,000 men might be re-embarked. But it certainly seemed that the whole of the French First Army and the whole of the British Expeditionary Force north of the Amiens-Abbeville gap would be broken up in the open field or else would have to capitulate for lack of food and ammunition. These were the hard and heavy tidings for which I called upon the House and the nation to prepare themselves a week ago. The whole root and core and brain of the British Army, on which and around which we were to build, and are to build, the great British Armies in the later years of the war, seemed about to perish upon the field or to be led into an ignominious and starving captivity.

That was the prospect a week ago. But another blow which might well have proved final was yet to fall upon us. The King of the Belgians had called upon us to come to his aid. Had not this Ruler and his Government severed themselves from the Allies, who rescued their country from extinction in the late war, and had they not sought refuge in what has proved to be a fatal neutrality, the French and British Armies might well at the outset have saved not only Belgium but perhaps even Poland. Yet at the last moment, when Belgium was already invaded, King Leopold called upon us to come to his aid, and even at the last moment we came. He and his brave, efficient Army, nearly half a million strong, guarded our left flank and thus kept open our only line of retreat to the sea. Suddenly, without prior consultation, with the least possible notice, without the advice of his Ministers and upon his own personal act, he sent a plenipotentiary to the German Command, surrendered his Army, and exposed our whole flank and means of retreat.

I asked the House a week ago to suspend its judgment because the facts were not clear, but I do not feel that any reason now exists why we should not form our own opinions upon this pitiful episode. The surrender of the Belgian Army compelled the British at the shortest notice to cover a flank to the sea more than 30 miles in length. Otherwise all would have been cut off, and all would have shared the fate to which King Leopold had condemned the finest Army his country had ever formed. So in doing this and in exposing this flank, as anyone who followed the operations on the map will see, contact was lost between the British and two out of the three corps forming the First French Army, who were still farther from the coast than we were, and it seemed impossible that any large number of Allied troops could reach the coast.

The enemy attacked on all sides with great strength and fierceness, and their main power, the power of their far more numerous Air Force, was thrown into the battle or else concentrated upon Dunkirk and the beaches. Pressing in upon the narrow exit, both from the east and from the west, the enemy began to fire with cannon upon the beaches by which alone the shipping could approach or depart. They sowed magnetic mines in the channels and seas; they sent repeated waves of hostile aircraft, sometimes more than a hundred strong in one formation, to cast their bombs upon the single pier that remained, and upon the sand dunes upon which the troops had their eyes for shelter. Their U-boats, one of which was sunk, and their motor launches took their toll of the vast traffic which now began. For four or five days an intense struggle reigned. All their armored divisions—or what was left of them— together with great masses of infantry and artillery, hurled themselves in vain upon the ever-narrowing, ever-contracting appendix within which the British and French Armies fought.

Meanwhile, the Royal Navy, with the willing help of countless merchant seamen, strained every nerve to embark the British and Allied troops; 220 light warships and 650 other vessels were engaged. They had to operate upon the difficult coast, often in adverse weather, under an almost ceaseless hail of bombs and an increasing concentration of artillery fire. Nor were the seas, as I have said, themselves free from mines and torpedoes. It was in conditions such as these that our men carried on, with little or no rest, for days and nights on end, making trip after trip across the dangerous waters, bringing with them always men whom they had rescued. The numbers they have brought back are the measure of their devotion and their courage. The hospital ships, which brought off many thousands of British and French wounded, being so plainly marked were a special target for Nazi bombs; but the men and women on board them never faltered in their duty.

Meanwhile, the Royal Air Force, which had already been intervening in the battle, so far as its range would allow, from home bases, now used part of its main metropolitan fighter strength, and struck at the German bombers and at the fighters which in large numbers protected them. This struggle was protracted and fierce. Suddenly the scene has cleared, the crash and thunder has for the moment—but only for the moment—died away. A miracle of deliverance, achieved by valor, by perseverance, by perfect discipline, by faultless service, by resource, by skill, by unconquerable fidelity, is manifest to us all. The enemy was hurled back by the retreating British and French troops. He was so roughly handled that he did not hurry their departure seriously. The Royal Air Force engaged the main strength of the German Air Force, and inflicted upon them losses of at least four to one; and the Navy, using nearly 1,000 ships of all kinds, carried over 335,000 men, French and British, out of the jaws of death and shame, to their native land and to the tasks which lie immediately ahead. We must be very careful not to assign to this deliverance the attributes of a victory. Wars are not won by evacuations. But there was a victory inside this deliverance, which should be noted. It was gained by the Air Force. Many of our soldiers coming back have not seen the Air Force at work; they saw only the bombers which escaped its protective attack. They underrate its achievements. I have heard much talk of this; that is why I go out of my way to say this. I will tell you about it.

This was a great trial of strength between the British and German Air Forces. Can you conceive a greater objective for the Germans in the air than to make evacuation from these beaches impossible, and to sink all these ships which were displayed, almost to the extent of thousands? Could there have been an objective of greater military importance and significance for the whole purpose of the war than this? They tried hard, and they were beaten back; they were frustrated in their task. We got the Army away; and they have paid fourfold for any losses which they have inflicted. Very large formations of German aeroplanes—and we know that they are a very brave race—have turned on several occasions from the attack of one-quarter of their number of the Royal Air Force, and have dispersed in different directions. Twelve aeroplanes have been hunted by two. One aeroplane was driven into the water and cast away by the mere charge of a British aeroplane, which had no more ammunition. All of our types – the Hurricane, the Spitfire and the new Defiant – and all our pilots have been vindicated as superior to what they have at present to face.

When we consider how much greater would be our advantage in defending the air above this Island against an overseas attack, I must say that I find in these facts a sure basis upon which practical and reassuring thoughts may rest. I will pay my tribute to these young airmen. The great French Army was very largely, for the time being, cast back and disturbed by the onrush of a few thousands of armored vehicles. May it not also be that the cause of civilization itself will be defended by the skill and devotion of a few thousand airmen? There never has been, I suppose, in all the world, in all the history of war, such an opportunity for youth. The Knights of the Round Table, the Crusaders, all fall back into the past – not only distant but prosaic; these young men, going forth every morn to guard their native land and all that we stand for, holding in their hands these instruments of colossal and shattering power, of whom it may be said that

      "Every morn brought forth a noble chance

      And every chance brought forth a noble knight,"

deserve our gratitude, as do all of the brave men who, in so many ways and on so many occasions, are ready, and continue ready, to give life and all for their native land.

I return to the Army. In the long series of very fierce battles, now on this front, now on that, fighting on three fronts at once, battles fought by two or three divisions against an equal or somewhat larger number of the enemy, and fought fiercely on some of the old grounds that so many of us knew so well – in these battles our losses in men have exceeded 30,000 killed, wounded and missing. I take occasion to express the sympathy of the House to all who have suffered bereavement or who are still anxious. The President of the Board of Trade[1] is not here today. His son has been killed, and many in the House have felt the pangs of affliction in the sharpest form. But I will say this about the missing: We have had a large number of wounded come home safely to this country, but I would say about the missing that there may be very many reported missing who will come back home, some day, in one way or another. In the confusion of this fight it is inevitable that many have been left in positions where honor required no further resistance from them.

Against this loss of over 30,000 men, we can set a far heavier loss certainly inflicted upon the enemy. But our losses in material are enormous. We have perhaps lost one-third of the men we lost in the opening days of the battle of 21st March, 1918, but we have lost nearly as many guns – nearly one thousand – and all our transport, all the armored vehi-

---

[1] Sir Andrew Duncan, now Minister of Supply.

cles that were with the Army in the north. This loss will impose a further delay on the expansion of our military strength. That expansion had not been proceeding as fast as we had hoped. The best of all we had to give had gone to the British Expeditionary Force, and although they had not the numbers of tanks and some articles of equipment which were desirable, they were a very well and finely equipped Army. They had the first-fruits of all that our industry had to give, and that is gone. And now here is this further delay. How long it will be, how long it will last, depends upon the exertions which we make in this Island. An effort the like of which has never been seen in our records is now being made. Work is proceeding everywhere, night and day, Sundays and week days. Capital and Labor have cast aside their interests, rights, and customs and put them into the common stock. Already the flow of munitions has leaped forward. There is no reason why we should not in a few months overtake the sudden and serious loss that has come upon us, without retarding the development of our general program.

Nevertheless, our thankfulness at the escape of our Army and so many men, whose loved ones have passed through an agonizing week, must not blind us to the fact that what has happened in France and Belgium is a colossal military disaster. The French Army has been weakened, the Belgian Army has been lost, a large part of those fortified lines upon which so much faith had been reposed is gone, many valuable mining districts and factories have passed into the enemy's possession, the whole of the Channel ports are in his hands, with all the tragic consequences that follow from that, and we must expect another blow to be struck almost immediately at us or at France. We are told that Herr Hitler has a plan for invading the British Isles. This has often been thought of before. When Napoleon lay at Boulogne for a year with his flat-bottomed boats and his Grand Army, he was told by someone, "There are bitter weeds in England." There are certainly a great many more of them since the British Expeditionary Force returned.

The whole question of home defense against invasion is, of course, powerfully affected by the fact that we have for the time being in this Island incomparably more powerful military forces than we have ever had at any moment in this war or the last. But this will not continue. We shall not be content with a defensive war. We have our duty to our Ally. We have to reconstitute and build up the British Expeditionary Force once again, under its gallant Commander-in-Chief, Lord Gort. All this is in train; but in the interval we must put our defenses in this Island into such a high state of organization that the fewest possible numbers will be required to give effective security and that the largest possible potential of offensive effort may be realized. On this we are now engaged. It will be very convenient, if it be the desire of the House, to enter upon this subject in a secret Session. Not that the Government would necessarily be able to reveal in very great detail military secrets, but we like to have our discussions free, without the restraint imposed by the fact that they will be read the next day by the enemy; and the Government would benefit by views freely expressed in all parts of the House by Members with their knowledge of so many different parts of the country. I understand that some request is to be made upon this subject, which will be readily acceded to by His Majesty's Government.

We have found it necessary to take measures of increasing stringency, not only against enemy aliens and suspicious characters of other nationalities, but also against British subjects who may become a danger or a nuisance should the war be transported to the United Kingdom. I know there are a great many people affected by the orders which we have made who are the passionate enemies of Nazi Germany. I am very sorry for them, but we cannot, at the present time and under the present stress, draw all the distinctions which we should like to do. If parachute landings were attempted and fierce fighting attendant upon them followed, these unfortunate people would be far better out of the way, for their own sakes as well as for ours. There is, however, another class, for which I feel not the slightest sympathy. Parliament has given us the powers to put down Fifth Column activities with a strong hand, and we shall use those powers, subject to the supervision and correction of the House, without the slightest hesitation until we are satisfied, and more than satisfied, that this malignancy in our midst has been effectively stamped out.

Turning once again, and this time more generally, to the question of invasion, I would observe that there has never been a period in all these long centuries of which we boast when an absolute guarantee against invasion, still less against serious raids, could have been given to our people. In the days of Napoleon the same wind which would have carried his transports across the Channel might have driven away the blockading fleet. There was always the chance, and it is that chance which has excited and befooled the imaginations of many Continental tyrants. Many are the tales that are told. We are assured that novel methods will be adopted, and when we see the originality of malice, the ingenuity of aggression, which our enemy displays, we may certainly prepare ourselves for every kind of novel stratagem and every kind of brutal and treacherous maneuver. I think that no idea is so outlandish that it should not be considered and viewed with a searching, but at the same time, I hope, with a steady eye. We must never forget the solid assurances of sea power and those which belong to air power if it can be locally exercised.

I have, myself, full confidence that if all do their duty, if nothing is neglected, and if the best arrangements are made, as they are being made, we shall prove ourselves once again able to defend our Island home, to ride out the storm of war, and to outlive the menace of tyranny, if necessary for years, if necessary alone. At any rate, that is what we are going to try to do. That is the resolve of His Majesty's Government—every man of them. That is the will of Parliament and the nation. The British Empire and the French Republic, linked together in their cause and in their need, will defend to the death their native soil, aiding each other like good comrades to the utmost of their strength. Even though large tracts of Europe and many old and famous States have fallen or may fall into the grip of the Gestapo and all the odious apparatus of Nazi rule, we shall not flag or fail. We shall go on to the end, we shall fight in France, we shall fight on the seas and oceans, we shall fight with growing confidence and growing strength in the air, we shall defend our Island, whatever the cost may be, we shall fight on the beaches, we shall fight on the landing grounds, we shall fight in the fields and in the streets, we shall fight in the hills; we shall never surrender, and even if, which I do not for a moment believe, this Island or a large part of it were subjugated and starving, then our Empire beyond the seas, armed and guarded by the British Fleet, would carry on the struggle, until, in God's good time, the New World, with all its power and might, steps forth to the rescue and the liberation of the old.

*Walter van Tilburg Clark*

# The Portable Phonograph

The red sunset, with narrow, black cloud strips like threats across it, lay on the curved horizon of the prairie. The air was still and cold, and in it settled the mute darkness and greater cold of night. High in the air there was wind, for through the veil of the dusk the clouds could be seen gliding rapidly south and changing shapes. A queer sensation of torment, of two-sided, unpredictable nature, arose from the stillness of the earth air beneath the violence of the upper air. Out of the sunset, through the dead, matted grass and isolated weed stalks of the prairie, crept the narrow and deeply rutted remains of a road. In the road, in places, there were crusts of shallow, brittle ice. There were little islands of an old oiled pavement in the road too, but most of it was mud, now frozen rigid. The frozen mud still bore the toothed impress of great tanks, and a wanderer on the neighboring undulations might have stumbled, in this light, into large, partially filled-in and weed-grown cavities, their banks channelled and beginning to spread into badlands. These pits were such as might have been made by falling meteors, but they were not. They were the scars of gigantic bombs, their rawness already made a little natural by rain, seed, and time. Along the road, there were rakish remnants of fence. There was also, just visible, one portion of tangled and multiple barbed wire still erect, behind which was a shelving ditch with small caves, now very quiet and empty, at intervals in its back wall. Otherwise there was no structure or remnant of a structure visible over the dome of the darkling earth, but only, in sheltered hollows, the darker shadows of young trees trying again.

Under the wuthering arch of the high wind a V of wild geese fled south. The rush of their pinions sounded briefly, and the faint, plaintive notes of their expeditionary talk. Then they left a still greater vacancy. There was the smell and expectation of snow, as there is likely to be when the wild geese fly south. From the remote distance, towards the red sky, came faintly the protracted howl and quick yap-yap of a prairie wolf.

North of the road, perhaps a hundred yards, lay the parallel and deeply intrenched course of a small creek, lined with leafless alders and willows. The creek was already silent under ice. Into the bank above it was dug a sort of cell, with a single opening, like the mouth of a mine tunnel. Within the cell there was a little red of fire, which showed dully through the opening, like a reflection or a deception of the imagination. The light came from the chary burning of four blocks of poorly aged peat, which gave off a petty warmth and much acrid smoke. But the precious remnants of wood, old fence posts and timbers from the long-deserted dugouts, had to be saved for the real cold, for the time when a man's breath blew white, the moisture in his nostrils stiffened at once when he stepped out, and the expansive blizzards paraded for days over the vast open, swirling and settling and thickening, till the dawn of the cleared day when the sky was thin blue-green and the terrible cold, in which a man could not live for three hours unwarmed, lay over the uniformly drifted swell of the plain.

Around the smoldering peat, four men were seated cross-legged. Behind them, traversed by their shadows, was the earth bench, with two old and dirty army blankets, where the owner of the cell slept. In a niche in the opposite wall were a few tin utensils which caught the glint of the coals. The host was rewrapping in a piece of daubed burlap four fine, leather-bound books. He worked slowly and very carefully, and at last tied the bundle securely with a piece of grass-woven cord. The other three looked intently upon the process, as if a great significance lay in it. As the host tied the cord, he spoke. He was an old man, his long, matted beard and hair gray to nearly white. The shadows made his brows and cheekbones appear gnarled, his eyes and cheeks deeply sunken. His big hands, rough with frost and swollen by rheumatism, were awkward but gentle at their task. He was like a prehistoric priest performing a fateful ceremonial rite. Also his voice had in it a suitable quality of deep, reverent despair, yet perhaps at the moment, a sharpness of selfish satisfaction.

"When I perceived what was happening," he said, "I told myself, 'It is the end. I cannot take much; I will take these.'"

"Perhaps I was impractical," he continued. "But for myself, I do not regret, and what do we know of those who will come after us? We are the doddering remnant of a race of mechanical fools. I have saved what I love; the soul of what was good in us is here; perhaps the new ones will make a strong enough beginning not to fall behind when they become clever."

He rose with slow pain and placed the wrapped volumes in the niche with his utensils. The others watched him with the same ritualistic gaze.

"Shakespeare, the Bible, *Moby Dick, The Divine Comedy*," one of them said softly. "You might have done worse, much worse."

"You will have a little soul left until you die," said another harshly. "That is more than is true of us. My brain becomes thick, like my hands." He held the big, battered hands, with their black nails, in the glow to be seen.

"I want paper to write on," he said. "And there is none."

The fourth man said nothing. He sat in the shadow farthest from the fire, and sometimes his body jerked in its rags from the cold. Although he was still young, he was sick and coughed often. Writing implied a greater future than he now felt able to consider.

The old man seated himself laboriously, and reached out, groaning at the movement, to put another block of peat on the fire. With bowed heads and averted eyes, his three guests acknowledged his magnanimity.

"We thank you, Doctor Jenkins, for the reading," said the man who had named the books.

They seemed then to be waiting for something. Doctor Jenkins understood, but was loath to comply. In an ordinary moment he would have said nothing. But the words of *The Tempest*, which he had been reading, and the religious attention of the three made this an unusual occasion.

"You wish to hear the phonograph," he said grudgingly.

The two middle-aged men stared into the fire, unable to formulate and expose the enormity of their desire.

The young man, however, said anxiously, between suppressed coughs, "Oh, please," like an excited child.

The old man rose again in his difficult way, and went to the back of the cell. He returned and placed tenderly upon the packed floor, where the firelight might fall upon it, an old portable phonograph in a black case. He smoothed the top with his hand, and then opened it. The lovely green-felt-covered disk became visible.

"I have been using thorns as needles," he said. "But tonight, because we have a musician among us"—he bent his head to the young man, almost invisible in the shadow—"I will use a steel needle. There are only three left."

The two middle-aged men stared at him in speechless adoration.

The one with the big hands, who wanted to write, moved his lips, but the whisper was not audible.

"Oh, don't!" cried the young man, as if he were hurt. "The thorns will do beautifully."

"No," the old man said. "I have become accustomed to the thorns, but they are not really good. For you, my young friend, we will have good music tonight."

"After all," he added generously, and beginning to wind the phonograph, which creaked, "they can't last forever."

"No, nor we," the man who needed to write said harshly. "The needle, by all means."

"Oh, thanks," said the young man. "Thanks," he said again in a low, excited voice, and then stifled his coughing with a bowed head.

"The records, though," said the old man when he had finished winding, "are a different matter. Already they are very worn. I do not play them more than once a week. One, once a week, that is what I allow myself.

"More than a week I cannot stand it; not to hear them," he apologized.

"No, how could you?" cried the young man. "And with them here like this."

"A man can stand anything," said the man who wanted to write, in his harsh, antagonistic voice.

"Please, the music," said the young man.

"Only the one," said the old man. "In the long run, we will remember more that way."

He had a dozen records with luxuriant gold and red seals. Even in that light the others could see that the threads of the records were becoming worn. Slowly he read out the titles and the tremendous dead names of the composers and the artists and the orchestras. The three worked upon the names in their minds, carefully. It was difficult to select from such a wealth what they would at once most like to remember. Finally, the man who wanted to write named Gershwin's "New York."

"Oh, no," cried the sick young man, and then could say nothing more because he had to cough. The others understood him, and the harsh man withdrew his selection and waited for the musician to choose.

The musician begged Doctor Jenkins to read the titles again, very slowly, so that he could remember the sounds. While they were read, he lay back against the wall, his eyes closed, his thin, horny hand pulling at his light beard, and listened to the voices and the orchestras and the single instruments in his mind.

When the reading was done he spoke despairingly. "I have forgotten," he complained; "I cannot hear them clearly.

"There are things missing," he explained.

"I know," said Doctor Jenkins. "I thought that I knew all of Shelley by heart. I should have brought Shelley."

"That's more soul than we can use," said the harsh man. "*Moby Dick* is better."

"By God, we can understand that," he emphasized.

The Doctor nodded.

"Still," said the man who had admired the books, "we need the absolute if we are to keep a grasp on anything.

"Anything but these sticks and peat clods and rabbit snares," he said bitterly.

"Shelley desired an ultimate absolute," said the harsh man. "It's too much," he said. "It's no good; no earthly good."

The musician selected a Debussy nocturne. The others considered and approved. They rose to their knees to watch the Doctor prepare for the playing, so that they appeared to be actually in an attitude of worship. The peat glow showed the thinness of their bearded faces, and the deep lines in them, and revealed the condition of their garments. The other two continued to kneel as the old man carefully lowered the needle onto the spinning disk, but the musician suddenly drew back against the wall again, with his knees up, and buried his face in his hands.

At the first notes of the piano the listeners were startled. They stared at each other. Even the musician lifted his head in amazement, but then quickly bowed it again, strainingly, as if he were suffering from a pain he might not be able to endure. They were all listening deeply, without movement. The wet, blue-green notes tinkled forth from the old machine, and were individual, delectable presences in the cell. The individual, delectable presences swept into a sudden tide of unbearably beautiful dissonance, and then continued fully the swelling and ebbing of that tide, the dissonant inpourings, and the resolutions, and the diminishments, and the little, quiet wavelets of interlude lapping between. Every sound was piercing and singularly sweet. In all the men except the musician, there occurred rapid sequences of tragically heightened recollection. He heard nothing but what was there. At the final, whispering disappearance, but moving quietly so that the others would not hear him and look at him, he let his head fall back in agony, as if it were drawn there by the hair, and clenched the fingers of one hand over his teeth. He sat that way while the others were silent, and until they began to breathe again normally. His drawn-up legs were trembling violently.

Quickly Doctor Jenkins lifted the needle off, to save it and not to spoil the recollection with scraping. When he had stopped the whirling of the sacred disk, he courteously left the phonograph open and by the fire, in sight.

The others, however, understood. The musician rose last, but then abruptly, and went quickly out at the door without saying anything. The others stopped at the door and gave their thanks in low voices. The Doctor nodded magnificently.

"Come again," he invited, "in a week. We will have the 'New York.'"

When the two had gone together, out towards the rimed road, he stood in the entrance, peering and listening. At first, there was only the resonant boom of the wind overhead, and then far over the dome of the dead, dark plain, the wolf cry lamenting. In the rifts of clouds the Doctor saw four stars flying. It impressed the Doctor that one of them had just been obscured by the beginning of a flying cloud at the very moment he heard what he had been listening for, a sound of suppressed coughing. It was not near-by, however. He believed that down against the pale alders he could see the moving shadow.

With nervous hands he lowered the piece of canvas which served as his door, and pegged it at the bottom. Then quickly and quietly, looking at the piece of canvas frequently, he slipped the records into the case, snapped the lid shut, and carried the phonograph to his couch. There, pausing often to stare at the canvas and listen, he dug earth from the wall and disclosed a piece of board. Behind this there was a deep hole in the wall, into which he put the phonograph. After a moment's consideration, he went over and reached down his bundle of books and inserted it also. Then, guardedly, he once more sealed up the hole with the board and the earth. He also changed his blankets, and the grass-stuffed sack which served as a pillow, so that he could lie facing the entrance. After carefully placing two more blocks of peat upon the fire, he stood for a long time watching the stretched canvas, but it seemed to billow naturally with the first gusts of a lowering wind. At last he prayed, and got in under his blankets, and closed his smoke-smarting eyes. On the inside of the bed, next the wall, he could feel with his hand the comfortable piece of lead pipe.

(1950)

## Dwight D. Eisenhower

# Farewell Address

Three days from now, after half a century in the service of our country, I shall lay down the responsibilities of office as, in traditional and solemn ceremony, the authority of the Presidency is vested in my successor.

This evening I come to you with a message of leavetaking and farewell, and to share a few final thoughts with you, my countrymen.

Like every other citizen, I wish the new President, and all who will labor with him, Godspeed. I pray that the coming years will be blessed with peace and prosperity for all.

Our people expect their President and the Congress to find essential agreement on issues of great moment, the wise resolution of which will better shape the future of the nation.

My own relations with the Congress, which began on a remote and tenuous basis when, long ago, a member of the Senate appointed me to West Point, have since ranged to the intimate during the war and immediate post-war period, and finally to the mutually interdependent during these past eight years.

In this final relationship, the Congress and the Administration have, on most vital issues, cooperated well, to serve the nation's good rather than mere partisanship, and so have assured that the business of the nation should go forward. So my official relationship with the Congress ends in a feeling, on my part, of gratitude that we have been able to do so much together.

We now stand ten years past the midpoint of a century that has witnessed four major wars among great nations—three of these involved our own country.

Despite these holocausts America is today the strongest, the most influential and most productive nation in the world. Understandably proud of this pre-eminence, we yet realize that America's leadership and prestige depend, not merely upon our unmatched material progress, riches and military strength, but on how we use our power in the interests of world peace and human betterment.

Throughout America's adventure in free government, our basic purposes have been to keep the peace; to foster progress in human achievement, and to enhance liberty, dignity and integrity among peoples and among nations.

To strive for less would be unworthy of a free and religious people.

Any failure traceable to arrogance or our lack of comprehension or readiness to sacrifice would inflict upon us grievous hurt, both at home and abroad.

Crises there will continue to be. In meeting them, whether foreign or domestic, great or small, there is a recurring temptation to feel that some spectacular and costly action could become the miraculous solution to all current difficulties. A huge increase in newer elements of our defenses; development of unrealistic programs to cure every ill in agriculture; a dramatic expansion in basic and applied research—these and many other possibilities, each possibly promising in itself, may be suggested as the only way to the road we wish to travel.

But each proposal must be weighed in the light of a broader consideration; the need to maintain balance in and among national programs—balance between the private and the public economy, balance between the cost and hoped for advantages—balance between the clearly necessary and the comfortably desirable; balance between our essential requirements as a nation and the duties imposed by the nation upon the individual; balance between actions of the moment and the national welfare of the future. Good judgment seeks balance and progress; lack of it eventually finds imbalance and frustration.

The record of many decades stands as proof that our people and their Government have, in the main, understood these truths and have responded to them well in the face of threat and stress.

But threats, new in kind or degree, constantly arise. Of these, I mention two only.

A vital element in keeping the peace is our military establishment. Our arms must be mighty, ready for instant action, so that no potential aggressor may be tempted to risk his own destruction.

Our military organization today bears little relation to that known of any of my predecessors in peacetime—or, indeed, by the fighting men of World War II or Korea.

Until the latest of our world conflicts, the United States had no armaments industry. American makers of plowshares could, with time and as required, make swords as well.

But we can no longer risk emergency improvisation of national defense. We have been compelled to create a permanent armaments industry of vast proportions. Added to this, three and a half million men and women are directly engaged in the defense establishment. We annually spend on military security alone more than the net income of all United States corporations.

Now this conjunction of an immense military establishment and a large arms industry is new in the American experience. The total influence—economic, political, even spiritual—is felt in every city, every state house, every office of the Federal Government. We recognize the imperative need for this development. Yet we must not fail to comprehend its grave implications. Our toil, resources and livelihood are all involved; so is the very structure of our society.

In the councils of Government, we must guard against the acquisition of unwarranted influence, whether sought or unsought, by the military-industrial complex. The potential for the disastrous rise of misplaced power exists and will persist.

We must never let the weight of this combination endanger our liberties or democratic processes. We should take nothing for granted. Only an alert and knowledgeable citizenry can compel the proper meshing of the huge industrial and military machinery of defense with our peaceful methods and goals, so that security and liberty may prosper together.

Akin to, and largely responsible for the sweeping changes in our industrial-military posture has been the technological revolution during recent decades.

In this revolution research has become central. It also becomes more formalized, complex and costly. A steadily increasing share is conducted for, by, or at the direction of the Federal Government.

Today the solitary inventor, tinkering in his shop, has been overshadowed by task forces of scientists, in laboratories and testing fields. In the same fashion, the free university, historically the fountainhead of free ideas and scientific discovery, has experienced a revolution in the conduct of research. Partly because of the huge costs involved, a Government contract becomes virtually a substitute for intellectual curiosity.

For every old blackboard there are now hundreds of new electronic computers.

The prospect of domination of the nation's scholars by Federal employment, project allocations and the power of money is ever present, and is gravely to be regarded.

Yet, in holding scientific research and discovery in respect, as we should, we must also be alert to the equal and opposite danger that public policy could itself become the captive of a scientific-technological elite.

It is the task of statesmanship to mold, to balance, and to integrate these and other forces, new and old, within the principles of our democratic system—ever aiming toward the supreme goals of our free society.

Another factor in maintaining balance involves the element of time. As we peer into society's future, we—you and I, and our Government—must avoid the impulse to live only for today, plundering, for our own ease and convenience, the precious resources of tomorrow.

We cannot mortgage the material assets of our grandchildren without risking the loss also of their political and spiritual heritage. We want democracy to survive for all generations to come, not to become the insolvent phantom of tomorrow.

During the long lane of the history yet to be written America knows that this world of ours, ever growing smaller, must avoid becoming a community of dreadful fear and hate, and be, instead, a proud confederation of mutual trust and respect.

Such a confederation must be one of equals. The weakest must come to the conference table with the same confidence as do we, protected as we are by our moral, economic and military strength. That table, though scarred by many past frustrations, cannot be abandoned for the certain agony of the battlefield.

Disarmament, with mutual honor and confidence, is a continuing imperative. Together we must learn how to compose differences—not with arms, but with intellect and decent purpose. Because this need is so sharp and apparent, I confess that I lay down my official responsibilities in this field with a definite sense of disappointment. As one who has witnessed the horror and the lingering sadness of war, as one who knows that another war could utterly destroy this civilization which has been so slowly and painfully built over thousands of years, I wish I could say tonight that a lasting peace is in sight.

Happily, I can say that war has been avoided. Steady progress toward our ultimate goal has been made. But so much remains to be done. As a private citizen, I shall never cease to do what little I can to help the world advance along that road.

So, in this, my last good night to you as your President, I thank you for the many opportunities you have given me for public service in war and in peace.

I trust that in you—that, in that service, you find some things worthy. As for the rest of it, I know you will find ways to improve performance in the future.

You and I—my fellow citizens—need to be strong in our faith that all nations, under God, will reach the goal of peace with justice. May we be ever unswerving in devotion to principle, confident but humble with power, diligent in pursuit of the nation's great goals.

To all the peoples of the world, I once more give expression to America's prayerful and continuing aspiration:

We pray that peoples of all faiths, all races, all nations, may have their great human needs satisfied; that those now denied opportunity shall come to enjoy it to the full; that all who yearn for freedom may experience its spiritual blessings, those who have freedom will understand, also, its heavy responsibility; that all who are insensitive to the needs of others, will learn charity, and that the sources—scourges of poverty, disease and ignorance—will be made to disappear from the earth; and that in the goodness of time, all peoples will come to live together in a peace guaranteed by the binding force of mutual respect and love.

Now, on Friday noon, I am to become a private citizen. I am proud to do so. I look forward to it.

Thank you, and, good night.

(1961)

# Inaugural Address

We observe today not a victory of party but a celebration of freedom, symbolizing an end as well as a beginning, signifying renewal as well as change. For I have sworn before you and Almighty God the same solemn oath our forebears prescribed nearly a century and three-quarters ago.

The world is very different now. For man holds in his mortal hands the power to abolish all forms of human poverty and all forms of human life. And yet the same revolutionary belief for which our forebears fought is still at issue around the globe, the belief that the rights of man come not from the generosity of the state but from the hand of God.

We dare not forget today that we are the heirs of that first revolution. Let the word go forth from this time and place, to friend and foe alike, that the torch has been passed to a new generation of Americans, born in this century, tempered by war, disciplined by a hard and bitter peace, proud of our ancient heritage, and unwilling to witness or permit the slow undoing of those human rights to which this nation has always been committed, and to which we are committed today at home and around the world.

Let every nation know, whether it wishes us well or ill, that we shall pay any price, bear any burden, meet any hardship, support any friend, oppose any foe to assure the survival and the success of liberty.

This much we pledge – and more.

To those old allies whose cultural and spiritual origins we share, we pledge the loyalty of faithful friends. United, there is little we cannot do in a host of cooperative ventures. Divided, there is little we can do, for we dare not meet a powerful challenge at odds and split asunder.

To those new states whom we welcome to the ranks of the free, we pledge our word that one form of colonial control shall not have passed away merely to be replaced by a far more iron tyranny. We shall not always expect to find them supporting our view. But we shall always hope to find them strongly supporting their own freedom, and to remember that, in the past, those who foolishly sought power by riding the back of the tiger ended up inside.

To those peoples in the huts and villages of half the globe struggling to break the bonds of mass misery, we pledge our best efforts to help them help themselves, for whatever period is required, not because the Communists may be doing it, not because we seek their votes, but because it is right. If a free society cannot help the many who are poor, it cannot save the few who are rich.

To our sister republics south of our border, we offer a special pledge: to convert our good words into good deeds, in a new alliance for progress, to assist free men and free governments in casting off the chains of poverty. But this peaceful revolution of hope cannot become the prey of hostile powers. Let all our neighbors know that we shall join with them to oppose aggression or subversion anywhere in the Americas. And let every other power know that this hemisphere intends to remain the master of its own house.

To that world assembly of sovereign states, the United Nations, our last best hope in an age where the instruments of war have far outpaced the instruments of peace, we renew our pledge of support: to prevent it from becoming merely a forum for invective, to strengthen its shield of the new and the weak, and to enlarge the area in which its writ may run.

Finally, to those nations who would make themselves our adversary, we offer not a pledge but a request: that both sides begin anew the quest for peace, before the dark powers of destruction unleashed by science engulf all humanity in planned or accidental self-destruction.

We dare not tempt them with weakness. For only when our arms are sufficient beyond doubt can we be certain beyond doubt that they will never be employed.

But neither can two great and powerful groups of nations take comfort from our present course—both sides overburdened by the cost of modern weapons, both rightly alarmed by the steady spread of the deadly atom, yet both racing to alter that uncertain balance of terror that stays the hand of mankind's final war.

So let us begin anew, remembering on both sides that civility is not a sign of weakness, and sincerity is always subject to proof. Let us never negotiate out of fear, but let us never fear to negotiate.

Let both sides explore what problems unite us instead of belaboring those problems which divide us.

Let both sides, for the first time, formulate serious and precise proposals for the inspection and control of arms, and bring the absolute power to destroy other nations under the absolute control of all nations.

Let both sides seek to invoke the wonders of science instead of its terrors. Together let us explore the stars, conquer the deserts, eradicate disease, tap the ocean depths and encourage the arts and commerce.

Let both sides unite to heed in all corners of the earth the command of Isaiah to "undo the heavy burdens . . . [and] let the oppressed go free."

And if a beachhead of cooperation may push back the jungle of suspicion, let both sides join in creating a new endeavor, not a new balance of power, but a new world of law, where the strong are just and the weak secure and the peace preserved.

All this will not be finished in the first one hundred days. Nor will it be finished in the first one thousand days, nor in the life of this Administration, nor even perhaps in our lifetime on this planet. But let us begin.

In your hands, my fellow citizens, more than mine, will rest the final success or failure of our course. Since this country was founded, each generation of Americans has been summoned to give testimony to its national loyalty. The graves of young Americans who answered the call to service surround the globe.

Now the trumpet summons us again—not as a call to bear arms, though arms we need; not as a call to battle, though embattled we are; but a call to bear the burden of a long twilight struggle, year in and year out, "rejoicing in hope, patient in tribulation," a struggle against the common enemies of man: tyranny, poverty, disease and war itself.

Can we forge against these enemies a grand and global alliance, North and South, East and West, that can assure a more fruitful life for all mankind? Will you join in that historic effort?

In the long history of the world, only a few generations have been granted the role of defending freedom in its hour of maximum danger. I do not shrink from this responsibility; I welcome it. I do not believe that any of us would exchange places with any other people or any other generation. The energy, the faith, the devotion which we bring to this endeavor will light our country and all who serve it, and the glow from that fire can truly light the world.

And so, my fellow Americans, ask not what your country can do for you; ask what you can do for your country.

My fellow citizens of the world, ask not what America will do for you, but what together we can do for the freedom of man.

Finally, whether you are citizens of America or citizens of the world, ask of us here the same high standards of strength and sacrifice which we ask of you. With a good conscience our only sure reward, with history the final judge of our deeds, let us go forth to lead the land we love, asking His blessing and His help, but knowing that here on earth God's work must truly be our own.

(1961)

*Eleanor Roosevelt*

# The Machinery for Peace

Humanity with all its fears
With all its hopes of future years
Is hanging breathless on thy fate.
           Henry Wadsworth Longfellow

Today, every human being in the world stands in constant peril from irresponsible use of nuclear power. But today, also, we have created the only machinery for peace that has ever functioned. That, of course, is the United Nations. The only real hope we can have of the survival of the human race lies in showing this new generation coming along how to improve that machinery to prevent our self-destruction.

If we go back in history we can find plenty of instances of civilizations that grew, flourished, and died. They died because human beings did not have the breadth of vision to understand the needs for human survival.

Because it is the work of men and women, of fallible human beings, the United Nations is not a perfect instrument. *But it is all we have.* If we are conscious of its imperfections then it is up to us, to every one of us, to try to find workable ways of improving it. I am reminded of Benjamin Franklin at the Constitutional Convention. There was, perhaps, not a single man there who approved wholeheartedly of that great document. But it was all they had. And Franklin begged any man who did not like some of its features to doubt his own infallibility a little and accept it.

One of the great stumbling blocks in the acceptance of our Constitution, of course, was the jealous clashes and distrust between state and federal groups. Everyone was afraid of having to give up a little.

At present the chief stumbling block in widespread backing of the United Nations is the fear each nation has that it will have to give up a little. In the case of our thirteen American colonies, years passed before the increased strength and benefits for all became truly evident and counteracted jealousy of individual rights and suspicions of group rights. It will doubtless take longer for us to lose our fear and distrust of other nations, other ways of life; to overcome our fear of losing some small part of our sovereignty for the common good, which means, as well, our own good and our own survival.

Suppose that the United States were to withdraw completely from world affairs. What then? Would we have assured our own independence and sovereignty and safety? Certainly not. Instead we would lose the only machinery for peace that exists, while the Communist tide would rise unchecked and the Bomb would still be there.

Any step, however small, that leads to international peace, to universal understanding, to strengthening the machinery of the United Nations is a good step. In fact, it seems to me that before we can ever hope to achieve universal disarmament we must create a climate of psychological disarmament. *The people must want peace* and they must put their weight behind achieving it. It is not alone the few warmongers who create the danger; it is, to a much greater extent, the apathetic.

"There have always been wars," say the cliché-minded. The implication is that wars must always occur in the future. But it would be equally sensible to say, "There have always been plagues and pestilence, smallpox and diphtheria, typhoid fever and other diseases." Yet we know that these are not inevitable and inescapable scourges. We have put our intelligence to work on known facts and consequently rid ourselves of these death dealers. When they occur now it is because of neglect and ignorance. But they do not need to occur at all.

It is curious to look back, from the standpoint of history and its teaching, at the wars that have engaged the Western world during the past two hundred years. As a result of those wars—and war always seems to me a temporary breakdown of civilized values—millions upon millions of human beings have died. And the more "advanced" we have become the more horribly many of them have died.

In each of these wars everyone, on each side, was persuaded that his was the cause of righteousness, that he was wielding a flaming sword against the forces of darkness. And the man against whom he fought stood for all the forces of evil.

But a war ends and there is a shuffle in the cards of power politics. The man who was our enemy is now our friend; the friend at whose side we fought so gladly and so proudly has now become the enemy. From a long-range viewpoint all this appears to be nothing but criminal stupidity.

I am aware that if we commit ourselves wholeheartedly to the strengthening of the United Nations—and I share the opinion of Clark M. Eichelberger that the United Nations should be the foundation of policy, not a diplomatic tool—there will be outcries from people complaining, "That is a risk."

Of course it is.

"How do we know," these people ask, "that the nations of the world will act wisely, that they will not all follow one ideology or another?"

Of course we don't know.

But there is no better course than to put our collective trust in a group of trained people such as one finds in the majority of cases in the United Nations.

In this public forum, whose actions and opinions are heard in every corner of the world, we can put before the world the alternatives and the choices that must be made. We can appeal always to the enormous strength and pressure of public opinion. And this, it seems obvious, is the best risk we could take.

It is the United Nations influence on the opinion of the world that has made the Soviets so determined to destroy its usefulness if they possibly can. Year after year, we have seen their efforts to render it impotent. Are we then to say meekly, "Oh, the Soviets don't want the United Nations to succeed; they are afraid of what it is accomplishing. Therefore, of course, we'll play along and pay no attention to it either. Let's let the whole thing go"?

In many respects, we still, in this nuclear age, live and think in terms of the past when it comes to international affairs. We are still trying to make the old balance of power work. And yet, under that system, there has not been a day in recorded history when at least a small war was not going on somewhere in the world. In other words, the old system does not work for peace and it is peace we want.

Since the United Nations was set up it has been possible to prevent the outbreak of World War III. In his report to the Fourth General Assembly Secretary-General Trygve Lie, said: "United Nations action in other parts of the world has also contributed to the progress made toward a more peaceful world by either preventing or ending wars involving 500,000,000 people."

The effect of collective security was shown by United Nations resistance to aggression at the 38th parallel in Korea. What might easily have turned into a chain of aggressions involving the whole East was prevented.

Now just as changing conditions brought about the need for amendments to our Constitution, so changing conditions altered many of the calculations on which the Charter of the United Nations was based, some of them almost before the ink was dry.

Chief of these, of course, was the dropping of the first atomic bomb on Hiroshima, which altered the original concept of security. A new and incalculable factor had entered the picture.

Little by little, however, the United Nations has proved its capacity for flexibility in coping not only with world conditions but with the recalcitrance of some of its own members, with the deliberate efforts to defeat its objectives, with the changes that have come in its own structure.

This flexibility of the United Nations Charter represents the same kind of strength and capacity for growth that our American Constitution has revealed in the face of change. Chief Justice Marshall wrote of our Constitution that "it was intended to endure for ages to come and to be adapted to the various crises of human affairs."

Like our Constitution, too, the United Nations Charter does not, again in Marshall's words, "attempt to provide, by immutable rules, for exigencies which, if foreseen at all, must have been seen dimly, and which can best be provided as they occur."

Clark M. Eichelberger summed up succinctly the situation as it existed in 1956: "The final break-up of the 5-power system in the United Nations occurred in 1956 when the United Kingdom and France vetoed a resolution in the Security Council over Suez, and the Soviet Union vetoed a resolution urging it to desist from armed intervention in Hungary. These vetoes led to two extraordinary and simultaneous sessions of the General Assembly in which the United States was the only great power willing to assume its Security Council obligations under the Charter in all circumstances."

Now the main point is this. Discouraging as all these circumstances were, did they render the United Nations impotent? Not at all. If the Security Council has declined in authority, the General Assembly has gained in power and influence. When the Security Council is unable to keep the peace because of a veto, the Uniting for Peace Resolution enables the General Assembly to take over.

In 1946, Ambassador Austin stated in an address to the General Assembly: "The General Assembly wields power primarily as the voice of the conscience of the world . . . we foresee a great and expanding area of operations for the General Assembly."

In 1961, Benjamin V. Cohen delivered a series of lectures on the United Nations at Harvard University. He summed up the situation in a telling way: "The effectiveness of the United Nations, however, depends not only on the lettered provisions of the Charter, but more importantly on the will and determination of the nations of the world to make it work, and upon the wisdom, imagination, and resourcefulness that their statesmen bring to that task."

Main sources of conflict in the United Nations obviously have been the admission of new nations and the disarmament problem as it has been complicated by the development of atomic power.

Let's take the difficulties presented by atomic fission first. The unpalatable fact with which we must start is this: If we want to save ourselves—and that means all the world, for fallout is no respecter of nations or of treaties—we must be willing to accept the restraints that would apply to all nations which have nuclear power. A taboo for one must be a taboo for all. It is fatuous blindness for anyone to assume that the United States or the Soviet Union should have special privileges; that they should be allowed unrestricted freedom in the control or use of this deadly power.

Indeed, we have only two major choices at this time. One is to continue to make bombs, to build nuclear strength for military purposes. Already enough bombs exist to destroy the whole world. We know that this multiplication of weapons of death solves nothing whatever.

The other choice is the complete end of the use of nuclear power for warfare. That means that the United States as well as the Soviets would have to stop building power for themselves.

There is, of course, a third alternative, but this seems to me incredible and unacceptable. It is the suggestion that we merely build bomb shelters and prepare to retire underground. Somehow, I can't see the American people crawling underground like moles looking for safety. I want to be out in the sun and the fresh air. I want everyone to be out there.

The only way we can free ourselves from the fear of the Bomb is to remove it as an instrument of war completely, and that can be done only by placing full control of all nuclear force and intelligence in the hands of an international power, the United Nations.

If the United Nations had control of nuclear weapons we would certainly all be better off than if the United States and the Soviet Union had that control. The United Nations is responsible to the world as a whole and I take it that the world as a whole will be consistently opposed to taking the risk of any kind of nuclear destruction.

But we must learn to swallow the bitter fact that if you want the threat of nuclear war to be controlled, you have to accept the risks of control. The trouble seems to be that while most human beings want peace, they also want to have everything their own way. Something has to give.

It was Bernard Baruch who first presented the plan of the United States for the regulation and control of atomic weapons. This was to be an International Atomic Development Authority, which would have a monopoly of the world's production of atomic energy. It would have the sole authority to engage in atomic research. No other nation at any time has ever made so broad a proposal for a world system of control.

The Soviets rejected the plan as "thoroughly vicious and unacceptable."

Today, however, when no single power can control the activities of the United Nations, it might be wise to press once more for this form of control, which would take atomic power forever out of the hands of belligerent nations interested primarily in their own increase of power and influence.

Today, the voice of the United Nations is heard in every corner of the world. Were the Soviets to reject this kind of control it would give the lie forever to their claims of peaceful intentions.

One thing should be obvious to everyone. We cannot discuss disarmament, we cannot provide for collective security in any meaningful sense as long as we continue to pretend that Red China does not exist. It contains one-fourth of the people of the world. It now has the secret of nuclear power and will, certain scientists have declared, have the Bomb itself—perhaps by the time this book is published.

It is therefore downright idiotic to continue to ignore the existence of this potentially dangerous power. No one can afford to disarm—and we all know it—while an aggressive military power like Red China remains outside a disarmament agreement. But if Red China were in the United Nations, if its point of view were on record, if it were bound by the same agreements as the other nations, if the peoples of the world were in a position to watch the choices the Chinese make, to see what they are doing, to hear what they are thinking, world opinion could be rallied on the side of peace.

I often wonder if the American people recognize the enormous impact of the United Nations on world opinion. This is the one body in the world where people of all nations and all shades of opinion can be heard, where problems can be discussed, where ways and means of handling them can be thrashed out. One of the chief reasons why the Soviets fear the United Nations and have, as Khrushchev demonstrated so dramatically, attempted to destroy its efficiency, is that when a man states his position in this place his voice is heard everywhere. His actions and his ethics and his motives are judged by peoples in every country. The obstructionist tactics of the Soviet delegates have caused them great loss of prestige among nations whom they hoped to influence by heavy barrages of propaganda.

In my opinion, every nation in the world should be admitted to the United Nations *for the protection of all.* For some years I have been bitterly attacked by people who called me a Communist because I advocate the admission of Red China to the United Nations. An editorial, this past summer, referred to my "friends, those thieves and murderers." The word *Communist,* of course, has become a rallying cry for certain people here just as the word Jew was in Hitler's Germany, a way of arousing emotion without engendering thought.

Those who oppose the admission of Red China take as their favorite point of view: "Look at the trouble we have with the Soviets and their continual *Nyet.* Naturally Red China and Russia will always vote together. They stand for the same thing."

But is this true? The increasing conflict of interest between the two great Communist nations, each of whom is constantly attempting to extend its sphere of influence, has become more and more apparent, in spite of friendly speeches occasionally made by their respective leaders.

One thing seems obvious to me. You can't fight Communism anywhere by pretending that it isn't there. And yet a portion of our country is still trying to do this. I can understand that these people feel that Communists give only lip service to many of the beliefs of the United Nations, and the resolutions passed by it. But even lip service is a help. Certainly when people are put in a public spot where they are exposed to world opinion and where they have to work with people of different points of view, it is bound in the end to broaden their outlook.

The main reason for looking realistically at the question of universal membership to the United Nations, the main reason for trying to influence Red China so that she will wish to join, is that every nation will eventually have the knowledge of nuclear fission. The only eventual security against nuclear weapons is disarmament. We cannot contemplate any kind of peace machinery that leaves out 650,000,000 militant people. Bluntly, to leave Red China outside such control agreements would be to give them control of whatever part of the world they want. A single great power left outside a disarmament agreement could determine the course of the whole world if it wished. This is the inescapable truth.

The United Nations is not a club of congenial people; it is, as it should be, a reflection of the whole world, with its turmoil, its conflicting interests, its diverse viewpoints. There has been a great deal said in certain areas of our country about the value of a council of nations all of whom think more or less alike. Mr. Herbert Hoover recently made a speech in which he suggested that we add a council of free states to function with the United Nations to preserve peace in the world. Here we find a failure to see that in the United Nations itself a revolution has been going on. Conditions have changed from the time when it was originally conceived. It is preposterous for us to believe that there are nations which would consent tamely to being left out of any matter that effects the world as a whole.

Frequently one encounters people who feel that there should be no more Communist nations in the United Nations, which would make nonsense of the whole UN concept. I wonder if they have ever added up the votes in the United Nations. So far as I can recall, the majority has always been against the Communist nations. What on earth are these people afraid of? How much faith do they have in the strength of their own cause?

In earlier days there was much fear that the emerging young nations in Africa would not be able to function satisfactorily in the United Nations, that they would have little if any interest in international questions. At first, this fear seemed justified. There was a tendency among certain groups to vote as a bloc, and to vote solely in the interests of African questions. But while the United Nations is serving as a forum for world opinion, it is also serving another purpose that few people appear to recognize. It is one of the most important schools in the world.

Over and over, I have watched the arrival of new delegates from new nations, which have only recently acquired their freedom from colonial rule. Now a fight for freedom in a nation is a domestic matter. When the delegates arrive here their interest is concentrated exclusively on their domestic problems. They have no interest whatever in the world outside. And here, I might point out, we are in no position to criticize. For many, many years after our own revolution, the American people remained stubbornly aloof from the world and a small nucleus still does so!

But I have studied the votes of these African representatives. Within an unbelievably short time, usually before the end of the first year, something happens to the point of view of the new delegate. For months he has been listening to the discussion of world problems. And he learns that the problems of his own country, like those of other nations, are not merely domestic in their scope. All of them have international repercussions, whether it is a matter of education, or the growing and acquiring of food, or the importation of machinery, or the building of dams. So the delegate learns to think, literally, like a man of the world.

Adlai Stevenson said not long ago: ". . . the peculiar merits of multilateral aid programs under United Nations auspices are being recognized more widely than ever. This is especially true in the new nations of Africa. I am told that the delegates to the recent meetings of the United Nations Economic Commission for Africa in Addis Ababa, were unanimous and emphatic in their desire to see the United Nations become a major partner in their development program."

One great strength of the United Nations is often not recognized; indeed, it is often regarded as a weakness. That is the amount of talk that goes on. Now the value of a public forum where people can protest their wrongs is enormous. In the first place, they are able to bring their problems and their complaints before world opinion; to arouse wide discussion about how their problems can be solved. But the second advantage is that talk is a wonderful way of letting off steam. It is a kind of safety valve. As long as men are arguing about the situation in words, they are not trying to solve it with bullets.

This reminds me of the conclusion of a very long talk which I had with Mr. Khrushchev in Russia, in the course of which we discussed a great many problems on which we were far apart. I can't, indeed, recall any point of agreement. When we parted he asked whether he could tell the press that it had been a friendly meeting.

"You can tell them," I suggested, "that we agreed to disagree."

"At least," he pointed out, "we weren't shooting at each other."

As long as talk goes on — at least we aren't shooting at each other.

It is up to every one of us as individuals to see what can be done, step by step, to create a climate of peace and to provide machinery for keeping it. Here, I feel, there is an urgent need for the women of America to work to strengthen the United Nations and to spread information about it, its functioning, its value, among the people of the country.

We should arouse public opinion to demand that, as far as possible, we work through the United Nations as part of a world team in dealing with foreign nations, and not by-pass it to act on our own.

Not long ago, I was talking with some of the women peace marchers. I said that I could understand why our youngsters wanted to demonstrate outside the White House. For those who were too young to vote this provided their only outlet, their only chance to express their opinions. But it seemed to me a futile action for grown women, a complete waste of energy.

Why, I asked them, instead of expending their energy in this pointless fashion, did they not devote it to trying to think out the first step we could take toward peace? *Because every step taken toward peace is a good step.*

One such step has occurred to me. It has been my experience that whenever I talk to foreign delegates they say: "You Americans do not really want a peaceful world and disarmament. If you stopped manufacturing munitions you would have a financial disaster. Your economy depends on war production, on not having peace."

Now they have a legitimate point. If we are going to convince the world that we are not merely paying lip service to the idea of disarmament, we must be able to answer this criticism satisfactorily. This means that it is our job, as individual citizens, to begin to educate our executives and our government representatives. We can call on them either at home or in Washington. We can suggest that the time has come, in this area as in others, to deal with the problem *by planning ahead.*

We might suggest that the President call a meeting of leaders in industry and labor and say to them something like this:

"Gentlemen, we must be prepared for disarmament. Let us together, or you by yourselves if you prefer, plan for such a situation. What would you convert to? How long would it take? What would you expect the government to do in the way of tax reduction or, perhaps, the retraining of labor in new skills?

"You labor people must think things through, too. Under automation, you must be aware that the workers will have to be better educated, more highly skilled. You must discuss this with industry and with government to see what can be done to prepare the worker for a peaceful world and industry for production without war contracts."

If this kind of thinking and planning were being done today we would be able to answer our doubting friends with perfect assurance. We could then tell them, "We have a plan. We know exactly what we will do and how long it will take and what it will require. So you see we do mean what we say when we talk about disarmament."

This would make clear to the Soviets, too, whose distrust of us is as deep as ours of them, that we are really devoted to the concept of world peace.

Certainly this is a positive first step, of more value than parading before the White House. Every such step is worth all the speeches and the gestures and the shoe banging in the world.

While we are appealing to industry, labor, and government in this country to plan for conversion to peaceful manufacture, we could go a step farther and carry the whole problem to the United Nations. We could explain what we have in mind, and how we plan to implement peace. We could ask the delegates from other nations: "How many of you will do this?"

This would be a direct challenge to the Soviets, who would have to face world opinion if they rejected the plan, and make clear that their propaganda about the warmongering Americans is utterly untrue.

A decision on our part to plan for conversion of defense manufacturing would have an impact on the neutral nations, particularly on those who get military assistance from us. We would have to tell them: "You understand that if we carry this plan through we must, of course, cut off our military aid to you. Can you prepare for this change in your own country? What kind of economic aid would you need to replace our defense material?"

People constantly ask how we can help to strengthen the United Nations. The way to do this is the strengthen our support here at home and to show by example that we are trying to live up to the ideals established by the organization. Our Bill of Rights is really the basis for the Universal Declaration of Human Rights but, as we know, we have not yet succeeded here at home in proving ourselves staunch advocates of civil liberties and equal rights for all human beings throughout the country. We must correct this situation if we are going to have something better than pure materialism to offer the world, something the Soviets can never offer because it is contrary to their whole system.

We have to work with the people as they are in this country, with all their shortcomings. But if we walk with heads erect and fight for the things we believe in, example will somehow affect every other nation as well as our own future and that of our children.

I remember clearly my husband's words in his last State of the Union address in 1945: ". . . in a democratic world, as in a democratic nation, power must be linked with responsibility and obliged to defend and justify itself within the framework of the general good."

(1963)

## Adlai Stevenson

# Speech on United Nations Charter Day

For me it is a two-fold honor to participate in these ceremonies marking the University of California's 96th Charter Day.

First, in honoring U Thant, Secretary General of the United Nations, you honor a man dedicated to the proposition that peace is nothing less than a human right. His dedication, I would add, is exceeded only by his labors to make that right universal. He is the symbol today of Lincoln's hope for a world in which right makes might. One cannot ask more of any man, and I am privileged to be here today in the company of a dear friend, a colleague and a great citizen of Burma and the world.

Second, coming as it does from a university that not only stands for, but has created some of the finest traditions of higher education, the degree you confer on me has meaning far beyond its flattering citation. I accept it with pride and gratitude.

This is by no means the first time I have spoken on the campus of the great university of my native state of California. And I well remember the last time. It was here in the Greek Theatre before a huge international conference of astronomers. Today, decorated with a Doctor's hood of the University of California, I feel even more — astronomical. I shall try to reciprocate by not abusing your kindness.

It was King Solomon who said, "Knowledge is a wonderful thing; therefore get knowledge; but with all thy getting, get understanding."

I could suggest no harder task, no greater challenge to a university in our complex world. And that is why we must see to it that no one, for whatever reason or in the service of whatever interest, diverts a university from its basic objective. For the university is the archive of the western mind, it is the keeper of the western culture; the fountain of of western culture is freedom — freedom to inquire, to speak, to write, to worship in security. Men may be born free, but they cannot be born wise. It is the aspiration of the university to make free men wise.

Thomas Jefferson proclaimed that the United States was the strongest nation on earth not because of its military might or its productive capacity, but because of its revolutionary ideas. The American Revolution, he said, is intended for all mankind. And I would remind you that there would have been no American Revolution had we not had men who were free and wise and, therefore, not afraid to stand up and rock the boat.

Such an audacious and revolutionary heritage poses certain dangers nowadays, especially in education. But education itself can be dangerous. My friend, Robert Hutchins, has pointed out that the only way to avoid this danger is an educational system in which the student is exposed to no ideas whatever. But that, I think, would be a greater danger by far.

So I am happy, Dr. Kerr, that in this great university on the rim of the Pacific, which is not pacific, faculty and students alike search for the truth and tackle the great ideas and tough problems of our time.

It is about some of these problems and ideas that I want to speak.

Chesterton once said that the trouble about truisms is that they are still true. No truisms have been more pitilessly overworked than those affecting our new post-scientific, post-technological world environment. How often are we told that space has been conquered, that communication from one end of the world to the other is instant! How often we hear about the interdependence of the world economy! Our ears have been all but stunned by reminders that a few nuclear bombs could finish off the human experiment. In fact, we are so stunned that, like Dr. Strangelove, we can learn to live with the bomb and stop worrying.

Repetition, reiteration, rhetoric have all rubbed off the cutting edge. What can one say to restore it, to discover once again the truth under the truism? Does it just add to the cozy fog to remind ourselves that year by year the proximity, the instant contact, the fateful inter-dependence actually grow by a sort of geometrical progression – each invention speeding the next, each advance mobilizing the means for more?

Ten years have passed, I recall, since I gave the Godkin Lectures at Harvard and tried to explore some of the implications of our narrowing world. Only ten years – and in that time we have halved our flight time within space and propose, within another decade, to halve it again. We have sent Telstar in the heavens. We have catapulted men into outer space. One man in 24 hours has lived through a dozen dusks and dawns and swung above our planet, seeing it for the first time for what it is – a little ball in infinite space – and seeing it perhaps with a new eye of understanding.

"Our Earth, how beautiful it is!" cried one of the Soviet Cosmo-nauts. Notice our Earth, mankind's Earth, the only little space in all infinity where man can breathe and live and sleep, the little space which now, with a casual flip of a switch, he can annihilate so that the breathing and the sleeping and the living come finally to their end.

If this interdependence – this interdependence of mutual destruc-tion – does not move us, what can, what will? We have to accept it as the new irrevocable environment of our age. And if there is one lesson above all that history should impress on us, it is that we ignore our envi-ronment at our peril.

From the origins of man, the collective group – call it tribe, call it state, call it nation – has battled with its neighbors, disputed the earth's surface, and in bloody engagement after bloody engagement marked the rise and fall of empires, confederacies, alliances and all kinds of dominations. It had one rationale. In the pre-scientific world, there were not enough resources to go round, and often the survival of one tribe meant the conquest of another's hunting grounds and the elimination of the other hunters. But however often and at whatever level this bit-ing struggle for survival was renewed – in little wars or big wars – there was no extermination. Other groups took up the burdens. The human experiment went on.

Today the supreme expression of historical irony is that the real war of extermination is possible, the final destruction of the human species, and just as the pressure of competitive need is withdrawn. We no longer need our neighbors' hunting grounds. The rationale of sepa-rate, desperate sovereignty has all but vanished in the last two or three decades. But just as the reason vanishes, the means take over. We can wipe out the children of God just at the moment when, at last, the possi-bility of nourishing all of them begins to dawn. Irony of ironies! – The scientific means to end the need for war are twisted to ensure that the war of final extermination at last becomes a possibility.

In theory, of course, we know how to break away from these old fatalities. Within wider and wider areas of the earth's surface, men have contrived to rise above the rule of force and grab. Our large, peaceful, domestic societies prove to us that man is not condemned forever to clan and vendetta. An impartial government which provides police protection and the means, by law courts, to settle disputes is not a pipe dream. We live with it every day, and here in America we do so within a continental federation. Within these wide frontiers of law and order, the economic life of the land may be competitive, but it is not lethal. There is no compulsion either to rob or kill or to starve.

In short, the ground rules of our domestic society are not bad guidelines for international order. And in a world where wars can exterminate and at the same time economic life can begin to feed everyone, the guidelines that have worked to give peace and some sufficiency over a whole continent are sign posts to an inter-continental world society.

Nor do they represent a shift of scope of anything like the proportions which, in physical terms, we begin to accept every day. For a world of instant communication and increasingly instant travel, a few enlargements in the concepts of government, law, police and the general welfare are still — or should still be — much less startling than jumping into outer space. Can we, then, seriously expect to modify everything except our institutions, and turn every physical habit upside down while preserving every political tradition unchanged?

Yet we must admit it. We are blinded to the over-arching facts of our new environment, because they still seem unfamiliar and we feel more at home, more cozy with the old lethal habits of the past. We love the poison that slays us. Twice in my lifetime our vaunted western world has plunged the globe into near total war. And in nazism it reached a pitch of hysteria which betrayed the fact that uncontrolled nationalism is now in many ways an incurably pathological condition.

Yet we still live with our passionate nationalisms. In fact, the last decade has seen such a flowering of new sovereignties that 113 states now make up the roster of the United Nations. Since we met here in San Francisco just 19 years ago it has more than doubled. Nor is this revival of nationalism simply a reflection of the ending of old imperialisms. The monolithic communist world has broken up into separate nationalisms. Our defensive alliance has been invaded by nationalism and is in disorder. The march toward European unity has been halted. And where do we, the United States, stand? What about us — the inescapable leader of the coalition of free men, the keystone of NATO's arch, the United Nations' chief backer, the largest contributor to the world's assistance programs, the nation whose retreat to isolationism — if it ever occurred — would destroy every one of the frail, halting experiments to build up some kind of post-national order to counter the blinding risks of our day?

We must face the fact. We live with divided minds on this great issue. With a prescience unmatched at the time, the founding fathers spoke not for Americans, but for mankind. They sought to set up a government based not on the affinities of blood and culture, but on the universal rights of man – the rights of all men – and believed indeed that they were setting new standards of rationality and legality for the whole human race. But in a world still so totally unready for their ideals, they believed that their best chance of preserving them was to avoid contamination. The spokesmen for humanity avoided "entangling alliances" and kept their new hemisphere out of the clutches of the old. The feeling of America as at once universal and also apart is as rooted in us as our constitution.

In our own day, the conflict between our traditions has come fully into the open, as it had to do once physical aloofness ceased to be a possible option. "Two souls – alas! – dwell in my breast" said Goethe, and of America it may be said that the soul of universalism and the soul of particularism, or isolation if you prefer, struggle for mastery in all our debates.

We are no longer alone in this dilemma and we see today the leaders of Russia and China struggling to reconcile their own national interests with their claim to speak for a communist future for mankind – with the added difficulty that the two variants of communism, the true and the false (we will leave them to decide which is which), are now in open conflict from one end of the world to the other. But we need not be concerned here with their dilemmas. What are we to do with our own?

Let me quickly remind you once more of the background to our conflict. It is the environment of the post-scientific era – of instant communication, near-instant travel, and of outer space. And every hour, the world draws in, draws closer still.

In this shrinking universe, we have considered and partly pursued three lines of policy since the war.

The first, now only the belief of an irrational but noisy minority, is based on pure American self-sufficiency and isolation. Intellectually, the majority no longer accept this, and the government does not nakedly proclaim it. But national interest is nonetheless invoked from time to time as though it were a factor unconnected with the dense web of others' national interests and with the high interdependence of the world's economic structure.

In a second strand – which has made up the bulk of our policy – we have abandoned aloofness and self-sufficiency to seek with friendly nations a common safeguard against communist pretensions. An alliance, largely conceived and generously executed, has entered into our policy making for the first time, and within it we have achieved many things which carry us beyond the day of national separatism. This alliance was not just a block against communism. It was a building block for future world order. It was a recognition of more than national interests. It was a method of organizing the underpinning of a world society in which even continental limits are beginning to look parochial.

Today, as I say, this alliance is in grave disorder. It is not simply a question of the reversion of a narrower nationalism on the part of a decisive partner. It is not simply the risk that the contagion of separatism may spread. It is that we can no longer rely on fear of the outward thrust of Stalinism to hold us together. Indeed, we may well confront one day a Mr. Khrushchev who has more in common with a contented, prosperous bourgeois west than with a racialist, radical, aggressive and impoverished far eastern rival.

What then should be our attitude now that the political landscape of the post-war world – the landscape of alliances and blocs – is changing before our eyes? I suggest to you that this spectacle only adds to the significance of the third strand in our post-war policy – the strand which both goes back to the earliest universal vision of the founding fathers and also accepts the newest, latest evidence of the world's inescapable interdependence, the strand with which we seek, patiently, soberly, one step at a time, to build up our international policy in tune with man's new technological and scientific environment.

There are traces and hints of this policy at every turn. Little by little, for instance, many international agencies are bringing wider vision into focus on economic development, aid, trade and the financing of all of them. All these activities have behind them the realization that no nation can subtract itself from the close mesh of economic interdependence, that in a world in which a small minority are growing steadily richer, while everywhere else the gap increases between rich and poor, elementary considerations of justice, even peace itself, demand a better sharing of the world's resources and solidarity on the part of those whom destiny has placed on the better side of the world's tracks.

But these first tentative steps towards the concept of the "general welfare" on a worldwide scale are concerned with the lesser part of the problems which confront us when we seek to live in a community. The most vital, the most dangerous, the most fateful issues concern our security, the settling of our disputes, the ability to give ourselves the pre-condition of civilized living – life without violence, life lived under agreed procedures of arbitration, conciliation, of law itself. Can we see much progress here? Are we not as immersed as ever in the age of arbitrary violence?

Here, too, I believe there is evidence of new beginnings, of a recoil from the nihilistic terror of war and of the escalation that leads to it. The Cuban Crisis has been followed, after all, by the partial test-ban treaty and a pause in the arms race. More than this, I see growing up in the interstices of the old power systems a new readiness to replace national violence with international peacekeeping. The Near East, Korea, Kashmir, Congo, now Cyprus, the various frontier forces and observer groups, none of them in themselves completely satisfactory or efficient, and yet adding up to peaceful means of policing, controlling and resolving disputes – to cease firing and start talking.

There is, I believe a rapidly increasing realization that nations, like individuals, are "part of the main," part of that wider family living so precariously on this planet, part of a human species whose sheer survival is now at stake.

So we have reached a sort of turning point. Many of the old pressures which kept our western alliance in being are losing strength. We are beginning to be confronted with a choice. Shall we go back to a senseless separatism and isolationism—made no less senseless by the high style and rhetoric of some of its contemporary practitioners. Or shall we reach out to the fuller vision of our greatest traditions—to the rights of all men, to a society based upon human brotherhood, to a worldwide peace secure in justice and ruled by law?

As I have said before, I believe that now as in the days of the founding fathers, even the faintest possibility of achieving such an order depends upon the steadfast faith of this country. In their day, too, democracy in an age of monarchs and freedom in an age of empire seemed the most remote of pipe dreams. Today, too, the dream of a world which repeats at the international level the solid achievements— of law and welfare—of our domestic society must also seem audacious to the point of insanity, save for the grim fact that survival itself is inconceivable on any other terms.

And once again we in America are challenged to hold fast to the audacious dream. If we revert to crude nationalism and separatism, every present organ of international collaboration will collapse. If we withdraw our support from the embryonic organs of world policing and world law, there will be no other sources of support. If we turn in upon ourselves, allow our self-styled patriots to entice us into the supposed security of an impossible isolation, we shall be back in the jungle of rampant nationalisms, baleful ambitions and irreconcilable conflicts which—one cannot repeat it too often—have already twice in this century sent millions to their deaths, and next time would—literally—send everybody to final destruction.

Thus the only sane policy for America—in its own interests and in the wider interests of humanity—lies in patient search for the interests which unite the nations, for the international instruments of law and security, for the institutions of a stable, working world society, for the strengthening of what we have already built inside and outside the United Nations.

If the United States does not press on, no one else will. If we falter, if we lay down this burden, the world, I believe without rhetoric or exaggeration, is lost.

So, in the words of the Scriptures, "Let us work while it is yet day." Honoring U Thant, Secretary General of the United Nations, today, you pay a fitting tribute to the leader of us all in this mighty work.

(1964)

*Wayne C. Booth*

# "Now Don't Try to Reason with Me!" Rhetoric Today, Left, Right, and Center

## 1

When I began teaching English twenty years ago, I saw myself as taking up the weapons of reason against a world committed to emotionalism, illogical appeals, and rhetorical trickery—a world full of vicious advertisers and propagandists who were determined to corrupt the young minds I was determined to save. Now, as a professor of rhetoric and dean of a liberal arts college, I may seem still to present myself in the same melodramatic light: the valiant champion of rationality against the forces of darkness. But bravely as I may try to hold my pose, both the world and the reasonings of men look more complicated than they did twenty years ago. Even as I turn my weapons on the enemies of reason, you will catch me revealing that I am not quite sure who they are, or whether I am qualified to challenge them.

But let me at least begin boldly, with a defense of reason that implies more clarity than I feel about how men ought to proceed when they set out to change each other's minds. The defense begins, quite properly, with the claim that we are in a time of intellectual crisis, a time when confidence in reason is so low that most men no longer try to provide good reasons for what they believe. Of course the very question of what constitutes a good reason is itself under debate, now as always—and I shall be returning to it later. But suppose we begin with the simple notion of proof—the presentation of evidence and arguments in a causal chain intended to pull the mind toward belief.

When we consider how much time teachers spend insisting that students exhibit genuine arguments in their papers, it is perhaps surprising to find the very notion that such forms of proof are desirable, or even obtainable, largely ignored in our public discourse. The simple painful task of putting ideas together logically, so that they track or follow each other, doesn't seem to appeal to many of us any more. I once heard Professor George Williamson of our English department explaining his standards for accepting articles for *Modern Philology*. "Considering the level of argument in the stuff that comes in, I can't really insist on anything that could be called a 'standard,'" he lamented. "I'm happy if I can find essays which show *some* kind of connection between the conclusions and the evidence offered."

You don't have to read much of what passes for literary criticism, or political argument, or social analysis, to conclude that the attention of most authors has not been primarily, or even secondarily, on constructing arguments that would stand up under close scrutiny. Leslie Fiedler spoke at Chicago a couple of years ago and said that the younger generation is really imitating Negro culture, and that the cultural warfare between what he calls palefaces and redskins accounts for our literature today. I protested to a student afterward that Fiedler had offered no evidence, no proof. "That doesn't matter," the student replied, "because it was so interesting."

But it is not simply that our practice is sloppy: open mistrust of rational argument is in the air. The first really modern form of this mistrust was Freud's claim that our conscious efforts at systematic thought are mere superstructures for the fundamental processes which are pre- or sub-logical. But Freud's own attack is, by recent standards, radically tainted with a faith in reason and logical argument. Norman O. Brown, one of the most widely quoted speculative anti-thinkers of the sixties, attacks psychoanalysis for relying on logical processes that alienate us from the realities of selfhood which, he says, are the only truths that we should care about. "The reality-principle," Brown says, "the light by which psychoanalysis has set its course, is a false boundary drawn between inside and outside, subject and object, real and imaginary, physical and mental. It gives us the divided world, the split or schizoid world." The psychoanalyst is, in Brown's view, simply using reason as a defense against the truths which can be found only by realizing the "surrealist" forces that lie too deep for reason.

Marshall McLuhan is an even better-known source of attacks on the intellect—or at least on that part of it that he calls "linear reasoning." Like Brown, McLuhan admits that most of our scientific, technological, and economic life depends on the linear thinking that was brought to its perfection with the invention of printing. But he says that the price we have paid for our "phonetic alphabet" is the diminished functioning of our senses of sound, touch, and taste. "Consciousness is not a verbal process," McLuhan says, with that blissful faith in half-truths which frequently illustrates his own theses. "Yet during all our centuries of phonetic literacy we have favored the chain of inference as the mark of logic and reason. In Western literate society it is still plausible and acceptable to say that something follows from something, as if there were some cause at work that makes such a sequence." McLuhan reminds us that Hume and Kant—or so he believes—both recognized that nothing ever *follows* as effect from something else as cause. Unfortunately, however, neither Hume nor Kant went far enough, McLuhan says, because they did not recognize that what had misled Western man into thinking that reasoning could be linear was the alphabet and printing!

The attack on "mere logic" in the name of intuitive truths that are deeper, more profound, and not amenable to logical testing is by no means a new thing in the world. Everyone who has ever really thought about it, from Plato to the present, has known that logic is by itself at best a weak though necessary tool—a tool that can be used by the devil as well as by angels. But if you read closely in McLuhan, Brown, and many others in recent years, you find that they are expressing a dissatisfaction with reason that goes far beyond a simple mistrust of logic or linear thinking. At its extreme it is a repudiation of anything that deserves the name "thought" at all, in favor of feeling or of the "wisdom of the body."

One of the most seductive expressions of this spirit is the development of what one might call the anti-essay. The word *essay* used to mean "an effort to try out," an attempt. One "essayed" to deal with a topic adequately. Today we have the anti-essay which is a non-attempt. Listen to how Susan Sontag introduces her famous non-essay into the regions of "camp":

> To snare a sensibility in words, especially one that is alive and powerful, one must be tentative and nimble. The form of jottings, rather than an essay (with its claim to a linear, consecutive argument), seemed more appropriate for getting down something of this particular fugitive sensibility. It's embarrassing to be solemn and treatiselike about Camp. One runs the risk of having, oneself, produced a very inferior piece of Camp.

We have grown used to such demurrers and to the kind of disjointed and self-contradictory "notes" she then offers: these are the marks, we tell ourselves, of a "nimble" mind. Surely it is not fair to ask whether the effort to grapple with the notion of Camp is really more difficult than the efforts of Plato and Hume and Kant to "snare" matters like justice and human understanding and the aesthetic order. But fair or not, the suspicion will not down: Miss Sontag simply has not done as much for us as she could have done by repudiating the fashion for non-attempts and pushing herself to some old-fashioned linear thought about how her genuinely clever "notes" relate to each other. She is capable of such thought; I have seen her do it. Why, then, should she deprive us of it?

But the truth is that Miss Sontag is coherence itself by comparison with some of her elders. If you want an interesting exercise in futility, just try sometime to construct an outline of one of McLuhan's chapters. As Edgar Friedenberg says of both Brown and McLuhan, their style "honestly derives from and expresses" their point of view.

I must confess that when I read what passes for argument in these attacks on traditional modes of arguing, I experience a succession of body blows that I'm sure would please these folks immensely. They would argue that my being offended by incoherence results from my bad upbringing: I am a product of an education oriented to print, to the visual, to the organized, the sequential, the analytical, the linear. They may be right. Some of us professors would no doubt be less ashamed if caught beating our wives than if caught in a logical fallacy. McLuhan would tell us all to stop worrying and relax: the time of linear thought, the time when "rational" meant "uniform and continuous and sequential," is over. We have entered a time of "creative configuration and structure," whatever that is, a time of the "inclusive form of the icon," a time when "the medium is the message," a time when what we say no longer matters but only how we say it.

Now I know that I'm being slightly unfair to McLuhan (though I think only slightly). On his descriptive side, as he points to what is happening to our minds under the non-verbal onslaught of the mass media, he is doing part of what must be done. The trouble—aside from his seeming pleasure in his *own* incoherence—is that in most of his recent utterances he seems to have stopped worrying about the loss of our traditional powers of reason. He says, in fact, that the new media, as "extensions of man," are capable of revealing synthetic, simultaneous truths perhaps more important than the old analytical hogwash. What I would want to insist on is that, even though the older forms of rationality are obviously limited, our need for them is as great as ever. To gloss over our need for defenses against irrationality with such phrases as "the medium is the message" is to sell out a major part of our humanity—even if the claim to bring to light neglected abilities proves justified.

2

Suppose we look at a bit of irrational message-mongering, done by one of the "new media," to see if we can be satisfied with saying that the content no longer matters. Everyone knows that journalism has been transformed in recent years, especially in the news magazines, from reportage into new forms of paralogical rhetoric: political argument disguised as dramatic reporting. It would be fun to spend the rest of my hour simply describing the new rhetorical devices, and the new twists on old devices, that *Time* magazine, only the most successful of many, exhibits from week to week, all in the name of news. Mr. Ralph Ingersoll, former publisher of the magazine, has described the key to the magazine's success as the discovery of how to turn news into fiction, giving each story its own literary form, with a beginning, a middle, and an end, regardless of whether the story thus invented matches the original event. Everyone I know who has ever been treated by *Time*—whether favorably or unfavorably—has been shocked by the distortions of fact for effect, and the more they know about a subject the more they are shocked. A doctor friend at the University says one cannot trust the medical reporting. Eric Bentley, the drama critic, says they cannot be trusted about drama. Igor Stravinsky says, "Every music column I have read in *Time* has been distorted and inaccurate."[1]

---

[1]As I read proof in May, 1970, I have an impression that *Time* has been somewhat improved lately. Am I simply reacting to the attacks on the "media" by Vice President Agnew? And to the fact that lately *Time*'s surreptitious editorializing is often employed against presidential policies and methods that I, too, deplore?

More important to us than all of this testimony is the *way* the distortions operate. Though much of the distortion is simply for the sake of being interesting, much of it is done to put across political and social viewpoints. I open an issue of *Time* at random to an attack on *Ramparts* magazine. It is of course not called an attack. It is made to look like a regular news account, objective, olympian. But it is a highly loaded attack, nevertheless. What troubles *Time* about *Ramparts*, amusingly enough, is that "*Ramparts* is slick enough to lure the unwary and bedazzled reader into accepting flimflam as fact" — a description which I would take as fitting *Time* exactly. "No other left-wing publication in the United States," *Time* says, "pursues shock more relentlessly or plays around more with fact." Now you may think, for a moment, that *Time* added that adjective "left-wing" in order to add one more charge to six other charges of leftism skillfully planted (to use a favorite *Time* word) in the account. But I prefer to think that *Time* is being unusually honest: by confining the competition for fact-distortion to left-wing magazines, *Time* has considerably ruled itself out of the running.

It is always instructive to follow *Time*'s shenanigans closely. Ask yourself, for example, how you would headline the following quotation, if you worked for *Time:* " 'Quite frankly,' says Hinckle, the publisher of *Ramparts,* 'there weren't enough Catholic laymen [we soon discovered] to write for and to buy the magazine. Besides, we got bored with just the church.' " Now think of a headline. Isn't it obvious? Your headline for this section will be "Bored With The Church." And that, of course, is the headline used, with an important shift in meaning.

Let's go on with the game. How would you describe where *Ramparts* is published? Where else but in "one of those topless streets in San Francisco's New Left Bohemia." What kind of humor does *Ramparts* publish? "Clever if sophomoric humor" — clever, or there would be no threat, sophomoric, or it might really be funny. How would you describe an article in *Ramparts* purporting to show that one million children have been killed or wounded in the Vietnam war? Could you do better than this: *Ramparts* "produced a mere juggling of highly dubious statistics." How would you describe the pictures of dead or wounded children? Why naturally as "a collection of very touching pictures, some of which could have been taken in any distressed country."

*Time* is, of course, only one example of a kind of nonrational persuasion that is practiced on us all the time, and *Ramparts* is also guilty of the disguised and dishonest rhetoric I am describing. Another good instance of this same kind of transformation of journalism into degraded rhetoric is *Fact*, the magazine from which I collected, perhaps somewhat naively, some of the testimony I earlier used against *Time*. I originally subscribed to *Fact* on the basis of a one-paragraph ad in the *New York Times;* it claimed that with so much editorializing in all other journals (that word "all" should have alerted me, perhaps) America needs a magazine devoted to objective reporting of the truth. I should have predicted what would come: a collection of shrill exposés, most of them with a touch of scandal and few of them providing enough solid evidence or argument to allow a reader to know whether there was anything to them or not. "A Psychoanalytical Study of Baseball," "A Study of Wife-Swapping in California," an argument that Dag Hammarskjold was a psychotic who committed suicide (*could* be, one says, but not on the basis of *this* evidence), another argument that Goldwater has been declared insane by thousands of psychiatrists (yet if you look closely at the evidence here it turns out to mean, at most, far less than the headlines claim)[2] – why, it's as hard to read *Fact* as it is to read *Time!*

The important point is that McLuhan's current cheerful response to such corruptions of the media is not enough. (He used to be much less complacent; now he says that TV advertising is the greatest art of our time. Even allowing for self-protective ambiguity, *what happened?*) To say that the medium is the message is entirely inadequate when a definite message has been sneakingly and very powerfully conveyed by the medium. The content of *Time,* and of *Ramparts,* and of *Fact* is very important indeed, once we have dug it out of the seemingly neutral prose. The medium is *not* the message nor is it that exciting new kind of "iconic presentation" that enables us "to live mythically and integrally." Rather, it is that very old-fashioned kind of manipulation of rhetorical distortions, skillfully placed in non-McLuhanesque sequences designed to take us in. And if we are not to be taken in, we must learn now as in the past to think *through* the medium *to* the message, to think critically about that message, to ask what reasons if any have been given to support it. In short, we must do exactly what McLuhan deplores: continue to *think* in what he calls the old, fragmented space and time patterns of the pre-electric age.

What I have been trying to suggest, with these examples, is that we live in a world in which men show little esteem for logic, little respect for facts, no faith in anyone's ability to use thought or discourse to arrive at improved judgments, commitments, and first principles. The consequences that one would expect in such a world, when honesty of observation, care with logic, and subtlety with dialectic have declined, can of course be seen wherever men try to change each other's minds. What is left to rhetoric when solid substantive argument is denied to it? Obviously only emotional appeal and appeal to the superior moral integrity and wisdom or cleverness of the rhetorician – what was formerly called "ethical appeal" (whether the appeal was moral or immoral). Emotional appeal and ethical appeal can never be expelled from the house of rhetoric; all the great rhetoricians are passionate in their rationalism. But when men are reduced to using these properly subordi-

---

[2]It was recently announced that Goldwater has won his libel suit against *Fact*. But of course in the four years since I wrote my preliminary verdict, the editor has gone on feeding his gulls – many of whom no doubt think of themselves as wise birds indeed.

nate appeals as if they were the sole means of persuasion, they produce the kind of rhetoric that we now find flowing at us, left, right, and center.

I have time only for two examples. They both will seem extreme and therefore unrepresentative to some of you, but the test is that they have apparently been effective on large numbers of Americans. Can you recognize who is speaking in the first quotation?

I can see a day when all the Americas, North and South, will be linked in a mighty system, a system in which the errors and misunderstandings of the past will be submerged, one by one, in a rising tide of prosperity and interdependence. We know that the misunderstandings of centuries are not to be wiped away in a day or an hour. But we pledge that human sympathy—what our neighbors to the south call an attitude that is "simpatico"—no less than enlightened self-interest will be our guide. I can see this Atlantic civilization galvanizing and guiding emergent nations everywhere. Now I know that freedom is not the fruit of every soil. I know that our own freedom was achieved through centuries by the unremitting efforts of brave and wise men. And I know that the road to freedom is a long and challenging road. And I know also that some men may walk away from it, that some men resist challenge . . .

No doubt you have placed the speaker by now in a general way. His is a political rhetoric appropriate to the campaign trail, and his platitudes are mostly the platitudes of the conservative center: the combination of human sympathy and self-interest building an Atlantic civilization (God knows how!) and the appeals to freedom might be offered by any Democrat or Republican of slightly jingoist cast. Only with the move toward the vaguely ominous charge that some men *resist challenge* do we suspect that this may be a different kind of conservative; we are thus not really surprised at the concluding phrase:

. . . accepting the false security of governmental paternalism.

The vapidities of a Goldwater, representing a nation that does not ask that its political candidates give reasons, are now clear! (I am not saying that only Goldwater could have written the passage, just that it is typical.)

Where on the left was I to find an equally revealing piece of bombast. It ought to be one that would make a few of my listeners mad—and a few more think. Obviously something by a student; obviously something from the new student left. Listen closely now to excerpts from a long "Letter to Undergraduates," by Bradford Cleaveland, former graduate student of the department of political science at Berkeley; it was written during the troubles of '64–'65.

Dear Undergraduates, . . . On the one hand there [is] substantial agreement that the University stamps out consciousness like a super-Madison Avenue machine;

on the other, people [are] saying, "So what?" or "Bring me a detailed and exhaustive plan." *But there is no plan for kicking twenty thousand people IN THEIR ASSES!* No plan will stop excessive greed, timidity, and selling out. At best the university is a pathway to the club of 'tough-minded-liberal-realists' in America, who sit in comfortable armchairs talking radical while clutching hysterically at respectability in a world explosive with revolution. At worst the university destroys your desire to see reality and to suffer reality with optimism, at the time when you most need to learn that painful art. . . .

. . . The first set of facts [is that in your undergraduate program] you are puppets. You perform. But when do you think? Dutifully and obediently you follow, as a herd of grade-worshiping sheep. If you are strong at all, you do this with some sense of shame, or if you are weak, you do it with a studied cynicism . . . as jaded youth with parched imaginations that go no further than oak-paneled rooms at the end of the line . . . BUT WHETHER YOU ARE STRONG OR WEAK YOU PERFORM LIKE TRAINED SEALS, AND LIKE SHEEP YOU FOLLOW . . . WITH THE THOROUGHBRED PHI BETA KAPPA SHEEP LEADING YOU!!! up the golden stairway to the omnipotent A, to the Happy consciousness, to success and a very parochial mind.

[The second set of facts is that the Charter Day is an unmerciful sham; an example of unparalleled demagoguery.]

Having elaborated these two sets of facts, which were of course not facts at all but deeply personal judgments, Mr. Cleaveland then moved to his clincher:

Dear Undergraduates!! I am no longer interested in cajoling you, arguing with you, or describing to you something you already know. I . . . entreat you to furiously throw your comforting feelings to duty and responsibility for this institution to the winds and act on your situation. . . . There is only one proper response to Berkeley from undergraduates: that you *organize and split this campus wide open!* From this point on, do not misunderstand me, my intention is to convince you that you do nothing less than begin an open, fierce, and thoroughgoing rebellion on this campus.

My point here is not to argue that Mr. Cleaveland was right or wrong in urging revolution. What interests me is the kind of reasons he felt were adequate to persuade undergraduates to strike against the university. The notion that thousands of highly selected American undergraduates should find this sort of thing appealing ought to frighten us all. Indeed, there is a kind of contempt for the intellect and its efforts running throughout the literature of the Berkeley revolt – and through other literature of the new left – which seems to me far more threatening to the future of the American left itself than has been generally recognized. When the left stops thinking, we should all know by now, it becomes as destructive of human values as the unthinking right – and I must say that there is a tone in much of this literature which suggests that thinking is itself a suspect activity. Cleaveland is fond of using the word "scholars" in quotation marks: he talks of "scholars" and "so-called liberals" who adopt "the hideous posture of studying" or analyzing the "problem."

Now I cannot really prove that these two rather special examples are in any way representative of right and left, or that their similar tendency to shout and chant rather than reason is representative of American rhetoric today. But I suspect that you have found, in your daily reading, enough that is like these two to bear out my hunch that there really is a predominance of irrational persuasion at work here. You may, in fact, have concluded – subjected to so much slick advertising and political propaganda as you are – that this is all there is to rhetoric, that in fact men cannot persuade each other rationally in such matters since, in matters of judgment and action, all choices are equally irrational.

And of course this is precisely why everyone in any academic community should be deeply disturbed whenever the Goldwaters and the Cleavelands begin to attract large numbers of listeners. We claim to be committed to free and honest and relentless inquiry. This almost everyone takes for granted; only a few on the extreme right and the extreme left have questioned this basic commitment of colleges and universities. What is not so frequently recognized is that the very notion of free inquiry depends on the possibility of valid, genuinely justified persuasion – that is, of a rhetoric not like Goldwater's and Cleaveland's but rather a rhetoric built on the use of reason to persuade men to believe one proposition – a true proposition – rather than another, a false or less adequate proposition.

### 3

My point is not, as I'm sure you realize by now, to indict either the left or the right, but to plead for what I take to be the very fragile twin values of honest inquiry and honest rhetoric. I have said so far that these values are under steady attack, both in theory and in practice, by men of both left and right – some of them presumably sincere, some of them no doubt knaves. Wherever men find themselves too impatient to think together about their problems, wherever immediate action based on "unity" becomes more important than men's determination to achieve genuine unity by discovering the truth together, my twin values disappear – often never to reappear in a particular society. They *always* risk annihilation in a major war, and it is not surprising that the Vietnam war, which seems to most of us self-evidently a horrible national disaster and which to many Americans seems self-evidently a righteous crusade, should have led us to shout rather than reason. My twin values disappear in any society whenever enough men decide that victory is worth whatever it costs. They disappear whenever men decide, as Bradford Cleaveland decided in California, that there is "only one proper response" to a political situation—the effort to destroy the opponent through force or political pressure. (I would not want to suggest that these twin values are the only values for mankind, or that I would never be willing to risk them for other values. Though it is fairly easy to show historically that most revolutionary efforts work more harm than good, I can think of situations when I would be forced to stop thinking and talking and start overthrowing: Nazi Germany, say, or *perhaps* Boston in 1775—but note how many of our revolutionaries managed to go on thinking as well as fighting. It is clear that the force of my plea for more reason and less shouting depends in part on my conviction that we are not yet in such an extreme situation. If you really believe that the only action possible in America is to choose one of two sides and then use violence to win, we may as well close the College and load our weapons.)

It is important to recognize that none of the attacks on reason—either theoretical or in the form of shapeless writing or biased reporting or open invitation to riot—none has pretended that reason is ineffective in dealing with practical, prudential affairs. Everyone admits that reason has produced fantastic results in science and technology. The protests seem, often enough, to be against the very success of rational calculation in the hands of statisticians, logicians, computer analysts, or army officers, when applied to human affairs without starting from humane premises. Atomic bombs and doomsday machines and calculations of overkill all seem to show what happens when reason is left to its own devices without the control of—of what?

Traditionally the answer might have been "the control of reason itself." Reason did not, in earlier centuries, mean simply logical calculation but rather the whole process of discovering sound first principles and *then* reasoning from them to sound conclusions. What seems distinctive in our time is the widespread conviction that our choice of first principles is itself irrational or capricious. Most teachers and students I talk with seem to have concluded that the choice of one's starting point is always an arbitrary act of faith, and that to debate about such choices is a mark of immaturity. After all, we have been shown in so many different ways that even in the physical sciences hypotheses are discovered intuitively; that the first principles are not subject to proof; that even the most seemingly objective knowledge is, as Michael Polanyi says, *"personal* knowledge"—infused with personal meanings and values and thus not really what we ordinarily mean by objective at all. Though most professional philosophers now as in all times are not relativists, the predominant lay philosophy is, I would say, a kind of relativism. Men make their own values; values change from society to society, and even from group to group within a society—"How can one reason about such things?" we seem to say to each other. It is not hard, in fact, to see why McLuhan and Brown and others feel that they must speak, even if in a distorted form, for truths that lie beyond reason.

The first part of my title comes from a *New Yorker* cartoon which showed a woman, quarreling with her husband, saying: "Now don't try to *reason* with me." The cartoon reflects, it seems to me, one of our attitudes toward reason. It is of course a male cartoon, and it betrays first of all the American male's traditional contempt for the female's unreasonableness. To be reasonable has in our folklore been the male's prerogative, one sign of his superiority. In this view, reason is of course a good thing to have; to be irrational, "like a woman," is somehow funny. But it is not hard to develop a different view of the cartoon; to think oneself into "the woman's point of view" and imagine how a brutal and irrelevant logical argument can cover up or violate fundamental needs or feelings while seeming to have all of the right on its side.

Man was traditionally known as the rational animal; in that view reason was of man's very essence. But it takes no great learning to remind us that much that we think of as distinctively human—love, poetry, martyrdom—can present itself in forms that seem to violate reason—or perhaps to transcend it. We can all quote Pascal, who said that the heart can be turned on by reasons that reason cannot dig—or words to that effect. Tertullian is supposed to have said that he embraced his religious belief just *because* it was absurd. In the last several centuries, many have seen man's peculiar humanity not in his rationality, not in the common grounds of truth and right action that reason leads to, but rather in his capacity for individual freedom, whether rational or mad. For them, the act of freely choosing an error or falsehood confers greater human dignity than the act of passively accepting that which reason seems to require and which many men consequently believe. Stephen Dedalus, in Joyce's *Portrait of the Artist as a Young Man,* is by no means the only literary portrait of a soul electing what he believes may be eternal damnation for the sake of doing things his own way, according to his own feelings. The romantic soul has for at least two centuries been shouting defiance at traditional reasonings, though one should hasten to add that the relation between reason and romanticism is laden with the same ambiguities as are our attitudes toward the coldly rational male and the weakly intuitive female: if the romantic hero can be portrayed as a representative of individualism gone mad, seeking what in modern jargon we might call a personalized truth which to everyone else will be damnable falsehood, he can also be portrayed in Faustian terms, as the man who is willing to violate intuition, love, and the value of religious faith and salvation all for the sake of knowledge—that is, for what reason reveals.

In either view, somehow, the Garden of Eden is threatened by man's quest for knowledge—not just knowledge of good and evil, but the whole search for intellectual mastery. A life led according to what the mind can test and prove seems somehow to threaten much that all of us hold dear. The young student who is impatient with the cautious weighings and probings and refusals of commitment that go on within every university is plainly in one great tradition of a mistrust of reason that all of us must feel at one time or another. Men are starving throughout the world; men's souls are being destroyed in Harlem and Mississippi; children are being bombed in Vietnam—and here you sit, training your intellects to savor the pleasures of art and literature and elegant argument!

**4**

So you see, we can make the emphasis fall either way: attacks on reason are vicious because reason, properly defined, is our most precious gift; or attacks on reason are needed, because no matter how you define a "reasonable life" much of what is most valued by men is left out. As a university professor I am committed to the supreme professional standard of rationality: insofar as I am an honest professor, worthy of my own respect, I am sworn to change my mind if and when someone shows me that there are *good reasons* to change my mind. But both as a man who loves art and literature that I cannot fully explain, and as a human being who holds to many values the correctness of which I cannot easily prove with unanswerable rational arguments, I know how much of my life is not readily explicable at the court of what is usually called reason.

The question is whether reasonable debate is in *any* degree possible about such basic commitments, political and moral and personal. What we call rhetoric is usually used only when scientific proof is not available—about such matters as whether to oppose or support the Vietnam policy, or whether to join a church or commit suicide, or whether to vote for Goldwater or join a strike against the University of California. Can such questions be debated rationally, or do we have available only those forms of persuasion used by Goldwater and Cleaveland—emotional appeals and appeals to the character of the speaker or references to the enemy's viciousness?

Though I have no time to undertake the difficult argument such a question demands, I should like to suggest that in losing our confidence in the possibility of finding genuinely good reasons for important human actions, in losing our belief in a reasonable rhetoric, we have laid ourselves open to the kinds of perverted rhetoric I have described. My main point is to argue that we must preserve and extend our capacity for a rational persuasion about the most important questions. If we don't, liberal education in any meaningful sense will die, leaving us at the mercy of propagandists and protected only by the superficial slogans of the propaganda analysts.

What has happened, I am convinced, is that we have fallen victims to an all-or-nothing kind of argument that we should be ashamed of. Of course we cannot find, in social and political and ethical questions, the degrees of certainty in proof that scientists – at least some of them – boast of. But does this mean that we are reduced to emotional appeal, shouting, lying, trickery, and ultimately, warfare? That it does not is in itself a conclusion to be proved with the kind of proof that is in question – and the intellectual problems are not simple. For now, perhaps you will be willing simply to record one man's strong conviction that a reasonable persuasion is not only possible but indispensable if we are to live well together.

Whatever such a rhetoric might be, it will not be a dry, unemotional kind of argument for the middle of the road. To believe in reason doesn't mean that one believes only in reason – one might recognize the truths of the heart without having to launch an attack on the head. The trouble with our present situation is that the defenders of logicality or rationality seem too often to be men who want to reason only about the means to unquestioned ends – they would "rationalize" society, make us efficient, lead us to social usefulness, rather than try to humanize us. This leaves the defenders of the heart to operate in a whirlwind of emotions, convinced that to be reasonable is somehow to be cold and calculating. Well, there *are* some causes worth dying for, and there are many causes not worth a hoot. I will not die for a cause unless I feel deeply about it. Imagine Churchill using only a chain of syllogisms trying to persuade the British to fight. But on the other hand I cannot distinguish the good causes from the circus acts unless I have learned to think about them, and the good rhetorician will, like Churchill during the war, show me by his arguments as well as by his character that he is on the right side.

## 5

We should be quite clear about what all this means to us. If we cannot find a defense of reason that makes of it something more than a useful weapon in the arsenal of each warring faction, if there is not some sense in which men can reason together about even their most precious commitment, if basic faiths and loves and first principles are entirely arbitrary and hence beyond discussion, then we may as well succumb to the McLuhanesque glow, or to the polymorphous perverse pleasures offered by Brown, or to the revolutionary inanities of Cleaveland. And, incidentally, we English teachers are on very shaky ground when we scribble in the margin "logic bad here" or "not clear how these propositions relate." We are on shaky ground in teaching *composition* at all. Who cares, after all, whether the logic is bad or good unless the conclusions that good writing might persuade to are in some sense superior to the conclusions produced by bad writing? But this can be true only if some first principles are themselves superior to others, only if they are in some sense *demonstrably* superior.

Plato said that the worst fate that can befall a man is to become a misologist, a hater of reason; for him it was clear that since man is essentially reasonable, when he ceases to reason he ceases to be a man. I happen to believe this unfashionable doctrine—assuming the broad definition of reason that I have been implying here. I also believe that when any society loses its capacity to debate its ends and means rationally, it ceases to be a society of men at all and becomes instead a mob, or pack, or a herd of creatures rather less noble than most animals. In America in recent years we have seen far too many such herds—self-righteous fanatics who know without listening that the speaker is wrong. There are many of our universities, so-called, where Karl Marx, say, or Miss Aptheker would be booed from the platform, even if the administration were to allow them to speak. And on the other hand there have been some disturbing instances lately of left-wing students in first-class universities coercing a speaker into silence. Whatever defenses may be offered for such rhetoric—the rhetoric of shouting a man down—it is not the rhetoric of a student, and those shouting mobs are not students, no matter what else they may be. It is one mark of an honest man, as it should be the mark of an educated man, that he tries not to use a double standard in judging his friends and his enemies. Self-righteous bullying fanatics are self-righteous bullying fanatics regardless of the cause they support, and they are as much a threat to the central values we defend when they bully on our side as when they bully on our enemy's. Men—at least some men—aspire to a life of sweet reasonableness, but all men seem engaged in a verbal warfare that leaves them perpetually teetering on the brink of actual warfare, local, national, and international. Our hold on reason is precarious; our institutions for giving it a chance are highly fragile. The very tradition out of which I speak of a rational rhetoric is itself fragile. It would not really be surprising if fifty years from now no one in America would even know what I'm talking about tonight—such a transformation would not be greater than many that history has known. Men in that time would know something that most of you do *not* know—what it *feels* like not to be *allowed* to follow a thought wherever it might lead, openly, publicly. Whether we move toward that genuine garrison state, that really total institutionalization of the mind, will depend in part, in very small but very real part, on how many of us here can manage—not in sermons like this, which are easy superficial substitutes for the day-by-day thinking that counts, but in our life as teachers and students—to reason together about what we care for most.

(1967)

*Jerry Rubin*

# A Yippie Manifesto

This is a Viet Cong flag on my back. During the recent hearings of the House UnAmerican Activities Committee in Washington, a friend and I are walking down the street en route to Congress—he's wearing an American flag and I'm wearing this VC flag.

The cops mass, and boom! all of a sudden they come toward us. I think: Oh, man, curtains. I am going to be arrested for treason, for supporting the enemy.

And who do the cops grab and throw in the paddy wagon?

My friend with the American flag!

And I'm left all alone in the VC flag.

"What kind of a country is this?" I shout at the cops. "YOU COMMUNISTS!"

Everything is cool en route to Canada until the border. An official motions me into a small room and pulls out a five-page questionnaire.

"Do you use drugs?" he asks quite seriously.

"Yeah," I say.

"Which?"

"Coca Cola."

"I mean DRUGS!" he shouts.

"Coca Cola is more dangerous for you than marijuana," I say. "Fucks up your body, and it's addictive."

"Have you ever advocated the overthrow of the Canadian government?" he asks.

"Not until I get into Canada."

"Have you ever been arrested for inciting to riot?"

I reply no, and it is true. In August I was arrested in Chicago for something similar, "solicitation to mob action," a violation of a sex statute.

Finally I ask the border official to drop out. "Man, your job is irrelevant," I say. "The Canadian-American border does not exist. There are no such things as borders. The border exists only in your head.

"No state has the right to ask me these questions. The answers are mine. Next thing I know you guys will be tapping my brain!"

I try to get the cat to take off his uniform right there. But he refuses, saying, "I've got a job to do and a family to support."

So goes the cancer of the Western world: everyone just doing his "job." Nobody learned the lesson of Eichmann. Everyone still points the finger elsewhere.

America and the West suffer from a great spiritual crisis. And so the yippies are a revolutionary religious movement.

We do not advocate political solutions that you can vote for. You are never going to be able to *vote* for the revolution. Get that hope out of your mind.

And you are not going to be able to buy the revolution in a supermarket, in the tradition of our consumer society. The revolution is not a can of goods.

Revolution only comes through personal transformation: finding God and changing your life. Then millions of converts will create a massive social upheaval.

The religion of the yippies is: "RISE UP AND ABANDON THE CREEPING MEATBALL!!"

That means anything you want it to mean. Which is why it is so powerful a revolutionary slogan. The best picket sign I ever saw was blank. Next best was: "We Protest—!"

Slogans like "Get out of Vietnam" are informative, but they do not create myths. They don't ask you to do anything but carry them.

Political demonstrations should make people dream and fantasize. A religious-political movement is concerned with people's souls, with the creation of a magic world which we make real.

When the national media first heard our slogan, they reported that the "creeping meatball" was Lyndon Johnson. Which was weird and unfair, because we liked Lyndon Johnson.

We cried when LBJ dropped out. "LBJ, you took us too literally! We didn't mean YOU should drop out! Where would WE be if it weren't for you, LBJ?"

Is there any kid in America, or anywhere in the world, who wants to be like LBJ when he grows up?

As a society falls apart, its children reject their parents. The elders offer us Johnsons, Agnews, and Nixons, dead symbols of a dying past.

The war between THEM and US will be decided by the seven-year-olds.

We offer: sex, drugs, rebellion, heroism, brotherhood.

They offer: responsibility, fear, puritanism, repression.

Dig the movie *Wild in the Streets!* A teenage rock-and-roll singer campaigns for a Bobby Kennedy-type politician.

Suddenly he realizes: "We're all young! Let's run the country ourselves!"

"Lower the voting age to 14!"

"14 or FIGHT!"

They put LSD in the water fountains of Congress and the Congressmen have a beautiful trip. Congress votes to lower the voting age to 14.

The rock-and-roll singer is elected President, but the CIA and military refuse to recognize the vote. Thousands of longhairs storm the White House, and six die in the siege. Finally the kids take power, and they put all people over 30 into camps and give them LSD every day. (Some movies are even stranger than OUR fantasies.)

"Don't trust anyone over 30!" say the yippies—a much-quoted warning.

I am four years old.

We are born twice. My first birth was in 1938, but I was reborn in Berkeley in 1964 in the Free Speech Movement.

When we say "Don't trust anyone over 30," we're talking about the second birth. I got 26 more years.

When people 40 years old come up to me and say, "Well, I guess I can't be part of your movement," I say, "What do you mean? You could have been born yesterday. Age exists in your head."

Bertrand Russell is our leader. He's 90 years old.

Another yippie saying is: "THE GROUND YOU STAND ON IS LIBERATED TERRITORY!"

Everybody in this society is a policeman. We all police ourselves. When we free ourselves, the real cops take over.

I don't smoke pot in public often, although I love to. I don't want to be arrested: that's the only reason.

I police myself.

We do not own our own bodies.

We fight to regain our bodies—to make love in the parks, say "fuck" on television, do what we want to do whenever we want to do it.

Prohibitions should be prohibited.

Rules are made to be broken.

Never say "no."

The yippies say: "PROPERTY IS THEFT."

What America got, she stole.

How was this country built? By the forced labor of slaves. America owes black people billions in compensation.

"Capitalism" is just a polite schoolbook way of saying: "Stealing."

Who deserves what they get in America? Do the Rockefellers deserve their wealth? HELL NO!

Do the poor deserve their poverty? HELL NO!!

America says that people work only for money. But check it out: those who don't have money work the hardest, and those who have money take very long lunch hours.

When I was born I had food on my table and a roof over my head. Most babies born in the world face hunger and cold. What is the difference between them and me?

Every well-off white American better ask himself that question or he will never understand why people hate America.

The enemy is this dollar bill right here in my hand.

Now if I get a match, I'll show you what I think of it.

This burning gets some political radicals very uptight. I don't know exactly why. They burn a lot of money putting out leaflets nobody reads.

I think it is more important today to burn a dollar bill than it is to burn a draft card.

(Hmmm, pretty resilient. Hard to burn. Anybody got a lighter?)

We go to the New York Stock Exchange, about 20 of us, our pockets stuffed with dollar bills. We want to throw real dollars down at all those people on the floor playing monopoly games with numbers.

An official stops us at the door and says, "You can't come in. You are hippies and you are coming to demonstrate."

With TV cameras flying away, we reply: "Hippies? Demonstrate? We're Jews. And we're coming to see the stock market."

Well, that gets the guy uptight, and he lets us in. We get to the top, and the dollars start raining down on the floor below.

These guys deal in millions of dollars as a game, never connecting it to people starving. Have they ever seen a real dollar bill?

"This is what it is all about, you sonavabitches!!"

Look at them: wild animals chasing and fighting each other for the dollar bills thrown by the hippies!

And then the cops come. The cops are a necessary part of any demonstration theater. When you are planning a demonstration, always include a role for the cops. Cops legitimize demonstrations.

The cops throw us out.

It is noon. Wall Street. Businessmen with briefcases and suits and ties. Money freaks going to lunch. Important business deals. Time. Appointments.

And there we are in the middle of it, burning five-dollar bills. Burning their world. Burning their Christ.

"Don't! Don't!" some scream, grasping for the sacred paper. Several near fist-fights break out.

We escape with our lives.

Weeks later *The New York Times* publishes a short item revealing that the New York Stock Exchange is installing a bulletproof glass window between the visitors' platform and the floor, so that "nobody can shoot a stockbroker."

(In Chicago 5,000 yippies come, armed only with our skin. The cops bring tanks, dogs, guns, gas, long-range rifles, missiles. Is it South Vietnam or Chicago? America always overreacts.)


The American economy is doomed to collapse because it has no soul. Its stability is war and preparation for war. Consumer products are built to break, and advertising brainwashes us to consume new ones.

The rich feel guilty. The poor are taught to hate themselves. The guilty and the wretched are on a collision course.

If the men who control the technology used it for human needs and not profit and murder, every human being on the planet could be free from starvation. Machines could do most of the work: people would be free to do what they want.

We should be very realistic and demand the impossible. Food, housing, clothing, medicine, and color TV free for all!!

People would work because of love, creativity, and brotherhood. A new economic structure would produce a new man.

That new structure will be created by new men.

American society, because of its Western-Christian-Capitalist bag, is organized on the fundamental premise that man is bad, society evil, and that: People must be motivated and forced by external reward and punishment.

We are a new generation, species, race. We are bred on affluence, turned on by drugs, at home in our bodies, and excited by the future and its possibilities.

Everything for us is an experience, done for love or not done at all.

We live off the fat of society. Our fathers worked all-year-round for a two-week vacation. Our entire life is a vacation!

Every moment, every day we decide what we are going to do.

We do not groove with Christianity, the idea that people go to heaven after they are dead. We want HEAVEN NOW!

We do not believe in studying to obtain degrees in school. Degrees and grades are like money and credit, good only for burning.

There is a war going on in the Western world: a war of genocide by the old against the young.

The economy is closed. It does not need us. Everything is built.

So the purpose of universities is: to get us off the streets. Schools are baby-sitting agencies.

The purpose of the Vietnam war is: to get rid of blacks. They are a nuisance. America got the work she needed out of blacks, but now she has no use for them.

It is a psychological war. The old say, "We want you to die for us." The old send the young to die for the old.

Our response? Draft-card burning and draft dodging! We won't die for you.

Young whites are dropping out of white society. We are getting our heads straight, creating new identities. We're dropping out of middle-class institutions, leaving their schools, running away from their homes, and forming our own communities.

We are becoming the new niggers.

I'm getting on a plane en route to Washington. An airline official comes up to me and says, "You can't go on this airplane."

"Why not?" I ask.

"Because you smell."

That's what they used to say about black people, remember?

They don't say that about black people anymore. They'd get punched in their fucking mouths.

Our long hair communicates disrespect to America. A racist, short-hair society gets freaked by long hair. It blinds people. In Vietnam, America bombs the Vietnamese, but cannot see them because they are brown.

Long hair is vital to us because it enables us to recognize each other. We have white skin like our oppressors. Long hair ties us together into a visible counter-community.

A car drives down the street, parents in front, and 15-year-old long-hair kid in back. The kid gives me the "V" sign! That's the kind of communication taking place.

Within our community we have the seeds of a new society. We have our own communications network, the underground press. We have the beginnings of a new family structure in communes. We have our own stimulants.

When the cops broke into my home on the Lower East Side to arrest me for possession of pot, it was like American soldiers invading a Vietnamese village. They experienced cultural shock.

Fidel Castro was on the wall. They couldn't believe it! Beads! They played with my beads for 20 minutes.

When the cops kidnapped me in Chicago, they interviewed me as if I had just landed from Mars.

"Do you fuck each other?"

"What is it like on LSD?"

"Do you talk directly with the Viet Cong?"

The two generations cannot communicate with one another because of our different historical experiences.

Our parents suffered through the Depression and World War II. We experience the consumer economy and the U.S.A. as a military bully in Vietnam.

From 1964 to 1968 the movement has been involved in the destruction of the old symbols of America. Through our actions we have redefined those symbols for the youth.

Kids growing up today expect school to be a place to demonstrate, sit-in, fight authority, and maybe get arrested.

Demonstrations become the initiation rites, rituals, and social celebrations of a new generation.

Remember the Pentagon, center of the military ego? We urinated on it. Thousands of stoned freaks stormed the place, carrying Che's picture and stuffing flowers in the rifles of the 82nd Airborne.

Remember the Democratic Convention? Who, after Chicago, can read schoolbook descriptions of national political conventions with a straight face anymore? The farce within the convention became clear because of the war between the yippies and the cops in the streets.

We are calling the bluff on the myths of America. Once the myth is exposed, the structure behind it crumbles like sand. Chaos results. People must create new realities.

In the process we create new myths, and these new myths forecast the future.

In America in 1969 old myths can be destroyed overnight, and new ones created overnight because of the power of television. By making communications instantaneous, television telescopes the revolution by centuries. What might have taken 100 years will now take 20. What used to happen in 10 years now happens in two. In a dying society, television becomes a revolutionary instrument.

For her own protection, the government is soon going to have to suppress freedom of the press and take direct control over what goes on television, especially the news.

TV has dramatized the longhair drop-out movement so well that virtually every young kid in the country wants to grow up and be a demonstrator.

What do you want to be when you grow up? A fireman? A cop? A professor?

"I want to grow up and make history."

Young kids watch TV's thrill-packed coverage of demonstrations — including the violence and excitement — and dream about being in them. They look like fun.

Mayor Daley put out this television film about Chicago. It had cops beating up young longhairs. In one scene, the cops threw a tear-gas canister into the crowd, and one demonstrator picked it up and heaved it right back.

Who do you think every kid in the country identified with?

Then the announcer said the chiller: "These demonstrations are Communist led! . . ."

Communism? Who the hell knows from Communism? We never lived through Stalin. We read about it, but it doesn't affect us emotionally. Our emotional reaction to Communism is Fidel marching into Havana in 1959.

There is NO WORD that the Man has to turn off your youth, no scare word.

"They're for ANARCHY!"

Damn right, we're for anarchy! This country is fucking over-organized anyway.

"DON'T DO THIS, DON'T DO THAT, DON'T!"

Growing up in America is learning what NOT to do.

We say: "DO IT, DO IT. DO WHATEVER YOU WANT TO DO."

Our battlegrounds are the campuses of America. White middle-class youth are strategically located in the high schools and colleges of this country. They are our power bases.

If one day 100 campuses were closed in a nationally coordinated rebellion, we could force the President of the United States to sue for peace at the conference table.

As long as we are in school we are prisoners. Schools are voluntary jails. We must liberate ourselves.

Dig the geography of a university. You can always tell what the rulers have up their sleeves when you check out the physical environment they create. The buildings tell you how to behave. Then there is less need for burdensome rules and cops. They designed classrooms so that students sit in rows, one after the other, hierarchically, facing the professor who stands up front talking to all of them.

Classrooms say:

"Listen to the Professor.

"He teaches you.

"Keep your place.

"Don't stretch out.

"Don't lie on the floor.

"Don't relax.

"Don't speak out of turn.

"Don't take off your clothes.

"Don't get emotional.

"Let the mind rule the body.

"Let the needs of the classroom rule the mind."

Classrooms are totalitarian environments. The main purpose of the school and education in America is to force you to accept and love authority, and to distrust your own spontaneity and emotions.

How can you grow in such an over-structured environment? You can't. Schools aren't for learning.

Classrooms should be organized in circles, with the professor one part of the circle. A circle is a democratic environment.

Try breaking up the environment. Scream "Fuck" in the middle of your prof's lecture.

So, we organize a University of the Flesh. Four of us go into a classroom. We sit in the middle of the class. The lecture is on "Thinking."

Thinking!

We take off our shirts, smoke joints, and start French kissing. A lot of students get nervous. This goes on for 10–15 minutes, and the professor goes on with his lecture like nothing is happening.

Finally a girl says, "The people there are causing a distraction, and could they either put their shirts back on or could they please leave."

And the prof says, "Well, I agree with that. I think that if you're not here to hear what I'm saying . . ."

We shout: "You can't separate thinking from loving! We are hard in thought!!"

And the prof says, "Well, in my classroom I give the lessons."

Scratch a professor deep and you find a cop!

Fucking milquetoast! Didn't have the guts to throw us out, but in his classroom, HE GIVES the lesson. So he sends his teaching assistant to get the cops, and we split.

We must bring psychological guerrilla war to the University.

The mind is programmed. Get in there and break that bloody program!

Can you imagine what a feeling a professor has standing in front of a class and looking at a room full of bright faces taking down every word he says, raising their hands and asking him questions? It really makes someone think he is God. And to top it off, he has the power to reward and punish you, to decide whether or not you are fit to advance in the academic rat race.

Is this environment the right one for teacher and student?

Socrates is turning in his grave.

I was telling a professor of philosophy at Berkeley that many of his students were wiser men than he, even though he may have read more books and memorized more theories.

He replied, "Well, I must take the lead in the transfer of knowledge."

Transfer of knowledge! What is knowledge?

How to Live.

How to Legalize Marijuana.

How to Make a Revolution.

How to Free People from Jail.

How to Organize Against the CIA.

When a professor takes off his suit and tie, and joins us in the streets, then I say, "Hey man, what's your first name? You're my brother. Let's go. We're together."

I don't dig the "professor" bullshit. I am more interested in a 15-year-old stoned dope freak living on street corners than I am in a Ph.D.

There is anti-intellectualism in America because professors have created an artificial environment. That is why the average working guy does not respect professors.

The university is a protective and plastic scene, shielding people from the reality of life, the reality of suffering, of ecstasy, of struggle. The university converts the agony of life into the security of words and books.

You can't learn anything in school. Spend one hour in a jail or a courtroom and you will learn more than in five years spent in a university.

All I learned in school was how to beat the system, how to fake answers. But there are no answers. There are only more questions. Life is a long journey of questions, answered through the challenge of living. You would never know that, living in a university ruled by the "right" answers to the wrong questions.

Graffiti in school bathrooms tells you more about what's on people's minds than all the books in the library.

We must liberate ourselves. I dropped out. The shit got up to my neck and I stopped eating. I said: NO. NO. NO!! I'm dropping out.

People at Columbia found out what it felt like to learn when they seized buildings and lived in communes for days.

We have to redesign the environment and remake human relationships. But if you try it, you will be kicked out.

You know what professors and deans will say? "If you don't like it here, why don't you go back to Russia!"

A lot is demanded of white, middle-class youth in 1969. The whole thing about technological and bureaucratic society is that it is not made for heroes. We must become heroes.

The young kids living in the streets as new niggers are the pioneers of tomorrow, living dangerously and existentially.

The yippies went to Chicago to have our own counter-festival, a "Festival of Life" in the parks of Chicago, as a human contrast to the "Convention of Death" of the Democrats.

I get a phone call on Christmas Day, 1967 from Marvin Garson, the editor of the *San Francisco Express-Times,* and he says, "Hey, it looks like the Peace and Freedom Party is not going to get on the ballot."

I say, "I don't care. I'm not interested in electoral politics anyway."

And he says, "Let's run a pig for President."

An arrow shoots through my brain. Yeah! A pig, with buttons, posters, bumper stickers.

"America, why take half a hog, when you can have the whole hog?"

At the Democratic convention, the pigs nominate the President and he eats the people.

At the yippie convention, we nominate our pig and after he makes his nominating speech, we eat him. The contrast is clear: Should the President eat the people or the people eat the President?

Well, we didn't kill our pig. If there is one issue that could split the yippies, it is the issue of vegetarianism. A log of yippies don't believe in killing and eating animals, so I had to be less militant on that point.

We bring Pigasus to Chicago, and he is arrested in Civic Center. The cops grab him. They grab seven of us, and they throw us in the paddy wagon with Pigasus.

The thing about running a pig for President is that it cuts through the shit. People's minds are full of things like, "You may elect a greater evil." We must break through their logic. Once we get caught in their logic, we're trapped in it.

Just freak it all out and proclaim: "This country is run on the principles of garbage. The Democratic and Republican parties have nominated a pig. So have we. We're honest about it."

In Chicago, Pigasus was a hell of a lot more effective than all those lackeys running around getting votes for the politicians. It turned out that the pig was more relevant to the current American political scene than Senator Eugene McCarthy. I never thought McCarthy could reform the Democratic party. Hell, McCarthy barely got into the convention himself. He had to have a ticket. That's how controlled the damn thing was. Finally, we forced McCarthy out into the streets with the people.

The election was not fair because every time we brought the pig out to give a campaign speech, they arrested him. It happened in Chicago, in New York, in San Francisco, even in London.

The yippies asked that the presidential elections be canceled until the rules of the game were changed. We said that everyone in the world should vote in the American election because America controls the world.

Free elections are elections in which the people who vote are the people affected by the results. The Vietnamese have more right to vote in the American elections than some 80-year-old grandmother in Omaha. They're being bombed by America! They should have at least some choice about if, how, and by whom they are going to be bombed.

I have nothing in particular against 80-year-old grandmothers, but I am in favor of lowering the voting age to 12 or 14 years. And I am not sure whether people over 50 should vote.

It is the young kids who are going to live in this world in the next 50 years. They should choose what they want for themselves.

Most people over 50 don't think about the potentialities of the future: they are preoccupied with justifying their past.

The only people who can choose change without suffering blows to their egos are the young, and change is the rhythm of the universe.

Many older people are constantly warning: "The right wing will get you." "George Wallace will get your momma."

I am so scared of George Wallace that I wore his fucking campaign button. I went to his campaign rally—all old ladies.

There are six Nazis who come with black gloves and mouthpieces, looking for a fight. And two fights break out. Two guys with long hair beat the shit out of them.

I am not afraid of the right wing because the right wing does not have the youth behind it.

"Straight" people get very freaked by Wallace. "Freaks" know the best way to fuck Wallace up. We support him.

At Wallace's rally in the Cow Palace in San Francisco, we come with signs saying "CUT THEIR HAIR!" "SEND THEM BACK TO AFRICA!" "BOMB THE VIETNAMESE BACK TO THE STONE AGE!"

When we arrive there is a picket line going on in front of the rally. I recognize it is the Communist Party picketing.

What? Picketing Wallace?

I walk up to my friend Bettina Aptheker and say, "Bettina, you're legitimizing him. You're legitimizing him by picketing. Instead, support him, kiss him. When he says the next hippie in front of his car will be the last hippie, cheer! Loudly!"

We have about two hundred people there, and we are the loudest people at the rally. Every five seconds we are jumping up and swearing, "Heil! Hitler! Heil! Hitler!"

Wallace is a sick man. America is the loony bin. The only way to cure her is through theatrical shock. Wallace is necessary because he brings to the surface the racism and hate that is deep within the country.

The yippie Fugs spearheaded the anti-war movement of the past five years by touring theaters and dance halls shouting into a microphone: "KILL, KILL, KILL FOR PEACE! KILL, KILL, KILL FOR PEACE!"

Wallace says aloud what most people say privately. He exposes the beast within liberal America. He embarrasses the liberal who says in one breath, "Oh, I like Negroes," and then in another breath, "We must eliminate crime in the streets."

Remember what Huey Long said: "When fascism comes to America, it will come as Americanism."

Wallace may be the best thing for those of us who are fighting him. You can only fight a disease after you recognize and diagnose it. America does not suffer from a cold: she has cancer.

The liberals who run this country agree with Wallace more than they disagree with him. George tells tales out of school. The liberals are going to have to shut that honest motherfucker up.

Do you dig that most cops support Wallace? Cops—the people who make and enforce the law in the streets! Wallace speaks FOR them.

Isn't that scary? Can't you see why blacks are getting guns and organizing into small self-defense units? Wouldn't you, if you were in *their* situation? Shouldn't *you* be?

Make America see her vampire face in the mirror. Destroy that gap between public talk and private behavior. Only when people see what's happening can they hear our screams, and feel our passion.

The Vietnam war is an education for America. It is an expensive teaching experience, but the American people are the most brainwashed people in the world.

At least the youth are learning that this country is no paradise— America kills infants and children in Vietnam without blinking. Only professional killers can be so cool.

If you become hip to America in Vietnam, you can understand the reaction against the red-white-and-blue in Latin America, and you can feel why China hates us.

They are not irrational—America is.

Wallace is a left-wing agitator. Dig him. He speaks to the same anxiety and powerlessness that the New Left and yippies talk about.

Do you feel overwhelmed by bigness, including Big Government?

Do you lack control over your own life?

Are you distrustful of the politicians and bureaucrats in Washington?

Are you part of the "little people"?

Wallace stirs the masses. Revolutions should do that too.

When is the left going to produce an inflammatory and authentic voice of the people? A guy who reaches people's emotions? Who talks about revolution the way some of those nuts rap about Christ?

Wallace says: "We're against niggers, intellectuals, liberals, hippies."

Everybody! He puts us all together. He organizes us for us.

We must analyze how America keeps people down. Not by physical force, but by fear. From the second kids are hatched, we are taught fear. If we can overcome fear, we will discover that we are Davids fighting Goliath.

In late September a friend calls and says, "Hey, I just got a subpoena from HUAC."

I say, "Yeah? I didn't. What's going on here? I'm angry. I want a subpoena too."

It's called subpoenas envy.

So I telephone a confidante to the Red Squad, a fascist creep who works for the *San Francisco Examiner,* and I say, "Hey, Ed, baby, what about HUAC? Are they having hearings?"

He answers, "Well, I don't know. Are they?"

"Well, my friend just got a subpoena," I say. "I'd like one, too. If you can manage it."

He says, "Call me back in a few hours."

I call him back that afternoon and he says, "Well, I just talked to HUAC in Washington, and you are right. They are having hearings, and they are looking for you in New York."

"In NEW YORK? I've been in Berkeley a week! You guys are sure doing a shitty job trying to save this country!"

We exaggerate the surveillance powers of cops. We shouldn't. They are lazy. Their laziness may be the one reason why America doesn't yet have a totally efficient police state.

The cops were not lazy in Chicago. They followed "the leaders" continuously, 24 hours a day. If you are trailed by four cops just six steps behind you, you can't do very much.

But the people really doing things – why, the cops didn't even know who they were!

Pigs cannot relate to anarchy. They do not understand a movement based on personal freedom. When they look at our movement, they look for a hierarchy: leaders, lieutenants, followers.

The pigs think that we are organized like their pig department. We are not, and that's why we are going to win. A hierarchical, topdown organization is no match for the free and loose energy of the people.

As the pigs check with their higher-ups to find out what to do next, we have already switched the tactics and scene of the battle. They are watching one guy over there, and it is happening over here!

I come to the HUAC hearings wearing a bandolero of real bullets and carrying a toy M-16 rifle on my shoulder. The rifle was a model of the rifles the Viet Cong steal and then use to kill American soldiers in Vietnam.

The pigs stop me at the door of the hearings. They grab the bullets and the gun. It is a dramatic moment. Press and yippies pack us in tightly. The pigs drag me down three flights of stairs and remove the bullets, leaving the gun, Viet Cong pajamas, Eldridge Cleaver buttons, Black Panther beret, war paint, earrings, bandolero, and the bells which ring every time I move my body. My costume carried a nonverbal message: "We must all become stoned guerrillas."

The secret to the costume was the painted tits. Guerrilla war is in America is going to come in psychedelic colors. We are hippie-guerrillas.

In HUAC's chambers Abbie Hoffman jumps up and yells out, "May I go to the bathroom?" Young kids reading that in their hometown papers giggle because they have to ask permission every time they want to go to the bathroom in school.

The message of my costume flipped across the country in one day: an example of our use of the enemy's institutions—her mass media—to turn on and communicate with one another.

I wore a Santa Claus costume to HUAC two months later in a direct attempt to reach the head of every child in the country.

Our victories are catching up with us: America isn't ready to napalm us yet, but the future doesn't look easy.

From June to November 1968, when I was helping to organize the demonstrations against the Democratic convention in Chicago, I experienced the following example of Americana:

New York pigs use a phony search warrant to bust into my apartment, question me, beat me, search the apartment, and arrest me for alleged felonious possession of marijuana; a pig in Chicago disguises himself as a biker to "infiltrate" the yippies as an agent provocateur and spy; he busts me on a frame-up, "solicitation to mob action," a felony punishable by five years in the pen; the judge imposes $25,000 bail and restricts my travel to Illinois; then the Justice Department in a document to a Virginia court admits that it maintains "electronic surveillance . . . of Jerry Rubin . . . in the interests of national security."

To try to suppress youth, Nixon will have to destroy the Constitution.

We will be presumed guilty until proven innocent.

Our privacy will vanish. Big Brother will spy on all of us and dominate our lives.

Every cop will become a law unto himself.

The courts will become automatic transmission belts sending us to detention camps and prisons.

People will be arrested for what they write and say.

Congress will impose censorship on the mass media, unless the media first censors itself, which is more likely.

To be young will be a crime.

In response, we must never become cynical, or lose our capacity for anger. We must stay on the offensive and be aggressive:

AMERICA: IF YOU INJURE ONE, YOU MUST FIGHT ALL.

If our opposition is united, the repression may backfire and fail. The government may find the costs too heavy.

Don't think, "They can never get ME."

They can.

You are either on the side of the cops or on the side of human beings.

YIPPIE!

(1969)

*Thomas Merton*

# Can We Survive Nihilism?

Poets and poetic thinkers—men who construct myths in which they embody their own struggle to cope with the fundamental questions of life—are generally "prophetic" in the sense that they anticipate in their solitude the struggles and the general consciousness of later generations. Rereading John Milton now, one cannot help realizing at once how close he is to us and how remote from us. He is remote, if you like, in his classic stamina—his capacity to develop his ideas in the longest and noblest periods. He is remote from us in his moral assumptions and his world view. Yet the ideas and experiences he develops are often (not always) strikingly contemporary.

For instance, his passionate concern with free speech in *Areopagitica*—an anti-Catholic tract if ever there was one—has borne fruit, through the effort of American Catholic bishops and theologians, in the Second Vatican Council's declaration on religious liberty. His concern with the dignity and liberty of the human being has now become everybody's cliché (though not everybody's dignity or liberty). As for *Paradise Lost,* without slandering the nobility of this great poem, we have to admit that there are times when it is structured like a movie or even like a comic strip. Milton sometimes had a very modern imagination. There are scenes in which Satan is Batman. More seriously, there are unquestionable affinities between John Milton's Satan and the Superman not of the comics but of Nietzsche.

Without falling into the romantic exaggerations of those "satanist" critics of Milton who see Satan as the true hero of *Paradise Lost,* we are forced to admit that Milton was, if not all, at least partly on Satan's side. The Satan of *Paradise Lost* is the embodiment of heroic energy, of obstinately futile resistance—a "freedom fighter," a loser who can't be kept down by superior odds. This is not to say that Milton approved of Satan or still less consciously sympathizes with him. But the element in Milton that was "modern," that which brings him close to us, was at work in the creation of this dynamic rebel, while the elements in Milton that were more remote—the classicist, the biblical thinker—disclaimed the rebel he had created. We are less disposed to see this because we have become habitually inattentive to the kind of cosmology and theology that Milton took for granted. The Satan of *Paradise Lost* is not for us part of a cosmic whole. He stands out against a background that does not concern us so much—a modern hero against the scenery of a baroque opera.

Milton's Satan can easily be seen as modern man; the activist, the tireless mover and shaker who acts and moves and shakes because these are his only resources. They make him seem able to tolerate an intolerable hell; they constitute for him a kind of freedom, a pretense of dignity. For this reason he is attached to them—in fact, he makes idols of them. They are his substitute for religion.

*Paradise Lost* opens with the fallen angels lying stunned in hell, where they have just made a crash landing. They do not stay that way for long. There is something curiously American about them. They get up and go. They go from a very hot part of hell to one that is slightly cooler and there, in order to make the best of things, build a devilish city and draw up a plan of action, a diabolical program, an energetically satanic way of life. The city is a secular city, and in many ways rather like New York, perhaps the New York of the Twenties and the Roxy theater rather than the New York of today.

Whatever this metropolis may be, the point is that they build it, and build it fast, by a brand-new method. Their work is itself a rebellion against inertia and defeat. Hence it is a kind of victory. And a special kind of victory at that, because it is gained entirely by their own ingenuity and their own resources. The unequaled verve of the first books of *Paradise Lost* enables us to surmise that Milton wrote these pages with special satisfaction, even though he was both emotionally and intellectually "against" this fantastic rebellion. But, in spite of himself, his own character—indeed, his own heroic struggle against the inertia imposed by blindness—disposed him to sympathize with this "sublimation" of beaten energies.

Yet at the same time these heroic energies are important. All the power, the splendor and the versatility of satanic technology remain illusory and pointless. One might almost say that, beneath his unconscious sympathy with the rebels, Milton realized even more deeply the finality of their despair. And this sense of futility is his final judgment on their rebellion—a fact which his superficial readers seem unable to realize.

There is ambivalence in Milton's Satan, and also in Milton's paradise. We cannot question the importance of the archetypal paradise myth
in *Paradise Lost*. The title itself states the problem: Man is created for
peace, delight, and the highest spiritual happiness. In traditional language, he is created for contemplation. Not a loss of self in mystical
absorption but self-transcendence in the dynamic stillness which, as
the Zen masters said, is found not in rest but in truly spontaneous
movement. But man's weakness and superficiality, his inordinate love
of a self metaphysically wounded with contingency, makes the paradise
life impossible. There is in Milton a tension between his desire of this
ideal and his feeling that it is unattainable. He never resolved the apparent contradiction. He could not find the secret of contemplation in
action and so saw, in practice, no solution but action without contemplation.

When he came to describe the ideal life of Adam and Eve in paradise, Milton was weak and unconvincing: The life is too contemplative
for him; there is too much leisure; there is apparently no room for inia-
tive; there is just nothing to *do*. E. M. W. Tillyard once compared Adam
and Eve in Milton to "old-age pensioners enjoying a perpetual youth"
because they have to live and work in a garden that of its own accord
produces more than they will ever need. Strangely enough, this is precisely the kind of society that seems to be resulting from the fantasti-
cally energetic and versatile progress of our technology. If inertia and
lack of outlet for creative energy create hell, then it appears that the
greatest threat to man is that he may succumb not to hostile nature or
to a stronger species, but to the explosive violence generated from the
utter boredom of his own conquests.

If Milton was an ambivalent activist, prone to sympathize with action and even rebellion for their own sakes, and unable to tolerate the
contemplation which he still believed to be best, his theology tends to
reflect these ambiguities, and here, too, he was modern. True, there can
be no question of the reality of God for Milton. He was not a God Is
Dead theologian before the time. Far from it. But his Pelagian taste for
action and his instinctive disposition to seek in man himself the solution to all man's problems make his Christ a rather incredible and superfluous saviour. True, the Divine Word in *Paradise Lost* is intended to
be even more heroically powerful than Satan in the poem—indeed, it
cannot be otherwise. But somehow, just because He *must* be more
powerful, His power is poetically less convincing. It can never be seriously challenged or tested: hence, a theological ambivalence that has
struck deep into the modern Christian consciousness and led eventually
to the poetic protest of nineteenth-century minds like Baudelaire and
Rimbaud which made explicit the contradictions which were as yet
only implicit in Milton.

There was in Milton a radical tension between his own psychology,
his heart, his character as formed in his own revolutionary struggle for

a republican England and then his battle with blindness, and the traditional structure of beliefs to which he consciously held. The traditional
structure was classic, static, and contemplative, while Milton was romantic, dynamic, and active. Milton was a romantic hero who wrote as a
great classical poet. These tensions doubtless help to account for his
greatness. But they have led astray all those who are able to see only one
side of the picture, who insist on taking one horn of the dilemma as the
answer to all the questions and dismissing the dilemma. Hence they
hail as power and truth what Milton saw to be impotence and illusion.

One modern mythology—which doubtless no longer refers consciously to Milton but still deals with much the same archtypal patterns—is filled with Milton's themes of power, rebellion, will, and the
drive to excel. But these themes have all undergone serious if not radical modification.

For one thing, the modern tendency is to interpret the dignity and
freedom of the person not as Milton did, but in a more frankly satanic
way. The freedom and dignity of the person, for most people, means in
fact the ability of the individual to assert himself forcefully, to get up
and overcome obstacles, to knock a few bystanders down if necessary,
and generally get everybody to recognize that he is around. One of the
cardinal satanic virtues is the absolute refusal to let anyone else
change your mind for you, by any means, reasonable or otherwise. This
means that you can never be prevented from being the boss at least in
your own small patch of hell. And this is freedom. "Better to reign in
hell than serve in heaven."

To assume that Milton endorsed such doctrine would be the most
monstrous misapprehension. He knew better than that what freedom
was and how liberty implied intelligence and adaptation to the objective realities of life. He rejected as impotence the completely irrational
misconception of freedom. This misconception is, first of all, purely
subjective and, secondly, a blind exercise of will. But a blind exercise of
will is doomed to frustration. When purely subjective whims encounter
the opposition of objective reality, there is only one way to overcome
them: Since intelligence will not serve, violence alone remains. But violence is self-destroying and hence absurd. The concept of freedom
which demands that one be one's own boss at all costs, that one should
never change his mind for anyone, is a concept that leads nowhere but
to blind addiction to violence and ultimately to willful self-destruction.
Much of the current talk of freedom today has no more validity than
this, and therefore it is a potential source of catastrophic madness.
What forms will this madness take? Anything is possible, from street
fighting to a nuclear *Götterdämmerung*.

In his *Myth of Sisyphus* Albert Camus re-created something similar to Milton's Satan in the "hero of the absurd" who resorts to a purely
"quantitative ethic." There are all kinds of affinities between Sisyphus

(or the other heroes of the absurd like Don Juan) and Milton's Demon Rebel. Again, there is a basically hopeless situation of stupefied inertia to be redeemed by action. What is fundamentally absurd (and hell is surely the realm of the absurd) cannot be made to make sense in itself. But one can seek to do *something* that makes sense. The will to make sense out of free action can counteract the absurd.

Though Camus more and more articulately disclaimed the title of "philosopher of the absurd" he is still stubbornly thought to have been preaching "the absurd" as a fundamental value—or as a heroically despairing antivalue. As a result of this, Camus's doctrine of revolt is sometimes turned upside down and stood on its head. In fact, Camus's study of the whole anatomy of revolution ends in a classic humanism, directly opposed to that nihilism which, he thought, is the automatic result of all absolute use of power whether in the spiritual or in the temporal orders. Thus, though a superficial reading of his early work seems to give some the impression that Camus advocated nihilism he was, on the contrary, a humanist and a moderate—a liberal who was left in the very uncomfortable position of rejecting all the facile and doctrinaire generalizations of the mass movements and finding his own way in solitude.

Yet Camus was no individualist. He knew the value of true solidarity and community, but he also knew the difficulty of finding them. Certainly the hopeful claims of movements and parties—and churches—did not seem to him to be automatic guarantees of communion in fruitful effort. But he did find true solidarity in the clandestine journalism of the French resistance, and later in the theater to which he devoted the best of his energies in the late Fifties, before his death.

Though Camus may have started with Sisyphus, a figure somewhat similar to Milton's Satan, he soon distinguished between liberty and anarchy, authentic rebellion and totalist nihilism, and in the end rejoined the kind of classic view of liberty which was the one Milton himself really held.

There are certain basic notions underlying Greek tragedy—notions about the meaning and moral structure of life. The most basic of these concepts are *hybris* and *nemesis*. When man, either through his own fault or simply through some chain of fatal circumstances, begins to defy the gods and assert his own power against the claims of a higher power (we would say "of reality"), he is permitted to get away with it for a while. But in the end the momentum generated by his rash and illusory self-confidence brings with it his own destruction. This does not mean that tragedy is always and simply a victory of the gods over man. On the contrary, the greatest tragedies are conflicts between the claims of various orders—various gods, perhaps—having almost equal rights. In this conflict, a character of true nobility can in fact emerge victorious, as Oedipus does in the final play of the Sophoclean trilogy, for example. Antigone is both ennobled and destroyed by a tragic dilemma:

her love for her brother or her obedience to the power of the state. Prometheus is caught between his love for man, his devotion to the older order of telluric gods, and the power of the new Olympians. Neither Prometheus nor Antigone can be said to be afflicted with *hybris*. But if even the guiltless or unconsciously guilty hero incurs destruction by defying certain forces, how much more will the natural tendency of ordinary man to *hybris*, or what we have described as satanic self-assertion, inevitably bring *nemesis* – a fatal retribution in which man's power becomes his own destruction.

Strictly speaking, neither Christ nor Satan in Milton's poem can be called a perfectly tragic figure because Satan's *hybris* has reached a kind of dynamic stasis in impotent and rebellious deadlock, while in Christ there is no defeat at all. Satan is always ruined, yet always comes back for more. Hence he is a figure not of tragedy but of melodrama – and, incidentally, since tragedy requires a single unified action, one can never have tragedy in a serial, however appalling it may be.

The Greek sense of measure, to which Camus ultimately appealed in his humanistic ethic, is built on a healthy fear of *hybris* and is something which apparently is entirely built on the fatality and destructiveness of *hybris*. A healthy fear of *hybris* is something which seemingly is completely lacking in the modern consciousness. We have swallowed without question the melodramatic values and dynamisms of a misunderstood Miltonic Satan and we have no tragic dread of *nemesis*. The Greeks, who were probably far wiser than we realize, were well aware that he who has no sense of *nemesis* is in fact very close to it. Those whom the gods would destroy, they first make mad – with self-righteous confidence and unquestioning self-esteem.

It might be interesting to refer in passing to Teilhard de Chardin, whose cosmic optimism restores all the dynamic energies and heroism of Milton's Satan to the Teilhardian Christ. Perhaps Teilhard was able to do this because his complete acceptance of evolutionism destroyed the tension and contradiction that were set up in Milton between his modern temper and his ancient world view. In Teilhard, the coincidence of the modern temper and a modern cosmology resulted in a convergence of energies that remained in unresolved conflict for Milton. Whether this convergence was too optimistic and too facile remains a point of controversy. But one thing is obvious: Teilhard's splendid poetic vision of his "Mass on the World" (in his *Hymn of the Universe*) strikingly resembles the splendid hymn to light at the opening of the third book of *Paradise Lost*. Teilhard is in many ways a Miltonic "epic poet" whose power depends precisely on the fact that he has, at least in his own creative experience, resolved the conflict which kept Milton's Christ such a dubious figure, and which made it impossible for Camus to become a Christian.

It is one thing to admire the literary power and ambiguity of Milton's Satan, but another to seek, unconsciously or otherwise, to make a satanic and activist nihilism one's way of life. Camus has shown in his study of revolt how this kind of nihilism has in fact entered into the very essence of all the modern power structures that are now in conflict. This leads to some frightening and salutary conclusions. The first and most important of these is that the satanic nihilism of the great modern power structures represents a fatal infestation of *hybris*. This leads infallibly to *nemesis* and to destruction if we cannot learn to do something about it. No free man can allow himself passively to accept and identify with any one of these power structures in an unqualified way. To do so means associating himself with its *hybris*, abdicating his moral and personal dignity, and participating in the cosmic witches' sabbath to which we are all now being invited.

Most of us seem to have accepted the invitation without stopping to reflect that there is a choice. Camus insisted that there is a choice: The choice is man himself. Man's true dignity must lead him, Camus thought, to a free rejection of any system which makes the power of state, money, or weapons absolute values in themselves. While we seem to be asked to choose between this or that ideology, this party or that, this power bloc or that, in reality the choice is quite different. If we examine all their claims, says Camus, we find that they eventually concur in placing ideologies above man himself—politics above humanity, nation, race, or party above truth, and power above everything.

Thus in every department of life the cart is before the horse, ends are sacrificed to means, man is alienated and destroyed in order to serve what is supposed to serve him. The state is theoretically for man, money is theoretically to help him live more easily, arms are supposed to protect him, and so on. But in fact man now lives and works in order to assemble and to stockpile the weapons that will destroy him, in an effort to serve a power structure which he worships as an end in itself and which makes his life more and more meaningless and absurd. Instead of using money to make life reasonable, man makes life unbearable by living for money. Everywhere we look we find the same contradictions and disorder—all symptomatic of one truth: Our seemingly well-ordered society is a nihilist city of pandemonium, built on *hybris* and destined for cataclysm.

Is this inevitable? Nothing is absolutely inevitable. Man is still free to make choices and he is even capable of making intelligent choices if he tries hard enough. But our future depends above all on this: the recognition that our present nihilistic consciousness is fatal, and the development of a totally new state of mind—a whole new way of looking at ourselves, our world, and our problems. Not a new ideology, not a new formula of words, not a new mystique; but as Tillich said, *a new man*. With a little humility, patience, native luck, and the grace of God, the hard years we are going to live through may teach us to open our eyes. Meanwhile, a more accurate understanding of Milton and Camus, perhaps a less naïve reading of Teilhard, may certainly help.

(1967)

# Alternate Table of Contents

## Speeches

## Essays and Other Prose Forms

# Short Stories

# Poetry

2 3 4 5 6 7 8 9 10 -KP- 80 79 78 77 76 75